NEW *Speaking Out: DSM in Context videos in Abnormal Psychology!*

BIPOLAR DISORDER

Interview with
FELIZIANO

Day in the Life:
FELIZIANO

POST TRAUMATIC STRESS DISORDER

Interview with
BONNIE

Day in the Life:
BONNIE

IMPULSE CONTROL DISORDER

Interview with
ED

Day in the Life:
ED

ANOREXIA NERVOSA DISORDER

Interview with
NATASHA

Day in the Life:
NATASHA

DEMENTIA DISORDER

Interview with
ALVIN

Day in the Life:
ALVIN

ASPERGER'S SYNDROME DISORDER

Interview with
DAVID

Day in the Life:
DAVID

MAJOR DEPRESSION

EVERETT

"You feel absolute
worthlessness.
You feel there is
no hope for the
future."

BULIMIA

JESSICA

"I started out with
a diet for me."

SCHIZOPHRENIA

LARRY

"My voices had
gotten the most
of me . . ."

SCHIZOAFFECTIVE DISORDER

JOSH

"When I was first
in the hospital,
I thought I was in
the middle of a
massacre . . ."

ADHD

JIMMY

"I think without it
(medicine) I would
be dreaming the
whole entire day."

AUTISM

XAVIER

"He is now talking,
which was
a blessing."

PLUS videos covering Obsessive-Compulsive Disorder, Hyphochondriasis,
Post Traumatic Stress Disorder, Social Phobia, HIV, Bipolar Mood Disorder with Psychotic Features,
Borderline Personality Disorder, Alcoholism, and Gender Identity Disorder.

abnormal PSYCHOLOGY

deborah c. **BEIDEL**
University of Central Florida

cynthia m. **BULIK**
University of North
Carolina at Chapel Hill

melinda a. **STANLEY**
Baylor College of Medicine

abnormal PSYCHOLOGY

Prentice Hall

Boston   Columbus   Indianapolis   New York   San Francisco   Upper Saddle River
Amsterdam   Cape Town   Dubai   London   Madrid   Milan   Munich   Paris   Montreal   Toronto
Delhi   Mexico City   Sao Paulo   Sydney   Hong Kong   Seoul   Singapore   Taipei   Tokyo

Editorial Director: Leah Jewell
Editor in Chief: Jessica Mosher
Executive Editor: Jeff Marshall
Editorial Assistant: Amy Trudell
Director of Marketing: Brandy Dawson
Marketing Manager: Nicole Kunzmann
Marketing Assistant: Laura Kennedy
Managing Editor: Michael Granger
Production Supervisor: Roberta Sherman
Text Permissions Research: Sue Brekka
Manufacturing Buyer: JoAnne Sweeney
Senior Art Director: Nancy Wells
Interior and Cover Designer: Anne DeMarinis

Manager, Visual Research: Beth Brenzel/
    Martha Shethar
Manager, Rights and Permissions: Charles Morris
Manager, Cover Visual Research & Permissions:
    Karen Sanatar
Cover Art: Anne DeMarinis
Media Director: Karen Scott
Senior Media Editor: Paul DeLuca
Editorial Production and Composition Service:
    Prepare Inc.
Printer/Binder: Courier Kendallville
Cover Printer: Lehigh-Phoenix Color/Hagerstown
Text Font: 10.5/14 Adobe Caslon Regular

Credits and acknowledgments borrowed from other sources and reproduced, with permission, in this textbook appear on appropriate page within text.

Photo Credits appear on page 589, which constitutes an extension of the copyright page.

Library of Congress Cataloging-in-Publication Data
Beidel, Deborah C.
Abnormal psychology / Deborah Beidel, Cynthia Bulik, Melinda Stanley.
    p. cm.
Include bibliographical references and index.
ISBN-13: 978-0-13-221612-8
ISBN-10: 0-13-221612-4
1. Psychology, Pathological. I. Bulik, Cynthia M. II. Stanley, M. A. (Melinda Anne) III. Title
RC454.B428 2010
616.89—dc22

2009034614

10 9 8 7 6 5 4 3 2   CIN   13 12 11 10

Prentice Hall
is an imprint of

www.pearsonhighered.com

Student Edition: ISBN-10: 0-13-221612-4
                  ISBN-13: 978-0-13-221612-8
Exam Copy: ISBN-10: 0-13-239796-X
                  ISBN-13: 978-0-13-239796-4

To our mentor, colleague, and friend,
SAMUEL MATHEW TURNER:
You knew when to push,
You knew when to pull us back,
And you never let us settle for less than our best.
Thank you for setting the bar so high
and for leading the cheer
when we cleared each new height.

brief contents

contents

CHAPTER 6

Mood Disorders 186

CHAPTER 7

Eating Disorders 224

CHAPTER 8

Gender and Sexual Disorders 256

CHAPTER 9

Substance Use Disorders 294

CHAPTER 10

Schizophrenia and Other Psychotic Disorders 332

CHAPTER 11

Personality Disorders 364

CHAPTER 15

Abnormal Psychology: Legal, Ethical, and Professional Issues 498

preface

Abnormal psychology is one of the most popular courses among undergraduate students and undergraduate psychology majors in particular. This no doubt is due in part to our endless fascination with human behavior and the forces that shape and act on it. A presidential proclamation declared that the 1990s would be known as the Decade of the Brain. In the year 2000, the American Psychological Association declared that the next decade would be the Decade of Behavior. While both of these decades witnessed exciting discoveries, we believe there is a fundamental flaw in dedicating separate decades to the brain and to behavior. Understanding human behavior requires us to integrate our understanding of both brain *and* behavior. In this volume, we integrate biological data with research from the social and behavioral sciences in order to foster the perspective that abnormal behavior is complex and subject to many different forces. Furthermore, we highlight how these variables often interact in a reciprocal fashion. Psychotherapy was built in part on the assumption that behavior could be changed by changing the environment, but science has now shown us that environmental factors can also change the brain. Similarly, new approaches to genetics, known as molecular genetics, have expanded our understanding of biological influences far beyond Gregor Mendel's experiments with peas. On the behavioral side, advances in computer technology such as virtual reality systems have provided enhanced therapeutic strategies for cognitive-behavioral treatments. Each new discovery raises new questions and unlocks new areas of exploration.

Despite the vast amount of knowledge yet undiscovered, the path to discovery is now much clearer. The integration of leading-edge biological and behavioral research, known as the translational approach, or "from bench to bedside," is what is needed to advance the study of abnormal psychology. We have followed this model in our book. We reach beyond the old clichés of nature or nurture, clinician or scientist, genes or environment, and challenge the next generation of psychologists and students to embrace the complexity inherent in replacing these historical "or's" with contemporary "and's." Only by reaching beyond one-dimensional explanations of human behavior will we achieve a more sophisticated appreciation of the causes of psychological disorders and develop innovative and effective approaches to prevention and treatment.

The Scientist-Practitioner Model

We take a *Scientist-Practitioner Approach* because we believe that abnormal psychology rests on knowledge generated through scientific studies and clinical practice. Many psychologists are trained in the scientist-practitioner model and adhere to it to some degree in their professional work. We live and breathe this model. In addition to our roles as teachers at the undergraduate, graduate, and postdoctoral levels, we are all active clinical researchers and clinical practitioners. However, the scientist-practitioner model means more than just having multiple roles; it is a philosophy that guides all of the psychologist's activities. Those familiar with the model know this quote well: "Scientist-practitioners embody a research orientation in their practice and a practice relevance in their research" (Belar & Perry, 1992). This philosophy reflects our guiding principles, and we wrote this text to emphasize this rich blend of science and practice. Because we are scientist-practitioners, all of the cases described throughout this text are drawn from our own practice, with the exception of a few quotes and newspaper stories designed to highlight a specific point. We have endeavored to "bring to life" the nature of these conditions by providing vivid clinical descriptions. In addition to the clinical material that begins our introduction to the topic, and the short clinical descriptions that are used liberally throughout each chapter, a fully integrated case study, drawn from one of our practices, is presented at the end of each chapter, again illustrating the interplay of biological, psychosocial, and emotional factors. Of course, details have been changed, and some cases may represent composites in order to protect the privacy of those who have shared their life stories with us throughout our careers.

We wanted to provide the student with something more than a dense review of the scientific literature, while maintaining a strong scientific focus. It is our view that neither a dense and cerebral scientific approach nor an overly popularized approach allows students to understand fully the essence of the psychological disorders we cover. In fact, in our experience, students respond positively to materials that make these conditions more understandable and vivid, and this is particularly true when the text is clear and easy to read. We wanted to "put a face" on these sometimes perplexing and unfamiliar conditions through the use of rich clinical material such as vignettes, case histories, and personal accounts. We hope that these illustrations will entice students to learn more about abnormal psychology while helping them acquire the important concepts. Thus, although the book represents leading-edge science, our ultimate goal is to portray the "human face" of these conditions. Our approach will appeal both to students who were attracted to the topic primarily from an interest in the clinical aspects of abnormal behavior and to students whose choice stemmed mainly from an interest in research. Each student will leave with an awareness that the best (and we believe only) approach to understanding abnormal behavior comes from the seamless combination of science and practice.

A Developmental Trajectory

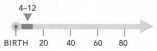

It has become increasingly clear that many types of abnormal behavior either begin in childhood or have childhood precursors. Similarly, without treatment, most disorders do not merely disappear with advancing age; in fact, several new disorders may emerge. Quite simply, as we grow, mature, and age, our physical and cognitive capacities affect how symptoms are displayed. Without this developmental perspective, it is easy to overlook important clues that indicate the presence of a particular disorder at a particular phase of life. Furthermore, the developmental focus is instrumental in helping students gain insight into the etiology of maladaptive conditions. In this text, when the same disorders exist in both childhood and adulthood, they are presented in the same chapter. In each chapter where we discuss psychological disorders, we also include a section called *Developmental Factors*, which highlights what is known about the developmental trajectory of each condition. In the margins of those pages, you will find the developmental trajectory icons, which indicate that important developmental features are discussed in that paragraph. In addition, two chapters (Chapter 12, Disorders of Childhood and Adolescents, and Chapter 13, Aging and Cognitive Disorders) are uniquely focused on disorders that exist at various developmental stages.

Sex, Race, and Ethnicity

In each chapter, we have attempted to describe what research has told us so far about how sex, race, or ethnicity affects a disorder's clinical presentation, etiology, and treatment. We carefully considered the terms used in the text to refer to these concepts. Indeed, the terms used to refer to sex, gender, race, and ethnicity are continually evolving, and the words that we use vary throughout the text. When we describe a particular study, we retain the categories that were used in the original publication (e.g., Afro-Caribbean, Caucasian, Pacific Islander). In order to create some consistency throughout the text, when we discuss general issues regarding race and ethnicity, we use standard terms (e.g., whites, African Americans, Hispanics). Although we are admittedly uncomfortable with calling groups by any labels, whether they refer to race, ethnicity, or diagnosis (e.g., blacks, whites, schizophrenics), in the case of race and ethnicity, for clarity of presentation and for parsimony, we opted for these categorical labels rather than the more cumbersome "individuals of European American ancestry" approach. Throughout the book, however, we have not labeled individuals who have psychological disorders with their diagnosis, as humans are far richer and more complex than any diagnostic label could ever capture. Moreover, referring to a patient or patient group by a diagnostic label is fundamentally disrespectful (e.g., bulimics, depressives, schizophrenics). People have disorders; they are not defined by their disorders.

Clinical Features

Consistent with our belief that the clinical richness of this text will bring the subject matter to life, each chapter begins with a clinical description that introduces and illustrates the topic of the chapter. These descriptions are not necessarily extensive case studies, but provide the reader with a global "feel" for each disorder. In addition, small case vignettes are used liberally throughout the text to illustrate specific clinical elements. Another important clinical element in our book is the "double case box," in which we illustrate the differences between typical human emotions (such as elation) and abnormal behavior (such as mania). We included these descriptions in selected chapters to emphasize that the difference between normal emotions and what we call psychological disorders is not simply the presence of emotion or specific behavior, but whether the behavior creates distress or impairs daily functioning.

NORMAL BEHAVIOR CASE STUDY
A Scary Event—No Disorder

Last month, Jamal was driving in a snowstorm. The road was icy, and Jamal regretted his decision to drive in the storm. But he wanted to get home to his wife and young son. As he was driving down the highway, his car hit a patch of ice and he began to skid off the road—sideways at first and then in a circle. It was a terrifying few moments, and images of his son and wife flashed before Jamal's eyes. The car landed in a ditch. Jamal was banged up but otherwise safe. That night, after he got home, he was unable to sleep—he kept going in to see his son sleeping in his crib. The next morning, his heart was pounding when he started his car, and for a few weeks afterward, he felt tense every time he drove past that ditch. ■

ABNORMAL BEHAVIOR CASE STUDY
Post-Traumatic Stress Disorder

In 1968, Jerry was drafted into the Army. In Vietnam, after a day-long firefight, Jerry was shot. His injuries were severe, and although he does not remember much of what happened after the bullet shattered his thigh bone, he does remember feeling extremely cold when he received a blood transfusion. Upon returning home, he was in the grocery store and walked down the frozen food aisle. The cold from the frozen food aisle precipitated a flashback, and Jerry thought that he was in Vietnam again. Now Jerry avoids the grocery store at all costs. Every time he hears a helicopter, he "hits the ground." Jerry has not been able to work since he came home from Vietnam. ■

Finally, each chapter concludes with a case study entitled *The Whole Story*, a clinical presentation, assessment, and treatment of a patient with a particular disorder, again drawn from the authors' own clinical files. Each concluding case study illustrates much of the material covered in the chapter and shows how a clinical psychologist approaches understanding, assessing, and treating the disorder. Furthermore, this concluding case study demonstrates how the clinician considers biological, psychological, environmental, and cultural factors in order to understand the patient's clinical presentation. Finally, the treatment program and outcome are described, highlighting how all of the factors are addressed in treatment. Through this process, the case study will allow the student to view "first-hand" the scientist-practitioner approach to abnormal behavior, dispelling myths often propagated through the media about how psychologists, think, work, and act.

examining the evidence

Is Trichotillomania a Variant of OCD?

The Facts Trichotillomania (TTM) is defined as repetitive hair pulling that results in noticeable hair loss. People affected with this repetitive behavior pull hair from their scalps, eyelashes, eyebrows, and even pubic areas. Sometimes people with TTM wear wigs, scarves, and false eyelashes to cover the damage. They want to stop pulling but feel powerless to do so. TTM is sometimes considered to be part of a spectrum of obsessive-compulsive behaviors (Stanley & Cohen, 1999), but are TTM and OCD the same?

Let's Examine the Evidence TTM and OCD have a number of common features:

1. Both are characterized by repetitive behavior over which people feel a lack of control.
2. Hair pulling and compulsions in OCD both decrease anxiety.
3. Some people with TTM have obsessive thoughts about hair pulling, wanting their hair to be symmetrical or free of aberrant hairs (that are too coarse, too short, or too wiry).
4. Both TTM and OCD are associated with high rates of coexisting anxiety and depressive disorders.
5. Higher rates of OCD occur in families of people with TTM.
6. Brain imaging studies have shown evidence of abnormal functioning in two areas of the brain, called the basal ganglia and the frontal lobe (see Chapter 2), in both TTM and OCD.
7. One antidepressant (clomipramine) and behavioral treatment are useful treatments for TTM and OCD.

TTM and OCD are different in many ways:

1. Hair pulling often occurs without focused awareness (i.e., people who pull often do so without paying attention to what they are doing); people with OCD are usually very focused on trying to reduce fears associated with obsessive thoughts.
2. Compulsions occur primarily in response to anxiety; hair pulling occurs in response to a wide range of negative moods (e.g., anger, boredom, sadness).
3. Hair pulling often produces feelings of pleasure; rituals do not.
4. Sensory stimuli (e.g., touching, feeling the hair) have an important role in hair pulling but not in compulsions.
5. Family members of people with OCD are more likely to have OCD than family members of people with TTM.
6. TTM is associated with lower rates of OCD symptoms and less severe anxiety and depression than OCD.
7. Serotonergic medications effective for the treatment of OCD do not work well for TTM.
8. Methods of behavioral treatment are quite different in TTM and OCD.

Conclusion TTM and OCD have some important common features and may share genetic influences. There may be a subtype of TTM that is very much like OCD, with hair pulling occurring in response to obsessive thoughts about hair. However, most studies suggest important differences in the clinical symptoms, neurobiological variables, and treatment procedures and responses for people with these two disorders. What factors do you think are most important in determining whether TTM is a form of obsessive-compulsive disorder?

THE WHOLE STORY: KERRY—TREATING SCHIZOPHRENIA

The Person: Kerry is 19 years old. He has always been a shy, quiet young man. Studious and respectful in high school, he had few friends and never dated. He was accepted at the state university, 100 miles from home.

The Problem: During his first semester, he became concerned that those who were living in his dorm were "out to get him." His concerns extended to an instructor who more a red shirt, which Kerry believed to be a sign of the devil. The archangel Michael began to speak to Kerry, commenting on his behavior and giving him instructions on how to behave. His roommate became alarmed, not only because Kerry accused him of inserting thoughts into his head but also because Kerry stopped eating (he thought the food might have been poisoned) and bathing (in case the water was contaminated).

Kerry stopped going to classes and was reluctant to leave his room, where he was constantly examining light fixtures and electrical outlets for listening devices planted there by the FBI. He would call his parents at odd hours of the night, crying and pleading with them to make the voices go away. The next day, he would call them and angrily accuse them of being in league with the devil, the FBI, or both. His bizarre behavior led to an inpatient hospitalization and a diagnosis of paranoid schizophrenia.

The Treatment: Kerry was treated with an atypical antipsychotic, which decreased his auditory hallucinations but did not eliminate them. Kerry was unable to tolerate the medication dosage considered necessary for optimal treatment outcome because of severe side effects, and he continued to express discomfort with auditory hallucinations. Kerry was treated with cognitive-behavior therapy (CBT) and felt that although he was better able to cope with the hallucinations on a daily basis, they still interfered with his ability to return to school or hold a job. Because he had achieved only a partial treatment response, Kerry had to take a leave of absence from school and returned home to live with his parents. The medical school near his parents' home was offering a research study using transcranial magnetic stimulation (TMS), and Kerry enrolled as a participant. TMS decreased the frequency of his symptoms such that he was then able to use the

coping skills he acquired through CBT to deal with the remaining hallucinations. Kerry's negative symptoms were also somewhat improved. Although he was not able to return to college full-time, he was able to maintain half-time employment as a dishwasher in a restaurant.

The Treatment Outcome: One year later, Kerry became depressed at his inability to return to his previous state of functioning. He stopped taking his medication and attempted to commit suicide by choking himself. He passed out before he suffocated and was hospitalized. After rehospitalization and reinstatement of his medication, Kerry was admitted to a partial hospitalization program, where he received group treatments such as social skills training and illness-management skills. Following his discharge, he was rehired at the restaurant and enrolled in one college course at a community college. Six months later, he moved out of his parents' house into a supported living facility, allowing him more independence. He continues to struggle with the hallucinations but has been able to use his coping skills to manage their severity.

Special Features

We would like to draw the reader's attention to three specific features that appear in each chapter. The first, *Examining the Evidence*, presents a current controversy related to the disorder under study in the chapter. However, we do not simply present the material. Rather, consistent with the scientist-practitioner focus of the book, we present both sides of the controversy and lead students through the data, allowing them to draw their own conclusions. Thus, *Examining the Evidence* boxes do not just present material, but foster critical thinking skills about issues in abnormal psychology. By considering both sides of the issues, students will become savvy consumers of scientific literature.

The second feature is called *Research Hot Topic*, which, at the time of publication, presents topical, leading-edge research. Consistent with the focus of this text, the *Research Hot Topic* boxes illustrate how science informs our understanding of human behavior, yet in a manner that is engaging to students (e.g., Virtual Reality Therapy for the Treatment of Anxiety Disorders"). As teachers and researchers who open our clinical research centers to undergraduate students, we know that many students think research is "dull." What they discover by participating in our research programs, and what students reading this text will discover, is that research is exciting.

Research HOT Topic

9/11—Trauma, Grief, PTSD, and Resilience

As currently defined, many stressors qualify as traumatic events and could result in a diagnosis of PTSD. Stabbings, shootings, and murder are common occurrences among inner-city adolescents (e.g., Jenkins & Bell, 1994). Natural disasters such as hurricanes, floods, and tornadoes also occur frequently and increase stress. However, merely experiencing a potentially stressful event does not mean that you will develop PTSD.

As recent research on loss and trauma illustrates, up to 90% of Americans report exposure to a traumatic event during their lifetime, but only 5 to 11% develop PTSD (Breslau & Kessler, 2001; Ozer et al., 2003). Even though witnessing a traumatic event may result in brief PTSD or subclinical stress (think about your own response on September 11, 2001), for most individuals,

these reactions disappear after a few months. Only a relatively small percentage of people exposed to a trauma actually develop PTSD. In the face of traumatic events such as the 9/11 terrorist attacks, the Oklahoma City bombing, or the Los Angeles riots, *recovery* (threshold or subthreshold psychopathology for a few months followed by a return to pretrauma levels) or *resilience* (maintaining a stable equilibrium in the face of the traumatic event) rather than PTSD was the predominant response (Bonanno, 2004). Researchers are now examining factors that predict (a) who will not recover, (b) what treatments are most likely to promote recovery, and (c) when those treatments should be applied.

What factors would you identify as important in the development of PTSD?

The third feature, *Real People, Real Disorders*, presents a popular figure who has suffered from the disorder discussed in the chapter. As we indicate in Chapter 1, although many people, including undergraduate students, suffer from these disorders, they often feel that they are alone or "weird." We wanted to break down the stereotypes that many undergraduate students have about people with psychological disorders. Using well-known figures to humanize these conditions allows students to connect with the material on an emotional, as well as an intellectual, level.

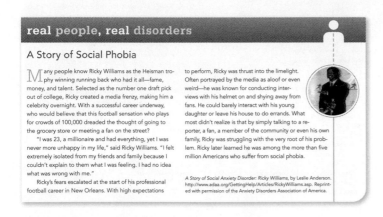

Intermediate and End of the Chapter Reviews

Finally, we would like to draw the reader's attention to the *Concept Checks* that are found throughout the chapter as well as the *Critical Issues to Remember* and *Test Yourself* sections at the end of each chapter. The *Concept Checks* provide quick reviews at the end of chapter sections, allowing students to be sure that they have mastered the material before proceeding to the next section. At the end of each chapter is *Critical Issues to Remember*, which provides an opportunity for us, as authors, to have a conversation with the students and to share what we see as the most important issues addressed in that chapter. Finally, *Test Yourself* provides another opportunity for students to review and master the material, using the format that they will most likely find on their class examinations.

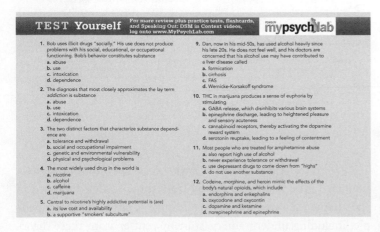

Teaching and Learning Package for Instructors

Test Item File authored by Christina Harnett at The Johns Hopkins University, this key support item has been rigorously developed to ensure the quality of both the questions and the answers. Each chapter includes a Total Assessment Guide (TAG) that lists all of the test items in an easy to use reference grid. The TAG organizes all test items by section so instructors can easily see the balance of questions available by subject and type (multiple choice, true/false, and essay).

MyTest The test item file comes with the NEW Pearson MyTest, a powerful assessment generation program that helps instructors easily create and print quizzes and exams. Questions and tests can be authored online, allowing instructors ultimate flexibility and the ability to efficiently manage assessments anytime, anywhere. For more information go to www.PearsonMyTest.com.

Instructor's Resource Manual authored by Ashlea R. Smith at Argosy University-Phoenix, offers an exhaustive collection of resources. Assets include: Lecture and Discussion suggestions, student activities, classroom demonstration ideas, handouts, and a full listing of readings, websites, and videos to integrate into your course, including the Speaking Out patient interview video segments.

Speaking Out: Interviews with People Who Struggle with Psychological Disorders, volumes I and II available now, volume III available spring of 2010.

This set of video segments allows students to see firsthand accounts of real patients with the various disorders described in their textbook. The interviews were conducted by licensed clinicians and range in length from 8 to 25 minutes. Disorders include major depressive disorder, obsessive-compulsive disorder, anorexia nervosa, PTSD, alcoholism, schizophrenia, autism, ADHD, bipolar disorder, social phobia, hypochondriasis, borderline personality disorder, aspergers, and much more. These videos are available on DVD for classroom use as well as through MyPsychLab. Volumes II and III now include both a patient interview as well as a second segment called "Day in the Life" which features interviews with friends, family, and co-workers to give a sense as to how the patient and loved ones deal with the disorder on a daily basis.

PowerPoint Lecture Slides with Classroom Response System Questions These slides are not only intended to be the basis for classroom lectures, but also for classroom discussions. The PPT slides concisely reinforce the content, and feature prominent figures from the text. The CRS questions are a great means to engage students in learning and facilitate the comprehension of text concepts.

All instructor assets are available in print and can also be found and downloaded from www.pearsonhighered.com/educator

MyPsychLab

This robust content management platform enables instructors to assign quizzes and tests, projects, and view those results online. Students also have access to a wealth of resources including chapter reviews, flashcards, research navigator, diagnostic tests, and the new Speaking Out: DSM in Context video product, which displays the Speaking Out videos and correlates the DSM criteria for that disorder. Students can better see the connection between the disorders and criteria as outlined by the DSM-IV. All instructor support materials can also be found on the "instructors" tab within MyPsychLab.

Resources for Students

MyPsychLab This exciting tool enables students to assess your understanding through a variety of pre and post tests along with chapter exams and get feedback immediately. Other resources to help you master the content include a dynamic ebook, flashcards, chapter summaries, and other media resources. In addition, students have access to the Speaking Out: DSM in Context video product, which displays the Speaking Out videos and correlates the DSM criteria for that disorder. Students can better see the connection between the disorders and criteria as outlined by the DSM-IV. Check it out at www.mypsychlab.com

Study Guide Authored by Jonathan R. Cook at the University of Missouri, this student resource includes numerous review and study questions along with other learning aids to help reinforce students' understanding of the concepts covered in the text.

Abnormal Psychology Casebook: A New Perspective (0-13-093787-8) This text, by Andrew R. Getzfeld, uses clear, accessible language and explanations, and features real cases based on a variety of psychopathologies—all involving patients/clients from a wide variety of cultural, ethnic, racial, religious, social, and socioeconomic backgrounds—and all based on the author's own experiences as a practicing social worker and psychologist.

Case Studies in Abnormal Behavior, 8/E (0-205-59416-6)
Robert G. Meyer, University of Louisville
L. Kevin Chapman, University of Louisville
Christopher M. Weaver, US Dept. of Veterans Affairs—Palo Alto & Stanford University
This rich collection of case studies integrates contemporary and recognizable classic cases to illustrate a wide range of clinical and legal issues related to abnormal psychology.

Case Studies in Abnormal Psychology bring the field of abnormal psychology to life for students with its rare combination of readability, humor, and strong scholarship.

To enable students to more fully understand the nature of the disorder, each case in this book contains the full background material relevant to etiological, diagnostic, and therapeutic considerations. Also, significant family and social history data are presented in order to give students a clear picture of how specific behavior patterns were generated and maintained.

CourseSmart eTextbook This new Pearson Choice offers students an online subscription to Abnormal Psychology, first Edition at a 50% savings. With the CourseSmart WebBook, students can search the text, make notes online, print out reading assignments that incorporate lecture notes, and bookmark important passages. Ask your Pearson sales representative for details, or visit www.coursesmart.com.

acknowledgments

This book began with the vision of our mentor and friend, Samuel M. Turner, Ph.D. He was the one who believed that the book could be written, convinced us to write it with him, and contributed substantially to the initial book prospectus. Following his untimely death, we asked ourselves if we could and should continue. We knew that Sam would not quit, and this book is our way of honoring him and his lasting influence on us.

We each met Sam and each other over 20 years ago when the three of us were in various stages of graduate training under his tutelage at Western Psychiatric Institute and Clinic (WPIC), University of Pittsburgh School of Medicine. We want to thank David Kupfer, M.D. who was Director of Research at WPIC at that time, for creating the cross-disciplinary and fertile research environment that allowed us to learn and grow. We are also grateful to the other scientist-practitioners who mentored us at various stages of our under-graduate and graduate careers: Alan Bellack, Michel Hersen, Stephen Hinshaw, Alan Kazdin, and Sheldon Korchin.

Second, we want to thank our editor, Jeff Marshall, for his enthusiasm, support, and patience throughout this process. He understood the personal loss of our friend but never doubted that we could still produce a quality book. He taught us much about the process and yet kept us true to our vision. Jeff's good humor was a constant source of support throughout the writing and editing process. A special thanks to Betty Gatewood, our developmental editor, who served as both task master and fairy godmother. When our scientist sides started to dominate, Betty helped us transform our stark scientific writing into readable and reachable language. Thanks to Rochelle Diogenes, Editor-in-Chief of Development, who also believed in us, always gave us the best advice and made sure we had the resources that we needed to deliver a quality project. We also thank the marketing, development, and production staff at Pearson—Brandy Dawson, Rebecca Dunn, Erin Grelak, Nicole Kunzmann, Leah Jewell, Maureen Prado-Roberts, Maureen Richardson, Martha Shearer, Roberta Sherman, and Amy Trudell; their first-class professionalism and devotion to this project was unbelievable. Thanks also to Anne DeMarinis, our book designer whose work can only be described by the words "visionary," "magnificent," and "cool."

Third, a big thank you to our students, colleagues, and friends who listened endlessly, smiled supportively, and waited patiently as we said once again "next month will be easier." In particular, thanks go to Diane Mentrikoski, Lindsay Scharfstein, Lauren Reba-Harrelson, Michelle Crisafulli, Xiaofei Mo, M. D., and Carole Chvarla, Ph.D., for their technical assistance on the book. To our colleagues, Candice Alfano, Ph.D., Armando Pina, Ph.D., Carl Lejuez, Ph.D., and Michael Kauth, Ph.D.—your professional contributions were immeasurable.

Fourth, we are grateful to our patients and their families whose life journeys or bumps along life's road we have shared. Good psychologists never stop learning. Each new clinical experience adds to our knowledge and understanding of the ill-nesses we seek to treat. We thank our patients and families for sharing their struggles and their successes with us and for the unique opportunity to learn from their experience. It is an honor and a privilege to have worked with each of them.

Fifth, we thank our spouses, Ed Beidel, Patrick Sullivan, and Bill Ehrenstrom, children (Brendan, Emily, Natalie, Brendan and Jacob), and families who waited patiently these last three years so we could bring this book to fruition. There are three names on the title page but without their love and support, that page would be blank.

As authors, each of us feels enormous gratitude to our co-authors for their tireless work and dedication to this project. Abnormal psychology is a broad topic, requiring ever-increasing specialization. Having colleagues who share an orientation but possess distinct areas of expertise represents a rare and joyful collaborative experience.

Text and Content Reviewers

We would like to thank the following colleagues who reviewed our manuscript and gave us a great many helpful suggestions: John Dale Alden, Lipscomb University; Rahan Ali, Penn State University; Jay Alperson, Palomar Community College; Jeffrey Baker, Monroe Community College; Rochelle Balter, John Jay College of Criminal Justice; Catherine Barnard, Kalamazoo Valley Community College; Keith Beard, Marshall University; Bethann Bierer, Metropolitan State College of Denver; Risa Blair, Miami Dade College; Rebecca Blais, University of Utah; Kathleen Bonnelle, Lansing Community College; Pamela Brouillard, Texas A&M Corpus Christi; Tracie Burke, Christian Brothers University; Mia Smith Bynum, Purdue University;

Glenn Callaghan, San Jose State University; Richard Cavasina, California University of PA; Amy Claxton, Arkansas State University; Lorry Cology, Owens Community College; Jonathan Cook, University of Missouri; Andrew Corso, Hofstra University; Pamela Costa, Tacoma Community College; Joseph A. Davis, Alliant University; W. Paul Deal, Missouri State University; Frederic Desmond, University of Florida; Michael DeVries, Trinity Christian College; Victor Duarte, North Idaho College; Brenda East, Durham Technical Community College; Diane Finley, Prince George's Community College; Linda Fleming, Gannon University; Michele Galietta, John Jay College of Criminal Justice; Anthony Goreczny, Chatham University; John C. Hallock, Pima Community College; Kevin Handley, Germanna Community College; Sheryl Hartman, Miami Dade College; Susan Hastings, Hope International University; Jim A. Haugh, Rowan University; Leo Herrman, Fort Hays State University; Julian Hertzdog, William Woods University; Jameson K. Hirsch, East Tennessee State University; Robert Hoff, Mercyhurst College; Debra Hollister, Valencia Community College; Robert C. Intrieri, Western Illinois University; George-Harold Jennings, Drew University; Jennifer Katz, SUNY Geneseo; Kevin Keating, Broward College; Scott Keiller, Kent State University-Tuscarawas; Lynne Kemen, Hunter College; Meredith Kneavel, Chestnut Hill College; Albert Lampasso, John Jay College of Criminal Justice; Jonathan S. Lang, Borough of Manhattan Community College, CUNY; Robert Lawyer, Delgado Community College; Trisha Lavigne, Glendale Community College; Freda Liu, Arizona State University; Marty Lloyd, University of Minnesota; Arthur Lurigio, Loyola University; Toby Marx, Union County College; Cathy McDaniels Wilson, Xavier University; Donna McEwen, Friends University; John McIlvried, University of Indianapolis; Michael McRae, UNC-Chapel Hill; Troy Melende, Arizona State University; C. Michael Nina, William Paterson University; Susan Nolan, Seton Hall University; Jill Norvilitis, Buffalo State College; Edward J. O'Brien, Marywood University; Theresa Odom, Burlington County College; Arthur Olguin, Santa Barbara City College; Augustine Osman, University of Northern Iowa; Crystal Park, University of Connecticut; Jeffrey J. Pedroza, Santa Ana College; Michelle Pilati, Rio Hondo College; Dongxiao Qin, Western New England College; Sean Patrick Reilley, Morehead State University; Liz Reiss, Baruch College; Karen Clay Rhines, Northampton Community College; Ken Rice, University of Florida; Kimble Richardson, University of Indianapolis; Vicki Ritts, St. Louis Community College—Meramec; Rochelle Robbins, Holy Family University; James Rodgers, Hawkeye Community College; Jennifer Rohling, University of South Alabama; Emily B. Russell, Loyola University New Orleans; Ronald A. Salazar, San Juan College; Shara Sand, LaGuardia Community College; Joseph D Sclafani, University of Tampa; Frances Shen, University of Illinois-Springfield; Erik Shumaker, Washington University; Nancy Simpson, Trident Technical College; Ashlea Smith, Phoenix College & Paradise Valley Community College; Jessica Snowden, Loyola University; Michael Spiegler, Providence College; George Spilich, Washington College; Amy Spilkin, San Diego State University; Mary Starke, Ramapo College; Stephanie Stein, Central Washington University; Lindsay Ross Stewart, Saint Francis University; Alexandra Stillman, St. Paul College; Debra Swodoba, York College (CUNY); Jennifer L. Tackett, University of Toronto; Ruddy Taylor, University of Alaska Anchorage; David Topor, The Warren Alpert Medical School of Brown University; Albert Tuskenis, Governors State University; Tina Pittman Wagers, University of Colorado Boulder; Rebekah Wanic, Cuyamaca College; Frederick Wassel, Quinsigamond Community College; Gordon Whitman, Tidewater Community College; Monica Williams, University of Pennsylvania; David Wolitzky, New York University; Anthony Zoccolillo, The College of NJ. Thank you for your constructive comments and for the time you took to review our work. We all have so much to do, and we are grateful that you gave of your time to make this a much better final product.

Focus Group Participants

Thank you to the following professors for participating in our focus groups: Jeffrey Baker, Monroe Community College; Rochelle Balter, John Jay College of Criminal Justice; Risa Blair, Miami Dade College; Pamela Brouillard, Texas A&M Corpus Christi; Amy Claxton, Arkansas State University; Andrew Corso, Hofstra University; Frederic Desmond, University of Florida; Michael DeVries, Trinity Christian College; Diane Finley, Prince George's Community College; Anthony Goreczny, Chatham University; George-Harold Jennings, Drew University; Sheryl Hartman, Miami Dade College; Jameson K. Hirsch, East Tennessee State University; Scott Keiller, Kent State University, Tuscarawas; Albert Lampasso, John Jay College; Trisha Lavigne, Glendale Community College; Freda Liu, Arizona State University; Cathy McDaniels Wilson, Xavier University; John McIlvried, University of Indianapolis. Troy Melende, Arizona State University; Crystal Park, University of Connecticut; Jeffrey J. Pedroza, Santa Ana College; Dongxiao Qin, Western New England College; Liz Reiss, Baruch College; Ken Rice, University of Florida; Rochelle Robbins, Holy Family University; Emily B. Russell, Loyola University, New Orleans; Shara Sand, LaGuardia Community College; Frances Shen,

College of Liberal Arts & Sciences; Ashlea Smith, Phoenix College & Paradise Valley Community College; Mary Starke, Ramapo College; Alexandra Stillman, St. Paul College; Jennifer L. Tackett, University of Toronto; Ruddy Taylor, University of Alaska Anchorage; Albert Tuskenis, Governors State University; Frederick Wassel, Quinsigamond Community College.

Cover Survey Respondents

Thank you to the following professors for participating in the cover survey: Kenneth Abrams, Kathy Adair, Regg Adkisson, Richard Alexander, Nicole Allgood, Kathryn Alves-Labore, Timothy Atchison, Lara Ault, Thomas Bailey, Michelle Barnett, Paul Bartoli, Michael Becker, Kelvin Bentley, Pam Birrell, Jerry Bockoven, Stephanie Boyd, Michael Boyle, Seth Brown, Tracie Burke, Regina Burkhart, Mandi Burnette, Krisanne Bursik, Maryann Bush, Mia Smith Bynum, Roxana Carlo, Sarah Cavanagh, Marc Celentana, Sharon Chacon-Mineau, Roger Chadwick, C. Charles, Kristen Cole, Lorry Cology, Melanie Conti, Patrick Courtney, Robert Cruickshank, William Deal, Kyle De Young, Marla Domino, Victor Duarte, Sarah Ducey, Stacey Dunn, Wendy Dunn, Yulia Dutton, Valerie Eastman, Penny Edwards, Runae Edwards-Wilson, Ron Eltzeroth, Kristi Erdal, Robert Fauber, Jeannine Feldman, Kathleen Felton, Pamela Fergus, Randy Floyd, Sue Frantz, Rhonda Frazelle, Roger Gaddis, Paul Galvin, Margaret Gleeson, William Gottdiener, Larry Grimm, Seth Grossman, Suzanne Gurland, John Gutowski, Ruth Hallongren, Kevin Handley, Susan Harvey, Mary Haskett, Susan Hastings, Kathleen Hathaway, William Hathaway, Steven Hayduk, Robert Hayes, Lynda Heiden, Peter Hendricks, Marc Henley, Leo Herrman, Melanie Hetzel-Riggin, Sam Hill, Michael Hillard, Sandra Hinko, Richard Hirschman, Mia Holland, Susan Howell, Peter Hurd, Khalil Islam-Zwart, Susan Jacobs, Patricia D. Johnson, Lance Jones, Samuel Jones, Jyotsna Kalavar, Yasmine Kalkstein, Paul Karoly, Kei Kawashiima-Ginsberg, Richard Kellogg, Kathryn Kelly, Mike Kelly, Hayden Kepley, Kenn Kerr, Ken Kikuchi, Rosalyn King, Ed Kingston, Meredith Kneavel, Mate-Kole, Radhika Krishnamurthy, Warren Lambert, Travis Langley, Cindy Lausberg, Trisha Lavigne, Richard Leavy, Penny Leisring, Sue Leung, Judith Levine, Heather Littleton, Kristi Lockhart, Dina Lofaro, Cynthia Lofaso, Kenneth Lombart, Chris Long, Sheryl Lozowski-Sullivan, Wade Lueck, Jason Lyons, Mikhail Lyubansky, Ricardo Machon, Michelle Majewski, John Malacos, Jeanne Marecek, Naomi Marmorstein, Monica Marsee, Toby Marx, Kevin Masters, Keith Matthews, Jack Maxfield, Susan McClenny, Donna McEwen, Mike McVay, Olivia Melroe, Jan Mendoza, Kanoa Meriwether, Terri Messman-Moore, Bryan

Midgley, Joni Mihura, Leslie Minor, Karen Miranda, Michael Miranda, Sarah Moesbergen, Janet Morahan-Martin, Robin Morgan, Rose Morgan-Woody, Karen Muir, Paulina Multhaupt, Karla Murdock, Robin Musselman, Kevin Myers, Jacquie Napurano, Lynn Neely, Paul Neunuebel, Carmelo Michael Nina, Matthew Nock, Susan Nolan, Jill Norvilitis, Peggy Norwood, Raymond Novaco, Claire Novosad, Carlota Ocampo, Laura Ochoa, Arthur Olguin, Patricia Oswald, Patricia Owen, Jelena Ozegovic, John Pachankis, Peggy Pack, Linda Palm, Robin Parritz, Joan Paterna, Jeffrey Pedroza, La Tania Peoples-Love, Rahsheda Perine, Greg Perlman, Kathi Peterson, L. Pfaff, Ralph Pifer, Lloyd Pilkington, Tina Pittman Wagers, Jeff Platt, Katherine Presnell, Susan Putnam, Kelly Quinn, Janice Rafalowski, Vi Rajagopalan, Kilduff Raymond, Lourie Reichenberg, Jacki Reihman, Sean Reilley, Karen Rhines, Nancy Rich, Raysa Richardson, Sabrina Rieder, Laura Ringer, Vicki Ritts, Keith Roach, Rochelle Robbins, Thomas Rodebaugh, James Rodgers, Kathleen Rogers, Mitchel Rose, Rosann Ross, Lindsay Ross-Stewart, John Rowe, Ron Salazar, Patricia Sandick, Stephen Saunders, Laura Scaletta, Anne Schell, Carrie Scherzer, Tom Schoeneman, Nadja Schreiber Compo, Mark Sciutto, Joe Sclafani, Gwendolyn Scott, William Scott, Sharon Sears, Sandra Sego, Larry Sensenig, Jennie Sharf, Vivian Shulman, Erik Shumaker, Mark Sibicky, Lee Skeens, Janet Smith, Laurie Smith, James Smolin, Jessica Snowden, Kandy Stahl, Stephanie Stein, Wayne Stein, Laura Stephenson, Betsy Stern, Xuan Stevens, Richard Stoner, Glenn Sullivan, Lynda Szymanski, Amber Tatnall, Andrew Terranova, Pamela Thacher, Rick Thompson, Tom Tiegs, Jeanne Tinsley, Sandra Todaro, Tanya Tompkins, Lucas Torres, Sarah Trost, Theresa Tylka, Karl Ullrich, Denise Valenti Hein, Karolyn Van Putten, Lora Vasiliauskas, William G. Vasquez, Steven Verney, Amber Vesotski, Paul Vonnahme, Marie Walker, Randall Walker, Michael Walraven, Anthony Walsh, Rebekah Wanic, Scott Weaver, Julia Whisenhunt, Ginger Wickline, Noelle Wiersma, Robert Wildblood, Jeff Willner, Steve Withrow, Katie Woehl, Susan Wolle, Pamela Woodruff, Lucinda Woodward, Jennifer Wright, Tuppett Yates, Mahbobeh Yektaparast, Kathleen Young, Peter Zachar, Robert Zettle, Anthony Zoccolillo, Valerie Zurawski.

Finally, we want to mention the students and instructors who will use this text. We hope you experience the joy and wonder that comes with learning about the challenging and intriguing topic of abnormal psychology. We are passionate about our field and compassionate with our patients. We are also dedicated educators. As such, we encourage you to contact us with comments, questions, or suggestions on how to improve this book. We value your opinions.

about the authors

DEBORAH C. BEIDEL received her Ph.D. in 1986 from the University of Pittsburgh, completing her predoctoral internship and postdoctoral fellowship at Western Psychiatric Institute and Clinic. Before joining the faculty at the University of Central Florida where she is Professor of Psychology and Director of the Doctoral Program in Clinical Psychology at the University of Central Florida, she was on the faculty at the University of Pittsburgh, Medical University of South Carolina, University of Maryland—College Park, and Penn State College of Medicine-Hershey Medical Center. Currently, she holds American Board of Professional Psychology (ABPP) Diplomates in Clinical Psychology and Behavioral Psychology and is a Fellow of the American Psychological Association, the American Psychopathological Association, and the Association for Psychological Science. She is a past Chair of the American Psychological Association's Committee on Accreditation, the 1990 recipient of the Association for Advancement of Behavior Therapy's New Researcher Award, and the 2007 recipient of the Samuel M. Turner Clinical Researcher Award from the American Psychological Association. While at the University of Pittsburgh, Dr. Beidel was twice awarded the "Apple for the Teacher Citation" by her students for outstanding classroom teaching. In 1995, she was the recipient of the Distinguished Educator Award from the Association of Medical School Psychologists. She is the Associate Editor of the Journal of Anxiety Disorders author of over 200 scientific publications, including journal articles, book chapters, and books, including *Childhood Anxiety Disorders: A Guide to Research and Treatment* and *Shy Children Phobic Adults: The Nature and Treatment of Social Anxiety Disorder*. Her academic, research, and clinical interests focus on child, adolescent and adult anxiety disorders, including their etiology, psychopathology, and behavioral interventions. Her research is characterized by a developmental focus, and includes high-risk and longitudinal designs, psychophysiological assessment, treatment development, and treatment outcome. She is the recipient of numerous grants from the National Institute of Mental Health and the Autism Speaks Foundation. At the University of Central Florida, she teaches abnormal psychology at both the undergraduate and graduate level.

CYNTHIA M. BULIK is the Jordan Distinguished Professor of Eating Disorders in the Department of Psychiatry in the School of Medicine at the University of North Carolina at Chapel Hill, where she is also Professor of Nutrition in the Gillings School of Global Public Health and the Director of the UNC Eating Disorders Program. A clinical psychologist by training, Dr. Bulik has been conducting research and treating individuals with eating disorders since 1982. She received her B.A. from the University of Notre Dame and her M.A. and Ph.D. from the University of California at Berkeley. She completed internships and postdoctoral fellowships at the Western Psychiatric Institute and Clinic in Pittsburgh, Pennsylvania. She developed outpatient, partial hospitalization, and inpatient services for eating disorders both in New Zealand and the United States. Her research has included treatment, laboratory, epidemiological, twin, and molecular genetic studies of eating disorders and body weight regulation. More recently, she has begun to explore innovative means of integrating technology into treatment for eating disorders and obesity in order to broaden the public health reach of interventions. She is the Director of the first NIMH-sponsored Post-Doctoral Training Program in Eating Disorders. She has active research collaborations throughout the United States as well as in Canada, New Zealand, Germany, Australia, Norway, Sweden, Finland, Holland, Spain, Italy, the United Kingdom, and Germany. Dr. Bulik has written over 300 scientific papers and chapters on eating disorders and is author of the books *Eating Disorders: Detection and Treatment* (Dunmore), *Runaway Eating: The 8 Point Plan to Conquer Adult Food and Weight Obsessions* (Rodale), and *Crave: Why You Binge Eat and How To Stop* (Walker). She is a recipient of the Eating Disorders Coalition Research Award, the Hulka Innovators Award, the Academy for Eating Disorders Leadership Award for Research, the Price Family National Eating Disorders Association Research Award, the Carolina Women's Center Women's Advocacy Award, and the Women's Leadership Council Faculty-to-Faculty Mentorship Award. She is a past President of the Academy for Eating Disorders, past Vice-President of the Eating Disorders Coalition, and past Associate Editor of the *International Journal of Eating Disorders*. Dr. Bulik holds the first endowed professorship in eating disorders in the United States. She balances her academic life by being happily married with three children and an ice dancer.

MELINDA STANLEY, Ph.D., is Professor and Head of the Division of Psychology in the Menninger Department of Psychiatry and Behavioral Sciences at Baylor College of Medicine. She holds The McIngvale Family Chair in Obsessive Compulsive Disorder Research and a secondary appointment as Professor in the Department of Medicine. Dr. Stanley is a clinical psychologist and senior mental health services researcher within the Houston Center for Quality of Care and Utilization Studies (HCQCUS), Michael E. DeBakey Veterans Affairs Medical Center, Houston, and an affiliate investigator for the South Central Mental Illness Research, Education, and Clinical Center (MIRECC). Before joining the faculty at Baylor, she was Professor of Psychiatry at the University of Texas Health Science Center at Houston, where she served as Director of the Psychology Internship program. Dr. Stanley completed an internship and postdoctoral fellowship at Western Psychiatric Institute and Clinic, University of Pittsburgh School of Medicine. She received a Ph.D. from Texas Tech University, an M.A. from Princeton University, and a B.A. from Gettysburg College, where she was a Phi Beta Kappa and summa cum laude graduate.

Dr. Stanley's research interests involve the identification and treatment of anxiety and depressive disorders in older adults. Her current focus is on the provision of services in primary care and the development of treatment modifications to meet the needs of patients with dementia and those in community settings where the mental health needs of older patients often remain unrecognized and undertreated. Some of this work includes the integration of religion and spirituality into therapy. Dr. Stanley and her colleagues have been awarded continuous funding from the National Institute of Mental Health (NIMH) for 14 years to support her research in late-life anxiety.

In 2008, Dr. Stanley received the Excellence in Research Award from the South Central MIRECC. In 2009, she received the MIRECC Excellence in Research Education Award. She has received numerous teaching awards and has served as mentor for five junior faculty career development awards. Dr. Stanley is a Fellow of the American Psychological Association, and she has served as a regular reviewer of NIMH grants. She is the author of over 150 scientific publications, including journal articles, book chapters, and books.

CHAPTER objectives

At the end of this chapter, you should be able to:

1 Explain the difference between behaviors that are different, deviant, dangerous, and dysfunctional.

2 Identify at least two factors that need to be considered when determining whether a behavior is abnormal.

3 Discuss spiritual/religious, biological, psychological, and sociocultural theories of the origins of abnormal behavior in their historical context.

4 Discuss the scientist-practitioner approach to abnormal psychology.

5 Describe the biological, psychological, social, and biopsychosocial perspectives on the origins of abnormal behavior.

abnormal psychology:
historical and modern perspectives

Steve was a Marine who served during the Vietnam War. He spent a year on patrol, constantly on lookout for the enemy. One night, the Viet Cong attacked his squad. During the firefight, the Marine next to him lost his arm. Steve got his buddy to the medic, but the horrific image never left him. He felt helpless and out of control. After returning from Vietnam, Steve had difficulty sleeping, lost interest in his hobbies, isolated himself from family and friends, and felt helpless and sad. Even 40 years later, he can still see himself in the rice paddy, watching in horror as the grenade hits his friend, amputating his arm. Every night he wakes in yet another cold sweat and with a racing heart—unable to breathe, as the nightmare occurs again. Steve cannot watch fireworks—he breaks out in a cold sweat and feels dizzy. He drops to the ground at the sound of a helicopter, reacting as if he were again under attack. He sleeps only 4 hours a night. Although employed for many years, he had many interpersonal conflicts with co-workers and his boss, and recently he was forced into early retirement. He has no friends except for his immediate family and other veterans who served in Vietnam.

Derek is 7 years old. From the time he was an infant, he was always "on the go." He has a hard time paying attention and has boundless energy. He is always in trouble, and his favorite expression is "but Mom, it was an accident" as he again breaks something because he is moving too fast. His parents compensate for his high level of energy by involving him in lots of physical activities (soccer, Tiger Cub Scouts, karate). He loves being with other children, but they often shun him because he cannot follow simple social rules. Derek had a wonderfully understanding first-grade teacher. Because he could not sit still, the teacher accommodated him with "workstations" so that he could move around the classroom whenever he felt the need. But now Derek is in second grade, and the new teacher does not allow workstations. She feels that he must learn to sit like all the other children. He visits the principal's office often for "out of seat behavior" and comes home crying because "none of the other kids like me." Although he seems intellectually bright and genuinely nice, he is failing in school and the teacher insists that he should be placed in a classroom for emotionally disturbed children.

Marcie just started college. She grew up in a small town but enrolled in a large university far from home. Her family has few financial resources, and a university scholarship was her only opportunity for college. She was reluctant to leave home, but her family and teachers encouraged her because it was a tremendous opportunity. Marcie is having difficulty adjusting to her new environment and describes herself as "severely homesick." She is very sad, cries for no reason, and has stopped attending classes. She believes that she is a failure for being unable to adjust and is afraid to tell her parents. She barely talks to her roommate, who is very concerned about the change in her behavior. Marcie no longer takes a shower. Sometimes she does not get out of bed and goes for several days without eating. She talks about being "better off dead."

The physical, cognitive, and behavioral symptoms displayed by Steve, Derek, and Marcie represent common emotional disorders. These behaviors are considered abnormal because most people do not want to take their life and they sleep more than 4 hours a night. Most children are able to sit still in a classroom. Though often unrecognized, psychological disorders exist in substantial numbers, across all ages, races, ethnic groups, and cultures, and in both sexes. Furthermore, they cause great suffering and impair academic, occupational, and social functioning.

Defining abnormality is challenging because behaviors must be considered in context. For example,

Donna and Matthew were very much in love. They had been married for 25 years and often remarked that they were not just husband and wife, but best friends. Then Matthew died suddenly, and Donna felt overwhelming sadness. She was unable to eat, cried uncontrollably at times, and started to isolate herself from others. Her usually vivacious personality disappeared.

When a loved one dies, feelings of grief and sadness are common, even expected. Donna's reaction at her husband's death would not be considered abnormal; rather, its *absence* at such a time might be considered abnormal. Consider how even though Donna and Marcie's depressive behaviors are similar, their circumstances are different. A theme throughout this book is that abnormal behavior must always be considered in context.

Normal vs. Abnormal Behavior

Sometimes it's fairly easy to identify behavior as abnormal, as when someone is still deeply troubled by events that happened 40 years ago or is feeling so hopeless that she can't get out of bed. However, in other cases it is not so easy. This is the challenge for those who attempt to define abnormal behavior. Put simply, abnormal means "away from normal," but that is simply a circular definition. By this standard, normal becomes the statistical average and any deviation becomes "abnormal." For example, if the average weight for a woman living in the United States is 140 pounds, then women who weigh less than 100 pounds or more than 250 pounds deviate significantly from the average. Their weight would be considered abnormally low or high. For abnormal psychology, defining abnormal behavior as merely being away from normal assumes that deviations on both sides of average are negative and in need of alteration or intervention. This assumption is often incorrect. Specifically, we must first ask the question, is simply being different abnormal?

IS BEING DIFFERENT ABNORMAL?

Many people deviate from the average in some way. Yao Ming is 7 feet 5 inches tall and weighs 295 pounds—far above average in both height and weight. However, his deviant stature does not affect him negatively. To the contrary, he is a successful and highly paid basketball player in the National Basketball Association. Mariah Carey has an abnor-

mal vocal range—she is one of a few singers whose voice spans five octaves. Because of her different ability, she has sold millions of CDs. Professor Stephen Hawking, one of the world's most brilliant scientists, has an intellectual capacity that exceeds that of virtually everyone else, yet he writes best-selling and popular works about theoretical physics and the universe. He does this despite suffering from Amyotrophic Lateral Sclerosis (ALS, also known as Lou Gehrig's disease), a debilitating and progressive neurological disease. Each of these individuals has abilities that distinguish him or her from the general public; that is, they are "away from normal." However, their "abnormalities" (unusual abilities) are not negative; rather, they result in positive contributions to society. Furthermore, their unusual abilities do not cause distress or appear to impair their daily functioning (as appears to be the case for Steve, Derek, and Marcie). In summary, being different is not equivalent to being psychologically abnormal.

Yao Ming, Mariah Carey, and Stephen Hawking differ from most people (in height, vocal range, and intelligence, respectively). However, these differences have resulted in positive contributions to society and are not abnormalities.

IS BEHAVING DEVIANTLY (DIFFERENTLY) ABNORMAL?

When the definition of abnormal behavior broadens from simply *being* different to *behaving* differently, we often use the term *deviance*. Deviant behaviors differ from prevailing societal standards.

On February 9, 1964, four young men from Liverpool, England, appeared on the Ed Sullivan Show and created quite a stir. Their hair was "long," their boots had "high (Cuban) heels," and their "music" was loud. Young people loved them but parents were appalled.

The Beatles looked, behaved, and sounded deviant in the context of the prevailing cultural norms. In 1964, they were considered outrageous. Today, their music, dress, and behavior appear rather tame. Was their behavior abnormal? They looked different and acted differently, but their looks and behavior did no harm to themselves or others. The same behavior, outrageous and different in 1964 but tame by today's standards, illustrates an important point—deviant behavior violates societal and cultural norms, but those norms are always changing.

Understanding behavior within a specific context is known as **goodness-of-fit** (Chess & Thomas, 1991). Simply put, a behavior can be problematic or not problematic depending on the environment in which it occurs. Some people will change an environment to accommodate a behavior in the same way that buildings are modified to assure accessibility by everyone. Derek's situation illustrates the goodness-of-fit concept. At home and in first grade, his parents and teacher changed the environment to meet his

goodness-of-fit the idea that behavior is problematic or not problematic depending on the environment in which it occurs

high activity level. They did not see his activity as a problem, but simply as behavior that needed to be accommodated. In contrast, his second-grade teacher expected Derek to fit an unadaptable environment. In first grade, Derek was considered "lively," but in second grade his behavior was considered abnormal. When we attempt to understand behavior, it is critical to consider the context in which the behavior occurs.

Group Expectations The expectations of family, friends, neighborhood, and culture are consistent and pervasive influences on why people act the way they do. Sometimes the standards of one group are at odds with those of another group. Adolescents, for example, often deliberately behave very differently from their parents (they violate expected standards or norms) as a result of their need to *individuate* (separate) from their parents and be part of their peer group. In this instance, deviation from the norms of one group involves conformity to those of another. Like family norms, cultural traditions and practices also affect behavior in many ways. For example, holiday celebrations usually include family and cultural traditions. As young people mature and leave their family of origin, new traditions from extended family, marriage, or friendships often become blended into former customs and traditions, creating a new context for holiday celebrations.

Often, these different cultural traditions are unremarkable, but sometimes they can cause misunderstanding:

Maleah is 12 years old. Her family recently moved to the United States from the Philippines. Her teacher insisted that Maleah's mother take her to see a psychologist because of "separation anxiety." The teacher was concerned because Maleah told the teacher that she always slept in bed with her grandmother. However, a psychological evaluation revealed that Maleah did not have any separation fears. Rather, children sleeping with parents and/or grandparents is normative in Philippine culture.

Culture refers to shared behavioral patterns and lifestyles that differentiate one group of people from another. Culture affects an individual's behavior but also is reciprocally changed by the behaviors of its members (Tseng, 2003). We often behave in ways that reflect the values of the culture in which we were raised. For example, in some cultures, children are expected to be "seen and not heard," whereas in other cultures, children are encouraged to freely express themselves. **Culture-bound illness** is a term that originally described abnormal behaviors that were specific to a particular location or group (Yap, 1967); however, we now know that some of these behavioral patterns extend across ethnic groups and geographic areas. How culture influences behavior will be a recurring theme throughout this book, and Maleah's behavior is just one example of how a single behavior can be viewed differently in two different cultures.

Development and Maturity Another important context that must be taken into account when considering behavioral abnormality is age. As a child matures (physically, mentally, and emotionally), behaviors previously considered developmentally appropriate, and therefore normal, can become abnormal.

Nick is 4 years old and insists on using a night light to keep the monsters away.

At age 4, children do not have the *cognitive*, or mental, capacity to understand fully that monsters are not real. However, at age 12, a child should understand the difference between imagination and reality. Therefore, if at age 12 Nick still needs a night light to keep the monsters away, his behavior would be considered abnormal and perhaps in need of treatment. Similarly, very young children do not have the ability to control their bladder; bedwetting is common in toddlerhood. However, after the child achieves a certain level of physical and cognitive maturity, bedwetting becomes an abnormal behavior and is given the diagnostic label of *enuresis* (see Chapter 12).

4–12
BIRTH   20   40   60   80

culture   shared behavioral patterns and lifestyles that differentiate one group of people from another

culture-bound illness   abnormal behaviors that are specific to a particular location or group

real people, real disorders

Ted Kaczynski (the Unabomber)

Over a period of 18 years (1978–1995), Theodore John (Ted) Kaczynski killed 3 people and wounded 29 others with a series of mail bombs. A brilliant mathematician, he became disillusioned with technology and moved to an isolated area of Montana where he lived in a cabin without electricity or running water (below). He justified the mail bombs as a fight against the evils of technology and progress. Although Kaczynski rejected the use of an insanity defense by his lawyer, a court-appointed psychiatrist diagnosed his behavior as *paranoid schizophrenia*, a serious mental disorder (see Chapter 10), but he was considered competent to stand trial. He was convicted and is serving life in prison without the possibility of parole. Leaving civilized society to live alone in a primitive cabin certainly could qualify as eccentric behavior, but does that mean that he was psychologically disturbed?

Kaczynski was academically gifted; he entered Harvard at age 16 and specialized in a field of mathematics few others understood. He was socially reclusive, unable to "connect" with others. Is merely preferring solitude rather than social interaction abnormal behavior?

Kaczynski believed that technical progress was undesirable and imposed unnatural demands on people. Living without modern technology would allow a happier, simpler life. Prepared to live out his life alone, he became angry as progress intruded into his wilderness area. So he decided to get revenge. Is this irrational thinking?

The targets of his bombs were professors, airline officials, computer stores, and an advertising executive, none of whom were responsible for the intrusion into his wilderness. Does this thinking and behavior cross the line between sanity and insanity?

From all accounts, Kaczynski was a social misfit, an eccentric, whose behavior evolved from behaving differently to behaving dangerously (perhaps as a result of disordered thinking). In this instance, his behavior was extremely harmful to others and could no longer be considered merely eccentric. It is also important to point out that most people who have psychological disorders are not dangerous and do not commit crimes or attempt to harm other people.

Eccentricity. What about the millionaire who leaves his entire estate to his dog? This behavior violates cultural norms, but it is often labeled eccentric rather than abnormal. Eccentric behavior may violate societal norms but is not always negative or harmful to others. Yet, as in the case of Ted Kaczynski (the Unabomber), sometimes behaviors that initially appear eccentric cross the line into dangerousness (see the box "Real People, Real Disorders: Ted Kaczynski").

IS BEHAVING DANGEROUSLY ABNORMAL?

The police arrive at the emergency room of a psychiatric hospital with a man and a woman in handcuffs. Jon is 23 years old. He identifies himself as the chauffeur for Melissa, who is age 35 and also in handcuffs. They are both dressed in tight leather pants and shirts, with unusual "spiked" haircuts and wearing leather "dog collars" with many silver spikes. Jon and Melissa live in the suburbs but spent a day in the city, buying clothes and getting their hair cut. As they were leaving the parking garage to return home, Melissa began to criticize Jon's hair. Jon became angry and ran the car (which belonged to

Melissa) into the wall of the parking garage—several times. When a clinician asked the police officer why they were brought to the psychiatric emergency room, the officer replied, "Well, would a sane person keep ramming a car into the wall of a parking garage?" Neither Jon nor Melissa had any previous history of psychological disorders. An interview revealed that Jon's behavior was the result of a lover's quarrel, and although their relationship was often volatile, they denied any incidents of physical aggression toward each other or anyone else.

Certainly, repeatedly ramming a car into the wall of a parking garage is dangerous, outside of societal norms, and could be labeled abnormal. Dangerous behavior can result from intense emotional states, and in Jon's case the behavior was directed outwardly (toward another person or an inanimate object). In other cases, dangerous behavior such as Marcie's suicidal thoughts may be directed toward oneself. However, it is important to understand that most people with psychological disorders do not engage in dangerous behavior (Linaker, 2000; Monahan, 2001). Individuals with seriously disordered thinking rarely present any danger to society, even though their behaviors may appear dangerous to others. Therefore, behavior that is dangerous may signal the presence of a psychological disorder, but dangerous behavior alone is not necessary or sufficient for the label of abnormality to be assigned.

IS BEHAVING DYSFUNCTIONALLY ABNORMAL?

Thus far, it is clear that simply being different, behaving differently, or behaving dangerously does not constitute abnormal behavior. A final consideration when attempting to define abnormal behavior is whether that behavior causes *distress* or *dysfunction* for the individual or others. Consider the examples of Robert and Stan (see Normal Behavior and Abnormal Behavior Case Studies below).

Both Robert and Stan engage in checking behaviors, but Robert's behavior falls into the category of what is called "normal checking" (Rachman & Hodgson, 1980). Stan's routine of checking the house before he leaves for work or goes to bed is *different* from the way in which most people lock up their house before going to work, so his behavior *deviates* from the norm. Even though simple deviance is not abnormal, Stan's behavior differs from Robert's in another way: Stan's checking occurs more frequently. Frequency alone does not mean a behavior is maladaptive, but frequency can lead to two other conditions: distress and dysfunction. Specifically, Stan's worries are so

---

NORMAL BEHAVIOR CASE STUDY
A Cautious Person—No Disorder

Robert is a very cautious person. He does not like to make mistakes and believes that the behavior standards that he sets for himself are high but fair. He is concerned about safety and worried that other people might take advantage of him if he makes a mistake. Before leaving his house or going to sleep, he walks through the house, checking to make sure that every door and window is locked and the oven and stove are turned off. This usually takes about 5 minutes. ∎

ABNORMAL BEHAVIOR CASE STUDY
Obsessive-Compulsive Disorder

Stan also is cautious and very concerned. When away from home, he worries that he forgot to lock a door and that his house has been robbed. Often he returns home to check that the house is locked. But even after he checks, he remains doubtful and spends hours each day checking and re-checking. He has an elaborate system of checking the locks, the doors, the garage door, and the burglar alarm system. He checks the stove seven times to make sure that the oven and the burners are off. Thoughts of a burglar in his house or his house burning down cause him great distress, sometimes interfering with his sleep. He is often late for work or for social engagements because he needs to go back to the house to check and re-check the locks. ∎

frequent and pervasive that they cause him to feel anxious and lose sleep at night. In this case, maladaptive behavior results in *distress;* Stan's worries result in a negative mood (anxiety) and cause him to lose sleep. Frequently, they also cause him to arrive late for work or for social engagements. Thus, his behaviors create occupational and social *dysfunction.* When one of these conditions is evident, the presence of a psychological disorder must be considered.

A DEFINITION OF ABNORMAL BEHAVIOR

To summarize, defining abnormal behavior requires the consideration of several factors. It is not merely being different or behaving differently, although the latter certainly might be a signal that something is wrong. Some abnormal behaviors are dangerous, but dangerousness is not necessary for a definition of abnormality. For the purposes of this book, **abnormal behavior** is defined as behavior that is inconsistent with the individual's developmental, cultural, and societal norms, creates emotional distress, or interferes with daily functioning.

The following chapters will examine many different types of abnormal behavior. As a guide, the behaviors are considered using the *Diagnostic and Statistical Manual of Mental Disorders*-Fourth Edition-Text Revision (American Psychiatric Association, 2000), commonly known as the DSM. This diagnostic system uses an approach that focuses on symptoms and the scientific basis for the disorders, including their *clinical presentation* (what specific symptoms cluster together?), *etiology* (how does the disorder begin?), *developmental stage* (does the disorder look different in children than it does in adults?), and *functional impairment* (what are the immediate and long-term consequences of having the disorder?). The DSM system uses a *categorical approach* to defining abnormal behavior. Although this method is somewhat controversial (see the box "Research Hot Topic: Categorical vs. Dimensional Approaches to Abnormal Behavior"), it remains the most widely accepted diagnostic system in the United States.

Abnormal Behavior in the General Population   Psychological disorders are common in the general population. Approximately 48% of adults in the United States have suffered from a psychological disorder at some time in their lives. During any one-year period, approximately 30% are suffering from one of these disorders (Kessler et al., 1994). The most commonly reported disorders in the United States are anxiety disorders and alcohol dependence (see Table 1.1). More than 17% of adults will suffer from

abnormal behavior   behavior that is inconsistent with the individual's developmental, cultural, and societal norms, creates emotional distress, or interferes with daily functioning

---

TABLE 1.1
Lifetime and 12-month Prevalence of Various Psychiatric Disorders

Disorders	Male		Female		Total	
	Lifetime	12 mo.	Lifetime	12 mo.	Lifetime	12 mo.
Depressive disorders	14.7%	8.5%	21.3%	12.9%	17.1%	10.3%
Anxiety disorders	19.2%	11.8%	30.5%	22.6%	24.9%	17.2%
Alcohol or drug use/dependence	35.4%	16.1%	17.9%	6.6%	26.6%	11.3%
Any disorder	48.7%	27.7%	47.3%	31.2%	48.0%	29.5%

Adapted from Kessler R. C., McGonagle K. A., Zhao S., Nelson C. B., Hughes M., Eshleman S., Wittchen H. U., Kendler K. S., "Lifetime and 12-month prevalence of DSM-III-R psychiatric disorders in the United States: results from the National Comorbidity Survey." *Archives of General Psychiatry* 51 (1), pp. 8–19, Table 2. Copyright © 1994 by the American Medical Association. Reprinted by permission of the publisher.

research HOT Topic

Categorical vs. Dimensional Approaches to Abnormal Behavior

The current diagnostic system, the *Diagnostic and Statistical Manual of Mental Disorders* (DSM), presents a *categorical* approach to understanding psychological disorders. The DSM assumes that a person either has a disorder or does not, just as one is either a boy or a girl. The current DSM is superior to previous diagnostic systems, which were tied to theory but not necessarily to data. However, two issues continue to present problems for a categorical approach: (a) symptoms rarely fall neatly into just one category; and (b) deciding when one has "enough" of a symptom to have a diagnosis.

In fact, people in psychological distress rarely have only one psychological disorder (Nathan & Langenbucher, 1999). A woman struggling with an eating disorder often feels depressed as well. Does she have two distinct disorders, or is her depression merely part of her abnormal eating pattern? Making these distinctions is more than just an academic exercise—it affects whether someone receives treatment. It may, for example, determine whether a psychologist decides to refer a depressed patient for medication treatment or just monitors her sadness to see if it disappears when the eating disorder is successfully treated.

The second issue—deciding when one has "enough" of a symptom to have a diagnosis—can be illustrated through the following example. Shyness and sadness are two behaviors that may be personality *dimensions* rather than a distinct category. When is one "sad enough" or "shy enough" to be diagnosed with a psychological disorder? Is shyness a personality feature or a psychological disorder? Currently, one is considered to have a psychological disorder when distress is severe enough or when functional impairment results. However, in many instances this is an artificial distinction and may deny people with moderate distress the opportunity to seek services. Scientifically, a *dimensional* approach would allow understanding of how abnormal behavior varies in severity over time, perhaps increasing and decreasing, or how behaviors change from one disorder to another.

Researchers continue to investigate the most accurate way to describe abnormal behavior. Determining the most appropriate way to describe psychological disorders will be a topic of research for many years in the future.

major depression, and more than 15% will struggle with alcohol dependence at some point in their lives. Social and specific phobias are also common disorders, affecting 13% and 11% of adults, respectively, during their lifetimes. Clearly, many people suffer from serious psychological disorders; this emphasizes the need for more understanding of these conditions and the development of effective treatments.

Factors Influencing the Expression of Abnormal Behaviors   Contextual factors play an important role when considering if and when abnormal behaviors may develop. Some factors include personal characteristics such as sex and race or ethnicity. For example, women are more likely to suffer from anxiety disorders (see Chapter 4) and mood disorders (see Chapter 6), and men are more likely to suffer from alcohol and drug abuse (see Chapter 9; Kessler et al., 2005). With respect to race and ethnicity, whites and African Americans suffer equally from most types of psychological disorders. Hispanics are more likely to have mood disorders such as depression than are non-Hispanic whites. In addition, as we shall see throughout this book, culture may influence how symptoms are expressed.

Socioeconomic status (SES), defined by family income and educational achievement, is another important factor that affects rates of psychological disorders among the general population. Except for drug and alcohol abuse, which occurs more often among those with the middle education level (a high school graduate but no college degree), psychological disorders occur most frequently among those with the lowest incomes and the least amount of education. A continuing debate is whether psychological disorders are the result of lower SES. Does more education and higher income serve to protect someone against psychological disorders by providing more supportive resources? An alternative hypothesis is that the impairment that *results* from a psychological disorder (inability to sleep, addiction to alcohol) results in job loss or limited educational achievement, a phenomenon known as *downward drift*. Another alternative is that a third factor, such as genetic predisposition, contributes both to the onset of a psychiatric disorder and to the inability to achieve academically or occupationally.

Few studies address the relationship of SES to psychological disorders specifically, but one study of the development of psychological disorders in children does help us understand this relationship. In this study, children were interviewed at yearly intervals, in some cases for 9 years. During that time, children from all SES groups *developed* psychological disorders at the same rate (Wadsworth & Achenbach, 2005). However, once the disorder was present, children from the lower SES category were less likely to *overcome* or recover from their disorder. Lower income usually means fewer economic resources and less access to treatment. Over time, this lack of recovery resulted in more children from the lower SES group with more psychological disorders.

As the above example illustrates, children as well as adults suffer from psychological disorders, and we know that age and developmental stage are important factors affecting abnormal behaviors. The Great Smoky Mountains Study examined the presence of psychological disorders in children, who were assessed yearly, in some cases for up to 7 consecutive years (Costello et al., 2003). Table 1.2 illustrates the prevalence of psychological disorders in children and adolescents.

It may be quite surprising that by age 16, one out of three children and adolescents (36%) has suffered from a psychological disorder. As illustrated in Figure 1.1, prevalence of disorders are highest among 9- to 10-year-old children, lower at age 12, and higher again in adolescence. Psychologists know that developmental maturity affects when and how symptoms develop, what types of symptoms develop, and even what kinds of disorders occur. The idea that the common symptoms of a disorder vary according to a person's age is known as the **developmental trajectory** (a *trajectory* is a path or progression). For example, compared with children who are diagnosed with

developmental trajectory the idea that common symptoms of a disorder may vary depending on a person's age

---

TABLE 1.2

Cumulative Prevalence of Psychiatric Disorders by Age 16

Disorder	Total	Girls	Boys
Any disorder	36.7%	31.0%	42.3%
Any emotional disorder	15.0%	17.1%	13.0%
Any anxiety disorder	9.9%	12.1%	7.7%
Any depressive disorder	9.5%	11.7%	7.3%
Any behavior disorder	23.0%	16.1%	29.9%
Conduct disorder	9.0%	3.8%	14.1%
Oppositional defiant disorder	11.3%	9.1%	13.4%
Attention-deficit/hyperactivity	4.1%	1.1%	7.0%
Substance use disorder	12.2%	10.1%	14.3%

From Costello, E. J., Mustillo, S., Erkanli, A., Keeler, G., & Angold, A., "Prevalence and development of psychiatric disorders in childhood and adolescence." *Archives of General Psychiatry*, 60, 837–844. Table 3. Copyright © 2003 by the American Medical Association. Reprinted by permission of the publisher.

FIGURE 1.1

Prevalence of Psychological Disorders in Children By Age and Sex

For boys, the prevalence of disorders peaks around age 9 or 10; for girls, prevalence peaks around age 16.

Adapted from Costello, E. J., Mustillo, S., Erkanli, A., Keeler, G., & Angold, A., "Prevalence and development of psychiatric disorders in childhood and adolescence." *Archives of General Psychiatry*, 60, 837–844. Figure 1. Copyright © 2003 by the American Medical Association. Reprinted by permission of the publisher.

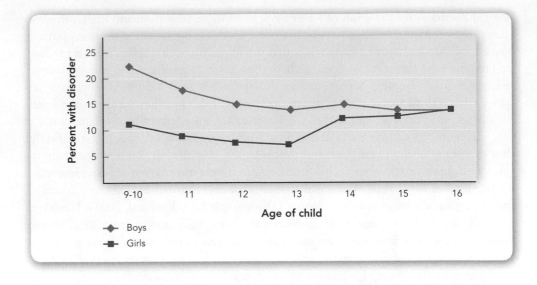

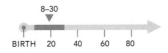

depression, adolescents with depression are more likely to feel hopelessness/helplessness, to lack energy or feel tired, to sleep too much, and to commit serious suicidal acts (Yorbik et al., 2004). Therefore, the symptoms of depression may change as a child matures. Even among adults, age also plays a role in the frequency of specific depressive symptoms. As adults mature, they are less likely to report feelings of sadness or negative thoughts about themselves or others (Goldberg et al., 2003). Therefore, even an emotion as common as sadness can appear differently at different ages.

Inattention to developmental differences may result in inaccurate detection of psychological disorders. For example, social phobia is characterized by a behavioral pattern of pervasive social timidity (see Chapter 4). Adults with social phobia report extreme fear when asked to give a speech. Young children rarely have to give a speech, and because they have no experience in the situation, they will deny fear of giving speeches. However, a similar childhood activity would be reading aloud in front of the class. Children with social phobia often report great fear when asked to read aloud. Therefore, accurately diagnosing social phobia depends on understanding not only the disorder, but how the disorder appears at different ages. Similarly, older adults with depression are less likely to report feelings of sadness and negative thoughts, but all adults (regardless of age) report physical symptoms of depression (inability to sleep or eat or being easily tired). Therefore, if a clinician assesses depression only by asking about sadness, depression in older adults may be overlooked. Throughout this book, we often will return to this issue of developmental psychopathology and how the same disorder may appear differently across the life span.

This developmental perspective also illustrates why the prevalence of psychological disorders vary by age (see Table 1.2). Certain disorders that are common in childhood (separation anxiety disorder, attention-deficit/hyperactivity disorder, bedwetting, and fecal soiling; see Chapters 4 and 12) become less common as children mature physically, cognitively, and emotionally. During adolescence, other disorders begin to emerge (depression, alcohol and drug use, eating disorders, panic disorder, and generalized anxiety disorder; see Chapters 4, 6, 7, and 9). The emergence of some disorders has practical and societal components (e.g., older adolescents are more likely to have access to alcohol, which is prerequisite to developing substance abuse). The emergence of other disorders coincides with cognitive maturity. Generalized anxiety disorder is defined, in part, by worry about future events (APA, 2000). This requires the ability to understand the concept of "future," a cognitive skill that usually emerges around age 12 (see Alfano et al., 2002). Therefore, although it is not impossible for younger children to suffer from generalized anxiety disorder, many more cases occur later, as cognitive maturity is achieved. Finally, biological changes also influence the emergence of psychological disorders. Hormonal changes associated with puberty may increase the likelihood of the emergence of eating disorders (anorexia, bulimia) in those who are at high risk for the development of these disorders.

---

concept CHECK

- Being different, or behaving differently, does not necessarily mean that someone is suffering from a psychological disorder. Determining the presence of abnormal behavior requires evaluation of the behavior in terms of its developmental, cultural, and societal contexts.

- In addition to determining context, the definition of abnormal behavior requires that the behavior create emotional distress or functional impairment.

- The current diagnostic system uses a categorical approach to classifying abnormal behavior. However, psychological symptoms rarely fall into one neat category. Furthermore, it is often difficult to determine the boundary between normal feelings such as sadness and psychological disorders such as depression. In these instances, a dimensional approach may be more useful.

APPLICATION QUESTION: At different ages, the same disorder may appear with very different symptoms. Young children are still developing in different ways. How might immature physical and cognitive development affect the emotional expression of psychological disorders?

Historical Views of Abnormal Behavior and Its Treatment

Throughout history, certain behaviors have been recognized as abnormal—often the same ones we recognize today. However, the explanations for these abnormal behaviors have evolved, ranging from an imbalance of bodily fluids to possession by demons, genetic abnormalities, and traumatic learning experiences. Today, new technologies allow us to watch the brain as it processes sights, smells, and sounds, solves problems, and experiences emotions. As this knowledge has grown, some of the earlier ideas about abnormal behavior seem outlandish or quaint. Here, we review those theories and show how scientific advances have changed our understanding of abnormal behavior.

ANCIENT THEORIES

Much of what we know about ancient theories of abnormal behavior is limited by available archeological evidence. Ancient cultures, such as ancient Egypt, believed in spirits who controlled much of the environment, including aspects of a person's behavior. Even before the Egyptians, some cultures engaged in a practice called **trephination**, whereby a circular instrument was used to cut away sections of the skull. One interpretation of trephination is that it was a treatment for abnormal behaviors. Opening up the skull, it may have been thought, released the evil spirits that had assumed control of the person (Selling, 1940). However, this is only an assumption, and there could have been other reasons for this practice, such as treating head wounds that might have resulted from warfare (Maher & Maher, 1985). Even today, we are not sure why trephination was practiced in ancient times.

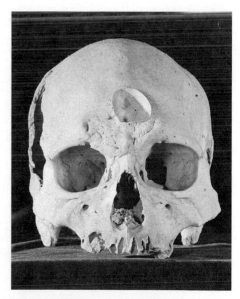

Trephination involved making a hole in the skull. It may have been a way that ancient peoples tried to release evil spirits from the body of an afflicted person.

trephination process whereby a circular instrument was used to cut away sections of the skull, possibly in an attempt to release demons from the brain

Hippocrates, the ancient Greek physician, believed that abnormal behaviors were caused by an imbalance in four bodily humours.

CLASSICAL GREEK AND ROMAN PERIOD

The ancient Greeks believed that abnormal behavior was controlled by the gods and that defiance of the deities could result in mental illness. Around the thirteenth century BC, the physician Melampus of Pilus introduced an organic model of illness to explain psychological symptoms and provided treatment using plants and other natural substances. He prescribed root extract for "agitated uterine melancholia" and iron powder for "traumatic impotence" (Roccatagliata, 1997). Another Greek physician, Asclepius, established the first sanctuary for mental disorders, offering biological (mandrake root and opium), physical (music, massage, drama), and psychological treatments (dream interpretation; Roccatagliata, 1997). During this period, mental illnesses were considered to result from either traumatic experiences or an imbalance in fluids (such as blood) found within the body. These fluids were called *humours*.

Often considered the father of medicine, Hippocrates (460–377 BC) was the most famous Greek physician. He produced both a diagnostic classification system and a model by which to explain abnormal behavior. Hippocrates identified common psychological symptoms such as *hallucinations* (hearing or seeing things not evident to others), *delusions* (beliefs with no basis in reality), *melancholia* (severe sadness), and *mania* (heightened states of arousal that can result in frenzied activity). All of these symptoms are still recognized today. He also introduced the term *hysteria*, now called *conversion disorder* (see Chapter 5). The term *hysteria* was used to describe patients who appeared to have blindness or paralysis for which there was no organic cause. Hippocrates, assuming incorrectly that the condition occurred only in women, attributed it to an empty uterus wandering throughout the body searching for conception. The external symptoms indicated where the uterus was lodged internally. He believed that the cure for hysteria was an environmental one: marriage or pregnancy. Of course, with advanced understanding of human anatomy and physiology, the "wandering uterus" theory was discarded. But even in very recent times, the term *hysteria* continued to describe an intense, dramatic pattern of behavior once associated with women.

Hippocrates believed that other abnormal behaviors resulted when environmental factors (changes of seasons) and/or physical factors (fever, epilepsy, and shock) created an imbalance in four bodily humours. In his model, the four humours were yellow bile, black bile, blood, and phlegm. Blood was associated with a courageous and hopeful outlook on life and phlegm was associated with a calm and unemotional attitude. Excessive yellow bile caused mania and excessive black bile caused melancholia, which was treated with a vegetable diet, a tranquil existence, celibacy, exercise, and sometimes bleeding (controlled removal of some of the patient's blood). Hippocrates advocated the removal of patients from their families as an element of treatment, foreshadowing the practice of humane treatment and institutionalization.

Another very influential Greek physician was Galen, who was the personal physician of the Roman Emperor Marcus Aurelius. Although the terms we use today were not the same ones used in ancient times, Galen's writings (which still survive today) indicate that his areas of expertise included many fields of medicine: neurophysiology and neuroanatomy, neurology, pharmacology, psychiatry, and philosophy (Raccatagliata, 1997; http://www.nlm.nih.gov/hmd/greek/greek_galen.html). An important distinction can be made between Hippocrates' and Galen's description of hysteria. Because Galen had studied human anatomy, he discounted the "wandering uterus" theory. Galen attributed hysteria to a psychological cause, believing it to be a symptom of unhappiness in women who had lost interest in and enjoyment of sexual activity.

After the fall of the Roman Empire, demonology again dominated theories of mental illness in Europe, but the enlightened thinking of Hippocrates and Galen remained influential in Islamic countries. There, Avicenna (980–1037; Namanzi, 2001), known as the "prince and chief of physicians" and "the second teacher after Aristotle," wrote approximately 450 works, including the *Canon of Medicine*, considered the most influential textbook ever written. Avicenna considered depression to result from a mix of humours, and he believed that certain physical diseases were caused by emotional distress. He stressed the beneficial effects of music on emotional disturbance. His approach to mental illness foreshadowed what would take an additional 600 years to appear in Europe—humane treatment of the mentally ill.

THE MIDDLE AGES THROUGH THE RENAISSANCE

In medieval Europe, demons were considered to be the source of all evil, preying on the "captive and outwitted minds of men" (Tertullian, in Sagan, 1996). There were many challenges to survival during the Middle Ages (wars, plagues, social oppression, famine), and people often sought reasons for these challenges. Church officials interpreted negative behavior as the work of the devil or as witchcraft, even when other, less dramatic, explanations existed. As a result of the church's powerful influence, witchcraft became a prominent theory to explain abnormal behavior. Over a 300-year period (1400s to 1700s), at least 200,000 people in Europe were accused of witchcraft and 100,000 were put to death, approximately 80 to 85% of whom were women (Clark, 1997). In fact, many of those accused probably suffered from psychological disorders (Zilboorg, 1939, cited in Clark, 1997). Once accused of being a witch, the person was tried and always found guilty. Accusations of witchcraft were not limited to European countries. "Witches" were also executed in Massachusetts in the seventeenth century. Thankfully, the Renaissance period brought new attitudes toward science and the church that challenged the reality of witches. However, as illustrated by today's stories of alien abduction (see the box "Examining the Evidence: Modern Witchcraft, Demons, and Alien Abductions"), beliefs in the supernatural/paranormal still exist in our modern world.

The Islamic philosopher and physician Avicenna wrote an influential medical text that recognized the interconnections between emotional distress and physical illness.

examining the evidence:

Modern Witchcraft, Demons, and Alien Abductions

One of the major tenets of Carl Sagan's book *The Demon Haunted World: Science as a Candle in the Dark* is that despite the technological advances of our society, many people do not understand the difference between pseudoscience, fundamentalist zealotry, and scientific evidence. Why else would so many people believe in alien abduction when there is no concrete evidence for it? Compare and contrast these two descriptions:

> *Succubi yield to males and receive their semen; by cunning skill, the demons preserve its potency, and afterwards, with the permission of God, then become incubi and pour it out into female repositories* (St. Bonaventura (1221–1274), cited by Sagan, 1996).

> *Betty and Barney Hill claimed to have been abducted by aliens on September 19, 1961. The abductions were remembered following a series of nightmares by Betty, who claimed that aliens stuck a needle in her belly button. Barney believed that the aliens took a sample of his sperm* (Carroll, 2003).

■ **The Facts** Over hundreds of years, many people have reported cases of spiritual visitation.

■ **The Evidence** There is no objective scientific evidence—only reports by those who claim they were visited. They usually say that the spirits or aliens come from the sky and need humans for reproductive purposes. Often those who report such experiences do so only under hypnosis, and many have other behaviors and beliefs that would be considered unusual.

■ **Let's Examine the Evidence** "Perhaps some day there will be a UFO or alien abduction case that is well-attested, accompanied by compelling physical evidence, and explicable only in terms of extraterrestrial visitation. It's hard to think of a more important discovery. So far, though, there have been no such cases, nothing that comes close. . . .Which then, is more likely: that we're undergoing a massive but generally overlooked invasion by alien sexual abusers, or that people are experiencing some unfamiliar internal mental state that they do not understand?" (Sagan, 1996).

During the Middle Ages, a common event was **mass hysteria**, in which a group of people shared a belief that they were affected or possessed by a demonic spirit (again, similar to beliefs regarding alien abduction). One of the first recorded cases (originating in Italy in the early thirteenth century) is known as *tarantism*, caused by the belief that the bite of a wolf spider (also known as a tarantula) would cause death unless a person engaged in joyous, frenetic dancing. Another form of the legend was that the spider's bite would cause frenetic dancing, jumping, or convulsing (Sigerist, 1943). In fact, the spider bite was harmless, and people's responses were fueled by mass hysteria. Another form of mass madness was *lycanthropy*, in which individuals believed that they were possessed by wolves. The belief was so strong that those affected would act like a wolf, even to the point of believing that their bodies were covered in fur.

There is a scientific basis for mass hysteria. **Emotional contagion** is defined as the automatic mimicry and synchronization of expressions, vocalizations, postures, and movements of one person by another (Hatfield et al., 1993). When these overt behaviors converge, emotions come together as well. These mimicking behaviors are not under voluntary control but nevertheless serve to influence behavior. Although many people may no longer believe that wolf or spider bites are responsible for abnormal behaviors, the process of emotional contagion remains a powerful influence on behavior (see the box "Examining the Evidence: Current-Day Mass Hysteria").

The Renaissance period (1400–1700) marked a second time of enlightenment in the treatment of mental illnesses in Europe. Much of this transformation can be traced back to the German physician Johann Weyer (1515–1588) and the Swiss physician Paracelsus (1490–1541). Weyer was the first physician to specialize in the treatment of

mass hysteria a situation in which a group of people share and sometimes even act upon a belief that is not based in fact (for example, tarantism and lycanthropy)

emotional contagion the automatic mimicry and synchronization of expressions, vocalizations, postures, and movements of one person by another

examining the evidence:

Current-Day Mass Hysteria

■ **The Facts** Although we tend to think of mass hysteria as occurring in an unenlightened era, episodes of mass contagion still occur today.

■ **The Evidence** In 1998, a teacher from Tennessee reported that she had a headache, nausea, shortness of breath, and dizziness, after she detected a "gasoline-like" smell in her classroom (Jones et al., 2000). The school was evacuated, and ultimately 80 students and 19 staff members went to the hospital emergency room with symptoms. When the school reopened, another 71 people went to the emergency room complaining of similar symptoms. Despite an exhaustive search, no medical or environmental reason was identified.

■ **Let's Examine the Evidence** Evidence that emotional contagion may have been the basis for the symptom reports includes the following:

1. Symptom onset occurred at 49 different locations in the school, even though many of these locations were served by totally independent air-handling systems.

2. Some individuals reported symptom onset outside of the school, at home, or when visiting others in the hospital.

3. Those who reported illness were more likely to be female, had more often observed another person who became ill, knew a classmate was ill, or reported an unusual odor at the school. All of these factors have been repeatedly associated with onset of mass psychogenic illness.

■ **Conclusion** It is important to note that the individuals experienced the symptoms they reported; it is incorrect to deny that the symptoms occurred. What is at issue however, is the cause of the symptoms. In the case of the Tennessee school, as in many others, after exhausting all possible environmental alternatives, the most likely explanation for the large outbreak of illness was emotional contagion, producing mass psychogenic illness.

mental illness, and Paracelsus refuted the idea that abnormal behaviors were linked to demonic possession. Paracelsus believed that mental disorders could be hereditary and that some physical illnesses had a psychological origin (Tan & Yeow, 2003).

These changing views toward mental illness changed treatment approaches as well. A movement arose that was genuinely concerned with providing help, and its goal was to separate those with mental illness from those who engaged in criminal behavior (Sussman, 1998). Beginning in the sixteenth century, people with mental illness were housed in asylums—separate facilities designed to isolate them from the general public. Though the concept of asylums was based on good intentions, the asylums quickly filled to capacity (and overcapacity). The lack of effective treatments turned the facilities into warehouses, often called *madhouses*. One of the most famous was St. Mary of Bethlehem in London. Treatment consisted of confinement (chains, shackles, isolation in dark cells), torturous practices (ice-cold baths, spinning in chairs, severely restricted diets), and "medical" treatments (emetics, purgatives, and bloodletting). For a small price, people in London could visit the asylum to view the inmates (Tan & Yeow, 2004). They called the place *Bedlam* (a contraction of "Bethlehem"), a word that came to describe chaotic and uncontrollable situations. Similar conditions existed in other parts of Europe as well as eventually in North America.

THE NINETEENTH CENTURY AND THE BEGINNING OF MODERN THOUGHT

A turning point for the medical treatment of mental illness occurred during the late eighteenth century when the French physician Philippe Pinel (1745–1826) and the English Quaker William Tuke (1732–1822) radically changed the approach to treating mental illness. In 1793, Pinel was the director of Bicêtre, an asylum for men. In his *Memoir on Madness,* he proposed that mental illness was often curable and that to apply appropriate treatment, the physician must listen and observe the patient's behavior, understanding the natural history of the disease and what events led to its development. He advocated calm and order within the asylum (Tan & Yeow, 2004). He removed the chains from the patients, both at Bicêtre and at the women's asylum known as Salpêtrière. Instead of using restraints, Pinel advocated daytime activities such as work or occupational therapy to allow for restful sleep at night.

At the same time, across the English Channel, William Tuke established the York Retreat (Edginton, 1997), a small country house deliberately designed to allow people with mental illnesses to live, work, and relax in a compassionate and religious environment. Instead of bars on the windows, Tuke used iron dividers to separate the glass window panes and even had the dividers painted to look like wood. The Retreat was built on a hill, and although it contained a hidden ditch and a wall to ensure confinement, the barriers could not be seen from the buildings; this gave the illusion of a home, rather than a place of institutionalization (Scull, 2004). The work of both Pinel and Tuke heralded *moral treatment,* "summed up in two words, kindness and occupation" (W.A.F. Browne, 1837, cited in Geller & Morrissey, 2004). Moral treatment was quite comprehensive. In the United States it included removal of the patient from the home and former associates, as well as respectful and kind treatment that included "manual labor, religious services on Sunday, the establishment of regular habits and of self-control, and diversion of the mind from morbid trains of thought" (Brigham, 1847, p.1, cited in Luchins, 2001).

Philippe Pinel, a French physician, released mental patients from their chains and advocated a more humane form of treatment.

Dorothea Dix of Massachusetts was a tireless reformer who brought the poor treatment of the mentally ill to public attention.

Moral treatment in the United States is most commonly associated with Benjamin Rush (1745–1813) and Dorothea Dix (1802–1887). Rush was a well-known physician at Pennsylvania Hospital and a signer of the Declaration of Independence. He limited his practice to mental illness, which he believed had its causes in the blood vessels of the brain (Farr, 1994). Although this theory was later disproved, Rush believed that the human mind was the most important area of study, and he became known as the father of American psychiatry (Haas, 1993).

In the United States, perhaps no name is more closely associated with humane care than Dorothea Dix, the Boston schoolteacher who devoted her life to the plight of the mentally ill and the need for treatment reform. Through her efforts, 32 institutions were established that included programs in psychiatric treatment, research, and education (Gold, 2005). Dix believed that asylums, correctly designed and operated, would allow for treatment and perhaps even cure. Although Dix brought the plight of the mentally ill to public attention, moral treatment alone did not cure most forms of mental illness. In fact, mental hospitals became associated with permanent institutionalization, custodial care, isolation, and very little hope.

During the late 1700s in Europe, the treatment of mental disorders went beyond providing rest and humane care. The Viennese physician Franz Anton Mesmer (1734–1815) hardly followed the conventional medical establishment. His academic thesis explored the clinical implications of astrology (McNally, 1999). Mesmer proposed that the body was a magnet and that by using the physician's body as a second magnet, a cure for mental illness could be achieved (Crabtree, 2000). Mesmer believed that a substance called **animal magnetism** existed within the body. When it flowed freely, the body was in a healthy state; however, when the flow of this energy force was impeded, disease resulted. The cure involved "magnetic passes" of the physician's hands over the body (McNally, 1999). Mesmerism was roundly criticized by a committee of scientists and physicians that included Benjamin Franklin and the noted French chemist Antoine Lavoisier.

Nonetheless, Mesmer's experiments constitute an important chapter in psychology. Although his theory of animal magnetism and his flamboyant cures (including a cape, music, magic poles used to touch various parts of the body, and magnetized water) were ultimately debunked, they illustrate the power of the **placebo effect**, in which symptoms are diminished or eliminated not because of any specific treatment, but because the patient believes that a treatment is effective. A placebo can be in the form of pills with inert ingredients such as cornstarch. A placebo can also be in the form of a therapist or physician who displays an attitude of caring about the patient. However, it is important to add that although placebos may change how patients feel, the effect is usually temporary. Placebos are not the same as actual treatment.

A significant event for establishing a biological basis for some psychological disorders occurred in the latter part of the nineteenth century. Scientists discovered that syphilis (a sexually transmitted disease caused by a bacterium) led to the chronic condition called general paresis, manifested as physical paralysis and mental illness, and eventually death. The discovery that a physical disease could cause a psychological disorder was a significant advance in understanding abnormal behavior, but we now know that bacteria are not the cause of most psychological disorders, even though in some cases, psychological symptoms may have a medical basis.

The work of the German psychiatrist Emil Kraepelin (1856–1926) was another important chapter in the history of abnormal behavior. During medical school, Kraepelin attended lectures in the laboratory of Wilhelm Wundt, the founder of modern scientific psychology (Decker, 2004). He applied Wundt's scientific methods to measure behavioral deviations, hoping to provide the theoretical foundations that he considered to be lacking in psychiatry (when compared with general medicine and psychology). On Wundt's advice, Kraepelin began to study "the abnormal" (Boyle,

animal magnetism a force that Mesmer believed flowed within the body and, when impeded, resulted in disease

placebo effect a condition in which symptoms of illness diminish or disappear not because of any specific treatment, but because the patient believes that a treatment is effective

2000). In 1899, after observing hundreds of patients, he introduced two diagnostic categories, based not just on symptom differentiation but also on the *etiology* (cause) and *prognosis (*progression and outcome) of the disease. **Dementia praecox**, now called **schizophrenia** (see Chapter 10), was Kraepelin's term for a type of mental illness characterized by mental deterioration. *Manic-depressive insanity* was defined as a separate disorder with a more favorable outcome. Kraepelin was best known for his studies of dementia praecox, which he believed resulted from *autointoxication*, the self-poisoning of brain cells as a result of abnormal body metabolism. Although a biological or metabolic cause for schizophrenia is not yet known, Kraepelin's contributions, both in terms of a classification system and a description of schizophrenia, cannot be overstated.

Another physician interested in the brain was Jean-Martin Charcot (1825–1893), who established a school of neurology at La Salpêtrière in Paris (Haas, 2001). Charcot was interested in hysteria, and he believed that it was caused by degenerative brain changes. However, at the same time, other researchers, Ambrose August Liébeault (1823–1904) and Hippolyte Bernheim (1837–1919), in Nancy, France, were conducting experiments to determine whether hysteria was a form of self-hypnosis. Debate raged between Charcot and the physicians collectively called the Nancy School. Eventually, most scientific data supported the views of the Nancy School. To his credit as a scientist, once the data were established, Charcot became a strong proponent of this view.

At about the same time, the Viennese physician Josef Breuer (1842–1925) was studying the effect of hypnotism. Breuer used hypnosis to treat patients with hysteria, including a young woman named Anna O., who had cared for her ailing father until his death. Shortly thereafter, she developed blurry vision, trouble speaking, and difficulty moving her right arm and both her legs. Breuer discovered that when under hypnosis, Anna O. would discuss events and experiences that she was unable to recall otherwise. Furthermore, after discussing these distressing events, her symptoms disappeared. Breuer called his treatment the **talking cure**, laying the foundation for a new approach to mental disorders.

THE TWENTIETH CENTURY

Although biological theories were still influential, the early part of the twentieth century was dominated by two psychological models of abnormal behavior: psychoanalytic theory and behaviorism. In this section, we examine the roots of these theories and how they set the stage for modern-day approaches to understanding abnormal behavior.

Psychoanalysis Sigmund Freud (1856–1939) was trained as a neurologist. His career in psychiatry began in France, where he worked with Charcot. After settling in Vienna, he published *Studies in Hysteria* in 1895 with Josef Breuer. He introduced **psychoanalysis**, a comprehensive theory that attempts to explain both normal and abnormal behavior. Freud's theory and practice were very controversial at the time. He believed that much of human behavior was controlled by unconscious, innate biological and sexual urges that existed from infancy. His theory that infants experienced sexual urges outraged Viennese Victorian society. Freud believed that one's experiences in the first 5 years of life were very important and could influence a person's behavior even as an adult. One of the first theoreticians to highlight the role of environmental factors in abnormal behavior, Freud considered this early environment to consist almost exclusively of the individual's mother and father. This belief sometimes led to detrimental and undeserved blaming of parents as the "root cause" of abnormal behavior. Freud believed that the key therapeutic ingredient was the achievement of *insight*. In other words, overcoming psychological difficulties meant understanding their causes and meaning. Unlike Breuer,

dementia praecox Kraepelin's name for a psychological disorder characterized by deterioration of mental faculties (now called schizophrenia)

schizophrenia a disorder involving serious abnormalities in thought, perceptions, and behavior

talking cure therapy in the form of discussion of psychological distress with a trained professional, leading to the elimination of distressing symptoms

psychoanalysis a theory of abnormal behavior originated by Sigmund Freud that was based on the belief that many aspects of behavior were controlled by unconscious innate biological urges that existed from infancy

Sigmund Freud introduced psychoanalysis, a theory that attempts to explain abnormal behavior as driven by unconscious biological and sexual urges.

Ivan Pavlov's pioneering experiments with dogs led him to discover classical conditioning, a process that underlies much normal and abnormal behavior.

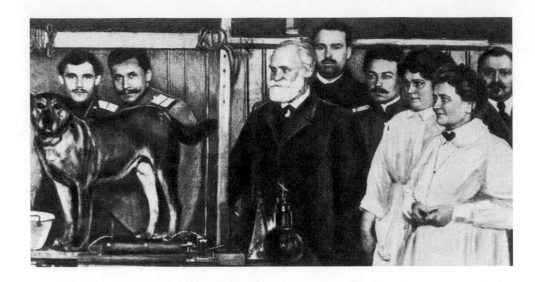

classical conditioning a form of learning in which a conditioned stimulus (CS) is paired with an unconditioned stimulus (UCS) to produce a conditioned response

behaviorism the theory that the only appropriate objects of scientific study are behaviors that can be observed and measured directly

John Watson introduced behaviorism, which in its strictest form asserts that all behavior is learned. With his student, Rosalie Rayner, he studied infants' emotional responses, showing that emotions could be acquired by classical conditioning.
Source: Archives of the History of American Psychology, The University of Akron.

Freud did not view hypnosis as necessary to achieve insight, but he did believe in the talking cure, a lengthy relationship between therapist and patient.

Behaviorism In 1904, Ivan Pavlov (1849–1936) received the Nobel Prize for his research on the physiology of dog digestion, which in turn led to his discovery of conditioned responses. A landmark moment for psychology was Pavlov's discovery of **classical conditioning**, in which an *unconditioned stimulus* (UCS) produces an *unconditioned response* (UCR). For example, you touch a hot stove (UCS) and you immediately withdraw your hand (UCR). A *conditioned stimulus* (CS) is something neutral that does not naturally produce the UCR. In the classical conditioning paradigm, the UCS is repeatedly paired with a CS, resulting in the UCR. After sufficient pairings, the CS, presented alone, becomes capable of eliciting a *conditioned response* (CR), which is similar in form and content to the UCR. In Pavlov's paradigm, food powder was the UCS that produced salivation (UCR) in his dogs. Pavlov paired a neutral stimulus, a ringing bell (CS), with the food powder. After a sufficient number of pairings, the CS (the bell alone) produced salivation (CR). This paradigm seems simple, but it is both powerful and more complex than it first appears. We will return to the conditioning theory of emotional disorders later in the chapter.

In 1908, John B. Watson (1878–1958), a well-known animal psychologist, joined the faculty of Johns Hopkins University. Watson believed that the only appropriate objects of scientific study were observable *behaviors*, not inner thoughts or feelings. This view, known as **behaviorism**, is based on principles that consider all behavior (normal or abnormal) to be *learned* as a result of experiences or interactions with the environment. Watson is most famous for his work with his student Rosalie Rayner. In 1920, they published the case of Little Albert, which demonstrated that emotional responses such as fear could be acquired through classical conditioning. In this case, Little Albert's fear of a white rat was established by pairing the white rat with a loud, aversive noise (Watson & Rayner, 1920). In addition, not only was an extreme emotional response established, but it generalized to other objects that, like the rat, were white and furry (a rabbit, a Santa Claus beard).

Unfortunately, Little Albert and his mother left Johns Hopkins soon after the experiments were completed, so whether his conditioned fear continued is unknown. However, 4 years later, another student of Watson's, Mary Cover Jones, used conditioning procedures to *extinguish* (eliminate) a fear of furry objects in a 2-year-old, Little Peter, who had been conditioned to fear these objects. Jones brought a rabbit into the room where Peter was playing. However, instead of trying to associate a neutral object with fear, she brought in other children who were not afraid of rabbits. When other children were in the room, Peter's fear of the rabbit seemed to decrease. Every time that Peter's fear lessened, she would bring the rabbit a little closer and wait for his fear to diminish again. Eventually, Peter was able to touch and play with the rabbit, which would suggest that he was no longer fearful. The research of Pavlov, Watson, Rayner, and Jones constituted powerful demonstrations that behaviors (even abnormal behaviors) could be learned and unlearned using conditioning principles. This view of abnormal behavior is very different from psychoanalytic theory. Yet, as we shall see, both theories continue to exert significant influence on our current views of abnormal behavior.

concept CHECK

- Ancient theories held that spirits controlled aspects of human behavior and that the biological seat of abnormal behavior was the brain.

- We know from writings from the classical Greek and Roman period that many psychological disorders that exist today were also present then. Hippocrates proposed that abnormal behavior resulted from an imbalance of bodily humours, indicating a biological cause. Other physicians, such as Galen and Avicenna, proposed that psychological factors also played a role.

- During medieval times, there was a return to theories of spirit possession, and charges of witchcraft were common. This was also the time when people with psychological disorders were locked up in institutional settings with little or no access to care.

- The nineteenth century marked the beginning of humane treatment advanced by leaders such as Pinel, Tuke, Rush, and Dix. During this time, Kraepelin also introduced a system for the classification of mental disorders and Charcot introduced psychological treatments.

APPLICATION QUESTION: Central figures in abnormal psychology during the twentieth century were Freud, Pavlov, and Watson. How does Freud's theory of the development of abnormal behavior differ from that of Pavlov and Watson?

Current Views of Abnormal Behavior and Treatment

This quick journey through history illustrates several important points about abnormal behavior. First, scientific advances lead to new and more sophisticated approaches to understanding human behavior. Research findings allow unsupported theories to be discarded and provide new hypotheses to be tested and evaluated. This is the core of a scientific approach to abnormal behavior. Scientists form hypotheses and conduct controlled experiments to determine whether their hypotheses are supported. If empirical evidence supports the hypotheses, then those theories continue. If the evidence does not provide support, the theory is discarded or changed, and the process begins again.

Second, scientific discoveries in areas other than psychology may later provide insight into abnormal behavior. For example, the Human Genome Project is dedicated to mapping all of the genetic material in the human body. As our understanding of this map develops, new genetic techniques (see Chapter 2) allow us to examine genetic abnormalities that may be associated with specific psychological disorders, such as schizophrenia and autism. Similarly, new technologies such as magnetic resonance imaging (see Chapter 2) lead us to examine the brain in ways never before possible. Although not initially developed to study abnormal behavior, these technologies help us to identify brain areas that we now know are involved in specific emotions such as sadness or fear. These examples illustrate how, as science advances, older theories such as demonology are replaced with newer insights and theories. Furthermore, as scientifically advanced as our current theories seem to be, they too will be revised or replaced as science continues to make new discoveries.

For the past 50 years, most psychologists who provide psychological services have been trained in the **scientist-practitioner approach** to psychology. The scientist-practitioner approach means that when the psychologist is providing treatment to people with psychological disorders, he or she relies on the findings of research. In turn, when conducting research, the psychologist investigates topics that help to guide and improve psychological care. Psychologists who utilize this perspective have a unique advantage because their scientific training allows them to differentiate fact from opinion when evaluating new theories, new treatments, and new research findings. This perspective also allows psychologists to apply research findings in many different areas to develop more comprehensive models of abnormal behavior. Critically applying a scientific perspective to theories of etiology and examining the evidence behind proposed theories prevent us from adopting explanations that are without a firm scientific basis (such as witchcraft or demonology). "Treatments" based on such ideas could have quite negative results and in some cases might even be deadly. As you read through this book, keep the scientist-practitioner model in mind.

For undergraduates, one of the most frustrating aspects of studying abnormal behavior is that psychologists often cannot provide a simple explanation for why a behavior occurs. What causes people to become so depressed that they commit suicide? Society often wants answers to these questions, but the answers are not simple. Unlike medical illness, abnormal behavior cannot be explained by bacteria or viruses that infect the body. Clinical descriptions and research findings have identified many different, and sometimes conflictual, factors that may be involved. The different findings have given rise to perspectives that try to weave coherent explanations from the clinical observations and research findings that are available. For psychological scientists, these perspectives are often known as *models* and consist of basic assumptions that provide a framework for organizing information and a set of procedures and tools that can be used to test aspects of that framework (Kuhn, 1962).

In this chapter, we introduce some of the different models that try to explain abnormal behavior. You might wonder why there are so many different approaches to understanding behavior. The answer, as you may recall from a point made earlier in this chapter, is that abnormal behavior is very complex, and as you will see, so far no one model appears capable of providing a comprehensive explanation. For example, some people develop a fear of driving after having been involved in a bad traffic accident; yet other people, who were in the same accident, do not develop a fear. If they were exposed to the same event, why do some people develop a fear and others do not? Using a scientific approach, researchers develop, examine, and discard models as new facts emerge. Below we examine some of the currently accepted models of abnormal behavior.

BIOLOGICAL MODELS

The biological model assumes that the major reason for abnormal behavior lies in the biological processes of the body, particularly the brain. Although long suspected to be the seat of abnormal behavior, only in the last 20 or 30 years have scientific advances allowed us to observe brain mechanisms directly. One area of scientific breakthrough has been in our understanding of genetics. As already noted, through genetic mapping, we are beginning to understand whether psychological disorders such as schizophrenia or manic-depressive disorder have a genetic basis, and if so, how that understanding might lead to better intervention and prevention efforts. Other technology breakthroughs such as Computerized Axial Tomography (CAT Scans) and Magnetic

scientist-practitioner approach an approach to psychological disorders based on the concept that when providing treatment to people with psychological disorders, the psychologist relies on the findings of research and in turn, when conducting research, the psychologist investigates topics that help to guide and improve psychological care

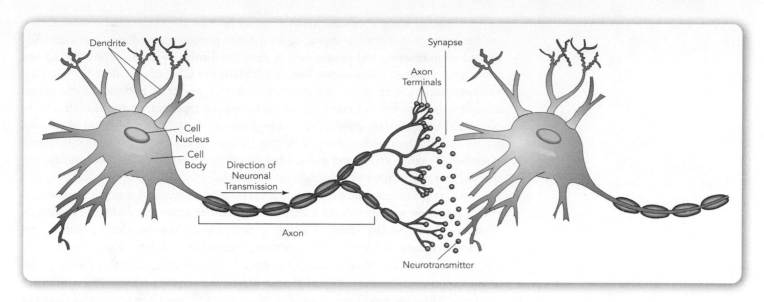

Dendrite

Cell
Nucleus

Cell
Body

Direction of
Neuronal
Transmission

Axon

Synapse

Axon
Terminals

Neurotransmitter

FIGURE 1.2

The Neuron Fires, Sending an Impulse to the Next Neuron

Each individual neuron transmits information that is vital for virtually every aspect of our functioning.

Resonance Imaging (MRI) allow direct examination of brain structure and activity. With this direct observation, we now have a much greater understanding of the role of the brain in abnormal behavior.

Although we often refer to the brain as if it were a single entity, it is a very complex organ. In fact, about 100 billion **neurons** (brain cells) make up the brain. Between the neurons are spaces known as **synapses**. Neurons (see Figure 1.2) communicate when **neurotransmitters** (chemical substances) are released into the synapse (i.e., the neuron fires) and land on a receptor site of the next neuron. That neuron then fires, sending an electrical impulse down the neuron to the axon, releasing neurotransmitters into the next synapse, and so the process begins again. Neurotransmitter activity is the basis for brain activity (thinking, feeling, and motor activity) and is related to many physical and mental disorders. Until recently, the activity of neurotransmitters in the brain had to be assessed indirectly from their presence in other parts of the body (blood or spinal fluid). However, it was always unclear how accurately chemicals in blood or spinal fluid really reflected neurotransmitter activity in the brain. Through advances in **neuroscience**, we now rely less on assumptions and indirect measures to understand the structure and function of the nervous system and its interaction with behavior. We can now directly observe many aspects of the brain's functioning, just as we do external behavior.

Imaging tests like the CAT and MRI examine the *morphology* (structure) of the brain and are used to determine whether parts of the brain are structurally different in those with and without psychological disorders. For example, the brains of patients with Alzheimer's disease have two structural abnormalities, *plaques* and *tangles,* which exist in far greater quantities than among older people without Alzheimer's disease (see Chapter 13). For other psychological disorders, the evidence is less definitive. In some disorders, such as post-traumatic stress disorder (PTSD, an anxiety disorder that occurs after a traumatic event), changes in the brain appear to be the result of, not the cause of, the disorder (Bellis, 2004). In other words, years of living with the disorder cause changes in the brain, a process sometimes known as **biological scarring**. In other instances, when compared to people with no disorder, the brains of people with schizophrenia show structural brain abnormalities that could occur before birth (Malla et al., 2002; Sallet et al., 2003; see Chapter 10). Although we do not know for certain how these structural abnormalities may influence behavior, they illustrate how our understanding of the brain and abnormal behavior has changed as a result of new technologies.

neurons nerve cells found throughout the body, including the brain

synapses spaces between neurons

neurotransmitters chemical substances that are released into the synapse and transmit information from one neuron to another

neuroscience the study of the structure and function of the nervous system and the interaction of that system and behavior

biological scarring the process whereby years of living with a disorder cause changes in the brain

Although some abnormal behaviors may be related to structural abnormalities, studies of brain *functioning* appear to be a more promising avenue of research. Advanced neuroimaging techniques such as Positron Emission Tomography (PET) and Functional Magnetic Resonance Imaging (fMRI; see Chapter 2) allow for mapping various areas of the brain, identifying brain areas that might be associated with various disorders. Differences in brain functioning have been reported for adults with schizophrenia (Holmes et al., 2005), depression (Holmes et al., 2005; Milak et al., 2005), adults and children with anxiety disorders (Baxter et al., 1992; Bellis, 2004), eating disorders (Wagner, 2005), and many other psychiatric disorders. These studies are numerous and will be reviewed throughout this book.

Although neuroscience data provide exciting new avenues for further research, it is still too soon to conclude that brain abnormalities cause psychological disorders. First, not all studies that compare people with and without a disorder find differences in brain structure or function. Furthermore, even when differences are detected, the abnormalities are not always found in a second trial, meaning that the abnormalities are not consistent. Second, to date, when differences exist, they are sometimes found in very different disorders. This means that whatever difference exists probably does not *cause* a specific disorder. Just like a fever that may be associated with many different physical illnesses, abnormal brain functioning may indicate that *something* is wrong, but not specifically what is wrong. Third, in most instances, few data indicate that these structural or functional abnormalities existed *before* the disorder occurred (schizophrenia and autism may be exceptions). It is just as likely that some disorders, such as post-traumatic stress disorder, may cause changes in brain functioning, if not necessarily brain structure. Over the next decade, continued research in these areas coupled with the development of even more sophisticated assessment devices and strategies may help clarify some of these issues.

The inheritance of physical traits such as hair color, eye color, height, and even predispositions toward some diseases (e.g., breast cancer, type I diabetes) is well established. It is perhaps less well known that some behavioral traits, both healthy traits and those that deviate from normal, are heritable. The field of **behavioral genetics** emerged with works by Sir Francis Galton (1822–1911) and his 1869 publication, *Hereditary Genius*. Since that time, behavioral genetics has explored the role of both genes and environment in the transmission of behavioral traits. Models of genetics research are presented in Chapter 2, and specific genetic theories for the various psychological disorders will be presented in other chapters.

Severe behavioral disorders, such as autism in children and schizophrenia in adults, have continued to defy simple explanations of biological or environmental etiology. Based on animal models that have found links between early viral infections and later behavioral changes, some researchers have proposed a **viral infection theory**. Specifically, during the prenatal period or shortly after birth, viral infections might cause brain abnormalities that later lead to behavioral abnormalities (see Chapters 10 and 12). However, we cannot yet say that this is a definitive cause, for the results of one study sometimes directly contradict another. Such contradictory findings are not unusual for psychology or any other science. As research continues, disparate findings are either reconciled or the theory is revised or discarded.

Even if future research confirms a relationship between viral infection and the onset of psychological disorders, there are still several different pathways that may produce this relationship. First, the virus may act *directly* by infecting the central nervous system (CNS). Similarly, infection elsewhere in the body could trigger the onset of a CNS disease. Second, viruses may act *indirectly* by changing the immune system of the mother or the fetus, thereby making one or both more susceptible to other biological or environmental factors. Third, both mechanisms may be involved (Libbey et al., 2005). Although some animal models suggest a possible relation between certain viruses and

behavioral genetics   field of study that explores the role of genes and environment in the transmission of behavioral traits

viral infection theory   the theory that during the prenatal period or shortly after birth, viral infections could cause some psychological disorders

changes in the brain, evidence that the virus *triggers* the onset of a disorder has proved elusive. The etiology of most psychological disorders is likely to be complex—not traceable to a single genetic, biological, or environmental factor. Other variables, yet to be discovered, may be responsible for triggering or modifying the course of illness.

PSYCHOLOGICAL MODELS

The biological model seeks the causes of abnormal behavior in the workings of the brain or body. By contrast, psychological approaches emphasize how environmental factors including parents and culture may influence the development and maintenance of abnormal behavior. In actuality, parental influence may be biological or psychological. Parents pass on their genes, but their influence is much broader. Parents can affect their children's behavior in at least four ways: through direct interaction, through their responses to a child's behavior, through modeling certain behaviors, or merely through giving instructions. Of course, a child's environment extends far beyond parents or even immediate family. The impact of other environmental factors, such as socioeconomic status, was illustrated earlier in the chapter. To provide another example, environmental events such as separation from biological parents increase the likelihood of depression in adolescents (Cuffe et al., 2005). Furthermore, in some cases, environmental and cultural influences may produce behavior that is considered abnormal in one culture but not in another, as in the earlier case of Maleah, where intergenerational bed-sharing was a commonly accepted practice in the Philippines. Cultural influences such as these are addressed below (see Sociocultural Theories).

Psychoanalysis   Sigmund Freud, the founder of psychoanalytic theory, believed that the roots of abnormal behavior could be found in events that occurred in the first 5 years of life. Because they happened so early, he believed that the person would retain no conscious memory of them—yet the unconscious memories would exert a lifelong influence on behavior. To understand the psychoanalytic perspective, it is necessary to examine three aspects of Freud's theory: the structure of the mind, the strategies used to deal with threats to the stability of the mind, and the stages of psychosocial development crucial for the development of normal (or abnormal) behavior.

In psychoanalytic theory, the mind consists of three regions: the id, ego, and superego. The *id* is the source of basic instinctual drives and the source of psychic energy, called *libido*. The id is pleasure-seeking, always seeking to gratify the libido's urges. The id is totally unconscious, so its urges and activities are outside our awareness. Think of the id as a professional athlete—"I want a big salary, I want a signing bonus." The *ego* develops from the id when the id comes in contact with reality. Think of the ego as a sports agent who mediates between the id's impulses (the athlete's desires) and the demands and restrictions of reality (the owner's contract offer). Rather than always seeking pleasure, the ego copes with reality, or as Freud put it, the ego obeys the reality principle. The ego has both conscious and unconscious components, so we are often aware of its actions. Finally, there is the *superego*, which is most similar to a conscience. The superego imposes moral restraint on the id's impulses (particularly those of a sexual or an aggressive nature). Think of the superego as the team owner or the league commissioner, who doles out monetary fines for breaking team or league rules. When moral rules are violated, the superego punishes with guilt feelings. Like the ego, the superego is partly conscious and partly unconscious. One function of the ego and superego is to manage or inhibit the id's impulses. Because these three intrapsychic forces constantly compete for expression, there is an ever-changing conflict, thus creating a dynamic, in this case, a *psychodynamic* system.

Another way the mind handles disruptive urges or unwanted feelings is by warding them off. For Freud, *defense mechanisms* keep unwanted thoughts and feelings from reaching conscious awareness. Through the use of these mechanisms, negative or distressing thoughts and feelings are expressed in a disguised, more acceptable form. Freud believed that some defense mechanisms prevented the onset of abnormal behavior. Other defense mechanisms (such as regression) may result in abnormal or age-inappropriate behaviors. Some of the defense mechanisms identified by Freud are presented in Table 1.3.

Almost as well known as the id, ego, and superego are Freud's stages of psychosexual development. In his theory, each person passes through these stages between infancy and 5 years of age. How a child copes with each stage has important effects on psychological development. The *oral phase* occurs during the first $1\frac{1}{2}$ years of life. Sucking and chewing are pleasurable experiences; aggressive impulses emerge after the development of teeth. The *anal phase* (from age $1\frac{1}{2}$ to 3 years) coincides with toilet training. During this time, parents emphasize discipline and control issues, and power struggles develop. Aggressive impulses on the part of the child could lead to

TABLE 1.3
Defense Mechanisms and Their Function

Defense	Function	Example
Denial	Dealing with an anxiety-provoking stimulus by acting as if it doesn't exist	Rejecting a physician's cancer diagnosis
Displacement	Taking out impulses on a less threatening target	Slamming a door instead of hitting someone
Intellectualization	Avoiding unacceptable emotions by focusing on the intellectual aspects	Focusing on a funeral's details rather than the sadness of the situation
Projection	Attributing your own unacceptable impulses to someone else	You make a mistake at work but instead of admitting it, you call a co-worker "incompetent"
Rationalization	Supplying a plausible but incorrect explanation for a behavior rather than the real reason	Saying you lost your job because you had a lousy boss when the problem was your poor work performance
Reaction formation	Taking the opposite belief because the true belief causes anxiety	Someone who is racially prejudiced overtly embraces that race to the extreme
Regression	Under threat, returning to a previous stage of development	Not getting a desired outcome results in a temper tantrum
Repression	Burying unwanted thoughts out of conscious thought	Forgetting aspects of a traumatic event (such as sexual assault)
Sublimation	Acting out unacceptable impulses in a socially acceptable way	Acting out aggressive tendencies by becoming a boxer
Suppression	Pushing unwanted thoughts into the unconscious	Actively trying to forget something that causes anxiety
Undoing	Attempt to take back unacceptable behavior or thoughts	Insulting someone and then excessively praising him/her

Adapted from *Psychology 101, Freud's Ego Defense Mechanism*. http://allpsych.com/psychology101/defenses.html. Copyright © 1999–2003, AllPsych and Heffner Media Group, Inc., All Rights Reserved.

personality traits of negativism and stubbornness, as well as the emergence of hostile, destructive, or sadistic behaviors. During the *phallic phase* (ages 3 to 5), psychosexual energy centers on the genital area; children derive pleasure from touching or rubbing the genital region. During this phase, children may develop romantic fantasies or attachments toward their opposite-sex parent. There are two additional psychosexual stages, *latency* and *genital* phases, although these are less often considered to play a role in abnormal behavior.

In psychoanalytic theory, disorders such as anxiety and depression are caused by negative experiences. Depending on the age at which the experience occurs, individuals become *fixated* (stalled) at a stage of psychosexual development, which leaves a psychological mark on the unconscious. For example, harsh parenting during toilet training results in a toddler who withholds his feces as a reaction. As an adult, this person will be stingy with money or gifts. In psychoanalytic theory, even though the individual is unaware of the early experience, it still influences daily functioning. In short, the individual behaves psychologically at the stage of development when the fixation occurred.

The goals of psychoanalysis, the treatment Freud developed, include *insight*, bringing the troubling material to consciousness, and *catharsis*, releasing psychic energy. Several techniques are used to achieve these goals. In *free association*, the person minimizes conscious control and without selection or censorship, tells the analyst everything that comes to mind, allowing the analyst to draw out information regarding unconscious conflicts. In *dream analysis*, individuals are encouraged to recall and recount their dreams, which are discussed in the analytic sessions. Freud called dreams the "royal road to the unconscious." He believed that dream content included many symbolic images that helped reveal the meaning of unconscious conflict. Another technique is *interpretation*, which Freud described as similar to the work of the archeologist or detective who attempts to reconstruct a past era or event through inferences from available fragments.

Modern Psychoanalytic Models   Freud's ideas have been carried on and revised by a number of other theorists. Initially, Freud named Carl Gustav Jung (1875–1961) as his successor. However, they disagreed over several key theoretical components, and Jung broke away to develop *Analytic Therapy*. Unlike Freud, Jung believed that behavioral motivators were psychological and spiritual (not sexual) and that behavior was motivated by future goals rather than determined by past events. Another former colleague, Alfred Adler (1870–1937), also broke with Freud to develop his own psychoanalytic school called *Individual Psychology*. Less comprehensive than Freud, Adler introduced several concepts that are part of everyday language and are associated with abnormal behavior: *sibling rivalry*, the importance of *birth order*, and the *inferiority complex*, where real or perceived inferiority leads to efforts to compensate for the deficiency.

More contemporary models of psychoanalysis, such as **ego psychology**, deviate from Freud by their greater focus on conscious motivations, healthy forms of human functioning, and the integrity of personality (rather than three distinct parts). *Object relations theory*, for example, addresses people's emotional relations with important *objects* (in this sense, people or things to which the person is attached). This theory emphasizes that people have a basic drive for social interactions and that motivations for social contact are greater than simply to satisfy sexual and aggressive instincts. Therapy uses the patient's relationship with the therapist to examine and build other relationships in their lives.

Behavioral Models   Unlike the psychodynamic perspective, where internal mental elements exert an influence on behavior, learning theory stresses the importance of external events in the onset of abnormal behaviors. According to learning theory, behavior is the product of an individual's learning history. Abnormal behavior is therefore

ego psychology   a form of psychodynamic theory that focuses on conscious motivations and healthy forms of human functioning

operant conditioning a form of learning in which behavior is acquired or changed by the events that happen afterward

reinforcement a contingent event that strengthens the response that precedes it

the result of maladaptive learning experiences. Behavioral theories do not ignore biological factors; instead, they acknowledge that biology interacts with the environment to influence behavior. Strict behaviorists focus on observable and measurable behavior and do not examine inner psychic causes, the internal structure of personality, and ongoing mental processes. They believe that abnormal behavior results from environmental events that shape future behavior, such as the conditioning events that led to Little Albert's fear. In contrast to psychoanalytic theory, for behavioral theory, significant experiences need not occur only during the first 5 years of life but rather can occur at any point in life.

Despite the pioneering work of Pavlov, Watson, Rayner, and Jones, behavior therapy remained in its infancy until the 1950s. Then a South African psychiatrist, Joseph Wolpe (1915–1997), dissatisfied with psychoanalysis, began to study experimental *neurosis* (anxiety) in animals. Using a classical conditioning paradigm, a dog learned that food followed the presentation of a circle but not an ellipse. Then, Wolpe altered the shape of the circle and the ellipse so that *discrimination* (and therefore, the signal for food) became increasingly difficult (is it a circle? is it an ellipse?). The dog struggled, became agitated, barked violently, and attacked the equipment, behaviors that would indicate the presence of negative emotions. Wolpe also observed that the severity of the fear was a function of the similarity between a new situation and the situation in which the fear was first acquired.

Once Wolpe demonstrated how classical conditioning principles could account for the development of anxiety, he applied the same principles to eliminate fear. In his landmark book *Psychotherapy by Reciprocal Inhibition* (Wolpe, 1958), Wolpe proposed that a stimulus will not elicit anxiety if an *incompatible behavior* (such as feeling relaxed) occurs at the same time. In other words, it is not possible to feel anxious and relaxed (or anxious and happy) at the same time; they are incompatible emotions. Mary Cover Jones treated Peter by selecting a situation that she thought would promote relaxation (other children playing in the room). In contrast, Wolpe specifically taught his patient how to relax. Then he deliberately paired relaxation (the incompatible response) with the fear-producing event. With repeated pairings, he eliminated anxiety.

Just as Jones began treatment of Little Peter by placing the rabbit at the opposite corner of the room and then moved it progressively closer, Wolpe used a *hierarchy*, in which elements of the anxiety-producing object are presented in a gradual fashion. For someone who fears flying, the hierarchy might include going to the airport, sitting in the boarding area, getting on the plane, taking off, and so on. Relaxation is paired with each step in the hierarchy. This therapy, called *systematic desensitization,* is very effective for a range of anxiety problems. Although used less frequently today than 30 to 40 years ago, systematic desensitization still forms the foundation for many current behavior therapy procedures.

"The more often I tell him to sit down, the more he stands up." This line, which could have been spoken by Derek's second-grade teacher, illustrates the powerful effect of attention. Sometimes yelling at a child for bad behavior actually increases it. To understand why, it is necessary to first understand the work of B. F. Skinner (1904–1990). Skinner observed that many behaviors occurred without *first* being elicited by a UCS. Rather, using animal models, he demonstrated that behavior could be acquired or changed by the events that happened *afterward.* Known as **operant conditioning**, these principles are relevant to the behaviors of individuals, groups, and entire societies.

The basic principle behind operant theory is **reinforcement**, which is defined as a contingent event that strengthens the behavior that precedes it. In its simplest form, a reinforcer may be considered to

B. F. Skinner explained how behaviors could be acquired or changed by reinforcement, a process called operant conditioning.

be a reward—a child does household chores and the reward is a weekly allowance. If the allowance is contingent upon (occurs only after) the completion of the chores, it is likely that the child will do chores again. The allowance is a *reinforcer* because it functions to increase behavior. Skinner identified several principles of reinforcement. First, reinforcers are always individual—what is a reinforcer for one person is not necessarily a reinforcer for another person (chocolate is not a reinforcer for everyone). Second, there are primary and secondary reinforcers. *Primary reinforcers* are objects such as food, water, or even attention. They have their own intrinsic value (that is, they satisfy basic needs of life or make one feel good). *Secondary reinforcers* are objects that have acquired value because they become associated with primary reinforcers. Money is a secondary reinforcer because it symbolizes the ability to acquire other reinforcers (heat in cold weather, a cold drink when thirsty). Much of Skinner's work was devoted to *schedules of reinforcement,* which established the "when" and "how" of reinforcement and set forth conditions under which behavior was more likely to be acquired or less likely to be extinguished. Skinner's work has applications for parenting, education, psychology, and many other aspects of behavior. How does Skinner's work apply to Derek? For children, adult attention is a powerful reinforcer. If every time Derek stands up, the teacher calls out his name (gives him attention) and asks him to sit down (or even worse, calls him aside and spends time asking him why he keeps standing up), this positive attention could be reinforcing, increasing the likelihood that when Derek wants attention, he will stand up again.

Children often learn behaviors by watching a model perform them, a process called vicarious conditioning.

Whereas reinforcement serves to increase the frequency of a behavior, **punishment** has the opposite effect: it decreases or eliminates a behavior. Punishment can be the application of something painful (spanking) or the removal of something positive (no television). Sometimes punishment is necessary to quickly eliminate a very dangerous behavior, as when a child with severe mental retardation engages in self-mutilating behaviors. The withdrawal of something positive, such as in a *time-out* (having a child sit in a corner for a few minutes), is often effective for behaviors such as tantrumming. Skinner advocated the use of reinforcement rather than punishment. Punishment suppresses a behavior, but if an alternative, substitute behavior is not acquired, the punished behavior reemerges. Therefore, when punishment is used to suppress a behavior, reinforcement of an alternative, positive behavior must also occur.

How do the dolphins at the aquarium learn to leap into the air, spin around three times, and then slide on a ramp to receive the applause of a human audience? The trainers use a procedure called *shaping,* a process whereby closer steps, or successive approximations, to a final goal are rewarded. Dolphin trainers begin by reinforcing (with food) any initial attempt or slight movement that resembles a turn. Gradually, the trainer requires a larger turn before providing reinforcement, until finally the dolphin must completely spin around before receiving reinforcement. Shaping is an effective procedure for the acquisition of new behaviors in children and adults and will be discussed in several other chapters in this book.

A third type of learning was described by Albert Bandura (1925–) and his colleagues at Stanford University during the early 1960s. **Vicarious conditioning** is characterized by *no trial learning*—the person need not actually do the behavior in order to learn it. Learning occurs when the person watches a model, that is, someone who demonstrates a behavior. Observation of another person can have a disinhibiting or inhibiting effect on current behaviors, or can teach new behaviors. This kind of *social learning* can explain the acquisition of abnormal behaviors such as aggression.

For behavior therapists, therapy focuses on the elimination of abnormal behaviors and on the acquisition of new behaviors and skills. Treatment targets the patient's

punishment application of something painful or the removal of something positive

vicarious conditioning a distinct type of learning in which the person need not actually do the behavior in order to acquire it

current symptoms. Although the past is considered important in understanding the present and the patient's current psychological distress, behavior therapy does not focus specifically on the early years of life. Furthermore, achieving insight is not considered sufficient to produce behavior change. Rather, behavior therapists focus directly on helping patients change their behavior in order to alleviate their psychological problems.

The Cognitive Model   The cognitive model proposes that abnormal behavior is a result of distorted cognitive (mental) processes, not internal forces or external events. According to cognitive theory, it is not situations and events that affect our emotions and behavior; rather, it is the way that we perceive or think about those events. Imagine that you fail the first test in your abnormal psychology class. If you think to yourself, "well, that was a hard test, but now I know what the instructor wants and I'll do better the next time," you are likely to feel okay about yourself and study harder for the next test. If however, after you fail the test you think, "I'm an idiot, why did I ever think I could be a psychologist," you may feel sad and lose your enthusiasm for the class. You may even decide that you should drop out. In each case, the situation was the same. It was what you thought about the situation, and yourself, that affected your mood and your future behavior. That is the core of cognitive theory. According to Aaron Beck (1921–), the originator of cognitive therapy, people with depression have three types of negative thoughts: a negative view of the self, the world, and the future. Beck called this the "negative cognitive triad." These negative assumptions are often called *cognitive distortions*. People may have many different types of distorted cognitive processes that affect their mood and behavior (see Table 1.4).

TABLE 1.4
Common Cognitive Distortions

Type	Example
All or nothing thinking	If I don't go to Harvard, I'll be a bum.
Overgeneralizing	Every thing I do is wrong.
Mental filtering	The instructor said the paper was good, but he criticized my example on page 6. He really hated the paper.
Disqualifying the positive	Sure I got an A but that was pure luck. I'm not that smart.
Jumping to conclusions	The bank teller barely looked at me. She really hates me.
Magnifying or minimizing	I mispronounced that word in my speech. I really screwed up. OR I can dance well but that's not really important—being smart is what's important and I'm not smart.
Catastrophizing	I failed this quiz. I'll never graduate from college.
Emotional reasoning	I feel hopeless, so this situation must be hopeless.
Making "should" statements	I should get an A in this class even though it is really hard.
Mislabeling	I failed this quiz. I'm a complete and total idiot.
Personalizing	We did not get that big account at work. It is all my fault.

Based on Burns, D. D. (1989). *The Feeling Good Handbook.* New York: William Morrow and Company.

In order to change abnormal behaviors, cognitive therapy is directed at modifying the distorted thought processes. Therapists assign "behavioral experiments" in which the patient engages in a certain activity and then examines the thoughts that accompany the activity. With therapist assistance, the patient learns to challenge negative thoughts, to assess the situation more realistically, and to generate alternative, more positive, thoughts. Cognitive therapy and behavior therapy share many similarities, but there are some differences. First, cognitive therapy is based on the assumption that internal cognitive processes must be the target of therapy, whereas behavior therapy assumes that changing behavior will lead to a change in cognitions. Second, cognitive therapy relies more on the use of traditional "talk" psychotherapy and insight than does traditional behavior therapy. Despite some theoretical differences, comparisons of behavior therapy and cognitive therapy suggest that they are equally effective treatments for most psychological disorders. In many cases, treatment procedures originally developed under one model or the other are now used together, thus the term *cognitive-behavior therapy*.

The Humanistic Model   Based on **phenomenology**, a school of thought that holds that one's subjective perception of the world is more important than the actual world, humanists believe that people are basically good and are motivated to *self-actualize* (develop their full potential). Abnormal behaviors occur when there is a failure in the process of self-actualization, usually as a result of people's failure to recognize their weaknesses and establish processes and strategies to fulfill their potential for positive growth.

The psychologist most closely associated with humanistic psychology is Carl Rogers (1902–1987). His theory of abnormal behavior begins with the assumption that psychopathology is associated with psychological incongruence, or a discrepancy between one's self-image and one's actual self. The greater the discrepancy, the more emotional and real-world problems one experiences. Incongruence results from the experience of *conditional* positive regard—a person is treated with respect and caring only when meeting the standards set by others (i.e., conditionally). The person comes to believe that he or she is worthy only when meeting those standards. Because this is an inaccurate, overly demanding image, emotional or behavioral problems result.

The goal of Rogers' psychotherapy, called *client-centered therapy,* is to release the individual's existing capacity to self-actualize (reach full potential) through interactions with the therapist. Therapy is based on three components. *Genuineness* refers to understanding the client's experiences both intellectually and emotionally. *Empathic understanding* means that the therapist understands the client's world as the client sees it. Finally, the therapist expresses *unconditional positive regard* by genuinely accepting the client with full understanding, trusting the client's resources for self-understanding and positive change. Whereas psychoanalytic therapy focuses on understanding the patient's past experiences, client-centered therapy focuses on present experiences, believing that the reestablishment of awareness and trust in that experience will lead to positive change.

SOCIOCULTURAL MODELS

All of the models of abnormal behavior discussed so far begin with the assumption that abnormality lies within the individual. Instead, **sociocultural models** propose that abnormal behavior must be understood within the context of social and cultural forces, such as gender roles, social class, and interpersonal resources. From this perspective, abnormal behavior does not simply result from biological or psychological factors but also reflects the social and cultural environment in which a person lives. Many social and cultural forces may influence behavior; we will discuss only a few here.

One well-studied social factor is *gender role*, defined as the cultural expectations regarding accepted behaviors for men and women, boys and girls. These differing role

phenomenology   a school of thought that holds that one's subjective perception of the world is more important than the world in actuality

sociocultural models   the idea that abnormal behavior must be understood within the context of social and cultural forces

Gender role expectations affect behavior. In Western cultures, showing emotion openly is more acceptable among females than among males

expectancies often exert a powerful influence on the expression of abnormal behavior. Consider the fact that girls (and women) are much more likely than boys (or men) to admit to having a phobia. Could gender role expectations, rather than biology, explain this difference? In Western cultures, girls are allowed to express emotions openly, whereas society discourages such behavior among boys—consider the phrases "boys don't cry" or "take it like a man." The implication is that showing emotion is not appropriate behavior for males and therefore not accepted in Western society. So boys learn to hide or deny emotions, such as fear. Other disorders possibly influenced by gender role are eating disorders, which are more common in girls and may be triggered by pervasive sociocultural pressures on women to be thin (see Chapter 7).

In addition to gender role, other social factors such as hunger, work, and domestic violence may make women more vulnerable to psychological distress (Lopez & Guarnaccia, 2000). More than 60% of women in developing countries do not have adequate food. In both developed and developing countries, women do not receive equal pay even when they are performing dangerous, labor-intensive jobs; and more often than men, they are victims of domestic violence. These factors, perhaps even in combination with others, are perceived to play a significant role in the development of psychological disorders, perhaps placing women at higher risk, not because of their biology but because of the social context in which they live.

Socioeconomic status is another social factor that may affect the development of psychological disorders. After Hurricane Andrew, rates of one type of psychological disorder, post-traumatic stress disorder (PTSD), were higher among African American and Hispanic children than among white children (LaGreca et al., 1996). On first glance, this difference might be attributed to race or ethnicity, but another important factor might be socioeconomic status (SES). Why might SES be an important factor? People from the lowest income bracket are more likely to live in housing that is easily damaged by strong winds and therefore are more likely to be homeless after a storm. Think back to Hurricane Katrina in 2005. Although all areas of New Orleans were affected by the storm, the areas of the city that were closest to the floodplain housed some of the city's poorest families. Coupled with the limited economic infrastructure that existed before the storm, these residents face continuing economic hardship and slow recovery (Meyers, 2008). With few social or economic resources, the likelihood of emotional distress and psychological disorders increases.

Interpersonal support is another social factor that helps people during times of emotional distress. Although many of the people most affected by Hurricane Katrina had few economic resources, they had deep neighborhood roots. Now, even years later, many remain displaced from their homes and their former social support systems, leading to the emergence of psychological disorders such as depression, anxiety, and post-traumatic stress disorder. As is obvious from this brief review, many different social factors can affect the onset of psychological distress, and throughout this volume, we will return to these issues as we attempt to understand abnormal behavior.

Along with social factors, the sociocultural model also includes cultural influences such as race and ethnicity. Historically, these variables were used unfairly to stereotype groups. In the early nineteenth century, for example, the brains of Africans, Native Americans, and Asians were considered to be simple and crude, leading to lower rates of insanity (Raimundo Oda et al., 2005). Insanity was believed to result from having to cope with the stresses of Western civilized life and was also thought to require a higher level of cognitive sophistication. Today, that explanation has been discarded but context and culture are still considered to be important influences on all types of behavior, including abnormal behavior.

Cultural factors may affect symptom expression and diagnosis. With respect to symptom expression, several different variables are important. First, are behaviors that are considered abnormal in one culture also considered abnormal in other cultures? In Puerto Rico, *dissociation* (a feeling of being detached from one's body—sometimes called an out of body experience) is considered a normal part of spiritual and religious experiences, but it would be regarded as abnormal in other Western cultures (Lewis Fernandez, 1998; Tsai et al., 2001). Similarly, behaviors that suggest extreme suspiciousness and mistrust of others may justifiably be labeled paranoia in white patients. Among other cultures and groups, however, these behaviors may simply be an adaptive response from people who have been marginalized because of sociodemographic factors or who have been the victims of stereotype or racial discrimination (Whaley, 1998).

Researchers with a sociocultural perspective examine how psychological disorders may express themselves differently in different cultures. Some of these different expressions are known as *culture-bound syndromes*, defined as certain conditions that are specific to a culture (Lopez & Guarnaccia, 2004; Miranda & Fraser, 2002). One such disorder, *ataque de nervios* (see Chapter 4), is found among Latinos, primarily those from the Caribbean. Although some symptoms of *ataque* (heart palpitations, trembling) are also found among non-Latinos, some are not (screaming uncontrollably, becoming physically aggressive). In addition, social forces also play a role with respect to when this disorder occurs. Specifically, *ataque* symptoms commonly occur as a result of social disruptions (changes in family status or close social networks; Guarnaccia et al., 1989).

Other cultural research examines whether psychological disorders that exist in one culture or country are also present in other cultures or countries, and what factors might account for these differences. For example, children in Thailand referred to a mental health clinic for treatment mostly display anxious and depressive symptoms, whereas children in the United States have more aggressive and conduct problems (Weisz et al., 1997). However, when researchers studied children in the community, rather than children referred to the clinic, there were no differences in the rates of aggression among U.S. and Thai children. The researchers explain these differences in terms of cultural factors. Specifically, religious and cultural practices in Thailand place a strong emphasis on self-control and restraint. Therefore, psychological distress in

Although Hurricane Katrina affected many residents of New Orleans, people pulled together to help one another, creating a social network that could prevent or lessen the hurricane's impact.

Among Hispanic families, "familism" may buffer people against stressful environments and events. Here a family participates in a cultural tradition. Quinceañera, a coming of age ceremony and celebration that occurs on a girl's fifteenth birthday, dates back to ancient native cultures of Central and South America, and Mexico.

Thai children may be modified by this cultural value and expressed in ways that do not involve aggression toward others. Yet, the distress is there, manifesting itself in "internal" symptoms of sad mood, fear, and anxiety, rather than aggressive behaviors.

As researchers gain a better understanding of the important roles that social and cultural factors play in the onset, expression, and treatment of psychological disorders, they are developing culturally sensitive treatments for many different disorders. These treatment approaches incorporate cultural values and expressions that may enhance the therapeutic process by increasing the number of people who seek, and benefit from, these enhanced interventions. Consider the cultural context that surrounds suicide. U.S.-born Latino adolescents are twice as likely to attempt suicide as foreign-born Latino youths (CDC, 2006). Although many factors are involved in the decision to attempt suicide, *familism* may be one factor to explain the higher rate of suicide attempts among Latino youth born in the United States. Familism is an orientation common in Latino cultures that emphasizes the centrality of, and obligation to, family over self or peers (Lugo et al., 2003). This orientation differs from that of mainstream U.S. teen culture, which emphasizes peer relationships, individualism, and moving away from the family (Goldston et al., 2008). It is possible that Latino teens (particularly those born in the U.S.) experience dissolution of the traditional familism when constantly exposed to the mainstream U.S. culture of individualism. The lack of emphasis on familial obligation may be a factor that leads to higher rates of suicide. It is also important to consider the family's significant role in Latino culture. Treatment may need to be modified to address this important cultural element. Currently, several interventions developed for depressed adolescents have been modified by including more direct involvement of parents in the treatment program. Although much more research is needed, culturally sensitive interventions are likely to increase the acceptance of, and therefore the effectiveness of, psychological interventions for psychological disorders.

THE BIOPSYCHOSOCIAL MODEL

In this chapter, we have examined biological, psychological, social, and cultural factors that affect the development and expression of abnormal behaviors. One reason there are so many different models is that no one perspective is able to explain all aspects of behavior and certainly not all cases of abnormal behavior.

Current approaches to physical medicine assume that all illnesses are based on biological processes that can be reduced to a biological cause, even if the specific physical process has not yet been determined. For example, we know that cancer occurs when abnormal cells develop and attack the body's systems, even though, as yet, we do not know what physical processes caused these cells to develop. In contrast, in the case of mental disorders, there is no single model of abnormal behavior, even though since the days of Hippocrates, scientists have searched for such single explanations (Lake, 2007). Instead, there are a diversity of models, and often the training backgrounds of mental health professionals result in different perspectives being emphasized. Modern scientists now recognize that (a) abnormal behavior is complex, (b) abnormal behavior cannot be understood using a single theoretical explanation, and (c) understanding abnormal behavior will advance only if we embrace and integrate the various conceptual models (Kendler, 2005). A significant challenge to understanding abnormal behavior

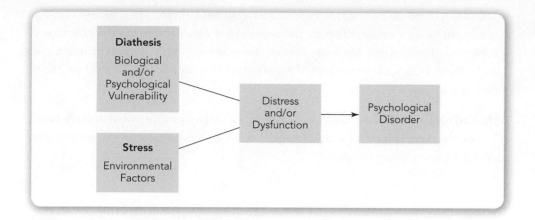

FIGURE 1.3
The Diathesis-stress Model

In this model, a *diathesis*, or vulnerability, interacts with individual stressors to produce a psychological disorder. The biopsychosocial model uses the concept of diathesis-stress to acknowledge that many different factors (biological, psychological, and social) may contribute to the development of a disorder.

is to understand how the mind and the brain interact and how to combine these very different perspectives to create a coherent theory of psychological disorders. In fact, modern scientists have moved past trying to reduce all behavior to one singular explanation. It is clear that causality can begin in the brain OR the mind, and can set off a chain of events that ultimately also affect the other component, leading to the onset of abnormal behavior (Kendler, 2005). Other researchers (Lake, 2007) have argued that integrating the perspectives of biomedicine, human consciousness, and neuroscience will lead to significant advances in understanding and treating psychological disorders.

Currently, most mental health clinicians subscribe to a **biopsychosocial perspective**, which acknowledges that many different factors probably contribute to the development of abnormal behavior and that different factors may be important for different people. This perspective utilizes a **diathesis-stress model of abnormal behavior**, which begins with the assumption that psychological disorders may have a biological basis (see Figure 1.3). The presence of a biological or psychological predisposition to a disease or disorder is called a **diathesis**. However, just having a *predisposition* for a disorder does not mean that a person will actually *develop* the disorder. Rather, the predisposition is assumed to lie dormant (as if it does not exist) until stressful environmental factors create significant distress for the individual. People react differently to stressful events. It is the combination of a biological predisposition and the presence of environmental stress that creates psychological disorders. The diathesis-stress model integrates biological, psychological, and sociocultural systems to provide explanations that are consistent with what we know are complex human behaviors. We will return to this biopsychosocial model and the diathesis-stress model many times throughout this volume.

concept CHECK

- The biological model of abnormal behavior assumes that abnormal behavior is rooted in a person's biology. The basis may be a genetic abnormality, abnormal brain structures, or abnormal brain functioning.

- Within the psychological model are several distinctive approaches, including psychoanalytic, modern psychoanalytic, behavioral, and cognitive models. Rather than looking to biology as the basis for psychological disorders, these models assume that environmental events, and how we interpret and react to those events, play a causal role in the onset of abnormal behavior.

- Sociocultural models are based on a broader perspective, proposing that broad social and cultural forces (not individual or unique environmental events) contribute to the onset of psychological disorders.

biopsychosocial perspective the idea that biological, psychological, and social factors probably contribute to the development of abnormal behavior and different factors are important for different individuals

diathesis-stress model of abnormal behavior the idea that psychological disorders may have a biological predisposition (diathesis) that lies dormant until environmental stress occurs and the combination produces abnormal behavior

- The biopsychosocial perspective incorporates a diathesis-stress model, wherein biology is thought to lay the foundation for the onset of the disorder through the presence of biological abnormalities. However, biology alone is insufficient; environmental, social, and cultural factors are always part of the equation that leads to the onset of psychological disorders.

APPLICATION QUESTION: Using a biopsychosocial perspective, what factors might influence the development of a psychological disorder in a member of the military who served in Operation Iraqi Freedom?

THE WHOLE STORY: MARCIE—HOW ONE DISORDER MIGHT HAVE BEEN UNDERSTOOD AND TREATED THROUGHOUT THE AGES

Feelings of depression have been documented since the beginning of recorded history, and depression is a common psychological disorder, affecting 17% of the general population.

The Patient: *Marcie just started college. She grew up in a small town but enrolled in a major state university far from home. Her family has few financial resources, and the university scholarship was her only opportunity for a college education. She was reluctant to leave home, but her family and teachers encouraged her because it was a tremendous opportunity. When Marcie was a child, she went to camp one summer and was very homesick for an entire week. Now Marcie is having those same feelings again as she tries to adjust to college life in a new town. She is very sad, cries for no reason, and has stopped attending classes. She believes that she is a failure for being unable to adjust and is afraid to tell her parents how she feels. She barely talks to her roommate, who is very concerned about the change in her behavior. Marcie no longer takes a shower, sometimes does not get out of bed, and will go for several days without eating. She talks about being "better off dead."*

Depression can be conceptualized from various perspectives, each of which would provide a unique approach toward treatment. If we were to convene a panel of experts to discuss various approaches to Marcie's treatment, we might hear the following perspectives:

Assessment and Treatment:

Hippocrates (380 BC): *"It is obvious that the patient is suffering from an excess of black bile, which causes feelings of melancholia. In order to restore the humours to a balanced state, she needs to eat a vegetable diet and engage in physical activity. She also needs a tranquil existence, which would include a period of celibacy."*

Roman Catholic priest (1596): *"Her symptoms are a direct result of possession by a demon, with whom she has engaged in illicit relations. Her failure to follow the rules of authority (go to class) and her wish to die are sinful acts and clearly indicate that she is in league with the devil. She may even be a witch."*

Phillippe Pinel, M.D. (1800): *"Mental illness is curable if we take the time to understand it. Marcie must be taken away from the environment that caused this problem and placed in the hospital, where she will be assigned to work in the garden. This physical activity will allow her to rest in the evening and her spirit will be restored."*

Sigmund Freud, M.D. (1920): *"Although on one level, Marcie is grateful for the opportunity to study at the university, on a deeper, more unconscious level, she may feel anger and resentment toward her parents for not having the resources to allow her to study at a more prestigious school that was closer to home. This anger was particularly scary as her mother was suffering from breast cancer. Her superego, whose job it is to keep these unacceptable emotions in check, turned the anger she felt toward her parents back onto herself, resulting in depression, which especially because of her mother's condition, is a more socially acceptable emotion."*

B.F. Skinner, Ph.D. (1965): *"Marcie has learned depressive behaviors through a series of reinforcing experiences. She probably receives significant attention from her family every time that she calls home and tells them she is homesick. She may feel sad, but the way to change emotion is to change behavior and the contingencies that control it. I suggest that all those who interact with her provide positive reinforcement for "nondepressive" behaviors (e.g., engaging in social activities, completing assignments) and extinguish, or ignore, depressive behaviors (e.g., not going to class, staying in her dorm room)."*

Cognitive Psychologist, Ph.D. (2005): *"Marcie's depression is the result of her negative perspective regarding herself and the world. All college students have trouble adjusting to new environments. However, Marcie's cognitive schema has falsely interpreted this adjustment difficulty as a sign of personal weakness and failure. In therapy, we will examine these dysfunctional beliefs and help Marcie develop a more positive, functional perspective."*

Biological Psychiatrist, M.D. (2006): *"This patient meets diagnostic criteria for major depressive disorder, single episode. She has no history of mania. Her family history is positive for depression (mother, maternal aunt, possibly grandmother), and her paternal grandfather committed suicide. Because her mother had a positive response to a selective serotonin reuptake inhibitor, I recommend a course of fluoxetine (Prozac) 20mg/day as an initial dose."*

Biopsychosocial Clinician (2008): *"Marcie's depression clearly shows how numerous factors combine to create her distress. Her family history indicates the presence of a genetic predisposition, leaving her vulnerable to the development of depression. However, she did not have any difficulties until she went to college, and the stress from (a) moving far away from home for the first time and (b) needing to keep her grades high so that she could maintain her scholarship are most likely environmental and social factors that triggered the actual onset of the negative mood. Medication may be useful in the short term, but Marcie needs to learn how to cope with stress so that she has the tools to counteract her biological predisposition and prevent future episodes because she will face stressors throughout her lifetime."*

CRITICAL ISSUES to remember

1. Abnormal behavior is sometimes difficult to define. It is not just behavior that is different, for certain differences can sometimes be positive for the individual and perhaps for society. Behavior that is deviant may be different but not necessarily abnormal. New trends often start as deviant but then become accepted by mainstream society. Dangerous behavior may be abnormal, but many individuals who have psychological disorders do not engage in dangerous behaviors. Dangerous behavior is not necessary or sufficient for the definition of abnormal behavior. Two primary considerations for determining whether a behavior is abnormal is whether it creates dysfunction (interferes with daily activities) and/or emotional distress.

2. Abnormal behavior is defined as behavior that is inconsistent with the individual's developmental, cultural, and societal norms, creates significant emotional distress, or interferes with daily functioning.

3. Behavior must always be considered in context. Context includes culture as defined by both individual and social spheres of influence as well as cultural traditions. It also includes consideration of developmental age, physical and emotional maturity, and socioeconomic status.

4. Historically, spirit possession was among the first proposed causes of abnormal behavior. However, as early as the classical Greek and Roman periods, biological and environmental explanations were given for some of the major psychiatric disorders (depression, schizophrenia). Such theories fell out of favor in Western Europe shortly afterward, although they continued to flourish in the Middle East. It was not until the Renaissance period that theories based on biology and environmental factors reemerged in Europe.

5. To understand abnormal behavior, it is a distinct advantage to adopt a scientist-practitioner approach. Critically applying a scientific perspective to theories of etiology and examining the evidence behind proposed theories prevent adhering to explanations that are without a firm scientific basis (such as witchcraft or pseudoscience). "Treatments" based on such ideas could have quite negative results and, in some cases, might even be deadly.

6. Today, biological, psychological, sociocultural, and biopsychosocial explanations dominate the explanations for the development of abnormal behavior. Each of the etiological theories has strengths and weaknesses, and each alone is inadequate to fully explain the presence of abnormal behavior. Determining abnormal behavior is complex, and it is likely that a combination of factors is responsible for any specific psychological disorder. There are many competing theories, and as science progresses, new theories will be developed and others will be discarded.

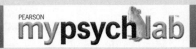

1. Abnormal behavior must always be considered in context because
   a. normal feelings, such as grief, can be mistaken for illness
   b. a person's cultural background may affect behavior
   c. a person's age may affect his or her symptoms
   d. all of the above

2. To be considered abnormal, a person's behavior must be "away from normal" and
   a. a violation of the individual's culture
   b. a cause of emotional distress and/or functional impairment
   c. a source of conflict with a person's peer group
   d. an embarrassment to the person's family

3. Contextual factors that should be considered in evaluating abnormal behavior include sex, race/ethnicity, and
   a. cognitive skills
   b. dimensional approaches
   c. personality problems
   d. socioeconomic status

4. It is important to consider a person's age and developmental stage when evaluating behavior because
   a. children have more serious disorders than adults do
   b. adults may not report all their symptoms
   c. developmental maturity affects what disorders occur and what symptoms are present
   d. disorders not treated during childhood will always persist throughout life

5. Our knowledge of early theories of abnormal behavior is limited because
   a. historical evidence is scanty
   b. modern technology cannot study demons and spirits
   c. only organic models were used before the modern era
   d. until recently, no records of patients' symptoms were kept

6. Hippocrates was an ancient Greek physician who
   a. produced a diagnostic classification system and a model by which to explain abnormal behavior
   b. identified common psychological symptoms such as hallucinations, melancholia, and mania
   c. introduced the term *hysteria*
   d. all of the above

7. In the Middle Ages, groups of people believed they were possessed by demons. Such episodes of mass hysteria are now explained by the concept of
   a. mimicry behavior
   b. emotional contagion
   c. alien abduction
   d. lycanthropy

8. Moral treatment, the eighteenth-century innovation of Philippe Pinel and William Tuke, was characterized by
   a. daily compulsory church attendance
   b. imposition of a work schedule to teach patients duty and productivity

   c. separation of patients from evil influences outside their homes
   d. kind treatment of patients and work to occupy their minds

9. When symptoms are diminished or eliminated not because of any specific treatment, but because the patient believes that a treatment is effective, we see the power of the
   a. therapeutic relationship
   b. placebo effect
   c. humane care movement
   d. animal magnetism effect

10. German psychiatrist Emil Kraepelin contributed to the study of abnormal psychology by
    a. observing hundreds of living patients
    b. introducing two diagnostic categories
    c. laying the groundwork for a classification system
    d. all of the above

11. The scientist-practitioner approach is important in the treatment of patients because patients are
    a. treated by clinicians who have developed models of human behavior
    b. taught how to evaluate research and choose treatments
    c. treated by clinicians who use empirical research to guide the treatment process
    d. able to help advance psychological research by being research subjects

12. The biological model seeks knowledge of abnormal behavior by studying
    a. the biology of the body, particularly of the brain
    b. biological scarring and structural abnormalities
    c. brain morphology as it affects bodily processes
    d. neuroimaging techniques

13. Biological scarring, or the process whereby years of living with a disorder causes changes in the brain, demonstrates the
    a. interaction among biopsychosocial factors
    b. importance of the psychoanalytic model
    c. interaction between psychological and social factors
    d. significance of downward drift

14. Compared with Freud, contemporary psychoanalytic theorists place less emphasis on psychosexual development and more importance on
    a. phenomenology
    b. sibling rivalry
    c. conscious motivation
    d. dream analysis

15. Pioneer behaviorist Joseph Wolpe discovered that a stimulus will not elicit fear or anxiety if
    a. conditioning prevents negative emotions
    b. operant conditioning reinforces relaxation
    c. discrimination becomes increasingly difficult
    d. incompatible behavior occurs at the same time

16. Behaviorist B. F. Skinner demonstrated that behavior could be changed by events that happened afterward, a phenomenon known as
    a. operant conditioning
    c. fear hierarchy
    b. systematic desensitization
    d. contingent reinforcement

17. Vicarious conditioning is different from other types of conditioning in that it involves
    a. shaping rather than punishment
    b. learning without punitive consequences
    c. learning without actually doing a behavior
    d. acquiring new behaviors by practice

18. The cognitive model is based on the idea that our
    a. perceptions and interpretations of events are more important than the events themselves
    b. cognitive abilities differ depending on our developmental stage
    c. brains are permanently affected by external events
    d. intelligence level determines which disorders we are prone to

19. A clinician who notes the role of a patient's sex, income level, and race in his or her problems is illustrating the influence of
    a. class differences
    b. sociocultural models
    c. symptom expression
    d. feminist psychology

20. When a clinician finds that several members of a patient's family have similar symptoms, he or she may suspect that the patient has a predisposition to illness known as a
    a. stressor
    b. biological model
    c. genetic abnormality
    d. diathesis

Answers: 1 d, 2 b, 3 d, 4 c, 5 a, 6 d, 7 b, 8 d, 9 b, 10 d, 11 c, 12 a, 13 a, 14 c, 15 d, 16 a, 17 c, 18 a, 19 b, 20 d.

CHAPTER
objectives

After reading this chapter, you should be able to:

1 Understand how research in psychology ranges from the cellular to the population level.

2 Recognize new techniques used to study abnormal psychology at the cellular or neuroanatomical level.

3 Understand the differences between behavioral genetics research (where genes are not studied directly) and molecular genetics research (where genes themselves are studied directly) and the strengths and limitations of both approaches.

4 Describe the strengths and limitations of case studies and single-case designs.

5 Understand the principles and applications of correlational research.

6 Describe the factors that influence outcomes of randomized controlled trials.

7 Recognize the principles and applications of epidemiological research as they relate to understanding abnormal behavior.

☑ ☑ ☑

research methods
in abnormal psychology

I was taking Introductory Psychology and we had the option of participating in research to get extra credit. There was an information board in the Department where we could read about studies and sign up. There were lots of studies we could choose from. I saw one that caught my interest and signed up.

The first thing I did was read the information sheet and fill in the consent form. On the first day, the researcher asked me all sorts of questions about my family history of alcohol use as well as how much I drink. I also had to fill out several questionnaires—mostly about alcohol and drug use.

She then scheduled me to come back the next day, and I was told not to eat for 1.5 hours before I came in and also not to smoke or brush my teeth!

The researcher then had me taste 10 different sweet solutions. She told me to sip the solution, swish it around in my mouth, and spit it out. Then I had to rate the solution, rinse my mouth with distilled water, and proceed to the next solution. For each solution, she asked me to rate how sweet and how pleasurable the taste was.

That was pretty much it. Afterward, the researcher told me that she was studying the association between a family history of alcoholism and sweet taste preference.

A few years later, I was checking around on the Internet to see if anything ever came of the study, and I typed in the researcher's name. To my surprise, she published a paper on the study and concluded that people with a family history of alcoholism actually do prefer sweeter tastes! It was pretty incredible to have been a participant in a study that actually got published.

Adapted from Kampov-Polevoy, A., Garbutt, J., & Khalitov, E. "Family history of alcoholism and response to sweets." *Alcoholism Clinical and Experimental Research*, 11, 1743–1749. Copyright © 2003. Reprinted by permission of Blackwell Publishing.

In introductory psychology classes, psychology is often described as the scientific study of behavior and mental processes. To understand human behavior, psychologists require research volunteers such as the participant described on page 41. Much of what we know about abnormal behavior is based on studies conducted using college students. Without such research, our understanding would be much more limited. In much research, investigators are looking at individual behavior. However, for abnormal psychology, a scientific approach requires research at all levels of human behavior. The National Institutes of Health (NIH) emphasizes the critical importance of understanding health and disease by conducting research at every level—from a single cell to society. **Translational research** is a scientific approach that focuses on communication between basic science and applied clinical research. The NIH has stated, "To improve human health, scientific discoveries must be translated into practical applications. Such discoveries typically begin at 'the bench' with basic research—in which scientists study disease at a molecular or cellular level—then progress to the clinical level, or the patient's 'bedside.' The translational approach is really a two-way street. Basic scientists provide new tools for use with patients, and clinical researchers make novel observations about the nature and progression of disease that often stimulate basic investigations. Translational research has proven to be a powerful process that drives the clinical research engine." Our introductory case illustrates one type of basic research—understanding how taste mechanisms may be related to alcoholism. This case illustrates another important point. The goal of most research is to publish the results so that other investigators can use the data to create new hypotheses and further the understanding of abnormal behavior. The lay public, those who don't do research, also need to be aware of research findings that have implications for their lives.

In line with a translational approach, this chapter begins with research strategies that focus on factors at the cellular and neuroanatomical level and that affect behavior in the entire organism. We then examine research at the individual and group level, where most scientific inquiry occurs. Finally, we turn to studies examining behavior at the population level. As we shall see, each approach provides a unique perspective on mental illness. Combined, they allow us to understand broadly the biological, psychological, and societal aspects of mental illness.

Research in Abnormal Psychology at the Cellular Level

Research at the cellular level is one of the newest and most exciting areas of study for abnormal psychology. Although the idea that the brain is the site of abnormal behavior dates back to prehistoric times, only recently have we had the tools to study the brain and the nervous system accurately. Before we discuss these new research findings, we need to review the workings of the nervous system and the other parts of the body that influence behavior.

NEUROANATOMY

The human nervous system has two main parts: the **central nervous system** (CNS) and the **peripheral nervous system** (PNS). The CNS consists of the brain and the spinal cord. As noted in Chapter 1, the brain contains approximately 100 billion nerve cells, or neurons. Each neuron extends along distinct and specific pathways, creating a complex but ordered web of neural circuitry. Typical neurons are composed of the *soma*, or the cell

translational research   a scientific approach that focuses on communication between basic science and applied clinical research

central nervous system   one part of the human nervous system that includes the brain and the spinal cord

peripheral nervous system   one part of the human nervous system that includes the sensory-somatic nervous system (controls sensations and muscle movements) and the autonomic nervous system (controls involuntary movements) and returns the body to resting levels after these systems have been activated

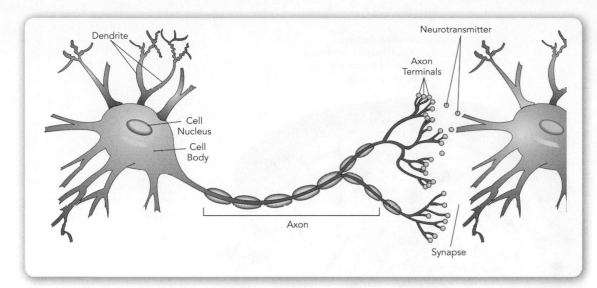

FIGURE 2.1
The Neuron

The cell body contains the nucleus and has projections called dendrites, which branch out and receive information from other neurons. Nerve impulses pass down the neuron. The gap between the axon terminals and the dendrites of the next neuron is called the synapse. Chemicals called neurotransmitters enable the nerve impulse to cross the gap to the receptors of the next neuron.

body, which contains the nucleus. The *dendrites* are finger-like projections that extend from the soma. Dendrites branch out and receive information from other neurons. The fiber through which a cell transports information to another cell is called the *axon*. *Axon terminals* are the branched features at the end of the axon that form *synapses* or points of communication with dendrites or cell bodies of other neurons (see Figure 2.1).

Having a general understanding of the structure of the brain is important because as we discuss the various psychological disorders, you will see that we are starting to understand how different parts of the brain play a role in different disorders. One way of looking at the brain's structure is through an evolutionary lens. This perspective helps us to understand which parts are oldest, govern the most basic aspects of our functioning, and appeared earliest in the evolutionary process.

Starting with the oldest parts of the brain, at its base is the **brain stem**, which controls most of the fundamental biological functions associated with living, such as breathing. The brain stem has several sections with separate functions (see Figure 2.2). At its base is the *hindbrain*, consisting of the *medulla*, *pons*, and *cerebellum*. These structures regulate breathing, heartbeat, and motor control. These functions are automatic activities required for life. You do not need to think about breathing or making your heart beat in order for those processes to occur. The term *lesion* refers to an area of damage or abnormality. We can tell a lot about the function of a particular brain structure by observing what happens to people when a specific structure is lesioned. For example, the cerebellum is critical for motor coordination. When lesions occur in the cerebellum, they result in disorders of fine movement, balance, and motor learning.

The **midbrain** portion of the brain stem has two important functions. First, it is a coordinating center bringing together sensory information with movement. It also houses the *reticular activating system*, which regulates our sleep and arousal systems.

Moving upward structurally and evolutionarily from the brain stem are the *thalamus* and the *hypothalamus* (see Figure 2.3). The thalamus can be considered as the brain's relay station, directing nerve signals that carry sensory information to the cortex (see below). A primary function of the hypothalamus is *homeostasis*, which is the regulation of bodily functions such as blood pressure, body temperature, fluid and electrolyte balance, and body weight.

brain stem   part of the brain, located at its base, which controls fundamental biological functions such as breathing

midbrain   a portion of the brain stem that coordinates sensory information and movement; includes the reticular activating system, the thalamus, and the hypothalamus

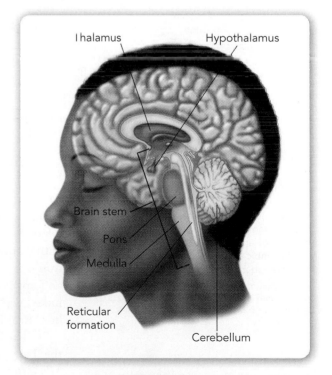

FIGURE 2.2
The Brain Stem

The oldest part of the brain, located at its base, controls most basic biological functions, such as breathing.

From Zimbardo, et al., *Psychology: Core Concepts*, 6e, (0-205-54788-5). Fig 2.9, p. 63. Copyright © 2009 Pearson/Allyn & Bacon. Reprinted by permission.

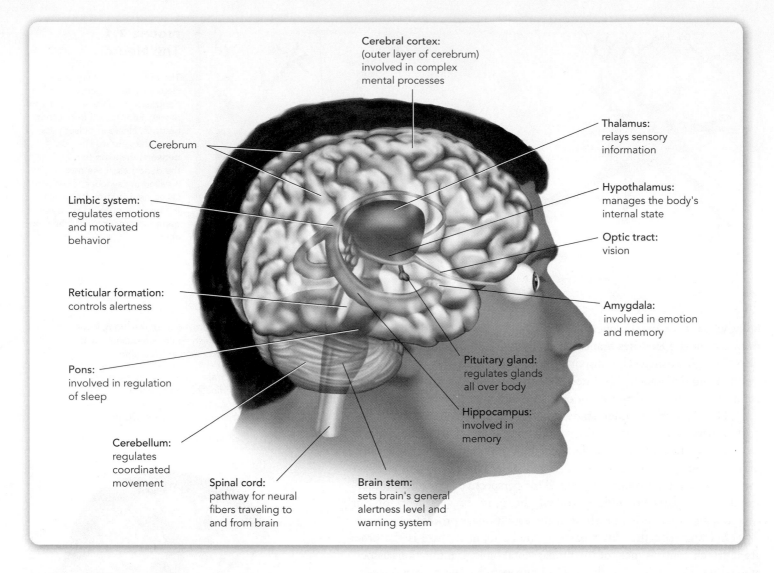

Cerebral cortex:
(outer layer of cerebrum)
involved in complex
mental processes

Cerebrum

Limbic system:
regulates emotions
and motivated
behavior

Reticular formation:
controls alertness

Pons:
involved in regulation
of sleep

Cerebellum:
regulates
coordinated
movement

Spinal cord:
pathway for neural
fibers traveling to
and from brain

Brain stem:
sets brain's general
alertness level and
warning system

Hippocampus:
involved in
memory

Pituitary gland:
regulates glands
all over body

Amygdala:
involved in emotion
and memory

Optic tract:
vision

Hypothalamus:
manages the body's
internal state

Thalamus:
relays sensory
information

FIGURE 2.3

The Thalamus, Hypothalamus, and the Limbic System

The thalamus is the brain's relay system, directing sensory information to the cortex; the hypothalamus regulates bodily functions; and the limbic system is a major center for human emotion.

From Zimbardo, et al., *Psychology: Core Concepts*, 6e, (0-205-54788-5). Fig 2.9, p. 63. Copyright © 2009 Pearson/Allyn & Bacon. Reprinted by permission.

forebrain part of the brain that includes the limbic system, basal ganglia, and cerebral cortex

cerebral cortex the largest part of the forebrain; contains structures that contribute to higher cognitive functioning including reasoning, abstract thought, perception of time, and creativity

Moving further up the evolutionary ladder from the midbrain to the **forebrain**, we find the *limbic system*, an umbrella term for several brain structures that are very important for the study of abnormal psychology. The limbic system includes the *amygdala*, the *cingulate gyrus*, and the *hippocampus*. The limbic system deals primarily with emotions and impulses. It is involved with the experience of emotion, the regulation of emotional expression, and the basic biological drives such as aggression, sex, and appetite. The hippocampus also has a role in memory formation and has been linked with the memory deficits that are characteristic of Alzheimer's disease (see the box "Real People, Real Disorders: Henry Gustav Molaison (H.M.)").

The *basal ganglia* are also at the base of the human forebrain. Structures within the basal ganglia include the *caudate, putamen, nucleus accumbens, globus pallidus, substantia nigra,* and *subthalamic nucleus.* In general, these structures are thought to inhibit movement. Diseases that affect the basal ganglia are marked by abnormal movements—these include Parkinson's disease (rigidity and tremor), bradykinesia (slow movements), and Huntington's disease (unconcontrollable dance-like movements of the face and limbs).

Moving even further up the evolutionary ladder, we encounter the largest part of the forebrain, the **cerebral cortex**, which contains the structures that contribute to the

real people, real disorders

Henry Gustav Molaison (H.M.)

The brain of Henry Gustav Molaison (H.M.) from Thibodaux, Louisiana, is believed to have been studied more than that of any person in history. For reasons of confidentiality, he was known to psychologists only as "H.M." until his death. Born in 1926 and raised in Connecticut, H.M. was an ordinary bicycle riding, ice skating boy. At age 9, he banged his head hard after being hit by a bicycle rider in his neighborhood. About age 16, he developed epilepsy and experienced many *grand mal* (severe) seizures. In 1953, he underwent major surgery in which parts of his medial temporal lobe were removed on both sides of his brain. His doctor, William Scoville, wanted to remove this part of the brain since it was where the seizures originated.

Two thirds of H.M.'s hippocampus was removed; leading neurologists assumed that this part of the brain was entirely nonfunctional. After the surgery, however, H.M. suffered from a form of amnesia in which he could not save new experiences as long term memories. Much to the joy of his doctors, H.M. was able to complete tasks that required recall from his short-term memory. He was also able to recall long-term memories of events that occurred before his operation. But he could not recall events that occurred after the operation.

Henry Molaison died on December 2, 2008, of respiratory failure in a nursing home in Connecticut. Although he was unsure of exactly how old he was, had to be reintroduced to his doctors every day, and repeatedly grieved when he heard about the death of his mother, he had a positive outlook on life. He was quoted as saying that he hoped his medical condition would help others and allow researchers to learn from his condition.

Scientific research has benefited greatly from H.M.'s experience. It has resulted in two key findings: short-term memories are not dependent on a functioning hippocampus, but long-term memories must go *through* the hippocampus in order to be permanently stored. These findings have forever changed the way scientists view the formation, retention, and recall of short- and long-term memory.

References: Corkin, 1968; Kolb & Whishaw, 1996; Smith & Kosslyn, 2007.

---

features that make us uniquely human, such as reasoning, abstract thought, perception of time, and creativity. The cerebral cortex is divided into two hemispheres. You may hear people talking about someone being either "left brained" or "right brained." How your brain works is definitely more complicated than just being left-handed or right-handed. Although the two hemispheres look structurally similar, they do appear to oversee different processes. Indeed, some people tend to favor one type of processing over the other.

The left hemisphere is primarily responsible for language and cognitive functions and tends to process information in a more linear and logical manner. The left hemisphere processes information in parts, sequentially, and uses both language and symbols (including numbers). The right hemisphere processes the world in a more holistic manner, in a spatial context, and is more associated with creativity, imagery, and intuition. There is considerable cross-talk between the hemispheres, and they can also "cover" for each other by stepping in if damage occurs on one side.

Each hemisphere consists of four lobes: temporal, parietal, occipital, and frontal (see Figure 2.4). The **temporal lobe** is associated with processing and therefore understanding auditory and visual information, and it plays a role in the naming or labeling of objects and verbal memory. The **parietal lobe** integrates sensory information from various sources and may also be involved with visuospatial processing. An example might be imagining rotating a three-dimensional object in space. The **occipital lobe**,

temporal lobe one of four lobes of the brain; associated with understanding auditory and verbal information, labeling of objects, and verbal memory

parietal lobe one of four lobes of the brain; integrates sensory information from various sources and may be involved with visuospatial processing

occipital lobe one of four lobes of the brain; located at the back of the skull; center of visual processing

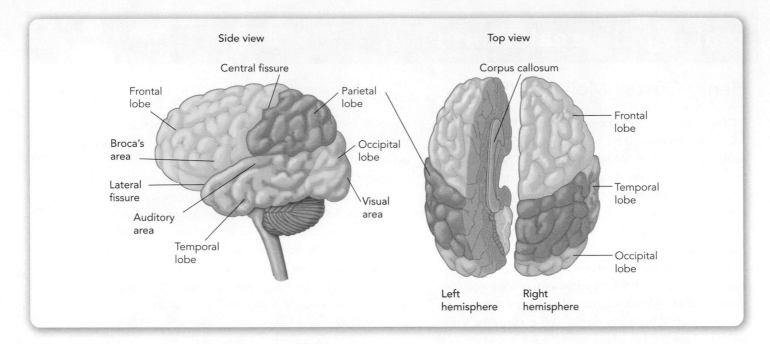

Side view

Central fissure

Frontal lobe

Broca's area

Lateral fissure

Auditory area

Temporal lobe

Parietal lobe

Occipital lobe

Visual area

Top view

Corpus callosum

Frontal lobe

Temporal lobe

Occipital lobe

Left hemisphere

Right hemisphere

FIGURE 2.4

The Cerebrum

The four lobes of the cerebrum (temporal, parietal, occipital, and frontal) control sensory, motor, speech, and reasoning functions. The outer ("gray matter") layer of the cerebrum is known as the cerebral cortex.

From Zimbardo, et al., *Psychology: Core Concepts*, 6e, (0-205-54788-5). Fig 2.9, p. 63. Copyright © 2009 Pearson/Allyn & Bacon. Reprinted by permission.

frontal lobe one of the four lobes of the brain; seat of reasoning, impulse control, judgment, language, memory, motor function, problem solving, and sexual and social behavior

endocrine system a system in the body that sends messages to the bodily organs via hormones

hormones chemical messengers that are released into the bloodstream and act on target organs

located at the back of the skull, is the center of visual processing. The **frontal lobe** is the seat of reasoning and is a critical factor in impulse control, judgment, language, memory, motor function, problem solving, and sexual and social behavior. Frontal lobes are instrumental in planning, coordinating, inhibiting, and executing behavior. The *corpus callosum* connects the two sides of the brain and allows them to communicate. A severed corpus callosum is not entirely incapacitating; however, it can lead to an inability to integrate certain brain functions. For example, if an image of a key is flashed in the right field of vision, the patient might *recognize* the image but not be able to correctly *name* it. A flash in the opposite field of vision could yield the correct *label*, but the individual could not discuss its *function*.

Beyond the brain and the spinal cord, which make up the central nervous system, the other major division of the human nervous system is the *peripheral nervous system* (PNS). The PNS is subdivided into the sensory-somatic nervous system and the autonomic nervous system. The *sensory-somatic nervous system* consists of the cranial nerves, which control sensation and muscle movement. The *autonomic nervous system* includes the sympathetic and parasympathetic nervous systems. The *sympathetic nervous system* (SNS) primarily controls involuntary movements. It serves to activate the body, creating a state of physical readiness. The SNS stimulates heartbeat, raises blood pressure, dilates the pupils, diverts blood away from the skin and inner organs to the skeletal muscles, brain, and heart, and inhibits digestion and peristalsis in the gastrointestinal tract, creating a bodily state of arousal that could indicate the presence of stress or anxiety (see Chapter 4). In contrast, the *parasympathetic nervous system* (PNS) returns the body functions to resting levels after they have been activated by the SNS.

Finally, the body's **endocrine system** regulates bodily functions but uses hormones to do so rather than nerve impulses (see Figure 2.5). Endocrine glands produce **hormones**, which are chemical messengers that are released directly into the bloodstream and act on target organs. The pituitary gland, located at the base of the brain, is known as the "master gland." It is under the control of the hypothalamus and controls many endocrine functions, including those central to the female menstrual cycle, preg-

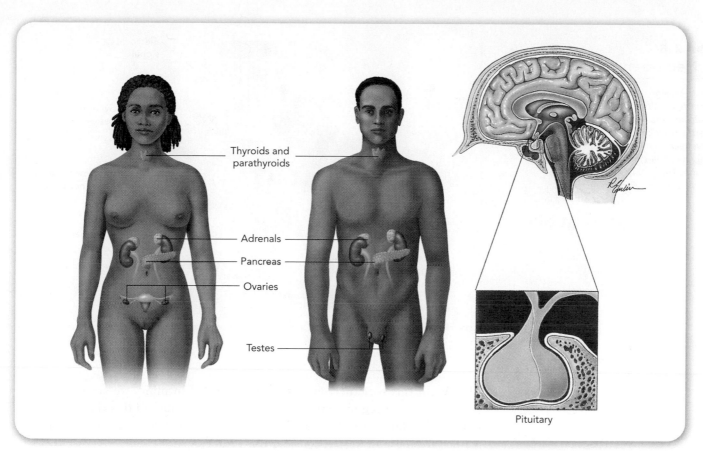

Thyroids and parathyroids

Adrenals

Pancreas

Ovaries

Testes

Pituitary

FIGURE 2.5
The Endocrine System

This system includes glands, such as the thyroid, gonads, adrenal, and pituitary glands, and the hormones they produce, such as thyroxin, estrogen, testosterone, and adrenaline. Hormones are chemical messengers that transmit information and instructions throughout the bloodstream, targeting cells that are genetically programmed to receive and respond to specific messages.

From Zimbardo, et al., *Psychology: Core Concepts*, 6e, (0-205-54788-5). Fig 2.9, p. 63. Copyright © 2009 Pearson/Allyn & Bacon. Reprinted by permission.

nancy, birth, and lactation. The adrenal glands (located on top of the kidneys) release epinephrine (adrenaline) in response to external and internal stressors such as fright, anger, caffeine, or low blood sugar. Thyroid hormones regulate metabolism, including body temperature and weight. The pancreas includes a gland (islets of Langerhans) that secretes insulin and glucagon to regulate blood sugar level. A number of studies have demonstrated that certain hormones (e.g., cortisol, prolactin) are elevated in people with depression, anxiety, and other psychological symptoms.

NEUROHORMONES AND NEUROTRANSMITTERS

Clearly, there are many different mini-systems within the overall nervous system. To understand human emotions, it is important to know how these various systems operate and cooperate. Communication in the nervous system is both electrical and chemical. Because neurons do not actually touch each other, chemicals called **neurotransmitters** relay the electrical signals from one neuron to the next (see Figure 2.6). When the electrical signal reaches the axon terminal, the neurotransmitters are released. They travel across the space between the neurons (called the synapse) and land on the surface of the neighboring neuron, at which point they trigger the second neuron to "fire," releasing the electrical impulse. Research on neurotransmitters has revolutionized psychiatry, as most drug treatments affect one or more of the core neurotransmitters by influencing their availability and/or their action in the brain. This highly active field of research is constantly identifying new substances that function as neurotransmitters. Specific neurotransmitter systems have been widely studied and will be discussed in the chapters on specific disorders.

neurotransmitters chemical substances that relay electrical signals between one neuron and the next

FIGURE 2.6
How Neurotransmitters Work

The electrical signal reaches the end of the first neuron, causing it to fire and release the neurotransmitters from their vesicles at the presynaptic membrane. The neurotransmitters travel across the synapse and land on receptors (holes) on the postsynaptic membrane. This initiates a signal in the second neuron, relaying the message.

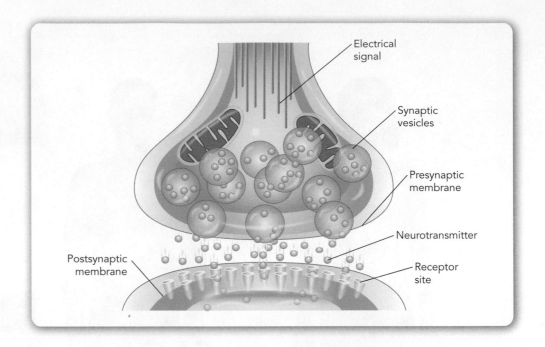

With this basic nervous system background in mind, we are ready to begin the journey from cell to society. In the remaining sections of this chapter, many different procedures used to study human behavior will be discussed. To provide a context for these strategies, consider this brief case.

Monica is 26 years old. She has been feeling sad, crying for no reason, feeling helpless and hopeless, and has had thoughts of taking her life. She cannot fall asleep at night and when she finally does, she wakes up several times. She has lost 20 pounds in two months because she does not feel like eating. Her primary care physician sent her to a psychologist who diagnosed her with depression.

Although the specifics regarding depressive disorders will be discussed in a later chapter, we will use this case example to explain different methodologies that are used for the scientific study of psychological disorders.

NEUROIMAGING

You may wonder how scientists know how the brain functions and which of its structures are responsible for human abilities and activities. Early on, much of our information came from unique cases such as accident victims or survivors of surgery (like H.M.) that allowed us to understand what functions were lost if a certain part of the brain was damaged or removed. More recently, understanding the structure and the function of the brain has been facilitated by advances in **neuroimaging** technology, which takes pictures of the brain. Tests such as *CT* or *CAT* scans (computerized axial tomography) and *MRI* (magnetic resonance imaging) provide static images, like snapshots, that allow detection of lesions or damaged areas. For a CAT scan, the patient is injected with a radioactive dye, and specialized X-ray equipment photographs the brain from different angles. The computerized images create a cross-sectional picture of the brain. MRI uses radiofrequency waves and a strong magnetic field to provide highly detailed pictures of the brain. MRI is superior to CT technology because it does not require the use of radiation. Instead, radiofrequency waves are directed at protons in a strong magnetic field. The protons are first "excited" and then "relaxed," emitting radio signals that can be computer-processed to form an image.

neuroimaging technology that takes pictures of the brain

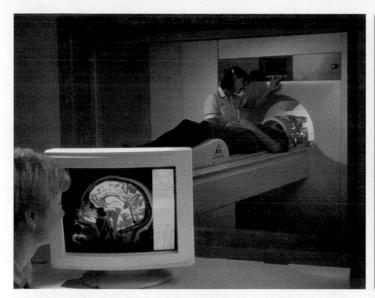
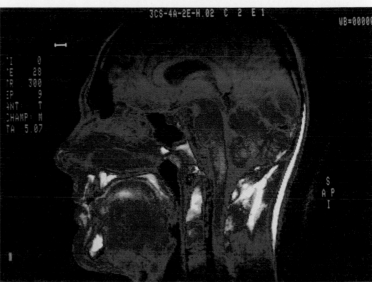

CAT and MRI scans, in which the brain is scanned by X-ray or radio waves, produce images that reveal brain anatomy.

CAT and MRI technology explores **neuroanatomy** (brain structure). Other technology exists that detects brain function. *Positron emission tomography* (PET scan) creates images based on the detection of radiation from the emission of positrons. In preparation for a PET scan, a patient is given a radioactive biochemical substance. As the radioactive isotope in the substance decays, it emits tiny particles that can be measured. PET brain imaging has enabled scientists to trace neurotransmitter pathways in the brain and from these data to determine the involvement of brain structures and pathways in human behavior.

Functional MRI (fMRI) identifies increases in blood flow that are associated with increases in neural activity in various parts of the brain. This technique allows not only a map of brain anatomy, but a map of brain function. fMRI allows the researcher to isolate specific brain activity in response to an event or stimulus (e.g., flashing an image of a spider to someone with a fear of spiders or examining the brain activity of someone experiencing auditory hallucinations, or "hearing voices").

Neuroimaging is an elegant, sophisticated, and expensive research tool. In typical clinical practice, neuroimaging is not needed to diagnose depression.

However, Monica and all those with psychological disorders are benefiting greatly from neuroimaging studies that help mental health professionals understand what brain structures and functions appear to be affected when someone is depressed. In turn, understanding altered brain functioning has helped with the development of interventions that target specific brain areas and functions.

GENETICS

Studies of brain structure and function provide new insights about the brain and its relationship to psychological disorders. However, merely knowing that there is altered brain activity does not fully explain why abnormal behavior occurs. Scientists must still explain how and why brain abnormalities exist. Applying genetics to the study of behavior has revolutionized abnormal psychology, and research on genetic factors now reaches from the cell to the population level. *Behavioral genetics* approaches include family, twin, and adoption studies and allow critical glimpses into whether certain behavioral traits or mental disorders run in families and the extent to which these familial patterns are due to genetics (are heritable) or environment. Modern molecular approaches to genetics and new methods of examining genetic associations have

neuroanatomy brain structure

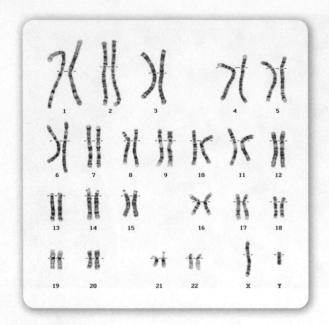

FIGURE 2.7
Human Chromosomes

A normal human being has 46 chromosomes—23 derived from each parent. Sex is determined by X and Y chromosomes; males are XY and females are XX.

allowed scientists to discover genetic *loci* (specific places on specific chromosomes) that are associated with many complex traits. We now know that behavioral traits and mental disorders are rarely caused by single genes. Commonly termed *complex traits*, most behavioral traits and disorders are thought to be influenced by many genes and environmental factors that exert small to moderate effects.

Genetics Basics   Recall from your high school biology class that the "building block of life" is *deoxyribonucleic acid* (DNA). The collection of DNA that exists in humans is called the human *genome*, and it contains approximately 20,000 to 25,000 genes. Each gene is a section of DNA, and together, genes make an organism unique. In humans, the genes are contained on 23 pairs of chromosomes—22 somatic (bodily) chromosome pairs and 1 sex chromosome pair, either XX (female) or XY (male) (see Figure 2.7). The mother always contributes an X chromosome to the sex chromosome pair. If the father's contribution is also an X chromosome, then the baby is a girl. If he contributes a Y chromosome, then the baby is a boy. Genes can exist in several different forms, called *alleles*, and it is specific alleles that create variation in species (e.g., height, hair color, eye color, personality, disease risk).

Genes follow several laws. Gregor Mendel (1822–1884), a Czech monk, working with the common garden pea, discovered two genetic laws of heredity. Although Mendel laid the foundation for our understanding of genetics, R. A. Fisher noted irregularities in the reporting of Mendel's findings. In 1936 he published a report suggesting that Mendel's observations were too close to expectation to be plausible (Fisher, 1936), an observation that has been revisited by several scientists subsequently. Nonetheless, understanding Mendel's laws is an important first step in understanding the basic principles of genetics. The *law of segregation* states that an individual receives one of two elements from each parent. One of the elements could be *dominant* (in which case the trait would be expressed in offspring), or the element could be *recessive* (genetically present but usually not expressed in offspring). If the child receives two recessive elements—one from each parent—then the recessive element or trait is expressed. In the case of eye color, brown is a dominant trait and blue is a recessive trait, so the only way to have blue eyes is to have two recessive elements.

Mendel's second law, the *law of independent assortment*, states that the alleles (variations) of one gene assort independently from the alleles (variations) of other genes. For example, the alleles for height and eye color do not always travel together. Not every short person has blue eyes. Short people may have brown eyes or hazel eyes. Similarly, people with blue eyes can be short, average, or tall. In short, genes for eye color and height assort independently.

Although the influence of genes on characteristics such as height, eye color, and various diseases has been known for generations, more recently, behavior geneticists have studied genetic effects on personality, attitudes, and abnormal behavior such as depression, extraversion, and schizophrenia. Over the past decade, the Human Genome Project has advanced our knowledge of genetics far beyond what Mendel discovered with his study of peas. What is very clear is that the human genome is a large space—approximately 20,000 to 25,000 genes. We now know that many parts formerly labeled "junk DNA" or "gene deserts" (because we had not identified specific genes in those areas) also contribute to many of the traits we express.

So with such a vast space, how do we even begin the search for genes that may increase the risk for developing certain psychological conditions? Behavioral genetics approaches examine physical and behavioral similarities among family members that would suggest that genes play a role in these familial similarities. More direct genetic approaches include three commonly used methods: genomewide linkage, candidate gene association studies, and genomewide association studies. But first, we turn our attention to behavioral genetics.

BEHAVIORAL GENETICS

The term *behavioral genetics* describes approaches to the study of behavior that do not examine genes directly but infer the action of genes and environment. Approaches in this category include family, twin, and adoption studies. Basically, these studies focus on whether traits and disorders run in families and why.

Family Studies One question commonly faced by researchers and clinicians is whether psychological disorders "run in families." In the classic family study, **familial aggregation** examines whether the family members of a person with a particular disorder (called the **proband**) are more likely to have that disorder than are family members of people without the disorder. If the disorder is more commonly found among the proband's family, the disorder is considered to be familial or to "aggregate in families." Family studies can take two forms. The *family history* method uses information from one or a few family members to provide information about other family members. You are probably familiar with this method if you have completed a checklist in your physician's office about your family medical history. The *family study* method involves direct interviews with each consenting family member. Because family members often do not disclose their psychological symptoms to one another, conducting separate interviews with each family member is considered to produce more reliable estimates of the actual traits or disorders that exist within the family.

In Monica's case, a clinician conducting a diagnostic interview might use the family history method to ask Monica about the presence of depressive symptoms in any members of her family. If Monica were participating in a family study about the causes of depression, the researchers might invite her relatives to participate in individual interviews to determine whether any of her relatives ever suffered from depression.

From a scientific perspective, determining whether symptoms "run in families" is an important first step in understanding whether a disorder might be influenced by genes. However, family members also share environmental experiences, and as discussed in Chapter 1, cultural contexts, including families, can have an important influence on behavior. Therefore, any observed familial aggregation could be due to either genetic *or* environmental factors, or most likely to some combination of these influences. One approach to disentangling genetic factors from environmental factors is through the use of adoption and twin study designs.

Adoption Studies Adoption creates a unique situation in which genetically related individuals do not live together and therefore do not share a common family environment. In adoptive families, babies who are adopted away from their biological parents live in a new and different environment. Therefore, similarities between sbiological parents and their adopted-away offspring are assumed to represent the genetic contribution to a given trait or behavior. By contrast, similarity between the adopted child and his or her adoptive parents measures the environmental contribution to parent-child similarity. This approximation holds only when the placement of the adopted child is not "selective" (e.g., when an upper middle class family of a certain religious persuasion requests that the adoptive family has a similar background). Adoption studies represent a middle ground when it comes to examining behavioral genetic models: they are more able to separate genetic from environmental effects than family studies, but they have their pitfalls and biases as well. One bias is that

familial aggregation process of examining whether family members of a person with a particular disorder are more likely to have that disorder than family members of people without the disorder

proband person with a particular disorder in a familial aggregation study

Identical (MZ) twins separated at birth and raised apart have been found to show strong similarities in adulthood.

adoption placement is not always random. Often babies will be placed with families that resemble their own on a number of dimensions such as race, religion, and socioeconomic status. With international adoptions increasing in popularity, additional issues are arising, including what sorts of conditions the adoptee faced before placement. Many of these conditions, such as placement in orphanages and lack of early attachment experiences, can lead to serious developmental consequences that can confound the interpretation of adoption studies.

Twin Studies   The scientific study of twins was another important step in understanding the contribution of genes and environment to abnormal behavior (Cederlof et al., 1982; Martin et al., 1997). These studies revolutionized our understanding of several major psychiatric conditions and modernized approaches to treatment. For example, three decades ago, it was widely believed that autism and schizophrenia (two disorders we examine in detail in later chapters) resulted solely from environmental trauma or parental deficits. However, based on a body of scientific evidence (Folstein & Rosen-Sheidley, 2001; Sullivan, 2008), we now know that these disorders have critically important genetic components.

Twin studies examine the similarities and differences between *monozygotic* (MZ or identical) and *dizygotic* (DZ or fraternal) twin pairs to identify genetic and environmental contributions to psychological disorders. MZ twins start out as a single embryo (fertilized egg). At some stage in the first 2 weeks after conception, the zygote (fertilized egg) separates and yields two embryos that are, for most intents and purposes, genetically identical. Therefore, behavioral differences between MZ twins, who essentially share all of their genes, provide strong evidence for the role of *environmental influences* (Plomin et al., 1994). By contrast, DZ twinning results from the fertilization of two eggs by different spermatozoa. DZ twins are no more similar genetically than other siblings and share, on average, one half of their genes. Thus, behavioral differences between DZ twins can result from genetic and/or environmental effects.

The most rigorous twin research design uses MZ twins who were separated in infancy and reared apart (that is, in different environments). In this case, genes and familial environment are distinctly separated. Two large studies of MZ twins reared apart in Minnesota (Bouchard et al., 1990) and Sweden (Pedersen et al., 1985) served as critical studies in demonstrating the strength of genetic factors in determining IQ. In addition, reunited MZ twins have discovered similarities on dimensions not usually considered to be under genetic control. For example, first-person accounts of reunited twins have included similarities on surprising dimensions, including where they have moles on their body, age they started balding, occupation, choice of cars and motorcycles, and even favorite beer.

MOLECULAR GENETICS

molecular genetics   the study of the structure and function of genes at a molecular level

genomewide linkage analysis   a technique that uses samples of families with many individuals who are ill with the same disorder or large samples of relatives who have the same disorder to identify genomic regions that may hold genes that influence a trait

Whereas behavioral genetic tools can tell us whether genes are involved in a particular trait or disorder, they do not tell us which of the 20,000 to 25,000 identified genes might be related to the presence of the disorder. To actually identify risk genes, research needs to drill down to the molecular level. **Molecular genetics** uses three primary methods: genomewide linkage analyses, candidate gene association studies, and a novel technique called genomewide association (Slagboom & Meulenbelt, 2002; Wang et al., 2005). **Genomewide linkage analysis** allows researchers to narrow the search for genes from the whole genome to specific areas on specific chromosomes. To conduct a linkage analysis, you either need large families in which many individuals have the disorder of interest or you need large samples of "affected relative pairs." That basically means pairs of relatives who both have the illness under study. You then cover the genome with markers and look for patterns that are different from what you would expect based on what we know about inheritance.

In a **candidate gene association study**, you compare specific genes in a large group of individuals who have a specific trait or disorder with a well-matched group of individuals who do not have that trait or disorder. In this approach, you choose one or several genes in advance based on some knowledge of the biology of the trait. For example, we know that serotonin may be involved in depression, so a candidate gene study might compare one or a few serotonergic genes in a large sample of people with the disorder (called *cases*) versus people who do not have the disorder but are similar in other ways to the cases (called *controls*). If you find that one variation of the gene is more common in the ill group, then you have some evidence that that gene might be associated with the illness. By and large, candidate gene studies tend to be initially very exciting when they emerge in the literature, but often other groups fail to replicate (repeat) the findings. For this reason the single-gene candidate gene approach is falling out of favor for larger, more powerful approaches.

Genomewide association (GWAS) also uses large samples of cases and well-matched controls. Unlike the candidate gene studies in which only one or a few genes are studied at one time, in GWAS hundreds of thousands of possible genetic variants scattered across the genome are tested for association in the same study. This is a key advantage of GWAS. In the candidate gene studies, you have to choose a gene or genes based on some prior knowledge of biology. GWAS does not require any such choice and yields a relatively unbiased search of the genome that can discover new genetic associations that you might not previously have considered. For many diseases, GWAS has unlocked new biological pathways that had not been considered in the past.

Studying Monica's genes would not be part of the usual clinical assessment to determine the diagnosis of depression. However, certain researchers (usually working in medical school settings) may be conducting a study on genetics and depression, and someone with symptoms like Monica's might be asked to participate by giving a sample of her blood or a scraping from the inside of her cheek—both of which contain DNA.

concept CHECK

- Research that teaches us about abnormal psychology can be conducted at the cellular or neuroanatomical level, with individual people or groups of people, or at the population level.

- When studying the brain from an evolutionary perspective, moving from the brain stem (which controls fundamental biological functions) to the forebrain (where higher cognitive functions occur) is a helpful way to understand mental disorders.

- New techniques in abnormal psychology research at the cellular level include neuroimaging (taking pictures of the brain), study of the function and interrelation of neurotransmitters (chemicals that relay electrical signals between the cells), and molecular genetics (identifying genes that are associated with clinical syndromes).

- Family, twin, and adoption studies are behavioral genetic methods that provide insight into how behavioral traits and mental disorders run in families and the extent to which familial patterns are due to genetics or environment.

candidate gene association study compares one or a few genes in a large group of individuals who have a specific trait or disorder with a well-matched group of individuals who do not have the trait or disorder

genomewide association study unbiased search of the human genome comparing cases and controls on genetic variants scattered across the genome for evidence of association

- Candidate gene, genomewide linkage, and genomewide association studies are more direct techniques that allow for the actual identification of genetic regions or actual genes associated with a trait or a disorder.

APPLICATION QUESTION If you conducted a family study and found that relatives of individuals with a disorder were three times more likely to have a particular psychiatric disorder than relatives of similar individuals without that disorder, why would it be incorrect to conclude that genetics were completely responsible for the development of that disorder?

Research in Abnormal Psychology at the Individual Level

Studies of brain structure and function and genetics are sophisticated research tools, but they are time consuming and not always cost effective. Most research in abnormal psychology has been based on comparing groups of people who have different characteristics, are tested in different ways, or receive different treatments. Conclusions are drawn based on the average responses for the group. Research at the individual level also helps identify general principles about abnormal behavior and its treatment. In fact, the practice of clinical psychology is generally directed toward the individual. Valuable information can be learned from intensive study of individual people, families, or small groups of people who can be considered a single unit. This research complements larger group-based studies by allowing for richer examination of details and the development of hypotheses and theories that can later be tested in group designs. At the individual level, there are two main methods of study: case studies and single-case designs.

THE CASE STUDY

The case study provides a detailed narrative of abnormal behavior and/or its treatment. It is sometimes accompanied by quantitative measurement (such as measuring the frequency of a problematic behavior), but it does not allow us to draw conclusions about causes of behavior. In the case study, nothing is manipulated by the observer; it is simply the recounting of a case or the telling of an individual's story. Nevertheless, case studies are useful for the study of abnormal behavior.

Benefits of Case Studies The brief description of H.M. presented earlier in the chapter is drawn from a **case study**, a comprehensive description of an individual (or group of individuals), using clinical data typically derived from a clinician's practical experience. Case studies can focus on the assessment and description of abnormal behavior or its treatment. In both instances, significant background material and detailed clinical information illustrate the complexity of the case. Gathering this detailed clinical material is not possible in group-based research where the focus is on group data.

As illustrated by H.M., case studies allow the examination of rare phenomena when group-based research would be nearly impossible, simply because not enough cases could be found (Kazdin, 2003). In *A Beautiful Mind*, Russell Crowe portrays John Forbes Nash, Jr., a mathematical genius who despite suffering from debilitating paranoid schizophrenia was awarded a Nobel Prize in Economics in 1994. Nash's story and the vivid portrayal by Crowe aroused public interest in schizophrenia and allowed millions to experience the psychological descent into paranoid thought first hand (see Chapter 10 for more information on John Nash).

Case studies can also generate hypotheses for group studies. In the true spirit of the scientist-practitioner model, clinical observations can lead to the development of testable theories and/or treatment using group designs. For example, John B. Watson's detailed study of Little Albert and Mary Cover Jones's report of Little Peter (see

Case studies are detailed descriptions of a single person that may help us understand a particularly rare behavior. A case study of the serial killer Theodore (Ted) Bundy for example, could shed light on the reasons that a person might engage is multiple murders.

case study comprehensive description of an individual (or group of individuals) that focuses on assessment or description of abnormal behavior or its treatment

Chapter 1) served as the basis for the development of treatments for anxiety disorders that have been tested scientifically and are still used today.

In addition, intensive case studies allow practitioners to be involved in research. Clinicians in full-time practice usually do not have the time or resources to develop and carry out research using large group designs. For the full-time clinician, detailed case notes can provide a scholarly report that informs others, illustrating how the scientist-practitioner model operates in the practice and study of abnormal behavior.

Finally, case studies illustrate important clinical issues that are not readily apparent in a group-based report. An example is a recent case report of five patients with both anxiety/depression and a lung disorder, chronic obstructive pulmonary disease (Stanley et al., 2005), who were participants in a much larger treatment trial. The case report provided more details about their specific clinical symptoms and their specific responses to treatment than was possible in the full clinical report (Kunik et al., 2008). This increased detail can be useful for clinicians who seek to use empirically supported treatments.

Variations and Limitations of Case Studies The amount and type of data included in case studies vary considerably. Some of these studies simply provide case descriptions. Others illustrate clinical points using standardized measures of behaviors or symptoms, allowing comparisons with other larger studies

Monica's symptoms of depression are more severe than those of patients included in large studies of depression treatments.

Scientifically rigorous case reports also attempt to standardize (keep consistent) the types of assessment and treatment procedures reported. By doing so, it is possible for other researchers or clinicians to replicate the same findings with another patient. Standardizing procedures for assessment or treatment also makes it possible to combine a small group of patients into a single report. In addition, standardized procedures make it easier to compare symptoms or the amount of change over time with what might be observed in studies of larger groups of patients.

Through the course of Monica's interview, her therapist discovered that Monica had eight brothers and sisters and that all of them suffered from major depression. This was highly unusual, and with her permission, the therapist decided to write a case study of Monica and her extensive family history of depression.

With all their advantages, however, case studies are limited in their ability to help us understand abnormal behavior. Most importantly, although case studies allow us to develop hypotheses about what might have caused certain symptoms or what type of treatment might be helpful, they do not allow us to make any firm conclusions about the cause(s) of symptoms or change following treatment. For example, improvement in a patient's symptoms could result from the specific treatment or from other factors that are unrelated to the actual treatment. These factors could include the simple passage of time, attention from a therapist, or subjective biases on the part of the patient or clinician.

In order to draw conclusions about the causes of symptoms or change, an *experimental control* condition is needed. In *controlled* scientific experiments, a comparison is made between at least two groups that differ only with regard to the variable being tested (often called the **experimental variable**). In the experimental group, the variable being tested is present; in the **control group**, this variable is absent. For example, a treatment for depression might be tested by giving the treatment to half of the depressed patients (experimental group) and not to the other half of patients (control group) who are similar to the experimental group in all other respects. If the experimental group then shows improvement, while the control group does not, we can infer that the treatment caused the improvement. Case studies, however, do not include control groups and thus cannot help us draw conclusions about causality.

experimental variable the variable being tested in an experimental study

control group comparison group for an experimental study; in this group, the variable to be studied is absent

SINGLE-CASE DESIGNS

Single-case designs are experimental studies conducted at the individual level (i.e., with a single person). This approach uses quantitative measurement and incorporates control conditions that allow clearer demonstration of causal relationships in a single individual.

Traditional research compares groups of similar patients before and after they receive different treatments. However, group-based research can make it difficult to observe individual behavior patterns. Also, group studies are expensive and time consuming (Morgan & Morgan, 2001). Single-case designs are essentially controlled experiments conducted with a single person. They control for alternative hypotheses (i.e., that something other than the treatment caused the change), and unlike case histories, they can lead to causal inferences. They require fewer resources and allow more detailed attention to individual patterns of change. In the single-case design, each person is a complete experiment, at various times participating in both the treatment and the comparison (or control) condition. The goal of the experiment is to examine whether behavior changes systematically, depending on whether the participant is in the treatment or the comparison phase.

Single-case design research begins with a baseline assessment that simply measures the behavior targeted for change (e.g., how often a child has a tantrum, how frequently panic attacks occur) before any experimental or control condition is implemented. An interesting challenge for this type of research is that sometimes merely asking a person to *monitor* a behavior may change how often or how long the behavior occurs. For example, asking a cigarette smoker to count the number of cigarettes smoked per day often results in a decrease in smoking. Why? Smokers are sometimes dismayed by the number of cigarettes they record and begin to decrease their smoking. Usually, however, behavioral change as a result of self-monitoring is only temporary. Therefore, baseline monitoring (i.e., assessment that occurs before beginning treatment) continues until the behavioral pattern is stable. Next, a treatment is applied and withdrawn, with *continuous assessment* of the target behavior. If the target behavior decreases with treatment and then returns to baseline when the treatment is withdrawn, the researcher can conclude that the treatment may have been effective (provided alternative explanations can be ruled out). If other researchers do similar research with the same results, the finding is *replicated* and confidence in it increases. Providing sufficient details about the patient, therapist, setting, and nature of the intervention aids replication of findings, which reinforces the study's conclusions. Regardless of the number of replications, however, the focus remains on describing individual patterns of behavior for one person, not aggregate data from multiple patients.

Design Strategies   The most common single-case design is known as the *ABAB* or *reversal* design, where A represents a baseline phase and B represents a treatment phase. In this model, the two phases are alternated to examine their impact on behavior. Behavior is first evaluated at baseline until stability is demonstrated (A). The treatment is then applied (B), and assessment continues until behavioral stability is achieved. Next, the treatment is withdrawn (A). If behavior returns to baseline during the second A phase, this is evidence that the treatment was the cause of the behavior change. Even more evidence for the power of the treatment is obtained when the intervention is applied again (another phase B) and another behavior change takes place. Each A-B sequence is considered a replication, and each time the "B" phase has the same effect, that is additional evidence that the treatment is the agent of change (Kazdin, 2003). The ABAB design can be used with patients of all ages, but it often is a particularly useful strategy to test the effects of behavioral treatments for children.

Caitlin is 3 years old. Since she was 15 months old, she has pulled out the hair on her head. Her pediatrician diagnosed her with trichotillomania, a disorder characterized by

Single case designs begin with self-monitoring. To help someone lose weight, a psychologist may begin measuring how many steps a person walks each day.

single-case designs   experimental studies conducted with a single individual

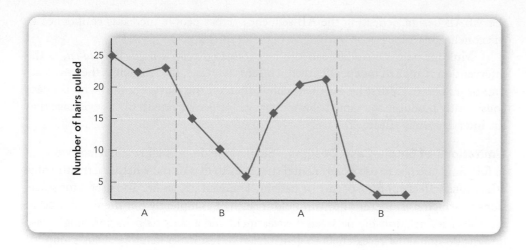

FIGURE 2.8
ABAB Research Design

Number of hairs pulled by Caitlin during baseline (A) and intervention (B) phases of behavioral treatment for hair pulling.

repetitive hair pulling that results in noticeable hair loss (see Chapter 4). He prescribed several medications, but none of them worked. A psychologist thought that Caitlin's hair pulling was reinforced by the substantial attention her parents gave her when they begged and pleaded with her to stop it. However, his instructions for them to stop paying attention to her hair pulling also were ineffective. Thus, he developed a behavioral treatment plan using a single-case design to try to stop this behavior.

Since most of Caitlin's hair pulling occurred at night, the psychologist directed her mother to collect the hair from her pillow each morning and put it in a plastic bag, labeled by the day of the week. The number of hairs pulled each night would be used to determine whether treatment was effective. The treatment plan was as follows:

Caitlin had a pair of pink mittens that she liked to wear, and her favorite food was cherry ice cream. If Caitlin wore her mittens all night (which would prevent her from pulling her hair), and they were still on her hands in the morning, she could have cherry ice cream for breakfast.

Using an ABAB design, the effectiveness of the treatment was evaluated (see Figure 2.8). The "A" phase was the baseline phase (no pink mittens or cherry ice cream). The "B" phase was the actual treatment (cherry ice cream for breakfast if Caitlin was wearing her mittens in the morning). Her mother continued to collect the hair each morning, and the average number of hairs pulled per night was recorded. Figure 2.8 shows the number of hairs on Catilin's pillow each morning (averaged over the week) during the treatment program. Each phase was three weeks in length. As Caitlin's hair began to return, the treatment program was gradually withdrawn. Six months later, she had a full head of hair.

In some cases, it is unethical or impractical to reverse a treatment. For example, it would be unethical to remove a treatment that reduces self-injurious behavior, such as head banging in children with developmental disabilities.

In Monica's case, it would be unethical to remove a medication that eliminated her depressive symptoms, including her suicidal thoughts.

Some interventions also produce learning that cannot easily be reversed. For example, relaxation training may produce changes in physical state (lower blood pressure) that do not quickly revert to baseline levels. When a behavior cannot be reversed, a *multiple baseline design* may be used (Morgan & Morgan, 2001). In this design, only one A-B sequence is applied, but the sequence is repeated across individuals, settings, or behaviors. When the *multiple baseline design* is conducted *across individuals*, the treatment is introduced at a different time. This is often done by varying the length of the baseline assessment for each person so that the cause of any improvement cannot be attributed to the duration of any standard baseline period. As in the ABAB design, repeating the AB sequence across people increases confidence in the conclusions.

Multiple baseline studies can also be conducted *with a single individual*, as the intervention is applied independently *across behaviors* (e.g., first smoking, then overeating) or *settings* (e.g., first home, then school, then on the playground). If the B phase consistently produces the same behavior change (or is replicated), this is evidence that the intervention is effective.

Limitations of Single-Case Designs   Single-case designs allow clinicians working in full-time practice to use experimental strategies to determine whether a treatment is efficacious (effective) for a particular patient. These strategies are also useful for situations in which it is unethical to withhold treatment completely but there is a need to test the causal relationship between the treatment and a person's behavior. Single-case designs do not allow researchers to generalize the results to heterogeneous groups of people, however. Furthermore, they do not address the impact of individual differences (related to age, sex, ethnicity), which may be very important in determining treatment response. Group-based research, discussed in the next section, is best suited to address these types of questions.

---

concept CHECK

- Case studies, which provide significant details about abnormal behavior or its treatment, allow us to study relatively rare psychological conditions and develop hypotheses for larger studies. Case studies do not, however, allow us to draw conclusions about causality.

- In order to draw causal conclusions, a research study needs to include an experimental control condition (in which the variable to be tested is absent).

- Single-case designs (e.g., the ABAB design, multiple baseline design) are studies of individual people that lead to conclusions about causality. They do not, however, allow us to generalize the results to heterogeneous groups of people, and they do not address the impact of individual differences.

APPLICATION QUESTION   Paul does not like school and throws a temper tantrum every day when it is time to walk to the school bus. If you were a therapist in private practice, how would you set up an experimental test to see if a treatment program you designed for Paul's parents was working to decrease the tantrums?

Research in Abnormal Psychology at the Group Level

Studies based on groups of people are the most common types of research used in abnormal psychology. Using groups allows researchers to draw conclusions based on the average performance across all participants. For example, an investigator recruits a large number of patients with depression for a study of a new treatment. The investigator measures depressive symptoms before and after treatment. After the experiment, depression decreases by 50%, suggesting that on average, patients who participated improved to that degree. The results do not mean, however, that each patient improved by 50%. Some patients benefited less from the treatment and others more. Because the results of the study are based on the average score of the group, they do not allow us to predict the behavior of any single individual. However, this type of research allows us to develop conclusions about important outcomes such as the impact of different treatments on different people and the prevalence of various disorders in different groups of people.

CORRELATIONAL METHODS

Group-based studies may be correlational or controlled in nature. Many important questions in abnormal psychology use **correlations**, or relationships, between different variables or conditions to understand aspects of behavior. Perhaps an investigator wants to know if the severity of depressive symptoms increases with age. To examine this relationship, subjects' ages and scores on a depression symptom inventory can be plotted graphically, with age on one axis (perhaps the *X* axis) and depression scores on the other (*Y*) axis. Then, using mathematical calculations, a line is fitted to the points to determine the degree of association (see Figure 2.9). A statistical concept known as a **correlation coefficient** indicates the *direction* and *strength* of the relationship. The direction of the relationship is considered positive or negative. When there is a *positive correlation*, an increase in one variable is associated with an increase in another variable (e.g., increased rates of smoking are associated with increased rates of heart disease; Neaton & Wentworth, 1992). By contrast, a *negative correlation* means that an increase in one variable is associated with a decrease in another variable (e.g., increased levels of education are associated with decreased rates of diagnosed dementia; Morris, 2005). The strength of a relationship is determined by the value of the correlation coefficient, which ranges from −1.0 to 1.0. Values close to those end points at 1.0 and −1.0 are indicative of a stronger relationship. A correlation of 0.0 indicates no linear relationship (see Figure 2.9). It is important to note that a strong relationship can be either positive or negative.

Interpreting the significance of a correlation depends on different factors. The first factor involves the size and heterogeneity of the study sample. If the sample of people studied is not sufficiently diverse with regard to the variables of scientific interest, the data may lead to inaccurate conclusions. For example, the relationship between age and memory would appear very different if data were collected from a sample of people between the ages of 18 and 85 compared with a sample between the ages of 60 and 70. In the latter group, the restricted age range would lead to correlations that did not represent the true relation between these two variables for the population as a whole.

Another factor important in interpreting correlational data is the way participants are selected. If study participants are chosen because they have a certain psychiatric disorder or because they come from a particular ethnic group, results will generalize only to that subset of people. The study findings may not be relevant for other diagnostic groups or other ethnicities.

Sometimes the relationship between two variables does not appear as a straight line. Some relationships are not linear in nature. For example, a popular theory about the association between stress and performance proposes an *inverted-U* relationship.

correlations relationships between variables

correlation coefficient statistical figure that describes the direction and strength of a correlation

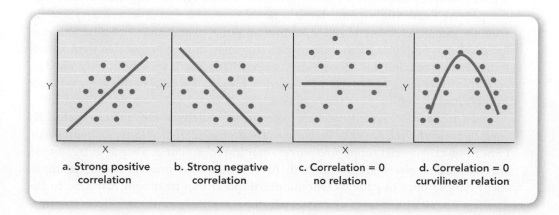

a. Strong positive correlation

b. Strong negative correlation

c. Correlation = 0 no relation

d. Correlation = 0 curvilinear relation

FIGURE 2.9
Examples of Correlational Relations

When data are graphed as points, the correlation (or lack of correlation) is revealed by the shape of the distribution.

Correlation is not causation. These two sisters have been having coffee together every day. Why should we not conclude immediately that drinking coffee leads to long life and happiness?

For testing situations or athletic performances, moderate levels of stress are associated with optimal performance. Much higher and lower levels of stress create poorer performance (Muse et al., 2003). This is known as a *curvilinear* relationship. Plotting a straight line through an inverted-U shape would yield a linear correlation coefficient near 0 (see Figure 2.9d). This would lead to a false conclusion that no relation exists between the two variables.

Correlation Is Not Causation   Often, correlations are inaccurately interpreted to imply a causal relationship. Correlations only explain the degree to which a change in one variable is associated with a change in the other; they do not allow you to conclude that one variable *causes* the second. A strong positive correlation between variables X and Y, for example, may be the result of X causing Y, Y causing X, or a third variable (Z) that influences both. In this example, the variable Z would be referred to as a *moderator* variable. For example, there is a significant correlation between moderate alcohol use (up to three drinks a day) and reduced risk of dementia in people age 55 and over (Ruitenberg et al., 2002). Often inaccurately reported in the media as causal (e.g., drinking moderately can prevent dementia), the data merely suggest that these two phenomena are related. In fact, moderate alcohol use may have a *direct* impact on cognitive functioning through the release of a neurotransmitter (acetylcholine or ACTH) in the hippocampus (a center for learning and memory). Alcohol use might also influence cognitive status *indirectly* through its effects on cardiovascular risk factors, decreasing the possibility of high blood pressure or stroke, both of which in turn could affect cognitive functioning. Other explanations might implicate different variables that could influence both alcohol use and the development of dementia (e.g., exercise level, education, genetic predispositions, type of dementia, etc.). Any of these alternatives could be the moderator variable (Z) that affects the relationship between alcohol and dementia.

It is even more tempting to assume a causal relationship when a significant correlation occurs between two variables that are measured at different points in time (for example, SAT scores and college grades). In these cases, terms like risk factor or *predictor* are used to describe this temporal relationship. For example, it is generally well known that cigarette smoking and lack of exercise are *risk factors* for elevated cholesterol and heart disease. However, other intervening factors may affect the relationship (e.g., nutrition). Since it would be unethical to do an experiment in which people were assigned to smoke a certain number of cigarettes per day, we can only understand these relationships through the use of correlational data.

Similarly, the severity of a disorder before treatment is often interpreted to *predict* treatment response. In most cases, more severe symptoms are associated with less positive treatment response, but it is not always clear that more severe symptoms *cause* the poorer response. This is an important point to understand because although "predict" may imply causality in everyday language, in psychology this term simply indicates that certain levels of variable X, assessed at Time 1, are significantly associated with certain levels of variable Y, assessed at Time 2. "Predict" in this sense does not mean "cause."

In treatment-focused research, correlational analyses can be very useful. By investigating the relationship between patient characteristics (e.g., demographics, clinical severity, social support resources) and improvement as a result of treatment, correlational analyses are useful both theoretically and practically. For example, identifying groups of patients who do not respond to a treatment may lead to the development of alternative treatments. Although correlational designs may yield important information, these studies can only measure covariation between predictors and outcomes. To draw conclusions about *causality*, controlled group designs must be used.

CONTROLLED GROUP DESIGNS

Most research in psychology uses **controlled group designs**, in which groups of participants are exposed to different conditions that are manipulated and controlled by the investigator. In these designs, participants in at least one *experimental group* are typically compared with at least one *control group*. These groups are usually designed to be highly similar with regard to as many variables as possible (e.g., age, sex, education) and to vary only on the **independent variable** (IV) that is controlled by the experimenter. For example, one group of depressed patients receives a treatment (the experimental group) and the other group does not (the control group), but in all other ways the groups are similar. The impact of the IV on some **dependent variable** (DV), or outcome measure, is then assessed. Statistical analyses examine whether group differences on the DV are greater than chance. If so, and if the groups differed only on the IV, one can conclude that the IV is likely to have caused the differences. The strongest inferences about causality come from randomized controlled designs.

Randomized Controlled Designs In this design, the most critical feature is **random assignment** of participants to groups. When assignment is truly random, each participant has an equal probability of being assigned to either group. In addition to random assignment, other features of randomized controlled designs can affect the study's conclusions. These include *participant selection procedures*, *internal and external validity*, and *assessment strategies*. When deciding how to select participants, an important consideration is whether to recruit an *analogue* or a *clinical* sample. *Analogue samples* (just like an analogy) are people who have the characteristics of interest and resemble treatment-seeking populations, but are not seeking clinical services. Researchers interested in social anxiety, for example, may recruit an analogue sample by placing an ad in the paper seeking people with public speaking anxiety. Analogue samples are most often recruited from college campuses or community groups. By contrast, *clinical samples* are people who are seeking services for a specific problem. A researcher in an anxiety disorders clinic may approach patients in the clinic to ask them to participate in a treatment study.

The decision to recruit an analogue or clinical sample is based on both theoretical and practical issues (e.g., what question will be addressed and what resources are available), but the decision has significant implications for the study's conclusions. Take, for example, an investigator who wishes to examine the efficacy of a treatment for depression in young adults. Conclusions may be dramatically different if the sample is recruited from a general college population (who may have a wide range of feelings of sadness) or from the student counseling center, where higher levels of depression may be more common (because the students are motivated to seek treatment). Results based on one sample simply may not *generalize* (be relevant) to the other.

Whether study findings can be generalized is also affected by the diversity and representativeness of the recruited sample. For instance, many studies fail to include a sufficient number of participants representing ethnic minority groups; findings therefore may not be relevant for large segments of the population. Guidelines from the National Institutes of Health, in fact, have emphasized the importance of including diverse groups of participants in clinical research to represent the population adequately in terms of age, gender, and ethnicity.

controlled group designs experiments in which groups of participants are exposed to different conditions, at least one of which is experimental and one of which is a control

independent variable the variable in a controlled experiment that is controlled by the experimenter

dependent variable the variable in a controlled experiment that is assessed to determine the effect of the independent variable

random assignment the most critical feature of a randomized controlled design wherein each participant has an equal probability of being assigned to each experimental or control condition

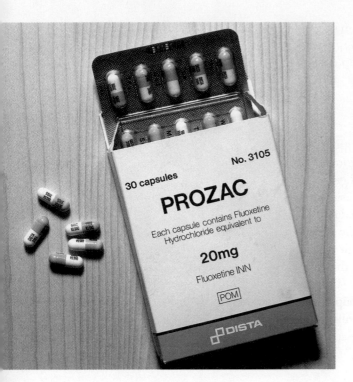

A research study is examining whether therapy is better than no therapy for the treatment of depression. Why would the internal validity of the study be threatened if some participants in the no therapy group started taking the antidepressant drug, Prozac?

Another issue of critical importance when examining the data from any study is the concept of validity. *Internal validity* is the extent to which the study design allows conclusions that the IV (intervention) caused changes in the DV (outcome). To increase internal validity, the researcher tries to control (keep constant) all variables except the one being tested (the IV). Limiting a study sample to women only, for example, increases internal validity and our ability to draw causal conclusions because potential differences in response based on sex need not be considered. To increase internal validity in a treatment study, a researcher would want to make sure that both subgroups of participants (those getting treatment and those not getting treatment) have exactly the same experiences over the course of the study with the exception of the actual treatment being tested. For example, in a study of depression treatment, to increase internal validity it would be important to ensure that participants in both groups receive no additional services or experiences that might reduce depression (e.g., support groups at church, medication from a primary care doctor) during the study period.

When internal validity increases, however, *external validity*, or the ability to generalize study findings to situations and people outside the experimental setting, often decreases. This is because study conditions that are well controlled often fail to represent the "real world." For example, results of a study based only on women participants may be relevant only to women and not to men, and studies of depression treatment that restrict participants' activities outside of the experimental treatment may not represent what happens in real life.

A major challenge for researchers is to strike an adequate balance between internal and external validity. Researchers want to be able to draw adequate conclusions about causal relationships, yet they also want results that are relevant to real-life phenomena. In treatment outcome research, internal and external validity are differentially emphasized in *efficacy* versus *effectiveness* research (Roy-Byrne et al., 2003). Efficacy research attempts to maximize internal validity, allowing the researcher to feel confident in identifying causal relationships. Patients are carefully selected to represent a *homogeneous group* (i.e., to have only the disorder the investigators want to study and no other conditions); specialized providers use a highly structured intervention; and comparison groups are chosen carefully to control for key elements of the treatment approach. These well-controlled studies allow the researcher to draw solid conclusions about the impact of the specific treatment, but sometimes the research procedures do not reflect real-world patients and clinics. In effectiveness research, which focuses more on external validity, patients are more heterogeneous (they often have more than one type of psychological disorder) and more similar to the kinds of patients treated in routine care. Treatment is often provided in typical health care settings (e.g., primary care) by clinicians who work in those settings; control conditions more often consist of the type of care typically offered in that clinic; and more emphasis is given to the cost-benefit ratio of treatment. These studies are sometimes less well controlled with respect to research design, but the results are more representative of what might happen when treatments are used in the "real" world. Efficacy and effectiveness designs are best viewed as complementary approaches to treatment research.

Conclusions from randomized controlled designs also depend on the assessment strategies researchers use. First and foremost, assessment instruments need to be *reliable* (measure a particular variable consistently over time and across patients) and *valid* (measure a variable accurately) (see Chapter 3 for more detailed information about reliability and validity). Using more than one assessment method is also important. For example, some measures of depression emphasize physical symptoms, such as sleep, whereas others emphasize difficulties in thinking, such as concentration and memory problems. Depression can be evaluated using self-report (typically through standardized questionnaires or surveys), global ratings by expert evaluators, direct observations of behavior, and psychobiological measures. Choosing measures that represent different methods of assessment also increases the confidence and generalizability of study findings.

Two other important issues related to our ability to draw conclusions from controlled research studies include the use of **placebo control** conditions and the consideration of *blinded* assessment. Even in controlled research, the expectations or biases of the researcher and the participants can affect study findings (participants who think they are getting a good treatment may get better just because they expect to do so). A placebo control group is one in which an "inactive" treatment is provided; all aspects of this treatment are like the experimental condition but without the "active ingredients" of the treatment. For example, in medication studies, the placebo control group receives a pill that looks exactly like the real medication, but in fact has no real medication (i.e., is more like a "sugar pill"). Because a significant proportion of patients get better with a placebo treatment (called *placebo response*), this kind of control condition allows the researcher to estimate what percent of improvement is actually due to expectation alone. Only if the experimental treatment produces greater response than the placebo can we say that the active ingredients of the treatment are important. In placebo-controlled studies, it is important for patients and any people who rate the degree of improvement to remain blinded to (unaware of) the condition to which the patient has been assigned.

For example, what if Monica agreed to participate in a research treatment study for depression, but she and the researchers knew that she had been assigned to the "placebo group"? How would Monica evaluate her improvement if she knew that she was not receiving active treatment?

To reduce bias that may influence study findings, it is important to keep research participants and evaluators blinded, or uninformed, about study goals and hypotheses, as well as their assigned treatment condition (active treatment, placebo, or no treatment control). Completely blind assessment is not always feasible, but this assessment strategy is helpful for enhancing study validity, as it reduces bias regarding treatment outcome.

Clinical vs. Statistical Significance   Clinical versus statistical significance is another important consideration when evaluating clinical research.

Suppose that after treatment, people in the treatment condition report that it now takes only 2 hours to fall asleep, compared with 2.2 hours for people in the control group.

Statistical significance refers to the mathematical probability that after treatment, changes that occurred in the treatment group did not occur by chance but were actually due to the treatment. Statistically significant findings show that the treatment changed the target behavior. But an equally important question is whether the significant findings have any practical or clinical value. Sometimes statistical significance indicates the presence of important clinical changes, but not always. In some studies, particularly those with large samples, statistically significant differences may actually be quite small (as in the sleep example above) and have no real implications for patient care.

placebo control   a control group in which an inactive treatment is provided

By contrast, *clinical significance* examines whether significant findings have practical or clinical value. For example, do treatments that reduce symptom severity have a meaningful impact on patients' lives?

Does a patient such as Monica, who was so depressed that she could not get out of bed before treatment, now not only feel less depressed but feel well enough to be able to return to work?

Clinical significance addresses whether the patient's functioning is improved as a result of treatment and the patient no longer has symptoms of a disorder. When statistically significant change occurs without major impact on patients' functioning, its clinical value is questionable. From a statistical perspective, various measures of the magnitude of the treatment effect are known as *effect sizes*. The larger the effect size, the more efficacious the treatment.

RACIAL, ETHNIC, AND CULTURAL GROUPS

As noted earlier, one major limitation of group-based research in abnormal psychology is the failure to include sufficiently diverse samples with regard to race, ethnicity, and culture. For many years, samples were also restricted with regard to sex and age. Much medical and clinical research conducted well into the 1980s, for example, excluded women. There are several reasons for this exclusion. One was the difficulty inherent in controlling for biological differences between the sexes, increasing the complexity and costs of any research design. Another concern, especially with medication trials, is the unknown effect of many new medications on the developing fetus and the difficulties inherent in ensuring that women participating in a clinical trial do not become pregnant during the course of the trial. Third, phase of the menstrual cycle can influence response to many interventions and is another variable that needs to be either incorporated into the study design or controlled. Although many of these reasons for exclusion are practical and defensible from a legal and ethical perspective, they have resulted in our knowing less about the efficacy of some medications in women. Older adults were often excluded from research as well, owing to the complex medical, psychological, and social changes that accompany aging. These kinds of exclusion criteria made it impossible to draw conclusions relevant to diverse groups of people. Similarly, the overabundance of research in abnormal psychology that has been conducted with white samples (often those attending college) may have little relevance for understanding abnormal behavior in people of other races, ethnicities, and cultures.

A growing body of research has begun to document differences in the expression, prevalence, and treatment response of mental health symptoms across different racial and ethnic groups, but it is still a challenge to recruit adequate samples. As a result of a series of unethical practices that occurred during the first half of the twentieth century (see Chapter 15), lack of trust and fear of stigmatization make some participants from ethnically diverse backgrounds reluctant to participate in research (Shavers et al., 2002). In addition, recruitment strategies often are inadequate for engaging minority participants (Sheikh, 2006). To encourage sex, age, racial, and ethnic diversity in research samples, the National Institutes of Health now require all grant applications to include specific recruitment plans targeting traditionally underrepresented groups. Increasing diversity in research samples will enhance the generalizability of study findings to more people. Furthermore, using a diverse sample provides a context for evaluating cultural differences that may affect assessment and treatment. Including diverse participants in research may require increased recruitment resources to target underrepresented groups. It also requires cultural sensitivity to explain the purpose of the research and ensure that assessment instruments are available for persons who speak different languages and come from different educational backgrounds.

The population sample used in research—whether similar or diverse—has great influence on the conclusions that can be drawn from a study.

CROSS-SECTIONAL AND LONGITUDINAL COHORTS

One question that has long fascinated researchers who conduct group-based research is how mental illness has changed in the population over time. It appears that some disorders are more common today than they once were, but how do we know this for sure? A related question is whether disorders occur only in one phase of life, such as childhood, or continue to be present once they appear. Specific types of group-based studies, often called **cohort studies**, can be used to answer these kinds of questions.

A school class is normally a birth cohort. If such a cohort is followed over the years, the result is a longitudinal study.

What Is a Cohort?   A **cohort** is a group of people who share a common characteristic and move forward in time as a unit. Examples include a *birth cohort* (e.g., all individuals born in a certain geographic area in a given year), an *inception cohort* (e.g., all individuals enrolled in a study at a given point in time based on a unifying factor such as place of work or school of attendance), and an *exposure cohort* (e.g., individuals sampled based on a common exposure such as witnessing the events of 9/11 or exposure to lead paint in childhood). Cohort designs are used to study incidence (onset of new cases), causes, and prognosis (outcome). Because they measure events in chronological order, they can help us to distinguish more clearly between cause and effect. For example, if we observe that experience of a traumatic event precedes the onset of post-traumatic stress disorder, we can be more confident that the traumatic events might play a causal role in the development of the disorder than if we had no information on which came first—the trauma or the symptoms. Cohort designs can include longitudinal studies to measure outcomes over time. Longitudinal designs measure the same cohort of individuals on several occasions (see below).

Cross-sectional Design   A **cross-sectional design** provides a snapshot in time. In its most basic form, participants in a cross-sectional design are assessed once for the specific variable under investigation. This design is efficient and can sample large numbers of individuals; however, cause and effect can rarely be determined. Expanding the design to include several cohorts of different ages who are assessed at the same point in time (e.g., all children enrolled in classes in a specific school district) provides a more complex picture of the variable of interest. The Youth Risk Behavioral Survey tracks cigarette use among youth in the United States. Table 2.1 gives the percentage of individuals across two high school cohorts (9th and 12th grades) who report cigarette use. This research design provides a cross-sectional landscape of high school students in one year, but it does not follow the same students throughout their high school years. This design does not identify changes that might occur in 9th graders as they proceed through high school.

Longitudinal Design   A **longitudinal** study takes place over time. This design includes at least two and often more measurement periods with the same individuals at different times. Many longitudinal studies have provided valuable data about the development of mental illness across the life span. Longitudinal cohorts can be assessed over the years, using measures that are age-appropriate at each measurement interval. A longitudinal birth cohort might sample all babies born during a certain month in a given area and follow those babies well into adulthood. Early assessments will be based on parental observations of the child, and later assessments will include age-appropriate assessments that the children complete themselves—as well as reports from parents and

cohort   a group of people who share a common characteristic and move forward in time as a unit

cross-sectional design   a research design in which participants are assessed once for the specific variable under investigation

longitudinal design   a research design in which participants are assessed at least two times and often more over a certain time interval

TABLE 2.1

Percentage of high school students who reported current cigarette use*
by sex, race/ethnicity[†], and grade—Youth Risk Behavior Survey—
United States 1991–2003[§]

Characteristic	1991 %	1995 %	2003 %
Sex			
Female	27.3	34.3	21.9
Male	27.6	35.4	21.8
Race/Ethnicity			
White, non-Hispanic	30.9	38.3	24.9
Female	31.7	39.8	26.6
Male	30.2	37.0	23.3
Black, non-Hispanic	12.6	19.2	15.1
Female	11.3	12.2	10.8
Male	14.1	27.8	19.3
Hispanic	25.3	34.0	18.4
Female	22.9	32.9	17.7
Male	27.9	34.9	19.1
Grade			
9th	23.2	31.2	17.4
12th	30.1	38.2	26.2

*Smoked cigarettes on ≥1 of the 30 days preceding the survey.
[†]Numbers for other racial/ethnic groups were too small for meaningful analysis.

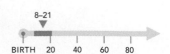

teachers. Outcomes measured in a longitudinal study may include incidence rates of disease, descriptions of the natural course of a variable of interest, and observations of risk factors. So, for example, in the birth cohort mentioned above, we could observe the incidence of autism (or the number of newly diagnosed cases during the observation period), the natural course of autism (how symptoms develop over the course of the 20-year observation period), and factors that were measured before the onset of the illness that are associated with those individuals who develop autism (e.g., older parents). Although longitudinal studies are slow and expensive to complete, their findings are valuable because they show us what happens to the same people over a long period of time.

In a longitudinal study, children who were diagnosed with depression between ages 8 and 13, were reassessed when they were between the ages of 19 and 21 (Kovacs et al., 2003). At this follow-up assessment, they were asked about additional episodes of depression and the presence of other psychological disorders. Teenage boys and girls continued to show symptoms of depression, but the study found that as they matured, girls with a history of childhood depression were more likely to develop eating disorders, whereas boys with a history of childhood depression were more likely to develop conduct or substance abuse problems. Another difference was that the depressive symptoms and eating problems occurred together in girls, whereas for boys, conduct and substance abuse problems occurred at times when boys were less depressed. When boys were more depressed, it seemed that their conduct and substance abuse problems decreased. Using this developmental design allows researchers to understand how symptoms such as depression can vary as a person matures. In addition, this longitudinal study illustrates how sex is related to the other types of psychological problems that may emerge when a teenage girl is depressed or when a teenage boy, with a history of depression, feels less depressed.

---

concept CHECK

- Correlational research tells us about the relationships between variables, but variables that are highly correlated (related) do not necessarily have a causal relationship (one of the variables does not necessarily cause the other).

- The outcomes of a randomized clinical trial are influenced by how participants are selected, the internal and external validity of the study design, and the types of measures used.

- Efficacy research attempts to maximize internal validity and the ability to draw causal conclusions, whereas effectiveness research emphasizes external validity and greater applicability to real-world patients and settings.

- Statistical significance refers to the mathematical probability that changes after treatment are due to the treatment itself. Clinical significance examines whether significant findings have practical or clinical value.

- Increasing the diversity of research participants with regard to race, ethnicity, and culture is essential for increasing the generalizability of study findings.

- Cohort studies can be used to study frequency, causes, and prognosis (likely outcome) of mental disorders.

APPLICATION QUESTION   In a new study, the investigators will examine the impact of cognitive behavior therapy (CBT) for depression in a group of children aged 7 to 17. Half of the children will receive CBT, and the other half will get "supportive treatment" (i.e., they will spend time talking to the therapist about whatever they want). The investigators are interested in how well the treatment affects depressive symptoms and quality of life. What are the independent and dependent variables in this investigation?

Research in Abnormal Psychology at the Population Level

When a researcher's goal is to understand abnormal psychology at the broadest possible level, the "group" of interest can become the general population. To achieve this bird's eye view, we use the research tools associated with epidemiological research, which examines abnormal behavior at its most global level, that of entire populations.

EPIDEMIOLOGY

Epidemiology focuses on disease patterns in human populations and factors that influence those patterns (Lilienfeld & Lilienfeld, 1980). As applied to abnormal psychology, epidemiology focuses on the occurrence of psychological disorders by time, place, and persons. Several terms are key to understanding epidemiological research. The first is **prevalence**, which is the total number of cases of a disorder in a given population at a designated time. *Point prevalence* refers to the number of individuals with a disorder at a specified point in time. *Lifetime prevalence* refers to the total number of individuals in a population known to have had a particular disorder at some point during their lifetimes. For example, the lifetime prevalence for major depression would be the number of people in the United States who have had an episode of major depressive disorder at any point in their lives. By contrast, **incidence** refers to the number of

epidemiology   a research approach that focuses on the prevalence and incidence of mental disorders and the factors that influence those patterns

prevalence   the number of cases of a disorder in a given population at a designated time

incidence   number of new cases that emerge in a given population during a specified period of time

Research HOT Topic

National Comorbidity Survey Replication (NCS-R)

How prevalent are mental illnesses in the United States? At what point will persons suffering from these disorders seek treatment? In 2005, four articles published in the *Archives of General Psychiatry* reported on a breakthrough national investigation of mental illness in the United States. The study is an extension of the 1990 National Comorbidity Survey, a landmark study that was the first to estimate the prevalence of mental disorders in a large, nationally representative sample.

A large sample size is one of the strengths of the NCS-R study: the researchers surveyed and collected data on 9,282 individuals living in the United States. To be considered for the study, participants had to be at least 18 years old, belong to a U.S. household, and speak English. Researchers used the International World Health Organization—Composite International Diagnostic Interview to determine which respondents met criteria for psychological diagnoses. Four categories of disorders were assessed: anxiety disorders, mood disorders, impulse control disorders, and substance use disorders. Researchers also collected information on treatment use, barriers to treatment, and satisfaction with treatment.

Results indicated that mental illnesses are common in the United States—26% of respondents met diagnostic criteria for a mental disorder within the past year. **Comorbidity** is the term used to describe the presence of at least two mental disorders affecting an individual. The NCS-R found that 45% of people with one mental disorder also met criteria for at least one other disorder. Unfortunately, the study revealed that there are often long time intervals between the time a person's mental disorder begins and his or her first attempt to seek treatment. Even more startling was the finding that only 41.1% of people with symptoms characteristic of a mental illness diagnosis received treatment. Untreated mental disorders were associated with problems in school, teenage pregnancy and unstable marriages, and unemployment later in life.

The findings in this study make it clear that although mental illnesses are common in American households, prompt and ongoing treatment is not. The NCS-R was conducted with a large representative sample and indicated that mental illnesses are highly comorbid; it also revealed that for most people symptoms of mental disorders begin appearing early in life. Because of the chronic nature and high prevalence of mental illness, it is imperative to expand and improve treatment for all persons in the United States who need it.

References: http://www.nimh.nih.gov/healthinformation/ncs-r.cfm
http://www.neuropsychiatryreviews.com/jul05/NCSRS.html

new cases that emerge in a given population during a specified period of time. An example of incidence could be the number of new cases of anorexia nervosa reported by pediatricians in the United States over the period of one year. Both incidence and prevalence are valuable in understanding patterns of occurrence of psychological disorders across time and across populations, and we will refer to these concepts throughout this book.

EPIDEMIOLOGICAL RESEARCH DESIGNS

Research designs used to study questions in epidemiology (e.g., how often do certain disorders occur in the population; are certain characteristics of people or places more likely to be associated with certain kinds of disorders; can we do anything to change certain patterns of prevalence and incidence?) can be observational (the researcher simply observes what is happening) or experimental (the researcher tries to change something and examine the effects).

comorbidity the co-occurrence of two or more disorders existing in the same person, either at the same time or at some point in the lifetime

Observational Epidemiology The most basic form of epidemiological research is *observational epidemiology*, which documents the presence of physical or psychological disorders in human populations. For psychological disorders, the most common method of documentation is to conduct diagnostic interviews, using a structured interview format in which all people interviewed are asked exactly the same questions. Using randomly selected segments of the population, this design allows researchers to determine the point or lifetime prevalence of various psychological disorders. Quite simply, it answers the questions, how many people suffer from a disorder (e.g., depression), and are certain subsets of the population (e.g., women) more likely than others to suffer from the disorder? Data from epidemiological studies were presented in Chapter 1, where we discussed rates of psychological disorders in the United States.

One highly informative study funded by the National Institutes of Mental Health, called the National Comorbidity Survey (1990–1992), was the first nationally representative mental health survey in the United States to use a standard set of questions to assess the prevalence and associated characteristics of psychological disorders. The cohort was first interviewed in 1990–1992 and then reinterviewed in 2001–2002 (NCS-2) to study patterns and predictors of the course of mental disorders. The study also evaluated whether certain primary mental disorders predicted the onset and course of secondary disorders (e.g., whether people with depression developed alcohol abuse). One of the subsequent studies was the NCS Replication (NCS-R), in which diagnostic interviews were conducted on a new sample of 10,000 respondents focusing on areas not covered in the original study (see the box "Research Hot Topic: National Comorbidity Survey Replication"). Another study was the NCS-A (adolescent), which interviewed 10,000 adolescents to determine the prevalence and correlates of mental disorders in youth. The NCS series has provided invaluable information for clinicians and policymakers by establishing the magnitude of the public health burden of mental disorders and documenting the need to plan services accordingly.

examining the evidence

Community Intervention Trial for Smoking Cessation (COMMIT)

■ **The Facts**   Intervention Programs are believed to keep smokers free. But do they?

■ **The Evidence**   The Community Intervention Trial for Smoking Cessation (COMMIT) was a large-scale study funded by the National Cancer Institute to assess a combination of community-based interventions designed to help smokers stop using tobacco. COMMIT involved 11 matched pairs of communities in North America, which were randomly assigned to an experimental condition offering an active community-wide intervention or a control condition (no active intervention). The 4-year intervention included messaging through existing media channels, major community organizations, and social institutions capable of influencing smoking behavior in large groups of people. The interventions were implemented in each community through a local community board that provided oversight and management of COMMIT activities.

■ **Let's Examine the Evidence**   Somewhat surprisingly, there was no difference in the average quit rate of heavy smokers in the intervention communities (18.0%) compared with the control communities (18.7%). The quit rates for light-to-moderate-smokers were statistically different: averages of 30.6% and 27.5% for the intervention and control communities, respectively. No significant differences in quit rates were observed between the sexes. Less-educated light-to-moderate smokers were more responsive to the intervention than were college-educated smokers with a light-to-moderate habit.

■ **Conclusion**   Extensive programs designed to encourage smoking cessation often have little effect.

Source: Community Intervention Trial for Smoking Cessation (COMMIT), 1991; 1995a; 1995b.

Experimental Epidemiology   In **experimental epidemiology,** the scientist manipulates exposure to either causal or preventive factors. A scientist might want to assess whether various environmental manipulations would be effective in producing weight loss (see the box "Examining the Evidence: Community Intervention Trial for Smoking Cessation (COMMIT)", page 69 for a similar approach to smoking cessation). The focus in this instance is on a weight loss for a community as a whole, not for any one individual person. Ten geographically separated communities could be randomly assigned to a community-based weight control program focusing on increasing walking to school, decreasing fast-food consumption, and decreasing videogame and TV time. The active intervention communities could be saturated with billboards, newspaper ads, local television commercials, and direct mailings, all promoting healthy approaches to weight control. The control communities would receive no intervention. Population-level outcomes would include the extent to which people were reached by the intervention and the extent to which the intervention was effective in producing both behavior and weight change.

---

concept CHECK

- Epidemiology in abnormal psychology research addresses the occurrence of psychological disorders and the factors that influence them.

- Prevalence refers to the total number of cases of a disorder that appears in a given population at a designated time. Incidence describes the number of new cases that emerge during a given period of time.

- The National Comorbidity Study and its Replication are longitudinal studies that have provided key information about the prevalence and correlates of mental disorders in adults and youth.

APPLICATION QUESTION   A researcher wants to design a study to determine how frequently anxiety occurs in adults and whether rates change as people get older. What kind of study would be best to conduct, and how might you design it?

experimental epidemiology   a research method in which the scientist manipulates exposure to either causal or preventive factors

---

THE WHOLE STORY: SUSAN, A PARTICIPANT IN A RANDOMIZED CONTROLLED TRIAL

Susan had been having episodes of depression and finally went to see her primary care doctor for advice. Her doctor had brochures about a therapy trial for depression at a nearby university and suggested that she might want to call for more information. The following describes Susan's experience as a participant in a clinical psychotherapy trial.

Screening Call: *Today I called the research coordinator for information. She told me that the study was for women between 20 and 40 and was designed to compare two different psychotherapies for depression. She described the two treatments to me—one was based on*

something called cognitive-behavioral therapy, and the other one was based on interpersonal psychotherapy. She explained that I would not be able to choose which treatment I received, that it would be decided by a procedure that was like a flip of a coin (randomization). She asked me a bunch of questions on the phone about my mood, how long I had been feeling this way, my sleep, appetite, energy levels, whether I was suicidal and whether I was on any medications. Then, based on my answers to those questions, she said we could set up an appointment for an initial evaluation.

Initial Evaluation: *I got to the clinic and was greeted by the research coordinator. She spent a lot of time explaining the study to me and presented me with an information sheet. I read it, and she asked if I had any questions. Then came all of the forms! First I filled out a* **consent form** *agreeing to the terms of the study and understanding my rights as a participant. I was assured that I could withdraw from the study at any time. Then I had to sign a* **HIPAA** *form, which was all about the privacy of my records and who could have access to them. This worried me a little bit because I certainly didn't want my boyfriend to find out, so I* talked with the research coordinator about it. She explained that HIPAA stood for the Health Insurance Portability and Accountability Act and that I could be completely assured that my boyfriend would not be able to have access to my records. Just when I thought I was done filling out forms, she gave me a packet of questionnaires that asked all sorts of questions—not only about my mood, but about anxiety, eating, my family, and all sorts of questions about what sort of person I am. Some of them were really hard to answer, but I had to choose yes or no. That took about an hour and a half.

Then I had a little break, and the coordinator explained that the next step would be a comprehensive evaluation by a psychiatrist. The psychiatrist, she explained, would not be the person who would be seeing me for therapy, but would conduct interviews with me throughout the study to see how I was progressing. The psychiatrist would not know which treatment I was receiving. In the evaluation, the psychiatrist asked a lot of the same questions that were on the questionnaire. This was a little irritating, but I guess the psychiatrist went into more depth than the questionnaires. She even asked about the first time I ever felt depressed when I was very young. She also asked questions about whether I heard voices or saw things that other people didn't see, asked about my drug and alcohol use (I was honest with her about almost everything—I just couldn't bring myself to tell her about that one experience with Ecstasy though—I barely know the woman and it was kind of embarrassing). She also asked all sorts of questions about my health and medications.

I met with the research coordinator again, she invited me into the study, then she got an envelope that had my participant number on it, opened it, and told me I was randomized to cognitive-behavior therapy.

Baseline Week: At the end of the evaluation day, the research coordinator instructed me on how to "self-monitor" my mood for the baseline week. She gave me a special personal digital assistant (PDA) that I was supposed to type in how depressed I felt every time it prompted me. I thought that was kind of cool—but worried about whether it would wake me up at night. She explained that the PDA was programmed for 8 a.m.–10 p.m. and that I would not be bothered by prompts any other time. So off I went with my PDA for a week of recording before my first appointment. I also left with the card of my therapist, Dr. McIntosh, whom I would see the following Thursday. For a week I dutifully responded every time it pinged me. It was kind of interesting, I noticed that my mood ratings always seemed to be worse in the afternoon.

Course of Therapy: I went to the clinic and was greeted by Dr. McIntosh. The first session went well. I liked her. She had a positive attitude and seemed like she really believed that the therapy had the potential to help. She took her time and explained everything clearly. She also told me that I needed to continue responding to the PDA throughout the study. For the first two weeks we met twice a week. She gave me a workbook and we worked through it step by step. Every session she started off reviewing how things had gone since the last session and whether I had done all of my self-monitoring and homework. It felt a little bit like school, but she really seemed to care about how I was feeling. She helped me start to recognize how negative my thinking was, and she challenged me to start doing some of those fun things that I had lost interest in recently. I never realized how much I catastrophized from the smallest of things or as Dr. McIntosh said, really made mountains out of molehills. I also hadn't realized how much my mood improved when I did some of the things on my fun list (even if I had to really push myself to do them in the first place). After the eighth session, I met with the psychiatrist again for another assessment. She went over many of the same questions as in the beginning, and I had to fill out MORE questionnaires. After eight sessions, I felt as if my mood was getting better. I still had some bad days, but it didn't feel like the same oppressive cloud that had been there before. I had eight more sessions—first once a week, then once every two weeks. Dr. McIntosh and I spent a lot of time working on strategies for what to do if I feel like my mood is slipping again—like identifying early warning signs and taking immediate action. By the end I really felt like I understood how much my own thinking patterns contributed to my staying depressed.

Follow-up: At the end of treatment I met with the psychiatrist again for an interview and I filled out more questionnaires. The research coordinator also asked me lots of questions about how I liked the treatment and whether I would have it again or recommend it to others. I came back at six months and one year for follow-up appointments when I met with the psychiatrist again and filled out more papers. Each time, the research coordinator checked in with me to see how things were going and to update my contact information. The second time, I ran into Dr. McIntosh. It was great to see her and to report that I was still feeling really well. When I look back on the whole experience of being in the study, honestly, I had been a little worried about being a "guinea pig," but truth be told, I felt really taken care of. So many people seemed to care about my well-being and they were all involved with my treatment. It was an amazing experience.

CRITICAL ISSUES to remember

1. Research on psychological disorders occurs on many levels, from the cellular or neuroanatomical to the individual or group levels, to the population level. Applying all of these approaches to the study of a single disorder allows for a comprehensive picture of the nature and course of a particular illness.

2. At the cellular level, we can understand mental disorders as we study the brain from an evolutionary perspective, which involves moving from the brain stem (which controls fundamental biological functions) to the forebrain (where higher cognitive functions occur). New techniques at the cellular level include neuroimaging (taking pictures of the brain), studying the function and interrelation of neurotransmitters (chemicals that relay electrical signals between the cells), and molecular genetics (identifying genes that influence risk for psychological disorders).

3. Substantial advances in the genetics of psychological disorders have been on the forefront of research over the past decade. Family, twin, and adoption studies are behavioral genetic methods that allow us to determine whether genes are likely to play a role. Candidate gene, genomewide linkage, and genomewide association studies are more direct techniques that allow for the actual identification of genetic regions or actual genes associated with a trait or a disorder.

4. Case studies, which provide significant details about abnormal behavior or its treatment, allow us to study relatively rare psychological conditions and develop hypotheses for larger studies. Case studies do not, however, allow us to draw conclusions about causality. Single-case designs (e.g., the ABAB design, multiple baseline design) are studies of individual people that lead to conclusions about causality. These studies do not, however, allow us to generalize the results to heterogeneous groups of people, and they do not address the impact of individual differences.

5. Correlational research tells us about the relationships between different variables. However, correlational research does not tell us about causality, since variables that are highly correlated (related) do not necessarily have a causal relationship with each other (i.e., one of the variables does not necessarily cause the other).

6. The outcomes of a randomized clinical trial are influenced by how participants are selected, internal and external validity of the study design, and types of measures used. Different kinds of clinical trials are designed to answer different questions. Efficacy research, for example, attempts to maximize internal validity and ability to draw causal conclusions, while effectiveness research emphasizes external validity and greater applicability to real-world patients and settings.

7. Epidemiology, or the study of populations, permits a bird's eye view of the study of causes, course, and outcome of psychological disorders. This type of research can tell us about the prevalence of disorders (the number of times the disorder appears in a population) and their incidence (the number of new cases that emerge during a given period of time), as well as whether certain subsets of the population are more likely to suffer from the disorder.

TEST yourself

For more review plus practice tests, flashcards, and Speaking Out: DSM in Context videos, log onto www.MyPsychLab.com

1. Researchers find that a chemical in a recently discovered rainforest plant significantly reduces appetite in laboratory mice. Other researchers then make the chemical into a drug and test it to see whether it helps obese people lose weight. This type of research is called
   a. bedside
   b. bench
   c. translational
   d. communication

2. Which of the following represents all of the different levels of research in abnormal psychology?
   a. cellular, individual, group, and population
   b. neuroanatomy, neurohormones, neurotransmitters, and genetics

   c. correlational, group, cross-cultural, and multiethnic
   d. cross-sectional, longitudinal, cohort, and epidemiological

3. The human nervous system has two main parts:
   a. the left and right cerebral hemispheres
   b. the central nervous system and the peripheral nervous system
   c. the upper and lower brain
   d. the cortex and the brain stem

4. A primary function of the hypothalamus is homeostasis and the regulation of
   a. thoughts and cognitions
   b. sleep/wake states and consciousness
   c. balance and many motor activities
   d. blood pressure, temperature, and weight

5. The autonomic nervous system includes the
   a. neurotransmitter and neurohormone system
   b. somatic and hormonal nervous system
   c. sympathetic and parasympathetic nervous systems
   d. midbrain and brain stem

6. Communication in the nervous system relies on signals transmitted by
   a. electrical impulses called action potentials
   b. chemicals called neurotransmitters
   c. an electrochemical process
   d. all of the above

7. Neuroscientists who want to see brain activity in people with a snake phobia would use which of the following imaging tests?
   a. CAT   c. fMRI
   b. MRI   d. PET

8. The indirect study of whether certain behavioral traits or mental disorders are heritable, or run in families, is called
   a. epidemiology
   b. behavioral ecology
   c. behavioral genetics
   d. homogeneous group design

9. Which of the following statements best describes what we know about how genes affect behavioral traits?
   a. a few genetic loci control all complex traits
   b. family studies show that genes are less important than environment
   c. behavioral traits are rarely caused by single genes
   d. complex traits exert only small effects

10. Twin studies have been of particular importance in the study of abnormal behavior because they have
    a. identified genetic vs. environmental contributions to psychological disorders
    b. examined similarities between twins from many different families
    c. shown that MZ twins in different environments develop different disorders
    d. shown that identical twins are never truly identical

11. We cannot infer the causes of behavior from case studies, but they do let us
    a. rule out subjective biases of the therapist
    b. rule out subjective biases of the patient
    c. control for the attention of the therapist
    d. objectively describe rare phenomena

12. When a treatment cannot be reversed, or if it would be unethical to withdraw a treatment, the single-case design strategy that should be used is called a(n)
    a. case study design   c. multiple baseline design
    b. AB design   d. ABAB design

13. A strong positive correlation between the number of cigarettes smoked and the amount of alcohol consumed per day can be interpreted to mean
    a. smoking leads to drinking
    b. drinking leads to smoking
    c. a third variable like stress increases both behaviors
    d. any of the above

14. The most common type of research in abnormal psychology is
    a. single subject design
    b. controlled group design
    c. longitudinal design
    d. epidemiological design

15. A researcher interested in social anxiety placed an ad in the paper seeking people with public speaking anxiety. People who volunteer for this type of study are part of a(n)
    a. analogue sample
    b. proband sample
    c. aggregate sample
    d. clinical sample

16. Research on an exciting new treatment that takes place with carefully selected patients at a world-renowned laboratory is less likely to have
    a. external validity
    b. external reliability
    c. internal validity
    d. internal reliability

17. In placebo-controlled studies, experts who rate the degree of patient improvement following treatment must be kept unaware of
    a. the funding source of the study
    b. which subjects were in the treatment group and which were in the control group
    c. who the authors of the study were and whether they implemented the treatment exactly as originally described
    d. whether enough subjects were recruited so that the study will have generalizable results

18. The meaningfulness of experimental results can be evaluated in several ways. The statistical significance of the results indicates the
    a. mathematical probability that the findings occurred by chance
    b. practical value of the findings
    c. clinical value of the findings
    d. all of the above

19. A criticism of early group-based research in abnormal psychology is that it
    a. regularly used samples that were too small
    b. failed to control for biological differences between the sexes
    c. stigmatized many of its subjects
    d. failed to include diverse samples

20. Children accidentally exposed to mercury when vaccinated are evaluated at one point in time. They are followed for 10 years and evaluated again. These children are part of a study called a
    a. group design
    b. longitudinal design
    c. comorbidity study
    d. randomized clinical trial

Answers: 1 c, 2 a, 3 b, 4 d, 5 c, 6 d, 7 c, 8 c, 9 c, 10 a, 11 d, 12 c, 13 d, 14 b, 15 a, 16 a, 17 b, 18 a, 19 d, 20 b.

CHAPTER objectives

After reading this chapter, you should be able to:

1 Understand the goals and uses of clinical assessment.

2 Name three important properties of psychological assessment instruments.

3 List and explain the function of different kinds of assessment instruments.

4 Explain why classification systems for abnormal behavior are valuable.

5 Recognize the importance of developmental and cultural variables that impact the experience and classification of abnormal behavior.

6 Discuss the pros and cons of dimensional models for understanding abnormal behavior that serve as alternatives to more traditional classification systems.

assessment and diagnosis

Pauline was 82 years old and functioned well for her age. She saw Dr. McGuire, a psychologist, every couple of weeks to help her manage anxiety and depression. Pauline had experienced anxiety and depression much of her life, and the coping skills she had learned in treatment were helping. She was active at church and with volunteer groups, traveled, and had many friends. Dr. McGuire, however, had recently started talking with her about the possibility of increasing memory problems. He had noticed that she was starting to repeat herself during their meetings and that she sometimes forgot major topics of their conversations from one session to the next. Pauline's daughter had also mentioned to her the possibility of memory problems, but Pauline didn't think her memory was that bad. Sure, she misplaced things—and people told her that she repeated herself—but at her age, who didn't? As long as she could stay active and involved, it didn't bother her that she might be having some minor memory problems.

One day before a scheduled appointment, Pauline called Dr. McGuire to say that she was in the hospital. She had suffered a bad fall the day before while walking in a shopping mall, and the doctors were running a series of tests. Dr. McGuire requested Pauline's permission to speak to her doctor and learned that there was some concern that Pauline might have had a minor stroke. They would conduct additional tests before she could be discharged.

When Pauline was released from the hospital, she went home with her daughter and followed up with her internist. She had not suffered a stroke, but the doctors were monitoring her symptoms because her blood pressure was high. She was more unstable on her feet and was using a cane. She was not allowed to drive. When Pauline came to her next therapy appointment with Dr. McGuire, her daughter came along. At this session, Pauline was quite confused. She could not recall many details about her hospitalization, and she repeated herself many times. She reported that she was taking pain medication as prescribed and that she would be seeing her internist the following day.

In the weeks that followed, Pauline began to regain some of her prior abilities, but her memory problems got worse and she was more depressed and anxious. She was more lethargic than usual, and worried more about the future and what might happen to her. Dr. McGuire became increasingly concerned about Pauline's ability to live independently and talked with Pauline and her daughter about the need for a more formal clinical assessment. There was a need to differentiate any medical, cognitive, and psychological reasons for Pauline's overall decline in functioning.

For Pauline and Dr. McGuire, many questions arose at this point. Did the fall result from some undiscovered medical problem? Was her pain medication creating more memory problems and depression? Might Pauline's fall and its consequences, such as losing independence, have produced increased worry and depression? Could Pauline's poorer functioning be the result of a progressive, deteriorating cognitive disease like dementia (see Chapter 13)? These questions, posed by Pauline, her therapist, and her family members, suggested the need for a clinical assessment to determine the nature and cause of her increasing difficulties, as well as to help guide future treatment. They also illustrate the complexity of the biological, psychological, and social factors that can affect psychological functioning.

Clinical Assessment

The **clinical assessment** of any psychological problem involves a series of steps designed to gather information (or *data*) about a person and his or her environment in order to make decisions about the nature, status, and treatment of psychological problems. Typically, clinical assessment begins with a set of *referral questions* developed in response to a request for help. Usually, the request comes from the patient or someone closely connected to that person, such as a family member, teacher, or other health care professional. These initial questions help determine the goals of the assessment and the selection of appropriate psychological tests or measurements. As in the case of Pauline, referral questions sometimes suggest the need for a thorough medical evaluation in addition to a psychological assessment.

GOALS OF ASSESSMENT

The process of assessment includes deciding what assessment procedures and instruments to administer, such as which measures of biological function, cognition, emotion, behavior, and personality style to use. Selection of assessment tools is determined to a large extent by the types of symptoms described and the age and medical status of the patient, but the theoretical perspective of the therapist may also play a role in the scope of the assessment (see Chapter 1). When evaluating a patient who is significantly depressed and anxious, for example, a behavioral psychologist focuses on measuring the environmental cues that produce the low moods, and the thoughts, behaviors, and consequences associated with them. A psychoanalytic psychologist, on the other hand, focuses more on assessing the patient's early childhood experiences and typical patterns of interpersonal functioning.

Later in this chapter, we describe some of the best known psychological tests and procedures used in the assessment process. Once an assessment is complete and all data are collected, the psychologist integrates the findings to develop preliminary answers to the initial questions. This information is typically given to the patient and any family members involved in the assessment and, with appropriate releases and permissions from the patient, to other health care providers who were part of the referral or assessment process. Although these discussions are still part of the assessment process, they often have therapeutic effects (Maruish, 1999). As people begin to have a better understanding of what is happening within and around them, they often experience improvement in their symptoms. A smoker is asked to count the number of cigarettes that are smoked each day and discovers that the number is far more than originally estimated. In some cases, this assessment serves as feedback, and the smoker decreases the number of cigarettes smoked even before formal treatment begins.

The value of assessment is not limited to answering a referral question. Assessment procedures can be useful even before a referral is provided, through the process of

clinical assessment the process of gathering information about a person and his or her environment to make decisions about the nature, status, and treatment of psychological problems

screening. Screenings can help identify people who have problems but who may not be aware of them or may be reluctant to mention them, and/or those who may need further evaluation. Clinical assessment also is useful at the end of the treatment process as a tool to measure progress or outcomes following intervention (see "Outcome Evaluation").

Screening   Screening assessments identify potential psychological problems or predict the risk of future problems if someone is not referred for further assessment or treatment. In a screening assessment, all members of a group (e.g., a community group, patients in a medical practice) are given a brief measure for which some identified cutoff score indicates the possibility of significant problems. For example, the Center for Epidemiologic Studies—Depression Scale [CES-D; (Radloff, 1977)] is a 20-item scale used in many community studies to screen people for depression and to estimate its prevalence. A score of 16 or higher on the CES-D indicates the possibility of significant depression and suggests that further evaluation is necessary (Derogatis & Lynn, 1999). Other screening instruments are more broad-based, covering many different psychological symptoms, including depression, anxiety, and social problems (e.g., the General Health Questionnaire [GHQ]; (Goldberg & Hillier, 1979). In most cases, when patients score above a certain cutoff number on a screening instrument, a more thorough evaluation can determine the nature and extent of their difficulties.

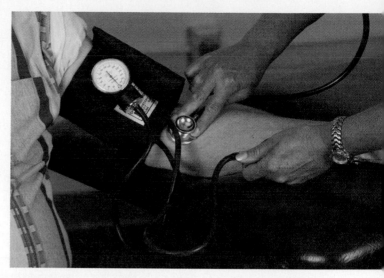

A quick blood pressure screening may be the first step in identifying serious medical problems. Similarly, mental health screenings may be key in the identification of psychological disorders.

Because many patients with psychological problems are more likely to see their physician than a mental health professional, brief methods for screening patients in medical settings have been developed. In fact, very simple two-item screening instruments have been used to identify medical patients with depression (Unutzer et al., 2002) or anxiety (Roy-Byrne et al., 2005) who might benefit from psychological or psychiatric treatment. To screen for depression (Spitzer et al., 1994), for example, a patient might be asked the following:

- During the past month, have you often been bothered by feeling down, depressed, or hopeless?

- During the past month, have you often been bothered by little interest or pleasure in doing things you normally enjoy?

Questions like these are particularly valuable because they require very little time to administer in a busy medical practice. An effective brief screen has also been developed for the presence of substance abuse problems (e.g., Alcohol Use Disorders Identification Test [AUDIT]; (Barbor et al., 2001).

To evaluate the usefulness of any particular screening measure, psychologists look for instruments that have strong sensitivity and specificity. *Sensitivity* describes the ability of the screener (or the instrument) to predict a problem that actually exists (e.g., the screener identifies depression and the person is actually depressed). *Specificity* indicates the percent of the time that the screener accurately predicts the absence of a problem (e.g., the cutoff score suggests no depression, and the patient truly is not depressed). *False positives* occur when the screening instrument indicates a problem when no problem exists (e.g., the patient's score exceeds the cutoff, but subsequent evaluation confirms the absence of depression). *False negatives* refer to instances in which the screening tool suggests there is no depression when the patient actually is depressed. Good screening tools have high specificity and sensitivity, but low false positive and false negative rates (see Figure 3.1).

Diagnosis and Treatment Planning   One of the major functions of assessment is to determine the **diagnosis** of an individual. Diagnosis refers to the identification of an illness. In some branches of medicine, diagnosis can be made on the basis of laboratory

screening   an assessment process that attempts to identify psychological problems or predict the risk of future problems among people who are not referred for clinical assessment

diagnosis   identification of an illness

FIGURE 3.1

Evaluating a
Screening Tool
for Depression

A good screening tool is sensitive and specific: it identifies
problems that do exist and
does not indicate problems
when none exist.

		Screening Results (Does the score on a depression measure indicate depression is present?)	
		Positive (Score suggests depression is present)	**Negative** (Score suggests depression is absent)
Actual Problem (Does the person have depression?)	Depression is present	Sensitivity (Test accurately identifies depression)	False Negative (Test suggests there is no depression, but patient is depressed)
	Depression is absent	False Positive (Test suggests patient is depressed, but patient is not depressed)	Specificity (Test accurately suggests depression is absent)

Note: The quality of the screening instrument is determined by the numbers in these cells.

tests. In psychology it is more complicated, and as you will see later in the chapter, diagnosis is based more on the presence of a cluster of symptoms. Typically, a diagnosis is made after a clinical interview with the patient. The term **differential diagnosis** is often used to weigh how likely it is that a person has one diagnosis as opposed to another. As we will see, however, patients often have sets of symptoms that require more than one diagnosis. The clinician, through his or her assessment, gathers a lot of data from the patient and often other sources (partner, parents, and teachers) to choose the diagnosis or diagnoses that fit the patient best. One of the central roles of diagnosis is that it facilitates communication across clinicians and researchers. Diagnostic systems for abnormal behavior include a specific library of diagnostic labels that increase understanding, facilitate communication, and help with treatment planning. Diagnostic assessments are more extensive than screens and are designed to provide a more thorough understanding of a person's psychological status. As we shall see later in the chapter, although diagnostic categories are not always the best way to describe certain conditions, they provide a standard that helps guide communication with patients and other providers.

Diagnoses are also critical for treatment planning. Just as it is important for a physician to determine an accurate diagnosis of a patient's headaches in order to prescribe an appropriate treatment, so it is important for a psychologist to make an accurate diagnosis of a patient's problematic behavior or mood. Inaccurate diagnoses may lead to inappropriate treatment (or lack of treatment entirely; see the box "Real People, Real Disorders: Cases of Misdiagnosis"). Finally, a diagnosis is often needed in order for a psychologist or other health care provider to be reimbursed by insurance companies.

A clinical assessment that leads to a diagnosis usually includes evaluation of symptom and disorder severity, patterns of symptoms over time (e.g., number, frequency, and duration of episodes), and patient strengths and weaknesses (Maruish, 1999). All of these characteristics are important for treatment planning. The assessment may also include personality tests, neuropsychological tests, and/or a behavioral assessment. A behavioral psychologist might also conduct a *functional analysis* of symptoms, which identifies the relations between situations and behaviors (e.g., what happens before, during, and after certain problem behaviors, moods, or thoughts) to aid in devising a treatment strategy.

Outcome Evaluation   Clinical assessments can be repeated at regular intervals during treatment to evaluate a patient's progress. Evaluating outcomes has always been part of clinical psychology as practiced from a scientist-practitioner perspective. Outcome evaluations help us know if patients are getting better, when treatment is

differential diagnosis   a process in which a clinician weighs how likely it is that a person has one diagnosis instead of another

real people, real disorders

Cases of Misdiagnosis

In some cases, insufficient assessment and inaccurate diagnosis can lead to inadequate or inappropriate treatment and disastrous consequences. The importance of careful assessment and diagnosis is illustrated in these real cases.

■ **Deafness, not Mental Retardation** Kathy Buckley, comedienne and inspirational speaker, has received numerous awards and accolades for her comic abilities and advocacy for persons with disabilities. However, her poor academic performance in the second grade led to a diagnosis of mental retardation and placement in a school for mentally and physically impaired children. It took professionals a year to determine that Kathy's academic difficulties were due to hearing loss, not mental incapacitation.

■ **Epilepsy, not Schizophrenia** A 46 year old woman was hospitalized in a university-affiliated facility with depressive symptoms and hallucinations that urged her to commit suicide (Swartz, 2001). Laboratory tests (e.g., electroencephalogram or EEG) revealed that she was having seizures characteristic of epilepsy. Antiseizure medication led to disappearance of symptoms. However, review of the patient's clinic records revealed that she had been given a diagnosis of schizophrenia (see Chapter 10) and treated as such for 10 years without alleviation of symptoms.

■ **Medication Reaction, not Depression** A 77-year-old woman developed symptoms of depression (e.g., fatigue, weight loss, motor slowing, and social withdrawal) one month after starting medication for congestive heart failure (digoxin). Antidepressant medication was given for 7 months, but her symptoms did not improve. When she was admitted to a hospital for further evaluation, medical tests revealed a very high level of digoxin. When the medication was discontinued, symptoms of depression improved rapidly (Song et al., 2001).

■ **Brain Tumor, not Anorexia Nervosa** A 19-year-old girl was admitted to the hospital with symptoms of anorexia nervosa (e.g., rapid weight loss of 16.5 pounds secondary to dieting, body dissatisfaction, and occasional binge eating). She was started on nasogastric feeding to increase her caloric intake as well as antidepressant medication to help control her anxiety. After the patient was discovered unconscious on the bathroom floor with symptoms consistent with a seizure, a brain scan revealed a brain tumor. Following surgical removal of the tumor, the patient's fear of weight gain and body distortion decreased, and two years later, she no longer showed any residual signs of an eating disorder (Houy et al., 2007).

"finished," or when we may need to modify an approach that is not achieving its aims. Outcome assessment may include evaluating patient satisfaction and providing data to support the marketing of treatment programs.

In order for outcome assessments to be useful, the same measures must be administered consistently over the course of treatment. The individual measures included in the assessment should represent a range of outcomes (e.g., symptom severity, treatment satisfaction, functioning, quality of life) and, when possible, a breadth of perspectives on outcome—not just the patient's viewpoint, but the therapist's perspective and perhaps that of family members or other closely involved parties (Lambert & Lambert, 1999). To be useful, the assessment measures must also be reliable and valid. To evaluate whether treatments have the desired effect, it is also important to assess both the amount of change and the patient's actual level of functioning at post-treatment. For example, imagine that you are very sick and have a fever of 104 degrees. You take some medicine, your fever goes down to 101 degrees, and you feel better. The reduction in your fever, from 104 to 101, is the amount of change from the medicine. But you still have a fever of 101, and so you are still sick—this is your actual level of functioning. In evaluating the outcome of psychological disorders, the goal may be to reduce symptoms and/or to eliminate the disorder.

The amount of change (how much a patient's symptoms have been reduced) is generally considered in terms of **clinical significance** (see Chapter 2). This means that the observed change actually is a meaningful improvement (e.g, social anxiety improves to the extent that the college student can now take courses that require oral presentations). A measure known as the Reliable Change Index (RCI) (Jacobson & Truax, 1991) is now frequently used to determine whether the degree of change from beginning to end of treatment is meaningful—for example, whether the change is more than we would expect based on normal changes that occur over time (see Reliability). Patients' scores on various measures after treatment are sometimes compared with scores of people without the disorder who have also completed the assessment to evaluate whether symptoms and functioning have moved into the normal range.

PROPERTIES OF ASSESSMENT INSTRUMENTS

The potential value of an assessment instrument rests in part on its various *psychometric properties*, which affect how confident we can be in the testing results. It is important to know, for example, how well the instrument measures the features or concepts it is intended to measure. For example, how well does a depression test actually measure depressive symptoms? An instrument's psychometric properties include standardization, reliability, and validity.

Standardization   To understand the results of clinical assessments, the score must be put in context. Think back to the concept of a fever. Why does a temperature of 104 degrees Fahrenheit create concern? Because it is so much higher than the body's normal temperature of 98.6 degrees Fahrenheit. Therefore, you use normal temperature to determine whether you are feverish and need medicine. In the same way, understanding the results of psychological assessment requires putting test results in context. Does a particular score indicate the existence of a problem, its severity, or its improvement over time? Standard ways of evaluating scores can involve normative or self-referent comparisons (or both). **Normative** comparisons require looking at a person's score as it compares with the scores of a sample of people who are representative of the entire population (with regard to characteristics such as age, sex, ethnicity, education, and geographic region) or with the scores of a subgroup who are similar to the patient being assessed. If we took the temperature of 100 adults, the average (mean) temperature would be 98.6 degrees. This is the normative body temperature for humans. If a person's score falls too far outside the range of the normative group, we can assume that a problem exists. To decide whether a score is too far outside the range of the normal group, we use a statistic called the *standard deviation* (*SD*) (see Figure 3.2). SD is a measure that tells us how far away from the mean (average) a particular score is. According to statistical principles, if a score is more than 2 SDs away from the mean, it is considered meaningfully different from what is normal. In comparing scores with normative groups, however, it is always important to consider the characteristics of both the patient and the group.

If Pauline's scores on the memory tests are low relative to those of the average middle-aged adult, but are the same as the scores of other people who are her age and education level, we would not be concerned about the presence of cognitive impairment. If, however, her scores are very low relative to people who are the same as Pauline in terms of age and education, we can conclude that she is experiencing significant cognitive difficulties.

Self-referent comparisons are those that compare responses on various instruments with the patient's own prior performance, and they are used most often to examine the course of symptoms over time. In the example of the fever, not everyone has

clinical significance   observed change that is meaningful in terms of clinical functioning

normative   a comparison group that is representative of the entire population against which a person's score on a psychological test is compared

self-referent comparisons   comparison of responses on a psychological instrument with a person's own prior performance

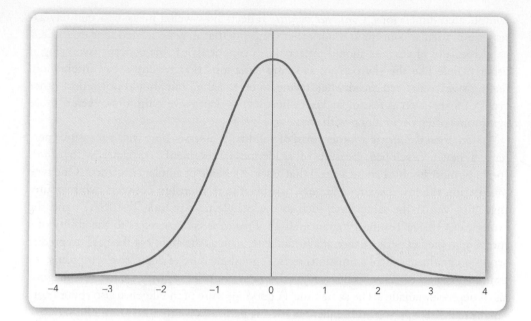

FIGURE 3.2
The Normal Curve

Numbers indicate standard deviations (SDs). A score more than two standard deviations away from the mean (the center point, 0) is considered meaningfully different from normal.

a standard body temperature of 98.6. Some people may have a usual body temperature of 99.2 degrees. In a self-referent comparison, we would compare the temperature of 104 to the person's usual body temperature of 99.2 degrees.

If Pauline's scores on measures of cognitive impairment turn out to be very low compared with how she performed 6 months ago, we would be concerned about a potentially deteriorating course of symptoms.

Self-referent comparisons are also used to evaluate treatment outcome. Over the course of treatment, we would of course hope to see self-referent comparisons that indicate improvement of symptoms and quality of life.

Reliability   The **reliability** of an instrument is its consistency, or how well the measure produces the same result each time it is given (Compas & Gotlib, 2002). Thermometers that measure your body temperature are generally quite reliable: they produce similar readings if you take your temperature now and again in 10 minutes. Psychological measures must also be reliable. If they do not produce consistent results, they are of no use. Reliability is assessed in many ways. **Test-retest reliability** addresses the consistency of scores across time. To estimate test-retest reliability, we administer the same instrument twice to the same people over some consistent interval, such as 2 weeks or 1 month. We then calculate a *correlation coefficient* (see Chapter 2) to estimate the similarity between the scores. Correlations of .80 or higher indicate that a measure is highly reliable over time.

Another measure of reliability, **interrater agreement**, is important for measures that depend on clinician judgment. When clinicians interview someone, they must decide whether the person's symptoms are severe enough to warrant a diagnosis or to provide treatment, and not everyone may judge a behavior in the same way. In these cases, we want to know that different clinicians would make the same judgment about symptom severity (i.e., ratings should reflect more about the person being interviewed than about the person doing the interviewing). To estimate interrater agreement, we ask two different clinicians to administer the same interview to the same patients.

Validity   A measure must not only be reliable but also valid. **Validity** refers to the degree to which a test measures what it was intended to assess. Much of what we measure in psychology reflects hypothetical or intangible concepts (e.g., self-esteem, mood, intelligence). The instrument's validity tells us how well we are assessing these

reliability   how well a psychological assessment instrument produces consistent results each time it is given

test-retest reliability   how well a test produces similar scores over time when given to the same individual(s)

interrater agreement   the amount of agreement between two clinicians who are using the same measure to rate the same symptoms in a single patient

validity   the degree to which a test measures what it is intended to assess

complicated dimensions. *Construct validity* reflects how well a measure accurately assesses a particular concept and not other concepts that may be related. For example, a valid measure of shyness should reflect the components of this concept (worrying if other people like the shy person, avoiding situations that require social interaction, feeling sweaty and red-faced when trying to be sociable) but should not reflect other types of fears (such as fear of snakes or needles) or depressive symptoms, even if those symptoms often occur along with shyness.

Criterion validity is another form of validity. It assesses how well a measure (perhaps a newly developed measure of academic achievement) correlates with others (perhaps more established measures) that assess the same or similar constructs. One type of criterion validity, *concurrent validity*, assesses the relationship between two measures that are given at the same time, such as the Scholastic Aptitude Test (SAT) and the American College Testing Program (ACT). *Predictive validity* refers to the ability of a measure to predict performance at a future date, such as the ability of the SAT to predict scores on graduate school admissions tests. A good measure of depressive symptoms, for example, should correlate well (have good concurrent validity) with a clinician's diagnosis of depression made at the same time. A good measure of intelligence also should correlate well with a person's subsequent academic performance (predictive validity).

Another issue related to validity is the accuracy of a psychologist's predictions or conclusions at the end of the assessment process. After all the assessment data are collected, a clinician is often asked to make a judgment: Does this person have major depression? Will a sex offender re-offend? What kind of treatment might be best for this person at this time? Is this student a good match for this academic program? Answering these questions is difficult, but we know from the results of many studies of health and behavior (Grove et al., 2000) that clinicians are more accurate if they base their conclusions on statistical instead of clinical prediction strategies. In *statistical prediction,* the clinician makes a judgment about someone based on data from large groups of people. Insurance companies, for example, decide how to price their policies using data from large studies that determine the probability of death or accidents based on certain identified risk factors, such as age, smoking history, and alcohol use (Compas & Gotlib, 2002). People with more risk factors pay more for their insurance. *Clinical prediction*, however, relies on the integration of data based on a clinician's judgment. Choosing new students for a graduate program based on the interviewer's impressions of the applicants' behavior during an interview rather than on established factors that predict good academic performance is an example of clinical prediction. In general, results of predictions based on the same patient data can be very different when these two different judgment strategies are used (Grove, 2005).

Paul Meehl, a leader in the field of psychological assessment, argued as early as 1954 that statistical predictions were far more accurate than clinician judgments. Data from over 136 studies have supported this conclusion (Grove et al., 2000). Statistical prediction is used in the practice of evidence-based medicine when data are available to predict who will benefit from which treatments. Clinical judgment, however, is useful when relevant statistical data do not exist and when new hypotheses need to be developed. Clinician judgment also plays a role in the use of the structured interview procedures discussed in the Clinical Interviews section of this chapter.

DEVELOPMENTAL AND CULTURAL CONSIDERATIONS

Many factors affect a clinician's choice of assessment techniques and instruments, but probably one of the most important factors is the patient's age and developmental status. The nature of the tests chosen, the normative values against which patient scores are compared, the people involved in the testing process, and the testing environment can vary significantly depending on whether the person to be assessed is a child or an adolescent, an adult, or an elderly person. The assessment of cognitive abilities in children who are too young to read, for example, requires different tests than those used with educated adults (Anastasi & Urbina, 1997). The abilities of older adults with significant cognitive impairment must also be assessed with unique instruments that capture more specific symptoms of problems like dementia (e.g., Dementia Rating Scale [DRS]; Mattis, 2001). Measures of psychological symptoms vary across age as well. Tests of psychological distress designed specifically for children, such as the Social Phobia and Anxiety Inventory for Children (SPAI-C) (Beidel & Turner, 1995) and the Children's Depression Inventory (CDI) (Kovacs, 1992) typically have different questions, fewer response choices, and simpler wording than adult measures because of children's limited (still developing) cognitive abilities. Unique measures of psychological symptoms also exist for older adults, such as the Geriatric Depression Inventory (GDS) (Sheikh & Yesavage, 1986), with content and response choice that better matches the experience and cognitive skill of older people.

Assessment must take into account a person's developmental age. Tests for children have simple wording and few response choices.

The assessment process itself may also vary depending on the patient's age. For example, different people may be involved in the assessment process if the patient is a child, an adult, or an elderly person with dementia. When assessing children, input from parents and teachers is essential. For older adults with cognitive limitations, it is helpful to obtain input from another adult who spends time with the patient. Children who are unable to read and older people with limited vision may also need more help completing self-report measures. Young children with limited attention capacity and older adults with cognitive and/or physical limitations may also need shorter testing sessions with more breaks.

The assessment process should also take cultural factors into account. Many measures used routinely in psychological evaluations, for example, were originally developed within the majority culture of the United States. Administering these measures to people with more diverse cultural backgrounds may produce biased results due to differences in educational backgrounds, language use, and cultural beliefs and values (Anastasi & Urbina, 1997). To address these issues, researchers have worked to develop "culture fair" assessments that take into account variables that may affect test performance. Many measures of psychological variables, for example, have been translated into other languages, and data from different minority groups have been collected (Novy et al., 2001). Simply translating measures into new languages, however, may not be sufficient to reflect other cultural influences. Thus, some measures of psychological performance have been developed that rely less on verbal than on nonverbal skill. For example, the Leiter International Performance Scale—Revised (Roid & Miller, 1997) is a nonverbal test of intelligence that requires no speaking or writing by either the examiner or the test-taker. Some of the tasks required of the test-taker include categorizing objects or geometric designs, matching response cards to easel pictures, and remembering and repeating sequences of objects in the correct order. Measures like this help to increase the cross-cultural utility of psychological assessments.

concept CHECK

- Clinical assessments are designed to gather information about a person's symptoms and to help clinicians make decisions about the nature, status, and treatment of psychological problems.

- Assessments can be used to screen people for psychological problems, diagnose problems, develop treatment plans, and evaluate outcomes.

- Assessment instruments must be standardized with normative or self-referent data to allow useful interpretation of scores.

- To be useful, assessment measures must produce reliable (consistent) scores across time and across assessors.

- Assessment materials and procedures must take into account the age and developmental level of the person being assessed, as well as cultural factors that may affect performance or scores.

APPLICATION QUESTION What are some of the ways that psychological tests might produce biased or inaccurate results? What are some ways this could be avoided?

Assessment Instruments

Psychologists can select from a wide range of assessment instruments when planning an evaluation. To an outsider, it may appear that there are far too many psychological tests and methods. However, having a large array of tests to choose from allows a psychologist to assess a patient's difficulties thoroughly and from many different perspectives. Failing to conduct a thorough assessment can have disastrous consequences (see the earlier box "Real People, Real Disorders: Cases of Misdiagnosis"). Choosing the best set of instruments depends on the goals of the assessment, the properties of the instruments, and the nature of the patient's difficulties. Some instruments ask patients to evaluate their own symptoms (*self-report measures*), and some require a clinician to rate the symptoms (*clinician-rated measures*). Some instruments assess *subjective responses* (what the patient perceives) and others *objective responses* (what can be observed). Some measures are *structured* (each patient receives the same set of questions), and others are *unstructured* (the questions vary across patients). When a number of tests are given together, the group of tests is referred to as a test battery. We incorporate discussion of these issues into our review here of the major categories of assessment instruments, including clinical interviews, psychological tests, behavioral assessment, and psychophysiological assessment.

CLINICAL INTERVIEWS

Clinical interviews consist of a conversation between an interviewer and a patient, the purpose of which is to gather information and make judgments related to the assessment goals. Interviews can serve any of the major purposes of assessment, including screening, diagnosis, treatment planning, or outcome evaluation. They also can be conducted in either an unstructured or structured fashion.

Unstructured Interviews In an **unstructured interview**, the clinician decides what questions to ask and how to ask them. Typically, the *initial interview* is unstructured to allow the clinician to get to know the patient and help determine what other types of assessment might be useful. Another purpose of the initial interview is for the clinician and patient to begin getting to know each other and develop a working relationship.

At the start of an initial interview, the clinician usually provides some education about the assessment process. The clinician then asks a series of questions about the patient's difficulties. These questions can be *open-ended*, allowing the patient flexibility to decide what information to provide (e.g., *Tell me about what brings you here today*), or *close-ended*, allowing the clinician to ask for specific information about a topic (e.g., *Have you been having crying spells?*). The content and style of the questions are guided by both the *presenting problem* (the identified reason for the evaluation) and the clinician's theoretical perspective. A psychodynamic therapist, for example,

clinical interviews conversations between an interviewer and a patient, the purpose of which is to gather information and make judgments related to assessment goals

unstructured interviews clinical interviews in which the clinician decides what questions to ask and how to ask them

might spend more time in an initial interview asking about the patient's early history, whereas a behavioral therapist might ask more questions about the sequence of events surrounding current symptoms. At the end of an initial interview, the clinician typically provides some summary of what has been learned and some guidelines about what will happen next.

The primary benefit of an unstructured interview is its flexibility: it allows the clinician to move in whatever directions seem most appropriate, following up the patient's comments. The major limitation is its potential unreliability. It is quite possible, for example, that two different interviewers could come to very different conclusions about the same patient if their interviews did not include the same topics or ask the same questions. For instance, if the interviewer does not ask questions about alcohol use and a patient is reluctant to bring up this topic, the interviewer may erroneously conclude that some other difficulty (e.g., depression) is the major cause of the presenting problem, when in fact the patient is drinking heavily, missing work, and feeling depressed because he is likely to lose his job. Structured interviews help to minimize such problems.

Structured Interviews In a **structured** or *semistructured* **interview**, the clinician asks each patient the same standard set of questions, usually with the goal of establishing a diagnosis. In the case of semistructured interviews, after the standard question, the clinician uses less structured supplemental questions to gather additional information as needed. Structured or semistructured interviews are used frequently in scientifically based clinical practice and in clinical research (Summerfeldt & Antony, 2002), and they increase the reliability of the interview process. Although a patient's scores still rely on clinician judgment, the consistency in content and the order of questions increases the likelihood of agreement across interviewers.

Many structured and semistructured interviews are available to help clinicians make diagnoses. Choosing one depends on the goal of the assessment, the clinician's knowledge of and training with the interview, and the properties of the interview itself (length, content focus, reliability, etc.). Some structured interviews are designed to be used with adults; others are intended for use with children. In some cases, structured interviews provide a broad overview of many diagnostic categories, while others are more focused on particular sets of diagnoses (e.g., anxiety, depression). Frequently, a more focused interview will be used after an unstructured screening interview indicates that certain diagnoses may be appropriate. These kinds of interviews can be useful in research settings, where it is often important to make sure that all patients in a study have similar diagnoses. They are also important in clinical practice so that a provider has sufficient details about diagnosis to design an appropriate treatment plan. The drawback of structured interviews is that the interviewer has less flexibility with regard to questioning.

PSYCHOLOGICAL TESTS

Psychological tests measure hundreds of dimensions, ranging from personality to intelligence to specific symptoms. In the following sections, we provide an overview of different kinds of psychological tests that measure dimensions such as personality characteristics, general levels of psychological functioning, intelligence, and behavior.

Personality Tests The choice of a **personality test** depends on its purpose and on whether one is assessing a healthy population or a clinical sample, although many personality tests measure overlapping concepts. Perhaps the best-known personality test is the *Minnesota Multiphasic Personality Inventory* (*MMPI*), developed in 1943 by

You may have participated in a market research survey, where someone stopped you in a public place and asked you a specific set of questions. Psychological structured interviews are conducted in the therapist's office but also consist of a series of questions designed to identify the person's symptoms.

structured interview clinical interview in which the clinician asks a standard set of questions, usually with the goal of establishing a diagnosis

personality test psychological test that measures personality characteristics

Starke Hathaway and J. Charnley McKinley, a psychologist and psychiatrist, respectively, from the University of Minnesota (Graham, 2000). To develop the 567-item, pencil-and-paper test, they used a then innovative technique that overcame some of the subjectivity of earlier scoring approaches. Using a method known as *empirical keying*, they developed statistical analyses to identify items and patterns of scores that differentiated various groups (e.g., patients with and without depression). Only items that differentiated the groups were retained. The MMPI also includes statistical scales to evaluate a number of test-taking behaviors. For example, a *Lie scale* identifies people who may not wish to describe themselves accurately. Other scales determine whether someone is "faking good" (describing oneself as more psychologically healthy than one is) or "faking bad" (presenting oneself as more psychologically distressed than is actually true), as well as many clinical scales to assess specific psychological characteristics.

A revised version of the MMPI, the MMPI-2, includes nine clinical subscales: Hypochondriasis, Depression, Hysteria, Psychopathic Deviance, Masculinity-Femininity, Paranoia, Psychasthenia (Anxiety), Schizophrenia, and Hypomania. The MMPI-2 is scored by a computer program that creates a profile that the testing psychologist can then interpret (see Figure 3.3). Serious concerns exist regarding the use of the MMPI-2 with ethnic minority samples, however, because the test was originally standardized on white samples (Butcher et al., 1989).

FIGURE 3.3

Sample MMPI Profile

The MMPI yields scores on several clinical subscales. It is scored by a computer that produces a personality profile.

Source: Excerpted from the MMPI®-2(Minnesota Multiphasic Personality Inventory®-2. Manual for Administration, Scoring, and Interpretation, Revised Edition. © 2001 by the Regents of the Univesity of Minnesota. Used by permission of the University of Minnesota Press. All rights reserved. *MMPI-2* and *Minnesota Miltiphasic Personality Inventory-2* are trademarks owned by the Regents of the University of Minnesota.

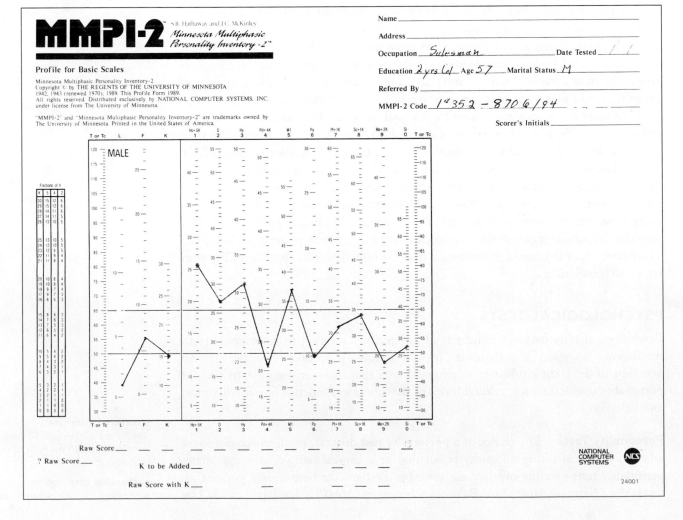

The Million Clinical Multiaxial Inventory (*MCMI*) is a 175-item true-false inventory that corresponds to eight basic personality styles (schizoid, avoidant, dependent, histrionic, narcissistic, antisocial, compulsive, passive-aggressive; see Chapter 11), three pathological personality syndromes (schizotypal, borderline, paranoid), and nine symptom disorders scales (anxiety, somatoform, hypomanic, dysthymia, alcohol abuse, drug abuse, psychotic thinking, psychotic depression, psychotic delusions). The MCMI has adequate reliability and validity, and clinicians sometimes prefer it to the MMPI because it requires less time to complete. There also are concerns, however, that the MCMI does not match well the categories of disorders as they are described in the DSM system and that this test also is culturally biased.

General Tests of Psychological Functioning   These assessments gather general information about the mental functioning of people who participate as healthy controls in a research study. They can also be used to compare general levels of functioning across groups or populations, or to test people before and after a specific event or intervention. They do not focus on one specific symptom area, such as depression or anxiety, but give a broad overview of how well a person is functioning psychologically.

The *Global Assessment of Functioning Scale* (see Figure 3.4), or the GAF, is a rating assigned by a clinician to describe a patient's overall functioning and well-being. The clinician chooses a number on a scale from 0 to 100 to indicate how well the patient is functioning. The rating includes consideration of both symptom severity and

---

FIGURE 3.4

Global Assessment of Functioning

91–100   Superior functioning in a wide range of activities, life's problems never seem to get out of hand, is sought out by others because of his or her many qualities, no symptoms.

81–90   Absent or minimal symptoms, good functioning in all areas, interested and involved in a wide range of activities, socially effective, generally satisfied with life, no more than everyday problems or concerns.

71–80   If symptoms are present, they are transient and expectable reactions to psychosocial stresses, no more than slight impairment in social, occupational, or school functioning.

61–70   Some mild symptoms OR some difficulty in social, occupational, or school functioning, but generally functioning pretty well, has some meaningful interpersonal relationships.

51–60   Moderate symptoms OR any moderate difficulty in social, occupational, or school functioning.

41–50   Serious symptoms OR any serious impairment in social, occupational, or school functioning.

31–40   Some impairment in reality testing or communication OR major impairment in several areas, such as work or school, family relations, judgment, thinking, or mood.

21–30   Behavior is considerably influenced by delusions or hallucinations OR serious impairment in communications or judgment OR inability to function in all areas.

11–20   Some danger of hurting self or others OR occasionally fails to maintain minimal personal hygiene OR gross impairment in communication.

1–10   Persistent danger of severely hurting self or others OR persistent inability to maintain minimal personal hygiene OR serious suicidal act with clear expectation of death.

0   Not enough information available to provide GAF.

Adapted with permission from the *Diagnostic and Statistical Manual of Mental Disorders, Text Revision*, Fourth Edition, (Copyright 2000). American Psychiatric Association.

level of impairment in social relationships and job or school performance. Comparing GAF scores can serve as a broad indicator of clinical improvement.

Another commonly used brief questionnaire is the 12-item *General Health Questionnaire* (GHQ) (Goldberg & Hillier, 1979). The GHQ gives a snapshot of mental health status over the previous weeks and can provide a meaningful change score. Each item is rated on a 4-point scale indicating degree of deviation from the individual's usual experience. Some example questions are: Have you recently: . . . Been able to concentrate on what you're doing? Lost much sleep over worry? Been able to enjoy your normal day-to-day activities? And been feeling reasonably happy, all things considered?

Neuropsychological Testing   Neuropsychological tests detect impairment in cognitive functioning using both simple and complex tasks to measure language, memory, attention and concentration, motor skills, perception, abstraction, and learning abilities. Performance on these tasks provides insight into the functioning of the brain.

One widely used battery to assess brain damage is the *Halstead-Reitan Neuropsychological Battery* (Reitan & Davidson, 1974), which evaluates the presence of brain damage. The battery differentiates healthy individuals from people with cortical damage and includes 10 measures of memory, abstract thought, language, sensory-motor integration, perceptions, and motor dexterity.

Another commonly used neuropsychological assessment is the *Wisconsin Card Sorting Test* (WCST), which measures *set shifting*, or the ability to display flexibility in thinking as the goal of the task changes (see Figure 3.5). Four stimulus cards are shown to the test-taker, each respectively displaying a red triangle, two green stars,

FIGURE 3.5

The Wisconsin Card Sorting Test

This test measures set shifting, the ability to display flexibility in thinking. It is used to test patients with brain disorders.

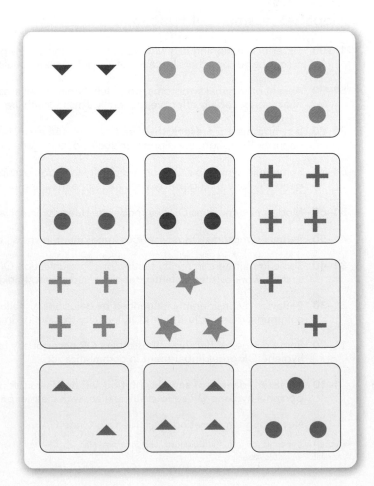

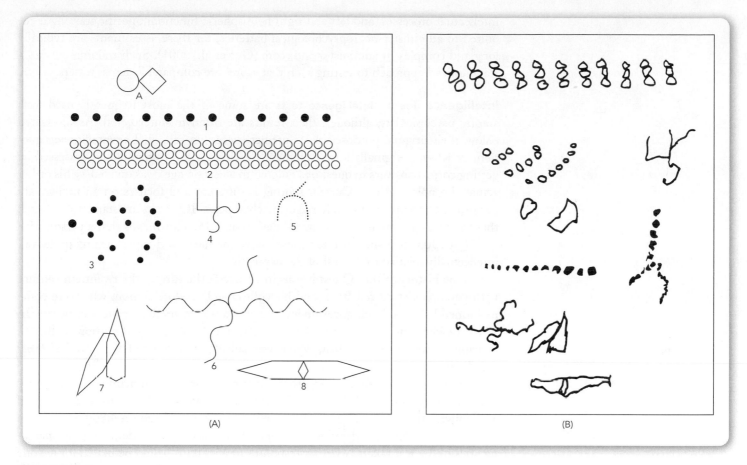

FIGURE 3.6

The Bender Visual Motor Gestalt Test

This is a neuropsychological test often used to detect brain damage or neurological impairment. The patient's attempts to copy the figures (A) show whether damage or impairment is present (B).

From Nevid/Rathus/Greene, *Abnormal Psychology in a Changing World*, 5e, p. 91. Copyright © 2008 Pearson/Prentice Hall. Reprinted by permission.

three yellow crosses, and four blue circles. Then, the test-taker is given additional cards and asked to match each to the original four stimulus cards. The examiner does not provide instructions on *how* to match the cards, but states whether the match is correct based on a specific rule that is chosen by the examiner. The rule is then changed based on the success of the test-taker, and the test continues for 128 trials or until all rule changes, or "achieved categories," have been completed (Resources, 2003). Completion of the card test requires attention, working memory, and visual processing. The WCST has been labeled a frontal lobe test because individuals with frontal lobe lesions do poorly on this test. The WCST discriminates between frontal and nonfrontal lesions and is often used for testing patients with schizophrenia, brain injuries, and neurodegenerative diseases such as dementia or Parkinson's disease (Resources, 2003).

Other commonly used neuropsychological assessments include the *Bender Visual Motor Gestalt Test* (see Figure 3.6), a simple screening tool often used to detect visual-motor development in children and general brain damage and neurological impairment (Piotrowski, 1995), and the *Luria-Nebraska Neuropsychological Battery* (Golden et al., 1980). The Luria is similar to the Halstead-Reitan test but is a more precise measure of organic brain damage. In contrast to many batteries, the Luria-Nebraska uses an unstructured qualitative method, generating 14 scores, including motor, rhythm, tactile, expressive speech, writing, reading, arithmetic, memory, intellectual processes, and left and right hemispheric function. Specific training is required to administer neuropsychological batteries, for these assessments are typically long and complex to administer and score (Gur et al., 2001). Such training ensures a standardized approach to testing such that scores are comparable across testers.

Intelligence Tests   Intelligence **tests** are some of the most frequently used tests among psychologists, although their results are often misinterpreted. As illustrated below, their original purpose was to predict success in school. The **intelligence quotient** or **IQ** was originally a measurement in which a child's mental age (assessed by getting correct answers to questions tailored to a certain age) was divided by his or her actual chronological age. Current scoring is different and focuses on an individual's performance relative to his or her age-matched peers. IQ scores are standardized such that the mean is 100 and the standard deviation is 15. This means that a person with an IQ of 130 is two standard deviations above the mean and is performing quite well intellectually relative to the rest of the population.

The history of the IQ test begins in France at the turn of the twentieth century with psychologist Alfred Binet and his colleague Theodore Simon, who were commissioned by the French government to create a test to predict academic success. In 1916, Lewis Terman, at Stanford University, translated a revised edition of Binet's instrument for use in English, which was subsequently named the *Stanford–Binet Intelligence Scale.*

Since its conception, the Stanford-Binet has gone through many revisions, and it is currently in its fifth edition. Subtests within the Stanford-Binet assess both verbal and nonverbal skills. The most recent version was standardized on 4,800 people, and the test items were considered for any kind of bias based on the demographic characteristics of the test takers (whether responses to any items would be biased for anyone based on sex, ethnicity, age, etc.). The test's validity was evaluated against other well-validated intelligence tests, including the previous editions of the *Stanford-Binet Intelligence Scale* and the *Weschler Adult Intelligence Scale,* a well-known intelligence test discussed below. Based on extensive research, the Stanford-Binet is believed to be appropriate for measuring intelligence among people with low intellectual functioning as well as among those at the highly gifted end of the continuum.

First published by David Wechsler in 1955 and currently in its fourth edition, the *Wechsler Adult Intelligence Scale* (WAIS-IV) (Wechsler, 2008) is one of the most commonly used general tests of intelligence to evaluate patients, students, employees, criminals, and other population subgroups. Initially adapted from the intelligence tests used by the Army, the test was based on Wechsler's definition of intelligence as "the aggregate or global capacity of the individual to act purposefully, to think rationally, and to deal effectively with his environment" (Weschler, 1939, p. 229).

The WAIS-IV produces four index scores: Verbal Comprehension Index (VCI), Working Memory Index (WMI), Perceptual Reasoning Index (PRI), and Processing Speed Index (PSI). These four index scores are combined to create a composite Full Scale IQ (FSIQ) score. The VCI and PRI can be used to create another global score, the General Ability Index (GAI). Each of the four index scores reflects a person's performance on a group of subtests that measure similar intellectual skills. Verbal Comprehension subtests, for example, measure comprehension through tests that are administered and answered verbally. Specific tasks on these subtests measure verbal reasoning (e.g., the ability to describe how are two objects alike), general fund of knowledge, the ability to define words, and understanding of social expressions (e.g., "killing two birds with one stone"). Working Memory subtests also are administered verbally, but these subtests more specifically assess attention, concentration, and mem-

intelligence tests   tests that measure intelligence quotient (IQ)

intelligence quotient   a score of cognitive functioning that compares a person's performance to his or her age-matched peers

ory by asking people to recall sequences of digits forward and backward, perform mental math problems, and remember sequences of letters and numbers. Perceptual Reasoning and Processing Speed subtests all require the test-taker to perform certain tasks as quickly as possible. Perceptual Reasoning subtests, for example, measure skills such as attention to detail (e.g., what is missing from a certain picture), nonverbal reasoning (putting puzzles together), and spatial perception (arranging blocks to match a printed design). Processing Speed subtests assess visual-motor coordination and visual perception by asking test-takers to determine whether a target symbol is in an array of symbols and to copy numbers that correspond with symbols into a grid. For these tasks, speed and accuracy are taken into account.

Taking a little over 60 minutes to administer, the WAIS-IV (Wechsler, 2008) assesses cognitive functioning in people aged 16 to 90, matched to the 2005 U.S. Census data with respect to sex, socioeconomic status, ethnicity, educational attainment, and geographical location. Under age 16, the Wechsler Intelligence Scale for Children (WISC-IV, 7–16 years) and the Wechsler Preschool and Primary Scale of Intelligence (WPPS-III, 2 1/2–7 years) are used.

The measurement of intelligence has always been controversial. This is one area in which the roles of nature and nurture have been hotly debated. In addition to questions about how these factors influence intelligence, our conceptualization of intelligence has changed over time. In contrast to Wechsler's early approach to measuring cognitive function, current tests of intelligence recognize and assess various subtleties and components of intelligence. Even more intriguing are advances in neuroscience that give us glimpses into the brain and the nature of brain activity associated with various tasks that reflect different aspects of intelligence.

Another controversy involves the bias of intelligence measures along the dimensions of sex, socioeconomic status, and racial, ethnic, and cultural background (Shuttleworth Edwards et al., 2004). There is a long standing contention that intelligence tests that are standardized primarily on white male populations are inappropriate for minority populations, including women, ethnic minorities, non-English speakers, and the physically challenged (Suzuki et al., 2001). Research is ongoing to develop tests that are not unfairly based on these factors.

Intelligence tests have additional pitfalls. Most importantly, they do not and cannot reflect all kinds of intelligence. Intelligence is a multifaceted and complex concept, and many believe that its measurement should not be limited to testing attention, perception, memory, reasoning, and verbal comprehension (Gottfredson, 1997). Such tests cannot capture other facets of intelligence such as Michael Jordan's skills on the basketball court or Shakespeare's literary genius. However, provided that an IQ score is not used as a measure of the broad concept of intelligence, it has useful applications, most notably the prediction of academic success and the assessment of performance deficits and inequalities, cognitive impairment, and mental retardation.

Projective Tests Projective testing emerged from psychoanalytic theory. Two widely used **projective tests** are the *Rorschach Inkblot Test* and the *Thematic Apperception Test* (TAT). The Rorschach, first published in 1921, was developed by a German psychiatrist, Hermann Rorschach. In this test, the patient is presented with increasingly complex and ambiguous inkblots (see Figure 3.7). The first blots are rather simple black and white images, and the later blots are more complex and colorful. The test's rationale is that when given such ambiguous stimuli, the patient "projects" a unique interpretation onto them that reflects his or her underlying unconscious processes and conflicts. One can immediately see how holding the Rorschach to our standards of reliability and validity would be a considerable task. Although Rorschach

projective tests tests derived from psychoanalytic theory in which people are asked to respond to ambiguous stimuli

FIGURE 3.7
An Inkblot Similar to Those in the Rorschach Inkblot Test

What does this look like to you?

died before he could develop a reliable scoring system, clinical psychologist John Exner constructed a rigorous system for standardized administration and scoring of the test known as the *Comprehensive System* (CS). The CS is a multivolume work that breaks the inkblot test into a complex matrix of variables. These variables are interpreted and scored to form a Structural Summary, which the clinician can use to understand the person's personality traits and psychological functioning (Exner, 2005). Despite these valiant attempts to impose structure on the Rorschach, many criticisms remain, rendering its usefulness highly questionable (see the box "Examining the Evidence: The Rorschach Inkblot Test").

The second popular projective test, the *Thematic Apperception Test* (TAT), was developed in 1935 by researchers at the Harvard Psychological Clinic. The assessment consists of 31 black and white pictorial cards, and the test-taker is asked to make up a story about the image. The examiner interprets the story without a formalized scoring system and is free to evaluate the response from within his or her own theoretical orientation. As with the Rorschach, it is believed that the descriptions that emerge provide insight into the psychological processes and unconscious of the test-taker. Given the qualitative nature of the test data and the absence of rigorous scoring and interpretation methods, the TAT remains a subjective test.

Despite their weaknesses, projective tests remain popular in some circles. Even when the tests are not used as part of an actual diagnostic battery, many clinicians will use them either in initial stages of therapy to "get the patient talking" or for patients who have difficulty discussing their emotions as a way to get them more in touch with what they are feeling.

Tests for Specific Symptoms   In addition to tests of general psychological functioning, we also need assessment tools that provide reliable and valid measures of specific types of symptoms, such as depression and anxiety. When testing treatments, we want to know how well certain treatments reduce symptoms of a particular disorder (e.g., which of two treatments better reduces the specific symptoms of depression). When a therapist treats someone for a particular problem, such as test anxiety, he or she may administer a questionnaire that measures severity of test anxiety over the course of treatment to see how well the intervention is working. Many scales have been developed for just this purpose. Some are clinician-administered assessments and others are self-report.

The Brief Psychiatric Rating Scale (BPRS) (Overall & Gorham, 1988) is a clinician-administered scale that assesses many different psychological symptoms, including bodily concerns, anxiety, emotional withdrawal, guilt feelings, tension, mannerisms and posturing, depressed mood, hostility, suspiciousness, hallucinations, motor retardation, uncooperativeness, unusual thought content, reduced emotional response, excitement, and disorientation. The BPRS assesses many specific symptoms. Other tests are more limited in scope, assessing the symptoms of one particular disorder. These disorder-specific scales exist for virtually every psychiatric disorder. Depressive symptoms, for example, are commonly assessed by the *Beck Depression Inventory-II* (BDI-II) (Beck et al., 1996), a 21-item self-report questionnaire. The *Beck Anxiety Inventory* (BAI) (Beck & Steer, 1993), is a 21-item self-report measure of anxiety that focuses on the severity of anxiety symptoms. The use of such specific scales by different

examining the evidence

The Rorschach Inkblot Test

■ **The Facts**   Despite some declining popularity in recent years, the Rorschach remains a frequently used psychological test that graduate students in clinical psychology are often trained to administer (Lilienfeld et al., 2000). Exner's Comprehensive System (CS) is the most commonly taught administrative and scoring procedure. The CS results in over 180 scores usually referred to as CS scores. However, the utility of the measure is a hotly contested issue in the psychological community, with many scientific articles praising or criticizing the test. Its proponents contend that it elicits a type of information from patients that is not obtained by other psychological measures and that is important for clinical decision making. Its critics point to three major limitations: the test's reliability, the adequacy of normative data, and the validity of scores. Is the Rorschach Inkblot Test useful? Let's examine the evidence.

■ **The Evidence**

1. As evidence of reliability, proponents note that 75% of CS scores have adequate interrater agreement (Wood et al., 2006), and the reliability of summary CS scores (based on sums of individual scores) is higher than the reliability of individual items (Hibbard, 2003).

2. As evidence for the adequacy of normative data, proponents note that data have been collected on approximately 600 people (including nonpatient adults, children, and various patient groups) and are adequate for interpretation in psychological assessment. The overdiagnosis of mental health problems in other groups when they are compared with the normative sample (a significant problem for this test) may be explained by the healthier nature of the normative samples, changes in scoring procedures since the original normative data were collected, increased psychopathology in society over time, and/or inadequate scoring in subsequent studies (Hibbard, 2003).

3. With respect to validity, proponents note that validity coefficients from research studies may underestimate the test's utility because the Rorschach is most useful when responses are integrated into an individualized assessment (Meyer et al., 2001). In other words, validity increases when clinicians use their clinical judgment to integrate Rorschach results with other assessment scores. This process may be too complex to be validated (Meyer et al., 2001).

■ **Let's Examine the Evidence**

1. What does it mean if 25% of CS scores do not meet traditional standards of interrater reliability (Wood et al., 2006)? In a test of this type, is the fact that only 75% of the scores are reliable "good enough"? Furthermore, test-retest reliability for most scores has not been adequately tested (Lilienfeld et al., 2000).

2. Normative data published by Exner and his colleagues are outdated. They were collected during the 1970s and 1980s and not consistently scored according to the most recently established procedures. This leads to overdiagnosis of individuals as having significant mental health problems when, in fact, they do not (Garb et al., 2005).

3. Adequate validity data exist for only 20 of more than 180 CS scores, including those that detect psychotic disorders, dependency, and treatment outcome. Another 160 CS scores have not yet been demonstrated to be valid, yet they continue to be used to make important judgments about people's psychological status (Wood et al., 2006).

■ **Conclusions**   Critics and advocates of the Rorschach agree that empirical data support the utility of some CS scores used for certain purposes. They also agree that many CS scores have not yet been studied adequately enough to evaluate their usefulness. Differences of opinion beyond these areas of agreement largely reflect the degree to which psychologists rely on empirical data versus clinician judgment in the assessment process (Garb et al., 2005). Scientifically based psychologists oppose the use of assessment tools that are not empirically validated, and therefore they do not support using unvalidated CS scores in the context of psychological decision making. People in this camp also point to the lack of evidence that clinical judgment improves predictions (see the discussion of clinical versus statistical prediction in this chapter). Yet proponents of the Rorschach, many of whom define themselves as scientist-practitioners, continue to argue for the clinical utility of patient responses even when relevant empirical data are not available. Yet others choose to hang inkblots on their walls as artistic mementos of psychology's past.

researchers has the added advantage of allowing comparisons of treatment effects across different studies and patient groups. Clinicians who use these measures are also better able to evaluate their patients' progress during treatment.

BEHAVIORAL ASSESSMENT

Carla had no idea when she first visited a behavior therapist to talk about her panic attacks that she would have "homework." Actually, the therapist assigned some at the end of the very first session! When their session was close to ending, he handed her some forms that he called practice records. He asked Carla to use these forms to record every panic attack she had during the next week and every time she avoided doing something that she thought might lead to a panic attack (e.g., going to grocery stores or movie theaters, driving on the freeway). The therapist also told Carla that he would be going with her to some of the frightening places that seemed to produce the panic so that he could learn more about her symptoms. That was a little scary, but she was glad that someone was finally going to help her figure out what was going on.

Many of the assessment instruments discussed so far measure internal, enduring states, such as intelligence and personality, that may underlie psychological problems. Behavioral assessment, however, is different. This approach relies on applying the principles of learning to understand behavior, and the ultimate goal is a functional analysis (Haynes et al., 2006). When conducting a **functional analysis** (also known as *behavioral analysis* or *functional assessment*), the clinician attempts to identify causal (or functional) links between problem behaviors and contextual variables (e.g., environmental and internal variables that have an impact on the problem behavior). Recalling the principles of classical and operant conditioning (see Chapter 1), we know that events that precede or follow certain symptoms or behaviors can have powerful effects in causing or maintaining those symptoms. Thus, to identify causal links, it is important to look at both *antecedents* and *consequences* of the behavior.

To identify antecedents and consequences of behavior, a behavioral assessment often starts with a behavioral interview. Here, the interviewer asks very specific questions to discover the full sequence of events and behaviors surrounding the patient's primary problems. In Carla's case, the therapist might ask her to describe in detail her most recent panic attack—where she was, who she was with, and what she was doing or thinking when she noticed the first symptoms. After those first symptoms, what did she think, feel, and do? What happened to the panic as a result of what she was thinking, feeling, and doing? What did other people do and when? All of these details might reveal that Carla was in the grocery store alone worrying about having a panic attack and monitoring her body for signs of one when she first noticed her heart rate increasing. She then might have pushed the cart to the side of the aisle and raced to the front door. After leaving the store so suddenly, she felt embarrassed, but also completely relieved that the symptoms of panic were subsiding. When she got home and told her husband, he felt sorry for her and gave her a big hug.

Learning about the specific sequence of events can help a clinician identify important functional relationships. In Carla's case, thoughts and expectations about panic may lead her to monitor her body for signs, perhaps noticing symptoms that are normal but that nonetheless frighten her because they have become a cue for panic. Noticing potential panic symptoms leads her to escape from the situation (leave the store), which reduces the panic symptom and reinforces her need to escape in order to control the symptoms. Her husband's comforting hug further reinforces her fear of panic. A good behavioral interview can uncover many different potential relationships. Other assessment tools used by behavior therapists include self-monitoring and behavioral observation.

functional analysis   also called behavioral analysis or functional assessment; a strategy of behavioral assessment in which a clinician attempts to identify causal links between problem behaviors and environmental variables

FIGURE 3.8

Awareness Practice Form

Patients use such forms to monitor and record their own behavior.

What <u>situation</u> created stress today?
_____

How did you <u>feel</u>?   What <u>physical signs</u> did you have?

[ ] anxious   [ ] fearful   [ ] muscle tension   [ ] shaking
[ ] worried, nervous [ ] angry   [ ] rapid pulse   [ ] sweating
[ ] embarrassed   [ ] sad   [ ] shortness of breath   [ ] other: _____
[ ] other: _____   [ ] butterflies in stomach

What <u>thoughts/worries</u> did you have? _____

What <u>actions</u> did you take to reduce anxiety? _____

Self-monitoring Carla's homework assignment to record her episodes of panic is an example of **self-monitoring**, a process in which a patient observes and records his or her own behavior as it happens (Compas & Gotlib, 2002). Psychological questionnaires are *retrospective*; that is, they ask about symptoms the patient may have had over the past week or past month. In contrast, self-monitoring requires patients to record their symptoms when they occur, allowing real-time information about the frequency, duration, and nature of the symptoms. Self-monitoring can contribute to a functional analysis if patients record contextual variables (aspects of the environment in which the behavior takes place) and sequences of events and behaviors (see Figure 3.8).

Self-monitoring can also create a record of how often problem behaviors are occurring before treatment begins and how symptoms change over time. For example, before treatment begins a woman who is monitoring her weight might record every single food or drink item that she consumed that day and be surprised to find that she has six "snacks" per day. As treatment progresses, the number of snacks she eats may decline to four, then to two, and finally to one snack per day. Self-monitoring is an important component of treatment because the act of recording symptoms by itself may increase patients' awareness of a problem behavior and reduce its frequency. For example, someone who begins to record the number of times he raids the refrigerator for food may be surprised by the frequency and without any specific treatment may begin to decrease the number of times he visits the kitchen for a snack. However, change produced in this fashion is typically only short-lived (Taylor, 2006).

Behavioral Observation **Behavioral observation** also involves measuring behavior as it occurs, but in this approach someone other than the patient monitors the frequency, duration, and nature of behavior. The first step is to define the behavior in a way that allows it to be clearly observed and reliably monitored. For a child with attention problems, for example, particular problem behaviors must be specified, such as leaving one's seat, speaking out of turn, and fidgeting (Compas & Gotlib, 2002). Simply asking raters to measure a global concept such as "inattentiveness" would lead to poor reliability across time and across raters.

Next, it is important to decide how to observe the behaviors of interest. *Event recording* involves monitoring each episode of the identified behavior, such as counting the number of times a child gets out of his or her seat, speaks out of turn, or fidgets during the school day (Compas & Gotlib, 2002; Tyron, 1998). Using *interval recording*, the behavioral assessor measures the number of times the identified behavior

self-monitoring a procedure within behavioral assessment in which the patient observes and records his or her own behavior as it happens

behavioral observation the measurement of behavior as it occurs by someone other than the person whose behavior is being observed

occurs during a particular interval of time (e.g., counting the number of times a child gets out of his seat during each 15-minute interval of a class period). Sometimes behavior can be observed in a *natural environment*. An assessor could go to a child's classroom to observe behavior, or a therapist could accompany a patient to the scene of a problem behavior. In other cases, behavior must be observed in an *analogue* fashion. In these instances, the assessor creates a situation similar to those in which the problem occurs to allow direct observation. For example, a patient with speech anxiety may be asked to stand up behind a desk or podium and give a speech. The therapist can count the number of times the patient stutters, the duration of silences in the speech, the amount of eye contact the patient makes, and the like.

Behavioral avoidance tests are often used to assess phobias and avoidance behavior by asking a patient to approach a feared situation as closely as possible (Compas & Gotlib, 2002). A patient with a height phobia, for example, might be asked to climb an outdoor set of stairs as high as possible. The observer measures how close the person can approach the feared situation. As is true for self-monitoring, behavioral observation strategies can be used to evaluate the severity of symptoms at baseline (before treatment begins), as well as to assess the degree of change after treatment.

PSYCHOPHYSIOLOGICAL ASSESSMENT

Psychophysiological assessment measures brain structure, brain function, and nervous system activity. This type of assessment measures physiological changes in the nervous system that reflect emotional or psychological events. Different types of measurements assess a range of biochemical alterations in the brain, or physiological changes in other parts of the body.

One of the oldest, most common, and least invasive types of psychophysiological measurements is *electroencephalography* (EEG). Researchers first measured and recorded brain waves in dogs in 1912, and by the 1950s, this method was used regularly throughout the United States (Niedermeyer, 1999). Electrodes are placed on the scalp, or in unusual circumstances, in the cerebral cortex, and differences in electric voltage between various parts of the brain are measured (Eisen, 1999). The output is called an electroencephalogram (EEG), which is an electrical signal. The EEG is a useful research tool because it is noninvasive and requires little effort from the participant. In some instances, the brain activity is recorded when the participant is engaged in cognitive processing related to the presentation of a simple, evoked stimulus, called an *event-related potential* (ERP). Changes in brain activity are recorded together with a time-stamped presentation of the stimulus, which can take many forms including auditory (sounds), visual (flashes of light or visual images), olfactory (smells), and more cognitive stimuli that can engage memory, pattern recognition, or emotional responses, for example.

Our understanding of EEG patterns has advanced considerably since the 1950s. In a healthy, relaxed adult, EEG activities typically appear to be a constant pattern of low-voltage changes, termed *alpha waves*. These patterns are altered by the presence of psychological or emotional factors, which can be observed in studies that compare the EEGs of individuals experimentally exposed to stressors with controls who are not exposed (Fein & Calloway, 1993). EEGs are useful tools for monitoring and diagnosing certain clinical conditions, such as a coma state and brain death, and for monitoring brain function while under anesthesia (Fein & Calloway, 1993). EEG recording is also one of the primary investigative tools used to identify seizure disorders. Observing quick and irregular spikes on an EEG of an awake individual may indicate the presence of a seizure and aid in distinguishing epileptic seizures from other types of nonepileptic brain dysfunction.

behavioral avoidance tests behavioral assessment strategies used to assess avoidance behavior by asking a patient to approach a feared situation as closely as possible

psychophysiological assessment assessment strategies that measure brain structure, brain function, and nervous system activity

EEGs can be recorded during sleep to reveal the rich and diverse types of brain activity that happen at night. While the EEGs are measuring brain waves, the electro-oculogram (EOG) records eye movements. Most people have heard about REM (rapid eye movement sleep), but the second broad sleep stage is non-REM sleep when the eyes are at rest. That complex state is actually made up of four stages, each marked by different types of wavelengths (Chockroverty, 1999). When we are awake, our brain activity is dominated by beta waves. As we relax or begin to fall asleep, alpha waves dominate. You can experience an alpha wave-rich state as you begin to doze off. The sleeper next moves into stages 1 and 2, which are marked by even slower theta waves, and then into stages 3 and 4, when even slower *delta waves* predominate. These are our deepest sleep stages—when awakened from these stages, we are likely to feel disoriented and groggy. Curiously, it is also during these stages that sleepwalking (*somnambulism*) and sleeptalking (*somniloquy*) occur (see Chapter 12).

The EEG is one of the oldest psychophysiological assessments, often used in research because it is noninvasive. It records changes in brain activity.

The EEG has several advantages as a tool for exploring brain activity. It allows the assessment of very fast responses—measured at the level of a millisecond rather than the second and minute level of other techniques. Moreover, EEG is the only measure that directly assesses electrical activity in the brain. Sometimes, however, an EEG may not be sensitive enough to detect specific neuronal activity or determine the specific neurotransmitter sending the signals (Koessler et al., 2007). In addition, compared with other functional brain imaging techniques, an EEG cannot determine functioning in a specific brain region. Although some people refer to an EEG as a brain function test, it is more accurately considered as a broad measure of brain activity (Eberwle, 2002) Accordingly, recent research has combined EEG with functional brain imaging techniques (Koessler et al., 2007).

Another type of psychophysiological assessment measure is *electrodermal activity* (EDA), which used to be called *galvanic skin response* (GSR). This measurement capitalizes on the fact that the sweat glands on the palms of the hands are controlled by the peripheral nervous system and thus react to emotional states. If you've ever experienced sweaty palms, you know this feeling. EDA measures the changes in electrical conductance produced by increased or decreased sweat gland activity. EDA is a window into the presence of stress or anxiety.

A common type of psychophysical assessment incorporating EEG or EDA strategies is *biofeedback* (see Chapter 14). The term *biofeedback* was first coined in the late 1960s. The goal of this assessment is to train patients to recognize and modify physiological signals. You probably use a form of biofeedback in your daily life. If you feel yourself getting anxious and your heart rate is increasing, you might start taking some deep breaths to calm yourself down. You recognize that your heart is beating fast, and you do something to try to reduce your arousal. Clinical biofeedback provides a bit more sophistication by using biofeedback machines that can detect and record physiological reactions and responses with great sensitivity. For example, bio-signals such as heart rate, blood pressure, or muscle tension can be detected and converted into a detectable signal, such as a light bulb flash every time a set threshold is met (e.g., every time the heart rate exceeds 90 beats per minute). The patient attends and responds to this visual signal by trying to relax tense muscles or slow the heart rate. Then the light flashes less often, signaling the patient's success (Association for Applied Psychophysiology and Biofeedback, 2007). Clinical biofeedback is used to treat various psychological conditions, including anxiety, panic, and attention-deficit/hyperactivity disorder. Other medical conditions for which this technique can be helpful include migraine headaches (Nestoriuc & Martin, 2007), Raynaud's disease (a circulatory disorder) (Karavidas et al., 2006), epilepsy, incontinence, digestive system disorders, high and low blood pressure, cardiac arrhythmias, and paralysis (Association for Applied Psychophysiology and Biofeedback, 2007). As you can see, biofeedback illustrates how feelings and emotions can affect bodily functions and how changing emotional states can change physical functioning. Biofeedback illustrates the complexity of a biopsychosocial approach to behavior. An exciting new area of research is how biological compounds (such as the medication oxytocin) may enhance someone's perceptual abilities, such as being better able to understand the emotions of others (see the box "Research Hot Topic: Oxytocin and 'Mind Reading'").

concept CHECK

- Clinical interviews usually occur early in the assessment process so that the clinician can begin to gather information and set assessment goals. These interviews can be administered in either unstructured or structured format.

- Psychological tests are used to measure personality, general and cognitive functioning, intelligence, and specific clinical symptoms.

Research HOT Topic

Oxytocin and "Mind Reading"

Assessment can take many forms. One fascinating advance is our ability to understand the association between underlying biology and observed social behaviors. Is it possible that the release of a hormone in the brain can affect our ability to form close relationships, to trust other people, and even to read minds? Researchers studying oxytocin, a naturally occurring substance in our bodies, have found that there may be such a link. For years, oxytocin was known only as a hormone involved in labor contractions and lactation. Now it appears that oxytocin can act as a neurotransmitter in the brain, where it is associated with many complex social behaviors. Animal studies have shown that oxytocin increases both maternal behavior and pair bonding (Carter, 1998; Young & Wang, 2004). A preliminary and intriguing study in humans found that after people took oxytocin, they were more likely to trust another person with their money (Kosfeld et al., 2005). This initial glimpse into the possible role of oxytocin led researchers to wonder whether a greater ability to "read" people was part of the mechanism responsible for the reduction in social stress and apprehension and increased attachment behavior associated with oxytocin.

The ability to detect another's thoughts and emotions purely through external observation, such as by noticing facial expression, is integral to human social interaction. Referred to as "mind reading," this practice of analyzing another's emotional state based on external cues alone is critical not only in conversation, but in the establishment and maintenance of trust as well.

Researchers (Domes et al., 2007) examined the effect of oxytocin on one's ability to "read minds." When asked to describe someone's thoughts or feelings based on a picture of their eyes alone, participants given oxytocin beforehand performed better than those not given any hormone. This ability to sense another's emotional state may facilitate social attachment and trusting behavior. Although the results must be viewed as preliminary, they provide an intriguing window into how our biology may influence our social functioning.

This information may also be useful in the future to researchers studying and treating patients with severe social impairments, especially autism (see Chapter 12). People with autism spectrum disorders have been shown to have a significant impairment in "mind reading" as well as low plasma oxytocin levels (Hill & Frith, 2003).

- Behavioral assessment, including self-monitoring and behavioral observation, is used to measure behavior and contextual (environmental) variables that cause and maintain the behavior.

- Psychophysiological assessment measures changes in the nervous system as they relate to psychological or emotional events. The most common form of psychophysiological assessment is the EEG, a measure of electrical signals in the brain.

APPLICATION QUESTION What tests might you choose to conduct a psychological assessment for a patient who is having severe headaches, anxiety, trouble concentrating, and difficulties in her marriage?

Diagnosis and Classification

A common language to describe observed clinical phenomena is critical to both clinical practice and research. The following discharge summary illustrates the use of such a common language as one clinician communicates to another clinician in a distant city as his patient is about to be transferred.

Between 2007 and 2010, I treated Susan intermittently for recurrent major depression together with her primary care physician, who managed medication. In that interval, Susan experienced three episodes of major depression lasting between 4 weeks and 4 months. Each time, she experienced marked low mood, anhedonia, agitation, early morning awakening, and problems with concentration. She reported frequent passive suicidal ideation, but no active suicidal intent or plan. She was prescribed 40 mg fluoxetine/day and remained on the medication throughout this interval. After her initial course of cognitive-behavioral therapy, we contracted that she would contact me for booster sessions each time she identified a lowering of her mood.

These common terms for symptoms and categories allow the new clinician to develop a relatively accurate picture of the patient. As we discussed earlier in this chapter, using diagnostic labels to describe sets of symptoms helps clinicians and researchers communicate about their patients. Deciding which diagnosis best fits a patient's pattern of symptoms also helps the clinician develop an appropriate treatment plan. However, this type of communication was not always the case in psychiatry. The classification of mental disorders has changed several times throughout history.

HISTORY OF CLASSIFICATION OF ABNORMAL BEHAVIORS

In 1952 the American Psychiatric Association (APA) adopted a classification system—the **Diagnostic and Statistical Manual of Mental Disorders** (DSM-I) (American Psychiatric Association, 1952)—from an earlier system developed in 1918 to provide the Bureau of the Census with uniform statistics about psychiatric hospitals. The 1952 DSM manual contained 106 categories of mental disorders (Grob, 1994). From that point forward, the DSM has expanded. Published in 1968, the DSM-II (American Psychiatric Association, 1968), listed 182 disorders in 134 pages and reflected the dominant psychodynamic perspective of the time. Symptoms were described as reflections of broad underlying conflicts or maladaptive reactions to life problems rather than in observable behavioral terms (Wilson, 1993). In 1974, the task force working to revise the DSM emphasized the importance of establishing more specific diagnostic criteria. The intention was to facilitate mental health research and to set up classifications that would reflect current scientific knowledge. In the DSM-III (American Psychiatric Association, 1980), which was a significantly

Diagnostic and Statistical Manual of Mental Disorders (DSM) a classification originally developed in 1952 to classify mental disorders; revisions have been made over subsequent years, and this document is a standard of care in psychiatry and psychology

different document than the DSM-II, categorization was based on description rather than assumptions about the causes of the disorder, and the psychodynamic perspective was replaced with a more biomedical approach (Wilson, 1993). The DSM-III was published in 1980 and consisted of 464 pages describing 265 diagnostic categories, an expansion that was controversial. There were many new diagnostic categories. For example, the former category of anxiety neurosis was divided into several different and distinct categories, including generalized anxiety disorder, panic disorder, and social phobia. Despite this controversy, all subsequent revisions have maintained the same structure as the DSM-III and have attempted to refine or improve this version rather than to overhaul the diagnostic system entirely. The next version, the DSM-III-R (American Psychiatric Association, 1987) included not only revisions but also renaming, reorganization, and replacement of several disorders, which yielded 292 diagnoses (Mayes & Horwitz, 2005). In 1994, DSM-IV listed 297 disorders. This revision emerged from the work of a steering committee, consisting of work groups of experts who (1) conducted an extensive literature review of their diagnoses, (2) obtained data from researchers to determine which criteria to change, and (3) conducted multicenter clinical trials (Schaffer, 1996). DSM-IV-TR (American Psychiatric Association, 2000), a "text" revision, was published in 2000, with most diagnostic criteria unaltered. This revision primarily provided updated information on each diagnosis and was more consistent with International Classification of Diseases-10 published by the World Health Organization (see below). As we continue to learn more about psychopathology, the DSM continues to evolve. The next version of the DSM, the DSM-V, is currently in production.

Although many valid criticisms have arisen as a reaction to the DSM system, at its most useful, it provides a framework and common language for clinicians and researchers. The DSM system helps clinicians examine presenting problems and associated features and to identify appropriate assessments and treatments. Moreover, accurate classification of mental disorders is a critical element of rigorous research. Ideally, as research in neuroscience and genetics progresses, we will see a greater reflection of underlying biology in the classification of mental disorders.

Most of the information presented in subsequent chapters of this book will cover the major clinical syndromes, or what are known in everyday language as mental disorders. The material will be organized mostly around disorders as they are defined in the DSM-IV-TR. Beyond listing diagnoses, however, the authors of the DSM wanted to devise a system that would offer more information about patients than a simple clinical diagnosis (e.g., depression). To do this, they created a **multiaxial system** that includes five dimensions or *diagnostic axes* on which patients' behavior and functioning can be classified. *Axis I* is the primary axis (dimension) on which clinical syndromes are diagnosed. These include many of the syndromes you will learn about in this book (depression, anxiety, eating disorders, substance abuse, etc.). *Axis II* is the dimension that addresses long-standing difficulties such as personality disorders, which will be described in Chapter 11 and developmental disorders, which will be described in Chapter 12. Diagnoses assigned on both Axes I and II include categories with explicit criteria and decision-making rules about what symptoms are required in order to assign the diagnosis. *Axis III* is the dimension on which medical problems are described. These are important given that many medical problems produce symptoms that overlap with or influence psychological symptoms. On *Axis IV* the clinician can record any psychosocial or environmental problems that may impact the patient's behavior or functioning (e.g., a recent life stage change such as divorce, death of a family member, or job change). *Axis V* requires a global assessment of functioning and is based on the GAF scale described earlier in this chapter (see Figure 3.9).

multiaxial system a system of diagnosis and classification used by the DSM that requires classifying a patient's behavior on five different dimensions

Figure 3.9 illustrates a full DSM-IV-TR diagnostic characterization of Pauline, the woman described in the case at the start of this chapter. She had already been seeing a psychologist for anxiety and depression, which are diagnosed on Axis I. A thorough neuropsychological evaluation revealed that she had significant cognitive impairment, which was defined as Dementia of the Alzheimer's Type (see Chapter 13).

An alternative to the DSM classification system is the **International Classification of Diseases and Related Health Problems (ICD)**. Published by the World Health Organization (WHO, 1992), the ICD uses a code-based classification system for physical diseases and a broad array of psychological symptoms and syndromes. The ICD system for diagnosing mental disorders was developed in Europe at approximately the same time as the original DSM was being developed in America, shortly after World War II. The first set of mental disorders was included in the ICD in 1948. The APA and WHO have worked to coordinate the DSM and the relevant sections of ICD, although some differences remain. Like the DSM system, the ICD is regularly revised; it is currently in its tenth edition [ICD-10 (1992)].

The ICD has become the international standard diagnostic classification system for epidemiology and many health management purposes. Beyond its use in classifying diseases and other health problems, the ICD is used for morbidity and mortality statistics for the WHO and for third-party payers and insurance companies (World Health Organization, 2007).

FIGURE 3.9
DSM Multiaxial Diagnoses for Pauline

Axis I: Generalized anxiety disorder

           Major depression

           Dementia of the Alzheimer'sType

Axis II: No diagnosis

Axis III: High blood pressure; Injury from fall

Axis IV: Recent fall

Axis V: Current GAF: 55

COMORBIDITY

As noted in Chapter 2, the term **comorbidity** refers to the presence of more than one disorder. As we have already noted, in many cases, a patient's symptoms cannot be fully characterized or diagnosed using a single category. For example, a patient with depression may also experience anxiety (panic) attacks and an eating disorder. When more than one disorder is diagnosed, the disorders are said to be *comorbid*. Almost half of people who have one mental disorder have symptoms that meet the criteria for at least one other disorder (Kessler et al., 2005).

The term *comorbidity* may be misleading because it is unclear whether the co-occurring diagnoses truly reflect the presence of distinct clinical disorders or whether they may actually be different manifestations of a single clinical disorder (Maj, 2005). However, the frequent co-occurrence of multiple psychiatric diagnoses cannot be ignored. Rates of comorbidity are high, and multiple theories exist to explain how the current diagnostic system may contribute to the common observation of comorbidity. For example, it may result from "the rule laid down in the construction of DSM–III that the same symptom could not appear in more than one disorder" (Maj, 2005; Robins, 1994). Given this rule, anxiety cannot appear in the criteria for depression, although the DSM acknowledges that patients with major depression are frequently anxious. Thus, the assessor is forced to turn to another diagnostic family in order to describe and record this prominent symptom. Another reason for increased comorbidity is the addition of new diagnostic categories with each new edition of the DSM. The DSM has nearly tripled in size since its first publication, encompassing more and more categories. If divisions between disorders are made with finer and finer distinctions (which may not actually reflect nature), it is logical that the likelihood of concurrent diagnoses will increase (Maj, 2005).

International Classification of Diseases (ICD) a classification system for mental disorders developed in Europe that is an international standard diagnostic system for epidemiology and many health management purposes

comorbidity the presence of more than one disorder

65–80

BIRTH 20 40 60 80

DEVELOPMENTAL AND CULTURAL FACTORS

As is true of assessment procedures, it is important to keep developmental and cultural variables in mind when assessment and diagnosis are considered. Diagnostic criteria may need to vary across the life span, for example. This issue is evident with childhood disorders (see Chapter 12), where separate DSM criteria describe patterns of abnormal behavior that are found primarily in childhood. Similarly, diagnostic criteria established for adults may not capture the experience of older people very well. We now use the same DSM criteria to diagnose many disorders in younger and older adults (see Chapter 13), yet we may need to create specialized criteria for the elderly, who tend to experience and describe psychological symptoms in unique ways (as do children). Some disorders, like dementia, occur primarily among older adults, but the possible role of developmental variables should be considered for all disorders. For example, specialized criteria have been proposed to diagnose anxiety disorders in older adults with dementia for whom the current DSM criteria may not be appropriate (Starkstein et al., 2007). Sometimes similar abnormal behaviors may be seen across the life span, but in other cases, important differences may emerge that impact understanding and treatment.

Different prevalences of psychological disorders are also consistently observed for men and women. As you progress through the chapters of this book, you will see repeatedly how men and women differ with regard to the prevalence and experience of various disorders. Women, for example, are more often diagnosed with depression and anxiety, whereas men are more often diagnosed with substance abuse. It is possible that men and women actually develop different disorders at different rates, perhaps with different genetic risk factors for certain syndromes. It is also possible that in some cases a similar underlying difficulty, such as stress, may be expressed differently for men and women.

Each chapter of this book also addresses differences in symptoms and disorders by race and ethnicity. In some cases, the prevalence of certain disorders varies according to ethnic and racial status, and symptoms may be different, too. You will see in some chapters, for example, that there are *culture-bound syndromes*, or sets of symptoms that occur together uniquely in certain ethnic or racial groups. *Ataque de nervios* is one example of an anxiety syndrome that occurs uniquely among Latinos (see Chapters 1, 4, and 13). Other such culture-bound syndromes will be discussed in various chapters.

Diagnostic criteria established for adults may not capture the experience of older people very well. They may have different symptoms or describe them differently than the way a younger person does.

In general, classification systems should take into consideration developmental, demographic, and cultural variables that affect the experience and description of abnormal behavior. Some symptoms are universally applicable, but others are not.

WHEN IS A DIAGNOSTIC SYSTEM HARMFUL?

A diagnostic system for mental disorders performs a necessary service by categorizing symptoms in a manner useful for clinical diagnosis, treatment, and research. However, there are also significant limitations to the current diagnostic approach. First, because many diagnostic categories require that a person have a specified number of symptoms from a longer list (e.g., four out of six symptoms listed might be required for a diagnosis), not all individuals with the same diagnosis will experience the same symptoms. In addition, most diagnostic classifications do not require that the symptoms be connected to a particular etiology (cause); therefore, different patients with the same disorder may have developed the symptoms in different ways. Finally, two people who have the same diagnosis do not necessarily respond to the same treatments.

Diagnostic categories also can encourage stereotyped conceptions of specific disorders. For example, imagine that a young woman has a grandfather who was diagnosed with bipolar disorder (see Chapter 6). He had a flagrant case marked by excessive spending, sexual indiscretions, and grandiosity (an inflated sense of one's own importance), leading to several hospitalizations and therapy. Although his granddaughter is beginning to experience less extreme signs and symptoms, she might hesitate to believe that she has the same disorder. In her mind, her symptoms don't fit the stereotype associated with the label of bipolar disorder or the behavior that she saw in her grandfather. Stereotyping by diagnosis can also lead a clinician to premature or inaccurate assumptions about a patient that prevent a thorough evaluation and comprehensive treatment plan (e.g., a patient who has a diagnosis of depression may be prescribed an antidepressant without sufficient evaluation of the need for nonmedication treatments to manage life problems). Similarly, labeling a patient with a diagnosis can lead to *self-fulfilling prophecies* (e.g., I have depression; therefore, I will never experience enjoyment like other people do) and create *stigmas* that impact the person's ability to function well at work or in social relationships (e.g., who wants to date a woman with depression?).

Another criticism of the DSM system is that its categories can reflect the beliefs or limited knowledge of an era. A good example was the inclusion of homosexuality as a mental illness before 1974. By being classified as a mental disorder, homosexuality was intrinsically defined as something that caused distress and impairment and that should be treated. This classification contributed substantially to the stigmatization of homosexuality, to homosexual persons' beliefs that there was something wrong with them psychiatrically, and to too many ill-conceived attempts to change their sexual orientation. Once research began to address homosexuality openly, empirical evidence did not support the claim that homosexuality was a form of mental illness or was inherently associated with psychopathology. After a majority vote, the American Psychiatric Association (APA) replaced the diagnosis of *Homosexuality* with *Ego-Dystonic Homosexuality* in the DSM-III (1980), referring to sexual orientation inconsistent with one's fundamental beliefs and personality. However, mental health professionals criticized this new diagnostic category as a political compromise designed to appease psychiatrists who still considered homosexuality pathological (APA, 2006). In 1986, the diagnosis was removed entirely from the DSM. In the current edition, DSM-IV-TR (APA, 2000), the only mention of homosexuality is found in the category *Sexual Disorders Not Otherwise Specified*. This category includes homosexuality that is marked by persistent and marked distress about one's sexual orientation, a category that may still reflect continued stigma. In 1992, the APA released the following statement:

> *Whereas homosexuality per se implies no impairment in judgment, stability, reliability, or general social or vocational capabilities, the American Psychiatric Association calls on all international health organizations and individual psychiatrists in other countries, to urge the repeal in their own country of legislation that penalizes homosexual acts by consenting adults in private. And further the APA calls on these organizations and individuals to do all that is possible to decrease the stigma related to homosexuality wherever and whenever it may occur.*

A final criticism of the DSM is that it simply includes too many disorders and that normal variations in human behavior have been overmedicalized by giving them diagnostic labels (see the box "Research Hot Topic: Too Many Disorders?"). Overall, although diagnostic systems that rely on classification of symptoms into disorders provide substantial benefits for patients, clinicians, and researchers, the limitations of these systems need to be considered. Alternative systems for discussing psychological problems have been developed that rely on dimensional models rather than categorical classification.

Research HOT Topic

Too Many Disorders?

A recent study by Ray Moynihan (Moynihan, 2006) published in the *British Medical Journal* on April 1, 2006 stated that "extreme laziness may have a medical basis." The authors called the new condition motivational deficiency disorder (MoDeD) and described its effects on daily life as being potentially fatal. In its most severe form, it could reduce the motivation to breathe. The article also discussed possible pharmaceutical treatments as well as criticism that "ordinary laziness" might be improperly diagnosed as MoDeD. Shortly thereafter, online blogs appeared to discuss MoDeD. People speculated about whether their symptoms "qualified them" for the disorder and where to go for treatment. News outlets quickly picked up the study as well, highlighting its results in their daily health columns.

Although this cleverly placed article was just an April Fool's joke, MoDeD's initial acceptance from the public highlights a larger issue that pervades society's concept of the human condition. *Are there too many disorders? Do we sometimes turn normal variations in human functioning into medical or psychiatric conditions?*

From 1952 to the present, the number of diagnostic categories in the DSM has expanded from 106 to 297. Could we really have discovered so many new psychological disorders in the last 60 years? In many cases, empirical data have been used to modify, add, or delete categories. In other cases, categories have been modified based largely on the consensus of clinicians who were part of the DSM Task Forces. Social, political, and economic variables may also play a role (e.g., there may be potential monetary gain from new drugs developed to treat new conditions). Nevertheless, research is needed to determine the validity of various "potential" diagnostic categories (e.g., premenstrual dysphoric disorder, depressive personality disorder). What is necessary for psychological distress to become a psychological disorder?

All health care professionals agree that it is essential to study the reliability and validity of a diagnostic category before establishing it as an official disorder. Much more controversial is the argument by some critics of DSM-IV (Chodoff, 2002) that we need clear biological markers that would differentiate psychological disorders from normal variations in human responses. Although some research is under way, the multitude of disorders listed in DSM-IV must still rely on "subjective checklists of a patient's history." An important research goal is to conduct carefully controlled studies to identify clusters or categories of symptoms that meaningfully describe true psychological disorders such as major depression but that do not pathologize normal human emotions such as grief following the death of a loved one. Until objective markers (biological or otherwise) are determined, we must carefully guard against MoDeD in all its variations.

DIMENSIONAL SYSTEMS AS AN ALTERNATIVE TO DSM CLASSIFICATION

The DSM and ICD are both based on categorical systems that classify sets of symptoms into disorders. As we have seen, such systems have advantages and disadvantages. One alternative to the DSM and ICD categorical diagnostic systems is a dimensional classification of abnormal behavior, which suggests that people with disorders are not qualitatively distinct from people without disorders. Rather, a dimensional model for understanding abnormal behavior suggests that symptoms of what are now called disorders are simply extreme variations of normal experience. Proponents of this model suggest that psychiatric illness is best conceptualized along dimensions of functioning rather than as discrete clinical conditions (Widiger & Samuel, 2005). Two features of mental illness that support the value of dimensional approaches are the high frequency of comorbidity (two or more disorders occurring together) and within-category variability (e.g., multiple people with the same diagnosis can have very different sets of symptoms and experiences). As we have already learned, comorbidity often occurs among people with psychological difficulties. When a person has one disorder (such as an anxiety disorder), there is a high likelihood that he or she will have a second disorder (such as depression). The current DSM-IV approach allows for the diagnosis of comorbid conditions, which is an important feature, as 45% of those with any mental disorder meet the criteria for two or more disorders (Kessler et al., 2005). Proponents of a dimensional model suggest that this alternative approach would allow for a richer description of patient difficulties across multiple areas of dysfunction. In a dimensional model, for example, a patient's functioning would be rated on a range of dimensions or traits (e.g., introversion, neuroticism, openness, conscientiousness, etc.) rather than simply on whether a set of symptoms was or was not present. This type of system also would lead to better categorization and understanding of a patient whose symptoms did not fall squarely into any existing category. In many cases, patients will report many symptoms of a particular disorder but not enough of them to actually meet diagnostic criteria. In a categorical system, these people are often considered to have *subthreshold* syndromes. A dimensional approach would allow us to describe all symptoms regardless of whether or not they actually met specified cut-offs or criteria.

A second proposed advantage of the dimensional approach is that the current categorical system leads to considerable within-category *heterogeneity* or variability. Despite the DSM's goal of creating relatively homogeneous diagnostic categories that would allow a "common language" of classification, individuals diagnosed with the same disorder actually may share few common features. For example, two people diagnosed with depression may have very different clinical presentations. While one may have depressed mood, crying, difficulty sleeping, fatigue, and difficulty concentrating, another may have loss of interest in things that used to bring pleasure, decreased appetite and weight loss, slowed motor behaviors, feelings of worthlessness, and recurrent thoughts of death. Both sets of symptoms would meet DSM criteria for Major Depression (see Chapter 6), but the primary complaints and targets for treatment would be quite different. Overall, this type of heterogeneity within diagnostic categories can adversely affect both clinical practice and research (Krueger et al., 2005). Dimensional proponents believe that their approach lends itself to a greater amount of relevant clinical information, which can have both clinical and research advantages (Watson, 2005).

Arguments against the dimensional model often focus on clinical utility. The categorical system offers a simple approach with a clear diagnostic label that provides an efficient way to share information. Dimensional models are innately more complex. For example, it is much simpler to explain to a patient that she has depression than to discuss with her where her symptoms lie along many dimensions of traits experienced by all people. The nature of clinical decision making (e.g., whether to hospitalize, which medication to use, whether to provide insurance coverage) is also facilitated by a simple, easily communicated categorical system. The complexity of sharing information that is organized along multiple dimensions would make communication with patients extremely difficult; communication across researchers and clinicians trying to share information about common clinical syndromes would also become more difficult. Furthermore, given that no single, accepted dimensional theory of psychopathology exists, there could be considerable difficulty achieving consensus on the type and quantity of dimensions required to capture the entire spectrum of mental illness (Blashfield & Livesley, 1999). Proponents of categorical approaches do concede that boundaries between most categories in the DSM-IV remain imprecise, and they also acknowledge that psychiatric classification needs further precision (Blashfield & Livesley, 1999).

---

concept CHECK

- The diagnosis and classification of psychological disorders are important for creating a common language for clinicians and researchers to facilitate communication about patients and psychological symptoms and syndromes. Diagnoses also help clinicians to develop appropriate treatment plans.

- The DSM system of classification is most often used in this country. An alternative classification system, the International Classification of Diseases (ICD), is used in Europe.

- Developmental, demographic, and cultural variables affect the nature and experience of abnormal behavior. These variables must be considered when evaluating the utility of diagnostic classification systems.

- A dimensional model for conceptualizing abnormal behavior has been suggested and debated as an alternative to traditional categorical classification systems such as DSM.

APPLICATION QUESTION What are some of the pros and cons for categorical versus dimensional models of classifying abnormal behavior?

THE WHOLE STORY: LIBBY—ASSESSMENT IN A CLINICAL RESEARCH STUDY

In this case study, we present the experience of Libby, a young woman with bulimia nervosa, an eating disorder that involves binge eating and purging (usually vomiting) (see Chapter 7). Libby is participating in a clinical trial that compares treatment based on medication (Prozac) to cognitive-behavioral therapy. The case is presented from the perspective of the participant, with commentary from the investigator about the purpose of each assessment.

I saw an advertisement on a local bus for free treatment for bulimia nervosa. I had been suffering for years but *had never had the funds to pay for treatment. All I was ever able to get was six sessions of counseling when I was an undergraduate. So I called the number for the study coordinator. She was a very nice woman, and she described the study to me. The first thing she did was ask me some questions on the phone—what was my age, current weight, lowest and highest past weight, and how often did I binge and purge.*

Researcher: This was the telephone screening. These questions were to determine preliminary eligibility for the study. We were looking for people *with current bulimia nervosa who were binge eating and purging at least twice per week for the past three months.*

The study coordinator set me up with an appointment for the following week and said she would send me a packet of information, a consent form, and some questionnaires in the mail. Three days later I received all of the information. The information sheet pretty much repeated what she had told me about the study—that there would be a randomization procedure (a flip of the coin) and I would receive either medication or group psychotherapy for bulimia.

I didn't really care what group I was in, I just wanted to get some proper treatment for this illness. I read through the consent form and signed on to participate in the study. Then I opened up the packet of questionnaires. I must have answered hundreds of questions. It took me over two hours. They ranged from eating behavior, to how I felt about my body shape and size, how depressed and anxious I was, and how much I drank alcohol, smoked cigarettes, and used drugs. There were also a bunch of questions about what kind of a person I was and another questionnaire that asked about the events that had happened in my life in the last year.

Researcher: The questionnaire battery included the Eating Disorders Examination Questionnaire to measure current eating symptoms, the Beck Depression and Anxiety Inventories to measure negative mood states that often accompany bulimia, the Fagerstrom Nicotine Tolerance Questionnaire to assess smoking and nicotine dependence, and measures of alcohol and drug use. The Life Events Schedule asks about significant environmental events that may have happened to the person in the last year. As part of a multiaxial diagnostic system, it is important to understand whether there are any significant stressors (such as financial difficulties) or important events (such as the death of a loved one) that could be influencing the person's thoughts or feelings. These were our baseline measures, many of which would be repeated at various times throughout the study.

When I arrived for my appointment, the researcher checked my consent form and checked through to make sure I answered all of the questions. I then had a rather extensive interview where the psychiatrist went into real depth about the history of the problems I have had with eating, depression, and anxiety. He also asked a lot about alcohol and drugs, but eventually he seemed to catch on that I was never into those things.

Researcher: We administered the baseline Structured Clinical Interview for DSM-IV to Libby in order to establish her baseline diagnosis and the Eating Disorders Examination Interview to get in-depth information about the nature of her eating disorder. According to our scoring, she met the diagnostic criteria for bulimia nervosa, major depression, and panic disorder. She was appropriate for inclusion into the study and was invited to participate.

The researchers welcomed me into the study. They then taught me how to self-monitor how often I binged and purged, which I had to do for a full week before starting therapy. I got randomized into the group cognitive-behavior therapy condition.

Researcher: For the next 12 weeks, Libby took part in cognitive-behavioral group treatment for bulimia nervosa. She continued to self-monitor her symptoms throughout the treatment. We could see from the text messages of her self-monitoring that her binge eating and purging behavior were improving by week 4.

I kept going to group and found the homework they gave me to be really helpful in starting to get a handle on my binge eating. It was also reassuring to share my experience with the other patients in the group. I had no idea that so many people faced the same hurdles that I did in keeping my bulimia under control. After 12 weeks of therapy, I was finally starting to feel like there was a light at the end of the tunnel.

Researcher: At the end of the 12 weeks, we asked Libby to fill out the same questionnaires she had at baseline to see how things had changed. We also readministered the Eating Disorders Examination Interview to get specific information about progress with her eating disorder. The psychiatrist who did the in-terview was unaware of her treatment group assignment. The interview revealed that she had been abstinent from binge eating for the past 4 weeks and had only purged once. This corresponded nicely with her self-monitoring data.

After the last interview, I set up my follow-up appointments. I was expected to return 3 months and 6 months after treatment. We had learned that relapse is common in bulimia and the best way to tell if a treatment works is to make sure that the changes we make actually stick. I was happy to return for the evaluations—especially since they assured me they would pay for parking and give me $50 for each session I attended!

Researcher: It is very important for us to make sure that the positive changes that we see persist. The only way to do this is by having scheduled follow-up assessments. Since many people do not return for their follow-ups, we have found that an excellent incentive to bring them back is to reimburse them for parking and provide a reasonable monetary incentive for their time. This is also an excellent opportunity for us to refer them for additional treatment if they are not doing well.

When I returned for my follow-up visits, the psychiatrist (who still didn't know which treatment I was in) asked me many of the same questions that she did at the start of the study. I could even tell how different my answers were thinking back to my first assessment. At this point, I was basically binge and purge free for the past 6 months with one exception. I went through a bad patch when I broke up with my boyfriend and I purged a couple of times, but I used the skills I had learned in therapy to get that behavior right back under control. Overall, I think being involved in a clinical trial was an interesting experience. Not only did I get great treatment, but the close follow-up helped me keep my symptoms under control.

CRITICAL ISSUES to remember

1. Clinical assessments can be used to gather information about a person's symptoms and to make decisions about the nature, status, and treatment of psychological problems. Assessments can be used for screening, diagnosis, treatment development, or outcome evaluation.

2. In order to determine the meaning of a score from a clinical assessment, it is important to compare the score with scores from other groups of people (called a normative comparison) or to a prior score by the same patient (self-referent comparison). The reliability of assessment measures refers to their ability to produce consistent scores across time and assessors. The validity of a test refers to the ability of scores to measure concepts accurately.

3. Clinical interviews usually occur early in the assessment process so that the clinician can begin to gather information and set assessment goals. These interviews can be structured or unstructured. Psychological tests measure personality, general and cognitive functioning, intelligence, and specific clinical symptoms. Behavioral assessment, including self-monitoring and behavioral observation, measures behavior and environmental variables that cause and maintain the behavior. Psychophysiological assessment measures changes in the nervous system as they relate to psychological or emotional events. The most common form of psychophysiological assessment is electroencephalography (EEG), which measures electrical signals in the brain.

4. Diagnosing and classifying psychological disorders is important for creating a common language for clinicians and researchers to facilitate communication about patients and psychological symptoms and syndromes. Diagnoses also help clinicians develop appropriate treatment plans. The DSM system of classification is most often used in the United States, but alternative models exist.

5. Assessment materials and procedures need to take into account the age and developmental level of the test-taker, as well as cultural variables.

6. A dimensional model for classifying abnormal behavior has been suggested as an alternative to more traditional categorical classification systems. This model suggests that abnormal behavior is better conceptualized along dimensions of functioning rather than in categories. Proponents of this system suggest that a dimensional model allows better attention to individual differences in symptoms that can occur for different patients with the same disorder. However, others argue that categorical systems are simpler and more efficient ways to share information.

TEST yourself

For more review plus practice tests, flashcards, and Speaking Out: DSM in Context videos, log onto www.MyPsychLab.com

1. Selection of assessment tools is largely determined by the patient's symptoms, age, and medical status. One other factor may be the
   a. early childhood experiences of the patient
   b. referral process
   c. environmental cues perceived by the therapist
   d. therapist's theoretical perspective

2. Physicians and other practitioners may choose to give new patients a screening assessment, which is
   a. a brief measure in which a cutoff score indicates the possibility of significant problems
   b. a test to determine whether the patient has a medical rather than a psychological condition
   c. a test to see whether the patient will benefit from psychotherapy
   d. a questionnaire that determines whether a patient needs to see a physician

3. With psychological disorders, the diagnosis given is primarily based on
   a. the therapist's theoretical perspective
   b. communication across clinicians

   c. a cluster of symptoms
   d. findings of laboratory tests

4. Diagnosis is important to physicians and psychologists because it facilitates
   a. treatment planning
   b. communication across clinicians and researchers
   c. understanding of a person's psychological status
   d. all of the above

5. A measure of clinical significance tells us that
   a. the patient is or is not satisfied with the treatment
   b. a patient's treatment is "finished"
   c. two clinical assessments are in agreement
   d. an observed change in a patient is a meaningful improvement

6. Comparing a person's score on a psychological test to the average scores obtained on that test from a large representative sample of people is a
   a. self-referent comparison
   b. psychometric comparison
   c. normative comparison
   d. clinical comparison

7. After an interview, a psychiatrist rates Jim's depression as severe. The next day a clinical psychologist also conducts an interview and rates Jim's depression as severe. The two clinicians are demonstrating
   a. interrater validity
   b. test-retest reliability
   c. interrater agreement
   d. test-retest validity

8. Dr. Smith develops the Smith Depression Inventory and gives it to hundreds of patients with depression. He also gives those patients the widely used Beck Depression Inventory. He finds that the average scores on the two questionnaires are highly correlated. Dr. Smith has demonstrated that the Smith Depression Inventory has
   a. concurrent validity
   b. predictive validity
   c. statistical prediction
   d. clinical prediction

9. A test publisher describes a psychological test as having extremely high predictive validity. This means the test
   a. has the ability to forecast particular outcomes
   b. has a high correlation with similar measures
   c. discriminates well between related concepts
   d. all of the above

10. Administering psychological tests to someone from another country may produce biased results if which of the following is not taken into consideration?
    a. the language in which the test was written
    b. the education of the person taking the test
    c. cultural beliefs and values of the person taking the test
    d. all of the above

11. Compared with unstructured interviews, structured interviews have several advantages, including
    a. avoidance of irrelevant questions
    b. briefer time frame
    c. identification of the best course of therapy
    d. increased reliability

12. Susan was sent to a neuropsychologist after a car accident left her having trouble concentrating and remembering things. The neuropsychologist gave her a battery of 10 measures assessing memory, abstract thought, language, sensory-motor integration, perceptions, and motor dexterity. This test battery is called the
    a. GAF
    b. WAIS
    c. Halstead-Reitan
    d. WCST

13. Although intelligence tests are controversial, they are useful in assessing
    a. genetics and its relative importance
    b. influences from a person's cultural background
    c. cognitive impairment
    d. nonverbal memory

14. Sally suffers from an eating disorder. The psychologist asked her to keep a diary and record what she eats, when she eats something, where she is when she eats, and what she is feeling right before, during, and after she eats. This is called
    a. behavioral application
    b. testing for specific symptoms
    c. self-monitoring
    d. self-report measuring

15. A patient has an extreme spider phobia. He is taken to a room with a cage of spiders against the opposite wall. He is asked to walk as close to the cage as he can. He takes two steps toward the cage and says he cannot go any closer. The psychologist measures the distance on the floor from the patient's feet to the cage. This is a
    a. continuous recording
    b. self-report measure
    c. natural environmental assessment
    d. behavioral avoidance test

16. The great advantage of the electroencephalogram (EEG) is that it
    a. can determine which neurotransmitters are active
    b. is the only measure that directly assesses electrical activity in the brain
    c. can identify functioning in a specific brain region
    d. is able to show specific neurons in the act of firing

17. The primary classification system used in the United States and published by the American Psychiatric Association is the
    a. ICD   c. Merck Manual
    b. DSM   d. Psychiatric Census

18. Psychosocial or environmental problems that may impact the patient's behavior or functioning is recorded on which of the following dimensions?
    a. Axis I   c. Axis III
    b. Axis II   d. Axis IV

19. The purpose of the multiaxial system is to
    a. let more than one clinician record information about a patient
    b. give a diagnosis that will be recognized internationally
    c. add an ICD diagnosis to a DSM diagnosis
    d. offer more information about patients than a clinical diagnosis alone

20. Dimensional classification is an alternative to categorical systems such as the DSM. One advantage of a dimensional system is
    a. better description of patients whose problems do not fit into a single category
    b. better use of a "common language" to classify patients
    c. simpler, clearer diagnostic labels for all conditions
    d. exclusion of all patients' comorbidity issues

Answers: 1 d, 2 a, 3 c, 4 d, 5 d, 6 c, 7 c, 8 a, 9 a, 10 d, 11 d, 12 c, 13 c, 14 c, 15 d, 16 b, 17 b, 18 d, 19 d, 20 a.

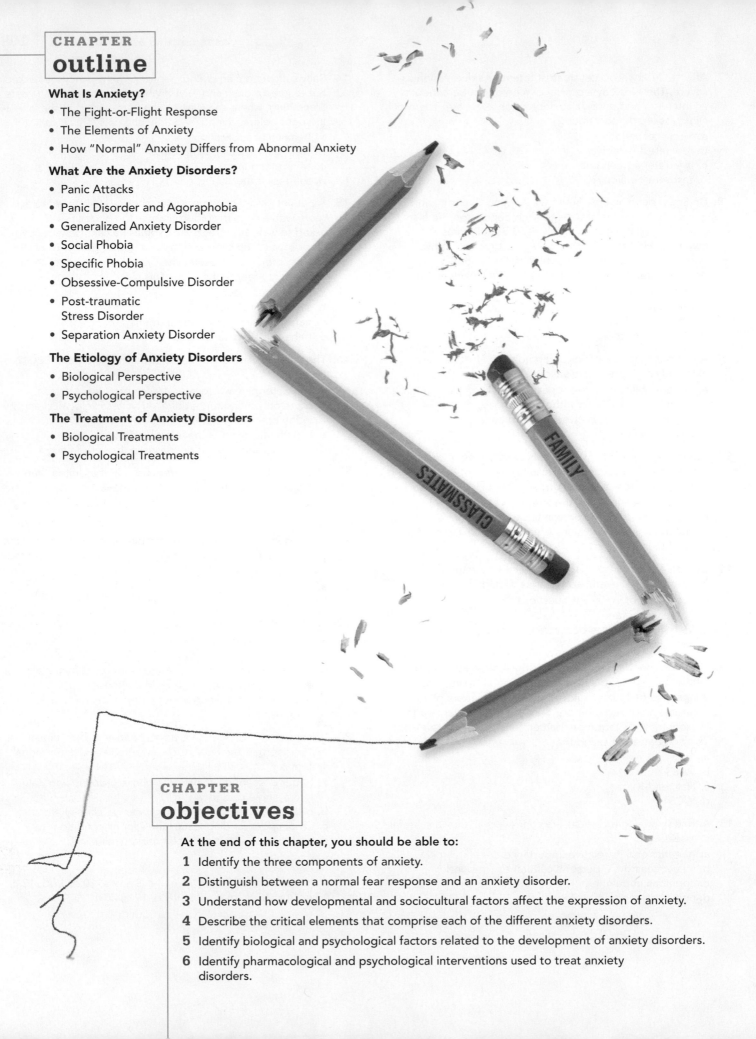

CHAPTER
objectives

At the end of this chapter, you should be able to:

1 Identify the three components of anxiety.

2 Distinguish between a normal fear response and an anxiety disorder.

3 Understand how developmental and sociocultural factors affect the expression of anxiety.

4 Describe the critical elements that comprise each of the different anxiety disorders.

5 Identify biological and psychological factors related to the development of anxiety disorders.

6 Identify pharmacological and psychological interventions used to treat anxiety disorders.

anxiety disorders

Greg is a third-year medical student about to begin his clinical training. Lately, he feels as if he cannot keep his head above water. His grades are still good, and he is looking forward to his clinical training, but he can't seem to shake the feeling that he just isn't doing well enough and that something serious is about to go wrong.

Greg was always a hard worker and very successful. As a child, he played sports, was in the band, and kept his grades high. He worried about whether he was doing well enough in school, whether his parents and teachers were pleased with his performance, whether his friends liked him, and whether he would become a doctor, but he was generally happy.

When he went to college, Greg started worrying more. College courses were more difficult, and he wanted to do well. Before big tests, he had trouble sleeping and sometimes found himself lying in bed, thinking over and over about whether he had studied hard enough. However, he did well on the tests and got into medical school. That next transition, though, seemed to set off a bigger set of worries. Medical school was extremely tough and very competitive, and Greg was worried that he would not do well enough to compete successfully for a residency. Now that he was going to be in the

hospital clinic treating patients, Greg was having even more trouble sleeping. Most nights, he had difficulty falling asleep, and he was sometimes awake for a few hours in the middle of the night, thinking about what he needed to do the next day. He noticed other worries popping up more often. He worried about his father, who was adjusting to a new job, and his younger sister, who was starting college and spending too much time socializing. He became more concerned about what his classmates thought of him. He began to have trouble concentrating. Perhaps because of his sleep problems, he was not paying attention in class, and he found himself needing to reread sections of his textbooks to make sure he understood the material. He also noticed that his neck and shoulders were tight—even painful at times—after long hours of hunching over books and worrying about grades. He became more irritated by his roommate, and he started to have a drink at the end of each day to take his mind off his worries and improve his sleep. However, this did not help: he continued to have trouble sleeping, and even though his last test scores were good enough, he was certain that his performance in the clinic would push him further down in the academic ranks.

Y ou can probably relate to aspects of Greg's distress. You may have had similar feelings on your first date, when you had to speak in public, or when you interviewed for a job. You worried about whether you would do well. Your heart raced, you felt tense, or perhaps your palms sweated. Maybe you had trouble sleeping the night before the event. All of these behaviors are typical of **anxiety**, a common emotion that is characterized by physical symptoms (faster heartbeat, feelings of tension) and thoughts or worries that something bad will happen.

What Is Anxiety?

Anxiety is a future-oriented response ("What if I mess up this speech? What if she does not like me?") and often occurs when people encounter a new situation or anticipate a life-changing event (starting college, getting married). In most instances, the anxiety that occurs in these situations is time-limited and leaves when the event is over. In some cases, however, anxiety spirals out of proportion to the actual situation; when this happens we say that a person suffers from an anxiety disorder. Before examining each specific anxiety disorder, it is first necessary to understand the nature of anxiety and a closely related emotion, fear.

THE FIGHT-OR-FLIGHT RESPONSE

You are walking in the park enjoying the solitude. You come upon two vicious-looking dogs that are fighting. You start to back away, but the dogs stop and come toward you. You know that you need to get out of there *fast*. Luckily, evolution has prepared you for this moment. Your *hypothalamus* (the part of your brain that is responsible for recognizing threatening situations and coordinating your response) sends a message to your *adrenal glands* to release the hormone *adrenaline*. You suddenly find yourself running faster and jumping higher than you ever thought possible. You did not even know that you could climb a tree, but you are doing it! Fortunately, the dogs soon get bored waiting for you to come down and they leave. Your body's response, called **fight or flight** was a general discharge of your **sympathetic nervous system** (SNS) (Cannon, 1929). The fight-or-flight response has been part of human behavior since prehistoric times (see Figure 4.1).

Your body's nervous system consists of two parts—the *central nervous system*, which includes your brain and your spinal cord, and the *peripheral nervous system*, which consists of all the other nerves in your body. The peripheral nervous system is further broken down into two parts—the *somatic sensory system*, which contains sensory and voluntary motor functions, and the *autonomic nervous system*, which controls involuntary movements. Finally, the autonomic nervous system also has two elements, the *sympathetic nervous system and the parasympathetic nervous system*. When activated by stress or fear, the SNS goes into overdrive. Your heart beats faster, supplying more blood to power the muscles. Your respiration rate increases, allowing more oxygen to get to your blood and brain. Whether it was prehistoric man trying to outrun a wooly mammoth or modern-day woman doing some fancy driving on an icy road to avoid careening off a bridge, this fight-or-flight response allows an optimal level of physical functioning in the face of threat.

Of course, such superhuman abilities are time-limited. After the SNS has been activated, the **parasympathetic nervous system** (PNS) returns your body to its normal resting state by decreasing your heart rate, blood pressure, and respiration. The fight-or-flight response is usually associated with the emotion that we call *fear*, a reaction to an existing or threatening event. The motivating power of fight or flight allows you to use all available resources to escape from a threatening situation. Some researchers have described this fight-or-flight reaction as an *alarm* to a present danger (Barlow, 2002).

anxiety   a common emotion characterized by physical symptoms, future-oriented thoughts, and escape or avoidance behaviors

fight or flight   a general discharge of the sympathetic nervous system activated by stress or fear that includes increased heart rate, enhanced muscle activity, and increased respiration

sympathetic nervous system   part of the autonomic nervous system that activates the body for the fight-or-flight response. When activated, the sympathetic nervous system increases heart rate and respiration, allowing the body to perform at peak efficiency

parasympathetic nervous system   part of the autonomic nervous system that counteracts the effects of system activation by slowing down heart rate and respiration, returning the body to a resting state

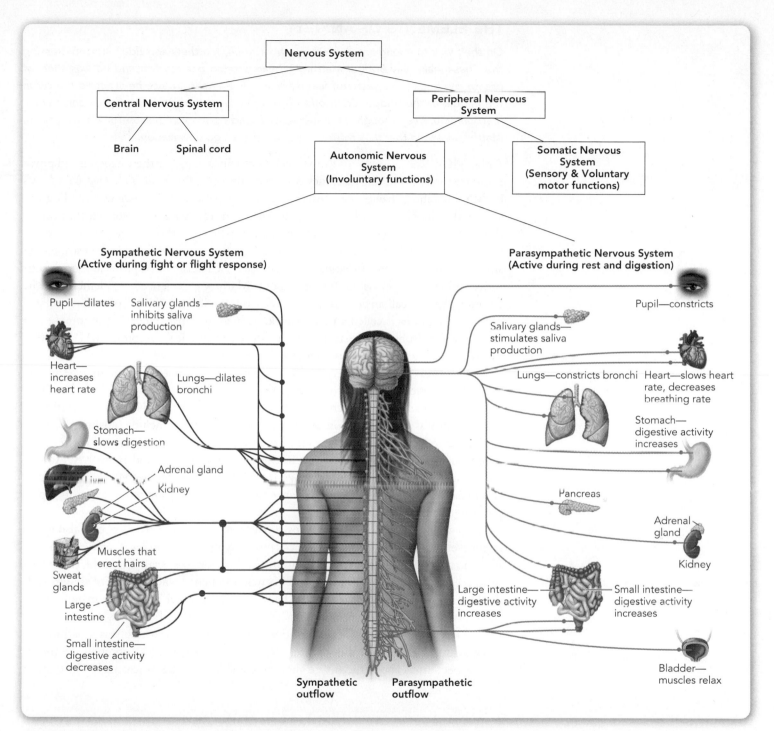

FIGURE 4.1

The Sympathetic and the Parasympathetic Nervous Systems

The sympathetic nervous system works to produce the fight-or-flight response, after which the parasympathetic nervous system returns the body to a normal resting state.

Adapted from Lilienfeld, et al., *Psychology: From Inquiry to Understanding* (p.121). Pearson/Allyn and Bacon. Copyright © 2009. Reprinted by permission of Pearson Education.

In contrast, anxiety, as we have already noted, is a future-oriented response and sometimes consists of lower levels of physical reactivity than the fight-or-flight response. Anxiety is also characterized by a thought pattern that is sometimes described as imagining the worst possible outcome. Anxiety is often present even when there is no real danger. In the next section, we examine the various components of anxiety.

THE ELEMENTS OF ANXIETY

On their way to a long-anticipated beach vacation, Matthew and Eden started crossing the Chesapeake Bay Bridge. Matthew's heart started beating fast and he was short of breath. He began to sweat and feel dizzy. Fearing a heart attack, he stopped the car in the middle of the bridge. Eden offered to drive but Matthew insisted that she call for medical help. Even though the paramedics found no medical reason for his symptoms, Matthew insisted that they return home rather than go on vacation.

Although he faced no obvious threat, such as a vicious dog, Matthew experienced physical symptoms, but in this case, they occurred unexpectedly or *out of the blue*. Matthew's body, mind, and behavior were affected by this experience. His *body* was sending out signals that he needed to leave (flee) the situation. His *mind* was worried that something was medically wrong, and so he called for help. Even though the paramedics said he was fine, he did not believe them. Because he felt so uncomfortable, he escaped the situation and went home (*behavior*), a place where he felt safe. The physical (body), cognitive (mind), and behavioral symptoms that Mathew experienced are elements of the emotion that we call anxiety. In Matthew's case, the intense "burst" of anxiety-related physical symptoms is called a **panic attack**, defined by a discrete period of intense fear or discomfort (subjective distress) and a cascade of physical symptoms (APA, 2000). We will return to panic attacks later in this chapter.

Emotions such as anxiety and fear have three distinct components (see Figure 4.2): physiological response, cognitive symptoms or subjective distress, and avoidance or escape. A panic attack such as Matthew's is a dramatic physical manifestation of anxiety, but it is not the only one. Other physical symptoms include blushing, buzzing or ringing in the ears, muscle tension, irritability, fatigue, gastrointestinal distress (indigestion, nausea, constipation, diarrhea), or urinary urgency and frequency. Among children, headaches and stomachaches (or butterflies in the stomach) are common complaints, although older children are more likely than younger children to report physical distress.

In addition to physical responses, anxiety includes subjective distress (also called cognitive symptoms). One type of cognitive symptom includes specific thoughts, ideas, images, or impulses. In some instances, the thoughts occur when the person affected sees a feared object or event, such as when someone who is afraid of spiders suddenly sees a spider ("What if that big hairy spider bites me?"). In other instances, the thoughts occur spontaneously ("What if I ran over a child when I was driving my car yesterday?"). A different type of cognitive symptom is worry, which was illustrated by Greg at the beginning of this chapter. **Worry** may be defined as apprehensive (negative) expectations about the future that are considered to be unreasonable in light of

panic attack a discrete period of intense fear or discomfort (subjective distress) and a cascade of physical symptoms

worry apprehensive (negative) expectations or outcomes about the future or the past that are considered to be unreasonable in light of the actual situation

FIGURE 4.2
The Three Components of Anxiety

Anxiety is considered to have three elements: physical symptoms, negative cognitions or subjective distress, and behaviors such as escape or avoidance.

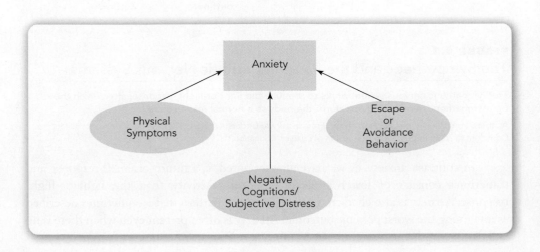

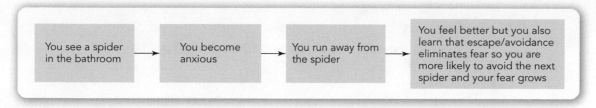

FIGURE 4.3

Negative Reinforcement Increases Avoidance Behavior and Anxiety

How feeling better can make your anxiety worse.

the actual situation. Consider Greg's worry. He always did well in school, and there was no reason to think that he would do poorly in the next part of his education. Yet he could not stop thinking about it—and his inability to stop his worry created emotional and physical distress. Worry exists among adults, adolescents, and some children. However, preadolescent children do not always report the thoughts and worries that are so commonly found in anxious adults (Alfano et al., 2006), perhaps reflecting their overall cognitive immaturity. Developmentally, young children do not yet have the ability to "think about thinking" (Flavell et al., 2001), a skill known as *metacognition*. Because of this difference, the cognitive symptom of worry is often absent in very young children. It appears only later, when children mature sufficiently to allow them to recognize and report their own thoughts.

The most common behavioral symptom of anxiety is escape from or avoidance of the feared object, event, or situation. A person who is afraid of elevators walks up the stairs. After the incident on the bridge, Matthew avoided driving. Avoidance can also take the form of overdoing certain behaviors. For example, fears of contamination may result in excessive behaviors such as washing or cleaning, designed to eliminate the feeling of contamination. Among children, unusual behaviors may be the first sign that a child is fearful. Children may play sick when it is time to go to school, cry, cling to a parent, or throw a tantrum. Some children are disobedient, refusing to follow instructions that involve contact with a feared event or object, even to the point of refusing to go to school.

Escape or avoidance behaviors bring temporary relief from distress, but they also reinforce behavioral avoidance through the process of negative reinforcement. Imagine that you are afraid of spiders. You see one in your bathroom and you run outside. You feel relieved because you are no longer in the same room as the spider. By running away, you removed a negative feeling of fear and you felt better. The feeling of relief that follows the removal of something negative is reinforcing; that is, this feeling increases the likelihood that the next time you see a spider, you will run away again. Therefore, eliminating distress by avoiding or escaping the situation can actually make the anxiety worse (see Figure 4.3). A primary goal of psychological treatment for anxiety is to reverse this pattern of negative reinforcement and eliminate avoidance of the feared situations.

HOW "NORMAL" ANXIETY DIFFERS FROM ABNORMAL ANXIETY

As we noted, it is normal to feel anxious from time to time, but when does *anxiety* become an *anxiety disorder*? The first factor to consider in making this decision is *functional impairment*. Remember Robert and Stan from Chapter 1? Before leaving home, both men walked through the house, checking to make sure that every door and window was locked and the oven was turned off. Robert did a quick 5-minute check, but Stan needed several hours to finish checking and as a result was sometimes late for work. Because his checking impaired his ability to get to work on time, Stan's behavior would meet the criteria for an anxiety disorder.

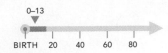

TABLE 4.1

Typical Fears at Different Developmental Ages

Age	Fears
Infancy	Loss of physical support
	Sudden, intense, and unexpected noises
	Heights
1–2 years old	Strangers
	Toileting activities
	Being injured
3–5 years old	Animals (primarily dogs)
	Imaginary creatures
	Dark
	Being alone
6–9 years old	Animals
	Lightning and thunder
	Personal safety
	School
9–12 years old	Tests
	Personal health
13 years and older	Personal injury
	Social interaction and personal conduct
	Economic and political catastrophe

Source: Ollendick et al., 1985.

A second factor that differentiates normal from abnormal anxiety is developmental age. Among children, fears are common, and they follow a developmental trajectory (Antony & Barlow, 2002). Two important aspects of the developmental model include the number and types of fears. The total number of fears declines as age increases. For infants and toddlers, so much of the world is new and initially scary that they are likely to have more fears. As illustrated in Table 4.1, different fears are also common at different ages (Barrios et al., 1981). As children mature physically and cognitively, they stop fearing loud noises (such as vacuum cleaners). They begin to understand that noisy things are not necessarily harmful. This *developmental hierarchy of fear* is not simply a matter of chronological age but involves cognitive development as well. When children are cognitively challenged (i.e., they may be 7 to 9 years old but have the cognitive ability of children ages 4 to 6), their fears usually reflect their *cognitive development*, not their chronological (actual) age (Vandenberg, 1993).

Sociodemographic factors (sex, race/ethnicity, and socioeconomic status) are a third consideration when differentiating normal from abnormal fears. In the general population, anxiety disorders are more common among females than males, sometimes at a ratio of 3 females to 1 male for any particular anxiety disorder. Why females report more fear than males is unclear, but it may reflect cultural and/or gender role expectations. Social acceptability may allow girls and women to *report* more fears, but they may not necessarily *have* more fears. For example, girls report more test anxiety than boys, but when physical symptoms (blood pressure and heart rate) are measured during an actual test, test-anxious boys and girls show equal increases (Beidel & Turner, 1998). Even though in the general population, more women than men report fears, the sex distribution is more equal among people who seek treatment. Therefore, when fears are severe, men and women are equally represented.

---

concept CHECK

- The fight-or-flight response is an activation of the sympathetic nervous system designed to allow the organism to fight off or flee from a perceived threat. In the case of anxiety disorders, this response may occur even when there is no real threat.

- Anxiety is usually considered to have three components: physiological reactivity (body), subjective distress/negative thoughts (mind), and escape or avoidance (behavior).

- In children, fears exist along a developmental hierarchy. At certain ages, fears are considered common and a normal part of development. At other ages, they are considered abnormal and in need of treatment.

APPLICATION QUESTION   Fears and anxiety disorders are more often reported by girls and women than men and boys. However, when placed in anxiety-producing situations, both sexes show equal physiological reactions. What societal factors might explain this difference?

What Are the Anxiety Disorders?

The **anxiety disorders** are a group of disorders that have in common the physical, cognitive, and behavioral symptoms described earlier. For each disorder, the anxiety is expressed in a different way or is the result of a different object or situation. Some people are anxious about public speaking, others do not like to fly on airplanes, and still others worry about contracting AIDS. Of course, some people are anxious in more than one type of situation, and in some cases they may have more than one anxiety disorder. The co-occurrence of two or more disorders existing in the same person (either at the same time or at some point in the lifetime) is called comorbidity. About 57% of people who are diagnosed with an anxiety disorder are comorbid for another anxiety disorder or depression (Brown et al., 2001). Therefore, although in the following sections we will discuss these disorders as distinct conditions, it is important to remember that often people who have one disorder may have additional disorders as well.

In the United States, 31.2% of adults suffer from an anxiety disorder at some time in their lives (Kessler et al., 2005), making these disorders one of the most common types among adults. Anxiety disorders are also common among children and adolescents, both in the United States and around the world. The prevalence of anxiety disorders among youth ranges from 8.6 to 15.7% (Costello et al., 2003; Essau, 2000). Most anxiety disorders develop early in life. The average age of onset is 11 years, one of the earliest for any psychiatric disorder (Kessler et al., 2005). Anxiety disorders occur with equal frequency across the three largest ethnic groups within the United States (Hispanics, non-Hispanic blacks, and non-Hispanic whites; Breslau et al., 2005). In addition to personal suffering, anxiety disorders compromise quality of life and social functioning (Mendlowicz & Stein, 2000), affect educational attainment (Kessler et al., 1995), and increase professional help-seeking and medication use (Wittchen et al., 1994). In addition to their serious and pervasive effect on the individual, anxiety disorders exert a substantial cost on American society. They produce a significant economic burden, costing society approximately $42.3 billion annually (Greenberg et al., 1999). Next, we examine the clinical picture of the various anxiety disorders.

anxiety disorders   a group of disorders characterized by heightened physical arousal, cognitive/subjective distress, and behavioral avoidance of feared objects/situations/events

PANIC ATTACKS

Remember when Matthew was driving across the bridge? He had a *panic attack*—a discrete period of intense fear and physical arousal. Panic attacks develop abruptly, and symptoms reach peak intensity in about 10 minutes (American Psychiatric Association [APA], 2000). Somatic and cognitive symptoms of a panic attack may include heart palpitations (pounding heart or accelerated heart rate), sweating, trembling, shortness of breath, choking, chest pain, nausea, dizziness, derealization or depersonalization (feelings of being detached from one's body or one's surroundings), fear of losing control or going crazy, fear of dying, paresthesias (tingling in the hands or feet), and chills or hot flushes. As many as 28.3% of adults have had a panic attack during their lifetime (Kessler et al., 2006), but just having a panic attack does not mean that you have a panic disorder or any other anxiety disorder. Although 28.3% of adults report having had a panic attack, only about 4.7% have panic disorder. Remember, in an anxiety disorder, the anxiety symptoms must cause distress or some form of functional impairment. Many people who have had a panic attack have had only one or a few and are not distressed or impaired by their rare occurrence.

When panic attacks are not isolated events, they may be a symptom of any of the anxiety disorders. Even though only a few anxiety disorders actually have the word *panic* in the title, panic attacks may be a symptom of another anxiety disorder, when a person is facing a frightening situation that is not a real threat to his or her physical well-being. A person who is afraid of snakes, for example, might have a panic attack if she sees a snake in a glass container at the zoo. In other cases, the anxiety reaction may be out of proportion to the object or situation. For example, you are flying and the airplane encounters mild turbulence, but you become very anxious and believe that you are going to die.

Panic attacks may be one of three types. *Situationally bound attacks* occur when a person confronts the feared object, such as when your friend who fears heights is suddenly confronted with the need to use a glass elevator. *Situationally cued attacks* occur in anticipation of a feared situation, as when someone with fears of public speaking has a panic attack a week before the speech. In other cases (such as Matthew's), the attack occurs unexpectedly, for no particular reason. People often say the attack came *out of the blue*. This represents the third type of panic attack, usually called uncued attacks. These uncued attacks are considered a *false alarm* (Barlow, 2002) because no object, event, or situation appears to precipitate the attack. Many times, people will misinterpret a panic attack as a heart attack and go to the hospital, which suggests just how frightening these symptoms can be. Yet, it is clear that panic attacks are common, occurring in people with various anxiety disorders and sometimes even in people who do not have an anxiety disorder.

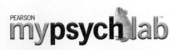

Panic Disorder

The Case of Jerry

"I was driving on an interstate. . . . And all of a sudden I got this fear."

www.mypsychlab.com

PANIC DISORDER AND AGORAPHOBIA

Panic attacks are the defining feature of two anxiety disorders: panic disorder without agoraphobia and panic disorder with agoraphobia. In **panic disorder without agoraphobia**, a person has had at least one panic attack and worries about having more attacks. The person also might worry about what a panic attack *means* ("am I developing a heart condition?" "am I losing my mind?") and may behave differently in response to the attacks, such as calling the doctor after every attack. Someone who has panic disorder without agoraphobia does not avoid situations (driving, shopping, getting on a bus) because of the fear that a panic attack might occur.

In **panic disorder with agoraphobia**, panic attacks are also a central feature. *Agoraphobia* (literally meaning "fear of the marketplace") is a fear of being in public places or situations where escape might be difficult or help unavailable if a panic attack occurs. People who have agoraphobia avoid public places, such as supermarkets,

panic disorder without agoraphobia a disorder in which the person has had at least one panic attack and worries about having more attacks

panic disorder with agoraphobia panic attacks combined with avoidance of places where escape (in case of a panic attack) may be difficult or impossible

DSM-IV-TR

Panic Disorder and Agoraphobia

Panic Disorder Without Agoraphobia   Recurrent unexpected panic attacks followed by 1 month of (a) persistent concern about having more attacks, (b) worry about the meaning of the attack or its consequences (e.g., losing control, having a heart attack, "going crazy"), or (c) a behavior change related to the attacks (going to a doctor's office or emergency room).

Panic Disorder With Agoraphobia   Recurrent unexpected panic attacks followed by 1 month of at least one of (a) persistent concern about having more attacks, (b) worry about the meaning of the attack or its consequences (e.g., losing control, having a heart attack, "going crazy"), or (c) a significant change in behavior related to the attacks (going to a doctor's office or emergency room) coupled with the presence of agoraphobia

Agoraphobia without History of Panic Disorder   The presence of agoraphobia related to fear of developing panic-like symptoms (e.g., dizziness or diarrhea) but the individual has never had panic disorder.

Adapted with permission from the *Diagnostic and Statistical Manual of Mental Disorders*, Text Revision, Fourth Edition, (Copyright 2000). American Psychiatric Association.

shopping malls, restaurants, churches, theaters, stadiums, riding in buses, cars, or planes, and traveling over bridges or through tunnels. Sometimes they are able to enter these situations but only with a trusted companion or by carrying certain items (such as a bottle of water) in case a panic attack occurs. In its most extreme form, people with agoraphobia may refuse to leave the house.

A related condition is **agoraphobia without history of panic disorder** (see the box "DSM-IV-TR: Panic Disorder and Agoraphobia"), where there is fear and/or avoidance of public places but the person has never had a panic attack. In these cases, the person fears the occurrence of incapacitating or extremely embarrassing physical symptoms such as dizziness or falling, losing control of the bowels or bladder, or vomiting (APA, 2000). Usually, these symptoms have never happened, at least not in public. Because people with this disorder rarely seek treatment, it has received very little attention from researchers.

In the general population, panic disorder without agoraphobia (3.7%) is the most common of the three disorders. About 1% have panic disorder with agoraphobia, and 1.4% have agoraphobia without history of panic (Kessler et al., 2005). Panic disorder is rare in young children and only slightly more common among adolescents. The disorder usually begins in early adulthood (McNally, 2001). More than 94% of people with panic disorder with or without agoraphobia seek treatment (Kessler et al., 2006). This is important because without treatment, symptom-free periods are rare. When a symptom-free period occurs, many people relapse within the year. Even with medication treatment, panic attacks often decrease in frequency but are not eliminated. Five years after receiving medication treatment, 85% of people no longer had *panic disorder*, although 62% still had occasional *panic attacks* (Andersch et al., 1997).

Women are more likely to experience panic attacks and panic disorder than men, and symptom variation exists across cultural groups. *Ataque de nervios*, discussed earlier in this book, is one example of a disorder that might be a cultural variant of panic disorder. Another is sleep paralysis, a condition that occurs more frequently among African Americans than whites (Paradis & Friedman, 2005). Sleep paralysis is a temporary state of paralysis experienced prior to falling asleep or upon wakening.

agoraphobia without history of panic
fear and/or avoidance of public places without any past occurrence of a panic attack

generalized anxiety disorder excessive worry about future events, past transgressions, financial status, and the health of oneself and loved ones

The person can open his or her eyes and is aware of the surroundings but otherwise cannot move (Cheyne, 2005). It is often accompanied by vivid and terrifying experiences called *hypnagogic* (the state between waking and sleeping) or *hypnopompic* (the state between sleeping and waking) hallucinations. Sleep paralysis often is associated with the presence of environmental stressors such as poverty or unemployment and is also more common among those with sleep disorders (see Chapters 12 and 14). Despite racial/ethnic group differences in its frequency in the United States, sleep paralysis appears to be a universal phenomenon, occurring in people from Guinea Bissau, the Netherlands, Morocco, and Surinam, among other places (deJong, 2005).

In addition to anxiety, people with panic disorder with or without agoraphobia often feel sad and depressed, in part because their anxiety limits their daily functioning (Stein et al., 2005), including the ability to work and socialize. About 50% of people with panic disorder rely on financial assistance either through unemployment, disability, welfare, or Social Security payments (Goisman et al., 1994). People with panic disorder and secondary (additional) disorders such as depression, eating disorders, and personality disorders may have suicidal thoughts or attempt suicide (Khan et al., 2002; Warshaw et al., 2000). Most researchers believe that the presence of the second disorder increases the likelihood of suicidal behavior.

GENERALIZED ANXIETY DISORDER

Greg, in the case that opened this chapter, illustrates the key feature of **generalized anxiety disorder** (GAD): excessive worry occurring more days than not and lasting at least 6 months. People with GAD worry about future events, past transgressions, financial matters, their own health and that of loved ones (APA, 2000). In addition to being out of proportion to the actual situation, the worry is described as uncontrollable and is accompanied by physical symptoms that include muscle tension, restlessness or feeling keyed up or on edge, being easily fatigued, difficulty concentrating, sleep disturbance, and irritability (see the box "DSM-IV-TR: Generalized Anxiety Disorder"). Cognitive symptoms include an inability to tolerate uncertainty (Ladouceur et al., 2000) and a belief that worrying may allow the person to avoid and/or prevent negative consequences (Borkovec et al., 2004). People with GAD often say, "I always find something to worry about," and they often have at least one other psychological disorder (Brawman-Mintzer et al., 1993; Bruce et al., 2001), usually another anxiety disorder or major depression. However, the worries of people with GAD are more severe, they complain more frequently of muscle tension, and they have lower levels of SNS arousal (Mennin et al., 2004) than people with other anxiety disorders. These factors often help clinicians decide whether someone has GAD or a different anxiety disorder.

People who face more real problems in living tend to have more reality-based anxiety than do people who live in more comfortable circumstances.

More adults than children have GAD (Wittchen & Hoyer, 2001), and the disorder most commonly starts in the late teens through the late 20s (Kessler et al. 2004). As Greg's case illustrates, GAD begins gradually and is usually a chronic condition. Even after pharmacological or psychosocial treatment, many people continue to have symptoms (Borkovec, 2002). Five years after it begins, 72% of people with GAD still suffer from the disorder (Woodman et al., 1999). Many people with GAD seek treatment from primary care physicians. In fact, up to 12% of people who seek treatment from their primary care physicians do so because of GAD symptoms (Wittchen & Hoyer, 2001).

DSM-IV-TR

Generalized Anxiety Disorder

Excessive anxiety and worry (apprehensive expectation) that is difficult to control, occurs more days than not and lasts for at least 6 months.

The worry encompasses many different events or activities (such as work or school performance, health, finances). Physical symptoms that accompany the worry include restlessness or feeling keyed up or on edge; being easily fatigued; difficulty concentrating; irritability; muscle tension; and sleep problems (difficulty falling or staying asleep, or restless unsatisfying sleep).

Adapted with permission from the *Diagnostic and Statistical Manual of Mental Disorders*, Text Revision, Fourth Edition, (Copyright 2000). American Psychiatric Association.

Many people suffer from GAD; prevalence estimates range from 5 to 10% of community and clinic samples (Maier et al., 2000; Wittchen & Hoyer, 2001). Among children, the prevalence is lower, affecting 3.6% of the general population (Bowen et al., 1990). Among children with GAD, feelings of tension and apprehension are common, as are a negative self-image and the need for reassurance (Masi et al., 2004). Children with GAD also have physical symptoms such as restlessness, irritability, concentration difficulties, sleep disturbance, fatigue, headaches, muscle tension, and stomachaches (Tracey et al., 1997). Adolescents report more physical symptoms than children, and headaches are more common among adolescents than young children (Tracey et al., 1997). GAD affects both sexes equally (Masi et al., 1999; Vesga-Lopez et al., 2008).

As with panic and agoraphobia, unexpected, negative, or very important life events are associated with the onset of GAD for both men and women (Kendler et al., 2003). When sociocultural factors are considered, GAD is more common among racial/ethnic minorities and people of low socioeconomic status (Kessler et al., 2004). It is important to remember that those with lower socioeconomic status may legitimately have more things to worry about (unsafe living conditions, lower income, poor health care, and therefore more medical conditions); thus, their worries may have a more realistic basis. Less certainty regarding the availability of basic necessities may play a role in the onset of GAD.

SOCIAL PHOBIA

The third most common psychiatric disorder in the United States (Keller, 2003), **social phobia** (also known as social anxiety disorder), is a severe fear of social or performance situations (APA, 2000). Social situations that create distress include speaking, eating, drinking, or writing in the presence of others, engaging in social interactions such as parties or meetings, and simply initiating or maintaining conversations (see the box "DSM-IV-TR: Social Phobia"). When in these situations, people with social phobia fear that others will detect their anxiety through their speech or behavior (forgetting a speech, mispronouncing a word, or shaking uncontrollably). Social phobia has two subtypes. The *nongeneralized or specific subtype* describes social fears that are limited to just a few social or performance situations (usually public speaking). People with the *generalized* subtype have fear in most social interactions (including public speaking, parties, and one-on-one conversation). Other differences also exist between the two subtypes; the generalized subtype is associated with more severe anxiety and depressive symptoms (Turner et al., 1992; Wittchen et al., 1999), an earlier age of onset (Wittchen et al., 1999), and a more frequent history of childhood shyness (Stemberger et al., 1995).

Social Phobia

The Case of Steve
"I imagine that people are watching me. They are watching me stumble in my efforts. . . ."
www.mypsychlab.com

social phobia a pervasive pattern of social timidity characterized by fear that the person will behave in a way that will be humiliating or embarrassing

DSM-IV-TR

Social Phobia

- A pervasive pattern of social timidity characterized by fear that the person will behave in a way that will be humiliating or embarrassing.
- The anxiety can become so intense that a panic attack may occur.
- Avoidance is not necessary for a diagnosis of social anxiety disorder—some patients engage in social encounters even though they experience significant emotional distress.
- In order for a child to receive this diagnosis, he or she must be capable of establishing age-appropriate friendships and the anxiety must occur when interacting with peers, not social relationships with familiar people, and the anxiety must occur in peer settings, not just in interactions with adults.
- Children may not have panic attacks but they may display distress by crying, tantrums, freezing, or shrinking from social situations with unfamiliar people.

Adapted with permission from the *Diagnostic and Statistical Manual of Mental Disorders*, Text Revision, Fourth Edition, (Copyright 2000). American Psychiatric Association.

In the introduction to this section, we noted that many people have more than one anxiety disorder. Over 50% of people with social phobia have additional anxiety disorders, such as GAD, agoraphobia, panic disorder, specific phobia, or post-traumatic stress disorder (Magee et al., 1996), as well as depression. Social phobia may substantially impair a person's ability to complete educational plans, advance in a career, work productively, and socialize with others (Zhang et al., 2004). People with social phobia often use alcohol to lessen their social distress, such as having a drink before a party, although there is little evidence that alcohol actually reduces anxiety (Carrigan & Randall, 2003). Even so, many people with both social phobia and alcohol dependence report that their substance abuse or dependence developed as a result of their attempts to reduce distress in social settings (Kushner, 1990).

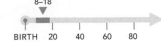

8–18

BIRTH 20 40 60 80

With an average age of onset between 11 and 13 years, social phobia is one of the earliest appearing psychological disorders (Kessler, 2003). Social phobia can be detected as early as age 8, and 8% of adults with social phobia report that their disorder began in childhood (Otto et al., 2001). When the disorder begins in childhood, it is not likely to remit without treatment. In fact, there is very little probability of spontaneous recovery when social phobia begins before age 11 (Davidson, 1993). Although social phobia rarely resolves without treatment, the symptoms may become better or worse depending on particular life circumstances. An episode of social phobia averages 18 years in length compared with 6 years for panic disorder and 1 year for major depression (Keller, 2003). However, more than 85% of those with social phobia recover with psychological treatment and remain symptom free 10 years later (Fava et al., 2001).

Approximately 3 to 4% of children and adolescents have social phobia (Beidel & Turner, 1998; Essau et al., 1999; Wittchen et al., 1999), as do 12 to 13% of adults (Kessler et al., 2005; Lecrubier et al., 2000). Even people who spend their lives in the public limelight can suffer from this disorder (see the box "Real People, Real Disorders: A Story of Social Phobia").

The situations feared by people with social phobia are similar regardless of age. Because social phobia is a chronic condition, its impact becomes more pervasive and creates significantly more dysfunction with age (see Table 4.2). This *negative developmental trajectory* begins in early childhood. If young children avoid social encounters with others, they are unlikely to learn appropriate social behaviors such as asking

real people, real disorders

A Story of Social Phobia

Many people know Ricky Williams as the Heisman trophy winning running back who had it all—fame, money, and talent. Selected as the number one draft pick out of college, Ricky created a media frenzy, making him a celebrity overnight. With a successful career underway, who would believe that this football sensation who plays for crowds of 100,000 dreaded the thought of going to the grocery store or meeting a fan on the street?

"I was 23, a millionaire and had everything, yet I was never more unhappy in my life," said Ricky Williams. "I felt extremely isolated from my friends and family because I couldn't explain to them what I was feeling. I had no idea what was wrong with me."

Ricky's fears escalated at the start of his professional football career in New Orleans. With high expectations to perform, Ricky was thrust into the limelight. Often portrayed by the media as aloof or even weird—he was known for conducting interviews with his helmet on and shying away from fans. He could barely interact with his young daughter or leave his house to do errands. What most didn't realize is that by simply talking to a reporter, a fan, a member of the community or even his own family, Ricky was struggling with the very root of his problem. Ricky later learned he was among the more than five million Americans who suffer from social phobia.

A Story of Social Anxiety Disorder: Ricky Williams, by Leslie Anderson. http://www.adaa.org/GettingHelp/Articles/RickyWilliams.asp. Reprinted with permission of the Anxiety Disorders Association of America.

others to play, making friends, and interacting in a socially appropriate manner. Because they are anxious and socially unskilled, they begin to avoid others and often are overlooked or invisible to their classmates. Avoidance leads to a vicious cycle whereby limited social abilities increase the likelihood of negative social interactions, which in turn increase avoidance, resulting in few opportunities to achieve important developmental milestones (e.g., dating, attending college).

Social phobia affects both sexes equally (Kessler et al., 2005), and within the United States, it occurs consistently across racial/ethnic groups (Bassiony, 2005;

TABLE 4.2

Developmental Differences in Distressful Social Situations

Social Situations	Children	Adolescents	Adults
Giving oral presentations	83%	88%	97%
Attending parties/social events	58%	61%	80%
Working in a group	45%	62%	79%
Initiating/maintaining conversations	82%	91%	77%
Dating	8%	47%	54%
Using public bathrooms	17%	30%	18%
Eating in the presence of others	16%	34%	25%
Writing in the presence of others	50%	67%	12%

Based on Rao et al., 2007.

Gökalp et al., 2001). A condition known as *taijin kyofusho*, found in Asian cultures, is sometimes considered a form of social phobia; it occurs most frequently among young men. Those with taijin kyofusho fear social interactions, but the underlying nature of the fear is different from that of social phobia (Kirmayer, 2001; Kirmayer et al., 1995). Whereas people with social phobia fear doing something that will embarrass themselves, people with taijin kyofusho fear offending and/or making others feel uncomfortable due to their inappropriate social behavior or perceived physical blemish/deformity. The focus on offending others may be based on Japanese culture, which emphasizes the importance of presenting oneself positively and the need for harmonious relationships and successful social negotiation (Kirmayer et al., 1995). Though found most frequently in Japan, the syndrome occurs in Korea and possibly other Asian countries (Chapman et al., 1995).

SPECIFIC PHOBIA

Ginny was a nurse who moved to the southeastern United States from Minnesota. She came to the clinic because she was about to quit her job and go back north. Ginny had rented an apartment, sight unseen, excited because she would be living on the intercoastal waterway. She had never seen "Palmetto bugs" (American cockroaches) before, but now she saw them on a daily basis, despite monthly exterminations. She was unable to sleep because she was afraid that a bug would crawl into her bed. She could not use the building elevator because there were bugs in it, so she walked up five stories even when carrying the grocery bags. Moreover, it was not just her apartment building—she saw the bugs everywhere. Despite having no job prospects in Minnesota, Ginny found that option preferable to "living with filthy bugs."

As Ginny's case illustrates, **specific phobias** (see the box "DSM-IV-TR: Specific Phobia") are severe and persistent fears of circumscribed events, objects, or situations that lead to significant disruption in daily functioning. A significant proportion of the general population admits to being fearful of something. You or someone close to you may be afraid of heights or snakes or flying or elevators. So when does a fear become a phobia? Two criteria determine when the term *phobia* should be applied to a specific fear. First, the symptoms cause significant emotional distress (even if one is able to do the task).

John had to give a presentation at a conference in a distant city, but he was afraid to fly. Since finding out about the presentation, he had not slept, worrying that the plane might crash. On the day that he was to leave for his trip, he was unable to eat. When he arrived at the airport, he was sweating profusely and his mouth was dry. He was exhausted by the time he arrived at the gate.

The second criterion is functional impairment.

John was not able to board the plane. His boss was very disappointed, and John was never asked to represent the company again. Soon John noticed that he was being "passed over" for promotions, which were being given to younger, less experienced workers.

Therefore, the answer to the question, "when does fear become a phobia?" is when it creates marked distress or impairs an aspect of life functioning.

Specific phobias usually fall into one of four groups: *animal phobias* (fear of animals or insects); *natural environment phobias* (fear of objects or events such as storms, heights, or water); *blood/injection/injury phobias* (fear of blood, injuries, or needles); or *situational phobias* (fear of situations such as public transportation, tunnels, bridges, elevators, flying, driving, or enclosed places; APA, 2000). Table 4.3 lists some common specific phobias among adults in the United States (Stinson et al., 2007).

specific phobias severe and persistent fears of circumscribed events, objects, or situations that lead to significant disruption in areas of functioning

DSM-IV-TR

Specific Phobia

- A severe fear that is excessive or unreasonable and occurs in the presence of, or in anticipation of, a specific object or situation.
- When in contact with the feared situation/object/event, anxiety occurs and may be so severe that a panic attack results.
- Children may express distress by crying, tantrums, freezing, or clinging.

Adapted with permission from the *Diagnostic and Statistical Manual of Mental Disorders*, Text Revision, Fourth Edition, (Copyright 2000). American Psychiatric Association.

People often have more than one specific phobia. Even though these disorders are severe and disabling, few people who suffer from them ever seek treatment unless the situation becomes extreme, as in the case of Ginny or John.

Animal phobias include fears of animals or insects. Ginny's case illustrates a phobia of cockroaches. Many children also exhibit animal fears.

Ronnie was 7 years old and had an extreme fear of dogs. He ran away whenever he saw a dog. Whenever he had to leave the house, he asked his mother if they might see a dog. He could not look at dogs in a pet store and turned off the television if there was a dog or a dog food commercial. The situation became so severe that Ronnie was refusing to visit his grandmother because her neighbor owned a dog.

Natural environment phobias include fears of objects or situations that are part of the environment. Situations such as heights or deep water are common, as are events such as electrical storms, hurricanes, or tornadoes.

Maura was 10 years old and had just moved to the Gulf Coast. Although she had never experienced a hurricane, she was terribly afraid that one would happen and would

TABLE 4.3
Percentage of Adults with a Specific Phobia

Type of Fear	Prevalence in the General Population
Insects, snakes, birds, or other animals	4.7%
Heights (tall buildings, bridges, or mountains)	4.5%
Storms, thunder, or lightning	2.0%
Being in or on the water	2.4%
Flying	2.9%
Being in closed places (cave, tunnel, or elevator)	3.2%
Being in a crowd	1.6%
Traveling in buses, cars, or trains	0.7%
Seeing blood or getting an injection	2.1%
Going to the dentist	2.4%
Visiting or being in the hospital	1.4%
Other specific objects or situations	1.0%

Adapted from Stinson F. S., Dawson D. A., Patricia Chou S., et al., "The epidemiology of DSM–IV specific phobia in the USA: results from the National Epidemiologic Survey on Alcohol and Related Conditions." *Psychological Medicine*, 37, 7, pp. 1047–1059, 2007 © Cambridge Journals, published by Cambridge University Press, reproduced with permission.

People who have phobias centered on the natural environment fear such things as storms, hurricanes, and tornadoes.

blow away her house. The television in Maura's room was constantly tuned to the Weather Channel so that she could monitor the potential for storms. She read the weather report in the newspaper every day. Her parents reported that she would not go outside on a cloudy day, fearing that a hurricane was developing. One evening, after hearing a report on hurricane preparedness, she counted the batteries in the house and concluded that there were not enough. She became hysterical and begged her father to go to the store that evening to get more, and he refused. Soon afterward, her parents took her to a psychologist for treatment.

Blood-injury-illness phobia is a common phobia, but it is different from other phobias in a significant way. Unlike other phobias in which associated physical responses reflect increased sympathetic nervous system activity, the characteristic response of blood-injury-illness phobias is dominated by parasympathetic activation. People with fears of needles, blood, or physical injury show **vasovagal syncope**, defined as *bradycardia* (slow heart rate) and *hypotension* (low blood pressure; Ost, 1996) that can lead to fainting (see Figure 4.4). The reason for this unusual physical response is unclear. It may be biologically determined, perhaps the remnant of an evolutionary response to a serious physical injury. When someone is injured, decreases in heart rate and blood pressure lead to decreased blood flow, which in turn enhances the person's chances of physical survival. This normal biological response is triggered inappropriately in those who fear blood or needles. This phobia can have serious consequences when it leads someone to avoid medical treatment.

Martha had a degenerative eye disease that if untreated by surgery would result in blindness. However, her fear of needles and injections was so intense that she had refused surgery; she even refused Novocain for dental procedures. She got dizzy and sweaty when she saw a needle and fainted on the only two occasions when she tried to give blood at the office blood drive. When she came to the anxiety clinic, she had already lost the vision in her left eye. She was seeking treatment for her phobia to save the vision in her right eye.

The fourth type of specific phobia is *situational phobia*. Fears of flying or enclosed places (sometimes called claustrophobia) are common situational phobias. John's fear of flying is an example of this phobia. Because people with agoraphobia also report fears and avoidance of certain situations, it is important to differentiate this disorder from specific phobias. People with a specific phobia are afraid of some aspect of the situation itself (e.g., having an accident while driving), whereas people with agoraphobia are afraid of having a panic attack while driving. Thus, although the physical and cognitive symptoms may be the same, the object or situation that precipitates the symptoms differs.

Specific phobia is a common anxiety disorder, affecting 12.5% of adults (Kessler et al., 2005) and 3.5% of children in the United States (Ollendick et al., 2004). It is also one of the most common disorders worldwide, affecting 4% of the general population in Mexico (Medina-Moira et al., 2005), 2.7% in Japan (Kawakami, et al., 2005), and 7.7% across six European countries (Belgium, France, Germany, Italy, the Netherlands, and Spain; ESMed/MHEDEA, 2004).

Most specific phobias develop during childhood, with an average age of onset of 7 years (Antony & Barlow, 2002; Kessler et al., 2005). Phobias are equally common among African Americans, Hispanic whites, and non-Hispanic white adults (Breslau 2006) and twice as likely to be found among adult women than adult men (Stinson et al., 2007). Specific phobias are more common among girls than boys and more common among young children than adolescents (Muris et al., 1999). Women account for between 74 and 90% of the adults with situational, animal, and natural environment phobias (Curtis et al., 1998). However, men and women are equally likely to fear heights and blood-injury-illness situations (Bienvenu & Eaton, 1998; Curtis et al., 1998).

vasovagal syncope a common physiological response consisting of slow heart rate and low blood pressure that sometimes occurs in people with blood-illness-injury phobias.

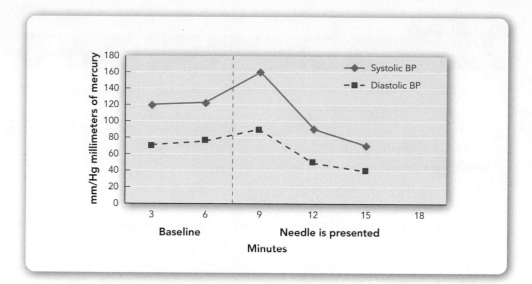

FIGURE **4.4**

Vasovagal Response in Blood-Injury-Illness Phobias

When in contact with blood, an injury, or the possibility of an injection, people with blood-injury-illness phobias may experience a physiological response known as vasovagal syncope. This sudden drop in blood pressure (BP) results in the person "feeling faint" or in actually fainting.

OBSESSIVE-COMPULSIVE DISORDER

Obsessive-compulsive disorder (OCD) consists of *obsessions* (recurrent, persistent, intrusive thoughts), often combined with *compulsions* (repetitive behaviors) that are extensive, time consuming, and distressful (see the box "DSM-IV-TR: Obsessive-Compulsive Disorder"). Obsessions are usually specific thoughts (e.g., "I will contract HIV if I touch a chair where an infected person sat"), but they may also be impulses (e.g., to jump off a high place) or images (e.g., stabbing a loved one). Defined as recurrent and persistent, obsessions are also intrusive, inappropriate, and often abhorrent, and they create substantial anxiety or distress (see "The Whole Story: Steve" at the end of this chapter). People with OCD recognize that their obsessions are the product of their own minds and not imposed upon them by someone else (as may occur in schizophrenia; see Chapter 10). Common obsessions include thoughts about dirt and germs (e.g., contracting cancer or another disease), aggression (a mother smothering her newborn baby with a blanket), failure to engage locks, bolts, and other safety devices (thereby putting an individual at risk for harm), sex (inappropriate sexual relationships such as molesting a child), and religion (thinking blasphemous thoughts).

Compulsions are the second part of OCD. They consist of repetitive behaviors that the person feels driven to do in response to obsessions or according to rigid rules (APA, 2000). Compulsions can be observable behaviors, such as repeatedly washing one's hands. They can also be unobservable, mental activities, such as silent counting. By completing the ritual, people with OCD feel that they can prevent their obsessions from becoming reality; "If I wash my hands for an hour, I won't get cancer." Compulsions are maintained by negative reinforcement. If you are afraid of contamination by "cancer germs," sanitizing your hands temporarily decreases the fear of contamination. Of course, that relief (removal of discomfort) temporarily feels good and increases the likelihood that the next time you feel contaminated, you will sanitize your hands again. In addition to hand-washing, common compulsions include excessive bathing, cleaning, checking, counting, and ordering possessions. Sometimes those with OCD are reluctant to discuss their obsessions and compulsions, even with members of their family. They perform their rituals in secret, often in the middle of the night. When the disorder is severe, the compulsions can dictate all of the person's activities.

More than half of people with OCD also have comorbid disorders such as depression, social phobia, specific phobia, GAD, and panic disorder (Antony et al.,

obsessive-compulsive disorder a condition involving obsessions (intrusive thoughts), often combined with compulsions (repetitive behaviors) that can be extensive, time consuming, and distressful

Obsessive-Compulsive Disorder

- This disorder is characterized by the presence of obsessions, compulsions, or both obsessions and compulsions.

- Obsessions are recurrent and persistent thoughts, impulses, or images experienced as intrusive and inappropriate, causing marked anxiety or distress.
  - They are not excessive worries about real-life problems.
  - Attempts to ignore, suppress, or neutralize them with some other thought or action is often futile.

- Compulsions are repetitive behaviors (e.g., hand washing, checking) or mental acts (e.g., counting, repeating words silently) that the person feels compelled to do as the result of an obsession, or according to rigid rules. The rituals are aimed at reducing distress or preventing some dreaded event/situation; however, they are not connected in a realistic way to the obsessions.

Adapted with permission from the *Diagnostic and Statistical Manual of Mental Disorders*, Text Revision, Fourth Edition, (Copyright 2000). American Psychiatric Association.

Obsessive/Compulsive Disorder:

The Case of Dave

"I knew in my heart of hearts that the water was turned off, but I had to go back and check it anyway."
www.mypsychlab.com

1998; Steketee & Barlow, 2002). Substance abuse may also coexist with OCD. Even when a comorbid disorder is present, the symptoms of OCD usually are most prominent and troubling. OCD is also often accompanied by a personality disorder (see Chapter 11); and in these cases, positive treatment outcome is less likely (Steketee & Barlow, 2002).

OCD is a chronic and severe condition that rarely remits without treatment. It usually begins between late adolescence and early adulthood (e.g., Nestadt et al., 1998; Rasmussen & Tsuang, 1986). Sometimes significant life events accompany the onset of OCD, including undesirable and uncontrollable events regarding health and bereavement (Khanna et al., 1988), accidents and serious mistakes (Rheaume et al., 1998), and pregnancy and childbirth (Wisner et al., 1999). Even when OCD begins in early adulthood, the person can often look back and see that elements of the disorder were present at an earlier age. When symptoms are present during childhood, OCD is more severe and results in greater impairment in daily functioning (Rosario-Campos et al., 2001; Sobin et al., 2000).

Among adults in the United States, the lifetime prevalence of OCD is 1.6% (Kessler et al., 2005), an estimate that is remarkably consistent across different countries (Weissman et al., 1994). Among children, prevalence estimates range from 1.9 to 4% (Geller et al., 1998; Valleni-Basile et al., 1994) and are consistent across world populations. It is important to understand that repetitive behaviors occur among people with psychological disorders other than OCD. For example, children with autism (see Chapter 12) often display repetitive behaviors such as spinning in a circle or flapping their hands. People with body dysmorphic disorder (see Chapter 5) have intrusive thoughts that center around their dissatisfaction with a body part, such as believing that their nose is very big and ugly. Because repetitive behaviors and intrusive thoughts exist in a number of different disorders, some researchers (e.g., Hollander et al., 2005; Stein, 2002) have proposed a diagnostic grouping called OCD spectrum disorders. In such a grouping, all disorders that included repetitive behaviors and intrusive ideas would be clustered together, regardless of whether they experience anxiety. In addition to OCD, autism and body dysmorphic disorder, OCD spectrum disorders would include other compulsive behaviors such as gambling, nail biting, and hair pulling (see the box "Examining the Evidence: Is Trichotillomania a Variant of OCD?"). At this

examining the evidence

Is Trichotillomania a Variant of OCD?

■ **The Facts** Trichotillomania (TTM) is defined as repetitive hair pulling that results in noticeable hair loss. People affected with this repetitive behavior pull hair from their scalps, eyelashes, eyebrows, and even pubic areas. Sometimes people with TTM wear wigs, scarves, and false eyelashes to cover the damage. They want to stop pulling but feel powerless to do so. TTM is sometimes considered to be part of a spectrum of obsessive-compulsive behaviors (Stanley & Cohen, 1999), but are TTM and OCD the same?

■ **Let's Examine the Evidence** TTM and OCD have a number of common features:

1. Both are characterized by repetitive behavior over which people feel a lack of control.
2. Hair pulling and compulsions in OCD both decrease anxiety.
3. Some people with TTM have obsessive thoughts about hair pulling, wanting hair to be symmetrical or free of aberrant hairs (that are too coarse, too short, or too wiry).
4. Both TTM and OCD are associated with high rates of coexisting anxiety and depressive disorders.
5. Higher rates of OCD occur in families of people with TTM.
6. Brain imaging studies have shown evidence of abnormal functioning in two areas of the brain, called the basal ganglia and the frontal lobe (see Chapter 2), in both TTM and OCD.
7. One antidepressant (clomipramine) and behavioral treatment are useful treatments for TTM and OCD.

TTM and OCD are different in many ways:

1. Hair pulling often occurs without focused awareness (i.e., people who pull often do so without paying attention to what they are doing); people with OCD are usually very focused on trying to reduce fears associated with obsessive thoughts.
2. Compulsions occur primarily in response to anxiety; hair pulling occurs in response to a wide range of negative moods (e.g., anger, boredom, sadness).
3. Hair pulling often produces feelings of pleasure; rituals do not.
4. Sensory stimuli (e.g., touching, feeling the hair) have an important role in hair pulling but not in compulsions.
5. Family members of people with OCD are more likely to have OCD than family members of people with TTM.
6. TTM is associated with lower rates of OCD symptoms and less severe anxiety and depression than OCD.
7. Serotonergic medications effective for the treatment of OCD do not work well for TTM.
8. Methods of behavioral treatment are quite different in TTM and OCD.

■ **Conclusion** TTM and OCD have some important common features and may share genetic influences. There may be a subtype of TTM that is very much like OCD, with hair pulling occurring in response to obsessive thoughts about hair. However, most studies suggest important differences in the clinical symptoms, neurobiological variables, and treatment procedures and responses for people with these two disorders. What factors do you think are most important in determining whether TTM is a form of obsessive-compulsive disorder?

time, however, OCD remains separate from these other disorders and in the category of anxiety disorders.

A small percentage of people with OCD have only obsessions or compulsions, but most adults have both. Among young children, rituals alone are common. Although adults clearly see that their rituals are responses to their obsessions, younger children usually do not know why they perform the rituals (Swedo et al., 1989). Furthermore, for children, it is important to view behavior through a developmental lens. Ritualistic behaviors alone do not automatically indicate that a child has OCD. Children with gastrointestinal diseases such as Crohn's disease and ulcerative colitis sometimes repeat certain behaviors, but these are the result of the self-care behaviors involved in their illnesses (Burke et al., 1989). As with fears in general, there appears to be a developmental trajectory for repetitive behaviors. Toddlers have many ritualistic behaviors (e.g., preparing for bedtime using a certain routine, eating food in a

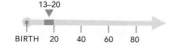

particular way, arranging stuffed animals, collecting or storing objects; Zohar & Felz, 2001). Over time, most children stop these behaviors because they lose interest in the activity. Only in certain instances do ritualistic and repetitive behaviors remain. As noted in Chapter 1, distress and functional impairment are important explanatory concepts for differentiating compulsions from "normal rituals." In comparison to children's typical ritualistic behaviors, compulsions develop at a later age, frequently persist into adulthood, are incapacitating and distressing, and interfere with normal development (King et al., 1995).

Men and women are equally likely to suffer from OCD, whereas among children, more boys than girls have the disorder (3:2 male-female ratio; Geller et al., 1989). In addition, boys develop OCD at a younger age and more often have another family member who suffers from the disorder (March et al., 2004; Tukel et al., 2005). The symptoms of OCD are similar across cultures, despite the fact that specific obsessions are sometimes culture-specific (e.g., fear of leprosy among those who live in Africa; Steketee & Barlow, 2002). Within the United States, some data suggest lower prevalence of OCD among African Americans than whites (Karno, 1988). However, this may indicate that African Americans may be more likely to seek treatment in traditional medical settings rather than mental health clinics. Repeated washing can result in severely rough and reddened skin, a condition known as contact dermatitis. People with this condition will seek treatment at a dermatology clinic rather than a mental health clinic (Friedman et al., 1995). However, because they often do not disclose why their skin is red and chapped, dermatological treatment is not successful. This delay in seeking appropriate treatment might explain why when African Americans patients are finally referred for psychological treatment, their symptoms are more severe (Chambless & Williams, 1995).

POST-TRAUMATIC STRESS DISORDER

post-traumatic stress disorder after an event that involved actual or threatened death, serious injury, or a threat to physical integrity, emotional distress leads to avoidance of stimuli associated with the trauma, feelings of emotional numbness, and persistent symptoms of increased sympathetic nervous system arousal

Post-traumatic stress disorder (PTSD) begins with a traumatic event such as military combat, assault, rape, or observation of the serious injury or violent death of another person. Later, when confronting events or situations that symbolize or resemble part of the trauma, such as a dark alley similar to the one where an assault occurred, the person may suffer an intense psychological and physiological reaction.

NORMAL BEHAVIOR CASE STUDY
A Scary Event—No Disorder

Last month, Jamal was driving in a snowstorm. The road was icy, and Jamal regretted his decision to drive in the storm. But he wanted to get home to his wife and young son. As he was driving down the highway, his car hit a patch of ice and he began to skid off the road—sideways at first and then in a circle. It was a terrifying few moments, and images of his son and wife flashed before Jamal's eyes. The car landed in a ditch. Jamal was banged up but otherwise safe. That night, after he got home, he was unable to sleep—he kept going in to see his son sleeping in his crib. The next morning, his heart was pounding when he started his car, and for a few weeks afterward, he felt tense every time he drove past that ditch. ■

ABNORMAL BEHAVIOR CASE STUDY
Post-Traumatic Stress Disorder

In 1968, Jerry was drafted into the Army. In Vietnam, after a day-long firefight, Jerry was shot. His injuries were severe, and although he does not remember much of what happened after the bullet shattered his thigh bone, he does remember feeling extremely cold when he received a blood transfusion. Upon returning home, he was in the grocery store and walked down the frozen food aisle. The cold from the frozen food aisle precipitated a flashback, and Jerry thought that he was in Vietnam again. Now Jerry avoids the grocery store at all costs. Every time he hears a helicopter, he "hits the ground." Jerry has not been able to work since he came home from Vietnam. ■

DSM-IV-TR

Post-traumatic Stress Disorder

- The person experienced, witnessed, or was confronted with an event or events that involved actual or threatened death or serious injury, or a threat to the physical integrity of self or others and responded with intense fear, helplessness, or horror.

- The traumatic event is persistently reexperienced through recurring intrusive distressing memories of the event, recurring distressing dreams about the event, acting or feeling as if the event were recurring, and intense physical and/or psychological distress when exposed to cues resembling part of the event.

- There is also persistent avoidance of stimuli associated with the trauma, numbing of general responsiveness, and persistent symptoms of increased sympathetic nervous system arousal.

Adapted with permission from the *Diagnostic and Statistical Manual of Mental Disorders*, Text Revision, Fourth Edition, (Copyright 2000). American Psychiatric Association.

A classic symptom of PTSD is *reexperiencing*, through recurrent and intrusive memories, thoughts or dreams about the trauma that occur repeatedly despite attempts to suppress them (see the box "DSM-IV-TR: Post-traumatic Stress Disorder"). The person suddenly acts or feels as if the event were occurring again. An interesting phenomenon in PTSD is that even though the memories can be intrusive (like the intrusive quality of obsessions), people sometimes cannot recall specific or important details of the traumatic event.

Another unique symptom of PTSD is *numbing*, which is an inability to feel emotions such as joy, surprise, or even sadness. People report a loss of interest in formerly enjoyable activities and a feeling of detachment from other people and the environment. They also describe a sense of a *foreshortened future* (a belief that they will not live a normal life span). Another common symptom is an overactive sympathetic nervous system, which creates a state of general and persistent arousal. This overarousal results in difficulty sleeping and concentrating, and creates emotional responses such as irritability or anger. In addition, people with PTSD report *hypervigilance* (a sense of being "on watch") and an *exaggerated startle response* (being easily startled).

Up to 92% of people with PTSD may have a comorbid psychological disorder, most commonly depression, other anxiety disorders, or substance abuse (Brunello et al., 2001; Perkonigg et al., 2000). Because PTSD is such a complex disorder with so many different symptoms, it is sometimes difficult to determine whether the sad mood or generalized anxiety is just part of the overall disorder or whether it represents a separate diagnosis. In either case, PTSD is one of the most difficult anxiety disorders to treat.

Because it begins with the occurrence of a traumatic event, PTSD can occur at any age (McNally, 2001). Among adults, it is usually categorized as either civilian PTSD or combat-related PTSD, depending on the event. Combat-related PTSD is usually more severe and less likely to respond to treatment. PTSD results in significant work impairment, with work productivity loss exceeding $3 billion per year (Brunello et al., 2001). It may also lead to reduced educational attainment, increased risk of bearing a child as a teenager, and more unstable marriages (Brunello et al., 2001). Approximately 6.8% of the adult U.S. population suffers from civilian PTSD (Kessler, 2005). The prevalence of combat-related PTSD is higher; up to 18.5% of veterans are diagnosed with PTSD (Hoge et al., 2007; Magruder et al., 2005; Seal et al., 2007; Tanielian & Jaycox, 2008).

Posttraumatic Stress Disorder

The Case of Bonnie

"I basically resigned myself to the fact that I was going to die."

www.mypsychlab.com

People who have developed PTSD as a result of experiences in war often find that their symptoms reemerge when they are confronted with stimuli reminding them of their initial trauma.

Historically, the onset of PTSD followed a life event defined as "out of the range of normal human experience" (combat, concentration camp imprisonment, natural disasters, assault or rape). More recent diagnostic criteria have expanded the list of "eligible" events to include many more human experiences, some of which are common (unexpected death of a loved one, serious illness in oneself such as cancer). Using these expanded criteria, one epidemiological survey reported that 89.6% of adults (92.2% of males and 87.1% of females) experienced a potentially traumatic event (Breslau & Kessler, 2001). However, despite almost universal exposure to a traumatic event, only 11.1% of the sample had PSTD. These different percentages illustrate a very important point: exposure to trauma alone does not automatically lead to PSTD. Events such as automobile accidents or the death of a loved one may result in temporary stress reactions (Keppel-Benson et al., 2002; Yehuda, 2002), but the typical response to a traumatic event is resilience, not PTSD (see the box "Research Hot Topic: 9/11—Trauma, Grief, PTSD, and Resilience").

Among children in the United States, the prevalence of PTSD is unknown because there are no controlled community investigations. Among German teens and young adults, 1% of males and 2.2% of females have PTSD (Essau et al., 2000). Among children actually exposed to a singular traumatic event (sniper shootings at school, earthquakes, boating accidents) estimates of PTSD range from 5.2 to 100% of those exposed (see Beidel & Turner, 2005). Prevalence estimates may vary because different investigators use different procedures (direct interviews of children vs. parent report, for example) to make the diagnoses. In addition, the emergence of PTSD depends on proximity to the event. The closer you are to the event, the more likely you are to develop PTSD. After an earthquake in Armenia (1988), for example, more children living at the earthquake's epicenter developed PTSD than did children living 50 miles away. One hopeful fact is that for many civilian traumas, PTSD cases decline with time (Yule et al., 2000).

Like the other anxiety disorders, symptoms of PTSD are different in children than in adults. Among children, reexperiencing may take the form of *traumatic play* in which the child reenacts relevant aspects of the traumatic event. However, it is important to avoid misinterpreting any behavior as indicating the presence of trauma or PTSD. Consider the following example. After the Oklahoma City bombing (1995), some children in the city built and destroyed buildings made of blocks (Gurwitch et al., 2002). Were all of these children suffering from PTSD? Developmentally, many children who have never been victims of bombings will build block buildings or sandcastles and then delight in knocking them down. Without knowledge of typical children's play, developmentally appropriate behaviors could be misinterpreted as indicating the presence of PTSD.

In addition to developmental differences in reexperiencing, other aspects of PTSD may differ by developmental age. Under age 6, bed-wetting, thumb sucking, fear of the dark, and increased difficulties separating from parents may be symptoms of PTSD, but they also occur in many children who have not been exposed to trauma (Fremont, 2004). Attentional problems, impaired school performance, school avoidance, health complaints, irrational fears, sleep problems, nightmares, irritability, and anger outbursts are common in children with PTSD, but they also occur in children with other disorders and sometimes in children with no disorder. Adolescents report symptoms more commonly found among adults: intrusive thoughts, hypervigilance, emotional numbing, nightmares, sleep disturbances, and avoidance. When a diagnosis of PTSD is a possibility, developmental factors must be considered.

Until very recently, PTSD among female military veterans was primarily the result of sexual assault or sexual harassment (Butterfield et al., 2000). However, the

After a trauma, children may engage in traumatic play, such as building a tower and knocking it down. However, engaging in this type of activity does not mean that a child was the victim of a trauma.

Research HOT Topic

9/11—Trauma, Grief, PTSD, and Resilience

As currently defined, many stressors qualify as traumatic events and could result in a diagnosis of PTSD. Stabbings, shootings, and murder are common occurrences among inner-city adolescents (e.g., Jenkins & Bell, 1994). Natural disasters such as hurricanes, floods, and tornadoes also occur frequently and increase stress. However, merely experiencing a potentially stressful event does not mean that you will develop PTSD.

As recent research on loss and trauma illustrates, up to 90% of Americans report exposure to a traumatic event during their lifetime, but only 5 to 11% develop PTSD (Breslau & Kessler, 2001; Ozer et al., 2003). Even though witnessing a traumatic event may result in brief PTSD or subclinical stress (think about your own response on September 11, 2001), for most individuals, these reactions disappear after a few months. Only a relatively small percentage of people exposed to a trauma actually develop PTSD. In the face of traumatic events such as the 9/11 terrorist attacks, the Oklahoma City bombing, or the Los Angeles riots, *recovery* (threshold or subthreshold psychopathology for a few months followed by a return to pretrauma levels) or *resilience* (maintaining a stable equilibrium in the face of the traumatic event) rather than PTSD was the predominant response (Bonanno, 2004). Researchers are now examining factors that predict (a) who will not recover, (b) what treatments are most likely to promote recovery, and (c) when those treatments should be applied.

What factors would you identify as important in the development of PTSD?

changing role of women in the military is likely changing the sex distribution of combat-related PTSD. Among civilian populations, some samples find that more females than males suffer from PTSD (Brunello et al., 2001), whereas others do not. Among women, about 50% of the cases of PTSD are associated with sexual assault (Brunello et al., 2001; Perkonigg et al., 2000).

There are also important sociocultural factors to consider when examining the prevalence of PTSD across racial/ethnic groups. As we noted in Chapter 1, after Hurricane Andrew devastated parts of Florida in 1992, African American and Hispanic children reported more traumatic distress than did white children (La Greca et al., 1996). However, as with many such differences, the important sociocultural factor may be socioeconomic status. After Hurricane Hugo in 1989, more African American than non-African American children reported fears but they also lived closer to the place where the storm came ashore. When demographic and proximity factors were controlled, the incidence of PTSD was not different (6.3 vs. 5.1%; Shannon et al., 1994). This highlights the importance of controlling for socioeconomic factors when investigating potential racial/ethnic differences in psychopathology. In many instances, it may not be the event itself but the ability to recover from the event that creates distress and precipitates the onset of PTSD. After a major hurricane, those with limited incomes have less ability to pay for needed repairs to homes and fewer personal resources to be able to start over. They are also more likely to work in minimum-wage jobs in businesses less likely to rebuild quickly after the storm. Therefore, group differences that appear to be based on racial or ethnic minority status may really reflect socioeconomic status.

SEPARATION ANXIETY DISORDER

Primarily affecting preadolescent children, **separation anxiety disorder** (SAD) is a severe and unreasonable fear of separation from a parent or caregiver. The child worries about being harmed or about a caregiver being harmed. Children may worry

separation anxiety disorder severe and unreasonable fear of separation from a parent or caregiver

DSM-IV-TR

Separation Anxiety Disorder

- Developmentally excessive and inappropriate anxiety concerning separation from an adult caregiver.
- Symptoms include:
  - Distress upon separation, persistent worrying about losing or harm befalling the caregiver
  - Persistent worry that an event such as a kidnapping will lead to separation from the caregiver
  - Reluctance to go to school or be alone
  - Reluctance to go to sleep without being near the caregiver
  - Repeated nightmares regarding themes of separation
  - Persistent physical complaints when separated from the caregiver

Adapted with permission from the *Diagnostic and Statistical Manual of Mental Disorders*, Text Revision, Fourth Edition, (Copyright 2000). American Psychiatric Association.

that they will be kidnapped or that a parent will be in an automobile accident or a plane crash. When the disorder is severe, the child may refuse to go to school or may not want to be physically separated from the parent, even at home. The child may insist on sleeping with the parent or may be unable to sleep overnight elsewhere. Children with this disorder will have nightmares with themes of separation. Physical symptoms often accompany the worry and most commonly include headaches or stomachaches.

About 3 to 5% of children may suffer from SAD (Silverman & Dick-Niederhauser, 2003), but many children recover within a short period of time (Foley et al., 2004). Girls are more likely than boys to report separation fears (March et al., 1997), and the disorder is more common among children than adolescents (Breton et al., 1999). White, African American, and Hispanic children are equally likely to suffer from SAD. In addition to refusing to attend school, children may refuse to attend social activities such as birthday parties or to participate in sports unless their parents accompany them and stay at the event.

Over the past 30 years, there has been continued speculation that childhood SAD and adult panic disorder may be developmentally different forms of the same disorder. Some adults with panic disorder report severe SAD when they were children. For some people, panic attacks begin after a major personal loss that results in separation (Klein, 1995). However, despite attempts to understand this relationship from different perspectives, the relationship between separation anxiety disorder and panic disorder is not clear (see the box "DSM-IV-TR: Separation Anxiety Disorder"). For example, although one longitudinal (4-year) study did not show a relation between SAD and the development of panic disorder in adolecents (Hayward et al., 2000), another longitudinal (4.5-year) study found that SAD in children predicted the later development of specific phobia, agoraphobia, panic disorder, and major depression (Biederman et al., 2007). When we use a developmental trajectory to understand these two different outcomes, it may be that SAD may precede the onset of many different types of anxiety disorders, and depression, not just panic disorder.

concept CHECK

- Panic attacks are defined as the presence of physical and cognitive symptoms of anxiety that occur suddenly. At least four symptoms must occur at the same time. Although the length of the attack may vary, it usually does not exceed an hour and is often much briefer. Panic attacks may be part of the clinical picture of any of the anxiety disorders.

- Panic disorder consists of sudden unexpected panic attacks accompanied by worry about when another attack will occur. When people with panic disorder begin to avoid places where they will be unable to get help, the avoidance is called agoraphobia.

- Specific phobias are the most common form of anxiety disorder. Although they may begin at any age, most specific phobias emerge during childhood. Specific phobias can create substantial functional impairment, but they respond well to psychological treatment.

- People with social phobia fear doing or saying something embarrassing in front of others. The most common age of onset for social phobia is midadolescence, although children also suffer from this disorder. Social phobia is one of the most chronic anxiety disorders, particularly when it occurs at an early age.

- The primary complaint among people who suffer from generalized anxiety disorder (GAD) is extensive worry about many different everyday events and activities, including finances, personal safety, health, future events, and past events. A range of physical symptoms is common; muscle tension is the most unique physical symptom of GAD relative to other anxiety disorders. GAD is a chronic anxiety disorder.

- Obsessive-compulsive disorder (OCD) affects people at any age and consists of obsessions (intrusive thoughts) and compulsions (ritualistic behaviors). OCD is one of the most chronic anxiety disorders and one of the most difficult to treat.

- When a traumatic event occurs, such as the September 11, 2001 attacks, stress reactions are common. For most people, this response is temporary, but a small number of people will develop post-traumatic stress disorder (PTSD), characterized by repeated reexperiencing of an event, numbing of emotional responses, and persistent autonomic arousal.

APPLICATION QUESTION Separation anxiety disorder primarily affects preadolescent children. Although the disorder may result in significant impairment, in many cases the condition is temporary in nature. What environmental factors or events might lead to the development of separation fears in young children?

The Etiology of Anxiety Disorders

How do anxiety disorders develop? As we saw in Chapter 1, Little Albert acquired a fear of a white rat after a series of conditioning trials in which the rat was paired with loud noises. This psychological model is very useful for understanding PTSD, which always develops after a traumatic conditioning experience. However, not every anxiety disorder can be traced back to a traumatic event, and not everyone who experiences a traumatic event develops an anxiety disorder. Just as people may fear many different objects or situations, anxiety disorders may develop in a number of different ways. In some instances, the cause is unknown. Biological and psychological causes have been identified, and the same disorder can develop in very different ways in different people. As will be evident at the end of this section, the biopsychosocial model may be the most comprehensive model of the etiology of the anxiety disorders.

BIOLOGICAL PERSPECTIVE

As we saw in Chapter 1, biological perspectives on abnormal behavior include investigations in genetics, family history, neuroanatomy, and neurobiology. Even when biological factors cannot fully explain the development of anxiety disorders, they may produce the vulnerability that "sets the stage" for other biological or psychological influences that can lead to the development of the disorder. Researchers have discovered several biological factors that play a role in the etiology of anxiety disorders.

Family and Genetic Studies   Are anxiety disorders inherited? These disorders do seem to run in families. Compared with relatives of people without a disorder, relatives (parents, brothers and sisters, aunts, and uncles) of someone with an anxiety disorder are also more likely to have an anxiety disorder (e.g., Hanna, 2000; Pauls et al., 1995). The same relationship occurs between parents and children. When a parent has an anxiety disorder, the child is more likely to have one, too (Beidel & Turner, 1997; Lieb et al., 2000). However, not every child in the family will develop anxiety; this means that genetics may play a role but does not provide the complete answer.

Twin studies also illustrate the role of genetics in the development of anxiety disorders. The concordance rate (see Chapter 2) for anxiety disorders among monozygotic twins (MZ) is twice as high as that of dizygotic twins (DZ) (34 vs. 17%; Andrews et al., 1990; Torgersen, 1983), but again, no specific gene or combination of genes have been identified. Another way to examine genetic contribution is through the concept of **heritability**, which is the proportion of variance in liability to the disorder accounted for by genetic factors. Heritability estimates have been reported for GAD (32%; Hettema, 2001), panic disorder (43%; Hettema, 2001), social phobia (20–28%; Kendler et al., 2001; Nelson et al., 2000), specific phobia (25–35%; Kendler et al., 2001), and obsessive-compulsive symptoms (27% to 47%; van Grootheest, 2005). One study of over 5000 twins (Hettema et al., 2005) revealed that one common genetic factor appears to influence GAD, panic disorder, and agoraphobia. A second genetic factor influences animal phobias and situational phobias. Social phobia appeared to be influenced by both genetic factors. However, all of the available genetic data indicate that genes do not tell the whole story. Given that none of the heritability estimates was 100%, environmental factors clearly also are important in the development of anxiety disorders.

The search for specific genes that influence vulnerability to anxiety disorders requires moving from twin studies to the newer area of molecular genetics. In mice, genetic influences for fear and anxiety have been found on 15 different chromosomes (e.g., Einat et al., 2005; Flint, 2002). In humans, studies have identified chromosomal *regions* that may be important, but specific *genes* have not yet been identified (Kim et al., 2005; Martinez-Barrondo et al., 2005; Olessson et al., 2005; Politi et al., 2006). Large studies of the entire human genome now underway may hold genetic keys to understanding OCD (Samuels, 2006) as well as other anxiety disorders, but the ultimate picture is likely to be a combination of several genes as well as environmental factors.

Based on the currently available data, what appears to be inherited is a *general vulnerability factor*, known as **trait anxiety** or anxiety-proneness (Hettema et al., 2001). Because these types of personality traits exist along a dimension, people can have different degrees of anxiety-proneness. Those high on this dimension are more "reactive" to stressful events and therefore more likely, given the right circumstances, to develop a disorder.

Carolyn and five of her friends were flying home from spring break. The plane flew through a thunderstorm, and wind shear caused the plane to drop suddenly and tilt at a 90-degree angle for approximately 10 seconds until the pilot regained control. The plane landed safely. Several months later, her friends wanted to fly to the Caribbean

heritability   the percentage of variance in liability to the disorder accounted for by genetic factors

trait anxiety   also called anxiety-proneness; a personality trait that exists along a dimension, with those high on this dimension being more "reactive" to stressful events and therefore more likely, given the right circumstances, to develop a disorder

but Carolyn declined. She was terrified to get on the plane. Despite their pleadings, Carolyn refused to go. Based on that one experience, Carolyn developed a specific phobia of flying.

Carolyn's case illustrates how anxiety-proneness might foster the development of fear. Even though all six women experienced the same environmental event, only Carolyn acquired a phobia. Perhaps Carolyn had a greater genetic vulnerability for the development of anxiety disorders.

Neuroanatomy Anxiety-proneness is a theoretical construct that is very useful in understanding the development of anxiety disorders. A *construct* is not something tangible; it only provides a frame of reference, such as the construct known as *free will*. Saying that someone is anxiety-prone does not explain what the abnormality is or where it is located. However, newly emerging CT, MRI, fMRI, and PET imaging data indicate that several areas of the midbrain are involved in anxious emotion. When someone is stressed, certain areas of the brain become more active, including the amygdala and the hippocampus (Uhde & Singareddy, 2002), as well as the limbic and paralimbic systems (Stein & Hugo, 2004). Because these neuroanatomical structures are important in processing emotion, they may also be involved in the development of fear and anxiety. For OCD, the orbital prefrontal cortex and the caudate nucleus are potentially important (Baxter, 1992). Using OCD as an example, we will illustrate how these brain regions may play a role in the onset of anxiety disorders.

Some OCD symptoms consist of impulses to blurt out words or the inability to control thoughts or behaviors. Neuroanatomical studies have shown that two regions, the prefrontal cortex and the caudate nucleus, make up a brain circuit that converts sensations into thoughts and actions (Stein, 2002; Trivedi, 1996). In fact, violent or sexual thoughts or impulses (often reported by people with OCD) appear to originate in the orbital prefrontal cortex. From there, the neuronal signals travel to the caudate nucleus, where normally they are filtered out. If they are not filtered out, the signals for these thoughts and impulses arrive at the thalamus, where the person experiences a drive to focus on the thoughts and perhaps to act on them.

From a scientist-practitioner perspective, this is a very interesting theory. Before we can accept it, however, we need a demonstration that brain activity in people with OCD is different from that in people with no disorder. One way to do this is to use *psychological challenge studies*. In this procedure, people confront objects or situations while PET methodology scans suspected areas of the brain for enhanced activity. In one study, when people with OCD and healthy controls were challenged (e.g., they were asked to touch "contaminated" objects), only people with OCD had enhanced brain activity in the orbitofrontal cortex, anterior cingulate, striatum, and thalamus areas (Trivedi, 1996). In other words, people with OCD responded differently when they touched these objects than did people without OCD. However, because the people already had OCD, we cannot know if this enhanced brain activity originally caused the disorder. Perhaps this activation exists only if the disorder is already present. Fully answering the question of etiology would require a longitudinal design. In one such study, we could define people at risk for OCD (perhaps a group that reacted with brain activation when touching contaminated objects but had no other OCD symptoms). We would assess this group on a regular basis for a few years to determine whether they later developed OCD. Another study might attempt to determine whether activation in these brain regions occurs only in people with OCD. Higher activation may

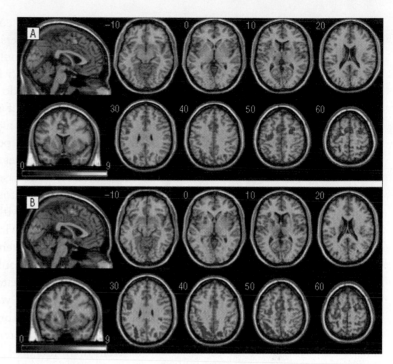

When engaged in a stressful mental task, people with OCD (panel B, below) show more areas of brain activity (shown by the red and yellow areas) than people with no anxiety disorder (panel A, above). fMRI studies help us understand how a psychological disorder, in this case OCD, influences, and is influenced by, brain functioning.

be common among people with many different anxiety disorders or even other types of psychological disorders. If the same brain activity occurs in people with many different disorders, then we could not conclude that it is a specific cause of OCD. Perhaps it is a general vulnerability factor for many different disorders.

Overall, there do appear to be differences in brain *functioning* between individuals with some types of anxiety disorders and those with no disorder. However, comparative studies examining brain *structures*, such as the size of the amygdala, do not reveal differences between people with anxiety disorders and healthy controls. Therefore, anatomical differences would not appear to be a factor in the development of anxiety disorders. In some cases, anxiety disorders may cause changes in brain function that then affect brain anatomy. Smaller hippocampal volumes have been consistently found in combat veterans with PTSD and in children who were sexually abused (Bremner et al., 1995, 1997; Gurvits et al., 1996; Stein et al., 1997). Although the full meaning of this important difference is not yet clear, this finding suggests that chronic environmental stress may result in neurochemical changes (brain functioning) that over time may change neuroanatomy (brain structure).

In Chapter 2, you learned that neurons in the brain use neurotransmitters—chemicals that exist throughout the nervous system—to carry messages from one neuron to another. Different neurotransmitters are primarily responsible for regulating different brain functions, such as movement, learning, memory, and emotion. The most consistently studied neurotransmitter is serotonin: it regulates mood, thoughts, and behavior and is considered to play a key role in anxiety disorders. Low serotonin levels in the cerebral cortex will prevent the transmission of signals from one neuron to the next, inhibiting the ability of the brain to effectively regulate mood, thoughts, and behavior.

What data support the hypothesis that serotonin is important in the anxiety disorders? First, compared with individuals with no psychological disorder, the cerebrospinal fluid (CSF) of people with GAD, panic disorder, PTSD, and OCD shows reduced levels of serotonin and its by-products. Although neurotransmitter levels in the spinal cord and the brain are not perfectly correlated, lower levels in the CSF suggest that these deficiencies may also exist in brain synapses (Stein & Hugo, 2004). Second, using a *biochemical challenge*, researchers give study participants a substance that alters their level of serotonin and analyzes how the biochemical change is related to increases or decreases in feelings of anxiety. Challenge studies help us understand how decreased serotonin levels may increase feelings of anxiety, but the results are not always consistent (Uhde & Singareddy, 2002). Third, medications known as selective serotonin reuptake inhibitors (SSRIs) *increase* serotonin in the neural synapses; people who are prescribed these medications report that their feelings of anxiety *decrease*. Working backwards, you might then conclude that less serotonin is related to increased anxiety. Together, all of these studies suggest that decreased serotonin at certain neural synapses is related to feelings of anxiety. However, many of the participants in these studies already had anxiety disorders, and that limits the conclusions that we can make. In order to conclude that low serotonin levels are a definitive cause of, rather than the result of, anxiety disorders, the studies would need to begin with people who did not have anxiety disorders and would have to manipulate the levels of serotonin in their bodies. Of course, it would not be ethical to conduct this type of study, which could deliberately create anxiety disorders in people.

Another neurotransmitter, gamma aminobutryic acid (GABA), inhibits *postsynaptic activity*; the reaction of the "receiver neuron" when a message is sent from one neuron to another. Reducing this postsynaptic activity inhibits anxious emotion. Thus, medications that allow GABA to inhibit postsynaptic activity more effectively are useful for the treatment of anxiety disorders (see the treatment section later in this chapter).

A substance called corticotrophin-releasing factor (CRF) also may be important for the development of anxiety disorders. CRF neurons are present in areas of the brain that regulate stress and process emotions (Heim & Nemeroff, 1999). When CRF is released

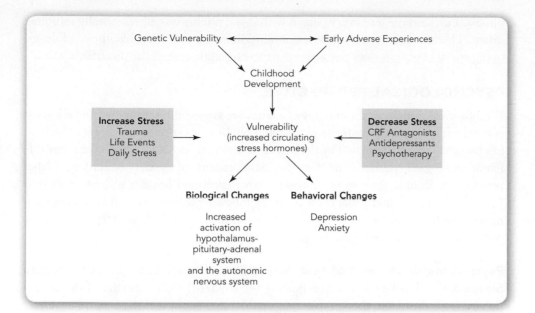

FIGURE 4.5
Stress May Affect Brain Functioning

Early adverse experiences can alter brain functioning, which may in turn increase the likelihood of developing an anxiety disorder.

Adapted from *Biological Psychiatry*, 46, Heim, C., & Nemeroff, C. "The impact of early adverse experiences on brain systems involved in the pathophysiology of anxiety and affective disorders." pp. 1509–1522, Copyright © 1999 Society of Biological Psychiatry with permission from Elsevier Science Inc.

by these brain areas, it stimulates production of chemical substances called adrenocorticotropic hormone (ACTH) and beta-endorphins. We know that when these chemicals are injected into the brains of mice, the animals behave in ways that suggest the presence of depression and anxiety. Similarly, when animals are placed in stressful conditions such as separation and loss, abuse or neglect, and social deprivation, they respond with heightened and persistent CRF activity in the hypothalamus and the amygdala (Heim & Nemeroff, 1999; Sanchez et al., 2001). These data suggest that early life experiences such as loss, separation, or abuse (environmental events) may change brain activity, making someone biologically vulnerable in the same way that genes produce vulnerability. In turn, when this chemical persists, overactivity persists (a biological contribution) and the person is at later risk for developing emotional disorders such as anxiety, and perhaps depression, depending on other biological or environmental contributors (see Figure 4.5).

Neuroscience offers exciting new ways to understand anxiety disorders. However, many challenges remain. Different technologies (CT, fMRI, SPECT, and PET) produce different images in the same brain region (Insel & Winslow, 1992; Trivedi, 1996). In addition, many studies compare people with anxiety disorders only to people with no disorder. This means that we can only conclude that healthy controls differ from people with an anxiety disorder. We cannot conclude that a particular brain abnormality is found only in people with anxiety disorders. To draw that conclusion, we would have to examine the brain activity of people with other types of disorders and determine whether people with other disorders (such as depression or eating disorders) did or did not have the same abnormality.

Temperament and Behavioral Inhibition Temperament describes individual behavioral differences that are present at a very early age, perhaps even at birth. **Behavioral inhibition**, a concept first proposed by Jerome Kagan (1982), is a temperamental feature that exists in approximately 20% of children. Children with behavioral inhibition withdraw from (or fail to approach) novel people, objects, or situations. They do not speak spontaneously in the presence of strangers, and they cry and cling to their mothers rather than approach other children to play. Children with behavioral inhibition are more likely to show anxiety reactions and are more likely to have childhood anxiety disorders, in particular phobias (Gladstone et al., 2005; Hayward et al., 1998). Behavioral inhibition, identifiable at 4 months of age, may be a unique risk factor for the later development of social phobia (Hirshfeld et al., 1992). However, this relationship is not absolute; not every infant with behavioral inhibition develops social

behavioral inhibition a temperamental feature characterized by withdrawal from (or failure to approach) novel people, objects, or situations

phobia. Furthermore, not every person with social phobia was a behaviorally inhibited infant. Therefore, although behavioral inhibition may increase the likelihood of developing social phobia, it does not account for every single case of the disorder.

PSYCHOLOGICAL PERSPECTIVE

Psychological theories of the etiology of anxiety are among the best known and the most researched. Most people understand fears and phobias by explanations that involve having previously been frightened by the object. A traumatic event is only one of many different etiological explanations for the development of anxiety disorders. Other perspectives include the role of individual experiences and broader influences such as family environment and social context. In the following section, we will examine explanations for the development of fear, based on established psychological theories such as psychoanalysis, behaviorism, and cognitive psychology.

Psychodynamic Theories of Fear Acquisition   The originator of psychoanalysis, Sigmund Freud, believed that free-floating (generalized) anxiety resulted from a conflict between the id and the ego (see Chapter 1). He thought that these conflicts resulted from sexual or aggressive impulses that overwhelmed the person's available defense mechanisms. Freud believed that the defense mechanisms of repression and displacement were operative in the development of phobias. A classic example of the psychoanalytic approach to the development of anxiety disorders is the case of Little Hans,

a 5-year-old boy born in nineteenth-century Victorian Europe. After watching a carriage-horse fall down and after playing horses with a friend who fell down, Hans developed a fear that a horse might fall down or bite him. This fear later extended to any horse-drawn vehicle, which he avoided at all cost. Hans refused to leave home when these vehicles might be present. Hans also was very concerned about his genitalia, fearing that his penis was not sufficiently large. His mother once told him not to touch his "widdler" or she would call a doctor to cut it off. Hans's father asked Freud for assistance. Using detailed information from conversations between Hans and his father (provided mostly by the father), Freud decided that Hans's fear and fixation on his genitalia represented his sexual feelings toward his mother, feelings that Freud called the Oedipus complex. Freud also noted that Hans was particularly afraid of horses with a black bit in their mouths, which Freud interpreted as a symbolic representation of his father's mustache. The horse, like Hans's father, was an object both admired and feared, and was obviously a rival for the affection of Hans's mother. Because he could not deal with them directly, Hans displaced all of these feelings onto horses, resulting in fear and avoidance.

Although there are many alternative theories explaining Hans's fears (e.g., classical conditioning, social learning theory—see Chapter 1), this case was extremely influential in the development of psychoanalytic theory in the early part of the twentieth century. Today, its overall influence has decreased markedly.

Behavioral Theories of Fear Acquisition   Conditioning theory has a prominent role in explaining fear acquisition, even though no single behavioral theory adequately accounts for the etiology of all anxiety disorders. Current behavioral theories are much more complicated than the story of Little Albert, the boy who learned to fear a white rat when it was paired with an aversive stimulus (see Chapter 1). The acquisition of fears through classical conditioning remains a primary explanation for the onset of anxiety disorders. However, classical conditioning theories cannot provide an explanation for all anxiety disorders, and thus, there are other behavioral explanations.

In addition to direct conditioning theory, people sometimes acquire fears through other forms of learning known as vicarious learning theory (see Chapter 1) and information transmission (Rachman, 1977). Consider the following example.

Justin has a fear of thunderstorms. He cries uncontrollably and hides in his closet whenever the skies darken. In a separate interview, his mother confided that she too had fears of thunderstorms, but never specifically told her son. Justin, however, told a different story. He knew thunderstorms were "scary" because Mommy would sit in a dark hallway whenever there was lightning and thunder. Clearly, without any traumatic event, Justin learned to fear thunderstorms.

Justin acquired his fear of thunderstorms just by observing his mother behaving fearfully. This process is known as *observational learning* or *vicarious conditioning*. Encouragingly, not everyone who experiences a traumatic event develops an anxiety disorder via direct conditioning. Remember Carolyn? She developed a fear of flying but her friends did not, even though they had the same experience on the plane. How does conditioning theory account for this difference? One explanation is that previous positive experiences with the same situation may protect against the later effects of a traumatic event. Positive experiences may provide immunity against anxiety disorders in the same way that a vaccination prevents children from acquiring the measles. Rhesus monkeys, for example, can be "immunized" against a fear of toy snakes (Mineka & Cook, 1986) by first observing other monkeys who were not afraid of a toy snake. Then, later when they saw monkeys who behaved fearfully in the presence of snakes, these "immunized" monkeys did not acquire the fear.

A third method by which anxiety disorders can occur is through information transfer, which means that a person instructs someone that a situation or object should be feared. Parents must instruct children about the dangers of crossing a busy street or the need to refrain from inserting objects (such as a knife) into an electrical outlet. When asked to report how their fears developed, a subset of children (39%) identified information transfer as the mechanism, as compared to direct conditioning (37%) and modeling (56%; Ollendick & King, 1991).

Current theories about the etiology of anxiety acknowledge that biological and psychological-environmental factors are both important elements. Contemporary models of learning theory acknowledge biological factors (genetics and temperament), environmental vulnerabilities (conditioning and social/cultural learning history), and stress factors (controllability and predictability of stressful events; conditioning experiences). All of these elements affect the quality and intensity of the conditioning event and therefore the anxiety and fear that develop as a result of the conditioning experience (Mineka & Zinbarg, 2006; see Figure 4.6).

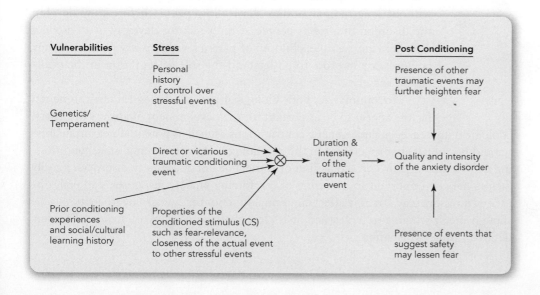

FIGURE 4.6

A Contemporary Theory of Fear Acquisition

Although early theories of learning did not adequately account for fear acquisition, revised models take into account the presence of biological and psychological vulnerabilities as well as environmental stressors that may be present before, during, or after the traumatic (conditioning) event.

Adapted from Mineka, S., & Zinbarg, R., "A contemporary learning theory perspective on the etiology of anxiety disorders: it's not what you thought it was." *The American Psychologist*, 61, 10–26. Copyright © 2006, American Psychological Association

Cognitive Theories of Fear Acquisition   As is the case with behavioral theories, there is no one cognitive approach to anxiety. However, all approaches assume that anxiety disorders result from inaccurate interpretations of internal events ("my heart is racing, I must be having a heart attack") or external events ("here I am giving a speech and my boss is yawning—I must be really boring"). Cognitive theories propose that people with anxiety disorders process information differently and this leads to the development of anxiety (McNally, 1995). Aaron Beck, perhaps the most dominant cognitive theorist, suggests that anxiety results from maladaptive thoughts that automatically interpret an ambiguous situation (e.g., I am short of breath) in a negative fashion (e.g., I must be having a heart attack; Beck & Emery, 1985). From a cognitive perspective, anxiety disorders develop because people misinterpret ambiguous situations as dangerous, resulting in physiological and cognitive distress. Because they never attempt to determine whether their beliefs are true, these negative thoughts maintain the presence of the disorder.

A second cognitive theory, and one relevant for panic disorder, is the *fear of fear* model (Goldstein & Chambless, 1978). This theory proposes that after the first panic attack, the person becomes sensitive to any bodily symptom and interprets any change in physiological state (e.g., a sudden heart flutter), as the signal of an impending panic attack (see Figure 4.7). This leads to a vicious cycle of worry, which then increases the likelihood of a panic attack and further increases worry. A third cognitive model is *anxiety sensitivity*, which is a belief that anxiety symptoms will result in negative consequences such as illness, embarrassment, or more anxiety (Taylor, 1995). Anxiety sensitivity is hypothesized to result from several factors, including previous panic attacks, biological vulnerability to panic, and personality needs (to avoid embarrassment or illness, or to maintain control). In this model, we see again how biology and learning interact to produce thoughts that lead to the inaccurate interpretation of future events.

Cognitive theories have evolved since their introduction 20 years ago, and most researchers now postulate that negative and/or distorted cognitions are important in the *maintenance* of anxiety disorders. There is less evidence that cognitions are the primary mechanism by which disorders initially develop. Models of panic disorder (fear of fear and anxiety sensitivity), for example, propose that an anxiety disorder develops when a person misinterprets the physical symptoms of a panic attack. However, these theories often do not adequately explain how those cognitive biases first came to exist. The specific contribution of cognitions to etiology is actually difficult to identify without longitudinal studies that follow people before they develop the disorder. Studies of people at high risk for developing an anxiety disorder (for example, children of parents with anxiety disorders) may be necessary in order to understand the role of cognition in the etiology of anxiety.

To summarize, both biological and psychological/environmental factors appear to be important for the development of anxiety disorders. Biological influences include genetic contributions as well as potential neurotransmitter and hormonal abnormalities. On the psychological/environmental side, conditioning experiences explain the acquisition of some, but not all, anxiety disorders. Family factors may be important in modeling or reinforcing anxiety responses, and environmental stressors may not only affect emotional functioning but also neuroanatomy. Although much remains to be learned, it is clear that the etiology of anxiety disorders defies a simple explanation.

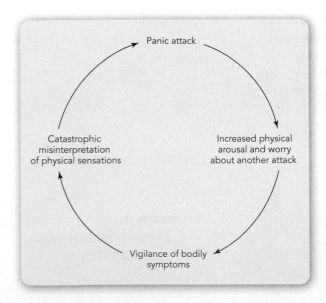

FIGURE 4.7

The Fear of Fear Model

After a panic attack, a person often worries about having another. This worry can create both physical and emotional arousal, which can result in overattention to normal physical symptoms. When these occur, they are overinterpreted as a signal of another panic attack.

- Biochemical theories regarding the etiology of anxiety disorders have investigated the role of many different neurotransmitters, but the strongest evidence exists for the neurotransmitter serotonin, which has an important role in the regulation of emotion.

- Twin and family studies support the role of genetics in the etiology of anxiety disorders although at the current time, the evidence suggests that an anxious temperament, not a specific anxiety disorder is most likely inherited.

- Strict psychoanalytic interpretations regarding the etiology of anxiety disorders have fallen out of favor.

- From a behavioral perspective, anxiety disorders may develop as a result of direct conditioning, observational learning, or information transfer.

APPLICATION QUESTION How do cognitive theories of the etiology of anxiety disorder differ from traditional behavioral theories?

The Treatment of Anxiety Disorders

There are several different approaches to the treatment of anxiety disorders, including biological, behavioral and cognitive-behavioral, and psychodynamic interventions. Psychodynamic theory is commonly applied in clinical settings but has not been the subject of much empirical research. In contrast, biological and behavioral or cognitive-behavioral approaches have substantial empirical support. All appear to be efficacious, resulting in remission rates of about 70% among those who are treated. In some instances, participants in research studies have a less complicated symptom pattern and do not have the comorbid disorders that are commonly seen in patients in nonresearch outpatient clinics. Because researchers are now only beginning to study how to implement the empirically supported treatments in traditional outpatient clinics, we do not know if these treatments are as successful when administered to people who have anxiety disorders together with other disorders, such as substance abuse.

BIOLOGICAL TREATMENTS

Today, biological treatments usually come in the form of medication, but, as we shall see, there are other treatments for anxiety disorders, including neurosurgery. You might recall from Chapter 1 that historically, somatic treatments consisted of bed rest, exercise, and work at simple tasks. Today, somatic treatments are based on modern knowledge of neuroanatomy and neurochemistry, allowing these interventions to target the brain directly.

Medication As we noted in the section on etiology, several anxiety disorders (panic disorder, GAD, PTSD, and OCD) are associated with the depletion of serotonin in the neural synapses, which in turn prevents the neurons from functioning properly. At the end of the presynaptic neuron are terminals that release serotonin into the synapse and other terminals that take the serotonin back up into the presynaptic neuron in a process called *reuptake* (see Figure 4.8). When the postsynaptic neuron receives enough serotonin, the neuron will fire, and the process continues. Without enough serotonin in the synapse, the signal does not pass to the next neuron as it should. One way to increase brain serotonin would be to stimulate the neuron to release more of the

FIGURE 4.8
How SSRIs Work

SSRIs block the neuron's normal reuptake mechanism, allowing serotonin to remain in the synapse and increasing the likelihood that it will land on the next neuron's receptor.

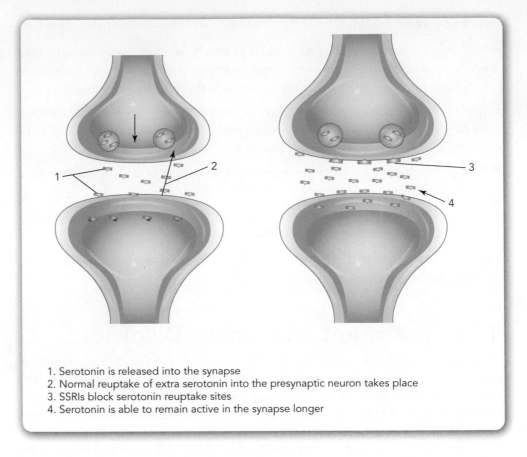

1. Serotonin is released into the synapse
2. Normal reuptake of extra serotonin into the presynaptic neuron takes place
3. SSRIs block serotonin reuptake sites
4. Serotonin is able to remain active in the synapse longer

neurotransmitter. An alternative is to block its reuptake, allowing the serotonin to remain in the synapse longer. Medications known as **selective serotonin reuptake inhibitors** (SSRIs) are thought to correct serotonin imbalances in this manner, by increasing the time that serotonin remains in the synapse.

SSRIs, such as Prozac, Luvox, and Zoloft, are now the biological treatment of choice for the anxiety disorders, with at least 40 studies demonstrating their efficacy compared with pill placebo. Positive treatment outcome has been demonstrated for panic disorder with or without agoraphobia (e.g., Pollack & Margol, 2000), social phobia (e.g., Stein et al., 2003), OCD (e.g., Marazzati et al., 2001), GAD (Rickels et al., 2000), and PTSD (Stein, 2000). The only exception is for specific phobia, for which there are no controlled studies (Antony & Barlow, 2002). Although the medications work better than placebo, they are not efficacious for everyone. Many people need to remain on these medications for an extended period of time and perhaps indefinitely, as relapse is common when the medication is withdrawn. Using these medications with children and adolescents requires extra caution. The Food and Drug Administration recently issued a warning regarding the possibility that among children, adolescents, and young adults with depression, SSRIs may increase the risk of suicidal thinking. Although no such increase has been reported in patients with anxiety disorders, children and adolescents should be monitored closely for the presence of any suicidal thoughts or plans.

GABA is another neurotransmitter that may be associated with anxiety disorders (Stein & Hugo, 2004), although the evidence is weaker for GABA than for serotonin. Drugs known as *benzodiazepines* (tranquilizers such as Valium and Xanax) allow GABA to transmit nerve signals more effectively, which in turn reduces anxiety. Benzodiazepines have efficacy for panic disorder with or without agoraphobia (e.g., Cross-National Collaborative Panic Study Second Phase Inves-

selective serotonin reuptake inhibitors drugs thought to correct serotonin imbalances by increasing the time that the neurotransmitter remains in the synapse

tigation, 1992), GAD (Rickels et al., 1993), and social phobia (Davidson et al., 1993). In the 1970s and 1980s, benzodiazepines were the treatment of choice for anxiety disorders, and they were prescribed quite freely. However, the drugs may cause physical and psychological dependence if they are used for a long period of time. These medications must always be withdrawn under a doctor's supervision because seizures may occur if the withdrawal is not done properly. Therefore, though efficacious, these medications are not considered the first choice for the treatment of anxiety disorders.

Psychosurgery   Before SSRIs and behavior therapy, OCD was considered to be resistant to treatment. As a last resort, surgery provided some relief of symptoms. In the past, surgery was imprecise, and the side effects included unresponsiveness, decreased attention, restricted or inappropriate affect, and/or disinhibition (inability to control emotion or behavior) (Mashour et al., 2005). Today, with the use of MRIs and the ability to destroy tissue with radiation (rather than needing to rely on surgery), there are many fewer side effects (although certainly no surgical procedure is without risk).

   Cingulotomy and *capsulotomy* are types of neurosurgery currently used to treat OCD. *Cingulotomy* is more common and involves inserting thin probes through the top of the skull into a portion of the brain called the cingulate bundle. The probes burn selective portions of the brain tissue (*Clinical Research News*, 2004). In *capsulotomy*, *gamma knife surgery* (a form of radiation treatment) makes precise lesions in brain tissue without the need for opening the skull. These surgeries are guided by the use of neuroimaging procedures such as MRI, allowing for surgical precision. Among people with OCD who were treated with cingulotomy, 45% of those unresponsive to pharmacological and behavioral interventions had at least a partial treatment response after neurosurgery (Dougherty et al., 2002). However, neurosurgery is only considered if the person with OCD has failed to benefit from medication and behavior therapy. Candidates for this surgery are always carefully screened because this surgery has risks, such as memory problems and personality changes. These negative outcomes occur less often than they did in the past because we now have more sophisticated neuroimaging and neurosurgery procedures (Dougherty et al., 2002).

Other Somatic Therapies   In addition to psychosurgery, new and potentially exciting interventions have been developed to treat anxiety disorders that are nonresponsive to traditional pharmacological and psychological treatments. These experimental procedures include transcranial magnetic stimulation (see Chapter 10) and deep brain stimulation (see Chapter 6). Although these treatments have shown promise (Mashour et al., 2005), many more research trials are needed before we can draw conclusions regarding their efficacy.

PSYCHOLOGICAL TREATMENTS

Psychological interventions were among the first treatments for anxiety disorders. Interventions are usually developed for adults and then adapted for children. However, in the case of anxiety disorders, some of the earliest case studies described successful treatment of children with phobias. Even so, today there is much more scientific evidence regarding the treatment of adults with anxiety disorders than there is with children. Below we describe psychodynamic and behavioral and cognitive-behavioral treatment for people of all ages.

Psychodynamic Treatment   Psychodynamic treatment uses free association and dream interpretation (see Chapter 1) as a reflection of the patient's experience in the outside world. As in the case of Little Hans, fears and phobias are considered merely signs of internal conflict. Treatment involves discovering and "working through" these conflicts. Some therapists still use psychoanalysis and psychodynamically oriented treatments to treat anxiety disorders. However, long-term psychodynamically oriented psychotherapy does not lend itself well to randomized controlled trial design. It is difficult both scientifically and ethically to assign someone to a placebo (i.e., no active treatment) or a wait list condition that would need to last a number of years. Therefore, we have little knowledge about the efficacy of psychodynamic therapy for the treatment of anxiety disorders. A review of controlled research examining psychodynamic psychotherapy (Leichsenring, 2005) revealed just two randomized controlled trials for anxiety disorders, only one of which reported a positive outcome. Modern adaptations of psychodynamically oriented treatments are now available and because they are briefer in length, they are more suitable for clinical trials. One form of psychodynamically oriented treatment is Interpersonal Psychotherapy (IPT; Klerman et al., 1984), which targets interpersonal disputes and conflicts, interpersonal role transitions, and complicated grief reactions (see Chapter 6 for an extensive description of this form of treatment). IPT has been tested in social phobia (Lipsitz, 1999) and PTSD (Bleiberg & Markowitz, 2005) with encouraging results. Larger controlled clinical trials are required before IPT can be recommended as a primary treatment for anxiety disorders.

Behavioral and Cognitive-Behavioral Treatment After 30 years of study, there are compelling empirical data that behavioral (BT) and cognitive-behavioral (CBT) interventions are the psychosocial treatments of choice for adults, adolescents, and children with anxiety disorders. There are many different forms of BT and CBT, but all incorporate a procedure known as **exposure** (i.e., facing your fears to get over them). For example, a person who fears dogs must have contact with a dog. Therapists make use of many different methods to provide exposure opportunities. For some fears, such as those of dogs or heights, exposure can occur through real-life experiences (called *in vivo exposure*). For other fears, such as being in a plane crash or becoming seriously ill from touching germs, conducting exposure involves instructing the person to imagine the feared event (*imaginal exposure*). To treat panic disorder, exposure therapy uses various exercises (e.g., running up and down the stairs) to create the physical symptoms of panic, such as shortness of breath and racing heart in the patient. In this way, the person is exposed to what he or she fears—physical symptoms associated with panic. Despite the seemingly simple nature of this treatment, determining exactly what the exposure situation should be, how long and how often it should occur, and who should conduct the sessions are all-important factors that contribute to its success. When done correctly, 70% of people with anxiety disorders show improvement (80% for specific phobia; Barlow, 2002; Compton et al., 2004). The only exception is combat-related PTSD, for which the rate is somewhat lower (Turner et al., 2005). Excluding combat-related PTSD, remission rates of 93% after 2 years and 62% after 10 years are common (Fava et al., 2001). Developing appropriate exposure situations has always been a challenge for therapists. New technologies such as virtual reality now allow therapists to expose people to commonly feared situations without having to leave their office (see the box "Research Hot Topic: Virtual Reality Therapy").

Sometimes the combination of exposure and other treatments enhances its effectiveness. Because people with social phobia avoid social interactions, they often do not have the basic skills needed for social communication (when it is a good time to talk to someone, how to be assertive without being aggressive). In this instance, social skills training (SST) is combined with exposure. SST teaches skills, usually conducted in a group setting, allowing for observation of the therapist, who models the skill, and then

exposure the crucial ingredient in behavior therapy, in which a person learns to overcome fears by actual or imagined contact with the feared object or event

Research HOT Topic

Virtual Reality Therapy

The most efficacious treatment for specific phobias is behavior therapy, in which the key component is exposure to the feared object, situation, or event. A person afraid of heights can be taken to a high place and can learn to lose this fear, using operant conditioning strategies (see Chapter 1). However, when the specific feared event is a plane crash, this event cannot be re-created. Therefore, therapists need an alternative means of exposure. Virtual reality is becoming a common tool for the treatment of certain specific phobias (heights, flying). The patient is fitted with a head-mounted display that has screens for each eye, earphones, and a device that tracks head, hand, and/or foot movements. When used to treat fear of flying (Rothbaum et al., 2002), scenarios consist of sitting in a passenger airline compartment during takeoff, flying in both calm and stormy weather, and landing. Noise and vibrations are added, as are voices of flight attendants, engine noises, and weather effects. Virtual reality therapy appears to be as effective as standard exposure treatments for phobias of heights and flying

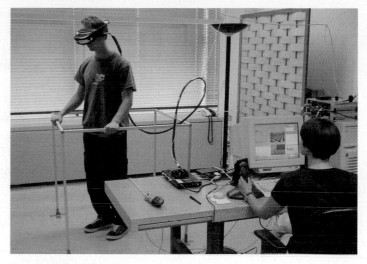

(see Rothbaum et al., 2002), and there is emerging evidence for social phobia and PTSD. With respect to the treatment of PTSD, virtual reality therapy is now being used to treat veterans returning from the conflicts in Iraq and Afghanistan.

practice with other group members, which allows for opportunities to rehearse skills in a safe, supportive setting.

Other treatments, such as relaxation training and cognitive-behavior therapy (CBT), can be combined with exposure to enhance treatment effects. *Relaxation training*, described in Chapter 1, may decrease general physical arousal and sometimes is the first step for the treatment of GAD. However, it is rarely used alone. A related intervention, *biofeedback*, combines the monitoring of physical behaviors such as blood pressure, pulse rate, or muscle tension, with relaxation training. The goal is to lower these levels of physical arousal by using relaxation. Feedback from the machines, in the form of signals that physical arousal is decreasing, provides cues that the person is being successful. It is believed that this feedback mechanism helps a person quickly learn what to do to lower his or her physical distress.

CBT combines exposure with cognitive restructuring in an attempt to change negative cognitions. In cognitive restructuring, a therapist asks the person to face an anxiety-producing event (a formal speech, for example) and to reflect on any negative thoughts that occur. For example, the thought might be "I'm going to mispronounce a word, make a fool of myself, and everyone will think I'm an idiot." The therapist then asks the person to enter the situation and see whether this "worst thing" actually happens. Of course, it does not happen. The therapist may also ask the patient to generate alternative positive or "coping" cognitions to counteract the negative thoughts; for example, "the audience knows that anyone can make a mistake—they will not see me as a complete fool." Over a series of exposure assignments, the patient's anxiety decreases and negative thoughts become less frequent.

Across all disorders, improvement rates for CBT, whether provided individually or in groups, average about 70% (e.g., Barlow, 2003). Despite what common sense would seem to suggest, more is not better. That is, combining behavioral and cognitive strategies does not seem to enhance their efficacy (Davidson et al., 2004; Hegel et al., 1994). Improvement rates remain in the 70 to 80% range. Reviews of the studies (Fairbrother, 2002; Rodebaugh et al., 2004; Zaider & Heimberg, 2003) that compare the impact of different treatment components (Hope et al., 1995; Salaberria & Echeburua, 1998), as well as statistical comparisons of different treatment outcome studies (Gould et al., 1997; Taylor, 1996; Wentzel et al., 1998), clearly indicate that exposure is the key ingredient. Other interventions may be used but do not necessarily increase response rates.

Combining BT or CBT with medication does not produce an enhanced effect in most instances. However, adding CBT to medication improves treatment outcome for patients with panic disorder who are treated in the primary care setting (Craske et al., 2005). BT and CBT have been used successfully to aid in benzodiazepine withdrawal for people with panic disorder (Otto et al., 1993).

concept CHECK

- Several different classes of medications are used for the treatment of anxiety disorders, but the first choice is the class known as the selective serotonin reuptake inhibitors (SSRIs).

- In addition to pharmacological treatments, other biological treatments for anxiety disorders exist. In severe cases of OCD, when behavior therapy and pharmacotherapy have been tried but were not efficacious, neurosurgical treatments such as cingulotomy and capsulotomy may provide some symptom relief.

- The combination of psychological and pharmacological treatments for anxiety disorders does not produce an outcome that is superior to either intervention when used alone.

APPLICATION QUESTION What is the common, and crucial, ingredient for behavioral and cognitive-behavioral therapy for anxiety disorders?

THE WHOLE STORY: STEVE—THE PSYCHOPATHOLOGY AND TREATMENT OF OBSESSIVE-COMPULSIVE DISORDER

The Person: Steve, age 20, was living in his parents' garage apartment. He was unemployed but occasionally worked odd jobs in his father's business.

The Problem: Steve washed his hands at least 30 times a day and had rigid behavioral rituals for showering, dressing, shaving, and brushing his teeth. If interrupted during a ritual, he had to start all over again. His morning ritual lasted over 3 hours each day. Steve was concerned that if he did not take care of his personal hygiene in exactly the right way, others would evaluate him negatively. To reduce his anxiety, Steve frequently checked his appearance in the mirror, glancing at his hands, clothing, and shoes to make sure everything was clean and neat. In total, he spent at least 5 hours a day doing cleaning and related checking rituals.

These symptoms took up so much time that Steve was unable to work. Furthermore, he was awkward in his social interactions. He had trouble carrying on a conversation, he fidgeted when he was talking to someone, and he was not able to look at people when interacting with them. When Steve came to the Anxiety Disorders Clinic, he spent most of his time alone.

Steve recalled that his parents also had problems with anxiety. As a child, Steve was shy, he worried a great deal, and had some rigid behaviors, such as keeping all of his stuffed animals in a very specific order. His obsessive-compulsive symptoms became a serious problem when he moved away from home to attend college. He sought treatment at the university counseling center, but weekly "talk therapy" just wasn't helping him. His grades continued to decline over three semesters, and he then moved back home.

The Treatment: Steve's treatment involved three major components: (1) a trial of medication; (2) behavior therapy to target OC symptoms; and (3) social skills training to improve his interpersonal functioning. He began treatment with a 3-month trial of an SSRI, which improved his mood. He was able to reduce the time spent doing daily rituals to 3 hours a day. He then began exposure and response prevention. His therapist created situations in which he felt "exposed" to negative evaluation while at the same time preventing the compulsions that he used. During exposure ses-

sions, Steve dressed in a way that he believed would produce negative evaluation from others (e.g., by choosing a shirt that wasn't a perfect match to his pants, "mussing" his hair slightly, pulling his tucked-in shirt up somewhat so that there was "extra" material showing, etc.) but would not make him look truly unusual. Steve was then asked to visit a public place (e.g., a bookstore, fast-food restaurant) where others would see him and to avoid "fixing" his appearance. At the start of each session, Steve's anxiety increased significantly. However, over the course of the session, his anxiety decreased, even when his appearance wasn't "perfect." Steve also was asked to begin reducing the time he spent at home with daily grooming. He and his therapist prepared a schedule with time limits. At the end of the time limit, Steve had to stop, regardless of whether he was pleased

with the result. Initially, this was extremely difficult. But with time, he further reduced the amount of time consumed with obsessions and compulsions. After another 3 months of treatment, Steve was able to get a part-time job working in a bookstore.

The third phase of treatment sought to improve Steve's social functioning. Using social skills training, Steve practiced making better eye contact, conversing more easily with strangers, and assuming a more relaxed body posture that put others more at ease.

The Treatment Outcome: As Steve's social skills improved, so did his mood. He made some acquaintances at work, and he even began to enjoy snack and lunch breaks with co-workers. Over time, Steve was able to increase his work hours, and he eventually obtained a full-time position as a manager in the bookstore.

CRITICAL ISSUES to remember

1. Anxiety consists of three components. The physiological components include sympathetic nervous system activation (e.g., cardiovascular and respiratory activation, gastrointestinal distress). The cognitive or subjective component consists of negative thoughts, impulses, or images and a subjective feeling of anxious distress. The behavioral component is defined by escape from or avoidance of objects, situations, or events that create anxious distress.

2. Anxiety is a common experience, and certain fears are common at various ages. However, to be considered an anxiety disorder, the fear or anxiety must cause significant distress and/or create functional impairment by interfering with common life activities.

3. A developmental hierarchy of anxious situations exists. This hierarchy is influenced by the child's cognitive maturity. Demographic factors such as gender, race/ethnicity, age, and socioeconomic status also influence the expression of anxiety. Women and girls seem to report fears at a rate much higher than men and boys, but sociocultural factors may also play a role.

4. There are different types of anxiety disorders. Some, like panic disorder with or without agoraphobia, consist of a fear of situations or places where escape may be impossible if a panic attack occurs. People who have agoraphobia without panic have fears and avoidance of the same situations or places, but they fear that physical symptoms such as nausea or gastrointestinal distress may occur. In the case of social or specific phobias, the anxiety is restricted to specific situations. Generalized anxiety disorder is characterized by pervasive worry about many different situations. People with obsessive-compulsive disorder suffer from intrusive thoughts and ritualistic behaviors that are distressing and difficult to control. After the occurrence of certain events such as a hurricane, rape, or other traumatic events, some people develop post-traumatic stress disorder, which consists of reexperiencing the event and physiological distress. Finally, separation anxiety is most commonly found in children and consists of anxiety surrounding separation from a caregiver.

5. Anxiety disorders develop in many different ways. Results of studies in molecular genetics, neurochemistry, and neuroanatomy are now allowing researchers and clinicians to make more advances in basic neuroscience and are providing unique insights into brain functioning. It is becoming clearer that anxiety and stress can alter brain chemistry and perhaps even some brain structures. In turn, these neuroanatomical and neurochemical alterations lead to the expression of anxiety disorders.

6. With respect to psychological etiologies, sometimes a conditioning experience takes place that clearly indi-

cates the etiology of the disorder. In most instances, however, the evidence is less clear, and a model that combines the influences of both biological and psychological/environmental factors may be the most appropriate.

7. Anxiety disorders are treatable. Pharmacological and behavioral/cognitive-behavioral interventions are both efficacious, but at this time combining them does not appear to provide any greater benefit. It is unclear whether other interventions also may be efficacious because they have not been subjected to empirical scrutiny.

TEST yourself

For more review plus practice tests, flashcards, and Speaking Out: DSM in Context videos, log onto www.MyPsychLab.com

 PEARSON mypsychlab™

1. The three elements of anxiety and fear are
   a. physiology, cognition, and behavior
   b. self-report, arousal, and worry
   c. worry, anticipation, and subjective distress
   d. escape, avoidance, and subjective distress

2. Sally was extremely apprehensive about her meeting next week with her boss to discuss her annual performance review, even though she had been doing well at work. She was experiencing excessive
   a. panic reactions
   b. compulsions
   c. worry
   d. phobic discharge

3. Sam has a spider phobia, and he has not gone to the woodshed since his wife complained of all the cobwebs in there. He has responded behaviorally with
   a. arousal   c. distress
   b. worry   d. avoidance

4. A normal source of anxiety for a 1- to 2-year-old child is
   a. loss of physical support
   b. strangers
   c. heights
   d. being alone

5. Which of the following is a major factor in distinguishing between normal anxiety and an anxiety disorder?
   a. developmental age
   b. functional impairment
   c. sociodemographics
   d. all of the above

6. Which of the following statements about anxiety disorders is *not* true?
   a. Most anxiety disorders develop in early adulthood.
   b. Comorbidity with depression and other anxiety disorders is common.
   c. Anxiety disorders are equally common among the three largest ethnic groups in the United States.
   d. Panic attacks may be a symptom of any anxiety disorder.

7. Heart palpitations (pounding heart or accelerated heart rate), sweating, trembling, shortness of breath, choking, chest pain, nausea, and dizziness are
   a. cognitive symptoms of panic attack
   b. behavioral symptoms of panic attack
   c. physiological symptoms of panic attack
   d. all of the above

8. Derealization or depersonalization (feelings of being detached from one's body or one's surroundings), fear of losing control or going crazy, and fear of dying are
   a. cognitive symptoms of panic attack
   b. behavioral symptoms of panic attack
   c. physiological symptoms of panic attack
   d. all of the above

9. Todd is afraid of flying. He is invited for a job interview that requires air travel. He has a panic attack while preparing for his interview a week before his flight. His panic attack is
   a. situationally bound
   b. situationally cued
   c. out of the blue
   d. uncued

10. Fear of being in public places or situations where escape might be difficult or help unavailable if a panic attack occurs is termed
    a. panic disorder
    b. social phobia
    c. generalized anxiety disorder
    d. agoraphobia

11. For the past year Mary has been experiencing uncontrollable worry about the future of her business, crime in the neighborhood, whether her husband truly cares for her, and her children's health. All of these concerns are out of proportion to the actual situation. She may be experiencing
    a. panic disorder
    b. agoraphobia
    c. generalized anxiety disorder
    d. social phobia

12. Stuart has never had a romantic partner. When he talks with his therapist, he says that he is afraid to ask anyone out because he becomes extremely anxious about initiating and maintaining conversations. He is likely to have
    a. panic disorder
    b. agoraphobia
    c. generalized anxiety disorder
    d. social phobia

13. Which of the following is not one of the four groups of specific phobias?
    a. agoraphobia
    b. natural environment phobia
    c. blood/injection/injury phobia
    d. animal phobia

14. Steve can't leave home without checking the doors and windows repeatedly to see that they are locked. When he finds that everything is locked, a sense of relief comes over him. Which of the following learning principles is likely to be maintaining his compulsive checking behavior?
    a. self-reinforcement
    b. negative reinforcement
    c. punishment
    d. positive reinforcement

15. Frank served in Iraq and fought in several difficult battles. Now, whenever he hears a car backfire, he jumps out of his chair thinking that he is under attack. Frank is showing a classic symptom of PTSD called
    a. lethargy
    b. reoccurring and intrusive memories
    c. reexperiencing
    d. behavioral disinhibition

16. Although PTSD affects people of all ages, sexes, and ethnic backgrounds, it is slightly different in children because
    a. symptoms such as bedwetting may be prominent
    b. the trauma may not be experienced firsthand, but through a significant other
    c. fewer traumatic events occur to children
    d. children engage in traumatic play

17. Parents go to a clinical psychologist asking about their child, who seems to worry all the time about being hurt. He refuses to go to school and won't sleep alone. On the way to school he often develops stomachaches or headaches. The clinical psychologist suggests that the child be evaluated for
    a. obsessive-compulsive disorder
    b. post-traumatic stress disorder
    c. separation anxiety disorder
    d. agoraphobia

18. The currently available data on the heritability of anxiety disorders suggest that
    a. a general vulnerability factor or anxiety proneness is what is inherited
    b. vulnerability to anxiety is likely to be controlled by a single gene
    c. genetic factors are only rarely involved in anxiety disorders
    d. four genetic factors are associated with GAD, panic disorder, and agoraphobia

19. Why do biological theories of anxiety disorders consider serotonin to be important?
    a. Serotonin is lower in the CSF of people with anxiety disorders
    b. Biochemical challenges that alter serotonin levels are related to increases or decreases in feelings of anxiety
    c. People who are prescribed selective serotonin reuptake inhibitors (SSRIs), which increase serotonin, report that their feelings of anxiety decrease.
    d. all of the above

20. The common ingredient in the most effective forms of behavioral and cognitive behavioral treatments of anxiety is
    a. exposure
    b. restructuring
    c. relaxation
    d. imagery

Answers: 1 a, 2 c, 3 d, 4 b, 5 d, 6 a, 7 c, 8 a, 9 b, 10 d, 11 c, 12 d, 13 a, 14 b, 15 c, 16 d, 17 c, 18 a, 19 d, 20 a.

CHAPTER objectives

After reading this chapter, you should be able to:

1 Understand how normal physical sensations can create abnormal concerns about somatic functioning.

2 Identify the contributions of biological, psychological, and environmental factors to somatoform disorders.

3 Understand the elements of dissociative experiences and the role of sociocultural factors in dissociative disorders.

4 Differentiate between the post-traumatic and iatrogenic models of dissociative identity disorder.

5 Understand the controversy surrounding repressed/recovered memories.

6 Differentiate somatoform, dissociative, and factitious disorders from the concept of malingering.

somatoform, dissociative, and factitious disorders

Lucy, who is married and age 50, feels awful. None of her doctors have helped her. About 10 years ago, she hurt her back while cleaning her house, and everything has gone "down hill" since that time. She has constant lower back pain and periodic neck pain despite operations to fuse together parts of her spine. Her left arm aches, but her doctor can't find a cause. She has numerous prescriptions for pain, including the powerful drug oxycontin. She complains of blood in her urine and pain during sexual intercourse.

Although her physician did not think it necessary, Lucy had a hysterectomy to reduce excessive menstrual bleeding. Despite this surgery, she recently called her gynecologist, worried that she had uterine cancer (even though her uterus had been removed). Now she believes that she has severe asthma and allergies. She has been taken by ambulance to the hospital emergency room for breathing treatments, and regularly uses two inhalers and three asthma medications. Yet allergy testing has revealed only moderate allergic reactions to pollen and dust mites. Several years ago, Lucy had extreme gastrointestinal pain. She complained of nausea, particularly after eating, and diarrhea. She sought out several physicians, but none could find anything wrong. After hearing that a friend had similar symptoms and had gall bladder surgery, Lucy convinced a physician that she too needed the surgery.

At the time of the psychological evaluation, Lucy had numbness in both legs. Her balance was affected, and she had difficulty walking. Last year, a niece was diagnosed with amyotrophic lateral sclerosis. Three physicians have told Lucy that she does not have amyotrophic lateral sclerosis, but she insisted on yet another MRI. Upon questioning by the psychologist, Lucy revealed contentious relationships with all of her family—her symptoms were always worse when she was fighting with her husband or her children.

Lucy's case is extreme, but we all have occasional aches and pains. In fact, 85 to 95% of the general population has at least one physical symptom every 2 to 4 weeks, and some people have unexplained symptoms as often as every 5 to 7 days (Katon & Walker, 1998). Common physical complaints include chest pain, abdominal pain, dizziness, headache, back pain, and fatigue, yet an organic cause is identified only 10 to 15% of the time. Clearly, many people have physical complaints for which there is no identified medical basis. Usually, physician reassurance that "everything is fine" allows people to resume their normal activities.

A few people, like Lucy, resist physician reassurance. Her case poses a challenge for health care professionals. How does one determine when physical symptoms result from psychological distress rather than organic illness? The answer is complex and requires consideration of three interrelated factors (Kirmayer & Looper, 2007). First, when are physical symptoms medically unexplained? Second, when is worry or distress about physical symptoms excessive? Third, when is physical distress considered to be caused primarily by psychological factors?

To answer the first question, physical complaints are considered to be medically unexplained when physical examination and diagnostic testing cannot determine any biological or physical cause. In Lucy's case, three different physicians could not diagnose her balance problems even when using the most sophisticated medical tests. Therefore, her symptoms were medically unexplained. To answer the second question, worry about physical health is excessive when it results in functional impairment or leads to medically unnecessary procedures (such as Lucy's gall bladder surgery). The answer to the third question, when does physical distress result from psychological factors rather than physical illness, is much more complicated. Its answer is the focus of this chapter. In fact, the interplay of physical symptoms, environmental stress, and emotional distress can create different types of psychological impairments known as somatoform, dissociative, and factitious disorders. We begin with the category of somatoform disorders.

Somatoform Disorders

Somatoform disorders are defined as conditions in which physical symptoms or concerns about an illness cannot be explained by a medical or psychological disorder (e.g., depression or anxiety). People who suffer from somatoform disorders experience real physical symptoms, but their physical pain cannot be fully explained by an established medical condition. The somatoform disorders can be a confusing diagnostic category because the individual disorders do not share an underlying emotion or a common etiology. Rather, all people with somatoform disorders are included in this category because of what is missing rather than because of what they have. Specifically, what the disorders share is the *lack* of a recognizable medical cause for their physical distress. There are six different somatoform disorders: somatization disorder, undifferentiated somatoform disorder, conversion disorder, pain disorder, hypochondriasis, and body dysmorphic disorder. Each is described in this section and in the box "DSM-IV-TR: Somatoform Disorders."

SOMATIZATION DISORDER

In 1859, the French physician Pierre Briquet (1796–1881) wrote an influential paper describing psychiatric patients with many somatic complaints that seemed to lack a physical cause. These patients were also likely to be depressed, and he noted that stressful life events could be particularly important in the onset and maintenance of their distress. This constellation of symptoms was once called *hysteria* or *Briquet's syndrome*, but

somatoform disorders conditions in which physical symptoms or concerns about an illness cannot be explained by a medical or psychological disorder

Somatoform Disorders

- **Somatization Disorder** Many varied physical complaints occurring over many years, resulting in numerous physician contacts and significant impairment in functioning. The symptoms cannot be explained by a known medical condition, or if there is a medical condition, the complaints and impaired function are excessive in nature.

- **Undifferentiated Somatoform Disorder** One or more physical complaints that cannot be explained by a known medical condition, or the symptoms/impairment are in excess of what would be expected from the medical condition. For example, a tension headache results in the need to stay in bed for 48 hours. The physical symptoms must last six months and must cause significant distress.

- **Conversion Disorder** Symptoms or deficits affecting voluntary motor or sensory function that suggest the presence of a neurological or medical condition. Onset or worsening of the symptoms is associated with psychological disorders, and the symptoms are not produced voluntarily. There is no general medical explanation, and the disorder causes distress or functional impairment.

- **Pain Disorder** Pain in one or more places in the body of sufficient severity that the person seeks clinical attention. The pain is not a function of a diagnosed medical condition, but causes clinical distress or functional impairment. Psychological factors are considered to have an important role in the onset, severity, maintenance, or exacerbation of the pain.

- **Hypochondriasis** Misinterpretation of bodily symptoms, resulting in a preoccupation with fears of having, or concern about having, a serious disease, despite the lack of medical evidence.

- **Body Dysmorphic Disorder** Preoccupation with an imagined defect in appearance or an excessive concern about a small physical defect. This preoccupation creates significant distress or functional impairment.

Adapted with permission from the *Diagnostic and Statistical Manual of Mental Disorders*, Text Revision, Fourth Edition, (Copyright 2000). American Psychiatric Association.

somatization disorder the presence of many symptoms that suggest a medical condition, but without a recognized organic basis

pseudoseizures sudden changes in behavior that mimic epileptic seizures but have no organic basis

these terms are no longer used because they carry negative connotations. Now known as **somatization disorder,** the condition is defined as the presence of many symptoms that suggest a medical problem, but have no recognized organic basis. As illustrated by Lucy, these physical complaints cluster into four categories (see Table 5.1). They do not necessarily occur at the same time, but all need to have been present at some time during the person's lifetime for the person to be diagnosed with somatization disorder.

Among all the symptoms presented in Table 5.1, the most frequently reported symptom is pain, including back pain (30%), joint pain (25%), arm or leg pain (20%), headache (19%), and abdominal pain (11%; Rief et al., 2001). Abdominal bloating (13%), food intolerance (12%), and heart palpitations (11%) are also common. Much less common but more dramatic are the *pseudoneurological* symptoms such as **pseudoseizures,** which are sudden changes in behavior that mimic epileptic seizures but have no organic basis (see "The Whole Story: Nancy" at the end of this chapter).

The diagnostic criteria for somatization disorder require that all four categories of symptoms must occur before age 30. In reality, symptoms often occur much earlier. In one sample, 55% of people suffering from somatization disorder had symptoms before age 15 (Swartz et al., 1991). Yet, even if somatization disorder begins in childhood, it often is not recognized until adulthood.

The French physician Pierre Briquet was first to identify a condition in which patients had many physical complaints without an obvious medical cause. This problem, once called Briquet's syndrome, is now called somatization disorder.

TABLE 5.1
Common Symptoms of Somatization Disorder

Category	Specific Complaints
Pain (in 4 areas of the body)	Head, abdomen, back, joints, and extremities. Pain during menstruation, urination, and sexual intercourse.
Gastrointestinal distress	Nausea, bloating, vomiting (when not pregnant), diarrhea, or food intolerance.
Sexual dysfunction	Disinterest, erectile dysfunction, ejaculatory difficulties, irregular menstruation, excessive menstrual bleeding, or vomiting throughout pregnancy.
Pseudoneurological	Impaired coordination, balance problems, paralysis or weakness, difficulty swallowing, aphonia (loss of voice), loss of feeling, blindness, deafness, seizures, amnesia, or loss of consciousness.

From APA, 2000.

UNDIFFERENTIATED SOMATOFORM DISORDER

Fortunately, few people have such varied physical complaints as Lucy, and somatization disorder is quite rare. Many more people have only a few, but very persistent, physical complaints, such as consistent nausea and stomach bloating. The symptoms are not explained by the presence of a medical condition and are not the result of an injury, substance use, or medication side effect. When such physical complaints are present for at least six months and cause distress or functional impairment, the person may be suffering from **undifferentiated somatoform disorder**. Although this disorder has the least specific diagnostic criteria, it is the most commonly diagnosed somatoform disorder (American Psychiatric Association [APA], 2000). It is considered a *residual diagnosis*, used when the person has long-standing and distressful physical symptoms that cannot be explained by a medical disorder or another psychological diagnosis (such as somatization disorder).

CONVERSION DISORDER

Somatization disorder and undifferentiated somatoform disorder are defined by the presence of different physical symptoms, including pseudoneurological complaints. A different somatoform disorder, **conversion disorder** consists solely of pseudoneurological complaints such as motor or sensory dysfunction. Symptoms of conversion disorder can be quite dramatic, such as sudden paralysis or blindness. They are not intentionally produced and cannot be fully explained by the presence of any medical condition (see "The Whole Story: Nancy" at the end of this chapter). Before assigning this diagnosis, a careful medical evaluation is necessary because about 10 to 15% of people originally diagnosed with conversion disorder will eventually be found to have a diagnosable medical condition (Binzer & Kullgren, 1998; Hurwitz & Pritchard, 2006). However, there is no way to determine which symptoms indicate a true neurological disorder. Therefore, therapists must strike a balance between excluding possible medical conditions and overdiagnosing and thereby reinforcing the behavior.

Symptoms of conversion disorder fall into three groups. The most common are *motor symptoms or deficits*, such as impaired coordination or balance, paralysis or weakness, difficulty swallowing, or a "lump in the throat," *aphonia* (loss of speech), or

undifferentiated somatoform disorder one or more physical complaints that are present for at least 6 months and cause distress or functional impairment

conversion disorder pseudoneurological complaints such as motor or sensory dysfunction

urinary retention. Within this group, muscle weaknesses, particularly in the leg, are most frequent (Krem, 2004). An unusual motor deficit is *globus hystericus*, which may include aphonia, sensations of choking, difficulty swallowing, shortness of breath, or feelings of suffocation (Finkenbine & Miele, 2004).

Hannah was a 28-year-old clerk at a car dealership. She had always been the "nervous" type and was very shy as a young girl. Sometimes when customers came in angry and complaining about their service, she started to feel a lump in her throat. She would put her hand up to her throat like she was choking, and when people asked if she was ok, she would gasp and say she couldn't get her breath. She would get more and more upset and was afraid she would suffocate. Sometimes the sensations would go away. At other times, Hannah would panic and call her doctor.

In many instances, globus hystericus goes away within a short period of time. However, if left untreated, it can lead to abnormal eating patterns or food avoidance.

Gina is 6 years old and has a history of fearful and inhibited behavior. She was referred by her pediatrician because she developed a fear of choking on food. Several weeks ago she was in a crowd of people and told her mother that she was choking. She was not, but her mother could only calm her down by taking her out of the crowd. Since that time, Gina has complained of a sore throat and an inability to eat solid foods. Gina's pediatrician ruled out any medical cause. This past week, her entire food intake consisted of milk, milkshakes, mashed potatoes, and yogurt.

Sensory deficits, a less common symptom group, include loss of touch or pain sensations, double vision or blindness, deafness, and hallucinations (APA, 2000). Movies sometimes portray people as having "hysterical blindness," but this condition is rarely documented. Also rare is the third symptom group, which consists of behaviors such as *seizures and convulsions.*

Symptoms of conversion disorder do not follow known neurological patterns, a factor that is often important in differentiating between a psychological or physical disorder. For example, a patient may complain of loss of sensitivity in the hand and wrist, a condition sometimes called *glove anesthesia* (see Figure 5.1). However, there is no anatomical combination of nerves in the hand and wrist that can explain this symptom pattern; this means that it is not a result of diseased neurons. The lack of a medical reason for this phenomenon suggests that the symptoms could have a psychological basis.

The classic description of conversion disorder includes a symptom called *la belle indifference* ("beautiful indifference"), defined as substantial emotional indifference to the presence of these dramatic physical symptoms. Even when unable to walk or move their arms, some people appear undisturbed by their paralysis. They deny emotional distress from their unusual symptoms and behave as if nothing is wrong. However, some people with conversion disorder are distressed by their symptoms (Kirmayer & Looper, 2007); thus la belle indifference, though often present, is not a necessary symptom of conversion disorder.

The label "conversion disorder" may seem to be an unusual term for a psychological disorder. If you recall the case of "Anna O" (see Chapter 1), you will remember that she had many symptoms of this disorder. Psychodynamic theorists, such as Freud and Breuer, theorized that Anna O was not directly expressing her psychological distress (the stress of taking care of her invalid father and his subsequent death). Instead, it was being expressed indirectly through physical complaints. Simply stated, they thought that her psychological distress was *converted* into physical symptoms. Although there is no strong empirical support for this theory, the term *conversion disorder* is still used to describe the presence of these symptoms.

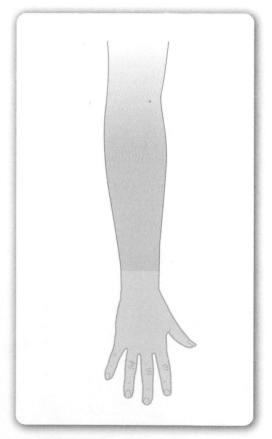

FIGURE 5.1
Glove Anesthesia

A person with conversion disorder might describe numbness in the entire hand or wrist, as shown here. However, this is not possible based on human neuroanatomy.

NORMAL BEHAVIOR CASE STUDY
Major Illness Reaction: No Disorder

Sharlene was diagnosed with breast cancer. She had surgery, radiation, and chemotherapy. About 6 months after she finished treatment, she felt a nagging pain in her upper back. It was not a sharp pain but a dull ache that would not go away. No matter what she did, the ache was there. Sharlene remembered that her mother, who died from breast cancer, had pain in her back too. It turned out that her mother's cancer had metastasized to her bones. Sharlene was worried, and the doctor ordered a bone scan. The results indicated that she did not have bone cancer. The doctor thought that the pain was the result of a muscle strain or injury. Sharlene felt better after she heard the results. Although the pain was still there and at times kept her from sleeping, she no longer worried about it. After a few months, the pain disappeared. ∎

ABNORMAL BEHAVIOR CASE STUDY
Pain Disorder

Margaret married right out of high school and did not have any special vocational skills. She recently divorced and had to take a job in a hospital cafeteria, and she hated it. On some days, she worked on the serving line—it was hot and her feet hurt from standing. On other days, she delivered food trays to patients—it was hard work and the patients did not seem appreciative. At work one day, she slipped and fell. Although the physician cleared her to return to work, Margaret reported severe and chronic pain in her lower back, and sometimes pain in her abdomen. An extensive diagnostic battery did not reveal any medical reason for her pain; yet it was so persistent that Margaret applied for disability. Her financial status was so negatively affected that she had to move in with her children. ∎

PAIN DISORDER

Pain, which is a common human experience, is frustrating to both patients and health or mental health professionals. Pain can contribute to the onset of psychological disorders or intensify conditions that are already present (Aigner et al., 2003). Margaret suffers from **pain disorder**, a condition characterized by persistent pain that defies medical explanation. Similarly, chronic pain may produce symptoms of depression, which further intensify feelings of pain (Verma & Gallagher, 2000). Distinguishing pain from pain disorder is necessary but not always easy to do. The person may have pain disorder if (a) the primary disorder is the presence of pain, not psychological symptoms such as low mood or anxiety, (b) medical problems do not exist, (c) the pain has lasted more than 6 months and affects the person's daily functioning, the person may have pain disorder. In some ways, pain disorder is similar to somatization disorder. However, somatization disorder has many different symptoms, but pain disorder consists solely of pain symptoms. Because the diagnosis is so difficult, and there are few empirical data on its symptoms and treatment, pain disorder will not be a primary focus of this chapter.

HYPOCHONDRIASIS

Have you ever read about an illness and then worried that you might have it? You may have mentioned your worry to someone who reassured you that you were fine, and so your worry disappeared. However, when fears or concerns about having an illness persist despite medical reassurance, the problem may be **hypochondriasis**. People with hypochondriasis do not necessarily suffer from physical symptoms. Rather, they have a dysfunctional "mind-set" that leads to worry about health, illness, and physical symptoms (Starcevic, 2006). They often elicit negative reactions from physicians because they cannot be reassured that they are well, and their behaviors are similar to the rituals found in obsessive-compulsive disorder (see Chapter 4). People with hypochondriasis constantly seek reassurance from physicians, spend time discussing their symptoms with family and friends, repeatedly check medical information sources, and monitor their own physical status (e.g., take their blood pressure). They also avoid situations associated with their fear (Taylor & Asmundson, 2004), such as refusing to go to a hospital for fear of catching an illness. These phobia-like behaviors have led some

pain disorder persistent pain that defies medical explanation

hypochondriasis fears or concerns about having an illness that persist despite medical reassurance

"But if you cure my hypochondria I won't have any hobbies."

experts to suggest that hypochondriasis should be renamed *health anxiety disorder* (e.g., Abramowitz & Moore, 2007), although currently the relationship of hypochondriasis to the anxiety disorders remains controversial.

Not all worries about illness warrant a diagnosis of hypochondriasis. Some people suffer from *transient hypochondriasis*, which may result from contracting an actual acute illness or a life-threatening illness, or even from caring for someone with a medical condition (Barsky et al., 1990b; Robbins & Kirmayer, 1996). Someone recovering from a heart attack may be reluctant to engage in physical activities, even though the physician has approved them. In contrast, people with traditional hypochondriasis have persistent fears of contracting an illness and are much more likely to have additional psychological diagnoses such as depression or an anxiety disorder. The high rate of comorbid anxiety and depressive disorders among people with hypochondriasis (perhaps as high as 78%) has led some clinicians and researchers to question whether hypochondriasis exists as a separate disorder (Robbins & Kirmayer, 1996). If the disorder does exist alone, it does so in only approximately 23% of people with hypochondriasis.

BODY DYSMORPHIC DISORDER

Also known as *dysmorphophobia*, **body dysmorphic disorder** (BDD) is an overwhelming concern that some part of the body is ugly or misshapen. Usually, if the concern is at all based in reality, it is an extreme exaggeration of a very minor flaw (e.g., a very small acne scar is described as a "huge crater on my face").

Amy is a 26-year-old Asian American woman who is convinced that her chin juts out terribly from the rest of her face. Actually an attractive young woman, Amy sees nothing but her chin when she looks in the mirror. She obsesses about how awful she looks—and what she believes others are saying behind her back. She is so distressed about her appearance that she refuses to go outside except to go to the store or see a doctor. When she goes out, she covers her chin with her hand and a tissue, actually making herself more noticeable to others. When at home, she checks herself in the mirror constantly. Each time, she hopes to see a different image staring back at her. But every time, all she sees is a huge chin, making her the ugliest person on earth.

Hypochondriasis

The Case of Henry

"I had a growth that I was worried about on my face."

www.mypsychlab.com

body dysmorphic disorder an overwhelming concern that some part of the body is ugly or misshapen

A patient with body dysmorphic disorder is convinced that some part of the body is ugly or misshapen. Worry about the "ugly" body part may become so intense that it approaches the point of a delusion.

Although any area of the body may cause concern, patients with BDD most commonly worry about their skin, hair, nose, and face, (e.g., size or symmetry of facial features, presence of wrinkles). Women with BDD are more likely to be preoccupied with their hips and their weight and more likely to pick at their skin and camouflage it with make-up. Unlike people with obsessive compulsive disorder and other anxiety disorders (see Chapter 4), people with BDD have very poor insight into their disorder. Sometimes their worry becomes so fixed and intense that it approaches the point of a *delusion* (e.g., a fixed but false belief that cannot be reasoned or argued away; see Chapter 10). Delusional beliefs were found among 36% of adults and 63% of adolescents in one sample of people with BDD (Phillips et al., 2006c).

People with BDD, especially those with delusional beliefs, are at high risk for suicide. In one sample, 78% considered suicide at some point during their illness, and 27.5% had a history of suicidal attempts (Phillips et al., 2005). These rates are at least 6 times higher than in the general population and higher than rates reported for people with schizophrenia or major depression. When followed prospectively for one year, 2.6% of people with BDD attempted suicide and 0.3% committed suicide (Phillips & Menard, 2006). There is a strong relationship between severity of suicidal ideation, severity of BDD symptoms, and functional impairment. People with the most severe symptoms and the most severe impairment are most likely to attempt suicide.

People with BDD are familiar patients in primary care, dermatology, and plastic surgery clinics. Up to 12% of dermatology patients and 16% of cosmetic surgery patients meet diagnostic criteria for BDD (Bellino et al., 2006; Thompson & Durrani, 2007). Even after undergoing dermatological and surgical treatment, they are rarely satisfied with the outcome (Phillips & Dufresne, 2002). In some instances, they focus on another "ugly" body part and begin the process all over again.

Like Amy, people with BDD frequently check their appearance to monitor changes. They often groom excessively or try to hide the offending feature. They may pick at their skin for hours each day, using their fingers, needles, pins, staple removers, razor blades, or knives to eliminate a blemish or scar (Phillips & Taub, 1995). The person's belief that he or she is ugly or has a physical deformity leads to occupational, social, and academic impairment. Concerns about appearance in BDD have some overlap with obsessions, leading to the suggestion that BDD is part of the obsessive compulsive spectrum disorders discussed in Chapter 4.

COMMON FACTORS IN SOMATOFORM DISORDERS

Despite individual differences in symptoms, all somatoform disorders share certain features. Approximately 33 to 40% of people with a somatoform disorder also have co-existing anxiety and/or depressive disorders (Barsky et al., 2005; Creed & Barsky, 2004; Krem, 2004; Phillips & Dufrense, 2002). Even among children, comorbid anxiety and mood disorders are common (Kozlowska et al., 2007). It is often a challenge to determine whether physical complaints represent a physical disorder, a psychological disorder such as depression, or the separate category of somatoform disorder.

FUNCTIONAL IMPAIRMENT

Somatoform disorders produce significant functional impairment (see Figure 5.2). Approximately 10 to 15% of adults in the United States report work disability as a result of chronic back pain (Von Korff et al., 1990). Among patients with conversion disorder, only 33% maintained full-time employment (Crimlisk et al., 1998). Similarly, people with somatization disorder worked fewer days per month (an average of 7.8 days) than people with no disorder (Guerje et al., 1997). Hypochondriasis and pain disorder raise the likelihood of physical disability, occupational impairment, and overutilization of health services (Aigner et al., 2003; Gureje et al., 1997). People with BDD report severe social impairment; they are very often single, avoid dating, and are socially isolated (Didie et al., 2006).

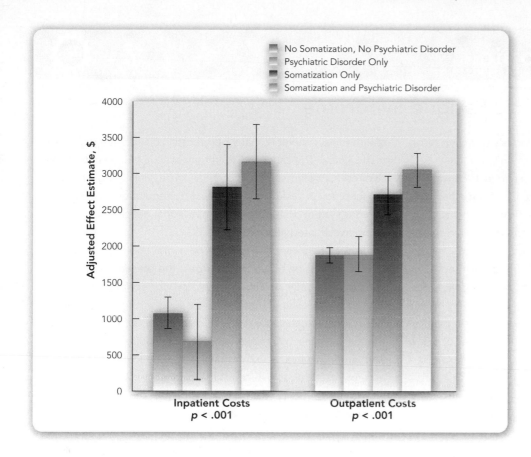

No Somatization, No Psychiatric Disorder
Psychiatric Disorder Only
Somatization Only
Somatization and Psychiatric Disorder

FIGURE 5.2

Somatization Increases Medical Use

As shown here, people with somatization disorder use more medical resources, and therefore have higher medical costs, than people with no disorders or people with psychiatric disorders (in this case, depression) alone. People with both mood disorders and somatization disorder have slightly higher costs than people with somatization alone.

From Barsky, A. J., Orav, E. J., & Bates, D. W., "Somatization increases medical utilization and costs independent of psychiatric and medical comorbidity." *Archives of General Psychiatry*, 62 (8), pp. 903–910. Copyright © 2005 by the American Medical Association. Reprinted by permission of the publisher.

In addition to causing functional impairment, somatoform disorders have a complex course. Hypochondriasis and BDD are severe and chronic conditions (Creed & Barsky, 2004), even when people receive mental health treatment (Phillips et al., 2006b). In contrast, undifferentiated somatoform disorder sometimes spontaneously remits (Kirmayer & Looper, 2007; Kroenke & Mangelsdorff, 1989), but it can be chronic when there are comorbid conditions such as anxiety and depression (Rief et al., 1995). Remission rates for somatization disorder are controversial. Early studies reported that less than 10% of people recover (Swartz et al., 1991), but more recent investigations report that between 30 and 50% of individuals recover one year later (Arnold et al., 2006; Creed & Barsky, 2004). Conversion disorder also appears to be an acute condition, with between 33 and 90% of patients remitted or significantly improved 2 to 5 years later (Binzer & Kullgren, 1998; Crimlisk et al., 1998; Kent et al., 1995). Of course, the more chronic cases are associated with greater functional impairment (Krem, 2004).

Although many physical complaints lack an organic basis, they still have an enormous impact on our medical system. Patients with medically unexplained physical symptoms constitute 15 to 30% of all primary care physician appointments (Kirmayer et al., 2004), and sometimes several different physicians evaluate the same patient complaint. Often, people with physical symptoms "doctor-shop" to find a physician who will provide a medical explanation, and in many instances, they receive different diagnoses from different medical specialists (Kirmayer & Looper, 2007). Some people remain unwilling to accept a psychological diagnosis; this leads to physician frustration, patient demoralization, and a continuing search for a physical explanation.

Patients with unexplained physical complaints are often seen in doctors' offices. They may even "doctor-shop" if they are told that their complaints have no medical cause.

Research HOT Topic

The Challenge of Chronic Fatigue Syndrome

Chronic fatigue syndrome (CFS) is a seriously disabling disorder that has puzzled the medical community for many years. The original medical diagnosis published in 1988 was lacking in validity, as it did not differentiate CFS from other types of unexplained fatigue, leading health professionals to call it a somatoform disorder. Revisions to the diagnostic criteria now yield a more reliable and valid diagnostic condition, requiring (1) severe chronic fatigue for at least 6 months with no known medical condition; and (2) four or more of the following symptoms: substantial impairment in short-term memory or concentration; sore throat; tender lymph nodes, muscle pain, multi-joint pain without swelling or redness; headaches of a new type, pattern, or severity; unrefreshing sleep; and postexercise tiredness lasting more than 24 hours.

CFS exerts a significant economic impact. The Centers for Disease Control reports that about 450,000 people may be affected by CFS, leading to a total annual loss of $9.1 billion—$2.3 billion from lost household productivity and $6.8 billion from lost labor force productivity (Reynolds et al., 2004).

Despite the increasing recognition of the disorder, some people with CFS cannot convince others that they suffer from a real medical condition; many people still consider it a psychosomatic illness. The cause of CFS remains unknown, despite intensive research efforts. Many potential causes, including viruses, immunological dysfunctions, cortisol dysregulation, autonomic nervous system dysfunction, and nutritional deficiencies have been investigated and ruled out.

Researchers continue to focus on a viral etiology because typical findings on blood tests suggest the presence of a viral infection. Recently, one investigative group reported that about 10% of people who contract the Ross River virus will develop CFS. Of course, this means that 90% of those with the virus will not. Other researchers have found similar results with Epstein-Barr virus, GB virus, human retroviruses, human herpes virus 6, enteroviruses, rubella, or candida albicans. In each case, a few individuals with CFS may have the virus, but the relationship is small and not statistically significant.

Researchers are continuing to pursue possible etiological factors, and they now believe that CFS may not have a single cause but may represent the final outcome of multiple precipitating somatic and/or psychological factors that act in combination, including viral infections, psychological stress, and toxins.

Doctor-shopping is just one example of how somatoform disorders increase medical utilization and costs. Over a one-year period, people with somatoform disorders average significantly more primary care visits, more specialty care visits, more emergency room visits, and more hospital admissions, as well as higher inpatient and outpatient care costs than the general population (Barsky et al., 2005; Robbins & Kirmayer, 1996). Determining a physical basis for these symptoms is quite costly (see the box "Research Hot Topics: The Challenge of Chronic Fatigue Syndrome"). In one sample, an average of $7,778 was spent to rule out physical causes for headache and $7,263 for back pain (Kroenke & Mangelsdorff, 1989). In all, treatment for somatoform disorders accounts for approximately 20% of all medical care expenses in the United States (Verma & Gallagher, 2000). Interestingly, and consistent with patients' belief that their physical ailment has a medical explanation, mental health care was the only form of health care that was not significantly higher in people with somatoform disorders.

EPIDEMIOLOGY

About 14 to 20% of the general population report worrisome physical symptoms that have no organic basis (Faravelli et al., 1997; Grabe et al., 2003). However, even though many people have these symptoms, few meet strict diagnostic criteria for a somatoform disorder. During any one year, 0.7 to 2.3% of people have BDD, 4.5 to 7.7% have hypochondriasis, 0.6% have pain disorder, 0.04% have conversion disorder, and 0.4 to 0.7% have somatization disorder (Creed & Barsky, 2004; Faravelli et al., 1997; Krem, 2004; Phillips & Dufresne, 2002).

SEX, RACE, AND ETHNICITY

Because these disorders are rare, we have very limited data on their interplay with variables such as sex, race, and ethnicity. We do know that somatization disorder is reported more frequently by women than by men (Creed & Barsky, 2004; Kroenke & Spitzer, 1998). Across racial and ethnic groups, the disorder affects 0.08% of Hispanics, 0.1% of non-Hispanic whites, and 0.45% of African Americans living in the United States (Swartz et al., 1991). These figures are consistent with estimates from around the world, which range from 0.1 to 3.0% across 13 cities in Europe, the Middle East, Asia, and Africa. In South America, the estimates are higher—8.5% to 17.7% (Gureje et al., 1997), but the reason is not clear. The higher prevalence may reflect cultural differences in how these disorders are understood, diagnosed, and treated.

As we noted earlier, people with somatoform disorders often reject psychological explanations. They feel that professionals are denying their real pain. Outside the United States, medical systems are more likely to use a sociocultural, rather than a psychological, explanation. Physicians discuss patients' physical distress in terms of family and community problems. When a sociocultural explanation is offered, people are more likely to acknowledge that stress, social conditions, and emotions can affect their physical status (Kirmayer et al., 2004).

One cultural variation in somatoform disorder is **shenjing shuairuo** (loosely translated, nerve weakness). In the early 1990s, approximately 80% of the people in China with a psychological disorder had this diagnosis (Chang et al., 2005). Symptoms of shenjing shuairuo include fatigue, poor memory, irritability, muscle aches, and sleep problems, symptoms that are also common among those who suffer from depression or anxiety. When DSM-IV diagnostic criteria were applied to people with a diagnosis of shenjing shuairuo, 55% of Chinese patients met criteria for a somatoform diagnosis (see Table 5.2). However, 45% of patients still had a disorder that seemed unique to Chinese patients.

People with shenjing shuairuo emphasize symptoms in the head, brain, and/or central nervous system (*shenjing*), perhaps translating emotional suffering into physical (neurological) symptoms (Chang et al., 2005). As understood by traditional Chinese medicine, the disorder is not simply a neurological disease (e.g., Lee, 1998). Fatigue, sleep disturbances, and dizziness are somato cognitive-affective symptoms that result from functional disharmony among interdependent vital organs. Thus, the subtlety of shenjing shuairuo is broader than the concept of somatoform disorders and may explain why all those who suffer from this disorder do not fit neatly into Western conceptualizations of psychological disorders (Chang et al., 2005).

shenjing shuairuo loosely translated, nerve weakness, a cultural variation of somatoform disorders found among the Chinese

---

TABLE 5.2

DSM-IV Diagnoses of Patients with Shenjing Shuairuo

Diagnosis	Percentage[1]
Undifferentiated somatoform disorder	31%
Pain disorder	22%
Somatization disorder	4%
Hypochondriasis	2%
No DSM-IV diagnosis	45%

From Chang, D. F., Myers, H. F., Yeung, A., Zhang, Y., Zhao, J., & Yu, S., "Shenjing shuairuo and the DSM-IV: diagnosis, distress, and disability in a Chinese primary care setting." *Transcultural Psychiatry*, 42 (2), pp. 204–218. Copyright © 2005 by Sage Publications. Reprinted by permission of SAGE.

[1] Numbers do not add to 100 because 2 patients had 2 diagnoses

DEVELOPMENTAL FACTORS

Diagnostic criteria for somatoform disorders are the same in children and adolescents as in adults, but the data that do exist indicate that somatoform disorders are rare before adulthood (Finkenbine & Miele, 2004; Kozlowska et al., 2007). As in adults, voluntary motor dysfunction was most common, followed by sensory dysfunction and pseudoseizures (Kozlowska et al., 2007). Body dysmorphic disorder appears to be particularly impairing for adolescents. They suffer significant distress, are highly likely to experience suicidal ideation (80.6%) and attempt suicide (44.5%), and have impaired academic, social, and occupational functioning (Phillips et al., 2006a). Like adults, adolescents with BDD were more likely to be female, and the most common areas of concern were skin (acne/scarring), hair (excessive body hair or balding), stomach, weight, and teeth. Both males and females worried equally about these areas. However, a greater proportion of adolescents than adults had worries about their appearance that reached the level of delusional thought.

13–18

BIRTH   20   40   60   80

ETIOLOGY

How somatoform disorders develop is poorly understood. Biological factors would seem to play a role, particularly when distorted perceptual processes, such as those found in BDD, are apparent. Yet, there are few controlled trials examining a biological cause for somatoform disorders. One small study found that female patients with somatization disorder or undifferentiated somatoform disorder ($n = 10$) had larger caudate nuclei volumes compared with healthy controls ($n = 16$; Hakala et al., 2004). How this larger brain structure might lead to excessive worry about physical symptoms is unclear, and the small sample size and the lack of a psychiatric control group prevent drawing conclusions. At this time, the body of etiological evidence lies in the realm of psychological factors, as reviewed in the following section.

Psychosocial Factors   Psychodynamic explanations for somatoform disorders propose that these disorders result from intrapsychic conflict, personality, and defense mechanisms. From a psychodynamic perspective, Anna O (Chapter 1) most likely had conversion disorder. She was probably emotionally stressed, and possibly resentful, because of the need to care for her father and because of his subsequent death. Anna O's psychological distress was unacceptable to her superego, and therefore her negative feelings were repressed and converted into physical symptoms—hence, use of the term *conversion disorder* to describe this condition.

Behavioral principles of modeling and reinforcement may also contribute to the development of illness behavior. Compared with healthy mothers, mothers with somatization disorder paid more attention to their children when they played with a medical kit than when they played with a tea set or ate a snack (Craig et al., 2004). This increased attention may lead to an increase in medical concerns, medical tests, or medical procedures in their children. Similarly, the more often adolescent girls were reinforced for expressing complaints about menstrual illness, the more often they had menstrual symptoms and disability days as adults. Also, childhood reinforcement of cold illness behavior significantly predicted cold symptoms and disability days for adults (Whitehead et al., 1994). In summary, there is strong support for the theory that reinforcing somatizing behaviors may increase the future likelihood of somatic complaints.

Other environmental factors also are associated with physical symptoms, distress, and somatoform disorders. Among adults, stress was temporally associated with 72% of somatoform disorders. In contrast, a history of sexual abuse was present in 28% of the cases (Singh & Lee, 1997). Among children (Kozlowska et al., 2007), family separation/loss was associated with the onset of the disorder in 34% of the cases. Family conflict/violence was associated in 20% of the cases, and sexual assault in only 4%. The

examining the evidence

Is Childhood Sexual Abuse Associated with Somatoform Disorders?

■ **The Evidence** Somatoform disorders (e.g., somatization disorder, conversion disorder) have been linked to physical and sexual abuse earlier in life (e.g., Bowman & Markand, 1996; Brown et al., 2005). Some theorists have used these observations to propose a causal relationship between abuse and somatoform disorders. What is the validity of this relationship?

Let's Examine the Evidence

■ **What Type of Research Designs Were Used in These Investigations?** The idea that physical and sexual trauma are factors in the onset of somatoform disorder is based on studies in which patients with somatoform disorder were interviewed. Only rarely is a control group of people with no disorder or another disorder included in the research design. Another consideration is that these studies also use correlational designs, and the data derived from them cannot support causality. In fact, two large prospective (longitudinal) studies challenge the association between somatoform disorders and sexual/physical abuse (Linton, 2002; Raphael et al., 2001). First, among adults with no history of back pain, self-reported history of *physical* abuse (not *sexual* abuse) predicted the development of back pain one year later. However, there was no relationship between physical or sexual abuse and the emergence of *new* pain when the person had back pain at baseline (Linton, 2002). In a second study, children documented to have early childhood abuse or neglect (n = 676) were compared with controls with no history of abuse (n = 520; Raphael et al., 2001). When followed into young adulthood where the number of medically explained and unexplained pain complaints was reported, physically and sexually abused and neglected individuals were *not* at risk for increased pain

symptoms. These prospective studies suggest that the previous correlational relationship between sexual and/or physical abuse and somatoform disorders may be simply a result of biased self-report based on retrospective data.

■ **What Other Factors Might Explain the Correlational Relationship?** In many instances, abusive acts occur in family environments where there are high levels of conflict, hostility, and aggression, as well as parent-child interactions that are cold, rejecting, and/or neglectful of children (Repetti et al., 2002). We know that these chronic stressors are related to abnormal neuroendocrine responses in the hypothalamic-pituitary-adrenal (HPA) axis (Mayer et al., 2001; see also Chapter 4), and this dysregulation may result in multiple somatic complaints (Heim et al., 2000).

■ **What Evidence Exists for This Relationship?** A carefully designed study examined not only the presence of physical and sexual abuse among people with somatoform disorders, but also measured hostile and rejecting family environments. The study did not find a relationship between abuse and somatic symptoms but did document an association between hostility/rejection by fathers and somatoform disorders in the children (Lackner et al., 2004).

■ **Conclusion** Family environments characterized by high conflict, hostility, and rejection may lead to a dysregulation of the neuroendocrine system that mediates stressful responses in the body. How could a chronic negative environment (in which abusive acts are more likely to occur) lay the foundation for the potential development of somatization symptoms and somatoform disorders?

relationship between somatoform disorders and childhood sexual abuse is controversial (Alper et al., 1993; Coryell & Norten, 1981; Morrison et al., 1989; see the box "Examining the Evidence: Is Childhood Sexual Abuse Associated with Somatoform Disorders?").

Distorted cognitions may also play a role in some somatoform disorders. In fact, somatization disorder may result from a cognitive process called *somatic amplification* (Barsky & Klerman, 1983), a tendency to perceive bodily sensations as intense, noxious, and disturbing. How this amplification occurs is unclear. This theory suggests that some people have heightened sensory, perceptual, and/or cognitive-evaluative processes that make them more sensitive to the presence of physical symptoms. This is an interesting theory, but few studies have assessed exactly how these perceptual processes contribute to the onset of somatoform disorders.

Other cognitive theories propose that somatoform disorders develop from inaccurate beliefs about (a) the prevalence and contagiousness of illnesses, (b) the meaning of bodily symptoms, and (c) the course and treatment of illnesses (Salkovskis, 1989). For example, someone with hypochondriacal fears about contracting breast cancer may hold inaccurate beliefs about the illness such as

- *so many women get breast cancer, it must be some type of unidentified virus,*
- *a pain in my chest is a signal that I may have breast cancer, and*
- *I have had this pain for some time.*
The cancer is probably throughout my body and no treatment will help me.

These beliefs may be activated by hearing or reading about breast cancer or after perceiving vague bodily sensations. As a result, the person becomes hypervigilant and worried about having, and perhaps dying from, the illness (Rode et al., 2001). Cognitive theories propose that it is not the symptoms but how the symptoms are interpreted that lead to the development of somatoform disorders. Although it is not clear how a person acquires these beliefs, they may result from the reinforcement and modeling theories discussed above.

An Integrative Model Understanding the interplay between psychological and somatic factors can be quite complicated. As illustrated by Figure 5.3, physical, psychological, and social factors probably play a role in the development of somatoform

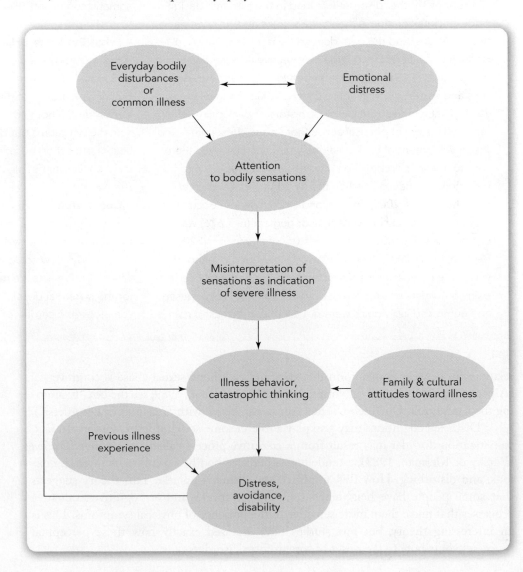

FIGURE 5.3
An Integrative Model of Somatoform Disorders

As illustrated in this model, biological, psychological, social, and cultural factors all play a role in the onset and maintenance of somatoform disorders.

Adapted from Kirmayer, L. J., & Looper, K. J., "Somatoform disorders." In *Adult Psychopathology and Diagnosis*, 5th Ed., by Hersen, M., Turner, S. M., & Beidel, D.C. (Eds.), pp.410–472. Copyright © 2007 John Wiley & Sons. Reproduced with permission of John Wiley & Sons, Inc.

disorders (e.g., Kirmayer & Looper, 2007). As we noted at the beginning of this chapter, transient aches and pains and bodily disturbances occur every day: you get a headache, a fleeting pain, or an upset stomach. The reason is not necessarily clear—perhaps you are unknowingly allergic to a certain food. Whatever the reason, your symptoms exist. Whether or not you pay attention to your symptoms depends on their intensity and also your learning history, including learning to interpret bodily symptoms as signs of a serious illness. The smallest sensation or change in your physical state may cause you to focus more intently on your body, looking for confirmation that something is wrong. Perhaps sensations such as ringing in your ears cause you to worry. If the ringing continues for some time, you may begin to worry intensely that something is wrong ("what if I have a brain tumor?"). This is normal illness behavior, and you may decide to see a physician.

A crucial factor is whether you are reassured by the physician's response ("There is no brain tumor") or whether you continue to worry, even though medical tests and physicians cannot find a reason for your distress. If you do continue to worry, your distress may become so severe that you change your lifestyle. Depending on your own cognitive schemas and learning history, your friends and family may support your "sick role" behavior or they may suggest you are a hypochondriac. The medical profession may also influence the course of your worry/somatoform disorder. If the physician conducts excessive and/or invasive testing, this may reinforce your belief that something is seriously wrong with you. When treating people with somatoform disorders, health care professionals must carefully convey understanding of the physical distress, yet help the patient understand the role of psychological stress in creating physical symptoms. Doing this successfully is the first step in the treatment of these disorders.

TREATMENT

The first challenge for treatment is the reluctance of people with somatoform disorders to reveal their worries to a professional. Among one sample of people with BDD, only 41% revealed their symptoms to their prescribing physician; instead many were being treated for a secondary disorder such as anxiety or depression. As noted earlier, a major challenge to successful treatment is the belief of many sufferers that they do not have a psychological disorder. They emphasize their physical symptoms and often resist a psychological intervention (Arnold et al., 2006). Since many patients with BDD see their problem as solely physical, they often seek and receive treatment from dermatological or surgical clinics. Often, they are displeased with the surgical outcome and may become angry and threatening toward the physician (Honigman et al., 2004).

There are relatively few controlled treatment studies for somatoform disorders. Antidepressants, particularly selective serotonin reuptake inhibitors (SSRIs, such as Prozac), may be effective for BDD when compared with placebo (Phillips et al., 2006b; Phillips & Dufresne, 2002). More controlled trials are necessary to determine whether the medication alters the core symptoms of BDD or the accompanying anxiety and depression. These drugs may help people with hypochondriasis (Greeven et al., 2007), but they may produce side effects that then lead to more worry about new symptoms (Barsky, 1996).

In some cases, basic education about the interplay of physical and emotional factors may reduce the symptoms and distress associated with somatoform disorders. Symptom-focused cognitive-behavior therapy (CBT) also may be helpful. As we noted earlier, people with somatoform disorders resist the notion that psychological factors play an important role in their disorder's onset or maintenance. Therefore, treatment focuses on teaching patients to cope with their symptoms by emphasizing how current psychological and social factors affect their symptoms without forcing people to accept a psychological basis for their disorder.

A patient undergoes relaxation training as part of cognitive-behavioral therapy. Relaxation helps the patient cope with troubling thoughts about the body and its symptoms.

CBT includes relaxation training, diverting attention away from the physical symptoms, response prevention (to prevent the checking of body parts that is common in BDD), and correction of automatic thoughts. CBT is efficacious for people with BDD or hypochondriasis (Buwalda et al., 2006; Greeven et al., 2007; Hiller et al., 2002; Looper & Kirmayer, 2002). For BDD, CBT in the form of modifying intrusive thoughts and overvalued beliefs about physical appearance, exposure to avoided body image situations, and response prevention to eliminate body checking has been found superior to no treatment (Rosen et al., 1995). Similarly, because somatization disorder is considered to result, at least in part, from environmental and personal stressors, teaching patients strategies to reduce stress may lessen their distress and lower the costs associated with their health care. To date, there are no controlled trials of CBT for conversion disorder, but a three-pronged approach is recommended: withdrawal of medical and social attention directed at the abnormality; physical and occupational therapy to retrain normal gait and movements; and psychotherapy to help the patient cope with stress (Krem, 2004). Similar behavioral approaches have been used to treat globus hystericus (Donohue et al., 1997).

---

concept CHECK

- Physical complaints are common and in many instances do not indicate the presence of a medical disorder.

- In some people, physical complaints that are severe, persistent, and without an organic basis may indicate the presence of a somatoform disorder. These can involve many different bodily systems (somatization disorder), one particular symptom (conversion disorder), concern that a body feature is ugly (body dysmorphic disorder), or worry that one might have contracted a certain disease (hypochondriasis).

- Although isolated physical symptoms without an organic basis are common among the general population, few people (either adults or children) meet strict diagnostic criteria for somatoform disorders. This limits our ability to understand the etiology of these disorders or to have large enough samples to conduct randomized, controlled trials.

- Despite our limited knowledge, we do know that the development of these disorders is quite complex, and includes physical, psychological, and environmental factors.

APPLICATION QUESTION Why could paying more attention to a toddler playing with a medical kit and ignoring play at other times lead to the development of a somatoform disorder?

Dissociative Disorders

There is perhaps no more controversial diagnostic group than the dissociative disorders. Mental health professionals cannot agree on the validity or even the existence of these conditions; 97% of a sample of psychologists who work in Veterans Administration hospitals believe that dissociative disorders exist (Dunn et al., 1994), but only 55% of Australian psychologists do (Leonard et al., 2005). In contrast, only 25% of American psychiatrists and 14% of Canadian psychiatrists felt that the diagnosis was supported by strong scientific evidence (Lalonde et al., 2001; Pope et al., 1999). These different percentages may reflect where mental health professionals work or the specific way in which the question is asked. However, as you will see, the issues run much deeper and have generated many interesting, and heated, debates.

In general, **dissociative disorders** involve "a disruption in the usually integrated functions of consciousness, memory, identity, or perception of the environment" (APA, 2000, p. 519). But what does this mean? Have you ever been so engrossed in reading something that you suddenly looked up and were startled to see your friend standing right in front of you? You were concentrating so hard that you were briefly unaware of your surroundings, a situation similar to a dissociative experience.

There are actually five types of dissociative experiences (Gleaves et al., 2001; Steinberg et al., 1993). *Depersonalization* is a feeling of detachment from one's body—experiencing the self as strange or unreal. Some people describe this feeling as if they were floating above their own body, watching themselves behave. *Derealization* is a feeling of unfamiliarity or unreality about one's physical or interpersonal environment. People describe feeling as if they were in a dream. *Amnesia* is the inability to remember personal information or significant periods of time. It is more than simply forgetting a name, where you put your keys, or what you had for dinner last Thursday night. *Identity confusion* describes being unclear or conflicted about one's personal identity. Finally, *identity alteration* describes overt behaviors indicating that one has assumed an alternate identity (Steinberg et al., 1993).

Isolated episodes of dissociation do not always indicate the presence of a dissociative disorder (e.g., Holmes et al., 2005). Your engrossment in your work is known as *absorption*, defined as fully engaging all your perceptual resources on one item, such that you are no longer attending to other aspects of the environment. Experiences such as absorption are common, and 46 to 74% of people without psychological disorders experience occasional episodes of derealization and depersonalization (Hunter et al., 2005). Furthermore, dissociative symptoms may occur in people with panic disorder, obsessive-compulsive disorder, agoraphobia, post-traumatic stress disorder, depressive disorder, bipolar disorder, and eating disorders (Holmes et al., 2005). When dissociative experiences are temporary, such as your momentary period of absorption, they create minimal, if any, distress. However, when they develop into chronic conditions, they are called dissociative disorders.

DISSOCIATIVE AMNESIA

Have you ever awakened in the morning and for a moment been unable to recognize your surroundings? Or have you ever found yourself driving and for a moment could not remember passing familiar landmarks? Your momentary forgetting/distraction may help you understand the concept of **amnesia**. This condition has many causes, including head injuries, epilepsy, alcoholic "blackouts," or low blood sugar. A temporary state of amnesia may also occur after a stroke or seizure, after electroconvulsive therapy (ECT) for depression, or as a result of drug toxicity or global dementia. Therefore, a medical evaluation is always the first step in the diagnostic process to rule out medical causes.

Dissociative amnesia is an inability to recall important information, usually of a personal nature. When it occurs following a stressful or traumatic event, its cause is considered psychological, not biological. There are several types of dissociative amnesia. Failure to recall events that occur during a certain period of time is known as *localized amnesia*, whereas *generalized amnesia* is a total inability to recall any aspect of one's life. A third type of amnesia is *selective amnesia*, in which the person forgets some elements of a traumatic experience. Dissociative amnesia is considered a reversible condition, and in many instances, people can later recall events, or parts of events, that they could not previously describe.

dissociative disorders a set of disorders characterized by disruption in the usually integrated functions of consciousness, memory, identity, or perception of the environment

amnesia inability to recall important information and usually occurs after a medical condition or event

dissociative amnesia an inability to recall important information, usually of a personal nature, that follows a stressful or traumatic event

dissociative fugue a disorder involving loss of personal identity and memory, often involving a flight from a person's usual place of residence

dissociative identity disorder presence within a person of two or more distinct personality states, each with its own pattern of perceiving, relating to, and thinking about the environment and self

Dissociative Identity:

The Three Faces of Eve
"Let us hear the various personalities speak . . ."
www.mypsychlab.com

DISSOCIATIVE FUGUE

Dissociative amnesia consists of a loss of personal memory, whereas **dissociative fugue** is a loss of personal identity as well as memory and is sometimes known as *psychogenic fugue*. In this disorder, people are found in a physical location away from their usual residence. "Fugue" means "flight." Fugue states may be associated with physical or mental traumas, depression, or legal problems (Kihlstrom, 2001). Patients in a fugue state may seek treatment if they become aware of their loss of personal identity and memory or if they come to the attention of the police (see the box "DSM-IV-TR: Dissociative Disorders").

DISSOCIATIVE IDENTITY DISORDER

In 1957, Hollywood released a film called *The Three Faces of Eve*, based on a nonfiction book of the same name. In the book and movie, Eve White is a housewife and mother, but when she is hypnotized as part of her psychotherapy, her psychiatrist discovers an alternate personality, Eve Black, who is outgoing and socially engaging, exactly the opposite of Eve White. Later, a third personality Jane, emerges. Although the book and movie contain a number of factual inaccuracies, the real Eve, Christine Costner-Sizemore, was able to integrate her personalities. *The Three Faces of Eve* introduced the term *multiple personality disorder*, now called **dissociative identity disorder** (or DID). Another example of DID is found in *Sybil*, where again a book, published in 1976, and a movie based on it, chronicled the treatment of a young woman who sought therapy for blackouts and "nervous breakdowns." In therapy, the psychiatrist discovers that Sybil has 16 different personalities (also known as alternative personalities or *alters*). The psychiatrist hypothesizes that these alters are the result of extreme physical and sexual abuse, what most people would describe as torture, by her mother, who suffered from schizophrenia. Christine Costner-Sizemore and Sybil are the two most familiar examples of dissociative identity disorder.

A graduate student in clinical psychology was conducting a study on bulimia nervosa (an eating disorder; see Chapter 7). Participant number 006 was a 32-year-old female with a 10-year history of bulimia nervosa. She had a tumultuous family history including sexual

abuse, physical abuse, and neglect. She binged multiple times per day and purged up to 10 times per day. She also abused laxatives and had comorbid alcohol and drug abuse. She felt that her disorder resulted from trauma inflicted by her parents, and she saw her eating disorder as a result of living in such an abusive family. She was angry, bitter, and deeply pessimistic about her future.

Later, the graduate student was contacted by another volunteer, number 026. The telephone number was the same as that of another participant, but the graduate student assumed that they were roommates. When participant 026 arrived, the graduate student was astonished to see participant 006 enter her office! Oddly, the participant did not seem to recognize her surroundings. She got lost on her way to the office and showed no recognition when she met the researcher. Although the student was sure that this was participant 006, the woman's personal and family history was completely different. The patient claimed that she had been bulimic for four years and before that had been overweight since childhood. She recalled her childhood as relatively happy and her parents as nurturing. Their only fault was that they frequently used food as a reward. Her first binge episode occurred after a breakup with a boyfriend, and she denied any history of anorexia nervosa, substance abuse, alcohol abuse, drug abuse, or physical or sexual abuse by her parents.

Curious about these two presentations, the researcher asked subject number 026 if she had ever been involved in research on bulimia nervosa. Astonishingly, she claimed that not only had she never been in a study but that this was the first time she ever told anyone that she had bulimia. To cover all her bases, the researcher asked subject 026 whether she had any siblings or if she had a twin. Subject 026 responded that she was an only child. Further inquiry into the patient's medical records and medical history revealed that this patient was known in the community to have dissociative identity disorder and possessed several alters. Needless to say, the researcher did not include this/these participant(s) in her final research sample.

DID is a fascinating topic that intrigues most abnormal psychology students. During the 1980s and early 1990s, some mental health therapists began to discuss DID with their patients and the media. An interesting phenomenon occurred. As the media attention increased, so did the number of people reported to be suffering from DID. However, even as therapists seemed to find case after case, the very existence of the disorder was called into question. Why? One of the primary criticisms surrounding DID is that, despite many published descriptions of the disorder, there are few quantitative studies and even fewer that constitute experimental research (Kihlstrom, 2001). In other words, the scientific status of DID as a diagnostic category is not well established. For example, it is unclear if DID can be reliably diagnosed. According to its proponents, its signs are intermittent and most DID patients do not recognize the existence of their alters before they begin therapy (see Piper & Mersky, 2004b). Therefore, unlike other disorders, in which people seek treatment because they are sad or anxious, the existence of alternate personalities is only discovered after the person is in therapy.

Another challenge for DID is that the terms used to describe the symptoms are difficult to define in a way that can be studied. There are no clear definitions of an alter or a distinct personality state. Furthermore, the number of alters seems to be increasing exponentially since the publication of the studies of Eve and Sybil. One descriptive study (Putnam et al., 1986) indicated that among 100 adults with DID, the average number of alternate personalities was 13.3, ranging from 1 to 60. Some therapists reported that their patients had too many alters to count. The most common alter was a child, aged 12 years or less. About half of the alters were of the opposite sex

Christine Costner-Sizemore, the real "Eve" portrayed in the famous film *The Three Faces of Eve.*

than the person seeking treatment, and most reported that the alter first made an appearance before age 12, even though the patient was unaware of its presence.

Similarly, there is no agreement on what defines "taking control of the person's behavior." As a result, each therapist can use *idiosyncratic* definitions. How does an alter take control? Does the alter simply have to speak to the therapist to be legitimate, or must the behavior be more complicated? Proponents of DID describe alters who engage in "doing schoolwork, selling illicit drugs, dancing in strip clubs, cleaning bathtubs" (Piper & Mersky, 2004a, p. 679). It is obvious that there are no clear answers to these questions. In the sections that follow, we will examine further the validity of DID. However, from the perspective of psychological science, one must question the reliability and validity of a disorder whose symptoms are not consistently present or cannot be independently verified.

DEPERSONALIZATION DISORDER

During times of heightened emotionality or stress (e.g., panic disorder, post-traumatic stress disorder, depression, or near-death experiences) or altered physical states such as substance abuse or head injury, many people report feelings of being detached from the body or feeling as if the world around them were unreal (Baker et al., 2003; Kihlstrom, 2001). In one group of people who reported these experiences, 62% had a documented medical condition, and 50% had a previous psychiatric diagnosis; most had depression and/or panic disorder (Baker et al., 2003). In some people, these experiences occur with great frequency and not necessarily in the context of emotional stress or physical illness.

Lucinda described multiple periods of time when the world suddenly felt unreal. Once, when she was with her friends, she felt as if they were in a movie and she was sitting in the audience, watching the others perform on the screen in front of her. Another time, she was walking and suddenly felt as if she were floating above the surface of the sidewalk.

When periods of dissociation are frequent and severe, the person may be suffering from **depersonalization disorder**, described as feelings of being detached from one's body or mind, a state of feeling as if one is an external observer of one's own behavior. The changes occur suddenly and are perceived as unreal and inconsistent with a person's prior experiences. People can experience either symptoms of depersonalization (being detached from one's body) or derealization (a feeling of unfamiliarity or unreality about one's physical or interpersonal environment). Most people with this disorder have symptoms of both types of dissociation (Baker et al., 2003).

In depersonalization disorder, a person feels detached from body or mind, as if observing his or her behavior from the outside. Or the person may feel that the external environment is unreal.

FUNCTIONAL IMPAIRMENT

There are few data examining the impact of dissociative disorders on social and occupational functioning (Johnson et al., 2005). In many cases, the presence of other, comorbid disorders does not allow a determination of whether the impairment is the result of another disorder, such as depression, or the result of dissociative disorders.

EPIDEMIOLOGY

There is great variability in the reported prevalence of dissociative disorders, depending on the characteristics of the sample (community sample or clinic sample) or the degree to which the interviewer believes in the diagnosis. In one epidemiological sample, 0.8% had depersonalization disorder, 1.8% had dissociative amnesia, and 1.5% had dissociative identity disorder (Johnson et al., 2006). Among inpatient samples, dissociative disorders affect from 4 to 21% of all psychiatric inpatients (Foote et al., 2006), with higher rates in settings specifically established for the treatment of these disorders. Data from outpatient samples are very limited. Among one clinic sample of inner-city outpatients, 29% had a dissociative disorder. However, they also had many other disorders, including depression, post-traumatic stress disorder, and anxiety disorders, and it is possible that depersonalization experiences were the result of one of those disorders. The issue of whether dissociative symptoms represent a primary disorder or are secondary to another disorder may seem to be simply an intellectual exercise. However, it is important for determining mental health policy, reimbursement for services, and approaches to treatment.

SEX, RACE, AND ETHNICITY

Both men and women suffer from dissociative disorders (e.g., Simeon et al., 2003). Worldwide prevalence estimates of dissociative disorders range from 18.5% of women in the general population of the Netherlands (Sar et al., 2007) to 8% of women in an inpatient sample in the same country (Friedl & Draijer, 2000). These estimates are higher than those reported in the United States, suggesting that some of these disorders may represent culture-bound syndromes. Dissociative symptoms, such as trance-like states, are a common part of religious experiences throughout the world. For example, in Uganda, dissociative amnesia and depersonalization were defined as psychological disorders much as they are in the United States (Van Duijl et al., 2005), whereas dissociative fugue and DID were considered to result from spirit possession.

Mary was born in Malaysia but moved to the United States when she was in her 30s. Shortly after she arrived, she received word that her mother, who still lived in Malaysia, had died suddenly. Mary was filled with grief. About 4 weeks after she received the news, she was waiting for the subway when someone suddenly bumped her on the platform. Mary became dissociated, alternating between talking incoherently and using foul language, pointing at what she said was a "snake." After about 5 minutes (during which time the police arrived), she became quiet and contemplative. She claimed amnesia regarding the event.

When Mary's husband arrived, he informed police that she had a long history of *latah*, a condition in which a person, after being startled by a sound or touch, suddenly falls into an altered state of consciousness during which he or she behaves as Mary did. The disorder occurs primarily among women from Malaysia, and those who are "latah" have numerous episodes, almost always precipitated by a sudden external event (Tseng, 2003). As this case shows, sociocultural factors may play a significant role in the experience of dissociative disorders.

DEVELOPMENTAL FACTORS

The average age of onset for depersonalization disorder ranges from 15.9 to 22.8 years (Baker et al., 2003; Simeon et al., 2003), although children as young as age 8 have been diagnosed with DID (Hornstein & Putnam, 1992). However, the children who were given this diagnosis also had many other psychological disorders as well as unusual beliefs (i.e., delusions), unusual perceptual experiences (hallucinations, such as hearing voices when no one is present), and histories of suicidal ideation and attempts. This means that, as with adults, DID, if it exists at all, rarely occurs alone, even in children (Putnam, 1993; Vincent & Pickering, 1988).

ETIOLOGY

Because dissociative disorders are very rare, there are few controlled trials examining their onset. Therefore, much of what has been written about the onset of dissociative disorders is based on clinical experience and impressions, not empirical data. In some instances, this theorizing has negatively impacted individuals, often the parents of those affected, by falsely accusing them of committing child abuse. As you read the examples in this section, consider whether some of these behaviors remind you of the concept of *emotional contagion*, which we discussed in Chapter 1.

Biological Factors   Neurological disorders, such as temporal lobe epilepsy, head injury, tumor, cerebral vascular accident (stroke), migraine, and dementia may produce symptoms such as blackouts, fugues, depersonalization, amnesia, anxiety and panic symptoms, and auditory, visual, and olfactory hallucinations (Lambert et al., 2002). Several empirical trials suggest that between 10 and 21% of patients with DID have abnormal brain activity (Sivec & Lynn, 1995). Therefore, although abnormal neurological function cannot account for the onset of all cases of dissociative disorders, some dissociative symptoms may result from neurological conditions.

Neuroanatomical and neurochemical studies of dissociative disorders are few (Sar et al., 2001; Simeon et al., 2001; Vermetten et al., 2006), and those that exist are limited by small sample sizes, lack of adequate control groups, or failure to exclude the presence of other disorders such as post-traumatic stress disorder (PTSD). Actually, when people with DID are compared with people with PTSD, there are few differences in brain anatomy and brain function (Loewenstein, 2005). The common denominator in both of these conditions may be chronic stress. As discussed in Chapter 4, the chronic stress associated with post-traumatic stress disorder can produce neuroanatomical changes in the hippocampus and amygdala, brain regions known to be involved in memory functions. Neurochemical changes may also occur. During periods of stress, the availability of neuropeptides and neurotransmitters (known collectively as *neuromodulators*) in these regions is altered, which affects establishing memory traces for specific events (Bremner et al., 1996). These neuromodulators may have both strengthening and diminishing effects on memory, based on the level of stress and the type of neuromodulator.

Psychosocial Factors   According to its proponents, DID is a failure of the normal developmental process of "personality integration." The failure is hypothesized to result from traumatic experiences and disordered caregiver-child relationships during critical developmental periods. This leads to the development and elaboration of distinct personality states (International Society for the Study of Dissociation, 2005). The traumas are most commonly incidents of physical and/or sexual abuse that occur during childhood.

As is true of the suggested association between abuse and somatoform disorders, data supporting the proposal that DID results from childhood trauma are correlational and based on samples of patients who are seeking treatment. Some proponents of this relationship assert that many or virtually all patients with DID were severely abused as children, but there are no controlled investigations to support these assertions. The available longitudinal studies of the adult effects of childhood sexual abuse do not include DID as one of the negative outcomes (e.g., Bulik et al., 2001; Piper & Merskey, 2004a). Of course, large epidemiological studies are sometimes conducted using telephone interviews, and researchers make decisions about how best to use the interview time. Sometimes rarely occurring disorders such as DID are not included in epidemiological surveys because they occur so infrequently. This means that the disorder may be present but undetected. However, even if some people who are sexually abused develop DID, this does not mean that all abuse victims develop DID or that

DID is the only result of sexual abuse. In one large twin study, a history of childhood sexual abuse was related to increased risk for many different outcomes, such as depression, suicide attempts, conduct disorder, substance abuse, social anxiety, adult rape, and divorce (Nelson et al., 2002). Therefore, childhood sexual abuse appears to increase the risk for adult psychopathology in general, but it does not appear to predict the development of any one particular disorder (Bulik et al., 2001).

Despite the lack of strong empirical data, clinicians who specialize in DID still propose that dissociation is used to cope with traumatic experiences, blocking painful events from awareness and allowing the person to function as if nothing traumatic had happened (Sivec & Lynn, 1995). Although blocking painful events might help someone cope in the short term, its repeated use results in functional impairments. However, here is where some theorists jump from a behavioral explanation to an etiological theory without the corroborating evidence. They conclude that anyone who experiences dissociative symptoms *must have been abused*. Significant gaps in childhood memories are considered evidence of repeated trauma (Bass & Davis, 1988). Patients are often encouraged to "remember" the trauma as a way of overcoming their symptoms. There is a fallacy in this reasoning, however, because these theories ignore the evidence that memory gaps before the age of 6 are common in the general population (Holmes et al., 2005). But what if people only "remember" abuse after a therapist explains that their symptoms are the result of unrecalled child abuse? Are these recovered memories or *false* memories?

The issue of *repressed memories* and *recovered memories* is an emotional and controversial issue for psychology and mental health professionals. Consider the following example:

In 1990, George Franklin, Sr., age 51, was found guilty of the murder of 8-year-old Susan Kay Nason. What made the case unusual was that the murder occurred more than 20 years earlier, and the primary evidence was the recovered memory of Franklin's daughter, Eileen, who was also 8 years old at the time. Eileen's memory of the murder did not return at once but in bits and pieces. By the time it had all returned, Eileen described witnessing her father sexually assault Susan in the back of a van and then kill her by smashing her head with a rock. Many people believed Eileen's account, even though many of the details could have been obtained from newspaper accounts. More disconcerting was the fact that many of the details she provided changed over time. For example, she initially stated that the event occurred in the morning. When later confronted with the fact that Susan had attended school that day, Eileen changed her testimony to state that the event occurred after school (from Loftus, 1993). Because of the inconsistency of Eileen's testimony, George Franklin's conviction was later overturned.

There is no way to determine whether Eileen's memories were fact or fiction, yet throughout the 1980s and 1990s, many people reported "recovered" memories, most often having to do with incidents of child abuse. Many therapists believed that these memories were absolute fact without considering that memory is fallible; in other words, memory can be inaccurate or even in some cases, completely made up.

To understand the recovered memory controversy, it is necessary to understand that memory is an active process. First, to remember something you must have paid attention to it.

Tom was walking down the street when he was physically assaulted. When describing the event to the police, he was unable to recall the face of his assailant.

Some theorists propose that such selective amnesia indicates the person's mind has actively blocked this aspect of the traumatic event. However, experimental data suggest that under conditions of high arousal, people pay attention to the central feature of an event at the expense of less important details (McNally, 2005). In the above instance, Tom may not have remembered the face of his attacker because his attention was focused on the perpetrator's gun.

Second, most people do not understand that "memory does not operate like a videotape recorder" (McNally, 2005, p. 818). Remembering is an active process and always involves reconstruction. Even very strong memories may change over time. The morning after the space shuttle *Challenger* exploded, undergraduate students were asked to write down where they were and what they were doing when they heard the news (Neisser & Harsch, 1992). Nearly 3 years later, they were interviewed again. The students were highly confident about the truthfulness of their memory, but the researchers detected many inaccuracies in their recall of the events, including very basic facts such as where they were and what they were doing. In short, memory changes as time progresses.

Just by asking a misleading question, memory researchers have demonstrated that eye witnesses can construct memories for events that did not occur. Ten months after a horrible plane crash that had national news coverage, people were asked "Did you see the television film of the moment that the plane hit the apartment building?" Actually, no such film was available, but when asked this question, more than 60% of the people responded that they had seen the film and were able to describe details of television coverage *that did not exist* (Cronbag et al., 1996). Other studies also illustrate that memories of entirely fictionalized events can be constructed. As part of a study of "childhood memories," adult subjects were provided with three true stories about their childhood as well as a fourth, false story (i.e., that at age 5, they were lost in a mall; Loftus & Pickrell, 1995). During follow-up interviews, when adults described everything they could remember about the four situations, 25% of the participants provided elaborate details about the event that never occurred.

What conclusions can we draw about the research on recovered/false memories? Even though a person provides a detailed memory and is confident that it is accurate, that does not always mean that the remembered event really happened (Laney & Loftus, 2005). The issue of recovered/false memories is not simply an intellectual curiosity but an important element in the controversy surrounding child abuse and by extension, DID. It is important to remember that (a) some children do suffer abuse, and (b) although some abused children may suffer from psychological disorders as adults, there is no clear link between abuse and DID. Furthermore, despite the disagreement regarding recovered memories, all mental health professionals agree on one key point: memories of childhood abuse that were always present are almost always authentic, as are those that are spontaneously remembered outside of a therapeutic setting (Holmes et al., 2005).

Even if we leave aside the issue of repressed/recovered memories, controlled clinical trials still provide only limited evidence for the relationship between abuse and DID. There are two reasons for this controversial relationship. First, the descriptions of abuse often are not objectively documented. Second, the definition of abuse can be quite variable. In some studies, it is limited to acts of physical or sexual abuse. In other studies, abuse is defined broadly to include emotional abuse and emotional/physical neglect, situations that are much more difficult to objectively define and quantify. In still other studies, the samples consist solely of individuals already diagnosed with dissociative disorders, with no adequate comparison groups, yet the results are described as "definitive" (Lewis et al., 1997).

With these limitations in mind, the data from controlled trials suggest that trauma exposure plays only a limited role. In one sample, trauma exposure accounted for only 4.4% of the dissociative symptoms (Briere et al., 2005). Emotional abuse plays an equally important, if not larger, role than sexual abuse (Simeon et al., 2001). More general environmental factors, such as a generally poor relationship between parent and child (even without specific acts of abuse) contribute more to the onset of these disorders (e.g., Nelson et al., 2002).

Therapists who adhere to a *post-traumatic model* of DID believe that a person "compartmentalizes" responses to trauma in the form of alternate personalities. They believe that different patient behaviors indicate the possible presence of alters, even if the person is unaware of their existence (Piper & Mersky, 2004b). Some therapists report that alters only emerge after repeated requests from the therapist. Could these actions actually cause DID? When the therapist or the therapy itself contributes to the onset of a disorder, the cause is said to be *iatrogenic*. An **iatrogenic** disease is one that is inadvertently caused by a physician, by a medical or surgical treatment, or by a diagnostic procedure. The *sociocultural model* postulates that DID is an iatrogenic disorder that develops using cues from the media, from therapists, as well as from personal experiences and observations of others who have enacted multiple identities. These experiences and cues are legitimized and maintained by social reinforcement in therapeutic settings (Spanos, 1994; see the box "Examining the Evidence: Can Therapy Cause Dissociative Identity Disorder?").

iatrogenic a term describing a disease that may be inadvertently caused by a physician, by a medical or surgical treatment, or by a diagnostic procedure

examining the evidence

Can Therapy Cause Dissociative Identity Disorder?

The number of cases of DID worldwide rose from 79 in 1970 to approximately 6,000 in 1986 (Elzinga et al., 1998), a period of time corresponding to the appearance of the book and movie, *Sybil*. By the year 2000, the number of cases was estimated to be in the tens of thousands (Acocella, 1998). The sociocultural model proposes that therapists (and the media) can influence people to develop alternate identities. Might these influences explain the dramatically increased prevalence of DID?

■ **The Evidence** Among DID patients, 80 to 100% have no knowledge of their alters before they began therapy (Dell & Eisenhower, 1990; Lewis et al., 1997; Putnam, 1989). As they continue in therapy, the number of alters reported by a person continues to increase (e.g., North et al., 1993). *Post-traumatic model* theorists address this phenomenon, explaining that patients with DID tend to hide their symptoms before treatment. Perhaps this is so, but are there alternative hypotheses?

■ **Let's Examine the Evidence** Several lines of evidence suggest that therapists may shape people to produce alternative personalities (Lilienfeld et al., 1999).

First, when people with no psychological disorders are given appropriate cues, they can successfully produce DID symptoms, including reports of physical, sexual, and satanic abuse rituals (Stafford & Lynn, 2002).

Second, both the increase in the number of patients with DID and the number of alters that appear during the course of treatment coincide with increased therapist awareness of the diagnostic features. In other words, the more the therapist believes in the diagnosis, the more likely the patients will be given the diagnosis.

Third, one DID expert recommends to novice therapists that when an alter does not emerge spontaneously, "asking to meet an alter directly is an increasingly accepted intervention" (Kluft, 1993, p. 29). Other advice includes giving the person the hypnotic suggestion that "everybody listen." Would such suggestions lead the patient to believe (i.e., shape the patient to believe) that other personalities must exist?

Such shaping did occur in the case of children's testimony during the McMartin preschool molestation trial in California in the 1980s, a notorious case in which a number of day-care workers were falsely accused and convicted of sexually molesting the children in their care. Later testimony refuted the original claims. Children who initially denied being molested by day-care workers were repeatedly interviewed until, as one child later reported, "Anytime I would give them an answer they didn't like, they would ask me again and encourage me to give them the answer they were looking for" (Zirpolo, 2005). In effect, children were encouraged to provide answers consistent with the therapist's preexisting beliefs.

■ **Conclusion** The post-traumatic model asserts that most therapists do not diagnose DID because they neglect to sufficiently probe for its features (Ross, 1997). However, both basic laboratory and behavioral observation data suggest that college students and patients may be vulnerable to therapists' expectations and may produce alters because of suggestions (or probing) by a therapist. This evidence indicates that iatrogenesis and the sociocultural model explanation for the existence of DID cannot be discounted.

TREATMENT

As noted, dissociative amnesia and dissociative fugue usually resolve without treatment. There are no controlled pharmacological trials for derealization disorder or DID, but clinical reports suggest that antidepressant medications may be helpful. It is unclear, however, whether these medications work on core dissociative symptoms or treat the associated anxiety and depression. The same conclusion may apply to cognitive-behavior therapy (CBT) approaches, which hypothesize that people with dissociative disorders misinterpret normal symptoms of fatigue, stress, or even substance intoxication as abnormal. CBT therapists challenge these misinterpretations by teaching the person to generate alternative explanations for their symptoms (a process known as cognitive restructuring). In some instances, people may avoid situations that elicit their symptoms, in which case exposure therapy (see Chapter 4) may help people enter these feared situations. CBT has been reported to be efficacious for depersonalization disorder, although controlled trials are not available (Holmes et al., 2005; Hunter et al., 2005).

---

concept CHECK

- Dissociative experiences occur in people with dissociative disorders, people with no psychological disorder, and people with many different types of psychological disorders.

- The existence of dissociative disorders as distinct psychological disorders is controversial, and among the entire group of disorders, DID is the most controversial.

- Despite its proponents, few data support the hypothesis that those who experience dissociative disorders are suffering from repressed memories or that when these memories are recovered through the therapeutic process, they are accurate in content.

- Similarly, few data indicate that childhood sexual or physical abuse is a frequent cause of dissociative disorder or that it is a unique etiological component.

APPLICATION QUESTION Most psychological disorders show a steady rise in prevalence from the mid-1980s throughout the year 2003. By contrast, the number of publications regarding dissociative amnesia and DID rose from low levels in the mid-1980s to a sharp peak in the 1990s followed by an equally sharp decline by 2003 (Pope et al., 2006a). Worldwide, in 2003, there were only 13 explicit cases of dissociative amnesia reported in the literature. How would you explain this phenomenon?

Factitious Disorders

There is a third group of disorders that involve the interplay of psychological factors and physical symptoms. **Factitious disorders** differ from somatoform and dissociative disorders in one very important way: physical or psychological signs or symptoms of illness are intentionally produced, in what appears to be a desire to assume a sick role. Unlike **malingering**, in which a person intentionally produces physical symptoms to avoid military service, criminal prosecution, or work, or to obtain financial compensation or drugs, symptom production in factitious disorders is not associated with any external incentives. People are aware that they are producing the symptoms and making themselves ill, but appear to be unaware of *why* they do it. People with factitious disorders may produce either primarily physical symptoms, primarily psychological symptoms, or both.

factitious disorders conditions in which physical or psychological signs or symptoms of illness are intentionally produced, in what appears to be a desire to assume a sick role

malingering a condition in which physical symptoms are produced intentionally to avoid military service, criminal prosecution, or work, or to obtain financial compensation or drugs

DSM-IV-TR

Factitious Disorders

- **Factitious Disorder**   The intentional production or pretending of physical or psychological signs or symptoms in oneself, the motivation of which is to assume a sick role. There are no external incentives for the behavior.

- **Factitious Disorder by Proxy**   The intentional production or pretending of physical or psychological signs or symptoms in another person. There are no external incentives for the behavior.

Adapted with permission from the *Diagnostic and Statistical Manual of Mental Disorders*, Text Revision, Fourth Edition, (Copyright 2000). American Psychiatric Association.

First described in 1951, factitious disorder was originally called *Munchausen syndrome*, named after Baron Karl Friedrich Hieronymus von Munchausen, an eighteenth-century German nobleman known for telling tall (and mostly false) tales. People with factitious disorder engage in deceptive practices to produce signs of illness. These behaviors include faking elevated body temperature, putting blood in urine to simulate kidney/urinary tract infections, or taking blood-thinning medications to produce symptoms of hemophilia. In addition, people with factitious disorder deliberately and convincingly fake chest pain or abdominal pain. They are also exceedingly willing to go through numerous invasive and dangerous diagnostic and therapeutic procedures. To convince physicians that they are physically ill, people with factitious disorder will manipulate laboratory results to substantiate their illness claims. Many of these manipulations are quite sophisticated, but Table 5.3 lists some of the simple things that patients do to convince health personnel that they are truly ill. Although patients with factitious disorders seek and often beg for medical intervention, they never reveal the fact that they are creating their own physical distress.

People with factitious disorder (see the box "DSM-IV-TR: Factitious Disorder") often go to emergency rooms during evenings and weekends when they are more likely to be evaluated by junior clinical staff (Ford, 2004). Furthermore, they sometimes invent false demographic information, including aliases and false information about

TABLE 5.3

Laboratory Results for Patients with Factitious Disorder

Presenting Complaint	Laboratory Evidence
Hematuria (blood in urine)	Red candy in urine sample
Nonhealing wound	Mouthwash found in wound
Diarrhea	Excessive ingestion of castor oil or laxatives
Pain from "kidney stones"	Glass fragments in urine
Anemia	"Self-induced" blood draws with substantial blood loss
Vomiting	Ipecac abuse

From Krahn et al., 2003 and Wallach, 1994.

their past (they may claim to be a Medal of Honor winner or a former football player). If hospital staff become suspicious, they sometimes get angry, threaten to sue the hospital, and leave.

Although most people with factitious disorder fabricate physical symptoms, some patients may fabricate psychological symptoms (see the box "Real People, Real Disorders: The Piano Man"). Common psychological symptoms include grief and depression over the recent death of a relative, such as a spouse or a child. Later, the "dead" person turns out to be alive or has been dead for a very long time (Ford, 2005). People may also fake other psychological disorders, including multiple personality disorder (see the box "Real People, Real Disorders: The Hillside Strangler" in Chapter 15), substance dependence, dissociative and conversion disorders, memory loss, and post-traumatic stress disorder.

Factitious Disorder by Proxy *The physicians were puzzled by 6-year-old Jenny's illnesses. The pieces just did not seem to fit together. Her mother had brought her to the emergency room at least once a month for the past year. Jenny complained of constant nausea, but there did not seem to be a medical reason. She had a multitude of gastrointestinal procedures—upper GI series, lower GI series, CT scans, and endoscopy. Her mother had taken her to seven different hospitals in the same state, and she insisted on the same tests at each hospital. Jenny saw numerous specialists, and on many occasions, her mother insisted that Jenny be hospitalized. The medical staff became suspicious when Jenny's nausea disappeared upon hospitalization. Their first thought was that there was conflict between Jenny and her mother, and Jenny was experiencing severe anxiety. In children, stomachaches are a common symptom of anxiety. Jenny's mother became angry at the suggestion. She would not consider the possibility that Jenny's distress was psychological. On the latest visit to the emergency room, her mother brought in Jenny's bloody stool sample. The medical staff was informed by the lab that there was definitely blood in the stool—but it was not Jenny's blood type.*

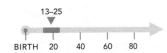

13–25

BIRTH 20 40 60 80

When one person induces illness symptoms in someone else, the disorder is known as **factitious disorder by proxy** or *Munchausen by proxy*. In most instances, a mother produces physical symptoms in the child, as in Jenny's case. After inducing the symptoms, the mother brings the child to the hospital and gives permission, or sometimes insists that the child undergo invasive and dangerous diagnostic procedures. There are few data describing the child victims of this disorder, but what exist indicates that children range in age from infancy through the teenage years and can have many different symptoms, including apnea (the child stops breathing), anorexia/feeding problems, diarrhea, seizures, cyanosis (turning blue from lack of oxygen), behavior problems, asthma, allergy, fevers, and pain (Sheridan, 2003). Child victims average 3.25 medical problems, ranging as high as 19 illnesses in a single child. Factitious disorder by proxy, when proved, is considered a form of child abuse, and the parent can be prosecuted. Occasionally, this disorder also occurs in nursing homes, where health care personnel inflict these physical symptoms on adult residents.

FUNCTIONAL IMPAIRMENT

People with factitious disorder often have numerous hospitalizations and can develop real disorders as a result of their self-administered injuries. For example, scar tissue may develop as a result of numerous surgical operations or self-injections. Sometimes a phenomenon known as *peregrination* occurs, in which the patient seeks treatment at different hospitals and sometimes travels from state to state or even country to country using false names. Factitious disorders are considered chronic, and although data from controlled trials are not available, it would appear that this disorder would affect social and occupational functioning.

factitious disorder by proxy a condition in which physical or psychological signs or symptoms of illness are intentionally produced in another person, most often in a child by a parent

real people, real disorders

The Piano Man—Dissociative Fugue, Factitious Disorder, or Malingering?

For a time, he was the world's most enigmatic young man—a haunted, gaunt figure known only as the "Piano Man." On April 7, 2005, police found him in Kent, England, soaking wet in a suit with the labels cut out. He had no passport, no credit cards, and no money. He was mute. Police put him in the care of psychiatrists, who gave him a pen and paper in the hope he would write his name. Instead, he drew a detailed sketch of a grand piano. When they brought him a piano, it was reported that he played for hours at a time. His condition set off a media frenzy in Europe, both to discover his identity and to determine his condition.

Many mental health professionals thought that he might have autistic disorder (see Chapter 12). His ability to play the piano was interpreted as an example of the highly specific talents often seen among people with this disorder. As discussed by a spokesperson for the National Autistic Society, the fact that he had ripped out the labels from his clothing and that he rarely made eye contact were further clues that he had autistic disorder. A clinical psychologist commented that the behaviors could also suggest schizophrenia. Depression or post-traumatic stress disorders were also possibilities. Medical administrators denied that he was faking his symptoms. He was described as very nervous and anxious.

Five months later, a nurse went into his room and said "Are you going to speak to us today?" He replied "Yes, I think I will." He told the staff that he was German, had been working in Paris but had lost his job, and after a broken love affair, had traveled by train to Great Britain. He was trying to commit suicide when the police picked him up on the beach. He had worked previously with mentally ill patients and had copied some mannerisms that successfully fooled the staff, including two very senior doctors. He said he drew a piano because that was the first thing that came into his head. Contrary to previous reports, he didn't play the piano; he just kept tapping the same key. After his revelation, he was sent home to Germany.

After you finish reading this chapter, decide for yourself. Did the Piano Man suffer from a dissociative fugue? Did he have factitious disorder? Did he have depression? Or was he malingering?

http://www.mirror.co.uk/news/headline=piano-man-sham

Among child victims of factitious disorder by proxy, 6 to 22% die as a result of the medical illnesses inflicted upon them, as do 25% of their siblings. The most common cause of death is suffocation or apnea (Ayoub et al., 2002; Sheridan, 2003). In one investigation (Sheridan, 2003), 7.3% of the child victims had long-term or permanent injuries.

EPIDEMIOLOGY

There are no known epidemiological data on the prevalence of factitious disorders in the general population. Among patients referred to one psychiatric consultation-liaison service, 0.8% of referrals over a 20-year period had factitious disorder (Sutherland & Rodin, 1990). At children's hospitals, the annual incidence was 2/100,000 or 0.002% (McClure et al., 1996 in Ford, 2005).

SEX, RACE, AND ETHNICITY

Although few data are available, factitious disorder is more likely to occur in women. When compared with men with the disorder, women in one sample were younger and more likely to have had health care training or health care jobs (Krahn et al., 2003). By contrast, those with the most severe disorder, including symptoms of peregrination and the adoption of aliases, are more likely to be male. Among people with factitious disorder by proxy, 77 to 98% are women, typically the child's biological mother, although fathers and foster mothers are also occasional perpetrators (Ayoub, 2006). There are no data available on race or ethnicity.

DEVELOPMENTAL FACTORS

Factitious disorder is most common in adults, but it does exist among children and adolescents as well. In one sample (Libow, 2000), children ranged in age from 8 to 18, and 70% were female. Children most commonly produce symptoms such as fever (heating the thermometer to fake a fever), diabetic insulin insufficiency (deliberately manipulating their insulin levels), bruises, and infections.

ETIOLOGY AND TREATMENT

Despite much speculation about the etiology of factitious disorders, few empirical data exist. Data from individuals suggest the presence of nonspecific neuroanatomical abnormalities, but in addition to lacking experimental controls, the findings are not consistent (Eisendrath & Young, 2005). Among the psychological theories, psychodynamic models explain factitious disorder as (a) an attempt to gain mastery or control that was formerly elusive, (b) a form of masochism (where pleasure occurs as a result of physical or psychological pain inflicted by oneself or another person), (c) the result of a deprived childhood, in which a child did not receive attention or care, or (d) an attempt to master trauma that was experienced as a result of physical or sexual abuse, with the physician unknowingly assuming the symbolic role of the abuser (Eisendrath & Young, 2005).

From a behavioral perspective, factitious behaviors are maintained because other people positively reinforce the person's illness behaviors or expressions. From a cognitive perspective, people with factitious disorders, through biased cognitive processes, misinterpret normal physical processes as indicators of physical illness; this cognitive perspective is similar to the hypotheses put forth to explain the etiology of somatoform disorders.

With respect to treatment, there are no controlled trials for factitious disorders. As we noted earlier, patients typically become angry when their manipulative behaviors are addressed by health or mental health personnel and they leave the treatment setting.

---

concept CHECK

- In contrast to somatoform or dissociative disorders, people with factitious disorders deliberately create physical symptoms in themselves or others.

- Whereas people who malinger do so for the purpose of compensation or to avoid a negative event, these factors are not apparent in people with factitious disorders.

- People can create symptoms of illness in themselves, as in factitious disorder, or can create illness in another person, as in factitious disorder by proxy.

APPLICATION QUESTION   What factors do you think would cause someone to decide to create illness symptoms in another person (as in a mother making her child/children ill) rather than creating those symptoms in herself?

THE WHOLE STORY: NANCY—A CASE OF CONVERSION DISORDER

The Patient: Nancy, 55 years old, comes to the psychiatric emergency room accompanied by her husband, George.

The Problem: Her complaint is as follows: "I have these fits and no one can find the cause." Nancy describes the sudden onset of seizures during which she falls down and shakes uncontrollably. She does not lose consciousness, and the seizures do not result in any injury. As a matter of fact, when she "falls," she usually falls slowly into a chair or onto the couch, suggesting some degree of control over her body movements. The last physician that she saw gave her husband some syringes with "antiseizure" medication, which he used to stop her seizures once they began.

The Diagnostic Assessment: After detailing the physical symptoms, the psychologist began to interview Nancy about her personal history. As a child, Nancy recalls her mother often taking her to the pediatrician. "My mother was very health conscious. She always worried about us when we were ill. If we had a fever or a headache, she would make us stay in bed, but she would stay in the room with us, playing games to keep us occupied. Once I was in the hospital to have my tonsils removed. This was before the time that parents were encouraged to stay in the hospital with their children. But my mother made such a fuss, the nurses let her stay. She showed me how much she loved me by refusing to leave me, even in the care of health professionals."

Nancy and George have been married for 35 years. She described her marriage as mediocre—she married George because she was pregnant. Her parents were both alcoholic, and as a child, she was subjected to a great deal of emotional abuse. Marriage was her way of getting out. George and Nancy have six children. Nancy never worked; her life revolved around her children. As a matter of fact, Nancy and George had nothing in common but their children. Recently, the youngest child moved out of the house. Now there was no one but Nancy and George, a marriage without communication or affection.

When asked how George was responding to her seizures, Nancy's face brightened. "It's the funniest thing" she said. "Ever since my seizures developed, George has become really attentive. He hasn't been this nice since I was pregnant. And I've been really lucky—George has been there every time that I've had a seizure to give me my medication. As soon as I get the injection, my tremors disappear." George had brought one of the syringes to the meeting. When he gave it to the psychologist, she could clearly see the words "saline injection" on the side. In fact, Nancy's antiseizure medication was salt water.

The Treatment: The therapist determined that Nancy was suffering from conversion disorder and that a number of environmental and social factors were maintaining her condition. However, because Nancy was convinced that her symptoms had a physical cause, the psychologist did not attempt to convince her otherwise. First, she had Nancy keep a log of what was happening every time that she had a "seizure." It became clear that her seizures occurred after conflict with her husband, children, and her sister. In most instances, the conflict centered on Nancy's inability to assert herself. Therefore, treatment focused on assertiveness training and general social skills training to increase her ability to express her wants and desires to her family. In addition, the therapist instructed George that when a seizure occurred, he should give Nancy her medicine but should not focus on or discuss the seizure in any way. This decreased family attention on this behavior. The therapist also gave George and Nancy homework assignments to do one pleasant thing per week—having dinner out with friends, going to a movie, taking a French cooking class.

The Treatment Outcome: After 6 months, Nancy's attacks had decreased from 3 times per week during the first month to only one in the past 8 weeks. She reported some increased marital satisfaction and was getting along better with her adult children. Her sister remained the only source of distress, but Nancy was vowing to continue to work on that relationship.

CRITICAL ISSUES to remember

1. Vague physical sensations, without any apparent organic cause, are common in the general population. These types of complaints are among the most common reasons for visits to primary care physicians. Among people who suffer from somatoform disorders, these symptoms create significant distress and cannot be reasoned away. It is important to understand that even if the cause of the physical symptoms is not organic, the pain and distress are very real.

2. Somatoform disorders are defined by the presence of physical symptoms or concerns about an illness that cannot be explained by an established medical or psychological disorder. Biological, psychological, and environmental factors may play a role in the onset of somatoform disorders. Environmental events, such as chronic stress, may create alterations in neurochemical response systems that automatically respond in times of stress. These altered responses may produce physical symptoms that cause psychological concern. Furthermore, reinforcement of the expression of physical complaints by parents or significant others may create physician-seeking or doctor-shopping as well as social and occupational impairment.

3. Dissociative disorders involve disruption in the integrated functions of consciousness, memory, identity, or perception, as in depersonalization, derealization, amnesia, or confusion or alteration of identity. Dissociative disorders are a controversial category of psychological dysfunction. Dissociative symptoms and disorders may represent culture-bound syndromes. Some researchers have suggested that DID is a culture-bound disorder that is limited to Western cultures.

4. Despite retrospective accounts of patients identified with these disorders, few empirical data support the post-traumatic hypothesis that childhood abuse is a major cause of dissociative disorders. By contrast, there are empirical data to support an iatrogenic model of dissociative identity disorder. It is very important to remember that an iatrogenic or sociocultural model does *not* mean that the disorder does not exist. Rather, it reflects an understanding of how these disorders are acquired.

5. The concept of repressed/recovered memories is inconsistent with current scientific knowledge regarding normal memory processes. Despite the existence of post-traumatic models, amnesia regarding activities before age 6 is common, and creating false memories, even of events as horrific as sexual abuse, is possible. This does not mean that childhood sexual abuse does not exist or is not a problem. However, most people who were abused as children remember it without prompting.

6. Malingering involves the creation of physical symptoms and illnesses for the purpose of gaining money or drugs, or avoiding negative events such as work, criminal prosecution, or military service. Factitious disorders involve the deliberate creation of physical symptoms or illness, but there is no apparent observable goal. In contrast, people with dissociative or somatoform disorders do not deliberately produce their physical symptoms and do not understand why the symptoms occur.

TEST yourself

For more review plus practice tests, flashcards, and Speaking Out: DSM in Context videos, log onto www.MyPsychLab.com

1. Julie has been diagnosed with a somatoform disorder. This means she is suffering from a condition in which her physical symptoms
   a. are faked in order to receive some type of external compensation
   b. can be explained by a psychological disorder
   c. cannot be explained by a medical or psychological disorder
   d. are confined to a part of her body that is particularly stressed

2. A patient with somatization disorder would, over the course of a lifetime, have which of the following categories of physical complaints?
   a. pain in the head, abdomen, back, joints, and extremities
   b. pain, gastrointestinal distress, sexual dysfunction, and pseudoneurological symptoms
   c. nausea, bloating, vomiting, diarrhea, and food intolerance.
   d. sexual disinterest, irregular menstruation, vomiting, and enuresis

3. Patients suffering from conversion disorder have symptoms that consist primarily of
   a. pseudoneurological complaints
   b. severe headaches
   c. unexplained pain
   d. gastrointestinal distress

4. Glove anesthesia is considered a classic conversion disorder. This is because glove anesthesia
   a. occurs in only one hand
   b. does not follow known neurological patterns
   c. follows known pain patterns
   d. occurs when the hand is in one position for a long time

5. Susan is always going to her doctor asking to be examined for cancer or heart disease even though she doesn't have any symptoms. Her physician says she has hypochondriasis. People with this disorder
   a. have anxiety about their health that leads them to deny their physical symptoms
   b. have a dysfunctional mind-set that leads them to worry excessively about their health
   c. avoid medical care because their symptoms aren't real
   d. are typically in poor health and should monitor their symptoms carefully

6. A patient who is successfully recovering from gall bladder surgery and is reluctant to engage in any physical activities even when approved by a physician may be suffering from
   a. hypochondriasis
   b. pain disorder
   c. la belle indifference
   d. transient hypochondriasis

7. A patient with body dysmorphic disorder (BDD) is best described as someone who
   a. has pain in many parts of his or her body
   b. has a delusional preoccupation with his or her body
   c. complains constantly of illness but is not sick
   d. experiences anxiety when undergoing medical procedures

8. One of the difficulties in making a diagnosis of somatoform disorder is that it is difficult to distinguish it from comorbid or coexisting conditions such as
   a. PTSD
   b. malingering and/or factitious disorders
   c. anxiety and/or depressive disorders
   d. hypochondriasis

9. The significance of *shenjing shuairuo* to the discussion of somatoform disorders across cultures demonstrates that
   a. there is significant cultural variation in the diagnosis
   b. there is little cultural variation in the diagnosis
   c. somatoform disorders are more common in Asian cultures
   d. somatoform disorders are more common in African cultures

10. Environmental factors often associated with somatoform disorders include
    a. country of origin
    b. time of year
    c. family conflict/violence
    d. presence of toxins in the soil

11. Which of the following cognitive factors have been associated with somatoform disorders?
    a. somatic amplification
    b. heightened sensory and perceptual sensitivity
    c. inaccurate beliefs
    d. all of the above

12. The first challenge in treating people with somatoform disorders is that they are often
    a. suffering from several serious medical conditions
    b. unwilling to consult only one doctor
    c. reluctant to consult a professional, especially a psychologist
    d. too depressed or anxious to seek treatment

13. One form of treatment that has been found to be very helpful with somatoform disorders is
    a. electroconvulsive therapy (ECT)
    b. symptom-focused cognitive-behavior therapy (CBT)

    c. MAO inhibitors
    d. recovered memory therapy (RMT)

14. A client goes to see a therapist with the following complaints: She feels detachment from her body and is experiencing herself as strange or unreal. In some situations she feels as if she were watching herself. The therapist says she is experiencing
    a. depersonalization
    b. amnesia
    c. multiple personalities
    d. post-traumatic stress disorder

15. A patient is referred to a neurologist for isolated memory loss; the diagnosis of dissociative amnesia is made. The most likely etiology in this patient is
    a. head injury
    b. repeated drug overdose
    c. extreme emotional trauma
    d. stroke

16. A man who owns a hardware store in a New England town mysteriously disappears. Years later the man is discovered in California. His name is changed, he has remarried, and he now works in a different occupation. He claims that he has no memory for his past life. The man may be suffering from
    a. psychogenic fugue
    b. depersonalization
    c. dissociative identity disorder
    d. post-traumatic stress disorder

17. Some experts argue that dissociative identity disorder, DID, is an iatrogenic disease, which means that it is caused by
    a. the interaction of biological, social, and environmental factors
    b. the experience of therapy itself
    c. repeated exposure to risk factors
    d. lifestyle factors that are difficult to change

18. The sociocultural model postulates that DID develops when individuals use cues from
    a. the media
    b. therapists
    c. other people who display multiple identities
    d. all of the above

19. Patients with factitious disorders have which of the following characteristics?
    a. brief medical histories
    b. self-administered injuries
    c. symptoms that consist primarily of pseudoneurological complaints
    d. extreme fear and avoidance of medical professionals

20. An 18-month-old infant in the pediatric ICU has been experiencing episodes of difficulty breathing and rapid heart rate with no apparent cause. All tests are negative. These symptoms only occur when the mother is with the child. The most likely cause of the infant's symptoms is
    a. congenital heart disease
    b. asthma
    c. factitious disorder by proxy
    d. seizure disorder

Answers: 1 c, 2 b, 3 a, 4 b, 5 b, 6 d, 7 b, 8 c, 9 a, 10 c, 11 d, 12 c, 13 b, 14 a, 15 c, 16 a, 17 b, 18 d, 19 b, 20 c.

CHAPTER objectives

At the end of this chapter, you should be able to:

1. Distinguish between normal sad mood and depression and between euphoria and mania.
2. Understand the differences between major depressive, dysthymia, bipolar I, and bipolar II disorders.
3. Discuss sex differences in the risk for depression.
4. Discuss factors associated with suicide and the relationship between depression and suicidal ideation and behavior.
5. Understand psychodynamic, behavioral, cognitive, and biological theories of the causes of depression.
6. Identify efficacious treatments for major depression and bipolar disorder.

mood disorders

Elaine and Zack met in college and fell in love. Inseparable for 4 years, they couldn't wait to get married and start a family. Zack studied accounting and Elaine majored in communications. Right after college they married and moved to Elaine's home town. Zack got a job with an accounting firm, and Elaine wrote news copy for a local TV station. They were very happy in their marriage, reveled in building their first home, and were already thinking about children.

One stormy evening while cooking dinner, Elaine got a phone call saying that her husband had been in an accident and that she needed to get to the hospital right away. She arrived too late; Zack had already been pronounced dead.

Elaine was inconsolable. At first, she couldn't believe what had happened. She kept expecting to see Zack again or that somehow she would wake up from this nightmare. When the reality of Zack's death finally registered, she cried for hours at a time, was unable to eat or sleep, and could barely get dressed. She saw no reason to live without him. None of the help her family and friends gave her could touch the pain she felt.

For the first 6 months, her grief was extreme. She went back to work and spent time with her family, but she felt she was just going through the motions. She would still come home and cry—surrounded by memories of the love of her life.

A year after Zack's death, Elaine's parents convinced her to sell their house and move somewhere where the memories were not so strong. This wise move helped Elaine begin to experience life again as more than just pain. Although the loss of her husband will always be part of her innermost being, and at times the pain returns, gradually, she has been able to begin to reengage in life and to live life the way Zack would have wanted her to.

Linda was a senior in high school. She had good grades (As and Bs), was involved in extracurricular activities, and played varsity sports. Although she was a worrier by temperament, she had friends and a busy high school schedule.

In her senior year she started losing interest in her activities. She quit the student newspaper and found it hard to drag herself to practice. All she wanted to do was stay at home in her room—she stopped seeing her friends and avoided their phone calls.

She went to bed at a decent hour but woke up first at 5 a.m. and then gradually earlier and earlier. Soon, she was wide awake at 3 a.m. and unable to fall back to sleep. She lost her appetite. Everything tasted like cardboard, and she lost 7 pounds that she didn't have to lose. She felt restless.

She was irritable with her younger brother and lashed out at her parents, which she had never done before. She stared at her homework for hours, reading the same paragraph again and again. Her grades plummeted and she became ineligible for athletics.

One of her teachers recommended that she see the school counselor, which she did grudgingly. Her thoughts became very dark, and she often felt there was no reason to live. She considered killing herself and had begun to explore how she might do it.

Linda had never felt this way before. She told the counselor that her maternal grandmother had been in a psychiatric hospital and that she had seen Prozac in her mother's medicine cabinet. The counselor contacted Linda's mother and helped her set up an appointment with a psychiatrist immediately. As it turned out, Linda's mother also had had several depressive episodes (often in the autumn months) and had been on medication for years. Linda started antidepressant medication and saw a psychologist for cognitive-behavioral therapy to help her develop skills to combat the negative thought patterns that often accompany depression.

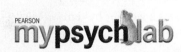

Depression

The Case of Helen
"I had electroshock treatments every other day for two weeks."
www.mypsychlab.com

Both Elaine and Linda had loss of energy and appetite, trouble sleeping, and very sad mood, but their stories illustrate vastly different sources of internal pain. Elaine was experiencing a classic grief reaction following the death of her husband, whereas Linda could not identify a cause for her depressed mood.

Linda's symptoms are a clear example of a mood disorder characterized most prominently by a pervasive and unshakable low mood. Linda's problems distressed her and bewildered those around her. Once a high-functioning and active girl both socially and athletically, she had become a social recluse. The cluster of signs and symptoms Linda experienced, including social withdrawal, lack of energy and interest, loss of appetite, insomnia, irritability, and restlessness, constitute a disorder known as major depression.

Major depression is just one type of mood disorder. Actually, mood disorders consist of several different conditions characterized by various degrees of depressed (low) or manic (high) moods. People with these syndromes have physical, emotional, and cognitive symptoms that may interfere with their ability to work, study, sleep, eat, interact with others, have sexual relations, and enjoy daily life. Although all of us have mood fluctuations from time to time, major depression is *not* the same as a transient "blue" mood or sad feelings, and mania is *not* the same as being elated. This chapter will examine how and why the mood disorders involve more than just bad (or good) moods.

What Are Mood Disorders?

As their name implies, **mood disorders** are syndromes whose predominant feature is a disturbance in mood. The disturbance can take the form of mood that is abnormally low or high. Mood that is abnormally low is known as **depression**, whereas mood that is abnormally high is known as **mania**. There are three distinct mood disorders: major depressive disorder, dysthymic disorder (or dysthymia), and bipolar disorder. These disorders are distinguished from each other by the presence of depressed or elated mood (or both) and by the length of time that the mood abnormalities persist.

mood disorders syndromes in which a disturbance in mood is the predominant feature

depression mood that is abnormally low

mania mood that is abnormally high

Major Depressive Episode

Major depression must include either depressed mood/irritability or loss of interest or pleasure (*anhedonia*) for at least 2 weeks. To meet criteria for major depression, at least three of the following symptoms must be present nearly every day for at least 2 weeks:

- significant weight loss when not dieting, or weight gain (change of more than 5% of body weight in a month), or decrease or increase in appetite
- insomnia or hypersomnia
- psychomotor agitation or retardation
- fatigue or loss of energy
- feelings of worthlessness or excessive or inappropriate guilt
- decreased ability to think or concentrate, or indecisiveness
- recurrent thoughts of death; recurrent thoughts of suicide without a specific plan, or a suicide attempt or a specific plan

Other symptoms may include:

- persistent anxious or "empty" mood
- feelings of hopelessness, pessimism, and helplessness
- changes in alcohol or drug use (prescription and nonprescription)
- crying spells
- decreased interest in sex
- physical changes such as headaches, digestive problems, and chronic pain that do not respond to treatment

Adapted with permission from the *Diagnostic and Statistical Manual of Mental Disorders*, Text Revision, Fourth Edition, (Copyright 2000). American Psychiatric Association.

MAJOR DEPRESSIVE DISORDER

The core symptom of **major depressive disorder** is persistent sad or low mood that is severe enough to impair a person's interest in or ability to engage in normally enjoyable activities. In adults, depressed mood is central to major depressive disorder, but in children, the persistent mood disturbance may take the form of irritability or hostility. Major depressive disorder can be extremely debilitating, in part because of other psychological, emotional, social, and physical problems that often accompany the persistent depressed mood. People with this disorder may feel completely worthless or extremely guilty, and they may be at risk for harming themselves. Major depressive disorder can affect a person physically by disrupting sleep, appetite, and sexual drive. Often, this means problems falling or staying asleep, feeling tired all the time, and having decreased appetite. However, about 40% of people diagnosed with major depressive disorder actually sleep and eat *more* than usual (a case referred to as "atypical depression"). Either way, the changes in sleep and appetite can lead to major problems with attention and concentration, and can increase an already overwhelming sense of inadequacy and inclination to withdraw from the world.

Major depression is an episodic illness. During their lifetime, some people have only one episode (*single episode*), but others suffer from multiple episodes separated by periods of normal mood (*recurrent*). Major depression is a prevalent psychological disorder: approximately 7 to 18% of the United States population experiences at least one episode of major depression by age 40. A single episode, according to the Diagnostic and Statistical Manual of Mental Disorders (DSM), lasts at least 2 weeks, but often episodes can persist for several months (see the accompanying DSM box). Figure 6.1 illustrates the course of the different forms of depression.

Inability to fall asleep or stay asleep is one of the symptoms of depression.

major depressive disorder persistent sad or low mood that is severe enough to impair a person's interest in or ability to engage in normally enjoyable activities

FIGURE 6.1
The Different Forms of Depression

Depression is not a single disorder, and its course and severity may differ depending on the specific condition. Contrast each of these patterns to normal mood fluctuations.

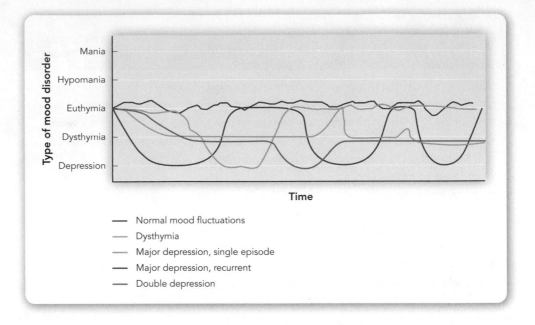

In addition to symptom duration of 2 weeks, another factor that distinguishes major depressive disorder from sad mood is that the symptoms must affect the ability to function in social or work settings. Symptoms of depression may sometimes result from physical disorders such as Cushing's syndrome (hypercortisolism, or too much of the hormone cortisol) and hypothyroidism (lack of sufficient thyroid hormone); however, a diagnosis of depression is not assigned if the symptoms are due to general medical conditions such as these. Nor is the diagnosis made if the depressed feelings result from a life event such as the death of a loved one, as was the case for Elaine (CenterWatch, 1995–2007; Ebmeier et al., 2006; Moore & Bona, 2001; Moore & McLaughlin, 2003; National Institute of Mental Health, 2000). Finally, depression can occur even after events that are not typically associated with sadness, such as after having a baby (we will consider depression following childbirth later in this chapter).

DYSTHYMIA

Not all depression is "major." **Dysthymia**, or *dysthymic disorder*, can best be conceptualized as a chronic state of depression (see the accompanying DSM box). The symptoms are the same as those of major depression, but they are less severe. Whereas major depression is an episodic disorder, dysthymia is persistent: by definition it lasts 2 or more years, and the individual is never without symptoms for more than 2 months (American Psychiatric Association, 2000). Dysthymia is a somewhat paradoxical condition: on a day-to-day basis, the symptoms are relatively mild, but because they are so persistent, they may lead to severe outcomes (e.g., social isolation, high suicide risk) that affect not only the sufferer but also extended family and friends. Because symptoms are generally less severe than those seen in major depression, people can suffer from dysthymia for years before seeking treatment. Meanwhile, friends and family may turn away, often mislabeling the person as too moody and difficult.

Louise was under a constant gray cloud. She felt as if she had lived through the marriage of her daughter and the birth of her first two grandchildren like a zombie. She felt no joy, no wonder, and would rather stay home and cry than visit and play with her grandchildren. When all of the other women at church beamed about the accomplishments of their families, she could only feel guilty for not being part of her own children's lives.

dysthymia a chronic state of depression; the symptoms are the same as those of major depression, but they are less severe

DSM-IV-TR

Dysthymia

Dysthymia is an overwhelming, chronic state of depression, characterized by continuous depressed mood for at least 2 years. (In children and adolescents, mood can be irritable and duration must be at least 1 year.) The condition also features the consistent presence of at least two of the following symptoms for at least two consecutive months:

- poor appetite or overeating
- insomnia or hypersomnia
- low energy or fatigue
- low self-esteem
- poor concentration or difficulty making decisions
- feelings of hopelessness

Adapted with permission from the *Diagnostic and Statistical Manual of Mental Disorders*, Text Revision, Fourth Edition, (Copyright 2000). American Psychiatric Association.

DSM-IV-TR

Manic Episode

A distinct period of abnormally and persistently elevated, expansive, or irritable mood, lasting at least 1 week or requiring hospitalization. During this time period, the person has three (or more) of the following symptoms:

- inflated self-esteem or grandiosity
- decreased need for sleep (e.g., feels rested after only 3 hours of sleep)
- greater talkativeness than usual or pressure to keep talking
- flight of ideas or subjective experience that thoughts are racing
- distractibility (i.e., attention too easily drawn to irrelevant external stimuli)
- increased goal-directed activity (either socially, at work or school, or sexually) or psychomotor agitation, or excessive involvement in pleasurable activities that have a high potential for painful consequences (such as unrestrained buying sprees, sexual indiscretions, or foolish business investments)

Adapted with permission from the *Diagnostic and Statistical Manual of Mental Disorders*, Text Revision, Fourth Edition, (Copyright 2000). American Psychiatric Association.

People with dysthymia may also have major depressive episodes (this is known as **double depression**). The combination of episodic major depressions superimposed on chronic low mood is often associated with poorer long-term outcome and higher relapse risk than either disorder alone (Keller et al., 1997). In many instances, dysthymia is undiagnosed until the person has a major depressive episode. When the person seeks help for the more severe depressive symptoms, the longer history of dysthymia is identified. Figure 6.1 presents the time course of dysthymia and double depression.

BIPOLAR DISORDER

As stated earlier, mood disturbance can include mood that is too low or too high, with the latter known as *mania*. Mania is different from elated mood, in which excitement and good feelings naturally match a happy or an enjoyable experience. Rather, mania is high mood that is clearly excessive and is often accompanied by inappropriate and potentially dangerous behavior, irritability, pressured or rapid speech, and a false sense of well-being

double depression combination of episodic major depressions superimposed on chronic low mood (see the accompanying DSM box). The case studies illustrate the contrast between normal elation and mania (see case study boxes). Because recurrent mania in the absence of any depressive episodes is extremely rare, the DSM does not recognize it as a separate disorder. Manic episodes almost always occur in tandem with episodes of depression, and a person who has only a single manic episode will very likely have depression as well. Generally, a person is said to suffer from **bipolar disorder** (formerly known as manic-depressive disorder) when both episodic depressed mood and episodic mania are present.

Bipolar disorder consists of dramatic shifts in mood, energy, and ability to function. It is a long-term episodic illness in which mood shifts between the two emotional "poles" of mania and depression. In a depressed period, a person may be all but immobile, feeling unable to get out of bed. By contrast, in a manic period, the same person may be so full of energy as to try to start a new business, buy a house, and plan a trip around the world in the same day. At either extreme, the person cannot cope with the demands of everyday life. Periods of normal feelings and energy commonly occur between these mood changes.

Bipolar disorder is commonly categorized as either **bipolar I** or **bipolar II** (see the accompanying DSM box). The main difference is the degree of mania. In bipolar I, full-blown mania alternates with episodes of major depression; it also includes a single manic episode with or without periods of depression. In bipolar II disorder, *hypomania* alternates with episodes of major depression. **Hypomania** is a mood elevation that is clearly abnormal but not severe enough to impair functioning or to require hospitalization. Behaviorally, a person in a hypomanic state may be overly talkative, excitable, or irritable, but there are no impulsive acts and gross lapses of judgment that are common during mania (such as telephoning Washington to tell the president how to run the country). Hypomania is "mild mania" and lasts at least 4 days (Berk & Dodd, 2005; Keck et al., 2001). More common than bipolar I, bipolar II disorder is defined by at least one episode of major depression and at least one hypomanic event. Bipolar II can be especially tricky to diagnose because a person experiencing hypomania may associate these episodes with periods of high productivity or creativity. The person may see these episodes as having positive rather than negative consequences and be much less likely to report them as distressing or problematic.

Jack felt on top of the world. He had never had his ideas flow so fast and furious. All week he needed only 2 hours of sleep per night, and he woke up totally refreshed and ready to go. He felt like a people magnet. He was funny, engaging, and full of energy. He was Instant Messaging people at all hours of the night and couldn't figure out why other people were signing off when he was in such good form. He wished this feeling could last forever.

bipolar disorder   both episodic depressed mood and episodic mania

bipolar I   full-blown mania alternates with episodes of major depression

bipolar II   hypomania alternates with episodes of major depression

hypomania   mood elevation that is clearly abnormal, yet not severe enough to impair functioning or require hospitalization

The frequency of mood elevations varies considerably across individuals and even within the same individual across time. Some people have episodes yearly or even less frequently. Mood shifts come out of the blue and are not necessarily in response to environmental events. In contrast, people with *rapidly cycling bipolar disorder* have four or more severe mood disturbances within a single year (American Psychiatric Association, 2000). Even less common is an extremely rapid cycling pattern in which multiple shifts between manic and depressed mood occur within a single day. Finally, people who have symptoms of mania and depression at the same time suffer from a **mixed state**; symptoms can include agitation, insomnia, changes in appetite, psychosis, and suicidal thoughts. A person in a mixed state can feel very sad and very energized at the same time. The episodic nature of bipolar I disorder, bipolar II disorder, and rapidly cycling bipolar disorder is illustrated in Figure 6.2.

mixed state symptoms of mania and depression that occur at the same time

NORMAL BEHAVIOR CASE STUDY
Elation Due to Academic Success

George was the first person in his family to go to college. His parents had immigrated to the United States from Cuba and had given him every possible advantage. He was valedictorian of his high school class and worked hard for the honor. He was never one to party or waste time—for him school was all about academics and sports. He lettered in baseball and led his school to the State Championships.

He got a full baseball scholarship to an Ivy League school. He was grateful for his athletic skills and was an All-American starting pitcher for the team, but political science was his first love.

George's teachers recognized that he had a keen sense of international relations, and they felt he had the potential to go far. Given his academic record and athletic success, they encouraged him to apply for a Rhodes scholarship. George thought that the son of immigrants would never have a chance at getting a Rhodes. He was so convinced of this that after he sent in his application, he put it out of his mind, forgetting about the decision date.

When the letter arrived in the mail, he remembered and his heart jumped into his throat. He talked himself down, reminding himself of the competition and his background. Then he opened the letter and found he had been selected. He started jumping up and down, knocking on everyone's dorm room, yelling "you're not going to believe this!" He jumped into the shower with his clothes on, shouting "omigod, omigod!" When he called his parents, he was talking so fast in a combination of Spanish and English that they could not understand him. He was positively over the moon! But after the news sank in, he came down to earth, thrilled and honored by the possibilities his future held. ■

ABNORMAL BEHAVIOR CASE STUDY
First Manic Episode

Alexis was walking the street in a short red dress, fashion gloves, and jewelry. Her face was completely and overly made up with gaudy red lipstick. She was approaching men she didn't know, asking for a light and coming on to them sexually. An older man, concerned for her well-being, notified the police.

In the psychiatric emergency room, she was fawning over the police officer, showing off her legs. She kept walking across the room to strike up conversations with other patients—the topics were inappropriate and flirtatious. Her energy had an edge. She kept asking when she was going to be seen, and "what's wrong with this joint that you can't get served."

Given her disruptive behavior, the attending psychiatrist and the resident evaluated her immediately. During the interview, she told the resident he was a hunk and asked him what he was doing later that night. Her speech was rapid and pressured, the doctors couldn't get a question in edgewise, and whatever answers she gave were not to the questions they asked. The attending physician gave her a medication to calm her down until her parents could arrive. As it turned out, she had just maxed out her credit cards buying all of the clothes, makeup, and jewelry she was wearing. Her parents had called in a missing persons report the previous evening and provided more information.

Her drug screen was negative, and there were no other medical reasons for her bizarre behavior. Her family history was positive for bipolar disorder, and this was her first manic episode. Alexis was admitted to the hospital and started a course of lithium medication. She also received psychoeducation about bipolar disorder and lithium and started psychotherapy to help her adjust to living with her diagnosis. ■

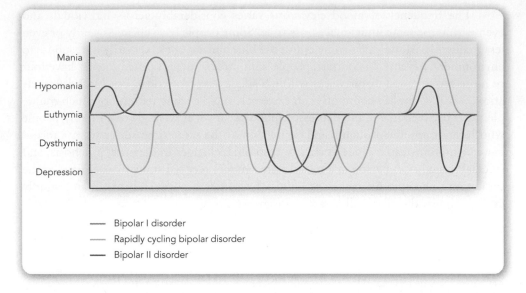

FIGURE 6.2

The Different Types of Bipolar Illness

Each type of bipolar disorder (bipolar I disorder, bipolar II disorder, and rapid cycling bipolar disorder) has a different course of illness.

Bipolar disorder requires lifelong treatment and clinical management (Depression and Bipolar Support Alliance, 2006, January 26, 2007). Although most people with bipolar disorder are free of symptoms between episodes, many have some continuing symptoms. Others, despite treatment, have chronic unremitting symptoms. Bipolar disorder is frequently depicted in literature as the mental illness that rests between the boundaries of creativity and madness, although this is not accurate. (See the box "Examining the Evidence: Is There a Link Between Art and Madness.")

Another disorder, **cyclothymic disorder**, is characterized by fluctuations that alternate between hypomanic and depressive symptoms. In cyclothymia, the episodes are not as severe as mania or major depression, but they persist for at least 2 years and as a result of the cyclical and often unpredictable mood changes, cause impairment (Winzelberg et al., 2000).

EPIDEMIOLOGY OF DEPRESSION

Major depression is the most common psychiatric disorder worldwide (Kessler et al., 1994b; Moore & Bona, 2001). Across various age, sex, and racial and ethnic groups in the United States (Kessler et al., 1994b, 2005; Regier et al., 1988), approximately 20.8% of people have a mood disorder during their lifetime (Kessler et al., 2005). For major depression, the prevalence ranges from around 5.8% (as assessed in the 1980s) to almost 17% (assessed in the 2000s) (Kessler et al., 2005). Dysthymia is less common, affecting between 2.5 and 6% of the general population (Kessler et al., 2005). Depression ranks fourth in terms of the global burden of disease (CenterWatch, 1995–2007; Moore & Bona, 2001). Disease burden uses an indicator called *disability adjusted life years (DALY)*, which measures the total amount of healthy life lost, to all causes, whether from premature death or disability. Clearly, major depression is a burden to both the individual and society.

In a manic state, people with bipolar disorder may act impulsively, such as spending excessive amounts of money.

SEX, RACE, AND ETHNICITY

Despite their commonality, mood disorders do not occur with equal frequency across all sex, racial, and ethnic groups. Although the precise reasons are unknown,

cyclothymic disorder condition characterized by fluctuations that alternate between hypomanic symptoms and depressive symptoms

examining the evidence

Is There a Link Between Art and Madness?

■ **The Facts** Throughout history there have been many remarkably talented artists who struggled through the tumultuous peaks and pitfalls associated with mood disturbances. In many cases, their personal experiences became the substance of their artistic expression: As Byron observed, "We of the craft are all crazy. Some are affected by gaiety, others by melancholy, but all are more or less touched." But is there really a relationship between art and madness?

■ **The Evidence** In *Touched with Fire*, Johns Hopkins Professor Kay Redfield Jamison examined the lives, works, and familial pedigrees of writers, poets, artists, and musicians and described a common thread among them: volatile cycles of compelling imagination, exuberance, and intelligence countered by periods of grim isolation and melancholy. Emily Dickinson, T.S. Eliot, Ernest Hemingway, Victor Hugo, Michelangelo, Charles Mingus, Georgia O'Keeffe, Sylvia Plath, Peter Tchaikovsky, Vincent van Gogh, and Virginia Woolf are just a few on Jamison's list with probable cyclothymia (cycling between dysthymia and hypomania), major depression, or manic-depressive illness. But without sound psychological and biological data to corroborate the diagnosis, these historical observations are not hard evidence that these individuals actually suffered from psychiatric illness. The question remains: what empirical evidence supports this link?

■ **Let's Examine the Evidence** In his research, University of Kentucky Professor Arnold Ludwig found that writers had much higher rates of depression and mania than matched controls. In his work *The Price of Greatness*, he writes that members of the artistic professions or creative arts are more likely than others to suffer from a lifetime mental illness. Similarly, in *The Hypomanic Edge*, Johns Hopkins psychologist John Gartner notes that hypomania may be a common (and potentially positive) trait among those who thrive in Western, bigger-better-faster culture. Yet not all individuals who have mood disorders are creative, and not all artists have mood disorders. So is there another variable that may be influential in this relationship?

■ **What Are Alternative Explanations for This Relationship?** Jamison suggests that mood disorders may foster imaginative thought, and she notes that diagnostic criteria for mania include "sharpened and unusually creative thinking." Combined with the breadth of deep emotions present in some mood disorders, such intellectual inspiration might lend itself to artistic creativity. "Ludwig speculates that those with mood disorders might be naturally drawn to artistic professions, given the potential normalization of the artistic temperament in such fields."

■ **Conclusion** The link between creativity and mood disorders is still not well understood but potentially has many implications for artists, medicine, and society. When creativity is a work source or is intrinsic to self-perception, what are the potential implications of dampening this temperament with pharmacology? Could this dampening of the creative spirit pose any barriers to efficacious treatment, and if so, what are the implications of untreated depression?

References: Gartner, 2005; Jamison, 1993, 1995; Ludwig, 1995.

some differences—especially the disproportionate number of women affected by depression—have consistently been observed and remain a topic of considerable scientific debate.

Depression in Women Across cultures, almost twice as many women (10 to 25%) as men (5 to 12%) suffer from major depression (Ebmeier et al., 2006; Kessler et al., 1994a), even though the exact ratio changes with age (Angold et al., 1991). Depressive symptoms are more common among women who have few financial resources, are less educated, and are unemployed (McGrath et al., 1990). Marriage seems to provide some protection for men, whereas married women have higher rates of depression than unmarried women (McGrath et al., 1990). Even among women, rates of depression vary by age. Reproductive events such as puberty, the premenstrual period, pregnancy, the postpartum period, and menopause all are risks for mood disturbances (Bennett et al., 2004; Driscoll, 2006; Evans et al., 2005; O'Hara & Swain, 1996), suggesting that the ebb and flow of female hormones may have some role. Yet the precise manner in which hormonal fluctuations influence risk for mood disorders remains unclear.

Postpartum Depression (PPD)

All of the books painted such a rosy picture—the happy mothers breastfeeding, talking with other moms, developing that special bond with their new babies. What is wrong with me? Why do I just want this child to stop crying and go away? I can't bear to have my husband touch me. What kind of a mother am I? All the baby does is scream. Help me! Where's the joy? Why can't I feel what they're feeling? —Susan, new mother

Approximately 10 to 17% of women experience depression during pregnancy, but as many as 80% of new mothers develop the "baby blues" within a few days of childbirth. These mild mood symptoms (tearfulness, sadness) generally subside 2 weeks postpartum (i.e., after childbirth). However, approximately 25% of women who report postpartum blues later develop more severe postpartum depression. In one of the most comprehensive studies conducted to date, 18% of Swedish women reported symptoms of depression 6 to 8 weeks postpartum, and 13% were still depressed 6 months postpartum. These rates have led some to call postpartum depression "the most common complication of childbirth." This disorder not only negatively affects mothers' functioning, but it is also associated with social, emotional, cognitive, and behavioral difficulties in the children (Josefsson et al., 2007; Larsson, et al., 2004; Moses-Kolko & Roth, 2004; O'Hara & Swain, 1996; Troutman & Cutrona, 1990). In very rare cases, women may suffer a different condition known as postpartum psychosis, which we discuss in chapter 10.

The "baby blues" are common among new mothers, but postpartum depression is a serious psychological disorder.

Depression in Racial and Ethnic Minorities and Across Cultures   In the United States, several studies found lower rates of depression among non-Hispanic black and Hispanic populations than among whites (Breslau et al., 2005). The National Health and Nutrition Examination study reported higher rates of major depression in whites (10.4%) than African Americans (7.5%) or Mexican Americans (8.0%), but higher rates of dysthymia in African Americans (7.5%) and Mexican Americans (7.4%) than whites (5.7%) (Riolo et al., 2005). Poverty was significantly associated with major depression in whites, and low levels of education were significantly associated with major depression for Mexican Americans. Intriguingly, major depression is reported at lower rates (0.8%) in Asian American populations (Jackson-Triche et al., 2000).

Understanding racial, ethnic, and cultural differences requires an appreciation of culture and language. Studies that have used similar methods—structured clinical interviews, for example—have identified vastly different prevalence figures across countries, with estimates of major depression nearing 20% in the United States in contrast to less than 5% in some countries in Asia (Tsai et al., 2003). Is it possible that specific factors related to race and ethnicity protect against the development of depression? In fact, two factors, ethnic identity (Herd & Grube, 1996; Mossakowski, 2003) and religious participation (Lee & Newberg, 2005; Varon & Riley, 1999; Wallace & Forman, 1998) seem to function as protective factors, lowering risk for depression.

A more fundamental question is whether the concept of depression is based primarily on a European (Western) understanding of mental illness. Many languages and cultures do not have words for depression, so simple translations of

Western interview questions can complicate the diagnostic process, yielding inaccurate diagnosis and incorrect prevalence data. Overall, individuals from various cultures report psychological and physical symptoms of depression (Cheng, 1989; Simon et al., 1999). Nonetheless, culturally appropriate terminology would ensure recognition of depression across cultures, races, and ethnic groups and also enhance treatment delivery and adherence (Patel, 2001).

EPIDEMIOLOGY OF BIPOLAR DISORDER

Bipolar disorder, which is much less common than major depression, has a lifetime prevalence of approximately 2 to 4% in North America (Grant et al., 2005; Schaffer et al., 2006). Bipolar disorder affects people of all ages. The average age of onset is in the early 20s, and the highest prevalence is among young adults ages 18 to 24. It is more common among those with low socioeconomic status, those who also have anxiety or substance use disorders, and those who have a close relative with the disorder. In the United States, the prevalence is highest among Native Americans and lowest among Asian Americans and Hispanics. Unlike major depression, bipolar disorder affects males and females equally, but there are a few sex differences. Men are more likely to have a manic episode first, whereas in women, the first episode is more likely to be depression (Winzelberg et al., 2000). Over the course of a lifetime, men are likely to have an equal or a greater number of manic episodes than women, whereas women have more depressive episodes (Winzelberg et al., 2000).

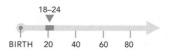

Bipolar Disorder

The Case of Feliziano
"Depression is the worst part. My shoulders feel weighted down, and your blood feels warmer than it is. You sink deeper and deeper."
www.mypsychlab.com

DEVELOPMENTAL FACTORS IN DEPRESSION

The peak age of risk for depression is between 25 and 44, with the most common age of onset around 32 years (Ebmeier et al., 2006; Judd et al., 1998; Moore & Bona, 2001). However, depression exists across all ages, and emerging data suggest that the risk of depression in children, adolescents, people with chronic illnesses, and the elderly (especially older people with health problems) is increasing (Moore & McLaughlin, 2003; National Institute of Mental Health, 2003).

An estimated 2.5% of children and 8.3% of adolescents in the United States report suffering from depression (National Institute of Mental Health, 2000). Although the diagnostic criteria are the same, the observable signs of depression may differ, and young people may lack the necessary vocabulary and insight to describe depressed mood. Warning signs can include nonspecific physical complaints such as headaches, muscle aches, stomachaches or tiredness, school absence or poor performance, unexplained irritability, crying spells, boredom, social withdrawal, alcohol or substance abuse, anger or hostility, relationship difficulties, and recklessness (National Institute of Mental Health, 2000). If untreated, depression in adolescence can lead to school failure, alcohol or other drug use, and suicide (U.S. Department of Health and Human Services, 2002).

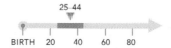

Children as well as adolescents and adults may suffer from depression, but the signs and symptoms of the disorder may be different in children.

Developmental factors also influence the sex ratio of depression. Throughout childhood, girls and boys are equally likely to have depression. However, around age 13, rates begin to climb for girls but remain constant or even decrease for boys (Cyranowski et al., 2000; Nolen-Hoeksema, 2001; Parker & Brotchie, 2004). By late adolescence, the 2:1 ratio (girls to boys) is established and thereafter remains fairly constant. As yet there is no clear explanation for this developmental sex difference, but biological, psychological, and environmental factors may be involved. These factors may include hormones, self-consciousness about bodily changes during puberty, poor sense of competence, socioeconomic disadvantage, victimization, chronic life stressors, lower self-esteem, and greater reactivity to stress. Any or all of these factors may converge to both increase risk and perpetuate mood disturbances in women (Nolen-Hoeksema, 2001; Parker & Brotchie, 2004).

In addition to female sex, high *neuroticism* (i.e., the tendency to be depressed, anxious, and emotionally reactive) is also associated with depression. Children high on the neuroticism trait may be more vulnerable to major depression (and anxiety disorders) (Parker & Brotchie, 2004). Using the biopsychosocial model (see chapter 1), hormonal influences on the female brain (the biological factor) may be particularly powerful in those with higher neuroticism (the psychological factor), thereby increasing their vulnerability to social stress (the social factor) and the likelihood of experiencing depression during and after puberty. Among children and adolescents, depression often goes unrecognized and untreated (Wang et al., 2005). This is unfortunate because early-onset depression often persists, recurs, and continues into adulthood (Weissman et al., 1999).

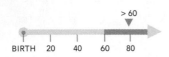

On the other end of the developmental spectrum, about 10.6% of those over the age of 60 suffer from depression (Baldwin et al., 2002) (see chapter 13), and approximately 1.3% suffer from dysthymia (NCS-R). We are already seeing the emergence of depression earlier in life; as the average age of the American population increases, researchers will be monitoring increases in the incidence of depression in late life (Kessler et al., 2005; Klerman & Weissman, 1989) (see chapter 13).

DEVELOPMENTAL FACTORS IN BIPOLAR DISORDER

Children suffer from bipolar disorder, but the symptoms may be very different from those seen in adults. Symptoms of mania are also somewhat different. In children, mania may be chronic rather than episodic, may cycle rapidly (Geller & Luby, 1997), or may appear as a mixed state. During a manic episode, they are more likely to display irritability and temper tantrums rather than a euphoric "high." These different symptoms make it difficult for mental health professionals to distinguish this disorder from other conditions such as attention-deficit/hyperactivity disorder, conduct disorder, oppositional defiant disorder, or even schizophrenia (National Institute of Mental Health, 2000; Weller et al., 1995) (see chapters 10 and 12). Accurate diagnosis is critical because the onset of bipolar disorder in childhood or early adolescence may represent a different and possibly more severe condition than the condition that develops in adulthood (Carlson & Kashani, 1988; Geller & Luby, 1997).

On the other end of the age spectrum, new cases of bipolar disorder occur in only 0.1% of adults over 65 (Robins & Regier, 1991) (see chapter 13). After that age, manic and depressive symptoms often develop in association with medical illness, especially stroke (Cummings, 1986; Van Gerpen et al., 1999). Older patients who may have had some elements of mania in younger years can experience manic symptoms later in life (Keck et al., 2001). Among older people, intervals between mania and depression are shorter and the episodes longer than among younger patients (Keck et al., 2001; Krauthammer & Klerman, 1978).

COMORBIDITY

Depression may co-occur with many medical conditions, including cardiovascular disease, central nervous system diseases, cancer, and migraines (Moore & Bona, 2001; Musselman et al., 1998). Coronary heart disease often coexists with depression, and depression can influence outcome from coronary illness (van Melle et al., 2004). Major depression also commonly coexists with other psychiatric conditions. Nearly three fourths (72.1%) of people with lifetime major depressive disorder had at least one additional disorder, including anxiety disorders (59.2%), substance use disorder (24%), and impulse control disorders (30%) (Kessler et al., 2005). In most cases, depression occurred before the other conditions.

Several strategies have examined the frequent co-occurrence of anxiety and depression. Perhaps most enlightening are twin studies that examine how the same genetic and environmental factors contribute to the two disorders. In fact, the genetic correlation between major depression and generalized anxiety disorder is 100% (Kendler, 1996; Kendler et al., 2007; Kendler et al., 1992), suggesting that the same genetic factors influence the risk for both disorders. Genetically vulnerable individuals may develop major depression, generalized anxiety disorder, or both, depending on their environmental experiences. In other words, genes provide the vulnerability to a negative mood state, and the environment shapes *which* negative mood state emerges. This conclusion—that depression and anxiety represent the same gene(s) but different environments—is one compelling explanation for why these two disorders co-occur so commonly. As yet, we have not unraveled the second part of the equation—namely, which environmental experiences result in depression, anxiety, or both?

concept CHECK

- Major depressive disorder is an episodic disorder and is marked by persistent low mood lasting at least 2 weeks. Dysthymia has a more chronic profile and consists of persistent low mood lasting a period of 2 years or more.

- Across the life span and across sexes, the prevalence of depression varies. Overall, depression is twice as common in women as in men.

- Bipolar I disorder is marked by the presence of manic episodes either with or without depressive episodes. Bipolar II is characterized by hypomanic episodes coupled with depression.

- Depression may look different in children and adolescents in part because of their level of cognitive development, insight, and available vocabulary to describe their feelings.

- Bipolar disorder in children is often marked by irritability rather than euphoria.

- Ethnic, racial, and cultural issues must be considered when determining the prevalence of depression across various groups.

APPLICATION QUESTION Depression in women is associated with both reproductive events and socioeconomic disadvantage. How would you go about determining the relative contribution of biology and environment?

Suicide

Although not all suicides are associated with depression, thoughts of suicide or of death are a frightening component of depression both for the sufferer and for family and friends. Suicide is one of the most perplexing of human behaviors and the most devastating outcome of depression. Its effects reach far beyond the person who dies and can have a deep and long-lasting impact on family, friends, the community, the nation, and sometimes even the world. Family members and friends may never understand what drove a person to suicide.

Suicide currently ranks as the eighth leading cause of death in the United States. It is estimated that between 2 and 5% of people in the United States attempt suicide sometime in their lives (Moscicki, 1999). The World Health Organization (WHO) estimates that worldwide about 873,000 people die by suicide every year. According to the Centers for Disease Control (CDC), in the 1990s suicide ranked sixth among causes of death in the 5- to 14-year age bracket, third in those 15 to 24 years, fifth in those between 25 and 44 years, and ninth in those between 45 and 64 years. It is commonly believed that suicide rates are underreported due to the misclassification of cause of death in situations such as single-vehicle car accidents. Rates differ across the world. According to the latest official figures released by WHO and the individual National Bureaus of Statistics, the highest rates of male suicide are found in Lithuania,

Firearms in the home increase the risk of suicide.

the Russian Federation, Latvia, Estonia, Belarus, and Hungary. In comparison, southern parts of Europe have low suicide rates. North America and Asia tend to fall between these estimates and generally have lower rates than most of the European countries. Except in selected rural and urban areas on mainland China, globally suicide rates are higher for males than for females (Heathcote et al., 1991).

SUICIDAL IDEATION, SUICIDE ATTEMPTS, AND COMPLETED SUICIDE

Suicidal ideation and behavior range from mere thoughts about suicide or death to plans about how to commit suicide to the completed act. Although varying in intensity, at each level these thoughts and behaviors should be taken seriously and should raise concern about the person's psychological well-being.

Thoughts of death, also known as **suicidal ideation**, may take different forms. *Passive suicidal ideation* is a wish to be dead but does not include active planning about how to commit suicide. *Active suicidal ideation* includes thoughts about how to commit the act, including details such as where, when, and how. Although some suicidal acts are impulsive, detailed suicidal plans are of considerable clinical concern because they indicate premeditation and determination to complete the act.

Suicidal acts are evaluated based on lethality and intent. Some acts, occasionally called *parasuicides*, are behaviors such as superficial cutting of the wrists or overdoses of nonlethal amounts of medications. These acts are unlikely to result in death. However, intent cannot necessarily be inferred from lethality. For example, a woman who takes some pills to end her life may be unaware that the dose was not lethal; she may have fully intended to die. In contrast, violent attempts such as hanging, self-inflicted gunshots, and jumping from a building are almost always associated with serious intent. Regardless of intent or lethality, up to 40% of individuals who commit suicide have made previous attempts (Zahl & Hawton, 2004). Previous attempts are a risk factor for later completed suicides. All attempts should be taken seriously and require immediate treatment.

WHO COMMITS SUICIDE?

In the United States, males are more likely to commit suicide than females, although females are more likely to attempt suicide (Moscicki, 2001). This difference exists across the age spectrum and may reflect the fact that males choose more lethal methods such as hanging or firearms. Among adolescent males, the greatest risk factors are mood disorders, previous suicidal attempts, substance abuse, conduct disorder, and presence of a gun in the home. In females, mood disorders, previous suicidal attempts, and presence of a handgun in the home increase risk (Brent et al., 1999; Shaffer et al., 1996). Youth from socially disadvantaged backgrounds (less education and lower socioeconomic status) are at elevated risk of serious suicide attempt (Beautrais et al., 1997, 1998) (see Figure 6.3). Other contributors are parental psychiatric illness, parental suicide attempt, a phenomenon called "drifting" (being generally disconnected from school, work, and family), sociodemographic disadvantage, and adverse family circumstances (Beautrais et al., 1997; Gould, 1990). In terms of immediate events likely to precipitate a suicide attempt, relationship breakdowns, interpersonal problems, and financial difficulties are most commonly reported in youth. However, fully one third of those attempting suicide do not identify any specific precipitating factor (Beautrais et al., 1997). Among the elderly, elevated risk of suicide is associated with chronic illness and decreasing social support (Conwell et al., 2002). For a discussion on suicide in the elderly, see Chapter 13.

Racial and ethnic groups also vary in their likelihood of committing suicide. In the United States, suicide rates are highest among whites and Native Americans, with African Americans and Hispanics showing lower rates (Centers for Disease Control and Preven-

suicidal ideation   thoughts of death

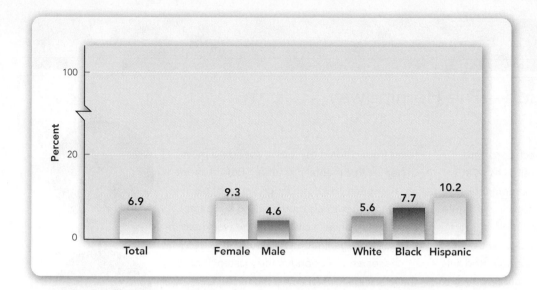

FIGURE 6.3
Percentage of High School
Students Who Attempted
Suicide, by Sex and
Race/Ethnicity

Serious suicide attempts are more frequent
among girls than boys and more common
among Hispanic adolescents than white or
black adolescents.

tion. National Center for Injury Prevention and Control. Web-based Injury Statistics Query and Reporting System (WISQARS) (Publication no. www.cdc.gov/ncipc/wisqars). Health, National Institute of Mental. (2007). *Suicide in the U.S.: Statistics and Prevention* (No. NIH Publication No. 06-4594): National Institutes of Health.).

RISK FACTORS FOR SUICIDE

When attempting to predict who is likely to commit suicide, a host of factors may increase or decrease the risk of acting on thoughts or impulses. Of these risk factors, a history of prior attempts remains one of the strongest predictors for a suicide attempt (Borges et al., 2006).

Family History   Suicidal behaviors run in families. This is demonstrated both by family studies and by highly visible cases in which multiple family members across generations have committed suicide (see the box "Real People, Real Disorders: The Heritability of Suicide"). However, as described in chapter 2, family studies are unable to disentangle the extent to which this familial factor is genetic or environmental. Adoption and family studies suggest a genetic effect that is independent of the genetic transmission of other psychiatric disorders, even those that tend to coexist, such as depression (Brent et al., 1996; Egeland & Sussex, 1985; Roy & Linnoila, 1986; Schulsinger et al., 1979). Twin studies show substantially higher concordance for monozygotic (MZ) than for dizygotic (DZ) twins (11.3% vs. 1.8%) (Roy et al., 1991), further supporting a genetic contribution. One study estimated the heritability of a serious suicide attempt to be approximately 55% (Statham et al., 1998).

Psychiatric Illness   Although suicide does not always occur within the context of mental illness, approximately 90% of attempted or completed suicides are committed by individuals who suffer from psychological disorders (Kessler et al., 2005). Of serious clinical concern is the relation between major depression and suicide (Kessler et al., 1994; Moore & Bona, 2001). Fully 80% of individuals with major depression have suicidal thoughts, and major depression is associated with a 15% lifetime risk for completed suicide (American Psychiatric Association, 2000; Moore & Bona, 2001). Depressed males are at particular risk, with a rate four times higher than that for women with major depression (National Institute of Mental Health, 2007). Suicide attempts in bipolar disorder are approximately 60 times higher than the international population rate; they tend to occur during severe depressive or mixed states and are often highly lethal (Baldessarini et al., 2006).

real people, real disorders

The Heritability of Suicide—The Hemingway and van Gogh Families

In the mid-nineteenth century, poet Alfred, Lord Tennyson, described multiple melancholic relatives as a "taint of blood" (Jamison, 1993). Perhaps a more striking reality is that suicide may also be heritable, as in the families of Ernest Hemingway and Vincent van Gogh.

Hemingway's family tree is tragically replete with suicide. Over two generations, four members committed suicide—the writer, his father, his brother, and his sister—and in 1996, the daughter of Ernest's oldest son, model Margaux Hemingway, died from a barbiturate overdose. Ernest was diagnosed with bipolar disorder, and a clear pattern of depression, rages, and mania exists in his family (Jamison, 1993; Lynn, 1987). Before the writer took his own life in 1961, he had been hospitalized and received electroconvulsive therapy for psychotic depression. The experience of his father's suicide was reflected in the author's writing: many of his characters come face to face with death and are admired for confronting death bravely and without emotional expression (Magill, 1983).

Suicide also runs strongly in the van Gogh family. Both Vincent van Gogh and his brother Cornelius took their own lives. Although Vincent van Gogh's condition has been debated for nearly a century, much evidence taken from letters and medical records suggests that the painter suffered from depression, and possibly manic-depressive illness (Jamison, 1993). His brother Theo also had psychotic and manic-depressive symptoms, and his sister Wilhelmina suffered from chronic psychosis, spending most of her life in a mental institution. Before shooting himself in 1890, van Gogh wrote of his illness in a letter to his brother Theo as "a fatal inheritance, since in civilization the weakness increases from generation to generation."

Research corroborates the existence of these suicidal clusters. Researchers in Denmark compared 4,262 people who had committed suicide with control subjects and evaluated their family histories of suicide and psychiatric illness (Qin et al., 2002). People with a family history of suicide were 2.5 times more likely to commit suicide than those without a family history. Other studies have found that the familiality of suicide might be genetically transmitted.

The heritability of suicide complicates the already difficult matter of coping with a family member's suicide—a process that can leave survivors with complex emotions, as well as a feeling of stigma surrounding the act of suicide. Given the seriousness of suicide, organizations such as the American Foundation for Suicide Prevention (AFSP) provide support and treatment resources to survivors. Joining these efforts, Mariel Hemingway, the granddaughter of the writer, has become an outspoken advocate for suicide prevention.

Other disorders associated with suicide attempts include substance use disorder, anxiety disorders, antisocial disorders, anorexia nervosa, and schizophrenia. Patients with schizophrenia may act on auditory hallucinations ("hearing voices") commanding them to kill themselves (Beautrais et al., 1996).

Biological Factors Scientific advances have increased our understanding of the neurobiology of suicide. In addition to genetics, neuroimaging and brain autopsy studies reveal very low levels of serotonin in the brains of people who have committed suicide (Mann et al., 2001). The biology and genetics of suicide appear to be at least partially independent of the biology of depression and other mental illnesses (Mann et al., 1986). In other words, depression alone does not lead to suicide, although it increases the risk. For example, behaviors such as impulsivity and pathological aggression, both of which are associated with low levels of serotonin, also may contribute to risk for suicidal behaviors.

UNDERSTANDING SUICIDE

It is impossible to completely re-create the thoughts, circumstances, and triggers that lead up to suicide. Although different approaches exist, they remain at best crude approximations of what actually occurs when the decision is made to end one's own life.

The Psychological Autopsy Piecing together the events leading to suicide is complicated. Between one fifth and one third of those who commit suicide leave suicide notes, but these notes are not typically detailed accounts of what led up to the act (Kuwabara et al., 2006). Putting together the information often involves a process known as a **psychological autopsy**. Clinicians interview family, friends, co-workers, and health care providers to identify psychological causes, in much the same way that a coroner searches for physical causes of death. A structured interview is sometimes used to reconstruct motives and circumstances. The interview addresses potential precipitants and stressors, motivation, lethality, and intentionality. For example, the interviewer may try to determine whether the person had distributed personal objects or written a will or other letters that would suggest deliberate suicidal intent.

Although this approach can help survivors understand factors that contributed to a suicide, it does little to diminish their anguish. Commonly, those left behind search for clues, and blame themselves for not noticing them in time. This is why comments about suicide or passive death wishes should always be taken seriously. Dismissing such comments as passing moods or cries for attention can be a devastating error. If a person is troubled enough to mention suicide, then something is wrong, and professional help is necessary.

PREVENTION OF SUICIDE

Since suicide is a final act, interventions must focus on prevention. Indeed, suicide prevention has served as a model for prevention in other mental illness fields, and prevention research has examined variables spanning the individual to the community level.

Crisis Intervention Suicide hotlines exist across the United States and are generally staffed by people with crisis intervention training. People with suicidal feelings are urged to call these hotlines to receive support, in the hope that a suicide attempt can be prevented. If the counselor determines that the caller is in immediate danger, the counselor attempts to locate the person and send help immediately. Because hotlines are anonymous, it is virtually impossible to assess their specific effectiveness on a population level. However, even if the hotline provides only a referral for further psychiatric care, it represents a meaningful component of suicide prevention.

Focus on High-risk Groups One approach to suicide prevention targets people with several known risk factors (Brent & Mann, 2005). The children of parents with mood disorders who have attempted suicide themselves are clearly an at-risk group. For those children, early detection and treatment of mood disturbances, substance abuse, and other comorbid symptoms could create an early connection with mental health professionals and provide parents and children with tools to deal with emerging symptoms before they become severe.

Societal Level Prevention Using teacher and peer support, societal approaches try to "reconnect" youth who are drifting with social and emotional supports, thereby improving both their school and family functioning (Eggert et al., 1995; Thompson & Eggert, 1999; Thompson et al., 2000). Other interventions try to eliminate access to methods of committing suicide such as detoxifying domestic gas and decreasing access to firearms (Brent & Mann, 2005). Effective strategies involve working directly with the gun owner to secure rather than remove the gun and providing psychoeducation

psychological autopsy interviews with family, friends, co-workers, and health care providers in an attempt to identify psychological causes of suicide

Suicide hotlines, staffed either by professionals or trained volunteers, provide counseling and support for people who believe that their only alternative is to commit suicide.

regarding the increased risk of suicide when there is a gun in the home. Some evidence exists that people who are determined to commit suicide will simply find alternative methods (Marzuk et al., 1992). It is not possible to eliminate every hazard (e.g., bridges and tall buildings), but limiting the availability of lethal weapons at least introduces a delay that creates an opening for intervention.

Preventing Suicidal Contagion   The media's portrayal of suicides of famous people has been associated with copycat suicides (Gould, 1990). The careless inclusion of details about suicide attempts and the portrayal of those who commit suicide as tragic or flawed heroes or martyrs can lead to a pathological obsession with suicide as a solution to life's problems—especially in youth. In addition, suicide clusters, suicide pacts, and Internet sites that function as how-to or support groups that encourage suicide are frightening and dark portrayals of youth whose thinking is detached from reality. When a youth commits suicide, schools often act immediately, intervening with *critical incident debriefing* (CID), a strategy whereby people who witnessed a trauma are brought together to talk about the event and their reaction to it. CID is a controversial intervention that when used incorrectly may do more harm than good (Bootzin & Bailey, 2005). However, when trained professionals join with school officials to administer CID appropriately, it may provide an outlet for expressing fears and grief by allowing youth to talk about the event, seek support, and take active steps toward closure (i.e., suggesting concrete ways of saying "goodbye" to the suicide victim). CID can also help to identify fellow students at risk for suicide, allow students to process the death of a peer, and provide an accurate and balanced (rather than glorified) account of the pain and futility of suicide (Macy et al., 2004; Meilman & Hall, 2006)

TREATMENT AFTER SUICIDE ATTEMPTS

Serious suicide attempts require immediate medical care; however, prolonged psychological care beyond the effects of the attempt is sometimes necessary.

Jackie was seriously depressed and felt that life was hopeless. She attempted suicide by jumping out of a fifth story window. Although she shattered almost every bone in her body, she did not die. Now, she faces a life with severe facial disfigurement, impaired ability to speak, and confinement to a wheelchair. All she thinks about is how to "finish the job." Jackie desperately needs help, now more than ever, to cope with and find some relief from her depressed mood and her physical ailments. But as long as she remains focused on ending her life, her mood is bound to stay depressed, making it very difficult for her to seek out and receive the help she deserves.

Deliberate self-harm is a major risk factor for suicide. Various psychological and psychosocial interventions reduce self-harm behavior and improve mood in people who previously attempted suicide. However, more studies are needed to determine the impact of these interventions in reducing subsequent suicide attempts or completed suicides (Hepp et al., 2004). Although it is recommended that all individuals receive follow-up psychiatric care after an attempt, data suggest that many people who attempt suicide fail to receive proper psychotherapeutic attention afterwards (Beautrais et al., 1997).

---

concept CHECK

- The best predictors of a future suicide attempt include a family history of completed suicide, the presence of a psychological disorder, and past self-harm behavior (including a previous suicide attempt).

- Women are more likely to attempt suicide, but men are more likely to complete suicide.

- Most individuals do not leave notes explaining why they committed suicide.

- Although not all those who commit suicide are seriously depressed, approximately 90% of individuals who commit suicide have a mental illness.

APPLICATION QUESTION Suicide is a uniquely human behavior. What features of humans as a species influence our ability to commit suicide?

The Etiology of Mood Disorders

An occasional feeling of low mood is a universal human experience, and usually, we can identify the reason. For example, if you missed going home for a holiday or if you didn't do well on an important exam, it would be reasonable to feel down for a day or two. Other events—such as losing a job or ending an important relationship—are more stressful and could lead to the onset of clinical depression. However, sometimes mood disorders can seem mysterious, and symptoms can turn into full-blown episodes with no obvious cause. Research provides valuable clues into the causes of mood disorders, even though no one perspective adequately explains its onset.

BIOLOGICAL PERSPECTIVE

With the adoption of new technologies and methods, studies of genetics and biological determinants have provided exciting new insights about depression's underlying causes and risk factors. Twin and adoption studies provide evidence of heritability. Neuroimaging studies map out brain circuitry and function that are altered in the context of mood disorders. These studies, in turn, help shape our understanding of how environmental and sociocultural factors influence the course of mood disorders. All this information is being synthesized to develop new interventions and strategies for treating and managing mood disorders.

Genetics and Family Studies   Genes influence the risk for major depression (CenterWatch, 1995–2007; Ebmeier, 2006; Moore & Bona, 2001), with evidence converging from family, twin, and genetic studies. Family studies illustrate how mood disorders track across generations. Twin studies can tell us to what extent a mood disorder is influenced by genetic or environmental factors. Molecular genetics studies help us identify the actual genes that code for proteins that influence risk for mood disorders.

Major depression runs in families. First-degree relatives of people with depression are two to three times more likely to suffer from depression than first-degree relatives of people without depression (Sullivan et al., 2000). In particular, the genetic predisposition appears stronger in those individuals who suffer from recurrent depression and when there is an earlier age at onset (Ebmeier et al., 2006). In addition to the family studies, twin studies estimate that the heritability of major depression is around 37% (Sullivan et al., 2000). That means that about 37% of liability to major depression is due to genetic factors, with the remaining risk due to environmental factors.

Family and twin studies suggest a genetic component. The next critical step in research on causes of depression is to identify the specific genes involved and determine their function. One approach, called a *linkage study*, narrows the search to particular areas on a chromosome or several chromosomes that have a higher likelihood of harboring risk genes (see Figure 6.4). Linkage studies are valuable because with over 20,000 genes in the human genome, this approach narrows the search. Based on linkage studies, it appears that risk genes for depression may lie on chromosomes 1, 3, 4, 6, 8, 11, 12, 15, and 18 (Levinson, 2005).

FIGURE 6.4
Chromosomes in a Linkage Study

Geneticists use a calculation known as a HLOD score (heterogeneity logarithm of odds) to determine whether a gene is related to a disorder. An HLOD score greater than 3 indicates areas of significant linkage. In this case, a linkage is shown between chromosome 12 and depression.

Reprinted from *American Journal of Human Genetics*, 73 (6), Victor Abkevich, et al., "Predisposition Locus for Major Depression at Chromosome 12q22-12q23.2" pp. 1271–1281. Copyright © 2003 with permission from Elsevier.

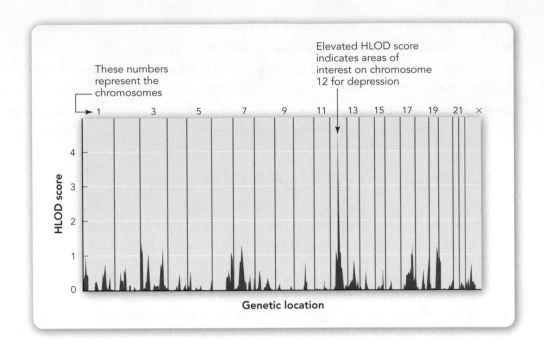

A second genetic approach, called an *association study*, starts by identifying a gene that is believed to be associated with a disorder and then examines whether genetic variations are more common among persons with a disorder (such as depression) than in controls without the disorder. For depression, association studies have focused on genes that regulate the *serotonergic system*. The serotonergic system is a network of neurons and neurotransmitters in the brain, one function of which is to regulate emotion (Levinson, 2005). Although several significant associations have been found, the available data do not yet solve the genetic puzzle.

Ultimately, understanding depression involves understanding both genetic and environmental factors. Exploring this interaction may help determine why some people are more vulnerable to environmental stressors (see the box "Research Hot Topics: The Interaction Between Genes and Environment"). New technologies and approaches will make it more likely that specific genes are identified. Future research may identify genetic variants that influence response to medication and perhaps to psychotherapy (Ebmeier et al., 2006; Malhotra et al., 2004), allowing mental health professionals to target treatment to an individual, enhancing its likelihood of success.

Bipolar disorder As illustrated by its complex clinical picture, multiple factors are implicated in the etiology of bipolar disorder (American Psychiatric Association, 2005; Berk & Dodd, 2005; Keck et al., 2001; National Institute of Mental Health, 2001; Perlis et al., 2006). Family, twin, and adoption studies all support a strong familial and genetic component (Hayden & Nurnberger, 2006; Keck et al., 2001; Perlis et al., 2006). Twin studies suggest that the heritability of bipolar disorder may be as high as 93% (Kieseppa et al., 2004).

Linkage studies have identified several areas of the genome that may hold susceptibility genes for bipolar disorder (Hayden & Nurnberger, 2006). Many genes have been implicated, but as yet there are no consistent findings. The next critical step in research into genetic factors that influence risk for bipolar disorder is to understand the function of suspected genes and how they may contribute to risk. Helping us address these questions are studies that use neuroimaging techniques to explain what happens in the brain of individuals with mood disorders.

Neuroimaging Studies   Several detailed studies of brain function have identified neurochemical pathways that may be dysfunctional in individuals with mood disorders (CenterWatch, 1995–2007; Ebmeier et al., 2006). Of particular interest are the norepinephrine and serotonergic systems, which are widely implicated in the etiology of depression (Delgado et al., 1990). Similarly, abnormalities in serotonin, norepinephrine, dopamine, acetylcholine, and other neurotransmitter pathways have been identified as potentially contributory factors for bipolar disorder (Keck et al., 2001). Dysfunctions in these systems affect neurotransmitter availability in the neural synapses, which in turn may cause the symptoms of mood disorders. Research on these systems has significantly advanced our understanding of etiology and contributed to the development of efficacious medications.

Neuroimaging studies (MRP, PET, fMRI) (see chapter 2) have identified several pathways in the brain that predispose individuals to develop mood disorders. For example, when compared with brain images from people without the disorder, areas of the brain, including the thalamus, hypothalamus, amygdala, caudate, prefrontal cortex, and cerebellum, are different in people with bipolar disorder (Keck et al., 2001; Soares & Mann, 1997; Strakowski et al., 2002). fMRI studies of people with bipolar disorder undergoing emotional and cognitive tasks have identified abnormal brain activity in frontal, subcortical, and limbic regions (Yurgelun-Todd & Ross, 2006). The sheer number of identified abnormalities makes it difficult to conclude that any one brain area is responsible for mood disorders. In fact, it appears that symptoms of mood disorder emerge from the dysfunction of interconnected brain networks (Adler et al., 2006). Though intriguing, these studies were conducted with people who had the disorder. Therefore, the data cannot be used to draw conclusions regarding causality. An alternative hypothesis is that differences in brain function may be the *result* of the disorder (i.e., *biological scarring*) rather than its cause. To ultimately determine the role of neurobiology, it will be necessary to conduct neuroimaging studies of individuals who are at risk for bipolar disorder but who do not yet show any symptoms (e.g., children of parents with bipolar disorder) and follow them over time. This research design could help determine whether any premorbid abnormalities exist and are associated with the development of mood disorders.

Environmental Factors and Life Events   Genetic studies suggest that biological factors play an important role in the etiology of mood disorders but biology is not the only factor—environment also plays an important role. Environmental factors that contribute to the onset of major depression include stress, loss, grief, threats to relationships, occupational problems, health challenges, and the burdens of caregiving (Brown et al., 1996; Kendler et al., 1998; Monroe et al., 2001). As discussed in chapter 4, stressors that occur early in life such as abuse, maternal deprivation, neglect, or loss may have enduring effects on brain regions that influence stress and emotion. These permanent brain changes, such as heightened stress responsiveness throughout life, may increase the risk for depression (Kaufman & Charney, 2001).

Understanding the role of life events requires determining whether the stressful event is truly independent of the mood disorder (e.g., one's house suddenly burns down—an independent life event) or whether the person's depression contributes to the emergence of the stressful life event (dependent life events).

Straight out of law school, John landed a prime job with a prominent law firm in his home city. The hours were grueling. At first he was energized by the challenge, but after months of getting by on four hours of sleep per night, he started to have pervasive self-doubts about his abilities, forget important facts about cases, and get into altercations with his colleagues. He was late for work and when he arrived, he looked disheveled and often disoriented. He was fired from his job and blamed his depression on this loss. In reality, the job stress precipitated the depression, and his job loss was a dependent life event.

Research HOT Topic

Gene x Environment Interaction

We know that both genes and environmental factors are involved in the onset of depression. One controversial study by Drs. Avshalom Caspi, Terrie Moffitt, and colleagues (Caspi et al., 2003) reported intriguing findings on a gene–environment interaction.

The Caspi study prompted headlines from newspapers worldwide, such as "Gene more than doubles risk of depression following life stresses." Specifically, the study showed that among people who suffered multiple stressful life events over 5 years, 43% with one version of a gene (the "short" version) developed depression, compared with only 17% with another version of the gene (the "long" version). Regardless of the number of stressful life events, people with the "long" or protective version had no more depression than people who were more stress-free. The gene studied in this investigation was responsible for programming the actions of a particular protein. That protein, in turn, was responsible for recycling the neurotransmitter serotonin after it entered the neural synapse. The most widely prescribed class of antidepressants acts by blocking this transporter protein. This allows more serotonin to stay in the synapse and to be available in pathways involved in regulation of the emotions. For this reason, the gene has been a prime suspect in mood and anxiety disorders.

The authors believed the key to understanding these findings was studying both genes and environment. Dr. Moffit stated: "We found the connection only because we looked at the study members' stress history." The study followed 847 Caucasian New Zealanders, born in the early 1970s, from birth into adulthood; 17% carried two copies of the stress-sensitive short version, 31% two copies of the protective long version, and 51% one copy of each version. Drawing on research done on animals, the researchers hypothesized that the interaction of genes and environment would be evident, and they therefore tallied life stresses on participants in the study. Although those with the short variant and at least four life events represented only 10% of the study sample, they accounted for nearly 25% of the cases of depression. Among those with four or more stressful life events, 43% of those with two copies of the short variant developed depression, compared with 17% of those with two copies of the long variant. After publication of this study, several groups attempted to replicate the findings. In 2009, a meta-analysis of over 14 studies that examined the association between the serotonin transporter gene, life events, and risk for depression showed no interaction of genotype and stressful life events on risk for depression. These results clearly illustrate the importance of replication in science and suggest caution when interpreting unreplicated findings.

References:

Risch, N., Herrell, R., Lehner, T., Liang, K. Y., Eaves, L., Hoh, J., Griem, A., Kovacs, M., Ott, J., Merikangas, K. R. Interaction between the serotonin transporter gene (5-HTTLPR), stressful life events, and risk of depression: a meta-analysis. *Journal of the American Medical Association, 301*, 2462–2471.

Source: Eureka Alert—http://www.eurekalert.org/pub_releases/2003-07/aaft-ghd070803.php

Although stressful life events are commonly reported in first episodes of major depression, over time, recurrent episodes seem to be more independent of life events (Kendler et al., 2000).

An important question is why stressful life events seem to lead to depression in some people but not in others. For example, women who are at greater genetic risk for major depression not only report a greater number of stressful life events (Kendler & Karkowski-Shuman, 1997; Kendler & Prescott, 1999), but they are also more sensitive to their effects (Kendler et al., 1995). This phenomenon is called *genetic control of sensitivity to the environment* (Kendler & Karkowski-Shuman, 1997). This basically means that two people can encounter the same stressful life event, but because of their genetic makeup, one person experiences that event as more stressful (see the box "Research Hot Topic: Genes and Environmental Interaction").

PSYCHOLOGICAL PERSPECTIVE

Long before we understood the role of biology, clinicians and researchers sought psychological explanations for mood disorders. Older psychological theories have evolved over time, and some factors, such as loss, are being consistently identified. Research has produced a complex picture that has questioned some early psychological theories and supported others. Nevertheless, these theories reflect our changing ideas of depression and provide a foundation for formulating new research questions and for designing new interventions.

Psychodynamic Theory Freud conceptualized depression as "anger turned inward" (Freud, 1917). The anger, he proposed, arises after the loss of an object—either real or imagined. In Freudian terms, an "object" is anything to which someone is emotionally attached (e.g., another person, an aspect of the self, an animal). The loss may be real, such as the death of a friend, or it may be a process that is completely contained in the unconscious—meaning below the patient's level of awareness. An unconscious loss might be the loss of some aspect of youth about which the person was not actively aware. In *Mourning and Melancholia* (Freud, 1917), Freud distinguished between these two terms. According to Freud, *melancholia* (a condition akin to major depression) is a "profoundly painful dejection, cessation of interest in the outside world, loss of the capacity to love, inhibition of all activity, and a lowering of the self-regarding feelings to a degree that finds utterance in self-reproaches and self-revilings, and culminates in a delusional expectation of punishment." To illustrate "anger turned inward," Freud noted that melancholics were often highly self-accusatory—usually in ways that were not realistic or justified. These accusations were misdirected against the self; Freud believed that they were actually directed against someone whom the patient loved. Freud focused on internal representations of our relationships in the external world. He emphasized that the loss of a person in the real world leads to an internal loss, which is experienced as a psychic wound or a lesion in one's self-esteem.

Psychodynamic theorists consider depression and mania as intricately interlinked. They view hypomania and mania as defenses against the unwanted and intolerable experience of depression. Exaggerated self-esteem and grandiosity protect the person against confronting the underlying distressing thoughts associated with low self-esteem or self-loathing.

Although the Freudian notions are colorful and intriguing, use of unconscious processes to explain these disorders means that the theory cannot be tested scientifically. However, the hypothesis that loss (as well as other stressful life events) can precipitate depression is supported by both clinical experience and research. Advances in psychodynamic theory focus more on the role of real-world relationships and loss in the emergence of depression than on unverifiable unconscious processes (Horner, 1974).

Attachment Theory Guided by data from animal studies, John Bowlby examined how disruptions in mother–infant attachment could lead to depression and anxiety. According to Bowlby, attachment has evolutionary significance for survival and is related to maternal protection of offspring from predators. Bowlby proposed that a child's response to maternal separation consists of three stages: (1) protest; (2) despair, pain, and loss; and (3) detachment or denial of affection for the mother. Others have expanded Bowlby's ideas to highlight how early attachment affects later life functioning and how disruptions in attachment lead to vulnerability to depression, anxiety, and problems with attachment in adulthood (Ainsworth, 1982).

Behavioral Theories *Charles is a widower. After his wife died, he decided to fill his time by volunteering at the hospital two blocks from his home. His volunteer work was fulfilling, and he won several hospital awards for his dedication to his work and the people whom he served. Financial pressures forced the hospital to close. Charles no longer felt comfortable driving, and there was no public transportation in his neighborhood. Now Charles had no way to occupy his time, no opportunity to feel needed, and no one to praise him for his work. Soon, Charles stopped getting dressed and told his children, who lived in another city, that there really was no reason to leave his house any more.*

Environmental factors, such as the loss of social support or social reinforcement, are a significant factor in the onset and maintenance of depressive episodes.

learned helplessness term meaning that externally uncontrollable environments and presumably internally uncontrollable environments are inescapable stimuli that can lead to depression

Behavioral theory (e.g., Skinner, 1953) proposes that depression results from the withdrawal of reinforcement (aspects of the social environment) for healthy behaviors. Changes in reinforcement may result from decreases in the number and types of reinforcing stimuli and/or the inability to obtain reinforcement due to a lack of social skills (Lewinsohn, 1974). For example,

Jenny was always shy but had a close circle of friends that she had to leave behind when she moved cross-country to a new city for what she thought would be a fabulous new job. Suddenly, there was no one with whom she felt close enough to go out to dinner or share her thoughts (there was a decrease in available social reinforcers). Her severe shyness prevented her from meeting new people (she was unable to obtain reinforcement because of a lack of social skills). Although she called her friends when she could, they could no longer drop by for a glass of wine or call her to go shopping. The longer she was in her new environment, the sadder she became. Her new colleagues saw a quiet person who did not smile, and they were not inclined to approach her.

Learned Helplessness   **Learned helplessness** is a theory that applied observations from experimental animal models to the understanding of human depression. Martin Seligman developed this theory by accident while exploring the effects of inescapable shock on avoidance learning (Kenyon, 1994–2007; Seligman, 1975). His experimental paradigm restrained dogs in a harness while several shocks (an unconditioned stimulus—UCS) were paired with a conditioned stimulus (CS), in this case a light. After the conditioning trials, the dogs were placed in a box where they could easily avoid a shock by jumping over a low barrier (see Figure 6.5). Surprisingly, most of the dogs failed to learn to avoid the shock. They remained sitting when the light came on, receiving shocks that they could easily have escaped. Seligman theorized that having been exposed to inescapable shocks interfered with the dogs' ability to learn that escape was possible in a new situation. However, about a third of the dogs learned to

FIGURE 6.5
Learned helplessness.

After being in an inescapable situation, the dog is put in a situation from which escape from painful shock is possible. However, because of prior learning, most of the dogs did not try to escape the shock by jumping over the very small barrier.

From Lilienfeld et al., (2009) *Psychology: From Inquiry to Understanding*, Allyn & Bacon. Copyright © 2009. Reprinted by permission of Pearson Education.

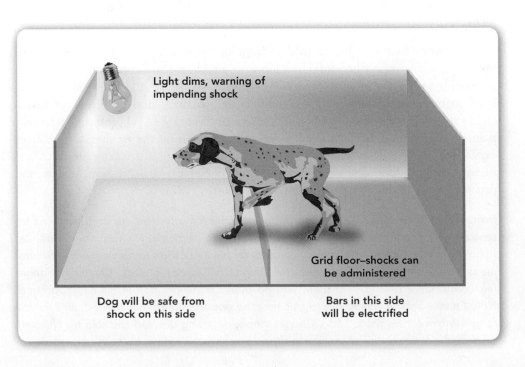

FIGURE 6.6
Common Thinking Errors

Dichotomous or "all or nothing" thinking: Thinking in "all-or-nothing" terms. *"If I can't do something perfectly, I may as well quit."*

Overgeneralizing: Condemning yourself as a total person on the basis of a single event. *"I got a C on a psychology test—I cannot be a psychologist."*

Selective thinking: Concentrating on your weaknesses and forgetting your strengths. *"It does not matter that I am a good singer. I cannot dance or act."*

Catastrophizing: Only paying attention to the dark side of things, or overestimating the chances of disaster. *"I didn't get into an Ivy League school. I'll never have a decent career."*

Personalizing: Taking things personally that have little or nothing to do with you. *"Jenny is so quiet. She must really be angry with me."*

Personal Ineffectiveness: Assuming you can do nothing to change your situation. *"Jack always criticizes me. I wish he would quit."*

escape, suggesting fundamental underlying differences in the likelihood of developing learned helplessness.

Learned helplessness proposes that externally uncontrollable environments (e.g. repeated abuse, failure at school or work, relationship failures) and presumably internally uncontrollable environments (e.g., pervasive low mood, thoughts of death) are inescapable stimuli that can lead to *dysphoria* (sadness or low mood) and major depression. Why some people develop learned helplessness and others do not may depend on whether the individual considers the situation as inescapable (Abramson et al., 1978, 2002). If the situation is attributable to an internal cause that is personal, pervasive, and permanent (e.g., I lost my job because I'm a jerk and I'll always be a jerk), then helplessness, hopelessness, and depression may result. In contrast, when negative events are given external and transient explanations (e.g., I lost my job because my boss is a jerk—in my next job I'll work for someone better), helplessness and depression are averted.

The parallels between learned helplessness in animals and major depression in humans provide one potential model for how *some* features of depression can develop in *some* people. It is highly unlikely that there is one single cause for major depression, but learned helplessness may represent one possible risk pathway. In addition, because we cannot probe the thoughts of animals, our animal models will, by definition, be only partial models. Nonetheless, these models can help us understand specific symptoms of major depressive disorder in humans.

Cognitive Theory   Aaron Beck, the father of cognitive therapy, proposed that thoughts cause feelings and behaviors and that *negative* thoughts can cause depressive feelings and behaviors. The theory proposes that *negative cognitive schemas* (patterns of negative thinking) can develop early in life and become part of an individual's self-concept (Beck, 1967; Sher, 2005). Negative schemas can be identified by the presence of "automatic thoughts." *Automatic thoughts* are dysfunctional thoughts and represent beliefs about the self that become a habitual pattern of thinking: "I'm a failure," "I have no willpower," and "I have no luck in love." Automatic thoughts tend to be extreme and counterproductive, and produce negative feelings. They go untested, become fixed, and lead to *self-fulfilling prophecies* (e.g., you expect to fail and so you do). Beck proposed that individuals with depression experience a *negative cognitive triad*—negative thoughts about the self, the world, and the future. He described a variety of thinking errors that sustain the negative thoughts in the triad (see Figure 6.6).

- Psychodynamic theories focus on the concept of "anger turned inward" and the role of loss in the etiology of depression.

- Behavioral theory focuses on the loss of reinforcement; depression results from the withdrawal of reinforcement (usually pleasant aspects of the social environment) that supports our participation in healthy behaviors.

- Learned helplessness theory focuses on perceiving uncontrollable environments as inescapable stimuli that lead to feelings of dysphoria and major depression.

- Cognitive theory focuses on the negative cognitive triad—negative thoughts about the self, the world, and the future.

APPLICATION QUESTION Mary started feeling depressed at the end of her first year of college. Earlier that year, she had injured her knee, which kept her sidelined from the varsity women's soccer team. After she got a C on an important exam in biology, she began to question her ability to enter medical school, her longtime goal. In the spring, her father died suddenly of a heart attack. How do you think each of these events might have contributed to her depression?

The Treatment of Mood Disorders

Several treatments are available for people who suffer from mood disorders, ranging from "talk" therapies to antidepressant medication and other biologically based treatments. Just as mood disorders may involve symptoms of the mind and body, treatment in some cases involves both psychotherapy and medication.

MAJOR DEPRESSION

Because many medical illnesses can masquerade as depression, an important first step in treatment is a comprehensive physical exam (American Psychiatric Association, 2000). In addition to ruling out a medical cause (such as cancer, malnutrition, mild stroke, certain metabolic disorders), a complete review of current medications is important because certain drugs can have side effects (such as fatigue or hyperactivity that disrupts sleep) that mimic depression. Once these possibilities are ruled out, the next step is selecting an appropriate treatment strategy. Surprisingly, only about half of those with major depression obtain professional treatment, and of these, only about 22% receive clinically adequate care (Kessler et al., 2003).

In part, this inadequate treatment is due to failure to recognize the symptoms, to the stigma associated with seeking care, or to the provider's lack of knowledge about evidence-based treatments. Having an established health care provider or health insurance significantly increases the likelihood of obtaining treatment (Ebmeier et al., 2006; Kessler et al., 1994a; Moore & Bona, 2001). Campaigns such as "Real Men, Real Depression" launched by the National Institute of Mental Health (http://menanddepression.nimh.nih.gov/) aim to improve mental health literacy by helping people recognize the signs of depression and providing a roadmap for seeking care.

There are many efficacious treatments for major depression. Psychotherapy helps people express distressing emotions and learn more effective ways to deal with factors that may have contributed to or resulted from depression. Medications and electroconvulsive therapy can help individuals who are too depressed to benefit from psychotherapy alone. Many choices exist, and often more than one approach is needed until an efficacious treatment is found (CenterWatch, 1995–2007; Ebmeier et al., 2006; Kessler et al., 1994a; Moore & Bona, 2001; Moore & McLaughlin, 2003).

Real Men. Real Depression.

It takes courage to ask for help. These men did.

Because men are less likely to admit feelings of sadness, the National Institute of Mental Health launched the "Real Men, Real Depression" campaign to help men understand and seek help for their symptoms of depression. This leaflet is part of their effort.

FIGURE 6.7
Thought restructuring record

After identifying a negative, automatic thought, a cognitive-behavioral therapist encourages the person with depression to replace that thought with a more positive idea. Reframing the situation in more positive terms often helps the person feel less negative about the self, the world, and the future.

Situation: Got a C on a test for which I studied really hard

Automatic Thought: I'm so stupid. I'll never get my degree

Emotion: Sad and discouraged

New Thought: This was the first test—next time, I'll be better prepared

Outcome: Concerned but motivated to continue in class

Psychological Treatments   Psychological treatments focus on understanding how thoughts, perceptions, and behaviors influence depressed mood and vice versa. They are generally delivered by a trained clinician (in most cases a clinical psychologist or licensed clinical social worker) in individual or group settings and are an essential component of a comprehensive treatment plan for depression.

Cognitive-behavioral therapy (CBT)   Cognitive-behavioral therapy (CBT) (Beck, 1979) is based on the premise that an individual can learn to think and behave differently, which can lead to improved mood. A key ingredient involves having patients record their thoughts, feelings, and behaviors (see Figure 6.7). Through this monitoring, patients identify situations or triggers for low mood as well as situations associated with improved mood. Once triggers are identified, the patient learns to recognize and modify automatic or distorted thoughts and change behaviors to improve mood and functioning.

After keeping her mood and thought records, Beverly noticed her moods were consistently worse as the weekends approached. Earlier in the week she was focused on work-related tasks, but then she noticed that around Wednesday she started having thoughts like "everyone else is making plans for the weekend and I'm going to be all alone as usual." By Friday morning she was consistently negative and the thoughts would get worse: "I am a complete loser." "No one wants to be around me." Working with her therapist, Beverly challenged her negative thoughts with other thoughts that were more balanced, less "all or nothing". For example, she replaced "No one wants to be around me" with "I haven't given people the chance to see who I am, I have to take initiative." Once she recognized the weekly pattern, she used the negative thoughts as calls to action rather than as signs of an inevitable slide into a weekend of misery and loneliness.

Interpersonal psychotherapy (IPT)   IPT is a focused time-limited therapy developed by Klerman and Weissman (Klerman et al., 1984). It has its roots in the work of Harry Stack Sullivan, who emphasized the importance of current interpersonal relationships for mental health. Its core principle is that interpersonal problems can trigger depression and depression itself can influence interpersonal functioning.

Sam had grown increasingly frustrated with his job since his new boss took over; they always disagreed about his effort, and his boss was constantly on his case. In addition, all of his co-workers avoided him in the break room, in large part because Sam always complained about the boss's heavy-handed tactics. He found himself having trouble getting up in the morning to go to work, and showing up late just led to more criticism. He withdrew from his co-workers and eventually from his wife, who was having trouble understanding Sam's sullen and angry mood. Losing his job was the last straw. He stopped coaching his son's baseball team because he was too ashamed to face the other dads, and he started staying out late at night to avoid the inevitably tough conversations with his wife about bills that were piling up.

IPT uses 12 to 16 sessions and focuses on an interpersonal problem area (grief, role transition, disputes, interpersonal deficits) that guides treatment. Therapeutic techniques include expression of mood, clarification of feelings, communication analysis, and behavior change. IPT is efficacious for mild to moderate depression and is also used to treat dysthymia, adolescent and late-life depression, anxiety, and eating disorders (Fairburn, 1993; Frank et al., 1991; Lipsitz et al., 2006; Mufson et al., 1994; Stuart, 1995). It has also been adapted for group use (Wilfley et al., 1993).

Behavioral activation Based on the theory that depression is maintained by a lack of positive reinforcement, early behavioral interventions focused on increasing access to pleasant, and therefore reinforcing, events through daily scheduling of pleasurable activities, social skills training, and time management strategies (e.g., Lewinsohn & Graf, 1973). *Behavioral activation treatment for depression* (BATD; Lejuez, Hopko, & Hopko, 2001) modifies this approach, emphasizing increased contact with positive reinforcement for healthy behaviors, thereby increasing positive mood. For example, for someone who is stuck in a "dead-end" job, therapy may include scheduling weekly trips to the library to read about career development. In BATD, the therapist and patient develop a comprehensive list of goals in major life areas. Each week, more specific goals and activities are developed jointly and completed by the patient (Hopko et al., 2003). As the patient completes the goals, increased positive reinforcement helps reduce depressive symptoms (e.g., Lejuez et al., 2001).

Biological Treatments Biological treatments are most often medications designed to alter mood-regulating chemicals in the brain (and body). These treatments are generally delivered by a psychiatrist, but may also be given by family practitioners (in part because of the stigma attached to seeking psychiatric care). These treatments are highly efficacious in reducing symptoms of depression, especially when combined with psychological treatment.

First-generation antidepressants—Tricyclic antidepressants and monoamine oxidase inhibitors The first drugs marketed to treat depression were the monoamine oxidase inhibitors (MAOIs) and the tricyclic **antidepressants** (TCA), sometimes called traditional or first-generation antidepressants. MAOIs treat depression by inhibiting (preventing) the action of the enzyme monoamine oxidase. Normally, this enzyme breaks down the neurotransmitters norepinephrine, serotonin, and dopamine in the brain. By preventing the enzyme from doing its work, the availability of these neurotransmitters in the neural synapses is increased, which is believed to cause the antidepressant effect.

These drugs are efficacious, especially in people who have depressive symptoms such as hypersomnia and weight gain (Thase & Kupfer, 1996). People who take MAO inhibitors need to refrain from eating foods containing the substance tyramine because the interaction of the drug and these foods can lead to a hypertensive crisis (extremely high blood pressure) and possibly death. Foods containing tyramine include smoked, aged, or pickled meat or fish; sauerkraut; aged cheeses; yeast extracts; fava beans; beef or chicken liver; aged sausages; game meats; red and white wines; beer; hard liquor; avocados; meat extracts; caffeine-containing beverages; chocolate; soy sauce; cottage cheese; cream cheese; yogurt; and sour cream. Owing to their potentially dangerous side effects, MAOIs are usually prescribed only if people do not respond to other medications.

antidepressants medications designed to alter mood-regulating chemicals in the brain and body that are highly effective in reducing symptoms of depression

Tricyclic antidepressants work by preventing the reuptake of various neurotransmitters in the brain—primarily norepinephrine and serotonin. By blocking their reuptake back into the neuron, it lengthens their availability in the synapse. The name of these drugs comes from the fact that they share a three-ring molecular structure. Countless randomized clinical trials document their efficacy compared to placebo controls. Typically, patients take the medication for 6 to 8 weeks. If the response is positive, the medication may need to be continued for many months to prevent a relapse (CenterWatch, 1995–2007; Ebmeier et al., 2006; Moore & Bona, 2001). It is extremely important that these medications not be stopped abruptly. First-generation antidepressants are often accompanied by multiple side effects, including dry mouth, constipation, bladder problems, sexual problems, blurred vision, dizziness, daytime drowsiness, and increased heart rate. Thus, they are no longer the first choice for pharmacologic treatment of depression (Gartlehner et al., 2005).

Second-generation antidepressants The second-generation antidepressants include **selective serotonin reuptake inhibitors (SSRIs)** and serotonin and norepinephrine reuptake inhibitors (SNRIs) (Hansen et al., 2005). Perhaps the best known antidepressant is fluoxetine (Prozac), which was approved in 1987 by the U.S. Food and Drug Administration (FDA). How most second-generation antidepressants work is not completely understood. In general, they act by selectively inhibiting the reuptake of serotonin at the presynaptic neuronal membrane, restoring the normal chemical balance. (See Figure 4.8 in chapter 4.) The SNRIs inhibit both serotonin and norepinephrine reuptake as well as that of dopamine to a lesser extent.

The SSRIs and other second-generation antidepressants appear to be as efficacious as the TCAs and MAO inhibitors (Gartlehner et al., 2005). Their advantage is that they have fewer and milder side effects than the TCAs (side effects may include sexual problems, headache, nausea, nervousness, trouble falling asleep or waking often during the night, and jitteriness) and are generally well tolerated by patients (Anderson, 2001; Hansen et al., 2005; Taylor et al., 2006).

In the early 2000s, concern was raised about a potentially lethal adverse effect of SSRIs. Several highly publicized cases led the FDA to issue a "black box" warning label, stating that antidepressants increased the risk of suicidal thinking in children and adolescents with major depressive disorder. This is the most serious warning the FDA can issue for a prescription medication. Youth treated with SSRIs need to be monitored very closely, especially during the first 4 weeks, for intensification of depression, emergence of suicidal thoughts or behavior, or behavioral changes such as sleeplessness, agitation, or social withdrawal. These substances have not been prohibited, despite their potentially dangerous side effects, because they provide substantial benefits for adolescents with moderate and severe depression, including many with suicidal ideation (National Institute of Mental Health, 2005).

The mechanism for increased suicidal ideation and behavior is unclear. Some suspect that SSRIs first improve physical symptoms before mood actually lifts. Thus, in the early stages of treatment, youth may feel more energy, and this increased energy and ongoing depressed mood increases the probability of acting on suicidal thoughts (Hall, 2006). A review of several studies, however, ultimately concluded that the benefits of SSRI treatment far outweigh the risks, although caution and careful monitoring are necessary (Bridge et al., 2007).

Electroconvulsive therapy Drug therapies are not the only biological treatment for major depression. **Electroconvulsive therapy (ECT)** is one of the most efficacious treatments for major depression, especially for persons who are severely

selective serotonin reuptake inhibitors (SSRIs) medications that selectively inhibit the reuptake of serotonin at the presynaptic neuronal membrane, restoring the normal chemical balance

electroconvulsive therapy (ECT) the controlled delivery of electrical impulses, which cause brief seizures in the brain and reduce depressed mood

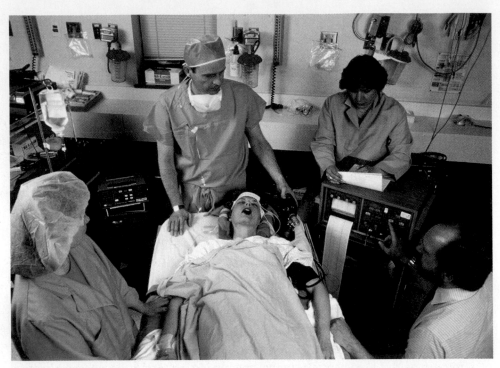

A medical team prepares a patient to undergo electroconvulsive therapy. Many precautions are taken to be sure that the patient is not injured and does not feel pain during the procedure.

depressed, who have not responded to medication or psychotherapy, who are unable to take antidepressants, or who are at serious risk of suicide. ECT can also be useful in the treatment of mania (Gitlin, 2006).

As used in the past, ECT was problematic, and fears based on reports from that era continue to concern some clinicians and patients today. Initially, ECT was used to treat psychotic disorders (Cerletti & Bini, 1938). Patients were not given muscle relaxants, which often led to injury from the violent seizures induced. In addition, the bilateral placement of electrodes often resulted in substantial and permanent memory loss. Modern approaches to ECT are safer and more humane than these early approaches and often lead to quicker symptom remission than either medication or psychotherapy (Husain et al., 2004). The current procedure involves administration of a muscle relaxant and a brief period of general anesthesia. Electrodes, placed at precise locations on the scalp, deliver electrical impulses, which cause brief seizures in the brain. Its precise mechanism of action remains a mystery. The seizures induced are not specific to one particular brain area and appear to influence the production of a number of neurotransmitters (Post et al., 2000).

Modern one-side (unilateral) approaches are equally efficacious and result in less memory loss. The most common side effects of the therapy as presently administered are confusion after the procedure and temporary amnesia (Ebmeier et al., 2006; UK ECT Review Group, 2003). ECT is usually administered several times a week for a number of weeks.

Light therapy for seasonal affective disorder Seasonal affective disorder **(SAD)** was first described by National Institute of Mental Health psychiatrist Norman Rosenthal in 1984. A subtype of major depression that afflicts millions of people worldwide, SAD is characterized by depressive episodes that vary by season. Though some patients experience summer depression, most are affected during December, January, and February. Symptoms of winter SAD include increased appetite, increased sleep, weight gain, interpersonal difficulties, and a heavy, leaden feeling in one's limbs.

Still not fully understood, the origins of SAD are largely, if not entirely, biological. Particularly interesting is the fact that its prevalence and severity tend to increase as one moves farther away from the equator (though leveling off beyond certain latitudes). Furthermore, especially sensitive people may experience more pronounced symptoms during prolonged cloudy weather. This suggests that decreased exposure to sunlight plays a part in the development of SAD, probably because of increased melatonin production. Melatonin, a hormone released by the pineal gland, increases during prolonged darkness. Exposure to light suppresses melatonin production.

Patients who are not severely suicidal or who are not able to take antidepressants may be treated with *light therapy*. This involves exposure to an artificial source of bright light, usually a light box, a light visor, or a dawn simulator. These devices produce light that is approximately 10 times brighter than regular household light bulbs. Light therapy sessions take place at the same time each day (usually in the morning) and generally last between 30 and 90 minutes. The patient sits by the light source, eyes open, so that light reaches the retina. Treatment usually begins with the onset of symptoms each winter and continues until spring.

Because full-spectrum light is not necessary to reap the benefits of light therapy, UV rays are filtered out to avoid damage to the eyes and skin. Nonetheless, there are occasional side effects, including photophobia (eye sensitivity to light), headache, fatigue, irritability, hypomania, and insomnia. In addition, light boxes are very expensive and often are not covered by insurance. Despite these potential drawbacks, light therapy appears to be effective in a substantial proportion of cases of SAD (Avery, 1998; Lam & Levitt, 1999; Rohan et al., 2004).

Light box therapy is sometimes used as a treatment for seasonal affective disorder (SAD).

Transcranial magnetic stimulation   *Transcranial magnetic stimulation* (TMS) uses a magnetic coil placed over the patient's head to deliver a painless, localized electromagnetic pulse to a part of the brain. Why the treatment works is not known; however, several clinical trials comparing it with a sham procedure have supported its use as a potentially effective alternative to ECT or medication (Ebmeier et al., 2006; Grunhaus et al., 2003; Janicak et al., 2002); see chapter 10 in this volume for a detailed description of TMS.

Deep brain stimulation   *Deep brain stimulation* (DBS) is a therapy targeting an area of the brain important for regulating negative mood changes, the subgenual cingulate region. It works by surgically implanting electrodes into specific, improperly functioning areas of the brain. These electrodes are attached by wire to a pulse generator (or "brain pacemaker") that is implanted into the chest wall. The electrodes continuously release tiny electrical impulses that deactivate (but do not kill) immediately surrounding brain cells. In this way, DBS inhibits abnormal activity in targeted parts of the brain and treats disorders characterized by overactivity. DBS has been approved by the FDA for use in treating Parkinson's disease and some types of bodily tremors. DBS has also been used to treat psychiatric disorders. In 2001, DBS was used to treat obsessive-compulsive disorder (OCD), leading to significant improvement in anxiety, compulsions, and comorbid depression (Greenberg et al., 2006).

In March 2005, DBS was used to treat six patients with long-standing, treatment-resistant depression (Mayberg et al., 2005). Several patients reported immediate mood changes: a sudden sense of intense calm and relief, a clearing of mental heaviness, the lifting of a black cloud, the disappearance of a void, and the fading of a burrowing dread in the pit of the stomach. In addition, researchers observed improved motor speed and higher rates of spontaneous speech. These results, though intriguing, remain preliminary and await confirmation with a larger controlled clinical trial.

seasonal affective disorder   subtype of major depression that is characterized by depressive episodes that vary by season

BIPOLAR DISORDER

Medications are the primary treatment for bipolar disorder; psychotherapy alone is insufficient (American Psychiatric Association, 2005). However, psychotherapy may provide emotional support to both the patient and family members and help the patient develop behavioral strategies to cope with symptoms and stabilize his or her mood. Psychotherapy reduces hospitalizations and improves daily functioning (Depression and Bipolar Support Alliance, 2006; National Institute of Mental Health, 2001). Different forms of psychotherapy are available to people with bipolar disorder, including cognitive-behavioral therapy, psychoeducation, family therapy, and interpersonal and social rhythm therapy (National Institute of Mental Health, 2001).

Psychological Treatments Psychological treatments are efficacious for bipolar disorder: they alleviate depressive symptoms and help patients recognize and respond to significant mood swings.

Cognitive-behavioral therapy (CBT) Cognitive-behavioral therapy (CBT) for bipolar disorder develops skills to change inappropriate or negative thought patterns and behaviors. CBT appears to decrease depressive symptoms (Zaretsky et al., 1999), improve outcome (Fava et al., 2001), and increase adherence to treatment recommendations (Cochran, 1984). Psychoeducation teaches the patient about bipolar disorder, its treatment, and how to recognize warning signs or precursors of mood shifts. Early recognition can prompt treatment seeking, reduce relapse risk, and improve social and occupational functioning (Perry et al., 1999). Education can also be informative for family and friends. Family-based treatment, sometimes initiated while an individual is still receiving inpatient care, focuses on developing strategies to reduce personal and familial stress (Glick et al., 1993).

Interpersonal and social rhythm therapy (IPSRT) Interpersonal and social rhythm therapy (IPSRT) (Frank et al., 1997) promotes adherence to regular daily routines (including regular sleep patterns). This treatment is based on interpersonal psychotherapy (Klerman et al., 1984), coupled with a *social zeitgeber* hypothesis (Grandin et al., 2006). This hypothesis states that the loss of *social zeitgebers* (a word that means "time givers" in German and that refers to persons, social demands, or tasks that set the biological clock) may result in unstable biological rhythms. In vulnerable individuals, this leads to manic or depressive episodes (Ehlers et al., 1988; Frank et al., 2005). Not getting enough sleep or getting too much sleep and not enough physical activity in one's day can both contribute to negative mood. Thus, patients treated under this therapeutic approach are coached to go to bed and get out of bed at the same time of day, every day. They are also advised to eat meals on a regular schedule during the day and to take breaks during long work days whenever possible. They are encouraged to keep a reasonable and consistent schedule of social events. IPSRT increases the regularity of social rhythms in individuals with bipolar disorder, which in turn is associated with decreased likelihood of new affective episodes (Frank et al., 2005).

Biological Treatments Bipolar disorder requires care by a psychiatrist and treatment with medication. A patient in a manic or depressive episode may need hospitalization to be safe and to receive needed treatment. The most commonly used medication is lithium (American Psychiatric Association, 2005; Berk & Dodd, 2005; Keck et al., 2001), which moderates mood swings from manic to depressive episodes. **Lithium** is a naturally occurring metallic element. Discovered by accident in the 1940s by John Cade, an Australian doctor, it was not widely used until the 1970s. For many years, lithium was used to treat bipolar disorder with no clear understanding of why it

lithium a naturally occurring metallic element used to treat bipolar disorder

worked. Then, in 1998, researchers at the University of Wisconsin discovered that a neurotransmitter called glutamate was the key to its efficacy. Too much glutamate in the synapse causes mania, whereas too little causes depression. Lithium moderates glutamate levels in the brain and thus serves as an efficacious treatment for people with bipolar disorder.

Lithium is intended as a long-term therapy and must be taken consistently. Often, when patients are *euthymic* (in a period of normal mood between depressive and manic episodes) or manic, they stop taking their medication either because they believe they are well or because they would like to keep experiencing some aspects of mania (e.g., increased energy, decreased need for sleep). If the patient discontinues the medication, however, clinical relapse often follows. Patients must be monitored carefully because if the dose is not exactly right, toxic levels of lithium may build up in the bloodstream.

In addition to lithium, anticonvulsant medications (normally used to treat epilepsy) are used for the management of bipolar disorders, sometimes in combination with lithium (American Psychiatric Association, 2005; Berk & Dodd, 2005; Keck et al., 2001). Other medications (such as atypical antipsychotics) may be added during depressive episodes (American Psychiatric Association, 2005; Berk & Dodd, 2005; Keck et al., 2001), but it is not clear if they are effective for children, adolescents, or older adults (Keck et al., 2001). Even though episodes of mania and depression can be controlled, bipolar disorder is a long-term illness that currently has no cure. It is important for patients to stay on their medications, even when well, to keep the disease under control and reduce the chance of recurrent, worsening episodes.

ECT can also be used in bipolar disorder, particularly for depressive episodes, extreme mania, or mixed episodes (Sikdar et al., 1994; Small et al., 1988; Thomas & Reddy, 1982). ECT is used primarily when medications and psychotherapy are not effective, when a person is at high risk for suicide, or when use of medications is contraindicated, such as during pregnancy (National Institute of Mental Health, 2001).

SELECTING A TREATMENT

With so many available options, clinicians and patients often feel challenged to determine the best treatment. The initial decision depends on several factors, including the nature and severity of symptoms, unipolar or bipolar features, psychotic features or suicidal intent, patient's age, preferences, tolerance of side effects, and treatments available in the patient's community.

Decades of placebo-controlled, randomized clinical trials indicate that unipolar depression responds to both psychotherapy and pharmacotherapy. Interpersonal psychotherapy and CBT have the strongest empirical support (National Institute of Mental Health, 2001), and IPT may have specific beneficial effects on interpersonal functioning (Weissman, 1994). But psychodynamic approaches have not proved to be very useful (American Psychiatric Association, 2005). CBT may be less efficacious than medication in people who are severely depressed (Thase & Friedman, 1999). Combining medication and psychotherapy provides only moderate additional benefit over either treatment alone (Hollon et al., 1992). Although approximately 60% of patients respond to psychotherapeutic interventions, relapse remains a concern—especially if treatment is not maintained and if symptoms are not entirely remitted at the end of treatment (Prien & Kupfer, 1986). For both pharmacologic and psychological interventions, continuation and maintenance treatment reduces relapse after the initial acute treatment phase ends. ECT is a viable option for individuals who are severely depressed or suicidal, or cannot tolerate antidepressants.

For bipolar disorder, medication with lithium or anticonvulsants is the treatment of choice. Although drug treatment is effective, many patients continue to experience breakthrough episodes or lingering symptoms (Gitlin, 2006). Psychotherapy alone is not effective for bipolar disorder. Family therapy, interpersonal and social rhythm therapy, and cognitive-behavior therapy in combination with medication can help the patient adjust to having a chronic illness, adhere to a treatment plan, and avoid relapses (Craighead & Miklowitz, 2000; Frank et al., 1999).

---

concept CHECK

- Many efficacious treatments are available for major depression, including psychotherapy, behavioral therapy, medication, electroconvulsive therapy, and light therapy.

- Psychotherapy helps patients become more effective in dealing with factors that contributed to or result from depression.

- Medications help regulate brain chemicals involved in emotion regulation.

- Psychotherapy alone may not be sufficient for more severe cases of depression; medication can be very efficacious in more severe cases but may cause side effects that can interfere with long-term use.

- Behavior therapy aims to restore patients' daily activity schedules (eating, sleeping, working, socializing) as a means of increasing the positive reinforcement of healthy behaviors.

- Electroconvulsive therapy (ECT) is particularly useful in cases of depression and bipolar disorder that do not respond to other treatments.

- Similar to ECT, transcranial magnetic stimulation (TMS) and deep brain stimulation (DBS) manipulate electrical activity in the brain, presumably counteracting existing abnormal patterns in key emotion-regulating brain regions.

- Light therapy is useful in the treatment of seasonal affective disorder.

APPLICATION QUESTION With only half of depressed individuals receiving health care and less than one quarter of them receiving adequate care, how could we improve health service delivery to individuals suffering from depression?

THE WHOLE STORY: LYNN—TREATMENT OF POST-PARTUM DEPRESSION

The Patient: Lynn was a 22-year-old senior at a college in the Northeast.

The Problem: She appeared at Student Health complaining of sadness and tearfulness, a drop in her grades, and a sense of being lost about her future. She awakened too early in the morning, had lost her appetite, and had lost interest in the things that she normally enjoyed. She sometimes thought it would be better if she were dead. Because of her religion, she stated that she would never commit suicide, but she wished that the Lord would take her life. She reported no symptoms of mania and no psychosis.

Lynn had been in a stable relationship for 3 years. She and Ted had been inseparable, and everyone, including Lynn, thought they would graduate from college, get married, and live happily ever after. It felt like a slap in the face when Ted announced a month ago that he no longer wanted to be in a serious relationship. Soon she saw him walking arm in arm with another woman. She was devastated. Even more important, she watched as her friends got jobs, chose their life paths after college, and after three changes of her major, she was lost and directionless.

Lynn came from a healthy and happy family. Her maternal grandmother, to whom she was quite close, had died one year ago. Lynn was not terribly independent, latching onto other people and following the crowd. Of note, her mother, two aunts, and her brother had all been treated with antidepressants. Lynn had never used drugs, drank alcohol oc-

casionally, and had only been drunk a few times. She was physically healthy. Her only medications were vitamins and the birth control pill.

The Treatment: The clinician diagnosed Lynn with major depression and recommended interpersonal psychotherapy (IPT). The therapist and Lynn together identified Lynn's main problem as role transitions; grief over Ted was secondary. Therapy focused on helping Lynn make the transition to independent life. She saw that she relied on others and that it was critical for her to make her own choices. With support from her therapist, she started to emerge from her depression after about 3 weeks and sought career counseling. After 8 weeks, her mood lifted. She started sleeping better, spent more time with her friends, and improved her grades.

Lynn completed graduate school and landed an excellent job as a media relations manager in a hospital associated with the university medical school. She married a supportive man, and all seemed well. Two months after the birth of her first child, at 27, Lynn was unable to shake a pervasive sense of feeling overwhelmed and was nearly incapacitated with depression. She cried all day, could barely muster the energy to shower, and was unable to care for her baby. When the baby cried at night, she would just bury her head under the pillow and lament what a horrible mother she was.

After a thorough evaluation, a psychiatrist diagnosed Lynn with postpartum depression. After 2 weeks on an

SSRI, she was able to play with her daughter. Her sense of humor came back, and her husband felt comfortable leaving Lynn with the baby. After 5 weeks, she felt much better—although she still was not back to her normal self. She saw a psychologist who specialized in postpartum depression and began a course of CBT. After a few weeks, Lynn could recognize the cycle of automatic thoughts that perpetuated her low mood. Whenever she perceived herself as failing at a task of motherhood, she would think "I'm a terrible mother." She worked to replace the thought with less self-deprecating thoughts. She eventually climbed back to her normal level of functioning and engaged in all aspects of mothering. After 12 weeks, she went back to work part time. She felt some pangs of regret about leaving the baby in day care, but she was glad to be back at work and continued to enjoy time with her daughter.

The Treatment Outcome: Lynn continued to take SSRIs for another year before the medication was gradually withdrawn. Her psychiatrist helped her to identify warning signs of depression because Lynn now had had two episodes in her lifetime. For Lynn, changes in sleep and appetite signaled a need to seek treatment immediately. Therapy gave her new tools for life. She began using them in other aspects of her life as well when she recognized dysfunctional cognitions.

CRITICAL ISSUES to remember

1. Distinctions must be made between transient changes in mood (either low or high) and more persistent and pervasive mood disturbances. Duration of the mood change and degree of impairment that results from the mood change are critical to making this distinction.

2. Depression is the most common psychiatric illness worldwide, although its expression may differ across cultures. Major depression is marked by either a single episode or recurrent episodes. The symptoms are persistent, lasting 2 weeks or more. Dysthymia refers to a more protracted, less severe course of low mood lasting 2 years or more. Bipolar I disorder is diagnosed in individuals who have experienced at least one episode of mania—regardless of whether a depressive episode has occurred. Bipolar II disorder includes depression and hypomania.

3. After puberty, depression is more common in females than in males. In addition, mood disturbances are greater during the premenstrual period, and mood disorders are more common during pregnancy, the postpartum period, and menopause.

4. Suicide risk is elevated in both major depression and bipolar disorder, and behaviors that suggest suicidal intent should always be taken seriously.

5. Both biology (genetics) and environment contribute to the risk for depression.

6. For major depression, both psychotherapeutic and pharmacologic options for treatment exist—either alone or in combination. Although the contribution of biology and genetics is clear, both CBT and IPT are highly effective treatments for major depression. Bipolar disorder generally requires medical management; however, psychotherapy can help the patient manage symptoms over time.

TEST yourself

For more review plus practice tests, flashcards, and Speaking Out: DSM in Context videos, log onto www.MyPsychLab.com

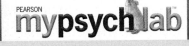

1. To be diagnosed with major depression, a person must have abnormally low mood that
   a. causes thoughts of suicide
   b. alternates with episodes of elevated mood
   c. affects the ability to function in social or work settings
   d. results from misfortune in life, such as a death in the family

2. People with dysthymia may also have major depressive episodes, a condition known as
   a. episodic depression
   b. double depression
   c. bipolar disorder
   d. chronic depression

3. Mania is not recognized in the DSM as a separate disorder because it
   a. is normal in conjunction with positive life events
   b. is an exciting and enjoyable experience
   c. is a less serious condition than hypomania
   d. almost never occurs without depressive episodes

4. The main difference between bipolar I and bipolar II disorder is the
   a. severity of the periods of mania
   b. interval between episodes of mania and depression
   c. severity of periods of depression
   d. level of medication necessary to treat the disorder

5. A person experiencing hypomanic episodes might not consider them problematic because they
   a. end very quickly
   b. are associated with a rapid cycling pattern
   c. are rare and part of a mixed state
   d. may be times of high productivity or creativity

6. Which of the following statements best describes the epidemiology of major depression?
   a. it is much more common among the elderly than among any other group
   b. it is less common worldwide than dysthymia
   c. it is the most common psychiatric disorder worldwide and affects far more women than men
   d. it is more common among blacks than among whites

7. Before age 13, girls and boys are equally likely to have depression. During adolescence, rates of depression climb for girls, possibly because of
   a. hormones
   b. self consciousness about bodily changes during puberty
   c. victimization
   d. all of the above

8. Passive suicidal ideation includes
   a. impulsive suicidal acts
   b. nonlethal attempts
   c. a wish to be dead
   d. all of the above

9. Suicide attempts, compared with completed suicides, are
   a. always preceded by a specific precipitating factor
   b. more likely in females than in males
   c. uncommon in adolescents
   d. less common in youth from a disadvantaged background

10. Which of the following is a *myth* about suicide?
    a. people who talk about committing suicide are never serious about it
    b. suicidal behavior runs in families
    c. most suicides are associated with psychological disorders
    d. most people who commit suicide do not leave notes

11. Which of the following is *not* considered a suicide prevention technique?
    a. portraying famous people who have committed suicide in the media
    b. targeting people with several known risk factors
    c. reconnecting youth who are drifting with social and emotional supports
    d. providing suicide hotlines

12. Neuroimaging studies of individuals with mood disorders have shown that
    a. dysfunction is linked to a single area of the brain
    b. no significant brain dysfunction is involved
    c. bipolar disorder cannot be linked to brain dysfunction
    d. mood disorders involve a number of brain abnormalities

13. Stressful life events seem to lead to depression in some people but not in others. A likely reason is
    a. stressful events in childhood do not lead to depression
    b. some people have more genetic sensitivity to life stress
    c. some people erroneously report more stress than they actually experience
    d. stress affects men far more seriously than women

14. In an interview with a clinician, a woman says, "I fail at everything I try." Such a statement is an example of
    a. learned helplessness
    b. major depression
    c. lack of positive reinforcement
    d. an automatic thought

15. One technique used in cognitive behavioral therapy for depression asks patients to
    a. record their thoughts, feelings, and behaviors
    b. recall any early childhood traumas
    c. examine role transitions in their life
    d. focus on communication analysis

16. In behavioral activation treatment for depression, the therapist and patient
    a. talk about a single behavior to be modified
    b. focus on uncontrollable activities that lead to helplessness
    c. participate in activating group therapy
    d. develop a comprehensive list of specific goals and activities in major life areas

17. Second-generation antidepressants are often preferred over first generation drugs because
    a. their mechanism of action is better understood
    b. they have fewer troublesome side effects
    c. they are not associated with suicidal thinking
    d. they can be used without careful monitoring

18. Electroconvulsive therapy is most appropriate for patients who
    a. need to take large doses of antidepressants
    b. have depression with a known biological cause
    c. have a specific abnormality on one side of the brain
    d. are severely depressed and who have not responded to other treatments

19. Which of the following is *not* a biological treatment for the mood disorders?
    a. electroconvulsive therapy
    b. transcranial magnetic stimulation
    c. deep brain stimulation
    d. neuroimaging

20. Seasonal affective disorder is often treated by means of
    a. first generation antidepressants
    b. transcranial magnetic stimulation
    c. exposure to bright light
    d. electroconvulsive therapy

Answers: 1 c, 2 b, 3 d, 4 a, 5 d, 6 c, 7 d, 8 c, 9 b, 10 a, 11 a, 12 d, 13 b, 14 d, 15 a, 16 d, 17 b, 18 d, 19 d, 20 c.

CHAPTER objectives

After reading this chapter, you should be able to:

1 Understand the features of anorexia nervosa, bulimia nervosa, binge eating disorder, and other eating disorders.

2 Discuss sex differences in the risk for eating disorders and why these differences exist.

3 Discuss developmental life course changes in the risk for eating disorders.

4 Explore psychodynamic, behavioral, cognitive, and biological theories on the causes of eating disorders.

5 Discuss personality features and comorbid conditions that are commonly associated with eating disorders.

6 Compare and contrast treatments for eating disorders.

eating disorders

Having excelled in middle school, Lauren was accepted into a prestigious boarding high school that focused on science and mathematics. Before school started, she had a physical exam. At the visit in early summer, her pediatrician (whom she had seen since childhood), weighed her and said, "My, you are filling out nicely." Embarrassed by this comment, Lauren went home and examined her body in the mirror. She saw her budding breasts and her expanding hips and didn't like it one bit. She turned sideways and looked at the protrusion where her flat stomach used to be and was determined to make it go away. Using all of her persistence and determination, she developed a strict regimen of running (2 miles in the morning, 5 miles in the evening) and a "healthy balanced diet" that followed the food pyramid in terms of nutrients but only contained 400 calories per day. She rationalized that if she got something from all the major food groups she'd be fine. Even so, the fats and oils made her very nervous. She told her parents that over the summer she would be preparing for this very competitive high school by developing the discipline she would need to excel. She started wearing layers and layers of clothes, checked her weight on the scales four times per day at regular intervals, felt her hip bones to make sure they were sticking out properly, and started skipping regular family meals.

At first her parents were proud that she was taking her educational opportunity so seriously, but then they started to worry as her temper began to flare. If they ran out of one of her regular foods, she would lash out at her mother for not having bought more at the last shopping trip. No substitutions were allowed. She became more and more rigid and added 300 sit-ups to her exercise regimen before bed to keep her abdomen toned. One day her mother accidentally walked into the bathroom as Lauren was getting into the shower and she was shocked by the emaciated body she saw. Ribs, vertebrae, a prominent clavicle. Her daughter looked like a concentration camp victim.

This discovery occurred two weeks before school was to start. Lauren's parents took her back to the pediatrician only to find that she had lost 30 pounds, dropping to 85 pounds at 5'5". Their daughter was severely underweight. Rather than starting school in the fall, Lauren spent two months on an inpatient eating disorders unit where her weight gain was carefully monitored by a dietitian and physicians and where she received the support that she needed to regain a healthy weight and to deal with the underlying anxiety she felt about her ability to succeed in the high-pressure environment of the math and science school.

St. Catherine of Siena was born in 1347, the 24th of 25 children. Her fasting, self-denial, and suffering bear close resemblance to modern-day anorexia nervosa.

Eating is so central to human nature that disturbances in normal eating behavior, like Lauren's, can be very hard to understand. For most people, food and eating are rich aspects of human existence. Our ethnic legacies are marked by certain dishes that are native to our ancestors; our family legacies are marked by traditional dishes that have been passed down for generations; holidays are celebrated with friends and family and always include food; and few social occasions occur without the involvement of food. But for those who are vulnerable to eating disorders, such seemingly harmless events can be devastatingly frightening. What would lead a healthy young woman like Lauren to restrict her diet so severely, resulting in a body weight far below what even the fashion industry might consider to be thin? In this chapter, we will examine psychological disorders in which the basic function of eating is disturbed.

Anorexia nervosa, the disorder from which Lauren suffered, was recognized in the medical literature in the late nineteenth century in both France (Lasègue, 1873) and Britain (Gull, 1874). Aware of the psychological or "nervous" components of the disorder, Gull highlighted the "perversion of the will" and focused on the role of starvation. Similarly, Lasèque emphasized the social and psychological factors associated with the disorder.

Although eating disorders have been widely recognized only in comparatively recent times, the historical record suggests that anorexia nervosa and other disorders occurred earlier. Bell (1985) provides vivid accounts of saints who starved themselves pursuing purity or devotion to God. Intriguingly, this is a classic example of how social context may alter the clinical expression of a disorder. The self-starvation mirrored the symptoms we see today in anorexia nervosa, yet the cultural context embedded the disorder in religion. Today, as in Lauren's case, we see the symptoms in a very different sociocultural context—one that involves a young woman's internalization of the ideal of extreme thinness.

Similarly, the behaviors associated with *bulimia nervosa*, an eating disorder which, as we will see, involves extreme overeating followed by vomiting or other purging behavior, were also seen in earlier times. Some Roman emperors, for example, appear to have engaged in frequent episodes of overeating and self-induced vomiting (Keel et al., 2005). Historical accounts also show us that eating disorders have not been confined to females. History is peppered with case reports of individuals who engaged in the perplexing behaviors associated with bulimia nervosa (e.g., binge eating or self-induced vomiting), although its recognition as a psychological disorder did not come until 1979 (Russell, 1979).

Today almost everyone knows someone or of someone who has suffered from an eating disorder—from actors to politicians to acquaintances and family members. Anorexia nervosa (see the box "DSM-IV-TR: Anorexia Nervosa") has the highest mortality rate of any psychological disorder, yet after decades of research, we understand strikingly little about the causes of this perplexing illness.

Anorexia Nervosa

Anorexia nervosa is a serious condition marked by an inability to maintain a normal healthy body weight. A person with anorexia may come to weigh less than 85% of ideal body weight. Younger patients fail to have the weight (and often height) increases expected as part of normal growth. Psychologists measure just how thin their patients

anorexia nervosa a serious condition marked by an inability to maintain a normal healthy body weight.

DSM-IV-TR

Anorexia Nervosa

Anorexia nervosa is marked by weight loss (or failure to gain weight in youth who are still growing) leading to a body weight of less than 85% of that expected. Despite low weight, individuals with anorexia nervosa have an intense fear of gaining weight or becoming fat. They may also:

- have a disturbance in the way in which they experience their body weight or shape.
- place extreme importance on their body weight or shape as measures of self-evaluation.
- deny the seriousness of their low body weight.
- stop having menstrual periods (amenorrhea) as a consequence of low body weight.

   In the *restricting type*, individuals do not engage in binge eating or purging behavior (i.e., self-induced vomiting or the misuse of laxatives, diuretics, or enemas). In the *binge eating/purging type*, people do engage in regular binge eating or purging behavior.

Adapted with permission from the *Diagnostic and Statistical Manual of Mental Disorders*, Text Revision, Fourth Edition, (Copyright 2000). American Psychiatric Association.

are by calculating **body mass index,** or **BMI.** Weight, in kilograms, is divided by height, in meters squared (kg/m²). Table 7.1 shows the cutoffs for underweight, normal weight, overweight, and obese. Table 7.2 gives examples of just what these measures mean in terms of a typical woman (5'6") and a typical man (5'11"). When measuring BMI in children, both sex and age need to be considered in order for BMI to be a meaningful measure.

   Anorexia nervosa is a visible eating disorder—patients are noticeably thin, although they may conceal their *emaciation* (severe underweight) by wearing layers of clothes or otherwise hiding their bodies. Anorexia nervosa has two subtypes, restricting and binge eating/purging. In the classic restricting subtype, patients maintain their low weight only by reducing their caloric intake and increasing their physical activity. In the binge eating/purging subtype, individuals may engage in either **binge eating**

body mass index or BMI   weight, in kilograms, divided by height, in meters squared (kg/m²)

binge eating   eating an unusually large amount of food in a short period of time and feeling out of control

TABLE 7.1

BMI Categories

BMI	Weight Status
Below 18.5	Underweight
18.5–24.9	Normal
25.0–29.9	Overweight
30.0 and above	Obese

TABLE 7.2

BMI to Weight Examples for Typical Woman and Man

BMI	Woman 5'6" Age 20 Weight (lbs)	Man 5'11" Age 20 Weight (lbs)
13	80	93
18.5	114	132
21	130	150
25	155	179
30	186	215
40	248	287

Even when extremely underweight, individuals with anorexia nervosa report seeing themselves as overweight. The mechanism for this distortion remains unknown.

(eating an unusually large amount of food in a short period of time and feeling out of control), **purging** [using self-induced vomiting, laxatives, or diuretics (water pill)], or both behaviors. Russell (1979) recognized the existence of binge eating in women with anorexia nervosa, and in early accounts these behaviors were seen to occur in over half of patients with anorexia nervosa at some point during their illness (Casper et al., 1980).

The second clinical feature of anorexia nervosa can be terribly perplexing to friends and families. This is an intense fear of gaining weight even though the person is already seriously underweight. Individuals with anorexia nervosa, even in the most extreme phases of emaciation, fear weight gain. They are not merely afraid of becoming fat; they are terrified by even the smallest amount of weight gain. This is commonly expressed as "feeling fat," although the precise meaning of that phrase differs by individual, as "fat" is not truly a feeling.

The third feature cluster includes three possible problems. Patients may have one, two, or all three of these features. The first problem is an actual *perceptual distortion* in which patients perceive their bodies as fat even when they are emaciated. The mechanism of this perceptual distortion remains unknown, but it may work in the same way that some people who have been overweight and lose weight still perceive themselves as overweight. Betsy recalls,

I remember during treatment when Anne, the dietitian, was working with me to include a muffin for breakfast. I put the muffin on my plate and just stared at it. It may as well have been a tarantula or a python. I took a bite and I could literally see my thighs getting fatter. The muffin was going straight to my thighs. After four bites I just panicked and threw the muffin away. I had to go running to get rid of it.

The second problem is *placing undue importance on weight and shape as a measure of self-evaluation.* People with anorexia nervosa are totally preoccupied by weight. In fact, their self-worth and self-esteem can be almost entirely determined by their weight. Slight increases can lead to a downward spiral of self-esteem.

The third problem in this cluster is *denial of illness.* Even when facing severe medical complications, individuals with anorexia nervosa insist that everything is fine. This creates considerable problems in reaching and accepting treatment and, on occasion, can result in patients being hospitalized involuntarily (see Chapter 15), as they are a clear danger to themselves.

Even at 70 pounds (BMI=12 kg/m^2) Betsy maintained her rigorous exercise schedule of running 5 miles per day, 400 sit-ups, and one hour on the exercise bike.

Finally, the official diagnosis of anorexia nervosa in females requires **amenorrhea,** or the absence of menstruation, for at least three consecutive months. Amenorrhea is a common response to starvation and weight loss as the body shuts down reproductive functioning in the face of famine. Interestingly, this diagnostic criterion is controversial, as there do not appear to be meaningful differences between individuals with anorexia nervosa who do and do not menstruate (Gendall et al., 2006; Watson et al., 2003). Girls and women who meet all of the diagnostic criteria for anorexia nervosa, but who continue to menstruate, are also seriously ill and require treatment.

In addition to the diagnostic features, anorexia nervosa is associated with a long list of associated psychological and medical features. Psychologically, depression and anxiety are commonly present. Medically, patients will often have slow heart rates, low blood pressure, and lowered body temperature (which might explain their tendency to wear layers of clothes even in warm temperatures). Table 7.3 presents additional clinical features associated with anorexia nervosa.

purging   using self-induced vomiting, laxatives, or a diuretic (water pill) in order to reverse the effects of a binge or to produce weight loss

amenorrhea   the absence of menstruation for at least three consecutive months

TABLE 7.3

Features Associated with Anorexia Nervosa

Physical Features	Psychological/Behavioral Features
Dehydration	Cognitive impairment
Electrolyte imbalances (sodium, potassium levels)	Body-checking (touching and pinching to measure fatness)
Osteoporosis	Depression
Lanugo hair (fine downy hair on body)	Anxiety
Dry brittle hair	Low self-esteem
Low body temperature	Self-absorption
Hypotension (low blood pressure)	Ritualistic behaviors
Bradycardia (slow heart rate)	Extreme perfectionism
Growth retardation	Self-consciousness
Bloating	
Constipation	
Fidgeting	
Loss of tooth enamel and dentin	

EPIDEMIOLOGY AND COURSE OF ANOREXIA NERVOSA

How common is anorexia nervosa? Based on the general population of girls and women between adolescence and young adulthood, between 0.3 and 1% suffer from anorexia nervosa (Hoek et al., 2003). That means that for every 100 girls or women in your class, one is likely to have the disorder at some point in her lifetime (Hudson et al., 2006). Many more girls and women (between 1 and 3%) suffer from less severe forms of anorexia nervosa (McKnight Investigators, 2003; Wittchen et al., 1998). Individuals with these *subthreshold conditions* can experience significant social and occupational impairment.

Anorexia nervosa is less common in boys and men. Females are about 9 times more likely to develop the disorder than males are. The disorder typically begins around adolescence (usually after puberty), but more recently, there have been reports of young children and older adults suffering from classic anorexia nervosa (Lask et al., 2000; Mangweth-Matzek et al., 2006).

Even though the media often make us think we are in the middle of an anorexia nervosa epidemic, we do not know whether the *incidence* (number of new cases) of the disorder has increased significantly over the past several decades. Some studies suggest that we are seeing more new cases (e.g., Eagles et al., 1995; Milos et al., 2004; Willi et al., 1983), and others report stable rates (Hall et al., 1991; Hoek et al., 1995). The discrepancy could result from how the studies were conducted and may also reflect the fact that many people (especially those with subthreshold anorexia nervosa) never seek treatment.

We do know that anorexia nervosa tends to cluster in certain segments of the population. These include the entertainment industry and sports, in which undue emphasis is placed on body shape and weight as part of performance. Actors, dancers, models, and athletes are at greater risk of developing the disorder. The accompanying box ("Real People, Real Disorders: Karen Carpenter") presents the well-known story of the death of the singer Karen Carpenter from anorexia nervosa.

Who develops anorexia nervosa, and what is life like during the illness and after recovery? Even after recovery, people who have suffered from anorexia nervosa tend to

real people, real disorders

Karen Carpenter—The Dangers of Syrup of Ipecac

Karen Carpenter and her brother, Richard, were a famous 1970s musical duo. The siblings won three Grammy awards during their career and performed at the White House. Their worldwide popularity earned them a star on the Hollywood Walk of Fame. In 1983, Karen Carpenter died from complications associated with the purging subtype of anorexia nervosa. Although her fans were aware of her diminishing size, her death came as a shock. It is believed that she died of heart failure caused by abuse of Ipecac syrup, which she used to induce vomiting. (Intended as a lifesaving remedy to induce vomiting in those who have ingested poison or overdosed on medication, syrup of Ipecac is toxic and can be deadly). After Karen Carpenter's death, the dangers of Ipecac were brought to public attention. One of Ipecac's major

dangers is that it is easily accessible. It is sometimes found in household first aid kits and can be bought in drugstores. When used properly, the syrup is a valuable medical tool, but when used repeatedly or in increasingly high doses it is highly toxic to the heart. Misuse of Ipecac syrup can lead to irregular heartbeat, seizures, dehydration, lethargy, respiratory complications, hemorrhaging, shock, electrolyte abnormalities, high blood pressure, cardiac arrest, and death.

Karen Carpenter's tragic story exemplifies the dangers of Ipecac abuse and has increased public awareness of the serious consequences of anorexia nervosa.

---

continue to have low BMIs (Sullivan et al., 1998). In addition, they can suffer from **osteoporosis** (decreased bone density) (Rigotti et al., 1991; Szmukler et al., 1985), major depression (Sullivan et al., 1998), and difficulties with fertility and childbirth (Bulik et al., 1999). The course of anorexia nervosa can be protracted and often includes periods of relapse, remission, and crossover to bulimia nervosa. Between 8 and 62% of people who start out with anorexia nervosa develop bulimic symptoms at some point during the course of their illness—usually during the first five years (Bulik et al., 1997; Eckert et al., 1995; Tozzi et al., 2005).

Many people are surprised to discover that anorexia nervosa has the highest mortality rate of any psychiatric disorder, estimated to be 5% per decade of follow-up (Sullivan, 1995). People with anorexia nervosa are 10.5 times more likely to die than their age- and sex-matched peers (Birmingham et al., 2005). The principal causes of death include both direct effects of starvation and suicide (Birmingham et al., 2005). For this reason, friends and family members always need to take anorexia nervosa seriously. Thinking that it is just a phase or that someone will "snap out of it" risks losing that person forever.

PERSONALITY AND ANOREXIA NERVOSA

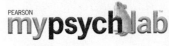

Anorexia Nervosa

The Case of Tamora

"If someone had told me how ugly I looked, being that thin, I wouldn't have done it. I mean, it was . . . part beauty and . . . part power."
www.mypsychlab.com

When we look back at Laura's case, we have to ask whether there are any hints in her personality that might hold the clue to why she developed this devastating illness. Some personality traits do seem to come before the eating disorder, get worse during the eating disorder, and often persist after recovery. The most important is *perfectionism*. People who develop anorexia nervosa are often described as model children and model students who set extremely high standards for themselves. They also apply that perfectionism to their pursuit of thinness and hold themselves to dieting standards above what others could possibly attain. Other common personality factors are *obsessionality* (going over and over things in their mind), *neuroticism* (being a worrier and having

osteoporosis decreased bone density

difficulty shaking things off), and low self-esteem (Wonderlich et al., 2005). This cluster of personality traits may help explain why adolescence and young adulthood are typical periods of risk for the development of eating disorders. Many of the developmental tasks of this life period involve substantial change and encounters with unfamiliar stimuli (e.g., leaving home for college, dating). Such transitions can be challenging even for healthy youth. People who are worriers, tend toward unwavering perfectionism, and find change difficult may experience this period of life as a trigger for an underlying predisposition to eating disorders. Addressing these fundamental underlying personality traits is often an important aspect of treatment.

COMORBIDITY AND ANOREXIA NERVOSA

As we have seen, people with anorexia often suffer from anxiety, depression, and other problems. Up to 80% of people with anorexia nervosa will suffer from major depression at some time during their lives (Halmi et al., 1991; Walters et al., 1995) and up to 75% from anxiety disorders (Bulik et al.,1997; Godart et al., 2002; Kaye et al., 2004), especially obsessive compulsive disorder (Kaye et al., 2004). It is particularly interesting that anxiety disorders are often present before an eating disorder develops (Kaye et al., 2004; Raney et al., 2008). To some, this suggests that anxiety may increase a person's risk for developing anorexia nervosa. If this is the case, early detection and treatment of anxiety disorders might be an effective way to prevent the development of eating disorders—at least for some people. Even after recovery, problems with depression and anxiety commonly persist (Sullivan et al., 1998). Effective treatment for anorexia nervosa must also address these additional disorders to completely restore healthy functioning.

| concept CHECK |

- Anorexia nervosa is a visible eating disorder marked by low body weight and fear of weight gain.

- Body mass index, or BMI, is a way of expressing both weight and height as one measurement.

- Anorexia nervosa is 9 times more common in females than males.

- The typical age of onset for anorexia nervosa is adolescence, although more and more cases are being reported in childhood and older adulthood.

APPLICATION QUESTION   How might the personality trait of perfectionism increase risk for the development of anorexia nervosa?

Bulimia Nervosa

Elisa was 21 years old, 5'10" and 144 pounds (BMI = 20.7 kg/m^2) when she first came to the eating disorders service. She reported 4 years of untreated binge eating and self-induced vomiting. Her high-risk binge times were in the evening, when she would close the blinds in her kitchen and, in her words "go hog wild." A typical binge included a gallon of ice cream, dry cereal straight from the box, and sometimes a whole package of cookies. Then she would switch from sweet to salty and start with chips and anything else she could find. In the last year, desperate to control her weight, she began taking laxatives. It started with some herbs from the health food store, but soon progressed to stronger laxatives. First she took the recommended dose, but then she needed more in order to get the desired effect. In the months before she sought treatment, Elisa lost her job and was basically housebound in her parents' home. She was binge eating and purging over 20 times per day and taking over 70 laxatives each night. She had developed large ulcers and scrapes in her throat because she was pushing objects down her throat

Bulimia Nervosa

Bulimia nervosa is marked by recurrent episodes of binge eating, characterized by eating, in a discrete period of time (e.g., within any 2-hour period), an amount of food that is clearly larger than most people would eat during a similar period of time and under similar circumstances. The person must also experience a sense of lack of control over eating during the episode and engage in recurrent inappropriate compensatory behaviors aimed at preventing weight gain. These can include:

- self-induced vomiting
- misuse of laxatives, diuretics, enemas, or other medications
- fasting or excessive exercise

Binge eating and compensatory behaviors must occur on average at least twice a week for three months, and the behaviors must not occur exclusively during episodes of anorexia nervosa.

There are two types of bulimia nervosa:

- in the *purging type*, the person regularly engages in self-induced vomiting or the misuse of laxatives, diuretics, or enemas
- in the *nonpurging type*, the individual uses fasting or excessive exercise, but does not regularly purge.

Adapted with permission from the *Diagnostic and Statistical Manual of Mental Disorders*, Text Revision, Fourth Edition, (Copyright 2000). American Psychiatric Association.

to induce vomiting. She had had two emergency room visits for dehydration. On one visit a blood test showed her potassium level to be dangerously low. After she was stabilized medically, she was admitted to a partial hospitalization program for eating disorders. She had difficulty adhering to the hospital's nonsmoking rules, and she frequently disappeared from the treatment facility during the day. When faced with the ultimatum of adhering to the program rules or being discharged against medical advice, she opted to leave. Two days later, Elisa was again in the emergency room with dehydration, an irregular heartbeat, and a low potassium level. This time she was admitted to a medical floor for monitoring, later to be transferred to an inpatient eating disorders program.

Unlike anorexia nervosa, **bulimia nervosa** (see the box "DSM-IV-TR: Bulimia Nervosa") is an invisible eating disorder, because patients are of normal weight or overweight. It is characterized by recurrent episodes of binge eating in combination with some form of *compensatory behavior* aimed at undoing the effects of the binge or preventing weight gain. Binge eating is the rapid consumption of an unusually large amount of food in a short period of time. Unlike simple overeating, the hallmark feature of a binge is feeling out of control. The person cannot stop the urge to binge once it has begun or has difficulty ending the eating episode even when far past being full. Some patients talk about a trance or a "binge mode" where everything else melts away during this time. The binge is usually stopped by running out of food, being interrupted by other people, or experiencing an extreme urge to purge.

Placing an actual caloric level on what constitutes a binge is difficult. Most agree that around 1,000 calories is the minimum amount to qualify as a binge—but in some cases, as many as 20,000 calories may be consumed. The way to judge is to ask whether the amount of food is more than a typical person would eat under similar circumstances. What is most important is whether overeating is coupled with a sense of loss of control. Indeed, some people (especially those with anorexia nervosa) might feel out of

bulimia nervosa a disorder characterized by recurrent episodes of binge eating in combination with some form of compensatory behavior aimed at undoing the effects of the binge or preventing weight gain

control even when they eat relatively small amounts of food. So, someone with anorexia nervosa might say she binged after eating two cookies. The term *subjective binge* defines eating a typical or even small amount of food (e.g., a cookie) coupled with the feeling that the eating is out of control. This is in contrast to the *objective binge*, which as described above is an unusually large amount of food plus feeling out of control.

The pattern of binge eating also varies. The frequency can range from occasionally to a few times per week to 20 or 30 times per day. Some people become locked in an entrenched binge–purge cycle, which comes to dominate their lives. For Elisa, evenings were clearly her high-risk times for binge eating, and she became locked into a vicious cycle of binge eating and purging that could not be interrupted.

Compensatory behaviors are any actions that are used to counteract a binge or to prevent weight gain. Compensatory behaviors to prevent weight gain include self-induced vomiting, misuse of laxatives, diuretics, or other agents, fasting, and excessive exercise. The *purging* subtype of bulimia nervosa includes those individuals who vomit or use laxatives, diuretics, or other agents. The *nonpurging* subtype includes those individuals who compensate via fasting or excessive exercise. It is important to note that some people purge in the absence of binge eating (see below under "Eating Disorders Not Otherwise Specified"). Compensatory behaviors are only partially effective in undoing the effects of a binge. As noted above, individuals with bulimia nervosa tend to be either of normal weight or overweight. Many calories associated with the binge get absorbed, and those calories lead to weight gain. Actually, laxatives are very ineffective compensatory agents. Because they work in the colon (after all of the nutrients have been absorbed in the stomach and the small intestine), only 5% of calories consumed are lost. Most of what is lost is water and valuable electrolytes (such as potassium), which is what makes laxatives so dangerous when abused.

In addition to the core symptoms of bulimia nervosa, many other physical and psychological features exist. Some are similar to those of individuals with anorexia nervosa, but others are quite distinct. Table 7.4 presents additional clinical features of bulimia nervosa.

TABLE 7.4
Features Associated with Bulimia Nervosa

Physical Features	Psychological/Behavioral Features
Dehydration	Depression
Electrolyte imbalances (sodium and potassium levels)	Low self-esteem
	Self-absorption
Acid reflux	Ritualistic behaviors
Ruptures of esophagus	Extreme perfectionism
Loss of tooth enamel and dentin	Self-consciousness
Swollen parotid glands	Anxiety
Gastrointestinal complications	Alcohol and drug abuse
Irregular menstruation	Irritability
Constipation	Impulsive spending
Bloating	Shoplifting

compensatory behaviors any actions that are used to counteract a binge or to prevent weight gain

EPIDEMIOLOGY AND COURSE OF BULIMIA NERVOSA

It's hard to know exactly how many people have bulimia nervosa. Many people with the disorder keep their behavior secret because of the stigma and shame attached to it. Recent estimates suggest that the prevalence is around 1 to 3% for women and 0.1 to 0.3% for men across westernized countries (Hoek et al., 2003; Hudson et al., 2006). When subthreshold forms of bulimia nervosa are included, the estimate is closer to 5 to 6%. This percentage range is probably more realistic because the frequency and duration criteria for bulimia in DSM are really just arbitrary cutoffs. In other words, even if a person doesn't meet all the diagnostic criteria, engaging in any binge eating and purging is unhealthful and potentially dangerous.

Is the incidence of bulimia nervosa rising? Few data exist to address this question, but individuals born after 1960 are at greater risk for the disorder (Kendler et al., 1991), suggesting that bulimia nervosa is a more "modern" phenomenon than anorexia. Some believe that bulimia nervosa is more of a culture-bound syndrome than anorexia nervosa (Keel et al., 2003), reflecting the trend that began in the 1960s toward thinner cultural ideals of beauty. Bulimia nervosa tends to be more common in urban than in rural areas (Hoek et al., 1995). This suggests that environmental exposure, social learning, or information transfer may play a role in the development of this disorder. Many patients state that they first got the idea to purge from something they read or even from a boyfriend on a wrestling team! However, virtually all young girls are exposed to this information at some time or another, so why do only 5% or so develop the disorder? This question is considered below in the section on genetics.

Who develops bulimia nervosa, and what is life like during the illness and after recovery? Like anorexia nervosa, bulimia nervosa is around 9 times more common in females than males. The disorder typically starts somewhat later than anorexia nervosa—in middle to late adolescence or early adulthood, although even later onset is not uncommon.

Although not typically associated with serious physical complications such as weight loss, those with bulimia nervosa commonly report physical symptoms such as fatigue, lethargy, bloating, and gastrointestinal problems. The disorder is hard on the body. Frequent vomiting leads to erosion of dental enamel, swelling of the parotid (salivary) glands, and calluses on the backs of the hands (Russell's sign, Figure 7.1) (Mitchell et al., 1991). Those who frequently misuse laxatives can have *edema* (bodily swelling), fluid loss and subsequent dehydration, electrolyte abnormalities, serious metabolic problems, and permanent loss of normal bowel function (Mitchell et al., 1991).

Mortality is uncommon in patients with bulimia nervosa, with rates as low as 0.5% (Keel et al., 1999). In one 10-year outcome study, 11% of individuals continued to meet full diagnostic criteria for bulimia nervosa and 18.5% met criteria for the residual diagnosis of eating disorders not otherwise specified (EDNOS); that is, their eating patterns were abnormal but did not actually fit the diagnostic criteria for any other eating disorder as defined in the DSM. Approximately one-half to two-thirds of patients eventually achieve full or partial remission (Herzog et al., 1999; Keel et al., 1997, 1999).

PERSONALITY AND BULIMIA NERVOSA

People with bulimia nervosa share some personality features with those who have anorexia nervosa, primarily perfectionism and low self-esteem, but differences also exist. Unlike the classic restricting subtype of anorexia nervosa, people with bulimia tend to be more impulsive (acting before thinking) and have higher *novelty-seeking* (stimulus or sensation-seeking) behavior (Bulik et al., 1995; Fassino et al., 2004; Steiger et al., 2004). These different personality factors are intriguing and reflect the symptom profiles of the disorders. Individuals with the restricting subtype of anorexia

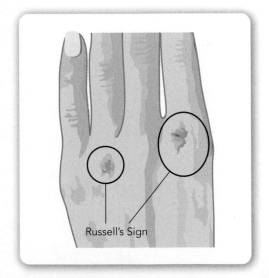

Russell's Sign

FIGURE 7.1

Russell's sign refers to scrapes on the knuckles caused by inserting the fingers down the throat to self-induce vomiting.

real people, real disorders

Elton John: Bulimia Nervosa and Drug and Alcohol Abuse

Critics have proclaimed Elton John to be the biggest pop music sensation of the 1970s, and his music can still be heard on the radio today. This legendary performer has spent much of his life in the spotlight. Fans worldwide have read about his turbulent addiction to cocaine and alcohol, as well as his love life, but what fans may be less aware of is his struggle with bulimia nervosa.

Born in 1947, Elton John was originally named Reginald Kenneth Dwight. By 11 he had been awarded a scholarship to the Royal Academy of Music. At the height of his career, he admitted to being bisexual, addicted to cocaine and alcohol, and suffering from bulimia nervosa. The world was shocked by his confession, particularly his struggle with bulimia, as it was unconventional at this time to hear of many men suffering from this disorder, much less a celebrity.

Not atypically, Elton John's road to recovery was difficult. He faced obstacles once he decided to seek treatment, because there were no Los Angeles clinics at the time that accepted patients needing rehabilitation for drugs and bulimia nervosa. In 1990, he checked into a Chicago hospital where he attended group therapy meetings, forged new friendships with other patients, and worked to overcome his problems. He declared himself recovered from bulimia nervosa later in 1990, ending his 14-year battle with the disease.

References: http://groups.msn.com/SilentStruggles/celebriteswhohavehadeds.msnw
Hillburn, R. (1992, August 30). Elton John on his days of drugs and despair. *Chicago Sun-Times*. Retrieved February 27, 2006, from http://www.vex.net/~paulmac/elton/articles/19920830_cst.html

nervosa display more rigid and obsessional personalities—congruent with their rigid eating patterns. By contrast, those with bulimia nervosa exhibit more erratic and impulsive traits—consistent with the impulsive and fluctuating nature of alternating starving, binge eating, and compensatory behaviors.

COMORBIDITY AND BULIMIA NERVOSA

Approximately 80% of patients with bulimia nervosa have another psychiatric disorder at some time in their lives (Fichter et al., 1997); this is a very high rate. Some individuals have several disorders at the same time, and some continue to suffer from other disorders even after they recover from bulimia nervosa. The most common comorbid psychiatric conditions include anxiety disorders, major depression, substance use, and personality disorders (see Chapter 11) (Braun et al., 1994; Brewerton et al., 1995; Bushnell et al., 1994). The accompanying boxes ("Real People, Real Disorders") present the story of Elton John, who suffered from comorbid bulimia nervosa and drug and alcohol abuse, and Diana, Princess of Wales, who suffered from depression and bulimia nervosa.

concept CHECK

- Bulimia nervosa is an eating disorder marked by binge eating and compensatory behaviors. Most patients are of normal weight or are overweight.
- Bulimia occurs more often in females than males and tends to begin in late adolescence or early adulthood.
- Bulimia has become more common since 1960 and is more common in urban than rural populations.

real people, real disorders

Princess Diana: Bulimia Nervosa and Depression

Being a princess is a common fantasy for young girls, but for Diana Frances Spencer being a princess was a reality accompanied by wealth, power, fame, and also private shame. After she married Charles, Prince of Wales, in 1981, Princess Diana became internationally known for her charm, commitment to charity, and passion for combating the AIDS epidemic. She emanated a high sense of style, beauty, and poise at all times. Her inner battles with depression and bulimia nervosa were topics of gossip among the public, but few people were aware of her private shame.

In 1992, Andrew Morton's book entitled *Diana: Her True Story* hit bookshelves around the world. Readers were shocked to learn that Princess Diana suffered from bulimia nervosa and was often overwhelmed by negative self images. She had kept her struggle with the disease a secret for years out of fear of the public's critical eye. In the next few years of her life, she surprised the royal family by repeatedly admitting to and discussing her bulimia nervosa with reporters. The public was stunned that a woman in such circumstances as Princess Diana suffered from such an unglamorous disease. It was a monumental year for eating disorder awareness, as Princess Diana helped remove the stigma attached to bulimia nervosa. Princess Diana helped thousands of other sufferers by admitting her private struggle.

References: http://cnnstudentnews.cnn.com/fyi/school.tools/profiles/princess.diana/student.storypage.html

- Comorbid depression, anxiety, and substance abuse are common in individuals with bulimia nervosa.

- Individuals with bulimia nervosa are perfectionistic and have low self-esteem, but they also tend to be more impulsive and have higher novelty-seeking behavior than people with anorexia nervosa.

APPLICATION QUESTION   How might cultural factors have led to an increase in bulimia nervosa since the 1960s?

Eating Disorders Not Otherwise Specified

As we've seen, the DSM criteria for anorexia nervosa and bulimia nervosa are very specific. In fact, most people who have eating disorders do *not* meet these criteria. Instead, they are given the diagnosis of **Eating Disorder Not Otherwise Specified (EDNOS)**. DSM-IV lists six examples of how the symptoms of EDNOS differ from those of the other disorders. Patients may have:

1. all features of anorexia nervosa except amenorrhea.

2. all features of anorexia nervosa except drastic weight loss.

3. all criteria for bulimia nervosa except frequency of binge eating or purging or duration of 3 months.

4. regular, inappropriate compensatory behavior after eating small amounts of food (purging disorder).

5. chewing and spitting out food.

6. binge eating disorder (binging without compensatory behavior).

Eating Disorder Not Otherwise Specified (EDNOS)   a residual diagnostic category for people who have eating disorders that do not match the classic profile of anorexia nervosa or bulimia nervosa

Since most people who seek treatment for an eating disorder receive a diagnosis of EDNOS (Fairburn et al., 2002; Turner et al., 2003), it is clear that the current classification system does not adequately capture eating-related pathology as it exists in the real world. Very little is known about most variants of EDNOS, except for binge eating disorder, which has received the most research attention.

BINGE EATING DISORDER

Lynette was a 42-year-old emergency room nurse. She had been overweight since childhood and was currently 5'5" and 195 pounds (BMI = 32.4 kg/m². Lynette's typical day started out late; she shunned both the scales and breakfast in the morning. She had to get the kids off to school and always prepared their breakfast, but she said her stomach didn't wake up until about 11 a.m. But then it woke up with a vengeance. On her 11 a.m. break, the vending machines "started calling her name." She started craving the prepackaged sandwiches she could get from the machines, loaded with packets of mayonnaise and relish. Once she got the salt cravings out of the way, she stopped by the candy machine. The best to satisfy the deep need inside of her was something with both chocolate and nuts—hit the sweet and salt cravings in one fell swoop. She had to get back to work in the afternoons, but she still had cravings. All she could think of was being alone in her kitchen after the kids were in bed and finally satisfying her needs. She would make it through the day with half of her mind on food the whole time. She fed the kids dinner, only eating a small salad herself. Once they were safely tucked in bed, she could have her "date with her pantry." Lynette said that food was her best friend. It was always there when she needed it. It was the only one that listened to her sadness, her loneliness, and her pain. For those few hours, surrounded by chocolate cupcakes, chips, chocolates, and ice cream, she felt comfort. She would be infuriated if one of the kids woke up and interrupted her binge. Most nights, she would retire to her bedroom in tears. Her "friend" had an edge. She would lie in bed with thoughts of failure running through her head, thinking she would never get her eating and her life under control. The next morning she would wake up with what she called a "food hangover" and start the process all over again.

Binge eating was first recognized in a subset of obese individuals by Stunkard in 1959. Binge eating disorder, though the subject of interest and research, is not yet an official psychiatric disorder. It is considered a classification requiring further study (Fairburn et al., 1993; Spitzer et al., 1993; Walsh, 1992). Basically, **binge eating disorder (BED)** is characterized by regular binge eating behavior, but without the regular compensatory behaviors that are part of bulimia nervosa.

Given that BED is a recent addition to the DSM, little is known about its morbidity and mortality. One study followed a clinical sample for 6 years after treatment; 57.4% of women had a good outcome, 35.7% an intermediate outcome, and 5.9% a poor outcome (Fichter et al., 1998). Only one patient had died. Six percent still had BED 6 years later, 7.4% had developed bulimia nervosa, and 7.4% continued to have some form of EDNOS. BED can be a chronic condition—the average length of time a person is ill is 14.4 years—suggesting that BED is not just a passing phase (Pope et al., 2006).

Since BED often occurs in people who are overweight or obese, one question is how obese people with BED differ from obese people without BED. Obese people with BED report that both their obesity and their dieting behavior started at an earlier age than obese people without BED (Spitzer et al., 1993). In addition, their weight yo-yo's (fluctuates) more throughout their lives (de Zwaan et al., 1994), they have more of the psychological features of eating disorders (Wilson, 1993), lower self-esteem and self-efficacy (Marcus et al., 1988), and more depression (Fichter et al., 1993; Marcus et al., 1988). They are also more likely to have depression and anxiety disorders at some

binge eating disorder (BED) a disorder characterized by regular binge eating behavior, but without the compensatory behaviors that are part of bulimia nervosa

DSM-IV-TR

Binge Eating Disorder (BED)

Binge-eating disorder is characterized by recurrent episodes of binge eating, defined as eating, in a discrete period of time (e.g., within any 2-hour period), an amount of food that is clearly larger than most people would eat during the same period under similar circumstances and sensing a lack of control over eating during the episode. Binge eating is associated with three (or more) of the following:

- eating much more rapidly than normal
- eating until feeling uncomfortably full
- eating large amounts of food when not feeling physically hungry
- eating alone because of being embarrassed by how much one is eating
- feeling disgusted with oneself, depressed, or very guilty after overeating

Individuals also report distress regarding the binge eating. The binge eating occurs, on average, at least 2 days a week for 6 months. The regular use of inappropriate compensatory behavior (e.g., purging, fasting, excessive exercise, etc.) does not occur and the individual does not have anorexia nervosa or bulimia nervosa.

Adapted with permission from the *Diagnostic and Statistical Manual of Mental Disorders*, Text Revision, Fourth Edition, (Copyright 2000). American Psychiatric Association.

time in their lives than do obese individuals who do not binge (Specker et al., 1994; Yanovski et al., 1993). In obese individuals, binge eating is associated with greater health dissatisfaction and higher rates of major medical disorders and physical and psychiatric symptoms (Bulik et al., 2002; Reichborn-Kjennerud et al., 2004).

As we have noted, BED is a provisional diagnosis, and as such it is still under investigation. But we do know something about how commonly it occurs. Around 3.5% of women and 2.0% of men in the general population meet criteria for BED (Hudson et al., 2006). BED is found in approximately 5 to 8% of obese individuals (Bruce et al., 1996). Therefore, if accepted as a diagnosis, BED might become the most common eating disorder. What we do not know is what impact the growing obesity epidemic will have on the incidence of this disorder.

concept CHECK

- EDNOS is a residual category for those who do not meet strict criteria for either anorexia or bulimia nervosa.

- Binge eating disorder (BED) is characterized by binge eating in the absence of compensatory behaviors.

- BED occurs commonly in individuals who are overweight or obese.

APPLICATION QUESTION How could BED contribute to the growing obesity epidemic, and how could treatment of BED be one approach to obesity prevention?

Sex, Race, Ethnicity, and Developmental Factors

Unlike some psychological disorders, eating disorders do not affect everyone equally, nor do they occur with equal frequency across the life span. Understanding eating disorders requires a careful understanding of who develops them and when.

EATING DISORDERS IN FEMALES AND MALES

As we mentioned earlier, anorexia nervosa is overwhelmingly more common in women and girls than in men and boys, with the official sex ratio being 9 to 1 (APA, 2000). Although the precise reason for this imbalance remains unknown, many theories have been suggested, including increased pressures on girls and women to attain a thin ideal, objectification of the female body, and the influences of female hormones on appetite and weight regulation (Klump et al., 2006; Striegel-Moore et al., 2007).

Although the sex ratio for bulimia nervosa is also approximately 9 to 1, women to men, the diagnostic criteria are somewhat sex-biased. This is because men tend to rely on nonpurging forms of compensatory behavior after binge eating, such as excessive exercise (Anderson et al., 2003; Lewinsohn et al., 2002). Changing our definition of bulimia nervosa may alter the sex ratio in this disorder (Anderson et al., 2003; Woodside et al., 2001). Male athletes are among those who feel strong pressure to remain slim and who may focus excessive attention on their weight and body shape.

Unlike anorexia and bulimia nervosa, the sex distribution of BED is fairly equal (Spitzer et al., 1992; Spitzer et al., 1993). Little is known about the other patterns of symptoms that fall under the heading of EDNOS.

RACE, ETHNICITY, AND EATING DISORDERS

It was once believed that eating disorders were restricted to white upper-middle-class girls. However, the picture is clearly not so simple. These early stereotypes more likely reflected who was able to access and afford treatment rather than who was actually suffering from the disorders (Smolak et al., 2001). Unfortunately, we do not have enough epidemiologic data to give us a clear picture of the racial and ethnic distribution of eating disorders and behaviors in the United States. One study (Striegel-Moore et al., 2003) assessing eating disorders in 2,054 young adult black and white women (average age 21 years) found higher rates of anorexia and bulimia nervosa among white than black women. Of particular interest, no black women were diagnosed with anorexia nervosa, compared with 1.5% of white women (Striegel-Moore et al., 2003). However, because the groups also differed on social class, it is not clear if the difference in prevalence was due to racial or socioeconomic differences, or both.

One group of researchers (Striegel-Moore et al., 2005) found different patterns of eating disorder symptoms across ethnic/racial groups. Binge eating in the absence of purging was more common in black women, whereas purging in the absence of binge eating was more common in white women. Several studies, however, did not find racial or ethnic differences in the prevalence of recurrent binge eating (Reagan et al., 2005; Smith et al., 1998; Striegel-Moore et al., 2001). Even less is known about the prevalence of eating disorders in other racial and ethnic groups. The lack of data about these disorders in the diverse U.S. population is a significant gap in our knowledge.

For binge eating disorder, fewer differences in prevalence exist across racial or ethnic groups (Yanovski et al., 1993). Preliminary data suggest that there may be increased risk for BED in lower socioeconomic classes (Langer et al., 1992; Warheit et al., 1993).

DEVELOPMENTAL FACTORS IN EATING DISORDERS

Despite the typical age of onset and the highly imbalanced sex ratio, principles of developmental psychology have not yet been adequately applied to examine the causes of eating disorders. Few studies have examined the relation between disturbed eating and childhood weight problems and the emergence of eating disorders in adolescence.

Anorexia nervosa in childhood is uncommon, although the incidence may be increasing (Lask et al., 2000). Bulimia nervosa before puberty is rarely reported (Stein et al., 1998). Clinical reports suggest that disordered eating behaviors and attitudes are clearly present in some preadolescent girls (Killen et al., 1994; Leon et al., 1993). In one study, childhood predictors of disordered eating behaviors included the mother's own body dissatisfaction, internalization of the thin body ideal (or how much they accepted society's pressure to be thin), bulimic symptoms, and maternal and paternal BMI, which predicted the emergence of childhood eating disturbance (Stice et al., 1999). The extent to which this familial relationship reflects environmental or genetic factors is unknown.

When anorexia nervosa begins in early adolescence, social and emotional development are clearly interrupted by its medical and psychological consequences (Bulik, 2002). The disorder itself and associated symptoms such as depression, anxiety, social withdrawal, difficulty eating in social situations, self-consciousness, fatigue, and medical complications can lead to isolation from peers and family. Often recovery requires facing challenges that normally would have been faced years before, such as establishing independence from family, developing trust in friendships, and dating and establishing romantic relationships. Although the physical toll of eating disorders is often emphasized, the social and psychological effects are equally disruptive. In addition, anorexia nervosa has dramatic effects on the family both emotionally and financially. Family meals often become battlegrounds marked by refusal to eat, power struggles about food, and frustration and tears. Parents struggle to understand as their child becomes increasingly unreachable and unable to think rationally about a function, eating, that to them seems a simple fact of life. The needs of siblings and other family members commonly become secondary to the demands of the eating disorder. This, coupled with the enormous expense of treatment, can wreak havoc on the most functional of families.

Addressing the issue of who develops bulimia nervosa, population-based studies of older children indicate that early menarche (onset of menstruation) may increase the risk for bulimia nervosa (Fairburn et al., 1997). Girls whose body fat percentage increases more rapidly and who develop mature figures earlier than their peers may develop greater body dissatisfaction. This may lead to earlier experimentation with behaviors designed to control eating and weight (Attie et al., 1989), which in turn increases the risk of developing eating disorders. For example, among middle school girls, higher body fat (an indication of maturational status) was associated with the development of eating problems two years later (Attie et al., 1989). Similarly, among 971 middle school girls (Killen et al., 1992), those who were more developmentally mature for their age were more likely to meet diagnostic criteria for bulimia nervosa. There may be important differences in family background as well. Compared with people with anorexia nervosa, the family background of individuals with bulimia nervosa also includes the same high achievement orientation. However, these families also have more problems with drug and alcohol dependence and greater frequency of sexual abuse than in anorexia nervosa. It is important to note, however, that sexual abuse is no more common in families of individuals with eating disorders than in families of individuals with other psychological illnesses.

We know even less about developmental factors associated with BED. Retrospective reports from obese women with BED indicate that binge eating before age 18 was associated with an earlier onset of obesity, dieting, and psychopathology (Marcus et al., 1995). Most studies indicate that BED generally begins in late adolescence or early adulthood (Hudson et al., 2006). Some people report that they began binge eating earlier in life (11 to 13 years old)—often before they even went on their first diet (Grilo et al., 2000). Among children aged 6 to 12, those who reported binge eating gained an additional 15% of fat mass compared with children who said they did not binge (Tanofsky-Kraff et al., 2006). Given its possible early childhood onset and potentially chronic nature, BED in children clearly needs further study aimed at identification and prevention of the disorder.

- Sufficient data do not exist to make definitive statements about racial and ethnic patterns in eating disorders. Some initial research suggests that anorexia is less common in black than in white women, although the extent to which this difference is related to social class is unknown. Less is known about bulimia nervosa, and BED seems to be more evenly distributed across racial and ethnic groups.

- Anorexia and bulimia nervosa are both much more common in females than males. Although the exact reason for this is unclear, several theories exist, ranging from sociocultural (increased emphasis on thinness for women) to hormonal (related to hormonal changes secondary to reproductive events). BED seems to be more equally distributed across sexes.

- Anorexia nervosa typically begins in early adolescence, and bulimia somewhat later. Childhood and later adult onsets also occur. Less is known about the developmental course of binge eating disorder.

APPLICATION QUESTION   How could early puberty influence body image and body dissatisfaction in young girls and thereby contribute to the development of eating disorders?

The Etiology of Eating Disorders

Although researchers have been studying eating disorders for decades, the causes are still elusive. Many theories have been proposed, ranging from purely sociocultural to purely biological. A complete understanding of the causes of eating disorders will no doubt require a reasonable synthesis of the different contributions of both biology and environment.

BIOLOGICAL PERSPECTIVES

Biological research has revolutionized our understanding of several psychological conditions. Classic examples are autism (once thought to be caused by cold and distant mothers) and schizophrenia (once thought to be caused by a "schizophrenogenic" mother). We now know that autism and schizophrenia are neurodevelopmental disorders. A neurobiological approach is now being used to help understand the biological basis of eating disorders. Our understanding of eating disorders has been enhanced considerably by the use of animal models. Observing animals in the lab is one way to understand the underlying biology of the core symptoms of eating disorders. This research focuses on those aspects of the illness for which animal analogues exist. Although we cannot develop animal models of some of the psychological components of eating disorders such as body dissatisfaction or body image distortion, we can develop models of more behavioral components such as food restriction and binge eating (see the box "Research Hot Topic: Do Animals Binge?").

Role of the Hypothalamus   We know from animal studies that the hypothalamus (a region of the brain that regulates certain metabolic processes and other autonomic activities) is influential in appetite and weight control. When researchers make surgical lesions in the *ventromedial hypothalamus* in mice, the mice overeat and become obese. In contrast, when lesions are made in the lateral hypothalamus, the mice reduce their food intake and lose weight. Therefore, the hypothalamus appears central to appetite and weight regulation in mice, but its function constitutes only one aspect of eating disorders. Furthermore, no evidence of consistent hypothalamic abnormalities has been observed in *humans* with eating disorders.

A ventromedially lesioned rat. The hypothalamus is central to weight and appetite regulation, and when the rat's hypothalamus is lesioned ventromedially, great weight gain results. If a rat's hypothalamus is lesioned laterally, the rat becomes extremely thin.

Activity-Based Anorexia Another animal model for anorexia nervosa focuses on the excessive hyperactivity seen in anorexic patients, which persists even in the underweight state. In this rodent model, unlimited access to a running wheel together with scheduled feeding leads to increased running wheel activity and decreased feeding. Under these conditions, rodents can lose over 20% of their body weight and can die from emaciation (Hillebrand et al., 2005; Routtenberg et al., 1967). This model is intriguing because it captures one perplexing symptom of anorexia nervosa (hyperactivity) and uses it to further understand its biological underpinnings and as a basis to understand pharmacological action (Kas et al., 2003). Breaking down complex psychological disorders into component parts and developing animal models for these component behaviors constitute a valuable scientific approach to understanding etiology.

Neuroendocrine and Neurohormonal Factors Other approaches to understanding biological causes focus on how the neuroendocrine and neurohormonal systems (see Chapter 2) affect feeding behavior and impulse control. Several neurotransmitter systems reviewed in Chapter 2 have been implicated in regulating feeding behavior. We will focus on the role of serotonin and dopamine, although several other neurotransmit-

Research HOT Topic:

Do Animals Binge?

What circumstances can lead a rodent to engage in what surely looks like binge eating behavior? Answering this question can help us understand some of the underlying biology of what may happen in people who binge.

Three major factors can lead to what appears to be binge eating in rodents—exposure to stress, periods of food deprivation, and "repeated intermittent exposure to delicious food and fluids" (Boggiano et al., 2005, 2006, 2007). These three factors sound curiously like human stress, dieting, and walking through the food court in the mall.

An interesting phrase has been coined in the animal literature called "binge priming." This refers to putting animals through repeated cycles of food deprivation followed by exposure to food that they consider to be delicious. This laboratory paradigm leads them to overeat—not only right after the food deprivation period but even after their weight is restored. So this "binge priming" has long-term effects on their eating behavior. This animal model mimics what we see in humans who go on a strict diet, then break the diet with a delicious food (it is unusual to break a diet with a low-calorie food like celery). This repeated pattern of food deprivation followed by a delicious falling off the wagon may in fact be priming the brain for binge eating.

Also of interest developmentally is that animals that go through these cycles of deprivation and exposure to delicious foods are also more likely to misuse drugs such as alcohol and cocaine. Apparently, this binge priming paradigm leads to

changes in the reward circuits in the brain and affects many of the neurotransmitters in the brain that are associated with the experience of pleasure and reward—for example, dopamine, acetylcholine, endogenous opiates, and cannabinoids.

Experts are especially worried about adolescents who undergo these repeated cycles of dieting and eating palatable foods because their brains are still developing and are more susceptible to reward (that, in addition to availability, is why adolescence is such a prime time for trying cigarettes, alcohol, drugs, and sex). The concern is that binge priming during this time might set them up not only for a lifetime vulnerability to binge eating but also substance abuse.

Stress and repeated food deprivation can lead to increased Oreo consumption.

ters may also have an influence on *feeding initiation* (starting eating), *satiety* (fullness), craving, and appetite (Badman et al., 2005; Gerald et al., 1996; O'Connor et al., 2005; Scammell et al., 2005). Serotonin and dopamine have been linked to changes in the psychological and behavioral features of eating disorders such as impulsivity and obsessionality (Roth et al., 2001; Simansky, 2005; Swerdlow, 2001). Indeed, serotonin has been directly related to the development of eating disorders (Brewerton et al., 1996; Jimerson et al., 1997; Kaye, 1997). In patients who have been free from anorexia or bulimia nervosa for more than a year, levels of serotonin remain high (Kaye et al., 1991, 1998). However, it is not clear whether this increased brain serotonin activity is the *result* of the disorder or if it was present earlier and could predispose someone to develop an eating disorder. In addition, abnormalities in serotonin might also contribute to some of the personality features of eating disorders, such as perfectionism, rigidity, and obsessionality in anorexia nervosa (Hinney et al., 1997; Kaye, 1997; Kaye et al., 2000). Moreover, the profile of individuals with anorexia suggests that they are able to maintain a state of denial and, with the exception of weight loss, find little pleasure in life. This led some researchers to suggest that dopamine, the primary transmitter for pleasure, might be involved. Data from PET studies indicates that individuals with anorexia might have a dopamine-related disturbance of reward mechanisms that contributed to their behavioral style of self denial (Frank et al., 2005).

Brain Structure and Functioning Studies   Structural brain abnormalities exist in patients with anorexia nervosa. Several measures suggest that when ill, these patients have reduced brain mass, including loss of gray matter (Muhlau et al., 2007) and larger brain ventricles (Dolan et al., 1988) (see Chapter 2). Structural brain changes have also been observed in individuals with bulimia nervosa, although these changes are less prominent in bulimia nervosa than in anorexia nervosa (Hoffman et al., 1989; Krieg et al., 1989). One long-term follow-up study has suggested that many of the structural brain differences seen in anorexia and bulimia nervosa normalize over time (Wagner et al., 2006).

No studies of individuals with anorexia and bulimia nervosa examine brain structure before patients develop eating disorders, so it is not known if these changes existed before the disorder developed or are the result of the condition. From a scientist-practitioner perspective, demonstrating that these changes persist after weight recovery does not provide evidence that these changes are causal. Indeed, starvation (or alternating starvation and binge eating) could cause lasting biological "scars," indicating that these changes were a result of the disorders, not the reason that they developed.

In terms of functional brain differences (see Chapter 2 on functional MRI), individuals with anorexia and bulimia nervosa have globally decreased brain glucose metabolism at rest (Delvenne et al., 1999) and increased serotonin activity in certain regions of the brain (Kaye et al., 2005; Wagner et al., 2005). These abnormalities are consistent with the rigid, inflexible, overcontrolled behavior seen in individuals with anorexia nervosa and some forms of bulimia nervosa.

Family and Genetic Studies   In Chapter 2, we discussed how understanding the role of genetics involves first asking whether a disorder runs in families and, if so, designing twin and adoption studies to determine the extent to which the familial pattern is due to genetic or environmental factors. Several family and twin studies have been conducted on eating disorders, although no adoption studies exist.

Family studies show that anorexia nervosa, bulimia nervosa, and BED clearly run in families. (See the box "Examining the Evidence: Genes or Environment in Anorexia Nervosa?".) Relatives of individuals with anorexia and bulimia nervosa have approximately 10 times the lifetime risk of having an eating disorder as do relatives of people without eating disorders (Hudson et al., 1987; Lilenfeld et al., 1998; Strober et al., 2000). However, family members do not necessarily share the same eating disorder;

examining the evidence

Genes or Environment in Anorexia Nervosa?

■ **The Facts**   Twin sisters Michaela and Samantha Kendall considered themselves to be overweight at age 14 and started dieting to lose weight. The notion that they were overweight wasn't their own idea. The girls were taunted and ridiculed by classmates (their mother estimated that they weighed nearly 200 pounds before they started dieting). Although the dieting began innocently, it ended up being devastating. The girls had no idea how controlling eating disorders could be. Samantha abused laxatives and eventually became unable to control her bowels. She soiled her bed sheets almost nightly. Both twins became pregnant at age 22 but had abortions for fear of getting fat. The twins attracted international media attention in the 1990s when they appeared on the Maury Povich show and shared their heartbreaking struggles with eating disorders. Both sisters eventually died from complications of anorexia nervosa. Michaela died first, lying next to her twin sister in bed. After Michaela died in 1994, Samantha tried desperately to turn her life around and recover. Unfortunately, the damage to her body had already been done, and although Samantha managed a short recovery period, she died in October 1997.

Is this just an example of the "fat phobic" environment terrorizing two young girls into anorexia nervosa, or could it be the manifestation of an underlying genetic predisposition?

Let's Examine the Evidence

■ **The Role of Environment**   The environment is a major contributor to eating disorders. Issues such as weight intolerance, teasing, fat phobia, and the societal pressure to be thin all contribute to young girls developing eating disorders. The teasing that the Kendall twins experienced was another powerful environmental influence: They made a pact never to be teased again. Twins also often have a special bond. In this case their pact to diet was so strong that they both eventually died. A rational approach to preventing eating disorders would include a focus on decreasing bullying and teasing in the schools as well as putting pressure on the media and the modeling industry to stop flaunting unrealistic ideals of thinness.

■ **The Role of Genetics**   The fact that the Kendall twins already weighed nearly 200 pounds by age 14 suggests that they were indeed biologically predisposed to eating and weight dysregulation. Although they were teased in school, countless overweight kids get teased in school and they never develop an eating disorder. The twins decided to go on their first diet together, and they never came off of it. Even though that first diet was a choice, once they were in negative energy balance (expended more calories than they took in), the anorexia took on a life of its own—because they were genetically predisposed. Why were they different? It was their bodies' response to starvation. Indeed, most teens who are overweight and go on a diet have a hard time losing weight and often become obese adults. In the Kendall twins' situation, their weight dropped like a stone, and they were able to maintain that frightening low weight until their death. In this case, their biology trapped them in the prison of anorexia nervosa. A rational approach to preventing eating disorders would be to identify the genes that predispose to anorexia nervosa and develop medications to counteract the biological factors that inhibit eating and enable maintenance of low body weight.

■ **Conclusion**   Not nature *or* nurture but nature *and* nurture. It is highly unlikely that either nature or nurture alone caused the Kendall twins' anorexia nervosa. Whereas countless adolescents are teased about their weight, only a small fraction ever goes on to develop anorexia nervosa. What made them more vulnerable? What made their bodies respond to dieting differently than the majority of their peers? It is very likely that their genetic predisposition rendered them more sensitive to negative energy balance than others. Their ability to maintain such low intake and low weight is testimony to the fact that they were biologically different from their peers. A rational approach to preventing eating disorders would be to identify high-risk individuals based on their genotype. These individuals could then be provided with strategies and tools to develop environments that would allow them to avoid situations of negative energy balance that could trigger an eating disorder.

References: http://www.anorexicweb.com/IdRatherBeDead/idratherbedeadtha.html

http://www.somethingfishy.org/memorial/memorial.php

Bateman, M. (1997, November 16). These are not just desserts. *The London Independent.*

rather, families often include members with anorexia nervosa, bulimia nervosa, and various types of EDNOS (Lilenfeld et al., 1998; Strober et al., 2000). BED also runs in families, independent of obesity (Hudson et al., 2006). Moreover, relatives of individuals with BED were 2.5 times more likely to be severely obese than were relatives of individuals without BED.

To what extent is this familial pattern due to genes, and to what extent can it be attributed to the environment or modeling of unhealthy behaviors? Twin studies consistently show that eating disorders and related traits are moderately genetic (Bulik et al., 2000; Wade et al., 1999). The heritability of anorexia nervosa is estimated to be around 60% (Bulik et al., 2006; Wade et al., 2000) and the heritability of bulimia nervosa between 28 and 83% (reviewed in Bulik, 2000). The remaining variance (in both disorders) is attributable to individual specific environmental factors (see Chapter 2). For BED, the best current estimate of heritability is approximately 41% (Reichborn-Kjennerud et al., 2004). As a result of the consistent replication across samples and across countries, it appears that eating disorders are indeed influenced by genetic factors.

Armed with the results of the twin studies, genetic studies of eating disorders have gone one step further and begun to examine closely areas of the genome that may influence the risk for anorexia and bulimia nervosa. To date, much less is known about the molecular genetics of BED or EDNOS, although these studies are currently underway. For anorexia nervosa, one area of interest is on chromosome 1 (Devlin et al., 2002; Grice et al., 2002). Two genes have been isolated in that area—one related to serotonergic function and one to dopaminergic function. Both are under study for their potential role in the development of anorexia nervosa (Bergen et al., 2003). Many other studies using the association approach (see Chapter 2) have explored genes that are known to influence appetite, weight regulation, and mood, again focusing on genes that influence the function of serotonin and dopamine and several other genes involved in functions central to the etiology of eating disorders.

For bulimia nervosa, a specific area of chromosome 10 has been identified as a "hot spot" for bulimia nervosa (Bulik et al., 2003). Intriguingly, this area was also identified as a "hot spot" in a genetic study of obesity (Froguel, 1998). Genetic studies using the association approach have focused on many of the same genes targeted in the study of anorexic nervosa. Of particular interest, one genetic variation associated with the serotonin system (Steiger et al., 2005) found a relationship with symptoms such as impulsivity, affective instability, and insecure attachment in women with eating disorders that included binge eating and purging.

Advances in the understanding of the genetics of eating disorders have been meteoric over the past decade; however, genes cannot paint the entire picture. The most likely causal explanations will involve an interaction between genes and the environment. Just having risk genes does not mean that someone will develop an eating disorder. In fact, someone with several risk genes may never develop a disorder if she is not exposed to environmental factors that trigger the genetic predisposition. Although our genes establish our baseline risk, our environment can be protective (buffering) and/or triggering (risk enhancing). As with so many psychological disorders, the complex interplay between genes and environment will be the key to understanding the emergence of these syndromes.

PSYCHOLOGICAL PERSPECTIVES

Several psychological theories attempt to explain eating disorders. These explanations dominated the field for decades, and many have offered useful insights about the role of families and culture. Many of these theories still contribute to our understanding of aspects of the disorders, but they are best considered together with what we know about biological risk factors as well.

Salvador Minuchin, an Argentinean psychiatrist who practiced at the University of Pennsylvania, championed the concept of the "psychosomatic family" and worked with families around the dinner table.

Psychodynamic Perspectives As we recall from Chapter 1, psychodynamic thinking focuses on the influence of early experience. Early psychoanalytic theory viewed anorexia nervosa as an attempt to defend against anxiety associated with emerging adult sexuality (Waller et al., 1940). Anorexia nervosa was considered an unconscious attempt to reverse or reject adult female sexuality via starvation to a prepubertal state (Dare et al., 1994). As psychoanalytic theory moved away from a narrow focus on sexuality, the explanation shifted to interpersonal relationships and the interpersonal context in which these disorders arose (Kaufman et al., 1964). One of the key clinicians and writers in the field, Hilde Bruch (Bruch, 1973, 1978), introduced rich clinical descriptions of patients with anorexia nervosa in her book *The Golden Cage*. Through her careful insights and keen ability to understand what motivated her patients to maintain such rigid control on food intake, she identified features such as body image distortion and a pervasive sense of ineffectiveness as core aspects of anorexic pathology.

Family Models of Eating Disorders Early family models of eating disorders, especially anorexia nervosa, focused on patterns of family dysfunction among patients who sought treatment. Perhaps best known is the work of Argentinean psychiatrist Salvador Minuchin (Minuchin et al., 1978), who identified four dysfunctional patterns. He noted enmeshment, rigidity, overprotectiveness, and poor conflict resolution as characteristic of what he referred to as psychosomatic families. The term **enmeshment** described the overinvolvement of all family members in the affairs of any one member. *Rigidity* described the difficulty families faced in adapting to the changing developmental needs of their children, for example, children's increasing need for autonomy. Rigid families have great difficulty maturing along with their children. *Overprotectiveness* meant that parents shielded children from age-appropriate experiences. Finally, *poor conflict resolution* reflected the difficulties these families had in dealing with problematic, negative situations.

According to Minuchin's theory, family pathology was expressed as a psychosomatic illness in one child (in this case anorexia nervosa). He used the family meal time to assess family functioning and as a therapeutic tool. His vivid examples of family meals provided insights into how families functioned at a high-risk time (namely, around food). Although his work brought the study of anorexia nervosa into the realm of scientific inquiry, his sample was biased toward families who could afford treatment at an academic center. Later studies suggested that his descriptions were oversimplified and that families of patients with anorexia nervosa were not so homogeneous.

Cognitive-behavioral Theories The cognitive-behavioral model focuses on distorted cognitions about body shape, weight, eating, and personal control that lead to and maintain unhealthy eating and weight-related behaviors. Consider the following classic example of a cognitive distortion. After eating one doughnut, someone with bulimia nervosa might think, "I've already blown it. I may as well go ahead and eat the whole dozen!" Proponents of a cognitive-behavioral model emphasize the power of thoughts to influence feelings and behaviors. In bulimia nervosa, distorted thoughts about food, shape, and weight lead to particular feelings and behaviors that then perpetuate the binge–purge cycle. Several cognitive-behavioral models of bulimia nervosa have been developed (Fairburn, 1981; Mitchell, 1990). We will address the specifics of cognitive-behavioral theory below as we describe the therapeutic approach that emerged from cognitive-behavioral theory.

Sociocultural Theories Sociocultural models emphasize the Western cultural preoccupation with thinness as beauty. The sociocultural model traces exposure to the

enmeshment overinvolvement of all family members in the affairs of any one member

ideal of thinness, to internalization of this ideal, observation of a discrepancy between actual and ideal, body dissatisfaction, dietary restraint, and restriction (Striegel-Moore et al., 1986). Since girls and women are often valued primarily for their appearance (Moradi et al., 2005), they are more likely to internalize the thin ideal.

Alone, sociocultural theory cannot account for the development of all eating disorders. Virtually all young girls are exposed to the thin ideal and many internalize it; yet only a few go on to develop full eating disorder syndromes (Striegel-Moore et al., 1986). Four lines of evidence provide partial support for the sociocultural model (Striegel-Moore et al., 2007). This evidence includes the imbalanced sex ratio in anorexia and bulimia nervosa, the increasing incidence of anorexia nervosa and bulimia nervosa in parallel with the decreasing body size ideal for women, cross-cultural differences in the incidence or prevalence of eating disorders with higher rates in cultures that value extreme female thinness, and the significant prospective relationship between internalization of the thin ideal and disordered eating.

As noted earlier, though highly plausible, the sociocultural model alone is an insufficient etiological explanation. Virtually all girls are exposed to the same societal images of ideal female body style, yet few develop eating disorders. Other factors probably contribute, and the leading candidates are genetic. A genetic predisposition may make an individual more vulnerable to behaviors such as dieting, which are triggered by exposure to sociocultural pressures toward thinness. Although the first diet may be nothing more than an unpleasant hunger-inducing experience for someone with low genetic vulnerability, for someone with high genetic vulnerability, the first diet may trigger the descent into full-blown anorexia nervosa. Another factor requiring further research is the role of increased average weight (average weight is increasing in children and young adults) and more frequent dieting (which starts earlier and affects many more people).

Barbies and GI Joes have unrealistic body proportions compared with actual human beings. Barbie's proportions have always been distorted, and over the years, GI Joe has morphed into proportions that no real man could attain.

---

concept CHECK

- Early psychodynamic models focused on anorexia nervosa as an escape from adult sexuality; later models focused on the interpersonal aspects of the disorder.

- Recent research highlights the role of neuroendocrine and neurohormonal systems in eating disorders.

- Eating disorders run in families and are moderately heritable; studies have identified areas on specific chromosomes for both anorexia and bulimia nervosa.

- Early family models focused on enmeshment, rigidity, overprotectiveness, and lack of conflict resolution as characteristic of families of individuals with anorexia; later models acknowledge that there is no "typical" family from which anorexia nervosa arises.

- Cognitive-behavioral models highlight the role of dysfunctional thoughts on the emergence and perpetuation of unhealthy eating and dieting behaviors.

- Sociocultural models focus on the ubiquitous pressure on girls and women to be thin and the internalization of the thin ideal.

APPLICATION QUESTION What are some of the ways in which biology and culture may interact to influence risk for the development of eating disorders?

The Treatment of Eating Disorders

Treatment goals for patients with anorexia nervosa, bulimia nervosa, and binge eating disorder differ somewhat, although there are commonalities. The normalization of eating behavior and weight is the central treatment goal for all disorders; however, the precise nature of the desired change differs. In anorexia nervosa, the initial goals are increased caloric intake and weight gain so that later stages of treatment can deal more effectively with the psychological aspects of the disorder. For bulimia nervosa, when weight is usually within the healthy range, the focus of treatment is on the normalization of eating, elimination of binge eating and purging episodes, and improvement in the psychological aspects of the disorder. In binge eating disorder, for patients who are overweight, the focus of treatment is on normalization of eating, elimination of binge eating, improvement in the psychological features of the disorder, and either weight stabilization or weight loss. The manner in which these goals are best achieved also differs by disorder.

INPATIENT TREATMENT OF ANOREXIA NERVOSA

Treatment for anorexia nervosa can be difficult and is best accomplished using a multidisciplinary team. The first and most critical step is weight restoration. Psychotherapy is difficult to conduct when the patient is acutely ill because her ability to think is impaired by starvation. Psychotherapeutic approaches include individual psychotherapy (cognitive-behavioral, interpersonal, behavioral, supportive, and psychodynamic), family therapy (especially for younger patients), and group therapy. Hospitalization is recommended for individuals who are below 75% of their ideal body weight (American Psychiatric Association Work Group on Eating Disorders, 2000).

Weight is not the only factor to consider when deciding on inpatient care. Other important factors to consider include medical complications, suicide attempts or plans, failure to improve with outpatient treatment, comorbid psychiatric disorders, interference with school, work, or family, poor social support, pregnancy, and the unavailability of other treatment options (American Psychiatric Association Work Group on Eating Disorders, 2000). Inpatient treatment involves highly specialized multidisciplinary teams, including psychologists, psychiatrists, internists or pediatricians, dietitians, social workers, and nurse specialists. At severely low weights, patients may be prescribed bed rest or have their activity limited for safety reasons and as a way to give their bodies a chance to start gaining weight. Typically, as patients eat and gain weight, they are given increasing privileges on the treatment unit. Often, a dietitian will choose menus for the patient initially. As she gets better and is able to make healthier choices, the patient takes on responsibility for food selections in order to continue her weight gain. Inpatient treatment for anorexia nervosa can be very difficult for patient and family. Treatment presents an unusual situation, in which the patient is deeply fearful of giving up her symptoms (starvation and low weight) and what the doctor has to offer as medicine is something the patient phobically avoids (food). Developing a collaborative relationship is critical to decreasing the patient's anxiety about weight gain and to making the hospitalization a success.

BIOLOGICAL TREATMENTS FOR EATING DISORDERS

Although medications are commonly prescribed for the treatment of anorexia nervosa, none has yet been identified as effective (Zhu et al., 2002). A recent report highlighted the critical need for developing medications that target the core symptoms of anorexia nervosa (Bulik et al., 2007). For bulimia nervosa, fluoxetine (Prozac) appears to reduce the core symptoms of binge eating and purging and associated psychological features such as depression and anxiety, at least in the short term (Shapiro et al., 2007). In 1994, the Food and Drug Administration (FDA) approved fluoxetine for the treatment of bulimia nervosa, and it remains the only approved medication for any eating disorder. Although fluoxetine reduces the core symptoms, it is still unclear whether its effects are long-lasting or associated with permanent remission. The optimal duration of treatment and the best strategy for maintaining treatment gains also remain unknown. For binge eating disorder, several medications that target the core symptoms of binge eating or weight loss, or both, have been tried, although none has yet received FDA approval (Brownley et al., 2007).

NUTRITIONAL COUNSELING

For all eating disorders, nutritional rehabilitation is a necessary but not sufficient intervention. Although patients with anorexia nervosa will often spend inordinate amounts of time pondering nutrition labels and counting calories, they are unable to apply this information to their own eating. Dietitians trained in the treatment of eating disorders can assess nutritional deficiencies in patients with anorexia nervosa, set appropriate goal weights, develop strategies for re-normalization of eating, and calculate caloric requirements for weight gain. For bulimia nervosa and binge eating disorder, dietitians can help the patient relearn appropriate portion sizes, eat meals in a normal way, and develop strategies for decreasing urges to binge. In addition, in binge eating disorder, the dietitian can help determine appropriate caloric intake for either body weight maintenance or weight loss. Although an important adjunct, nutritional therapy is ineffective as a sole intervention and is unacceptable to patients as reflected in high dropout rates when delivered as the only intervention (Hsu et al., 2001).

COGNITIVE-BEHAVIORAL THERAPY

As we have seen in earlier chapters, cognitive-behavioral therapy (CBT) helps patients change patterns in thinking that contribute to their problems. The application of CBT to the treatment of eating disorders focuses on faulty cognitions about body shape, weight, eating, and personal control that lead to and perpetuate the dysfunction in eating and weight. The therapist addresses both relatively easily accessible thoughts, called *automatic thoughts*, which are often evaluative in nature, and deeper *core beliefs*, which are the guiding principles or self-truths of the individual. CBT involves identifying and challenging distorted cognitions about food, eating, and body shape and weight, and replacing them with health-promoting alternatives. Studies that have dismantled the cognitive and behavioral components of CBT have shown that the cognitive component appears to be most critical in effecting behavior change.

Recovery rates with CBT vary from 35 to 75% at five or more years of follow-up (Fairburn et al., 2000; Fichter et al., 1997; Herzog et al., 1999). The rates differ in part because of varying definitions of recovery. However, approximately 33% of individuals with bulimia nervosa relapse, and the risk is highest during the year following treatment (Herzog et al., 1999; Keel et al., 1997).

For anorexia nervosa, preliminary evidence suggests that CBT may reduce relapse in adults after weight has been restored (Pike et al., 1996). It is unclear how effective CBT can be when patients are extremely underweight, however. Given that this therapy requires active cognitive effort, patients whose cognitive processing is impaired by self-starvation may not be able to benefit from CBT during the acute stage of their illness (McIntosh et al., 2005). What we know about the efficacy of CBT for anorexia nervosa is limited to adults, for no studies have adequately evaluated developmentally tailored cognitive-behavioral treatments for adolescents.

The cornerstone of CBT for bulimia nervosa is self-monitoring. Patients keep track of what they ate, whether it was a binge or purge episode, the situation they were in, who else was present, and their thoughts and feelings (see Figure 7.2). By analyzing

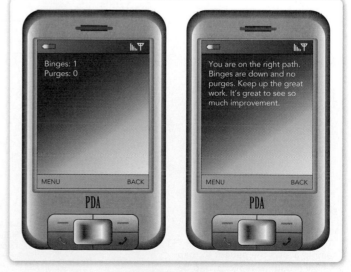

FIGURE 7.2
Self-Monitoring Via Text Message

The patient types in her status and receives a return message from her therapist.

the data, the patient and therapist can identify patterns of unhealthy behavior, including high-risk times and situations for binge eating and purging, which serves as a first step in establishing healthier behavior patterns. More recently, modern information technology has been adapted for self-monitoring, including the use of personal digital assistants (PDAs) and cell phone-based text-messaging.

The next steps involve mastering the language and concepts of CBT, including recognizing thoughts, feelings, and behaviors that are associated with unhealthy eating behavior; learning to recognize cues for and consequences of disordered eating; learning to control automatic thoughts; and learning to restructure distorted cognitions that perpetuate unhealthy eating behaviors. Finally, CBT focuses substantial attention on relapse prevention—again providing tools for maintaining healthy behaviors (see Figure 7.3).

CBT is also effective in the treatment of binge eating disorder (Brownley et al., 2007). Of interest, in the United Kingdom, self-help, often incorporating CBT principles, is recommended as an initial step in the treatment of this disorder (National Institute of Clinical and Health Excellence, 2004). Patients with binge eating disorder might first be offered a self-help book or an on-line cognitive-behavioral program to use at their own pace. For some, this approach might be enough to put them on the path to recovery. At the next check-in, if doing well, they might be encouraged to continue. If they have made no progress or if their condition has deteriorated, they are referred for specialist treatment as a second step in care.

By extension, dialectical behavioral therapy (DBT) focuses on emotional dysregulation as the core problem in eating disorders, with symptoms viewed as attempts to manage unpleasant emotional states. A small study of DBT for bulimia showed that patients receiving DBT had significantly greater decreases in binge eating and purging than did those on a waiting list and that abstinence was greater after DBT treatment than in the waiting list group (Safer, 2001). DBT is also being explored as an intervention for anorexia nervosa (McCabe, 2002) and binge eating disorder (Chen, 2008).

FIGURE 7.3

A Behavioral Chain

Chaining allows the patient to map out how thoughts, feelings, and behaviors cascade to unhealthy consequences. The object of the technique is to help the patient learn strategies to break the chain at every link.

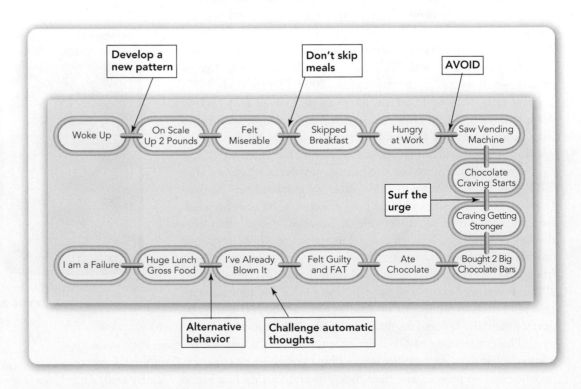

INTERPERSONAL PSYCHOTHERAPY (IPT)

IPT is a brief, time-limited psychotherapy that was initially developed for the treatment of depression (Klerman et al., 1984). IPT is based on the theory that regardless of their cause, the current depressive symptoms are "inextricably intertwined" with the patient's interpersonal relationships. The goals of IPT for depression are to decrease depressive symptoms and to improve interpersonal functioning by enhancing communication skills in significant relationships. The adaptation of IPT for the treatment of bulimia nervosa (Fairburn, 1993), anorexia nervosa (McIntosh et al., 2000), and binge eating disorder (Wilfley et al., 1993) applies the same principles, focusing on the reduction of eating disorder related symptoms. IPT for eating disorders intervenes at the symptom and social functioning levels by addressing one of four problem areas: interpersonal disputes, role transitions, abnormal grief, or interpersonal deficits.

For anorexia nervosa, IPT has been found to be less effective than a manual-based specialist supportive clinical management (a therapy based on supportive psychotherapy and sound clinical management) or CBT (McIntosh et al., 2005). For bulimia nervosa, IPT has been found to be as efficacious as CBT, but CBT shows more rapid decreases in bulimic symptoms (Fairburn et al., 1991, 1993). IPT, delivered both individually and in group therapy, has also shown preliminary efficacy in binge eating disorder (Wilfley et al., 1993). It is interesting that a treatment that does not directly address the core symptoms of the eating disorder (especially bulimia and binge eating disorder), but focuses solely on current interpersonal relationships, produces results equivalent to CBT, which focuses specifically on the disordered eating and body image issues. The mechanism of action of IPT for bulimia nervosa and binge eating disorder is unknown. Clearly, eating disorders often have profound effects on interpersonal relationships, and IPT highlights the many ways in which the eating disorder disrupts social functioning.

FAMILY-BASED INTERVENTIONS

Based on early family theories of anorexia nervosa, Minuchin and Palazzoli have advocated therapy aimed at changing the dysfunctional family system (Minuchin et al., 1978; Palazzoli, 1978), modifying dysfunctional transactional family patterns, and reorganizing the family around healthier and more open communication (Minuchin et al., 1978). There is no question that family involvement is critical in the treatment of anorexia nervosa—especially in young patients who are not chronically ill (Russell et al., 1987). However, the early observations by Minuchin and others of the "typical" anorexia nervosa family have not been substantiated. Indeed, there is no one prototypic anorexic family. Modern approaches to family therapy for anorexia nervosa include conjoint family therapy, where all family members are treated together; separated family therapy, in which parents are treated separately from their ill child; parent training, in which parents are provided with psychoeducation and tools to manage their child's eating disorder (Zucker et al., 2005); and a popular approach, the Maudsley method, which focuses on parental control of the initial stages of renutrition (Lock et al., 2002). The Maudsley approach hinges on seven principles:

1. Work with experts who know how to help you.
2. Work together as a family.
3. Don't blame your child or yourself for the problems you are having. Blame the illness.
4. Focus on the problem before you.
5. Don't debate with your child about eating—or weight-related concerns.
6. Know when to begin backing off.
7. Take care of yourself. You are the child's best hope.

The Maudsley approach empowers parents to take an active role in achieving successful treatment. This approach also includes therapist-assisted family meals.

Although family therapy is effective with adolescents, as currently conceptualized it does not appear to be efficacious for adults with anorexia nervosa (Bulik et al., 2007). No studies have yet explored alternative forms of family therapy (i.e., with partners and children of individuals with anorexia nervosa). One clinical trial has shown initial promise for family-based treatment of bulimia nervosa (le Grange et al., 2007). There have been no clinical trials of family therapy for binge eating disorder.

---

concept CHECK

■ Renutrition is a critical first step in the treatment of anorexia nervosa. Inpatient treatment may be necessary to help the patient gain adequate weight.

■ Fluoxetine (Prozac) is the only FDA-approved treatment for any eating disorder (bulimia nervosa).

■ Cognitive-behavioral therapy is effective in the treatment of bulimia nervosa and may be beneficial for adults with anorexia nervosa after they have gained weight.

■ Interpersonal psychotherapy is also effective for bulimia nervosa, although symptom change comes about more slowly than with CBT.

■ Family therapy is effective for the treatment of adolescents with anorexia nervosa but has not yet been shown to be effective with adults.

APPLICATION QUESTION   How could family therapy be adapted for use for older patients?

THE WHOLE STORY: LISA—DETECTION AND TREATMENT OF ANOREXIA NERVOSA IN A STUDENT ATHLETE

The Person: *Lisa loved to run. In elementary school she outran the boys. In middle school she joined the cross-country team, was team captain, and won the conference championships. Running was her life and she was good at it. She ran cross country and the 3000 throughout high school, racking up state championships in both. But that was just like Lisa—she was always driven to do her best, whether it was academics or athletics. Even in first grade, she often cried and would tell her mother that she was worried that she did not do her best—and she had to be the best. So she was*

thrilled when she was awarded full athletic scholarships to two excellent universities. She chose a university that was two states away that excelled in women's track and field.

The Problem: *The cross-country season started off well her freshman year, but she had tendonitis problems during indoor track season. The trainers had her sit out the season so that she would be ready for outdoor track season. Not competing caused her great distress. She watched her teammates at home meets, listened to their tales of victory at away meets, and she longed to be out*

there with them. She found it difficult to concentrate on her school work. Previously an A student, she started to get Cs in chemistry and calculus. Not only that, but she started to gain weight. Even though she was swimming and cross training to try to stay in shape, it wasn't the same as being on the team. Carrying around an extra 10 pounds made her feel like she didn't belong. She felt fat and disgusting. With only one month to go before outdoor season, she felt desperate to get back into shape. She was limiting herself to 300 calories per day and she was exercising about 6 hours a day—swimming, elliptical machine, running, doing hundreds of crunches on her dorm room floor—she never sat still. Her tendonitis improved a little, and she was able to start training with the team again—but she didn't stop her extra exercising. She was quickly back to her training weight, but the coach noticed that her running wasn't quite back to her previous outstanding level. He assumed that it was just from the time off and worked with her to increase her miles and try to improve her overall conditioning. The attention paid off, her running improved, she took second at the relays and she was contributing to the team's success. But she started looking really thin. Her teammates noticed her in the locker room and were shocked that they could count every rib and vertebrae. They went to the coach with their concerns. The coach listened but had a dilemma. NCAA finals were coming up and they were well positioned to win, but not without Lisa. Could he wait until after the finals to talk to Student Health? He decided to sit on it for a couple of days and then decide.

The Treatment: Two days later, he got a call from EMS. One of his athletes had collapsed during a 15-mile training run and was being transported to the Emergency Room. He rushed to the ER and found Lisa hooked up to an IV, exhausted and dehydrated. She was tearful and determined to go to the finals, saying she was letting everyone down.

The coach told Lisa about the conversation he had had with her teammates. Avoiding talking about the finals, he told her that he would do whatever he could to work with her to get healthy and that was the only goal right now. The coach agonized over not having approached her immediately. Waiting two days could have meant her life.

At first, Lisa's treatment focused on support while she was being renourished. Her weight had dropped to 78 pounds and she was 5'5" (BMI = 13 kg/m^2). Her therapist noted that her thinking was very negative. It was unclear whether she was also suffering from depression or if her low mood and negative thoughts were simply secondary to starvation. She continued to believe that she had let down the team, the school, her family, and herself. She also believed that she could only run well if she were the thinnest girl on the team. Initially, Lisa was afraid that the therapist's only goals were to make her fat and to keep her from running. However, Lisa began to see that the therapist would indeed work with her to get her back to her sport but only after she was fully recovered. As her thinking cleared, her therapist began self-monitoring—not only of her food intake, but of her urges to exercise and her thoughts. They worked together to ensure that she was eating properly and not engaging in unhealthy exercise that would make weight gain nearly impossible. She began to recognize patterns in her urges to exercise as well as some of the automatic thoughts that had maintained the eating-disordered behaviors. She realized that every time she saw a female athlete in revealing clothing she started to feel as if she needed to get back to her waiflike weight. She would develop an overwhelming urge to go running or punish herself in the gym. Her therapist helped her to unpack the distorted thinking that fueled that urge ("I'll only be a successful runner if I am back to my previous low weight") and helped her integrate the realization that her low weight actually interfered with her running rather than helping it. Gradually, she became more and more confi-

dent in her ability to resist the urge to exercise, although she still felt waves of envy as she saw the thinner girls. As she gained weight, her mood improved, so her physician saw no immediate need for medication. However, she did continue to monitor Lisa's mood over time to see if the depression would return and medication might be required.

The Treatment Outcome: The following year before cross-country season, with Lisa's permission, a meeting was set up with Lisa, her parents, her coach, her trainer, and her therapist. Together they developed a plan for Lisa's competitive season, including reasonable training schedules and procedures for action if warning signs emerged. Lisa also talked openly about her struggle with her teammates, who were supportive of her efforts toward recovery.

In many ways Lisa was a highly successful young woman—academically and athletically. The transition from high school to college, though exciting, posed significant challenges for her. Two states away from home, she was on her own in a highly competitive Division I school. Precisely those traits (competitiveness and determination) that made her a great success were her undoing after her injury. Lisa didn't have the personal tools to deal with this setback in a healthy way; instead, she went overboard with exercise as a means of feeling a sense of control over her situation. Once she was able to engage in a supportive relationship with her therapist, she was able to change her behavior, although clearly there were many cues in the environment that led to urges to exercise. With the support of her family, therapist, trainer, coach, and teammates, Lisa was able to finish her competitive college career successfully.

CRITICAL ISSUES to remember

1. Anorexia nervosa is marked by extreme low weight, fear of gaining weight, and undue emphasis on shape and weight as part of self-evaluation. Bulimia nervosa is seen in individuals who are of normal weight or overweight and is marked by binge eating and compensatory behaviors such as self-induced vomiting or laxative abuse. Binge eating disorder also includes binge eating behavior but without compensatory behaviors.

2. Anorexia nervosa and bulimia nervosa are 9 times more common in females than in males. Binge eating disorder has a more even sex distribution.

3. Anorexia nervosa typically begins in early adolescence, with bulimia somewhat later. Child and later adult onsets also occur. Less is known about the developmental course of binge eating disorder.

4. Many theories of the causes of eating disorders exist, among them psychodynamic, biological/genetic, cognitive-behavioral and sociocultural. A complete appreciation of the factors that cause and maintain eating disorders will probably involve a combination of genetic and environmental factors.

5. Depression and anxiety are commonly comorbid with anorexia and bulimia nervosa. Personality styles characteristic of both disorders include perfectionism; however, bulimia also tends to be associated with more impulsive features.

6. The initial and critical step in the treatment of anorexia nervosa is renutrition and weight gain in a supportive environment. Family involvement is critical for younger patients. Cognitive-behavioral therapy may be helpful after weight restoration. For bulimia nervosa, both cognitive behavioral therapy and fluoxetine (Prozac) have been shown to be effective in reducing binge eating and purging behavior, although the long-term efficacy of medication treatment is unknown.

TEST yourself

For more review plus practice tests, flashcards, and Speaking Out: DSM in Context videos, log onto www.MyPsychLab.com

1. Which of the following criteria is necessary for a diagnosis of anorexia nervosa?
   a. a body weight of less than 85% of that expected for height and sex
   b. a BMI of 20–22
   c. a history of purging behaviors
   d. recent weight loss

2. Even at a very low body weight, a person with anorexia nervosa will experience
   a. lack of concern about physical appearance
   b. complete absence of appetite
   c. intense fear of gaining weight
   d. unusually high self-esteem

3. The attitude most difficult to overcome in patients with anorexia nervosa is their
   a. rationalization of any weight gain
   b. acceptance of obese family members
   c. denial that a problem exists
   d. preoccupation with fashion

4. The two subtypes of anorexia nervosa are
   a. EDNOS and BED
   b. restricting and binge eating/purging
   c. typical and atypical
   d. objective and subjective

5. The physical effects of anorexia nervosa after recovery may include
   a. osteoporosis
   b. decreased intellectual ability
   c. poor integration into society
   d. occupational disability

6. Anorexia nervosa is considered a very serious psychological problem primarily because
   a. it often includes periods of relapse
   b. it has the highest mortality rate of any psychological disorder
   c. it is routinely ignored by patients' families
   d. patients deny their condition and are reluctant to get help

7. The diagnosis of bulimia nervosa requires the presence of
   a. strict eating patterns
   b. alternating purging and nonpurging behaviors
   c. binge eating, alternating with compensatory behaviors
   d. behaviors designed to ensure weight loss

8. The hallmark feature of a binge is the
   a. perceived number of calories
   b. type of food
   c. length of time
   d. perceived lack of control

9. A patient with bulimia nervosa who sometimes eats a typical or even small amounts of food, but still feels that the eating is out of control, is experiencing
   a. excessive guilt
   b. subjective binge eating
   c. compensatory behavior
   d. objective binging

10. People seeking treatment for an eating disorder are most commonly diagnosed with
    a. anorexia nervosa
    b. bulimia nervosa
    c. eating disorder not otherwise specified
    d. binge eating disorder

11. Miguel has become morbidly obese. He regularly eats at restaurants that serve meals buffet style. He prefers to eat alone, however, and he often eats until he is uncomfortable. He does not purge. He may be suffering from
    a. binge-eating disorder
    b. bulimia nervosa
    c. compensatory behavior disorder
    d. anorexia nervosa—binge eating type

12. The incidence of bulimia nervosa in men may be underestimated because
    a. it is socially unacceptable for men to admit to having emotional difficulties
    b. men tend to use other compensatory behaviors besides purging, such as exercise
    c. few studies have been conducted with men
    d. it is associated with illegal steroid use

13. Susan is going through puberty before most of her middle school classmates. Susan may be at
    a. greater risk for developing an eating disorder
    b. lower risk for developing body dissatisfaction
    c. greater risk for being sexually abused
    d. less risk for being underweight

14. In animal studies, surgical lesions in the brain indicate that the neuroanatomical center for appetite and weight control is the
    a. pituitary gland
    b. occipital lobe
    c. hypothalamus
    d. frontal lobe

15. The obsessionality and rigidity associated with eating disorders have been associated with what aspect of brain functioning?
    a. serotonin and dopamine levels
    b. glucose absorption
    c. plaque formation
    d. synaptic efficiency

16. What structural brain abnormalities are seen in patients with anorexia nervosa?
    a. frontal lobe distortion
    b. decrease in ventricle size
    c. loss of gray matter and reduced brain mass
    d. all of the above

17. According to the early family model, patients who seek treatment for anorexia nervosa are members of families who are experiencing enmeshment. This means that the family is
    a. having difficulty dealing with problematic, negative situations
    b. overinvolved in the affairs of the patient
    c. not adapting to the changing developmental needs of the children
    d. excessively shielding the children from age-appropriate experiences

18. The multidisciplinary team's critical first step in the treatment of anorexia nervosa is
    a. prescribing medication
    b. encouraging a realistic body image
    c. ensuring renutrition
    d. promoting healthy family communication

19. Which component of CBT appears to be the most effective in promoting behavioral change?
    a. forming a therapeutic alliance
    b. changing thinking patterns
    c. increasing personal control
    d. increasing self esteem

20. The most effective way to approach the treatment of anorexia nervosa is with
    a. nutritional counseling
    b. conjoint family therapy
    c. interpersonal psychotherapy
    d. a multidisciplinary team

Answers: 1 a, 2 c, 3 c, 4 b, 5 a, 6 b, 7 c, 8 d, 9 b, 10 c, 11 a, 12 b, 13 a, 14 c, 15 a, 16 c, 17 b, 18 c, 19 b, 20 d.

CHAPTER objectives

After reading this chapter, you should be able to:

1 Understand that "normal sexual behavior" is difficult to define and depends on biological and cultural factors.

2 Identify the characteristics of gender identity disorder and understand how it relates to transsexualism and transvestic fetishism.

3 Recognize that men and women exhibit different patterns of sexual behavior and identify the role of gender in the definition and development of sexual dysfunction.

4 Understand the biological and psychological complexities involved in the etiology and treatment of sexual dysfunction.

5 Identify the three types of paraphilias and give examples of each type.

6 Identify the most promising biological and psychosocial treatments for the paraphilias and the ethical issues that affect the conduct of clinical research.

gender and sexual disorders

Steven and Alice, both 48 years old, have been married for 25 years. They have three children, aged 20, 18, and 15. They sought out a therapist because their marriage was in trouble—they were both experiencing sexual difficulties. Alice said that she was just not interested in sex any more. She denied depression and had no history of sexual abuse. She was still menstruating every month, so hormonal changes accompanying menopause could not completely explain her lack of desire. Alice loved Steven, but her lack of desire was highly frustrating to him.

Steven was a senior stockbroker in a major brokerage house, and he was working 16 hours a day. He was stressed and anxious much of the time. Steven loved Alice but was frustrated that their sex life had not been good for some time. About 6 months ago, Steven had a heart attack and afterward had difficulty with sexual performance. Although he still had sufficient sexual desire, once he initiated sexual activity, he worried that he was straining his heart. Added to this, Alice was not responsive when they did have intercourse, so he felt pressure to "get it over with." Now he had developed a pattern of premature ejaculation.

Alfred Kinsey was one of the first scientists to investigate the sexual behaviors of men and women in the United States.

Steven and Alice are suffering from sexual dysfunctions, and their situation highlights many of the issues that we will address in this chapter. First, many people, even those in a committed, loving relationship, can be sexually dissatisfied. Second, difficulties in sexual performance never occur in isolation. Biological, psychological, interpersonal, and environmental factors often contribute to the development and persistence of sexual dysfunction. Steven and Alice are unusual in one respect—they consulted a therapist. Many people suffer from sexual dysfunctions, but few seek treatment.

Sexual dysfunctions are one of the three types of disorders discussed in this chapter. They consist of difficulties with sexual performance. Another category, *gender identity disorder*, involves psychological dissatisfaction with one's biological sex. It is not dissatisfaction with a sexual behavior or attitude; it is dissatisfaction with and distress over one's entire identity as male or female. *Paraphilias* are yet a different category and consist of sexual arousal to inappropriate objects, situations, or individuals. As these disorders illustrate, sexual behavior is complex and multifaceted. It is also the subject of frequent misunderstandings and misconceptions. To understand these behaviors and their impact, we first review how, historically, we understand sexual function and dysfunction.

Human Sexuality

Perhaps because the subject is highly personal and often considered taboo, people find it difficult to discuss sexual attitudes and behaviors. This leads to many misconceptions about normal sexual functioning. One of the first formal attempts to understand sexual behavior occurred in 1938, when Alfred Kinsey, a professor of biology at Indiana University, interviewed Americans about their sexual practices. Kinsey published his findings in *Sexual Behavior in the Human Male* in 1948 and *Sexual Behavior in the Human Female* in 1953. The books created public and scientific controversies. The most serious scientific criticism was that Kinsey's samples were not representative of the general population in the United States. Nevertheless, over the course of his career, Kinsey and his staff interviewed approximately 18,000 Americans about their sexual practices, and his groundbreaking work was a significant force in the scientific study of sexuality.

Shortly after Kinsey's publications, William Masters, a gynecologist, and his wife, Virginia Johnson, a psychologist, began their own research program in human sexuality. In addition to interviews, Masters and Johnson actually recorded the physical responses of more than 700 adults as they engaged in sexual activity. They published their research in their books, *Human Sexual Response* (1966) and *Human Sexual Inadequacy* (1970). In these books, they described the physical and psychological bases of sexual response, measured the body's sexual responses, examined deviations from normal sexual functioning, and developed treatments to address dysfunction. Much of what we know about the physical responses leading to orgasm stems from the work of Masters and Johnson.

William Masters and Virginia Johnson observed sexual interactions of men and women, recording physiological responses during different phases of sexual activity.

SEXUAL FUNCTIONING

The basis of sexual functioning is the human sexual response cycle. Originally, Masters and Johnson described four stages of sexual functioning: arousal, plateau, orgasm, and resolution (Masters & Johnson, 1966). Helen Singer Kaplan, a psychotherapist who specialized in sex therapy, described sexual response as consisting of desire,

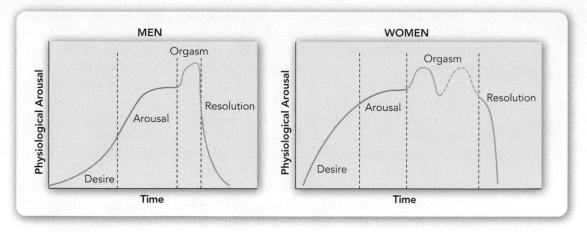

FIGURE 8.1

The Human Sexual Response Cycle

The sexual response cycle typically consists of four phases. In contrast to men, women may have more than one orgasm prior to the resolution phase.

excitement, and orgasm (Kaplan, 1979). Most contemporary explanations incorporate some combination of these terms, conceptualizing four phases of sexual response (see Figure 8.1). First is the *desire phase*, which begins in response to external or internal cues. This is followed by the *arousal phase*, characterized by physical and psychological signs of sexual arousal. In men, the most overt response is *penile tumescence*, which occurs as blood flow to the penis increases. In women, arousal is marked by *vasocongestion* (swelling of the blood vessels) in the genital area and vaginal lubrication. Psychologically, there is a positive emotional response. Next is the *orgasm phase*. For men, there is a feeling of the inevitability of ejaculation followed by actual ejaculation of seminal fluid. For women, there are contractions in the outer third of the vagina. Both men and women also experience a strong subjective feeling of pleasure that is based in the brain rather than the genitalia. The *resolution phase* is more common in men than women. There is a decrease in physical arousal, followed by a refractory (resting) period during which penile erection cannot occur. Women may experience two or more orgasms before experiencing a resolution phase. As you will see later in the chapter, health and mental health professionals use this model of sexual response to understand sexual dysfunctions. However, as illustrated below, this model of sexual response may not be an equal "fit" for understanding sexual behavior in men and women.

SEX DIFFERENCES IN SEXUAL RESPONSE

All surveys of sexual practices indicate that men engage in more frequent sexual activity than do women. Does this mean that males have a stronger biological **sex drive**, defined as craving for sexual activity and pleasure (Baumeister et al., 2001)? Most people assume that the answer is "yes," but that is not necessarily true. Men think about sex more often, are more frequently sexually aroused, have more frequent and different fantasies, desire sex more often, desire more partners, masturbate more often, are less able or willing to go without sex, more often initiate sex, less often refuse sex, use more resources to get sex, make more sacrifices for sex, have a more favorable attitude toward, and enjoy a wider variety of, sexual practices, and rate themselves as having stronger sex drives than women (Baumeister et al., 2001). However, women have a higher capacity for sex, are biologically capable of engaging in sexual behavior for a longer period of time, are capable of more orgasms than men, and do not have a refractory period (Baumeister et al., 2001).

sex drive physical and/or psychological craving for sexual activity and pleasure

There are also differences in how each sex defines sexual drive. For many men, sexual desire is defined primarily by physical pleasure and sexual intercourse. However, women appear to define sexual desire more broadly and include in their definition the need for emotional intimacy (Basson, 2002; Peplau, 2003). Female sexual responses may be more complicated than a biological-affective drive marked by sexual thoughts, fantasies, and a conscious urge to engage in sexual activity (Tiefer, 2001). Thus, sexual desire may exist equally in both sexes when different definitions are applied. Understanding these differences is important because as we will illustrate, the current diagnostic system has evolved from a model of male sexual functioning and may not appropriately identify sexual dysfunction in women.

Biological sex also interacts with age to affect sexual behavior. In men, the effects of age are most apparent in genital response (inability to achieve an erection) whereas in women, the effects of age are most apparent in declining sexual interest (Bancroft et al., 2003). There is also a psychological difference. Unlike men, many women do not consider normal age-related changes in their sexuality or sexual practices to be problematic.

UNDERSTANDING SEXUAL BEHAVIOR

Since the time of Kinsey and Masters and Johnson, there has been increased research aimed at understanding sexual behavior. Over the past 20 years, there have been several large well-controlled surveys—one targeted men aged 20 to 39 (Billy et al., 1993), a second targeted college-age women (Debuono et al., 1990), and a third targeted adults aged 40 to 80 (Nicolosi et al., 2006). Surveys of typical sexual practices provide a context for understanding the deviations that are the topics of this chapter.

Over a 12-month period (see Figure 8.2), 95% of males between the ages of 18 and 30 and 87% of females between the ages of 18 and 22 years had vaginal intercourse (Billy et al., 1993; Debuono et al., 1990). In addition, 74% of men and 86% of women orally stimulated the genitalia of their partner, and 79% and 65% were the recipients of oral stimulation by a partner, respectively. In contrast, only a minority (20% of males and 9% of females) engaged in anal intercourse during a 12-month period.

Indeed, adults of all ages are sexually active. One of the largest surveys assessed 27,900 people aged 40 to 80 in 29 countries. This study found that in this large group, 82% of men and 76% of women believed that "satisfactory sex is essential to maintain a relationship" (Nicolosi et al, 2006). As Figure 8.3 shows, although there is a decline with age, 48% of men and 25% of women age 70–79 think about sexual activity at least several times per month (Nicolosi et al., 2006). In fact, 22% of men aged 70 to 79 reported still thinking about sex every day. Furthermore, only 17% of men and 23% of women between the ages of 40 and 80 believed that older people no longer want sex.

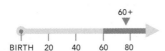

FIGURE 8.2
Sexual Activity of Males Between Ages 18 and 30 and Females Between 18 and 22

As this graph shows, both young men and women engage in a variety of different sexual behaviors, although the percentages differ by sex and by type of behavior.

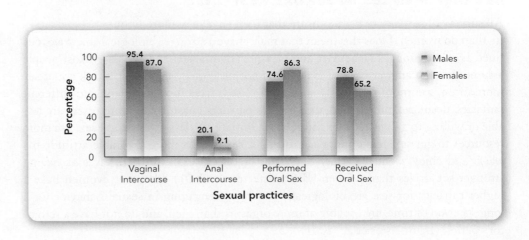

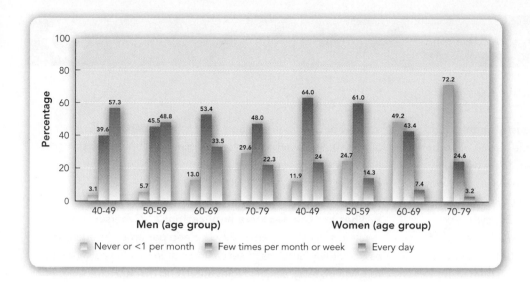

FIGURE 8.3
Frequency with Which Men and Women of Various Ages Think About Sexual Activity

Across English-speaking populations, there is a decline in the frequency with which men and women think about sexual activity on a daily basis, but even at advanced ages, interest in sex does not disappear.

From "Sexual activity, sexual disorders and associated help-seeking behavior among mature adults in five Anglophone countries from the Global Survey of Sexual Attitudes and Behaviors (GSSAB)," by A. Nicolosi, et al., *Journal of Sex & Marital Therapy*, 32, 331–342. Copyright © 2006 Taylor & Francis Group, reprinted by permission of the publisher (Taylor & Francis Group, http://www.informaworld.com).

Clearly, satisfactory sexual functioning is important to many middle-aged and elderly adults. Consistent with their belief in its importance, 93% of men aged 40 to 49 are sexually active, as are 53% of men aged 70 to 80 years (Nicolosi et al., 2004). For women aged 40 to 49, 88% were sexually active, as were 21% of women aged 70 to 80. As with younger adults, middle-aged and older men were more likely to think about and engage in sexual activity than were women.

Within the United States, studies of sexuality and sexual behaviors have often neglected cultural considerations, particularly among Hispanic and Asian populations (Meston & Ahrold, 2007). Whereas sexual experiences among Hispanic undergraduate students in the United States appear to be on a par with those of non-Hispanic whites (Cain et al., 2003), Asian students report less participation in intercourse, masturbation, oral sex, and petting (Meston et al., 1996), and Asian women reported lower frequencies of these behaviors than non-Asian women or Asian men. Similarly, Hispanic men had higher levels of sexual permissiveness than Hispanic women (Cain et al., 2003). Furthermore, African American women were more likely than white women to endorse the statement that engaging in sexual activity was important, whereas Japanese and Chinese women were less likely than white women to agree with the idea that sex was important (Cain et al., 2003).

What constitutes sexuality and sexual behavior varies a great deal across cultures (Nieto, 2004). Some researchers have suggested that sexual attraction is not simply biological or sociocultural—it is an integrated response (Tolman & Diamond, 2001). We have already noted one biological factor, age, that may affect sexual functioning. Within a sociocultural context, sexual relationships exist within societies that in turn exist within a larger culture and also within a historical context (recall from Chapter 1 how Freud "shocked" Victorian society by suggesting that young children had sexual feelings and desires). Yet among the Khumbo of Nepal, children are considered sexual beings at age 5, when they must begin to cover their genitalia with clothing, behavior that is expected of adults but not the younger children (Nieto, 2004). Therefore, there is no universal standard of "normal" sexuality or sexual behavior. In fact, one new type of sexual behavior, called *cybersex*, is becoming more common, as more and more people have access to the Internet (see the box "Research Hot Topic: The Internet and Cybersex").

Appropriate dress for girls and women is dictated by culture. Above, typical dress for American teenagers. Below, typical dress for women in Esfahan, Iran.

Research HOT Topic

The Internet and Cybersex

Internet sex sites are the third largest industry on the World Wide Web (Carnes et al., 2001). A Google search of "cybersex" yielded over 5 million hits. In contrast, there were only 143 hits using a scientific search engine (Pub Med), and only 22 were controlled research studies. Clearly, public interest in cybersex far outstrips scientific knowledge. But cybersex can result in personal distress and negatively affect areas of functioning. Researchers are beginning to study this increasingly common behavior.

■ **How do we define cybersex?** Currently, there is no accepted definition. Some researchers include all Internet sex activity as cybersex. Others distinguish between *online sexual activity*, which may include searching for information about sexual dysfunctions or sex therapy, and cybersex, defined as interchanges with a partner for the purpose of sexual pleasure (Southern, 2008). Still others break down cybersex participants into three subgroups: recreational users, sexually compulsive users, and at-risk users (Cooper et al., 2004).

■ **How many people engage in cybersex?** A Swedish study indicated that 30% of men and 34% of women had engaged in at least one cybersex experience (Daneback et al., 2005); 38% were between the ages of 18 and 24, and 13% were over age 50. When questioned about their ability to control their online sexual activity, 19% of respondents to an online survey admitted being unable to stop their behavior (Cooper et al., 2004). Still another study determined that perhaps as many as 11.8 million people have problems controlling online sexual behavior (Goldberg et al., 2008).

■ **What are the negative implications?** Cybersex use can result in changes in personality or sleep patterns, disregard for responsibility, and loss of sexual interest in real-life partner sex, real-life infidelity, sexual exploitation, and divorce (Goldberg et al., 2008; Schneider, 2003; Southern, 2008). If sites charge a fee, users may incur huge debts. Employee productivity is at risk; 70% of Internet sexual activity occurs on weekdays between 9 a.m. and 5 p.m. (Southern, 2008). Downloading sexual material from certain sites may lead to charges of trafficking in child pornography (Cooper et al., 2004).

■ **Who is at risk for overuse of cybersex?** One of the most pressing research issues is identifying who might be at risk for these behaviors. However, there are no empirical data available addressing this issue.

In summary, it is clear that cybersex is an emerging problem, but as yet our knowledge is based on clinical reports and survey research. However, its increasing prevalence and potentially harmful effects are motivating mental health professionals to initiate research in order to better understand and therefore be able to treat this behavior, if it rises to the level of an addiction.

People may engage in sexual behavior with someone of the opposite sex (heterosexuality), someone of the same sex (homosexuality) or in some instances, partners of either sex (bisexuality). Until about 25 years ago, many people considered a homosexual orientation to be a mental disorder, but for a long time it was not clear how many people engaged in sexual behaviors with someone of the same sex. One reason was that, given how difficult it is to get people to discuss sexuality, questions about same-sex practices were rarely included in surveys of adult sexual behaviors. In one of the first surveys (Billy et al., 1993), 2.3% of young men aged 20 to 39 reported that they had engaged in same-sex activity. This rate was consistent with a survey of men and women in the United States aged 18 to 70; 2% reported exclusive same-sex activity or sexual activity with both sexes (Leigh et al., 1993). These rates are also consistent with other Western countries. Population surveys of adults in Britain and France revealed that 3.6% of British men had engaged in sexual activity with another man on at least one occasion, as had 4.1% of French men (Bajos et al., 1995).

Overall, it appears that between 2 and 5% of men and 1 and 2% of women are exclusively same-sex attracted (Diamond, 1993; Laumann et al., 1994; Wellings et al., 1994). These rates appear to be consistent worldwide, although cultural customs and sanctions often dictate the frequency of same-sex *behavior*, as opposed to a gay/lesbian or bisexual *identity*. In other words, people may feel sexual attraction toward someone of the same sex, but they may not act on that emotion because of religious or cultural practices. As with heterosexual attraction, there are sex differences in the strength of same-sex attraction; men are more likely to be exclusively attracted to the same sex, and women are more likely to describe themselves as attracted to both sexes (Bailey et al., 2000). This sex difference may reflect greater erotic plasticity among women (Rahman & Wilson, 2003); their sex drive is more likely to be influenced by cultural and social factors. In addition, these differences may also reflect different etiological pathways by which sexual orientation develops.

The development of sexual orientation appears to be biologically based. In fact, over half a century of research has not provided any support for etiology based on psychological theories (Rahman & Wilson, 2003). Homosexual or same-sex orientation appears to be at least in part genetically determined (Kendler et al., 2000; Kirk et al., 2000). In one study, the heritability estimates for homosexuality were between 50–60% for females and 30% for males (Kirk et al., 2000). However, further efforts are needed to understand the basis of the genetic contribution in determining sexual orientation.

Other attempts to understand the biology of sexual orientation have focused on the role of sex hormones, called *androgens*. Atypical levels or timing of androgens during fetal development (high or low, early or late) do not always create differences in secondary sexual characteristics, genital anatomy, or gonadal function, but they may affect sexual orientation. Some researchers have examined the relationship between homosexuality and (a) non-righthandedness, (b) differences in the ratio of the second (index) finger to the fourth (ring) finger, and (c) symmetry in patterns of fingerprint ridges. In the latter two cases, gay men show patterns more like heterosexual women than they do heterosexual men. Although these three differences may be related to abnormal levels of androgens during prenatal development (Rahman & Wilson, 2003), the data so far are not conclusive because the sample sizes in these studies are small. Also, the methods of determining a relationship are indirect. Specifically, this research uses physical features of adults to hypothesize about the presence of *prenatal hormones*, present when the fetus was in the uterus (i.e., in utero). More direct, and perhaps more conclusive, evidence would come from directly measuring these hormones in utero.

More conclusive data have been reported for fraternal birth order in males. Across numerous and diverse samples (Gooren, 2006), gay men had a greater number of older brothers than did heterosexual men. One explanation for this phenomenon is that there is an incompatibility between the mother's immune system and the androgens that are in the male fetus. The mother's body responds to the presence of male androgens with an immune response, in the form of antibodies (to fight off the androgens). These antibodies cross the placental barrier and affect fetal hormonal level. As the number of male-offspring pregnancies increases, this immunological response becomes stronger and may affect fetal brain masculinization, although it is unclear whether the entire brain is affected or only certain specific areas (Blanchard & Bogart, 2004; Blanchard et al., 2006; Kauth, 2005). Estimates of risk indicate that each older brother increases a younger brother's risk by 33 to 48%, but overall, this accounts for only a small increase in overall prevalence. Furthermore, not all gay men have older brothers, and, of course, the theory cannot account for homosexuality or bisexuality among women (Gooren, 2006). Therefore, although this androgen theory may explain the origin of sexual orientation for some gay men, it will most likely remain only one of many potential etiologies.

---

concept CHECK ───

- The work of Kinsey and Masters and Johnson provided the impetus for studying sexual behavior scientifically.

- The human sexual response consists of four phases: desire, arousal, orgasm, and resolution.

- Although sexual behaviors decline in frequency with age, satisfactory sexual functioning is considered important by people at any age.

- Sexual orientation appears to be biologically based, with both genetic and prenatal hormonal influences. However, this research is still in its infancy, and emerging theories appear to account for only a small percentage of people who experience an exclusive same-sex attraction, highlighting the need for further research.

APPLICATION QUESTION If sexual desire is defined in terms of a craving for sexual activity or pleasure, men have a stronger sex drive than women. However, women have a greater capacity for sexual activity than do men, and for women, the concept of sexual drive includes emotional intimacy in addition to sexual activity and pleasure. How might such different concepts of "sex" affect our interpretations of emotional states such as "love" and "commitment"?

Gender Identity Disorder

William is 23 years old. He came to the psychology clinic after hearing one of the psychologists talking about depression on TV. He thought that the psychologist seemed very understanding, leading him to seek treatment. William felt sad, but his real reason for coming to the clinic was that he "no longer wanted to be a man." Ever since he was a young child, William had felt like a girl. His happiest time was sneaking into his sister's room and putting on her pink dancing costume. In fact, he coveted any of his sister's clothing. His father was horrified and forced William to play with guns, a football, anything that would help him "be a man." William tried, but he always felt as if he were pretending. He felt that he was a woman trapped in a man's body.

How does a child know if he is a boy or a girl? The answer seems obvious but it is not. Traditionally, *sex* was considered to be determined by genes, hormones, and physical genitalia, whereas *gender* could be defined as categories of male or female defined by cultural role expectations. Some researchers consider these definitions to be very simplistic (Lyons & Lyons, 2006), and the complex issue of defining these terms is outside the scope of abnormal psychology. But what if you have male genitalia yet you feel like a girl? To understand William's behavior and feelings, it is necessary to introduce the term *gender identity*, which is the personal understanding of oneself as male or female. Gender identity typically develops by age 3 or 4 (Bradley & Zucker, 1997). Usually, biological sex and gender identity match—boys who are genetically male describe themselves as boys, and girls who are genetically female describe themselves as girls. However, in some cases, as with William, biological sex and gender identity do not match, leading to distress and impairment. In such cases, the person is considered to have a **gender identity disorder** (GID).

Gender Identity Disorder

A strong and persistent cross-gender identification (not simply a desire for the cultural advantages of the other sex) and persistent discomfort with one's own sex or sense of inappropriateness in the gender role of one's sex.

Adapted with permission from the *Diagnostic and Statistical Manual of Mental Disorders*, Text Revision, Fourth Edition, (Copyright 2000). American Psychiatric Association.

GID (see the box "DSM-IV-TR: Gender Identity Disorder") is not simply a momentary wish to be the opposite sex because of cultural or social advantages (e.g., "men have all the power"). It is strong and persistent cross-sex identification—a person's biological sex is inconsistent with his or her gender identity. Among children, GID is apparent in repeated statements that the child *wants* to be the opposite sex or *is* the opposite sex; cross-dressing in clothing stereotypical of the other sex (as with William); persistent fantasies of being the opposite sex or persistent preference for cross-gender roles in pretend play; a strong desire to participate in games and activities usually associated with the opposite sex; and strong preference for playmates of the opposite sex.

In addition to identifying with the opposite sex, people with GID have persistent discomfort with their own sex. Boys express disgust about their penis or testes, state that the penis will disappear or that it would be better not to have a penis. They avoid "rough-and-tumble" play or stereotypically male activities. Girls express persistent discomfort by refusing to sit on the toilet to urinate, stating that they have a penis or will grow one, stating that they do not want to grow breasts or begin menstruation, and demonstrate aversion to female clothing (refusing to wear dresses). Among adolescents and adults, this is called **transgender behavior**. There may be attempts to pass as the opposite sex through cross-dressing, disguising one's own sexual genitalia, or changing other sexual characteristics.

It is important to differentiate between the terms **transsexualism** and *transvestic fetishism*. The latter is the desire and perhaps even the need, among heterosexual men, to dress in women's clothes (Bradley & Zucker, 1997), but not the abhorrence of one's own sex or the wish to *be* the opposite sex (Sharma, 2007). We will discuss transvestic fetishism later in this chapter in the section on paraphilias.

Because it is so rare, GID is not a disorder that is included in epidemiological investigations, making it difficult to determine its prevalence. The most commonly reported prevalence estimates are 1 in 30,000 to 37,000 for men and 1 in 100,000 to 107,000 for women (Brotto & Klein, 2007). As illustrated by William, feeling trapped in one's body can lead to feelings of depression. In fact, people with GID often have other psychiatric disorders, most commonly anxiety, depression, and personality disorders (Cohen-Kettenis et al., 2003; Hepp et al., 2005; Meyer, 2004; Taher, 2007; Zucker, 2004). However, these disorders do not occur more frequently among people with GID than people with other psychiatric disorders (Cohen-Kettenis et al., 2003). They are also not the cause of GID (Meyer, 2004). Rather, these anxiety and depressive symptoms are a response to the condition and to the ridicule that people with GID often face as a result of their behavior. Cross-gender identification sometimes becomes so strong that people have **sex reassignment surgery**, a series of procedures that matches their physical anatomy and their gender identity (see the box "Real People, Real Disorders: Renee Richards' Second Serve").

gender identity disorder strong and persistent cross-gender identification and persistent discomfort with one's own biological sex

transgender behavior behavioral attempts to pass as the opposite sex through cross-dressing, disguising one's own sexual genitalia, or changing other sexual characteristics

transsexualism another term for gender identity disorder, commonly used to describe the condition when it occurs in adolescents and adults

sex reassignment surgery a series of behavioral and medical procedures that matches an individual's physical anatomy to gender identity

real people, real disorders

Renee Richards' Second Serve

Richard Raskind was a Yale University graduate, an officer in the Navy, a well-respected ophthalmologist, and an amateur men's tennis champion. He also suffered from GID. In 1975, at age 40, he underwent sex reassignment surgery and became Dr. Renee Richards, reestablishing her life and her ophthalmology practice in Southern California. She also began to compete in women's tennis tournaments. When a reporter revealed the 6'2" tennis player's former identity, she was barred from the game. Dr. Richards attracted international attention when she successfully challenged the United States Tennis Association's sanctions against her in court. Once she was allowed to participate, 25 other female players withdrew from one tournament in protest. They felt that her presence was unfair—that despite her surgery, she still had the muscular advantages of a male and genetically remained a male. Dr. Richards disagreed. She had a new name, a new sex, and all of her official papers (passport, medical license) bore her new identity. Dr. Richards did not change her sex to be a tennis superstar. For her, participation in the women's bracket was an issue of human rights. A court order allowed her to play in the 1977 United States Open. In the first round, she was defeated by Wimbledon champion Virginia Wade.

Even with the strong conviction that she was a woman, Dr. Richards was initially very conflicted about sex reassignment surgery. In the late 1960s, Dr. Richards received female hormone treatments for the first time and traveled to Casablanca for sex-change surgery, but stopped at the hospital doorstep and did not go through with the operation. Subsequently, Dr. Richards had breast reduction surgery, married, fathered a child, and divorced. Yet the discomfort never left, and eventually she chose sex reassignment surgery. In 1975, Dr. Richards became legally female.

Although never regretting the surgery, Dr. Richards wished at times that it had not been necessary. "What I said was if there were a drug, some voodoo, any kind of mind-altering magic remedy to keep the man intact, that would have been preferable, but there wasn't," Dr. Richards says. "The pressure to change into a woman was so strong that if I had not been able to do it, I might have been a suicide." Now living in New York, at age 72, Dr. Richards no longer plays tennis—her great passion is golf.

Richards, Renee (1983). *Second Serve.* Lanham, MD: Madison Books. http://www.nytimes.com/packages/html/sports/year_in_sports/08.27.html http://www.nytimes.com/2007/02/01/garden/01renee.html?ex= 1181966400&en=654550bf545eba8d&ei=5070 February 1, 2007

FUNCTIONAL IMPAIRMENT

Among young children, cross-gender behaviors are common, and their presence alone does not seem to create significant distress. However, these behaviors may result in peer rejection or social isolation, which can in turn lead to negative mood states (Bartlett et al., 2000). Sometimes the distress associated with GID is not found in the child, but in his or her parents. As one mother reported,

He was very excited about [putting on a blouse of mine] and leaped and danced around the room. I didn't like it and I just told him to take it off and I put it away. He kept asking for it. He wanted to wear that blouse again (Green, 1987, p. 2).

Among children with GID, distress does not result from cross-gender behaviors, but from being *prevented* from engaging in the desired behaviors.

SEX, RACE, AND ETHNICITY

Occasional cross-gender behavior is common among elementary school children (Sandberg et al., 1993) and does not automatically indicate the presence of GID. When present, GID is usually first detected between ages 2 and 4. The earliest signs include persistent cross-gender dressing and play. Verbal wishes to be a member of the other sex do not usually occur before age 6 or 7 (Bartlett et al., 2000). Before puberty, there are 5 to 7 preadolescent boys for every 1 preadolescent girl evaluated and treated for GID (Bradley & Zucker, 1997; Zucker, 2004). By contrast, in adolescence, the ratio of boys to girls with GID is virtually equal (Bradley & Zucker, 1997; Zucker, 2004).

In certain Arab countries, GID exists even when contradicted by religious, moral, and social values (Taher, 2007). Sometimes, transsexual individuals do not self-identify unless they know that sympathetic health professionals and treatment are available. For example, once sex reassignment surgery was available in Singapore, transsexuals of Chinese, Malaysian, and Indian ethnicity began to seek treatment (Tsoi & Kok, 1995). The appearance of these patients contradicted previously held beliefs that transsexualism was rare among the Chinese (Tseng, 2003).

Although Western cultures recognize two gender categories, other cultures have a greater number of classifications. For example, in India, a third gender is known as the *hijra* (Nanda, 1985). Although most are biologically male, hijra are not considered to be male or female but to possess elements of both sexes. They usually dress as women and refer to themselves as female.

Hijra are found in different cultures and are considered a third gender, neither masculine nor feminine.

ETIOLOGY

There are a number of theories about the etiology of GID, but virtually no empirical data to support many of them. On the biological side, some hormonal data provide intriguing but nonspecific evidence for a biological contribution to the development of this disorder. Psychosocial theories have examined the role of family, particularly parent-child relationships.

Biological Theories Neuroanatomical research has identified differences in the brains of men and women (Michel et al., 2001). One study found that the brains of male transsexuals were similar in size and shape to those of heterosexual women and unlike the brains of heterosexual men (Zhou et al., 1995). Why the brain structure of the transsexual male should be different is not clear, but may be the result of prenatal hormonal imbalances. Although these findings are intriguing, they require much replication before firm conclusions can be drawn.

A hormonal condition that may contribute to the development of GID is *congenital adrenal hyperplasia* (CAH). Boys and girls with CAH are missing an enzyme necessary to make the hormones cortisol and aldosterone. As a result, the body produces too much of the male hormone androgen, causing early and inappropriate male sexual development in both sexes. At birth, girls with CAH have ambiguous genitalia, often appearing more male than female. As they grow, these girls develop male secondary sexual features such as a deep voice and facial hair. Boys begin puberty as early as 2 to 3 years of age.

In addition to physical differences, girls with CAH display more cross-gender role behaviors than girls without this condition (Berenbaum et al., 2000; Cohen-Bendahan et al., 2005; Zucker, 2004). They do become more feminine with age, but some adult women with CAH (particularly those with the most severe form) have less heterosexual interest and are less feminine than those with no hormonal disorder (Hines et al., 2004; Long et al., 2004). We still do not know if CAH, or any other hormonal imbalance, leads to the development of GID. We do know that this condition affects prenatal hormonal levels, the development of physical sex characteristics, and gender behaviors. Understanding CAH may help us understand the development of GID in girls, but not in boys.

Psychosocial Theories Psychoanalysts postulate that parental rejection may play a role in the onset of GID. For example, if parents really wanted a girl but had a boy instead (Sharma, 2007), they may reject their son. That rejection may cause the boy to try to please the parent by behaving like a girl. Although parents who reinforce masculine or feminine behaviors will increase the frequency of those behaviors, it does not appear that simple reinforcement alone can affect gender identity. One well-known case (Green & Money, 1969) suggests that biology is stronger than environmental forces.

John and his brother were identical twins. During their circumcision, the physician's hand slipped and ablated (cut off) John's penis. After much discussion, the physicians and John's parents agreed that he should be raised as a girl, and he was renamed Joan. His parents dressed and treated Joan as a girl, and at adolescence, Joan was given female hormone replacement therapy to encourage the development of secondary female sexual characteristics (breast development). Despite all the efforts, Joan never felt like a girl and often rebelled against adult efforts to make her behave like a girl. Finally, at age 14, her parents told her the truth. Interestingly, John recalled that he had suspected that he was a boy beginning in the second grade. In adulthood, John had sex reassignment surgery, lived as a man, married, and adopted three children (Diamond & Sigmundson, 1997). However, this story does not have a happy ending. John suffered from depression and in 2004, at age 39, he committed suicide.

The reasons for John's suicide are unknown but probably include his unusual childhood and a strong family history of depression—John's mother and twin brother suffered from depression (Colapinto, 2004). His twin brother died from an overdose of antidepressants, and John had twice attempted suicide when he was in his 20s. Although John's story has a sad ending, it provides us with an important insight: environmental efforts alone cannot overcome biology and establish or change gender identity.

TREATMENT

There are few longitudinal studies of children with GID, but the studies that are available suggest that only a minority of children who originally receive this diagnosis continue to be distressed about their gender into adulthood (Zucker, 2008). In two follow-up studies conducted 10 to 15 years after the original diagnosis, between 12 and 27% of individuals were still classified as gender dysphoric (Drummond et al., 2008; Wallien & Cohen-Kettenis, 2008). In those studies, children who had the most severe symptoms of GID were the ones still likely to have the disorder and most likely to have a homosexual or bisexual orientation. Among the adults who no longer had gender dysphoria, half of the boys and all of the girls had a heterosexual orientation (Wallien & Cohen-Kettenis, 2008).

Perhaps because the disorder is quite rare, there are no controlled trials for treatments of GID. Clinically, there are several different treatment approaches, some of which are available only in specialized clinics. The most common procedure for adults is surgical reassignment.

Sex Reassignment Surgery   Historically, treatment for adults with GID attempted to change the person's social and sexual behaviors to match his or her biological sex. Currently, treatment focuses on helping adults live as their chosen gender identity, maximizing their psychological and social adjustment. There are three phases to the intervention: living as the desired gender, hormone therapy, and sex reassignment surgery (Meyer et al., 2001). Not every person who begins treatment completes the sex reassignment surgery phase.

In the first stage, the person lives in the new gender role for at least two years (Meyer et al., 2001). The person dresses and socializes consistent with the desired gender role, allowing the person to examine how this change affects every aspect of life.

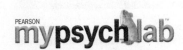

Gender Identity Disorder

The Case of Denise

"My earliest memories, back when I was about 4 years old . . . I remember cross-dressing back then, all the way until really around my puberty."

www.mypsychlab.com

This step is considered absolutely necessary for the treatment program. The second step is hormone therapy. Testosterone is given to biological females and estrogen to biological males, reducing unwanted secondary sex characteristics and leading to the secondary sexual characteristics of the preferred sex. The third and final phase is the actual surgery. For males transitioning to females, this includes surgical removal of the penis and the creation of a clitoris, labia, and artificial vagina. For females transitioning to males, it includes removal of the breasts, vagina, and uterus and the formation of a scrotum, testicular prostheses and the creation of a neophallus (an artificial penis). The goal is to try to preserve sexual functioning in order to achieve optimal quality of life (Lawrence, 2003).

Compared with treatments for other psychological disorders, sex reassignment surgery is an extensive and radical procedure (Smith et al., 2005). Although early studies suggested that a percentage of those who had surgery were not satisfied with the results, more recent and longer term follow-up data indicate that the outcome has become more positive (Landén et al., 1999). Sex reassignment surgery eliminates gender dysphoria (Lawrence, 2003; Smith et al., 2005), improves body satisfaction and interpersonal relationships, and reduces anxiety and depression (Smith et al., 2001, 2005; Weyers et al., 2008). In one long-term follow-up (Weyers et al., 2008), the participants did endorse some difficulties with sexual arousal, lubrication, and pain. Across different studies, more than 95% of patients reported satisfaction with sex reassignment surgery (Lawrence, 2003; Smith et al., 2005). A few patients were dissatisfied; most commonly, those individuals lacked family support and/or had additional psychological disorders affecting overall functioning (Eldh et al., 1997; Landén et al., 1998).

Some adolescents with GID seek sex reassignment surgery, and it is reasonable to question whether adolescents can make such an irreversible decision. Early sex reassignment surgery may prevent gender dysphoria during adolescence (Delemarre-van de Waal & Cohen-Kettenis, 2006), and the physical outcome is more satisfactory when secondary sex characteristics have not yet developed. However, such surgery requires absolute certainty because the intervention is nonreversible. Only a small number of adolescents receive sex reassignment therapy, and many questions remain about the procedure, including at what age the surgery should occur and whether those who have surgery continue to feel positively about the procedure as adults.

Psychological Treatment   There are no randomized controlled trials of psychosocial interventions, but case reports and single-case design studies indicate that behavioral, psychoanalytic, and eclectic approaches have been used with children. These approaches all focus attention and reinforcement on same-sex activities and friendships, spending time with the same-sex parent, and having play dates with same-sex peers (Bradley & Zucker, 1997). In a case series of boys with gender identity problems (Rekers & Lovaas, 1974; Rekers et al., 1974; Rekers & Mead, 1979), same-gender behaviors were rewarded (prizes given) and cross-gender behaviors were punished (prizes removed). The intervention was efficacious for a number of children, but recently, these behavioral approaches have been criticized for forcing specific gender stereotypes (i.e., stereotypical masculine behaviors) (Bryant, 2006) onto young children. Certainly, the treatment's moral and ethical ramifications deserve consideration.

concept CHECK

- Gender identity disorder, sometimes called transsexualism in adults, is the sense that one's biological sex does not match one's gender identity.

- The disorder appears to be more common in males than females among adults and can have a pervasive effect on all aspects of functioning.

- The cause of GID is unknown but may be related to hormonal imbalances that begin prenatally.
- Sex reassignment surgery is a long-term process that culminates in irreversible surgery to match the person's physical anatomy with their gender identity.

APPLICATION QUESTION Children with the most severe symptoms of GID may continue to have gender dysphoria as an adult, but this outcome occurs in a minority of people with this disorder. Furthermore, the distress associated with GID is often that of the parent and not the child. Applying what you know about diagnosis and treatment, would you recommend treatment to a parent of a child who has GID symptoms?

Sexual Dysfunctions

As we illustrated in the opening section of this chapter, many factors contribute to sexual performance, including age, sex, and culture. Therefore, the diagnostic criteria for all **sexual dysfunctions** consist of an absence or an impairment of some aspect of sexual response *that causes significant distress and/or functional impairment and includes consideration of age, sex, and culture.* In some instances, the prevalence of a disorder changes when these factors are considered. In addition, a person's life circumstances, such as physical illness or physical separation from the sexual partner, must be considered when determining the presence or absence of a sexual dysfunction. With these issues in mind, we turn our attention to disorders of sexual functioning, which are classified as disorders of sexual desire, sexual arousal, orgasm, and pain.

SEXUAL DESIRE DISORDERS

Sexual desire is defined as interest in sexual activity or objects, or wishes to engage in sexual activity. Disorders of sexual desire, as illustrated by Alice at the beginning of the chapter, are defined as diminished or absent interest in sexual activity, and consist of one of two subtypes: *hypoactive sexual desire disorder* and *sexual aversion disorder.*

Hypoactive sexual desire disorder is defined as reduced or absent sexual fantasies, reduced sexual behavior with a partner, and reduced sexual behavior through masturbation (Maurice, 2005). (See the box "DSM-IV-TR: Sexual Desire Disorders.") Factors often associated with decreased sexual desire include low sexual satisfaction, the presence of another sexual dysfunction (such as pain), negative thoughts about sexuality, and other forms of psychological distress such as depression, anxiety, and couple distress (Trudel et al., 2001).

Approximately 15% of men and 30% of women aged 19 to 59 in the United States experience hypoactive sexual desire disorder (Laumann et al., 1999). Similar rates are found for men and women from the Middle East (21% and 43%, respectively) and from Southeast Asia (28% and 43%, respectively; Laumann et al., 2005). Across cultures, this disorder is more frequent in women than men. However, because men and women may have different sexual goals and define sexual desire differently, we must be careful not to overinterpret these data. Patterns of male sexuality, for example, are not necessarily the best standard by which to compare the behaviors of females.

Although listed in DSM-IV, there is little information about **sexual aversion disorder.** Defined as persistent or extreme aversion to, and avoidance of, genital contact with a sexual partner, people with this disorder rarely seek treatment. Clinical reports suggest that this dysfunction affects many aspects of interpersonal functioning, not simply sexual interactions (Brotto & Klein, 2007). For example, someone with sexual aversion disorder may avoid social relationships, as they might lead to an expectation of sexual activity.

Monica was 28 and a newlywed. She loved Alex and he was so gentle and patient. She told him that she wanted to be a virgin on her wedding night and he agreed they would wait. There was only one problem—Monica did not like sexual activity. She did not under-

sexual dysfunctions absence or impairment of some aspect of sexual response that causes distress or impairment considering age, sex, and culture

hypoactive sexual desire disorder reduced or absent sexual desires or behaviors, either with a partner or through masturbation

sexual aversion disorder persistent or extreme aversion to, or avoidance of, genital contact with a sexual partner

DSM-IV-TR

Sexual Desire Disorders

Hypoactive Sexual Desire Disorder Consistently deficient or absent sexual fantasies or sexual desire, taking into account factors such as age and life circumstances.

Sexual Aversion Disorder Consistently extreme aversion to and avoidance of all (or almost all) genital sexual contact with a partner.

Adapted with permission from the *Diagnostic and Statistical Manual of Mental Disorders*, Text Revision, Fourth Edition, (Copyright 2000). American Psychiatric Association.

DSM-IV-TR

Sexual Arousal Disorders

Female Sexual Arousal Disorder Consistent inability to attain or maintain an adequate lubrication-swelling response until the completion of sexual activity. The disorder can be physical or psychological in nature or a combination of the two.

Male Erectile Disorder Consistent inability to attain or maintain an adequate erection until completion of sexual activity.

Adapted with permission from the *Diagnostic and Statistical Manual of Mental Disorders*, Text Revision, Fourth Edition, (Copyright 2000). American Psychiatric Association.

stand other people's interest in sex and had never liked being touched in a sexual way. She thought that on her wedding night, with Alex, it would be fine. But as he approached her, she got very nervous, and not in a good way. As Alex attempted sexual intercourse, Monica screamed and ran, spending the rest of her wedding night locked in her bathroom. The next day she told Alex that she was not interested in a sexual relationship and soon afterwards, Alex asked for a divorce.

SEXUAL AROUSAL DISORDERS

The second category of impaired sexual functioning, sexual arousal disorders (see the box "DSM-IV-TR: Sexual Arousal Disorders"), has separate categories for females (female sexual arousal disorder) and males (male erectile disorder).

Female sexual arousal disorder is a persistent or recurrent inability to maintain adequate vaginal lubrication and swelling response until the completion of sexual activity. Symptoms can be primarily psychological or primarily physiological (Basson et al., 2003). When primarily psychological, the condition is sometimes called *subjective sexual arousal disorder*. In these cases, there may be a physical response to sexual stimulation (for example, vaginal lubrication), but no subjective feeling of sexual excitement or sexual pleasure. In contrast, when primarily physiological (also called *genital sexual arousal disorder*), there are subjective feelings of sexual desire but no physiological response. The third subgroup, *combined sexual arousal disorder*, includes lack of both subjective and physiological response.

Female sexual arousal disorder is a controversial diagnosis. It is commonly reported in gynecological settings—up to 75% of women seeking routine care in one sample (Nusbaum et al., 2000). However, this disorder may not exist independently of disorders of sexual desire or orgasmic disorder.

Male erectile disorder is a common male sexual dysfunction known in the media as erectile dysfunction (formerly known as *impotence*). It is the persistent and recurrent

female sexual arousal disorder   persistent or recurrent inability to maintain adequate vaginal lubrication and swelling response until the completion of sexual activity

male erectile disorder   persistent and recurrent inability to maintain an adequate erection until completion of sexual activity

inability to maintain an adequate erection until completion of sexual activity. Important elements of this definition are the words "persistent" and "recurrent." Most men experience an occasional episode of erectile dysfunction, usually caused by fatigue, stress, or anxiety. The diagnosis is not given unless there is consistent inability to achieve an erection or maintain it until cessation of sexual activity. There also must be significant distress and/or interpersonal difficulty.

ORGASMIC DISORDERS

The third group of sexual dysfunctions are orgasmic disorders, including female orgasmic disorder, male orgasmic disorder, and premature ejaculation (see the box "DSM-IV-TR: Orgasmic Disorders"). The diagnostic criteria for female or male orgasmic disorder are very similar, but we will discuss them separately. **Male orgasmic disorder**, sometimes known as *delayed ejaculation* or *retarded ejaculation*, is the delay of or inability to achieve orgasm despite adequate sexual stimulation. This disorder is not as common as premature ejaculation. Some men might consider delayed ejaculation to be an advantage as it could increase the sexual pleasure of a partner. In these cases, a diagnosis may not be warranted because there would not be any distress or functional impairment. However, some men who suffer from retarded ejaculation report frustration, distress, and sometimes pain (Brotto & Klein, 2007).

Female orgasmic disorder is also defined as persistent and recurrent delay or absence of orgasm following the normal excitement phase. Sometimes called *anorgasmia*, lack of orgasm is a common complaint among women. Before making a diagnosis, it is necessary to consider age, adequacy of sexual stimulation, and sexual experience. Interestingly, unlike most other sexual disorders, female orgasmic disorder is most common among younger women (Laumann et al., 1999).

Premature Ejaculation   Sometimes known as rapid ejaculation (see "The Whole Story: Michael"), **premature ejaculation** is the most common male dysfunction, affecting approximately 30% of men (Laumann et al., 1999). The process of ejaculation consists of four phases. *Erection*, or penile tumescence, is the first phase and is controlled by the parasympathetic nervous system. The second phase is *emission*, in which semen is collected and transported in preparation for the third stage, *ejaculation*, which is the release of seminal fluids out of the penis. This occurs when signals from nerves in the urethra reach the spinal cord and cause a reflex response. The sympathetic and somatic branches of the nervous system (see Chapter 2) are responsible for stages 2 and 3. The final stage, *orgasm*, is the subjective feeling of pleasure associated with ejaculation and is believed to be a cortical (brain) experience (Metz et al., 1997).

Premature ejaculation has been defined in different ways. In some instances, it is a specific number of minutes between vaginal entry and ejaculation, although there is no commonly accepted time interval. Among self-identified premature ejaculators, 90% ejaculated within 1 minute of vaginal insertion and 80% ejaculated within 30 seconds (Waldinger, 2002). In contrast, other samples of men who described themselves as premature ejaculators reported ejaculation that occurred before vaginal insertion or as long as 10 minutes after insertion, although most (79%) reported ejaculation ranging from before insertion to 2 minutes after penetration (Symonds et al., 2003).

A different definition involves an inability to inhibit ejaculation long enough for a partner to reach orgasm 50% of the time (Masters & Johnson, 1970). The advantage of this definition is that it is not tied to a specific number of minutes, but the disadvantage is that it depends on the partner's sexual response (Metz et al., 1997). This definition acknowledges that often sexual dysfunction may be a dysfunction of the couple, not of a single person, such as we saw earlier in the case of Steven and Alice.

Still other researchers (e.g., Kaplan, 1974) define premature ejaculation as simply a lack of control over ejaculation. To come to some consensus, the International Society

male orgasmic disorder   sometimes known as delayed ejaculation or retarded ejaculation; the delay of or inability to achieve orgasm despite adequate sexual stimulation.

female orgasmic disorder   persistent and recurrent delay or absence of orgasm following the normal excitement phase. Sometimes called *anorgasmia*

premature ejaculation   consistent ejaculation with minimal sexual stimulation before, immediately upon, or shortly after penetration and before the person wishes it

Orgasmic Disorders

Orgasmic Disorder (Female or Male) Consistent delay in, or absence of, orgasm following a normal sexual excitement phase, taking into account factors such as age, sexual experience, and adequacy of sexual stimulation.

Premature Ejaculation Consistent ejaculation with minimal sexual stimulation before, immediately upon, or shortly after penetration and before the person wishes it, taking into account factors such as duration of excitement phase, age, novelty of the sexual partner, and recent frequency of sexual activity.

Adapted with permission from the *Diagnostic and Statistical Manual of Mental Disorders*, Text Revision, Fourth Edition, (Copyright 2000). American Psychiatric Association.

Sexual Pain Disorders

Dyspareunia Consistent genital pain associated with sexual intercourse that occurs in either men or women.

Vaginismus Consistent involuntary spasms of the musculature of the outer third of the vagina that interfere with sexual intercourse.

Adapted with permission from the *Diagnostic and Statistical Manual of Mental Disorders*, Text Revision, Fourth Edition, (Copyright 2000). American Psychiatric Association.

for Sexual Medicine held a meeting of experts in the field. They agreed on the following definition of premature ejaculation for heterosexual males: "always or nearly always occurring before or within one minute of vaginal penetration, and the inability to delay ejaculation on all or nearly all vaginal penetrations, and negative personal consequences such as distress, bother, frustration and/or the avoidance of sexual intimacy" (p. 347, McMahon et al., 2008). As can be seen, the majority of research in this area has been conducted with heterosexual couples. More work is required to determine the extent to which patterns of dysfunction are similar in homosexual or bisexual individuals.

Premature ejaculation is considered *primary* when a man has suffered from this condition since his first sexual encounter. The above definition of premature ejaculation was limited to primary (or lifelong) premature ejaculation. *Secondary* premature ejaculation is the term used when a man initially had no difficulty controlling ejaculation but now ejaculates prematurely (such as Steven). Among men with secondary premature ejaculation, 75% have a physical disease that might account for it, while the other 25% do not have a physical disorder but do report relationship problems (Metz et al., 1997).

SEXUAL PAIN DISORDERS

The fourth category of sexual dysfunctions is sexual pain disorders (see the box "DSM-IV-TR: Sexual Pain Disorders"). Both men and women may experience **dyspareunia** (consistent genital pain associated with sexual intercourse), but one particular form of sexual pain, vaginismus, is specific to women. Compared with other disorders, there is comparatively little research regarding the symptoms, etiology, and treatment of these diagnostic categories.

Among men in Western countries, 3 to 5% report the presence of dyspareunia (Laumann et al., 2005). Among gay men, 14% suffer frequent and severe pain during receptive anal sex, a condition known as *anodyspareunia* (Damon & Rosser, 2005).

dyspareunia consistent genital pain associated with sexual intercourse

Among women seeking routine gynecological care, 72% report pain from sexual activity (Nusbaum et al., 2000). Even minimal attempts at sexual intercourse can result in dyspareunia, leading to severe distress and avoidance of sexual behavior.

Marianne is a college freshman, and she is in love with Jeff. After several months of dating, they want to become sexually intimate. They have tried on several occasions but every time, Marianne feels her vaginal muscles contract and she cries out in pain. It is not just being physically intimate with Jeff that causes pain. She has never been able to insert a tampon into her vagina. The physician wanted to perform an internal exam to rule out the presence of infection, which could cause pain. Although he tried to insert a speculum, Marianne cried out and asked to discontinue the examination.

Marianne's pain is called **vaginismus**, unwanted involuntary spasms of the vaginal muscles that interfere with intercourse or vaginal insertion. As with other categories of sexual pain disorder, few empirical studies have addressed the validity of this diagnosis. Subjective experience of a vaginal spasm does not always correlate with actual spasms measured during gynecological examination (Reissing et al., 2004), indicating the importance of psychological factors in this diagnosis. Furthermore, most women who report vaginismus also report the presence of dyspareunia (de Kruiff et al., 2000).

FUNCTIONAL IMPAIRMENT

Any sexual dysfunction can lead to dissatisfaction. Depending on the particular complaint, between 65 and 87% of people with a sexual dysfunction report dissatisfaction (Fugl-Meyer & Sjögren Fugl-Meyer, 1999). Furthermore, sexual difficulties between partners are common. Among men with erectile dysfunction, lower sexual desire affected 60% and lack of sexual arousal affected 44% of their partners (Sjögren Fugl-Meyer & Fugl-Meyer, 2002). In addition, when there is a sexual dysfunction, whether in one's partner or oneself, both individuals' sexual well-being is affected. However, sexual disorders may sometimes affect sexual functioning without impacting overall functioning. Men who report premature ejaculation indicate that fulfilling a partner's need is an important part of their own sexual satisfaction (Rowland et al., 2004). While their disorder may affect their own self-esteem and ongoing sexual relationship, it does not always impact their overall relationship (Byers & Grenier, 2003). In one study, only 6% of men with premature ejaculation reported that they declined an opportunity for sexual intercourse because of their disability, and even this occurred only rarely (Grenier & Byers, 2001).

Reflecting society's reluctance to talk about sex is the fact that less than 19% of adults with sexual dysfunctions have ever sought professional help (Moreira et al., 2005). Even when the problem was frequent, 36% did not seek any advice. Among those who did, 55% sought support from family or friends, 19% went to media sources, and 32% sought medical advice (Nicolosi et al., 2006). When asked why they did not consult with a professional, 72.1% said that they did not consider the behavior to be a problem, 53.9% did not think it was a medical problem, 22.7% were embarrassed to talk about it, and 12.2% did not have access to medical care. These data, once again, illustrate two important points. First, what one person considers a problem is not necessarily a problem for someone else. Second, even those who are frequently bothered by sexual dysfunctions may not realize that the problem can be treated or are reluctant to discuss it with a professional.

EPIDEMIOLOGY

One of the most comprehensive studies of sexual dysfunction in the United States is the National Health and Social Life Survey, which used a sample of 3,159 Americans aged 18 to 59 years (Laumann et al., 1999). This study included face-to-face

vaginismus unwanted involuntary spasms of the vaginal muscles that interfere with intercourse or any attempt at vaginal insertion

TABLE 8.1

Prevalence (%) of Sexual Difficulties in Men Aged 18 to 59

Sexual Difficulty	Age			
	18–29	30–39	40–49	50–59
Lack of interest in sex	14	13	15	17
Unable to achieve orgasm	7	7	9	9
Climax too early	30	32	28	31
Sex not pleasurable	10	8	9	6
Anxious about performance	19	17	19	14
Trouble maintaining or achieving an erection	7	9	11	18

From Brotto & Klein, 2007; Laumann et al., 1999.

TABLE 8.2

Prevalence (%) of Sexual Difficulties in Women Aged 18 to 59

Sexual Difficulty	Age			
	18–29	30–39	40–49	50–59
Lack of interest in sex	32	32	30	27
Unable to achieve orgasm	26	28	22	23
Experienced pain during sex	21	15	13	8
Sex not pleasurable	27	24	17	17
Anxious about performance	16	11	11	6
Trouble lubricating	19	18	21	27

From Brotto & Klein, 2007; Laumann et al., 1999,

interviews and questionnaire data and found that sexual dysfunction existed among 43% of women and 31% of men. Tables 8.1 and 8.2 illustrate the prevalence of common sexual difficulties in men and women.

As depicted above in Tables 8.1 and 8.2, the presence of some sexual *dysfunctions* (consistent difficulties with sexual performance that create distress or impairment) increases with age. Problems with erectile dysfunction in men and difficulty with vaginal lubrication in women appear to become more prevalent with increasing age (Fugl-Meyer & Sjőrgren Fugl-Meyer, 1999; Laumann et al., 1999).

SEX, RACE, AND ETHNICITY

Sexual dysfunctions occur across race and ethnicity. Comparisons of African American and white women indicate that, in general, African American women reported lower levels of sexual desire and pleasure than did white women, whereas white women were

FIGURE 8.4

Prevalence of Erectile Dysfunction by Race and Socioeconomic Status

Although simply examining the data by race/ethnicity would suggest group differences in the prevalence of erectile dysfunction, these differences disappeared when the researchers controlled for the men's socioeconomic status.

From V. Kupilian, et al., "Socioeconomic status, not race/ethnicity, contributes to variation in the prevalence of erectile dysfunction," *Journal of Sexual Medicine*, 5, 1325–1333. Reprinted by permission of Blackwell Publishing.

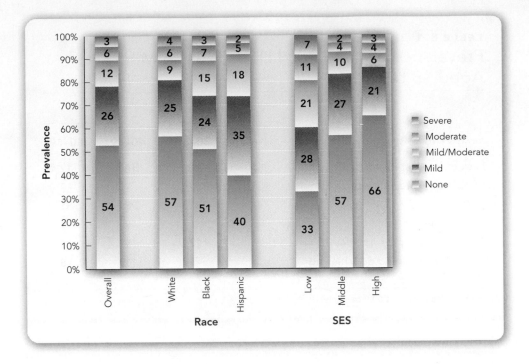

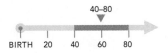

more likely to have pain. Both white and African American women reported more sexual difficulties than did Hispanic women (Laumann et al., 1999). In men, the results of the Boston Area Community Health Survey (BACH) indicate that 24.9% of African American and 25.3% of Hispanic men reported erectile dysfunction, compared with 18.1% of white men (Kupelian et al., 2008) (see Figure 8.4). Although this would appear to suggest a higher prevalence of erectile dysfunction in the first two groups, these racial/ethnic differences appeared to be the result of socioeconomic differences. This suggests that rather than looking at factors within each group that might account for these differences, researchers need to pay attention to social and environmental factors such as employment status, income, and living accommodations that might predispose one to poor health.

In the Global Study of Sexual Attitudes and Behaviors, which assessed 27,500 adults between the ages of 40 and 80 in 29 countries, 28% of the men and 39% of the women reported ever having a sexual dysfunction (Nicolosi et al., 2004). Among men, 28% had at least one sexual dysfunction; premature ejaculation was most common (14%) followed by erectile difficulties (10%; Nicolosi et al., 2004). Among women, 39% had at least one sexual problem; lack of sexual interest was most common (21%), with 16% reporting inability to achieve orgasm and 16% reporting vaginal lubrication difficulties. Across cultures, prevalence of erectile dysfunction is higher in Eastern Asia and Southeastern Asia (27.1% and 28.1%) than in Western countries. Men in Southeastern Asia also had higher prevalence of retarded ejaculation (Laumann et al., 2005). Similarly, women from Southeast Asia had the highest prevalence of female orgasmic disorder (41.2%; Laumann et al., 2005).

DEVELOPMENTAL FACTORS

There are few epidemiological data on the prevalence of sexual dysfunctions among young adults; most studies have focused on various sexual practices and risky sexual behaviors such as those that might lead to HIV infection. The few available data indicate that premature ejaculation is the most common complaint among adolescent and young adult men. This problem is usually the result of limited sexual experience or feelings of fear, guilt, or anxiety accompanying sexual activity (Seftel & Althof, 2000). In another sample, problems with low sexual desire were reported by 7% and 16% of 30-year-old men and women, respectively (Ernst et al., 1993).

ETIOLOGY

Some sexual dysfunctions are related to medical conditions, and a physical examination is necessary to rule out physical causes. In addition, medications for physical disorders such as hypertension and for psychological disorders such as depression may lead to sexual dysfunction, as can the use of illicit drugs.

Biological Factors   Biological conditions may affect sexual desire. Hormonal imbalances, such as hypothyroidism and hypogonadism (Maurice, 2005) can occur at any age and may decrease sexual interest directly by lowering the amount of sex hormones in the body. They may also function indirectly by causing negative mood states, which in turn decrease sexual desire. Other hormonal imbalances are age-related. Menopausal changes in women reduce estrogen, which affects vaginal lubrication and vaginal tissue elasticity, which in turn results in discomfort and possibly dyspareunia. In men, testosterone levels decrease with age (beginning in the 30s and 40s). How this decline decreases sexual desire and performance is unclear (Isidori et al., 2005), but decreases in testosterone can lower sexual desire and produce erectile dysfunction.

Physical disorders, such as cardiovascular disease, hypertension, diabetes, kidney failure, and cancer can decrease sexual desire or performance. Among men treated for diabetes, 28% have erectile dysfunction (Feldman et al., 1994). Men who have had surgery for prostate cancer may subsequently suffer from erectile dysfunction (Stanford et al., 2000). Alternatively, physical illness may impair sexual arousal indirectly by causing psychological distress, which may in turn decrease desire.

Androgens contribute to feelings of sexual desire in women as well as in men, although their specific effect on female sexual functioning is not yet known (Brotto & Klein, 2007). Women who have had their ovaries removed have lower levels of androgens, and this can decrease sexual desire. In addition, pelvic surgery, chemotherapy, and radiation treatment have been associated with dyspareunia, vaginal dryness, and hypoactive sexual desire (Amsterdam et al., 2006).

Alcohol and drugs can create temporary sexual dysfunction, including premature ejaculation and retarded ejaculation in men and orgasmic disorders in men and women. Drugs that block dopamine receptors or serotonin reuptake in the brain can also retard ejaculation (Metz et al., 1997; Waldinger 2002). Antidepressant medications, such as the selective serotonin reuptake inhibitors (SSRIs), improve mood but produce significant sexual side effects (Ferguson, 2001). They decrease physical response, inhibit the ability to achieve orgasm, and retard ejaculation in males, although they may improve psychological desire or arousal (see "Biological Treatments" under "Treatment" below).

Psychosocial Factors   Negative emotional states such as depression may be associated with sexual dysfunction. College women who were depressed were more likely than nondepressed women to report difficulties with sexual arousal, inability to achieve orgasm, and painful intercourse (e.g., Cyranowski et al., 2004; Frolich & Meston, 2002). In addition, they reported less satisfaction with their sexual relationship and less pleasure during sexual activity. Among normally aging men (aged 40 to 70), depression and erectile dysfunction were strongly correlated, and this effect was independent of aging, health status, medication use, and hormones (Araujo et al., 1998). It is unclear if low sexual desire is a cause or a result of depression—and the relationship may be different for different people.

Behavior theorists, as well as sex therapists (Masters & Johnson, 1970), propose that anxiety and stress play a role in sexual dysfunction, as both anxiety and premature ejaculation are associated with the sympathetic nervous system. Performance anxiety appears to be a major cause of erectile dysfunction and can be a cause of other sexual dysfunctions as well. If a man experiences temporary dysfunction as a result of alcohol, stress, or anxiety, the temporary problem may become a concern, and erectile dysfunction may become a self-fulfilling prophecy. Sex theorists also suggest that premature ejaculation results from conditioning experiences involving the need to ejaculate quickly, such as hurried sexual contacts in parked cars (see "The Whole Story: Michael"), sex with prostitutes, and engagement with sexual partners with whom there is a lack of intimacy (Metz et al., 1997). Although such patterns are sometimes present in the history of men with premature ejaculation, few empirical data address this issue (Grenier & Byers, 2001).

Factors such as couple distress or negative life events may result in temporary changes in sexual functioning in both sexes (Bancroft et al., 2003). Environmental events such as sexual assault may result in cases of vaginismus (Weijmar Schultz & Van de Wiel, 2005). Such dysfunctions do not indicate permanent changes in biological functioning, in contrast to those caused by aging.

TREATMENT

It is unfortunate that some people who are distressed by their sexual functioning never seek treatment because of ignorance or embarrassment. There are many available treatments with documented efficacy for improving sexual functioning.

Biological Treatments Because low levels of certain hormones, particularly testosterone, may affect sexual functioning, physicians may prescribe testosterone replacement therapy. Available as an injection, patch, or gel, replacement therapy is efficacious for men with low testosterone and sexual desire (Isidori et al., 2005). Testosterone patches may also improve sexual desire and satisfaction among women who have undergone *hysterectomy* (removal of the uterus) or *oophorectomy* (removal of the ovaries) (Braunstein et al., 2005; Buster et al., 2005; Kingsberg, 2007; Shiren et al., 2000).

The relationship between depression and sexual functioning is complicated. Depression can decrease sexual desire. As noted earlier, some antidepressants that improve depressed mood (e.g., SSRIs) increase sexual *desire* but impair sexual *performance* by delaying ejaculation and inhibiting orgasm. The side effect of delayed ejaculation means that some men may be reluctant to take the medication to treat their depression. However, this side effect means that SSRIs may be a useful treatment for premature ejaculation, delaying ejaculation for several minutes (Kara et al., 1996; Strassberg et al., 1999). This illustrates how a medication's negative effect in one context may be a positive therapeutic effect when used differently.

We noted at the beginning of this section that people with sexual dysfunctions often fail to seek treatment because they do not know that help is available. However, this cannot be said about pharmacological treatments for erectile dysfunction. In fact, it is difficult to watch television or read a newspaper without seeing an advertisement for Viagra, Levitra, or Cialis. The blockbuster drug Viagra (generic name sildenafil) was approved in early 1998 for the treatment of erectile dysfunction. Tadalafil (Cialis) and vardenafil (Levitra) soon followed. These drugs are known as phosphodiesterase type-5 (PDE5) inhibitors. PDE5 is a molecule found in the *corpus cavernosum*, which is the spongy erectile tissue in the penis and the clitoris. PDE5 is involved in *detumescence* (loss of erection), so PDE5 inhibitors allow penile erection to occur. Since the introduction of these drugs, thousands of studies have examined the efficacy of PDE5 inhibitors for erectile dysfunction. All three drugs are more efficacious than placebo, with 43 to 80% efficacy depending on the reason for the dysfunction (Lewis et al., 2005; Osterloh & Riley, 2002; Porst et al., 2001). The success of the PDE5 inhibitors for male erectile dysfunction has encouraged clinical trials of Viagra as a treatment for female sexual arousal disorder (see the box "Examining the Evidence: Viagra for Female Sexual Arousal Disorder").

Before the introduction of PDE5 inhibitors, erectile dysfunction was treated with a substance known as prostaglandin E1, which was either injected into the penis or inserted into the urethra. Positive effects ranged from 70 to 87% (Linet & Ogrinc, 1996; Padma-Nathan et al., 1997). However, the discomfort associated with the drug's administration makes many men unwilling to use it. A cream version of prostaglandin E1, applied externally to treat female sexual arousal disorder, does not appear to be better than placebo (Padma-Nathan et al., 2003).

examining the evidence

Viagra for Female Sexual Arousal Disorder

The success of Viagra in treating erectile dysfunction invariably led to questions about whether this medication might help other sexual dysfunctions. For example, given the high prevalence of sexual dysfunctions among women, would Viagra be a useful treatment for female hypoactive sexual desire disorder or female sexual arousal disorder?

■ **The Evidence** PDE5 inhibitors block a molecule in the corpus cavernosum (spongy tissue) that creates detumesence in the penis. Corpus cavernosum tissue is also present in the clitoris of females. Six placebo-controlled trials have studied the efficacy of Viagra for women. Two studies (Berman et al., 2003; Caruso et al., 2001) reported positive effects (enhanced orgasm, improved sexual satisfaction). However, four other studies (Basson & Brotto, 2003; Basson et al., 2002; Berman et al., 2003; Kaplan et al., 1999) did not find any positive effects, including a very large multicenter trial that had a sample of 788 women (Basson et al., 2002).

■ **Let's Examine the Evidence** There were differences between the studies that found positive outcomes for Viagra versus those that found no effects.

First, positive effects occurred when the sample consisted of women with female sexual arousal disorder. No effects were found for samples of women with more heterogeneous sexual dysfunctions (such as hypoactive sexual desire disorder or both hypoactive sexual desire disorder and female sexual arousal disorder).

Second, in one of the two positive trials (Caruso et al., 2001), women received both the active drug and the placebo (though at separate times), and each condition was compared with the baseline condition (no pill). When someone takes an active drug and later a placebo (or vice versa), the side effects of the medication may "unblind" the patients. Side effects, more likely to accompany active medication, allow participants to correctly guess which substance they are taking. When the dependent variable is a subjective report, such as "feel more aroused," knowing when you are taking the active medication could influence your judgment of how well the pill worked.

Third, in one of the positive studies, positive effects were found on two specific questions on a self-report measure of sexual satisfaction, but not on the overall score. While an entire self-report inventory may be reliable and valid, the same psychometric properties cannot be said to apply to a single question. Therefore, conclusions based on a positive response to a single item must be regarded cautiously.

■ **Conclusion** In contrast to the thousands of studies examining the efficacy of Viagra for erectile dysfunction, the few studies examining its effect on women present a mixed picture. Although the same biological tissue exists in both sexes, it appears that Viagra works for only a few women. What hypothesis might you suggest to account for these differences?

Finally, there are physical treatments for erectile dysfunction. Penile implants are prosthetic devices that consist of a pump placed in the penis or scrotum that forces fluid into an inflatable cylinder, producing an erection. Similarly, vacuum devices consist of a plastic cylinder and a constriction ring that is placed around the penis. A vacuum is created using a pump, which produces an erection. The cylinder is then removed. Physical treatments are common when there is a physical reason for erectile dysfunction, such as diabetes or prostate surgery. Though efficacious and without side effects, they are awkward to use and do not always produce satisfactory results.

Psychosocial Treatments   First developed in the 1970s and 1980s, psychosocial treatments for sexual dysfunctions are efficacious (Hawton, 1995; Heiman, 2002), but many have only been studied in randomized, controlled trials more than 20 years ago (Brotto & Klein, 2007). Although further and more sophisticated research is necessary, below we review the available and empirically supported treatments.

Sex therapy (Masters & Johnson, 1970) consists of teaching couples about sexual functioning, enhancing communication skills, and eliminating performance anxiety through specific couples' exercises. Using *sensate focus and nondemand pleasuring*, treatment focuses on decreasing performance anxiety and increasing communication. There are three steps in sensate focus. Both partners must become comfortable at each level of intimacy before proceeding to the next step. The first step focuses simply on pleasurable, nonsexual touching. Partners take turns touching the other's body, but they are prohibited from touching the genitals and breasts. During the second step, partners touch any part of the other's body, including the genitals and breasts. The focus remains on the sensation of touching. Intercourse is not allowed. The third step involves mutual touching, eventually leading to sexual intercourse. Sex therapy is most effective for vaginismus and erectile dysfunction that are psychological in origin (Hawton, 1995), and for female hypoactive sexual desire disorder (Trudel et al., 2001). The long-term outcome is variable. In some instances, initial treatment effects are not maintained when patients are followed up several years later (Brotto & Klein, 2007).

Used by Masters and Johnson (1970) and Kaplan (1979), the *"stop-squeeze" technique* (Semans, 1956) is highly efficacious for premature ejaculation. In this treatment, the sexual partner stimulates the penis until an ejaculatory urge occurs. At that point, sexual stimulation stops and the partner squeezes the glans of the penis (the tip) until the urge disappears. This sequence is repeated until the interval between initial sexual stimulation and ejaculatory urge lengthens. Then the couple practices briefly inserting the penis into the vagina without thrusting, and the practice continues until the man is able to control the timing of ejaculation and the couple reports sexual enjoyment. This treatment can be adapted for a man to use alone (see "The Whole Story: Michael"). The "stop-squeeze" technique has a success rate of about 60% (Althof, 2006; Metz et al., 1997), although positive long-term outcome is achieved in only a minority of cases (Metz et al., 1997).

For female orgasmic disorder, *directed masturbation* (Heiman & LoPiccolo, 1987; Masters & Johnson, 1970) is commonly prescribed by therapists. Women focus on sexually erotic cues and use graduated stimulation to the genital area, particularly the clitoris. Allowing the woman to focus on sexual stimulation that is effective for her without worrying about a partner's behavior enables her to more effectively communicate her wishes to a partner. Approximately 90% of women treated with directed masturbation become orgasmic after this treatment (Heiman & LoPiccolo, 1987).

Treatment for vaginismus is based on standard systematic desensitization (see Chapter 4) and uses different-sized vaginal dilators. Using a hierarchical approach, the dilators are inserted into the vagina, either by the woman or her partner, while she practices relaxation. Over time, a woman becomes comfortable engaging in sexual activity. This procedure, sometimes coupled with cognitive-behavior therapy to challenge irrational beliefs such as "intercourse will always be painful" is a highly successful treatment (Kabakçi & Batur, 2003; Leiblum, 2000; ter Kuile et al., 2007).

Vaginal dilators, of increasing sizes, are used to treat vaginismus.

---

concept CHECK

- Sexual dysfunctions encompass a broad range of sexual behaviors and include disorders of sexual desire, arousal, orgasm, and pain.

- Sexual dysfunctions may affect as many as 31% of men and 43% of women.

- Diagnoses of sexual dysfunctions must include consideration of distress and impairment as well as age, sex, and prior sexual experience.

- Sexual dysfunction may result from physical diseases, psychological disorders, or environmental events. Sexual dysfunction may also be a contributing factor to psychological disorders.

APPLICATION QUESTION There are efficacious pharmacological and psychosocial treatments for men with sexual dysfunctions and efficacious psychosocial treatments for women. Since talking about sex has become more common among young adults in Western cultures, how might this affect our understanding of the prevalence and treatment of sexual dysfunctions? Do you think that this new "openness" would affect males and females in the same way?

Paraphilias

Paraphilias are intense, persistent, and frequently occurring sexual urges, fantasies, or behaviors that involve unusual situations, objects, or activities (APA, 2000). Paraphilias are a very mixed group of disorders, but all involve a behavior that society considers unusual (or out of the norm). The public sometimes associates paraphilias with criminal activity, but the relationship is not so simple. Some paraphilias, such as *transvestic fetishism*, are unusual but do not involve criminal activity. Other paraphilias, however, such as *exhibitionism* or *pedophilia*, may result in criminal charges. In addition, there are sexual offenders, such as rapists, who do not commit that act because of a paraphilia (McElroy et al., 1999). Therefore, not every paraphilic activity is criminal, but some may lead a person to engage in criminal acts.

There are three categories of paraphilias: sexual arousal toward nonhuman objects, sexual arousal toward children or nonconsenting individuals, and sexual arousal related to suffering or humiliation of oneself or others. Defining the limits of a paraphilia is difficult because some behaviors (such as physical restraint during sexual activity) do not necessarily cause distress or functional impairment for some adults (Krueger & Kaplan, 2001). Therefore, before any behavior is labeled a paraphilia, its impact in terms of distress and functional impairment must be considered.

SEXUAL AROUSAL TOWARD NONHUMAN OBJECTS

In some instances, sexual urges, fantasies, or behaviors are associated with inanimate objects rather than people (see the box "DSM-IV-TR: Sexual Arousal Toward Inanimate Objects"). Many different objects may be associated with sexual arousal, although certain categories, such as women's lingerie, occur more frequently. However, it is important to remember that not everything that a person identifies as "sexy" indicates the presence of deviant sexual arousal. A young man may find that seeing his girlfriend wearing lacy underwear enhances his sexual desire for her, but a person with a paraphilia would find the underwear alone arousing.

paraphilias intense, persistent, and frequently occurring sexual urges, fantasies, or behaviors that involve unusual situations, objects, or activities

fetishism sexual arousal (fantasies, urges, or behaviors) that involves nonliving objects (not limited to female clothing used in cross-dressing)

transvestic fetishism sexual arousal in men that results from wearing women's clothing and is accompanied by significant distress or impairment

Fetishism *Micky was referred to the clinic after his arrest for shoplifting. A high school senior who was a loner for most of his school career, Micky was overweight, clumsy, and had bad acne. He had mediocre grades and was the classic "last kid to get picked for the team." He never had a girlfriend. Micky loved to cook. He spent hours in the kitchen baking, as his goal was to become a pastry chef. This was Micky's second shoplifting offense. The first time, he was caught stealing a pair of red underpants from the women's lingerie department. He avoided charges by telling the security guard that he wanted to buy his girlfriend a birthday present but didn't have enough money. The guard felt sorry for him and let him go. The second time, he wasn't so lucky. He had taken a bag of women's panties and was caught on the security camera masturbating with them in one of the men's changing rooms. When the store security guard called his mother, she was horrified. She searched his room and found stashes of women's underwear in the back of his drawers and under his bed. At the court-ordered assessment, Micky was reluctant to discuss his sexuality at all. He seemed indifferent to his fetishism and only hoped that this arrest would not interfere with his ability to get into a culinary academy.*

Sexual arousal (fantasies, urges, or behaviors) that involves nonliving objects (not limited to female clothing used in cross-dressing) is known as **fetishism**. It would be impossible to provide a complete list of fetish objects, but the most common are female underwear, stockings, footwear, or other apparel (APA, 2000). Sexual arousal may occur after looking at or fondling the object, rubbing, licking, or smelling the object, seeing someone else wearing the object, or manipulating the object by cutting or burning it (Chalkley & Powell, 1983). There are virtually no empirical data on this disorder, although those who engage in fetishism are primarily men, and once established, the disorder is chronic (Brotto & Klein, 2007).

Transvestic Fetishism *Bill is a successful physician with a big secret. It started when he was a teenager. His sister had hung her bra over the shower rod. He was curious—how did girls wear them? What did it feel like? He found himself getting excited at the thought of the lacy bra against his skin. One day he took the bra and matching panties out of the fresh laundry. His sister never noticed. Whenever he wore them, he felt sexually aroused. Bill was shy and awkward around girls. He rationalized that he did not have time for girls— he had to study if he wanted to become a doctor. All through high school, college, medical school, and residency, he satisified his sexual urges by wearing women's underwear underneath his shirt and pants. Now he was a physician and he was interested in marrying and settling down. He was seeking treatment because he was quite distressed; he wanted to ask out an attractive nurse who seemed interested in him. But he did not feel the same sexual excitement thinking about her that he did when he thought about wearing the lacy underwear.*

Cross-dressing may provide sexual gratification for some men, whereas male entertainers sometimes dress as females to entertain the public.

Also known as *cross-dressing*, **transvestic fetishism** is sexual arousal that results from wearing women's clothing, and is accompanied by significant distress or impairment. Not every man who cross-dresses suffers from transvestic fetishism. Female impersonators, for example, wear women's clothing to impersonate female singers or actresses on stage; these performers are not necessarily sexually aroused when wearing the clothing or performing. Transvestic fetishism occurs only among heterosexual men. Among one sample of cross-dressers, 60% were married and 83% of the wives were aware of their husband's activities (Docter & Prince, 1997). Among the wives, 28% were completely accepting of their husband's behavior, whereas 19% were described as completely antagonistic. The rest were reported to have less clear feelings.

Sexual Arousal toward Inanimate Objects

Both of these conditions must exist for at least six months for the diagnosis to be given:

Fetishism The person has consistent and intense sexually arousing fantasies, sexual urges, or behaviors involving inanimate objects such as women's undergarments.

Transvestic Fetishism A heterosexual male has consistent intense sexually arousing fantasies, sexual urges, or behaviors involving cross-dressing.

In both instances, there must be distress or impairment as a result of the behaviors.

Adapted with permission from the *Diagnostic and Statistical Manual of Mental Disorders*, Text Revision, Fourth Edition, (Copyright 2000). American Psychiatric Association.

SEXUAL AROUSAL TOWARD CHILDREN AND NONCONSENTING ADULTS

Unlike fetishism and transvestic fetishism, sexual arousal toward children and non-consenting adults (see the box "DSM-IV-TR: Sexual Arousal toward Children and Nonconsenting Adults") involves unwilling victims, in most cases, women or children. Some behaviors in this category, such as exhibitionism, may elicit temporary startle reactions or annoyance from the victims, whereas in other cases, such as child abuse, long-term and serious detrimental effects may occur. In addition, all of the behaviors in this category are not only deviant sexual behaviors but they are also criminal offenses, although the extent of the legal implications varies with the particular activity.

Exhibitionism *Max was not sure why he did it, but boy, it sure felt good. He experienced a tremendous urge that could not otherwise be satisfied—nothing else felt the same. When he felt the urge, he would dress in only a dark raincoat and ski mask. Right before dusk, he would drive to a part of town where he was not known. He would hide in the bushes until a woman walked by—he would jump out and open his raincoat, exposing his genitals. Usually the woman would scream. For Max, the possibility of being caught naked and the surprise of the victim were important elements of his sexual satisfaction.*

Defined as recurrent fantasies, urges, or behaviors involving exposing one's genitals to an unsuspecting stranger, **exhibitionism** may also include the act of masturbation in front of a stranger. The shock of the victim is sometimes the sexually arousing component. Most often the perpetrator is male (Federoff et al., 1999), and most victims are female. Exhibitionism is a "high victim" crime. Among 142 people with a history of exhibitionism, there were a total of 72,074 victims (Tempelman & Stinnett, 1991). People who engage in exhibitionism are not different from the general population in terms of academic achievement, intelligence, socioeconomic status, or emotional adjustment (Brotto & Klein, 2007). They are more likely than people with other types of paraphilias to be in committed relationships. They also are less likely than others to see their behavior as harmful to the victim (Cox & Maletzky, 1980).

Frotteurism *Nate is a 20-year-old college student. Socially introverted since middle school, he has a few male friends and has had a few dates with girls. Around age 13, Nate realized that he became sexually aroused by fantasies about women he saw in the mall, at sports games, or the movie theatre. He had no interest in meeting them, but he was sexually aroused by the idea of rubbing his body against them. When Nate was 17, he began to act on this urge. On a crowded morning subway ride, Nate would brush his body up against women. He'd say "excuse me," as if he intended to pass them, but he'd linger for*

exhibitionism recurrent fantasies, urges, or behaviors involving exposing one's genitals to an unsuspecting stranger

Sexual Arousal toward Children and Nonconsenting Adults

All of these conditions must exist for at least six months for the diagnosis to be given:

Exhibitionism   The person has consistent and intense sexually arousing fantasies, sexual urges, or behaviors involving the exposing of the genitals to an unsuspecting person.

Frotteurism   The person has consistent and intense sexually arousing fantasies, sexual urges, or behaviors involving touching and rubbing against a nonconsenting person.

Voyeurism   The person has consistent intense sexually arousing fantasies, sexual urges, or behaviors centered on observing an unsuspecting person who is naked, disrobing, or engaging in sexual activity.

Pedophilia   The person has consistent and intense sexually arousing fantasies, sexual urges, or behaviors involving sexual activity with a child or children not yet 14 years old. The person is at least 16 years old and at least 5 years older than the child or children. This diagnosis does not include an older adolescent involved in an ongoing sexual relationship with a 12- or 13-year-old.

Adapted with permission from the *Diagnostic and Statistical Manual of Mental Disorders*, Text Revision, Fourth Edition, (Copyright 2000). American Psychiatric Association.

a few seconds to press his penis up against the woman's derriere or hip. Soon he was not satisfied just doing it once; by age 18, he was spending hours on the subway each day. He began to have fantasies of exclusive, caring relationships with his female victims. Once at college in a rural area, he worried that he would not be able to fulfill his sexual urge. He tried to stop and began dating a woman. However, his sexual compulsion was so powerful that actual romantic interactions with a partner left him unfulfilled. Nate was very distressed. Then, in an abnormal psychology class, he heard the word frotteurism. Nate was astonished, ashamed, but also somewhat relieved—he was not the only one with this secret behavior.

Sexually arousing urges, fantasies, or behaviors that involve touching or rubbing against a nonconsenting person are known as **frotteurism**. The word comes from the French word *frotter*, meaning "to rub." As illustrated by Nate, the behavior occurs in public places such as crowded buses or subways. Areas of contact are primarily thighs, buttocks, genitals, or breasts. Usually the person fantasizes about a positive emotional relationship with the victim (APA, 2000). What few data exist suggest that the disorder occurs almost exclusively in adolescent or young adult men who have many victims, are rarely arrested, and when arrested, serve minimal sentences (Krueger & Kaplan, 1997).

Voyeurism involves sexually arousing urges, fantasies, and behaviors that are associated with seeing an unsuspecting person naked, undressing, or engaging in sexual activity (APA, 2000). To be considered a disorder, there must be significant distress or actual voyeuristic acts. Although there are few empirical data, people with voyeurism are thought to have limited social skills, limited sexual knowledge, and problems with sexual dysfunction and intimacy (Marshall & Eccles, 1991).

Pedophilia is characterized by sexual urges, fantasies, or actual behavior directed toward a prepubescent child (see the box "DSM-IV-TR: Sexual Arousal toward Children and Nonconsenting Adults" for the required ages of perpetrators and victims). The sexual arousal may be toward girls, boys, or girls and boys. For this disorder, if the

frotteurism   consistent and intense sexually arousing fantasies, sexual urges, or behaviors involving touching and rubbing against a nonconsenting person

voyeurism   consistent intense sexually arousing fantasies, sexual urges, or behaviors centered on observing an unsuspecting person who is naked, disrobing, or engaging in sexual activity

pedophilia   consistent and intense sexually arousing fantasies, sexual urges, or behaviors involving sexual activity with a child or children not yet 14 years old. The person is at least 16 years old and at least 5 years older than the child or children.

person has acted on the urges or fantasies, the diagnosis is appropriate, even if the perpetrator denies distress or functional impairment (APA, 2000). Although the terms *pedophile* and *child molester* are sometimes used interchangeably, they are not synonymous. Someone with pedophilia could have urges or fantasies involving sexual activity with a child but never act on them. That person would not be a child molester. Yet much of what we know about pedophila comes from samples of convicted child molesters and does not describe all those who suffer from the disorder.

The most common pedophilic acts are fondling and genital exposure. Intercourse (oral, vaginal, or anal) is less common, and rape or abduction are the least common (Fagan et al., 2002). Perpetrators can be familial or nonfamilial. Among one offending group, 29% of offenders were natural parents, 29% other parents, and 40% other caretakers (Sedlak & Broadhurst, 1996). When the offender and the child are related, pedophilia is called *incest*. Although incest perpetrators share many similarities to perpetrators who abuse biologically unrelated children, incest victims are usually at the age of puberty. Younger children are most often the victims of nonbiologically related males with pedophilia (Rice & Harris, 2002).

Girls are more often the victims of pedophilia than are boys, although a perpetrator who prefers boys will often have a much higher number of victims (Abel & Oxborn, 1992). Table 8.3 illustrates the difference between those who have heterosexual pedophilia and homosexual pedophilia. These differences include the number of victims involved, where the offenses occur, the sex and age of the victims, and whether the perpetrator is also sexually attracted to adults. Initially considered to be a disorder of men, there now is evidence that some women suffer from pedophilia (Brotto & Klein, 2007; Fagan et al., 2002). Clearly, those who qualify for a diagnosis of pedophilia are not a homogeneous group.

Pedophilia is defined as sexual attraction to prepubescent children. Having fantasies or impulses about engaging in sexual behavior with children is not considered criminal unless the person acts on the sexual urges. In that case, the behaviors do constitute a crime and may bring the individual to the attention of the criminal justice system. Criminal behaviors are not simply limited to sexual acts with a minor child. Possessing sexual images of children (child pornography, even when obtained over the

---

TABLE 8.3
Men's Pedophilic Acts with Boys and Girls

Male Perpetrator/Female Victim	Male Perpetrator/Male Victim
Few victims	Many victims (up to hundreds)
Offends repeatedly with same victim	Offends only once with a victim
Offenses occur in victim's home	Offenses occur away from victim's home
Mean age of victim is 8 years	Mean age of victim is 10 years
Offender also attracted to older women	Offender not attracted to adults of either sex
Offender commonly married	Offender single
Behavior began in adulthood	Behavior began in adolescence
Low income, unemployed, alcoholic, lower IQ, psychopathic	Stable/employed, average IQ, "immature," prefers company of children to adults

From McConaghy, 1993.

Internet) is a criminal offense. Because epidemiological studies do not include questions about pedophilic fantasies and behaviors, the prevalence of pedophilia in the general population is not known (Fagan et al., 2002). Furthermore, the percentage of child abusers who suffer from pedophilia is also unknown.

SEXUAL AROUSAL INVOLVING SUFFERING OR HUMILIATION OF ONESELF OR OTHERS

The terms *masochist* and *sadist* are commonly used in our society and do not always refer to sexual behaviors. However, sexual masochism and sexual sadism are diagnostic categories that involve pain and humiliation during sexual activity (see the box "DSM-IV-TR: Sexual Arousal Involving Suffering or Humiliation of Oneself or Others"). It is important to understand that it is not a specific behavior that defines these disorders but the fact that the resultant pain, humiliation, or suffering creates sexual arousal.

Jack had a secret. He experienced intense sexual arousal and orgasm when his supply of oxygen was cut off during sexual activity. When he could not find a partner willing to choke him while they engaged in intercourse, Jack would "do it himself"—using a chair and a rope to briefly hang himself while he masturbated. He was always extremely careful to have an escape route. One day he did not show up at a meeting. It was not like Jack to miss meetings, and his concerned colleagues went to his office. They found Jack, naked and dead, hanging from a ceiling beam, an overturned ladder nearby.

Sexual masochism is sexual arousal that occurs as a result of being humiliated, beaten, bound, or otherwise made to suffer. The events actually occur and are not simulated. Pain may result from being slapped, spanked, or whipped. Humiliation may result from acts such as wearing diapers, licking shoes, or displaying one's naked body. Other acts might include being urinated or defecated on, self-mutilation, or, as in Jack's case, being deprived of oxygen (Brotto & Klein, 2007). Males and females who engage in sexual masochism may do so by mutual agreement and use a safety signal when they want to stop. Yet in some cases these activities lead to injury or death, as happened to Jack.

Sexual sadism also involves the infliction of pain or humiliation, but in this case the physical or psychological suffering is inflicted on another person. The disorder is found primarily among males. Serious injury or death can occur, and over time those who engage in sexual sadism tend to increase the severity of their sadistic activities (APA, 2000). Furthermore, in some instances, the sadistic acts may be nonconsensual, resulting in the crime of sexual assault.

Many of those who engage in sexual sadism formerly engaged in sexual masochism (Baumeister, 1989). In some individuals, sexual fantasies and behaviors alternate between sadism and masochism (Abel et al., 1988; Arndt et al., 1985).

FUNCTIONAL IMPAIRMENT

People who have paraphilias often have more than one. Among one group of sex offenders with a paraphilia, 29% had two paraphilias and 14% had three paraphilias. Specifically, 81% met criteria for pedophilia, 43% for frotteurism, 19% for sexual sadism, 14% for voyeurism, and 14% for paraphilia not otherwise specified (McElroy et al., 1999).

Despite their unusual sexual practices, people with paraphilias are often indistinguishable from other people in nonsexual areas of functioning. They do not seek out pain or humiliation in other types of activities. They are described as well-adjusted, successful, and above the norm on assessments of mental health (Brotto & Klein, 2007). Men with transvestic fetishism are happy with their biological sex and gender identity. Their behaviors, occupations, and hobbies are typical of those found in other heterosexual males (Buhrich & McConaghy, 1985; Chung & Harmon, 1994). However, accidental deaths, such as Jack's, sometimes occur from oxygen deprivation. In the

sexual masochism consistent intense sexually arousing fantasies, sexual urges, or behaviors involving actual acts of being humiliated, beaten, bound, or otherwise made to suffer

sexual sadism consistent sexual arousal that occurs when acts of humiliation, beating, bondage, or acts of suffering are inflicted on another person

DSM-IV-TR

Sexual Arousal Involving Suffering or Humiliation of Oneself or Others

Sexual Masochism and Sexual Sadism   Over at least a six month period, the person has consistent intense sexually arousing fantasies, sexual urges, or behaviors involving actual acts of being humiliated, beaten, bound or otherwise made to suffer (sexual masochism) or finds these acts, when inflicted on another person, to be sexually exciting (sexual sadism).

Adapted with permission from the *Diagnostic and Statistical Manual of Mental Disorders*, Text Revision, Fourth Edition, (Copyright 2000). American Psychiatric Association.

United States, England, Australia, and Canada, one or two deaths from this cause occur per one million people each year (APA, 2000).

SEX, RACE, AND ETHNICITY

As noted, most epidemiological surveys of psychological disorders do not ask questions about paraphilias. Most people find these behaviors difficult to discuss, and it is highly unlikely that they would admit them to a stranger. Furthermore, in some instances, these behaviors could lead to criminal charges, making it even more unlikely that people would admit to them. Therefore, most of what we know about paraphilias comes from those who seek or are referred for treatment or who have been apprehended as a result of their sexual behavior. This results in confusing and conflicting prevalence estimates. At this time, the most accurate statement is that paraphilias are probably rare, but their actual prevalence remains unknown.

Almost all people with paraphilias are men, but females with pedophilia have been reported (Krueger & Kaplan, 2001). Sexual masochism is also found among women, although the ratio is still approximately 20 males to 1 female (APA, 2000). Another sex difference is that women prefer less pain than men during sexually masochistic activities (Baumeister, 1989).

Cultural factors are particularly important to consider in the case of paraphilias. For example, exhibitionism is considered a paraphilia when cultural norms require wearing clothing that covers the genitalia. When exposure of the genitals is the norm, as in some tropical areas where clothing is not traditionally worn, the diagnosis of exhibitionism may not be appropriate (Tseng, 2003).

DEVELOPMENTAL FACTORS

The most common age of onset for all paraphilias is adolescence to young adulthood (Abel et al., 1985; APA, 2000), although the disorders may begin at any age. Particularly in the case of pedophilia, we usually think about children as the victims. However, young boys (some as young as age 4) have been known to commit acts of pedophilia by sexually molesting even younger children. In one sample, boys who abused younger children were an average of 8 years old at the time that they committed their first offense, and the victims averaged 6 years of age (Cavanagh-Johnson, 1988). The perpetrators used coercion to commit the offenses and knew the children that they victimized.

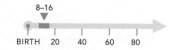

Across one sample of sex offenders, the average age of onset for a paraphilia was 16 years but ranged from 7 to 38 years (McElroy et al., 1999). Compared with sexual offenders without paraphilias, sexual offenders with a paraphilia were significantly younger when they committed their first sexual offense, had offended for a longer period of time before being arrested, had had more victims, and were significantly more likely to suffer from anxiety, depressive, substance abuse, and impulse-control disorders (Krueger & Kaplan, 2001).

ETIOLOGY

The etiology of paraphilias is unknown (Krueger & Kaplan, 2001), although various theories have been proposed. With respect to biology, several studies have examined the role of endocrine abnormalities in paraphilias, but data have failed to document differences in those with paraphilias (Krueger & Kaplan, 2001). Similarly, neuroanatomical and neurochemical studies have not detected specific brain abnormalities (Hucker et al., 1988; O'Carroll, 1989; Tarter et al., 1983). Similarly, there are few data supporting a role for genetics in the onset of paraphilias (Krueger & Kaplan, 2001).

With respect to psychosocial theories, a commonly held belief is that people who abuse children were abused themselves. However, the available data do not support this contention. If estimates of abuse are correct, as many as 1 in 10 children may be sexually abused before the age of 18, but the vast majority of these children do not develop pedophilia (Murphy & Peters, 1992). Research tells us that a history of child abuse is not necessary or sufficient for the development of pedophilia. In one sample, 28% of sex offenders reported a history of sexual abuse as children, compared with 10% among a nonoffending community sample (Hanson & Slater, 1988). Although the rate among offenders is higher, it still means that almost 3 out of 4 offenders did not have a history of childhood sexual abuse.

Behavioral conditioning theories have been proposed to explain the development of paraphilias, but there are few empirical data. For example, if a person engages in a paraphilia and achieves sexual release, engaging in that behavior is reinforced and likely to be repeated. In a similar vein, negative family environments and disrupted family structures have been hypothesized to play an etiological role, but these hypotheses are based primarily on isolated case reports with few supporting data (Brotto & Klein, 2007).

TREATMENT

Again, it is important to note that a diagnosis requires significant distress or functional impairment. People with paraphilias often are not motivated to change because the sexual behavior is very reinforcing. It creates a pleasurable state and therefore is likely to be repeated. When individuals do seek treatment, it is usually mandated by the legal system, and individuals often discontinue treatment once legal oversight is terminated. Some investigators consider pedophilia to be a chronic disorder, with treatment directed toward stopping abuse and helping the perpetrator learn to control his deviant behavior (Fagan et al., 2002). Sometimes treatments are combined to achieve optimum results. Positive outcomes have been reported for these treatments, but the available data are few and the sample sizes are small and far from conclusive.

Determining the efficacy of interventions requires accurate assessment of the problem before and after treatment. This is particularly difficult in the case of paraphilias, as most people are reluctant to discuss these behaviors. Furthermore, admitting to certain sexual behaviors may have legal consequences. Therefore, many researchers and some clinicians depend on objective measures of sexual arousal known as **plethysmography**: penile plethysmography for males and vaginal photoplethysmography for females. Most research has been directed at the *penile plethysmograph*, considered a reliable and valid form of assessing sexual arousal, including deviant sexual arousal. The penile plethysmograph measures changes in penile tumescence when the man is shown sexually arousing or nonarousing stimuli. The stimuli usually consist of photographs of males and females, of all ages, against a plain background. The man is instructed to look at the slide, and his erectile response is recorded.

By identifying deviant patterns of sexual arousal, penile plethysmography can distinguish between sexual and nonsexual offenders (although it is more accurate in detecting those who did not commit a sexual offense than those who did commit an offense) and between rapists or child molesters and nonoffenders (Barbaree & Marshall, 1989; Barsetti et al., 1998). It also predicts violent recidivism among sexual offenders, and

plethysmography a method to measure sexual arousal in men or women informs clinicians and researchers about the efficacy of treatment (Lalumière & Quinsey, 1994; Seto, 2001). In the section on psychosocial treatment below, we will also show how penile plethysmography can assess treatment outcome.

Despite the advances in understanding sexual deviations made possible by plethysmography, there are a number of ethical, social, and medical concerns about its use (Abel et al., 1998). Because the assessment uses nude photographs, one concern is the potential exploitation of children. Even when the photos are used solely for purposes of assessment and treatment, transporting them across state lines can result in arrest for trafficking in child pornography. Second, researchers must be concerned about the transmission of HIV/AIDS when the plethysmograph is used. Third, the device is very intrusive because it must be placed on the penis, and sometimes a technician's assistance is required. This raises questions about its use with adolescents, who later could accuse the technician of abuse. Finally, although it is difficult, some men can "beat the machine" and control their physiological response to appear less aroused than they actually are.

In response to these concerns, a new assessment strategy, the *visual reaction time task*, has been developed. This procedure measures the length of time that people look at slides of males and females (of all ages) who are wearing bathing suits. The theory is that people will look longer at the pictures that they find sexually arousing (e.g., heterosexual women should look longer at slides of adult males, rather than children of either sex or adult females). The visual reaction time task appears to be as reliable and valid as penile plethysmography (Abel et al.; 1988, 2004) and is more acceptable for use with adolescents (Abel et al., 2004).

Biological Treatment   Surgical castration, though efficacious for some people, is no longer used to treat paraphilias due to obvious legal and ethical constraints (Rösler & Witztum, 2000). Phamacological interventions include SSRIs and antiandrogens. Because some forms of paraphilia are considered to be compulsive in nature, the SSRIs were initially considered to have some promise due to their efficacy in treating obsessive-compulsive disorder (see Chapter 4), but to date, their efficacy for paraphilias is not established (Gijs & Gooren, 1996; Rösler & Witztum, 2000).

The primary goal of *antiandrogen medications* is to reduce the sexual drive. Medroxyprogetertone acetate (Depo-Provera) and leuprolide acetate (Depo-Lupron) are testosterone-lowering medications currently used in the United States. Cyproterone acetate is available in Canada and Europe. These drugs inhibit *lutenizing hormone secretion*, which in turn is responsible for decreasing testosterone levels (Rösler & Witztum, 2000). Depending on the dosage used, there often is still enough testosterone for erectile function to allow sexual intercourse with an appropriate partner (Fagan et al., 2002). The drug controls behaviors such as pedophilia, exhibitionism, and voyeurism as long as the patient continues to take the medication, but there are significant side effects and a high recidivism rate (an average of 27%) that limit its usefulness (Rösler & Witztum, 2000).

Psychosocial Treatment   Behavioral and cognitive-behavioral treatments for paraphilias are the most common psychosocial intervention and at this time are considered the most efficacious (Krueger & Kaplan, 2002). Treatments based on learning theory have been applied to the treatment of paraphilias since the 1970s and usually involve two parts: decreasing sexual arousal to inappropriate sexual stimuli and enhancing appropriate sexual behavior.

Eliminating or Decreasing Inappropriate Sexual Arousal   Treatments based on classical and operant conditioning (see Chapter 1) have been successfully developed for various paraphilias. **Satiation** involves exposing the person to the arousing stimuli and continuing that exposure for an extended period, until the stimuli no longer produce positive, erotic feelings. For example, a man who fantasizes about exposing his genitals to adolescent females would be asked to imagine that fantasy and

satiation   a treatment that uses prolonged, imaginal exposure to arousing sexual stimuli until it no longer produces positive, erotic feelings.

masturbate for an extended period of time (perhaps for 2 hours) until he reports an absence of sexual arousal or perhaps even aversion to the idea. A number of sessions must be conducted until even any initial sexual arousal is eliminated. **Covert sensitization** is a similar procedure in which the individual is asked to imagine doing the deviant act but also visualize the negative consequences that result from it. The scene is presented to the patient for a period of time, over repeated sessions, until the patient reports that urges to engage in the deviant behavior are eliminated.

For example, a patient who is troubled by urges to expose himself might be presented with the following:

You hear the teenage babysitter next door playing outside with the children. You feel the urge to stand in front of a window that faces that house and expose yourself. If you stand on a chair, you can expose your genitals and no one will see your face. You know it is wrong, but the urge keeps getting stronger. You climb into the window and pull down your pants. You hear the babysitter gasp—her voice trembles as she tells the children to get into the house. You feel so good. But before you can pull up your pants, the door opens and your mother screams. "Ben, what are you doing? How could you do this?" She is crying and you struggle to pull up your pants. Soon there is a pounding at your door— and when your mother opens it, still crying and screaming "what's wrong with you," the babysitter is at the door with a policeman. You stand there embarrassed and humiliated as the girl watches you, standing in your underwear, being arrested for exhibitionism. As you are taken away, the entire neighborhood sees you being handcuffed and put into a police car, wearing just your underwear. You are humiliated, your mother is humiliated, and tomorrow everyone will know what a pervert you are.

Olfactory aversion is the pairing of noxious but harmless odors (such as ammonia) with either sexual fantasies or sexual behaviors. It is an application of classical conditioning theory. Typically, the person is presented with deviant sexual stimuli and then inhales the ammonia fumes, which cause burning and watering eyes, runny nose, and coughing. With repeated pairings, the deviant sexual behavior is suppressed, usually within a few weeks (Laws et al., 2001).

Cognitive-behavioral group therapy is the treatment of choice for those who suffer from pedophila. The intervention includes psychoeducational groups, anger management, assertiveness training, human sexuality, communication training, control of deviant sexual arousal, and relapse prevention, in which participants are educated about identifying high-risk relapse situations (Studer & Aylwin, 2006). Cognitive-behavioral treatments include *cognitive restructuring*, in which distorted or faulty cognitions ("I'll never be normal") are identified and more adaptive positive thoughts are substituted ("I can change"). A second cognitive-behavioral treatment is *empathy training*, in which offenders are taught to recognize the harmful aspects of their behavior and put themselves in the place of the victim to build empathy toward the victim. As noted, behavioral and cognitive-behavioral treatments are efficacious, but it is not clear that they produce permanent behavioral change for paraphilias (Laws et al., 2001). Booster sessions are probably needed. In addition, these interventions are only one aspect of an overall treatment plan (Krueger & Kaplan, 2002).

Enhancing Appropriate Sexual Interest and Arousal Sex is a biological drive, and eliminating deviant sexual urges, fantasies, or behavior will be ineffective unless the person finds a more appropriate sexual outlet. To address this dimension of functioning, clinicians utilize interventions such as *social skills training*, in which the person is taught basic social conversation skills, including initiating and maintaining conversations, assertive behavior, and dating skills in order to establish relationships with appropriate adults. When the person with a paraphilia is in an established adult

covert sensitization a treatment that uses prolonged, imaginal exposure to engagement in a sexually deviant act but also imagining the negative consequences that result from it.

olfactory aversion a treatment pairing an extremely noxious but harmless odors (such as ammonia) with either sexual fantasies or sexual behaviors

relationship, the patient's aberrant sexual behavior may severely strain the relationship, particularly if there are legal complications. Therefore, *couples therapy* may be necessary. Finally, people with paraphilias often lack a basic understanding of sexual behavior, particularly appropriate adult sexual behaviors, and treatment may therefore need to include *sex education* (Krueger & Kaplan, 2001).

---

concept CHECK

- Paraphilias are defined as intense sexual fantasies, urges, or behaviors directed toward inanimate objects, situations, or activities.

- *Paraphilia* and *pedophilia* are sexual disorders. *Sexual offender* and *child molester* are terms applied to people whose behaviors involve criminal sexual activities.

- Paraphilias, compared with other forms of psychological disorders, are an under-researched area.

- Behavior therapy is the most empirically supported treatment for paraphilias.

APPLICATION QUESTION In Shakespeare's play *Romeo and Juliet*, some scholars have set Romeo's age as an adult and Juliet is stated to be age 13 (McConaghy, 2001). If Romeo were an adult, would he be guilty of pedophilia? Why or why not?

THE WHOLE STORY: MICHAEL—TREATMENT OF SEXUAL DYSFUNCTION

The Person: *Michael is 21 years old. His first real girlfriend just broke up with him, and he is sure it is because of his inadequate sexual performance. Michael is very shy around girls, and he admits that he does not even know how to talk to them. Furthermore, he has had few sexual experiences. He lost his virginity in the backseat of a car, and he said "it was over before I knew it."*

The Problem: *Until now, his sexual experience consisted of visits to local prostitutes, where he always felt rushed both by the woman and by the thought that he might get caught in a police raid. With his first real girlfriend, he often ejaculated before intromission. His girlfriend kept saying that it did not matter, but he knew that it did. His friends told him to think about baseball when having sex, in an effort to delay ejaculation, but that did not work. Michael was desperate to get help.*

The Treatment Plan: *The psychologist knew that premature ejaculation could* *be treated by the stop-squeeze technique, but Michael did not have a partner. The therapist began by explaining the rationale to Michael and educated him about the normal male sexual response cycle and the four-step process of ejaculation. This was important because Michael needed to learn to recognize the plateau phase in order to implement the procedure correctly. Once Michael understood these biological processes, the therapist taught him to use the procedure himself through masturbation. In session, the therapist discussed the procedure and used drawings to show Michael where and when to squeeze. The therapist developed a self-monitoring sheet so that Michael could track his progress. Michael was instructed to practice the procedure each day, trying to lengthen the time between his initial erection and ejaculation.*

Treatment Progress: *At each treatment session, Michael reported on his progress. In session, the therapist focused on social* *skills training, particularly heterosocial interactions and dating skills. As Michael's confidence grew, he was able to invite a girl to a movie. He did not attempt to engage in a sexual relationship at once, but waited until he felt very comfortable. He continued to practice the stop-squeeze technique and did not visit any prostitutes in order not to impede his progress.*

Treatment Outcome: *After three months of dating, Michael and his girlfriend became sexually intimate. Michael reported that the first time was "not very long"— only about three minutes after intromission. His girlfriend attributed it to the fact that they had had a lot of wine that evening and told him not to worry. Because he did not feel rejected, Michael was able to try again. At the end of treatment, Michael was engaging in vaginal intercourse for about five minutes before ejaculation. He also had increased confidence in his ability to interact socially, not just sexually, with women.*

CRITICAL ISSUES to remember

1. The term *normal sexual behavior* is hard to define. The human sexual response cycle consists of four phases: desire, arousal, orgasm, and resolution. Vaginal intercourse is the most frequently practiced sexual activity. Yet biological (age, sex) and cultural factors play a role in how frequently sexual activity occurs and what type of sexual behaviors are practiced.

2. Gender identity disorder (GID), also known as transsexualism in adults, is a strong and persistent cross-gender identification and persistent discomfort with one's own sex. Transsexualism differs from transvestic fetishism, which occurs only in heterosexual males and consists of sexual arousal that occurs when dressing in female clothing.

3. Sexual dysfunction occurs in both men and women, but the nature of the dysfunction differs by sex. Whereas deficits in sexual performance are most common in men, lack of sexual desire is often the most common complaint among females. There are also differences between the sexes in the degree to which males and females perceive their sexual behavior to be problematic.

4. Sexual dysfunctions may have a biological basis, including hormonal imbalances, physical illnesses, and surgical complications. Psychological factors may also lead to sexual dysfunction and in turn, sexual dysfunction can lead to psychological distress. Treatment is also complex and can include biological or psychological interventions, both of which have established efficacy. However, treatments that work with one sex are not always efficacious for the other sex.

5. Paraphilias consist of intense, persistent, and frequently occurring sexual urges, fantasies, or behaviors that involve unusual objects, situations, or activities. A person who has a paraphilia is not necessarily a sexual offender, which is a term restricted to those who are arrested and convicted of a sexual offense. In some cases, a paraphilia such as pedophilia can result in conviction of a crime. However, those with sexual urges or fantasies to commit acts such as exhibitionism or voyeurism, but who do not act on those urges, have not committed a sexual offense.

6. Psychological interventions are the most efficacious treatment for paraphilias, but many who suffer from these disorders are either reluctant to seek treatment or do not see the need for treatment. Often, they participate in treatment only when required by court order and quit when they are no longer compelled to go. Furthermore, because paraphilias are unusual and often misunderstood, those who suffer from these disorders rarely seek treatment. This makes it difficult to conduct the clinical trials necessary to fully determine the efficacy of these treatments.

TEST yourself

For more review plus practice tests, flashcards, and Speaking Out: DSM in Context videos, log onto www.MyPsychLab.com

1. One of the first formal attempts to study human sexuality using extensive surveys of thousands of Americans was conducted by
   a. B. F. Skinner
   b. Masters and Johnson
   c. Alfred Kinsey
   d. Helen Singer Kaplan

2. Masters and Johnson's studies of human sexuality differed from those of other researchers because they
   a. interviewed adults instead of conducting survey-based research
   b. interviewed couples together instead of separately
   c. observed and recorded psychosexual development and social attitudes
   d. observed and recorded the physical responses of their subjects while they engaged in sexual activity

3. According to contemporary theories, which of the following is *not* considered one of the four phases of the sexual response cycle?
   a. refractory
   b. desire
   c. resolution
   d. orgasm

4. Surveys of sex practices show differences in males and females. Women have a greater
   a. capacity for sex
   b. need for a resolution phase
   c. variety of sex practices
   d. number of fantasies

5. Which of the following statements accurately reflects our understanding of sexual functioning in middle-aged and elderly adults?
   a. Most men and women between the ages of 40 and 49 are no longer sexually active.
   b. Satisfactory sexual functioning is important to most adults over 40.
   c. Middle-aged and older women generally don't regard satisfactory sex as essential to maintaining a relationship.
   d. Men's sexual interest declines sharply after middle age.

6. Which of the following statements best characterizes what we know about the development of sexual orientation?
   a. In cultures that frown on same-sex behavior, homosexual orientation is rare.

b. Worldwide, about 5% of men and women develop same-sex orientation.

c. Sexual orientation appears to be biologically based.

d. There is greater erotic plasticity among men than among women.

7. Congenital adrenal hyperplasia is a hormonal condition in which too much of the hormone androgen is produced during the prenatal period and the first few years of life. This condition causes

   a. transvestism in boys as early as 4–6 years of age

   b. extremely feminine behavior in young boys

   c. hyperfeminine behavior in young girls

   d. early and exaggerated male sex characteristics in both sexes

8. Louis called his co-workers together for a meeting at the end of the week and explained that beginning the following week he would be coming to work dressed as a woman and that he wanted to be called Louise. He described this as the start of a process of treatment for his

   a. homosexual disorder

   b. gender fetish disorder

   c. gender identity disorder

   d. hermaphroditic disorder

9. Larry has been experiencing high levels of stress because of increased layoffs at work. He and his partner Bernard have had a satisfying sexual relationship until recently. Now Larry typically experiences an ejaculation within a minute of initiating sex. Larry is likely to be suffering from

   a. homosexual disorder

   b. gender identity disorder

   c. primary premature ejaculation

   d. secondary premature ejaculation

10. Susan cannot have sexual intercourse with her boyfriend due to pain in the outer part of her vagina. Susan's gynecologist cannot perform a pelvic exam because she cannot insert a speculum without causing Susan extreme pain from muscle spasms. Which of the following disorders is Susan likely to be suffering from?

    a. dyspareunia

    b. dyspepsia

    c. vaginismus

    d. anorgasmia

11. Which of the following statements best reflects what has been learned about sexual dysfunction from population surveys?

    a. Sexual dysfunctions decrease with age for both sexes.

    b. Sexual dysfunctions are rare among young people but begin to appear in middle age.

    c. Only a small minority of the population ever experiences a sexual dysfunction.

    d. Sexual dysfunctions are fairly common, and many people do not seek help for their problems.

12. The sexual dysfunction most often responsive to pharmacologic treatment is

    a. hormonal insufficiency

    b. erectile dysfunction

    c. female sexual arousal disorder

    d. vaginismus

13. Psychosocial treatments for sexual dysfunctions have been shown to be effective. Among these techniques are

    a. sensate focus

    b. the stop-squeeze technique

    c. nondemand pleasuring

    d. all of the above

14. Transvestic fetishism is the desire to dress in clothes of the opposite sex for sexual gratification. This disorder is

    a. diagnosed in men

    b. found in both men and women

    c. common in homosexuals

    d. diagnosed in transsexuals

15. The most common pedophilic acts are

    a. intercourse and rape

    b. voyeurism and frotteurism

    c. incest and use of pornography

    d. fondling and genital exposure

16. The most common age of onset for paraphilias is

    a. adolescence to young adulthood

    b. adulthood to middle age

    c. middle age to later in life

    d. childhood

17. The argument that one of the most frequent reasons people abuse children is that they were abused when they were young

    a. reflects numerous epidemiological studies of sex offenders

    b. fails to consider that the vast majority of abused children do not become pedophiles

    c. fails to consider the changing societal and cultural definitions of child abuse

    d. explains why child abuse is a self-perpetuating problem

18. The device that measures physical changes in the penis when a man is shown sexually arousing or nonarousing stimuli is called the penile

    a. volumetric gauge

    b. tumesograph

    c. photoplethysmograph

    d. plethysmograph

19. Antiandrogen medications are used to treat some forms of paraphilia. Their mechanism of action is to

    a. lower the recidivism rate through selective sedation

    b. decrease the sexual drive by reducing testosterone levels

    c. eliminate recidivism through chemical castration

    d. increase normal heterosexual behaviors by decreasing lutenizing hormone levels

20. Treatments for paraphilias that eliminate or decrease inappropriate sexual arousal include

    a. rational emotive and cognitive-behavioral therapy

    b. social skills training, couples therapy, and sex education

    c. satiation, covert sensitization, and olfactory aversion

    d. stop-squeeze technique and sensate focus

Answers: 1 c, 2 d, 3 a, 4. a, 5 b, 6 c, 7 d, 8 c, 9 d, 10 c, 11 d, 12 b, 13 d, 14 a, 15 d, 16 a, 17 b, 18 d, 19 b, 20 c.

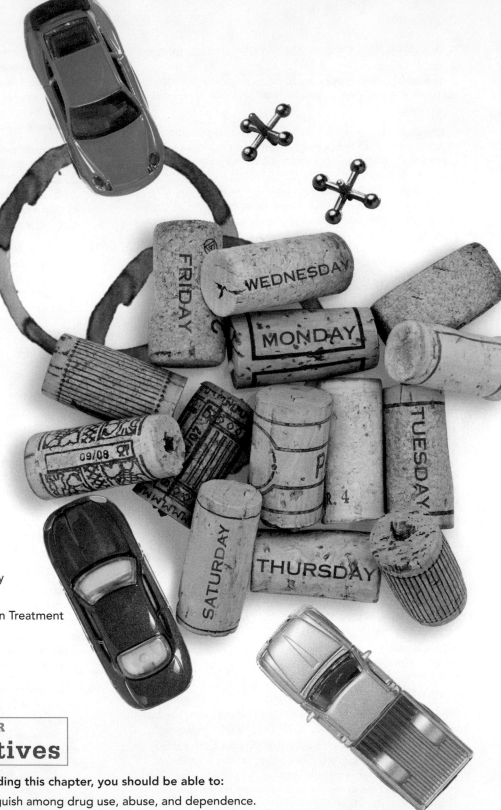

CHAPTER objectives

After reading this chapter, you should be able to:

1 Distinguish among drug use, abuse, and dependence.

2 Understand the principles of tolerance and withdrawal and how they differ across various classes of drugs.

3 Appreciate how various drugs act in the body to produce their characteristic effects.

4 Describe the short- and long-term negative psychological and health consequences of various types of substance abuse and dependence.

5 Understand the contributions of biological, genetic, behavioral, cognitive, and sociocultural theories to understanding substance abuse and dependence.

6 Compare and contrast treatments for various types of substance abuse and dependence.

substance use disorders

Karen wasn't sure this was the life she wanted. Before the kids, she and her husband had a really equal relationship—Scott helped with the cooking, she helped with the cars—but now they had a traditional sex-role relationship, and she felt there was no way out. She agreed to stay home with Danny, age 2, and Timmy, age 6, until they started school, while Scott pursued a partnership at his law firm. Karen was a good mom, but when her third child, Joey, was born, she felt like she was losing control. Making matters worse, Timmy was becoming jealous of the attention his new brother was getting and was becoming a terror on wheels.

Karen tried to talk with her husband, but he didn't understand. Timmy did not talk back to his dad, and when Scott got home from work, Timmy was usually so tired that he'd just sit with dad quietly. When Karen asked for help, Scott agreed, but he continued to work late every night.

Karen tried to talk with her mom and the other moms at the playground, but they rattled off advice that felt very judgmental to Karen. One day after talking to her mom, she was exasperated. She put the kids up for their nap and decided to have a glass of wine to relax. What started out as an "innocent" drink in the afternoon soon snowballed into a full bottle by the time Scott came home. At first she carefully hid the bottles, but she soon realized that he wasn't paying any attention anyway. At this point, she stopped caring what he thought. Wine became her support system.

She rationalized her drinking and took steps to be safe. She did her errands in the morning and only started drinking around noon. However, things got worse after she hurt her back. Her doctor prescribed some Vicodin (a narcotic painkiller) and recommended physical therapy. She passed on the therapy, but Vicodin made her feel as if nothing mattered—and her back stopped hurting! So, still drinking her bottle of wine, she would now also pop a pill or two as needed. Sometimes she would pass out in bed.

One afternoon while she was dozing on the couch, Timmy threw something at his baby brother that cut his forehead. Panic stricken, Karen strapped the kids in their car seats and drove to the emergency room. It was raining and she lost control of the car. When she woke up, everyone was safe, but she was in the hospital with her arm in a sling. She was ok, but because of her blood alcohol content of .12 she was charged with driving under the influence. Scott demanded that she stop drinking immediately. He was surprised to hear her say she didn't think she could stop. He realized that they needed to come together and get Karen professional help.

How Severe Is the Problem?
Use, Abuse, and Dependence

In Karen's case, what started out as one "innocent" drink soon progressed to a serious problem that jeopardized her children's safety. Karen found that she needed to drink more and more—one glass of wine no longer allowed her to relax. Known as tolerance, this is one property of substances that can propel a person from use to abuse and ultimately drug dependence. How does this process occur? Why can some people stop at just one drink while others lack the internal "brakes" that keep them from spiraling into addiction? In this chapter, we discuss how biology, psychology, and culture interact to influence the development of substance abuse and dependence.

Whether the drug is caffeine, nicotine, alcohol, or heroin, most people use substances at some point during their lifetime. **Substance use** refers to low to moderate use experiences that do not produce problems with social, educational, or occupational functioning (American Psychiatric Association, 2000). Drinking caffeinated sodas daily, drinking a beer or two at weekend parties, having wine with dinner, or smoking marijuana occasionally all qualify as *substance use*—although some substances are legal and some are illegal. The definition of use makes no claims as to the legality of the behavior.

The effect of substance use varies from mild (perking up after morning coffee) to extreme, which is known as **substance intoxication** (American Psychiatric Association, 2000). The definition of intoxication includes several concepts. First, intoxication is reversible (one comes down from the intoxicated state) and substance-specific (the features of intoxication vary with the substance ingested). In addition, intoxication results in maladaptive behavioral or psychological changes associated with the central nervous system. Finally, the effects of intoxication emerge during or shortly after drug use. Consider the sports fan who has had too much to drink at a game or someone who is unable to walk a straight line in a sobriety test. These individuals are experiencing intoxication. Intoxication can be an isolated event, or it can be a recurring state in a substance abuse disorder.

Distinguishing between substance use and abuse can be complicated. Indeed, cultural norms vary—what is viewed as use in one culture may be regarded as abuse in another. Even legal ramifications differ across cultures. For example, Table 9.1 presents

Drawing the boundaries between alcohol use, abuse, and dependence requires knowledge of the frequency, duration, and severity of the behavior.

substance use low to moderate use experiences with a substance that does not produce problems with social, educational, or occupational functioning

substance intoxication the acute effects of substance use

TABLE 9.1
Legal Blood Alcohol Limits Around the World

Country	BAC limit (%)
Pakistan, Saudi Arabia	0.00
Norway, Sweden	0.02
China, India, Japan	0.03
Argentina, Australia, Finland, France, Germany, South Africa, Switzerland	0.05
Brazil, Canada, Chile, Fiji, Ireland, New Zealand, Singapore, United Kingdom, United States	0.08

http://www.driveandstayalive.com/articles%20and%20topics/drunk%20driving/artcl-drunk-driving-0005--global-BAC-limits.htm

DSM-IV-TR

Substance Abuse

A maladaptive pattern of substance use leading to clinically significant impairment or distress that can include:

- failure to fulfill major role obligations at work, school, or home
- use in situations in which it is hazardous (e.g., driving an automobile or operating heavy machinery)
- substance-related legal problems
- continued use despite persistent or recurrent social or interpersonal problems caused or exacerbated by the substance use.

Adapted with permission from the *Diagnostic and Statistical Manual of Mental Disorders*, Text Revision, Fourth Edition, (Copyright 2000). American Psychiatric Association.

DSM-IV-TR

Substance Dependence

A maladaptive pattern of substance use, leading to clinically significant impairment or distress accompanied by at least 3 of the following:

- tolerance
- withdrawal
- using the substance in larger amounts or for longer than originally intended
- a persistent desire for the substance or unsuccessful efforts to cut down
- spending significant time trying to obtain the substance
- effects on important social, occupational, or recreational activities
- continued use despite persistent or recurrent physical or psychological problems (such as smoking even though one has lung cancer).

Adapted with permission from the *Diagnostic and Statistical Manual of Mental Disorders*, Text Revision, Fourth Edition, (Copyright 2000). American Psychiatric Association.

the legal blood alcohol limit across a number of countries showing varying tolerances of alcohol behind the wheel.

According to the DSM (see the box "DSM-IV-TR: Substance Abuse"), use becomes **substance abuse** when ingesting the substance leads to disruption in social, educational, or occupational functioning. Examples of disruption include missing class and seeing grades fall because of too much partying; having numerous relationship breakups caused by alienating partners by repeated drug use; or being arrested for drunk driving.

Whereas substance abuse focuses on observable and maladaptive consequences, **substance dependence** goes one step further and includes attention to the physiological actions of the substance (see the box "DSM-IV-TR: Substance Dependence"). Substance dependence most closely approximates the lay term *addiction* and is characterized by two distinct factors, *tolerance* and *withdrawal*.

First, **tolerance** is the diminished response to a drug after its repeated use. This means that over time, a person needs to use more of the drug to achieve the same "high." Karen's increasing wine consumption is an example of tolerance. **Withdrawal** is

substance abuse ingestion of a substance that leads to disruption in social, educational, or occupational functioning

substance dependence a condition characterized by two distinct factors, tolerance and withdrawal

tolerance diminished response to a drug after repeated exposure to it

withdrawal symptoms associated with physical dependence on a drug that occur when the drug is no longer taken

associated with physical dependence on a drug. Once there is physical dependence, attempts to abstain from the drug result in highly unpleasant physical symptoms. Withdrawal symptoms vary by drug class and lead to renewed use of the drug to alleviate the symptoms. At this point, the drug is not only being used to achieve the "high" but also to remove the negative effects of withdrawal.

In addition to tolerance and withdrawal, the behavioral features of substance dependence include using larger amounts than intended; desiring or attempting to cut down; spending time trying to acquire the substance; giving up social, occupational, or recreational activities because of substance use; and continuing use despite known physical or psychological problems caused by or exacerbated by the substance use.

Factors affecting the likelihood that a person will become dependent include the drug's addictive potential as well as user characteristics (what is known as liability to dependence). Some drugs such as heroin and alcohol produce more withdrawal symptoms. Some users are more prone to substance problems because of their genetic makeup, ongoing life stress, or immersion in a subculture that involves drug use (Daughters et al., 2007). Liability to dependence therefore is determined by a combination of genetic and environmental factors. These factors are discussed later in this chapter in the sections on individual substances as well as in the section on etiology.

---

concept CHECK

- Substance *abuse* is ingestion of a substance that leads to disruption in social, educational, or occupational functioning.

- Substance *dependence* includes two additional factors, *tolerance* and *withdrawal*. Tolerance is a diminished response to a drug after repeated exposure to it. Withdrawal occurs after someone becomes physically dependent on a drug, when his or her attempts to abstain produce highly unpleasant withdrawal symptoms.

APPLICATION QUESTION Many students are exposed to underage drinking in college. What factors do you think contribute to whether students engage in that behavior? What are some of the genetic and environmental factors that influence whether underage college drinking becomes a regular event or remains rare event?

Commonly Used "Licit" Drugs

We focus first on three very common legal drugs widely used in our society—caffeine, nicotine, and alcohol. Although there are no formal restrictions on the sale of caffeine, there is some general understanding that it is not a good source of energy for young children. Nonetheless, children are introduced to caffeine very early in life through carbonated beverages. In contrast, there are age restrictions on the purchase and use of nicotine and alcohol, with penalties applicable to both the buyer and the seller. We start with these legal substances as they illustrate the widespread and accepted use of psychoactive substances in our society.

CAFFEINE

"One doppio espresso, one grande latte . . . two shots, one espresso macchiato." Orders like this are heard every morning at countless coffee bars. **Caffeine** is a central nervous system (CNS) stimulant with a kick that boosts energy, mood, awareness, concentration, and wakefulness. Caffeine may be consumed quite safely in moderation to produce these positive effects. Coffee, a robust source of caffeine, has become an important part of our culture and often serves as a backdrop for socializing.

caffeine a central nervous system stimulant that boosts energy, mood, awareness, concentration, and wakefulness

Although less harmful than most other substances, caffeine, like other stimulants, affects multiple organs within the body, and withdrawal after regular use produces short-term effects such as a "crash." There are also long-term effects, including tolerance, dependence, and withdrawal. One diet soda a day can escalate to 10 during exam time to get the same level of alertness. If you then celebrate the end of exams with a back-to-nature camping trip, you might find yourself with a blistering caffeine-withdrawal headache. Caffeine's other side effects include agitation or "jitteriness," headaches, mood lability (changeability), rebound fatigue, and insomnia (Silverman et al., 1992). Although caffeine's precise mechanism of action remains unknown, the neurotransmitters adenosine and serotonin have been implicated in its effect on the brain (Carrillo & Benitez, 2000). Caffeine has a long half life (it stays in the bloodstream a long time). Some people can experience its effects 6 hours or more after their last dose.

Functional Impairment   Because caffeine consumption is almost universal and is considered normal, its potential health effects are often overlooked. Over time, caffeine may contribute to cardiovascular disorders, reproductive problems, osteoporosis, cancer, and psychiatric disturbances (Barone & Grice, 1994; Carrillo & Benitez, 2000; Garattini, 1993; Massey, 1998). For some people, the equivalent of 5 to 8 cups of coffee per day may lead to anxiety and to respiratory, urinary, gastric, and cardiovascular distress (Carrillo & Benitez, 2000). In people who are particularly anxiety prone, even small doses can trigger intense feelings of anxiety, fear, or panic (Charney et al., 1985). Consumption of large amounts of caffeine can produce acute caffeine intoxication, which includes physical symptoms such as restlessness, nervousness, excitement, insomnia, flushed face, diuresis (increased urination), gastrointestinal disturbance, muscle twitching, rambling flow of thought and speech, fast or irregular heartbeat, periods of inexhaustibility, and psychomotor agitation. Although rare and requiring extremely high doses (roughly 50 to 100 8-ounce cups of coffee per day), caffeine-associated death can occur. Unfortunately, this outcome is increasingly likely with the trend toward high-dose beverages that contain caffeine far in excess of a regular cup of coffee. Several deaths due to accidental caffeine supplement overdose have been reported (Holmgren et al., 2004; Kerrigan & Lindsey, 2005; Mrvos et al., 1989).

Caffeine is the most widely used drug in the world. The manner in which it is consumed is often colored by cultural conditions.

Epidemiology   Caffeine is the most widely used drug worldwide. Over 80% of the world's population consumes it daily (James, 1997). In one large epidemiological study ($N = 15,716$), 87% of adults in the United States consumed food and beverages containing caffeine, with coffee (71%), soft drinks (16%), and tea (12%) being the primary sources (Frary et al., 2005). Sodas typically have between 2 and 5 mg of caffeine per ounce, ranging from Coke at the lower end and Mountain Dew at the higher end (ranging from about 25 to 60 total mg in a 12-ounce serving). Tea ranges from about 5 mg per ounce (about 60 total mgs in a 12-ounce serving), coffee ranges from about 7 mg per ounce in instant coffee and lattes to over 20 mg per ounce in stronger brews (ranging from about 80 mg to well over 200 mg in a 12-ounce cup), and espresso, which is about 50 mg per ounce (about 150 total mg in a double 1.5-ounce serving; http://www.energyfiend.com/the-caffeine-database). An emerging trend, especially among adolescent boys and young men, is the use of highly caffeinated energy drinks. Energy drinks typically start at around 10 mg per ounce and can exceed 100 mg per ounce at the high end (often referred to as energy shots, which are recommended for dilution but often are taken in their packaged form). These drinks have now joined coffee as a legal drug that many use at moderate levels to boost energy but that also have the potential to produce negative side effects. They may provide a false sense of wakefulness that might replace adequate sleep, which may have especially problematic health consequences for developing adolescents (http://www.marininstitute.org/alcopops/resources/EnergyDrinkReport.pdf).

NICOTINE

John looked around the group as the therapist said, "Congratulations. If you are going to quit, you'll need to plan for events that trigger your urge to smoke. So I'd like everyone to think about an upcoming situation when you will really need a cigarette." John almost laughed. Quitting smoking would be easy. He wouldn't even be here if his wife, Sandra, who was quitting with him, hadn't insisted John come with her. Sheila described how she liked to blow off steam at happy hour, drinking and smoking the stress away. Oscar described trying to drink his morning coffee without a cigarette. Mikey talked about how his work "smoke break" was the only way he managed to calm down and not strangle his boss. Cheryl, a high-powered lawyer, described how, after a big win, she would sit outside on "her bench" and smoke in celebration. When it was Sandra's turn, John was in a cold sweat and could barely concentrate. All this talk about smoking made him think he needed one right now. When the group leader called his name, he blurted out, "right now, my trigger is right now!"

Especially for people who are genetically susceptible, **nicotine** is a highly addictive drug (Benowitz, 1988; United States Surgeon General's Report, 1988). Its most common source is the plant, *Nicotiana tabacum*, which has been chewed and smoked for centuries. Cigarettes are the most common method of delivery, but other methods such as cigars, pipes, and smokeless tobacco are widely available.

Nicotine can enter the bloodstream via the lungs (smoking), mucus membranes of the mouth or nose (chewing tobacco, using snuff), and even the skin (using a transdermal nicotine patch). Nicotine is both a stimulant and a sedative; its rapid action (8 to 10 seconds) and rapid effect are part of what makes the drug so rewarding or reinforcing. Many smokers report that nicotine produces temporary tension relief and helps with alertness and concentration. Furthermore, nicotine has strong social determinants. Indeed, subcultures centered on cigars and smokeless tobacco are common, and cigarette smoking provides an instant social affiliation, from smokers asking each other for a light at a bar to a few strangers standing outside in the cold, chatting while they smoke.

Nicotine also has pervasive physical effects (see Figure 9.1). It stimulates the adrenal glands, causing a discharge of epinephrine (adrenaline), leading to a feeling of a "rush" or a "kick." This stimulation also leads to glucose release and increases blood pressure, respiration, and heart rate. Nicotine affects the pancreas by suppressing insulin secretion, leading to mild hyperglycemia (elevated blood sugar) in smokers. Central to its highly addictive potential, nicotine releases dopamine, directly affecting the brain's pleasure and motivation centers. The release of dopamine is believed to underlie the pleasurable sensations described by many smokers (National Institute on Drug Abuse, 2001).

Functional Impairment Frequent use of nicotine leads not only to addiction, but also to acute drug tolerance. Highly dependent smokers identify the first cigarette of the day as the hardest one to give up. Overnight, withdrawal has begun, and by morning the "craving" is quite strong. Moreover, smoking cessation leads to withdrawal symptoms that can last up to a month or more, making quitting very difficult. These symptoms may include depressed mood, insomnia, irritability, frustration or anger, anxiety, difficulty concentrating, restlessness, decreased heart rate, increased appetite, and weight gain.

Tobacco use is the largest preventable cause of death in the world (Centers for Disease Control and Prevention, 2002; Fiore, 2000). In 1964, the United States Surgeon General's Advisory Committee on Smoking and Health first identified smoking as a leading contributor to preventable illness and premature death. Subsequent Surgeons' General reports underscore the severe impact of cigarette smoking, including increased risk for many types of cancer, cardiovascular disease, and respiratory illnesses. Smoking during pregnancy is related to pregnancy complications, premature birth, low-birth-weight infants, stillbirth, and sudden infant death syndrome (SIDS) (Office

The plant *Nicotiana tabacum* is dried and processed into cigarettes, cigars, pipe tobacco, and smokeless tobacco for consumption.

nicotine   a highly addictive component of tobacco that is considered to be both a stimulant and a sedative

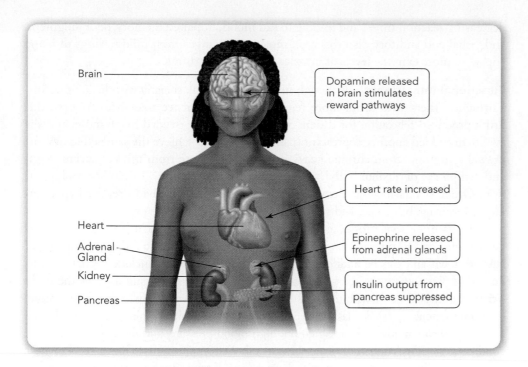

FIGURE 9.1
The Effects of Nicotine on the Body

Nicotine affects many bodily systems, including the brain, the adrenal glands, and the pancreas, influencing the central nervous system, the respiratory system, the cardiovascular system, and the digestive system.

of the U.S. Surgeon General, 2004). Concerted efforts to promote quitting have been partially successful: smoking rates have declined dramatically in the United States in the past 40 years (Centers for Disease Control and Prevention [CDC], 1994, 2004a). Most smokers are aware of the deleterious health effects, and it is estimated that 70% of smokers actually want to quit (CDC, 1994). However, while over 46% make an active attempt to quit each year, only 2.3% achieve sustained abstinence (CDC, 1994).

Epidemiology In the past decades, there have been dramatic declines in the number of people who smoke, although statistics vary by demographic group. In 2004, 21% of adults in the United States smoked cigarettes, 23.4% of men and 18.5% of women. Similarly, the number of high school students who had smoked in the past month declined from 36% in 1997 to 22% in 2003. Despite these promising trends, 44.5 million adults and 3 million adolescents still smoke. Smoking cuts across all ethnic and racial groups and across all socioeconomic strata, although research indicates that African American adolescents start smoking at a later age than other groups (Kelder et al., 2003). There is some evidence that smoking relapse during a cessation attempt is more likely for women and racial/ethnic minorities (Doolan & Froelicher, 2006); however, more recent studies indicate no reliable sex or ethnicity differences when comprehensive behavioral treatments are provided (Velicer et al., 2007).

ALCOHOL

As we saw in the case that opened this chapter, Karen initially used alcohol to relax, but her drinking eventually endangered her own and her children's health. Although many people find a drink stimulating, alcohol is actually a depressant. The active ingredient in any alcoholic drink, *ethyl alcohol*, is quickly absorbed via the stomach and intestines into the bloodstream. Then it is distributed throughout the body and quickly acts to depress the central nervous system. Although alcohol affects many neurotransmitter systems, its effect on receptors in the brain's *gamma aminobutyric acid (GABA)* system are particularly noteworthy. GABA is the brain's primary inhibitory neurotransmitter. So, by increasing GABA firing, alcohol inhibits other brain activity. This explains why alcohol is called a "depressant." Continued drinking leads to a slowing (depression) of the central nervous system, impairing motor coordination, decreasing reaction times, and leading to sad mood, impaired memory, poor judgment, and visual and auditory disturbances. Impairment ranges from mild feelings of being "tipsy" to more extreme levels of intoxication, or being drunk.

Functional Impairment   Although many people drink socially with little or no impairment, others who drink more regularly may experience tolerance. At first, one drink produced relaxation for Karen. Soon, however, she needed much more, and she eventually added another depressant (pain medicine) to achieve the same effect. Withdrawal symptoms from chronic heavy drinking can range from mild to severe. Signs and symptoms of alcohol withdrawal include tremors, anxiety, irritability, and agitation. Other effects include a craving for alcohol, insomnia, vivid dreams, hypervigilance, vomiting, headache, and sweating.

In its most severe form, alcohol withdrawal includes hallucinations (false sensory perceptions) and seizures. Alcohol hallucinations begin within 1 to 2 days of stopping or cutting down and can be auditory, visual, or tactile. They may include a phenomenon known as *formication*, the sensation of having ants or bugs crawling all over the body. Seizures may also occur within 1 to 2 days of cessation. Another withdrawal symptom, **delirium tremens** (DTs), can last up to 3 to 4 days after stopping drinking. DTs are characterized by disorientation, severe agitation, high blood pressure, and fever. This is a severe condition; 5% of individuals die from these metabolic complications (Trevisan et al., 1998).

Depending on its severity, withdrawal can be treated with either careful monitoring (if mild) or the administration of benzodiazepines (see Chapter 4). Benzodiazepines can help decrease neuronal hyperactivity and reduce withdrawal symptoms as well as the risk of seizures and DTs. Alcohol and benzodiazepines have similar mechanisms of action, so individuals become *cross tolerant*—that is, their tolerance to one drug translates to tolerance of the other.

Although alcohol withdrawal can be associated with medical complications, excessive consumption of alcohol can also cause serious long-term health effects. **Alcohol cirrhosis** is a liver disease that occurs in about 10 to 15% of people with alcoholism. Cirrhosis is the slow deterioration and malfunction of the liver due to chronic injury. In the case of alcoholism, the injury is from alcohol exposure. Chronic alcohol consumption can impair the liver's ability to detoxify the blood, leading to the development of scar tissue. In turn, scar tissue obstructs blood flow and impairs the liver's function.

Long-term alcohol abuse also harms the brain. **Wernicke-Korsakoff syndrome** is caused by deficiencies in thiamine secondary to alcohol dependence. The syndrome is characterized by a cluster of symptoms including confusion, *amnesia* (see Chapter 13), and *confabulation*, an adaptation to memory loss in which the individual "fills in blanks" with made-up information. *Wernicke's encephalopathy* includes short-term memory loss, paralysis of the eyes, and unsteady gait. Because people with Wernicke-Korsakoff syndrome lose the ability to learn from experience, they almost always require custodial care, and 80% of individuals with this condition will not regain full cognitive function.

Fetal alcohol syndrome (FAS) (Jones & Smith, 1973), another severe consequence of alcohol use, occurs when a pregnant woman drinks alcohol and it passes through the placenta and harms the developing fetus. Children with FAS have classic identifiable facial anomalies, including short palpebral fissure lengths (distance from the inner to outer corner of the eye) a smooth philtrum (area between the nose and upper lip) and a thin upper lip. There may also be neurodevelopmental abnormalities including small head size, structural brain abnormalities, and neurological problems such as impaired fine motor skills, hearing loss, poor eye-hand coordination, and abnormal gait. As the child develops, there may be other problems, including learning difficulties, poor school performance, and impulse control problems. A primary determinant of the severity of FAS is how much and how frequently the mother drinks (Abel & Hannigan, 1995).

PEARSON

Alcoholism

The Case of Chris

"Toughest thing I ever did was admitting I had a problem."

www.mypsychlab.com

delirium tremens   a symptom characterized by disorientation, severe agitation, high blood pressure, and fever, which can last up to 3 to 4 days after stopping drinking

alcohol cirrhosis   a liver disease that occurs in about 10 to 15% of people with alcoholism

Wernicke-Korsakoff syndrome   a syndrome caused by deficiencies in thiamine secondary to alcohol dependence

fetal alcohol syndrome   a syndrome in babies that occurs when pregnant mothers drink alcohol and it passes through the placenta and harms the developing fetus

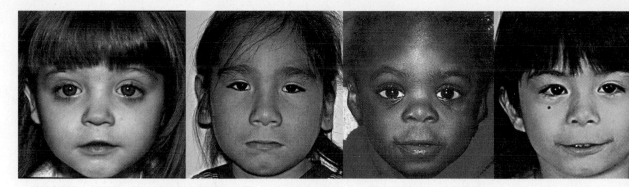

Characteristic features of fetal alcohol syndrome include a short palpebral fissure length (the distance from the inner to outer corner of the eye), a smooth philtrum (area between the nose and upper lip), and a thin upper lip.

Epidemiology, Sex, Race, and Ethnicity   After caffeine, alcohol is the most commonly used psychoactive substance (American Psychiatric Association, 2000). In a large nationwide study using face-to-face interviews of 43,093 individuals in 2001–2002, the prevalence of alcohol abuse was 4.65% and dependence was 3.81%. One intriguing question is whether these diagnoses remain stable over time. One longitudinal survey (Hasin et al., 1990) found that four years after initial diagnosis, 15% of individuals continued to meet the criteria for alcohol abuse, and 39% no longer met the diagnostic criteria for any alcohol-related disorder, although it is unclear whether these people were able to continue with more sustained abstinence. The persistence of alcohol problems seems to be best predicted by the frequency of intoxication and the frequency of heavy drinking (more than 5 drinks a day) (Dawson, 2000).

Considerable differences exist in patterns of alcohol abuse and dependence across sex and racial/ethnic groups. Abuse and dependence are more common among males (6.93%) than females (2.55%), a ratio of about 2.72 (Grant et al., 2004). Although men are at greater risk for alcohol use disorders, women may be more vulnerable to the negative health consequences of heavy drinking (Dawson & Grant, 1993). In terms of race and ethnicity, the prevalence of abuse is greater among whites than among African Americans, Asians, and Hispanics. The prevalence of dependence is higher in whites, Native Americans, and Hispanics than Asians (Grant et al., 2004).

---

concept CHECK

- Caffeine, a CNS stimulant, is the most widely used drug in the world. Some people develop tolerance and have difficulties with withdrawal; caffeine intoxication is rare but possible.

- Nicotine is highly addictive and is considered to be both a stimulant and a sedative. It produces its effects via the release of dopamine in the brain.

- Alcohol is a CNS depressant that affects gamma aminobutyric acid (GABA) receptors in the brain. Extensive alcohol use can lead to serious withdrawal symptoms, such as delirium tremens or DTs, and prolonged abuse can be associated with serious consequences, such as Wernicke-Korsakoff syndrome.

APPLICATION QUESTION   In Western cultures, the use of caffeine, nicotine, and alcohol is common. What do these drugs contribute to our culture, and how would the Western world differ in the absence of these drugs?

Illicit Drugs

Each year, new and often dangerous drugs make their way into the population. Entry points vary from the drug underworld to the doctor's prescription pad—yet the desire for new mind-altering substances continues. Illicit drug use comes with steep emotional, social, legal, and financial costs, but for many individuals, the strong pull of the physiological high and/or the escape from the real world make long-term abstinence difficult. In this section, we begin with marijuana. Although illegal in the United States, it is legal in some other countries, such as the Netherlands, and is continuously under scrutiny for decriminalization, especially for medical use. We then examine other classes of drugs that have primary effects on the central nervous system—stimulants, depressants, and hallucinogens. Finally, we review inhalants and prescription medicines.

MARIJUANA

Marijuana comes from the *Cannabis sativa* plant, which also produces the fiber known as hemp. Its leaves can be dried and used in food and drink, or—most frequently—smoked. Marijuana is the most commonly used illicit drug in the United States (Substance Abuse and Mental Health Services Administration, 2006). The active ingredient is **tetrahydrocannabinol**, or THC. When marijuana is smoked, THC immediately enters the brain, and lasts for 1 to 3 hours (National Institute on Drug Abuse, 2005b). The user usually experiences a pleasant state of relaxation, intensified color and sound, and slowed perception of time. Mild effects include dry mouth, increased hunger ("the munchies") and thirst, trembling, fatigue, depression, and occasional anxiety or panic. The effects of marijuana depend on the dose and the characteristics or sensitivity of the user. Also, THC content varies across preparations and methods of delivery. While low doses are commonly associated with relaxation, higher doses are associated with visual and auditory activity and fascination, increased heart rate and blood pressure, bloodshot eyes, and occasionally anxiety, panic, and paranoia.

marijuana a drug derived from the *Cannabis sativa* plant that produces mild intoxication

tetrahydrocannabinol the active ingredient in marijuana

NORMAL BEHAVIOR CASE STUDY
Marijuana Use—No Disorder

Meghan was from a small town and arrived at the state university for her freshman year. She so wanted to fit in. Her roommate was from New York City—very sophisticated. They really hit it off, even though her roommate disliked sports. That weekend, they went to their first college party. Meghan was amazed to find everyone drinking alcohol and smoking marijuana. Meghan's roommate passed her a joint. Meghan held it for a minute, while everyone stared at her. Her roommate said "Meghan's from a small town—we might have to show her how to inhale." So Meghan inhaled just to fit in. She did not want to make a scene. She partied hard that night and felt so sophisticated. This was college life. Then Meghan started track, and her teammates invited her to a party. Some people were drinking alcohol, but many had soft drinks. No one pushed her to do drugs. Meghan invited her roommate to the track parties, but her roommate found them dull—not enough "partying." For the rest of the semester, Meghan split her time between partying with her roommate's crowd, where she smoked to "fit in" and hanging out with her track buddies, where she drank Coke when she felt like it. At the end of the semester, she moved in with her track buddies, leaving the drugs behind. ∎

ABNORMAL BEHAVIOR CASE STUDY
Marijuana Abuse—Disorder

That summer, Matt went to wrestling camp, and his buddies stayed home. Matt found his passion and his buddies found marijuana. At his welcome-back party, Ronnie offered him a joint. Matt's coach said that he would kick anyone off the team if he found them using drugs, so Matt refused. The guys teased, but they didn't push too hard. During wrestling season, Matt was around less, partly because he was busy and partly because he was afraid the coach would find out about the drugs. Over time, his friends became increasingly angry at Matt's success and his "holier than thou" attitude about drugs. They made a big deal each time he refused. One night Matt couldn't take it any more—he grabbed the joint and inhaled deeply. It didn't taste or feel good, but it was a relief getting everyone off his back. He soon started smoking with his friends and then began using regularly. Soon, he lost his motivation for wrestling. He trained with less intensity and began to feel the physical effects of regular marijuana use. At the State Championships he wrestled someone he had beaten handily at the start of the season. Matt started off well but as the match continued he found himself short of breath. Before he knew it, he was flat on his back. ∎

How does marijuana produce these effects? Its active ingredient, THC, is received by special brain receptors called *cannabinoid receptors*, which influence pleasure, learning and memory, higher cognitive functions, sensory perceptions, and motor coordination (National Institute on Drug Abuse, 2005a). Like most drugs of abuse, THC activates the brain's reward system by stimulating the release of dopamine, leading to the feelings of euphoria associated with being "high."

Functional Impairment Heavy marijuana use results in persistent memory loss; impairment of attention, learning skills, and motor movement; addiction; chronic respiratory problems; and an increased risk of head, neck, and lung cancer. However, THC has medicinal effects as well. It is useful in the treatment of nausea in cancer chemotherapy, glaucoma, and appetite stimulation in AIDS, with new treatment avenues currently being investigated (Felder et al., 2006). (See the box "Research Hot Topic: Medical Uses of Marijuana.")

Research HOT Topic

Medical Uses of Marijuana

Most people agree that illegal substance use is personally and socially hazardous, but the past decade has witnessed an intensified movement in favor of the use of marijuana for medical purposes. Although marijuana has been considered illegal since 1937, its illegal status became official in 1970. In that year, the Controlled Substances Act divided all drugs into five categories. Marijuana was placed in Schedule I—high potential for abuse, no currently accepted medical use in the United States, and lack of accepted safety for use under medical supervision. According to federal law, it is illegal for physicians to prescribe marijuana and other Schedule I drugs to patients, under penalty of prosecution and loss of the license to prescribe drugs.

Some states exempt patients who use medical marijuana with physician supervision from criminal prosecution: Alaska, Arizona, California, Colorado, Maine, Montana, Nevada, Oregon, and Washington. Two states have medical marijuana laws: Hawaii and Vermont. The Hawaii bill protects seriously ill patients who use marijuana for medical purposes from local and state criminal prosecution. The Vermont bill legalized medical marijuana for seriously ill persons suffering from AIDS, cancer, or multiple sclerosis.

Researchers believe that marijuana has many therapeutic applications, including relief from nausea and appetite loss, reduction of pressure within the eye, reduction of muscle spasms, and relief from some forms of chronic pain. Studies indicate that marijuana can be beneficial for symptoms associated with AIDS, cancer, glaucoma, epilepsy, and multiple sclerosis and perhaps chronic pain such as migraine headaches, menstrual cramps, and arthritis. In 1997, the National Institute of Health formed a group of eight clinical trials experts. The group concluded that much of the existing evidence for medical marijuana use was anecdotal and that controlled clinical trials were necessary. They noted that there was enough scientific research to suggest that marijuana might have a positive medical role in some areas.

The value and safety of medical marijuana use is severely compromised when the drug is used in an unregulated manner and in the most common method of administration when not prescribed—smoking. Specifically, smoking marijuana is not particularly safe and can be ineffective for medicinal purposes for several reasons. First, medications work best when they are taken in an appropriate dose. Smoking does not provide a precise and controlled dose, even under the best of circumstances when the percentage of active ingredient is clear. When obtained through nonregulated sources, there is never a guarantee of purity. A more problematic risk is smoking as a means of drug administration. It is a misconception that only cigarettes impair health; many of the same risks, as well as a few others, are evident when smoking marijuana. Ongoing research must address both the benefits and risks associated with marijuana for medicinal purposes. The scientific process should be allowed to evaluate the potential therapeutic effects of marijuana for certain disorders, apart from the societal debate over the potential harmful effects of nonmedical marijuana use.

References: http://www.nih.gov/news/medmarijuana/MedicalMarijuana.htm
http://www.norml.org/index.cfm?Group_ID=3376

Marijuana Policy Project. (2006, February). Medical Marijuana Briefing Paper. Retrieved on March 13, 2006 from http://www.mpp.org/medicine.html.
http://www.medmjscience.org/Pages/reports/nihpt1.html

FIGURE 9.2
Use of Illicit Drugs

During 2006, persons aged 12 or older used a broad variety of different illicit drugs.

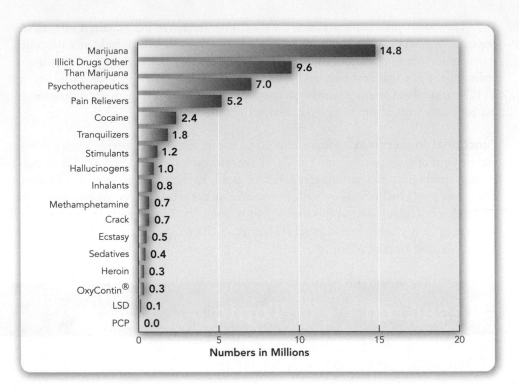

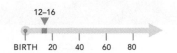

Evidence regarding tolerance to cannabis is unclear. Some studies report tolerance, while others do not report a need for increased doses to achieve the same high. Craving for marijuana and withdrawal symptoms can make it difficult to quit (Budney et al., 2003). Withdrawal symptoms include restlessness, loss of appetite, trouble sleeping, weight loss, and shaky hands, irritability, and anxiety (Budney et al., 2001; Haney et al., 1999; National Institute on Drug Abuse, 2005a).

Epidemiology   Marijuana is the most frequently used illicit substance, with 14.8 million users (6.1% of the population age 12 and older) in one month in 2004 (Substance Abuse and Mental Health Services Administration, 2006) (see Figure 9.2). The average age at which people first use marijuana is about 18 years. More males (8.3%) than females (4.3%) use marijuana (Substance Abuse and Mental Health Services Administration, 2005). Among all illicit drug users in one study, 76.4% used marijuana; 56.8% used only marijuana, 19.7% used marijuana and another illicit drug, and 23.6% used an illicit drug other than marijuana in the preceding month (Substance Abuse and Mental Health Services Administration, 2005). Among U.S. adults (Compton et al., 2004), data from large surveys in 1991 and 2001 indicated little change over that decade (4.0% reported use during 1991 to 1992 and 4.1% in 2001 to 2002). Although the prevalence of marijuana use has remained relatively stable over the past decade, the prevalence of marijuana abuse and dependence has increased significantly, possibly because the potency of THC in marijuana has increased (Compton et al., 2004).

CNS STIMULANTS

Tammy was an adult from an early age. Her mother was an alcoholic who brought home different men. When Tammy was 13, one of the men molested Tammy while her mother lay passed out on the sofa. These experiences took a toll on Tammy. She had trouble making friends, and she was incapable of romantic intimacy. At 17, she worked at a clothing store. There she met Margaret, who was fun and easy going, all the things Tammy wasn't. One night after work, Margaret offered her a ride home and talked her into stopping at this rave. Margaret bought some pills and gave one to Tammy. After about

30 minutes, Tammy felt a wave come over her. The experience was unbelievable. She felt free and wanted to be intimate and close with those around her. The next day she slept through her shift at work. She had already missed several shifts because of her mother, and she was fired. She thought about going back to work to beg for her job, but instead she called Margaret to see if she had any more pills.

Having already discussed two widely used legal stimulants (nicotine and caffeine), we now turn to cocaine and amphetamines, whose commonly reported effects include euphoria, increased energy, mental alertness, and rapid speech. Some people also feel a sense of power and courage, the ability to tackle otherwise daunting tasks, and increased feelings of intimacy and sexual arousal. There are, however, serious short- and long-term adverse effects associated with cocaine and amphetamines, including dangerous elevations in blood pressure and heart rate and cardiovascular abnormalities, potentially leading to heart attack, respiratory arrest, and seizures. These stimulants disrupt the normal communication among brain circuits by increasing dopamine, which leads to elevated mood and increased alertness. In high doses, increased dopamine and norepinephrine can lead to hallucinations, delusions, and paranoia (see Chapter 10).

Amphetamines come in many forms. Legitimate uses include the treatment of asthma, nasal congestion, attention-deficit/hyperactivity disorder (see Chapter 12), and narcolepsy (a sleep disorder). These drugs prolong wakefulness (and thus are sometimes used by people who need to stay awake—pilots on long flights, truckers, students studying for exams) and suppress appetite (and thus are sometimes used by dieters). Amphetamines, also known as uppers, bennies, and speed, are produced in laboratories, and on the street are often cut (mixed) with dangerous toxic substances such as cyanide or strychnine. Three different preparations of amphetamines include *amphetamine* (Benzedrine), *dextroamphetamine* (Dexedrine), and *methamphetamine* (Methedrine). These drugs, swallowed in pill form or injected for a quicker kick, increase the release of dopamine, norepinephrine, and serotonin in the brain.

Other manufactured amphetamines, sometimes referred to as designer drugs, often spread rapidly throughout the community across sex, race, and socioeconomic status. One example, *methylenedioxymethamphetamine* (MDMA), interferes with the reuptake of serotonin. Initially used as an appetite suppressant, the pill form of MDMA (**Ecstasy**) has become a common "club" drug and a frequent trigger for emergency room visits. Similarly, **crystal methamphetamine** (ice, crank) is a form of methamphetamine that produces longer lasting and more intense physiological reactions than the powdered form. It is smoked in glass pipes or injected—the high is rapid and intense and can last for 12 hours or more.

Functional Impairment In addition to increased heart rate and blood pressure, amphetamines can damage blood vessels in the brain, causing stroke. Users can develop paranoid anxiety, confusion, and insomnia—and the psychotic symptoms can persist and recur even months and years after drug use has ended. Over time, users can become violent and aggressive and suffer from emaciation and malnutrition due to appetite suppression. Tolerance develops rapidly, often leading to rapid dose escalation. Withdrawal from prolonged highs produces "crashes" marked by depression, irritability, and prolonged periods of sleep.

Epidemiology In 2006, an estimated 1.2 million Americans ages 12 years and older were using amphetamines and methamphetamines (Substance Abuse and Mental Health Services Administration, 2006). For stimulants, prevalence is approximately equal by sex (0.5% in both males and females in a one-month period) (Substance Abuse and Mental Health Services Administration, 2006). Among persons admitted for treatment of substance abuse in 2001, approximately 6% (98,000 cases) were

amphetamines stimulant drugs that prolong wakefulness and suppress appetite

ecstasy the pill form of *methylenedioxymethamphetamine* (MDMA) a common "club" drug and a frequent trigger for emergency room visits

crystal methamphetamine a form of methamphetamine that produces longer lasting and more intense physiological reactions than the powdered form

considered primary amphetamine users. Most people (71.0%) who are treated for amphetamine abuse do not use another substance. When they do report polydrug use, it is usually marijuana (47%), alcohol (36%), or cocaine (10%). Although data are limited, evidence suggests significantly greater use among whites than other groups (Hopfer et al., 2006).

COCAINE

Louisa was an up-and-coming model. At age 16 she traveled all the time. When she wasn't shooting or preparing for a shoot, she was exercising or working with her tutor trying to keep up with her school work. What worried her most, however, was the pressure to stay impossibly thin. Louisa was constantly hungry. Before fashion week, an older model saw her struggling, smoking cigarette after cigarette to curb her appetite. She introduced Louisa to cocaine, snorting lines in the dressing room saying "This is the only way to get through the week . . . and you won't feel hungry at all!" She was right. For the next two days, Louisa had a lot more energy. She seemed on top of everything else including her school work. And then she crashed. Things spiraled out of control. One night right before a big show, she could barely move from exhaustion.

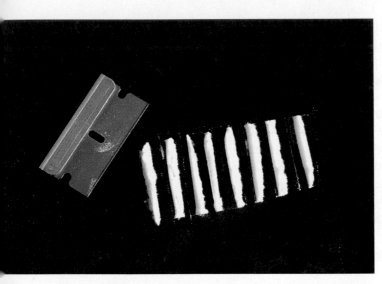

Characteristic lines of cocaine cut with a razor in preparation for inhalation, known as "snorting."

Cocaine, which comes from the leaves of the coca plant, is indigenous to South America. Coca leaves have been chewed for centuries to provide relief from fatigue and hunger. Cocaine's introduction to the United States in the late 1800s was as a legal additive to cigars and cigarettes, and believe it or not, to Coca Cola. Cocaine was also used as a painkiller because of its anesthetic effects. Once its addictive properties became known, this use declined.

The powdered form of cocaine can be snorted or dissolved in water and injected. Crack cocaine is a smoked form of rock crystal cocaine that is highly addictive, delivers large amounts of drug quickly via the lungs, and produces an immediate euphoric effect. The term *crack* refers to the crackling sound it makes when heated (National Institute on Drug Abuse, 2004b). (www.drugabuse.gov/infofacts/cocaine.html).

Functional Impairment   Cocaine is highly addictive. Its powerful stimulant effects are thought to be caused by inhibiting the reabsorption of dopamine by nerve cells. When more dopamine is available in the synapses, there is more stimulation of the brain reward pathways and therefore more positive feelings. When tolerance develops, use increases in order to get the initial euphoric effects. When users take larger doses, their exposure to the drug is increased and they are more sensitive to its dangerous effects, such as anesthetic and convulsant effects. This phenomenon may account for reported deaths after relatively low doses (www.nida.nih.gov/researchreports/cocaine/cocaine.html).

Epidemiology   In 2006, 2.6 million individuals 12 years or older were estimated to have used cocaine and 467,000 used crack (see Figure 9.2). An estimated 1.5 million Americans 12 years or older could be considered to be abusing or dependent on cocaine in the past 12 months (Substance Abuse and Mental Health Services Administration, 2003). This increased to 1.6 million in 2004. More than 90% of cocaine users reported use of marijuana before they tried cocaine. More males (18.9%) than females (11.2%) reported cocaine use, and the same imbalance was noted for crack (4.8% versus 2.5%) (Substance Abuse and Mental Health Services Administration, 2003). The highest rate of cocaine use was observed in American Indians/Alaska Natives (2.0%), followed by 1.6% of African Americans, 0.8% of non-Hispanic whites and Hispanics,

cocaine   a stimulant that comes from the leaves of the coca plant, indigenous to South America

0.6% of Native Hawaiian or other Pacific Islanders, and 0.2% of Asians (Substance Abuse and Mental Health Services Administration, 2003).

SEDATIVE DRUGS

Leila, a nurse, was energetic and loved her work. A fellow nurse suggested having a poker night. Leila had never gambled, but that first night she cleaned up. After doing it again, she found herself enjoying gambling. As a nurse she kept unusual hours and came home late at night stressed and looking for a way to relax. Unlike games with her friends, the internet casino was always available. At first she was so excited about her wins and worried about getting back her losses that she hardly missed the sleep. Soon, however, she was cutting everything and everyone else out of her life. As her losses grew, she opened up new credit cards to get more money to win back her losses. She was convinced that she just needed one good streak to get everything back. When she could no longer open any more credit cards, she followed the advice of another nurse on an Internet gambling site and stole painkillers and Xanax from work to get some quick cash. At first, Leila just took a few pills. After an especially big loss, she felt suicidal. To calm down, she took one Xanax. This helped her walk away from the computer for a while and relax. Over time she needed more and more pills to sell and to take for herself, until the hospital found out what she was doing and fired her.

Sedative drugs include two general classes—**barbiturates** and **benzodiazepines**, both of which are central nervous system *depressants*. This means that their mechanism of action is the opposite of the CNS *stimulants* discussed above. Initially used to treat anxiety and insomnia, barbiturates are now less commonly prescribed than benzodiazepines due to the high risk of abuse, dependence, and overdose.

Barbiturates or "downers" act on the GABA-ergic system in a manner similar to alcohol. Common barbiturates include amobarbital (Amatol), pentobarbital (Nembutal), and secobarbitol (Seconal). They can be swallowed or injected and are often used to counteract the effect of "uppers" or amphetamines. Initial benefits at low doses include disinhibition and euphoria, helping to alleviate feelings of anxiety. In the short term, barbiturate use leads to slurred speech, decreased respiration, fatigue, disorientation, lack of coordination, and dilated pupils. At higher doses, users can experience impaired memory and coordination, irritability, and paranoid and suicidal ideation.

Benzodiazepines were originally prescribed (widely) for the treatment of anxiety; they can be used responsibly and effectively for short-term treatment of anxiety and insomnia. At high doses, the drugs produce lightheadedness, vertigo, and muscle control problems. However, their prolonged use or use without a prescription is of considerable concern. Valium, commonly known as "mother's little helper," would have been a drug that Karen might have been prescribed in the 1960s to deal with the stress of caring for young children. Other benzodiazepines include Xanax and Halcion. Although generally considered to be safer than barbiturates and to have lower potential for abuse and dependence when used as prescribed, they are not completely benign. One powerful benzodiazepine, Rohipnol ("roofies" or "date rape drug"), is available by prescription in many countries but not the United States. This drug is 7 to 10 times more potent than Valium and causes partial amnesia—which means that people given the drug often cannot remember certain events when they were intoxicated. It is this feature and its powerful effects that earned it the reputation of being associated with date rapes.

Functional Impairment If overused, both barbiturates and benzodiazepines can result in oversedation and problems in thinking and interacting with others. Although the drugs are legal if prescribed, their use by those without a prescription or their

sedative drugs barbiturates and benzodiazepines, which are central nervous system depressants and cause sedation and decrease anxiety

barbiturates sedatives that act on the GABA system in a manner similar to alcohol

benzodiazepines sedatives that can be used responsibly and effectively for the short-term but still have addictive properties

misuse by people for whom they are medically inappropriate often leads to theft and other dangerous strategies for obtaining the drug. With barbiturates, tolerance develops rapidly, producing a high risk for overdose. Death results from depression of the brain's respiratory center. Withdrawal from barbiturates produces tremors, increased blood pressure and heart rate, sweating, and seizures. Tolerance and withdrawal also occur with benzodiazepines. Withdrawal mirrors alcohol withdrawal and includes anxiety, insomnia, tremors, and delirium. Although benzodiazepines can be overused with problematic consequences, they have largely replaced barbiturates due to less potential for dependence and fewer side effects.

Epidemiology   The average age of onset for unprescribed benzodiazepine use is around 25 years (Substance Abuse and Mental Health Services Administration, 2005). Because these drugs are prescribed, much of what we know about their abuse comes from hospital admissions. From this perspective, over half of benzodiazepine-related admissions (59%) are female. The drugs tend to be abused secondary to other drugs (usually alcohol), most commonly by whites and by individuals who have higher levels of education. Users of benzodiazepines are more likely to have another psychiatric diagnosis than those who are admitted for abuse of other drugs (http://www.oas.samhsa.gov/2k3/benzodiazepine/benzo.htm). National epidemiological data suggest that approximately 4.2% of males and 7.9% of females reported nonmedical use of anti-anxiety drugs, including benzodiazepines (Simoni-Wastila, 2000; Simoni-Wastila et al., 2004). The preponderance of abuse by women may in part be due to the fact that these drugs are more frequently prescribed to women than to men (Simoni-Wastila et al., 2004).

Barbiturate use in the United States has varied over the past several decades. In 1975, its use in the United States peaked at 10.7%, but by 1992, only 2.8% of high school seniors reported using a barbiturate in the past year. Unfortunately, there has been a resurgence in "popularity" of barbiturates among youth, with the estimated prevalence of use for 12th graders in 2005 at about 7.0%.

OPIOIDS

Dennis had no idea what a panic attack was, but he knew that sometimes his heart would race and he'd think he was losing his mind. Dennis mentioned this to his cousin one day at a family BBQ. Dennis's cousin, who playfully referred to himself as a street pharmacist, suggested that he might have something that would help take the edge off. Dennis wasn't crazy about sticking a needle in his arm, but he trusted his cousin. The drug gave him a calm feeling, making him numb to his usual feeling of hyperarousal.

Opium, used primarily to relieve physical pain, has been used and appreciated in various forms and cultures throughout history. Drugs such as heroin, morphine, and codeine are derived from the opium poppy and are classified as **opioids**. There are also synthetic opioids such as methadone. Thus, this class of drug spans the spectrum from legal and medically prescribed (though carefully controlled) drugs, such as codeine and morphine, to highly illegal and dangerous drugs, such as heroin.

Opioids produce pain relief, euphoria, sedation, reduced anxiety, and tranquility. Their effect stems from activation of the body's natural opioid system. In order to produce their characteristic high, they mimic the effect of the body's natural opioids, *endorphins* or *enkephalins*, which are released in the body in response to pain. Depending on the drug, dose, and method of delivery, opioids produce a broad range of effects. Besides pain relief and sedation, they cause narrowing of the pupils, constipation, flushed skin, itching, lowered blood pressure, slow heart rate, and low body temperature. Opioids can be smoked, snorted, injected beneath the skin ("popped"), or mainlined (injected into the bloodstream).

PEARSON

Substance Abuse

Therapist Jean Obert
"Being addusted to heroin is one of the most difficult things to kick."
www.mypsychlab.com

opioids   drugs derived form the opium poppy, such as heroin, morphine, and codeine

Functional Impairment   Tolerance to opioids develops very rapidly, often after only 2 or 3 days. Users often increase their dosage, and when taking preparations of unknown strength (as in the case of street drugs), they can unwittingly self-administer lethal doses. Similarly, administering a previously tolerated dose after a period of abstinence can lead to death from overdose. (See the box "Real People, Real Disorders: Kurt Cobain—A Tragic End to a Life of Substance Abuse.") Heroin is dangerous not only because of its pharmacologic effects, but also its underworld association with drug trafficking. This can include tainted preparations (to increase volume and profits), medical risks associated with sharing needles, and violence. All contribute to high mortality. Early withdrawal symptoms, which may appear as soon as 4 to 6 hours after stopping the drug, include rapid breathing, yawning, crying, sweating, and a runny nose. Withdrawal symptoms worsen with chronic use and may include hyperactivity, intensified awareness, agitation, increased heart rate, fever, dilated pupils, tremors, hot and cold flashes, aching muscles, loss of appetite, abdominal cramps, and diarrhea (Merck & Co. 1995–2006). Symptoms can continue for 1 to 3 days, complicating the addict's task of quitting.

When opiates are popped or mainlined with shared or unsterilized needles, medical complications may include viral hepatitis and liver damage, infections at the injection site, and transmission of the human immunodeficiency virus (HIV), which

real people, real disorders

Kurt Cobain—A Tragic End to a Life of Substance Abuse

Kurt Cobain (1967–1994) was the lead singer, guitarist, songwriter, and co-founder of the band Nirvana. Haunted by a troubled childhood, Cobain often expressed his past in his aggressive, dark, and distinctive music and was a seminal sound in the grunge rock movement of the late 1990s. Critics of popular music consider Cobain one of the most important musicians of his time. His career ended early; after a long battle with substance abuse, he committed suicide at the age of 27.

In 1986, Cobain began to use heroin sporadically. By the end of 1990, he was addicted. In 1992, he responded to his band's concern about him: "I mean, what are they supposed to do? They're not going to be able to tell me to stop. So I really didn't care. Obviously to them it was like practicing witchcraft or something. They didn't know anything about it so they thought that any second, I was going to die." The same evening, Cobain overdosed.

Over the next two years, the cycle continued: overdoses, hospitalizations, and short remissions were followed by withdrawal symptoms, then subsequent abuse and more overdoses. Believing his last overdose was a suicide attempt, his wife, Courtney Love, called on their close friends to intervene. While Nirvana's manager described

Cobain as "den[ying] that he was doing anything self-destructive," urged by his friends, he entered a detox program the following day. The next night, however, he left the center without telling anyone. On April 8, 1994, Cobain was found dead at his Seattle home with a shotgun at his side. Cobain's death was a result of a self-inflicted shotgun wound to the head.

Sadly, Cobain's story is not unique. About 25% of completed suicides occur among drug and alcohol abusers. The suicide rate of people under age 30 is increasing, and suicide is among the most significant causes of death in both male and female substance abusers. In the months before their suicides, people who abuse substances like Cobain often see a doctor or are hospitalized for psychiatric problems. Helping a person at risk of suicide to get treatment for mental health and substance use problems, as well as increasing social support from family, friends, and health-care professionals, is integral to reducing the risk of suicide.

References: www.cobain.com
mentalhealth.samhsa.gov/suicideprevention/http://www.nimh.nih.gov/publicat/harmsway.cfm

causes AIDS. Lung and immune system problems can develop, as can neurologic problems due to insufficient blood flow to the brain, potentially resulting in coma. Opioid use during pregnancy is particularly dangerous and can result in significant morbidity and mortality for mother and baby (Kaltenbach et al., 1998).

Epidemiology   Patterns of opiate use vary by age, socioeconomic status, education, and type of drug used. Many national surveys that target heroin use may underestimate prevalence because of the difficulty of surveying current users due to living situation, failure to disclose, or health status secondary to the dangers of sharing needles (i.e., HIV, AIDS, hepatitis). Use has been relatively stable since 2002, with only 0.1% of the population considered to be current users (having used heroin at least once in the past month) (Substance Abuse and Mental Health Services Administration, 2005).

Opiates are also commonly prescribed for pain relief (codeine, morphine). However, when not taken as directed, these prescribed drugs can also be abused. Of the 1.8 million hospital admissions for substance abuse treatment in 2003, 18% involved opiates as the primary illicit drug of abuse. Of these 324,000 admissions, 84.3% involved heroin while the remainder were for nonheroin opiates.

LSD AND NATURAL HALLUCINOGENS

Hallucinogens produce altered states of bodily perception and sensation, intense emotions, detachment from self and environment, and, for some users, feelings of insight with mystical or religious significance. The effects are caused by a disruption of the nerve cells that influence the transmission of the neurotransmitter serotonin (National Institute on Drug Abuse, 2005b), resulting in an experience of the world that is very different from reality.

As with marijuana, the perceptual changes are often intensified experiences in which people become fascinated by minute details. Objects can become distorted and appear to shift and change shape. All five senses can be affected. Depending on the situation and the person, such "trips" can be experienced as pleasant and fascinating or deeply disturbing and frightening.

Many naturally occurring and synthetic hallucinogens exist. Naturally occurring hallucinogens include *psilocybin* (magic mushrooms) and *mescaline* (a product of the peyote cactus). The most widely known synthetic hallucinogen, **d-lysergic acid diethylamide (LSD)**, gained notoriety in the 1960s counterculture movement, when the drugs were believed to "expand the consciousness." LSD was first synthesized in the laboratory by Swiss chemist Albert Hoffman in 1938. His self-testing of the compound led to the following observations:

Last Friday, April 16, 1943, I was forced to stop my work in the laboratory in the middle of the afternoon and to go home, as I was seized by a peculiar restlessness associated with a sensation of mild dizziness. On arriving home, I lay down and sank into a kind of drunkenness which was not unpleasant and which was characterized by extreme activity of imagination. As I lay in a dazed condition with my eyes closed (I experienced daylight as disagreeably bright) there surged upon me an uninterrupted stream of fantastic images of extraordinary plasticity and vividness and accompanied by an intense, kaleidoscope-like play of colors. This condition gradually passed off after about two hours. http://www.drugtest.org/library/psylib/hofmann.htm

Functional Impairment   Psychological symptoms such as emotional swings, panic, and paranoia can lead to bizarre or dangerous behavior. Tolerance builds up rapidly but fades after a few days. Hallucinogens do not produce classic withdrawal symptoms and are not physically addictive. However, a condition known as *hallucinogen persisting perception disorder* is a long-term condition that may affect some users. In this condition

hallucinogens   drugs that produce altered states of bodily perception and sensations, intense emotions, detachment from self and environment, and, for some users, feeling of insight with mystical or religious significance

d-lysergic acid diethylamide (LSD)   a synthetic hallucinogen, first synthesized in 1938

people experience perceptual distortions (e.g., hallucinations) long after all traces of the drug have left the system, perhaps as a result of stress or fatigue. The hallucinations and distortions can be persistent or come in periodic short bursts, or "flashbacks."

Epidemiology Unfortunately, information on the epidemiology of hallucinogen use is even more sparse than for other illicit drugs. Data from a national survey indicate that an estimated 934,000 persons initiated use of a hallucinogenic drug in the preceding year (Substance Abuse and Mental Health Services Administration, 2005). Hallucinogen use is apparently more common in males (17.7%) than in females (11.7%) (Substance Abuse and Mental Health Services Administration, 2006).

INHALANTS

The drugs most commonly used by teenagers, **inhalants**, include substances such as cleaning fluid, gasoline, paint, and glue that are used as a source of inhalable fumes (Substance Abuse and Mental Health Services Administration, 2003). Inhalants are attractive because their effect is immediate and lasts between a few minutes and a few hours. The reinforcing effects include rapid onset of sedation, euphoria, and disinhibition, as well as the sensation of heat and excitement believed to enhance sexual pleasure. Their immediate adverse effects include dizziness, drowsiness, confusion, slurred speech, and impaired motor skills. Other immediate, and potentially fatal, effects include irregular heartbeat and respiratory failure (Maxwell, 2001). Inhalants act by quickly entering the bloodstream, dispersing throughout the body, and impacting the central nervous system and peripheral nervous system. Many different chemicals can be inhaled, so it is difficult to generalize about their effect. However, the vaporous fumes can change brain chemistry and may permanently damage the brain and central nervous system. Some of the chemicals that are inhaled include toluene (paint thinner, rubber cement), butane and propane gas (lighter fluid, fuel), fluorocarbons (asthma sprays), chlorinated hydrocarbons (dry-cleaning agents, spot removers), and acetone (nail polish remover, permanent markers).

Inhalants are often the drug of choice for youth of poor socioeconomic status around the world.

Functional Impairment Chronic exposure to fumes, regardless of the type, can cause severe damage to all vital organs, including the brain and bone marrow, leading to compromised red blood cell production and anemia. Inhalants can also have a profound effect on nerves. Nerve damage and other neurological problems may be due in part to the damage that inhalants cause to the protective fatty tissue that surrounds and protects nerve fibers (myelin). Myelin assists with the rapid communication necessary for nerve fibers. Damage can lead to muscle spasms and tremors, causing permanent interference with basic functions such as walking, bending, and talking. In inhalant abusers, magnetic resonance imaging (MRI) studies show observable changes in brain structure, including shrinkage of the cerebral cortex, cerebellum, and brain stem, leading to permanently impaired motor and cognitive abilities (Sherman, 2005). Withdrawal symptoms do occur when people stop using inhalants, including weight loss, muscle weakness, disorientation, inattentiveness, irritability, and depression (National Institute on Drug Abuse, 2004a).

Epidemiology Inhalants are often one of the first illicit drugs used by youth, and together with tobacco, alcohol, and marijuana round out the top four drugs used by youth in America (Centers for Disease Control and Prevention, 2004b). However, data are not plentiful. According to a national survey in 2003, 10.7% of youth aged 12 to

inhalants vapors from a variety of chemicals that yield an immediate effect of euphoria or sedation and can cause permanent damage to all organ systems including the brain

17 years used an inhalant at least once in their lifetime (Substance Abuse and Mental Health Services Administration, 2003). The use of inhalants is more common in youth owing to their easy availability (they often are present in the household, are inexpensive, and can be bought legally) (Centers for Disease Control and Prevention, 2004b).

A comprehensive study in the American Midwest documented clear sex differences in inhalant use, with males more likely to try inhalants (21.7%) and more likely to use them on a monthly basis (9.4%), whereas comparable figures for females were 13.5% and 5.8%, respectively (Ding et al., 2007). These data are consistent with national surveys (Substance Abuse and Mental Health Services Administration, 2006). Consistent patterns have also emerged for ethnicity and inhalant use, with whites and Hispanic youth being more likely to use inhalants and African Americans having the lowest rates (Centers for Disease Control and Prevention, 2004b; Ding et al., 2007).

SEX, ETHNICITY, EDUCATION, AND ILLICIT DRUG USE

Research has been insufficient to provide us with clear information on sex and ethnic differences among individuals with substance use disorders. This is particularly unfortunate as any efforts to prevent or treat substance use disorders need to be tailored to the needs of the population. We do know that the pathway to drug addiction is different for women and men. Although women are less likely to be substance abusers and tend to become abusers at later ages, they often become dependent more quickly and experience more severe consequences of drug use over shorter periods of time (e.g., Hser et al., 2004). Substance use in women is also often associated with relationship issues; women with substance use disorders are more likely to have a partner who also uses illicit drugs (Westermeyer & Boedicker, 2000). They also more commonly turn to drugs when dealing with the break-up of a relationship (Amaro, 1995). Women who use substances also have greater psychiatric comorbidity compared with male substance users, with rates approximating 20% greater than in men (Kessler et al., 1997). The disorders include anxiety, depression, borderline personality disorder (see Chapter 11), and post-traumatic stress disorder (Brooner et al., 1997; Cottler et al., 2001; Trull et al., 2000).

When attempting to understand the role of ethnicity, two problems arise. First, relatively little research has been conducted explicitly on the topic of ethnicity and drug use. Second, in most research, the role of ethnicity is confounded with low socioeconomic status. So the relative impact of low socioeconomic status, poverty, and ethnicity must always be kept in mind when considering these data. Studies do indicate unique risks and needs among many minority individuals who misuse drugs. People from minority groups who reside in inner-city areas are particularly vulnerable to drug use as a result of higher levels of poverty, violence, and availability of street drugs (e.g., Avants et al., 2003). The prevalence of illicit drug use has been reported to differ across racial and ethnic boundaries. Specifically, in 2006, among persons aged 12 or older, the rate was lowest among Asians (3.6%). Rates were 13.7% for American Indians or Alaska Natives, 9.8% for blacks, 8.9% for persons reporting two or more races, 8.5% for whites, 7.5% for Native Hawaiians or other Pacific Islanders, and 6.9% for Hispanics (Substance Abuse and Mental Health Services Administration, 2006). Among youth aged 12 to 17, the rates of current illicit drug use among American Indians and Alaska Natives were around twice the overall rate (18.7 vs. 9.8%, respectively), suggesting a need for prevention and treatment efforts in those populations.

Education level is also associated with illicit drug use—it is lower among college graduates (5.9%) than among those who did not graduate from high school (9.2%), high school graduates (8.6%), and those with some college (9.1%) (Substance Abuse and Mental Health Services Administration, 2006).

- Marijuana is derived from the *Cannabis sativa* plant; its active ingredient is THC; cannabinoid receptors in the brain influence pleasure, learning and memory, higher cognitive functions, sensory perceptions, and motor coordination.

- CNS stimulants including cocaine and methamphetamine prolong wakefulness and suppress appetite. They also influence dopamine levels and produce dangerous elevations in blood pressure and heart rate and cardiovascular abnormalities, potentially leading to heart attack, respiratory arrest, and seizures.

- Sedative drugs include barbiturates and benzodiazepines. They are central nervous system depressants and cause sedation and decrease anxiety.

- Hallucinogens include mescaline, LSD, and psilocybin (mushrooms). They produce altered states of bodily perception and sensations, intense emotions, detachment from self and the environment, and, for some users, feelings of insight with mystical or religious significance.

- Inhalants, which are inhalable vapors from a variety of chemicals, yield an immediate effect of euphoria or sedation and can cause permanent damage to all organ systems including the brain.

APPLICATION QUESTION   Given that the various substances often lead to quite different "highs," what factors might influence drug choice across individuals?

Etiology of Substance-Related Disorders

Friends and family often cannot understand why someone continues to use drugs when so much is at stake. A husband whose marriage is in jeopardy apparently "chooses" to return to drinking knowing divorce will be the consequence. A man who has had one warning at work for a positive urine screen smokes marijuana on a week night knowing that another positive test means he's out of work. A pregnant woman continues to smoke even while reading the warning label on the cigarette pack. What drives people to make these self-destructive choices? They were once blamed on moral weakness or depravity, but today our understanding has become increasingly sophisticated and acknowledges the contribution of biological, behavioral, and sociocultural factors.

BIOLOGICAL FACTORS

Although the impact of social factors such as poverty and peer influences on drug use is often emphasized, biological influences also affect drug use. In order to understand the biology of substance use, one must appreciate not only the effect of each substance on biology, but also the effect of an individual's biology on his or her potential to abuse alcohol or drugs.

Family and Genetic Studies   A substantial body of family, twin, adoption, and molecular genetic research has determined that both genes and environment affect the likelihood of substance abuse. After analyzing more than 17,500 MZ and DZ twin pairs from 14 different studies, researchers concluded that both genetic and environmental factors influence whether you ever start smoking, whether you keep smoking, and whether you become dependent on nicotine (Sullivan & Kendler, 1999). Environmental factors seem to be particularly important in determining whether a person starts smoking (especially among adolescents), and genetic factors are more prominent in influencing whether the smoker progresses to nicotine dependence. In addition, studies are underway to identify areas of the genome and specific susceptibility genes that may be important in nicotine dependence (Gelernter et al., 2004; Straub et al., 1999) Most genetic association studies have examined the dopaminergic system. Identified associations include dopamine receptor genes, transporter genes, and other genes in the dopaminergic system, but not all results have been replicated.

For alcohol dependence, in both men and women, genetic factors account for about 50 to 60% of the variance in liability (Prescott, 2001). The search for candidate genes has focused on many systems including the dopamine, serotonin, and GABA pathways. Studies are underway to further explain how genes influence alcohol dependence. It is perhaps no coincidence that some overlap has been observed in the genes that influence both nicotine and alcohol dependence. Indeed, both disorders often co-occur, and at least some of the same genes may influence the risk of developing each type of dependence (Grucza & Beirut, 2007).

Family, twin, and adoption studies are more difficult to conduct with illicit drug users because people who abuse substances are reluctant to report their use and to participate in research. However, we do know that genetic factors play a substantial role. In a large Norwegian twin study, Kendler et al. (1997) reported heritability estimates for a range of illicit drug use (e.g., cannabis, stimulants, opiates, cocaine, and psychedelics) from 58 to 81%. The remaining variance was attributable to individual-specific environmental effects.

What remains unknown is precisely what is inherited. We have not yet identified specific genes to explain why some people become addicted to substances while others do not. Although the complete picture remains unclear, neurobiology, cognition, personality, and behavior may all contribute to addiction liability.

Neurobiology   From a neurobiological perspective, alcohol and drugs act on the part of the brain that is involved with processing pleasurable feelings (the reward system). The reward circuitry includes the ventral tegmental area and the basal forebrain (see Figure 9.3). By using neuroimaging technology, we can observe how this pathway gets activated in response to drug administration. Importantly, although dopamine is commonly considered the "pleasure" neurotransmitter, other transmitters are also involved in the development and maintenance of addictive behaviors including the opioid, serotonergic, and GABA systems.

FIGURE 9.3
The Brain's Reward System

The dopaminergic system is the primary reward system in the brain. Major structures in the system are highlighted, including the ventral tegmental area (VTA), the nucleus accumbens, and the prefrontal cortex. Information travels from the VTA to the nucleus accumbens and then up to the prefrontal cortex.

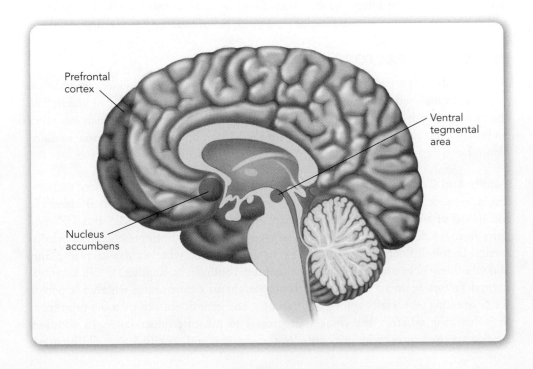

The endogenous opioid system is clearly involved in the reinforcing effect of opiates, as well as that of alcohol and nicotine. This system is directly involved in how pleasurable we perceive the drug to be. As we will see in the treatment section, administering an *opiate receptor antagonist*, which blocks the positive effect of the drug, is effective in decreasing alcohol use in humans (Garbutt et al., 1999). Serotonin appears to be associated with alcohol use (LeMarquand et al., 1994) and may also be associated with the reinforcing properties (positive effects) of cocaine (White & Wolf, 1991). Sedative drugs may act primarily through the GABA system.

Thus, several neurotransmitters are involved with the experience of reinforcement and reward associated with drug and alcohol use. In addition, genetic and environmental factors may combine to determine who is most vulnerable to the lure of such rewards. One hypothesis is that people at risk for drug and alcohol dependence have deficits in their brain reward pathway. One example is a person with "low dopamine or hypodopaminergic" traits, meaning that the brain of such a person requires a dopamine "fix" to feel good (Blum et al., 2000). This deficit could lead the person to seek a drug that would provide that good feeling. Maladaptive behaviors that could develop in an attempt to boost dopamine include addictive, impulsive, and compulsive behaviors. Although further research is required to verify this model, conceptualizing substance use as the result of a chronically underrewarded brain system can be a useful way for family and friends to understand the challenges of abstaining from alcohol and drugs. It also may help in developing approaches to treatment for substance dependence that focus on finding alternative rewarding experiences to replace those provided by drugs.

PSYCHOLOGICAL FACTORS

Although biology plays a central role, psychological factors also influence critical aspects of drug use, such as the decision to try a drug (initiation), the decision to continue using the drug, the frequency with which a drug is used, and cessation of drug use.

Behavioral Factors—Drugs as Reinforcers Drugs are reinforcing in several ways, and operant conditioning helps explain the role of drugs as reinforcers. First, drug-induced euphoria produces positive physical feelings and increases the likelihood that the drug will be used again. This is positive reinforcement. Drug use is also maintained by negative reinforcement, in which repeated drug use removes an unpleasant state. If you are feeling tired and lethargic and grabbing a cup of coffee removes that lethargic state, this is negative reinforcement. Positive reinforcement processes are more directly implicated in the initial stages of addiction, with negative reinforcement mechanisms playing an increasingly important role as addiction progresses.

Conditioning through positive or negative reinforcement involves more than the simple act of using the drug. Environmental aspects such as settings in which the drugs are taken, the people with whom drugs are used, or the paraphernalia used to administer the drugs themselves become cues (signals) to begin drug use (Caprioli et al., 2007). This is why, for example, some people who are trying to quit smoking say, "I do OK till I go into a bar—once I start to drink, I really need a cigarette." This fits well with classical conditioning models of substance use (Domjan, 2005). In these models, external stimuli that have been paired with drug use produce some of the same bodily sensations that previously have been caused by the drug itself (i.e., the conditioned and unconditioned responses are similar). In this way, stimuli that previously had signaled the arrival of a drug (the sight of a person or passing a particular street corner) seem to set off a whole host of feelings and reactions that trigger drug use. In the case of drug-compensatory conditioned responses, regulatory bodily changes occur in the presence of conditioned stimuli (e.g., drug paraphernalia, fellow drug users) to counteract the anticipated effects of drugs or alcohol (Siegel et al., 2000). If the individual does not engage in substance use following these compensatory bodily changes, he or she feels considerable pain and discomfort (i.e., withdrawal). As a result, the individual may engage in substance use as a form of escape or avoidance from withdrawal symptoms (Domjan, 2005).

Laboratory paradigms can test the reinforcing effects of various drugs from both operant and classical conditioning perspectives. For example, laboratory animals can be given either free access to alcohol or drugs, or can be trained to work (press a lever) in order to receive a drug. Changing the reinforcement schedule (free versus work) helps the researcher determine how reinforcing the drug is to the animal, allowing comparisons of the relative reinforcing value of two drugs, for example, alcohol versus nicotine. Another approach—*conditioned place preference*—initially exposes the animal to two distinct but neutral environments (cage A or cage B). Then a drug is repeatedly paired with one of the environments (cage A, for example). After the conditioning trials, the amount of time the animal spends in the "drug" environment helps establish its positive effects.

Cognitive Factors   Cognitive theories are based on the premise that how a person interprets a situation influences the decision to use a drug (Beck et al., 1993). A social setting may activate the thought, "I am much more relaxed after I have a beer," or "A line of cocaine will make me more sociable," and make the person more likely to use the substance. Cognitions can also affect a person's reaction to physiological symptoms associated with anxiety and craving (Beck et al., 1993). A thought such as "I cannot stand not having a cigarette" will increase awareness of cravings and enhance the reaction when craving occurs.

Based in social learning theory (Bandura, 1977a, 1977b), Bandura's social cognitive approach (Bandura, 1999) explores biased belief systems that maintain substance abuse. Briefly, substance use disorders are initiated and maintained by positive drug outcome expectancies (e.g., this drug will make me feel good), minimal negative expectancies (e.g., I have never gotten caught), and poor self-efficacy beliefs regarding one's ability to cope without drugs (e.g., I don't think I can survive another day of school without marijuana). Although empirical studies have demonstrated a relation between positive outcome expectancies and substance use, such approaches rely on self-report of cognition, which is subject to bias.

Behavioral and cognitive theories focus on how expectations of outcome are associated with actual outcomes (i.e., relaxation, pleasure). The associations arise directly from the drug's effects as well as from environmental factors that are paired with those positive feelings. Repeated exposure to the drug and the associated cues biases the information that you recall about drug use (i.e., you remember the buzz but not the hangover) (McCusker, 2001). Lapses and relapses occur when the cues for use outweigh the positive features of abstinence (e.g., keeping a relationship).

SOCIOCULTURAL, FAMILY, AND ENVIRONMENTAL FACTORS

Among the factors associated with substance abuse, sociocultural dimensions are critical. Social, family, and environmental variables all combine with genetic predisposition to contribute to substance-related disorders. Many researchers have studied the contribution of family, peer, and socioeconomic factors to the development of substance-related disorders. In studies of both adolescents and adults, family and peer influence (Wang et al., 2007), trauma (Wills et al., 2001), and economic factors (Black & Krishnakumar, 1998; Boles & Miotto, 2003) have all demonstrated an association with increased substance use and abuse. Although these relationships highlight the importance of environmental variables, the exact manner in which they interact with genetic predisposition remains unknown.

Cultural, family, and social factors also may buffer or protect against substance abuse. The use of alcohol and nicotine has been found to be strongly and inversely related to dimensions of religiosity (Kendler et al., 1997). Although these relationships—both risk and protective—highlight the role of environmental variables, our understanding demands an integrated perspective on the roles of genes and environment. However, it is also important to consider that substance use may play an important role in some cultures.

DEVELOPMENTAL FACTORS

Many adolescents experiment with drugs, but most do not progress to abuse or dependence (Newcomb & Richardson, 1995). Earlier age of substance use initiation and heavy use during adolescence are two risk factors (Kandel & Davies, 1992). Further, drug-related problems (i.e., experiencing some symptoms without meeting full diagnostic criteria) in adolescence predict future substance use disorders, elevated levels of depression, and antisocial and borderline personality disorder symptoms (see Chapter 11) by age 24 (Rohde et al., 2001).

Drug involvement is typically progressive, beginning with substances that are legal for adults (e.g. alcohol, nicotine), followed by marijuana, and then other illicit drugs (Anthony & Petronis, 1995). For this reason some argue that adolescent marijuana use is a gateway to other drug use, but this statement often is misinterpreted. Marijuana is the initial illicit drug used before the use of other more harmful drugs (Daughters et al., 2007). However, "gateway" is usually interpreted to mean that marijuana use somehow precipitates the use of other drugs. Precipitating factors might include environmental factors, such as increased access to other drugs, or pharmacological factors, in which case marijuana use might make one vulnerable to developing dependence on other drugs. It is also important to note that many people never "graduate" past marijuana at all and others may briefly experiment with other drugs but not progress to regular use (Tarter et al., 2006).

Regardless of whether marijuana is a gateway drug, more direct developmental consequences are associated with its use. Any drug can have damaging effects if it is used chronically, with biological consequences such as compromised brain development. There are also social consequences such as "arrested development," where normal developmental experiences and growth opportunities may be missed due to excessive marijuana use. Many individuals who use substances throughout their adolescence will simply stop using on their own as they enter adulthood. For those who reach the point of substance dependence, however, recovery is more difficult even with treatment. For this reason prevention efforts are especially relevant for adolescents. The most effective approaches focus on skills-based programs as opposed to providing information or using scare tactics (Nation et al., 2003).

Low socioeconomic conditions and the absence of alternative reinforcers can increase the risk of engaging in substance abuse.

concept CHECK

- Genetic factors contribute to alcohol and drug use disorders, although the specific way in which genes influence substance abuse remains unknown.

- Most drugs of abuse either directly or indirectly stimulate the "reward center" of the brain, located in the ventral tegmental area.

- Although dopamine is often highlighted as the neurotransmitter involved with pleasure or reward, the serotonergic, GABA, and opioid systems are also involved in the experience of reward associated with drug use.

- Euphoria, excitement, relaxation, and feelings of intimacy all are part of the positive reinforcement that may be experienced when using illicit drugs.

- Cognitive factors, including expectancies and self-efficacy, influence a person's ability to remain drug-free.

APPLICATION QUESTION Although we discuss how genes and environment interact to influence the risk for drug abuse, can you describe a situation in which someone who is at low genetic risk might develop drug abuse solely due to environmental exposures? Similarly, can you describe a scenario in which someone with very high genetic liability would never develop a drug abuse problem?

Treatment of Substance Abuse and Dependence

The choice of treatment is based on several factors, including which drug is being abused and the person's particular characteristics and resources. Although many factors determine treatment success, treatment should be multifaceted and individually tailored. Medical treatment both for detoxification and for reduction of substance cravings and use may be useful, but the best evidence is for behavioral treatment approaches. For these disorders, treatment should be as intense and long lasting as possible. For severe substance use problems, residential treatment may help people recover away from potential substance use triggers. Less intensive options, such as day hospitalization or outpatient treatment, are also possible. Although treatment is available across all ages and social strata, there is evidence that minority individuals from low-income settings sometimes have difficulty finding adequate specialized treatments. We will cover the treatment of substance abuse broadly, highlighting evidence-based approaches when they exist.

Judging the effectiveness of an intervention is complex. For some drugs, such as heroin and amphetamines, the goal might be total abstinence and no relapse. For other drugs, such as alcohol, some researchers have argued that drinking moderately, and in a controlled way, may be an acceptable goal (see the box "Examining the Evidence—Controlled Drinking?," page 326). Thus, evaluating treatment efficacy can be daunting—especially when comorbid psychopathology, or legal or financial complications, may interfere with treatment success.

Thirteen principles of effective treatment must be considered before deciding on a specific treatment approach. Figure 9.4 presents these guiding principles and provides a framework for approaching intervention as well as a glimpse into the complexity of treating these often intractable disorders. Keeping these critical factors in mind, we will now explore the various types of interventions.

THERAPIES BASED ON COGNITIVE AND BEHAVIORAL PRINCIPLES

Interventions based on cognitive and behavioral principles are efficacious in treating substance use (Dutra et al., 2008). Although we will cover several different approaches in this section, it is important to recognize that each strategy targets the function of substance use and uses interventions that focus on the cognitive, behavioral, and or environmental factors maintaining substance use.

FIGURE 9.4
Principles of Effective Treatment for Substance Abuse

Because people abuse so many different substances and people who abuse substances have so many different characteristics, substance abuse treatment must be multifaceted.

Adapted from the National Institute on Drug Abuse (2000)

1. No single treatment is appropriate for all individuals.

2. Treatment needs to be readily available.

3. Effective treatment attends to multiple needs of the individual, not just his or her drug use.

4. An individual's treatment and services plan must be assessed continually and modified as necessary to ensure that the plan meets the person's changing needs.

5. Remaining in treatment for an adequate period of time is critical for treatment effectiveness.

6. Counseling (individual and/or group) and other behavioral therapies are critical components of effective treatment for addiction.

7. Medications are an important element of treatment for many patients, especially when combined with counseling and other behavioral therapies.

8. Addicted or drug-abusing individuals with coexisting mental disorders should have both disorders treated in an integrated way.

9. Medical detoxification is only the first stage of addiction treatment and by itself does little to change long-term drug use.

10. Treatment does not need to be voluntary to be effective.

11. Possible drug use during treatment must be monitored continuously.

12. Treatment programs should provide assessment for HIV/AIDS, hepatitis B and C, tuberculosis and other infectious diseases, and counseling to help patients modify or change behaviors that place themselves or others at risk of infection.

13. Recovery from drug addiction can be a long-term process and frequently requires multiple episodes of treatment.

References

http://www.springerlink.com.libproxy.lib.unc.edu/content/lx2823g88243520t/fulltext.pdf
http://www.nida.nih.gov/PODAT/PODATindex.html

Avoidance of the Stimulus   In some treatments for substance abuse, people may be instructed to avoid stimuli that are related to past drug use (e.g., fellow drug users, drug paraphernalia) (Read et al., 2001). Evidence for this strategy comes from studies of returning Vietnam veterans who were addicted to heroin while in Vietnam and treated before returning home (Robins & Slobodyan, 2003). The rate of relapse for these soldiers was significantly less than for comparable groups of civilians whose experience with heroin was on their home territory. One reason for the reduced relapse in veterans may have been their removal from the environment in which heroin use occurred. Although avoidance of drug-related stimuli can prevent the occurrence of cravings and relapse, many remain skeptical about the value of this approach. Long-term avoidance of all drug cues is virtually impossible for most people, and complete avoidance of drug-related stimuli fails to teach individuals more adaptive behaviors that are incompatible with taking drugs (Rohsenow et al., 1990).

Relapse prevention A widely used cognitive-behavioral intervention is **relapse prevention (RP)**, (Marlatt & Gordon, 1985). RP uses *functional analysis* (see Chapter 3) to identify the antecedents and consequences of drug use and then to develop alternative cognitive and behavioral skills to reduce the risk of future drug use. Working together, the therapist and patient identify high-risk situations and the (1) trigger for that situation, (2) thoughts during that situation, (3) feelings experienced in response to the trigger and thoughts, (4) drug use behavior, and (5) positive and negative consequences of drug use. After analyzing this behavior chain, the therapist and patient develop strategies for altering thoughts, feelings, and behaviors to help avoid or manage situations that threaten the patient's commitment to abstinence (Wheeler et al., 2006).

In this model a *lapse* is a single instance of substance use and a *relapse* is a complete return to pretreatment behaviors. A core feature of RP, **abstinence violation effect**, focuses on a person's cognitive and affective responses to engaging in a prohibited behavior. How a person responds to the lapse, and not the lapse itself, determines whether the lapse becomes a relapse (Collins & Lapp, 1991; Curry et al., 1987; Larimer et al., 1999; Shiffman et al., 1997). For example, if after having one drink the recovered alcoholic says, "I'm a failure, I'm an incurable addict, I may as well give up," his chances of progressing to a relapse are greater than someone whose response is "I had one drink, but that doesn't mean I have to have two. I can stop now, pour the rest of this away and still be successful in my commitment to quit." The abstinence violation effect acknowledges that a person can have positive affective responses to a lapse independent of the cognitions (e.g., "that scotch felt good going down") (Hudson et al., 1992; Ward & Hudson, 1996). Attention to these cognitions is essential to successful relapse prevention. In other words, we cannot ignore the fact that drug use simply might be pleasurable. Acknowledging these positives can be explored in functional analysis or problem-solving therapy, focusing both on finding other pleasurable activities and other strategies aside from seeking pleasure to cope with negative events.

MOTIVATIONAL ENHANCEMENT THERAPY

Despite the severe impairment in social and occupational functioning that substance abuse causes, a drug's reinforcing effect can be so strong that the desire to use it overshadows any negative consequence. Two critical questions are how to motivate people to enter treatment, and how to tailor treatment to the motivational level of the individual. The **transtheoretical model** (TTM) proposes a five-stage sequential model of behavioral change (Prochaska & DiClemente, 1983). *Precontemplation* is characterized by limited awareness of the problem, few emotional reactions to substance abuse, and resistance to change. Individuals in the *contemplation* stage are more aware of the problem and weigh the positive and negative aspects of their substance abuse. The *preparation* stage is marked by a decision to take corrective action (within the next month), and the *action* stage is characterized by actual attempts to change environment, behavior, or experiences. Once entering the *maintenance* stage, individuals are acquiring and engaging in behaviors that are designed to prevent relapse. Evidence strongly supports this model and its relevance for treating substance use disorders (Migneault et al., 2005).

Stages of Change and Motivational Enhancement Therapy (MET) Motivational interviewing begins by identifying each person's place on the TTM model as the entry to motivate people to change. This approach differs greatly from more traditional approaches that are more confrontational and require a patient to be ready to quit for therapy to proceed. Motivational interviewing (Miller, 1983; Miller & Rollnick, 1991) uses principles of motivational psychology to produce rapid, internally motivated change and to mobilize the patient's own resources for change. This may include focusing on patient strengths as opposed to weaknesses, and getting the patient to

relapse prevention treatment approach that uses functional analysis to identify the antecedents and consequences of drug use and then develops alternative cognitive and behavioral skills to reduce the risk of future drug use

abstinence violation effect the core feature of relapse prevention, which focuses on a person's cognitive and affective responses to re-engaging in a prohibited behavior

transtheoretical model a five-stage sequential model of behavioral change

collaborate in the selection of goals and how to achieve them. The goal of MET is to help the individual move through the stages of change swiftly and effectively in order to achieve sustained treatment response. MET can be used as a singular treatment or as preparation for other interventions. It is effective for adults across a wide range of substances (Tait & Hulse, 2003), but may be especially relevant for adolescents where ambivalence about abstinence may be more common (Grenard et al., 2006; Tevyaw & Monti, 2004).

Skills training Skills training is an important part of cognitive-behavioral therapy. Skills training approaches are based on the idea that substance users may lack some of the basic skills that are necessary for everyday coping. For this reason, these approaches are sometimes called coping skills interventions. Approaches targeting coping and social skills training are among the most widely used (O'Leary & Monti, 2002). According to this approach, interpersonal, environmental, and individual skill deficits pose a challenge to sobriety, and the goal is to teach the basic skills that enable substance users to manage problematic aspects of their life. The Community Reinforcement Approach (Hunt & Azrin, 1973; Meyers et al., 2003) is based on the same principles and includes a broad range of skills training including vocational counseling, but is especially targeted at identifying and building the substance user's social network and other support systems. Data support this approach both as a stand-alone treatment and as an adjunct to medication and other treatment approaches (Read et al., 2001).

Although complete abstinence is a goal of most approaches, treatments for alcoholism such as behavioral self-control training focus on strategies to help the individual control alcohol use. Strategies include goal setting, self-monitoring, efforts to limit use, rewards for achieving goals, functional analysis of drinking situations, learning alternate coping skills, and relapse prevention. Considerable evidence supports the use of this approach (Walters, 2000).

Behavioral therapies based on classical and operant conditioning Although many interventions include both behavioral and cognitive components, several are rooted more specifically in behavior theory. Some behavioral interventions are focused on classical conditioning and center on the physiological aspects of substance use. One prominent example is **aversion therapy** (also known as aversive conditioning). As we have noted, in most cases substance use is associated with positive sensations. In aversion therapy, drug or alcohol use is paired repeatedly with an aversive stimulus (e.g., electric shock) or images (e.g., having patients imagine unpleasant images each time they visualize drug use). Although questions remain regarding its efficacy, especially when used alone, it may be an important element of a comprehensive treatment program (Howard et al., 1991; Rimmele et al., 1995; Upadhyaya & Deas, 2008). Similarly, behavioral interventions such as relaxation training and biofeedback can help the individual minimize and overcome physiological urges to use substances as well as reduce stress and tension for which substance use may be a coping strategy.

Some behavioral interventions focus more directly on operant conditioning. For example, inpatient and residential treatment programs (and some outpatient programs) implement **contingency management approaches** (Prendergast et al., 2006) in which rewards (either concrete reinforcers such as money or intangible reinforcers such as program privileges) are provided for treatment compliance, such as negative urine screens for drugs. Compared with 12 weeks of usual treatment alone, adding contingency management for methamphetamine users resulted in less drug use and longer periods of abstinence (Roll et al., 2006). This finding suggests that contingency management holds promise as a component of treatment for methamphetamine use.

aversion therapy a treatment approach in which drug or alcohol use is paired repeatedly with an aversive stimulus or images

contingency management approach treatment approach in which rewards are provided for treatment compliance

Group meetings help people struggling with substance abuse find support and accountability.

Twelve-Step Approaches   If you've ever seen a discreet advertisement for a meeting of "Friends of Bill W," you saw a notice for an Alcoholics Anonymous (AA) meeting. Established in 1935 by "Bill W." Wilson and Robert Hilbrook Smith, AA's twelve-step approach (see Figure 9.5) is based on the need for abstinence. It begins with the realization that the individual is powerless over the addiction, and it provides a structured approach to remaining sober. There are regular meetings and a sponsor who can be called if a member is feeling unable to maintain sobriety or is in need of support. Acknowledgment is made for each year of sobriety, and social support is crucial. Based on the popularity of AA, additional twelve-step approaches have been developed, including NA (Narcotics Anonymous) and OA (Overeaters Anonymous).

You can see the conflict between behavioral and cognitive-behavioral approaches, which focus on developing skills to control addiction, and the twelve-step approach, which emphasizes an unmanageable life, an inability to control addiction, and participants' belief that only a Higher Power can cure them of their addiction. Although the evidence base is not extensive, some studies suggest that AA is effective. Personal testimonies also attest to its power (Ouimette et al., 1997), as well as other aspects common to more empirically based treatment reviewed above such as structure, social support, and identification of nonsubstance rewards (Moos, 2008).

Opinions remain divided on twelve-step approaches. For people who have found the focus on God inconsistent with their own beliefs, variations have emerged that provide a more non-religious set of steps (e.g., Rational Recovery). Even without an extensive evidence base, if the twelve-step programs are efficacious for only a percentage of addicted individuals, they deserve a place among available treatments.

FIGURE 9.5
Twelve Steps of Alcoholics Anonymous

1. We admitted we were powerless over alcohol—that our lives had become unmanageable.

2. Came to believe that a Power greater than ourselves could restore us to sanity.

3. Made a decision to turn our will and our lives over to the care of God as we understood Him.

4. Made a searching and fearless moral inventory of ourselves.

5. Admitted to God, to ourselves and to another human being the exact nature of our wrongs.

6. Were entirely ready to have God remove all these defects of character.

7. Humbly asked Him to remove our shortcomings.

8. Made a list of all persons we had harmed, and became willing to make amends to them all.

9. Made direct amends to such people wherever possible, except when to do so would injure them or others.

10. Continued to take personal inventory and when we were wrong promptly admitted it.

11. Sought through prayer and meditation to improve our conscious contact with God as we understood Him, praying only for knowledge of His will for us and the power to carry that out.

12. Having had a spiritual awakening as the result of these steps, we tried to carry this message to alcoholics, and to practice these principles in all our affairs.

BIOLOGICAL TREATMENTS

As mentioned earlier, biological interventions play an important role in the treatment of substance abuse and dependence. They can be used as the sole intervention or as an adjunct to psychological or community interventions.

Withdrawal symptoms can be severe and occasionally lethal. **Detoxification**, medically supervised drug withdrawal, is necessary to treat substance dependence—but it is only the first step. Medications can reduce withdrawal symptoms and decrease the likelihood of adverse effects. For example, benzodiazepines can be administered to reduce the likelihood of an alcoholic developing DTs.

Agonist substitution is a type of therapy that substitutes a chemically similar safe medication for the drug of abuse. Chemically safe means several things. First, the substitute drug binds with the same receptors as the target drug, thereby preventing any pharmacological effect ("high") of the target drug. Although the substitute shares many similarities with the target drug, it also differs in several key ways. The substitute works more slowly and has fewer acute pharmacological effects, with no resulting high and subsequent crash. Although there may be some potential for drug dependence, it typically is far less severe than with the target drug. People taking an agonist substitution drug are still taking a drug regularly, but with few of the social, occupational, and physical impairments associated with the target drug. The most widely known agonist substitute is **methadone**, used as a replacement for heroin. Distributed under controlled conditions in "methadone clinics," methadone removes the substantial risk associated with obtaining and injecting heroin. Some individuals continue on methadone therapy indefinitely, but considerable evidence suggests that coupling methadone with counseling, individual psychotherapy, or contingency contracting improves treatment outcome (O'Brien et al., 1995).

Nicotine Replacement Therapy Whereas methadone replacement substitutes one drug for another, some replacement therapies vary the *method* of drug delivery rather than the drug itself. **Nicotine replacement therapy (NRT)** is safe and effective when used as part of a comprehensive smoking cessation program. NRT is available over the counter as gum or a patch and by prescription as a puffer or inhaler or sublingual (under the tongue) lozenges. NRT replaces nicotine from cigarettes, reduces withdrawal symptoms, and helps the patient resist the urge to smoke. NRT approaches increase the odds of quitting approximately 1.5- to 2-fold both with and without additional counseling (Silagy et al., 2004).

Antagonist Treatments Since the positively reinforcing effects of drugs appear to be a major factor in their use, could drug use be discontinued if these sensations were blocked by a drug that *antagonized* (acted against) the action of the drug of abuse? Several studies have examined the efficacy of the opioid antagonists *naltrexone* and *nalmefene* to treat alcohol abuse. Naltrexone reduces the risk of relapse to heavy drinking and the frequency of drinking when compared with placebo, but it does not substantially enhance abstinence (Garbutt et al., 1999). More recently, long-acting injectible preparations of naltrexone were found to reduce heavy drinking among alcohol-dependent patients during 6 months of therapy (Garbutt et al., 2005). Although antagonist drugs do not miraculously reverse drug use, they are a valuable pharmacologic tool worthy of further investigation.

Aversive Treatments Similar to aversion therapy, aversive pharmacologic interventions pair ingestion of the substance with a noxious physical reaction. The best known substance is *disulfiram* or **Antabuse**. Disulfiram prevents the breakdown of *acetaldehyde* (found in alcohol), and the buildup of this substance in the body produces the noxious feelings. While taking Antabuse, people who consume alcohol experience nausea,

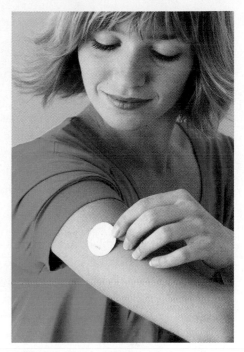

The nicotine patch allows for controlled release of nicotine into the body and helps with smoking cessation.

detoxification medically supervised drug withdrawal

agonist substitution a type of therapy that substitutes a chemically similar medication for the drug of abuse

methadone the most widely known agonist substitute, used as a replacement for heroin

nicotine replacement therapy (NRT) a safe and effective therapy used as part of a comprehensive smoking cessation program

antabuse aversive medication that pairs the ingestion of a drug with a noxious physical reaction

examining the evidence

Controlled Drinking?

■ **The Facts** Many conceptualizations (disease model) and treatment approaches (AA, therapeutic communities) for alcohol are based on the idea that complete abstinence is the only acceptable approach to overcoming alcohol dependence. Over the last half century researchers have begun to question this all-or-nothing approach.

■ **The Evidence** Mark and Linda Sobell conducted the best known study of what is now called controlled drinking (Sobell & Sobell, 1973). Results indicated that people receiving behavioral treatment for alcoholism combined with learning skills to engage in nonproblematic drinking had significantly more "days functioning well" during a two-year follow-up period than those receiving a treatment aimed at abstinence (Sobell & Sobell, 1973; Sobell & Sobell, 1978). Can alcoholics be taught to control their drinking?

■ **Let's Examine the Evidence** Although this research was well received, it also had detractors (Pendery et al., 1982) and inspired spirited criticism in sources such as the *New York Times* and the television news show *60 Minutes,* suggesting that the research was both flawed and potentially fraudulent. However, an independent investigation of the Sobells' research supported the integrity of this work on all counts. Alan Marlatt, a leading researcher in alcohol, suggested that the media closely covered the critiques of the Sobells' work, but paid little attention to the evidence supporting its integrity and validity (Marlatt et al., 1993). The controversy over controlled drinking still continues, but it has taken its toll on the scientific community, and research directly bearing on this question has been pursued less frequently than might be expected (Coldwell & Heather, 2006).

■ **What Are Alternative Explanations for This Controversy?** Probably the clearest finding from this research is that controlled drinking approaches may be especially suited to individuals with less severe drinking problems (Sobell & Sobell, 1995), although other researchers question the apparent consensus that it is not a suitable approach for more severely dependent drinkers (Heather, 1995). Today, the spirit of controlled drinking lives on, but the name largely has not survived. "Harm reduction" is the most common name now used (Marlatt et al., 1993). Although harm reduction shares many of the same goals as controlled drinking, it has received less critical attack and initial evidence is encouraging (Witkiewitz & Marlatt, 2006). Furthermore, treatment approaches such as motivational interviewing (Miller, 1983) place the client's preferences and goals at its center, and allow patients to choose controlled drinking as a strategy for treatment. Yet, it is notable that in many cases even motivational interviewing is conducted within settings favoring an abstinence-only approach (Coldwell & Heather, 2006).

■ **Conclusion** Although no one would argue that abstinence is bad, researchers in the tradition of controlled drinking hope to provide alternatives for people who may be able to attain a normal and healthy life without complete avoidance of alcohol.

vomiting, and increased heart rate and respiration. Controlled studies of disulfiram reveal mixed results. Drinking frequency is reduced, but minimal evidence has been found to support improved continuous abstinence rates (Garbutt et al., 1999). Discontinuing the drug is all that is required to return to drinking without the noxious symptoms.

Vaccines A truly novel approach to treatment is *immunopharmacotherapy*—or vaccination against drug use. By giving someone a vaccine, antibodies are produced that bind to the targeted drug before it reaches the brain and therefore block its positive, reinforcing effects. By attaching drugs to proteins from the blood, an immune response can be triggered, and the body generates antibodies against them. As early as 1974, it was discovered that when rhesus monkeys already addicted to heroin were vaccinated, the monkeys significantly reduced their lever pressing for heroin, indicating that the vaccine blocked the heroin high (Bonese et al., 1974). Since then, animal models have been developed for immunization against cocaine, nicotine, hallucinogens, and methamphetamine, suggesting the potential efficacy of these treatments in humans. Human clinical trials are currently underway for vaccines against cocaine and nicotine (Meijler et al., 2004). If effective, this intervention could have intriguing social ramifications. Will parents vaccinate their children against nicotine, alcohol, marijuana, and other drugs, just as we do against polio, measles, and mumps? Will the tobacco companies resist the vaccines because they will infringe on the free market? Will incarcerated individuals who have committed drug-related crimes be vaccinated against their will? Many important ethical and social questions will arise as the efficacy of the immunopharmacotherapy approach becomes clear.

SEX AND RACIAL/ETHNIC DIFFERENCES IN TREATMENT

Women face unique barriers to obtaining treatment for substance abuse, which may account for findings suggesting that women are less likely to enter treatment then men. For instance, limited access to child care and society's punitive attitude toward mothers who abuse drugs can keep them from admitting that they have a problem and seeking help (Allen, 1995). Women also differ from men in their response to treatment, although the data are inconsistent. Several studies have reported that women are more likely than men to drop out of substance abuse treatment, although this finding is far from conclusive (Bride, 2001; Joe et al., 1999; McCaul et al., 2001; Simpson et al., 1997).

In addition to sex differences, treatment studies also suggest that ethnic and racial minorities are less likely to complete and/or seek treatment, to receive treatment services, and to achieve recovery (Jerrell & Wilson, 1997; Rebach, 1992). Importantly, however, several studies indicate that minority clients do not differ from nonminority clients in their response to treatment (Pickens & Fletcher, 1991). Clearly, additional research is needed to clarify which factors predict poor or favorable treatment outcomes among minority individuals. Lundgren and colleagues (Lundgren et al., 2001) found that different racial and ethnic groups enter different types of drug treatment; specifically, Latino drug users were a third less likely than white drug users to enter residential treatment, and African American drug users were half as likely as white drug users to enter methadone maintenance treatment. Another critical factor is that minority groups may receive inferior treatment, based on reduced effectiveness and treatment costs allocated per patient (Schulman et al., 1999).

It is clear that our ability to truly understand how best to prevent and treat substance use disorders will need to be built on a solid foundation of research that considers the specific needs and challenges associated with sex, ethnicity and race, and socioeconomic status. Considerable care must be taken not to assume that any particular conclusion applies to all groups.

---

concept CHECK

- Substance use disorders are difficult to treat. However, as part of multifaceted interventions, behavior therapy procedures such as contingency management therapy and aversion therapy play a prominent role.

- Relapse prevention strategies focus on the cognitive responses to lapses and relapses and help the patient maintain abstinence after successful treatment.

- Twelve-step programs focus on powerlessness over the addictive process and on complete abstinence from the substance.

- Antagonist treatments use one drug to block the reinforcing properties of another drug, thus reducing its pleasurable effects and lessening the risk of relapse.

- Aversive medications such as Antabuse pair the ingestion of a drug with a noxious physical reaction.

- Vaccines are being developed to eliminate the positive and reinforcing physical response to various drugs.

APPLICATION QUESTION   With some psychiatric illnesses, the patient and the therapist are "on the same side." They both want to take the symptoms away (e.g., "Doctor, please help me get rid of the phobia that interferes with my life"). With substance abuse, this is often not the case. If you are the therapist, what are the therapeutic challenges of working with a patient whose goals may differ from yours?

THE WHOLE STORY: GLORIA—TREATING POLY-SUBSTANCE ABUSE

The Person: Gloria, 36 years old, was mandated by the court to 30 days of residential treatment at a community center.

The Problem: At the time of her arrest, she was living with her boyfriend of three years, their 2-year-old son, and one child from a previous relationship. Gloria dropped out of high school and got her GED. She had a series of low-paying jobs and most recently lost her job as a cashier at a diner after she stole money from the cash register. She was financially dependent on her boyfriend, whose source of income was unknown. When she arrived at the facility, she denied substance use within the prior 24 hours and reported some physical and psychological discomfort due to withdrawal. She was agitated, her speech was pressured, and her thoughts and speech were disorganized. She denied any hallucinations or delusions.

At intake, she met the criteria for current crack/cocaine dependence and alcohol abuse. In the past, she had used marijuana, amphetamines, and heroin. A previous HIV test was negative. Her family history was positive for heroin and cocaine dependence (father), alcoholism (mother), and death by heroin overdose (brother). Her boyfriend was a crack user

who was not interested in receiving treatment, and he had interfered with her earlier attempts to get sober. She worried that her older daughter was using drugs and engaging in unsafe sexual activity, which concerned her greatly, as she hoped her daughter could escape the cycle of high-risk behaviors that characterized her family.

The Treatment: Gloria was mandated to treatment following her arrest for stealing from the diner. This was her only arrest. She had had three previous contacts with the legal system, when neighbors, fearing for her children, called the police in response to loud yelling and throwing of objects against the wall. On each occasion, the police left, giving the couple a warning only. She denied any abuse or imminent danger to herself or her children.

The only hint that Gloria was interested in treatment for her addictions was her concern about her older daughter and worry that her baby would be placed in foster care. Although she was clear that her boyfriend was not supportive of her treatment, she did mention a sister who she felt would support her as well as the backing of members of her church.

In addition to her substance abuse problems, Gloria reported a period lasting for about the past two months when her mood had been consistently low. She reported decreased appetite and poor sleep.

Following review of her initial assessment, a preliminary treatment plan was developed. The team identified four targets—treat her crack/cocaine dependence, treat her alcohol abuse, further evaluate her depression, and mobilize social support for continued abstinence. Her team felt that even though the treatment was court mandated, Gloria was sufficiently concerned about her children that they could enhance her desire to change her behaviors.

A complete behavioral analysis identified the triggers associated with her cocaine and alcohol use. Her boyfriend, a drug dealer, was a major trigger in her use. Remaining financially dependent on him would seriously increase her risk of relapse.

During her residential treatment, Gloria learned skills for resisting urges to use. She worked through lapse and relapse scenarios and planned strategies for remaining clean. She had several family meetings with her sister and brother-in-law to mobilize family support. The team also helped her mobilize her faith and organized several outings to her church to meet with people who knew her situation and would provide support after treatment. Gloria also attended AA meetings regularly while in treatment and planned to continue attendance after discharge. While in treatment, she was trained in parenting skills. Her older daughter, who had indeed started using drugs herself, was referred for treatment. Her social worker helped her with job placement and with finding low-cost housing.

The Treatment Outcome: At the end of the 30-day treatment, Gloria was afraid to be discharged. She felt as if she had only started to get clean, and she did not know what she would do without the daily support of the center staff. When she was admitted, she feared that 30 days was a life sentence, but now she knew that it was really too short a time for true recovery. She was realistic about her chances of staying sober. She knew that the thought of financial security would tempt her to go back to her dealer boyfriend, but each time she considered that she had to pair that desire with her concern for her children's welfare. She was stepped-down to weekly sessions with her social worker to provide ongoing support and early identification of any lapses or relapses. Gloria continued to attend AA meetings at her church. Her sister helped out by providing child care while Gloria worked. In return, Gloria helped her sister with her housekeeping job.

At the one-year anniversary of her discharge, Gloria was still sober. She managed to continue to attend AA, had become a regular member of her church community, and had become a better mother to her daughter, who had also remained drug-free since her intervention. She continued to have fluctuations in her mood, and noted honestly that at times she felt ill-equipped to put the required energy into remaining sober. However, her children remained her primary motivator, and her social and family supports helped carry her through the times of highest risk.

CRITICAL ISSUES to remember

1. Drug use refers to moderate use of a substance without impairment in social, occupational, or educational functioning. Abuse occurs when use leads to disruption in these domains, and dependence incorporates physiological responses to the substance, including tolerance and withdrawal.

2. Tolerance refers to needing a markedly increased amount of the substance to achieve the same effect, and withdrawal symptoms occur when a dependent person attempts to cut down or abstain from regular drug use.

3. Drugs have specific mechanisms of action to produce their effects. For example, nicotine achieves its rewarding effects through the dopamine system; alcohol modulates receptors in the GABA system; opioids mimic the body's natural opioids; and hallucinogens disrupt serotonergic function and cause the user to experience unusual sensations.

4. Caffeine produces rapid alertness; nicotine is highly addictive and associated with a rapid pharmacologic effect; alcohol creates a sensation of being more relaxed, outgoing, and social; marijuana is associated with an intensified experience of color and sound and a slowed perception of time; cocaine and methamphetamine are CNS stimulants that can result in dangerous elevations of cardiovascular function; opioids reduce pain; hallucinogens can cause the user to experience unusual sensations; inhalants produce a rapid high but can lead to permanent organ and brain damage.

5. Drug and alcohol abuse emerge from a combination of genetic and environmental factors. Environmental factors can serve either to increase risk or to protect an individual from substance abuse.

6. No one treatment exists for substance abuse—both pharmacologic and behavioral approaches can be combined into a comprehensive treatment program that includes considerable attention to motivation and relapse prevention.

TEST yourself

For more review plus practice tests, flashcards, and Speaking Out: DSM in Context videos, log onto www.MyPsychLab.com

1. Bob uses illicit drugs "socially." His use does not produce problems with his social, educational, or occupational functioning. Bob's behavior constitutes substance
   a. abuse
   b. use
   c. intoxication
   d. dependence

2. The diagnosis that most closely approximates the lay term *addiction* is substance
   a. abuse
   b. use
   c. intoxication
   d. dependence

3. The two distinct factors that characterize substance dependence are
   a. tolerance and withdrawal
   b. social and occupational impairment
   c. genetic and environmental vulnerability
   d. physical and psychological problems

4. The most widely used drug in the world is
   a. nicotine
   b. alcohol
   c. caffeine
   d. marijuana

5. Central to nicotine's highly addictive potential is (are)
   a. its low cost and availability
   b. a supportive "smokers' subculture"
   c. its direct influence on the brain's pleasure centers
   d. its suppression of insulin production, producing hyperglycemia

6. Susan has smoked for 10 years but has decided to quit. According to the Centers for Disease Control, what is the likelihood that she will have achieved sustained abstinence at the end of a year?
   a. 2.3%
   b. 18.5%
   c. 46%
   d. 70%

7. Although alcohol affects many neurotransmitters, its effect is particularly powerful on the neurotransmitter
   a. serotonin
   b. GABA
   c. dopamine
   d. epinephrine

8. In its most severe form, alcohol withdrawal can include which of the following symptoms?
   a. hallucinations and formication
   b. seizures and metabolic complications
   c. delirium tremens
   d. all of the above

9. Dan, now in his mid-50s, has used alcohol heavily since his late 20s. He does not feel well, and his doctors are concerned that his alcohol use may have contributed to a liver disease called
   a. formication
   b. cirrhosis
   c. FAS
   d. Wernicke-Korsakoff syndrome

10. THC in marijuana produces a sense of euphoria by stimulating
    a. GABA release, which disinhibits various brain systems
    b. epinephrine discharge, leading to heightened pleasure and sensory acuteness
    c. cannabinoid receptors, thereby activating the dopamine reward system
    d. serotonin reuptake, leading to a feeling of contentment

11. Most people who are treated for amphetamine abuse
    a. also report high use of alcohol
    b. never experience tolerance or withdrawal
    c. use depressant drugs to come down from "highs"
    d. do not use another substance

12. Codeine, morphine, and heroin mimic the effects of the body's natural opioids, which include
    a. endorphins and enkephalins
    b. oxycodone and oxycontin
    c. dopamine and ketamine
    d. norepinephrine and epinephrine

13. Alcohol and drugs act on the brain's reward circuitry, which includes the
    a. medial cortex of the prefrontal lobes
    b. ventral tegmental area and the basal forebrain
    c. basal ganglia and hypothalamus
    d. Wernicke-Korsakoff's area

14. Harry is getting ready for a date. Before he leaves his apartment, he smokes some marijuana, which he believes helps him to be more charming and interesting. Which theoretical perspective best explains Harry's actions?
    a. behavioral
    b. psychodynamic
    c. cognitive
    d. sociocultural

15. Chronic use of illicit drugs during adolescence may result in "arrested development," which is
    a. slowed brain development resulting from metabolic changes
    b. inhibited physical maturation due to a decrease in sex hormones
    c. delays in emotional maturation due to incarceration
    d. missed social experiences and emotional growth opportunities

substance use disorders 331

16. Michelle quit smoking 6 months ago. She went out drinking with an old friend and had a few cigarettes with her. The next day she bought a pack of cigarettes, saying to herself, "I just won't ever have any willpower." This illustrates the
    a. inescapable cycle of addiction to nicotine
    b. weakness of an unsystematic cessation program
    c. application of controlled smoking
    d. abstinence violation effect

17. What is the fundamental difference between the cognitive-behavioral approach and the 12-step AA approach to the treatment of alcohol abuse?
    a. cognitive-behavioral approaches emphasize skills to control addiction rather than always requiring complete abstinence
    b. 12-step programs reject the disease or medical model of addiction
    c. cognitive-behavioral approaches lack the empirical support that AA programs have established
    d. there is no fundamental conflict; both approaches are often used successfully in conjunction with one another

18. In agonist substitution, a chemically similar safe medication is substituted for the drug of abuse. The most common drug used in this manner is
    a. naltrexone   c. disulfiram
    b. methadone   d. acetaldehyde

19. As in aversion therapy, aversive pharmacologic interventions pair ingestion of the substance with a noxious physical reaction. The best known substance used in this manner is
    a. naltrexone   c. disulfiram
    b. methadone   d. acetaldehyde

20. Controlled drinking approaches may be especially suited to individuals who have a
    a. less severe drinking problem
    b. severe dependence on drinking
    c. strong religious orientation
    d. history of failure in response to other treatments

Answers: 1 b, 2 d, 3 a, 4 c, 5 c, 6 a, 7 b, 8 d, 9 b, 10 c, 11 d, 12 a, 13 b, 14 c, 15 d, 16 d, 17 a, 18 b, 19 c, 20 a.

CHAPTER objectives

After reading this chapter, you should be able to:

1 Distinguish between a psychotic experience and the psychotic disorders.

2 Understand that schizophrenia is *not* a condition involving "split personality," nor does it usually involve violent behavior toward others.

3 Identify the positive, negative, and cognitive symptoms of schizophrenia.

4 Understand how culture plays a role in the expression and treatment of schizophrenia and other psychotic disorders.

5 Discuss the neurodevelopmental model of schizophrenia.

6 Understand the interplay of genetic, biological, psychological, and environmental factors in the etiology of schizophrenia.

7 Identify effective pharmacological and psychological treatments for schizophrenia.

schizophrenia and other psychotic disorders

What I remember most is how disoriented and frightened I felt. With little warning, my world had simply shifted under my feet. Over a period of several months, I began to believe that messages were being left for me in graffiti across campus. I also began to believe that my phone was being tapped. My friends insisted I was mistaken. But no one knew enough to realize anything was wrong. And then one day everything changed. One afternoon I realized the people on the radio were talking to me, much the way one has an intuition about a geometry proof, a sudden dawning of clarity or understanding. This clarity was more compelling than reality. It took me several weeks to put the pieces together. What I had known all my life was wrong. My friends were not real friends: at best they were neutral, at worst they were spies for the CIA. Graduate school was a luxury I was no longer allowed. There was a secret history of the world to which I now became attuned. It involved the NSA, the CIA, and the stealth bomber, which flew just out of sight in order to register details regarding my movements. An evil dictator was gathering power to himself and he meant to perpetuate a holocaust on the Nation. Only the American resistance, of which I was now a part, stood in his way. As time passed I became proficient at reading code. Most of my days were spent reading and responding to the newspaper so that the resistance could gather its military and economic resources to retake territory that had been lost. I learned to communicate by deciphering bits of conversation, reading newspaper articles, and listening to songs on the radio. Everyone could read my mind, so unless I was engaged in conversation, I spoke mostly in my head. I could not read anyone else's mind so I remained dependent on the media for information.

Within 6 months, I became adept at coordinating different avenues of information. However, I was living a nightmare. When I shut my eyes, I saw neon-colored cartoon characters that zoomed in and out of my field of vision. They were so bright it hurt. At night I would keep my eyes open until I fell asleep from exhaustion. I also lived in terror of the evil dictator and his minions. I never knew where they might be or how to evade them. I begged my superiors to have me killed. When it became clear that this was not going to happen, I took matters into my own hands. Within the course of a week, I tried to commit suicide four times.

Psychotic Disorders

Psychotic disorders are characterized by unusual thinking, distorted perceptions, and odd behaviors. People with a psychotic disorder are considered to be out of touch with reality and to be unable to think in a logical or coherent manner. They sometimes behave oddly, talking or mumbling to themselves or gesturing at someone that no one else can see. There are several different psychotic disorders; some are serious and chronic while others are temporary states of confusion. Before we discuss the different disorders, it is first necessary to understand the abnormal cognitive, perceptual, and behavioral symptoms that define these conditions.

WHAT IS PSYCHOSIS?

Delusions and hallucinations are characteristic of schizophrenia. The person who experiences them is in poor touch with reality and often behaves in ways that seem strange or bizarre.

Psychosis is a severe mental condition characterized by a loss of contact with reality. This usually takes the form of a **delusion** (a false belief) or a **hallucination** (a false sensory perception), or both. Both of these phenomena are illustrated in our opening case, which involves several false beliefs (being spied on, being part of a resistance movement) and false sensory perceptions (seeing cartoon characters that were not there). Such a dramatic loss of contact with reality can be quite frightening and can affect every aspect of functioning, even leading the affected person to behaviors as extreme as attempting suicide.

Although psychotic symptoms can be quite disturbing, hallucinations or delusions alone do not necessarily mean that a psychotic disorder, such as schizophrenia, is present. Psychotic symptoms may also occur among adults with other psychological disorders, including bipolar disorder, major depression, posttraumatic stress disorder, and substance abuse disorders. Children with bipolar disorders, obsessive-compulsive disorder, autistic disorder, and conduct disorder (see Chapter 12) also may have psychotic symptoms (Biederman et al., 2004).

Psychotic experiences such as delusional thinking and hallucinations may also occur in people with physical illnesses such as brain tumors, Alzheimer's disease, and Parkinson's disease, and after physical damage to the brain such as brain injuries or exposure to toxic substances. When psychotic experiences occur suddenly, the presence of a serious brain-related medical condition must first be considered.

Finally, psychotic experiences sometimes occur even when no psychological disorder is present. Brief or limited psychotic experiences are common, occurring in 2 to 12% of adults (Hannsen et al., 2005; Sidgewick et al.,1894, cited in Johns & van Os, 2001) and may include thoughts of persecution, a feeling that someone is stealing or manipulating one's thoughts, or hearing voices or sounds no one else can hear. One important difference is that individuals without psychotic disorders report that the voices are positive; they were not upset by the presence of the voices and felt in control of the experience (Honig et al., 1998). In contrast, those suffering from psychosis perceive the voices as negative and do not feel in control of the experience.

Psychotic symptoms may thus occur across many different physical conditions and psychological disorders, and even at times among people with no apparent physical or psychological disorder. However, psychotic symptoms are most often considered as one of the defining characteristics of schizophrenia.

WHAT IS SCHIZOPHRENIA?

Schizophrenia is a severe psychological disorder characterized by disorganization in thought, perception, and behavior. People with schizophrenia do not think logically, perceive the world accurately, or behave in a way that permits normal everyday life and work. They may worry that the government is spying on them, that voices on the radio are speaking directly to them—giving them instructions about how to behave or transmit-

psychosis a severe mental condition characterized by a loss of contact with reality

delusion a false belief

hallucination a false sensory perception

schizophrenia a severe psychological disorder characterized by disorganization in thought, perception, and behavior

ting messages only they can understand. As a result of these delusions and/or hallucinations, they behave oddly, appearing to others to be talking to themselves or doing such things as barricading themselves inside their apartments to prevent being kidnapped by an unseen enemy. Schizophrenia is a serious psychological disorder, as the condition creates severe impairment and it is often chronic, even with the best available treatments.

As discussed in Chapter 1, schizophrenia was first defined over 100 years ago by the German psychiatrist Emil Kraepelin and the Swiss psychiatrist Eugen Bleuler. Kraepelin called this disorder **dementia praecox** to highlight its pervasive disturbances of perceptual and cognitive faculties (*dementia*) and its early life onset (*praecox*), and to distinguish it from the dementia associated with old age. Bleuler focused on four core symptoms of the disorder: ambivalence, disturbances of affect, disturbance of association, and preference for fantasy over reality (Tsuang et al., 2000). Bleuler renamed the condition schizophrenia, combining the Greek words for split (schizo) and mind (phrene), to highlight the splitting of thought, affect, and behavior that occurs among those with this disorder.

Because almost everyone has felt sad at some time in their life, it is easy for most people to understand that depression is "extreme" sadness. However, it is difficult for people to understand the unusual symptoms of schizophrenia, a disorder that challenges mental health professionals as well. Yet, during the last 100 years, our understanding of the clinical presentation, etiology, and treatment of schizophrenia has improved substantially. Before examining its symptoms, it is important to clarify several common misconceptions about schizophrenia.

Perhaps because it is so difficult to understand the experience of schizophrenia, there are many mistaken ideas about this disorder. This lack of understanding has led to many inaccurate media and literary portrayals of schizophrenia. Robert Louis Stevenson's *The Strange Case of Dr. Jekyll and Mr. Hyde* is a classic description of two contradictory personalities that exist within the same individual. Dr. Henry Jekyll is sensitive and kind; Mr. Edward Hyde is a violent murderer. Even today the term *Jekyll and Hyde* is used to describe behaviors that appear to be polar opposites, yet exist within the same person. However, those with schizophrenia do *not* have "split personalities." The Greek word "schizo" describes the split between an individual's thoughts and feelings, not the splitting of the personality. However, this misunderstanding is common. According to a Harris Poll conducted for the National Organization on Disability in the USA, about two-thirds of people surveyed believe that "split personality" is part of schizophrenia (http://www.abc.net.au/science/k2/moments/s1200266.htm).

A similar misconception is that schizophrenia involves multiple personalities. As discussed in Chapter 5, there does exist a condition called dissociative identity disorder (DID). People with DID are considered to have two or more distinct personalities, each with its own thoughts, feelings, and behaviors. As illustrated by novels such as *The Three Faces of Eve* and *Sybil*, one personality may be unaware of the other's behavior. However, each personality perceives, deals with, and interacts with the environment successfully. This ability to successfully negotiate with the environment is what differentiates people with schizophrenia from people with DID. Schizophrenia results in an inability to perceive the environment appropriately or deal with it adequately. In short, people with schizophrenia do *not* have split or multiple personalities.

SCHIZOPHRENIA IN DEPTH

Schizophrenia has three symptom categories: positive symptoms, negative symptoms, and cognitive impairments (see the box "DSM-IV-TR: Schizophrenia"). In the case of schizophrenia, the term *positive* does not mean optimistic or upbeat; it denotes the *presence* of an abnormal behavior within the individual. **Positive symptoms**, the behaviors that people most often associate with schizophrenia, consist of unusual thoughts, feelings, and behav-

dementia praecox original name for schizophrenia, coined by Kraepelin, to highlight its pervasive disturbances of perceptual and cognitive faculties (*dementia*) and its early life onset (*praecox*), and to distinguish it from the dementia associated with old age

positive symptoms a group of schizophrenic symptoms including unusual thoughts, feelings, and behaviors that vary in intensity, and in many cases are responsive to treatment

People with schizophrenia sometimes believe that their thoughts are being tampered with—being removed from their heads or broadcast on TV, for example. This is a *delusion*, a false belief.

iors. They vary in intensity and in many cases are responsive to treatment (Tirupati et al., 2006).

One positive symptom of schizophrenia is the presence of delusions, beliefs that are not based in fact (see Table 10.1). **Persecutory delusions** are the most common. These consist of the belief that someone is harming or attempting to harm the person. Other delusions consist of the belief that the person is a special agent/individual (as in our opening case) (Appelbaum et al., 1999). Although most delusions are distressing in nature, sometimes the delusion is grandiose, with negative events occurring when others do not act in accord with the delusional content.

Kim was a college student of Korean descent and was hospitalized after he was found wandering around on the city streets, yelling at strangers because they did not bow when he walked by. Upon questioning, Kim revealed that he was the emperor of Korea and that those on the street were not giving him the deference appropriate to his royal status.

Other common delusions are **delusions of influence**, which include beliefs that one's behavior or thoughts are controlled by others. People with schizophrenia often believe that their thoughts are being manipulated by processes known as thought withdrawal, thought broadcasting, or thought insertion. People with delusions of influence believe that the government is inserting thoughts into their head or that evil forces, such as alien invaders, are "stealing" thoughts out of their head. In thought broadcasting, the person believes that his or her private thoughts are being revealed to others, usually by being transmitted over the radio or television.

A second positive symptom is hallucinations (hearing voices when no one is there, seeing visions that no one else sees; see Table 10.1). Auditory hallucinations are most common (experienced by 71% of one sample; Mueser et al., 1990) and can range from simple noises to one or more voices of either gender. Voices are most commonly negative in quality and content, but on occasion can be comforting or kind (Copolov et al., 2004). Auditory hallucinations that appear to be exclusive to people with schizophrenia are voices that keep a running commentary on the individual's behavior or several voices that have a conversation. Visual hallucinations are less common (14% in one sample) but do occur, often in those with the most severe form of the disorder (Mueser et al., 1990). Common examples of visual hallucinations include seeing the devil or a dead relative or friend. About 15% of hallucinations are *tactile* (touch). *Olfactory* (smell) and *gustatory* (taste) hallucinations are the least common type (11%).

John was diagnosed with schizophrenia. Despite medication, he continued to have auditory hallucinations, consisting of voices that talked to him or directed him to do certain things. John talked back to the voices or laughed aloud at something that they said. Each day, John came to the local mental health clinic for the free coffee provided to patients waiting for an appointment. He rarely had an appointment, but the staff was sympathetic toward him and would let him sit in the waiting room and drink coffee. He was never violent, but his behavior often disturbed the clinic patients unfamiliar with schizophrenia. On many occasions, John's behavior became too upsetting to the other patients, and the staff had to ask him to leave. Even though he was hallucinating, a staff member would approach him and say, "John, it is time to go now." Immediately, John would look up, greet the staff member by name, say, "Sure, see you tomorrow," and calmly leave the clinic.

John's behavior illustrates a very important point about people suffering with schizophrenia. Hallucinations may persist despite adequate medication dosages, but many patients are able to function at some level and maintain some contact with reality even while hallucinating.

persecutory delusions beliefs that someone is persecuting the patient or that the individual is a special agent/individual

delusions of influence beliefs that one's thoughts or behaviors are being controlled by others

TABLE 10.1
Types of Delusions and Hallucinations Found in People with Schizophrenia

Symptom	Example
Delusions	
Influence	Beliefs that behavior or thoughts are controlled by others, including thought withdrawal, broadcasting, or insertion, or mind reading by another person
Self-Significance	Thoughts of grandeur, reference (random events, objects, and behaviors of others have a particular and unusual significance to oneself—such as the messages left in graffiti in the introductory case), religion (believing that one is a supreme being), guilt, or sin
Persecution or Paranoid	Thoughts that others are out to harm the person
Somatic	Belief that one's body is rotting away
Hallucinations	
Auditory	Noises or voices, perhaps speaking to or about the person
Visual	Visions of religious figures or dead people
Olfactory	Smells
Gustatory	Tastes
Somatic	Feelings of pain or deterioration of parts of one's body or feeling that things are crawling on, or are in, the skin or the body

From Kimhy et al., 2005; Mueser et al., 1990.

One aspect of the catatonic subtype of schizophrenia is *waxy flexibility*, in which a person's limbs can be "posed" by someone else. The person will remain in that position until she is moved again.

Another positive symptom is abnormality of speech. When untreated, individuals with schizophrenia usually show strange speech patterns that indicate deterioration in their cognitive functioning. Some examples of this cognitive deterioration include **loose associations,** or thoughts that have little or no logical connection to the next thought (e.g., "I once worked at an Army base. It is important to soldier on. The Middle East— I like to travel, my favorite place is Arizona"). Another symptom is **thought blocking,** exemplified by unusually long pauses in the patient's speech that occur during a conversation. A third symptom is called **clang associations,** in which speech is governed by words that sound alike, rather than words that have meaning (e.g., "I have bills, summer hills, bummer, drum solo"), rendering communication meaningless.

Yet another positive symptom is the unusual, sometimes bizarre, behaviors exhibited by people with schizophrenia. **Catatonia** is a condition in which a person is awake but is nonresponsive to external stimulation. During a catatonic state, the patient may not move or make eye contact with others. He or she may be *mute* (without speech) or muscularly rigid (like a statue). When there is **waxy flexibility,** parts of the body (usually the arms) will remain frozen in a particular posture when positioned that way by another person.

Positive symptoms may be quite dramatic, but they alone are not sufficient for a diagnosis of schizophrenia. A second symptom category necessary for the diagnosis are the negative symptoms. In this case, the term *negative* does not refer to bad or horrific content. It refers to the *absence* of behaviors that exist in the general population. In schizophrenia, **negative symptoms** are behaviors, emotions, or thought processes (cognitions) that exist in people without a psychiatric disorder but are absent (or are

loose associations thoughts that have little or no logical connection to the next thought

thought blocking unusually long pauses in the patient's speech that occur during a conversation

clang associations speech governed by words that sound alike rather than words that have meaning

catatonia condition in which a person is awake but is nonresponsive to external stimulation

waxy flexibility a condition in which parts of the body (usually the arms) will remain frozen in a particular posture when positioned that way by another person

negative symptoms behaviors, emotions, or thought processes (cognitions) that exist in people without a psychiatric disorder but are absent (or are substantially diminished) in people with schizophrenia

substantially diminished) in people with schizophrenia. Common negative symptoms include *blunted affect, anhedonia, avolition* or apathy, *alogia*, and *psychomotor retardation*.

Blunted affect describes diminished or immobile facial expressions and a flat, monotonic vocal tone that does not change even when the topic of conversation becomes emotionally laden. This inconsistency between a schizophrenic patient's facial expression and vocal tone and the content of his or her speech is one example of why Bleuler used the word "split" to describe this disorder—for example, the patient may describe horrific thoughts with very little emotional expression in the face or voice. **Anhedonia** refers to a lack of capacity for pleasure—the person does not feel joy or happiness. **Avolition**, or apathy, is an inability to initiate or follow through on plans. Often, relatives of people with schizophrenia interpret this apathy as simple laziness or a deliberate unwillingness to improve their life—an erroneous interpretation that can create distress and discord in the family environment (Mueser & McGurk, 2004). **Alogia** is a term used to describe decreased quality and/or quantity of speech. **Psychomotor retardation** describes slowed mental or physical activities. When psychomotor retardation affects cognition, for example, speech can be slowed to the point that it is difficult or impossible for others to follow the conversation. Unlike positive symptoms, which can be largely controlled by medication, negative symptoms like these are treatment-resistant; they tend to persist (Fenton & McGlashan, 1991) and restrict the person's ability to hold a job, go to school, or even take care of personal responsibilities such as bathing or dressing.

The third main category of symptoms among people with schizophrenia is **cognitive impairment**. Deficits in cognitive abilities include impairments in visual and verbal learning and memory, inability to pay attention, decreased speed of information processing (how fast information is understood), and impaired abstract reasoning and executive functioning (ability to solve problems and make decisions; Green et al., 2004). To illustrate cognitive impairments, consider the following example of impaired abstract reasoning. People without schizophrenia interpret the phrase, "People who live in glass houses should not throw stones," to mean that one should not criticize others when they themselves also may have faults or flaws. However, many individuals with schizophrenia interpret that statement as follows: "It means that you should build a house with bricks because stones cannot break bricks." Cognitive deficits are one of the earliest signs of schizophrenia (Kurtz et al., 2005). Like negative symptoms, cognitive deficits are long-lasting and strongly correlated with functional impairment. However, for some people with schizophrenia, many aspects of cognitive functioning can remain in the normal or even the above-normal range (see the box "Real People, Real Disorders: John Nash—*A Beautiful Mind*").

blunted affect diminished or immobile facial expressions and a flat, monotonic vocal tone that does not change even when the topic of conversation becomes emotionally laden

anhedonia a lack of capacity for pleasure; the person does not feel joy or happiness

avolition an inability to initiate or follow through on plans

alogia decreased quality and/or quantity of speech

psychomotor retardation slowed mental or physical activities

cognitive impairments impairments in visual and verbal learning and memory, inability to pay attention, decreased speed of information processing, and impaired abstract reasoning, any or all of which may be found in different psychotic disorders

real people, real disorders

John Nash—A Beautiful Mind

John Forbes Nash Jr. (1928—) created the influential mathematical theory known as game theory. In his early thirties, at the height of his career, he experienced a psychotic episode and was diagnosed with schizophrenia. He claimed that aliens were communicating with him and that he was their special messenger. Over the next 30 years, he was hospitalized many times. He returned to the Princeton faculty in 1960, while he was still undergoing treatment. A campus legend, Nash became "The Phantom of Fine Hall" (Princeton's mathematics center), a shadowy figure who would scribble arcane equations on blackboards in the middle of the night. A proof he had written at age 20 ultimately became a foundation of modern economic theory. In 1994, as Nash began to show signs of emerging from his delusions, he was awarded a Nobel Prize in Economics along with two other game theorists. Currently in remission, Nash takes care to manage his disorder and continues to hold an appointment in mathematics at Princeton. While cautious with people he does not know, he is said to have a dry sense of humor. He is best known in popular culture as the subject of the movie, *A Beautiful Mind*, about his mathematical genius and his struggles with mental illness. Although there are several inaccuracies depicted in the movie (e.g., Nash's hallucinations were exclusively auditory, not both visual and auditory), the movie is a powerful illustration of the impact of schizophrenia and Nash's triumph over this severe and debilitating disorder.

http://nobelprize.org/nobel_prizes/economics/laureates/1994/nash-autobio.html
http://www.pbs.org/wgbh/amex/nash/filmmore/index.html
http://www.sane.org/content/view/390/0/

In addition to general cognitive impairment, people with schizophrenia have a deficit in *social cognition*, which is the ability to perceive, interpret, and understand social information, including other people's beliefs, attitudes, and emotions. People with schizophrenia are often deficient in the basic skills necessary for positive social interactions (Bellack et al., 1990; Penn et al., 2001), including the ability to perceive social nuances and engage in basic conversation. This limits their ability to relate well to others and socialize appropriately, a skill that is necessary for effective academic, social, and occupational functioning (see "Treatment of Schizophrenia and Other Psychotic Disorders" later in this chapter).

Although a diagnosis of schizophrenia requires the presence of symptoms from each of the three symptom categories, each person will have a different set of symptoms. Certain symptoms cluster together in what are known as subtypes. Table 10.2 lists the different subtypes of schizophrenia and their primary symptoms.

People with schizophrenia often have additional psychological disorders as well. Depression affects as many as 45% of people with schizophrenia (Leff et al., 1988) and approximately 5% commit suicide (Inskip et al., 1998; Palmer et al., 2005). Suicide rates are much higher during the initial onset of the disorder (Malla & Payne, 2005) and immediately before or after any inpatient hospitalization (Qin & Nordentoft, 2005). Acts of self-harm do not occur at any greater frequency for people with schizophrenia than for those with other psychological disorders. Factors that increase the likelihood of self-harm include previous depressed mood or previous suicide attempts, drug abuse, agitation or restlessness, fear of mental deterioration, or delusions or hallucinations that encourage such behavior (Symonds et al., 2006; Tarrier et al., 2006).

Approximately 47% of people with schizophrenia also have anxiety disorders (Kessler et al., 2005). Because their disorder leaves schizophrenic patients vulnerable to victimization and violence as a result of poor living conditions or homelessness,

TABLE 10.2

Schizophrenia Subtypes

Type	Primary Symptoms
Paranoid	Delusions/hallucinations of a persecutory and frightening nature; cognitive and negative symptoms are less prominent
Catatonic	Behavior that is extreme in either dimension: diminished motor activity—immobility (rigid posture, waxy flexibility) and/or mutism unresponsive to commands or suggestions OR excessive motor activity and/or **echolalia** (repeating verbatim what others say) that is purposeless in nature
Disorganized	Verbalizations that are without form or understandable content (giggling constantly for no reason) and/or behavior that is repetitive, purposeless, or silly
Undifferentiated	Symptoms of schizophrenia are present but do not fall neatly into one of the above categories
Residual	Only negative symptoms are present or previous positive symptoms have lessened in severity or frequency

Schizophrenia

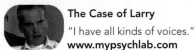

The Case of Larry
"I have all kinds of voices."
www.mypsychlab.com

post-traumatic stress disorder (PTSD) is quite common, occurring in at least 43% of patient samples (Mueser et al., 2002). Substance abuse occurs among approximately 50% of individuals with schizophrenia (Regier et al., 1990). Among one group of patients with both schizophrenia and substance abuse, alcohol was the most commonly abused drug (89%), followed by marijuana (27%), and benzodiazepines (13%; Erkiran et al., 2006). Substance abuse results in greater impairment in daily functioning than when schizophrenia occurs alone; people with both disorders are more likely to relapse and have to be rehospitalized, to be homeless, and to be noncompliant with their treatment (Drake & Brunette, 1998).

Could the use of alcohol or drugs by people with schizophrenia be a strategy to cope with or escape from negative symptoms such as the inability to feel pleasure (Khantzian, 1987)? This is known as the self-medication hypothesis and has been the subject of much debate and controversy. A recent meta-analysis (i.e., a statistical procedure that analyzes the results of many different research studies) suggests that patients with both schizophrenia and substance use disorders have *fewer* negative symptoms than patients who do not abuse substances (Potvin et al., 2006). However, before concluding that substance abuse decreases symptoms (a cause-and-effect model), remember that all of these data are cross-sectional and correlational in nature (see Chapter 2). Actually, there are two ways to interpret the relationship between substance abuse and schizophrenia. First, substance abuse might relieve negative symptoms such as anhedonia or apathy, providing support for the self-medication hypothesis. Alternatively, those with fewer negative symptoms may simply be less likely to abuse these substances. Experimental and longitudinal designs, rather than correlational studies, are necessary to disentangle this issue.

concept CHECK

- Schizophrenia is a serious psychological disorder that is characterized by disorganization in thought, perception, and behavior. People with schizophrenia do not think logically, perceive the world accurately, or behave in a way that permits normal everyday life and work.

- Symptoms of schizophrenia are divided into three groups. There are positive symptoms, such as hallucinations and delusions; negative symptoms, such as blunted affect and anhedonia; and cognitive impairments, such as impaired reasoning.

echolalia   repeating verbatim what others say

■ Patients with schizophrenia often have other psychological disorders as well. Post-traumatic stress disorder, substance abuse, anxiety, and depression are common. These complicate the patient's long-term adjustment and the likelihood of an optimal treatment outcome.

APPLICATION QUESTION Your friend is also in your abnormal psychology class. She was robbed at gunpoint the other day, and she confides to you that every time she walks down the street where the robbery occurred, she thinks that she sees the man who robbed her. Then the image disappears. She is afraid that she is developing schizophrenia. What would you tell her?

Functional Impairment *Dorrie was always shy and did not make friends easily. She was very bright and graduated summa cum laude from a local college in the Southeast. She was admitted to a prestigious Master's Program in Business Administration in the Northeast. Soon after she arrived, she became very concerned about her safety and worried that others were out to harm her. She began to spend more and more time alone and she bought a gun for her personal safety. One day, the school called her parents—Dorrie was walking around campus threatening to shoot the "undercover CIA agents." She was dismissed from the program, and her parents took her home. Her symptoms are now partially controlled by medication. She works part-time in the elementary school cafeteria, but may never be able to live independently or fulfill her former academic potential.*

The more severe the symptoms of schizophrenia, the more severe is the impairment in the person's ability to function. Any delay in receiving treatment increases the severity of the functional impairment. Although long-term outcome is significantly worse when the illness is untreated for one year (Harris et al., 2005), even smaller delays seriously affect the possibility of being able to live and function independently again. This means that treatment should begin as soon as possible in order to limit the chronic nature of the disorder.

Schizophrenia takes a significant human toll on the individual and his or her family. Its social and economic burden makes it one of the 10 most debilitating (medical or psychological) conditions in the world in terms of disability-adjusted life years (Mueser & McGurk, 2004). Among psychological disorders, schizophrenia is one of the most serious conditions and 100 years ago was considered to have a progressively deteriorating course, with little to no chance for recovery (Bleuler, 1911; Kraepelin, 1913). As a result of the discovery of effective treatments beginning in the 1960s, positive symptoms such as hallucinations and delusions may lessen and intensify in severity over an individual's lifetime, resulting in periods of remission followed by relapse. Although the situation has improved somewhat since that time, the long-term outcome of schizophrenia is still quite poor. Twenty-five percent of all psychiatric hospital beds are occupied by patients with schizophrenia (Geller, 1992) and in 2002, the estimated cost of this disorder was $62.7 billion (Wu et al., 2005). In one longitudinal study of adults with schizophrenia, only 20% had a good outcome when reassessed after 2 to 12 years (Breier et al., 1991). During this interval, 78% had a relapse requiring hospitalization, 38% had attempted suicide, and 24% had an episode of depression or bipolar disorder. Like substance abuse, coexisting depression increases the chance of a poorer overall outcome. Those who have both schizophrenia and depression are likely to be frequently hospitalized and to be unemployed (Sands & Harrow, 1999). Poorer general physical health and excessive medical morbidity (rates of illness) are also common among people with schizophrenia (Brown et al., 2000; Osby et al., 2000), including increased risk of infectious diseases (Rosenberg et al., 2001), physical injury as a result of violent victimization (Walsh et al., 2003), and smoking-related and other illnesses (deLeon et al., 1995).

Cultural factors play a role in the course of schizophrenia; positive outcomes are more often found in developing countries than in developed nations. This may seem contradictory to what one would expect but may be the result of fewer social supports for people in more industrialized countries. In industrialized nations, people often leave home and family for better economic opportunities in a distant city, but in turn have limited family support when illness occurs. Cultural factors that are more prominent in developing countries and appear to be associated with better outcome for patients include differences in social structure, the more central role of the family in caring for psychiatrically ill patients, and differing beliefs about the etiology of the disorder (Tseng, 2003). For example, people in developing nations are more likely to accommodate deviance by a member of the community. They are more likely to keep a person with mental illness at home rather than seek hospitalization. People in developing countries have a relatively simpler lifestyle, making it easier for a patient with cognitive impairments to negotiate the environment. All of these factors have been associated with a more positive patient prognosis (Sartorius et al., 1978), and more recent studies continue to support the role of the family and community in affecting the outcome for people with schizophrenia (Tseng, 2003).

A common misconception about schizophrenia is that it is associated with violence. In fact, the rate of violent acts committed by people with schizophrenia (and other serious mental disorders) is higher than rates of violence for the general population (Hodgins et al., 1996). However, it is not higher (and in some cases, it is lower) than among patients with other serious disorders such as depression and bipolar illness (Monahan et al., 2001). Among patients with schizophrenia recently discharged from a psychiatric hospital, 8% committed a violent act during the first 20 weeks after hospitalization and 15% committed a violent act after the first year (Monahan et al., 2001). Many different behaviors are included in definitions of violence, some of which are considered minor acts (simple assault without injury or weapon use), whereas others represent more serious violence (assault using a lethal weapon, assault resulting in injury, threat with a lethal weapon or sexual assault; Swanson et al., 2006). When examined by type of violence, the overall rate of violent acts committed by people with schizophrenia during a 6-month period was 19.1%, but only 3.6% were serious acts of violence. An additional factor is that violent acts of any type are more often perpetrated by people with both schizophrenia and substance abuse than by people with schizophrenia alone (Erkiran et al., 2006).

People with schizophrenia are often the victims of violence. In some instances, their impaired cognitive and emotional status makes them easy targets. However, people with schizophrenia are also at risk for violence because their disorder limits their occupational choices and their income. Thus, their lower socioeconomic status means that they often live in neighborhoods where crime is common. Furthermore, some people with this disorder are homeless, and living on the streets also increases the likelihood of being a crime victim. Overall, the percentage of individuals with schizophrenia who are victimized (from crimes such as assault, rape, and robbery) ranges from 16% over a one-year period (Walsh et al., 2003) to 34% when the time period is expanded to three years (Brekke et al., 2001). As with violence perpetration, most people with schizophrenia are the victims of nonviolent rather than violent crimes (Fitzgerald et al., 2005; Hiday et al., 2002).

People with schizophrenia are at risk for victimization by others. They often live in unsafe conditions, and their cognitive impairments make them easy targets.

People with schizophrenia are significantly impaired in many aspects of life functioning, including self-care, independent living, interpersonal relationships, work, school, parenting, and leisure time (Mueser & McGurk, 2004). Not every person with this disorder is impaired in each of these areas, and in many instances, it is not the presence of positive symptoms (which can be controlled with medication) that is associated with functional impairment. Rather, the disorder's cognitive deficits limit the ability to function effectively. Even a behavior as simple as getting dressed requires several different cognitive abilities (Bellack, 1992). *Executive functioning* (the ability to make decisions) is required to initiate the process of getting dressed, *memory* is required to recall where clothing articles are kept (drawers, closets), and *attention* is required in order to complete the process of getting dressed (not being distracted and therefore, not finishing the process; Velligan et al., 2000).

Delusions and hallucinations distract people with schizophrenia, leaving them with only a limited ability to attend to their environmental surroundings. For example, people with schizophrenia are unable to observe or detect the social cues of other people, leading to awkward social interactions. Finally, deficits in memory and concentration may affect the ability to hold a job (Velligan et al., 2000). Work performance suffers when workers are unable to remember job assignments or follow instructions (e.g., "Mary, sweep the floor once an hour and every 30 minutes check to make sure the hair stylists have clean towels for their stations").

Epidemiology Schizophrenia is recognized around the world and the prevalence is approximately the same in all cultures. The lifetime prevalence of schizophrenia averages 1%, ranging from 0.3 to 1.6% of the general United States population (Kessler et al., 2005). This percentage is consistent across different populations, cultures and level of industrialization (WHO, 1973). In any given year, between 16 and 40 of every 100,000 people develop schizophrenia (Jablensky, 2000), making it a very significant public health problem in terms of both its frequency and its disabling effects. Its onset can be either acute or gradual, and in many instances, *premorbid* (before the illness) features exist for many years before the actual psychotic symptoms emerge.

When the onset is gradual, the person often has some deterioration of functioning before the positive symptoms of the disorder emerge. In the *prodromal* phase, there may be social withdrawal or deterioration in personal hygiene, such as not bathing or not changing clothes. The person may also have difficulty functioning properly at work or school. As the disorder progresses, the person enters the *acute* phase. Here, the person exhibits the positive symptoms, including hallucinations, delusions, and thought disorder. Negative symptoms are also present, but they are overshadowed by the psychotic behaviors. After the acute episode, some people with schizophrenia have a *residual phase*. The psychotic symptoms are no longer present, but the negative symptoms often remain. The continuing presence of negative symptoms sometimes prevents the person from being successfully employed or having satisfying social relationships.

Sex, Race, and Ethnicity There are significant differences between the sexes with regard to the age of onset for schizophrenia, as well as its course and prognosis. Women tend to develop schizophrenia at a later age than men do. Perhaps because of this difference, women often have a milder form of the disorder, with fewer hospital admissions and better social functioning (Mueser & McGurk, 2004). When the disorder develops later, there is more opportunity to achieve adolescent and young adult developmental milestones and develop better social functioning (e.g., graduating from high school or college or getting married). Of course, just finding a difference between the sexes does not explain why that difference exists. The sex difference in age of onset may be related to hormonal and/or sociocultural factors. For example, the female hormone estrogen has a strong protective influence on brain development and is hypothesized to lessen the abnormal brain development commonly seen among those with schizophrenia (Goodman et al., 1996; see also "Etiology of Schizophrenia" later in this chapter).

With respect to sociocultural factors, females are socialized from a very early age to be more socially competent than males, and they have more extensive social networks (Combs & Mueser, 2007). As is true for other areas, the answer to why sex differences exist may not be as simple as social competence or more extensive social networks. Both factors appear to be important influences in lessening the overall impact of schizophrenia among women.

Within the United States, symptoms of psychosis are consistent across various racial and ethnic groups, including Korean Americans, African Americans, Latinos, and Euro-Americans (Bae & Brekke, 2002). Similarly, data from the World Health Organization (WHO, 1973) reveal that the clinical symptoms of schizophrenia are consistent worldwide. Across all cultures, paranoid schizophrenia is the most common type (39.8%), whereas the catatonic subtype is found least often (6.7%).

Although the *symptoms* of schizophrenia are common across racial and ethnic groups, rates at which a *diagnosis* of schizophrenia is given are not equally common, at least within the United States. African Americans are far more likely to receive a diagnosis of schizophrenia than are whites (e.g., Barnes, 2004; Bell & Mehta, 1980; Lawson et al., 1994) and Latino patients (Minsky et al., 2003), particularly when the diagnosis is based on unstructured clinical interviews. Members of other ethnic groups, even when expressing very similar symptoms, are more frequently diagnosed with psychotic depression. Factors such as racial and ethnic biases, misinterpretation of patient reports due to a lack of understanding of cultural features, or racial differences in the presentation of psychiatric symptoms may bias clinicians' interpretation of patient symptoms (Barnes, 2004). For example, among some African Americans the phrase "the witch is riding me" describes episodes of *isolated sleep paralysis*, a variant of panic disorder. However, the phrase is less familiar to white clinicians, who sometimes misinterpret this statement as a delusional belief. Such cultural insensitivity leads to misinterpretation of symptoms and inaccurate diagnosis (Minsky et al., 2003).

Even if not deliberate, racial bias appears to be a very real factor in the diagnosis of schizophrenia. Most diagnoses are based on interviews in which the clinician and patient meet face to face, so the patient's race is known to the evaluator. Determining diagnoses based solely on a person's symptoms (without knowing race) could eliminate potential racial bias. When clinicians make a diagnosis based on a written transcript of a diagnostic interview, rather than conducting an actual interview, African Americans are no more likely than European Americans to receive a diagnosis of schizophrenia (Arnold et al., 2004). These data suggest that the characteristics of a patient (in this case, race), not just the symptoms, may play an important role in determining a diagnosis. This is a very important issue because the label of schizophrenia still carries a negative connotation and a poor prognosis. A mistake in diagnosis may result in unsuitable treatment, with powerful medications being used inappropriately.

Inaccurate diagnosis may also result from inattention to cultural differences in behavior, lack of cultural competence among clinicians, language barriers and few bilingual therapists, and diagnostic errors as a result of inadequate clinical interviews conducted in busy outpatient clinics (Minsky et al., 2006). Eliminating racial and ethnic biases poses a significant challenge. Clinicians who are of the same race or ethnicity as the patient could reduce misunderstanding of cultural factors, but there are too few minority mental health professionals in the United States for that to be the single answer. Increasing cultural sensitivity and awareness of the issue is also important.

Developmental Factors As children, adults who develop schizophrenia may have situational anxiety, nervous tension, depression, and "psychotic-like" experiences such as perceptual disturbances, magical thinking, and referential ideas (Owens et al., 2005). *Magical thinking* describes the belief that thinking about something can make it happen. For example, after you wish your parents were dead, they are involved in a serious car accident, and you conclude that your thoughts caused the accident. If you have *ideas of reference*, you interpret casual events as being directly related to you. For example, you walk by two people and they start to laugh—you wonder if they are laughing at you. If you had *delusions of reference*, you would be sure that they were talking about you. These abnormalities in mood and perceptions have been reported consistently in childhood and suggest that some aspects of schizophrenia are present, though often undetected, long before the onset of the more dramatic positive symptoms.

Patients' childhood histories are usually collected retrospectively; that is, once the disorder is diagnosed, patients (or perhaps their parents) are asked to recall "how they were" before the symptoms began. These descriptions are compared with descriptions of people who do not suffer from the disorder. From a scientific perspective, this retrospective design is better than nothing at all, but it has a serious limitation. The cognitive deficits common among people with schizophrenia may limit the ability to recall premorbid functioning accurately. In addition, parents' recall of an adult child's early history may be affected by his or her more recent behaviors. Thus, any recollection of previous events may be biased by the current illness. A prospective research design that would assess premorbid behaviors objectively before an illness developed would be the preferable approach.

In one well-designed prospective study (Schiffman et al., 2004), Danish youth aged 11 to 13 were videotaped under *standardized* (identical) conditions while they were eating lunch at school. Observers rated the children's behavior for sociability (smiles, laughs, initiates or responds to conversations), involuntary movements (right or left hand, facial movement, other abnormal movements), and general neuromotor signs (raised elbows, eye movements, other abnormal movements). Nineteen years later, when the participants were between the ages of 31 and 33, they were interviewed by individuals unaware of their earlier behavioral ratings. Twenty-six children had developed schizophrenia. Their behaviors at age 11 to 13 were compared with those of adults who had other disorders and to adults who had no disorder. When compared with both groups, adults with schizophrenia were significantly less sociable when they were children. Furthermore, when compared with people who had a different psychiatric disorder (such as depression), people who developed schizophrenia had more subtle general neuromotor abnormalities as children. Because this study was prospective in design (not retrospective), included the entire birth registry of all children born in Denmark during a specific time (therefore there was no selection bias that might have influenced the results), used objective measures (rather than subjective report), and included a psychological comparison group, these results provide strong evidence that poor sociability and abnormal motor functioning may be factors uniquely related to the onset of schizophrenia.

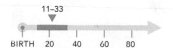

Schizophrenia usually begins in late adolescence or early adulthood, but approximately 23% of patients develop the disorder after age 40 (Harris & Jeste, 1988; see also Chapter 14). About 1% of adults have schizophrenia (Mueser & McGurk, 2004), but only 0.01% of people under age 18 suffer from this disorder. Within this group, more adolescents than children suffer from schizophrenia. When the disorder begins in childhood or adolescence (usually considered before age 18), it is called **early-onset schizophrenia (EOS)**, and has severe biological and behavioral consequences.

Biologically, children with EOS lose more cortical gray matter than children without a psychological disorder (Kranzler et al., 2006) over a five year period. This loss occurs on both sides of the brain and progresses from front to back (Vidal et al., 2006), indicating significant biological deterioration in brain functioning. Behaviorally, only between 8% and 20% of those with EOS ever achieve full symptom remission; most have persistent symptoms throughout their lifetimes (Eggers & Bunk, 1997; Röpcke & Eggers, 2005). Even when compared with patients with adult-onset schizophrenia or children with other forms of psychoses, patients with EOS are more impaired; they have additional psychotic episodes, are in need of more continuing psychiatric care, and

early-onset schizophrenia (EOS)
schizophrenia that develops in childhood or adolescence (usually before age 18)

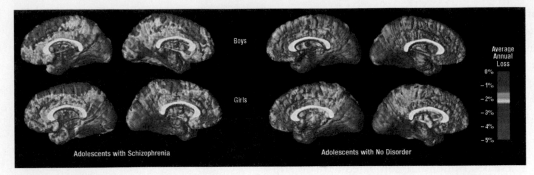

All adolescents undergo synaptic pruning. However, as the fMRI images above show, the rate is far advanced in children who have early-onset schizophrenia. The magenta color indicates the areas of greatest neuronal loss and violet the areas of least neuronal loss.

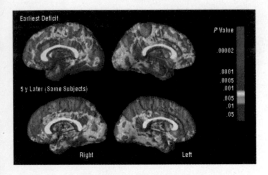

In the upper row of images (age 13), the areas of greatest neuronal loss are in the frontal lobe, the area commonly associated with reasoning and problem solving. Five years later, at age 18 (bottom), the areas of neuronal loss are more pervasive, encompassing virtually all areas of the brain.

brief psychotic disorder the sudden onset of any psychotic symptom that may resolve after one day and does not last for more than one month

schizophreniform disorder a condition with symptoms that are identical to those of schizophrenia except that the duration of the illness is shorter (less than 6 months) and there is less impairment in social or occupational functioning

are more impaired in the area of social functioning and independent living (Hollis, 2000; Kranzler et al., 2006). Perhaps the only positive factor for children with EOS is that their IQ scores remain stable even 13 years after the disorder's onset (Gochman et al., 2005). Clearly, this is one disorder where the earlier the onset, the more severe the outcome.

The long-term outcome is little better when the onset of schizophrenia occurs in adolescence. More than 10 years later, 83% of one sample had at least one additional episode that required inpatient treatment, and 74% were still receiving psychiatric treatment (Lay et al., 2001). Impairments in life functioning were common: 57% did not achieve their premorbid educational and occupational goals, 66% were socially disabled (were socially isolated, avoided social activities, were unable to do typical household chores, lived without a sexual relationship), and 75% were financially dependent on their parents or public assistance. People with EOS have also been found to be less likely to marry or remain married (Eaton, 1975; Munk-Jørgensen, 1987), especially if they were male, and less likely to go to college (Kessler et al., 1995).

Even before delusions and hallucinations begin, children and adolescents with EOS are socially withdrawn, have difficulty interacting with peers, and have school adjustment problems (McClellan et al., 2003; Muratori et al., 2005). Because early onset does not allow much opportunity for normal social development, it is not surprising that the long-term outcome for those with EOS is worse than when schizophrenia begins in adulthood. Outcome is extremely poor when the disorder begins before age 14 (Remschmidt & Theisen, 2005).

OTHER PSYCHOTIC DISORDERS

Schizophrenia is the most common type of psychotic disorder and the one that has been most thoroughly studied. However, psychotic experiences do not always mean that the person is suffering from schizophrenia. There are several other types of psychotic disorders.

Brief psychotic disorder is the sudden onset of any psychotic symptom, such as delusions, hallucinations, disorganized speech, or grossly disorganized or catatonic behavior. As indicated by its name, this disorder may resolve after one day and does not last for more than one month. After the disorder remits (resolves itself), the person returns to a normal level of functioning. Often, the disorder's onset is associated with significant psychosocial stressors, such as the death of a loved one or birth of a child (see the box "Real People, Real Disorders: Andrea Yates and Postpartum Psychosis").

The symptoms of **schizophreniform disorder** are identical to those of schizophrenia with two exceptions. First, the duration of the illness is shorter, ranging from at least 1 month to less than 6 months. In a few instances, the symptoms seem to just disappear. In other instances, a person is treated successfully and never has another episode, although why treatment is successful in any particular case is not known.

The second difference between people with schizophrenia and those with schizophreniform disorder is that in the case of schizophreniform disorder, impaired social or occupational functioning is a possibility, but some people can still conduct their daily activities. For example,

Jack was suspicious that his neighbors were listening in on his telephone conversations or were keeping a record of when he entered and left his apartment. However, he did not harbor those same suspicions about co-workers. Therefore, although he would not

real people, real disorders

Andrea Yates and Postpartum Psychosis

Andrea Yates methodically drowned her five children (ages 6 months to 7 years) in the family bathtub on June 20, 2001. From all accounts, she was suffering from a severe case of recurrent postpartum psychosis, a condition for which she had been treated in the past. After drowning her oldest son, she called the police, was arrested, and confessed to the crime. Her defense asserted postpartum psychosis as the reason for the killings. Yates told her jail psychiatrist, "It was the seventh deadly sin. My children weren't righteous. They stumbled because I was evil. The way I was raising them they could never be saved. They were doomed to perish in the fires of hell." Although all agreed that Mrs. Yates was psychotic, she was found guilty of the crime and sentenced to prison. However, her conviction was overturned, and in her second trial, the jury found her not guilty by reason of insanity. She was com-

mitted to a mental institution until she is no longer in need of treatment.

The birth of a baby is usually a happy and eagerly anticipated event. Yet, postpartum psychosis occurs in 1 or 2 women out of every 1000 who give birth (Robertson et al., 2005). Research suggests that both stressful life events and/or a preexisting psychological disorder (schizoaffective disorder, major depression, bipolar disorder) may be related to its onset (Kumar et al., 1993; Robertson et al., 2005). In some instances, hormonal changes that commonly occur a few days after childbirth also may contribute to the onset of postpartum psychosis, particularly in women who had a psychological disorder before they became pregnant (Kumar et al., 1993). As in other disorders, both biological and psychosocial factors appear to play a role in postpartum psychosis.

---

answer his telephone (because his neighbors might be listening) and was reluctant to leave his apartment (because the neighbors would mark down the time), he did leave once a day to go to work.

Individuals with **schizoaffective disorder** might be considered to have both schizophrenia and a depressive disorder. That is, in addition to all of the symptoms of schizophrenia, the patient also suffers from a major depressive, manic, or mixed episode disorder at some point during the illness. Schizoaffective disorder is a controversial diagnosis. It has been considered to be a type of schizophrenia, a type of mood disorder, or an intermediate condition between the two. When comparisons of patients with schizophrenia, schizoaffective disorder, and mood disorders were made, positive symptoms were more severe in people with schizophrenia than in people with schizoaffective disorder, but both groups had equally severe cognitive impairments (Evans et al., 1999). Other investigators, examining many different variables, suggest that schizoaffective disorder should be renamed *psychotic mood disorder*, due to the presence of the mood symptoms (Lake & Hurwitz, 2006). In some instances, diagnostic decisions are made on which group of symptoms (psychotic or mood) is considered to be more severe or more impairing.

Delusional disorder consists of the presence of a nonbizarre delusion (defined as an event that might actually happen; see Table 10.3).

Janice does not believe that she needs to see a mental health professional. She is confident that, despite all medical evidence to the contrary, she has contracted cancer. Her belief is based on the fact that she can actually feel the cancer cells eating away at her body. She sits in the psychologist's office, calmly relating the fact that she has consulted at least 20 physicians, all of whom are wrong. Her family physician told her that he would not see her anymore unless she consulted a mental health professional.

Schizoaffective Disorder

The Case of Josh

"I looked out the window and saw this guy with a machete chasing one of the psychiatrists."

www.mypsychlab.com

schizoaffective disorder a condition in which, in addition to all of the symptoms of schizophrenia, the patient also suffers from a major depressive, manic, or mixed episode disorder at some point during the illness

delusional disorder a condition in which a person has a nonbizarre delusion, no other psychotic symptoms, and few changes in overall functioning other than the behaviors immediately surrounding the delusion

TABLE 10.3

Common Delusional Themes among Those with Delusional Disorder

Type	Content
Erotomanic	Another individual, usually of higher status, is in love with the person (sometimes found among "celebrity stalkers")
Grandiose	The person has feelings of inflated worth, power, knowledge, identity, or special relationships to a deity or famous person
Jealous	The person's sexual partner is unfaithful
Persecutory	The person (or someone close to the person) is being badly mistreated
Somatic	The person has a medical condition or physical defect for which no medical cause can be found

People with delusional disorder do not have other psychotic symptoms except perhaps hallucinations that are directly related to the delusion (such as Janice's report of feeling the cancer cells eating away inside her). Also, in contrast to schizophrenia, there are few changes in the person's overall functioning other than the behaviors immediately surrounding the delusion (Janice's "doctor-shopping" to find someone who will treat her cancer). Because people with delusional disorder do not believe that they need treatment, it is unclear how many people suffer from this disorder.

When two or more individuals who have a close relationship share the same delusional belief, the disorder is known as **shared psychotic disorder** (folie à deux).

Allen was a successful businessman. His cognitive faculties began to fade as he approached retirement. He had difficulty with daily activities, and his wife, Alicia, began to have cognitive problems as well (as a result of a mugging incident in which she sustained head injuries). Family members, concerned about their safety, moved them to an assisted living environment where their activities were monitored by a medical staff. Allen began complaining that he was being held against his will, that the staff was stealing his belongings, that his food was being poisoned, and that his family was trying to kill him. Initially, Alicia tried to convince him that none of this was real, but after a few weeks, she became convinced that her husband's beliefs were true. Alicia needed surgery and was transferred to a medical center and then to a rehabilitation center for physical therapy. As a result of her separation from Allen, her delusional beliefs quickly disappeared.

Shared psychotic disorder begins when one person (sometimes termed the "inducer" or "the primary case") develops a psychotic disorder with delusional content. The "inducer" is the dominant person in the relationship with a second individual (usually related by blood or marriage and living in close physical proximity) and over time, imposes the delusional system on the second person, who then adopts the belief system and acts accordingly. If the relationship is interrupted (as happened for Allen and Alicia), the delusional beliefs of the second person quickly disappear. Shared psychotic disorder is equally common among males and females, and affects both younger and older patients. Among one sample, 90% of those suffering from this disorder were married couples, siblings, or parent-child dyads (many of whom were socially isolated from others). Dementia, depression, and mental retardation were common features among those with this disorder (Silveira & Seeman, 1995).

shared psychotic disorder   a condition in which two or more persons who have a close relationship share the same delusional belief; also known as folie à deux

- The consequences of schizophrenia are more serious and long-lasting when the disorder begins in childhood, a condition known as early-onset schizophrenia (EOS).

- In contrast to schizophrenia, which is considered to be a chronic disorder, other forms of psychosis may be time-limited. Brief psychotic disorder, for example, may last for only one day. Schizophreniform disorder lasts no more than 6 months.

- Schizoaffective disorder is a condition in which psychotic symptoms and major depression are equal in severity and frequency. In this group of patients, the positive symptoms of psychosis are less severe than in those with schizophrenia alone.

APPLICATION QUESTION   The case of Andrea Yates illustrates how a biological event (the birth of a baby) can result in the onset of a very serious psychological disorder (postpartum psychosis). Does this mean that childbirth is the reason for this disorder? Why or why not?

Etiology of Schizophrenia

Schizophrenia is a complex disorder. Its symptoms are quite dramatic and not easily understood by the general public. Many different theories about its development have been offered, and in some cases, discarded. Overall, a century of research has been more successful in ruling out than in establishing causes of schizophrenia. For example, it is now clear that this disorder is not caused by "poor" or "bad" parenting—a relief to families who have to cope with someone struggling with this disorder. It is now quite clear that schizophrenia probably involves many different elements. In this section we examine the biological, psychological, and social/environmental factors that may play a role in the onset of schizophrenia.

BIOLOGICAL FACTORS

There is a growing consensus, based on research done over the past 50 years, that schizophrenia is a neurodevelopmental disorder. Research has established that this disorder has a genetic component and that abnormalities exist in both brain structure and brain function. This does not mean that we now thoroughly understand this complex disorder—there is much that we still have to learn. However, we now know that there are no simplistic explanations and no single biological factor. The following will describe what we know so far.

Neurotransmitters   The three different symptom categories that make up schizophrenia might suggest abnormalities in several different neurotransmitter systems. By far the most attention has been paid to neurotransmitters associated with the dramatic positive symptoms. For more than 50 years, schizophrenia has been considered to be a disorder associated with an excess of the neurotransmitter *dopamine*. The **dopamine hypothesis** emerged from clinical observations that chemical compounds such as amphetamines and *levadopa* (also called L-dopa, a drug used to treat Parkinson's disease) increase the amount of dopamine available in the neural synapse, which, in turn, can lead to the development or worsening of psychotic symptoms. In contrast, substances that decrease dopamine seem to be associated with the lessening of psychotic symptoms.

  We use the term *associated with* above because a causal relationship between dopamine and schizophrenia has not been clearly established, and three possibilities must be considered. First, excessive dopamine could lead to the development of

dopamine hypothesis   the theory that a cause of schizophrenia is the presence of too much dopamine in the neural synapses

schizophrenia. Second, the chronic stress created by a disorder as serious as schizophrenia may create many different brain abnormalities, including excess dopamine. Finally, both excess dopamine and schizophrenia could result from some third, currently unknown, variable. Although the direction of this relationship remains uncertain, the existence of abnormal dopamine levels in the neural synapses of patients with schizophrenia has been established. The relationship is far from simple, however. It appears that *too much* dopamine in the limbic area of the brain may be responsible for positive symptoms (i.e., overactivity of behavior and perception), whereas *too little* dopamine in the cortical areas may be responsible for negative symptoms (i.e., impaired cognitive abilities and motivation; Davis et al., 1991; Moore et al., 1999). Therefore, dopamine abnormalities are not simply a matter of too much or too little in the brain. They may take the form of both excesses and deficits within the same individual. This finding may explain why medications that block dopamine levels reduce positive symptoms but do not change negative symptoms (see the section "Treatment of Schizophrenia and Other Psychotic Disorders").

As you will recall, the second category of symptoms found in people with schizophrenia are the negative symptoms, which are defined as an absence of behaviors that are found in people without the disorder. In many ways, the negative symptoms of schizophrenia (e.g., slowed speech, apathy) are similar to the psychomotor retardation symptoms found in depression. In Chapter 6, we learned that these symptoms of depression may be related to the limited availability of *serotonin* (a different neurotransmitter) in certain neural synapses. It appears that serotonin deficits may also be present in the same brain areas in people with schizophrenia (Horacek et al., 2006). Finally, there is a third set of neurotransmitters, *GABA and glutamate*, and there is evidence in both animals and humans that these substances play an important role with respect to learning and remembering new material. Therefore, deficits in these neurotransmitters may be associated with some of the cognitive impairments (the third category of symptoms) found among people with schizophrenia (Addington et al., 2005).

Genetics and Family Studies Determining that too much dopamine exists in the limbic system of patients with schizophrenia may explain some of the disorder's symptomatology, but it does not explain how or why the neurotransmitter abnormalities exist. Genetics may be one explanation (Sullivan, 2005). As with some other psychological disorders, schizophrenia seems to "run in families." But again, just because a parent has schizophrenia does not mean that the child will also develop the disorder. Genetically, the risk of developing schizophrenia is 15% if one parent has the disorder and 50% if both parents have the disorder (McGuffin et al., 1995). Rates of *concordance*, both twins having the disorder, are higher among monozygotic (MZ, or identical) twin pairs, ranging from 60 to 84% (Cardno et al., 1999). Modern genetic approaches have made significant progress in *mapping* (identifying) specific genes that may be associated with schizophrenia. Nine chromosomes and seven candidate genes have been identified (Harrison & Owen, 2003) as potentially contributing to the development of schizophrenia through at least two possible pathways: direct transmission of the actual disorder from one family member to another or indirect transmission by affecting the functioning of neurotransmitters such as dopamine (Norton et al., 2006).

With respect to direct transmission of schizophrenia, there appears to be a positive genetic relationship between areas on one gene (known as GAD1) with family members who have early-onset schizophrenia (Addington et al., 2005). However, linkage studies are not precise (not everyone with the genetic abnormality develops the disorder). Furthermore, the results are not always replicated when a second study sample is examined. The genetics of schizophrenia has been the subject of considerable research; over 3,000 potential genes and genetic abnormalities have been identified (Lewis et al., 2003), but few of these studies have consistently identified the same gene (Norton et al,

The Genain quadruplets were four identical sisters brought up together who all developed schizophrenia as young adults. However, their age of onset and their symptoms differed.

examining the evidence

Genetics and Environment in the Development of Schizophrenia

Because MZ (genetically identical) twins are not 100% concordant for schizophrenia, a strict genetic etiology is unlikely. In fact, 80% of those with psychotic symptoms do not have a parent with the disorder, and in 60% of the cases, no family history can be identified (Gottesman, 2001). Therefore, other factors must contribute to this disorder. One such factor now receiving increased attention is the family environment.

■ **The Evidence**   In Finland, a national sample of children adopted away at birth whose mothers had schizophrenia was compared with children who were also adopted away but whose mothers did not have schizophrenia (Tienari et al., 2004). The family environment in the adoptive family was classified as disordered (high in criticism, conflict, constricted affect, and boundary problems) or healthy (low in criticism, conflict, constricted affect, and boundary problems). The offspring were interviewed at age 23 and again at age 44. As adults, 36.8% of the biological children of schizophrenic mothers who were raised in a "disordered" family environment developed a "schizophrenic spectrum disorder," whereas only 5.8% of children of schizophrenic mothers who were reared in a "healthy" family environment developed one of these disorders. In contrast, the adoptive family environment was not a factor for those children whose mother did not have schizophrenia; 5.3% of children raised in disordered environments developed a schizophrenic spectrum disorder, as did 4.8% of children raised in healthy family environments.

■ **Examining the Evidence**   These results suggest that a family environment high in conflict and criticism and low in expressions of emotion may be an important factor in the development of schizophrenia *but only when the child has a parent with schizophrenia*. Whereas, overall, about 15% of offspring develop schizophrenia if one parent has the disorder, that percentage is doubled when the children are raised in a "disordered" family environment, even when they are not raised by a parent with the disorder.

■ **What do these data illustrate about the role of genetics?**

1. Even when a person has a "genetic predisposition" to develop schizophrenia (mother has the disorder) and is raised in an environment that is not "healthy," 63.2% do *not* develop a schizophrenic spectrum disorder.
2. Although 36.8% developed a schizophrenic spectrum disorder, only 5.1% developed schizophrenia; many of the others had psychotic disorders or depression with psychosis. This means that what appears to be inherited is a general risk factor for psychosis, not necessarily for schizophrenia.

■ **What do these data illustrate about the role of the environment?**

1. A conflictual or disorganized environment appears to increase the risk for a psychotic disorder, but only among those who have relatives with schizophrenia.
2. Even with no genetic risk and a "healthy family environment," 4.8% of individuals still developed a schizophrenic spectrum disorder.

■ **Conclusion**   The answer is not simple, as both biological and environmental factors appear to play a role. If you were a psychologist, how would you explain the outcome of this study to your female patient with schizophrenia who wants to have a child?

2006; Sullivan, 2005). Until outcomes are consistently replicated, it is difficult to determine the actual contribution of particular genes. Most scientists agree that if a genetic basis exists for schizophrenia, it probably involves the action of numerous genes (polygenetic influence). With respect to indirect transmission, scientists believe that genes that produce general changes in dopamine levels alone may be insufficient for development of the disorder. However, they may provide a biological vulnerability that, when combined with other biological abnormalities and environmental stressors (such as those described below), may result in the development of schizophrenia.

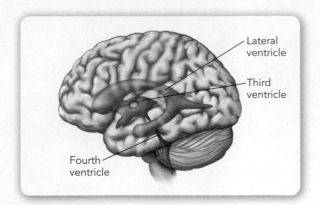

FIGURE 10.1
Ventricles of the Brain

The brain's ventricles contain cerebrospinal fluid, which helps cushion the brain against injury. Compared with people with no disorder, people with schizophrenia have enlarged ventricles. Although the exact meaning of this difference is not clear, it is one bit of evidence suggesting a neurodevelopmental basis for the disorder.

Neuroanatomy The dramatic abnormalities in perception, thought, and behavior found among people with schizophrenia lead naturally to consideration of brain abnormalities, which may be structural or functional. One consistent neuroanatomical abnormality found among people with schizophrenia is enlargement of the brain *ventricles* (Wright et al., 2000). The ventricles are cavities in the brain that contain cerebrospinal fluid (see Figure 10.1), which acts as a cushion to prevent brain damage if there is a blow to the head. In addition to enlarged ventricles, people with schizophrenia have a reduction in cortical (gray matter) areas of the brain (Andreasen et al., 1994) compared with those with no disorder. Based on MRI data, it is clear that these structural brain abnormalities are present at the onset of the disorder (Vita et al., 2006). These same abnormalities exist in the non-ill parents of adults with schizophrenia (Ohara et al., 2006), the children of adults with schizophrenia (Diwadkar et al., 2006), and other non-ill relatives (McDonald et al., 2002). The consistency of these abnormalities, coupled with their existence among people who do not show symptoms of the disorder (but who have a relative with the disorder), indicate that these abnormalities are not the result of the illness but are present before the positive symptoms emerge.

Abnormal brain structure exists not only at the macro level of enlarged ventricles and decreased cortical size. Differences are also evident at the basic cellular level of the brain. Brain abnormalities that appear specific to people with schizophrenia (compared with those with no psychiatric disorder or a different disorder) include mild structural disorganization at the level of the individual brain cells (evident at autopsy) and altered neuronal connections in multiple brain areas (Opler & Susser, 2005). This type of cellular disorganization cannot happen as a result of brain deterioration or aging; it can only occur early in the process of brain development (before birth). Studies of cerebral development indicate that this phase of cortex development occurs during the second trimester of pregnancy. Therefore, it is clear that these abnormalities develop long before the onset of the observable symptoms of schizophrenia.

Viral Theories and Other Prenatal Stressors There are now sufficient data, including the neuroanatomical data presented above, to conclude that structural and functional brain abnormalities exist among people with schizophrenia. Genetics may contribute to this abnormal development, but genetics alone cannot account for the onset of schizophrenia. Another aspect that may affect fetal brain development is the prenatal environment. Prenatal factors identified as potentially associated with the later onset of schizophrenia include maternal genital or reproductive infections during the time of conception (Babulas et al., 2006), influenza during the first or second trimester period (Brown et al., 2004), nutritional deprivation during early gestation (Susser et al., 1996), lead exposure during the second trimester (Opler & Susser, 2005), bleeding during pregnancy (Cannon et al., 2002), and severe prenatal maternal stress (King et al., 2005).

Among all of these prenatal risk factors, one of the most thoroughly investigated is maternal exposure to the influenza virus during pregnancy. In an initial report (Mednick et al., 1988), children of mothers who were exposed to an influenza virus during their second trimester (the second three months) of pregnancy were at greater risk of developing schizophrenia when they became adults. Since the publication of this study, the relationship of influenza and schizophrenia has been an area of continuous controversy. About 50% of the research literature confirms this initial relationship, but the other 50% is unable to detect any increased risk for schizophrenia following influenza exposure. One reason for these inconsistent findings is that, in many instances, determining whether the mother was exposed to influenza depended on the mother's recall rather than objective medical data. In one of the few studies where objective evidence exists, exposure to influenza, documented by presence of the virus in the mother's blood, resulted in a sevenfold increase in the risk of developing schizophrenia, when exposure occurred during the first, but not the second, trimester (Brown et al., 2004).

How could exposure to influenza be related to the development of schizophrenia? Since the influenza virus does not cross the placenta, the virus itself is not responsible for any abnormal brain development. However, when a pregnant woman (or anyone) contracts influenza, the immune system produces antibodies (in this case, IgG antibodies) to fight the infection. These antibodies cross the placental barrier and react with fetal brain *antigens* (a substance that stimulates production of antibodies), producing an immunological response that disrupts fetal brain development. In turn, abnormalities in *structural* brain development may then trigger *functional* abnormalities that in turn result in the onset of schizophrenia (Wright et al, 1999). Think about an automobile engine. If it is not built (structured) correctly, it will not run (function) correctly.

Although no direct studies in humans are available to support this hypothesis, the offspring of pregnant mice that are deliberately exposed to the influenza virus have a reduced number of cells in the cortex and hippocampal areas of the brain. This is a significant finding because these are the same neuroanatomical areas that have been identified as abnormal in patients with schizophrenia (Fatemi et al., 1999). Given the complex nature of schizophrenia, it is far too simplistic to conclude that it is caused simply by exposure to the influenza virus. Its etiology is probably much more complicated. Furthermore, it is important to note that many pregnant women are exposed to influenza each year and only 1% of adults develop schizophrenia. Therefore, other factors must play a role.

Many obstetrical complications have positive but weak relationships to schizophrenia, but these do not appear to play a major role (Cannon et al., 2002). Overall, the definition of obstetrical complications is very broad, and when applied across the general population, 25 to 30% of all pregnancies have some type of complication. So again, you cannot conclude that all children born to women with pregnancy complications will develop schizophrenia (Rapoport et al., 2005). It is more likely that these complications signal the presence of other factors with a more direct role, or indicate a general vulnerability to the development of various mental illnesses. In the case of schizophrenia, it is possible that these factors, when combined with a genetic predisposition, may be the initial triggers leading to the development of the abnormal brain structures we have discussed.

A Neurodevelopmental Model of Schizophrenia

From a biological perspective, schizophrenia is best conceptualized as a neurodevelopmental disorder. Genetic and prenatal or perinatal (occurring at the time of birth) risk factors may set the stage for a disease process that encompasses biological, cognitive, and social changes that occur over time and result in schizophrenia (see Figure 10.2). Longitudinal studies using repeated fMRI neuroimaging (Rapoport et al., 2005) show that people with schizophrenia lose significant gray matter during adolescence through a normal biological process known as **synaptic pruning** (weaker synaptic contacts in the brain are eliminated and stronger connections are further strengthened). For people with schizophrenia, synaptic pruning occurs at a rate faster than it does in people without schizophrenia, beginning in childhood and accelerating in adolescence. The timing of this acceleration coincides with the emergence of subtle behavioral, motor, and cognitive abnormalities (Jones et al., 1994; Walker et al., 1994). Impaired peer relationships, enhanced social isolation and social anxiety, disruptive behaviors in preadolescent boys, and

synaptic pruning a process in which weaker synaptic contacts in the brain are eliminated and stronger connections are further strengthened

FIGURE 10.2

Neurodevelopmental Model of Schizophrenia

In this general neurodevelopmental model, many different biological and environmental factors are shown that probably contribute to the onset of schizophrenia.

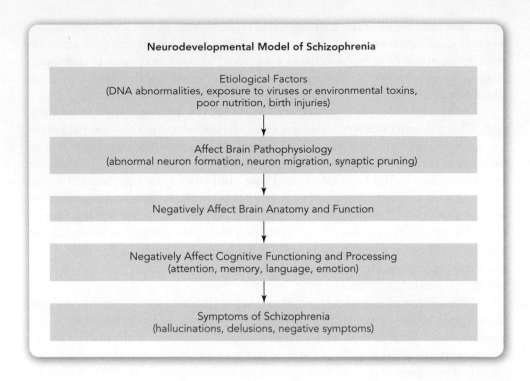

Neurodevelopmental Model of Schizophrenia

Etiological Factors
(DNA abnormalities, exposure to viruses or environmental toxins, poor nutrition, birth injuries)

↓

Affect Brain Pathophysiology
(abnormal neuron formation, neuron migration, synaptic pruning)

↓

Negatively Affect Brain Anatomy and Function

↓

Negatively Affect Cognitive Functioning and Processing
(attention, memory, language, emotion)

↓

Symptoms of Schizophrenia
(hallucinations, delusions, negative symptoms)

withdrawal behaviors in preadolescent girls also emerge during this time. All of these behaviors are associated with, but not specific to, the onset of schizophrenia in adulthood (Done et al., 1994). However, schizophrenia is not simply a biological process; some of the brain abnormalities seen in people with schizophrenia also occur in their relatives, who never develop the disorder. This means that other factors, such as psychological and environmental influences, probably contribute as well.

FAMILY INFLUENCES

Historically, the "schizophrenogenic mother" was considered as an environmental factor representing either a cause and/or a response to the presence of schizophrenia in a child (Parker, 1982), even an adult child. This concept emerged from the clinical observations of mental health professionals who worked with families of patients with schizophrenia and who described patients' mothers as dominant, overprotective, and rejecting. However, controlled scientific investigations (including longitudinal designs) did not confirm the existence of such a behavior pattern (Hartwell, 1996). How do we reconcile the clinical observations with the empirical data? One explanation is that the concept of the "schizophrenogenic mother" was based in part on observations or descriptions of family interactions when the patient already had schizophrenia. However, when a psychological disorder is present, particularly one that affects cognition and behavior as seriously as does schizophrenia, family interactions are also affected. In many cases, parents must assume substantial responsibility for their children—even their adult children—and this could result in parents acting in a domineering and overprotective fashion, perhaps out of necessity given their child's disorder. However, this does not mean that parents behaved in this way *before* the patient developed the disorder.

Ruling out poor parenting or a "bad" family environment highlights an important point: what science has determined is (or is not) the cause of a disorder is not necessarily the same as what people believe is responsible for their suffering. Earlier, we noted how culture may affect the expression and interpretation of the symptoms of schizophrenia. Similarly, culture may also shape explanations of its etiology. Whereas white patients born in the United Kingdom (UK) gave a biological explanation for their illness (e.g., it is the result of physical illness or substance use) (McCabe & Priebe, 2004), second-generation UK residents of African-Caribbean, Bangladeshi, or West African descent were more likely to provide a social explanation (e.g., interpersonal problems/stress/negative childhood experiences) or a supernatural one (e.g., magic spells/evil forces).

Returning to our examination of familial factors, even though the notion of a "schizophrenogenic mother" is no longer accepted, environmental factors such as family interaction remain the subject of scientific scrutiny. The concept known as **expressed emotion** (EE) describes a family's emotional involvement and critical attitudes that are found among people with a psychological disorder, in this case, schizophrenia. Patients with schizophrenia who live in family environments that are high on EE variables (which include high levels of emotional overinvolvement and critical attitudes) are more likely to relapse and have higher rates of rehospitalization (e.g., Butzlaff & Hooley, 1998). High EE is an environmental stressor that may increase the likelihood of relapse among those with schizophrenia. However, a treatment designed to increase communication and problem-solving skills among families of a patient with schizophrenia was no more effective than the control condition of monthly family visits (Schooler et al., 1997). This means that although high EE may predict relapse, it may not be possible to change these family patterns once they are established.

Unlike the study presented in "Examining the Evidence: Genetics and Environment in the Development of Schizophrenia" (which was a prospective study), the relationship between high EE and relapse is based mainly on correlational data. Therefore, no conclusions about the role of EE as a *causal* factor are available. It is possible that high levels of emotional involvement and critical family attitudes emerge *after* the onset of the patient's disorder. Coping with someone with schizophrenia can be very stressful, creating financial and emotional burdens as well as negative health consequences for family members (Dyck et al., 1999). In fact, the family interaction patterns identified as characteristic of EE have been identified with other disorders, such as drug and alcohol abuse. High EE may reflect the emotional toll of living with a family member with any type of severely impairing mental disorder.

The relationship of EE to relapse and rehospitalization may be unique to whites. Whereas low levels of criticism and fewer intrusive behaviors by relatives were associated with better patient outcome for white patients, high levels of critical and intrusive behavior were associated with better outcomes for African American patients (Rosenfarb et al., 2006), illustrating once again the need to consider culture, race, and ethnicity when studying abnormal behavior. Given these differences, the role of EE in the course of schizophrenia requires further study and should include attention to other racial and ethnic groups as well.

We noted that schizophrenia "runs in families." In some instances, the relatives of patients with schizophrenia also have schizophrenia; in other instances, they may have some behaviors associated with the disorder, such as exaggerated distrust of strangers, but not at a level that produces impairment. These relatives possess *traits* associated with schizophrenia, such as a deficit in social cognition. Although definitions of this construct differ, it is useful to think of social cognition as the "mental operations underlying social interactions, which include the human ability and capacity to perceive the intentions and dispositions of others" (Brothers, 1990, p. 28). Social cognition, sometimes called social perception, includes skills such as the ability to perceive when someone is interested in conversation or to interpret eye contact or a smile from a stranger.

Melanie, age 20, was diagnosed with paranoid schizophrenia. She was hospitalized after she went to the local FBI office demanding the surveillance tapes that she believed they

expressed emotion a concept used to describe the level of emotional involvement and critical attitudes that exist within the family of a patient with schizophrenia

had collected regarding her daily activities. When Melanie's mother, Linda, came to the unit for a consultation with the social worker, the social worker noticed that Linda did not make eye contact and asked the social worker at least 12 times who would have access to her daughter's hospital records.

Although Linda had never been treated for schizophrenia, her behavior indicated deficits in social cognition. A **gene–environment correlation** means that the same person who provides a patient's genetic makeup also provides the environment in which that person lives. Thus, individuals who are at increased genetic risk for schizophrenia may also be exposed to environments that may also increase risk of developing symptoms of schizophrenia. Did Linda's mother contribute to her daughter's condition by virtue of shared genes or by fostering an environment limited in appropriate social cognition? In such a case, it is difficult to disentangle genetic and environmental influences on the development of a disorder—they are deeply intertwined.

concept CHECK

- Advances in neuroscience have allowed for a much better understanding of structural and functional brain abnormalities. Only ventricular enlargement has been a consistently reported structural abnormality in schizophrenia, although many different abnormalities have been hypothesized.

- To date, there is some evidence for a genetic contribution to the development of schizophrenia, but it may not be as a result of direct transmission of specific genes. Genes may also affect the expression of schizophrenia indirectly by affecting the functioning of neurotransmitters such as dopamine.

- Twin and family studies illustrate the complex roles of genes and the environment in contributing to the development of schizophrenia. Concordance rates (both twins having schizophrenia) are higher among monozygotic (MZ) than dizygotic (DZ) twin pairs. Furthermore, not every child whose parent has schizophrenia will develop the disorder, and many people develop schizophrenia even though neither of their parents has ever had the disorder.

- The neurodevelopmental model of schizophrenia suggests that genetics and prenatal and/or perinatal risk factors may set the stage for a disease process that encompasses biological, social, and cognitive changes. An important concept is synaptic pruning, whereby weaker synaptic contacts are eliminated and stronger ones are further strengthened. In people with schizophrenia, this process is accelerated and is associated with behavioral, motor, and cognitive abnormalities.

APPLICATION QUESTION A viral model for the development of schizophrenia is illustrated by studies examining exposure to the influenza virus in pregnant women. Given the number of people who catch the flu each year, how strong is the evidence for this theory?

Treatment of Schizophrenia and Other Psychotic Disorders

Much of the historical treatment of mental illnesses discussed in Chapter 1 actually describes treatment of psychotic disorders such as schizophrenia. Until the last 50 years, institutionalization and humane treatments such as those proposed by Pinel, Tuke, Rush, and Dix (see Chapter 1) were among the few courses of action available to treat these disorders or at least separate people suffering from psychological disorders from the rest of society. Surgical treatments, in the form of primitive lobotomies, were also done, but primarily these were attempts to decrease a patient's agitated, aggressive, or violent be-

gene–environment correlation the same person who provides a patient's genetic make-up also provides the environment in which that person lives

havior. *Lobotomies* involved first administering anesthesia and then entering the person's brain either through a hole drilled in the skull or by inserting a device similar to an ice pick above the eyeball. The rationale for these procedures was that emotions were seated in the brain and that removing some of the brain matter would alleviate suffering (similar to *trephination* discussed in Chapter 1). The outcomes of lobotomies were generally negative, and included cognitive and emotional deficits and in some cases death. The situation has changed dramatically; several effective treatments are now available for people with schizophrenia. These treatments are far from universally or uniformly effective, but they constitute a great advance over what was available 100 years ago.

PHARMACOLOGICAL TREATMENT

Pharmacotherapy (medication) is the treatment of choice for schizophrenia. The most common medication class is the **antipsychotics**, which block dopamine receptors at four different receptor sites labeled D1, D2, D3, and D4 (Horacek et al., 2006). However, blocking the receptor is not simply an "all or nothing" process. Depending on the particular drug, blocking may be temporary, permanent, partial, or complete, and the type of blocking affects how well the drug works. Antipsychotics have only limited effects, however. They do not improve the negative symptoms or the cognitive deficits found among people with schizophrenia. Antipsychotics are efficacious at decreasing positive symptoms and consist of two types—typical and atypical.

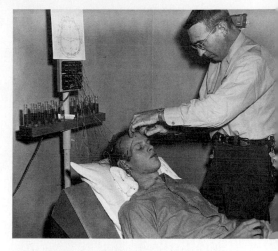

In the 1940s and 1950s, many people who were considered to have uncontrollable behavior were given a surgical treatment called a lobotomy. Although there were different procedures, all were designed to sever some neuronal connections in the brain.

Typical Antipsychotics Before the 1990s, the available antipsychotics (now called **conventional** or **typical antipsychotics**) effectively reduced the positive symptoms of schizophrenia but produced serious side effects. These included muscle stiffness, tremors, and **tardive dyskinesia**, a neurological condition characterized by abnormal and involuntary motor movements of the face, mouth, limbs, and trunk (Gray et al., 2005). The most common symptoms of tardive dyskinesia are movements of the tongue (lip licking, sucking, smacking, and fly-catching movements), jaw (chewing, grinding), face (grimacing, tics), and eyes (blinking, brow arching). Unfortunately, tardive dyskinesia appears to be a fairly common condition; after 15 years of treatment with typical antipsychotics, about 52% of patients will develop this side effect (Kane et al., personal communication, cited in Tarsy & Baldessarini, 2006). Tardive dyskinesia may begin months or years after the start of the medication (Margolese & Ferreri, 2007). Although it is not clear why this syndrome occurs, one possibility is that the typical antipsychotics create "supersensitivity" of the dopamine receptors, leading them to "overreact" and produce these abnormal movements (e.g., Dean, 2006). Unfortunately, discontinuation of the medication does not eliminate tardive dyskinesia, and it is likely that once the receptor sensitivity is altered, it cannot be easily reversed.

Atypical Antipsychotics Since the 1990s, a newer group of medications called the **atypical antipsychotics** are preferred for the treatment of schizophrenia in both adults and youth (Kranzler et al., 2005; Mueser & McGurk, 2004). These medications are considered as effective as traditional antipsychotics in treating positive symptoms, and they are much less likely to produce tardive dyskinesia. They also have some effects on negative symptoms and cognitive impairments (Mallinger et al., 2006). The medications do not help everyone, and one study found that over an 18-month period more than 60% of patients who were prescribed one of these medications discontinued them due to side effects or lack of effectiveness (Lieberman et al., 2005). Still, the atypical antipsychotics may represent an improvement over their predecessors because they help reduce negative symptoms and produce fewer side effects (Fleischhacker & Widschwendter, 2006). Although they are less likely to produce tardive dyskinesia, they have their own significant side effects including producing diabetes and high

antipsychotics a class of medications that block dopamine receptors at neuron receptor sites

conventional or **typical antipsychotics** medications that effectively reduce the positive symptoms of schizophrenia but produce serious side effects

tardive dyskinesia a neurological condition characterized by abnormal and involuntary motor movements of the face, mouth, limbs, and trunk

atypical antipsychotics medications that effectively treat positive symptoms, are much less likely to produce tardive dyskinesia, and have some effect on negative symptoms and cognitive impairments

triglycerides (a type of fat found in the blood). The most dangerous side effect is *agranulocytosis*, which is a lowering of the white blood cell count that could be fatal if not detected in time. Weight gain (sometimes severe) is another side effect that occurs in both children and adults (Kranzler et al., 2006). Therefore, although the atypical antipsychotics are now the most commonly prescribed medication for people with schizophrenia, whether they represent a *significant* improvement remains controversial (Lieberman et al., 2005). Newer biological treatments such as transcranial magnetic stimulation attempt to change brain functioning through procedures other than medications (see the box "Research Hot Topic: Transcranial Magnetic Stimulation").

As illustrated in the sections on symptoms and etiology, cultural factors play a role in the treatment of schizophrenia. White patients more frequently preferred medication and counseling treatments (McCabe & Priebe, 2004). In contrast, patients of Bangladeshi descent preferred a religious activity or no treatment at all, consistent with their beliefs that the cause of their illness was societal or spiritual in nature. Despite their different cultural backgrounds, all patients (white, Bangladeshi, and African-Caribbean and West African) were equally likely to comply with their prescribed treatment. Therefore, different cultural preferences did not affect their willingness to accept offered treatments.

In addition to different treatment preferences, racial disparities exist in the frequency with which atypical antipsychotics are prescribed, with whites approximately six times more likely to receive these medications than African Americans (Mallinger et al., 2006), who are more likely to receive the typical antipsychotics. The reasons for the different prescription rates are unclear, because the symptoms of schizophrenia do not differ in these two groups. One factor to consider is the difference in the rate of side effects—African American patients may be at increased risk for medication-induced diabetes and agranulocytosis (Moeller et al., 1995), side effects more commonly found with the atypical antipsychotics. This might make some psychiatrists less likely to prescribe these medications to African Americans, but this alone would not seem to account for such a large disparity.

One of the greatest challenges to effective pharmacological treatment for people with schizophrenia is medication compliance. Approximately 50% of patients never take their medication or do not take it as prescribed (Fenton et al., 1997). Medication noncompliance is associated with high relapse rates and poorer treatment response (Ilott, 2005; Yamada et al., 2006). Noncompliance occurs among chronic patients and those recovering from their first episode (Kamali et al., 2006). The reasons for noncompliance are varied but include distress about side effects and embarrassment or stigma (Perkins et al., 2006; Yamada et al., 2006), more severe positive symptoms, lack of insight regarding symptoms, alcohol and drug abuse (Kamali et al., 2006), and lack of belief in the need for treatment or the benefit of medication (Perkins et al., 2006). Psychoeducation programs aimed at enhancing patients' understanding of medication compliance have produced only moderate results (Ilott, 2005). Interventions may need to tailor the education to each patient's specific concerns rather than just provide general information.

PSYCHOSOCIAL TREATMENT

Antipsychotic medications are considered the treatment of choice for patients with schizophrenia. However, drugs do not completely eliminate the symptoms of this disorder, and psychosocial strategies are used as *adjunctive* (supplemental) interventions that aim to further reduce primary symptoms as well as to decrease daily stress on the patient and/or family, increasing the patient's social skills, and helping the patient find and maintain employment when possible.

Psychoeducation   Schizophrenia is hard on the patient and the family. Positive symptoms often require hospitalizing the patient, and negative symptoms strain family relationships and cause considerable conflict. For example, a patient who withdraws

Research HOT Topic

Transcranial Magnetic Stimulation

Transcranial magnetic stimulation (TMS) is a new, noninvasive biological treatment approach used to treat several psychological disorders, including depression, obsessive-compulsive disorder, and schizophrenia. The goal of TMS is to provide stimulation to a targeted area of the cerebral cortex to change brain activity. Using a small coil placed over the scalp, a brief but powerful magnetic current passes through the scalp and skull. This induces an electrical current that produces *depolarization* (neuronal discharge) in the area beneath the coil and in functionally related areas (Hoffman et al., 2003). Based on the magnetic frequency used, the stimulation can produce an excitatory or inhibitory effect on the specific neurons (Saba et al., 2006). Although there is some variation in the actual treatment regimen, one treatment involves 8 minutes of stimulation on day 1, 12 minutes on day 2, and 16 minutes on the next 7 days (Hoffman et al., 2003). Side effects appear to be minimal and include brief headaches that are treated with standard over-the-counter medication, and concentration and memory difficulties that last no more than 10 minutes after treatment (Hoffman et al., 2003).

The use of TMS in schizophrenia is based on neuroimaging studies that show specific areas of brain activity during auditory hallucinations. For example, areas important for speech perception become activated during periods of hallucinations (Hoffman et al., 2003). These findings have produced several hypotheses regarding the neuroanatomical basis of auditory hallucinations, including (a) the hallucinated voice is the patient's inner speech that is misperceived as coming from outside the brain; or (b) the hallucination is the result of a malfunction of the speech perception system—in effect, the system creates speech without any input from the outside (Lee et al., 2005). TMS changes the activity of these neurons, thereby decreasing (at least temporarily) the frequency of hallucinations.

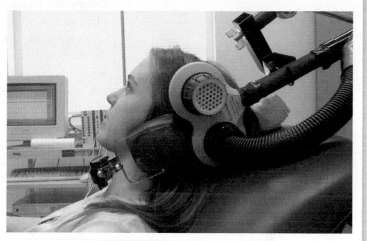

Although this technique has not been intensively studied yet, available data suggest that TMS is more effective than *sham TMS* (using the coil but not delivering the current) in reducing auditory hallucinations that are resistant to medication. When compared with sham TMS, patients who received actual TMS reported reduced frequency of voices, reduced distraction when the voices did occur (Hoffman et al., 2003), and reduced scores on self-report of positive symptoms (including hallucinations; Lee et al., 2005). However, TMS does not appear to reduce delusions (Saba et al., 2006). Also, its effects are time-limited, and it is unclear whether more extended treatment courses could produce more lasting effects.

As discussed in Chapter 2, many differences in available experiments including sample sizes, strength of an intervention (in this case, strength of the magnetic field), and different outcome variables (in this case, hallucinations vs. delusions) make it difficult to determine whether TMS is really effective for schizophrenia. Further studies are needed. However, given the impairing nature of residual schizophrenic symptoms, this promising treatment is sure to be the object of much further study.

from family activities and neglects personal hygiene may face hostile criticism from family members. Since family environments characterized by high levels of emotional involvement and critical attitudes toward the patient (high EE) are associated with higher rates of relapse and higher rates of rehospitalization for some patients (e.g., Butzlaff & Hooley, 1998), an important treatment component is psychoeducation of the family and significant others. **Psychoeducation** is a process by which patients and family members are educated about the disorder, receiving the same type of information that is found in this chapter. The goal is to reduce family members' distress and

Psychoeducation patient and families are educated about the disorder in order to reduce familial distress and equip them to work effectively with the patient

allow them to work more effectively with the patient and caregiver. These programs reduce relapse rates and shorten length of hospitalization (Motlova et al., 2006; Pitschel-Walz et al., 2001). Although family psychoeducation does not affect the symptoms of the disorder directly, it helps family members understand and deal with the patient and the illness.

Cognitive-Behavioral Treatment   Between 20 and 50% of people with schizophrenia continue to have hallucinations despite taking antipsychotic medication (Newton et al., 2005), creating continuing distress and negatively affecting social and occupational adjustment. Psychologists have used behavioral and cognitive-behavioral therapy (CBT) to reduce or eliminate psychotic symptoms, although its use is not common. The literature describing the efficacy of behavior therapy for schizophrenia dates back 35 years (e.g., Glaister, 1985; Nydegger, 1972), and CBT appears effective in reducing psychotic symptoms that remain even with the proper use of medication (Butler et al., 2006; Cather et al., 2005; Gaudiano, 2006). CBT consists of psychoeducation about psychosis and hallucinations, exploration of individual beliefs about hallucinations and delusions, education in using coping strategies to deal with the symptoms, and improving self-esteem (Wykes et al., 2005). Patients take medication while participating in CBT. In one investigation, group CBT significantly reduced the severity of hallucinations (compared with a control group), but only when the therapy was delivered by very experienced group therapists (Wykes et al., 2005). Group CBT for psychotic symptoms appears to be more effective when it is delivered early in the course of the illness (i.e., within the first three years of onset; Newton et al., 2005). Further research is now examining why these two factors (very experienced therapists and treatment delivered within the first three years of symptom onset) may be so important.

Social Skills Training   Impaired social functioning is a core symptom of schizophrenia, and behaviors such as social isolation and withdrawal often occur before psychotic symptoms appear. The inability to interact with others in a socially acceptable way interferes with social, occupational, and vocational functioning. Effective social skills are needed to interview for a job, maintain employment, establish social support networks, or go to college. Social skills training teaches the basics of social interaction, including nonverbal skills such as eye contact, vocal tone, and voice volume, and verbal skills such as initiating and maintaining conversations, expressing feelings, and acting assertively. Although not a comprehensive treatment for schizophrenia, social skills training has a long and successful history improving the social functioning of people with this disorder (Bellack, 2004), even those who are middle aged or older (Granholm et al., 2005), and who have had the disorder for many years.

Supported Employment   The ability to maintain full-time competitive employment is associated with higher rates of symptom improvement, enhanced leisure and financial satisfaction, and enhanced self-esteem (Bond et al., 2001a). However, few patients with schizophrenia (between 10 and 20%; Mueser & McGurk, 2004) are able to work full time. For many people with schizophrenia, the disorder begins during the transition from adolescence to adulthood, before they have experience with adult work activities. Supported employment is a psychosocial intervention that provides job skills to people with schizophrenia. The program includes a rapid job search approach; individual job placements that match patient preferences, strengths, and work experience (if any); follow-along support (continued contact with therapists and job counselors); and integration with the treatment team (Bond et al., 2001b). Such programs help people with schizophrenia find and maintain competitive employment, but there are not yet enough programs for all the people who could benefit from them.

- Pharmacological treatment is the primary treatment for schizophrenia, particularly the class of medication known as the atypical antipsychotics, which appear to help with both the positive and the negative symptoms.

- Use of the typical antipsychotics has declined, as they are associated with an irreversible side effect known as tardive dyskinesia.

- Some hallucinations are resistant to medication treatment, in which case cognitive-behavioral treatment may have some positive effects.

APPLICATION QUESTION   Given that medications have side effects so severe that a subset of patients discontinues taking medication, why is cognitive-behavioral treatment not used first to treat the positive symptoms of schizophrenia?

THE WHOLE STORY: KERRY—TREATING SCHIZOPHRENIA

The Person: *Kerry is 19 years old. He has always been a shy, quiet young man. Studious and respectful in high school, he had few friends and never dated. He was accepted at the state university, 100 miles from home.*

The Problem: *During his first semester, he became concerned that those who were living in his dorm were "out to get him." His concerns extended to an instructor who wore a red shirt, which Kerry believed to be a sign of the devil. The archangel Michael began to speak to Kerry, commenting on his behavior and giving him instructions on how to behave. His roommate became alarmed, not only because Kerry accused him of inserting thoughts into his head but also because Kerry stopped eating (he thought the food might have been poisoned) and bathing (in case the water was contaminated).*

Kerry stopped going to classes and was reluctant to leave his room, where he was constantly examining light fixtures and electrical outlets for listening devices planted there by the FBI. He would call his parents at odd hours of the night, crying and pleading with them to make the voices go away. The next day, he would

call them and angrily accuse them of being in league with the devil, the FBI, or both. His bizarre behavior led to an inpatient hospitalization and a diagnosis of paranoid schizophrenia.

The Treatment: *Kerry was treated with an atypical antipsychotic, which decreased his auditory hallucinations but did not eliminate them. Kerry was unable to tolerate the medication dosage considered necessary for optimal treatment outcome because of severe side effects, and he continued to express discomfort with auditory hallucinations. Kerry was treated with cognitive-behavior therapy (CBT) and felt that although he was better able to cope with the hallucinations on a daily basis, they still interfered with his ability to return to school or hold a job. Because he had achieved only a partial treatment response, Kerry had to take a leave of absence from school and returned home to live with his parents. The medical school near his parents' home was offering a research study using transcranial magnetic stimulation (TMS), and Kerry enrolled as a participant. TMS decreased the frequency of his symptoms such that he was then able to use the*

coping skills he acquired through CBT to deal with the remaining hallucinations. Kerry's negative symptoms were also somewhat improved. Although he was not able to return to college full-time, he was able to maintain half-time employment as a dishwasher in a restaurant.

The Treatment Outcome: *One year later, Kerry became depressed at his inability to return to his previous state of functioning. He stopped taking his medication and attempted to commit suicide by choking himself. He passed out before he suffocated and was hospitalized. After rehospitalization and reinstatement of his medication, Kerry was admitted to a partial hospitalization program, where he received group treatments such as social skills training and illness-management skills. Following his discharge, he was rehired at the restaurant and enrolled in one college course at a community college. Six months later, he moved out of his parents' house into a supported living facility, allowing him more independence. He continues to struggle with the hallucinations but has been able to use his coping skills to manage their severity.*

CRITICAL ISSUES to remember

1. A psychotic experience is a single event that involves a loss of contact with reality and usually consists of a delusion or a hallucination. Psychotic experiences occur in people without any psychiatric disorder, people with medical illnesses, and people with many of the different psychological disorders discussed in this book. When psychotic experiences become frequent or continuous and create distress and/or functional impairment, they are called psychotic disorders.

2. Terms such as *multiple personality* and *split personality* are *not* synonyms for schizophrenia. The term *schizophrenia* describes the "disconnect" among an individual's thoughts, feelings, and behavior, not the existence of one or more complete personalities within a single person.

3. The positive symptoms of schizophrenia consist of hallucinations, delusions, and bizarre behaviors such as catatonia and waxy flexibility. Negative symptoms consist of affective flattening, anhedonia, alogia, and avolition. Cognitive symptoms consist of deficits in visual and verbal learning and memory, ability to pay attention, speed of information processing, and abstract reasoning and executive functioning.

4. Race, culture, and ethnicity play a role in the diagnosis, etiology, and treatment of schizophrenia. Within the United States, there are no differences in the symptom pattern of people with schizophrenia among various racial and ethnic groups. However, African American men appear to be diagnosed with schizophrenia at a higher rate than African American women or whites of either sex. When compared with people with schizophrenia who live in developed countries, people with schizophrenia who live in developing nations often have a more positive treatment outcome, possibly because their families are more supportive of, and play a more supportive role in, the patient's care.

5. The neurodevelopmental model of schizophrenia is based on research indicating that the brain abnormalities commonly associated with schizophrenia occur early in the course of human development, sometimes prenatally. Genetic alterations, prenatal environmental factors, or obstetrical complications may begin an ongoing developmental process that encompasses biological, cognitive, and social changes occurring throughout a lifetime. An accelerated process of synaptic pruning in the brain may also be an important factor in the disorder's etiology.

6. Biological factors may combine with environmental influences such as a disordered family environment to finally produce schizophrenia. Prenatal events associated with the disorder include biological factors such as exposure to influenza and environmental stressors such as maternal malnutrition. Environmental factors that are influential after birth include the family. For example, children of mothers with schizophrenia are more likely to develop the disorder themselves if they are "adopted away" into a disordered family environment. Psychological factors such as family support may help prevent relapse and rehospitalization.

7. Schizophrenia is a chronic disorder, and full symptom remission is rare. Treatment utilizes both medication and psychological methods. The medications of choice are the atypical antipsychotics, which are effective at reducing or eliminating positive symptoms and have some effect on the negative symptoms. Psychological interventions such as social skills training, cognitive-behavioral treatment, and supported employment are effective *adjunctive*, or additional, treatments that may reduce negative symptoms, reduce medication-resistant hallucinations and delusions, and enhance employment skills.

TEST yourself

For more review plus practice tests, flashcards, and Speaking Out: DSM in Context videos, log onto www.MyPsychLab.com

1. Psychotic experiences are characteristic of schizophrenia, but they also occur in people with other disorders. Of the following, they are *least* likely to occur in people with
   a. brain tumors
   b. mood disorders
   c. substance use disorders
   d. specific phobias

2. The psychiatrist who introduced the term *dementia praecox* was
   a. Emil Kraepelin
   b. Benjamin Rush
   c. Eugen Bleuler
   d. Philippe Pinel

3. Persecutory delusions, auditory hallucinations, and unusual behaviors are examples of
   a. positive symptoms
   b. negative symptoms
   c. cognitive deficits
   d. catatonia

4. Frank has a diagnosis of schizophrenia. When his case manager asked what time he went to bed last night, he said, "2 o'clock frick frock tick tock and I won't be wearing a mock." This is an example of
   a. loose association
   b. thought blocking
   c. clang association
   d. alogia

5. Blunted affect, anhedonia, avolition, and psychomotor retardation are examples of
   a. positive symptoms
   b. negative symptoms
   c. cognitive deficits
   d. catatonia

6. The third category of schizophrenia symptoms is cognitive impairment, which includes
   a. delusions and hallucinations
   b. personality and affect splits
   c. attention and memory deficits
   d. anhedonia and avolition deficits

7. James has schizophrenia. At times, he maintains a rigid posture and is unresponsive to vocal commands. At other times, he repeats what other people say to him. Which subtype of schizophrenia does James most likely have?
   a. paranoid
   b. undifferentiated
   c. catatonic
   d. disorganized

8. People with schizophrenia who live in developing countries have a better outcome than do people in developed countries because
   a. the United States ranks 39th in mental health service provision worldwide
   b. the chronic nature of schizophrenia is relatively unknown in developing countries
   c. alternative folk medicine is as effective as modern medical methods
   d. smaller communities and less complex environments offer more social support

9. African Americans are more likely to be given a diagnosis of schizophrenia because
   a. they are more likely than white people to suffer from the disorder
   b. clinician bias leads to misinterpretation of symptoms
   c. they more often report episodes of sleep paralysis, which is associated with the disorder
   d. all of the above

10. In one prospective study, Danish youth were videotaped in a school cafeteria when they were 11 to 13 years old. Twenty-nine years later as adults, some of these individuals had developed schizophrenia. As children, the adults who developed the disorder were
    a. less social and exhibited subtle neuromotor abnormalities
    b. eccentric or odd, but without delusions or hallucinations
    c. showing early signs of split personality
    d. not different from the other children

11. Schizophrenia usually begins at what stage of life?
    a. early childhood
    b. middle childhood
    c. early adulthood
    d. early middle age

12. Shortly after Lucinda was told by the police that her 12-year-old daughter was killed by a hit-and-run driver, she went into a catatonic state. A few hours later she began to hear voices, and her speech became disorganized. She said that an angel had come to visit her. These symptoms stopped after several days. Lucinda was suffering from
    a. catatonic schizophrenia
    b. residual schizophrenia
    c. schizophreniform disorder
    d. brief psychotic disorder

13. Individuals diagnosed with schizoaffective disorder might be considered to have
    a. both schizophrenia and a depressive disorder
    b. only the negative symptoms of schizophrenia plus a mood disorder
    c. a nonpsychotic mood disorder
    d. a brief psychotic disorder

14. The finding that genetically identical twins are not 100% concordant for schizophrenia strongly implies that
    a. a uniquely genetic etiology for schizophrenia is unlikely
    b. environmental factors must be the cause of schizophrenia spectrum disorders
    c. family conflict cannot cause schizophrenia because twins are usually raised in the same family environment
    d. mothers must unconsciously treat twins differently and this leads to vulnerability to schizophrenia

15. Among possible prenatal risk factors for schizophrenia, one of the most thoroughly investigated is
    a. genital or reproductive infections
    b. nutritional deprivation during early gestation
    c. severe prenatal maternal stress
    d. maternal exposure to the influenza virus

16. High levels of emotional involvement, intrusiveness, and critical attitudes among family members of people with schizophrenia may negatively affect treatment outcome. This theory is known as
    a. expressed emotion
    b. emotional scapegoating
    c. family enmeshment
    d. emotional stigmatization

17. Jeff has schizophrenia and has developed some unusual movements and tics in his face, mouth, and hands. This condition, called tardive dyskinesia, is caused by
    a. exposure to the influenza virus in utero
    b. high EE in a patient's family
    c. treatment with typical antipsychotic drugs
    d. a lowering of the white blood cell count

18. One of the greatest challenges to effective pharmacological treatment of schizophrenia is
    a. correct diagnosis of the condition in the first place
    b. medication noncompliance
    c. provision of the correct medication, typically an atypical antipsychotic
    d. all of the above

19. When patients and their families learn about schizophrenia in order to reduce family distress and help the patient cope, the process is known as
    a. psychoeducation
    b. cognitive-behavior therapy
    c. social skills training
    d. psychotherapy

20. Training that teaches nonverbal skills such as eye contact, vocal tone, and voice volume, and verbal skills such as initiating and maintaining conversations, expressing feelings, and acting assertively, is called
    a. psychoeducation
    b. cognitive-behavior therapy
    c. social skills training
    d. psychotherapy

Answers: 1 d, 2 a, 3 a, 4 c, 5 b, 6 c, 7 c, 8 d, 9 b, 10 a, 11 c, 12 d, 13 a, 14 a, 15 d, 16 a, 17 c, 18 b, 19 a, 20 c.

CHAPTER
objectives

At the end of this chapter, you should be able to:

1. Discuss how personality disorders differ from other disorders discussed in this book.

2. Describe the three clusters of personality disorders and the disorders within each cluster.

3. Appreciate the complex nature of personality disorders.

4. Understand the role biology may play in the origin of personality pathology.

5. Discuss psychodynamic and cognitive-behavioral theories of personality disorders.

6. Discuss treatment approaches to personality disorders.

personality disorders

Jeff would be happiest if his life never varied. He is a 52-year-old married statistician with three children ages 18, 16, and 12. Every day for the past 15 years, he has risen at 5:30, exercised for 30 minutes while reading the paper, had two cups of coffee, a bowl of cereal, and a piece of fruit, and caught the same train to work. Each time that train was delayed, he anxiously looked at his watch, bemoaned the transit system, and fretted about lost time in the office. Even when the kids were younger, if one was sick on a school day, he still kept to his schedule. He insisted that the household be run to his specifications. If the kids were asked to fold laundry, it had to be done right. If they did it wrong, he gave them one chance to fix it, and if they still did it wrong, he did it himself. His motto was, "if you want something done right, you have to do it yourself." He reviewed his children's homework fastidiously and grilled them if their grades slipped. Dinner was expected at 6:30. He played tennis on Tuesday and Thursday evenings. Other evenings he worked in his study. His office was a shrine of order and organization. Color-coded post-it notes contained lists of what he and his team had to accomplish for various projects. But he was a prisoner of his lists. At times, he would sit at his desk, three different colored lists in front of him, faced with scores of e-mails, and simply not know where to begin. How should he optimize his to-do list to maximize his productivity? He would get lost in looking for the algorithm that could make him more efficient. As the lists became longer and the inbox fuller, he could become paralyzed by anxiety. He had long stopped supervising graduate students. Several had dropped out, unable to deal with his exceedingly high expectations and constant criticism. One evening he developed chest pains on the tennis court, and his partner drove him to the ER. It wasn't a heart attack, but his blood pressure was sky high. He was referred to his family doctor for follow-up. His doctor called him on the carpet. She had warned him countless times about his lifestyle, pressure, and anxiety, but he never listened. She called this his wake-up call. She gave him medications for the blood pressure and the name of a psychologist to help him deal with his driven and obsessive- compulsive personality style.

Personality traits are observable from the early years. Many of our perceptions of others are based on our impressions of their personalities. From this picture, whom would you choose as "most likely to succeed in business"? "Most likely to graduate from college"? "Most likely to lead a protest march"?

Personality Trait versus Personality Disorder

What is the difference between a personality *trait* and a personality *disorder*? All people can be described in terms of specific patterns of personality, but not all have a disorder. We commonly use adjectives to describe someone's typical behaviors: Jan is rigid and controlling, Kiara is outgoing and optimistic, Liza is flitty and distractible, Ty is condescending and arrogant, Jack is self-interested and untrustworthy. So when does behavior cross the line from trait to disorder? In some people, characteristic ways of seeing, interpreting, and behaving in the world develop over time in a way that is inflexible and maladaptive. If someone cannot adapt his or her characteristic approach to the world when necessary, and that approach causes significant psychological distress either to the person or to others, then these *traits* may have crystallized into a personality *disorder*. Differentiating between traits and disorders is crucial for both diagnosis and treatment. It is important, though not always easy, to recognize at what point a personality style has become rigid and maladaptive.

A second relevant dimension to consider is that of clinical *state* versus a personality *trait*. A *state* refers to the expression of a personality characteristic that is related to a specific circumstance, clinical condition, or period of time. For example,

Juan, who is usually even-tempered and easy-going, becomes emotionally unstable whenever he is under stress. He lashes out at people and vacillates between being nice and barking at people.

Juan's behavior is a function of his current life events and would be considered a state-dependent change—not his characteristic way of approaching the world. His behavior would be considered *ego-dystonic*, or distinctly different from his typical characteristics.

Conversely, a *trait* refers to the specific and characteristic way someone approaches the world. It is unlikely to change across situations, time, and events. For example, if Juan's behavior tends to fluctuate unpredictably most of the time, and others describe him as "dramatic" or "Jekyll and Hyde," this behavior would be considered a personality trait. It is *ego-syntonic*, or related directly to his core personality.

If we observe Juan at any one time and note that his emotions vacillate more often than those of his peers, there may be several possible explanations. First, his emotional vacillation may not create any significant psychological distress for him or those around him, but may simply reflect a colorful aspect of his unique personality. Alternately, our observation may not have detected important contextual information, namely, that Juan is very upset lately because he's been having problems at work. After a comprehensive clinical evaluation, he may receive a diagnosis of major depression. A third possibility is that Juan's vacillation reflects an ingrained way that he interacts with the world, one that has caused him to lose relationships, jobs, and ties with his family. In this case, we would say that he has a *personality disorder*.

These three alternative explanations highlight several important aspects of a personality disorder diagnosis. First, it is critical to differentiate between a personality trait and a personality disorder. Second, personality disorders should never be diagnosed after a single brief behavioral observation, as they represent enduring ways of dealing with the world. Third, personality disorders should not be diagnosed in the absence of a surrounding context. What is meant by context? In Chapter 3, we discussed the five-axis diagnostic system used in the DSM to categorize behavior. *Axis I* is the dimension on which all of the disorders that we have discussed in this book so far can be found. Axis I disorders are clinical syndromes, such as depression, anxiety, eating disorders, and substance abuse. Think about Axis I disorders in the same way that you think of general medical illnesses. In contrast, *Axis II* is the dimension that addresses long-standing difficulties such as mental retardation (see Chapter 12) or personality disorders, which are the focus of this chapter. A person can have an Axis I disorder, an Axis II disorder, or both. It is even possible that in one's life, one may be diagnosed with an Axis II disorder that is stable throughout one's lifetime and have Axis I disorders that come and go at different times. When we say that deciding if someone has a personality disorder needs to consider the surrounding context, we mean that one must be careful not to assume that a behavior indicates the presence of a personality disorder when a person may be suffering from an Axis I disorder. For example, many people may seem to have a personality disorder (be very emotional, be abusing substances) when they are in the throes of an acute episode of an Axis I disorder (such as major depression). It may be necessary to wait until the Axis I disorder remits and then determine whether the troubling behaviors are still present. This example illustrates how difficult it is to diagnose a personality disorder: if Juan seeks treatment, the evaluating clinician must consider that his current state does not necessarily reflect his typical behavior. So, given that we all have distinctive personality traits, how do we know when a personality state constitutes a maladaptive personality disorder? Because there is no strong evidence supporting a clear boundary between personality traits and personality disorders, the latter may be best understood as pathological amplifications of underlying traits.

Determining whether a behavior should be labeled a disorder must include consideration of impairment and distress. This is a particular challenge for the category of personality disorders, where symptoms are difficult to quantify. Furthermore, personality disorders have few biological or observable signs. Personality disorders can't be detected with a blood test, for example. They also must be distinguished from the Axis I disorders in the book. You might think of the Axis I disorder in the same manner as an acute medical illness that afflicts a person who functions relatively well in many aspects of life. In contrast, a personality disorder is not a dramatic or acute illness, but a long-term, chronic, pervasive pattern of inflexible and maladaptive functioning. Personality disorders are not so much illnesses as a "way of being." They are typically apparent in late adolescence or early adulthood and may persist throughout life.

One particularly difficult distinction is between personality disorders and Axis I disorders that have a prolonged course, such as dysthymic disorder (see Chapter 6). In terms of impairment, what separates the distress caused by disorders described in other chapters from the difficulty created by personality disorders? As we describe the various personality disorder clusters, we will illustrate the ways in which these disorders can impair social and occupational functioning. One interesting characteristic of these disorders is that they often cause more distress to other people than to the person with the disorder. Some people with personality disorders may feel very little distress or even none at all.

One way to understand what distinguishes personality disorders from the other disorders in this book is "the three P's." These disorders are patterns of behavior that are *persistent* (over time), *pervasive* (across people and situations), and *pathological* (clearly abnormal). A **personality disorder**, therefore, is "an enduring pattern of inner experience and behavior that deviates markedly from the expectations of the individual's culture, is pervasive and inflexible, has the onset in adolescence or early adulthood, is stable over time, and leads to distress and impairment" (APA, 2000, p. 685). Definitions of personality disorders have always highlighted symptom stability—these are not transient moods or temporary quirks of behavior, but persistent behavioral features.

The DSM divides personality disorders into three clusters: **Cluster A**, "odd or eccentric," **Cluster B**, "dramatic, emotional, or erratic," and **Cluster C**, "anxious or fearful." These labels do not relate directly to the names of the individual disorders within the clusters but describe an overall style of behavior that cuts across the individual disorders. However, some researchers and clinicians question the validity of these clusters. Why? Because, as we've seen, personality traits are common to everyone—we all may have enduring tendencies to be somewhat eccentric, emotional, or fearful—and exactly at what point do these traits turn pathological?

According to the DSM categories, one either has or doesn't have a particular personality disorder. This is known as the *categorical* model of personality. Many researchers emphasize that a better model would use a *dimensional* approach, one that captures the full range of a trait. A dimensional approach would consider personality to be on a continuum, for example, socially outgoing people on one end and extremely shy people on the other. (See Chapter 3 for more discussion of categorical versus dimensional classification.) Since the DSM approach is currently dominant, we will focus first on its classification system in our discussion of the disorders, followed by an examination of alternate dimensional approaches to personality.

| concept CHECK |

- Distinguishing between personality traits and disorders is critical and must include a careful consideration of interpersonal and environmental contexts.

- Personality disorders represent characteristic but maladaptive and inflexible ways of seeing, interpreting, and behaving that have developed over time.

APPLICATION QUESTION In an assessment, what kinds of information would a psychologist want to know if he or she wanted to determine whether a patient's problem involved a personality disorder?

Personality Disorder Clusters

Most mental health professionals follow the DSM categorical approach when characterizing, communicating about, and treating personality disorders. In the following sections, we present both a clinical description and a clinical example of each personality disorder. Keep in mind that impairment is the hallmark of these disorders and that in many instances, impairment is judged from the perspective of others who are affected by the person's personality disorder. Also, remember the three P's (persistent, pervasive, pathological). In the following box, "DSM-IV-TR: General Diagnostic Criteria for a Personality Disorder," we present general criteria for a personality disorder in order to provide the scaffolding around which the specific personality disorder profiles are constructed. Regardless of the specific nature of the personality disorder, they all meet the fundamental criteria outlined here.

personality disorder an enduring pattern of inner experience and behavior that deviates from the norm, is pervasive and inflexible, has an onset in adolescence or early adulthood, is stable across time, and leads to distress or impairment

Cluster A a group of personality disorders that include characteristic ways of behaving that can be viewed as odd, quirky, or eccentric; includes paranoid, schizoid, and schizotypal personality disorders

Cluster B a group of personality disorders that include characteristic ways of behaving that can be viewed as exaggerated, inflated, dramatic, emotional, or erratic; includes antisocial, borderline, narcissistic, and histrionic personality disorders

Cluster C a group of personality disorders that include characteristic ways of behaving that are marked by considerable anxiety or withdrawal; includes avoidant, dependent, and obsessive-compulsive personality disorders

DSM-IV-TR

General Diagnostic Criteria for a Personality Disorder

Experience and behavior that deviates markedly from the expectations of the individual's culture. The pattern includes two (or more) of the following areas:

- cognition (perception and interpretation of self, others, and events)
- affectivity (the range, intensity, lability [changeability], and appropriateness of emotional response)
- interpersonal functioning
- impulse control.

The pattern is inflexible and pervasive across several personal and social situations and leads to clinically significant distress or impairment in social, occupational, or other important areas of functioning. The pattern is stable and long-standing and its onset can be traced back at least to adolescence or early adulthood. It cannot be accounted for by another mental disorder or the direct effects of substance use or a general medical condition such as head trauma.

Adapted with permission from the *Diagnostic and Statistical Manual of Mental Disorders*, Text Revision, Fourth Edition, (Copyright 2000). American Psychiatric Association.

CLUSTER A: ODD OR ECCENTRIC DISORDERS

The common features of Cluster A (see the box "DSM-IV-TR: Cluster A Disorders") are characteristic behaviors that can be viewed as odd, quirky, or eccentric by an external observer (APA, 2000). Disorders in Cluster A include features similar to those seen in psychosis and schizophrenia (see Chapter 10). Indeed, the dividing line between psychosis and Cluster A personality disorders is unclear. For example, family members of people with schizophrenia have higher rates of Cluster A personality disorders—suggesting possible continuity between Axis I psychotic disorders and Axis II Cluster A disorders (Kendler et al., 1993).

Paranoid Personality Disorder Paranoid **personality disorder** is a pervasive distrust and suspiciousness of others such that their motives are interpreted as malevolent (APA, 2000). While a little bit of paranoia can be adaptive in some situations (e.g., protecting oneself from dishonest individuals), paranoid personality disorder is characterized by unjustified and pervasive distrust. People with this disorder, without any evidence, believe that others are out to exploit, harm, or deceive them; bear grudges and are unforgiving of perceived insults; and are hypervigilant for signs of disloyalty or untrustworthiness in friends, family, and acquaintances (APA, 2000). Typical beliefs of individuals with paranoid personality disorder may include, "I cannot trust other people," "Other people have hidden motives," "If other people find out things about me, they will use them against me," "People often say one thing and mean something else," and "A person to whom I am close could be disloyal or unfaithful." Unfortunately, this distrust can extend to friends and family members and potentially damage relationships. In paranoid personality disorder, the suspiciousness does not extend to delusional thoughts. If delusions are present, there is probably a more serious condition, such as delusional disorder or paranoid schizophrenia.

Arun had done reasonably well as an undergraduate biology major and was now a graduate student in genetics. He was often concerned that fellow students were stealing his

Paranoia can include distrust and suspiciousness of family and friends (movie still from the film *Paranoid Park*).

paranoid personality disorder a pervasive distrust and suspiciousness of others such that their motives are interpreted as malevolent

DSM-IV-TR

Cluster A Disorders

Paranoid personality disorder is characterized by a pervasive distrust and suspiciousness of others and includes at least four of the following:

- believing that others intend harm or deception
- questioning the loyalty or trustworthiness of others
- fearing that information will be used against him or her
- reading negative meanings into benign comments
- being quick to rebut in an angry manner
- suspecting infidelity in a sexual or romantic partner without reason.

Schizoid personality disorder is a pervasive pattern of social detachment and a limited expression of emotion in interpersonal contexts. It includes at least four of the following:

- lack of desire for relationships, few friends
- preference for isolation
- lack of enjoyment in activities
- being neutral regarding praise or criticism
- a general lack of emotionality.

Schizotypal personality disorder is a consistent pattern of social problems marked by significant deficits in the ability to maintain close relationships and by distortions in thoughts and idiosyncratic behavior marked by at least five of the following:

- ideas of reference (excluding delusions of reference);
- abnormal beliefs or magical thinking (e.g., thinking about an event can make it happen)
- unusual perceptual experiences
- odd thinking and speech
- suspiciousness or paranoia
- inappropriate emotional expression
- odd, eccentric, or peculiar behavior or appearance
- limited number of friends or relatives; excessive social anxiety and paranoia.

Adapted with permission from the *Diagnostic and Statistical Manual of Mental Disorders*, Text Revision, Fourth Edition, (Copyright 2000). American Psychiatric Association.

ideas or cheating off his papers, but he never filed any formal complaints. He had gone to a university close to home as an undergraduate and had lived with his parents. Grad school was the first time he was truly away from home. Arun's research focused on a specific gene associated with a rare form of deafness. He started suspecting that his supervisor had brought him to the university to take credit for his work and claim it as his own. One day, Arun gave his mentor a contract guaranteeing that the supervisor would not steal any of Arun's intellectual property. When the supervisor wouldn't sign, Arun was convinced that he was out to get him. Arun wanted to go to the Dean, but he knew that the Dean and his supervisor were friends and were probably in cahoots anyhow. Arun started locking up his written work and bought extra security for his laptop. He even developed second datasets that were inaccurate so that if his supervisor stole the data and published it, the theft would be evident.

When his supervisor confronted him about how he was feeling, Arun interpreted it as yet another attempt to get access to his work. He began writing letters to the Chancellor of the university, the governor of the state, and various state legislators apprising them of the situation. When the Chancellor contacted the Dean, who then called Arun's supervisor, it became clear that Arun was disturbed. He was taken to Campus Health services, where he was evaluated and diagnosed with paranoid personality disorder.

Arun's case illustrates several features of paranoid personality disorder. First, Arun's pervasive suspiciousness led him to believe that conspiracies existed all around him. He questioned the loyalty and trustworthiness of fellow students and even departmental faculty. Arun had no evidence that others were trying to steal his data, but he nonetheless persisted in his beliefs. People around him would invariably have perceived him as abrasive, accusing, and suspicious. At first, his faculty adviser and chancellor may have been willing to listen to and investigate his concerns, perhaps wondering if he had had a bad experience elsewhere that made him protective of his work. However, they might soon realize that Arun was suspicious of them as well. They realized that Arun's reality was different from their own.

A classic example of the interpersonal difficulties that accompany paranoid personality disorder is the suspicion of infidelity in a partner. At first, it looks like routine jealousy, but then it becomes clear that the suspicion goes far beyond any rational thought and there is nothing the partner can do to dispel the fears. Another common feature of paranoid personality disorder is interpreting innocent events as being personally relevant or having personal meaning. For example, getting stuck in the longest line in the grocery store or being singled out for security screening in the airport could be viewed as a personal attack.

Schizoid Personality Disorder   **Schizoid personality disorder** is a pervasive pattern of detachment from social relationships and a restricted range of emotional expression in interpersonal settings (APA, 2000). People with schizoid personality disorder may be introverted, solitary, emotionally unexpressive, and isolated. They derive little enjoyment from or show little interest in belonging to families or social groups. Often absorbed in their own thoughts and feelings, they can be afraid of relationships that require closeness and intimacy. People with this disorder also appear to be indifferent to others' opinions and frequently prefer tasks without human interaction (e.g., laboratory or computer tasks). They seem to experience few emotional extremes such as anger or joy. Instead, they hover indifferently in the middle range of emotion. This disorder is also associated with the absence of enjoyment of sensory, bodily, or interpersonal experiences (APA, 2000). Sometimes the detachment experienced by people with this disorder can lead to impairment in both social and occupational functioning. Often oblivious to normal social cues, they cannot engage in the normal social discourse that maintains relationships and supports occupational success. The lack of social skills can be misinterpreted as aloofness. However, people with schizoid personality disorder usually do not have the hallucinations, delusions, or the complete disconnection from reality that occurs in untreated (or treatment-resistant) schizophrenia, although they may experience brief psychotic episodes especially in times of stress.

Zack was a 24-year-old stable hand and was most comfortable when alone with the horses and mucking stalls. He came in early in the morning, did his work, left late at night, and barely spoke to anyone. New people would try to engage him in conversation, but he just wasn't interested. People would sometimes interpret his lack of interest as arrogance and wonder what made him feel so special, but more often they would wonder how anyone could go so long without talking to anyone. A new young rider brought her horse to the stables and took a liking to Zack. Even though he seemed really distant, she thought he was attractive. She asked him out, but he just seemed to have absolutely no interest

Chloe O'Brian, played by Mary Lynn Rajskub in the television program "24," showed a pervasive pattern of detachment from social relationships and a restricted range of emotions in interpersonal settings. These aspects of personality characterize schizoid personality disorder.

schizoid personality disorder   a pervasive pattern of social detachment and a limited expression of emotion in interpersonal contexts

in her—or anyone else. Zack would visit his parents about once a month. His mother was a seamstress and his father delivered mail. When he went home, he sometimes helped his mother rip out seams of articles she was sewing, but they all basically sat there in silence or worked while the TV was on.

In lay terms, Zack would be called a loner or a hermit. He was not concerned by his lack of relationships and showed almost no emotional response when the young rider showed interest in him. His work reflected his preference for being alone. The horses placed no social demands on him. Yet it did not appear that his job gave him pleasure. In fact, it seemed routine and rote. If he was praised for his work, he would take tips, but he seemed to garner no sense of pride in his work or appreciation for their kind words. The image of Zack and his parents sitting around watching TV and barely talking suggests that a schizoid style might run in the family and reflects the general lack of emotionality and engagement seen in these individuals.

Schizotypal Personality Disorder   **Schizotypal personality disorder** is a pervasive pattern of social and interpersonal deficits marked by acute discomfort, reduced capacity for close relationships, cognitive or perceptual distortions, and behavioral eccentricities (APA, 2000). Symptoms of schizotypal personality disorder are best described as a cluster of idiosyncrasies. People with this disorder may have offbeat, peculiar, or paranoid beliefs and thoughts. Moreover, they have difficulty forming relationships and have extreme social anxiety. During interpersonal interactions, people with this personality disorder may react inappropriately, show no emotion, or inappropriately talk to themselves. Another feature is "magical thinking," an erroneous belief that one can foretell the future or affect events by thinking certain thoughts. People with schizotypal personality disorder may harbor *ideas of reference.* These are incorrect interpretations that events around them have specific and unusual personal meaning. These interpretations are not as severe as *delusions of reference* (see Chapter 10), in which beliefs develop a delusional pattern. People with schizotypal personality disorder also report unusual perceptual experiences or have odd patterns of thinking and speech. Some people with this disorder display suspiciousness or paranoia, and their emotional expressions can be inappropriate and excessive or severely restricted.

The oddities found in people with schizotypal personality disorder are not restricted to thinking and behavior. Individuals may also have an odd, eccentric, or peculiar physical appearance as reflected in their clothing and personal hygiene, and these oddities, in addition to their excessive social anxiety and paranoia, may result in limited social relationships.

Everyone on campus knew him as "the pigeon man." When students first saw him, they avoided him by crossing the street. Here was some guy talking to himself (without an earbud!). He slept at the local shelter, where the workers saw him as harmless. In fact, they told people that the pigeon man was more afraid of them than they should be of him. He rarely washed, had holes in his shoes, and held all of his possessions close to his body in a burlap bag when he slept at night. During the day, he dug scraps out of the trash, sat in the park on a bench surrounded by pigeons, fed them, and carried on extended conversations with the birds. Sometimes he laughed and other times he looked positively angry at the birds. When he was done, he retreated back into his own little world, walking up and down the streets, until it was time to go back to the shelter for a meal. His case manager confirmed that he did not have hallucinations or delusions and had never met diagnostic criteria for schizophrenia. Yet this odd pattern of behavior had been with him since middle school, where his yearbook caption called him "bird boy."

The pigeon man's history of eccentric behavior around birds existed from childhood. Thus, his symptoms were persistent. Keeping his possessions in his burlap bag

schizotypal personality disorder   a consistent pattern of social problems marked by significant deficits in the ability to maintain close relationships and by idiosyncratic behavior and distortions in thoughts

close to his body clearly reflected suspiciousness or paranoia about his belongings. Although he was not dangerous, he caused uneasiness in others, probably because of his personal appearance and his erratic behaviors. Clearly, the pigeon man's experience with reality was not shared by those around him—he saw the world differently, although he never had a psychotic episode. Nonetheless, his sustained odd and eccentric behavior was sufficiently extreme to lead others to avoid him.

CLUSTER B: DRAMATIC, EMOTIONAL, OR ERRATIC DISORDERS

The common features of Cluster B are behaviors that are viewed as exaggerated, inflated, dramatic, emotional, or erratic (APA, 2000) (see the box "DSM-IV-TR: Cluster B Disorders"). The four disorders in this cluster are marked by extreme and often colorful patterns of behavior. Other common features are the fluctuating nature of symptoms—often vacillating between extremes. These patterns can be particularly disrupting interpersonally, as the cases below illustrate.

Antisocial Personality Disorder   **Antisocial personality disorder** (ASPD) is a pervasive pattern of disregard for and violation of the rights of others (APA, 2000). It is more common in males than in females. This personality disorder has been known throughout history, literature, and the legal system by many names, including psychopathy, sociopathy, and dyssocial personality disorder. This diagnosis is reserved for individuals who are at least 18 years old and who had symptoms of conduct disorder before age 15 (see Chapter 12), illustrating how the pattern of antisocial behavior begins in childhood, then crystallizes and intensifies over time. Common behaviors in youth include cruelty to animals and people, destruction of property, deceitfulness or theft, or serious violations of rules (APA, 2000).

Antisocial personality disorder often has its roots in childhood, with antisocial behaviors such as theft and vandalism.

ASPD is somewhat easier to diagnose than other personality disorders because of its flagrant behaviors. Fundamentally, people with ASPD fail to conform to social norms, which often leads to legal difficulties including arrests. They often lie, use aliases, con others for profit or enjoyment, destroy property, harass others, and engage in behaviors and actions that violate the basic rights, wishes, safety, and feelings of others (APA, 2000) (see the box "Real People, Real Disorders: Jeffrey Dahmer: Antisocial Personality Disorder"). Associated features include being highly impulsive and engaging in problematic activities on the spur of the moment. This can result in physical fights, temper outbursts, physically abusive behavior, changes in residence, reckless driving, and other impulsive high-risk behaviors that threaten their own safety and well-being (e.g., high-risk sexual behavior, motor vehicle accidents caused by reckless driving or driving while intoxicated, drug use). Another common feature is irresponsibility, exhibited by unemployment, underemployment, or poor and erratic job performance and financial irresponsibility, including bad debts and failure to support their families or children. In addition, individuals with ASPD fail to take responsibility for their own actions and commonly blame the victims for inciting their behavior. Examples include saying that a rape victim deserved the assault because of her sexy clothes or blaming physical fights on the other guy (e.g., "he had it coming to him"). Perhaps most disconcerting is the tendency to minimize the consequences of their actions and the tendency to feel no remorse. Indeed, they may be completely indifferent to the consequences of their actions.

antisocial personality disorder   a pervasive pattern of disregard for and violation of the rights of others

DSM-IV-TR

Cluster B Disorders

Antisocial personality disorder is a consistent pattern of disregard for and violation of the rights of others, as indicated by the following:

- failure to conform to social norms with respect to lawful behavior, arrest, lying, use of aliases, or conning others
- impulsivity or lack of planning skills; irritability and physical fighting; disregard for the safety of self or others
- regular irresponsibility
- age at least 18 with evidence of conduct disorder before age 15.

Narcissistic personality disorder is a pervasive pattern of grandiosity, need for admiration from others, and lack of empathy. Characteristics include the following:

- grandiose sense of self-importance; preoccupation with success and power
- a belief that one is "special" and unique
- need for excessive admiration; a sense of entitlement
- exploitation of others for personal ends; a lack of empathy
- envy of others or the belief that others are envious of oneself
- arrogant, haughty behaviors or attitudes toward others.

Borderline personality disorder is characterized by a pervasive pattern of instability in interpersonal relationships, self-image, and affect, and marked impulsive features such as frantic efforts to avoid real or imagined abandonment. Characteristics include five or more of the following:

- a pattern of strained interpersonal relationships characterized by fluctuating extremes of idealization and devaluation
- significant, consistent, unstable self-perceptions
- impulsivity in at least two potentially destructive areas (other than suicidal or self-mutilating behaviors)
- recurrent suicidal behavior, gestures, or threats, or self-mutilating behavior
- emotional instability due to a significant reactivity of mood
- chronic feelings of emptiness
- inappropriate irritability or expression of anger
- stress-related paranoid thoughts or severe dissociative symptoms.

Histrionic personality disorder is characterized by a pervasive pattern of excessive emotionality and attention seeking. Characteristics include at least five of the following:

- being uncomfortable when not the center of attention
- showing inappropriate sexually seductive or provocative behavior
- displaying quickly changing and superficial expression of emotions
- using physical appearance as a means of getting attention
- speaking in an impressionistic and simplistic manner
- showing extreme emotionality and theatricality
- being easily influenced by others
- perceiving relationships as more intimate than they are in reality.

Adapted with permission from the *Diagnostic and Statistical Manual of Mental Disorders*, Text Revision, Fourth Edition, (Copyright 2000). American Psychiatric Association.

real people, real disorders

Jeffrey Dahmer: Antisocial Personality Disorder

Jeffrey Lionel Dahmer (1960–1994), one of the most infamous serial killers in American history, murdered at least 17 men and boys between 1978 and 1991. Dahmer's killings were notably abhorrent, involving violent sodomy, necrophilia (sex with dead bodies), dismemberment, and cannibalism.

What causes someone to commit such heinous acts of violence against humanity? Insanity? Psychiatric illness? Evil? Any combination of these? In the case of Jeffrey Dahmer, several forensic experts addressed this question during his famous court case. While never formally diagnosed by expert witnesses, Dahmer appeared to have classic features of antisocial personality disorder. He showed no remorse for his crimes against others and acted in an impulsive, callous, manipulative, aggressive manner that reflected a failure to accept social norms. Moreover, many red flags appeared to be present in his childhood.

As a child, Dahmer reportedly dissected already dead animals. At age 14, he began drinking alcohol, and at 18, soon after his parents' divorce, Dahmer committed his first murder. Dahmer invited the victim to his house and killed him because he "didn't want him to leave." By the summer of 1991, Dahmer was murdering approximately one person per week, and in a typical antisocial manipulation, used his charismatic nature to attract his victims, homosexual men and boys.

Commenting on this magnetism, Anne Schwartz, who covered the Dahmer story for the *Milwaukee Journal*, stated, "The day Jeffrey Dahmer was sentenced, I heard him read his statement to the court calmly and eloquently, and I wondered how easily I could have been conned." She continued, "He was an attractive man when he laughed. . . . I could see how so many were taken in by him."

With evidence overwhelmingly against him, Dahmer chose to plead not guilty by reason of insanity, arguing that his necrophiliac urges were so strong that he could not control them. The court found Dahmer guilty on 15 counts of murder and sentenced him to 15 life terms, totaling 937 years in prison. Dahmer served his time until late 1994, when he was beaten to death by a fellow inmate while on work detail in the prison gym.

Jeffrey Dahmer is an extreme example of how features of antisocial personality disorder can be associated with criminality. While all individuals who engage in antisocial behaviors are not criminals, 40% of convicted felons do meet the criteria for an antisocial personality disorder. The line between mental illness and criminal behavior is not clear in this instance, and the distinction between illness and evil will no doubt be debated far into the future in hospitals, jails, and courtrooms.

References: http://www.criminalprofiling.com/Psychiatric-Testimony-of-Jeffrey-Dahmer_s115.html
http://www.crimelibrary.com/serial_killers/notorious/dahmer/19.html
http://www.tornadohills.com/dahmer/life.htm

Brandon was raised in a family that included his father, mother, and a younger sister, but he did not have a close relationship with anyone. Without parental supervision or involvement, Brandon was often in trouble at school for inappropriate conduct, even at an early age. Despite being very bright, his grades were poor because "he just doesn't care." At 13, he was sent to a youth detention center for breaking into a neighbor's house while high on marijuana, and soon after being released he began car-jacking.

At age 19, he was sent to state prison for 18 months for a felony. In prison, Brandon gained a reputation as a "gangsta" for his ability to intimidate other prisoners by physical force, and he had small tear drops tattooed onto his cheek. After he was released, he was arrested as an accomplice to murder in a drive-by shooting in a neighboring state. He was sent back to jail, then transferred to a federal prison.

In prison, Brandon often bragged about his ability to seduce women, always using fake names, and after gaining their trust, taking a good deal of their money. Brandon had no regrets about his behaviors. If anything, he viewed each incident as another notch in his

belt. He could not communicate with others without ultimately resorting to violence. In the beginning, Brandon gained clout with other prisoners with his devil-may-care attitude, but other than a few individuals whom he seemed to have under his cunning influence, most of the other prisoners were fearful of his ruthlessness.

The developmental nature of the disorder can be seen in the early misbehavior evident in childhood and adolescence. The severity of the misbehavior intensified as Brandon matured. He lacked empathy for his victims and had no remorse for his behavior. Although not all individuals with antisocial personality disorder end up in prison, in Brandon's case his early conduct problems were the first steps on a path to a lifetime of criminal behavior.

Narcissistic Personality Disorder   **Narcissistic personality disorder** is a pervasive pattern of grandiosity (in fantasy or behavior), need for admiration, and lack of empathy (APA, 2000). People with this disorder have an exaggerated sense of self-importance and are often absorbed by fantasies of limitless success. Secondary to this preoccupation with their own superiority, they seek constant attention and may try to win admiration from others by flaunting or boasting about their perceived special abilities. This behavior often masks fragile self-esteem. Constant external praise or admiration allows them to continue to bolster their own grandiose sense of self.

People with narcissistic personality disorder often express a sense of entitlement—or a belief that they deserve only the best of everything and should only associate with others who are of similarly high caliber. For example, someone with narcissistic personality disorder might be unlikely to settle for just any doctor. She might seek out the top doctor, the best stylist, or the most famous lawyer. The mundane will not do.

A corollary to this overestimated sense of accomplishment is the converse—namely, a devaluation of what others do or what others have accomplished. Those with narcissistic personality disorder can come off as haughty and arrogant as they constantly flaunt their superiority. Their attitudes toward others can be patronizing and disdainful. People with narcissistic personality disorder are often so self-absorbed that they have a complete lack of empathy for others. They may be so preoccupied with their own need for praise and admiration that they are unable to understand other people's desires, needs, or feelings. People around them often come to feel ignored, devalued, or used.

Stephān (originally Steven) had always been outwardly confident in his small town high school. He felt that he transcended his Midwestern environs because he had traveled to Europe as a child. His edgy, electronic music and his interest in water polo were not as popular at his public high school as in the upper-crust private schools he had read about in the New York Times Sunday Edition. Stephān felt that he was unique compared with other students. Generally looking down on what he thought were the "common" tastes of his school, he had few friends and generally kept his high self-opinion to himself. However, during his first year at a prestigious East Coast liberal arts college, Stephān's belief in his own uniqueness became intensified. He sought out friends based on whether he had seen them in the society columns of magazines or knew their parents were significant donors to the university; he was aloof and rude to professors and students in classes that he was "forced" to take due to university standards, and complained of "wasting time in subjects that have nothing to do with being a CEO of a Fortune 500 company!" While quite charismatic, eloquent, and intelligent in his business courses, he often lied that his knowledge of economics came from his father, a prominent businessman who wrote for the Wall Street Journal (in reality his father was a convenience store owner). While quite successful in his academic pursuits, when faced with group projects, his peers perceived Stephān as a nightmare to work with—always blaming them when he

narcissistic personality disorder   a pervasive pattern of grandiosity, need for admiration from others, and lack of empathy *made small errors, or pitting students against each other and then standing back to watch the arguments. Stephān rarely wrote his own papers, saying "Why waste my time when I can easily persuade one of the naïve, previous-valedictorian freshmen to do it for me?" While Stephān desperately sought and often believed he had the admiration, attention, envy, or even fear of those around him, he was often seen as arrogant and obnoxious by his classmates.*

As illustrated by this case, Stephān created a persona that was legendary in his own mind. He considered himself vastly superior to others and grossly overestimated his abilities and prospects for the future. There was a deep disconnect between his beliefs (i.e., that everyone around him admired and respected him) and reality (i.e., that everyone around him found him to be quite insufferable and arrogant).

Although superficially confident, people with narcissistic personality disorder can experience extremes in mood and self-esteem. When their needs for admiration are not met, they may, at least temporarily, feel injured or defeated, resulting in low mood and social withdrawal.

Borderline Personality Disorder   **Borderline personality disorder** is a pervasive pattern of unstable interpersonal relationships, self-image, affect, and impulsivity (APA, 2000). Its symptoms can be severe and rapidly fluctuating. Intense bouts of anger, depression, and anxiety may last for hours, or as long as a day. Other behaviors include impulsive hostility, self-injury, and drug or alcohol abuse. Cognitive distortion and an unstable and conflicted sense of self and self-worth can lead to frequent changes in long-term goals, career plans, jobs, friendships, gender identity, and values. Individuals may feel misunderstood, ill-treated, bored, empty, and have an unstable self-identity. At extreme times, the identity disturbance can be so severe that individuals with borderline personality disorder may feel as if they do not exist at all.

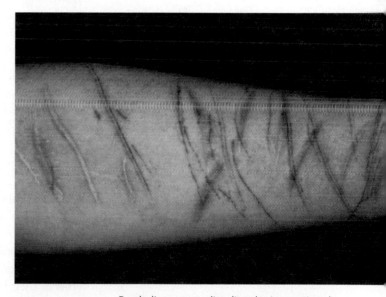

At the core of borderline personality disorder is a deep fear of abandonment. Minor separations or endings are misinterpreted as signs that they are being abandoned, left alone, or rejected and can lead to desperate attempts to remain connected and in contact with others. Examples include a therapist going on vacation or a partner having to go out of town for work. To prevent such separations, a person with borderline personality disorder may engage in impulsive and desperate behaviors such as self-mutilation or suicide attempts to keep the person near (see the case below).

Borderline personality disorder is associated with multiple impulsive behaviors, including self-harm.

These destructive behaviors and personality style can lead to highly unstable social relationships. Idealization (intense positive feeling) is quickly replaced by devaluation (intense anger and dislike). A person with borderline personality disorder may immediately form an attachment to another person and idealize him or her. Then, when a minor conflict occurs, there can be a rapid swing to the other extreme, and strong negative emotions toward the person develop. Impulsivity is another hallmark symptom and may include binge eating, shoplifting, gambling, irresponsible spending, unsafe sexual behaviors, substance abuse, or reckless driving.

People with borderline personality disorder are also at a high risk for suicide and self-harm (Paris, 2002; see also "Treatment of Personality Disorders" later in this chapter). As mentioned above, self-harm and suicide attempts can result from perceived abandonment or from feelings of emptiness and nothingness. Self-mutilation can include cutting, burning, punching, and a variety of other behaviors that cause bodily injury. These can occur during *dissociative episodes* (in which there is a temporary

borderline personality disorder   a pervasive pattern of instability in interpersonal relationships, self-image, and affect, with marked impulsive features such as frantic efforts to avoid real or imagined abandonment

detachment from reality). Some individuals report that self-harm releases underlying mounting tension. Others say that it helps them know that they can still experience feelings, and still others claim that it helps counteract a belief that they are somehow evil or tarnished.

At a large state university, far away from her parents in Philadelphia, Sophia was a college sophomore who didn't know if she would ever finish spring semester. She was so sick of her mother, e-mailing her once a week to ask her how things were going—wasn't this why she left Pennsylvania in the first place, Sophia thought, to get far away from her idiotic and annoying parents? She thought they were "so attached to all of that whole community, family crap of 'the old country'—don't they know they're in America now!" When her mother sent an e-mail to simply say hello, Sophia immediately thought, "I hate her so much, she is so intrusive and horrible," and responded to her e-mail with a scathing account of how she wished her mother "would f#*king get out of her face!" As had happened so many times before, when something triggered Sophia—whether a seemingly friendly e-mail from her parents, a negative comment from her boss, or anything else that perturbed her—her reaction was fast and extreme. Sometimes it was an emotional, verbal outburst, but other times she would turn on herself: making small cuts on her upper, inner thigh, where she could hide the wounds so no one would hassle her. After she flared, she felt alone, powerless, helpless, and empty. She would e-mail her mother back, apologizing, saying how much she needed her love, and confessing that she was "a horrible, selfish person who doesn't deserve to live." Then she would get down on herself for being "a Pollyanna, a suck-up." Sophia was stuck in a vacillating cycle that left her emotionally and physically injured, drained, constantly bouncing between opposing thoughts, and unavailable to sustain relationships.

When people learn about borderline personality disorder, their first question is often "the borderline of what?" Historically, the term refers to the border between neurosis and psychosis, acknowledging that some, but not all people with this disorder can experience transient psychotic episodes. Being around or in relationships with people with borderline personality disorder can be challenging. Friends and partners feel like they are on an emotional rollercoaster or that their value rises and falls like the stock market. Sophia's mother would often say to her husband that she could never predict which Sophia was going to come home from school or be on the phone, the loving and adoring one or the resentful, hateful one. The inconsistent sense of self that is experienced by the sufferer is also experienced by those around him or her. The person is often considered exhausting and "high maintenance." Fostering a sense of stability both in terms of their internal experience and their network of social relationships is critical to leveling out the complex emotions of individuals with borderline personality disorder.

Histrionic Personality Disorder Histrionic personality disorder is a pattern of excessive emotion and attention-seeking behavior. *Histrionic* means "dramatic" or "theatrical," and people with this disorder incessantly "perform" and draw attention to themselves (APA, 2000). At first, they are attractive and magnetic as they draw attention by their liveliness, colorful behavior, and flirtatiousness. Yet when no longer the center of attention, they engage in behaviors that draw the limelight back to them. Physical appearance or provocative and seductive behavior are often used to draw people into their circle, causing disruption in a variety of social and occupational settings.

Their emotional expressions are pronounced but lack depth and shift rapidly. These changeable, shallow emotions create an impression of not being genuine and of faking or putting on their feelings. Histrionic speech also has a dramatic and shallow flair. Someone with this disorder might speak in lavish and colorful terms, express strong opinions, and behave in a dramatic manner, yet her actions seem overblown and insincere.

histrionic personality disorder a pervasive pattern of excessive emotionality and attention seeking

People with histrionic personality disorder consider relationships to be closer or more intimate than they actually are. Coupled with their dramatic flair for language, they may refer to a casual acquaintance as "one of my closest friends in the whole wide world" or describe degrees of closeness in relationships that are in reality quite distant (e.g., seeing a celebrity in a restaurant and subsequently stating that they frequently dine together at their favorite bistro).

When she entered the party with her partner, Susan, Destiny was vibrant, gregarious, and the center of attention. She was in her element. At first it was very charming: she easily told stories to complete strangers as if she had known them her whole life. But after four hours of Destiny's theatrical socializing and flirtatious behavior, Susan grew tired and started to feel like an accessory. This was the fourth party this week and Susan felt disrespected by Destiny's flirting with others." One of Destiny's biggest concerns was what other people thought of her, and when she felt insecure, she lost her temper. It was often directed at Susan, who had become increasingly tired of bearing the brunt of her behavior. With Destiny always needing to be in control and calling the shots—fluctuating from enraged to content based on the circumstances—Susan had thought of leaving her many times. Two weeks ago, Destiny grabbed a glass vase and threw it at the floor, screaming in a fit of rage when Susan suggested that they not go out to dinner because she had a stressful day at work. After the fight, Destiny withdrew from contact and didn't speak for days. When she became less angry, she was extremely sweet and solicitous toward Susan. Destiny's inexorable theatrics and need to be the center of attention eventually led to the end of the relationship.

Living with someone with histrionic personality disorder can take a toll on interpersonal relationships. Although initially alluring, Destiny, with her constant need to be the center of attention and her flirtatiousness with others, was unable to engage in a healthy and trusting emotional relationship with Susan. As evidenced by this case, behavior that is overly dramatic and demanding can be destructive to relationships.

CLUSTER C: ANXIOUS OR FEARFUL DISORDERS

The common features of Cluster C are characteristic behaviors marked by considerable anxiety or withdrawal (APA, 2000). The three disorders in this cluster share features that reflect some form of anxiety-social anxiety, obsessionality, or fear of independence. As we will see with each disorder, distinctions must be made between the personality disorder and Axis I disorders that share some of the same clinical features. Again, recalling the distinction between "ways of being" versus illness can guide diagnostic decisions.

Avoidant Personality Disorder Avoidant personality disorder (see the box "DSM-IV-TR: Cluster C Disorders") is a pervasive pattern of social inhibition, feelings of inadequacy, and hypersensitivity to negative evaluation (APA, 2000). People with this disorder avoid social or occupational interactions for fear of rejection, criticism, or disapproval. Common patterns include being excessively shy and uncomfortable in social situations and worrying that what they say will be considered foolish by others. Other fears include blushing or crying in front of others, and becoming very hurt by any real or perceived disapproval by others.

People with avoidant personality disorder may entirely avoid making new friends unless they have complete assurance that they will not be rejected. A common concern is that others will be critical or disapproving unless proved otherwise. This personality disorder can lead individuals to avoid intimate relationships entirely because of worries about being accepted. Avoidant individuals are hypervigilant to signs of rejection or criticism and may over- or misinterpret other peoples' comments about themselves.

avoidant personality disorder a pervasive pattern of social inhibition, feelings of inadequacy, and hypersensitivity to negative evaluation

DSM-IV-TR

Cluster C Disorders

Avoidant personality disorder is a pervasive pattern of social shyness, feelings of inadequacy, and taking criticism in a personal and hypersensitive manner. Characteristics include at least four of the following:

- avoidance of occupational activities involving other people because of fear of rejection
- avoidance of interaction with others unless sure of being accepted and liked
- avoidance of intimacy in close relationships for fear of being rejected
- preoccupation with fears of being negatively evaluated or rejected in social settings
- discomfort in new social interactions due to fear of criticism
- feelings of social inferiority and inadequacy
- reluctance to engage in new social activities for fear of embarrassment.

Dependent personality disorder is a pervasive and excessive need to be taken care of by others that leads to dependency and fears of being left alone. Characteristics include at least five of the following:

- indecisiveness and need for excessive reassurance from others
- need for others to be responsible for most aspects of his or her life
- difficulty communicating disagreement for fear of being abandoned or rejected
- difficulty initiating self-directed activity due to a lack of self-confidence
- going to extremes to garner caring or approval from others (e.g., such as doing unappealing tasks)
- feelings of discomfort or helplessness when alone
- need to seek out a new relationship quickly when a close relationship ends
- preoccupation with fears of being independent.

Obsessive-compulsive personality disorder is a pervasive preoccupation with orderliness, perfectionism, and mental and interpersonal control to the point of distress. Characteristics include at least four of the following:

- losing the point of an activity by being preoccupied with rules, orderliness, structure, etc.
- perfectionism that interferes with task completion
- extreme devotion to productivity to the exclusion of social and leisure activities
- rigidity and stubbornness
- extreme conscientiousness and strictness about morality and values (other than for cultural or religious reasons)
- inability to discard old, useless objects even when these lack sentimental value
- reluctance to delegate tasks or to work with others unless in strict control
- miserliness, with money strictly saved for future catastrophes.

Adapted with permission from the *Diagnostic and Statistical Manual of Mental Disorders*, Text Revision, Fourth Edition, (Copyright 2000). American Psychiatric Association.

Lou was a 35-year-old mechanic who rarely came out from under a car. Ever since he can remember he was basically terrified of talking to other people. Even though his grades were acceptable throughout high school, he was afraid that people would think he was "simple" because he never knew what to say. He avoided all school social events and group projects, and would not attend graduation. He stayed in the garage all day working on cars. He quit work in one garage because he had to "cover" the front counter when the clerk went on breaks or lunch. He could not deal with the phones and the customers. Lou would be under the cars worried that the phone would ring or he'd hear the bell on the counter. He did excellent work and was offered several promotions that would require him to supervise others, but he refused because he did not know how to handle teams of people. To this day, Lou has never gone on a date. He eats alone in his house in front of the television every night and avoids all social contacts. When Lou's mother found out he had refused promotions, she decided she had "had it" with his "ridiculous shyness" and brought him in for psychotherapy. Lou has been working for over a year with a therapist trying to develop skills to overcome his pervasive anxiety about the social world.

The core of avoidant personality is shyness and a sense of inadequacy that leads to significant impairment in life both socially and occupationally. People with this disorder may completely avoid talking about themselves or be very withdrawn or restrained due to their potential fear of criticism or disapproval. Others would describe them as quiet, shy, or "wall flowers." People perceive themselves as socially inadequate, inferior, and inept at social interaction. Social self-esteem and self-efficacy tend to be quite low. (See the box "Examining the Evidence: Generalized Social Phobia vs. Avoidant Personality Disorder.")

Dependent Personality Disorder   **Dependent personality disorder** is a pervasive and excessive need to be taken care of, which leads to submissive and clinging behavior and fears of separation (APA, 2000). People with dependent personality disorder often have great difficulty making the simplest of everyday decisions, let alone larger life choices. This can result in a pattern of relying on others to make decisions and becoming paralyzed if advice and assistance are not available (e.g., not being able to leave the house without advice on which coat to wear). People with this disorder may become passive participants in the world and often allow others to take over responsibility for planning all aspects of their life. The degree of dependency is disproportionate to age-related norms and does not include situations in which depending on others is essential for survival (e.g., medically related dependence).

People with dependent personality disorder may also have trouble starting projects on their own. Having low confidence in their own ability and a chronic need to check with others for guidance and reassurance, they would rather follow than lead. Because of their exaggerated fears about their incompetence or inability to function or survive independently, a sense of helplessness can develop when they are left alone.

After the break-up of a significant relationship, people with dependent personality disorder quickly rebound into another relationship. They find it difficult to tolerate periods of independence and will desperately embark on another dependent relationship in order to minimize intense anxiety and fears associated with being alone. They may become so preoccupied with fears of being left alone that they go to extreme measures to arrange situations where they will have assurance of care.

Donna was the younger of two sisters and her mother's favorite "because she was prettier." As a child, Donna was indeed lovely, but she was very shy and clung to her mother's apron strings. She wet the bed until the age of 13 and only had sleepovers at her closest

dependent personality disorder   a pervasive and excessive need to be taken care of by others that leads to dependency and fears of being left alone

examining the evidence

Generalized Social Phobia vs. Avoidant Personality Disorder

Since 1987, both the Axis I diagnosis of social phobia and the Axis II diagnosis of avoidant personality disorder have been defined by fears of criticism and avoidance of activities that involve many different social interactions, not merely fears of pubic speaking (see Chapter 4). Both avoidant personality disorder and generalized social phobia involve restraint in and avoidance of social situations. Given that there is such overlap in the diagnostic criteria, are generalized social phobia and avoidant personality disorder really two separate conditions?

■ **The Facts** Only one criterion, "is reluctant to take personal risks or engage in new activities," appears to differentiate the diagnostic criterion of avoidant personality disorder from generalized social phobia. In 1992, based on several carefully controlled studies, it was concluded that avoidant personality disorder and the generalized subtype of social phobia were overlapping constructs (Widiger, 1992). Yet, the two categories continue to exist, suggesting that some view these conditions as qualitatively distinct. Why?

■ **Let's Examine the Evidence** Early studies (Herbert et al., 1992; Holt et al., 1992; Turner et al., 1992) examined a host of variables, including the core characteristics of the disorders, the associated symptoms (such as depression), and etiology. Data from all these studies indicated that across all measures, individuals diagnosed with avoidant personality disorder had more

severe problems, but the differences were quantitative, not qualitative. In other words, the difference appeared to be one of simple severity, not the qualitative distinction one would hope to find for these separate groups. More recent studies (Chambless et al., 2008; Huppert et al., 2008; Rettew, 2000) continue to search for qualitative distinctions, examining the same variables as the earlier studies but also including variables related to treatment outcome. Although statistical analysis appeared to be able to categorize people as either suffering from generalized social phobia or avoidant personality disorder, the distinction disappeared when the severity of social phobia symptoms was statistically controlled. In other words, classification was still based solely on symptom severity. In each case, those with avoidant personality disorder had more severe symptoms and more functional impairment. In many studies, so many people qualified for a diagnosis of both disorders that classification appeared meaningless (Rettew, 2000).

■ **Conclusion** Even though several controlled studies have tried to find qualitative differences between the Axis I condition of generalized social phobia and the Axis II condition of avoidant personality disorder, few clear distinctions can be found. The primary difference remains the quantitative distinction of clinical severity, illustrating how early-onset anxiety disorders can become so pervasive that they can affect every aspect of daily functioning.

friend's house, since she understood the problem and knew why she brought a plastic sheet. Donna's mother was very opinionated and domineering. When she drank alcohol, she would get very loud. Donna was always the one to quietly and gently ask her to be a little quieter. In high school, when Donna's friends began dating, her mother always disapproved of the boys they dated. No one would EVER be good enough for her Donna. Donna did date a few boys, but none met with her mother's approval. When it was time to decide about college, despite Donna's good grades, her mother told her that college was a waste of time and suggested she get her realtor's license—that way she could live at home, save money, and make a good living. Donna agreed and did as her mother suggested. Indeed, she was relieved because she was terrified of having to live alone or in a college dorm. She still went shopping for her mother and did errands for her parents regularly. At 37, she was still living at home. Her sister was married with children and constantly hassled her about "getting a life." Donna loved playing with her little niece, because Lily loved her unconditionally. Some of Donna's brief relationships with men had bordered on the abusive. She never felt like she had the right to stand up for herself and thought she didn't really have opinions about anything. At least the men were there to care for her if she needed them. Whenever she brought one home to meet her parents, her mother never failed to find fault and interfere in the relationship. Donna couldn't stand up to her mother or break away and become independent. She spent evenings in her room in tears worrying about her future and what would happen if her mother died and was no longer able to look after her.

Despite the uncomfortable aspects of her life, Donna remained at home with her mother where she felt someone would look after her and help her make critical decisions. She was preoccupied with worries about her future and fears about being unable to care for herself if her mother was no longer available. Donna's degree of dependence had nothing to do with any physical condition or actual need for dependency on others and was clearly age inappropriate.

Obsessive-Compulsive Personality Disorder **Obsessive-compulsive personality disorder** is a pervasive pattern of preoccupation with orderliness, perfectionism, and mental and interpersonal control at the expense of flexibility, openness, and efficiency (APA, 2000). People with this personality disorder are classic examples of being unable to see the forest for the trees. Being hyperfocused on rules, trivial details, lists, or procedures can lead to losing sight of the overarching activity. A common behavior is checking and rechecking work to ensure complete accuracy. A strong feeling of self-doubt can lead to missing important work or school deadlines. This disorder is defined by the aspiration for perfection, which sometimes backfires. For example, an individual may become so preoccupied with the details of perfecting part of a task that he never "pulls it all together" and does not complete the entire task. Students may recopy an assignment over and over in search of the "perfect" report, but consequently not finish on time and miss the assignment deadline.

This quest for perfection can often lead to a preoccupation with and devotion to work that leaves little or no time for leisure activities, pleasurable activities, or friendships and relationships. This is quite evident in the case that begins this chapter, in which Jeff's entire life is focused on his work schedule. Anxiety increases if there is not a goal or a structure to activities, and people with this disorder may even turn to structuring leisure time for themselves or their children. "Chilling" or "kicking back" is not in their vocabulary and indeed would be highly uncomfortable and even anxiety provoking. Others perceive them as rigid or stubborn.

Another common feature of obsessive-compulsive personality disorder is overconscientiousness and strict moral and ethical values that go beyond what is appropriate or normative for the person's cultural background or religious affiliation. This can result in holding oneself (and others) to extraordinarily high standards of moral and ethical conduct and merciless self-punishment if a rule is transgressed.

Other associated features include being "pack rats," unable to discard things that have no use or apparent sentimental value. Hoarded objects may seem completely useless (e.g., old cell phones, old junk mail). Delegation of work to others can also be a challenge, and the belief might be, like Jeff's, "if you want something done right, you have to do it yourself." This leads to feelings of being overwhelmed and unable to accomplish all of the tasks on the list. Rigidity and control may also extend to the financial area, where people may feel compelled to pinch pennies or save for a rainy day, depriving themselves or their family. The first purchases to be rejected are any that are associated with pleasure or leisure and do not contribute in a direct or meaningful way to the accomplishment of tasks on the list. Like Jeff, the individual with obsessive-compulsive personality disorder is a prisoner of lists and "shoulds."

While obsessive-compulsive disorder is marked by obsessions and compulsions (such as excessive hand washing), obsessive-compulsive personality disorder is marked by traits such as orderliness, perfectionism, and rigidity.

obsessive-compulsive personality disorder a pervasive preoccupation with orderliness, perfectionism, and mental and interpersonal control to the point of distress

OTHER PERSONALITY DISORDERS

Although the three clusters capture a broad range of personality disturbance, they are far from comprehensive. Sometimes people clearly have a personality disturbance (in that the traits are pervasive, persistent, and pathological and are more a "way of being" than an illness). Yet, they do not fit tightly into one of the disorder boxes. These individuals are given a diagnosis of personality disorder—not otherwise specified, which indicates that their symptoms may be a mixture of several disorders. Of all of the personality disorders, this is the most frequently used Axis II diagnosis in clinical practice (Verheul et al., 2007; Verheul & Widiger, 2004). Some people meet the criteria for more than one personality disorder (e.g., dependent and histrionic or obsessive-compulsive and paranoid).

Although it may be easy and diagnostically convenient to think of mental disorders as clear-cut categories, sometimes they are not. Research is a shifting construct, and there is continuing debate within the field about how personality disorders should be understood. Rather than a categorical model, some theorists propose a dimensional model of personality (see Chapter 3). One well-known dimensional model is the five-factor model (FFM). In this model, behavior is classified along five different dimensions—neuroticism, extraversion, openness, agreeableness, and conscientiousness—and a person would be rated as being maladaptively high or low on each dimension (see Figure 11.1). Integrating these dimensional factors of personality into current DSM-IV diagnoses may make these diagnostic categories more descriptive. For example, a person with schizoid personality disorder would score maladaptively low on extraversion, while someone with borderline personality disorder would score maladaptively high on neuroticism (anxiousness). Proponents of a dimensional model (Widiger & Lowe, 2008) believe that it would provide a more comprehensive picture of personality and would eliminate the need to give several personality disorder diagnoses in order to adequately describe behavior. Because this approach highlights personality strengths, it could also reduce the stigma of labeling someone with a personality disorder.

FIGURE 11.1

The Five-Factor Model of Personality

This model posits five primary dimensions of personality: extraversion, neuroticism, conscientiousness, agreeableness, and openness to experience.

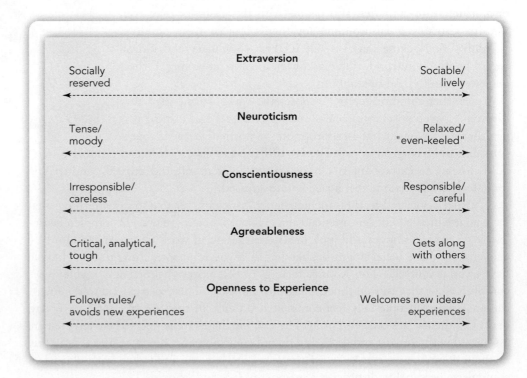

Beyond the debate between categorical versus dimensional systems, the personality disorders described in DSM-IV may only capture a fraction of the personality-related problems of interest to patients and clinicians (McCrae et al., 2001). In one study (Westen & Arkowitz-Westen, 1998), 60% of patients treated for personality-related problems and distress did not meet criteria for a DSM-IV personality disorder. Yet, personality problems, such as perfectionism and shyness, were among the reasons patients sought treatment. As mentioned above, it is the rare case that someone seeking treatment fits perfectly into one of the personality disorder categories. More often than not, people will have a varied collection of symptoms that cut across not only disorders within a cluster, but also sometimes across clusters. The psychologist's job is to evaluate and treat the complexity of the personality disturbance as it exists in the person and not to have his or her perspective limited by the published boundaries of any set of diagnostic criteria.

DEVELOPMENTAL FACTORS AND PERSONALITY DISORDERS

The DSM multiaxial system (see Chapter 3) helps clinicians make distinctions about the patient's current state in contrast to lifetime patterns of behavior, but the distinctions are not always entirely clear. For example, how long must a personality disturbance persist to qualify for a personality disorder diagnosis? When significant personality pathology exists in individuals under age 18, is a personality disorder diagnosis appropriate if personality is theoretically still under formation? While a diagnosis may be appropriate if the features are present for at least a year, diagnosing personality disorder in someone under age 18 remains controversial given the effects of brain maturation on the course of personality maturity (Ceballos et al., 2006).

From a developmental perspective, many manifestations of personality disorders represent typical (although transient) childhood and adolescent behaviors. Dependency, anxiety, hypersensitivity, identity formation problems, conduct problems, histrionics, and testing the limits occur commonly during childhood and adolescence. In general, longitudinal follow-up studies show that such behaviors decrease over time, although higher rates of personality disorder-type symptoms during childhood and adolescence are associated with greater risk for Axis I and Axis II disorders later in life. More flagrant symptoms (such as harming animals or risky sexual behavior) may be more serious red flags for later personality disturbance. As our understanding of personality formation emerges, evidence has accumulated that personality disorders originate very early in life and may, at least in part, be programmed at the genetic level. Elements of later personality may even be foreshadowed in the simple behaviors exhibited by babies and toddlers (De Clercq & De Fruyt, 2007). As we watch personality emerge in children, the difference between healthy development of individual personality features and the earliest symptoms of personality pathology remains unclear.

In community and clinical samples, adolescent personality disorders are associated with emotional distress and psychological impairment. In the Children in the Community study (Johnson et al., 2006)—a prospective longitudinal investigation of 593 families at four time points from childhood to adulthood—low parental affection or nurturing was associated with elevated risk for antisocial, avoidant, borderline, paranoid, schizoid, and schizotypal personality disorders among adult offspring. Aversive parental behavior (e.g., harsh punishment) was associated with an elevated risk for borderline, paranoid, and schizotypal personality disorders among adult offspring. As this study controlled for offspring behavioral and emotional problems and parental psychiatric disorder, these findings suggest that parental rearing styles may affect the development of personality disorders in children. The clearest case of progression from adolescence through adulthood is with conduct disorder and antisocial personality disorder (Johnson et al., 2006).

Longitudinal studies such as the Block Project can trace childhood personality features into adulthood to identify early indicators of later psychopathology. Here, researchers stand surrounded by years and years of collected data.

Adolescent personality disorders are also associated with the presence of Axis I disorders. A young woman who shows persistent dependent traits throughout adolescence may find herself at greater risk for developing major depression during adulthood when she experiences loss. Applying dimensional approaches to understanding personality development in children may yield richer information. One longitudinal cohort study, called the "Block Project," has followed 100 children since the age of 3 well into adulthood. The Block Project found that characteristic childhood personality and behavioral patterns predicted the later development of problems such as dysthymia. Boys who developed dysthymia by age 18 were observed to be more aggressive, self-aggrandizing, and undercontrolled at age 7. Girls with later depressive tendencies were self-critical and overcontrolling as children (Block et al., 1991). Therefore, personality differences that exist in early childhood were associated with the later development of disorders such as depression, but different behaviors were important for boys and girls. However, we need to be careful that we do not immediately assume that every unusual childhood and adolescent behavior represents a risk factor for the emergence of a later psychological disorder. We do not yet fully appreciate the clinical significance of personality traits during childhood and adolescence.

COMORBIDITY AND FUNCTIONAL IMPAIRMENT

As each case in this chapter indicates, personality disorders produce substantial functional impairment, most obviously in interpersonal relationships. The person with borderline personality disorder alienates her friends and lovers with her rapidly fluctuating moods of adoration and hatred; the obsessive-compulsive father alienates his family with his rigid approach to the world; the son with schizoid personality disorder abandons his siblings and has few ties to the rest of the world. Perhaps not surprisingly, people with personality disorders create considerable distress for people around them and are often the topic of conversation because of the unusual and extreme aspects of who they are.

Occupational functioning is also often deeply affected. From the person with avoidant personality disorder who passes on promotions to avoid interpersonal contact, to the person with antisocial personality disorder who moves irresponsibly from job to job, to the person with histrionic personality disorder who flirts inappropriately to gain attention from coworkers, personality disorders can lead to occupational problems and failures. Needless to say, managers do not necessarily have the psychological background to understand that these patterns of behavior are secondary to a personality disorder. These behaviors result in poor or inappropriate performance and potentially loss of employment.

In addition to their problems with social and occupational functioning, people with personality disorders, in general, are at higher risk than other people for many (Axis I) psychiatric disorders. Paranoid and schizoid personality disorders have been most strongly associated with dysthymia and mania (Grant et al., 2005). Avoidant and dependent personality disorders show strong associations with major depression, dysthymia, and mania (Grant et al., 2005). Avoidant personality disorder is also strongly associated with social phobia (Mattik & Newman, 1991). Borderline personality disorder is commonly comorbid with major depression (Sullivan et al., 1994), bulimia nervosa (Rosenvinge et al., 2000), and substance use disorders (Dulit et al., 1993; Skodol et al., 1999). Antisocial personality disorder often occurs within the context of substance abuse and other impulse control disorders (APA, 2000; Dulit et al., 1993; Goldstein et al., 2007). These high rates of comorbidity suggest that the clinical presentation and functional impairment of personality disorders can be compounded by the presence of Axis I disorders. Furthermore, the combination results in significant personal distress and poses considerable treatment challenges. As noted later in this chapter, intervention must address not only the pervasive personality pathology but also the acute symptoms associated with comorbid Axis I disorders.

EPIDEMIOLOGY

There are few epidemiologic data on the prevalence of personality disorders. One reason is that personality disorders cannot be reliably diagnosed in a single setting. Most epidemiologic studies rely on a single diagnostic interview (at best) and a series of self-report questionnaires (most commonly). Capturing the complexity of personality disorder diagnoses in cross-sectional epidemiological studies is a daunting and potentially unreliable task. This caveat must be kept in mind when considering the data that do exist.

In the general U.S. adult population, prevalence estimates for specific cluster A disorders range from 0.5% to around 4% (Grant et al., 2004). Results from the 2001–2002 National Epidemiologic Survey on Alcohol and Related Comorbidities revealed that as many as 14% of adult Americans meet criteria for at least one personality disorder (Grant et al., 2004). The specific prevalences reported in this study were obsessive-compulsive 7.8%, paranoid 4.4%, antisocial 3.6%, schizoid 3.1%, avoidant 2.3%, histrionic 1.8%, and dependent 0.5%.

SEX, RACE, AND ETHNICITY

Our understanding of sex differences in personality disorders comes from epidemiological studies and from studies of clinical populations. However, sex differences reported in clinical studies can be biased and may reflect the likelihood of the different sexes to seek treatment (or be brought in for treatment) rather than true sex differences. When we compare results across epidemiologic studies, two constant patterns emerge. First, antisocial personality disorder is consistently more common in males (Grant et al., 2004). Second, dependent and avoidant personality disorders tend to be more common in females (Grant et al., 2004; Torgersen et al., 2001). Although in clinical settings, histrionic personality disorder tends to be diagnosed more often in females and narcissistic personality disorder in males, this pattern is observed in some (Torgersen et al., 2001) but not all (Grant et al., 2004) epidemiologic studies. Beyond those differences, few consistent patterns emerge in terms of sex differences in personality disorders.

There are few population-based data on racial and ethnic differences in personality disorders. In one longitudinal study of white, African American, and Hispanic participants, borderline personality disorder was significantly more common in Hispanic than in white and African American patients, and schizotypal personality disorder was more common in African American than white participants. Data from the Epidemiological Catchment Area (ECA) study (Robins et al., 1984) indicated similar estimates of histrionic personality disorder among African Americans and whites (Nestadt et al., 1990). Borderline personality disorder may be more common in nonwhite individuals belonging to lower socioeconomic groups (Swartz et al., 1990), and similar estimates of antisocial personality disorder were found among Mexican Americans, Puerto Ricans, and non-Hispanic whites (Canino et al., 1987; Karno et al., 1987).

The existing data on racial and ethnic factors in personality disorders must be viewed with considerable caution. We simply do not have adequate large-scale culturally sensitive studies that will shed enough light on racial and ethnic differences in either the prevalence or differences in clinical presentation of these disorders.

- Cluster A, the "odd or eccentric" cluster, includes features reminiscent of those seen in psychosis and schizophrenia. This cluster includes paranoid, schizoid, and schizotypal personality disorders.

- Cluster B, the "dramatic, emotional, or erratic" cluster, tends to be marked by dramatic or exaggerated personality features. This cluster includes borderline, narcissistic, histrionic, and antisocial personality disorders.

- Cluster C, the "anxious or fearful" cluster, includes dependent, avoidant, and obsessive-compulsive personality disorders.

- Personality disorders are often associated with substantial functional impairment, especially in the realm of interpersonal relationships.

- Of the personality disorders, antisocial personality disorder has the clearest developmental roots, with origins often clearly traced back to childhood and evidence of conduct disorder before age 15.

APPLICATION QUESTION   Sometimes defining the boundaries between personality disorder and criminal behavior found in someone like Jeffrey Dahmer can be a daunting task. If you were asked to think about where to draw that line, what issues would you consider?

The Etiology of Personality Disorders

What causes a persistent and maladaptive way of dealing with the world? Are there indicators early in life that predict the emergence of personality pathology? Can we use the same tools that we use with Axis I disorders to understand the causes of personality disorders? These are all critical and current questions that are being addressed with active research within the personality disorders field. As with Axis I disorders, neither genetic underpinnings, nor chemical imbalances, nor psychological features, nor problematic social environments alone account for the development of personality pathology. Critical to understanding personality pathology is the convergence of both a biopsychosocial perspective and a full understanding of the developmental context. In the remaining sections of this chapter, we outline what is known about biological, psychological, and social factors and how they interact to result in disturbances in personality function.

BIOLOGICAL PERSPECTIVES

Ask any mother with more than one child and she will tell you that her babies had distinct and often quite different personalities from birth—and sometimes even from before birth (see the box "Research Hot Topic: Tracking Temperament from Childhood into Adulthood").

In contrasting her children, Lashanda said, "Ronnie was a holy terror from the day he was born. He would scream and scream and nothing could soothe him. In fact it went back even further than that. Seems whenever I wanted to sleep when I was pregnant, he wanted to play. I didn't get a minute's rest for nine months. It's amazing I had another one! Then came Jake. When I was pregnant, he slept when I slept. After he was born, I kept expecting him to be like Ronnie—throwing tantrums in the middle of the night—unable to be consoled. He might yell a little, I would come into his room, rub his back, he would pass a little gas, sigh, smile, roll over and fall back to sleep. Those boys had different wiring!"

Temperament is influenced by genetics and may account for some of the variability in personality traits. It refers to personality components that are biological or genetic in origin, observable from birth (or perhaps before) and relatively stable across time and across various situations (Buss, 1999). For example, some children are born fussy and

Temperament, a part of personality that is believed to be biologically based, is apparent early in life.

temperament   personality components that are biological or genetic in origin, observable from birth (or perhaps before) and relatively stable across time and situations

Research HOT Topic

Tracking Temperament from Childhood into Adulthood

Temperament refers to the stable moods and behavior pro-files first observed in infancy and early childhood. Two of the most extensively studied aspects of childhood temperament are the behavioral tendencies to approach or withdraw from un-familiar stimuli. Some children cower behind their mother when confronted by a stranger (behaviorally inhibited children), while others eagerly engage and approach the stranger (uninhibited children). Jerome Kagan and his colleagues have followed a cohort of children who were categorized as inhibited or uninhibited within the first two years of life. In addition to the observed differences in approach/withdrawal, major differences were also found in the children's underlying biological reactions when they were confronted with unfamiliar individuals. Inhibited children showed faster heart rates and greater heart rate vari-ability, pupillary dilation during cognitive tasks, vocal cord ten-sion when speaking under moderate stress, and salivary cortisol levels. Intriguingly, these differences remained throughout later childhood and adolescence. But what happens when the chil-dren become adults? Do they "grow out of" their biology and their tendency to approach or avoid?

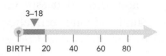

Schwartz, Wright, and colleagues tracked down 22 adults (mean age 21.8 years) from this study who had been catego-rized in the second year of life as inhibited ($n = 13$) or uninhibited ($n = 9$). Using functional magnetic resonance imaging (fMRI), they measured the response of the amygdala (a central mecha-nism in our brain that controls arousal) to novel versus familiar

faces. Amazingly, the biological footprint of being inhibited or uninhibited was still there. The adults who had been character-ized as inhibited as children had greater amygdalar activation to unfamiliar faces than the adults who had been classified as uninhibited. These findings show that some of the basic brain properties relating to temperament are preserved from infancy into early adulthood.

References: Kagan, 1994; Schwartz et al., 2003.

---

irritable, and others are mellow and calm. Even mothers of twins will point out funda-mental differences in the temperament of babies who shared a womb. Temperament is evident across the life span as well as across cultures. When these innate biological components interact with the outside world (i.e., experience), personality emerges (Cloninger et al., 1993). Thus, personality traits are a combination of temperament and experience. Personality disorders represent a dysfunctional outcome of this process when these traits become exaggerated and are applied in maladaptive ways.

The links between various personality dimensions and underlying biological or genetic markers remain theoretical. In 1993, Cloninger proposed that there were asso-ciations between dimensions of temperament and specific neurotransmitter systems (Cloninger et al., 1993). As our understanding of temperament and neurobiology has progressed, it is clear that any one trait–one neurotransmitter theory will be replaced by more sophisticated models that account for complex biological underpinnings.

Family and Genetic Studies   Family and twin studies clearly indicate that both personality disorders (Kendler et al., 2008; Reichborn-Kjennerud et al., 2007) and personality traits (Jang et al., 1996; Rettew et al., 2008) are familial and influenced primarily by genetic factors. As with all complex traits, a single gene is not responsible for a single temperamental trait; the trait probably results from variations in several genes coupled with environmental influences.

Ongoing studies have explored genetic and environmental factors in personality disorders. Large twin studies indicate that paranoid, schizoid, and schizotypal personality disorders are all moderately heritable (Kendler et al., 2007, 2008). A large multivariate twin study yielded heritability estimates across personality disorders ranging from the lower end (20.5% schizotypal and 23.4% paranoid) to the most heritable (borderline 37.1%, avoidant 37.3%, and antisocial 40.9%).

The Role of Traumatic Events   Although one might consider traumatic events as transient environmental factors (and indeed they are), we now know that especially during critical developmental windows, they can have profound and long-term effects on brain biology (Goodman et al., 2004). A childhood history of physical and/or sexual abuse has been associated with personality disorders (Herman et al., 1989; Ogata et al., 1990; Zanarini et al., 1989). People with personality disorders report increased rates of childhood emotional abuse, physical abuse, and neglect (Battle et al., 2004; Bierer et al., 2003). These associations provide an important clue to the biological mechanisms underlying the development of personality disorders. Early maltreatment is associated with problems in basic attachment. Attachment is one of the processes that provides the foundation for our later ability to relate to others interpersonally. Poor attachment is believed to interfere with brain structures that underlie development of the ability to think about the mental states of others, called *mentalization* (Fonagy et al., 1991). Early trauma and the subsequent disruption in attachment may lead to neurodevelopmental deficits in interpersonal functioning and create a pathway to the development of severe personality disturbance.

Good attachment between parent and child is important to personality development. Poor attachment may play a role in the etiology of personality disorders.

A person's neurobiological responses to threat stimuli may be changed after traumatic events, including childhood traumatic experiences. Alterations in arousal, fear conditioning, and emotional regulation have been observed in people who have a history of traumatic events (Arnsten, 1998; Bremner, 2007; Bremner et al., 1999; Mayes, 2000; Shin et al., 2005). These shifts in brain functioning are adaptive in the context of real danger, which requires a rapid automatic response to ensure survival. However, early trauma may permanently impair the biology of arousal regulation and fear conditioning, causing an inappropriate reaction even when danger is not imminent. Thus, trauma might lead to "overperceiving" and "overresponding" to threats. Early childhood trauma may have a permanent effect on brain development, which can set the stage for the emergence of maladaptive personality traits. Because many personality disorders represent maladaptive, and in many cases, exaggerated responses to seemingly innocuous interpersonal events, these fundamental neurobiological disturbances may well underlie the erratic and dysregulated responses to the world commonly seen in people with personality disorders.

Brain Structure and Functioning Studies   With the advantage of assessment tools such as fMRI and PET scans, we are now able to examine the neurobiology of some personality disorders. Behaviorally, people with schizotypal personality disorder show the same psychotic-like cognitive and perceptual symptoms and cognitive disorganization as people with schizophrenia. However, biologically, these two groups show similarities and dissimilarities. Structurally, both schizotypal and schizophrenic individuals show abnormalities in *temporal lobe* volume (Siever et al., 2002). However, the decrease in brain volume that is found in the *frontal lobe* in people with schizophrenia is not found in people with schizotypal personality disorder. Functionally, there are also subtle biological differences. Whereas both groups show decreased brain activity in the frontal cortex, only people with schizotypal personality disorder appear to be able to activate other regions of their brain as a way to compensate for this deficit (Siever et al., 2002).

With Cluster B disorders, studies examining people with borderline and antisocial personality disorders have focused on brain regions that control rage, fear, and impulsive automatic reactions (the prominent symptoms of the disorders). It appears that the hippocampus and amygdala may be as much as 16% smaller in people with borderline personality disorder than in people with no personality disorder. Traumatic experiences, which are common in people with borderline personality disorder, may create these neuroanatomical changes (Driessen et al., 2000). Neurobiological theories on antisocial personality disorder focus on individual differences in arousal or detection. One theory suggests that people at risk for antisocial personality disorder are in a chronic state of underarousal and that their behavior represents misguided attempts to seek stimulation (Quay, 1965). Another theory focuses on the apparent fearlessness of people with antisocial personality disorder and hypothesizes that they have a higher fear detection threshold than other people (Lykken, 1982). This difference in detection of fear allows them to enter calmly into situations that others would find overwhelmingly fear-inducing.

PSYCHOLOGICAL AND SOCIOCULTURAL PERSPECTIVES

Personality development has long been the territory of psychological theories. An entire branch of psychology (personality psychology) deals with the psychological processes underlying healthy and maladaptive personality traits. For decades, various psychological theories dominated our understanding of their etiology. The two most prominent theories, which we review here, are the psychodynamic and the cognitive-behavioral perspectives.

Psychodynamic Interpretations   Most psychodynamic theories focus on early parental interactions that shape behavioral traits that become personality disorders. For example, borderline personality disorder was believed to emerge when lack of parental acceptance damaged self-esteem and led to fears of rejection (Gunderson, 1984). Indeed, this theory is generally consistent with the high rates of abuse and neglect reported by people with borderline personality disorders (Herman et al., 1989; Ogata et al., 1990). According to these theories, people tend to internalize negative parental attitudes, leaving them vulnerable to fears of abandonment and to self-hatred. In addition, they tend to treat themselves as they were treated by their parents. These attitudes prevent the development of mature, consistent, and positive perceptions of themselves and others, and lead to a severe inability to regulate mood when faced with disappointment, and difficulty in taking another's point of view. These theories are especially applicable to borderline personality disorder.

One influential theory developed by the psychiatrist Otto Kernberg (1975) proposes a continuum of psychopathology, from persistent, severe psychosis to severe personality disorders through neurotic to healthy functioning. Kernberg's work focused primarily on the development of borderline personality disorder but also encompassed other personality disorders. For example, people with narcissistic personality disorder construct a largely inflated view of themselves in order to maintain their self-esteem. On the outside, these individuals appear grandiose, but inside they are often very sensitive to even very minor attacks on the self. They create this enlarged perception of themselves in order to match the grandiose perception of their ideal in their own mind's eye. When events happen that make them feel as if they are not meeting this ideal, they then experience shame, sadness, and a sense of failure. Thus, grandiosity protects against these negative emotions.

Cognitive-behavioral Theories Cognitive-behavioral theory proposes that learning is at the basis of personality, which is also substantially molded by an individual's unique environment. From a cognitive perspective, personality evolves from an interaction between a person's environment and the way he or she processes information. Cognitive-behavioral theory and therapy have enriched our understanding of personality disorders, contributing concepts such as goals, skills, self-regulation, and schemas, or core beliefs (e.g., I am an unlovable person) (Bandura, 1986; Mischel, 1973; Mischel & Shoda, 1995). Considerable focus on how people learn to regulate moods (Linehan et al., 1993) and their development of core beliefs about themselves and their worlds (Beck et al., 2003) has transformed the theory into cognitive-behavioral treatments for personality disorders (see "Treatment of Personality Disorders").

Sociocultural Theories Sociocultural theories of personality go beyond the study of the individual to include a broader contextual view of personality development, including culture as a critical element in the shaping of personality. Miller (1997) describes culture and personality as "mutually constitutive phenomena" and views them as integral to each other. Fundamental cultural differences can deeply influence the concept of personality. For example, consider the differences in the concept of "self" in Japanese and Western cultures. In Japanese culture, "self" includes both the personal self and that of the surrounding cultural community; in dominant Western culture, the self is considered independent and not contingent upon others (Markus & Kitayama, 1991). Clearly, this core conceptual difference could influence perceptions of what constitutes abnormal behavior.

An additional factor that influences cross-cultural studies of personality is language. Classic Western personality measures may not capture cultural nuances of expression and language, such as the Japanese term *amae*, or the need for dependency (Doi, 1973), and the Hindu term *anasakti*, or nonattachment, a freedom from dependency that is associated with greater peace and mental health (Pande & Naidu, 1992). The "similarities" in personality disorders that we observe across cultures may simply reflect the imposition of Western language on non-Western cultures. Therefore, although the dimensional aspects of personality appear consistent across cultures, there will also be cultural differences that will enrich our understanding of personality disorders (Poortinga & Van Hemert, 2001).

Across cultures, different ideas of basic human concepts such as "self" may lead to very different conceptualizations and treatments of personality disorders. In Japan, the "self" is a broader concept than the individual "self" in the United States.

---

concept CHECK

- Temperament refers to biological features of personality that are present at birth. The interaction between temperament and environmental experience leads to the development of personality.

- Personality traits and personality disorders run in families and have been shown to be moderately heritable.

- Traumatic events, especially during critical periods of development, can have profound and long-term effects on brain biology that influence personality development.

- Freudian psychodynamic theories explored the impact of early interactions with parents on later personality organization.

- Cognitive-behavioral theory holds that personality emerges from learning and an individual's unique environment. How the individual processes and interprets information about the self and the world is central to the development of personality.

APPLICATION QUESTION Imagine a scenario in which two children with very different personalities (one highly neurotic and one highly extraverted) experience a traumatic event (a drive-by shooting in which a stranger is killed). How might their responses differ?

Treatment of Personality Disorders

Treating long-standing patterns of behavior is inherently different from treating acute disorders. There is no magic pill to change a person's personality style. Both patient and therapist have to make subtle distinctions between healthy and maladaptive behavior patterns. The patient has to understand the perspective of other people whom their disorder affects adversely. In addition, since these behavior patterns are long-standing, one cannot expect rapid improvement—particularly if they reach back to early childhood and involve changes in brain functioning. Other significant challenges include just getting patients with personality disorders into treatment. Often, the people around them are more interested in getting them treatment than the patients are themselves. Finally, the treatment can be especially complicated when people have more than one personality disorder and also have an acute Axis I illness such as major depression, bipolar disorder, bulimia nervosa, or substance abuse. Such complications can pose treatment challenges for the most dedicated clinician. Patience, consistency, and persistence are valuable therapist characteristics that can facilitate treatment of personality disorders.

Only recently have we witnessed a surge of randomized controlled trials investigating the treatment of personality disorders. Although the overall amount of research remains small, recent studies have explored the efficacy of dynamic therapy, cognitive-behavioral therapy, or their variants. The quality of the research varies, because some studies focus on specific personality disorders, others on the personality disorder clusters, and still others on personality disorders in general. This makes the results of the studies difficult to interpret.

Most studies on specific personality disorders have focused on borderline or antisocial personality disorder. Although avoidant personality disorder and Cluster C disorders have received some research attention, there is a dearth of data on the treatment of Cluster A disorders. With this background in mind, we describe various treatments for personality disorders, their empirical basis, and the limitations of the available research. Given the broad and heterogeneous nature of this area, we present treatment approaches and data related to personality disorders generally and borderline personality disorder specifically.

Despite a limited number of treatment studies, recent data support the importance of psychotherapy in the treatment of personality disorders. While pharmacotherapy may help manage associated symptoms such as anxiety or depression, psychosocial treatments and excellent communication among all those delivering care are required for optimal management of personality disorders.

Early treatments for personality disorders were rooted in dynamic psychotherapy and adapted psychoanalytic techniques in long-term therapeutic approaches. Current treatment approaches differ somewhat according to disorder and often include components to address concurrent comorbid Axis I disorders.

For Cluster A disorders, treatment can be challenging. When their core problem is distrust, it can be particularly difficult for people with paranoid personality disorder to trust the motives of a therapist. People with schizoid personality disorders have little desire for social interaction, so it is difficult to convince them that social interactions are often necessary and positively reinforcing (Freeman, 2002). People with schizotypal personality disorder often benefit from cognitive-behavior therapy that helps them develop appropriate thoughts and eliminate or modify odd or eccentric cognitions (Beck et al., 2003).

There is a form of cognitive behavioral therapy specially developed to deal with the challenges inherent in treating people with the rapidly fluctuating symptoms of borderline personality disorder. This approach, *dialectical behavior therapy* (DBT), has considerable empirical support (Binks et al., 2006; Linehan et al., 2006). DBT is based on the premise that borderline personality disorder is defined by a failure to regulate emotions, probably due to a biological vulnerability combined with an environment in which the child's private experiences were denied, contradicted, or punished by significant others. The treatment emphasizes discussion and negotiation between therapist and patient, with a balance between the rational and the emotional, and between acceptance and change. A hierarchy of treatment goals is established, with elimination of self-harm behaviors taking priority. Learning new skills is a core component of the intervention, including mindfulness (being aware of one's emotional state), interpersonal effectiveness, distress tolerance, and observing, describing, and participating in emotional response. These approaches help the patient calm down what can feel like a chaotic internal state, pay attention to emotionally driven behavior, and develop skills to manage feelings and impulses more effectively.

When compared to treatment as usual (what we call "talk therapy"), DBT and partial hospitalization produce superior treatment results (Brazier et al., 2006). Moreover, DBT may be more cost-effective than traditional therapy for borderline personality disorder. Other treatment strategies that are sometimes efficacious for borderline personality disorder include inpatient therapy (Dolan et al., 1997) and what are known as step-down programs, which are characterized by short-term inpatient treatment followed by longer-term outpatient and community treatment (Chiesa et al., 2006; Chiesa et al., 2004).

Medications, including antidepressants, mood stabilizers (drugs that even out the highs and lows seen in mood disorders), and antipsychotics, are often prescribed for borderline personality disorder. These drugs target sudden mood swings, impulsivity, and aggression. Although currently few data exist, initial research indicates that the drugs might be helpful (Bellino et al., 2008). The atypical antipsychotics (see Chapter 10) may be helpful for patients with borderline personality disorder who have psychotic-like, impulsive, or suicidal symptoms (Grootens & Verkes, 2005). It is critical to understand that remission from borderline personality disorder does occur. In a six-year prospective outcome study (Zanarini et al., 2003), 34.5% of patients met criteria for remission at 2 years, 49.4% at 4 years, 68.6% at 6 years, and 73.5% over entire follow-up. Moreover, only 5.9% of patients who remitted had symptoms that reoccurred at a later time.

Dialectical behavior therapy blends Zen practice with CBT and teaches concepts such as "mindfulness," or being aware of one's experiences and emotional state. Here, Dr. Marsha Linehan (the developer of DBT) and her students, Trevor Schraufnagel and Andrada Neacsiu illustrate mindfulness practice of therapists at start of DBT team meetings.

concept CHECK

- Personality disorders are difficult to treat. People who suffer from personality disorders often do not see the effect of their behavior on others. Treatment is often slow because the maladaptive behaviors have existed for decades. Finally, people with personality disorders often have Axis I disorders as well, making treatment more complicated.

- Although medications may help manage associated symptoms such as anxiety or depression, psychotherapeutic interventions are the treatment of choice for personality disorders.

- Dialectical behavioral therapy that focuses on the central role of emotion regulation has been shown to be efficacious in the treatment of borderline personality disorder.

- Therapeutic communities that include individual or group psychotherapy are also efficacious in the treatment of personality disorders.

APPLICATION QUESTION   If a patient is suffering from alcohol dependence and a personality disorder, which problem might you consider treating first, and why?

THE WHOLE STORY: ROBIN—LIFE TRANSITIONS AND BORDERLINE PERSONALITY DISORDER

The Person: *Robin was a senior in high school when she began to worry her parents and friends. Her family had moved to a new state in the summer before her senior year. In her previous school she had been relatively popular, very involved with acting and student government, and according to her mother a well-behaved, though a sensitive and moody girl. She desperately did not want to move. She had a circle of friends and was worried that the new high school would be filled with cliques and she would have trouble making friends.*

The Problem: *Soon after they moved, there was a dramatic transformation in Robin. She dyed her hair black, started wearing black eye makeup and black clothing, and rarely spoke at home. She would come home from school, throw her books down, and hide out in her room. She avoided meals with the family and always seemed to be brooding. Whenever anyone showed concern for her well-being, she returned their concern with anger and pushed them away. On the night of her referral she came running into her mother's bedroom screaming that she was afraid she was going to die. Blood poured from her right arm. Her mother bandaged her up to stop the bleeding and took her directly to the emergency room. There she discovered that this wasn't the first time Robin had cut herself. Under her long black sleeves and skirt, her arms and thighs were covered with cuts. Tonight she had just gone too deep and she was scared.*

The Treatment: *Robin was admitted to the inpatient unit for evaluation. The psychiatrist diagnosed her with major depression and borderline personality traits and recommended medication and psy-*

chotherapy. She also cautioned Robin about drinking and using drugs while taking the medication and warned her of the potential negative interactions. She referred Robin to a therapist who specialized in dialectical behavioral therapy (DBT).

Robin desperately did not want to go into therapy and on the first day adopted a stance that the therapist called "I dare you to care about me" and clearly intended to test all the limits. The therapist was no stranger to this personality style and recognized how chaotic and nonconstant the world must seem from Robin's eyes. She knew the key was consistency and firm compassion.

They established a therapeutic contract that centered around honesty. The DBT approach used a broad array of cognitive and behavioral strategies to help Robin learn to accept herself just as she was, within the context of trying to teach her how to change, starting with her self-harming cutting behavior. The therapist took a firm problem-solving stance, but as is typical with DBT, the therapist recognized that it would be too much to try to get all the skills training accomplished in one individual session per week. She therefore contracted for additional weekly group therapy. The group focused on the development of skills in emotion regulation, distress tolerance, interpersonal effectiveness, self-management, and core mindfulness (a way of learning how best to observe, describe, and participate in the world around you). As she learned these skills in group, Robin's individual therapy could focus on ways to best integrate these skills into daily life. Though reluctant at first to attend a group with "a bunch of 'emo's'," Robin signed a contract with

her therapist promising to attend. Robin's therapist agreed to continue working with her in individual therapy only if Robin would also attend weekly groups for the following year, as well as follow some of the basic rules of therapy. After a rollercoaster of emotions about what she was undertaking, Robin signed the contract. The therapist told her that the therapy was very structured and specific in terms of what was considered most important to talk about. If Robin was feeling suicidal or performing any life-threatening or self-damaging behaviors, such as cutting, her therapist wouldn't allow her to address anything else. The next important issue was focusing on anything that got in the way of therapy. For example, about 6 months into therapy, Robin brought in a gift for her therapist. It was a button that read, "Your caring about me is starting to piss me off." Sometimes it was really hard for Robin to accept the compassionate side of her therapist's stance. Deep down, she feared she wasn't worth being cared about. With the message inherent in the gesture, the focus of the therapy shifted directly to targeting Robin's feelings about the therapist and her ability to accept being cared for.

As therapy progressed, there were numerous ups and downs. Two trips to the emergency room for cutting returned the focus to the self-destructive behaviors. Gradually, Robin was able to apply the emotion regulation skills she had learned in group at the times when cutting seemed like the only option. She was able to begin to focus on thoughts or behaviors that got in the way of developing a reasonable quality of life, behavioral skills, and finally, self-validation and self-respect.

All of the "rules" frustrated Robin at first, but after she got used to this type of therapy, she understood that the rules existed because if she were injured or dead, or doing things to interfere with her therapy, there was little point in working on the rest. Moreover, she really wanted to work on other issues, which provided the motivation for her to work on "first things first." After a lot of advances and steps backward over the course of a year and a half of therapy, Robin began to accept herself for who she was, while working on changing some of her unhealthy ways of dealing with problems by putting her DBT skills to use.

The Outcome: *Robin graduated from high school and was accepted at the local college. No longer on her parents'* insurance, she transferred her care to the Campus Health Services, where she kept up with both individual and group therapy. The therapist occasionally wondered how she fared in the transition to college and after leaving the group. Several years later, an e-mail arrived in the therapist's inbox announcing her college graduation and her plans to become a high school counselor.*

CRITICAL ISSUES to remember

1. It is critical to differentiate between a personality trait and a personality disorder. A personality disorder is an enduring pattern of inner experience and behavior that deviates from the norm, is pervasive, persistent, and pathological, has an onset in adolescence or early adulthood, is stable across time, and leads to distress or impairment.

2. The personality disorders are grouped into three clusters based on core features: Cluster A, "odd or eccentric," includes paranoid, schizoid, and schizotypal personality disorders, Cluster B, "dramatic, emotional, or erratic," includes antisocial, narcissistic, borderline, and histrionic personality disorders, and Cluster C, "anxious or fearful," includes avoidant, dependent, and obsessive-compulsive personality disorders. Although this is the dominant model, many prefer a more dimensional approach to capturing the essence of personality.

3. Personality disorders are complex phenomena with roots in childhood and adolescence. They are marked by individual experiences that deviate from normative experience and behaviors that are perceived by others as deviant. Given the nature of personality disorders, they often lead to difficulties with interpersonal functioning.

4. Personality traits and disorders are heritable. Some personality disorders may be related to early trauma, which may lead to structural changes in the brain associated with traits such as hypervigilance and impulsivity.

5. Psychological theories of personality disorders include the psychodynamic, focusing on the impact of early relationships with the parents on later personality organization, and cognitive-behavioral, focusing on the emergence of personality from learning and the environment and the way in which the individual processes and interprets information about the self and the world.

6. Treatment for personality disorders can be particularly challenging, as it must address long-standing patterns of behavior, subtle distinctions between healthy and maladaptive behavior patterns, and the perspective of other people whom the disorder affects adversely. In general, psychotherapeutic approaches are recommended; medication can be included to manage comorbid Axis I disorders or symptoms.

TEST yourself

For more review plus practice tests, flashcards, and Speaking Out: DSM in Context videos, log onto www.MyPsychLab.com

1. A personality trait is defined as a behavior pattern that is
   a. inflexible regardless of context within a situation
   b. consistent across situations
   c. emotionally expressive over time within a situation
   d. maladaptive across situations

2. A personality trait may become a personality disorder when
   a. its symptoms can be quantified
   b. it becomes a dramatic, acute illness
   c. it becomes inflexible and maladaptive
   d. it does not reflect a person's typical behavior

3. According to the DSM-IV-TR, personality disorders are usually apparent in
   a. periods of high stress
   b. adolescence or early adulthood
   c. infancy or early childhood
   d. major developmental transitions

4. Cluster A personality disorders are characterized by which of the following?
   a. odd, quirky, or eccentric behaviors
   b. social anxiety, obsessionality, and fear of independence

c. emotional and erratic behaviors, and the absence of remorse

d. all of the above

5. Which of the following symptoms differentiates paranoid personality disorder from paranoid schizophrenia?
   a. believing that others intend harm or deception
   b. delusional thinking
   c. reading negative meanings into benign comments
   d. doubting the loyalty or trustworthiness of others

6. Schizoid personality disorder is characterized by which of the following?
   a. social detachment and a general lack of emotionality
   b. clinging to family members
   c. overvaluing the opinions of others
   d. unpredictable emotional lability

7. A characteristic that differentiates schizotypal personality disorder from paranoid or schizoid personality disorder is
   a. social detachment
   b. suspiciousness of others
   c. questioning the loyalty of friends
   d. eccentric appearance and behavior, and magical thinking

8. Mr. Cistern opened up a financial services company in a small close-knit retirement community. He promised large returns and little risk using his special investment system. He convinced many retirees to invest their entire savings. After several months he suddenly disappeared with all of the firm's assets. After an investigation, it was revealed that Mr. Cistern had done this many times in the past. Mr. Cistern might have
   a. narcissistic personality disorder
   b. borderline personality disorder
   c. antisocial personality disorder
   d. histrionic personality disorder

9. Persons diagnosed with narcissistic personality disorder need constant praise because
   a. it helps them cope with their fragile self-esteem
   b. they need to have social interaction reinforced or they withdraw
   c. without praise, they lose motivation
   d. praise keeps them from being self-absorbed

10. What feeling is characteristic of persons with borderline personality disorder?
    a. an overinflated sense of self-worth
    b. devaluation of others
    c. lack of empathy for others
    d. fear of abandonment

11. Dawn is a theater major in college. Her counselor has recently diagnosed her with histrionic personality disorder. What characteristics of this diagnosis make this major a relatively good choice for her?
    a. her boundless energy to devote to her roles and her need for little sleep
    b. her ability to form close relationships with other cast members
    c. her demonstrative and attention-seeking style
    d. her attention to detail and skill at easily memorizing scripts

12. Cluster C personality disorders are characterized by which of the following?
    a. excessive guilt and remorse
    b. lack of emotional expressiveness
    c. distorted thinking and cognition
    d. anxiety and social withdrawal

13. Avoidant personality disorder can be easily confused with which Axis I disorder?
    a. depression   c. generalized anxiety disorder
    b. generalized social phobia   d. Alzheimer's disease

14. Although Christine's boyfriend is physically abusive toward her, she worries that he will leave her. This fear leads her to be very submissive to him. Christine may be suffering from
    a. borderline personality disorder
    b. histrionic personality disorder
    c. narcissistic personality disorder
    d. dependent personality disorder

15. A person with obsessive-compulsive personality disorder may exhibit
    a. mental and interpersonal overcontrol
    b. unrealistic perfectionism
    c. inability to discard things of no use
    d. all of the above

16. Which childhood behaviors are strongly associated with the development of antisocial personality disorder?
    a. identity formation problems and dependency
    b. separation anxiety and hypersensitivity
    c. histrionics and testing the limits
    d. risky sexual behavior and harming animals

17. Which infant/toddler behavior is strongly associated with inhibited temperament?
    a. withdrawal from unfamiliar stimuli
    b. intense interest in novel sounds and sights
    c. attention to faces resembling the mother's
    d. attention to sounds resembling human speech

18. Personality disorders may develop as the result of
    a. genetic predisposition
    b. physical and/or sexual abuse
    c. disruption in the attachment phase of development
    d. all of the above

19. To successfully treat patients with personality disorders, therapists need
    a. high intelligence and problem-solving ability
    b. excellent diagnostic skills
    c. patience, consistency, persistence, and dedication
    d. the ability to recognize unconscious conflicts in others

20. The treatment that emphasizes discussion and negotiation between the therapist and patient, balancing the rational and the emotional, and balancing acceptance and change, is called
    a. dynamic psychotherapy
    b. cognitive-behavior therapy
    c. psychoanalytic therapy
    d. dialectical behavior therapy

Answers: 1 b, 2 c, 3 b, 4 a, 5 b, 6 a, 7 d, 8 c, 9 a, 10 d, 11 c, 12 d, 13 b, 14 d, 15 d, 16 d, 17 a, 18 d, 19 c, 20 d.

CHAPTER
objectives

At the end of this chapter, you should be able to

1 Describe how basic physical, cognitive, and emotional development during childhood and adolescence affects the expression of psychological disorders.

2 Identify psychological disorders that emerge primarily during childhood and adolescence.

3 Understand etiological factors that contribute to the development of disorders of childhood and adolescence.

4 Identify positive and negative aspects of pharmacological treatments.

5 Identify psychosocial treatments for the disorders of childhood and adolescence.

6 Describe the unique role of parents in the treatment of children and adolescents.

disorders of childhood and adolescence

Jeremy is 12 years old and in seventh grade. He is doing well academically but has significant difficulty with social relationships. He is unaware of social conventions and does not make eye contact with other people. He speaks loudly, often asks inappropriate questions, and makes inappropriate, and often irrelevant, statements or noises. When conversing, Jeremy engages in lengthy monologues on topics that interest him (dinosaurs, plumbing, and cars) and fails to pick up on others' lack of interest. He has no friends and is often ridiculed and rejected by peers. He sometimes behaves in ways that are self-injurious, pulling his hair, picking his skin, and hitting himself in the head.

Jeremy first displayed unusual behaviors at 18 months of age. He licked the pavement, chewed on rocks, and put "strange" things in his mouth. He did not like to be hugged and pushed his parents away if they attempted any physical contact. At age 2, he did not yet speak. He simply grunted or led his mother by the hand to communicate. He began speech therapy shortly thereafter, and by age 3 was talking in complete sentences. As a young child, Jeremy lined up toy cars. He never played with the entire car but would spin the wheels over and over. He did not play with other children but stood alone watching them. Now, at 12, Jeremy becomes upset by any change in routine, insisting on dressing in a certain order (e.g., socks, then pants, then shirt). He is also hypersensitive to sound; he can hear a siren miles away and covers his ears in crowded noisy places such as shopping malls.

Throughout this book, we have used a developmental perspective to understand abnormal behavior, and this perspective informs our understanding of psychological disorders in two ways. First, it is important to understand that childhood and adolescence are stages of life characterized by critical physical, cognitive, and emotional development. With respect to physical development, infants first acquire the ability to raise their head, then roll over, sit up, crawl, and finally walk. Physical maturation also includes brain development. The human brain triples in weight during a child's first two years, reaching 90% of its adult weight by the time the child is 5. Along with brain size, there is an increase in the child's *cognitive abilities*. Children learn to think and solve problems, and their memory improves. During adolescence, they develop the cognitive abilities to understand and use abstract concepts (e.g., justice, beauty), to engage in hypothetical thinking (e.g., what is the worst thing that could happen), and to use *metacognition* (the ability to think about thinking—e.g., what is the best way to solve a problem).

Along with physical and cognitive maturity, children also develop *emotionally*. Early in elementary school, children understand basic emotions (happy, sad, mad, scared), but they often attribute facial expression to an external event (e.g., "she's smiling because she's holding a puppy") rather than to an internal emotional state (e.g., "she's smiling because she is happy"). With increasing maturity, adolescents recognize more subtle emotions, such as disgust, worry, and surprise, and associate facial expressions with internal emotional states.

How does understanding this path of human development help us understand psychological disorders in childhood? Quite simply, until children have achieved basic physical, cognitive, and emotional developmental milestones, psychological disorders may express themselves differently in childhood than they do in adulthood. We have seen examples of this in the areas of anxiety, depression, and schizophrenia, among others. For example, young children cannot *worry* about future events until they have the ability to *think* about future events. Because of these developmental differences, mental health professionals acknowledge that although many psychological disorders may have roots in childhood, they are not often fully manifested until late adolescence or even adulthood.

Using this same developmental perspective, we find that other psychological disorders are more common in children than adults. They are present at birth or emerge during childhood and present significant challenges for those who suffer from them. Some of these disorders may continue to exist throughout adulthood, such as mental retardation or autism. In other instances, physical, cognitive, and/or emotional maturation may function to change the symptoms, lessen their impact, or even make them disappear. This often happens with disorders of feeding and elimination, for example. Many different disorders exist within the broad category of disorders of childhood and adolescence. Some, such as learning disorders, affect specific aspects of functioning such as academic achievement. We begin, however, with mental retardation, a common disorder that affects many different aspects of functioning.

Mental Retardation

Most people understand mental retardation to mean below-average intellectual functioning (see the box "DSM-IV-TR: Mental Retardation"). How we measure what is average or below average, however, is quite controversial. When psychologists measure intelligence, they use a standardized, individualized test and calculate an intelligence quotient (IQ) score. The IQ score is calculated as the ratio of measured intellectual ability to a person's expected performance based on his or her age. When psychologists talk about average intelligence, they are referring to the range of test scores that falls one standard deviation above or below the mean IQ score of 100. Therefore, people with IQ scores between 85 and 115 are considered to have average intelligence (as measured by that particular test). Although there is controversy regarding the meaning of IQ scores and when an IQ score indicates the presence of mental retardation, the DSM-IV-TR uses an IQ score of less than 70 in its diagnostic criteria for mental retardation. (See Chapter 3 for more on intelligence testing.)

Therefore, the first criterion for a diagnosis of mental retardation is significantly subaverage intelligence. However, a diagnosis of mental retardation requires more than below-average intelligence—the person's *functional abilities* must be below the level expected for his or her age and culture (Szymanski & King, 1999). Functional abilities are the skills that allow us to adapt and cope with life's basic demands—bathing, dressing, eating appropriate foods, and so on. Therefore, a person with **mental retardation** has both below-average measured intelligence (IQ less than 70) and deficits in adaptive functioning. The onset of mental retardation is always before the age of 18.

The term *significant subaverage intellectual functioning* describes a range of cognitive abilities that can be divided into one of four subtypes. *Mild mental retardation* represents intellectual functioning measured as an IQ score between 50–55 (lower limit) and 69 (upper limit). *Moderate mental retardation* represents intellectual functioning measured as an IQ score between 35–40 (lower limit) and 50–55 (upper limit). *Severe mental retardation* includes intellectual functioning measured by an IQ score between 20–25 (lower limit) and 35–40 (upper limit), and *profound mental retardation* describes intellectual functioning represented by IQ below 20 to 25.

The second criterion necessary for a diagnosis of mental retardation is *concurrent deficits or impairment in functioning*. On average, the lower the IQ score, the more impaired is the child's ability to adapt and function independently, although the relationship is not always simple and there are always individual differences.

Cathy's latest intelligence testing indicated that her measured IQ was 60. Cathy was a pleasant young woman of 24 years with appropriate skills for everyday social interaction. Although she was able to shower independently, someone had to first check the water temperature because otherwise she would burn herself. Although she understood that hamburgers (her favorite food) had to be cooked before eating, her only attempt to cook independently had set the kitchen on fire. As a young woman, she was interested in men, but did not understand basic concepts of sexual reproduction.

mental retardation significantly subaverage intellectual functioning *and* deficits or impairment in at least two areas of life functioning

Mainstreaming children with Down syndrome into regular classroom settings helps develop acceptance and understanding of individual differences.

Clearly, Cathy had great difficulty functioning independently in the areas of self-care, home living, and health and safety, and she had been this way even as a child.

In addition to the core diagnostic features of lower intellectual functioning and diminished ability to function independently, children with mental retardation are five times more likely than other children to have any of the psychological disorders in this book (Bregman, 1991; Rutter et al., 1976) with the possible exception of schizophrenia or substance abuse disorders (Kerker et al., 2004). Physical disorders are also common among people with more severe or profound mental retardation; 15 to 30% have seizure disorders, 20 to 30% have motor handicaps such as cerebral palsy, and 10 to 20% have visual and auditory impairments (McLaren & Bryson, 1987).

FUNCTIONAL IMPAIRMENT

As we have noted, adaptive impairment is necessary for a diagnosis of mental retardation, but the extent and type of impairment is variable. Adults with mild to moderate mental retardation function in the community with minimal to moderate support. They might live in a group home, where a small number of adults live together under supervision of a counselor. Some adults are also able to hold traditional jobs in the community, such as working in a grocery store. Sometimes an intervention known as *supported employment* provides training and a job coach to help people succeed in meaningful jobs (Hill et al., 1987; McCaughrin et al., 1993; Revell et al., 1994; see Chapter 10). Adults with more significant cognitive impairments may work in a *sheltered workshop*, which is usually a free-standing workplace where workers perform tasks for other businesses, such as sending out large mailings, packing items for shipment, or assembling certain products. People who work in sheltered workshops are paid wages and learn job skills such as coming to work on time, completing a task assignment, and taking direction from a supervisor.

In schools, *mainstreaming* could be considered supportive education for children with mental retardation. Mainstreaming means that whenever possible, children with disabilities are included in regular classroom settings, allowing participation in typical childhood experiences. Whereas children with mental retardation may need separate classroom instruction for mathematics, they may take the same physical education classes as the general student body. Inclusion in regular classroom settings promotes acceptance of people with mental retardation and enhances their own self-esteem.

About 1% of the general population has mental retardation (American Psychiatric Association, 2000), although the specific number of people affected may vary slightly depending on the particular IQ test used. The majority of people with a diagnosis of mental retardation—about 85%—have IQ scores in the mild category (Szymanski & King, 1999). The number of American children with mental retardation, by sex and race/ethnicity, is depicted in Table 12.1. It is important to emphasize that differences based on race and/or ethnicity may be misinterpreted if socioeconomic status is not considered. There is a strong positive relationship between socioeconomic status and IQ—generally, the lower the socioeconomic status, the lower the IQ. Worldwide, more children with mild mental retardation are from the lower socioeconomic strata. This type of mental retardation, as we shall see, is less likely to have a biological basis (Leonard & Wen, 2002).

There is continuing controversy regarding the relationship of lower IQ scores and racial or ethnic minority status in the United States. Many IQ tests do not consider cultural differences in verbal expressions of ideas, language, and behaviors. When assessed by nonverbal tests, which are less dependent on language and culture, differences in IQ based on race/ethnicity are much reduced (Sternberg et al., 2005).

More boys than girls have a diagnosis of mental retardation, but these sex differences are primarily among those with the mild type and may result from differences in

TABLE 12.1
Rates of Mental Retardation by Sex and Ethnicity

Sex	Ethnicity	% Identified With Some Form of Mental Retardation
M	Native American	1.62
M	Asian/Pacific Islander	0.54
M	African American	3.15
M	Hispanic	0.96
M	White	1.36
F	Native American	1.26
F	Asian/Pacific Islander	0.44
F	African American	2.10
F	Hispanic	0.74
F	White	1.05

Used with permission of the American Association on Intellectual and Developmental Disabilities, from "Impact of sociodemographic characteristics on the identification rates of minority students as having mental retardation," by Oswald, D. P., Coutinho, M. J., Best, A. M., & Nguyen, N. in *Mental Retardation (Intellectual and Developmental Disabilities)*, 39, 2001; permission conveyed through Copyright Clearance Center, Inc.

children's verbal abilities. At younger ages, girls have superior verbal language skills (Harasty et al., 1999; Joseph, 2000), and this may affect their test performance. No sex differences are found among those with the more severe forms of mental retardation (Richardson et al., 1986).

ETIOLOGY

Throughout this book, we have often introduced discussions of etiology with cautionary statements that the cause of a disorder is unknown. However, there are numerous known causes for mental retardation. Many are biological, and others are environmental. For about 35% of people with MR, the cause is one of the disorders identified in Table 12.2. Many genetic disorders may produce mental retardation (Walker & Johnson, 2006). When there is a genetic cause, the disorder is apparent at birth or shortly thereafter. In other cases, mental retardation may result from environmental factors, a number of which are preventable. Below, we examine the best known causes of mental retardation, beginning with the biological factors.

Genetic Factors Named for the British geneticist John Langdon Haydon Down (Czarnetzski et al., 2003), **Down syndrome** (*Trisomy 21*) describes the unusual condition in which there are three chromosomes (i.e., trisomy) in a set, rather than the usual set of two. This error occurs during cell division of a sperm or ovum—the chromosome pair does not divide as it should. Instead, the chromosomes "stick together." Later, when the sperm fertilizes the ovum, rather than each (sperm and ovum) contributing one chromosome to the 21st pair, three are present. People with Down syndrome have three #21 chromosomes in every cell in their body, giving them a total of 47, rather than the usual 46, chromosomes. Other trisomy conditions exist (Trisomy 13, Trisomy 18) and may also result in mental retardation, but Down syndrome is by far the most common condition.

Down syndrome a genetic form of mental retardation caused by the presence of three chromosomes rather than the usual two on the 21st pair

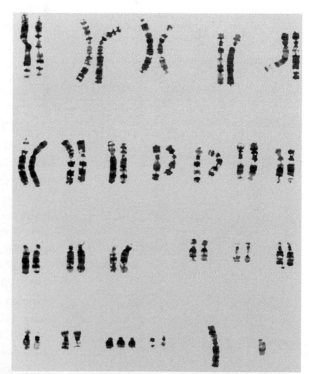

Down syndrome is a chromosome abnormality that results in three chromosomes on the 21st pair—the third group from the left in the bottom row. The 23rd pair (bottom right) is an XY, so this is a boy.

TABLE 12.2

Identifiable Causes of MR and Estimated Frequency

	Example
Prenatal Causes	
Genetic disorders (32%)	Down syndrome
	Tuberous Sclerosis
	Phenylketonuria
	Fragile X
	"Familial MR"
	Williams syndrome
	Praeder-Willi syndrome
Malformation of Unknown Causes (8%)	Neural tube defects
	Cornelia de Lange syndrome
External Prenatal Causes (12%)	Human Immunodeficiency Virus (HIV) infection
	Fetal alcohol syndrome
	Prematurity
Perinatal (birth) causes (11%)	Encephalitis
	Neonatal asphyxia
	Hyperbilirubinemia
Postnatal causes (8%)	Encephalitis
	Lead poisoning
	Deprivation
	Trauma, tumor
Unknown Causes (25%)	

From: "Practice Parameters for the Assessment and Treatment of Children, Adolescents, and Adults With Mental Retardation and Comorbid Mental Disorders" *Journal of the American Academy of Child and Adolescent Psychiatry*, Volume 38(12) Supplement. December 1999. 5S–31S. Copyright © 1999 American Academy of Child and Adolescent Psychiatry. Reprinted by permission.

Children with Down syndrome have distinctive facial features including oblique eye fissures (slanted eyes), epicanthic eye folds (folds of skin in the corner of the eye), a flat nasal bridge, protruding tongues, short stocky stature, a very short neck, and small ears. Virtually every person with Down syndrome has mental retardation, mostly in the mild to moderate range, meaning that they are able to attend school, learn basic living skills, and function in a structured environment. Children with Down syndrome may also have numerous medical problems, including heart defects, intestinal abnormalities, visual and hearing impairments, and respiratory ailments (Roubertoux & Kerdelhué, 2006). About 1 out of every 1000 children is born with Down syndrome, although the specific rate varies with maternal age; much higher rates occur among older mothers (see Table 12.3). It is not clear why older mothers are more likely to have children with Down syndrome. One hypothesis is that because all of a woman's ova are formed at the same time, those released later in life have more opportunity to be exposed to radiation and toxins, and thus are susceptible to a higher rate of cell and chromosome abnormalities.

In children with Down syndrome, almost all brain structures are smaller than normal (Roubertoux & Kerdelhué, 2006; Teipel et al., 2004). Another characteristic is the presence of plaques and neurofibrillary tangles, usually found among adults with Alzheimer's disease (see Chapter 13). In children with Down syndrome, this deterio-

TABLE 12.3

Maternal Age Risks for Down Syndrome

Maternal Age	Risk at Birth
15 to 24 years	1 out of 1300
25 to 29 years	1 out of 1100
35 years	1 out of 350
40 years	1 out of 100
45 (and older)	1 out of 25

From Hook E.B., Cross P.K., Schreinemachers D.M. "Chromosomal abnormality rates at amniocentesis and in live-born infants." *Journal of the American Medical Association* 1983, 249(15):2034–38. Copyright © 1983 by the American Medical Association. Reprinted by permission of the publisher.

ration begins at about age 8 and progresses, accelerating rapidly between the ages of 35 and 45 (Lott & Head, 2005). The result is that almost all people with Down syndrome have some evidence of Alzheimer's disease by age 40.

Phenylketonuria (PKU) is a genetic disorder in which the body cannot break down the amino acid *phenylalanine* because an essential enzyme is absent. Without the enzyme, phenylalanine accumulates in the body, causing mental and physical abnormalities (dos Santos et al., 2006). PKU occurs in about .01% of the population, with large variations by race and ethnicity. Whites and Native Americans have the highest rate, with much lower rates among African Americans, Hispanics, and Asians (Hellekson, 2001). In the United States, every infant is screened at birth for PKU, resulting in few untreated cases of the disorder. Treatment requires daily dietary supplements and a severely restricted low-protein diet. Milk and dairy products, meat, eggs, wheat, beans, corn, peanuts, lentils, and other grains are prohibited (dos Santos et al., 2006), and compliance with these restrictions can be quite poor. This diet must be continued until at least age 8 to prevent mental retardation; discontinuation of the diet after the age of 12 does not seem to lower IQ score (Hellekson, 2006).

Fragile X syndrome (FXS) is the most commonly inherited cause of mental retardation (Sundaram et al., 2005; Valdovinos, 2007) and occurs when a DNA series makes too many copies of itself and "turns off" a gene on the X chromosome. When the gene is turned off, cells do not make a necessary protein, and without the protein, FXS occurs. In addition to mental retardation, children with FXS have behavioral disorders such as hyperactivity, temper tantrums, irritability, poor eye contact, self-stimulation, and self-injurious behaviors (Crawford et al., 2002; Valdovinos, 2007). Perhaps because girls have 2 X chromosomes (that is, they have a "spare" X chromosome) they are only half as likely as boys to have FXS (1 out of 4000 males and 1 out of 8000 females).

Other genetic disorders that can result in mental retardation include *tuberous sclerosis complex (TSC)* and *Lesch-Nyhan syndrome*. Resulting from mutations on at least two different genes (Sundaram et al., 2005), TSC affects 1 in every 30,000 people in the U.S. In TSC, benign tumors affect all body organs, including the brain, and result in developmental delays, seizures, and learning disabilities. About 50% of people with TSC have mental retardation (Leung & Robson, 2007). Lesch-Nyhan syndrome is a rare genetic disorder that is transmitted on the X chromosome. Because it is a recessive trait, it occurs only in boys. Girls, who have two X chromosomes, are protected from the disorder. Like PKU, this disorder involves a missing enzyme. When the genetic defect is present, excess uric acid accumulates throughout the body. Lesch-Nyhan syndrome causes many different behavioral problems, including

phenylketonuria a genetic disorder in which the body cannot break down the amino acid *phenylalanine;* if untreated, leads to the development of mental retardation

fragile X syndrome the most commonly inherited cause of mental retardation; occurs when a DNA series makes too many copies of itself and "turns off" a gene on the X chromosome. When the gene is turned off, cells do not make a necessary protein, and without it, FXS occurs

fetal alcohol syndrome leading known preventable environmental cause of mental retardation; results from drinking alcohol during pregnancy

cognitive dysfunction, mental retardation, and aggressive and impulsive behaviors. Mental retardation is usually moderate, but it can range from profound to mild (Olson & Houlihan, 2000). Nearly all children with this disorder develop persistent and severe self-injurious behavior, sometimes with permanent physical damage.

Environmental Factors When genes are not the cause of mental retardation, factors such as the prenatal or postnatal environment may be responsible. Prenatal influences associated with the presence of mental retardation include uterine environmental toxins (maternal alcohol use, infections), premature birth, hypoxia (lack of oxygen to the brain, often during birth), or fetal malnutrition. Postnatal factors include malnutrition, bacterial and viral infections, lead exposure, and social factors such as poverty, low environmental stimulation, and maternal education (Walker & Johnson, 2006). However, it is important to understand that unlike genetic disorders such as Down syndrome, the presence of these environmental factors does not automatically lead to mental retardation. For example, many children live in impoverished environments, yet have average or above-average IQs.

The leading known preventable environmental cause of mental retardation is drinking alcohol during pregnancy, which can result in **fetal alcohol syndrome** (FAS; West & Blake, 2005) (see Chapter 9). According to the Centers for Disease Control, rates of fetal alcohol syndrome vary widely, ranging from 0.2 to 1.5 per 1,000 live births in different areas of the United States. Drinking alcohol during pregnancy can affect the physical development of the fetus, including brain development. In addition to mental retardation, fetal alcohol syndrome is associated with birth defects, abnormal facial features, growth problems, central nervous system abnormalities, memory problems, impaired academic achievement, vision or hearing impairment, and behavioral problems (see Figure 12.1).

Another preventable environmental cause of mental retardation is exposure to lead, which can enter the bodies of young children in different ways. First, many older homes contain lead-based paint, which can peel off and be eaten by young children, who have a tendency to put many things in their mouth. Also, when the paint becomes old and worn, the chips may be ground into tiny particles that mix with dust, which are then inhaled. Ingestion or inhalation leads to a buildup of lead in the body (Brown

FIGURE 12.1

Parts of the Brain That Can Be Affected by Maternal Alcohol Consumption

When a woman drinks during pregnancy, many parts of the fetal brain can be damaged.

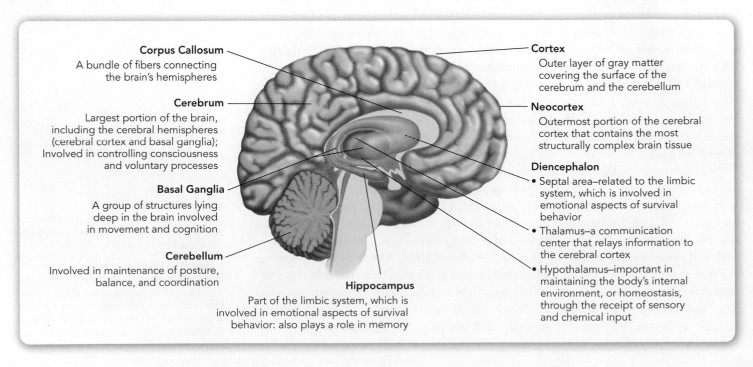

Corpus Callosum
A bundle of fibers connecting the brain's hemispheres

Cerebrum
Largest portion of the brain, including the cerebral hemispheres (cerebral cortex and basal ganglia); Involved in controlling consciousness and voluntary processes

Basal Ganglia
A group of structures lying deep in the brain involved in movement and cognition

Cerebellum
Involved in maintenance of posture, balance, and coordination

Hippocampus
Part of the limbic system, which is involved in emotional aspects of survival behavior; also plays a role in memory

Cortex
Outer layer of gray matter covering the surface of the cerebrum and the cerebellum

Neocortex
Outermost portion of the cerebral cortex that contains the most structurally complex brain tissue

Diencephalon
• Septal area–related to the limbic system, which is involved in emotional aspects of survival behavior
• Thalamus–a communication center that relays information to the cerebral cortex
• Hypothalamus–important in maintaining the body's internal environment, or homeostasis, through the receipt of sensory and chemical input

et al., 2006). Even low levels of exposure to lead in childhood are associated with low intelligence. Greater exposure is associated with substantially lower IQ scores (Needleman & Gatsonis, 1990). Even years later, adults who were exposed to lead in childhood still had academic difficulties and behavior problems (Needleman et al., 1990). For more information on lead exposure in houses, see Chapter 15.

In many cases of mild mental retardation, the specific cause is unknown. **Cultural-familial retardation** is defined as "retardation due to psychosocial disadvantage" (Weisz, 1990). Whereas severe mental retardation exists across all socioeconomic levels, mild mental retardation is more common among children in the lower socioeconomic classes (Stromme & Magnus, 2000), which include residents of poverty-stricken inner-city areas, poor rural areas, and migrant workers. Among the lowest socioeconomic classes, the prevalence of mild mental retardation ranges from 10 to 30% of the American school-age population (Popper et al., 2004). However, sociocultural retardation is not limited to the United States—the same factors have been identified in European countries as well (Gillerot et al., 1989).

The reason for the association between lower socioeconomic status and mild mental retardation is unclear, but both biological and environmental factors may contribute. In the early years of life, the brain is still developing. Environmental factors such as poor nutrition, lack of access to early educational enrichment (e.g., preschool, educational toys), or restricted access to medical care may negatively affect brain development, leading to lower IQ scores.

> **cultural-familial retardation** mild mental retardation that is more common among children in the lower socioeconomic classes and is considered retardation due to psychosocial disadvantage

TREATMENT

Until recently, many people with mental retardation were housed in institutions. Few community resources were available, and parents were encouraged to institutionalize their child where it was felt that the necessary extensive care would be available. There was even hope that proper environmental care might reduce deficits, even though leaving the institution was not a long-term goal of placement (Brosco et al., 2006). In fact, most people who were institutionalized remained there for the rest of their lives. Today, about 90% of people with mental retardation live with families or in community placements, such as group homes. Mental retardation is not reversible, but many children can learn basic academic and adaptive functioning skills. Psychological treatments focus on teaching skills that facilitate community adjustment, such as self-care, independent living, and job maintenance. Behavioral procedures such as *shaping* (rewarding successive approximations of desired behavior) and *chaining* (teaching small, discrete behaviors and then putting them together), allow children with mental retardation to learn simple tasks such as putting on a pair of pants or more complicated behaviors such as going to the bank and cashing a check.

Medical treatments to reduce diseases that cause mental retardation have decreased its general prevalence. The number of children with mental retardation as a result of measles and whooping cough has decreased since the introduction of successful vaccinations for these diseases (Brosco et al., 2006) (see Figure 12.2). Medication does not treat the core symptoms of mental retardation but is sometimes used for coexisting psychological disorders such as attentional or aggressive behaviors. Overall, people with mental retardation respond to medication in the same way as others, but rates of response are poorer and side effects more common (Handen & Gilchrist, 2006).

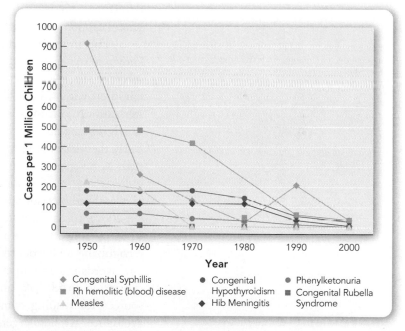

FIGURE 12.2

Prevalence of Specific Causes of Mental Retardation over Time

During the past 50 years, advances in medical science have decreased the prevalence of mental retardation.

From Brosco et al, (2006) Impact of specific medical interventions on reducing the prevalence of mental retardation. *Archives of Pediatric and Adolescent Medicine*, 160, 302-309, Figure 1. Copyright © 2006 by the American Medical Association. Reprinted by permission of the publisher.

concept CHECK

- Mental retardation is defined as significantly subaverage intelligence and deficits or impairments in adaptive functioning. Intellect and adaptive functioning exist along a continuum and can range from mild to severe or profound.

- There are many different causes of mental retardation, both biological and environmental.

- Some causes of mental retardation are preventable but once it occurs, available treatments do not reverse the condition. Behavioral and pharmacological treatment may improve functioning and associated conditions.

APPLICATION QUESTION A significant proportion of mild mental retardation has a cultural-familial etiology. Can you identify two factors leading to this type of mental retardation, and if you had unlimited resources, how would you eliminate these causes?

Learning Disorders

A universal task of education is to teach children basic skills such as reading, writing, and mathematics. Yet a number of public school children in the United States have at least average intelligence but have difficulty mastering these basic academic tasks (American Psychiatric Association [APA], 2000). Collectively known as **learning disorders** (see the box "DSM-IV-TR: Learning Disorders"), these conditions are defined by academic achievement below expectations for age, years in school, and IQ score. Affecting both sexes, these disorders can result in demoralization, low self-esteem, and school dropout rates higher than those in the general population.

The most common type of learning disorder is *reading disorder*, sometimes known as *dyslexia*. Reading disorder is defined as reading achievement scores that are substantially lower than expected for the child's age, IQ, and/or educational level. Children with reading disorder may display oral reading errors such as distortions, substitutions, or omissions of words. Silent reading disabilities include reading very slowly and making comprehension errors. They often also have difficulty with spelling. Early theories of reading disorder emphasized vision and visual perceptual difficulties such as reversal of letters. However, advances in neurobiology and neuropsychology indicate that reading disorders most likely result from a diminished ability to recognize and produce sounds (*phonemes*) that when put together form words (Shaywitz et al., 2007). Instruction in reading is based on phonics, the process of "sounding out" a word by converting its visual representation into the appropriate sounds. Difficulty recognizing and articulating sounds leads to a cascade of negative events. "Sounding out" words is slow and effortful; thus, reading is less fluent. It also requires more concentration to identify and pronounce difficult words, leaving fewer attentional resources for reading comprehension and leading to mental fatigue and behavioral avoidance (Kronenberger & Dunn, 2003).

Another learning disorder is *mathematics disorder*, sometimes called *dyscalculia*. Mathematics disorder is a diminished ability to understand mathematical terms, operations, or concepts, recognize numerical symbols or arithmetic signs, or copy numbers or figures correctly. Difficulty performing mental calculations may lead affected children to rely on external devices, such as counting on their fingers. They also often have difficulty with the logic of word problems.

The third learning disorder, *disorder of written expression*, also called *dysgraphia*, is more than sloppy handwriting. It includes difficulty composing grammatically correct sentences; frequent grammatical, punctuation, or spelling errors; and diminished ability to organize coherent written paragraphs. Effective writing requires different cognitive, visual, and motor skills, including knowledge of vocabulary and grammar, eye-hand coordination and hand movement, and memory (Pratt & Patel, 2007).

learning disorders conditions involving academic achievement below expectations for age, years in school, and IQ score

Deficits in any of these areas can lead to impairment. Children with writing disorder have no trouble presenting material orally but struggle with putting those same ideas into written form. Their written sentences are short, difficult to understand, and riddled with spelling and grammatical errors.

Between 5 and 10% of school children, perhaps up to 4 million children, may suffer from a learning disorder. The most common is reading disorder (Kronenberger & Dunn, 2003; Pratt & Patel, 2007; Shaywitz et al., 2007), which may affect between 2 and 8% of all children. Reading disorder is more common in boys, but the reason is not clear. One hypothesis is that it may not be more common but *more commonly identified* because associated behavioral disorders, such as attention-deficit/hyperactivity disorder, lead to a referral to a mental health professional. During that evaluative process, the reading disorder is identified. Difficulty with phonics and reading may lead to the identification of reading disorder as early as the preschool years. By contrast, disorder of written expression is often not apparent until third or fourth grade, when there are increased demands to present ideas in writing.

FUNCTIONAL IMPAIRMENT

Approximately 40% of children with learning disabilities eventually drop out of school, limiting their opportunities for employment (APA, 2000). They also often feel demoralized by their disabilities and report low self-esteem. Children with learning disorders may also have other emotional and behavioral problems of childhood such as attention-deficit/hyperactivity disorder, conduct disorder, depression, and anxiety disorders.

Children with mild symptoms may be difficult to identify and may be described by parents or teachers as messy, unfocused, or disorganized (Pratt & Patel, 2007). As adults, they compensate by developing a working vocabulary in their occupational area that allows them to function effectively. However, they still have difficulty with unfamiliar words. Their reading may be accurate but not fluent or automatic (Shaywitz et al., 2007).

ETIOLOGY

The etiology of learning disorders is unclear. These disorders probably do not arise from a single neurological impairment but from the inability of several brain areas to work together.

Much more is known about the etiology of reading disorder than about other learning disabilities. Structural and functional magnetic imaging studies and positron emission tomography (PET) studies have identified various areas of the brain that appear to be important for reading (Shaywitz et al., 2007) (see Figure 12.3). Again, why a child would have abnormal brain functioning is not entirely clear, but genetics appears to play a significant role. Concordance rates for reading disorder are 71% for

FIGURE 12.3

Areas of the Brain Involved in Reading Disorder

Reading is a complex process that involves several areas of the brain.

From Shaywitz, S., *Overcoming Dyslexia: a new and complete science-based program for reading problems at any level.* New York: Alfred A. Knopf, 2003, p. 34, Copyright © 2003 Sally Shaywitz. Reprinted by permission of the publisher.

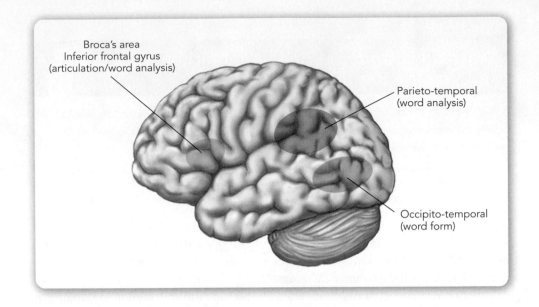

monozygotic twins and 49% for dyzygotic twins (Castles et al., 1999). Although there is some variability, between 23 to 65% of children who have a parent with a reading disorder also have the disorder (Scarborough, 1990). There is much yet to learn about the biological basis of reading disorders, but what is clear at this time is that the disorder does not result from the inheritance of one single gene. It is likely that a number of different genes are involved.

TREATMENT

Treatment for learning disorders usually occurs in the educational setting. Intervention for reading disorder begins early and focuses on developing the skills necessary for phonological processing and fluent reading, with later emphasis on reading for comprehension (Kronenberger & Dunn, 2003). Figure 12.4 illustrates the trajectory of reading scores for good and poor readers. As illustrated, poor readers can make significant progress in their reading skills, but they never achieve the skill level possessed by

FIGURE 12.4

Reading Skills in Good Readers Compared with Those Who have Reading Disorder

Over time, deficits in reading skills in good readers (children without reading difficulties) and poor readers (those with reading disorder, or dyslexia) remain constant. This shows that children with reading disorder are not just "slow" at acquiring skills but have a specific reading deficit.

From Shaywitz, S., *Overcoming Dyslexia: a new and complete science-based program for reading problems at any level.* New York: Alfred A. Knopf, 2003, p. 34, Copyright © 2003 Sally Shaywitz. Reprinted by permission of the publisher.

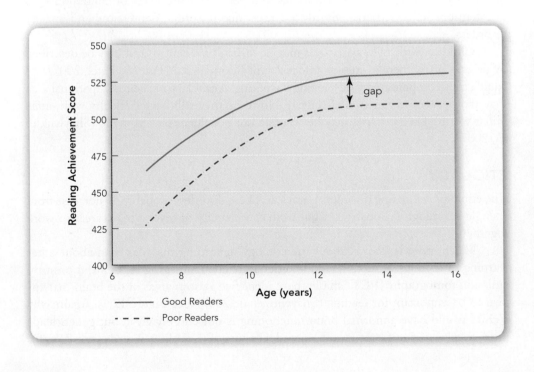

good readers at the same age. As children mature and gains are consolidated, intervention shifts to disability accommodation (Pratt & Patel, 2007), such as more time for reading and test taking, the use of computers, tape recorders, or recorded books to allow effective functioning in academics and occupational environments.

Treatment for mathematics disorder includes arithmetic drills and memorization. Because writing disorder is considered to result from difficulties in the written expression of ideas, children first engage in simple writing tasks such as keeping a diary. As their basic writing skills improve, they are given more challenging writing tasks.

---

concept CHECK

■ Learning disorders are defined as academic achievement that is lower than expected given the child's age, years of schooling, and measured IQ. There are three types of learning disorders: reading disorder, mathematics disorder, and disorders of written expression.

■ Reading disorder is most common and most likely represents a difficulty in phonological processing, resulting from abnormalities in different areas of the brain.

■ Genetics appear to play a major role in the etiology of reading disorder. The etiology of mathematics disorder and disorder of written expression is unknown.

APPLICATION QUESTION Treatment for learning disorders occurs in educational settings and consists of attempts to teach academic skills. At later ages, treatment takes the form of accommodations to deal with remaining deficits. Based on your knowledge of brain development, why would this radical change in treatment approach occur?

Pervasive Developmental Disorders

We saw in the case of Jeremy, at the beginning of this chapter, that some childhood behavioral abnormalities are evident very early in life. Most children spontaneously say "mama" or "dada" before age 1. But Jeremy did not speak until age 3 when he had speech therapy. Jeremy also had unusual social behaviors. He refused to make eye contact, spoke too loudly, asked inappropriate questions, and made inappropriate statements or noises. In addition to holding his toy car and spinning the wheels over and over, he showed other stereotyped behaviors. (These are repetitive behaviors that serve no observable social functions, such as hand flapping, spinning, and ritualistic pacing.) Such behaviors are characteristic of **pervasive developmental disorders** (PDD), disorders that consist of serious impairments in a child's reciprocal social interaction and communication, together with the presence of stereotypical behavior, interests, and activities (APA, 2000). PDD consists of five different disorders. The most common ones, *Autistic Disorder* (see the box "DSM-IV-TR: Autistic Disorder"), *Asperger's Disorder*, and *PDD–Not Otherwise Specified (PDD-NOS)*, will be discussed here. They are collectively labeled **autism spectrum disorders**. (Two other disorders, Rett's Disorder and Childhood Integrative Disorder, are very rare and will not be discussed here.)

In 1943, the psychiatrist Leo Kanner described children with *autistic disturbances of affective contact*, highlighting behaviors that are central to this disorder and are apparent before 30 months of age (Rutter, 1978). One key feature of **autistic disorder** is *deficits in social relatedness* (Klin, 2006), including the inability to make eye contact and to recognize facial expressions, and a lack of interest in social interaction. The second criterion, *impairment in communication*, includes delays in acquiring spoken language. Approximately 20 to 30% of children with autistic disorder do not speak at all (Klin, 2006).

pervasive developmental disorders serious impairments in a child's reciprocal social interaction and communication, and the presence of stereotypical behavior, interests, and activities

autism spectrum disorders a group of disorders consisting of autistic disorder, Asperger's disorder, and pervasive developmental disorder not otherwise specified

autistic disorder disorder characterized by qualitative impairment in social interactions and communication, and a pattern of restricted and stereotyped behaviors, interests, and activities

DSM-IV-TR

Autistic Disorder

- Qualitative impairment in social interactions including lack of eye contact or facial expressions, failure to develop peer relationships, inability to seek or share enjoyment, interests, or achievement, inability to reciprocate in social or emotional interactions.
- Qualitative impairment in communication including delay of spoken language, impaired ability to maintain a conversation, stereotyped or repetitive use of language, lack of spontaneous make-believe or imitative play.
- Restricted and stereotyped behaviors, interests, and activities such as preoccupation with interests that are abnormal in intensity or focus, inflexibility with respect to routines or rituals, and stereotyped or repetitive motor mannerisms, such as hand or finger flapping, or preoccupation with parts of objects.
- In most, but not necessarily every child with this disorder, there are deficits in intellectual functioning.

Adapted with permission from the *Diagnostic and Statistical Manual of Mental Disorders*, Text Revision, Fourth Edition, (Copyright 2000). American Psychiatric Association.

Other deficits include the inability to start or continue a conversation, and stereotyped or unusual language, such as *echolalia*, the repetition of the last word, sound, or phrase that was heard.

The third criterion, *restricted, repetitive, and stereotyped behavior patterns*, includes intense preoccupation with a particular interest.

Adi has a fascination with pipes and turbines. When he encounters one, he stops and stares, refusing to leave. His parents often him find in the basement staring at the furnace. He knows everything about the mechanics of large machinery and talks incessantly about the advantages and disadvantages of various systems, types of piping, etc.

Repetitive and stereotyped patterns also include intense adherence to routines (e.g., eating or bedtime rituals) and self-injurious behaviors (e.g., eye gouging, head banging, hand biting). Why children engage in these behaviors is unclear; but some clinicians hypothesize that these behaviors allow the child to stop an aversive environmental stimulus such as a hug (Matson et al., 1996).

Infants who develop autistic disorder are often described as being "too good" and never crying. They lack social interest, do not play interactive or imitative games (such as peek-a-boo), are extremely sensitive to touch and sound, and have abnormal sleep patterns with nighttime awakenings that last for several hours. They also have rigid eating behaviors, refusing to eat certain foods because of the smell, texture, or taste.

Children with **Asperger's disorder** (see the box "DSM-IV-TR: Asperger's Disorder"), first described by pediatrician Hans Asperger in 1944, have the same social impairments and stereotyped behaviors as children with autistic disorder. They do not have difficulties with verbal language, but often have poor eye contact, a monotone voice, and do not understand social cues (e.g., looking at one's watch is a signal to end a conversation). They also have intense specialized interests and often appear clumsy.

Not all mental health professionals consider Asperger's disorder as a separate psychological disorder (Klin, 2006). Sometimes called "high-functioning autism," it may be a variation of autistic disorder, in which children have normal intelligence and acceptable communication skills. The rising number of children with Asperger's disorder concerns mental health clinicians, who wonder if too many children are being given this diagnosis (Klin, 2006). Although both disorders will be discussed in this

Autism

The Case of Xavier
"He'll watch a DVD, same scene over and over and over again."
www.mypsychlab.com

Asperger's disorder qualitative impairment in social interaction, restricted and stereotyped behaviors, interests, and activities, but no deficits in communication and at least average intellectual functioning

section, it is important to remember that Asperger's, as a distinct psychological disorder, is still controversial.

The third diagnostic category within the autism spectrum category, **pervasive developmental disorder not otherwise specified** (PDD-NOS), is assigned when children have *some* but not *all* of the behaviors that characterize autistic disorder (Barbaresi et al., 2006). Although it is the most common diagnosis in the autism spectrum disorders category, its diagnostic criteria have not been validated (Scheeringa, 2001), and we will not discuss PDD-NOS separately from the other disorders.

Approximately 60 to 75% of children with autistic disorder or PDD-NOS have IQs below 70 (Barbaresi, 2006; Bethea & Sikich, 2007). Behavioral problems such as hyperactivity, impulsivity, social anxiety, general anxiety, irritability, and aggression are common (Bethea & Sikich, 2007), as are depression and phobias (Matson & Nebel-Schwalm, 2007).

FUNCTIONAL IMPAIRMENT

Autistic disorder is a life-long impairment that affects the entire family; only about one third of all people with this disorder are ever able to live independently (Klin, 2006). However, deficits in the core areas do improve with age, and there are always exceptions to this generally bleak outlook (see the box "Real People, Real Disorders: Temple Grandin, Ph.D.").

Children with Asperger's disorder are socially isolated, desiring social interaction but seeking it inappropriately: interrupting others, engaging in one-sided conversations about a favorite topic, speaking too loudly and too rapidly. Unlike children with autistic disorder, who usually require special classroom placement, children with Asperger's disorder are able to function academically in traditional classroom settings. However, because of their social difficulties, these children are often bullied, teased, or ignored by their classmates, resulting in social isolation at school.

The prevalence of autism spectrum disorders has increased dramatically in recent years (see the box "Examining the Evidence: Do Vaccines Cause Autism?"). Before 1994, the median prevalence of autism was 0.05% (Fombonne, 2005). The most recent estimate is that 1 in every 152 children (0.6% of the general population) may have an autism spectrum disorder (CDC, 2007). When broken down by diagnostic group, 0.1% have autistic disorder, 0.03% have Asperger's disorder, meaning that PDD-NOS, with its limited diagnostic validity, is the largest single group. However, the increased *prevalence* (proportion of people in the general population who have a disorder) of autism spectrum disorder cannot be attributed to an increase in *incidence* (number of new cases of a disorder during a given time interval). It is likely that the addition of two new diagnostic categories (Asperger's disorder and PDD-NOS), changes in diagnostic criteria, diagnostic practices, special education policies, and the availability of diagnostic services are contributing factors (Fombonne, 2005; Klin, 2006).

Asperger's Disorder

The Case of David
"It's grueling to think about what to say, what not to say."
www.mypsychlab.com

pervasive developmental disorder not otherwise specified a diagnosis assigned to children who have *some* but not *all* of the behaviors that characterize autistic disorder

real people, real disorders

Temple Grandin, Ph.D.

Temple Grandin, Ph.D., is a professor of animal science at Colorado State University. She obtained her B.A. at Franklin Pierce College, her M.S. in Animal Science at Arizona State University, and her Ph.D. in Animal Science from the University of Illinois. She has written more than 300 articles and several books. One book, *Animals in Translation*, was a *New York Times* best-seller. Her writings on animal grazing behaviors have helped reduce stress on animals during handling, and in North America, about half the cattle in livestock yards are handled in a system that she designed.

Dr. Grandin has autistic disorder. She didn't speak until she was three and a half years old, communicating by screaming, peeping, and humming. In 1950, she was labeled "autistic," and professionals recommended that she be institutionalized. The book she eventually wrote,

Emergence: Labeled Autistic, stunned the world. Until then, most people assumed autistic disorder prevented achievement or productivity in life. She speaks about her disorder because, she says, "I have read enough to know that there are still many parents, and, yes, professionals, too, who believe that 'once autistic, always autistic.' This dictum has meant sad and sorry lives for many children diagnosed, as I was in early life, as autistic. To these people, it is incomprehensible that the characteristics of autism can be modified and controlled. However, I feel strongly that I am living proof that they can."

(Taken from *Emergence: Labeled Autistic*).
http://www.harcourtbooks.com/AnimalsInTranslation/extendedbio.asp
http://www.grandin.com/index.html

Autistic disorder is more common among boys than among girls, with 3.5 to 4 boys for every 1 girl diagnosed (Bethea & Sikich, 2007). Asperger's disorder also appears to be more common among boys than girls, although there are few actual empirical data. Currently, there are no data to indicate that of the prevalence of autistic disorder or Asperger's disorder differ by race, ethnicity, or social class (Fombonne, 2005; Klin, 2006).

The onset of autistic disorder is always before age 3, and the core features are often clearly present by age 2 (Lord et al., 2006). Parents sometimes recognize that something is wrong at a much earlier age, perhaps as early as 12 to 18 months. However, as children grow, their symptoms may change dramatically between infancy and early childhood, particularly among children initially diagnosed with PDD-NOS (Charman et al., 2005; Lord et al., 2006). Although it is possible that autism can be reliably detected at 18 to 24 months (Lord et al., 2006), symptoms are more stable beginning at age 3, allowing for a more accurate diagnosis.

The long-term outcome of autistic disorder is variable. In one controlled longitudinal study (Eaves & Ho, 2008), 46% of children who were diagnosed with autistic disorder had a poor outcome as young adults, 32% had a fair outcome, and 21% had a good to very good outcome. IQ remained stable from childhood to adulthood. Emotional problems were present among 62% of the sample, most commonly obsessive-compulsive disorder or another anxiety disorder. Only 27% had ever been employed, for an average of 5 hours per week and most often in a sheltered workshop. Over half of the adults were living at home (56%) or in a group home or foster care (35%). Despite these figures, some adults with autistic disorder, such as Dr. Temple Grandin, do achieve success.

examining the evidence

Do Vaccines Produce Autism?

■ **Fact #1**   Forty years ago, 4 out of every 10,000 children were diagnosed with autism. The rate now is 1 out of 152 (CDC, 2007).

■ **Fact #2**   Childhood inoculations (measles-mumps-rubella, or MMR, vaccine) occur between 12 and 18 months of age.

■ **Fact #3**   Some children with autism appear to develop normally until around age 2, when developmental regression appears.

■ **Possible Conclusion?**   Because the incidence of autism appears to have increased when the MMR vaccine became common, the vaccine caused the rise in rates (Wakefield, 1999). Let's examine the evidence.

■ **Let's Examine the Evidence**   Wakefield (1999) described a *correlational relationship* between vaccination and autism, but it was wrongly interpreted as causation. Other studies appeared to confirm this parallel upward trend. However, the studies did not manipulate the variable of interest (MMR vaccine), which would be necessary to conclude causation. When researchers examined variations in the diagnosis of autistic disorder *before* and *after* the termination of a vaccine program (Honda et al., 2005), rates rose when the vaccine was administered. However, *rates continued to rise* after the vaccine was discontinued. If the MMR vaccine were responsible, the rate should have *decreased* once the program was discontinued (but it did not).

■ **What are possible alternative explanations for the increased rate of autistic disorder?**
1. **Change in diagnostic practices.**   Until recently, a child with mental retardation was not given a second diagnosis of autism, even if autistic behaviors were present. Now, both diagnoses can be given, leading to a rise in the total number of autism diagnoses.
2. **Changes in diagnostic criteria.**   Forty years ago, autism was a single diagnosis. Now, there are two other disorders in the category of autism spectrum disorder: Asperger's disorder and PDD-NOS. All are considered under the broader diagnostic category of autism spectrum disorders (Rutter, 2005), leading to a rise in the total number of children with one of the disorders.

■ **Conclusion**   Environmental or biological contributors to autism cannot be discounted, but current data do not support a causal role for MMR vaccinations (Rutter, 2005; Taylor, 2006). The National Academy of Science's Institute of Medicine concludes that future research should be directed "toward other lines of inquiry that are supported by current knowledge and evidence. . . . The vaccine hypothesis doesn't offer that promise" (Meadows, 2004).

ETIOLOGY

Autistic disorder is a neurodevelopmental disorder associated with the presence of different genetic syndromes and chromosomal abnormalities (Barbaresi et al., 2006). Even though its specific genetic mechanism is not yet known, the estimated heritability is greater than 90% (Gupta & State, 2007). Interestingly, whereas advancing maternal age is associated with Down syndrome and mental retardation, advancing paternal age may be associated with an increased prevalence of autistic disorder (Reichenberg et al., 2006). However, as with Down syndrome and maternal age, it is not clear how a father's advanced age might lead to development of the disorder.

One indication of the neurodevelopmental basis of autistic disorder is unusually accelerated head and brain growth during the first few years of life. At birth, children later diagnosed with autistic disorder have a head circumference at the 25th percentile for all infants. Between 6 and 14 months of age, head circumference and brain size reaches the 84th percentile, far exceeding the growth rate for typically developing children (Bethea & Sikich, 2007; Courchesne & Pierce, 2005).

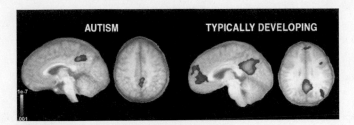

AUTISM   TYPICALLY DEVELOPING

In response to viewing faces of familiar people and strangers, brain activity occurs in both people with autism and people with no disorder. However, when the two groups are compared, there is stronger activation in people with no disorder and more areas of the brain are activated.

In addition to the abnormal growth rate, diagnostic imaging (MRI, fMRI, and PET scans) provides data that suggest subtle structural and organizational abnormalities in the brains of at least some children with autistic disorder. Particularly affected is the anterior cingulate cortex, an area that integrates verbal information with emotional tone and observation of personally important faces. When shown pictures of familiar and significant faces, children without autistic disorder show activation in the anterior cingulate cortex, while children with autistic disorder do not (Pierce et al., 2004). This would suggest that children with autistic disorder do not have the same neurochemical reaction when they see familiar faces as do typically developing children.

Another area of the brain that appears to be underactivated in children with autistic disorder is the fusiform gyrus (Pierce et al., 2001). This area is important in the recognition of facial expression. Severe underactivation of this area appears to be related to severe social impairment (Schultz et al., 2001). This would suggest that there could be a biological basis for this social impairment. If the part of the children's brain that recognizes faces is not functioning properly, children miss social cues that are "automatically" used by others to engage in pleasurable social interactions. It is not yet clear if therapy can change this biological deficit.

There are many avenues of exciting new research about the neurological bases of autistic disorder, but there are many medical misunderstandings about its causes. One theory is that autistic disorder is caused by the measles-mumps-rubella vaccine (see the box "Examining the Evidence: Do Vaccines Produce Autism?"). Another theory without empirical support is that autistic disorder is caused by thimerosal (a mercury-containing preservative used in vaccines). Why would such theories develop if no evidence supports them? One reason is that parents, in a desperate search for explanations, often misinterpret or overinterpret research data in their quest to find a cause for autistic disorder. Despite the current lack of evidence, some parents refuse to allow their children to be vaccinated for childhood medical disorders, thereby exposing their children to diseases that may result in physical handicaps such as blindness, mental retardation, or even death.

Throughout history, there have also been psychological misunderstandings about the etiology of autistic disorder. In the 1950s and 1960s, psychosocial theories proposed that "refrigerator mothers" (parents who were emotionally unresponsive to their infants) were responsible for its development (Klin, 2006). This concept was discredited in the 1970s when it became clear that the roots of the disorder were neurobiological. Parents do play a critical role in the early detection and treatment for children with this disorder (see the Treatment section), but they do *not* cause autism.

TREATMENT

Early and intensive behavioral treatment improves the long-term outcome for children with autistic disorder (Barbaresi et al., 2006). Behavioral interventions typically target five groups of problem behaviors: aberrant behaviors, social skills, language, daily living skills, and academic skills (Matson et al., 1996; Williams White, 2007). For all categories except aberrant behaviors, treatment consists of *positive reinforcement and shaping*, which teaches new and needed behaviors (such as saying a word, putting on clothes, completing homework). Clinicians teach parents to train their children in these skills. *Applied behavior analysis* (ABA) is a behavioral intervention that uses shaping and positive reinforcement to improve social, communicative, and behavioral skills by intensively training (shaping) and rewarding (reinforcing) specific behaviors. Introduced by O. Ivar Lovaas (1987), applied behavior analysis (conducted for 40 hours per week for more than two years) improved the behaviors in 9 out of 19 children with autistic disorder (47%), such that they were indistinguishable from children without the disorder. Although subsequent studies did not replicate this high success rate, empirical data show that ABA is effective, particularly when provided individually, for at least 20 hours per week and started before age 4 (Barbaresi, 2006).

In the case of aberrant behaviors, self-injury is an unfortunate part of the clinical syndrome and must be treated quickly or serious and permanent injury or even death may result. Mildly *aversive procedures* (e.g., a short spray of warm water to the face) quickly and painlessly disrupt such behaviors. When such treatments are combined with positive approaches to behavior change, self-injurious behaviors can be reduced or eliminated (Matson et al., 1996). Aversive procedures are used (a) in very specific instances, (b) when the child's health or welfare is at risk, and (c) under the supervision of a qualified professional. Furthermore, aversive procedures such as a spray of warm water or placing lemon juice on the tongue are quite effective. Mild electric shocks were used in the past but are now used rarely, if at all, and only when less aversive procedures are not effective and there is danger of severe physical damage (such as brain injury as a result of repeated head banging). Decisions about aversive procedures should never be made by a single person, but only after consultation with other professionals and perhaps an ethics committee.

No medications are efficacious for the social or communication deficits found in children with autistic disorder (Barbaresi et al., 2006). Atypical antipsychotic drugs (see Chapter 10) may manage behaviors such as tantrums, aggression, and self-injurious behavior (McCracken et al., 2002) and improve restricted, repetitive, and stereotyped patterns of behaviors, interests, and activities (McDougle et al., 2005). Stimulants reduce hyperactivity but are not as effective as they are in children with attention-deficit/hyperactivity disorder (Research Units on Pediatric Psychopharmacology, 2005). Selective serotonin reuptake inhibitors (SSRIs) are safe, but it is not clear if they are really effective. They may decrease repetitive behaviors (Hollander et al., 2005) but increase behavioral agitation in a population already prone to this behavior (Kolevzon et al., 2006).

concept CHECK

- Autism spectrum disorders, which include autistic disorder, Asperger's disorder, and pervasive developmental disorder not otherwise specified, are life-long conditions.

- All three disorders are characterized by deficits in social interaction as well as restricted and stereotypic behaviors, interests, and activities. Children with autistic disorder also have impairments in communication.

- Our increasingly sophisticated understanding of genetics now offers more detailed explanations to families of children with autism spectrum disorders. Despite increased understanding, we cannot yet offer treatments that entirely reverse the effects of these conditions. Early and intense interventions can produce symptom improvement and enhance the long-term outcome.

APPLICATION QUESTION Pervasive developmental disorders are neurobiological in nature and appear to have a genetic basis. When looking at faces, certain areas of the brains of children with autism spectrum disorders, such as the fusiform gyrus, do not appear to have the same level of reactivity as the brains of children with no disorder. How does this neurobiological finding relate to the clinical condition of Asperger's disorder?

Attention Deficit and Disruptive Behavior Disorders

Being active is part of childhood, whether it is playing games at recess, being involved in organized sports, or just wrestling with a sibling. An important developmental process involves the ability to control physical activity and direct it toward the achievement of identified goals. Most children achieve this developmental milestone. However, for a subset of children, physical activity is not goal-directed or at least not toward socially sanctioned goals. Some children and adolescents exhibit out-of-control behaviors such as temper tantrums and disobedience, behaviors that are characteristic of *oppositional defiant disorder*. In other instances, the behaviors are more socially deviant and illegal, such as fire-setting, assault, or burglary. In these instances, the child may be suffering from *conduct disorder*. In a third group of children, the behaviors are not goal-directed but just excessively overactive, resulting in negative outcomes such as household disruption, academic underachievement, and poor social relationships. These children suffer from *attention-deficit/hyperactivity disorder*, a common disruptive behavior disorder to which we now turn our attention.

ATTENTION-DEFICIT/HYPERACTIVITY DISORDER

Ronnie had a situational problem that was resolved by proper school placement and a challenging curriculum. Jason has **attention-deficit/hyperactivity disorder (ADHD)**, (see the box "DSM-IV-TR: Attention-Deficit/Hyperactivity Disorder"), a prevalent, early-onset childhood disorder that affects many aspects of functioning. The symptoms of ADHD fall into three categories. First are symptoms of *inattentiveness*, such as daydreaming, distractibility, and an inability to focus on or complete a task. The second component is *hyperactivity*, excessive energy, restlessness, excessive talkativeness, and an inability to sit still (Biederman, 2005). The third component, *impulsivity*, includes blurting out answers, interrupting others' conversations, and inability to take turns. Some children have the inattentive subtype (only showing inattention symptoms), and others have the hyperactivity subtype (only showing hyperactive/impulsive symptoms). Still other children have the combined subtype, with symptoms from all three components.

attention-deficit/hyperactivity disorder (ADHD) a common childhood disorder characterized by inattentiveness, hyperactivity, and impulsivity

---

NORMAL BEHAVIOR CASE STUDY
Boyish Exuberance

Ronnie is 6 years old. He has older brothers and loves "rough and tumble" play. He has broken a few family possessions but not more than his brothers. He does not like to sit quietly for a long period of time; reading has never been his favorite activity. However, 90% of the time he finishes activities that he starts. He was eager to start first grade. He gets good grades and has only been sent to the principal once, for talking out of turn. Sitting still in first grade is hard—he says school is boring. Psychological testing revealed a superior IQ score, and when he started the gifted and talented program, his out-of-seat behavior disappeared and he no longer found school boring. ■

ABNORMAL BEHAVIOR CASE STUDY
Attention Deficit Hyperactivity Disorder

Jason is 7 years old. He has trouble at school academically and complains that he hates school. He has no friends and is constantly picked on by the other children. He wants to socialize, but he always ends up fighting. He is genuinely puzzled about why other children do not like him. Jason is impulsive—he interrupts others, butts in line, and disrupts organized games. He cannot sit still, does not pay attention in class, and will not follow the rules at home. His mother reports that he has been a "wild child" since age 3. During the clinic interview, Jason does not sit in the chair. At times, he lies down on the floor and a few moments later, he is standing on the window sill. ■

DSM-IV-TR

Attention-Deficit/Hyperactivity Disorder (ADHD)

ADHD is a pervasive pattern of inattentiveness and/or hyperactivity/impulsivity that is more frequent and severe than expected given a child's developmental age.

- Inattention includes (a) failure to attend to detail, schoolwork, work, or activities, (b) difficulty with attention, listening, finishing, or organizing activities, (c) avoidance or reluctance/dislike of tasks that involve sustained mental effort, (d) being easily distracted or forgetful.

- Hyperactivity includes (a) fidgeting with hands or squirming when seated, running or climbing inappropriately, (b) inability to remain seated or quietly engaging in tasks, or (c) often being "on the go" or "driven by a motor", talking excessively.

- Impulsivity includes blurting out answers before questions are completed, having difficulty taking turns, interrupting, or intruding on others.

Adapted with permission from the *Diagnostic and Statistical Manual of Mental Disorders*, Text Revision, Fourth Edition, (Copyright 2000). American Psychiatric Association.

Children with ADHD are impulsive (cannot inhibit responses, do not wait to generate a plan before they act), inattentive (cannot pay attention in order to store information), and unable to concentrate (cannot focus on one particular idea or activity in order to develop a plan of action or way to behave). They are described as having a deficit in *executive functioning*, which are defined as cognitive abilities needed to formulate a goal, plan a series of actions to achieve the goal, and maintain the plan in memory in order to carry it out (Lesaca, 2001; Sergeant et al., 2002; Willcutt et al., 2005). However, not every study reports the same deficit pattern.

ADHD is most commonly diagnosed in early elementary school. Establishing the diagnosis earlier (i.e., the preschool years) is challenging because many symptoms (short attention span, difficulty sitting still, high activity level) are developmentally appropriate during toddlerhood (Blackman, 1999). When ADHD is diagnosed at the preschool age, the combined type is most common (Lahey et al., 1998; Wilens et al., 2002). When diagnosed at this early age, children continue to have ADHD symptoms during the elementary school years (Lahey et al., 2004).

Until about 20 years ago, ADHD was thought to disappear at or shortly after puberty (Smith et al., 2000). It is now clear that adolescents and adults also suffer from ADHD (Biederman, 2005). Some adults were diagnosed in childhood, but a substantial number are diagnosed for the first time in adulthood. Determining ADHD in adults is a challenge and is controversial. Some of the diagnostic criteria (unable to sit still in class, has difficulty playing quietly) are obviously not valid for adults. Also, deciding whether an adult had such symptoms before age 7 is difficult, as it is often based solely on retrospective self-report (McGough & Barkley, 2004). The diagnostic criteria for ADHD have never been validated for adults.

Children and adults with ADHD often have other disorders, including conduct problems (Wilens et al., 2002), mood disorders, anxiety disorders, and learning disabilities (Biederman, 2005). Similarly, among adults with ADHD, anxiety disorders are most common, followed by mood disorders, substance abuse, and antisocial personality disorder.

PEARSON
mypsychlab

Attention-deficit/Hyperactivity Disorder (ADHD):

The Case of Jimmy
"Sometimes I just drift off."
www.mypsychlab.com

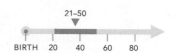

21–50

BIRTH   20   40   60   80

Functional Impairment   Children with ADHD have more accidents and injuries (perhaps as a result of poor motor coordination), poorer peer relationships, and more academic underachievement, sleep problems, and family stress (Biederman, 2005; Daley, 2006) (see Figure 12.5). Among adolescents, school delinquency, failure to graduate from high school, smoking, and substance abuse are common (Biederman & Faraone, 2005; Smith et al., 2000). Perhaps because of inattentiveness and impulsivity, adolescents with ADHD have a higher risk of injury and are more likely to have automobile accidents and to be involved in criminal behavior (Smith et al., 2000).

The course of ADHD is variable. At midadolescence, 20% of boys who had ADHD as children had poor academic, social, and emotional functioning (Biederman et al., 1998). However, 20% were functioning well, and 60% had an intermediate outcome (doing poorly in some areas and well in others).

Across cultures, about 5% of children have ADHD (Biederman, 2005; Canino et al., 2004; Costello et al., 2003; Graetz et al., 2001; Rohde et al., 2005; Wolraich et al., 1998). Many more boys (4.7%) than girls (1.1%) have ADHD (Costello et al., 2003). Boys with ADHD may have more severe symptoms or may suffer more impairment, making it more likely that their parents will seek treatment. Compared with boys, girls with ADHD have different impairments. They are more likely to have the predominantly inattentive subtype, less likely to have a learning disability, less likely to have problems in school or in their spare time, and less likely to have comorbid depression or disruptive disorders (oppositional defiant disorder, conduct disorder; Biederman et al., 2002; Spencer et al., 2007). Teachers rate boys with ADHD as more inattentive and hyperactive/impulsive than girls with this disorder (Greene et al., 2001; Hartung et al., 2002).

Symptoms of ADHD appear to improve at different rates. Symptoms of inattention decline only minimally as children mature, while hyperactivity/impulsivity symptoms show a much greater rate of decline, particularly from elementary school through midadolescence (Spencer et al., 2007). About 50% of children diagnosed with ADHD will continue to have the disorder during adolescence (Smith et al., 2000). The outlook is even better for adults. Most adults who had ADHD as children will no longer have the disorder by age 30 to 40, but about 50% will still have some functional impairment (Biederman & Faraone, 2005).

Etiology   ADHD may be best described as a neurobehavioral disorder with genetic, biological, and environmental influences. Like many other disorders, ADHD "runs in families," with between 20 and 25% of family members of someone with ADHD also

FIGURE 12.5
ADHD and Childhood Injuries

Compared with children with no disorder, children with ADHD are at higher risk for bicycle and pedestrian injuries.

From DiScala, C., et al. "Injuries to Children with Attention Deficit Hyperactivity Disorder," *Pediatrics*, December 1998, 102 (6): 1415–1421. Reprinted with permission from Pediatrics, Vol. 102 (6), pp. 1415–1421, Copyright © 1998 by the AAP

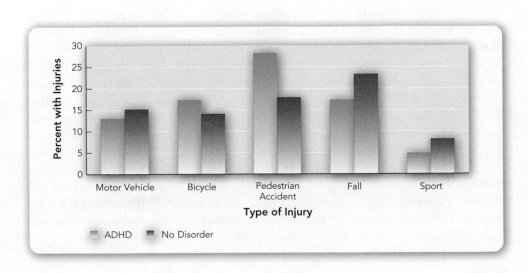

having symptoms. Twin studies also support its heritability, with a mean heritability of 77% (Biederman, 2005), suggesting a substantial genetic influence. Genetic studies have identified at least seven different genes thus far that may be associated with ADHD. The contribution of these genetic abnormalities is not yet known, but they may influence the levels or functioning of neurotransmitter systems that are important for symptoms of inattention, impulsivity, and hyperactivity (Biederman, 2005). For example, genetics or other prenatal factors may affect fetal or neonatal brain development. Structural brain imaging studies (i.e., MRI) reveal abnormalities in the frontal cortex, cerebellum, and subcortex when children with ADHD are compared with children who have no disorder (Castellanos et al., 2002). These structural abnormalities are stable, nonprogressive, and unchangeable even with medication.

Other potential contributory factors include lead contamination, maternal smoking and/or alcohol use during pregnancy, pregnancy and delivery complications (Biederman, 2005, Biederman & Faraone, 2005), and psychological risk factors such as marital discord, lower socioeconomic status, larger family size, foster care placement, paternal criminality, maternal psychological problems (Rutter et al., 1976). It is clear that the etiology of ADHD is complex and is probably influenced by many different factors, each of which makes a single, small contribution (Faraone et al., 2005).

Treatment   The decision to treat ADHD must consider the child's age (3-year-old children should not be expected to sit still for the same length of time as 10-year-olds) and level of functional impairment at home, school, and other activities. Treatment should aim at restoring behavior to age-appropriate standards (Chronis et al., 2006).

Both pharmacological and behavioral interventions have been used effectively to treat ADHD. Stimulant medications, such as Ritalin, have a 40-year record of efficacy for ADHD's core symptoms (Biederman & Faraone, 2005). The drugs work by enhancing the neurotransmission of dopamine and norepinephrine (Spencer et al., 2004), allowing these chemicals to remain in the synapses for a longer period of time, increasing their availability for neurotransmission. Stimulants are short-acting medications and may need to be taken several times a day, sometimes making compliance difficult. These drugs decrease ADHD's core symptoms, but whether they affect other areas of functioning, such as academic achievement, is less clear (Hechtman & Greenfield, 2003; Wells et al., 2000).

The use of stimulants to treat ADHD is controversial. First, up to 30% of children may not respond to stimulant medication (Chronis et al., 2006). Second, stimulant medication may affect physical stature. Children who take stimulants grow more slowly than other children. However, their average final height is not different from children who do not take stimulants, if the medication is discontinued during adolescence (Klein & Manuzza, 1988).

Effective behavioral treatments for ADHD include behavioral parent training, classroom behavioral management (daily report cards), social skills training, and an intensive outpatient/summer treatment program (Chronis et al., 2006; Smith et al., 2000). *Behavioral parent training* teaches parents how to reward positive behaviors and decrease negative behaviors. In addition to improving core ADHD symptoms and sometimes classroom behavior (Chronis et al., 2006; Pelham et al., 1998), behavioral parent training improves parenting behavior, and in some cases decreases stress on parents (Chronis et al., 2004). The *Daily Report Card* is a classroom behavioral management program that targets school-relevant goals such as homework completion and staying in one's seat (Chronis et al., 2006; Smith et al., 2000). Teachers record classroom behavior on a report card and parents use a reward system to reinforce positive school behaviors. A third behavioral treatment, social skills training, teaches children with ADHD to interact appropriately with others (taking turns, allowing others to decide which game to play). Social skills training appears to be particularly efficacious when combined with behavioral parent training (e.g., Pfiffner & McBurnett, 1997).

Because of the range and severity of their behavioral problems, children with ADHD may require intensive and comprehensive treatment programs. The Summer Treatment Program (Pelham et al., 2000) is an 8-week, all-day program that includes a point system, daily report cards, social skills training, academic skills training, problem-solving training, and sports training in a day camp atmosphere. There is also weekly Parent Management Training. The Summer Treatment Program is an efficacious intervention for children with ADHD, decreasing symptoms and increasing associated behavioral functioning (e.g., Pelham et al., 2000, 2004).

The Collaborative Multimodal Treatment Study of Children with ADHD (MTA) is the largest controlled clinical trial comparing behavioral treatment (using the components described above), medication (primarily stimulant medication), a combination of behavioral treatment and medication, and standard community care for preadolescent children with ADHD. At the end of the treatment program, all four treatments improved children's symptoms, but children in the medication only and children in the combined group showed significantly more improvement than children in behavioral treatment alone or community care (MTA Cooperative Group, 1999). Do the results of this study mean that behavioral intervention is not useful for ADHD or at the least, that it does not add value over medication? When an alternative method of data analysis was used, children who received medication and behavior therapy had a superior outcome over medication alone, which contradicts the original outcome (Conners et al., 2001). Thus, even though this was the largest child treatment study ever funded by the National Institute of Mental Health, its results are unclear and subject to various interpretations.

Children with conduct disorder often engage in behaviors such as vandalism, theft, and destruction of property.

conduct disorder continuous and repeated pattern of violating the basic rights of others or breaking societal rules, including aggression toward people or animals, destruction of property, deceitfulness or theft, and serious rule violations

CONDUCT DISORDER AND OPPOSITIONAL DEFIANT DISORDER

In addition to ADHD, two other disruptive behavior disorders are *conduct disorder* and *oppositional defiant disorder*. Although considered separate disorders, both are characterized by deviant, and sometimes unlawful, behaviors. They are among the most difficult disorders to treat, are the most common reason that a child is brought to a mental health clinic (Loeber et al., 2000), and often lead to incarceration in the juvenile justice system.

Conduct disorder (see the box "DSM-IV-TR: Conduct Disorder"), by far the more serious disorder, is a continuous and repeated pattern of violating the basic rights of others or breaking societal rules. Behaviors fall into four different categories: aggression toward people or animals, destruction of property, deceitfulness or theft, and serious rule violations.

The first category, *aggression toward people and animals*, includes what is commonly known as bullying behavior—threats or intimidation directed toward others, such as initiating physical fights, stealing, or forcing someone to engage in sexual activity. Such children are also physically cruel toward people and animals. The second category is *destruction of property*, such as vandalism or deliberate fire-setting. It is important to emphasize that this is a behavioral pattern—not simply an isolated incident of property destruction, as often happens when siblings fight. The third component is *deceitfulness or theft*, and includes activities such as breaking into houses or cars, lying, and nonconfrontational theft—shoplifting or forgery. The fourth component includes *serious violations of rules*, such as breaking parental curfews, running away from home overnight, and school truancy.

Conduct Disorder

A consistent and pervasive pattern of behavior that ignores the rights of others or violates major, age-appropriate behavioral norms. The pattern includes aggression toward people and animals, destruction of property, deceitfulness or theft, and serious violation of rules.

Adapted with permission from the *Diagnostic and Statistical Manual of Mental Disorders*, Text Revision, Fourth Edition, (Copyright 2000). American Psychiatric Association.

Oppositional Defiant Disorder

A pattern of negative, hostile, or defiant behaviors, such as losing one's temper, arguing with adults, defying or refusing adult requests, annoying people, blaming others for his/her mistakes, being easily annoyed, angry and resentful, spiteful and vindictive.

Adapted with permission from the *Diagnostic and Statistical Manual of Mental Disorders*, Text Revision, Fourth Edition, (Copyright 2000). American Psychiatric Association.

Cecily is 8 years old. Her mother describes her as a "behavior problem." Specifically, Cecily often loses her temper and throws tantrums, particularly when she does not get her own way. She is not physically aggressive but argues with her parents whenever they ask her to do something and is constantly disobedient. She refused to clean up her room unless her parents gave her $10.00. She deliberately teases her baby brother and then laughs when he cries. Her mother describes her as spiteful. Her older sister received an award for an art project. The day after her sister brought the trophy home, it was discovered broken in half and the art project destroyed. When her mother confronted Cecily about it, Cecily blamed it on her one-year-old brother.

Cecily's behaviors are characteristic of **oppositional defiant disorder** (ODD), another disruptive behavior disorder. Whereas the behaviors that are part of conduct disorder (deliberate fire-setting, armed robbery, deliberate cruelty to people or animals) are inappropriate at any age, some behaviors that are part of ODD must be considered within a developmental context. For example, temper tantrums are common among 2-year-olds. However, Cecily was not 2 years old, and her temper tantrums were not simply toddler frustration. Also, one temper tantrum is not sufficient for a diagnosis of ODD. Rather, there must be a repeated and consistent pattern of negative, hostile, and defiant behaviors.

The average age of onset for ODD is about age 8 (APA, 2000), and it almost always begins before early adolescence. Unlike ADHD and conduct disorder, where disruptive behaviors occur in several settings, it is common for children with ODD to behave negatively only at home. Because both of these disorders have at their core a pattern of negative behaviors directed against people and society, we will examine them together throughout the remainder of this section.

Many children with ODD and conduct disorder have additional disorders, and the combination negatively affects outcome. Coexisting ADHD is common in boys (Hinshaw, 1994). Commonly co-occurring disorders among girls include anxiety and mood disorders, and girls with both conduct disorder and depression are at increased risk for suicidal behaviors (Keenan et al., 1999). Substance abuse is a common problem

oppositional defiant disorder negative, hostile, or defiant behaviors that are less severe than those found in conduct disorder

Less likely than boys to engage in physical aggression, girls with conduct problems often engage in relational aggression—such as teasing and ostracizing other girls.

among children with conduct disorder (Keenan et al, 1999; Loeber et al., 2000). For girls, conduct disorder is also associated with early pregnancy (Keenan et al., 1999). As adults, some children with either ODD or conduct disorder will have antisocial personality disorder.

The prevalence of conduct disorder and ODD is higher among children from lower socioeconomic classes and higher in the worst inner-city neighborhoods (see Loeber et al., 2000). Boys are more likely to have a diagnosis of ODD than girls (13.4% vs. 9.1%, respectively, by age 16; Costello et al., 2003). Conduct disorder is more common among boys (14.1%) than girls (3.8%; Costello et al., 2003) in community settings, whereas the ratio is more equal in clinical settings. Initially, conduct disorder in girls was relatively understudied because so few girls engage in physical fights. However, it is now clear that girls engage in *relational aggression*, which includes peer alienation, ostracism, manipulating social networks, circulating slanderous rumors, and character defamation (Ehrenssaft, 2005; Keenan et al., 1999). When physical aggression does occur, boys target strangers and girls target family or intimate partners (Ehrensaft, 2005).

From a developmental perspective, some mental health clinicians have questioned whether preschool children can be diagnosed with ODD or conduct disorder. Preschoolers do not have access to knives or guns, but they might use sticks or stones for weapons (Keenan & Wakschlag, 2002). Similarly, older children may steal cars, whereas preschool children may steal candy. Behaviors that are part of ODD and conduct disorder may change again when adolescents reach adulthood, where the diagnosis is antisocial personality disorder (see Chapter 11). Clearly, disruptive behavior disorders exist at all ages, even if expressed differently at various developmental stages.

Etiology   Little is known about the cause of ODD, as virtually all of the research on genetics, neuroanatomy, and neurochemistry has been directed at conduct disorder. There is some evidence for a familial relationship between conduct disorder and adult antisocial personality disorder, but to date, genetic studies have not provided specific clues (Burke et al., 2002). Potential environmental causes include prenatal factors such as maternal smoking or substance abuse, pregnancy and birth complications, and postnatal environmental toxins such as lead. Psychological disorders in parents, poor parenting behaviors, child abuse, and socioeconomic status may also play a causal role. Any of these factors may be associated with conduct disorder or ODD, but it is highly unlikely that any one factor will be identified as important for all children with disruptive disorders (Burke et al., 2002).

Treatment   Most mental health clinicians agree that psychosocial interventions should be the first line of treatment. Medication, particularly when used alone, has been unsuccessful for treating the core symptoms of ODD and conduct disorder (Bassarath, 2003) (see the box "Research Hot Topic: Psychiatric Medication Use in Children"). There are very few controlled treatment trials for children with ODD or conduct disorders and even fewer with samples in which the children do not also have other disorders. However, given those limitations, atypical antipsychotic agents such as risperidone reduce symptoms of aggression in children with ODD and conduct disorder (Bassarath, 2003; Pandina et al., 2006).

An effective behavioral treatment for ODD and conduct disorder is parent management training (Patterson & Gullion, 1968), which was described in the section on ADHD treatment (behavioral parent training). For ODD and conduct disorder, parent management training is more efficacious than treatment as usual or no treatment (Brestan & Eyberg, 1998; Farmer et al., 2002; van den Wiel et al., 2002;

Research HOT Topic

Psychiatric Medication Use in Children

Psychiatric medications are one of the largest groups of drugs manufactured by pharmaceutical companies. Most medications undergo rigorous development, and data are collected by controlled trials, such as those described throughout this book. Some research examines whether people can tolerate the medication and determines its most effective dose. If successful, active medication is compared with placebo to determine efficacy. In many instances, medication trials use adult samples. If approved by the Food and Drug Administration (FDA), the drug may be given to children, even if it was not tested on children.

Over the past two decades, an increasing number of children have been prescribed medication for behavioral or emotional disorders. Between 1987 and 1996, total psychotropic medication use for youth increased two- to threefold, and by 1996, these medications were prescribed for children as often as for adults (Magno-Zito et al., 2003). This dramatic increase occurred even though there were still relatively few clinical data from studies of children. Perhaps even more troubling is that

medication prescriptions for preschoolers also increased dramatically between 1991 and 1995 (Magno-Zito et al., 2000). Rarely, if at all, are preschool children included in clinical trials. Some children are taking two or more medications, with empirical data about the drugs based almost exclusively on case reports and small, nonblinded trials (Safer et al., 2003). Thus, these powerful medications are being prescribed to children with few if any empirical data to back their use.

In 1997, the FDA offered a six-month extension on a drug company's patent if pharmaceutical manufacturers provided data on pediatric populations. More recently, the Pediatric Research Equity Act (2003) gave the FDA the authority to mandate pharmaceutical research on children (Magno-Zito et al., 2004). Hopefully, this law will encourage pharmaceutical manufacturers and independent investigators to conduct research with children, which will provide clinicians with important and very necessary data on their safety and efficacy in youth.

Webster-Stratton et al., 1988). Particularly efficacious for preadolescent children, it may reduce criminal arrests, decrease time spent in institutions, and decrease self-reported delinquency compared with usual care or no treatment (Woolfenden et al., 2002).

A community-based intervention for ODD and conduct disorder is Multisystemic Therapy (MST), an intensive case management approach to treatment (Henggeler et al., 1998). MST includes interventions conducted in the clinic, at home, at school—wherever the need exists. The choice of treatment is flexible—individual therapy, family therapy, social work interventions to assist in family functioning, and therapists always "on call" to provide needed services. MST, provided primarily to adolescent populations, is an efficacious intervention that not only decreases symptoms of conduct disorder but also decreases incarceration in both hospitals and juvenile justice settings (Henggleler et al., 1999).

concept CHECK

- ADHD has variable symptoms and a complicated and complex etiology. The disorder creates significant functional impairment in many aspects of life.

- ADHD, once considered a disorder that affected only children, is now understood in some cases to continue into adolescence and adulthood. Both pharmacological and behavioral interventions are efficacious for the treatment of this disorder.

- Conduct disorder and ODD might be considered to be disorders of "misbehavior"— and include activities such as disobedience, lying for no apparent reason, truancy, and other delinquent activities. Some children with ODD may develop conduct disorder as adolescents. Conduct disorder exists in girls but is sometimes overlooked if clinicians do not look for evidence of relational, rather than physical, aggression.

- The causes of ODD and conduct disorder are unknown and complex. Treatments must likewise be multifaceted.

APPLICATION QUESTION A friend in your abnormal psychology class thinks that he has ADHD, but he was never evaluated or diagnosed as a child. How would he go about collecting empirical evidence to demonstrate he had the disorder as a child, which is necessary for a diagnosis?

Childhood Disorders of Eating, Sleeping, and Elimination

Basic physical functions such as eating, sleeping, and elimination would seem to come naturally to children. In much the same way that we breathe without thinking about it, eating and sleeping are activities that are considered innate, not specifically learned. Although children must be taught to use the toilet for elimination, most children learn to control their bowels and bladder with very little effort and minimal instruction.

However, some children do not easily acquire these behaviors, or they may lose control over behaviors previously achieved. Children who once controlled their bladder may begin to "wet the bed." In other instances, children exhibit behaviors that resemble eating but the substance consumed is not food. In this section, we will discuss disorders of eating, sleeping, and elimination, paying particular attention to those disorders that have their onset in childhood.

FEEDING AND EATING DISORDERS

Many children, particularly infants and toddlers, are "picky eaters."

Sarah was 5 years old. Although she had no medical problems, her height and weight were at the 2nd percentile for her age. Sarah refused to eat any foods except peanut butter sandwiches and candy. When offered other foods, she would cry and hold her breath until her mother gave her a peanut butter sandwich.

Sarah had no need to eat other foods—when she held her breath, she got her way. Treatment consisted of offering Sarah other foods and teaching her mother to ignore her tantrums. In Sarah's case, abnormal eating was the result of environmental factors and was not really dangerous. But other disordered eating behaviors, *pica* and *rumination*, are conceptually more perplexing and difficult to treat (see the box "DSM-IV-TR: Disorders of Eating, Sleeping and Elimination").

Pica is the recurrent, compulsive consumption of nonnutritive items. The term comes from the Latin word for "magpie," a bird that voraciously consumes food and nonfood substances (Stiegler, 2005). According to one parent, "Over the last couple years we have pulled out of [our son's] throat: a set of keys, large bulldog clips, sticks, rocks, wads of paper, open safety pins, wire (from the screen, etc.). Plus all the stuff that he gets down before we can get it out: magnets from the fridge, Barbie parts, paper, money, paper clips, etc." (Menard, 1999, cited in Stiegler, 2005). Although children with developmental disabilities (such as Jeremy) constitute the largest group of people with pica, the disorder also occurs in people with mental retardation, schizophrenia, and sometimes people with no psychological disorder.

Pica occurs in various socioeconomic groups, both sexes, and all ages (Stiegler, 2005), but may be more common among women, children, and those of lower socio-

pica recurrent, compulsive consumption of nonnutritive items

economic status (Rose et al., 2000). Pica can result in serious health consequences, including lead poisoning, parasitic infections, malnutrition, dental trauma, oral lacerations, gum disease, and erosion of tooth enamel (Stiegler, 2005). Consuming safety pins, glass, or nails can obstruct or perforate the esophagus, stomach, or intestines. Finally, the ingestion of certain items may repulse caregivers or peers, leading to social isolation and/or rejection (Stiegler, 2005).

Cultural pica occurs in many countries. Women in India consume soil and by-products (mud, clay, ash, lime, charcoal, and brick) in response to pregnancy cravings (Nay, 1994). East African women consume soil for purposes of fertility (Abrahams & Parsons, 1996). Certain cultures in South America eat clay for its purported medicinal value (Rose et al., 2000). In the United States, eating kaolin (also known as white dirt, chalk, or white clay) occurs in the Piedmont region of Georgia (Grigsby et al., 1999) and parts of Mississippi (Ali, 2001).

A rare eating disorder is **rumination disorder**, where recently eaten food is effortlessly regurgitated into the mouth, followed by rechewing, reswallowing, or spitting it out. Rumination disorder occurs in both sexes and may begin in infancy, childhood, or adolescence (Chial et al., 2003; O'Brien et al., 1995). Episodes may occur several times per day and may last for over an hour (Chial et al., 2003; Soykan et al., 1997). Because rumination resembles vomiting, some people are initially diagnosed with bulimia nervosa or gastroesophageal reflux disease. They sometimes undergo gastrointestinal surgical procedures and consult multiple physicians before getting a correct diagnosis (O'Brien et al., 1995).

Etiology and Treatment   Pica has many different causes. Iron and/or zinc deficiencies may result in the urge to ingest certain foods or substances, but many people without these conditions also engage in pica. Environmental factors (stress and impoverished living environments) or developmental disorders are important causal factors (Stiegler, 2001). Among people without psychological disorders, pica sometimes begins after stressful events such as surgery or the loss of a family member (Soykan et al., 1997).

Medications are not efficacious for the treatment of these feeding disorders. Behavioral interventions such as habit reversal, relaxation training, and cognitive-behavioral therapy are efficacious for rumination disorder (Chial et al., 2003; Soykan et al., 1997). *Habit reversal* is a behavioral treatment in which a problem behavior is eliminated by consistently using a competing (i.e., alternative) behavior. In the case of rumination, the patient is taught *diaphragmatic* (deep) breathing, a competing response that eliminates rumination in most patients (Chial et al., 2003).

Behavioral interventions, such as overcorrection, also are effective for pica. If such procedures are done repeatedly and consistently, pica can be eliminated or greatly reduced (Foxx & Martin, 1975).

Leslie was 14 years old and had moderate mental retardation. When not closely monitored, she would eat any foreign object that she found on the floor. The psychologist developed an overcorrection program that consisted of Leslie spitting out the object and throwing it away. Then she would be led to the bathroom to brush her teeth for 10 minutes using an antiseptic toothpaste. After one week of consistent overcorrection, Leslie's pica was reduced by 60%.

SLEEP DISORDERS

People of all ages may have sleep disturbances, sometimes in conjunction with another psychological disorder and sometimes not. Like other aspects of physical development, sleep patterns change as a person matures. Among children, occasional *sleepwalking*

rumination disorder   regurgitating recently eaten food into the mouth, followed by either rechewing, reswallowing, or spitting it out

Although we think of sleep as restful, parasomnias can disrupt sleep and create distress for children and their parents.

(sitting up in bed, getting out of bed, and walking during sleep), *sleep terrors* (expression of fear, a loud scream, and rapid heartbeat), and *nightmares* (very vivid, frightening dreams) are common. When these behaviors occur frequently, the child may have sleepwalking disorder, nightmare disorder, or sleep terror disorder. Together, sleep problems are called **parasomnias** (see the box "DSM-IV-TR: Disorders of Eating, Sleeping and Elimination") They are transient conditions, common in children and usually disappear in adolescence (Laberge et al., 2000; Thiedke, 2001).

Parasomnias occur in "bursts"—several nights in a row, followed by quiet periods of up to several weeks (Guilleminault et al., 2004). They also occur at predictable times during the sleep cycle (Thiedke, 2001). One particular type of parasomnia is **sleep terror disorder**. Also known as night terrors, it most often occurs during the first 90 minutes of sleep. The child suddenly sits up, screams, and cannot be consoled. Physical symptoms include rapid heartbeat, rapid breathing, trembling, pupil dilation, and sweating (Mason & Pack, 2005). The episode usually lasts only a few minutes but can extend to 30 minutes before the child falls back to sleep (Thiedke, 2001).

Sleepwalking disorder (also known as *somnambulism*) consists of sitting up in bed with eyes open but "unseeing" (Thiedke, 2001). In some instances, the child may get out of bed and walk through the house. Sleepwalking is sometimes accompanied by sleeptalking (*somniloquy*), but speech is rarely intelligible. Both sleepwalking and sleep terror disorder are states of confusion and partial arousal, and in both disorders there may be no memory of the event (Guilleminault et al., 2004).

Nightmare disorder consists of repeated episodes of long, frightening dreams that usually involve a physical threat to survival and produce vivid imagery. The child awakens from the dream and can recall its content (Agargun et al., 2004).

Parasomnias can disrupt the sleep of various members of the household. The child is often the least affected, whereas parents may suffer significant distress and lack of sleep. Sleepwalking does have the potential for physical injury, such as falls. Before age 13, between 2 and 5% of children sleepwalk regularly (Agargun et al., 2004; Klackenberg, 1987), and 6.3% between age 6 and 11 have more than five sleep terror episodes per month (Goodwin et al., 2004).

Sleepwalking and sleep terrors are common in both sexes and across cultures (Agargun et al., 2004; Goodwin et al., 2004; Laberge et al., 2000). Although cross-cultural data are few, these disorders are equally common in Hispanic and non-Hispanic white children in the United States (Goodwin et al., 2004). Comparisons among other ethnicities have not been studied.

There is little information on the etiology of parasomnias. Because they almost always disappear by adolescence, one hypothesis is that parasomnias may result from an immature central nervous system. Other biological hypotheses stem from reports that children with parasomnias often have parents with sleep disorders (Guilleminault et al., 2004, Mason & Pack, 2005). Environmental factors related to the onset of sleep terrors have been identified and include stress or fatigue (Mason & Pack, 2005; Thiedke, 2001). Parasomnias are frightening to parents, but reassurance that children will outgrow them is usually the only intervention required.

ELIMINATION DISORDERS

An important aspect of physical development is controlling bladder and bowel functions, which usually happens in the preschool years. Lack of control past this age may indicate the presence of enuresis or encopresis (see the box "DSM-IV-TR: Disorders of Eating, Sleeping and Elimination"). **Enuresis** is the voiding of urine into one's clothing or bedding. It may occur during the day (diurnal enuresis), at night (nocturnal

parasomnias unwanted physical events that happen during sleep

sleep terror disorder a type of sleep disorder in which the child suddenly sits up, screams, and cannot be consoled

sleepwalking disorder also known as somnambulism, this disorder consists of sitting up in bed with eyes open but "unseeing" and sometimes getting out of bed and walking through the house

nightmare disorder repeated episodes of long, frightening dreams that usually involve a physical threat to survival and produce vivid imagery

enuresis voiding of urine into one's clothing or bedding

Disorders of Eating, Sleeping, and Elimination

Pica   Repetitive consumption of nonfood objects, despite efforts not to do so. The behavior is not developmentally appropriate (the person is more than 18 months of age) and is not culturally sanctioned.

Rumination Disorder   Repeated regurgitation and rechewing of food without the presence of a gastrointestinal disorder. The rumination does not occur only during episodes of anorexia nervosa or bulimia nervosa.

Nightmare Disorder (Dream Anxiety Disorder)   Repeated awakenings with detailed recall of dreams that are extended and extremely frightening.

Sleep Terror Disorder   Recurrent, abrupt awakening from sleep that begins with a panicky scream; occurs during the first third of sleep.

Sleepwalking Disorder   Recurrent episodes of getting out of bed and walking around, occurring during the first third of sleep time.

Enuresis   Repeated pattern of daytime and/or nighttime urinary voiding into clothing or bed clothes.

Encopresis   Repeated passage of feces on or into inappropriate places (floor or clothing), whether intentionally or voluntarily, by someone over the age of 4 years.

Adapted with permission from the *Diagnostic and Statistical Manual of Mental Disorders*, Text Revision, Fourth Edition, (Copyright 2000). American Psychiatric Association.

enuresis), or both times (diurnal and nocturnal). *Primary* enuresis describes a condition in which a child has never achieved urinary continence (voiding urine is fully under the child's control), while *secondary* enuresis occurs if a child who was once fully continent loses that control. Primary nocturnal enuresis, or bed-wetting, is the most common form of the disorder. **Encopresis** is the repeated elimination of feces on or into inappropriate places such as the floor or clothing by someone over age 4. Encopresis can be intentional or accidental and, like enuresis, may be primary or secondary.

Each year, approximately 15% of children with enuresis recover without treatment (Forsythe & Redmond, 1974; Jalkult et al., 2001). Although enuresis may distress children and parents, there is little actual research examining this problem. In contrast, children with encopresis often feel ashamed and avoid social interaction. They may be ostracized by peers and be the target of anger, punishment, and rejection by others, including family (APA, 2000). When compared with children with no disorder, children with encopresis had higher parent and teacher ratings of anxiety, depression, and behavioral problems, but only 20% had significant functional impairment or substantial distress (Cox et al., 2002).

Enuresis occurs worldwide, with prevalence estimates ranging from 3.1 to 7.3% depending on age (Costello et al., 1996; Jalkut et al., 2001; Wille, 1994; Yeung et al., 2006). About 1% of children suffer from encopresis (APA, 2000), but they account for 3% of all pediatric appointments and 25% of pediatric gastroenterology appointments (Brooks et al., 2000). Among white children, boys were three times more likely than girls to be diagnosed with either enuresis or encopresis (Costello et al., 1997).

encopresis   repeated elimination of feces on or into inappropriate places such as the floor or clothing by someone over age 4

An alarm device is often used in the treatment of enuresis. A moisture sensor is attached to the child's underwear and detects moisture, triggering an alarm that awakens the child to get up and use the toilet.

Despite many years of study, it is not clear whether children with enuresis have weaker bladders than other children (Jalkut et al., 2001; Wille, 1994). Enuresis does run in families. Between 30 and 40% of children with enuresis have parents who had primary nocturnal enuresis (Jalkut et al., 2001), and monozygotic twins are twice as likely to be concordant for enuresis as dizygotic twins. Multigenerational family studies have implicated areas on four different chromosomes that may hold genes contributing to the cause of enuresis (see Mikkelsen, 2001). However, psychosocial and environmental factors cannot be overlooked (von Gontard et al., 2001).

Environmental and psychological factors that may contribute to the development of secondary enuresis include behavioral disturbances, stressful life events, and delayed achievement of initial bladder control (Eidlitz-Markus et al., 2000; Fergusson et al., 1990; Jalkut et al., 2001), suggesting that both genetic and environmental factors may be the most appropriate model for understanding the development of enuresis. The etiology of encopresis is rarely studied. About 80% of children with encopresis have chronic constipation, and in 90% of all cases of chronic constipation, there is no obvious medical or functional cause (Issenman et al., 1999; van Dijk et al., 2007). Encopresis is often the result of withholding the stool, perhaps as a result of previous painful defecation experiences or extremely hard stools. This leads to chronic constipation and subsequent involuntary leakage of feces as a result of stool impaction (van Dijk et al., 2007).

For enuresis, the most empirically supported treatment is the *enuresis alarm* (Mikkelsen, 2001), initially known as the *bell-and-pad* method when it was introduced in 1902 (Pander, 1902, cited in Jalkut et al., 2001). The system consists of a battery-operated alarm or vibrator that is connected to a thin wire attached to the child's underwear, sleeping pad, or bedding. When urination begins, the alarm awakens the child, who then goes to the toilet. Over time, the child becomes sensitized to the sensations of a full bladder and awakens before urination. The average success rate for enuresis alarms, defined as 14 consecutive dry nights, is 65% (Butler & Glasson, 2005), but the average relapse rate is 42%. Relapse rates are higher when the intervention is short (less than seven weeks).

Currently, the most common medication for enuresis is desmopressin acetate (DDAVP), which reduces nighttime urinary output and the number of enuretic episodes. However, the reduction in enuretic episodes varies greatly, and only a small percentage continue to "stay dry" once the medication is withdrawn. Medical treatment for encopresis consists of enemas to clear the bowel and laxatives to deal with constipation. However, this intervention is usually considered to be only the first stage and is followed by behavioral interventions to "promote proper toileting behavior" (daily toilet sitting and use of positive reinforcement; see "The Whole Story: Jake" at the end of this chapter). The medical-behavioral intervention is superior to medical treatment alone (Brooks et al., 2000), with improvement rates ranging from 65% to 78% (Borowtiz et al., 2002; Cox et al., 1998).

concept CHECK

- Pica is the consumption of nonnutritive and, in some cases, dangerous substances. It is most commonly found among people with developmental disorders. Pica may sometimes be a culturally sanctioned practice.

- Rumination disorder is a rare condition involving effortless regurgitation of food. It can have serious medical consequences.

- Parasomnias consist of sleep terror disorder, sleepwalking disorder, and nightmare disorder. These disorders are common in children but usually disappear by adolescence.

- Enuresis appears to have a genetic component, although specific genes have not been identified. Encopresis often results from medical problems such as constipation, which may in turn be caused by poor diet.

APPLICATION QUESTION   Enuresis and encopresis are responsive to behavioral interventions, which are considered the treatment of choice. Given that these problems appear medical in nature, how would you explain the success of behavioral interventions to the parents of a 9-year-old with enuresis?

THE WHOLE STORY: JAKE—THE TREATMENT OF ENCOPRESIS

The Person: *Jake is 7 years old. He lives with his parents and a 3-year-old brother. He soils his underwear one or two times per day, always during the daytime. Jake refuses to sit on the toilet, and he shows other oppositional behaviors as well. He interacts well with his peers and is a good student.*

The Problem: *Jake has been soiling for more than four years. He was never adequately toilet trained and describes defecation as very painful. He does not change his soiled underwear unless he is told to do so. There are no behavioral consequences for soiling; as a matter of fact, his mother leaves a stack of his clean underwear in the bathroom. His father tries to pressure Jake to use the toilet.*

The Assessment: *Before beginning psychological treatment, Jake had a medical evaluation. An X-ray showed impacted stool in his bowel. The condition was so severe that it required a hospital-administered enema. The treatment was successful; however, following the hospitalization, his soiling increased to 12 times per day and occurred at school and home. The psychologist conducted a thorough assessment of Jake's difficulties. During the diagnostic interview, it was clear that his parents had difficulty getting Jake to behave in areas other than toileting. Jake often did not follow his parents' instructions, and as illustrated*

by their different approaches to his soiling, his parents had different ideas about parenting.

The Treatment: *Initially, the treatment plan (Weeks 1 and 2) consisted of asking Jake to sit on the toilet for 10 minutes once a day. While on the toilet, Jake's father would read a story (to make the time enjoyable and not seem like a punishment). The psychologist made a sticker chart and Jake got a sticker for every day that he "did his minutes." It is important to note that Jake was reinforced for merely sitting on the toilet, not for having a bowel movement. If Jake got four stickers a week, he got a prize.*

As usually happens, the first two weeks of this treatment revealed an important point. Ten minutes was too long for a 7-year-old boy to sit on the toilet! Therefore, during Weeks 3 and 4, Jake sat on the toilet for 5 minutes twice per day. His father read a story, and Jake got a sticker for every time that he "did his minutes." If he earned 10 stickers per week, Jake got a prize. His parents noticed that some of Jake's other behaviors were changing—for example, he was changing his soiled pants without being prompted.

The psychologist noted that Jake's diet contained very little fiber, and she discussed dietary factors leading to constipation, fecal impaction, and the painful

bowel movements. She encouraged his parents to include more fiber in the family's diet during Week 5. Jake's treatment still included a sticker for sitting on the toilet for 5 minutes twice per day, and he earned two stickers if, when on the toilet, he defecated in the toilet. Instead of getting a prize, "special parent time" was the reward for earning stickers. Jake's soiling behavior was completely eliminated at Week 6.

The Treatment Outcome: *At Week 10, Jake wanted the door closed when he was sitting on the toilet, and although his father was still going in to read, during Week 10 and 11, Jake sat alone for the last 2 minutes (which was when his bowel movements were most likely to occur). During Weeks 12 to 14, Jake was sitting alone for 4 minutes, soiling was eliminated, and the parents reported satisfaction with Jake's behavior.*

The case study illustrates the interplay between biological, psychological, and environmental factors. Before initiating any psychological/behavioral intervention that may involve a medical problem, it is important that the patient first be evaluated medically, as Jake was. Furthermore, environmental interventions included the use of dietary changes as well as changing the child's behavior and the parents' response to those behaviors.

CRITICAL ISSUES to remember

1. Physical, cognitive, and emotional growth during childhood and adolescence affect the development and expression of psychological disorders. It is necessary to understand behavior within the context of normal development rather than immediately assuming that it is abnormal. As children mature and achieve developmental milestones, behavior once considered appropriate may become symptomatic of a behavioral or an emotional disorder.

2. A number of behavioral and emotional disorders emerge during infancy and childhood and are more common among children and adolescents than adults. These include mental retardation, learning disorders, pervasive developmental disorders, disruptive behavior disorders and disorders of eating, sleeping, and elimination.

3. Both biological and environmental factors may contribute to the etiology of disorders of childhood and adolescence. A substantial number of biological disorders and conditions contribute to the development of mental retardation. Similarly, a number of genetic variations appear relevant to the onset of autism spectrum disorders. In the case of other disorders, biological, psychological, and/or environmental factors are equally important. Furthermore, these factors operate in a complex fashion. Not all children with a particular disorder have the same *type* of disorder, and in many instances the symptoms are not the same for all children. Therefore, multiple and different factors may eventually lead to the development of the same disorder.

4. For the disorders in this chapter, pharmacological interventions appear to be most efficacious for treating the core symptoms of ADHD. For other disorders, medication may control some of the associated features (e.g., aggression), but it is not effective for the core symptoms and is not considered to be useful as a single treatment.

5. For many disorders (e.g., ADHD, conduct, ODD), the primary psychological intervention is behavioral in nature and is directed at the parents, rather than at the child with the disorder. Although behavioral theories do not necessarily propose that abnormal parent-child interactions are the cause of the psychological distress, they may be a maintaining factor and therefore must be targeted in a comprehensive treatment program. Furthermore, even when the child is the focus of treatment, parents play an important role in helping their child carry out the treatment program.

6. Teaching parents the basic skills necessary to effectively manage their children's behavior is a highly efficacious treatment and is the treatment of choice for many of the disorders in this chapter. In the case of conduct disorder or ADHD, comprehensive psychosocial interventions such as summer treatment programs or Multisystemic Therapy offer great promise, not only in decreasing core symptoms but in improving overall functioning.

TEST yourself

For more review plus practice tests, flashcards, and Speaking Out: DSM in Context videos, log onto www.MyPsychLab.com

1. Micha is 13 years old. She has a heart defect, very poor eye-hand coordination, and she cannot dress herself. She speaks in simple sentences and can follow only simple instructions, but she is good-tempered and friendly. Micha's IQ is 55. In addition to her intellectual deficit, Micha also has
   a. functional deficits
   b. social deficits
   c. attentional deficits
   d. emotional deficits

2. Down syndrome is caused by
   a. plaques and neurofibrillary tangles
   b. the absence of an essential enzyme
   c. the presence of an extra chromosome
   d. a break in a specific chromosome

3. The rate of Down syndrome as a proportion of live births increases with
   a. alcohol abuse   c. malnutrition
   b. the mother's age   d. smoking

4. A form of mild retardation resulting from both biological and environmental factors associated with psychosocial disadvantage is called
   a. Lesch-Nyhan syndrome
   b. environmental deprivation syndrome
   c. FAS
   d. cultural-familial retardation

5. Two behavioral procedures that allow children with mental retardation to learn simple tasks are
   a. shaping and chaining
   b. affirmation and role playing
   c. psychoeducation and questioning
   d. covert sensitization and modeling

6. Learning disorders are probably the result of
   a. an inability to digest milk products
   b. brain trauma during birth or infancy
   c. biological toxins that affect brain functioning
   d. the inability of several brain areas to work together

7. The major difference between autistic disorder and Asperger's disorder is that in Asperger's there are no
   a. restricted and stereotyped behaviors and activities
   b. difficulties with eye contact
   c. impairments in social interaction
   d. deficits in communication

8. The recent increased prevalence of autism spectrum disorders may be due to
   a. increases in the incidence of maternal exposure to toxic chemicals
   b. the increased number of required childhood vaccines
   c. changes in diagnostic criteria, special education policies, and the availability of diagnostic services
   d. the availability of insurance coverage for expensive treatment, which justifies giving this diagnosis

9. One indication of the neurodevelopmental basis of autistic disorder is
   a. excess activation in several parts of the brain
   b. excessive crying and fussing in infancy
   c. unusually fast head and brain growth in infancy
   d. significant retardation evident shortly after birth

10. The treatment approach that uses shaping and positive reinforcement to improve social, communicative, and behavioral skills by intensively shaping and rewarding specific behaviors used to treat autism disorders is called
    a. applied behavior analysis
    b. cognitive-behavior therapy
    c. sensory integration therapy
    d. chelation therapy

11. Ted has been diagnosed with ADHD. Which behavior is not likely to be a problem for him?
    a. inattention
    b. hyperactivity
    c. impulsivity
    d. isolation

12. Which of the following reasons explains why ADHD is most commonly diagnosed in early elementary school?
    a. children develop the disorder around age 7
    b. many symptoms are developmentally appropriate in younger children
    c. children cannot complete the complicated diagnostic assessments until they can read
    d. it is necessary to observe the child's behavior in a school setting to make a definitive diagnosis

13. Adolescents with ADHD have more car accidents. This is most likely due to
    a. inattentiveness and poor motor coordination
    b. co-occurring substance abuse problems
    c. medications used to treat the condition
    d. sleep deprivation

14. Stimulant medications such as Ritalin work to reduce the core symptoms of ADHD by
    a. stimulating the cerebral cortex to create new neural pathways
    b. stimulating the "learning center" of the brain
    c. enhancing the neurotransmission of dopamine and norepinephrine
    d. enhancing the release of serotonin and GABA

15. Joey has a long history with local law enforcement officers. He's been picked up several times for vandalism. His latest arrest is for deliberately setting fire to his stepfather's storage unit. Joey has also been arrested in the past for putting a cat in a dryer. The most likely diagnosis he would receive for his behavior might be
    a. ADHD
    b. conduct disorder
    c. autism spectrum disorder
    d. oppositional defiant disorder

16. Kaylee is a sweet-tempered 5-year-old who once had such a severe temper tantrum that she broke her finger when she punched a wall. The emergency room physician diagnosed Kaylee with oppositional defiant disorder. This may be an inappropriate diagnosis because
    a. the diagnosis requires a repeated pattern of negative and defiant behaviors
    b. she is older than the typical patient diagnosed with ODD
    c. temper tantrums are a symptom of ADHD
    d. ODD is a diagnosis primarily given to adolescent males

17. Unlike boys with conduct disorder, girls with conduct disorder engage in more
    a. retail theft
    b. hair-pulling fights
    c. relational aggression
    d. cruelty to animals

18. Steve is 9 years old and has been diagnosed with a pervasive developmental disability. He has been observed eating dirt and tree leaves. Steve's behavior is known as
    a. enuresis
    b. delusional behavior
    c. rumination
    d. pica

19. Parasomnias are unwanted events that happen during sleep. These events can occur
    a. several nights in a row, followed by quiet periods of up to several weeks
    b. at predictable times during the sleep cycle
    c. with physical symptoms such as rapid heartbeat and breathing
    d. all of the above

20. Kim was toilet trained by the time she was 3 years old. Now, at age 6, she is wetting the bed three nights per week. Kim has
    a. primary enuresis
    b. secondary enuresis
    c. primary encopresis
    d. secondary encopresis

Answers:: 1 a, 2 c, 3 b, 4 d, 5 a, 6 d, 7 d, 8 c, 9 c, 10 a, 11 d, 12 b, 13 a, 14 c, 15 b, 16 a, 17 c, 18 d, 19 d, 20 b.

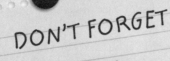

CHAPTER objectives

At the end of this chapter, you should be able to:

1 Recognize geropsychology as an emerging area of psychological research and practice.

2 Understand the ways in which aging may impact the expression and treatment of psychological symptoms and disorders in older adults.

3 Recognize the unique symptoms and issues that affect diagnosis and treatment of depression, anxiety, substance abuse, and psychosis in older adults.

4 Distinguish between dementia and delirium, two cognitive disorders that are common among older adults.

5 Understand the etiological factors affecting psychological and cognitive disorders of later life.

6 Identify empirically supported treatments for psychological and cognitive disorders among older adults.

aging and cognitive disorders

Ernest is a 73-year-old African American male who was the pastor of a small, rural church for 30 years before he retired 10 years ago. Ernest married for the first time when he was 25 years old and had three children. His wife left their family, however, when the children were 7, 5, and 4 years old. Ernest raised the children on his own, with help from his sister, who lived nearby. At age 60, when he was nearing retirement, he married a woman who was 10 years younger. He and his new wife developed an active retirement life filled with traveling, visiting relatives and friends, and playing bridge. About four years ago, however, Ernest began to have memory problems. He regularly lost his keys and glasses, and he began to rely more on lists when he went about his daily chores and errands. Over time, he became more confused, and he had trouble keeping his lists organized. He began to have difficulty finding the right words to express his thoughts, and his wife noticed that he often re-peated himself, telling her the same things several times a day. Ernest had always been very quick with numbers and calculations, but he began to have trouble keeping his mind focused on balancing his checkbook. He made calculation errors and couldn't remember where to record various pieces of financial information. He also got more and more confused as he continued to play bridge with his wife and friends. As Ernest developed more serious cognitive limitations, he started to feel anxious and depressed. He had always been a cheerful man who was full of life. But over the years, he started to withdraw from social engagements at church and in the community because he was worried that others would notice his problems in thinking. He also felt less interested in activities that he used to enjoy. His wife was quite worried about him and how she would be able to continue to care for him if he got more confused.

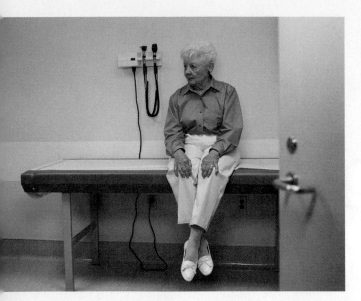

The elderly population is growing rapidly, but the number of health professionals available who specialize in geriatric care lags far behind.

geropsychology a subdiscipline of psychology that addresses issues of aging, including normal development, individual differences, and psychological problems unique to older persons

Symptoms and Disorders of Aging

Like Ernest, many older adults experience cognitive decline and psychological symptoms as they age. However, despite what many people believe, problems like Ernest's are not a normal part of aging. As we shall see in this chapter, the experience and expression of psychological symptoms may be different in older than in younger adults, in part because of the physical, cognitive, and social changes that accompany aging. Understanding the issues that are unique to aging provides an important context for helping us to identify and treat problems that arise for older people.

GEROPSYCHOLOGY AS A UNIQUE FIELD

The population of older adults in the United States is growing rapidly (see Figure 13.1). As the baby boom generation (those born between 1945 and 1964) approaches retirement, this trend will accelerate. Census projections indicate that there will be more than 50 million adults age 65 or older in the United States by 2010 (www.census.gov). This represents more than a 20% increase in the population of older people since 2000. By 2030, 20% of the U.S. population will be in this age group. With so many older adults in our society, we need to better understand the issues that confront older people. As we age, changes occur in our physical functioning (more medical problems, decreased sensory capacity), social functioning (retirement, reduced social networks as friends and family face health challenges), and cognitive abilities (changes in attention, learning, and memory). All of these are important factors that provide a unique sociocultural context by which to understand abnormal behavior in older adults.

Geropsychology is a subdiscipline of psychology that addresses issues of aging, with particular attention to patterns of normal development, individual differences, and psychological problems that are unique to older persons (usually considered age 65 or older). It has long been recognized that childhood is a developmental stage with particular challenges and that there are disorders specific to childhood and unique ways that children experience and express psychological symptoms. Geropsychology expands this developmental approach to include the challenges and psychological symptoms faced by older adults, such as physical changes, lifestyle shifts, and role changes.

The field of geropsychology is expanding rapidly, with increasing numbers of professional organizations and training programs (Qualls et al., 2005) that focus on

FIGURE 13.1

The Aging Population of the United States

The population of older adults in the United States is growing rapidly. The steep rise starting around 2015 reflects the aging of the baby boom generation.

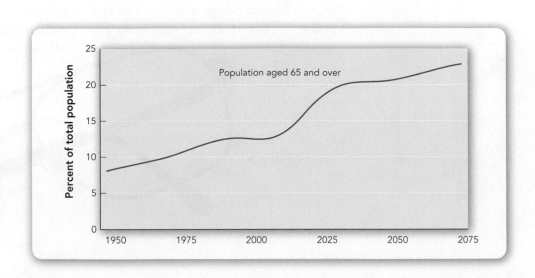

providing services to meet the needs of older people. Research efforts are also increasing as we strive to understand patterns of typical late-life development, unique problems experienced by older adults, and strategies for improving their quality of life. Nevertheless, there are still tremendous gaps in our knowledge of psychological symptoms and disorders among older people and in our ability to identify and treat them. Furthermore, the number of researchers, educators, and health care professionals with specialized training and expertise in geriatrics is insufficient to meet the needs of this growing segment of our society. In keeping with the developmental focus of this book, we hope to identify some of the unique ways in which psychological problems affect people in the later decades of life.

SUCCESSFUL AGING

Leonard is the picture of successful aging. He is 89, lives alone in the same house where he has lived for the last 40 years, and periodically drives almost 80 miles to visit his son.

Leonard retired many years ago, but he continues to spend time in his home office every day. He checks the Internet to keep up with current events, maintains e-mail contact with friends and college classmates, and writes a regular column for his university's alumni magazine. Leonard is also active in a number of civic organizations, takes a nap every day, and enjoys a cocktail before dinner. When his wife died two years ago, Leonard was sad, but he began to spend more time with friends and neighbors, inviting them to his home for afternoon visits. Over time, his home became a center for neighborhood socializing. The neighbors listen to his stories about life during World War II, enjoying his sense of humor and positive attitude. Leonard also continues to take a short walk each evening. Although he can't go very far now that his hip hurts, he always has a smile for any neighbor who is passing by. Leonard's optimism about life is infectious; his neighbors often remark that he is more energetic and positive than they are, although many are 50 years younger. Leonard has some "rules" for aging well. A few of these include: (1) use your brain every day, (2) stay active, and (3) socialize with younger people and entertain younger ideas.

Although Leonard is not a psychologist, his philosophy and lifestyle reflect much of what is known about *successful aging.* Approximately one-third of older adults are judged to be aging successfully (Depp & Jeste, 2006), but there is as yet no consistent definition of this term. In fact, Depp and Jeste identified 29 different definitions of successful aging in 28 studies! Common themes across these definitions include perceived good health and an active lifestyle, continued independence in functioning, lack of disability, absence of cognitive impairment (which may be impacted by higher education and increased mental activity), and positive social relationships (Blazer, 2006; Phelan & Larson, 2002). Theories of positive aging also focus on a theoretical model known as *selective optimization and compensation* (Baltes & Baltes, 1990; Schultz & Heckhausen, 1996), meaning that people age more successfully when they modify their goals and choices to make best use of their personal characteristics. These adjustments often require compensating for age-related limitations that reduce one's ability to reach previously valued goals.

Max is an aging fisherman who used to be out on a boat every weekend. He can't fish any longer, but he can spend time reading magazines about fishing, watching television shows about fishing, and trading old fishing stories with his buddies at the local coffee shop.

Leonard also made choices that make the most of his ability to engage in rewarding activities and optimize his social, mental, and physical functioning.

About one-third of older adults continue to experience good health and active lives in their later years. Successful aging is encouraged by positive social relationships and continuing mental activity.

PSYCHOLOGICAL SYMPTOMS AND DISORDERS AMONG OLDER PEOPLE

In the United States, 20 to 30% of older adults have a psychological disorder (American Association of Geriatric Psychiatry, 2006; Jeste et al., 1999; Lyness et al., 1999). Even more have significant problems that do not meet the diagnostic criteria for a psychological disorder but nonetheless create unnecessary distress, reduce functional ability, and result in poorer quality of life. The prevalence of psychological disorders is even higher among homebound elderly (Bruce & McNamara, 1992), patients with chronic medical illness (Kunik et al., 2005), and people who live in nursing homes (Gurland, 2004; Junginger et al., 1993). The personal and societal costs associated with psychological symptoms in the elderly are high, and there are simply not enough appropriately trained professionals available to help (Bartels & Smyer 2002; Jeste et al., 1999).

Only about half of the older adults who report mental health problems receive treatment. Many older people with psychological symptoms do not seek treatment because they fear that others will think they are "crazy," because they lack sufficient resources (money, ability to find a therapist), or because of logistic limitations (an inability to drive to the clinician's office). Those who do seek help typically go to general medical settings like their doctor's office instead of specialized mental health clinics. Unfortunately, many psychological symptoms and disorders go unrecognized in medical settings (Jeste et al., 1999). Even when problems are identified, treatment is often inadequate (Roundy et al., 2005). One reason for inadequate recognition and treatment is the limited time physicians now spend with patients during office visits, resulting in insufficient time for assessing and treating mental health problems. **Ageism**, however, is an equally serious issue. Many older adults and their doctors consider psychological distress to be a normal part of aging (Gallo et al., 1999) and therefore not something that requires treatment. Reactions like the following are common:

- *Of course you feel down. You were recently diagnosed with a serious heart condition. It is normal for you to feel less energetic.*

- *I, too, would feel anxious if I had been forced to retire and didn't have enough money to support my wife and myself into older age. Who wouldn't be anxious in this situation?*

- *Oh, yes, I understand your concerns about your memory—I lose things all the time!*

These comments ignore the fact that psychological symptoms and disorders are *not* a normal part of aging. Many emotional disorders experienced by older adults are treatable, and even when the progressive, neurobiological disorders associated with aging cannot be reversed (e.g., Alzheimer's disease, Parkinson's disease), quality of life can be improved.

It is commonly recognized that the symptoms of a disorder may be different for adults and children. Only now are clinicians and researchers beginning to understand how aging may also affect the expression of psychological symptoms. Older adults often report less negative mood and distress than younger adults (Goldberg et al., 2003; Lawton et al., 1993), although it is not entirely clear whether these differences reflect different experiences or simply different expressions of mood. In Chapter 4, for example, you learned that boys and girls differ in how much fear they *express*, not how much fear they *experience*. Similarly, older adults often focus more on physical symptoms than on psychological symptoms of distress, and this may be another reason why they seek treatment from primary care physicians rather than mental health clinicians.

ageism tendency to attribute a multitude of problems to advancing age

Eloise denied feeling anxious but reported that her back and neck muscles were tight all the time, so much so that they hurt. She wasn't able to sit comfortably for long periods anymore, and her stomach "acted up" frequently when stressful events occurred. She was hoping for some help to decrease her muscle pain and reduce her acid indigestion and occasional diarrhea.

Focusing on physical symptoms complicates the identification of psychological disorders in older people, particularly for primary care physicians, who are less experienced in this area. The diagnostic challenge is further complicated by increased medical problems as people age. Many medical diseases and treatments create symptoms that mimic psychological disorders. For example, symptoms of diabetes include weight loss and lethargy, which are also symptoms of depression. Even something as seemingly harmless as decongestants can cause nervousness, sleeplessness, and increased blood pressure or heart rate, which are also symptoms of anxiety. When older adults have both medical and psychological difficulties, recognizing psychological problems is a huge challenge.

Although psychological difficulties in older age are often thought to be mainly cognitive (e.g., dementia), many of the disorders that older people face are the same ones that affect younger people, such as depression, anxiety, and substance abuse (Gurland, 2004; Lyness et al., 1999). Accordingly, we will discuss these problems first in the chapter before we consider the very serious problem of dementia, which is not a normal part of aging. Within each category of difficulties experienced by older people, understanding normal age-related changes in physical, social, and cognitive functioning is necessary to provide a developmental context for evaluating these disorders. As with other age groups, *comorbidity* (multiple disorders occurring together) also occurs.

concept CHECK

- The field of geropsychology addresses normal development, individual differences, and psychological problems unique to aging.
- Psychological symptoms are not a normal part of aging.
- As many as 20 to 30% of older adults have a psychological disorder.
- Most older adults with psychological problems do not seek help from mental health specialists.
- Psychological problems are sometimes difficult to identify in older adults.

APPLICATION QUESTION What are some of the factors that influence the experience and expression of psychological problems in older adults?

Depression and Anxiety in Later Life

Aging is associated with various types of loss (e.g., death of a loved one, changes in job or financial status, deterioration in physical abilities) and uncertainty about the future (e.g., ability to retain independence, future changes in health status, death). Therefore, it should not be surprising that depression and anxiety disorders are among the most common psychological problems that older adults face. However, depression and anxiety are not a natural consequence of growing old. Only recently has research begun to address the nature, etiology, and treatment of these problems in older adults, blending theories and strategies derived from younger adults and emerging ideas that are unique to aging populations.

UNIPOLAR AND BIPOLAR DEPRESSION

Jean devoted her life to being a wife and mother. She raised five children and supported her husband through a very busy career. When Tom retired three years ago, Jean expected to spend the rest of her life traveling with him and visiting her children and grandchildren, who lived across the country. However, Tom died suddenly of a heart attack just 6 months after he retired. Jean felt lost. She had no one with whom to share her thoughts. Her friends, whose husbands were still living, called less often. When she did go out with them, she felt like a "fifth wheel." She traveled alone to see her children, and that wasn't enjoyable either. Jean found herself feeling apathetic about life in general, but she didn't know why. Since Tom died, she had also developed a number of medical problems. Her heart pounded often, she felt full and bloated even when she ate small amounts of food, she was tired most of the time, and she lay awake much of the night, thinking about all sorts of things. Her family thought she ought to get more involved in the church, but she just didn't have the energy. Her daughter thought she was depressed, but Jean knew she wasn't crazy. She was just getting older and adjusting to life as a widow.

Most depressive disorders are diagnosed in older and younger adults using the same criteria. However, as Jean's case illustrates, older adults are often reluctant to acknowledge psychological symptoms, not wanting to be viewed as "crazy." Also, they often report symptoms differently than younger adults, and because symptoms of depression overlap with symptoms of common medical illnesses, current diagnostic categories may not be the most useful for older adults. In fact, depression among older people often includes cognitive difficulties such as problems with attention, speed of information processing, and **executive dysfunction** (difficulty planning, thinking abstractly, initiating and inhibiting actions, etc.). These symptoms can occur as part of depression even when dementia is not present (Kindermann et al., 2000; Lockwood et al., 2000). **Reversible dementia** or **pseudodementia** (see the section on Dementia later in this chapter) occurs when the full syndrome of dementia appears to be present but resolves after appropriate treatment for depression.

Medical disorders can also produce depressive disorders that are unique to older adults. For example, **vascular depression** is a mood disorder that occurs in the context of cerebrovascular disease (disease of the arteries that supply blood to the brain). Symptoms of vascular depression include increased difficulties with language (e.g., speaking fluently, naming objects), increased apathy and slowed movements, and less agitation and guilt than patients with other forms of depression (Alexopoulos, 2004). In a person who has Alzheimer's disease, depression is diagnosed when the symptoms are present for at least 2 weeks (Olin et al., 2002).

The possibility of suicide associated with depression is a particular concern for older persons. Americans over the age of 65 commit suicide at a rate twice that of younger adults (McIntosh et al., 1994). Older white men are at highest risk for completing suicide, although women attempt suicide more frequently (Alexopoulos, 2004). This pattern is consistent with the data for younger adults (Figure 13.2). Most older adults who commit suicide have seen their physician within a few months of their death (Frierson, 1991), suggesting that many suicides may be preventable. Risk factors for suicide in older people overlap with those for younger adults and include depression and anxiety, loneliness, financial problems, poor medical health, and reduced social support (Alexopoulos, 2004; Bartels et al., 2002).

Few adults develop mania or bipolar disorder after the age of 65. Many adults who do show initial signs of bipolar disorder in later life have a history of major depression. Similarly, older patients who have manic symptoms later in life may have had elements of the disorder earlier in life (Keck et al., 2002). When bipolar disorder occurs in older patients, the intervals between manic and depressive shifts are shorter, and the episode duration is longer relative to younger patients (Keck et al.,

executive dysfunction difficulty planning, thinking abstractly, initiating, and inhibiting actions

reversible dementia also known as **pseudodementia**, occurs when the full syndrome of dementia appears to be present but resolves after appropriate treatment for another disorder

vascular depression a mood disorder that occurs in the context of cerebrovascular disease

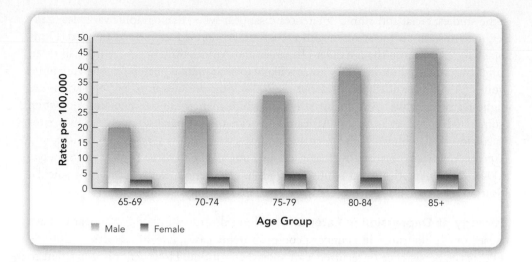

FIGURE 13.2
Suicide Rates Among Older Americans

Suicides are much more common among older men than women, and the rates increase with increasing age.

2002). After the age of 65, medical illnesses, especially stroke, and other medical causes, such as medications are more likely to be associated with the onset of bipolar disorder than the genetic factors proposed for younger adults (Van Gerpen, Johnson & Winstead, 1999; Weller & Weller, 1991).

Prevalence and Impact   In the general population, major depression and dysthymia affect approximately 1% and 4% of older adults, respectively (NIH consensus conference, 1992; Steffens et al., 2000). These percentages are lower than those found among younger adults, although up to an additional 15% of older people have depressive symptoms that fail to meet diagnostic criteria but still create significant distress and impairment (NIH consensus conference, 1992). Depressive disorders and symptoms are also more common when surveys are conducted in medical settings (Kunik et al., 2005; Lyness et al., 1999) and among older adults who are homebound (Bruce et al., 2002) or have cognitive impairment (Alexopoulos, 2004). In these populations, the prevalence of major depression is as high as 14%, and up to half of patients have clinically significant depressive symptoms.

Mood disorders and symptoms can affect daily functioning and even survival in older adults, much as they do in younger adults. Consider two older adults with the same medical condition, one of whom also has depression and the other does not. The patient with both a medical disorder and depression has an increased risk of death, and not simply because of the increased likelihood of suicide. Depression significantly affects the outcome of medical disease. People with depression and medical illness recover less well, use more health care services, and create greater costs for the health care system (Callahan et al., 1994; Luber et al., 2000). Late-life depression also decreases quality of life (Unutzer et al., 2000), increases physical disability, and reduces the ability of patients to care for themselves (Bruce et al., 1994; Steffens et al., 1999).

As noted earlier, few older adults suffer from bipolar disorder, with a prevalence of only 0.1% in one epidemiological sample (Robins & Regier, 1990, ECA). Mortality rates among older adults with bipolar disorder are elevated, and perhaps even higher than among older people with unipolar depression (Shulman et al., 1992), although the reason for the higher rate is not yet known.

Sex, Race, and Ethnicity   As is true of younger adults, depressive disorders among older people occur more often in women than in men (Gonzalez et al., 2001; Steffens et al., 2000). But in contrast to younger adults, depressive symptoms and disorders are more common among African American and Hispanic older adults, particularly those who are least acculturated in American society (Blazer et al., 1998; Gonzalez et al., 2001). In

life-span developmental diathesis-stress model   considers the role of biological predispositions, stressful life events, and personal protective factors in the etiology of depression

some studies, racial and ethnic differences disappear when demographic variables (gender, marital status, living status, health status) and economic factors are controlled (Dunlop et al., 2003). Even though older Hispanics and African Americans are more likely to suffer from mood disorders, they are less likely to seek mental health care than are older whites (Alvidrez et al., 2005; Blazer et al., 2000). Suicide rates in older populations are highest among white men, followed by nonwhite men, white women, and nonwhite women (McIntosh et al., 1994). African American and Hispanic adults have lower rates of suicide than whites. Rates of suicide among Asian adults (Japanese, Chinese, and Korean Americans) increase with age and are comparable to those of Whites (Sakauye, 2004). Asian American and white older adults also report elevated levels of suicidal ideation relative to African American older people (Bartels et al., 2002).

Etiology of Depression in Later Life   Mood disorders in late life appear to have causes much like those in younger people. In many cases, late-life depression simply reflects the persistence or recurrence of an earlier episode. However, it is important to identify the original age of onset for mood disorders (early versus late) because it may have treatment implications (McMahon, 2004). Older adults with *early-onset depression* (typically defined as onset before age 35 or 45) more often have a family history of depression, probably reflecting the genetic contributions discussed in Chapter 6 (Alexopoulos, 2004). In contrast, people with *late-onset depression* are more likely to have coexistent cognitive impairment and more evidence of brain abnormalities, suggesting the presence of brain deterioration (Alexopoulos, 2004). They more often have a family history of dementia as well (van Ojen et al., 1995). Late-onset depression seems to occur more often in the context of vascular, neurological, or other physical diseases that are associated with genetic causes, such as Parkinson's disease, cerebrovascular disease, and Alzheimer's disease. For those with late-onset depression, symptoms of mood disorders sometimes precede diagnosis of the medical condition by months or years (McMahon, 2004).

Researchers are examining the role of specific genetic factors in the emergence of late-life depression. Some studies have shown a correlation between a gene, the *apolipoprotein (APOE) e4 allele*, and late-life depression (Zubenko et al., 1996), although the finding has not always been replicated. We also need to remember that this correlation (between the gene and depression) may merely reflect an underlying and stronger association between *APOE4* and dementia (see "Dementia") (Plassman & Steffens, 2004). That is, the gene may be related to the onset of dementia, and the mood disorder may result from the dementia and not the effects of the gene.

Aging is associated with both personal and environmental challenges, and unique environmental stressors may influence the onset of depression among older adults. A number of stressors, for example, often accompany retirement and/or a loved one's death. These secondary effects include an increased sense of loss, decreased social status, and reduced income. Physical activity is beneficial for mild to moderate levels of depression, but older adults may face limitations in physical activity. However, older adults have the benefit of increased maturity and life experience, which may better equip them to handle challenging life events.

Biological and environmental factors likely interact to contribute to the onset of late-life depression. A **life-span developmental diathesis-stress model** considers the role of *biological predispositions* (biological variables that carry increased risk for depression such as genetics, medical disease, etc.), stressful life events (typically those that are unique to older people), and personal *protective factors* (e.g., maturity and previous life experiences) that reduce the potential negative impact of biological and environmental risk factors (Gatz, 2000). In this model, the impact of biological and personal protective factors increases with advancing age, while the impact of stressful events remains constant. (See Figure 13.3.)

With increasing age come increasing challenges for older adults—friends pass away and children move to distant cities, potentially creating an environment that can lead to loneliness and depression.

Psychological Theories Psychological theories of depression etiology also apply to older adults. Recall the aging fisherman who could no longer go out on a boat to fish but found alternative ways to enjoy his hobby? Without such alternatives, loss of pleasant activities and environmental reinforcement could lead to depression-related avoidance and withdrawal behaviors. Older adults also experience learned helplessness; they often feel a loss of control over their environments, and suffer from erroneous thinking that is common in depression. Look for etiological factors that may contribute to Walter's depression:

Walter (age 87) and his wife (age 85) recently moved to an assisted living facility. The responsibilities of keeping up their house had become too much for them. Cleaning the house, mowing the lawn, and doing small repairs were no longer easy chores. Running errands had even become difficult given the limitations in Walter's vision that resulted from eye disease. Although Walter and his wife hated to move from the house and neighborhood where they had lived for over 50 years, their children convinced them that moving into a smaller place where they would have day-to-day help was better. After the move, though, Walter never seemed to regain his strength. He began to feel tired most of the time, and his energy and interest in socializing decreased. He played cards with other residents occasionally, and he went out to lunch when his daughter came to visit. But he missed his old neighborhood and church friends. He was only able to attend church services occasionally, when someone came to get him, and he just didn't enjoy it the way he used to. He felt old and not very useful. His spirits perked up when his grandchildren come to see him, but they never stayed very long, and he had trouble hearing them because they talked too fast. Walter's wife became concerned when he started to lose weight and just didn't seem hungry most of the time. He also never slept very well any more, except when he took sleeping pills. He often felt that he was just waiting to die.

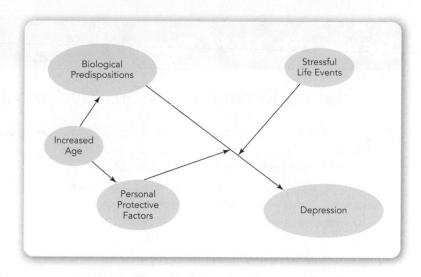

FIGURE 13.3

Life-span Diathesis-stress Model

This model suggests that advanced age increases the influence of biological variables (e.g., genetics, medical diseases) and personal protective factors (e.g., maturity, life experience) on stress. In this model, however, the impact of stressful life events remains constant across the life span.

Treatment of Depression in Older Patients Because depression can accompany so many medical diseases, treatment must begin with a physical evaluation to rule out any medical causes, such as thyroid abnormalities, anemia, or diabetes. Once a diagnosis of depression is established, treatment options include pharmacological and psychological interventions.

Medications used to treat depression in younger adults (see Chapter 6) are effective with older patients (Alexopoulos, 2004; Shanmugham et al., 2005). Approximately 60% of older adults with depression improve with pharmacological treatment, which is significantly higher than the 30% who respond to placebo (Schneider, 1996). Age-related changes in the body's response to medications increase older adults' sensitivity to drugs, both in terms of positive response and side effects. As a result, doses are typically increased more slowly and the dosage necessary for a positive response is lower than in younger adults. Electroconvulsive therapy (ECT) is used infrequently, but is valuable for patients who have such severe symptoms that they cannot wait for the medication to have an effect or for those who fail to respond to alternative treatments.

Lithium is used as a treatment for bipolar disorder, but doses for elderly patients are typically one-half to two-thirds of those used in younger patients (Alexopoulos, 2004). Because lithium can worsen cognitive impairment and create delirium (a syndrome described in more detail below), it must be used carefully (Young, 2005). ECT is also highly effective for mania, with up to 80% improvement reported (Alexopoulos, 2004).

Psychological treatments also are efficacious for late-life depression (Mackin & Arean, 2005). The greatest amount of empirical support exists for behavioral and

Research HOT Topic

Translating Research in Geropsychology to the "Real World"

Much is now known about the treatment of depression and other mental health problems among older adults based on controlled clinical trials conducted in academic clinical settings (medical school psychiatry clinics, university psychology clinics, etc.). Patients who participate in those studies, however, are often not representative of older adults in the "real world." They are often healthier, better educated, and mostly white, calling into question how the outcome of the study relates to more diverse groups of older adults. Furthermore, many older people never seek mental health services from specialized psychiatry, psychology, or other mental health settings. More often, they are treated by their primary care physicians, where depression, anxiety, or other psychological problems are often unrecognized. Still other older people are too fragile and unhealthy even to get to a medical clinic, and either receive no care or obtain home health care through a community-based agency, where again psychological problems can be overlooked. Even when depression or other mental health problems are recognized in these more nontraditional mental health settings, care is often inadequate or substandard relative to evidence-based standards. Current priorities for federal research funding, there-fore, are focused on developing strategies to test evidence-based practices in more real-world settings (e.g., primary care, community-based home health care) and to increase the accessibility of mental health services in the context of other ongoing care.

A number of large clinical trials have recently addressed these issues. Two particularly noteworthy studies, Project IMPACT (Improving Mood: Promoting Access for Collaborative Treatment) and Project PEARLS (Program to Encourage Active, Rewarding Lives for Seniors), show that evidence-based interventions are effective in community practice settings. (Ciechanowski et al., 2004; Unutzer et al., 2002). In Project IMPACT, problem-solving therapy and pharmacotherapy for depression, delivered by trained professionals, were effective for older adults in primary care, with no differences in outcomes for African Americans and Latinos (Arean et al., 2005). The PEARLS project established the effectiveness of home-based problem-solving therapy for dysthymia and minor depression, again delivered by trained professionals. Similar studies have examined the utility of evidence-based treatments for late-life anxiety in primary care (Stanley et al., 2009).

cognitive-behavioral treatments (CBT). CBT is consistently superior to wait list or placebo control conditions, and there is some evidence that it is better for older adults than alternative psychological approaches. A variation of CBT called problem-solving therapy is useful for older adults with dysthymia or minor depression, common conditions in older age groups (Mackin & Arean, 2005). Other psychological treatments that appear beneficial for late-life depression are interpersonal therapy and brief psychodynamic therapy (see Chapter 6). *Reminiscence therapy*, used more uniquely with older adults, focuses on patients' recall of significant past events and how they managed distress. Reminiscence therapy may reduce late-life depression, although effects are not as strong as for CBT and we do not know exactly how this treatment works (Gum & Arean, 2004).

ANXIETY

As with depression, the diagnostic criteria for anxiety disorders are consistent across the life span (see Chapter 4), but there are important differences in the nature of anxiety and worry among older adults. These differences include developmental/life-cycle issues, attitudes about mental health problems, *cohort differences* (differences that occur because people are born in different generations), and the presence of medical disorders that can complicate differential diagnosis.

With respect to life-span issues, worries reported by older people reflect the problems that arise in later stages of life. For example, older people tend to worry more about health and less about work relative to younger and middle-age adults. Older adults often worry about stressful life transitions (e.g., retirement, widowhood), added care-giving responsibilities (when spouses or aging parents require significant assistance), and economic and legal issues associated with reduced income, increased health care costs, and end-of-life planning (American Psychological Association, 2003). Other potentially stressful events include changes in physical health, vision, and hearing, sleep, continence, energy levels, memory, and increased disability (Brenes et al., 2005; Lenze et al., 2001). Anxiety can result from these physical changes or may contribute to worsening physical symptoms and lead to poorer physical health, sleep disruption, and memory problems.

Older adults use fewer psychological terms to describe anxiety (e.g., shame, guilt) (Kogan et al., 2000; Lawton et al., 1993) and prefer words such as "fret" or "concern" to describe worry or anxiety (Stanley & Novy, 2000) possibly because they are uncomfortable with more psychologically oriented terms. Older adults also emphasize physical symptoms (Lenze et al., 2005); this makes recognition of anxiety disorders particularly difficult when medical illnesses are present. Many medical problems have physical symptoms that are common in anxiety (e.g., shortness of breath, chest pain, muscle pain or stiffness, gastrointestinal distress), and many medications produce anxiety-related side effects. For example, some drugs for high blood pressure can create heart rate abnormalities, and bronchodilators that treat breathing disturbance can create nervousness, trembling, and increased heart rate.

Anxiety overlaps significantly with depression among people of all ages, but this overlap is even more common among older adults (Beekman et al., 2000; Lenze et al., 2000; van Balkom et al., 2000). In most cases where overlap exists, symptoms of anxiety are present before symptoms of depression emerge (Lenze et al., 2000; Schoevers et al., 2005; Wetherell et al., 2001), suggesting that early treatment of anxiety may prevent depression, at least in some cases.

Along with depressive disorders, anxiety and worry are common psychological symptoms among older people, who may have health problems, disabilities, caregiving responsibilities, reduced income, or other sources of concern.

Prevalence and Impact Although anxiety disorders receive less attention than depression, they are one of the most common and significant mental health problems affecting older adults. Approximately 3.5% (Bland et al., 1988) to 10.2% (Beekman et al., 1998) of older adults suffer from anxiety disorders. In many cases, their prevalence is twice as high as that of depression (Regier et al., 1988; Weissman et al., 1985). As with depression, anxiety is more common among homebound elderly (Bruce & McNamara, 1992) and those living in nursing homes (Junginger et al., 1993). The reported prevalence is also higher in medical settings (Kunik et al., 2005; Tolin et al., 2005).

Among the anxiety disorders, specific phobias and generalized anxiety disorder (GAD) are most common in late life (Beekman et al., 1998), although post-traumatic stress disorder also exists among older adults with histories of war trauma, experiences with natural disasters, or assault (Averill & Beck, 2000). Most research has focused on GAD, which occurs in approximately 7% of the general population (Beekman et al., 1998) and 11% of patients in medical clinics (Tolin et al., 2005). Clinically significant anxiety that does not meet diagnostic criteria is even more common (20–40%) (Brenes et al., 2005; Kunik et al., 2003; Mehta et al., 2003; Wittchen et al., 2002). Available figures may underestimate its true prevalence since anxiety can be difficult to recognize, particularly in medical settings (Stanley et al., 2001). GAD may be the most difficult anxiety disorder to diagnose because its physical symptoms (sleep disturbance, fatigue, restlessness, difficulty concentrating) overlap the most with symptoms of normal aging, medical conditions, and medications that are common in later life.

Anxiety in older adults is associated with less physical activity and poorer functioning, more negative perceptions of health, decreased life satisfaction, and more loneliness (Cully et al., 2006; De Beurs et al., 1999; Kim et al., 2000). Older adults with anxiety have more physical disabilities (Brenes et al., 2005; Lenze et al., 2001) and poorer quality of life (Wetherell et al., 2004). They also use more health care services (De Beurs et al., 1999; Stanley et al., 2001) and are more dependent on others to function (Naik et al., 2004). Older men with anxiety are at increased risk of death (Kawachi et al., 1994; van Hout et al., 2004). As in other age groups, anxiety disorders are associated with significant distress and impaired functioning.

Sex, Race, and Ethnicity   As with younger adults, anxiety disorders are more common among women (Beck & Averill, 2004), although women have longer life expectancies, and some studies have not considered this factor when determining prevalence. Furthermore, not all community data indicate that sex is a significant risk factor for anxiety in later life (Beekman et al., 1998). Thus, it is unclear whether the differences in its prevalence are accurate or merely reflect the greater number of women in the older population.

The prevalence of late-life anxiety disorders differs based on race and ethnicity, although many studies do not include sufficient numbers of ethnic minority patients to establish firm conclusions. Available data, however, suggest that GAD is more common among older African American women (3.7%), followed by non-African American women (2.7%), non-African American men (0.7%), and African American men (0.3%; Blazer et al., 1991). GAD also occurs frequently among older Puerto Rican medical patients (11%; Tolin et al., 2005), and anxiety disorders in this population are associated with more depression, higher levels of suicidality, poorer self-perceptions of health (e.g., a view of oneself as "sickly"), and increased use of health services (Diefenbach et al., 2004). Older African Americans with GAD report more somatic symptoms than whites (Kraus et al., 2005).

Gloria was a 58-year-old Puerto Rican woman who attended a Hispanic women's support group. During one meeting, she shared significant distress about her daughter, who was in a stormy dating relationship and moving away from family values in her behavior. Gloria was very upset with the way things were going. After the topic of group discussion changed, Gloria fell on the floor and began shaking violently, as if she were having a seizure. However, her face wasn't turning blue, she didn't lose bowel or bladder control, and she wasn't biting her tongue. The group leader was unable to console Gloria or decrease her symptoms. The ambulance was called to take Gloria to the ER.

Culture-bound syndromes (see Chapter 4) also occur among older adults. They may be more common among older people due to lower education, less assimilation to the majority culture, and higher rates of foreign-born adults (Sakauye, 2004). In one study, *ataque de nervios*, which Gloria experienced, was reported by 26% of older Puerto Rican primary care patients. *Ataques* in this sample were associated with both anxiety and depressive disorders, particularly GAD and major depression, and they were characterized by anger, anxiety, dissociation, yelling or screaming, losing control, and seeking medical attention (Tolin et al., 2006).

Etiology of Anxiety in Later Life   Among both community and clinical samples, the onset of GAD can be either early or later in life (Beck & Averill, 2004; Stanley, 2003). Many older adults report long-term or lifetime symptoms of anxiety, whereas others indicate a more recent onset. In the latter cases, stressful life events (financial stress, increased physical disability, loss of social support, etc.) may play a unique role (Ganzini et al., 1990). Some studies suggest no differences in clinical symptoms related to age of onset (Beck et al., 1996), but other data indicate more severe symptoms among patients with earlier onset and more serious functional limitations due to physical problems among those with later onset (Le Roux et al., 2005).

Certainly, the biological and psychological theories reviewed in Chapter 4 are relevant, particularly for older people who have suffered from anxiety since their younger years. Although little research has specifically addressed the etiology of anxiety in older adults, a recent large twin study demonstrated that approximately 25% of the variance in liability for GAD among older adults (ages 55 to 74) resulted from genetic factors (Mackintosh et al., 2006). Diathesis-stress hypotheses proposed for late-life depression are also relevant for anxiety for the same reason; biologically inherited vulnerability factors and stressful life experiences probably interact to create these disorders.

Biological factors in late-onset anxiety disorders require serious consideration because anxiety symptoms overlap with those of various medical diseases. Anxiety may be a psychological response to medical illness (Flint, 2004), a part of the medical picture, or a separate psychological syndrome. Consider chronic obstructive pulmonary disease (COPD), a common lung disease in later life with symptoms including shortness of breath and catastrophic thoughts about physical symptoms. These same symptoms are also characteristic of panic disorder. COPD-related symptoms may precipitate anxiety syndromes in chronically ill people who worry excessively about medical symptoms and associated difficulties.

Curtis had severe COPD that required oxygen therapy 24 hours a day. He was concerned about his medical condition whenever he went on an outing with his family. Even mild shortness of breath during an outing caused Curtis to feel panicky—thinking that he might not be able to breathe and that he might die. As he became more worried, his breathing worsened and he sometimes experienced dizziness, sweating, and shakiness. Doctors told Curtis and his family that not all of these symptoms would be expected based on his COPD and current treatments, but Curtis worried that the doctors might be missing something. He also began to feel concerned that he was slowing his family down when they were out, and he chose to stay home alone more often. As a result, Curtis felt depressed and even more anxious about going out.

Treatment of Anxiety in Older Patients As with depression, it is necessary to rule out physical illnesses that may be producing anxiety-like symptoms. If an anxiety disorder exists, treatments are similar to those used for younger people, with most research examining pharmacological and psychosocial (primarily cognitive behavioral) treatments.

Because older adults often seek help for mental health problems in a medical setting, most treatment for anxiety involves the use of medication. Among older adults, benzodiazepines are prescribed most frequently; they are given to as many as 43% of patients with persistent anxiety (Schuurmans et al., 2005). Although some data indicate that these medications are superior to placebo (Bresolin et al., 1988; Frattola et al., 1992; Koepke et al., 1982), benzodiazepines can create serious side effects for older adults, including memory problems and slowing of motor behaviors. These effects can lead to negative consequences such as decreased ability to drive safely, increased risk of hip fractures due to falls, and significant memory problems. As such, alternative medications are preferred.

Antidepressants, such as selective serotonin reuptake inhibitors (SSRIs), are effective for older adults with anxiety disorders (Katz et al., 2002; Lenze et al., 2009; Schuurmans et al., 2006). These medications have fewer side effects than benzodiazepines and are recommended as the first-line pharmacological treatment. Even antidepressants have side effects, however, and older patients often prefer psychosocial treatment over pharmacotherapy when they are given a choice (Gum et al., 2006; van Hout et al., 2004; Wetherell et al., 2004).

Cognitive-behavioral group therapy is effective for older adults with mood or anxiety disorders.

Most studies of psychological treatments have examined cognitive-behavior therapy (CBT), which is considered to be well suited for older patients because it is time-limited, directive, and collaborative (Zeiss & Steffens, 1996). CBT is efficacious for patients with GAD (Nordhus & Pallesen, 2003; Stanley et al., 2009) but fewer older adults respond positively to CBT compared with younger patients (Wetherell et al., 2005). Modifying the treatment (slowing the pace, using different learning strategies to teach skills, etc.) may be necessary for older patients. CBT also appears useful for other anxiety disorders (panic disorder, social phobia) (Barrowclough et al., 2001; Schuurmans et al., 2006; Thorp et al., 2009).

---

concept CHECK

- Approximately 1 to 4% of older adults meet the criteria for major depression and dysthymia; but up to 15% more have depressive symptoms that create significant distress.

- Older white men are at highest risk for completing suicide.

- Medication and psychological treatments are effective for depression and anxiety in older adults.

- Older adults often describe anxiety differently than younger adults, with fewer psychological terms and more emphasis on physical symptoms.

- The most prevalent anxiety disorders in older adults are GAD and specific phobias.

APPLICATION QUESTION Why do depression and anxiety so often remain undiagnosed and/or untreated in older adults? And why do you think that most older adults prefer therapy over medication for treating anxiety or depression?

Substance Abuse and Psychosis in Later Life

When most people think of older adults with psychological problems, they may not picture an older man who goes to bed drunk at night or a woman with paranoid delusions. Yet, older people suffer from substance abuse problems and from psychotic disorders just as some younger people do. As with depression and anxiety, less is known about these disorders among older people than among younger adults. Nevertheless, substance use and psychotic symptoms can affect the quality of life and functioning of older people, and research is beginning to address the unique nature, causes, and treatment of these problems.

SUBSTANCE ABUSE

Harold was a 72-year-old divorced man who always enjoyed social events. He could have a few drinks, smoke a few cigarettes, enjoy his friends, and wake up feeling fine the next day. Even as he got older, he could "hold his own" at a party. One night when he was driving home from a gathering, he swerved to miss a car that he thought was too close to the line and ran off the road. His car suffered some damage, and he hurt his back and neck. The doctor gave him some pain medication, which made things much easier. He was already taking a mild tranquilizer for his nerves—but that was from a different doctor. He was sure there would be nothing wrong with adding one pill a day. When he started to have more trouble sleeping because of the pain, he decided to take one extra pill—and sometimes added a beer. That made it even easier to relax. Before long, Harold couldn't get to sleep without the tranquilizer, a double dose of pain medication, and a beer.

Alcohol, prescription medications, and tobacco are the substances most commonly abused by older adults.

Alcohol and other substance abuse disorders are an underappreciated problem for older adults. Overuse of alcohol, misuse of prescription medications (e.g., benzodiazepines, sedatives, narcotic painkillers), and tobacco abuse are the most common problems (Atkinson, 2004). Although the diagnostic criteria are the same as for younger adults (see Chapter 9), the symptoms are not always consistent. Among older people, alcohol abuse is less often associated with antisocial behavior, legal problems, unemployment, and lower socioeconomic status than among younger adults. Instead, problematic substance use in older adults may be recognized only as they grow increasingly dependent on others (who then have more opportunity to observe patterns of use) and/or as substance use affects medical illnesses and their treatment (Blazer, 2004) or patient safety (car accidents, falls, etc.).

The National Institute on Alcohol Abuse and Alcoholism (NIAAA) recommends that adults age 65 and over have no more than 1 drink per day, or 7 drinks per week, with no more than 4 drinks in any 1 day (Oslin, 2004). However, as with younger adults, alcohol abuse in late life is defined not simply by the number of drinks but by use that has adverse consequences (medical, social, or psychological) and that negatively impacts functioning. Determining adverse consequences may be challenging, as older adults may have fewer obligations outside the home and fewer social contacts.

Bill reported drinking five glasses of wine each evening, but he drank at home and did not drive. He also no longer had to get up early in the morning to get to work. As such, he denied any problems due to alcohol use.

Is Bill abusing alcohol?

Similarly, overuse of prescription drugs may develop gradually and go unrecognized. Patients may be prescribed medications by multiple physicians, who are unaware of other medications a patient may be taking. Many older adults tend to take less medication than they are prescribed. However, patients who are more passive and compliant may take multiple medications without questioning their potential overlap (Blazer, 2004). Over-the-counter medications can complicate drug interactions even further. In many cases, prescription abuse among older adults is noticed only when signs of toxicity or withdrawal occur.

Prevalence and Impact   Tobacco is the most commonly abused substance in older adults, even though the prevalence of tobacco dependence is lower than among younger people. Nevertheless, over 17.1 million adults over the age of 50 reported smoking within the previous month (National Survey on Drug Use and Health:

Substance use among older adults: update, 2006). The serious negative health consequences of smoking are well known (cancer, heart disease, COPD, osteoporosis, etc.), and tobacco use disorders account for more disability and mortality among older adults than all other substance use disorders combined (Atkinson, 2004).

In the United States, prevalence estimates for alcohol abuse and dependence among older adults range from 1.9 to 4.6% for men and 0.1 to 0.7% for women (Atkinson, 2004; Myers et al., 1984; Grant et al., 2004). These estimates are lower than among younger adults, although many cases go unrecognized in older patients. The prevalence is also likely to rise as baby boomers age (Patterson & Jeste, 1999). Current cohorts of older adults were raised at a time when temperance was highly valued (Blazer, 2004). In fact, 50% to 60% of older adults report abstinence (Oslin, 2004). Younger and middle-aged adults, however, grew up with easier availability and wider use of alcohol and other substances. Whether the prevalence of abuse among older populations will be higher as younger adults reach older adulthood is not yet known.

Problematic or risky drinking (excessive alcohol use that may not meet diagnostic criteria for substance abuse) occurs more frequently than alcohol abuse, perhaps affecting as many as 15% of men and 12% of women (Blazer, 2004). Approximately one-third of older adults with alcohol use problems develop the disorder in later life, but many of these individuals may have been risky drinkers in their earlier years. When the disorder begins later in life, symptoms are typically milder and more circumscribed, and less family history is reported. Late onset occurs more often among women (Atkinson, 2004).

Admitted drug abuse is rare among older adults, with prevalence estimates near 0% (Atkinson, 2004). However, older people take 25% of the medications consumed in the United States (Blazer, 2004) and are particularly likely to be prescribed benzodiazepines. Up to 15% of older people at any one time have such a prescription (Atkinson, 2004). Although there is little misuse, physical and psychological dependence can result from long-term use (4 to 12 months). When these drugs are used for chronic insomnia, tolerance may be particularly problematic, although most surveys of substance use do not consider this type of dependence.

Despite low rates of abuse, alcohol and other substances can have significant detrimental effects. Of particular concern are age-related physical changes (decreased lean body mass and total body water related to total fat, increased central nervous system sensitivity, etc.) that decrease the body's ability to *metabolize* (break down) drugs. This age-related decline increases the potential for side effects and toxicity from alcohol and other substances. The same amount of alcohol, for example, produces higher blood alcohol levels and more impaired performance in older adults than it does in younger people (Atkinson, 2004). Therefore, continuing to drink the same amount of alcohol can lead to increased problems of abuse as a person ages. Excessive alcohol use can result in falls and other accidents, decreased sexual interest and impotence, medical problems, and increased risk of delirium, dementia, dehydration, and gait problems (Oslin, 2004). In addition, abuse increases the risk of problematic drug interactions (Oslin, 2004) and can interfere with the treatment of chronic medical problems, such as hypertension and diabetes.

Sex, Race, and Ethnicity   Older men use alcohol at twice the rate of women, and they are up to six times more likely to be problem drinkers. These differences are consistent across various ethnic and racial groups (Atkinson, 2004). Illicit drug use is more common in older men, but women use more prescription medication for nonmedical reasons (National Survey on Drug Use and Health: Substance use among older adults: 2002 and 2003 update, 2006).

There are no consistent differences in substance abuse based on ethnicity. Some data suggest that the prevalence of alcohol use disorders is equal across ethnic groups

(Myers et al., 1984), but other studies report a higher prevalence of disorders and use among whites compared with African Americans (Ruchlin, 1997) or Hispanics (National Survey on Drug Use and Health: 2002 & 2003 update, 2006). Drinking is uncommon among older Chinese Americans (Kirchner et al., 2007). Non-Hispanic African Americans (23%) smoke more cigarettes than non-Hispanic whites and Hispanics (National Survey on Drug Use and Health: Substance use among older adults: update, 2006).

Etiology   Theories regarding the development of alcohol and substance use disorders in younger adults also apply to older patients, particularly when the disorder starts early in life. Across the life span, some people have a steady use pattern, whereas others use alcohol and substances more progressively or variably. When the onset of abuse occurs later in life, there is less evidence that genetic factors are operative, but there is often a personal history of habitual use and/or risky drinking (Atkinson, 2004; Blazer, 2004). Vulnerability to abuse also increases with medical frailty and the need for multiple medications. Likewise, benzodiazepine overuse increases when patients have a history of alcohol abuse or dependence.

Treatment of Substance Abuse   Most of the research on treating substance abuse in older adults focuses on risky or problematic drinking (Oslin, 2004). Treatment is aimed at both prevention and early intervention. *Brief alcohol counseling (BAC)* may reduce at-risk drinking and prevent more extensive alcohol-related difficulties (U.S. Preventive Services Task Force, 2004). BAC typically provides family support and education, including direct feedback about problematic drinking and specific advice about reducing alcohol use. *Behavioral self-control procedures* (e.g., keeping a drinking diary, behavioral contracting) are also sometimes used. In primary care settings, BAC (using either one or four brief patient contacts) has had positive results for at-risk drinking in older adults (Fleming et al., 1999; Oslin, 2005a).

For older adults with diagnosed alcohol or substance abuse rather than risky drinking, treatment outcomes are comparable across age groups when older and younger adults are treated together (Atkinson & Msra, 2002). Older patients, however, tend to be more adherent to treatment recommendations (Oslin et al., 2002) and have better outcomes when treatment is age-specific (Kashner et al., 1992). Age-specific treatment may foster better peer relationships and longer retention in treatment, which may enhance treatment outcomes (Atkinson, 2004).

Medications such as naltrexone (see Chapter 9) are safe and beneficial for the treatment of late-life alcohol abuse (Oslin et al., 1997). Another drug, disulfiram (Antabuse), is commonly used to prevent drinking in younger adults. However, this drug can be dangerous for older patients if they drink while taking the medication (Atkinson, 2004). Antidepressant medication can be useful for reducing drinking if patients experience depression along with alcohol abuse.

Benzodiazepine dependence is usually treated by gradual discontinuation of the drug. However, the outcome is poor if the drug has been used for a long time. When treatment is successful, cognitive functioning improves and anxiety, depression, and insomnia symptoms are reduced. Some symptoms may remain, and older adults are at increased risk for return usage (Atkinson, 2004). Finally, smoking cessation treatments that are efficacious for younger adults (e.g., brief interventions in primary care, transdermal nicotine patch therapy) also are efficacious for older patients (Atkinson, 2004).

PSYCHOSIS

Older adults, like those who are younger, can experience some of the most severe psychological disorders, the psychoses. In many cases, the diagnostic categories used to describe these disorders are the same for older and younger adults (see Chapter 10).

Schizophrenia in older adults is usually a continuation of a disease process that began at an earlier age. It is far less likely, but not impossible, for schizophrenia to begin at older ages.

We focus here on different characterizations of schizophrenia that are used to describe subgroups of older patients and on psychotic symptoms that arise in the context of Alzheimer's disease and other forms of dementia.

In 80% of older adults with schizophrenia, the onset occurs in young adulthood and continues into older age (Jeste et al., 2004a). For 60% of these adults, the disorder is relatively stable over their lifetimes. Another 20% experience worsening of symptoms, and 20%, such as John Nash (see Chapter 10), show symptom improvement and even remission in later life. Generally, the symptoms are the same for older and younger adults, with one exception. As adults with schizophrenia age, cognitive performance deteriorates, but the rate of decline is no different than among adults without schizophrenia (Eyler et al., 2000).

When the disorder begins late in life, there is a unique pattern of related symptoms (Howard et al., 2000). **Late-onset schizophrenia** first appears after age 40. Many characteristic risk factors (family history, genetic risk, and childhood maladjustment) are similar to earlier onset (Jeste et al., 2004a), but people with late-life schizophrenia have a higher prevalence of the paranoid subtype and more auditory hallucinations. They also have fewer negative symptoms and less impaired cognitive skills (e.g., learning, ability to abstract, and flexibility in thinking). When the disorder begins later in life, patients report higher premorbid functioning (better functioning before the disorder started) and more successful occupational and marital histories (Jeste et al., 2004a).

Very-late-onset schizophrenia-like psychosis is a heterogeneous category that develops after age 65. In the very-late-onset subgroup, psychotic symptoms follow a stroke, tumor, or other *neurodegenerative* change. Because these symptoms occur after a period of normal neurobiological development, very-late-onset schizophrenia differs from all other forms of schizophrenia, which are considered *neurodevelopmental* (e.g., Jeste et al., 2004b, see Chapter 10). Very-late-onset schizophrenia-like psychosis is associated with less genetic susceptibility, less evidence of childhood maladjustment, and fewer negative symptoms (Jeste et al., 2004a).

Approximately 30 to 50% of patients with Alzheimer's disease develop psychotic symptoms (Jeste & Finkel, 2000), usually 3 to 4 years after the Alzheimer's diagnosis. The psychotic symptoms are very different from those in late-life schizophrenia (Jeste & Finkel, 2000). In psychosis that occurs with Alzheimer's disease, patients more often report simple and concrete delusions.

Betty repeatedly told her daughter that the man across the hall in her assisted living community was stealing from her. She was certain that he came into her room when she was sleeping and took her things.

Misidentification of a caregiver also is common.

Grace regularly referred to her daughter, with whom she lived, as "that woman who lives here and cleans the house."

Auditory hallucinations are rare, but visual hallucinations are more common.

When she was awake in the middle of the night, Hazel frequently looked out her window and saw fires burning and children dying, but no one would come to help.

A past history of psychosis is rare in patients who develop psychotic symptoms during the course of dementia, and these symptoms often remit during later stages. Compared with dementia patients without psychosis, patients with both disorders show increased aggressive behavior, wandering, agitation, family problems, and lack of self-care (Jeste et al., 2004b).

late-onset schizophrenia   schizophrenia that first appears after age 40

very-late-onset schizophrenia-like psychosis   a schizophrenic-like disorder, but with symptoms that do not include deterioration in social and personal functioning

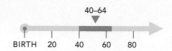

Prevalence and Impact   Schizophrenia occurs in 0.6% of people age 45 to 64 and in 0.1 to 0.5% of people age 65 and older (Jeste et al., 2004a, 2004b). Up to 29% of patients with schizophrenia report onset after age 40, and up to 12% report onset of symptoms after age 60 (Jeste et al., 2004a). Psychotic symptoms are more common among patients who are hospitalized or living in nursing homes. Schizophrenia in later life is tremendously debilitating, with significant impact on functioning, quality of life, health care use and costs, and mortality (Van Critters et al., 2005). Poorer functioning is associated with worse cognitive performance, less education, and more severe negative symptoms (Evans et al., 2003).

Sex, Race, and Ethnicity   Late-onset schizophrenia is more common among women, but begins at an earlier age for men (Jeste et al., 2004b). Neuroendocrine changes, greater longevity of women, and differential psychosocial stressors may explain these sex-related differences. Estrogen, for example, may serve as an *endogenous antipsychotic* (a naturally occurring substance that functions in the same way as an antipsychotic medication). In this instance, until menopause, estrogen may prevent psychotic symptoms in women who are biologically at risk for schizophrenia (Seeman, 1996).

As noted in Chapter 10, the symptoms of psychosis and schizophrenia are common across racial and ethnic groups of younger adults, although the higher prevalence of schizophrenia diagnoses among African Americans is well documented. Likewise, psychosis and inaccurate diagnoses of schizophrenia are more common among African American older adults (Faison & Armstrong, 2003). Contributing factors include clinician bias, lack of culturally appropriate assessment instruments, and misinterpretation of psychotic symptoms.

Spirituality and witchcraft are often used to explain these unusual symptoms among African American, Hispanic, and Native American populations (Sakauye, 2004). Hallucinations with religious content actually may represent normal religious experience in some cultures (Faison & Armstrong, 2003), and thoughts that might be classified as paranoid for some patients actually may represent "healthy" or "normal" reactions to discrimination-related trauma or immigration experiences. Finally, herbal medications used in some cultures can cause psychotic symptoms when combined with some antidepressant or antipsychotic medications.

Etiology   Late-onset schizophrenia shares many possible etiological factors with schizophrenia that begins earlier in life. Genetic factors may play a role in 10 to 15% of patients with late-onset schizophrenia who have relatives with the disorder (Jeste et al., 2004b). Brain abnormalities are similar to those in patients with earlier onset, including enlarged ventricles, increased density of dopamine receptors, and reduced size of the superior temporal gyrus (see Chapter 10). People with late-onset schizophrenia have better premorbid social functioning than those who develop it earlier, but their social adjustment is poorer and they display more eccentric behavior (Jeste et al., 2004b).

Some etiological factors, such as hypothesized differences in hormonal changes and psychosocial stressors, may produce later onset in women. In addition, late-onset schizophrenia is associated with deficits in hearing and vision. Although the exact nature of this relation is not clear, symptoms may arise from inadequate correction of these impairments, such as not getting the appropriate glasses (Jeste et al., 2004b).

As noted earlier, very-late-onset schizophrenia-like psychosis is generally associated with neurological damage, such as a stroke or tumor. In these cases, there is no evidence of a direct genetic role, although both genetic and environmental factors may contribute to medical conditions, such as stroke, that then produce psychotic symptoms. When psychosis occurs in people with Alzheimer's disease, more severe cognitive

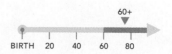

impairment is present (see "Dementia"). Patients with both disorders have greater degeneration in the brain, increased levels of norepinephrine, lower levels of serotonin, and other problems, such as tremors, muscle rigidity, and slowed movement, as in Parkinson's disease (Jeste, 2004a).

Treatment of Psychosis As with younger adults, the primary treatments for schizophrenia for older adults include the typical and atypical antipsychotic medications. However, treatment response may differ across age groups. Physical and emotional differences in cognitive and social functioning, age-related changes in metabolism and neurotransmitter receptor sensitivity, medical illnesses, and use of other medications may affect response to antipsychotic medication. Little research has examined the efficacy of antipsychotic medications specifically in older adults, but available data suggest modest improvements in a range of symptoms (Van Citters et al., 2005). The atypical antipsychotics produce better outcome and fewer side effects than do the typical antipsychotics. Because older adults show increased medication sensitivity and much higher rates of movement-related side effects (e.g., tardive dyskinesia, see Chapter 10), medication doses are typically 25% to 50% lower for them than for younger adults (Jeste et al., 2004b).

When psychosis occurs in the context of Alzheimer's disease or other dementias, antipsychotic medications produce modest effects, with atypical variants performing best (Schneider et al., 2006; Weintraub & Katz, 2005). As age increases, medication dosage decreases. Because psychotic symptoms frequently remit in the later stages of dementia, long-term use of medications is often not necessary (Jeste et al., 2004a). Patients with dementia are particularly sensitive to medication side effects, and even the atypical antipsychotic medications can produce sedation, fluctuation in blood pressure, and even increased risk of mortality (Schneider et al., 2005).

Only a small number of studies have tested the utility of psychological treatments for schizophrenia in older adults, but skills training and CBT in various combinations have positive effects (e.g., Granholm et al., 2005). These interventions help patients challenge their delusional beliefs and change behaviors related to medication noncompliance and health care management. Patients also learn social, communication, and life skills (e.g., organization and planning, financial management) aimed at improving overall functioning. Among patients with psychosis and dementia, family support and education are important, as well as caregiver coping skills training and behavioral management of problematic behaviors, such as aggression toward caregivers.

---

concept CHECK

- Alcohol, prescription medications, and tobacco are the most commonly used substances among older people, but in old age, problem drinking is more common than alcohol dependence.

- Brief alcohol counseling includes education about the effects of drinking, direct feedback about problematic drinking, and advice about reducing alcohol.

- Patients with late-onset schizophrenia have more frequent auditory hallucinations, fewer negative symptoms, less impaired cognitive skills, and better functioning earlier in life.

- Psychosis that occurs with dementia is uniquely defined by simple and concrete delusions, misidentification of a caregiver, and visual hallucinations.

- Atypical antipsychotic medications are associated with increased risk of mortality in patients with psychosis and dementia.

- Nonmedication treatment can be helpful for older adults with schizophrenia.

APPLICATION QUESTION Why are alcohol and substance abuse such serious problems for older adults even though prevalence is lower among them than among younger people?

Cognitive Disorders

Remember Ernest from the beginning of this chapter? The symptoms he experienced, which are common in dementia, are affecting growing numbers of older people and their families. Dementia and other cognitive disorders (disorders of thinking) affect older adults more than the other syndromes discussed in this chapter. As older people live longer and the population of older people continues to increase, more and more people will suffer from these cognitive dysfunctions. Some level of cognitive decline (e.g., in memory, attention, speed of processing information) is associated with normal aging. However, **delirium** and **dementia** are two disorders that represent deficits in cognitive abilities that significantly affect older people.

DELIRIUM

Elizabeth was an 86-year-old widow with a diagnosis of dementia; her children became concerned when she started to lose interest in her usual activities. She was less alert and attentive than usual, cried more often, had little appetite, and wasn't sleeping well. Her children worried that she was depressed. She also had many medical problems, including high blood pressure, chest pain, congestive heart failure, arthritis, cataracts, and "seizures" during which she seemed to go blank and mumbled. Her children believed that these problems were all controlled as well as possible with medications prescribed by her internist and various specialists. When the psychiatrist examined her, she was cooperative and pleasant, but she cried occasionally, even when she wasn't talking about anything sad. She was slow to respond, and her voice often trailed off and became inaudible. At these times, her words were jumbled. Her daughter reported that episodes like this were common and usually worse at night. The psychiatrist learned that Elizabeth was taking eight different medications. The rationale for each of these medications was reviewed, and the psychiatrist made a provisional diagnosis of medication-induced delirium. Over the next 2 months, six of the medications were discontinued, and many of Elizabeth's symptoms improved.

The primary feature of delirium (see the box "DSM-IV-TR: Delirium") is an alteration in consciousness that typically occurs in the context of a medical illness or after ingesting a substance (such as a drug). Altered states of consciousness can range from decreased wakefulness and stupor (*hypoactive type*) to severe insomnia and hyperarousal (*hyperactive type*). The onset of delirium is sudden, typically within hours or days, but it can be slow and progressive among older adults (Raskind et al., 2004). Symptoms of delirium can persist for months in older patients (Levkoff et al., 1992), in contrast to young adults, where they typically disappear after only a short time.

DSM-IV-TR

Delirium

A disturbance of consciousness (reduced clarity of awareness of the environment) and decreased ability to focus attention. Symptoms are accompanied by

- a change in cognitive functioning (e.g., memory difficulties, disorientation, language disturbance), or
- development of delusions or hallucinations not accounted for by dementia or any other previously existing condition.

Delirium typically starts suddenly and fluctuates over the course of the day, and there is usually evidence from the patient's history or medical tests that the delirium is caused by a medical condition.

Adapted with permission from the *Diagnostic and Statistical Manual of Mental Disorders*, Text Revision, Fourth Edition, (Copyright 2000). American Psychiatric Association.

---

delirium alteration in consciousness that typically occurs in the context of a medical illness or after ingesting a substance

dementia different syndromes characterized by persistent and multiple cognitive difficulties that create significant impairment in social or occupational functioning

Prevalence and Impact Delirium is common in general hospitals, where the prevalence ranges from 11% to 16% (Liptzin, 2004). Delirium can be present at hospital admission, or onset can occur 1 to 3 days after surgery. The disorder is common in hospitalized patients with acquired immunodeficiency syndrome (AIDS; 30-40%) and among terminally ill patients who are near death (80%). In the general community, the prevalence is close to 1% (Folstein et al., 1991). Over the past 10 years, prevalence estimates have been increasing, perhaps as a result of briefer hospital stays that do not allow sufficient time for full recovery from surgery (Liptzin, 2004). Over 20% of patients with Alzheimer's disease have episodes of delirium during the course of their disorders (Lerner et al., 1997). Delirium is associated with longer hospital stays for medical patients (Ely et al., 2001; Thomason et al., 2005), increased health care costs (Franco et al., 2001), more complications following surgery, poorer posthospitalization functioning, and increased risk of institutional placement (Liptzin, 2004).

Sex, Race, and Ethnicity Men are at greater risk for delirium than women (Liptzin, 2004). There is no evidence that age, race, or sex influences the prevalence of incorrect diagnosis. However, incorrectly diagnosed women more often receive a diagnosis of depression, and misdiagnosed men are more frequently given no diagnosis (Armstrong et al., 1997).

Etiology Delirium is associated with a range of biological and environmental factors (Liptzin, 2004; Raskind et al., 2004), but it is most often brought on by a serious systemic medical illness, such as AIDS, congestive heart failure, infection, or toxic effects of a medication, as illustrated by the case of Elizabeth. Medication toxicity occurs more easily among older adults since they metabolize drugs differently and often take multiple medications that could interact to produce adverse drug effects. Other biological causes of delirium include metabolic disorders (e.g., hypothyroidism or hypoglycemia), neurological disorders (e.g., head trauma, stroke, seizure, or meningitis), malnutrition or severe dehydration, and alcohol or drug intoxication or withdrawal. The risk of delirium increases with age and cognitive impairment. In some cases, episodes of delirium may be the first symptom of an underlying dementia (Raskind et al., 2004).

A diathesis-stress model may be the most likely explanation for the onset of delirium (Inouye et al., 1993; Inouye & Charpentier, 1996). Environmental factors that increase the risk for delirium during hospitalization include the use of physical restraints, use of more than three medications, and use of a bladder catheter (Weber et al., 2004). Risk factors that contribute to dehydration, poor nutrition, and sleep deprivation are also important. How these factors interact is not entirely clear, but delirium is associated with dysfunction in the prefrontal cortex, thalamus, and basal ganglia. Furthermore, a number of neurotransmitters may be involved (e.g., dopamine, serotonin, GABA, acetylcholine) (Liptzin, 2004; Trzepacz et al., 2002). In summary, the onset of delirium is complicated, but determining its origin is necessary because for some older adults, appropriate intervention (rehydration, stopping medication) may reverse its symptoms.

Delirium is a disturbance in consciousness that may lead to unusual behaviors. One common cause is the toxic effects of medications.

Treatment Delirium is often not recognized or is inadequately treated (Weber et al., 2004). As a first step, screening for known risk factors (e.g., dementia, substance use) is necessary. Precautions to minimize delirium include monitoring medications, ensuring proper nutrition and hydration, and managing the patient's sleep-wake cycle (Liptzin, 2004; Weber et al., 2004). When symptoms occur despite prevention strategies, early detection is important to reduce the duration and impact of the episode.

In general, treatment strategies include medication, environmental changes, and support for both the patient and family (Trzepacz et al., 2002). Low-dose antipsychotic medications can help keep the patient safe and reduce symptoms. When delirium is due to withdrawal of alcohol or other sedatives, short-acting benzodiazepines may be used (Liptzin, 2004). Education and supportive care provide information about symptom course, allowing family members to remain with the patient. Beneficial environmental manipulations include reducing sensory stimulation, providing orientation through visual cues such as family pictures and clocks, and maintaining a regular day-night routine with open blinds, limitations for daytime sleeping, and minimization of nighttime wakening for vital signs and other medical procedures (Liptzin, 2004).

DEMENTIA

Dementia is a devastating disease: it gradually robs patients of their ability to function independently, and it creates significant emotional problems for patients and their families, who suffer with them through sometimes long periods of increasing dysfunction. Treatments are available to slow progression of the disease and improve quality of life, but dementia remains one of the most common and debilitating disorders of older age.

Types of Dementia   The term *dementia* describes different syndromes characterized by persistent and multiple *cognitive difficulties* that create significant impairment in social or occupational functioning. Dementia is different from delirium. In dementia, cognitive difficulties are not accompanied by changes in consciousness or alertness. The central feature of dementia is memory impairment, and cognitive difficulties in at least one additional category are necessary for a diagnosis (e.g., difficulties with understanding or using words, inability to carry out motor activities, failure to recognize or name objects, or deficits in executive abilities). (See the box "DSM-IV-TR: Dementia.")

Dementia is typically diagnosed only after extensive interviews and history taking with the patient and close relatives or friends, cognitive testing and observation, a thorough medical evaluation, and often a neuroimaging test (e.g., CT or MRI), although the cost-effectiveness of neuroimaging has been questioned (Raskind et al., 2004). To diag-

Dementia

The Case of Alvin

"That's one of the real difficulties. There's no sign that goes off and says, Yes, he's understanding, or No, he's not understanding it."
www.mypsychlab.com

dementia due to other general medical conditions cognitive impairment related to HIV, head trauma, Parkinson's disease, and Huntington's disease, or other medical illness

Alzheimer's disease the most common form of dementia, characterized by a gradual onset and continuing cognitive decline, which includes memory loss, difficulties with language and decision making, and ultimately inability to care for self

neurofibrillary tangles twisted protein fibers within neurons found in the brains of patients with Alzheimer's disease

cerebral senile plaques deposits of beta-amyloid protein that form between the cells found in the brains of patients with Alzheimer's disease

nose dementia, cognitive difficulties are compared with prior levels of functioning. Understanding the potential etiology is important because reversible causes, though infrequent (9%) (Clarfield, 2003), can include vitamin deficiency (particularly B-12), thyroid dysfunction, drug toxicity, and normal pressure hydrocephalus (an abnormal increase of cerebrospinal fluid in the brain's ventricles, or cavities). In most cases, however, dementia reflects a progressive pattern of cognitive disability and functional impairment.

There are four major categories of dementia (DSM, 1994). *Dementia of the Alzheimer's Type* (commonly known as Alzheimer's disease) has a gradual onset and continuing cognitive decline. *Vascular dementia* is diagnosed when cerebrovascular disease, such as stroke, is a potential cause of cognitive dysfunction. *Substance-induced dementia* reflects cognitive impairment associated with substance use (a drug of abuse or a medication). **Dementia due to other general medical conditions** includes symptoms thought to be related to HIV, head trauma, Parkinson's disease and Huntington's disease, or other medical illness. Finally, some people may have a diagnosis of dementia due to multiple etiologies.

Alzheimer's disease is by far the most common subtype of dementia, accounting for up to 75% of all patients with dementia (Chapman et al., 2006). It has a slow and progressive course of cognitive decline. Early signs may be subtle and not dramatically different from what is seen in normal aging (Backman et al., 2005). The first noticeable signs include forgetting recent events or names, repeating statements or questions, getting lost while driving in familiar places, and experiencing difficulty with calculations (Chapman et al., 2006; Raskind et al., 2004). A diagnosis of Alzheimer's disease at this early stage does not imply cognitive incompetence, and many people with Alzheimer's disease are able to maintain a positive quality of life for a number of years after diagnosis (see Treatment; Morris, 2005). Over the next 5 to 15 years, Alzheimer's disease results in more severe impairments in the ability to use language, make decisions, and engage in self-care (see the box "Real People, Real Disorders: Ronald Reagan, Decreasing the Stigma of Alzheimer's Disease"). Behavioral problems also occur and include disrupted sleep, wandering, irritability, and aggression. The rate of progressive deterioration in cognitive capabilities and functioning increases as the severity of the disease worsens (Morris, 2005).

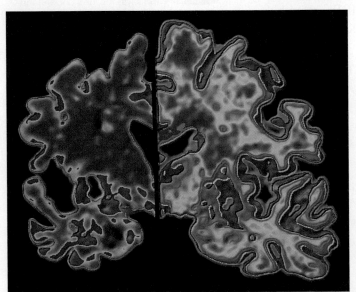

At left, a brain slice from a patient with Alzheimer's disease; at right, the brain of someone without this disorder. The brain on the left is shrunken, due to the death of nerve cells.

Virginia's difficulties were subtle at first. In fact, only her husband and best friend ever seemed to notice. She was able to hide her memory and language difficulties using jokes about her increasing age and self-imposed memory strategies (e.g., writing notes to herself; sticking to usual routines). However, as time went on, these strategies were less effective, and people began to notice how much trouble she was having. Virginia's husband started to notice that she was losing more abilities almost every week.

A long period of gradual deterioration such as Virginia's is typical of this disease and can be devastating to family and friends of the person affected. As one nurse and patient advocate has written: "Alzheimer's can be called the long good-bye. You grieve about the loved one from the moment you begin to observe the gradual loss of memory and the speech and personality changes, because they are incurable. The person you love is gradually changing before your eyes. You say good-bye many times until the final good-bye at death." —Norma Wylie, 1996 (in *Sharing the Final Journey: Walking with the Dying*).

We now know that Alzheimer's disease involves the presence of **neurofibrillary tangles** (NFT; twisted protein fibers within neurons) and **cerebral senile plaques**

real people, real disorders

Ronald Reagan: Decreasing the Stigma of Alzheimer's Disease

"My fellow Americans, I have recently been told that I am one of the millions of Americans who will be afflicted with Alzheimer's disease. . . . Nancy and I had to decide whether . . . we would make this news known in a public way. . . . In opening our hearts, we hope that this might promote greater awareness of the condition. . . . At the moment I feel just fine. . . . Unfortunately, as Alzheimer's disease progresses, the family often bears a heavy burden. I only wish there was some way I could spare Nancy from this painful experience . . . I now begin the journey that will lead me into the sunset of my life." Ronald Reagan, November 5, 1994, letter to the American public.

Alzheimer's disease impacts people without discrimination. Ronald Reagan (1911–2004), the 40th president of the United States (1981–1989), is probably the best known sufferer. He was diagnosed in 1994 and died in 2004. Even before he was diagnosed, however, he may have known something was wrong. In a regular medical check-up, he may have only partly joked when he said to his doctor,

"I have three things that I want to tell you today. The first is that I seem to be having a little problem with my memory. I cannot remember the other two."

His friends noticed signs of the disease in the early 1990s, but even after his diagnosis in 1994, Reagan continued to exercise, play golf, and go to his office. As his condition deteriorated, however, his life became more reclusive, and he was unable to remember that he had ever been president. The strain on his family was tremendous, despite their many advantages and the best care available. Nevertheless, Reagan and his family did much to increase public awareness and decrease the stigma of Alzheimer's disease through the public disclosure of his condition and their continued efforts to educate the public and encourage continued fundraising and research.

Sources:
http://www.cnn.com/SPECIALS/2004/reagan/stories/speech.archive/alzheimer.announcement
http://www.pbs.org/theforgetting/experiences/index.html
http://www.washingtonpost.com/wp-dyn/articles/A39072-2004Jun13.html

---

(SP; deposits of beta-amyloid protein that form between the cells) in the hippocampus, cerebral cortex, and other regions of the brain (Chapman et al., 2006; Morris, 2006). Increased frequency of NFTs and SPs accompanies normal aging, but people with Alzheimer's disease have excessive amounts. Autopsies indicate that current clinical procedures for diagnosing Alzheimer's disease are 90% accurate (Morris, 2005).

Vascular dementia is diagnosed when a patient's history, laboratory tests, and/or brain imaging studies indicate cognitive impairment as a result of cardiovascular disease, such as stroke, transient ischemic attack (TIA or mini-stroke), coronary artery disease, or untreated high blood pressure. In these conditions, blockages of blood vessels result in tissue death, or *infarction*, in the brain. Damage may be to a single, major vessel or to a number of smaller ones, in which case **multi-infarct dementia** is diagnosed (Morris, 2005). Vascular dementia has different clinical features than Alzheimer's disease, including more sudden onset, more focal or "patchy" cognitive deficits, and more stepwise progression of cognitive difficulties (Chapman et al., 2006). Vascular dementia rarely occurs alone. In many cases, symptoms of Alzheimer's disease are also present (Morris, 2005). Vascular tissue death may lower the threshold for Alzheimer's disease, even though some causes of vascular dementia are modifiable (e.g., untreated hypertension).

vascular dementia cognitive dysfunction that occurs as the result of cerebrovascular disease

multi-infarct dementia cognitive dysfunction that occurs as the result of several small strokes

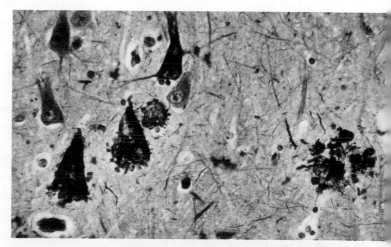

A microscopic examination of brain tissue taken from a patient with Alzheimer's disease reveals the neurofibrillary tangles (dark triangular shapes at left) and cerebral senile (amyloid) plaques (dark round shape at right) associated with this disorder.

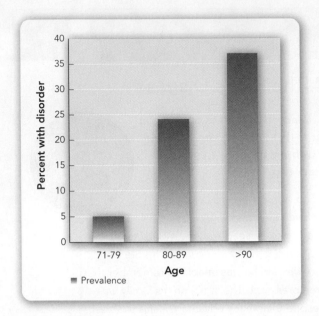

FIGURE 13.4

The Prevalence of Dementia Increases With Age

Although individual studies report different prevalence estimates, all research shows that dementia becomes more prevalent as people get older.

substance-induced dementia cognitive impairment associated with substance use

subcortical dementia condition involving damage primarily in the inner layers of the brain and found frequently during the later stages of HIV and in Parkinson's disease and Huntington's disease

Substance use, in particular alcohol abuse, can lead to dementia that is difficult to differentiate from Alzheimer's disease. In **substance-induced dementia**, however, abstinence may stop or even reverse cognitive decline and cortical damage (Atkinson, 2004). Substance use also may increase vulnerability to other forms of dementia and increase the risk for other contributing factors, such as head trauma, infectious disease, and vitamin deficiency.

A number of medical conditions are also associated with dementia. These are the syndromes referred to as *Dementia Due to Other Medical Conditions.* **Subcortical dementia** (where damage occurs primarily in the inner layers of the brain) occurs frequently during the later stages of HIV and in Parkinson's disease and Huntington's disease. There are other dementias caused by medical conditions, but these forms are very rare.

Prevalence and Impact Progressive dementia occurs in 5 to 10% of adults age 65 and over (Chapman et al., 2006; Gurland, 2004). Although figures vary across studies, all data suggest that the prevalence of dementia increases dramatically with advancing age (Figure 13.4). As noted earlier, Alzheimer's disease is the most common type, diagnosed in up to 75% of cases. Despite these high prevalence figures, many patients with dementia remain undiagnosed and untreated (Morris, 2005).

The impact of dementia on patients, their families, and the health care system is enormous.

Gene finally had to move in with his daughter, Sarah, and her family because he just couldn't function independently anymore. Although Sarah knew this was the right thing to do, it was hard on everyone. Someone had to be with him most of the time, and it was hard for everyone to observe Gene, who had once been a vibrant man with many interests and skills, gradually deteriorate to a point where he couldn't remember their names.

As cognitive abilities and functional capacity deteriorate, negative emotional, social, and behavioral outcomes occur (Gurland, 1980; Kunik et al., 2003). In the early stages, social and emotional withdrawal is common. Remember how Ernest started to withdraw from activities at church and in the community for fear that people would notice his memory problems? Up to 30% of patients with Alzheimer's disease also have major depression (Gurland, 1980), and as many as 70% have anxiety symptoms (Seignourel et al., 2008; Teri et al., 1999). These figures are not surprising given the significant distress patients experience when they hear they have this deteriorating, debilitating condition. Anxiety and depression in addition to Alzheimer's disease, however, result in more behavioral problems and greater limitations in daily activities (Teri et al., 1999). The combination also increases social disability, decreases independence (Porter et al., 2003; Schultz et al., 2004), and increases risk of nursing home placement (Gibbons et al., 2002).

People with dementia have more frequent coexisting medical conditions and reduced life expectancy. Dementia may exceed heart disease, stroke, diabetes, and cancer as a predictor of mortality in patients age 65 and older (Tschanz et al., 2004; Alzheimer's Association, 2009). Dementia also affects the treatment of medical conditions. Cognitively impaired patients are often unaware of changes in symptoms and treatment needs, and they have limited capacity to participate in health care decision making, self-care, or other health care plans (Boise et al., 2004; Brauner et al., 2000).

As Gene's memory and ability to express himself decreased, Sarah had to accompany him to all his doctors' appointments and coordinate all of his medical care.

Dementia also affects family caregivers. Wives, daughters, and daughters-in-law have the greatest burden of care, including assistance with nutrition and exercise, memory aids and activities of daily living, and behavioral plans to manage associated mood and behavior problems (Chapman et al., 2006). Caregivers are at increased risk themselves for depression, stress, deterioration in health, and increased role and interpersonal strain (e.g., strained family relationships) (Schulz et al., 1990).

For Sarah, taking care of her father was a full-time job. It limited the amount of time she could give to her children, making her feel guilty and sad. It was also hard to remain patient when she had to answer the same questions over and over.

Family caregiver stress is the most common reason people with dementia are placed in nursing homes (Wright et al., 1993). Use of health services and health care costs are also significantly greater for patients with dementia than for nondemented patients with similar chronic conditions (Bynum et al., 2004; Hill et al., 2002). In fact, dementia increases the total cost of health care by over $20,000 per year or three times the cost for people without dementia (Alzheimer's Association, 2009).

Sex, Race, and Ethnicity   Alzheimer's disease is more frequent in women than men (Reisberg et al., 2003). Higher rates are sometimes, but not always, found in African American and Hispanic groups (Gurland, 2004; Sakauye, 2004; Sink et al., 2004). These inconsistent findings may result from differences in testing and diagnostic procedures or inadequate sampling strategies. They may also result from inattention to factors such as education, language or literacy, comorbid psychiatric or medical illnesses, and culturally biased measures of cognitive functioning. Incidence rates (number of new cases diagnosed) may be equal across races, but differential survival rates may affect prevalence (total number of cases at a given time) (Jarvik & Mintzer, 2000). In addition, genetic factors may vary across racial groups; the presence of a specific genetic allele (*APOE*) is associated more strongly with whites and Japanese patients than with African American or Hispanic groups (Farrer et al., 1997). Among Koreans, Japanese, and Chinese, cases of Alzheimer's disease and vascular dementias have increased over the past 25 years, and the most likely factors are the environmental or dietary changes associated with increased Westernization (Sakauye, 2004).

Etiology of Dementia   Genetic factors appear to play a large role in the development of irreversible, progressive dementia. Early-onset Alzheimer's disease (before age 55), which accounts for 1% of all Alzheimer's disease cases, is associated with mutations in at least one of three different genes (Morris, 2005a). In most cases, signs and symptoms arise after age 55. Increasing age itself is one of the strongest predictors of dementia, with risk increasing by 0.5 to 1.0% per year after the age of 70 (Tsuang & Bird, 2004). Later-onset Alzheimer's disease (age 65 or over) is significantly associated with a specific mutation (e4) of the *APOE* gene (Morris, 2005; Tsuang & Bird, 2004), and people with a condition known as *mild cognitive impairment* who also have the risk variant of the *APOE* gene are at increased risk for developing dementia (see the box "Examining the Evidence: Is Mild Cognitive Impairment (MCI) a Precursor of Dementia or a Separate Syndrome?"). However, this mutation is neither necessary nor sufficient; only 50% of people with Alzheimer's disease have this gene variant. In addition, many people with this gene variant do not have any cognitive impairment; therefore, there is no one-to-one relationship between the presence of the gene form and Alzheimer's disease. As with all complex conditions, dementias most likely result from multiple genetic and environmental factors.

A diathesis-stress model is also relevant for understanding the onset of dementia. Genetic factors appear to be less important after age 85 (Silverman et al., 2003). Other forms of dementia are less clearly linked to genetic causes. To summarize, the most well-established risk factors for a diagnosis of dementia appear to be age, family history, and the presence of the e4 variant of the *APOE* gene (Table 13.1).

Amnestic MCI mild cognitive impairment in which cognitive complaints focus on memory difficulties

examining the evidence

Is Mild Cognitive Impairment (MCI) a Precursor of Dementia or a Separate Syndrome?

■ **The Facts: A Definition of MCI** MCI is characterized by (Chapman et al., 2006; Petersen et al., 2001):

1. Subjective cognitive complaints (usually memory, but not always), preferably verified by someone who knows the patient well enough to provide meaningful information about his/her condition.
2. Objective evidence of cognitive difficulties as measured by neuropsychological tests.
3. Adequate ability to perform activities of daily living.
4. Criteria for dementia not met.

Amnestic MCI is a subtype of MCI in which cognitive complaints focus on memory difficulties (Petersen et al., 2001). There has been great interest of late in the concept of MCI and whether it is a precursor of Alzheimer's disease or other forms of dementia, or whether it is a variation of normal aging. Determining the nature and predictive value of MCI may be important for establishing early treatment for dementia, although ethical issues arise with the notion of diagnosing a condition about which little is known (Petersen et al., 2001). MCI occurs in 19% of people younger than age 75 and in 29% of people older than 85 (Lopez et al., 2003).

■ **What Data Support MCI as a Precursor of Dementia**

1. People with MCI progress to a diagnosis of AD at a rate of 10 to 15% per year, relative to rates of 1 to 2% in people without cognitive difficulties (Petersen et al., 1995; Tierney et al., 1996).

2. People with MCI and the *APOE4* allele gene are at increased risk for developing dementia (Petersen et al., 1995).
3. Neuroimaging and neuropathology studies suggest that people with MCI share features with Alzheimer's disease, including hippocampal atrophy and neurofibrillary tangles (Petersen et al., 2001).

■ **What Data Refute MCI as a Precursor of Dementia?**

1. Some people with MCI never progress to any state of significantly worsened cognitive functioning (Petersen et al., 2001).
2. *Conversion rates* (the rates at which people with MCI progress to a diagnosis of dementia) vary widely across studies, perhaps due to difficulties in diagnosing MCI. It is often difficult to evaluate the extent to which cognitive difficulties interfere with daily functioning.
3. MCI can result from many different causes, including depression, substance abuse, side effects of medications, and the like (Morris, 2005).

■ **Conclusions** Like dementia itself, there are likely many forms of MCI, and a full evaluation of all possible medical and psychological causes for declining cognitive symptoms needs to be done. Amnestic MCI is probably a significant risk factor for the development of Alzheimer's disease (Morris, 2005; Petersen et al., 2001; Tabert et al., 2006). All people with suspected MCI should be monitored regularly for any worsening of symptoms. There is as yet no evidence that treatments demonstrated useful for dementia also are useful for MCI, but a number of studies are ongoing (Petersen et al., 2001).

Engaging in activities such as taking college classes, playing a musical instrument, or doing crossword puzzles may offer older adults some protection against Alzheimer's disease.

Certain *protective factors* may reduce the risk of cognitive decline. Advanced education seems to reduce the risk of Alzheimer's disease, vascular dementia, and alcohol-related dementia (Gurland, 2004) by creating cognitive reserves such as increased coping skills that in turn minimize the impact of cognitive deterioration (Stern et al., 1994). Advanced education may also increase neuronal connections that counterbalance noticeable changes as NFTs and SPs develop (Bourgeois et al., 2003). In addition, older adults with increased education may use more of their frontal lobes, suggesting the availability of neurobiological reserves that facilitate coping with cognitive deterioration (Springer et al., 2005). Other potentially protective biological and environmental variables include dietary factors (e.g., increased intake of omega-3 polyunsaturated fatty acids, decreased fat and cholesterol intake, vitamins C and E), moderate use of alcohol, use of nonsteroidal anti-inflammatory drugs (NSAIDs), and increased engagement in mental activities (e.g., playing games, puzzles, and playing a musical instrument) (Chapman et al., 2006; Morris, 2005).

Treatment of Dementia and Related Difficulties   As already noted, in most cases, dementia cannot be reversed or cured. Treatment targets delaying disease progression, prolonging independent functioning, improving quality of life, managing associated emotional and behavioral symptoms, and providing support and assistance to caregivers (AAGP Position Statement, 2006). Treatments include pharmacological and nonpharmacological approaches. Medications known as cholinesterase inhibitors (CEIs; e.g., Aricept) appear to slow cognitive decline and improve global functioning (relative to placebo) for patients with mild to moderate Alzheimer's disease (Chapman et al., 2006; Morris, 2005). Alzheimer's disease is associated with the destruction of neurons that release the neurotransmitter acetylcholine. Since it is not yet possible to regenerate these acetylcholine-producing neurons, CEIs block the enzyme that breaks down this neurotransmitter. This process increases the remaining level of acetylcholine in the brain. CEIs do not reverse the damage to the neurons; they merely allow whatever neurotransmitter is left to function more effectively. Improvements with these drugs are greatest in the early stages of Alzheimer's disease, before extensive neurobiological damage has been done. The use of CEIs may delay nursing home placement (Geldmacher et al., 2003), although it is not entirely clear that the medications reduce the costs of caring for patients (Morris, 2005).

As the severity of Alzheimer's disease increases, another medication (memantine or Namenda) can be added to block overproduction of the neurotransmitter glutamate (Reisberg et al., 2003; Tariot et al., 2004), which plays a role in learning and memory. High doses of vitamin E also appear to slow the progress of symptoms in moderate to severe dementia, but very high doses of vitamin E may increase mortality (Miller et al., 2005). Medications can also control the noncognitive symptoms of dementia, including emotional disturbance, aggression, agitation, psychotic symptoms, and sleep disturbance. Antidepressant medications are useful to treat depression and other emotional symptoms (Weintraub & Katz, 2005). Antipsychotic medications can reduce delusions, hallucinations, agitation, and aggression. Because these drugs can have very serious side effects (increased risk of seizures, tardive dyskinesia, cardiovascular adverse events, increased mortality), they should be used cautiously (Katz et al., 2002; Schneider et al., 2005; Weintraub & Katz, 2005).

Nonmedication interventions do not affect disease progression directly but may minimize its impact. These strategies include changing the environment to ensure patient safety (e.g., walking aids to prevent falls, driving limitations or discontinuation), structuring daily routines, and facilitating appropriate nutrition, exercise, and social engagement. Caregivers play a major role in helping patients make these changes. Cognitive functioning can also be affected by cognitive training strategies that enhance comprehension, learning, and memory even among people with severe dementia (Bayles & Kim, 2003; Bourgeois et al., 2003; Brush & Camp, 1998; Sitzer et al., 2006). Behavioral interventions may reduce agitation (Teri et al., 2000), anxiety (Kraus et al., 2008) depression (Teri et al., 1997, 2003), and behavioral problems (Burgio et al., 2001, 2002). Caregivers may also require cognitive-behavioral interventions to manage stress, increase coping skills and decrease depression (Akkerman & Ostwald, 2004; Gallagher-Thompson et al., 2003; Teri et al., 1997).

---

concept CHECK

- Delirium can arise from serious medical illness or toxic effects of a medication.

- The first step in the treatment of delirium is early detection. The next steps can include medications, environmental changes, and support.

- Dementia, characterized by multiple cognitive impairments, is a tremendously debilitating disease for patients and one that places great stress on their families.

- The most common form of dementia is Alzheimer's disease, which is characterized by insidious onset and progressive course.

- Alzheimer's disease is associated with a variant of the *APOE gene (e4)*, but only 50% of people with this disorder have this gene variant.

- Medications used to treat Alzheimer's disease do not reverse damage to neurons, but they may delay disease progression. Nonpharmacological treatments can also reduce the impact of dementia.

APPLICATION QUESTION   How does the type of dementia impact the nature and treatment of symptoms?

THE WHOLE STORY: CHARLOTTE—THE PSYCHOPATHOLOGY AND TREATMENT OF ANXIETY DISORDER IN AN OLDER PATIENT

The Patient: *Charlotte is a 78-year-old widow who was always a worrier and a perfectionist. Her parents were loving but often critical when her school performance or other behavior wasn't perfect. Charlotte was very successful in her early years. She completed a college degree and worked as a bank teller and supervisor for eight years before she married and had children. She stopped working when she had her first baby, but she remained busy with volunteer work during the years when she raised her three children. Throughout her life, despite outward success, Charlotte was always worried that things might not turn out well enough. She was concerned that her children were not doing well enough in school, that she was not a good enough mother, that her home wasn't clean and orderly enough, and that she and her husband might not have enough money to support them as they got older.*

The Problem: *Despite this persistent worry over the years, Charlotte functioned well in her roles as wife, mother, and volunteer. When her husband died five years ago, however, she realized just how much she had relied on him for reassurance. Without him around to remind her that she was doing a good job and that their children were well adjusted, she had more trouble easing her mind of the worries. She began to spend many hours a day worrying about various things—whether people liked her, how well her grandchildren were doing in school, whether she was doing enough to help at church, and how she would be able to support herself if she developed serious medical problems.*

Charlotte also began to experience significant sleep difficulties. She fell asleep easily, but she woke up frequently during the night, sometimes to go to the bathroom, but always with many worries on her mind. Her arthritis also seemed to be getting worse, possibly because of increased muscle tension, and she developed serious problems with back and neck pain. Charlotte also found herself more irritable and snappy with her children, and she noticed difficulties with her memory and concentration. She misplaced things regularly and spent a lot of time looking for her keys, purse, and calendar. She also had difficulty concentrating when she sat down to read, and her children noticed that she was irritable and preoccupied much of the time.

The Diagnosis: *Charlotte initially contacted the clinic for an evaluation of her memory. She was worried that she might have Alzheimer's disease. As part of Charlotte's initial evaluation, she also was assessed for the full range of possible psychiatric disorders. Cognitive evaluations showed no excessive deficits in her memory or thinking, but her symptoms met the criteria for generalized anxiety disorder. She also had symptoms of depression, but not with sufficient severity for a diagnosis of major depression.*

The Treatment: *Initial treatment strategies involved teaching Charlotte how to identify different symptoms of anxiety— for example, physical tension, worry-related thoughts, and behavioral avoidance. Simple self-monitoring forms were created that included spaces for recording various symptoms. As Charlotte became more familiar with her anxiety symptoms, she realized just how often she worried about things. She also learned how to identify physical symptoms of anxiety (e.g., muscle tension) that she had never noticed before.*

Next, Charlotte began to learn skills to reduce her anxiety. The goal of this phase of treatment was to give her a "toolbox" of skills to choose from to manage anxiety. The first skill that she learned was deep breathing. Charlotte used this skill to decrease her anxiety when she noticed her body tensing up. She also learned how to identify and challenge her worry-related thoughts (e.g., "I am a terrible grandmother; my grandchildren don't think I'm any fun.") and substitute more realistic thoughts (e.g., "My grandchildren love me. We usually have fun together. It is okay if sometimes they prefer to spend time with someone else."). She also learned how to solve problems instead of just worrying about them and how to push herself to face her worries (e.g., leading prayers at church even though she was afraid she'd say the "wrong" words).

The Treatment Outcome: *Over a period of 3 months, Charlotte learned many skills, and she began to worry less and felt that her life was more fulfilling.*

CRITICAL ISSUES to remember

1. Geropsychology is a subdiscipline of psychology that focuses on issues of aging, in particular, patterns of normal development, individual differences, and psychological problems that are unique to older adults.

2. Approximately 20 to 30% of older adults have a psychological disorder. Psychological symptoms often go unnoticed in older adults, and many people never receive treatment. Older adults with psychological disorders often describe symptoms differently than younger adults do, making recognition difficult. Overlapping medical problems also make the diagnosis of emotional problems difficult among older patients, particularly in medical settings where older adults most often go for help.

3. Older adults with depression and anxiety often focus on somatic rather than psychological symptoms. Symptoms of depression and anxiety often overlap with cognitive impairment and medical diseases. The presence of serious medical illness and cognitive impairment puts older adults at increased risk for anxiety and depression. Overuse of alcohol, misuse of prescription medications, and tobacco abuse are the most common substance use problems in older adults. For most older adults, schizophrenia onset occurs in young adulthood. Late-onset schizophrenia is associated with fewer negative symptoms and less impaired cognitive skills, but higher prevalence of paranoia and more auditory hallucinations. Very-late-onset schizophrenia-like psychosis usually occurs after stroke, tumor, or other neurodegenerative change.

4. Dementia and delirium are two major cognitive disorders that impact older adults. Although both involve difficulties in thinking, delirium is associated with a change in consciousness or alertness. Dementia is not. Delirium often occurs as a result of serious illness or toxic effects of a medication or multiple medications. Alzheimer's disease, the most common type of dementia, has a slow and progressive course that involves difficulties with memory, language, decision making, and ultimately self-care.

5. Biological and psychological variables often interact in the development of emotional and cognitive disorders in older people. Most often, data point to the possibility of a diathesis-stress model that suggests an integrated impact of biological vulnerabilities (e.g., genetic predispositions) and environmental stressors (e.g., death of a loved one, change in occupational or social status). Psychological disorders with onset in later life are less likely to be associated with a family history of the disorder.

6. Most of the interventions that are used to treat younger adults with anxiety, depression, substance abuse, and psychosis are also efficacious in adults, although there may be a need to adjust medication dosages and the manner in which psychological interventions are conducted. With respect to empirically supported treatments, medication and cognitive-behavioral treatment have the most research support. Medications can slow the progression of dementia and psychological treatments can improve quality of life, but damage to neurons is not reversed.

TEST yourself

For more review plus practice tests, flashcards, and Speaking Out: DSM in Context videos, log onto www.MyPsychLab.com

1. The subdiscipline of psychology that addresses issues of aging, with special attention to psychological problems that are unique to older persons, is
   a. geriatric psychiatry
   b. gerontology
   c. geropsychology
   d. generational psychology

2. Treating the elderly on the assumption that psychological and medical problems are a normal part of aging is associated with what characteristic in the health care provider?
   a. experience
   b. ageism
   c. acceptance
   d. pessimism

3. Which of the following factors complicates the identification of psychological disorders in older people?
   a. Symptoms of many medical diseases mimic psychological disorders.

b. The elderly are often very tolerant of psychological symptoms.
   c. Older adults express their psychological distress to others very readily.
   d. Psychological disorders are relatively rare in the elderly and thus are easily missed.

4. Executive dysfunction occurs when a person has difficulty
   a. driving and performing simple self-care activities
   b. remembering past tasks and activities
   c. planning, thinking abstractly, initiating and inhibiting actions
   d. following instructions from a health care provider

5. Shui-bian was concerned that his mother was suffering from dementia. She had gotten lost at the shopping center, misplaced objects, and forgotten names of friends and acquaintances. Her symptoms gradually disappeared after her physi-

cian put her on antidepressant medication. Her diagnosis was most likely
a. Alzheimer's disease
b. vascular depression
c. Parkinson's disease
d. pseudodementia

6. Harold is a depressed widower who went to a psychologist who specialized in working with the elderly. The psychologist asked Harold to talk about significant events in his life and how he managed his loneliness in the past. The type of therapy used by this psychologist is called
a. reminiscence therapy
b. cognitive-behavioral therapy
c. geriatric psychotherapy
d. problem-solving therapy

7. Anxiety may be difficult to diagnose in older people because
a. clinicians assume it is rare in the elderly
b. worry about life problems is normal in old age
c. many medical conditions have symptoms that are common in anxiety
d. older adults are often confused about their symptoms

8. Over 40% of the elderly who suffer from persistent anxiety are given benzodiazapines, such as Valium. This is remarkable because such medications cause
a. loss of bowel and bladder control
b. memory problems and slowing of motor behaviors
c. manic and hypomanic reactions
d. elevated heart rate and blood pressure

9. Cognitive-behavior therapy for anxiety disorders may need to be modified for older patients. The primary adaptation is that
a. the therapist must speak louder and use simple language
b. the pace is slowed, and different learning strategies are used
c. discussion of certain topics such as sexuality and death is avoided
d. all of the above

10. Substance abuse is often only recognized in the elderly when
a. it affects a medical condition or causes accidents
b. symptoms of withdrawal occur
c. employment or social life is affected
d. dementia symptoms are made worse

11. The most commonly abused substance in older adults is
a. over-the-counter medication
b. benzodiazapines
c. tobacco
d. alcohol

12. As people age, there is a decrease in the body's ability to metabolize alcohol, prescribed medication, and illegal drugs. This means
a. larger amounts are needed to obtain the same effect
b. it is more difficult to detect the substance in the blood and urine
c. a very small amount of a substance causes acute illness
d. toxic levels are reached more rapidly

13. The loss of clarity, attention, and awareness that is often brought on by a serious medical illness, such as AIDS, congestive heart failure, infection, or toxic effects of a medication, is called
a. delirium
b. dementia
c. stupor
d. euphoria

14. Mr. Jones had a stroke and no longer recognized the faces of people he knew or common objects that he encountered. He even had difficulty recognizing his wife and children until he heard their voices. This is termed
a. aphasia
b. apraxia
c. agnosia
d. amnesia

15. The presence of neurofibrillary tangles and cerebral senile plaques in the hippocampus, cerebral cortex, and other regions of the brain is most often associated with which disorder?
a. Huntington's disease
b. Parkinson's disease
c. HIV
d. Alzheimer's disease

16. Vascular dementia can be distinguished from other types of dementia on the basis of the
a. sudden onset and more stepwise progression of cognitive difficulties
b. possibility of remission following proper diagnosis and treatment
c. gradual onset and gradual progression of cognitive difficulties
d. comorbidity with traumatic brain injuries due to falls and accidents

17. Progressive dementia occurs in what percentage of adults age 65 and over?
a. 5 to 10 %
b. 10 to 15 %
c. 15 to 20 %
d. 20 to 30%

18. Later onset AD (age 65 or over) is significantly associated with what specific genetic factor?
a. trigene 21
b. mutation of the APOE gene
c. a missing MCI gene
d. at least seven different genes

19. What protective factor appears to reduce the risk of cognitive decline in AD and other dementias?
a. advanced education
b. increased intake of omega-3
c. moderate use of alcohol
d. all of the above

20. The family doctor has told Stacey that she believes that her mother is showing early signs of AD. The doctor would like to start Stacey's mother on Aricept, a medication used in the early stages of AD. Aricept is a (an)
a. glutamate blocker
b. antidepressant
c. cholinesterase inhibitor
d. nutritional supplement

Answers: 1 c, 2 b, 3 a, 4 c, 5 d, 6 a, 7 c, 8 b, 9 b, 10 a, 11 c, 12 d, 13 a, 14 c, 15 d, 16 a, 17 a, 18 b, 19 d, 20 c.

CHAPTER
objectives

After reading this chapter, you should be able to:

1 Define health psychology and the roles of a health psychologist.

2 Describe mind-body dualism and its significance for health psychology.

3 Define stress and describe how it is measured.

4 Describe the impact of stress on health and the immune system.

5 Recognize a range of behaviors that may affect health and how health psychologists help people change behaviors to maintain health.

6 Identify factors that affect adjustment to chronic illness and strategies to improve adjustment and quality of life for people with a chronic disease.

health psychology

Joe was 42 years old, a successful business-man with a demanding career, a wife with a demanding career, and three high-achieving children. Joe was constantly "on the go." He traveled quite a bit for work, was president of the local Rotary Club, and was considering running for a local public office. On weekends, he coached his youngest son's soccer league, and when soccer was not in season, he coached his daughter's basketball team. Joe was also active in his church. His wife was equally involved in the community and the lives of their children. Joe and his wife often joked about needing a "date night" in order to connect. But they could never seem to find the time to go out for a quiet dinner. Lately, Joe had been experiencing some episodes of dizziness when he stood up. He was not too worried, however. He thought he probably just needed more sleep—or a vacation—but he could not find the time.

One day at work, Joe was rushing from his office to an important meeting when he suddenly lost all feeling on the right side of his body. He stumbled, losing his balance, and fell against the receptionist's desk. A co-worker rushed to his side and asked him if he was OK, but his speech was so garbled the co-worker could not understand him. The receptionist called 911, but during the ambulance ride Joe's symptoms disappeared and he began arguing with the paramedics about his need to return to his job and the important meeting. He promised to see his physician, and he did so later that week because the symptoms really scared him. A series of tests revealed hypertension as well as other early signs of cardiac disease. Joe's physician told him that he had experienced a transient ischemic attack (TIA), also known as a mini-stroke. The physician called it a wake-up call and told Joe that he had a choice—change his lifestyle or be at high risk for a major stroke, which could leave him paralyzed and without speech.

Although you may not be 42 years old, you can probably relate to many aspects of Joe's life—too many demands and too little time. Stress seems to have become a way of life for many Americans, and too often, healthy behaviors that actually help us to manage stress (exercise, relaxation, time to ourselves, eating "right") are the first behaviors that we eliminate from our daily routines as we try to control our chaotic environment. Perhaps every "wake-up call" is not as dramatic as Joe's, but the impact of environmental factors on physical and psychological health is an important area of study for psychologists. The focus of this chapter is on health psychology—the study of the complex relationships between physical and psychological health and dysfunction.

Health Psychology: Defining the Field

Good physical health is maintained at least in part by attitudes and behaviors, making health psychology an important subdiscipline of psychology. **Health psychology** uses the principles and methods of psychology to understand how attitudes and behaviors influence health and illness. Health psychologists study how people develop positive and negative health habits (e.g., exercise, eating, smoking), how stress and health are related, and which psychological variables affect the onset and treatment of medical illnesses. Health is defined today as it was in 1948 by the World Health Organization as a state of mental, social, and physical well-being, not just the absence of illness (World Health Organization, 1948). In addition to health psychology, related fields of study include **behavioral medicine**, an interdisciplinary field (not just psychology) that studies the relation between behavioral and biomedical science, and **medical psychology**, the study and practice of psychology as it relates to health, illness, and medical treatment. At the heart of health psychology is the **biopsychosocial model**, which suggests that health is determined by complex interactions among biological, psychological, and social factors. This model is in contrast to a **biomedical model**, in which illnesses are explained solely by biological processes. Over the years, however, and across different disciplines, the relation between mind and body has not always been well understood.

THE MIND-BODY RELATIONSHIP

Although in some earlier periods of human history there was occasional recognition that mind and body were profoundly linked (see Chapter 1), until very recently our thinking has been dominated by the idea of **mind-body dualism**. This concept, which is associated with the French philosopher René Descartes, holds that the mind and body function independently, although they may interact. With the Renaissance, advances in medical technology emphasized identifying physiological explanations for physical illness. Until the present day, a philosophy of mind-body dualism has persisted, as illustrated by significant efforts to identify biological causes for medical illness and the relative neglect of mental health care (Belar & Deardorff, 1995). Only recently has psychology had any role in treating medical illness. Now, psychologists routinely offer services related to the prevention, treatment, or management of physical health problems (such as smoking cessation treatment for patients with respiratory or cardiac diseases, or relaxation training to help diabetic children reduce their fear of injections). Later in this chapter, we will review some of these treatments.

In the first half of the twentieth century, the idea of mind-body dualism began to be challenged. Freud linked the mind and body to explain *hysteria* (now known as conversion disorder), a condition in which he believed that unconscious psychological conflicts caused unexplained physical complaints, such as physical weakness and paralysis (see Chapter 1, the case of Anna O.). In the 1930s and 1940s, psychiatrists Flanders Dunbar and Franz Alexander proposed associations between certain

health psychology a subfield of psychology that uses its principles and methods to understand how attitudes and behaviors influence health and illness

behavioral medicine an interdisciplinary field that studies the relation between behavioral and biomedical science

medical psychology the study and practice of psychology as it relates to health, illness, and medical treatment

biopsychosocial model a theoretical perspective that suggests that health is determined by complex interactions among biological, psychological, and social factors

biomedical model a perspective that explains illnesses solely by biological processes

mind-body dualism a belief that the mind and body function independently, associated with the French philosopher René Descartes

personality patterns and specific medical illnesses (e.g., an *ulcer-prone personality*). At this time, there were new ideas about the relationship between psychological conflicts and physical illness that implicated the autonomic nervous system. In this view, psychological conflicts produce anxiety, which causes the nervous system to create an organic problem (e.g., an ulcer) (Taylor, 2006). From these influences came the development of *biopsychosocial models* of physical illness, which recognize the contributions of body, mind, and the social environment to the development of illness (see Figure 14.1).

PSYCHOLOGICAL INFLUENCES ON HEALTH

It is now widely accepted that psychological variables (such as health habits, attitudes, and personality characteristics) and social factors (such as stress and social support) affect physical health. Similarly, medical illness can affect psychological health and social functioning. For example, anxiety and depression are more common among people with medical illness than among healthy controls (see Chapter 13 for a discussion of this issue among older adults). When medical illness and psychological problems coexist, functioning is even more impaired. The treatment of medical disease, especially chronic medical illness (such as diabetes and hypertension, which develop slowly and often persist for a lifetime), is also influenced by psychological and social variables. These include such factors as the doctor-patient relationship, expectations for treatment outcomes, and psychological coping and adjustment. This chapter will focus on three primary topics: the role of stress in physical and mental health, the impact of psychology and behavior on medical illness and its treatment, and the nature and impact of psychological treatments for health-related conditions

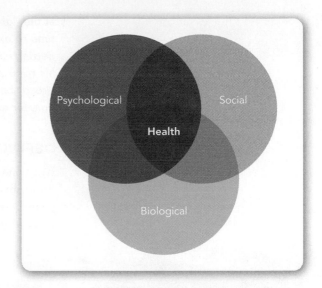

FIGURE 14.1

The Biopsychosocial Model of Health or Illness

Mind, body, and the social environment all contribute to health or to the development of illness.

---

concept CHECK

- Health psychology uses the principles and methods of psychology to understand the effects of attitudes and behaviors on health and illness.

- Health is defined as a state of mental, social, and physical well-being, not just a lack of illness.

- Mind-body dualism suggests that mind and body function independently. This point of view is not supported by current empirical research.

APPLICATION QUESTION Although research clearly suggests that psychological and biological variables affect one another, why do you think that a mind-body dualism perspective persists in medical research and health care?

The Role of Stress in Physical and Mental Health

Chris just couldn't believe how stressful it was to be a college freshman. He had really looked forward to moving away and starting this new chapter in his life, but he wasn't at all prepared for how difficult it was to be away from his family and his girlfriend, who was attending college in a different state. He was also shocked at how much work was required for his classes—huge amounts of reading, projects due in different classes every week, tests that covered way too much material. And Chris was having a hard time making new friends. He came from a small town where everyone knew everyone else. Here, just walking on campus felt like he was in a huge city—and he was lost about where and how to meet people. He also wasn't eating well—it was too hard to get to the cafeteria at the right times and much easier to grab fast food in between classes. Chris didn't have time to exercise like he used to, and he didn't sleep well in the noisy dormitory. It was getting harder to concentrate in class because he was so tired and there was so much on his mind and his "to do" list. He just wasn't sure if he would make it or not. He had already been to the infirmary twice, once for a bad cold that wouldn't go away and another time for recurrent headaches.

DEFINING STRESS

Everyone experiences stress—it is impossible to get through life without it. However, the events that cause stress and the symptoms that accompany stress vary greatly across people. **Stress** is defined broadly as any negative emotional experience that is accompanied by biochemical, physiological, cognitive, and behavioral responses that attempt to change or adjust to the stressor (Baum, 1990). A **stressor** is any event that produces tension or another negative emotion like fear (DiMatteo & Martin, 2002) and that prepares the organism for a *fight-or-flight* response (see Chapter 4). Stressors can be physical (a medical disease or physical injury), environmental (natural disaster, high level of noise, change in living situation), interpersonal-social (break-up of a relationship, argument with a family member), or psychological (sudden realization that a final exam is tomorrow instead of the day after). The characteristics of an event affect the probability that it will produce stress. Perceived stress is more likely if an event has a negative outcome, but positive outcomes also can produce stress. The idea that positive life events or experiences can create stress may seem contradictory, but you can probably recall a time in your life when a positive event created stress for you (e.g., planning for or going on a big trip; starting a new relationship).

Everyone experiences stress—even school-children. Stress can only be understood individually, however, as what is stressful for one person may not be for another.

Stress is also more likely when the event is perceived as uncontrollable, unpredictable, or ambiguous (in which case the person has no clear idea what action to take) or when it has an impact on a major area of life, such as parenting, personal relationships, or achievement (Taylor, 2006). Because people may react differently to the same event, a stressor can only be understood fully when the interaction between an event and a person is considered. For example, some people are energized and better able to focus on a task when the deadline is near. Others feel so pressured that they lose their ability to concentrate and complete a project. Remember Chris? He had significant stress after leaving home for college. Other college freshmen, however, thrive on the changes that occur at this life stage.

After a stressful event, an interactive **appraisal process** occurs in which a person assesses whether he or she has the resources or coping skills to deal with the event (Lazarus & Folkman, 1984) (see Figure 14.2). First, the person assesses potential harm or threat (*primary appraisal*). Perceptions of threat are heavily influenced by many psychological and social variables, such as a person's beliefs and values, that give meaning to the event and its expected outcomes (Lazarus, 1999; Thompson & Van-Loon, 2002). For example, losing a job will be perceived as a much greater threat by a middle-aged man who is supporting a family of four than by a college student who is working part-time for extra money. Next, the person identifies available skills to cope with or overcome the possible negative outcomes (*secondary appraisal*). Coping strategies fall into two broad categories. *Problem-focused coping* is acting to reduce possible negative outcomes (looking for a new job). *Emotion-focused coping* is acting to reevaluate the personal meaning of the situation (losing my job doesn't mean I am a bad worker) (Thompson et al., 2002). Stress occurs when a person feels that his or her coping skills are inadequate to manage a potentially harmful or threatening event.

stress any negative emotional experience that is accompanied by biochemical, physiological, cognitive, and behavioral responses that are aimed at changing or adjusting to the stressor

stressor any event (or stimulus) that produces tension or other negative emotion, such as fear

appraisal process a person's assessment of whether he or she has the resources or coping skills to meet the demands of a situation

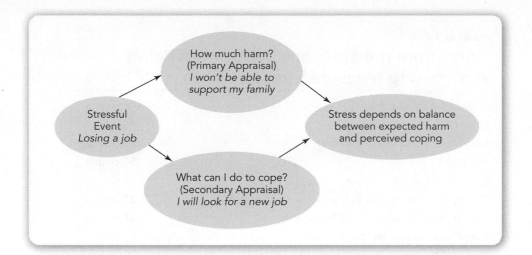

FIGURE 14.2
The Appraisal Process
Following a Stressful Event

After a stressful event, the person assesses the potential harm or threat and his or her ability to cope with it. Stress occurs when a person feels unable to cope with the possible threat.

There are many forms of stress. *Acute stress* occurs when a potentially threatening event and the associated reaction last for only a brief time—for example, a burglary. *Chronic stress* develops when a threatening event continues over time, as with a chronic illness, excessive work demands, or long-term poverty, and/or when a person consistently feels inadequate to deal with ongoing negative outcomes (DiMatteo et al., 2002). *Daily hassles*, or minor aversive events that occur day-to-day (the coffee pot breaks in the morning, the dog has an accident on the rug, a meeting runs overtime and makes you late for class) can accumulate to create stress. Finally, *major life events* that affect the way a person lives, such as starting college, marriage, divorce, job change or home relocation, or diagnosis of a major illness, can produce stress. Under any of these conditions, perceived or actual inability to cope results in a *stress reaction*, with symptoms of a *fight-or-flight* response (e.g., increased blood pressure, heart rate, sweating, respiration rate). Adaptive responses help the person react quickly and positively to potentially harmful events (e.g., helping a child who is choking). Detrimental responses disrupt functioning (e.g., stress about a class project leads to poor sleep and missed classes). Detrimental responses also potentially set the stage for poorer health (Taylor, 2006).

Daily hassles are minor aversive events that are sources of stress. This type of stress is usually brief and manageable.

MEASURING STRESS

Various procedures are used to evaluate acute stress, major life events, and daily hassles. Acute stress is often measured with an **acute stress paradigm**. Short-term stress is created in the laboratory, and its effect on physiological, neuroendocrine, and psychological responses is measured. Stress can be created in different ways. A participant may be asked to solve a frustrating math problem, to deliver an impromptu speech, or be administered a mild electric shock (Martin & Brantley, 2004; Taylor, 2006). This approach allows researchers to carefully examine biological responses (heart rate, blood pressure, blood chemistry) and psychological variables as measured by interviews and questionnaires (level of chronic stress, personality style) at the same time. When acute stress is measured in the laboratory, researchers must carefully consider the ethical issues involved in placing participants in a stressful situation (e.g., could participants be harmed in any way?). In addition, laboratory stressors (for example, mild electric shock) are not usually the same as those commonly experienced in everyday life, and this limits the usefulness of data collected by such procedures.

Measuring the impact of life events is common in stress research. In 1967, researchers studying stress (Holmes & Rahe, 1967) created the *Social Readjustment Rating Scale* (SRRS), which is still used today (see Table 14.1). The SRRS lists 43 potentially stressful life events, each of which has a numerical rating that estimates how

acute stress paradigm a procedure in which short-term stress is created in the laboratory and its impact on physiological, neuroendocrine, and psychological responses is measured

TABLE 14.1

Items from the SRRS and Associated Points Assigned to Measure Stress

Death of a spouse	100 points
Divorce	73 points
Death of a close family member	63 points
Marriage	50 points
Sexual difficulties	39 points
Taking out a mortgage or loan for a major purchase	31 points
Beginning or ceasing formal schooling	26 points
Major change in living conditions	25 points
Major change in working hours or conditions	20 points
Major change in sleeping habits	16 points
Vacation	13 points

much life "readjustment" is related to the event. The list includes both positive and negative events, both of which may cause stress and affect health.

The SRRS is a simple way to evaluate the relationship between life events and health, and it generalizes well to "real life" because people rate their real experiences. However, its reliance on people's recall of events may introduce memory bias. Also, measuring the effect of life events with the SRRS does not take into account individual differences (how various life events affect different people in different ways), nor does it differentiate the impact of positive and negative life events.

The *Hassles Scale* (Kanner et al., 1981) measures the frequency and severity of day-to-day stressors, whereas the *Uplifts Scale* (Kanner et al., 1981) assesses day-to-day events that counteract the negative effects of stress. For both measures, people rate the frequency of daily hassles, which include events such as misplacing or losing things or being interrupted. They also rate uplifts, such as completing a task, being complimented, or laughing at a joke. The severity of hassles is also rated, and intensity scores are calculated for both hassles and uplifts. Like the SRRS, however, these scales rely on people's ability to recall activities, and people who tend to feel easily stressed and anxious may rate the severity of daily hassles differently than other people, creating problems for studies that examine the relation between stressors and health.

When people feel stressed, they may stop taking care of themselves. They may get less sleep, smoke or drink more, or eat irregular or unhealthful meals.

THE IMPACT OF STRESS ON HEALTH

However we measure it, we know that stress can impact health *indirectly* and *directly*. When people feel stressed, they often stop taking care of themselves and develop poor health habits. Like Chris, people under stress get less sleep, exercise less, change eating habits in unhealthy ways (e.g., eat more fast food, have more irregular meals), and drink more alcohol. These poor health habits can produce negative health consequences that are *indirectly* related to stress (DiMatteo et al., 2002). Other indirect pathways between stress and health include injuries, which are more frequent among people who are under stress (e.g., at work, during sports activities, or while driving), and adoption of a "sick role" to avoid obligations and situations when people feel unable to cope. However, stress can have a more *direct* impact on physical functioning and health. It can cause changes in the nervous and endocrine systems and affect the immune system.

Physiology of Stress In the 1930s, Walter Cannon described the body's well-known flight-or-flight response that occurs during stress (see Chapter 4) (Cannon, 1932). This response prepares any organism to escape or engage in conflict when a potentially dangerous stimulus/event occurs. Physical responses include increased *sympathetic nervous system* activity—increased blood pressure, more rapid heart and respiration rates, increased blood sugar levels, sweaty palms, and muscle tension. Cannon proposed that continual or chronic physical stress responses could break down a person's ability to fight illness. In the 1950s, Hans Selye proposed a related theory called the **General Adaptation Syndrome (GAS)** (Selye, 1956), which has three stages: (1) *Alarm*, when the body mobilizes to meet a threat (with increases in activity within the sympathetic nervous system); (2) *Resistance*, when the individual attempts to cope with or resist the threat; and (3) *Exhaustion*, when continued efforts to overcome the threat deplete physical resources. In this third stage, a person becomes increasingly vulnerable to illness. As you will see through the remainder of this chapter, we now know that chronic stress is associated with increased rates of serious medical illnesses such as hypertension, cardiovascular disease, diabetes, and arthritis (DiMatteo et al., 2002; Taylor, 2006).

Although both the fight-or-flight and GAS theories propose similar methods by which stress influences physiology and health, they do not address the psychological and social variables that affect the *appraisal process* described earlier. For example, divorce is stressful for most people. However, for those in a very conflictual or abusive marriage, divorce may actually produce less stress than the marriage. Remember—the same event is not equally stressful to everyone.

When stress does occur, the stress responses affect two major systems: the **sympathetic-adrenomedullary system (SAM)** and the **hypothalamic-pituitary-adrenocortical (HPA) axis**. These two systems have different functions. The "revved up" feeling is the *SAM response*—increased adrenal gland stimulation results in the secretion of epinephrine and norepinephrine. Continuous and long-term SAM activation can suppress immune functioning (see "Stress and the Immune System," below) and produce changes in resting blood pressure, heart rate, and heart rhythms. The second response, the *HPA response*, involves the hypothalamus. During stress, the hypothalamus increases production of corticotrophin-releasing factor (CRF), which causes increased secretion of adrenocorticotropic hormone (ACTH) and increased cortisol (another hormone). Increased cortisol helps the body store carbohydrates, reduce inflammation, and return the body to a steady state after stress (Taylor, 2006). Repeated HPA stimulation can change daily cortisol patterns, compromising immune functioning and impairing memory and concentration.

Stress and the Immune System

Clara was a stellar musician throughout high school. She dreamed of attending Juilliard and having a career as a concert violinist, so she was extremely disappointed when her first application was rejected. After 2 years of college elsewhere, however, she applied again and was granted an audition. Clara was thrilled, but also overwhelmed at the prospect of the interview. She prepared intensely and had trouble thinking of anything else during the days before she was to travel. To top it all off, the audition was going to occur right before final exams and right after a major project was due. It was too much all at once, but there was nothing more important in her life. The morning of her flight, Clara woke up with a cough, a terrible sore throat, and a fever. How could she possibly do her best now that she was sick? She just couldn't afford to be ill at this critical moment in her life.

To understand how Clara's stress contributed to her physical symptoms on the morning of her audition, we need to understand how the immune system works and how stress can change its functioning. The immune system protects the body against bacteria, viruses, and carcinogens in both *specific* and *nonspecific* ways. (DiMatteo et al., 2002; Martin et al., 2004; Taylor, 2006). **Specific immune system** responses protect us

General Adaptation Syndrome (GAS)
a three-stage process of stress adaptation, including alarm, resistance, and exhaustion

sympathetic-adrenomedullary system (SAM) a system that responds to stress in which increased adrenal gland stimulation results in the secretion of epinephrine and norepinephrine

hypothalamic-pituitary-adrenocortical (HPA) axis a system that responds to stress in which the hypothalamus produces increased corticotrophin-releasing factor (CRF), which in turn causes increased secretion of adrenocorticotropic hormone (ACTH) and increased cortisol

specific immune system protection against specific infections and diseases as a result of natural or artificial processes

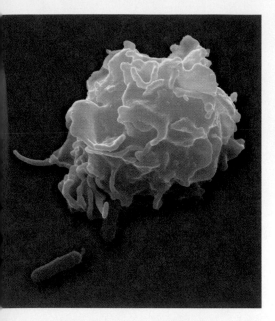

A white blood cell, hugely magnified, engulfing a pathogen. Stress can interfere with the functioning of the immune system, which means that stressed-out people are more likely to become ill.

against specific infections and diseases, such as chicken pox and tuberculosis. These responses can be the result of natural or artificial processes. Natural immunities are acquired through breast milk or as a result of having a particular disease (once you have had chicken pox, you are no longer susceptible to it). Artificially produced immunities are acquired through vaccinations or inoculations.

Nonspecific immune system responses offer general protection against infections and diseases in four different ways. First, *anatomical barriers*, such as the skin and the mucous membranes in the nose and mouth, prevent microbes from getting into the body. Second, a process called *phagocytosis* leads to the production of more white blood cells that destroy invaders. Certain white blood cells called *T-lymphocytes* (T-cells) are particularly important because they secrete chemicals that attack and kill invading microbes. Some T-cells are *killer cells* (T_c), and others are *helper cells* (T_H). Still other cells known as *natural killer* (NK) cells are also active in this process. Third, other white blood cells known as *B-lymphocytes* secrete antibodies or toxins into the blood to kill invading bacteria and viruses. Last, *inflammation* at the site of an infection, which produces swelling and increased blood flow, allows more white blood cells to move in and attack pathogens.

Psychological and social variables may complicate the functioning of the immune system. **Psychoneuroimmunology** is the study of the relations among social, psychological, and physical responses. We now know that people (like Clara) who are under severe and/or chronic stress are more likely to catch a cold, develop an upper respiratory infection, or get the flu (Cohen et al., 1998; Ironson et al., 2002). Stress *suppresses* the ability of the immune system to function adequately and increases people's susceptibility to bacteria and viruses. When people are under stress, wounds heal more slowly (Marucha et al., 1998), chronic diseases progress more rapidly, and vaccinations are less effective (Ironson et al., 2002; Martin et al., 2004).

As noted earlier, stress increases epinephrine and cortisol levels (the SAM and HPA responses discussed above), and this decreases the activity of the helper T-cells and lymphocytes that are important for killing bacteria and other toxins. Among medical students, academic stress at exam time was associated with lower T-cell activity and fewer NK cells and activity (Glaser et al., 1985; Kiecolt-Glaser et al., 1984). People or animals under stress develop fewer antibodies following immunization for flu, hepatitis, and tetanus (Ironson et al., 2002), meaning that these vaccinations are likely to be less effective. However, the relationship between stress and cell activity is not simple. Many variables affect this relationship, including how much time has elapsed since the stressor occurred, how much control people believe they have over the stressor, the person's age, and time of day (Delahanty et al., 2000; Miller et al., 2007; Peters et al., 1998). Interpersonal interactions also affect cell activity and immune functioning. Hostility between spouses, for example, is associated with suppressed (reduced) immune functioning (Kiecolt-Glaser et al., 1998). Loneliness, or perceived social isolation, is also associated with many indicators of poorer immune functioning (Hawkley & Cacioppo, 2003), and positive social support benefits immune functioning (Uchino et al., 1996).

The Psychological Impact of Stress   Stress and poorer immune functioning are associated with increases in negative moods, including depression, anxiety, hostility, and anger. People who are depressed have reduced NK cell activity, lower lymphocyte response, and more white blood cells (suggesting that the body is trying harder to fight infection) (Herbert & Cohen, 1993). These associations appear stronger for older people and those who are hospitalized. Other negative moods, including anger, hostility, and anxiety, are also associated with reduced NK cell activity and immune system suppression (DiMatteo et al., 2002). On the other hand, positive mood is linked to lower stress, increased NK cell activity, and increased antibody levels, all of which indicate better immune functioning and ability to ward off disease (Stone et al., 1994; Valdimarsdottir & Bovbjerg, 1997).

nonspecific immune system   general protection against infections and diseases provided by anatomical barriers, phagocytosis, B-lymphocytes, and inflammation

psychoneuroimmunology   the study of the relations between social, psychological, and physical responses

Several psychological disorders are associated with physical stress responses. Depression, alcoholism, and eating disorders are linked to increased HPA activity (Ehlert et al., 2001). Elevated HPA activity also exists among women who were abused as children, and this relationship is particularly strong when symptoms of depression and/or anxiety are present (Heim et al., 2000). Of course, one of the most extreme psychological responses is post-traumatic stress disorder (PTSD; see Chapter 4), which consists of vivid and intrusive memories of the trauma, avoidance of people and things that signify the trauma, significant physiological arousal, and emotional numbness. People with PTSD have more physical health problems, particularly more frequent cardiovascular, gastrointestinal, and musculoskeletal disorders, and they use medical health services more often than those without the disorder (Jankowsi, 2006).

Moderators of Stress   Variables that affect how stress is experienced and how it affects health and other aspects of functioning are called **stress moderators**. We consider here internal and external variables that may moderate the link between stress and health.

We already mentioned the possible role of *personality* in health problems. Characteristic patterns of behavior, thinking, and feeling can increase or decrease the effect of stress on health. One of the best-known personality styles is the **Type A behavior pattern**, which has been linked to increased risk of coronary heart disease (CHD). The Type A behavior pattern (Friedman & Rosenman, 1974) describes behaviors that are associated with consistent strivings for achievement, impatience and time urgency, and aggressiveness toward others.

Robert, a middle-aged father of two boys, aged 12 and 14, worked for an oil company. His job was important to him; he supervised a large group of engineers, and he worked hard. He got to work early, completed projects ahead of deadlines, and was always on time for meetings. Robert's co-workers, however, were not as timely or efficient, and it made him angry when they missed deadlines or asked for extensions. He also became irritated with his sons when they didn't seem to be doing their best. Sometimes they just seemed to be "goofing off," and he didn't understand why they weren't more competitive. He also couldn't stand to get behind a slow driver. He could feel his blood pressure rise when he got stuck behind someone who seemed to be out for a "country drive" on the freeway. In fact, lately it seemed that he was angry all the time. He argued more with his wife, yelled too often at his children, and got into disagreements at work.

Robert's personality could place him at risk for health problems. People with a Type A behavior pattern, like Robert, tend to feel chronically aroused (always keyed up) and have difficulty relaxing. Other Type A dimensions include a sense of time urgency and competitiveness. However, it is the feelings of anger and hostility associated with a Type A style that are more important for predicting increased risk of CHD and heart attack (Gallacher et al., 2003; Moller et al., 1999). In addition, people who are hostile and distrustful, even if they do not have the full Type A pattern, have an increased risk for cardiovascular problems (Taylor, 2006). Levels of hostility are higher in men than women, and this may partially explain the increased risk of CHD in men (Matthews et al., 1992).

Other personality characteristics (internal moderators) such as *negative affectivity* (the tendency to experience negative mood, including anxiety, depression, and hostility), a *pessimistic explanatory style* (the tendency to blame negative outcomes on some stable characteristic of oneself), for example, "I didn't get that promotion because I am just not very good at my job.", and *optimism* (the tendency to expect positive outcomes) may affect how stress influences health. Negative affectivity and/or a pessimistic style have been linked to poorer immune functioning (van Eck et al., 1996), poorer response to surgery (Duits et al., 1997), more physical complaints even when actual symptoms are not worse (Cohen et al., 2003), and poorer long-term physical

stress moderators   variables that affect how stress is experienced and how it affects health and other aspects of functioning

Type A behavior pattern   a personality pattern associated with the onset of coronary heart disease, associated with consistent strivings for achievement, impatience and time urgency, and aggressiveness toward others

Social support can reduce the impact of stress when people are confronted with a challenge, such as a natural disaster.

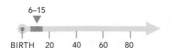

6–15

BIRTH 20 40 60 80

health (Maruta et al., 2002). Optimists, on the other hand, are sick less often (Cohen et al., 2003) and have lower blood pressure and less risk of CHD (Kubzansky et al., 2001; Raikkonen et al., 1999). They also function better in the presence of pain (Brenes et al., 2002) and have improved outcomes following surgery (Scheier et al., 1989). Optimists may have better health outcomes because they are better at solving problems, seeking social support, and emphasizing the positive aspects of a situation (Scheier et al., 1986).

External moderators, such as resources and social support, also influence the impact of stress. People with greater external resources, such as more time and money, a higher level of education, a better job, and a higher standard of living, function better when faced with stress (Taylor, 2006). One of the most important predictors of health is *socioeconomic status*, which is influenced by variables such as education, income, and occupation. People with higher socioeconomic status have fewer medical and psychological disorders, and they even live longer (Adler et al., 1993). Greater social support from family, significant others, friends, and others in the community also reduces the negative effects of stress. People with more social support are less distressed, have reduced risks of illness or death, and adjust better to chronic diseases (Martin et al., 2004; Taylor, 2006). Even "social" support from animals, particularly dogs, can lower heart rate and blood pressure (Allen et al., 2002) and reduce levels of stress-related hormones (Odendaal & Meintjes, 2003).

There are at least three types of social support. *Tangible support*, such as financial help, goods (food), and services (child care, transportation), can reduce the impact of a stressful event. *Informational support*, which involves the sharing of information to reduce stress, can help solve problems and manage stressful situations. *Emotional support*, such as the provision of caring, can provide reassurance during periods of high stress. Social support may reduce the impact of stress directly (e.g., by improving available coping resources) or indirectly (e.g., by making potentially stressful situations seem less threatening). There is still much to learn about the ways that social support moderates the relationship between stress and health.

SEX, RACE, AND DEVELOPMENTAL ISSUES

In comparison to adults, much less is known about children's responsiveness to stress. Clinically, we know that many children express distress through physical complaints such as headaches and stomachaches. Recurrent abdominal pain (RAP) is among the most common complaints of childhood. Occurring in approximately 10% of children, RAP consists of at least three bouts of pain that are so severe as to impede daily functioning (Ramchandani et al., 2005). A physical cause is identified only in 10 to 15% of cases of RAP. Psychologically, children with anxious temperament and anxiety disorders are overrepresented. Because the pain comes and goes, stressful events are assumed to be associated with the pain episodes; however, there has been little systematic research on the topic.

Although the basic physical response to stress is similar for men and women, men may have greater cortisol and immune system stress responses than do women (Kirschbaum et al., 1999; Rohleder et al., 2001). Recent research also reveals different coping styles. Men are more likely to use *problem-focused coping*, doing something to change stressful conditions. Women more often use *emotion-focused coping*, expressing feelings and seeking social support to cope with stress (Martin et al., 2004). Women are more likely to use a "tend and befriend" strategy instead of the "fight-or-flight" response (Taylor et al., 2000). Early studies of stress assessed mostly male participants to avoid the need to control for greater cyclical variation in hormone responses (due to the reproductive cycle) among women. Recent animal and human research, however, indicates that women tend to care for and affiliate with others during times of stress (i.e., tending and befriending) (Taylor et al., 2000). This difference may reflect evolutionary influences that dictated different parental roles. Motherhood, for example, requires protecting offspring, getting them out of the way, and calming them down rather than attacking predators and leaving young ones unprotected (Taylor et al., 2000). This different response may reflect different hormones found in males and females.

Little research has examined differences in stress responses among different racial and ethnic groups. Among the few existing studies, factors such as socioeconomic status or sex have typically not been controlled. As noted earlier, lower socioeconomic status is associated with higher levels of stress and disease, possibly as a result of discrimination or differential coping and social support (Gallo & Matthews, 2003). Despite these limitations, race and ethnicity may play a role in the relationship between stress and physical outcomes. For example, chronic exposure to discrimination, both racial and other types, may be related to the amount of coronary artery calcification in African American women (Lewis et al., 2006), and increased chronic stress tends to differentially alter daytime cortisol response in Hispanic relative to non-Hispanic women (Gallagher-Thompson et al., 2006). Racial or ethnic background also may moderate the impact of social support and other potentially important variables such as religion and spirituality (see the box "Research Hot Topic: Religion, Stress, and Health"). Asians and Asian Americans, for example, seem to benefit more from *implicit social support* that does not require disclosure of personal information, whereas European Americans benefit more from explicit social support that involves receiving advice and emotional support from others (Taylor et al., 2007). Certain racial or ethnic groups also may rely more heavily on religion and spirituality to reduce the impact of stress.

Women may use a "tend and befriend" strategy rather than a "fight-or-flight" response when confronted with stress. This may reflect the influence of evolution—motherhood more often requires protecting offspring than fighting predators directly.

concept CHECK

- The level of stress is determined by an interaction between a person and an event. The person first perceives the level of harm associated with an event (primary appraisal) and then assesses his or her ability to cope (secondary appraisal).

- Stress can be acute (short-term) or chronic (long-term) and can be caused by daily hassles or major life events.

- Stress can be measured in the laboratory, where its impact on physiological, neuro-endocrine, and psychological responses can be assessed, or by questionnaires that ask people about major events and daily hassles.

- The impact of stress on health can be indirect (by means of changes in health-related behaviors) or direct (by physical changes in SAM, HPA, and immune functioning).

- *Psychoneuroimmunology* is the study of relations among psychological and social variables, immune system functioning, and disease.

- Moderators of the impact of stress on health include personality style (such as the Type A behavior pattern), economic resources, and social support.

APPLICATION QUESTION How would you design a study to test the impact of stress on test performance? How would you measure stress? How would you be able to tell if there was a causal link between stress and performance?

Research HOT Topic

Religion, Stress, and Health

In recent years, there has been a dramatic increase in research into the role of religion and spirituality in physical and mental health. Most people in the United States believe religion is important. They believe in God, pray, and attend church (Powell et al., 2003; Taylor, 2006). Thus, research examining the effects of religious beliefs and behaviors on health outcomes is of significant interest. A number of studies have demonstrated that religion, defined by regular attendance at church services, is associated with reduced mortality in healthy people (Powell et al., 2003). Other studies have found that religion and spirituality may improve the ability to cope with stress (Graham et al., 2001; Koenig et al., 1988), reduce depression (Braam et al., 2004), decrease engagement in adolescent sexual behavior (Rotosky et al., 2004), and improve cognitive functioning among older adults (Hill et al., 2006). Although specific findings vary across studies, higher levels of religion and spirituality are also associated with reduced blood pressure and hypertension (Krause et al., 2002; Steffen et al., 2001), lowered cortisol response following stress (Tartaro et al., 2005), and less rapid progression of cancer (Kinney et al., 2003). The health benefits of religion may be due to a number of variables, including the social support that often accompanies religious involvement, healthy behaviors promoted by various religions (e.g., less smoking, alcohol use, etc.), and beliefs that help people cope with difficult situations (Taylor, 2006).

Most of this research is *correlational*, making it very difficult to draw conclusions about the *cause* of improved health among people with greater religious involvement. In addition, not every study finds positive health outcomes associated with increased religion/spirituality. Some studies have suggested, for example, that religion and spirituality do not slow the progression of cancer, protect against cancer mortality, or improve recovery from acute illness when other important variables are taken into account (e.g., preexisting health conditions, other health behaviors, etc.) (Powell et al., 2003). Findings also sometimes differ with regard to ethnicity and gender. In many cases, more carefully designed studies are needed. Definitions of religion and spirituality, for example, are not consistent across studies. In some cases, religion is defined by service attendance; in other cases, the definition relies on religious-related beliefs or self-reported religious identity. There also are few standardized questionnaires available to assess involvement in religion or spirituality, and many studies do not include sufficiently diverse samples to generate broadly applicable findings. Future research is sorely needed, with careful attention to a variety of variables.

Psychology and Behavior in Medical Illness

At age 45, Sharon was married and worked as an office manager at a local doctor's office. Although her husband was physically active, she led a fairly sedentary life and had gained a lot of weight over the past 10 years. For the past year, she had felt consistently tired and had difficulty sleeping. She scheduled a visit with her internist (whom she hadn't seen in a couple of years) and was diagnosed with type II diabetes. As part of her treatment, Sharon was asked to start an exercise program, lose weight, modify her diet, and manage her stress. Whew! What a tall order—much easier said than done. However, she started walking 3 times a week and changed her eating habits, counting carbohydrates and limiting sweets. Over a couple of months, she saw her glucose levels drop, and she began to feel better in many ways. As time went on, however, she noticed that whenever she had a stressful week at work, her glucose levels were more unstable. During those difficult times, she found it harder to maintain healthy behaviors. Managing diabetes and sticking to healthy eating and exercise was going to be a lifelong task.

BEHAVIOR AND HEALTH

Maintaining a healthy diet and weight, getting enough sleep, exercising regularly, limiting alcohol use and smoking, using sunscreen, and wearing seat belts are all ways to prevent illness and accidents. Many of these health behaviors (sometimes called *health habits*) are established early in life, when people are not yet worried about their health. However, data clearly link health behaviors and health status (e.g., illness, disability) and even mortality. Given their significant roles in reducing the risk of cardiovascular disease, diabetes, cancer, obesity, and osteoporosis—healthy eating, regular exercise, and not smoking are three important components of healthy behavior.

Healthy Eating   Dietary habits play a particularly important role in the development of coronary heart disease, hypertension, and some forms of cancer. However, fewer than 33% of people in the United States eat the daily recommended servings of fruits and vegetables (Centers for Disease Control, 2007). Many biological, demographic, psychological, and social-cultural variables affect eating behaviors. Genetic, cultural, and social variables, for example, have a significant effect on taste preferences and food choice. People make food choices based on both innate and learned taste preferences, the foods that are commonly available (e.g., in rural versus urban settings, in ethnic minority vs. majority families, in settings where financial resources are abundant or limited, etc.), and according to their attitudes, knowledge, and beliefs (West et al., 2004). Stress, anxiety, and depression are also associated with less healthy eating patterns (Taylor, 2006). When stressed, people may have trouble monitoring their food intake and its consequences (Ward & Mann, 2000), and stress can be associated with either increased or decreased eating. People who are anxious or depressed also have difficulty maintaining special diets, such as those implemented to reduce cholesterol (Stilley et al., 2004). In general, recommended dietary changes for healthier eating are very effective, but they are often difficult to implement due to expense, extra time required for shopping and/or food preparation, and so forth.

Exercise and Physical Activity   The benefits of exercise are well known. Greater physical activity is associated with decreased resting heart rate, lower blood pressure, improved sleep, lower rates of obesity and cardiovascular disease, and increased longevity (Taylor, 2006). Regular exercise and increased activity are also associated with improved mood and well-being (Hansen et al., 2001), lower levels of depression (Lindwall et al., 2007), and reduced perception of pain (Hoffman & Hoffman, 2007). Nevertheless, many people are not active enough to stay healthy. Insufficient physical activity is related to a variety of social, demographic, and psychological variables. People who exercise less have lower incomes and less education and social support (Dubbert et al., 2004). Less physical exercise also is associated with increasing age and ethnic minority status. Physical inactivity, for example, is more common among older than younger adults and in African American and Hispanic adults than Caucasians (Lee & King, 2003). Women also are less physically active than men. Similar patterns occur among adolescents. Boys are more physically active than girls, and minority youth are less active than non-Hispanic white adolescents. Some of these observations, however, may be explained by socioeconomic differences between ethnic groups (Dubbert et al., 2004).

Healthy eating habits can be an important factor in fighting stress and disease.

About 50% of people who start an exercise program continue for up to 6 months. Psychological variables such as *self-efficacy* (the belief that one is capable of exercising regularly) affect the ability to maintain an exercise program. Most commonly, people report that stress and lack of time are the primary reasons for giving up on exercise (Taylor, 2006). However, people who exercise cope better with stress (Brown & Siegel, 1988), and we shall see later that exercise is an important component of stress management treatments.

Smoking Another major modifiable risk factor for poor health, smoking, is associated with significant increases in rates of lung cancer, cardiovascular disease, emphysema and other respiratory problems, and death. Smoking also increases the risk of accidents and injuries at work and poses health risks for the smoker's family members and co-workers (Taylor, 2006). Although overall rates of smoking are declining in the United States (Centers for Disease Control & Prevention, 2003), significant numbers of Americans continue to smoke. What do we know about psychological and social variables that lead people to smoke? First, smoking is more common among poorer people and those with less education. Previously more common among males than females, smoking rates are now similar among adult men and women and adolescent boys and girls (Fisher et al., 2004). Most people begin smoking before the age of 18, and starting to smoke is often associated with higher levels of stress and anxiety, increased contact with peers who smoke, and parental modeling (Fisher et al., 2004). Attitudes and knowledge about associated health effects also are important. Adolescents, in particular, are less concerned about the potential health risks associated with smoking and are more susceptible to initiating the behavior (Chassin et al., 2001). Advertising and marketing campaigns that target adolescents have significant effects on smoking initiation and continued use.

PSYCHOLOGICAL FACTORS AFFECTING PHYSICAL CONDITIONS

We have examined how the mind-body connection affects the experience and outcomes of stress, the functioning of the immune system, and the maintenance of health. Psychological, behavioral, and social factors also influence the development, course, and treatment of medical illnesses and other physical conditions. We have examined the impact of stress and personality factors on respiratory illness and cardiovascular problems. Here, we address the role of psychological, behavioral, and social factors in other medical illnesses such as HIV/AIDS, cancer, chronic pain, insomnia, and chronic fatigue. Certainly, psychological factors can affect many other physical conditions, but we focus here on this subgroup of illnesses.

HIV/AIDS The human immunodeficiency virus (HIV) destroys the body's ability to fight infection and some types of cancer. Early symptoms of HIV infection include fever, headache, and fatigue. These symptoms, however, generally disappear after a short time and may not return in a chronic or severe fashion for as much as 10 years (DiMatteo et al., 2002). Yet the virus continues to grow in the body. Acquired immunodeficiency syndrome (AIDS) is diagnosed when HIV-infected people have a particularly low number of T-cells or when one of 26 clinical conditions appears as a result of *opportunistic infections* (infections that do not usually cause disease in healthy persons). The first case of AIDS in the United States was diagnosed in 1981. Since then, over 900,000 cases have been reported (www.niaid.nih.gov/factsheets/hivinf.htm), although millions of people worldwide are living with HIV/AIDS.

HIV is spread through unprotected sex, contact with infected blood, sharing of contaminated needles or syringes, and from mother-to-child. People with other sexually transmitted diseases are more susceptible to HIV infection, and rates of HIV are growing rapidly among minority groups and women. Although African Americans constitute only about 13% of the U.S. population, they account for 49% of people with HIV/AIDS (www.cdc.gov/hiv/topics/aa/index.htm). Among African Americans, the progression from HIV to AIDS occurs more rapidly, mortality rates are higher, and survival time is shorter. In fact, HIV/AIDS is now a leading cause of death

real people, real disorders

Magic Johnson—Living with HIV

On November 7, 1991, Magic Johnson shocked the world with an announcement that he was HIV positive and was retiring from an amazing basketball career. He was tested during a routine exam, and was suddenly faced with a life-threatening illness and fear for his wife, who was pregnant at the time. Her test came back negative, but his adjustment was difficult. He missed playing basketball and suffered from medication side effects, stress, and mood swings. Nevertheless, Johnson has survived long and well (over 18 years), probably as a result of his excellent physical condition, his daily "multidrug cocktail," and the role he has assumed in the fight against AIDS. Magic Johnson has used his celebrity status and financial advantages to reduce stigma (AIDS isn't just a "gay disease"), educate the public about risks (with particular focus on black men and women, among whom prevalence is high), and support AIDS research.

(http://www.usatoday.com/news/nation/2006-11-30).

among African Americans. In 2004, Hispanics accounted for 18% of new HIV/AIDS diagnoses, and increasing rates also are reported among women, particularly African American and Hispanic women. Women now account for over 25% of new HIV/AIDS diagnoses, and 80% of these women are African American or Hispanic.

High-risk behaviors that facilitate susceptibility to HIV and its transmission are affected by many social and psychological variables, including knowledge, attitudes, social support, and self-efficacy (perceived ability) for changing risky behavior (Taylor, 2006). Even in our current information technology age, many people remain uninformed about HIV and AIDS. Risky behaviors are still common. They are influenced by mood, cultural values, social pressure, and modeling. The stigma of AIDS and potential negative reactions directly affect the willingness to get tested, which then affects early detection and treatment (Herek et al., 2003). Education about the disease, modes of transmission, and risky/safe behaviors is a useful secondary prevention effort targeted to at-risk groups (Weinhardt et al., 1999).

People with HIV face many challenges, including gradual deterioration of health and cognitive abilities, potential loss of employment, increased reliance on others, and stigma, fear, and prejudice. Depression, anxiety, and substance abuse are common (Pence et al., 2006) and occur more often among patients with poor social support or severe medical symptoms (Heckman et al., 2004). However, the impact of physical symptoms on negative mood can be reduced when people see some benefit from the illness, as in the case of Magic Johnson who has taken an active role in the fight to reduce stigma and increase research (Siegel & Schrimshaw, 2007) (see the box "Real People, Real Disorders: Magic Johnson—Living with AIDS"). Social support is particularly important because it helps the patient adjust to the disease and get appropriate treatment.

Depression, stress, and social support also affect disease progression and adjustment (Cruess et al., 2004). Negative beliefs about oneself, the future, and disease course are associated with decreased T-cell counts and more rapid progression from HIV to AIDS (Taylor, 2006). Higher levels of stress reduce immunity to infection and increase the rate of progression from HIV to AIDS (Leserman et al., 2000), although social support can mitigate the effects of stress (Cruess et al., 2000). Depression also increases disease progression and mortality rates in both men and women (Ickovics et al., 2001; Mayne et al., 1996). Bereavement-related depression is a key issue. People with HIV/AIDS frequently live in communities where disease risk is high and where loss of important relationships is frequent.

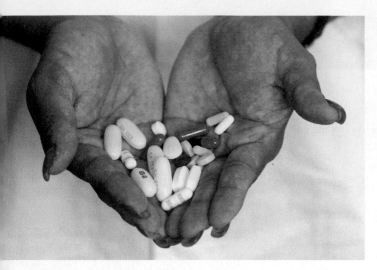

One day's dose of HIV medications.

A number of medicines are now available to slow HIV progression and reduce AIDS-related deaths. These drugs are expensive and have significant side effects, including decrease in red or white blood cells, pancreatic inflammation, nerve damage, and gastrointestinal symptoms. HIV/AIDS is now often a chronic disease (i.e., many people like Magic Johnson live with the disease for a long time), but long-term management requires complicated drug treatment. Adhering to these drug regimens is very difficult, particularly when other stressors are also present. Depression and reduced social support are associated with poorer treatment adherence in HIV positive men and women (Gonzalez et al., 2004), whereas education, stress management, and social support may increase adherence and promote better health.

Demographic variables also affect treatment, as minority patients (African American and Hispanic) are less likely than Whites to get newer medications quickly, and people with higher socioeconomic status have greater access to treatment programs (Taylor, 2006). Treatment programs, in general, need to be sensitive to the specific needs of demographic and cultural groups that vary with regard to beliefs, self-perceptions of risk, and common behaviors (Taylor, 2006).

Cancer   Cancer is the second leading cause of death in the United States (following heart disease). Cancer rates have declined in recent years, probably as a result of decreased smoking and improved treatments. However, over one million people per year are diagnosed, and more than 500,000 per year die from the disease (see Table 14.2) (National Cancer Institute, seer.cancer.gov/statfacts/html/all.html). The effects of cancer are even more widespread because family and friends of the patient also suffer through the disease and its treatment.

Although genetic factors play a role in the development of many kinds of cancer, some biological and lifestyle variables are also important. Socioeconomic status, for example, plays a role in cancer prevalence (Downing et al., 2007), and economic variables influence the use of cancer screening tools such as mammography (McAlearney et al., 2007). Unhealthy behaviors such as unprotected sun exposure, smoking, alcohol

---

TABLE 14.2

Incidence of a Cancer Diagnosis by Race/Ethnicity and Age (2001–2005)

Race/Ethnicity	Incidence Rates by Race	
	Male	**Female**
All Races	549.3 per 100,000 men	411.0 per 100,000 women
White	551.4 per 100,000 men	423.6 per 100,000 women
Black	651.5 per 100,000 men	398.9 per 100,000 women
Asian/Pacific Islander	354.0 per 100,000 men	287.8 per 100,000 women
American Indian/ Alaska Native	336.6 per 100,000 men	296.4 per 100,000 women
Hispanic	419.4 per 100,000 men	317.8 per 100,000 women

National Cancer Institute, seer.cancer.gov/statfacts/html/all.html.

use, and fatty diet without sufficient fruits and vegetables also are linked to increased cancer risk (DiMatteo et al., 2002; Taylor, 2006). Early detection through self-examination or medical testing may also improve outcomes and reduce mortality. As discussed above, these behaviors are in turn influenced by many psychological and social factors, including knowledge and beliefs, peer pressure, and stress (Henderson & Baum, 2004). Although not all data are consistent, there is some evidence that depression increases the risk of developing cancer (Carney et al., 2003; Henderson et al., 2004), possibly by altering cortisol, noreprinephrine, and the immune system. There are also small but significant links between cancer and a *cancer-prone personality style* (sometimes referred to as Type C personality), which describes people who are cooperative, unassertive, compliant, and do not express anger (McKenna et al., 1999). These studies are primarily correlational. Prospective studies that assess people over time are needed to determine potential causal links to cancer onset. Similarly, prospective studies are needed to examine the relationship between cancer and increased stress or lack of social support (Henderson et al., 2004; McKenna et al., 1999).

Many of the variables that are linked to cancer onset also affect its progression and course, as well as patient adjustment to the disease. Depression, pessimism, negative expectations, and an avoidant coping style (one that involves failure to confront the disease and/or express negative feelings) are associated with more rapid disease progression (Brown et al., 2003; Schulz et al., 1996). Similarly, increased stress and reduced social support are associated with more rapid physical deterioration and increased rates of recurrence (Henderson et al., 2004; Kerr et al., 2001). Although the effects may vary across different forms of cancer, stress and reduced social support affect natural killer cell activity, which decreases the body's ability to fight virus and tumor growth.

Because many patients diagnosed with cancer survive for many years, adjustment to cancer as a chronic illness is an important issue. Patients deal with many significant challenges, including fatigue, physical limitations and pain, decreased immune function and increased susceptibility to other infections, surgical removal of organs, body image difficulties, and prostheses. Emotional reactions such as depression, anxiety, and hopelessness, as well as changes in interpersonal relationships, are also common (e.g., marital and sexual relationships may change after breast cancer or prostate cancer treatment). Children may develop symptoms of PTSD as a result of their diagnosis and treatment (Somerfield et al., 1996). When parents are ill, children may have significant fears, and changes in family roles and interaction patterns can be quite stressful (e.g., older children may take on more responsibility at home or have less time with either parent when one parent is ill). Children's adjustment to their parent's cancer is influenced to some degree by family communication and by their mother's depression and level of adjustment (Osborn, 2007).

Predictors of adjustment to cancer overlap with factors that influence its onset and course. Interpersonal support is important, particularly from a spouse or partner. Married patients actually survive longer than single, divorced, or separated patients (Lai et al., 1999), and good marital adjustment predicts less distress from the diagnosis (Banthia et al., 2003). Active conversations about the disease and problem solving between partners are particularly useful (Hagedoorn et al., 2000). Optimism, active coping, feelings of control, and finding meaning in the experience also enhance adjustment and in some cases improve immune functioning and physical health (Barez et al., 2007; Taylor, 2006) (see the box "Real People, Real Disorders: Lance Armstrong, Cancer Survivor"). There is also some evidence that psychosocial treatments, including cognitive-behavior therapy, supportive treatments, and exercise programs improve adjustment and coping for patients and their partners (Badger et al., 2007; Mutrie et al., 2007) and possibly even survival.

real people, real disorders

Lance Armstrong, Cancer Survivor

Lance Armstrong was born in September 1971. He competed successfully as a triathlete from the age of 15, but he won world renown in his cycling career, winning the Tour de France seven consecutive times between 1999 and 2005. He returned to professional cycling in 2009. In October 1996, 3 years before his first Tour de France win, Armstrong was diagnosed with testicular cancer that had metastasized to his abdomen, lungs, and brain. He was given less than a 50% chance of survival, a figure that was elevated over real expectations to give him hope. Armstrong underwent chemotherapy and surgery, recovered within a year, and went on to achieve a cycling record that surpassed all prior accomplishments. How did he do it? What psychological and behavioral factors played a role in his successful recovery and survival? Part of his miraculous recovery was attributed to his unusual physical attributes, including top aerobic fitness and an ability to endure an inordinate amount of physical stress. Armstrong also has

an extraordinary level of tenacity. He pushed himself toward greatness and toward recovery from cancer. Some of his tenacity may have come from the teachings and behavior of his mother, who was his most ardent supporter through health and illness. She worked two jobs to care for him when he was young and taught him to treat adversity as a challenge to be overcome. During his illness and recovery, Armstrong had the support of an excellent medical team, his mother, and a girlfriend, and he never allowed himself to believe that he would die. He also used his experience with cancer to perceive life as a gift that carried with it an obligation to other cancer patients and survivors. Like Magic Johnson, he established a foundation that offers support and encouragement for cancer survivors.

Sources: www.unitedathletes.com/english/profiles/larmstrong.html
www.college.hmco.com/psychology/resources/students/shelves

Chronic Pain

When Howard woke up, he knew immediately that it was the beginning of another 2- to 3-week bout of back pain. He had played golf the day before after a morning of yard work, and it must have been too much strain. Howard was only 50, but he had been dealing with chronic back pain ever since he hurt himself playing football when he was 30. He'd also had surgery for a ruptured disc 3 years ago and now regularly had episodes of pretty severe pain. As he tried to roll over in bed, he thought about what was ahead. He wouldn't be able to play golf for at least a few weeks, and he would need to increase his daily dose of anti-inflammatory medication. He also wouldn't be able to sit at his desk for very long or play catch with his kids. Sleep wouldn't be easy either; he knew he would be up walking the floor when the pain got bad. Howard knew he needed to get back on track with the exercises the physical therapist had recommended. When he did those regularly, his back was better, but he was just too busy lately. He was really tired of dealing with this ongoing problem. It made him tired and grumpy and even a little depressed.

As we learned in Chapter 5, pain disorder is diagnosed when a patient's primary complaint is persistent pain that occurs without sufficient medical explanation. In Howard's case, however, persistent back pain had a medical explanation and did not qualify for a DSM diagnosis. Nevertheless, his symptoms produced ongoing distress and dysfunction. Chronic back pain like Howard's is one of the most common causes of disability in the United States. Up to 85% of people have back pain at some point, and arthritis pain and chronic headaches affect millions of people every year (Taylor, 2006). Pain is useful when it provides feedback about changes that are needed to keep the body healthy or safe (e.g., when to change positions, exercise, or move away from a potential danger like intense heat). However, there is not always a direct correlation between the location of the pain and its source, making its diagnosis and management a very complex issue. Pain is a huge source of disability, reduced productivity, and cost. It is the reason for at least 10% of physician visits in the United States, and associated costs to society are over $70 billion each year as the result of increased health care needs and reduced productivity (Gatchel & Maddrey, 2004). Pain is such a common problem that it is now considered the "fifth vital sign," in addition to pulse, blood pressure, body temperature, and respiration in medical evaluations.

Pain is generally classified as acute (lasting less than 6 months) or chronic (lasting 6 months or more). Acute pain usually occurs as a result of injury and resolves when the body heals. Chronic pain can be ongoing, as with chronic back pain, or associated with recurrent episodes of acute pain, as with migraines. Some chronic pain gets progressively worse over time, as with rheumatoid arthritis. Biologically, pain involves transmission of information from nerves at the injury site through the spinal cord and to the cerebral cortex. Other messages then go back to the site of the injury and other body parts where physical changes (e.g., muscle contractions, breathing changes) occur to help block the pain (Taylor, 2006).

The experience of pain is not always tied directly to the severity of a medical illness or other biological process. Many environmental, psychological, and social-cultural factors are involved. For example, the situation in which pain occurs affects its meaning and interpretation, which in turn influences the amount of distress and interference. Psychological variables are also important. Depression and anxiety commonly accompany pain and worsen its experience (Dickens et al., 2003; Vowles et al., 2004). People in pain feel unable to do things they used to enjoy, have decreased feelings of control, and worry about what will happen if the pain gets worse.

Pain is also common among people with depression and predicts poorer response to treatment (Bair et al., 2004). Negative thoughts (e.g., "I'll never get better"; "Things are only going to get worse") and unnecessary withdrawal from pleasurable activities (e.g., "I'd better not go to that basketball game; sitting on those bleachers will be too hard on my back" "I just can't be around people anymore—it's too hard to concentrate on what they are saying when I am in so much pain all the time") worsens depression and limits the efficacy of treatment (Bishop & Warr, 2003; Severeijns et al., 2004). The experience and expression of pain are sometimes reinforced by people or events. People who express pain through words or behavior sometimes get more attention, are relieved of responsibility, and receive financial compensation. These environmental reinforcers can be powerful motivators for the continued experience and/or expression of pain.

There also are individual differences in the frequency with which people report pain, seek help from their doctors, and respond to pain treatments (Turk & Monarch, 2002). These differences are not always related to actual physical conditions, but can be influenced by biological factors, learning history, and sociocultural variables. Women, for example, are typically more sensitive to pain than men (Gatchel & Maddrey, 2004), and they visit their doctors more often in response to pain (Kaur et al., 2007). Even among women, however, cultural variables affect the pain experience. Cultural expectations and attitudes about childbirth influence both pain experience and speed of recovery (Taylor, 2006). Pain prevalence and experience also are related to racial and ethnic differences. African American and Hispanic patients, for instance, show more pain sensitivity and less pain tolerance than non-Hispanic whites do, although these differences are also influenced by variables such as education, income, and racial/ethnic identity (Cano et al., 2006; Deyo et al., 2006; Rahim-Williams et al., 2007). Race and ethnic status also affect pain treatment. African Americans and Hispanics are less likely to receive adequate treatment for pain than whites (Cintron & Morrison, 2006), although these differences may be influenced to some extent by economic variables. Hispanic and non-Hispanic white women with private insurance, for example, are more likely to receive pain medication during childbirth than women from these same racial-ethnic groups who have no insurance (Glance et al., 2007). For black women, however, rates of pain medication were lower than for the other ethnic groups regardless of insurance status.

The goals of pain treatment may be to eliminate pain, reduce pain, or improve function in the face of some pain. Treatment includes both medical (medication, surgery, etc.) and nonmedical (acupuncture, psychological) approaches, although medication is used most often. Significant amounts of money are spent each year on over-the-counter and prescription pain medications. The most popular prescription medication is morphine, although this and other **analgesic medications** in the opioid family (e.g., codeine, hydrocodone [Vicodin]; oxycodone [OxyContin]) can cause dependence (see Chapter 9), leading to significant controversy over their use (see the box "Examining the Evidence: Are Opioid Medications Useful or Too Risky in the Treatment of Pain?"). Anti-inflammatory drugs and antidepressants can also reduce pain. Antidepressant drugs reduce anxiety and depression and also act on neural pathways that relay pain information. Anti-inflammatory drugs reduce pain but do not change mood. Nonmedical treatments for pain include relaxation training, biofeedback, and hypnosis. During **biofeedback**, patients learn to modify physical responses such as heart rate, respiration, and body temperature. During **hypnosis**, patients are taught to relax, a trance-like state is induced, and hypnotic suggestions are used to reduce pain and change pain-related thoughts. All of these interventions show positive effects, although the additional value of biofeedback over relaxation alone is not well established (Taylor, 2006). Cognitive-behavioral treatments that involve relaxation, imagery (imagining a positive scene to induce relaxation or picturing cancer as an enemy to be destroyed), cognitive therapy (changing thoughts about pain), and behavioral changes (becoming more active in managing one's own pain, engaging in positive behaviors despite pain) also can be useful. Typically, both medical and nonmedical strategies are integrated into a pain management program that is individually tailored to meet a patient's needs (Gatchel & Maddrey, 2004).

Insomnia   Certainly, you can recall times when you failed to get enough sleep—before a big test or when something stressful was going on in your life. Well, you are not alone. Up to 30% of people report some type of sleep disruption (National Institute of Health, 2005). This figure rises to 50% of patients in medical clinics (Pegram et al., 2004). Difficulty sleeping can be an acute problem, such as when better sleep returns after a major exam is over, or a chronic condition, defined as sleep problems that last anywhere from 30 days to 6 months.

Although the DSM-IV-TR lists diagnostic criteria for insomnia (see the box "DSM-IV-TR: Insomnia"), researchers who study this disorder may not use these exact criteria. In most cases, the definition includes persistent sleep difficulties over

analgesic medications   medications that reduce pain

biofeedback   process in which patients learn to modify physical responses such as heart rate, respiration, and body temperature

hypnosis   a procedure for treating pain during which patients relax, a trance-like state is induced, and hypnotic suggestions are used to reduce pain

primary insomnia   difficulty initiating or maintaining sleep, or nonrestorative sleep, over a period of at least 1 month and with significant distress and/or interference with functioning

DSM-IV-TR

Insomnia

Primary insomnia is difficulty initiating or maintaining sleep, or nonrestorative sleep, over a period of at least one month, with significant resultant distress and/or interference in functioning. The difficulties are not the result of an alternative sleep disorder (e.g., narcolepsy), a substance (e.g., a medication), or another medical or psychological problem (e.g., depression).

Adapted with permission from the *Diagnostic and Statistical Manual of Mental Disorders*, Text Revision, Fourth Edition, (Copyright 2000). American Psychiatric Association.

examining the evidence

Are Opioid Medications Useful or Too Risky in the Treatment of Pain?

■ **The Facts**   Opium, derived from the seedpod of poppies, was used to treat pain and other illnesses thousands of years ago. Opium-derived drugs became very popular in the nineteenth century, although concerns about misuse and overuse led to serious controls over their legal use by the 1940s (Ballantyne & Mao, 2003). Legal penalties for inappropriate use are severe, and many physicians are reluctant to prescribe these drugs. Are physicians correct to limit their use of opioids for the treatment of pain? Does caution lead to inadequate treatment for many pain sufferers? Can these drugs be used appropriately to manage pain without addiction?

■ **What Evidence Suggests that Use of Opioids Is Too Risky?**

- Opioids are the most commonly abused prescription drug. Rates of opioid abuse increased significantly from 1994 to 2000 (Atluri et al., 2003).

- Human and animal studies suggest that long-term use can increase sensitivity to pain (Ballantyne & Mao, 2003).

- Opioid use is sometimes accompanied by problematic or illegal behavior, including escalating doses without physician recommendation, requesting multiple prescriptions from different providers, and requesting refills without a physician visit (Webster & Webster, 2005).

- Rapid dose increases can create life-threatening respiratory depression (although this occurs rarely).

■ **What Evidence Supports the Value of Opioid Medications for Pain Treatment?**

- Studies show that opioid medication is effective for reducing pain in short-term and longer-term (up to 32 weeks) treatment (Ballantyne & Mao, 2003), although mixed results occur with regard to how these medications improve functioning.

- Approximately 15% of cancer patients and 80% of non-cancer patients with chronic pain fail to receive adequate treatment for pain (Chapman & Gavrin, 1999).

- Addiction occurs infrequently when opioid medications are used to treat pain (Atluri et al., 2003; Taylor, 2006).

- If one particular medication no longer manages pain, switching to an alternative opioid medication may be of value (rather than increasing the dose of a current drug) given that all types of opioids do not act on the same pain receptors (Ballantyne & Mao, 2003).

■ **Conclusions**   Consensus statements from experts suggest that opioids can be used appropriately to manage pain when guidelines about recommended drugs, doses, and duration of treatment are followed. Generally, a full medical examination is conducted before an initial prescription is given, as well as a careful review of the benefits and risks of opioid use (e.g., the risk of overuse increases if the patient has a personal or family history of substance use and/or if a psychiatric disorder is diagnosed). Patients appropriate for opioid medication are those whose symptoms have not improved with alternative approaches and who have limited risk factors for abuse. Opioids may even be prescribed, however, when risk factors for abuse are present but the pain is sufficiently severe that treatment of both pain and abuse are necessary. Patients prescribed opioids should work solely with one physician and one pharmacy, and careful follow-up and monitoring are needed to check for signs of overuse or abuse (e.g., requests for early refills, requests for refills without a physician visit, etc.).

some specified time interval that are associated with impairment in daily functioning (Nau et al., 2005; Pegram et al., 2004). Sleep difficulties can include problems falling asleep or staying asleep, waking up too early in the morning, and feeling fatigue upon awakening (often the result of what is called *nonrestorative sleep*). Insomnia can result in problems such as daytime sleepiness, impaired work or school performance, and cognitive impairments such as difficulties with attention, concentration, and memory. People with insomnia also have symptoms of depression and anxiety, increased risk for medical illness, poorer immune functioning, and greater risk of automobile accidents (Taylor, 2006). Significant economic costs also are incurred as a result of poorer productivity at work and related health care costs (Smith et al., 2002).

Sleep problems are common, even among young people. Lack of sleep can have a significant impact on daily functioning, including academic achievement.

Sleep problems are associated with several demographic variables. Women, for example, have significantly more sleep problems than men do (Morin et al., 2006; Nau et al., 2005), with differences beginning to emerge at menarche (Johnson et al., 2006). Older adults also have more sleep difficulties than middle-aged adults (Nau et al., 2005), although the relationship between sleep and age varies with ethnicity. African American adults, for example, sleep more poorly and have more insomnia than white adults overall, but for African Americans, prevalence peaks in middle, rather than older adulthood (Durrence & Lichstein, 2006). Again, ethnic differences in sleep symptoms and patterns may actually reflect socioeconomic differences between ethnic groups (Roberts et al., 2006). Similarly, among older adults increased sleep difficulties may not result from age alone, but from changes in circadian rhythms, increased prevalence of medical illnesses, medications that affect sleep, and psychosocial factors associated with age (Ancoli-Israel & Cooke, 2005). At the other end of the developmental spectrum, adolescents can develop sleep difficulties as they experience increased social pressures and greater demands at school (Pegram et al., 2004). Thus, normal age-related sleep changes occur through the life span (Pegram et al., 2004), but at all ages, a diagnosis of insomnia considers how sleep difficulties affect daytime functioning.

Insomnia can result from stress, anxiety, or depression. In fact, sleep difficulties are part of the diagnostic criteria for depressive disorders and generalized anxiety disorder. Sleep problems also may result from medical problems such as pain, gastrointestinal reflux, and sleep apnea (a condition in which air passages are blocked and disrupt sleep). Poor sleep habits such as drinking caffeine and exercising too close to bedtime may disrupt sleep. Other poor sleep behaviors include irregular sleep schedules and excessive napping. People can also learn to associate being in bed with tossing and turning instead of sleeping (an example of classical conditioning). At a very early age, children can learn poor sleep patterns if they are consistently "helped" to fall asleep (e.g., *Jacob cannot fall asleep at bedtime or after wakening in the middle of the night unless Mom rubs his back*) or when patterns of nighttime behaviors do not foster relaxation and sleep (e.g., the last activity before bedtime involves rough-housing with Dad) (Ferber, 1985).

Understanding how people learn poor sleep habits suggests behavioral interventions to improve sleep. For example, teaching parents how to change bedtime routines and respond to nighttime awakenings can help children learn to comfort themselves and get to sleep on their own (Ferber, 1985). For adults, behavioral treatment involves teaching new sleep habits such as using the bed only for sleep (e.g., getting up out of bed when one can't sleep and reading quietly until feeling tired again), setting a regular bedtime that doesn't vary more than 30 minutes or so even on weekends, limiting naps, and restricting alcohol and nicotine intake (Morin & Espie, 2003) (see Table 14.3). Relaxation training and cognitive therapy (changing beliefs about sleep) also can help. These behavioral and cognitive treatments are effective for both middle-aged and older adults (Irwin et al., 2006; Morin et al., 2009) even when sleep difficulties are secondary to a chronic medical illness (Rybarczyk et al., 2005).

Medications often used to treat sleep difficulties include benzodiazepines (e.g., temazepam [Restoril] flurazepam [Dalmane]), newer drugs that are not benzodiazepines but act on the same receptors (e.g., zolpidem [Ambien]; eszopiclone [Lunesta]), antidepressants, and nonprescription antihistamines (National Institute of Health, 2005). These treatments work more quickly than behavioral approaches, with less patient effort. Improvements in sleep are comparable following cognitive-behavioral and pharmacological treatments (Morin et al., 2009; Smith et al., 2002). However, long-term dependence and tolerance are a concern for some medications, particularly for older adults who have frequent sleep problems. They are also more likely to suffer problematic side effects such

TABLE 14.3

Good Sleep Habits

S = Set a regular bedtime and wake time

- It's helpful to go to bed at the same time and wake up at the same time.

L = Limit the use of the bedroom

- Limit the use of the bedroom/bed for sleep or sex.

E = Exit the bedroom if you are not asleep in 15–20 minutes

- When you go to bed at your regular time, but don't feel sleepy within 15–20 minutes, you should get up and go into another room until you feel sleepy again.
- This rule can be used throughout the night—if you get up in the middle of the night and can't get back to sleep in 15–20 minutes, then move to another location until you are sleepy.

E = Eliminate naps

- Naps can be disruptive to nighttime sleeping. If you are unable to avoid a nap mid-day, limit it to one hour and do not sleep after 3:00 P.M.

P = Put your feet on the floor at the same time every morning

- It is important to wake up at about the same time every morning, give or take 30 minutes. Setting an alarm can help this pattern.

as cognitive impairment and problems with balance and walking that increase the risk of falls and other accidents. There is also the need to consider the phenomenon of medication-dependent insomnia, which is defined as more intense sleep difficulties and anxiety when medications are withdrawn (Smith et al., 2002). Interestingly, behavioral and cognitive treatments can help reduce medication use as well as improve sleep for chronic users of benzodiazepines (Morin et al., 2004).

concept CHECK

- Many behaviors have a significant impact on health, including eating, sleeping, exercise, use of alcohol and nicotine, level of sun exposure, and risky sexual behaviors.
- Poorer health habits are typically seen in people with lower education and income, as well as in those with increased depression and anxiety.
- Anxiety and depression are common correlates of serious medical illnesses like HIV/AIDS and cancer, and variables such as negative beliefs, poor social support, and increased stress can accelerate the progression of medical symptoms.
- Pain is such a common problem that it is now considered the "fifth vital sign" in medical evaluations.
- The experience of pain is not always directly related to severity of a medical illness or injury. Many psychological, environmental, and cultural factors influence the perception of pain. A diagnosis of pain disorder is not appropriate when chronic pain has a medical explanation.
- Insomnia can be defined by any of a number of sleep difficulties, including trouble falling asleep, staying asleep, waking too early, or feeling tired upon waking.

APPLICATION QUESTION Your roommate drinks caffeinated soft drinks all the time. After her morning classes, she takes a nap for several hours, and she often stays up all night trying to catch up on schoolwork. Today, she tells you that for the last week she has had trouble falling asleep. What can you tell her to help her understand how some of her behaviors might be affecting her sleep?

Psychological Treatments for Health-Related Conditions

The first part of this chapter has illustrated the important role that psychological factors play in health and illness. In the following section, we discuss how psychologists and psychological interventions may help in the overall treatment program for many health problems. Treatment may occur in private practice, in a medical setting such as an outpatient clinic or hospital, or within an organization, such as a workplace or school that offers health and wellness programs. Before examining what health psychologists do, we first define a health psychologist.

THE ROLE OF A HEALTH PSYCHOLOGIST

A health psychologist typically has a doctoral degree (Ph.D. or Psy.D.) in psychology (clinical, counseling, social, cognitive, or physiological areas) and specialty training in medical/health issues, completed during doctoral training (e.g., a specialized Health Psychology track) and/or during postdoctoral work. Most health psychologists are trained in the scientist-practitioner model, with combined expertise in clinical care and research. In clinical settings, health psychologists work with a patient or medical team to change behaviors, attitudes, or beliefs to promote health and improve adjustment to illness. They may work with patients individually or in groups, and they sometimes provide assistance to family members. Health psychologists in research careers typically work in university or medical school settings, where they conduct research examining the relations between psychological and physical variables or the effectiveness of interventions to improve health and quality of life.

HEALTH PSYCHOLOGY INTERVENTIONS

In earlier sections, we reviewed strategies that health psychologists might use to help patients manage pain and improve sleep. Here, we review other interventions that focus on increasing healthy behaviors, managing stress, and adjusting to chronic illness.

Increasing Healthy Behaviors It might be interesting to take stock of your own inventory of healthy behaviors. Do you:

- Eat a balanced diet and exercise regularly?
- Sleep at least 7 hours a night?
- Smoke? Drink too much alcohol?
- Always wear your seatbelt? Use sunscreen?

If you have ever tried to change your behavior in these areas, you know that it is not always easy. Certainly, it is easier to prevent poor health habits than to change them. Increasing healthy behaviors among people without disease is called **primary prevention** (DiMatteo et al., 2002). Developing a program to prevent smoking in teens is an example of this approach.

Secondary prevention includes health-promotion programs for people at increased risk for health problems, such as people with a family history of stroke or heart attack. Initiating a low-cholesterol diet and exercise program for someone whose parent died young from a heart attack is an example of a secondary prevention strategy. The goal is to help people initiate or change behaviors to improve health.

One of the first steps to increase healthy behaviors is education and awareness. Public education campaigns can increase healthy behaviors. For example, in the mid-1960s, there was a mass media campaign to educate the public about the hazards of smoking. This campaign had a significant influence on attitudes and beliefs about

primary prevention   intervention programs that focus on increasing healthy behaviors among people without disease

secondary prevention   health-promotion programs for people at increased risk for health problems

smoking (Taylor, 2006). Education also occurs individually when doctors explain the importance of certain health-related behaviors to their patients (e.g., when pediatricians advise parents about a balanced diet and healthy exercise program for their child). Education is sometimes combined with self-monitoring or keeping daily records of health-related behaviors. For example, modifying one's diet might involve first keeping daily records of food intake. Sometimes the simple act of monitoring behavior can lead to positive changes, although often other strategies are also needed.

Other interventions are based on classical conditioning or operant conditioning. **Stimulus control** is a behavior change strategy based on classical conditioning. It involves modifying behavior by changing the stimuli that bring on the behavior. For example, changing one's diet is much easier if unhealthy "stimuli" like cookies and chips that provoke more snacking (the unhealthy behavior to be changed) are removed from the home. Learning to eat only when sitting down at the table (and not when watching television or standing in front of the refrigerator) is another way to control stimuli associated with eating. **Contingency contracting** is a strategy that relies on setting up a reinforcement program to encourage healthier behavior. For example, a family might set up a program for a child with poor eating habits by offering tokens that can be exchanged for a special (nonfood) treat, such as a trip to the zoo.

Increasing healthy behavior sometimes requires changing attitudes such as *self-efficacy* (how much someone believes he or she can do something). We know that self-efficacy can affect people's ability to maintain exercise programs. Thus, health behavior plans that involve changing beliefs about abilities can be important for improving health.

Stress Management   Remember that important relationship between stress and health? If stress can negatively affect health, then programs to help people manage stress can help people stay healthy. Stress management skills, such as biofeedback, relaxation, and meditation, can be taught individually or in group or classroom-type settings at the workplace, school, or other community site. Stress management successfully reduces blood pressure in patients with hypertension (Linden et al., 2001), improves anxiety and T-cell counts for patients with HIV (Antoni et al., 2000), improves health status for patients with arthritis (Parker et al., 1995), and reduces risk factors in patients with coronary heart disease (Daubenmier et al., 2007).

As with increasing healthy behaviors, the first step in stress management is education and awareness. People learn to identify personally stressful situations and how they respond to these situations. Self-monitoring is one good strategy for increasing awareness. Keeping daily records helps patients understand their personal stressors and the thoughts, feelings, behaviors, and coping patterns that are part of their stress response. Remember Chris? He had difficulty adjusting to the stresses associated with beginning college, such as being away from home, having a much heavier school workload, and making new friends. His typical coping patterns included eating fast food to save time and reducing the amount of time he spent exercising. He also stayed up late trying to keep up with reading and studying.

When Chris went to the infirmary the third time, the nurse suggested that he consider taking a stress-reduction class. He decided to give it a try. When he started paying closer attention, he realized just how tense his body was in many situations and how often he had negative thoughts about himself when he was under stress ("I am just not smart enough to succeed here." "I must be the only one here who is homesick. What a wimp I am.") Chris also began to realize that he actually wasn't very good at managing his study time. School had always been easy for him before, so he never had to spend much time planning his studies. Now things were different.

Yoga and meditation can be learned individually or in classes and are effective stress management techniques.

stimulus control   modifying behavior by changing the stimuli that bring on the behavior

contingency contracting   strategy that relies on setting up a reinforcement program to encourage healthier behavior

Once someone is aware of stress-producing situations and responses, the next step is to learn new coping skills such as improving diet and increasing exercise. Exercise training appears to increase resistance to stress (Salmon, 2001). Other coping skills include relaxation training, learning time management skills, and changing thoughts.

For Chris, learning to stop and take a deep breath during stressful situations was very useful.

More structured strategies like progressive deep muscle relaxation can also help reduce stress (see Chapter 4) as can goal-setting and changing thoughts.

Chris also benefited from learning how to plan ahead and set specific goals for studying each day. This helped him feel less overwhelmed by the increased academic load. He also learned how to think differently about himself. Instead of cutting himself down when he was under stress, he learned to say things like: "College is tough, but I am doing ok." "My grades don't have to be as good as they were in high school as long as I am doing my best."

Adjusting to Chronic Illness   As we have seen, people with chronic illness, such as HIV/AIDS, cancer, chronic pain, diabetes, and coronary heart disease experience many changes, including decreased physical capacity, altered relationships with family and friends, financial strain, and high rates of anxiety and depression. How does a health psychologist help people cope with these changes? First, we know that good social support can improve disease outcomes. We also know that stress and negative beliefs about the disease, oneself, and the future predict poorer outcomes. Therefore, adjustment to chronic illness might involve continuing social interaction, managing stress, and modifying beliefs. Encouraging patients to seek social support and providing education and support to family members enhances everyone's adjustment. Some patients and families also benefit from formal support groups that provide emotional support and information about ways that others have coped successfully.

In many ways, coping with a medical illness is similar to coping with other stressful experiences, suggesting that stress management can be useful. Learning about the disease (e.g., what to expect in terms of progression, what treatment choices are available) and identifying potential stressors (e.g., trips to the doctor, changing medication) are important first steps. Relaxation and exercise can also improve adjustment, and patients with chronic disease often learn new skills to effectively integrate ongoing medical care into their lives. For example, they may need to learn to eat differently and change their routines to make time for complicated medical treatments (e.g., insulin shots for diabetes before every meal; chemotherapy treatments that affect functioning for days or weeks at a time). Health psychologists help patients integrate long-term medical care into their lives while helping them maintain their identities as parents, spouses, co-workers, and friends (DiMatteo et al., 2002).

Behaviors and thoughts that encourage feelings of control over illness can be helpful. Self-efficacy or confidence can affect health behaviors. Increased feelings of self-efficacy and control are associated with better adjustment to chronic illnesses such as chronic obstructive pulmonary disease (Kohler et al., 2002), sickle cell disease (Edwards et al., 2001), and chronic pain (Turner et al., 2007). Therefore, treatments that increase confidence and control can help people adjust to chronic disease. Magic Johnson and Lance Armstrong illustrate the importance of finding benefit or meaning in the experience of disease. Health psychologists can help patients identify positive outcomes associated with their disease and positive ways to use their experiences to help others.

Support groups, such as the Livestrong Army, help patients with chronic and life-threatening diseases feel empowered.

- Health psychologists work to help people change behaviors, attitudes, or beliefs in ways that promote health and adjustment to illness.
- The first step toward increasing healthy behavior involves education about the way behaviors can affect health and gaining awareness of one's own health-related behaviors.
- Stress management can improve the health of patients with medical problems such as cancer, HIV/AIDS, and coronary heart disease.
- Strategies for reducing stress and coping with chronic illness include relaxation, changing behaviors, and changing thoughts.

APPLICATION QUESTION   What behaviors could you change to improve your health?

THE WHOLE STORY: SANDY—VICTORY OVER CANCER

The Patient: *Sandy is 37 years old. She has a great career and a wonderful family. She exercises three times per week. She does not really watch her diet, but her weight is well within the normal range. People tease Sandy all the time, calling her a "Type A personality without the hostility."*

The Problem: *When Sandy was 16 years old, her mother (who was 37) was diagnosed with breast cancer. Despite treatment, her mother died about 10 years after her diagnosis. Because of her mother's history, Sandy's physician insisted that she start having mammograms at a very early age. Sandy just thought of them as routine—surely the same thing would not happen to her. But now, at age 37, Sandy's mammogram showed a suspicious spot and a biopsy confirmed it— Sandy had breast cancer. She could not believe it—she felt absolutely healthy. How could she have such a life-threatening disease? Sandy cried for two days— then she decided to do something about it. With the help of a friend, she found the nearest breast cancer treatment center, met with a surgeon, and had the surgery to remove the cancer.*

The Treatment: *Following her surgery, Sandy had many choices—radiation therapy, chemotherapy, hormonal therapy. Everything was happening fast, and it* seemed overwhelming. Sandy was not sure what to do. She felt that her life was out of control. Her family, though emotionally supportive, seemed unable to help her make decisions or chart a course. One member of the comprehensive treatment team at the breast cancer center was a health psychologist. Sandy asked to meet with her—to discuss her concerns and fears, and to find a way to cope with the overwhelming nature of the disease.

The health psychologist had several recommendations. First, it was clear that throughout Sandy's life, she had responded to adversity with problem-focused coping strategies. So the psychologist decided to build on these strengths by helping Sandy find more functional ways of coping with her current stress. Sitting around crying, her health psychologist pointed out, was completely natural in the circumstances but would not be very helpful. She assigned Sandy tasks to enhance her coping style. For example, Sandy investigated various forms of breast cancer therapy. Second, because she was such an active person, the health psychologist (after consultation with Sandy's surgeon) asked Sandy to re-start her exercise program. Not only did this reduce her stress level, it helped restore her energy and hastened her reha- bilitation from surgery. Third, to deal with Sandy's feelings of being out of control, the health psychologist encouraged her to return to work—on a part-time basis at first and then full-time. The health psychologist suggested that Sandy consider a breast cancer support group. Sandy attended one session but did not go back. The women in the group, though nice, spent a lot of time talking about breast cancer but did not seem interested in figuring out what to do about it. Instead, Sandy joined more "active" support groups—participating in the Komen Foundation "Race for the Cure" and the LIVESTRONG Foundation. These organizations were much more consistent with her coping style.

The Treatment Outcome: *Sandy began to realize that although she might not have complete control of the cancer that was in her body, she still had control over other aspects of her life. Finally, the health psychologist helped Sandy break down her upcoming course of treatment into a series of smaller steps. By focusing on these short-term goals, Sandy felt more capable of dealing with the long treatment course ahead of her. Sandy's family remained an important source of emotional support, cheering her on as she overcame each hurdle and remained cancer-free.*

CRITICAL ISSUES to remember

1. Health psychology uses the principles and methods of psychology to understand the effects of attitudes and behaviors on health and illness. Health psychologists study how people develop positive and negative health habits (e.g., exercise, eating, smoking, etc.), how stress and health are related, and which psychological variables affect the onset and treatment of medical illnesses.

2. Mind-body dualism suggests that mind and body function independently. This point of view is not supported by current empirical research, which demonstrates that psychological and social variables have a significant impact on health and physical functioning.

3. Stress is determined by an interaction between a person and an event. Stress can be *acute* (short-term) or *chronic* (long-term) and can be caused by *daily hassles* or *major life events*. Stress can be measured in the laboratory, where its impact on physiological, neuroendocrine, and psychological responses can be assessed, or by questionnaires that ask people about major events and daily hassles.

4. Stress has been linked to an increase in unhealthy behaviors, a higher rate of accidents, greater frequency of anxiety and depression, and poorer immune functioning (e.g., reduced resistance to disease). Variables that affect the role of stress in health include personality style, such as the Type A behavior pattern, economic resources, and social support.

5. Behaviors that have a significant impact on health include eating, sleeping, exercise, use of alcohol and nicotine, level of sun exposure, and risky sexual behaviors. People with lower education and income, as well as those with depression and anxiety, have poorer health habits. Health psychologists can help people develop healthier patterns of eating and exercising, as well as reduce harmful behaviors such as smoking.

6. Anxiety and depression occur commonly in patients with serious medical illnesses like HIV/AIDS and cancer. Variables such as negative beliefs, poor social support, and increased stress can accelerate the progression of medical symptoms. Many psychological, environmental, and cultural factors also influence the perception of pain. Health psychologists work to help people change behaviors, attitudes, or beliefs in ways that promote health and adjustment to illness. Strategies for reducing stress and coping with chronic illness include relaxation, changing behaviors, and changing thoughts.

TEST yourself

For more review plus practice tests, flashcards, and Speaking Out: DSM in Context videos, log onto www.MyPsychLab.com

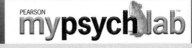

1. The subdiscipline of psychology that studies the interactions among biological, psychological, and social factors is called
   a. developmental psychology
   b. medical psychology
   c. social psychology
   d. health psychology

2. In 1948 the World Health Organization defined health for the first time in terms of
   a. a lack of illness, disease, or suffering
   b. both physical and mental illness
   c. positive lifestyle values
   d. mental, physical, and social well-being

3. The person most associated with the concept of mind-body dualism is
   a. Flanders Dunbar
   b. Franz Alexander
   c. René Descartes
   d. Sigmund Freud

4. Stress is most likely to be present when an event
   a. has an anticipated negative outcome that affects the family
   b. is unpredictable or ambiguous with no clear plan of action
   c. generates an intense emotional reaction
   d. requires a specific set of coping skills

5. Kevin was delayed on his way to a movie by road construction. As he approached the box office, he noticed that the person in front of him was purchasing tickets for a large school group. When he finally got to the ticket agent, he realized he did not have cash and the theater did not take credit or debit cards. These events represent
   a. daily hassles
   b. acute stress
   c. chronic stress
   d. continuous negative outcomes

6. Which of the following is not one of Hans Seyle's General Adaptation Syndrome stages?
   a. adaptation
   b. alarm
   c. resistance
   d. exhaustion

7. Bodily responses to stress, such as increased blood pressure, rapid breathing, and sweaty palms, indicate
   a. extreme emotion-focused coping
   b. increased sympathetic nervous system activity
   c. overwhelming daily hassles
   d. detrimental responses to chronic stressors

8. Inflammation in the body is a sign that
   a. a specific immune system response has been triggered by disease
   b. natural immunity has been triggered by stress
   c. the nonspecific immune system is at work
   d. all normal bodily systems have been overwhelmed by stress

9. Depression, alcoholism, and eating disorders have all been linked to elevated
   a. T-cell secretion
   b. phagocytosis
   c. HPA activity
   d. natural killer cell reuptake

10. The Type A characteristic that predicts an increased risk of cardiovascular disease and heart attack is
    a. anger and hostility
    b. time urgency and impatience
    c. sensation and stimulus seeking
    d. competitiveness and achievement orientation

11. Recent research suggests that men and women tend to use different coping styles when under stress. Women more often use
    a. religion and spiritual coping
    b. problem-oriented coping
    c. emotion-focused coping
    d. humor and distraction coping

12. Approximately what percentage of people who start an exercise program continue it for up to 6 months?
    a. 80%
    b. 70%
    c. 60%
    d. 50%

13. African Americans and other minorities account for a disproportionate percentage of the deaths from HIV/AIDS because
    a. they have acquired immunological vulnerabilities
    b. culturally specific practices make the disease progress rapidly
    c. they are less likely to receive newer medications and have less access to medical treatment
    d. all of the above

14. The psychological disorder that some evidence has associated with an increased risk for cancer is
    a. depression
    b. anxiety
    c. anorexia nervosa
    d. substance abuse

15. The oncologist described Sarah, a newly diagnosed patient with lung cancer, as having the classic Type C personality. Sarah is likely to be
    a. uncooperative, hostile, and oppositional
    b. assertive, extroverted, and achievement oriented
    c. hostile, angry, and extremely vocal
    d. cooperative, unassertive, and compliant

16. Which of the statements below most accurately characterizes the relationship between pain and psychological disorders?
    a. Psychological problems seldom have much influence on physical pain
    b. Pain is linked to psychological distress regardless of person or context
    c. Pain must be treated and reduced before psychological problems are addressed
    d. Pain may cause psychological distress, and psychological distress may make the experience of pain worse

17. Physicians are often reluctant to prescribe opiate medications for patients with severe chronic pain because opiates
    a. significantly decrease sexual desire and performance
    b. are more expensive than synthetic alternatives available
    c. quickly lose their effectiveness in relieving chronic pain
    d. are the most commonly abused prescription drugs

18. Which of the statements below about insomnia is true?
    a. Most insomnia is caused by medical illness, not stress
    b. Insomnia is a chronic problem that affects over 50% of the population
    c. Insomnia is more common among women and the elderly than other groups in the population
    d. Sleep difficulties are always a normal part of adolescence

19. Paul has a desk job and is overweight. Because several members of Paul's family have diabetes, the doctor recommended a program for Paul emphasizing healthy diet and exercise. This program focuses on
    a. primary prevention
    b. secondary prevention
    c. coping skills
    d. psychological medicine

20. Using self-monitoring, biofeedback, coping skills, and relaxation techniques to improve health is known as
    a. restorative health counseling
    b. primary prevention
    c. stress management
    d. psychosomatics

Answers: 1 d, 2 d, 3 c, 4 b, 5 a, 6 a, 7 b, 8 c, 9 c, 10 a, 11 c, 12 d, 13 c, 14 a, 15 d, 16 d, 17 d, 18 c, 19 b, 20 c.

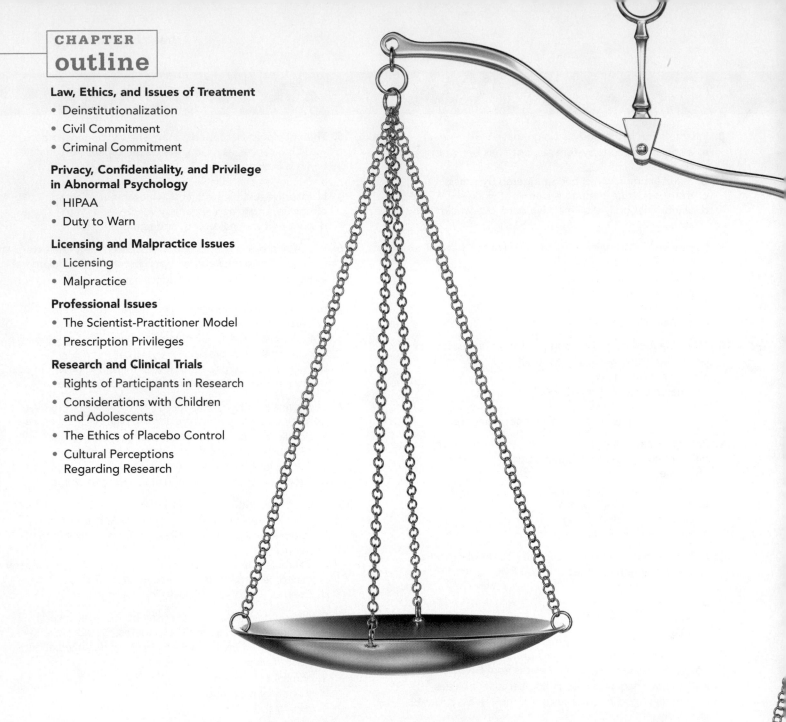

CHAPTER objectives

After reading this chapter, you should be able to:

1 Understand legal, ethical, and professional issues related to the practice of psychology.

2 Discuss the positive and negative aspects of deinstitutionalization.

3 Understand the difference between criminal and civil commitment.

4 Identify the reasons for involuntary commitment for psychiatric services.

5 Describe documents crucial to the development of rights for research participants.

6 Give reasons why some cultural groups may be reluctant to participate in research.

abnormal psychology:
legal, ethical, and professional issues

Colorado therapists Julie Ponder and Connell Watkins were convicted of reckless child abuse and sentenced to 16 years in prison after a young girl died during a "rebirthing" therapy session in April 2000. During the "rebirthing" session, 10-year-old Candace Newmaker was wrapped tightly in a blanket and pushed on with pillows, in an effort to re-create the birth process. Watkins, who was neither licensed nor registered to conduct therapy, held the rebirthing session in her home. At the trial, jurors saw and heard Candace on video begging for her life from under her fabric "womb." Excerpts of dialogue from the video were published by the *Denver Rocky Mountain News* and provide a first-hand account of Candace's last hour of life. Throughout the 70-minute tape, Candace begs the therapists to get off of her and let her breathe. At one point, as she cries and pleads for her life, the four adults present pushed even harder on the girl, putting all their adult weight on top of the 70-pound fourth-grader. Here are excerpts from the tape:

CANDACE NEWMAKER: I can't do it. (Screams) I'm gonna die.

JULIE PONDER: Do you want to be reborn or do you want to stay in there and die?

CANDACE NEWMAKER: Quit pushing on me, please. . . . I'm gonna die now.

JULIE PONDER: Do you want to die?

CANDACE NEWMAKER: No, but I'm about to. . . . Please, please I can't breathe. . . .

CANDACE NEWMAKER: Can you let me have some oxygen? You mean, like you want me to die for real?

JULIE PONDER: Uh huh.

CANDACE NEWMAKER: Die right now and go to heaven?

JULIE PONDER: Go ahead and die right now. For real. For real.

CANDACE NEWMAKER: Get off. I'm sick. Get off. Where am I supposed to come out? Where? How can I get there?

CONNELL WATKINS: Just go ahead and die. It's easier. . . . It takes a lot of courage to be born.

CANDACE NEWMAKER: You said you would give me oxygen.

CONNELL WATKINS: You gotta fight for it. . . . (Candace vomits and defecates.)

CONNELL WATKINS: Stay in there with the poop and vomit.

CANDACE NEWMAKER: Help! I can't breathe. I can't breathe. It's hot. I can't breathe. . . .

CONNELL WATKINS: Getting pretty tight in there.

JULIE PONDER: Yep. . . . less and less air all the time.

JULIE PONDER: She gets to be stuck in her own puke and poop.

CONNELL WATKINS: Uh huh. It's her own life. She's a quitter.

CANDACE NEWMAKER: No. . . . (This is Candace's last word.)

The women's lawyers tried to convince the jury that Candace was a severely troubled young girl and was lying when she said she could not breathe. Watkins stated in a message to her supporters saying that "some-how the 10-year-old inexplicably stopped breathing." A day after the verdict, Colorado became the first state to make re-birthing therapy illegal. The court case did not address the issue that in Colorado a license is not required to practice psychotherapy.

Based on a report by Benjamin Radford, Managing Editor of the SKEPTICAL INQUIRER. COPYRIGHT 2001 Committee for the Scientific Investigation of Claims of the Paranormal

The tragic case of Candace Newmaker illustrates what can happen when untrained (or undertrained) therapists use a treatment for which there is no scientific support. Why would these therapists use such a dangerous procedure? There are many reasons why therapists use dangerous or untested treatments. These include lack of clinical experience, inability to appropriately evaluate the supporting research, and mistakes about treatment efficacy because of conclusions based on correlational, not causal, data (Doust & Del Mar, 2004). Some therapists deny that empirical data alone should be used to determine whether a therapy works. They argue that *clinical expertise* is equally important (American Psychological Association Task Force on Evidence-Based Practice, 2005). However, from the scientist-practitioner perspective that we have used throughout this book, clinical experience alone is no substitute for data that emerge from well-controlled, internally and externally valid, empirical studies.

In this chapter, we will examine legal, ethical, and professional issues relevant to understanding abnormal behavior and its treatment. Why do we include these issues in a book on abnormal psychology? Quite simply, by offering clinical services or conducting research, psychologists assume obligations to patients, to research participants, and to society. To the person seeking treatment, psychologists have the responsibility of practicing in their area of expertise; using treatments that are not harmful (and that preferably have a strong scientific basis); and never doing anything that will sacrifice their patient's health and safety. Although they were not psychologists, Candace Newmaker's therapists violated all of these guidelines.

There are additional ethical guidelines as well. Patients have the right to choose whether to participate in treatment, to choose the type of treatment (pharmacological, psychological), and to expect that their participation in therapy will remain confidential. In a research study, participants have the right to be fully informed of all study requirements and the right to refuse to participate. Their participation in a project must clearly involve more benefits than risks, and their rights and dignity must be respected.

In some cases, society has determined that protecting the public from potential risk is more important than respecting the rights of an individual in treatment or research. Protections for society include the psychologist's responsibility to inform appropriate third parties if a patient threatens bodily harm to others and the forced medication of people with mental illness arrested for a crime. In these instances, basic rights such as the right to confidentiality and the right to refuse treatment are compromised in order to protect society. In the next section, we examine society's laws and psychologists' ethical obligations when they provide clinical services.

Law, Ethics, and Issues of Treatment

Many laws regulate everyday activities such as driving a car, getting married, and purchasing and consuming alcohol. Other laws strictly prohibit actions such as driving while intoxicated, breaking and entering, and assault. Still other laws regulate the practice of various professions, such as psychology, to protect vulnerable people from unqualified practitioners (see the section on licensure in this chapter).

In contrast to laws, **ethics** are accepted values that provide guidance in making sound moral judgments (Bersoff, 2003). Unlike laws, ethics are developed by a profession or group, not a branch of government. In psychology, the American Psychological Association's code of ethics guides the behavior of most psychologists. The code of ethics covers five core values: beneficence and nonmaleficence, fidelity and responsibility, integrity, justice, and respect for people's rights and dignity (American Psychological Association, 2002; see Table 15.1).

When psychologists join a professional organization such as the American Psychological Association or the Association for Psychological Science, they agree to behave in a manner consistent with the association's code of ethics. Failure to do so could result in expulsion from the association. Read the paragraph below and identify which ethical principles were violated.

Dr. Smith is conducting research on psychotherapy. He recruits his students to participate in the research project, promising them extra credit in class. He promises that any information they provide will remain confidential. After looking at the videotapes, he realizes

---

TABLE 15.1

The Five Aspirational Goals Related to the Science and Practice of Psychology

Aspirational Goals	Definition
Beneficence and nonmaleficence	Psychologists always work to benefit their patients and are always careful not to do anything that causes harm.
Fidelity and responsibility	Psychologists seek to establish relationships of trust and are aware of their responsibilities to patients, colleagues, and society in general.
Integrity	Psychologists promote honesty and truthfulness in their science, teaching, and practice.
Justice	Psychologists promote fairness and equality for all persons. Everyone has equal access to psychology's contributions and services.
Respect for people's rights and dignity	Psychologists value the worth of everyone and uphold rights to privacy, confidentiality, and self-determination.

ethics accepted values that provide guidance to make sound moral judgments

deinstitutionalization release of inpatients from hospitals to community treatment settings

that responses illustrate "classic" responses, and he decides to use the tapes in a professional workshop he will do next month.

Other guidance on professional practice comes from state laws. Each state has a licensing board that sets the criteria for who can practice as a psychologist. When psychologists apply for a license, they must agree to adhere to the state's code of ethics (similar to that of many professional organizations), as well as its laws and statutes. If they fail to do so, the state could revoke the psychologist's license, resulting in an inability to practice. Both licensing laws and codes of ethics promote positive behavior, and psychologists adhere to both sets of standards.

An important issue with which both psychologists and society struggle is how to provide optimal treatment to those with psychological disorders. Throughout history, there have been many shifts in the favored approach to treatment. One of the most dramatic changes has been the shift in views regarding the need for institutionalizing patients. Currently, we are in a phase of deinstitutionalization, and it is to this issue that we now turn.

DEINSTITUTIONALIZATION

As you learned in Chapter 1, since the time of Hippocrates, physicians have advocated removing patients from society and housing them in environments where treatment can be provided in a humane setting. This idea was behind the nineteenth-century "humane movement," which advocated the *removal* of mentally ill persons from the community to hospital-like or residential settings where they could receive appropriate and adequate care. Ironically, such hospitals and residences eventually came under such criticism that a twentieth-century movement arose to get the patients out of institutions and back into the community. At the time, the idea was that needed care would be provided there, where patients could live with fewer restrictions.

Confining patients in hospitals was common mainly because until the 1960s, there were few effective treatments to control aggressive behaviors, making institutionalization the simplest way to protect the public. Institutionalization was also common for people with schizophrenia and mood disorders, because effective medications for serious psychological disorders had yet to be discovered. In the United States, state hospitals cared for increasing numbers of people with psychological disorders from their inception in the 1800s to their peak in 1955. At that time, there were 559,000 beds in psychiatric institutions, and institutionalization was the most common form of psychological treatment (Talbott, 1979/2004). By mid-century, however, it was the institutional setting that was considered inhumane. Hospitals were grossly understaffed, treatment was primarily limited to medications, and few, if any, patients were ever discharged. Few psychosocial treatments were available, and most patients spent their days in their beds or watching television. Discharging patients from these institutions so that they could obtain better care in the community was promoted as the humane alternative.

Beginning in the 1960s, effective medications became available, and treatment options expanded dramatically. With improved medication treatment, it was recognized that people with psychological disorders could function outside the institutional setting if there was appropriate medical and community support. So began the process of **deinstitutionalization**, the release of inpatients from hospitals to community treatment settings. Proponents of deinstitutionalization argued that community care would be better and cheaper than institutional care, particularly when medications constituted at least part of the treatment. Although medications were not always effective in "curing" mental illness, they could control seriously disordered behavior, allowing some

Until the late 1960s, people with psychological disorders were hospitalized in restrictive settings, and most were simply confined without treatment. Few efficacious psychotherapies or medications existed at that time.

people to leave the locked wards and contribute to society in a positive manner (see the case of John Nash in Chapter 10). Considered in terms of overall reductions in numbers of hospitalized patients, the deinstitutionalization movement was very successful. In the year 2000, only 59,403 state mental hospital beds remained available in the United States (Lamb & Weinberger, 2005), a decrease of about 90% in the last 30 years. Another similar deinstitutionalization effort in 2001 pressed states to provide alternative community settings for persons with mental retardation, as their continued institutionalization was viewed as unjustified and as a form of discrimination (Lakin et al., 2004).

Looking back through a 50-year lens, deinstitutionalization reduced the number of people involuntarily housed in state mental hospitals. Despite the good intentions behind this idea, however, as early as 1979 there were emerging concerns that the community care solution would fail (Talbott, 1979/2004). For example, the total number of people hospitalized for reasons of mental illness decreased during this time, but the number of persons with mental illness in state and federal prisons, local jails, and other locked settings increased dramatically (Lamb & Weinberger, 2005). These data suggest that the movement never achieved its original objective—to allow those with psychological disorders to reintegrate into the community.

Why did the deinstitutionalization movement fail? There are many reasons, but an important one was that after discharge, many patients did not receive the outpatient care and supervision they needed. Outpatient clinics, many of which were state funded, were understaffed and could not provide the treatment needed by patients with severe and chronic disorders. Furthermore, the available staff was often inadequately trained to deal with people suffering from severe psychological disorders. Patients with schizophrenia, for example, did not keep clinic appointments and stopped taking their medication, allowing their psychotic symptoms to reemerge. Without continued treatment, their mental status deteriorated and many patients became a danger to themselves and society, once again necessitating forced removal from the community.

The lack of appropriate follow-up care for deinstitutionalized patients illustrates the basic flaw in the deinstitutionalization process—it involves much more than just unlocking the doors of the hospital and allowing the patient to leave. It is a process of social change that has many secondary positive and negative consequences (Lamb & Bachrach, 2001). In addition to the increasing incarceration of people with psychological disorders, another negative effect of deinstitutionalization is homelessness, now a major social problem in many cities.

In a group home, people with psychological disorders can live in a less restrictive environment and learn skills necessary to stay in the community.

Homelessness One of the most negative effects of deinstitutionalization was that many people with psychological disorders ended up living on city streets. Their disheveled appearance and active psychotic symptoms created concern and sometimes fear among community residents (Talbott, 1979/2004), despite the fact that people with mental disorders are much more likely to be victims of violence than perpetrators (Brekke et al., 2001). Depending on the particular sample, 32.7 to 73% of those who are homeless have psychological disorders (Cougnard et al., 2006; Langle et al., 2005; Mojtabai, 2005), rates that are higher than the rate in the overall population (15.7%: Cougnard et al., 2006).

Because of the serious nature of their psychological disorders and the fact that they often stop taking their medication once they leave an institutionalized setting (see Chapter 10), people with schizophrenia are at high risk for homelessness. Among one sample of patients with schizophrenia who were discharged from hospitals to the community, 7.6% were homeless at some point during the three months after discharge (Olfson et al., 1999). The risk of homelessness is higher when there is comorbid drug abuse or persistent psychiatric symptoms and more impaired global functioning.

When people with psychological disorders are released from institutions but not given appropriate social supports, they may have difficulty coping with the demands of everyday life. A significant number become homeless.

Homelessness among patients with severe mental illness is not a problem unique to the United States. In rural China, 7.8% of people with schizophrenia were homeless at some point during a 10-year period (Ran et al., 2006). People most likely to be homeless had ramshackle or unstable housing, a family history of schizophrenia, no income, and were unmarried. Among French patients with schizophrenia, those who were homeless were more likely to be male and single, to abuse drugs, and to have had more frequent hospitalizations (Cougnard et al., 2006). Across cultures, poor social support and substance use increase the likelihood of homelessness among the mentally ill.

If we consider deinstitutionalization as a process rather than a singular event, it appears that homelessness among people with psychological disorders is not a problem of deinstitutionalization per se but of the way in which the process is implemented. Successful deinstitutionalization requires more than an adequate treatment plan. The process will not work unless patients' skills and resources for living independently are considered (Lamb & Bachrach, 2001). Among a group of patients discharged from a locked psychiatric unit, 56% did not have the minimal abilities necessary to function in the community (Lamb & Weinberger, 2005). During their first 12 months in the community, they spent at least 90 days in locked or structured institutions (including jail) and had to be rehospitalized at least five times. Despite an adequate community treatment plan, they had chaotic lives and interpersonal conflicts. For the entire sample, only 33% were living stable lives in the community and did not require rehospitalization. These outcome data pose a challenge for clinicians working with seriously mentally ill populations. There is a need to find a better way to identify which patients need which resources to make a successful transition from hospital to community. When patients with psychological disorders are unable to care for themselves in the community or if they become a danger to themselves or others, they may have to be institutionalized against their will, a process known as civil commitment.

CIVIL COMMITMENT

Miguel was brought to the psychiatric emergency room by ambulance. His landlord called the police because smoke was coming from under his apartment door. When the police finally broke down the door, they found Miguel was burning the furniture. He explained that about a month ago, he became suspicious about his co-workers. He feared that they were reading his mind. So he quit his job. Without any other source of income, he was unable to pay his bills and the electric company shut off his heat. To stay warm, he was burning his furniture in the fireplace, creating a significant fire hazard to everyone in the building.

Miguel's behavior (burning furniture in the fireplace) constituted a danger to himself and to others living in the building. **Civil commitment** is a state-initiated procedure that forces involuntary treatment on people who are judged to have a mental illness who present a danger to themselves (including an inability to care for themselves) or others (Appelbaum, 2006) and who refuse to participate in treatment voluntarily. During the early twentieth century, civil commitment usually meant inpatient hospitalization, and sometimes it still does. However, with the deinstitutionalization movement, there has been a shift to **outpatient commitment**, defined as "a court order directing a person suffering from severe mental illness to comply with a specified, individualized treatment plan that has been designed to prevent relapse and deterioration. Persons appropriate for this intervention are those who need ongoing psychiatric care owing to severe illness but who are unable or unwilling to engage in ongoing, voluntary, outpatient care" (Lamb & Weinberger, 2005, p. 530). Outpatient commitment

civil commitment a state-initiated procedure that forces involuntary treatment on people who are judged to have a mental illness, who present a danger to themselves (including an inability to care for themselves) or others

outpatient commitment a court order that directs a person to comply with a specified, individualized outpatient treatment plan is considered more coercive than voluntary treatment but less coercive than inpatient hospitalization (Swartz & Monahan, 2001) because the person remains in the community with continued access to social supports.

In some instances, outpatient commitment is a condition for being discharged from a hospital. It is also an alternative to hospitalization for people who are currently in the community and whose condition is deteriorating. Outpatient commitment also may be used as a preventive measure for people considered to be at high risk for psychological deterioration and possible hospitalization (Monahan et al., 2001). It is not clear whether outpatient commitment has produced positive treatment outcomes for most patients (Steadman et al., 2001; Swartz et al., 2001). It does appear to have a higher chance of success when it is sustained (commitment lasts for more than 6 months) and intensive (approximately seven contacts per month). With this type of planning, hospital admissions were reduced by 57% among one sample of people with serious psychological disorders (Swartz et al., 1999).

Nevertheless, outpatient commitment is a very controversial issue (Monahan et al., 2001; Petrila et al. 2003). The American Psychiatric Association considers outpatient commitment a "useful tool in an overall program of intensive outpatient services aiming to improve compliance, reduce rehospitalization rates, and decrease violent behavior among a subset of the severely and chronically mentally ill" (Gerbasi et al., 2000). However, some members of the public, mental health law advocates, and clinicians oppose treatment coercion of any type, considering it an infringement of civil liberties, an extension of social control, and the alienation of the mentally ill from treatment (Swartz & Monahan, 2001). In some instances, patients may only receive social entitlements (welfare benefits and subsidized housing) if they agree to participate in treatment. In other instances, patients must agree to outpatient commitment in order to avoid more severe restrictions (jail, inpatient hospitalization). As we have noted, forcing someone to participate in treatment raises ethical concerns for many people (Monahan et al., 2001). However, in instances such as Miguel's, his right to refuse treatment ended when his actions (burning furniture in his fireplace) put the public (others in the building) at risk.

Miguel was hospitalized for a week, at which time he denied the presence of hallucinations or delusions. He was discharged to a group home, where his medication compliance could be monitored by the group home staff.

To ensure that he continued to comply with all aspects of this treatment, Miguel was under an outpatient civil commitment order.

CRIMINAL COMMITMENT

Whereas civil commitment is a response to behavior that poses a danger to self or others, **criminal commitment** occurs when a person with a psychological disorder commits a crime. Within the courtroom, those who are criminally committed may be judged not guilty by reason of insanity, guilty but mentally ill, or incompetent to stand trial. Court cases often involve high-profile media events, such as the trials of Andrea Yates and Ted Kaczynski. However, there are many misconceptions regarding the use and purpose of what is commonly referred to as the insanity defense.

Mental Illness vs. Insanity   *On March 30, 1981, John W. Hinckley, Jr., attempted to assassinate President Ronald Reagan. Hinckley was obsessed with the actress Jodie Foster and was stalking her for some time. He made numerous attempts to gain her attention, including trying to assassinate the president. Hinckley claimed that he had repeatedly watched the movie* Taxi Driver, *in which a disturbed man plots to assassinate a presidential candidate. Hinckley shot and severely injured President Reagan, Reagan's press secretary James Brady, a police officer, and a Secret Service agent. A jury found*

criminal commitment   a court-ordered procedure that forces involuntary treatment on a person with a psychological disorder who commits a crime

John Hinckley, who attempted to assassinate President Ronald Reagan, was found not guilty by reason of insanity. He remains institutionalized in a psychiatric hospital.

Hinckley not guilty by reason of insanity, and for the past 25 years, he has been confined to Saint Elizabeth's Hospital in Washington, D.C., for treatment of depression and psychosis.

For a person to be found guilty of a crime, the state must demonstrate that the accused person committed the illegal act and behaved with criminal intent (Borum & Fulero, 1999). **Not guilty by reason of insanity** (NGRI) is a legal decision that describes people who commit a crime but who are prevented by a psychological disorder from understanding the seriousness and illegality of their actions. Therefore, they are considered not to have criminal intent. Andrea Yates, for example, was initially convicted of murdering her five children, but in a second trial she was found not guilty by reason of insanity. A jury found her incapable of understanding her actions because of her psychotic illness. Not every state allows for a not guilty by reason of insanity defense, and historically, medical professionals have long been divided on whether those with psychological disorders who commit crimes should be held accountable.

Charles Julius Guiteau shot President James Garfield in 1881. Garfield did not die until 80 days later, as a result of infection rather than the gunshot itself. Guiteau appeared to be delusional, yet he was tried and executed for the assassination despite the protests of some medical professionals. His autopsy revealed chronic brain inflammation and other symptoms consistent with a diagnosis of neurosyphillis, a neuropsychological disorder (Paulson, 2006).

It is important to understand that insanity is a *legal* term, not a psychological disorder. Determining whether a person is sane or insane occurs as a result of legal proceedings. How such a determination is made differs by state, but in most cases it is based on one of two insanity rules (Borum & Fulero, 1999). The first is the **M'Naghten Rule**, established in England in 1843.

Daniel M'Naghten, possibly as a result of paranoid schizophrenia, believed that the English Tory party was persecuting him. He planned to kill the British prime minister but killed his secretary instead.

He was tried for the crime, but the court ruled that he was not responsible for his actions if (a) he did not know what he was doing, or (b) he did not know that his actions were wrong.

There have been several changes to the standard originally established by the M'Naghten Rule. In 1929, the District of Columbia added an "irresistible impulse" test, allowing consideration of whether the defendant suffered from a "diseased mental condition" that did not allow the resistance of an irresistible impulse, acknowledging the idea of volition (freedom to choose or the ability to control behavior). The standard was changed again in 1954 when a judge in the U.S. Court of Appeals created the *Durham Rule*, which held that an accused person is not criminally responsible if the unlawful act was the result of a mental disease (Lehman & Phelps, 2004). Because of this rule, the court decision hung on the testimony of an expert witness—if the witness said the person had a mental disease, the court had little choice but to find the defendant not criminally responsible. Therefore, the Durham Rule was discarded and replaced by the American Law Institute (ALI) model penal code definition (American Law Institute, 1962). This states that a person is not responsible for criminal acts if the psychological disorder results in the inability to appreciate the wrongful conduct *or* if the person is unable to conform his conduct to the requirement of the law (i.e., the person cannot control his or her behavior). Finally, the *Insanity Defense Reform Act* of 1984 states that as a result of mental illness, the defendant lacks the capacity to appreciate the nature and quality or wrongfulness of the act. Compared with the M'Naghten

not guilty by reason of insanity a legal decision that describes people who commit a crime but who are prevented by a psychological disorder from understanding the seriousness and illegality of their actions

M'Naghten Rule a legal principle stating that a person is not responsible for his actions if (a) he did not know what he was doing, or (b) he did not know that his actions were wrong

test, which is based solely on a cognitive standard (did the person understand his or her actions and know they were wrong?) the more recent criteria consider cognition *or* volition (Borum & Fulero, 1999).

Committing an illegal act is not the same as committing a crime. To be convicted of committing a crime, a person must possess **mens rea**, which is Latin for a guilty mind or criminal intent. To be considered guilty of committing a crime, the person must engage in illegal behavior and have *criminal intent*. In many instances, people with psychological disorders lack the intent to commit the crime with which they are charged.

Eric Clark had been acting oddly for years, convinced that Flagstaff, Arizona, was populated by hostile space aliens. He slept surrounded by a burglar alarm made from fishing line and wind chimes. He decided that the police were aliens as well, and when he was stopped for driving erratically through a residential neighborhood, he shot and killed a Flagstaff police officer (Appelbaum, 2006).

Clark's lawyers contended that he lacked *mens rea* (criminal intent) because his delusions interfered with his ability to recognize that the victim was a police officer, not a hostile space alien. Unfortunately, Arizona law does not allow the introduction of mental illness when juries consider criminal intent. Thus, without being able to introduce his psychotic disorder, Clark was convicted and sentenced to 25 years in prison.

Eric Clark's inability to use the insanity defense is a situation that is more common than most people believe. There are actually many misconceptions about the plea of NGRI (Borum & Fulero, 1999). One of the most common misconceptions is that NGRI is overused. In fact, NGRI is used in less than 1% of all felony cases and is successful only 15 to 25% of the times that it is used. This means that very few people successfully use an insanity defense (see the box "Real People, Real Disorders: Kenneth Bianchi, Patty Hearst, and Dr. Martin Orne").

Another common misperception is that people who are acquitted as NGRI are simply set free. In fact, most people who are acquitted as NGRI are hospitalized for periods of time as long as, and sometimes longer than, they would have served if found guilty of the crime, as has happened to John Hinckley. Finally, the NGRI defense is not limited to murder cases, and despite public opinion, people who are acquitted are no more likely to be re-arrested than those who are convicted felons (Pasewark et al., 1982; Steadman & Braff, 1983).

It is important to remember that NGRI is an affirmative defense. If it is successful, the individual is not subject to criminal incarceration but is subject to civil proceedings regarding confinement (Borum & Fulero, 1999). In contrast, when a person is found **guilty but mentally ill** (GBMI) or *guilty except insane*, the person is considered criminally guilty and is subject to criminal penalties such as incarceration in a penal institution. The addition of "but mentally ill" acknowledges the presence of a psychological disorder when the offense was committed, but does not change the person's criminal responsibility. Although proponents of GBMI hoped that it would address some of the public's concerns regarding NGRI, it has not done so. Specifically, GBMI has not reduced the number of NGRI acquittals (perhaps because that number is so small to begin with). Of even more concern to mental health professionals, GBMI has not ensured that the defendant receives any additional treatment or even any treatment at all while in prison (Borum & Fulero, 1999).

Incompetence to Stand Trial

Elizabeth Ann Smart, age 14, was kidnapped from her bedroom on June 5, 2002. She was found alive nine months later not far from her home in the company of two homeless adults, Brian David Mitchell and Wanda Ileen Barzee. It was alleged that Mitchell and Barzee kidnapped Elizabeth to be Mitchell's second wife. After his arrest, a psychological competency evaluation revealed that

mens rea Latin term for guilty mind or criminal intent

guilty but mentally ill a legal decision in which a person is considered criminally guilty and is subject to criminal penalties. The addition of the phrase "but mentally ill" acknowledges the presence of a psychological disorder when the offense was committed, but does not change the person's criminal responsibility

real people, real disorders

Kenneth Bianchi, Patty Hearst, and Dr. Martin Orne

In October 1977 and February 1978, ten women were found tortured, strangled to death and abandoned in the hills surrounding Los Angeles, thus giving the offender the name The Hillside Strangler. The police finally arrested cousins Kenneth Bianchi and Angelo Buono, both of whom had committed the crimes. After his capture, Bianchi claimed that he had a multiple personality (MPD—now renamed DID, dissociative identity disorder; see Chapter 5) and that he was insane. Two experts in the disorder examined Bianchi and reported the existence of a second personality, Steve. Both experts agreed that Bianchi was insane, even though people with multiple personality usually have at least three separate personalities and Bianchi did not.

Martin Orne, M.D., Ph.D. (1927–2000) was a preeminent scientist who conducted research in many different areas of psychology, including hypnosis, memory, and lie detection. Because of his expertise in basic studies of memory and lie detection, Dr. Orne had developed procedures to determine when people were faking a diagnosis or faking being hypnotized.

Called by the prosecution to conduct an additional examination of Mr. Bianchi, Dr. Orne first discussed multiple personality disorder with him. Bianchi told Dr. Orne about Steve. Dr. Orne told Bianchi that it was rare for someone with MPD to have only two personalities—most people had at least three. Dr. Orne then hypnotized Bianchi, and suddenly a third personality named Bill appeared. In his court testimony, Dr. Orne pointed out that he was not better than the other clinicians, but he showed that Bianchi faked a third personality because of Dr. Orne's prehypnotic suggestion. Dr. Orne also pointed out another clue that Bianchi was faking MPD. During his initial examination of Mr. Bianchi, Dr. Orne asked him, under hypnosis, to imagine that his lawyer was sitting in the room—Bianchi actually stood up, walked across the room, shook hands with the imagined attorney, and insisted that Dr Orne had to be seeing the attorney as well. Dr Orne testified that people under deep hypnosis do not get out of their seats and attempt to shake somebody's hand unless told by the hypnotist to do so. Dr. Orne did not tell Bianchi to do that. Furthermore, deeply hypnotized subjects do not insist that others also see the image. Later, police discovered that Bianchi had numerous books on psychology, diagnostic testing, hypnosis, and criminal law in his home, suggesting that he could have studied how to present himself in an "insane" manner.

Dr. Orne was not always a witness for the prosecution. In 1976, Patricia Hearst, the heiress who was abducted by the Symbionese Liberation Army (SLA), was arrested and tried for participating in a bank robbery. Hearst's lawyers said that her abduction and torture were responsible for her actions, whereas the prosecution suggested that Hearst's appearance during the robbery (she was casually holding a gun) suggested that she was there of her own free will. Although initially concerned that she was faking, Dr. Orne conducted numerous tests, giving her many opportunities to exaggerate or fabricate her story. Unlike Bianchi, Ms. Hearst never picked up on any cues, and according to Dr. Orne "really, simply didn't lie" (Woo, 2000). In summary, Dr. Orne was a scientist-practitioner who developed scientific methods in a laboratory setting that he then applied in clinical and legal settings, thereby demonstrating how the work of psychologists contributes to society.

Mitchell suffered from a delusional disorder. Although he understood the charges against him, he had an impaired capacity to (a) disclose to counsel pertinent facts, events, and states of mind, and engage in reasoned choice of legal strategies and options; (b) manifest appropriate courtroom behavior; and (c) testify relevantly. During court appearances, Mitchell would begin to sing and had to be forcibly removed from the courtroom. His disorder substantially interfered with his relationship with counsel and his ability to participate in the proceedings against him. On July 26, 2005, he was found incompetent to stand trial and was committed to the custody of the executive director of the Utah Department of Human Services for treatment intended to restore him to competency (http://www.utcourts.gov/media/news/archives/StatevMitchell-Ruling).

Brian David Mitchell was judged by the court to be incompetent to stand trial for the crime of kidnapping and imprisoning Elizabeth Ann Smart.

When an accused person, such as Mitchell, is so mentally disordered that he or she cannot assist in his or her own defense, the person is considered incompetent to stand trial. Under our system of justice, in order for an accused person to receive a fair trial, it is important that the accused person have a rational and factual understanding of the procedures and be able to consult with his lawyer and assist in the defense. The determination of incompetency is the result of an evaluation in which a specially trained mental health professional assesses the person's competency to assist in his or her defense. Although few empirical data exist, 77.5% of the individuals in one sample who were referred for evaluation were determined to be incompetent (Stafford & Wygant, 2005). People determined to be incompetent were more likely to have a psychotic diagnosis than people found to be competent. Psychiatric treatment restored competency in 47% of the individuals initially determined to be incompetent so that they could later stand trial. However, medicating patients just so that they can be tried for illegal behaviors they committed when they lacked criminal intent raises serious ethical issues.

The Right to Refuse Medication/Treatment When faced with serious, disabling, or terminal illnesses, people often make choices about treatments. Sometimes people refuse treatments that produce serious side effects or do not improve their quality of life. The right to refuse treatment is accepted in United States law, and the wishes of competent individuals are respected. The use of an *advance directive* (a document that specifies in advance the types of treatment a patient wishes to receive or not receive) allows family members or others responsible to act in accord with the person's wishes. In some states, advance directives exist for the treatment of mental illness as well. But does that right extend to someone who committed a crime but was found to be incompetent to stand trial as a result of a psychological disorder?

Dr. Charles Sell was charged with Medicaid fraud, mail fraud, and submitting false insurance claims. Dr. Sell had a 20-year history of abnormal behavior, beginning with his belief that communists had contaminated the gold that he used for filling teeth. Over the years he suffered from many different psychotic symptoms. He had occasionally been treated with antipsychotics but stopped taking the medication. He continued to have hallucinations and delusional beliefs, including telling the police that "God told me every [FBI] person I kill, a soul will be saved" (Appelbaum, 2003). In 1999, Sell was examined and found mentally incompetent to stand trial. He was hospitalized to determine whether there was a probability that he would ever become competent. After two months, the staff recommended that he take antipsychotic medication. Dr. Sell refused and the medical staff went to court to administer antipsychotic medication against his will (Annas, 2004).

It is important to note that patients in mental hospitals are often medicated against their will if they are a danger to staff or other patients. This was not the case for Dr. Sell. He was not a danger to hospital personnel, so forcible medication was solely to restore his competence for trial. The United States Supreme Court ruled in this case that someone could be involuntarily medicated solely for the purpose of restoring competency only if (a) important governmental interests were at stake (e.g., having a fair but speedy trial); (b) forced medication made it "substantially likely that the defendant will be competent" and "substantially unlikely that the drug will have effects that renders the trial unfair"; (c) no less intrusive means were available; and (d) the medication is "medically appropriate" (Annas, 2004). What did this ruling mean for Dr. Sell? He could not be forced to take medication until these issues were resolved, and his legal status remains unclear. Should a patient be forced to accept treatment if his behavior is not harmful to himself or others? When psychologists participate in these proceedings, they must balance society's rights with the ethical principles of beneficence and nonmaleficence, as well as respect for people's rights and dignity.

concept CHECK

- As members of society, psychologists are bound to abide by laws and codes of ethics.

- The Code of Ethics of the American Psychological Association covers the core values of beneficence and nonmaleficence, fidelity and responsibility, integrity, justice, and respect for people's rights and dignity.

- The deinstitutionalization movement developed to stop the process of hospitalizing psychiatric patients for the rest of their lives. However, despite the promise of deinstitutionalization, one unfortunate outcome has been the lack of appropriate living arrangements for those with psychological disorders. The result is that many people with severe psychological disorders are homeless or in jail.

- Outpatient commitment can be used as a condition for release from an inpatient unit, as an alternative to hospitalization, or as a way to provide intensive treatment in order to prevent inpatient hospitalization.

- Insanity is a legal term, not a psychological disorder. In rare instances, patients with serious psychological disorders are found to be not guilty by reason of insanity, whereas in other instances they are found guilty but mentally ill.

APPLICATION QUESTION   The right to refuse treatment is valued by patients and mental health professionals alike. The interesting paradox is that even when it is clear that patients lack the capacity to understand their actions, their negative behavior so horrifies the public that there is pressure to restore their mental faculties so that they can be imprisoned for their actions. In such instances, society's need for patients to be accountable for their actions appears to override patients' right to refuse treatment. Is it ethical to treat people who are criminally insane in order to punish them for the commission of a horrific crime?

Privacy, Confidentiality, and Privilege in Abnormal Psychology

Annie has obsessive-compulsive disorder. She has many intrusive thoughts, but the most frightening is that when using a sharp knife, she will lose control and stab her son, severely injuring or perhaps even killing him. Annie loves her son and she is a good mother. She is horrified about these thoughts and does not want to act on them. Yet, she is so afraid that she will lose control that she has taken all the knives out of the house (including the butter knives). She has also removed all the scissors. She made an appointment to see a psychologist, but she is worried. What if the psychologist thinks she is crazy?

As we have noted throughout this book, psychological disorders are accompanied by significant emotional distress. Part of this distress relates to patients' concerns that they are "crazy" or that others will think that they are "crazy." To help patients feel comfortable, mental health professionals agree that what is discussed within the therapy session will not be revealed to others. The terms *privacy, confidentiality*, and *privilege* all describe environments that provide protection against unwilling disclosure of patient information. There are, however, certain conditions in which the therapist must violate these protections, and we will address these exceptions later in the chapter when we examine the issue of duty to warn.

The concept of privacy has a long history in the United States and is the basis for many laws. The right to privacy limits the access of other people to one's body or mind, including one's thoughts, beliefs, and fantasies (Smith-Bell & Winslade, 1994).

Annie has not told anyone about her intrusive thoughts. At this time, her thoughts are private.

Privacy is a right of the individual, who alone can give it away. When a person reveals thoughts, behavior, and feelings to another person, privacy is lost. In the context of therapy, the private information shared with a therapist is considered confidential. **Confidentiality** is an agreement between two parties (in this case, the therapist and patient) that private information revealed during therapy will not be discussed with others.

Although it makes her quite uncomfortable, Annie tells the psychologist, Dr. Jones, about her thoughts. Because she and her therapist have established a therapeutic relationship, the content of her intrusive thoughts is now considered confidential. Dr. Jones may not disclose it to others.

Psychologists are covered by the concept known as privilege. Even if called to testify in court, they cannot be compelled to reveal what a client told them in a therapy session.

The psychologist agrees to keep confidential the information that the patient reveals. Even if the patient decides to discuss that information, the psychologist still is bound by confidentiality.

The third concept is **privilege**, a legal term that prevents a therapist from revealing confidential information during legal proceedings. You may have heard the term *privileged communication*, which is often used to describe conversations between a lawyer and client. Sometimes physicians and psychologists hold privilege, meaning that they are legally protected against being forced to reveal confidential information in a legal proceeding. If communication is privileged, the psychologist cannot be compelled to reveal it in court (or any other legal setting). Privileged communication is not an automatic right of the therapist or the patient. Whereas confidentiality is considered to be an ethical commitment, privilege is established by state law. For mental health clinicians, privilege extends to therapists who are licensed to practice therapy in a particular state.

Dr. Jones is a licensed psychologist. Therefore, should she ever be subpoenaed in a court case, Dr. Jones would not have to testify about Annie's mental status or the nature of the treatment because that is privileged information.

Although confidentiality is often assumed to be absolute, there are certain situations in which it does not apply. Psychologists discuss these situations with the patient at the start of treatment. For example, a graduate student in clinical psychology in training to provide therapy requires supervision by a senior psychologist. In supervisory sessions, the trainee shares patient information with the supervisor to make sure that the treatment is conducted appropriately. In this case, the supervisor is bound by the same confidentiality standard as the therapist.

Other situations that require or call for exceptions to confidentiality include instances in which patients make their mental health an aspect of a lawsuit or a criminal defense strategy (such as insanity pleas or malpractice lawsuits). In these cases, neither confidentiality nor privilege applies, as the case cannot be decided without knowledge of the situation. Confidentiality is also limited when health insurance companies require information about diagnosis and aspects of treatment (number of sessions, frequency of sessions) to provide payment for mental health treatment.

confidentiality agreement between two parties (in this case, the therapist and patient) that private information revealed during therapy will not be discussed with others

privilege legal term that prevents a therapist from revealing confidential information during legal proceedings

When treating a child, confidentiality issues become more complicated. Some information must be shared with parents, whereas other information remains confidential.

Disclosing confidential information is also necessary during civil commitment proceedings, when involuntary treatment is necessary because the individual presents a danger to self (such as wanting to commit suicide) or others (a deliberate expression of intent to harm another person).

Annie denied any thoughts of hurting herself. She vehemently denied that she wanted to harm her son and in fact, had taken steps to make sure that it would not happen (removing the knives and scissors from the house).

Therefore, she was not in need of involuntary commitment, and the psychologist did not have to violate confidentiality. Finally, confidentiality must also be breached when adults admit that they are physically or sexually abusing children or elders, in which case the therapist must report the abuse to the appropriate state authorities.

When the patient is a minor child or an adolescent, other exceptions to confidentiality apply, and again, therapists discuss these issues at the start of treatment so that the minor and the parent or guardian can make an informed decision about participating in therapy. With respect to children and adolescents, all mental health clinicians, including psychologists, are required by state law to report physical, sexual, or emotional abuse to the proper state authorities, thereby violating confidentiality. State laws may cover other behaviors (such as substance abuse) where parents have a right to information about their child's treatment. Each state has its own guidelines, and in some cases, different clinics in the same state may have different guidelines (Gustafson & McNamara, 1987). Exceptions to confidentiality also apply when a child or an adolescent is actively contemplating suicide or homicide, as is the case for adults. Psychologists violate confidentiality in order to keep their patients and others physically safe. In certain instances, breaking confidentially is a medical or legal necessity. In other cases, unfortunately, it can occur as a result of carelessness. To help safeguard patient confidentiality, the federal government recently enacted a law known as HIPAA.

HIPAA

When you check in at your doctor's office, particularly if you are a new patient, you sign various consent forms that include the abbreviation **HIPAA**, which stands for **Health Insurance Portability and Accountability Act**. Although HIPAA was originally designed to protect Americans who were previously ill from losing their health insurance when they changed jobs, HIPAA also provided a uniform standard for transmission of health care claims forms, thereby streamlining the health care system. Legislators took the opportunity to include safeguards to protect patients' confidential health information. HIPAA is a complicated system of laws and regulations, but two of its components, security and privacy, have implications for psychological treatment as it relates to protected health information.

The HIPAA security rule attempts to assure patient confidentiality by securing administrative, physical, and technical office procedures. Psychologists and physicians restrict information to only those people who have a right to know it. The security rule also requires keeping information received on fax machines, written on telephone message pads, and even on sign-in sheets from being viewed by an unauthorized person, usually defined as someone who does not work in the office.

Protected Health Information (PHI) is information about your health or health care that is maintained as a medical record or transmitted to another person. The HIPAA privacy rule requires that psychologists must obtain a patient's consent before using any PHI to carry out treatment, payment, or health care operations. In other words, when you sign the HIPAA consent form, you agree to allow your clinician to share your health information with (a) other health care professionals who may be involved in your

Health Insurance Portability and Accountability Act (HIPAA) system of laws and regulations that protect the security and privacy of health information

treatment; (b) companies responsible for billing your insurance or paying your physician for services; and (c) companies responsible for arranging medical or legal reviews of services and auditing of medical care facilities. It also covers some other business-related functions, but these are less relevant to psychology. HIPAA consent does not include permission to share records with an employer or a school. Similarly, the psychologist's patient notes (called psychotherapy notes or process notes) are not considered part of the information included in the general HIPAA consent.

Therefore, although many people believe that everything said in therapy is confidential, this is not always the case. When a patient expresses a threat or desire to hurt others, the confidentiality of the therapeutic relationship becomes secondary to a *duty to warn* the third parties who may be at risk.

DUTY TO WARN

In 1969, University of California student Prosenjit Poddar sought therapy with a psychologist at the university's student health center because a young woman named Tatiana Tarasoff had spurned his affections. The psychologist believed that Poddar was dangerous because he had a pathological attachment to Tarasoff and because he told the psychologist that he had decided to purchase a gun. The therapist notified the police both verbally and in writing. He did not warn Ms. Tarasoff because that would have violated patient–psychologist confidentiality. Poddar was questioned by the police, who found him to be rational. They made him promise to stay away from Tarasoff. Two months later, however, on October 27, 1969, Poddar killed Tarasoff. The Supreme Court of California found that the defendants (the Regents of the University of California) had a **duty to warn** Ms. Tarasoff or her family of the danger. In a second ruling, the court charged therapists with a duty to use reasonable care to protect third parties against dangers posed by patients. In short, the court found that a patient has no right to confidentiality when the patient's actions might put the public at risk.

More than 30 years later, the Tarasoff decision (as it is known) still has broad implications for the mental health profession. One is that society does not hold confidentiality in the same high esteem as do therapists and patients. Society dictates that safeguarding the public welfare, particularly in the case of potential homicide, is more important than confidentiality. However, duty to warn is a slippery slope. What if the potential threat is not outright death, as was the case for Tatiana Tarasoff, but bodily infection?

Michael is 33 years old. He has been married for 8 years and has two children. He had an affair with a neighbor several years ago. His wife never knew about the affair. Michael recently discovered that the neighbor died of AIDS. Michael had an HIV test, which was positive. Michael told his therapist that he has no intention of telling his wife about his test results (Chenneville, 2000).

If Michael were your patient, what would you counsel him to do? The laws are not clear in this type of situation. Depending on the particular state, the therapist may be *permitted* to make a disclosure to the health department or Michael's spouse, *required* to make a disclosure to the health department or Michael's spouse, or *required* to maintain confidentiality at all costs. Depending on the law in the state where Michael lived, the psychologist might have to follow any one of these three options.

Prediction of Dangerousness   The psychologist's duty to warn is based on the belief that mental health clinicians have the ability to predict human behavior. Psychologists and psychiatrists are often asked to determine how likely it is that a person will become violent when the need for civil commitment is at issue (Skeem et al., 2006). In the past, mental health professionals were unable to predict patient dangerousness at a rate higher than chance alone (Steadman, 1983). In some instances, clinical intuition may help predict dangerousness. In an emergency room, male patients who worried clinicians

duty to warn   therapists' duty to use reasonable care to protect third parties from dangers posed by patients

(based on a diagnostic evaluation but no real empirical data) were more likely to subsequently commit violent acts and be involved in serious violence (Lidz et al., 1993).

Over the past decade, there has been a significant improvement in the ability of mental health clinicians to predict patient violence through the use of *actuarial* (quantitative) prediction measures, particularly when the prediction is based on specific psychological *symptoms* (such as anger or sadness) and not psychological *disorders* (major depression, schizophrenia; Skeem et al., 2006). In particular, anger/hostility is predictive of violence over both short-term (1 week) and long-term (6 month) follow-up periods (Gardner et al., 1996; Skeem et al., 2006). Other symptoms such as anxiety, depression, or delusional beliefs did not predict acts of violence, at least not in the short term (Skeem et al., 2006).

---

concept CHECK

- When a person reveals private thoughts to a psychologist, the information is considered confidential. When the therapist is a licensed psychologist, the information is also considered privileged.
- Sometimes confidentiality must be violated. Such cases include behaviors that are considered dangerous to the patient or others, abuse of children or elders, or substance abuse by children or adolescents.
- If a patient threatens to harm another person and that person can be identified, the psychologist has a duty to warn the threatened person as well as the police.
- Actuarial predictions allow psychologists to predict violence at levels better than chance alone. One factor that appears to play a role is patients' anger and hostility.

APPLICATION QUESTION Remember Michael, who did not want to tell his wife that he had HIV? What if instead of being married, Michael were single, had gotten HIV as a result of a single encounter with someone he had met in a bar, and now was so angry that he told his therapist that he intended to go out and infect every woman that he could? Does a psychologist have a duty to warn?

Licensing and Malpractice Issues

Licensing psychologists, social workers, and mental health counselors in order to allow them to provide psychological services serves several functions, including setting minimum standards of training and education to protect the public from unskilled or dangerous mental health services or providers. Insurance companies recognize the importance of licensing: they usually will not pay for psychological services unless the professional has a license.

LICENSING

As noted earlier in this chapter, states have laws that govern the practice of certain professions, such as medicine, law, and teaching. Psychologists who wish to provide therapy must be licensed by the state in which they practice. Psychologists who do not provide therapy (cognitive psychologists, biological psychologists, or social psychologists, for example) are not required to be licensed. State law specifies who can use the word "psychologist," who can provide specific psychological services, and what type of training a person must have in order to practice psychology. Licensure laws vary by state, and there are many ways that nonqualified individuals can practice what some consider a form of therapy. In some states, people who are not psychologists but who wish to provide therapy can do so by avoiding the use of the words *psychology and psychologist*, instead using the term *psychotherapy*.

State laws protect the public by setting forth the minimal acceptable level of training and experience necessary for the practice of psychology. Most states have very similar requirements, including a doctorate in psychology and two years of postdoctoral experience (or one year predoctoral internship and one year postdoctoral experience). The psychologist must also pass a national exam and a state exam. Once licensed, psychologists must adhere to the laws and the code of ethics. Failure to do so could result in loss of the license or claims of malpractice. Furthermore, in order to maintain their license, psychologists must engage in *continuing education*, whereby they continue to attend workshops, read articles, and participate in other professional activities to refine and improve their knowledge and skills in psychology.

MALPRACTICE

Malpractice is defined as "professional misconduct or unreasonable lack of skill" (Black, 1990, p. 959). The psychologist's work, like that of all professionals, must meet certain standards, defined as "that degree of care which a reasonably prudent person should exercise in same or similar circumstances" (Black, 1990, p. 1405). Although the law does not require all psychologists to use the same form of therapy, the care must meet commonly accepted professional standards (Baerger, 2001). If care is not consistent with standards, the psychologist may be guilty of malpractice. Although psychologists are less likely to face malpractice claims than are physicians, the number of lawsuits filed against psychologists increases each year. Candace Newmaker's therapists were convicted of reckless child abuse, but fortunately this is a very rare form of malpractice.

Studies of malpractice offenses committed by mental health clinicians (either psychiatrists or psychologists) are few. In one anonymous survey, 3.5% of psychologists engaged in an inappropriate relationship; the majority were male psychologists who established a relationship with former female patients (Lamb et al., 2003). The American Psychological Association prohibits interpersonal relationships between psychologists and patients until at least two years after the termination of therapy and only when a number of other conditions can be fulfilled. It is difficult to meet all of the criteria in the ethical code, and most psychologists never engage in any type of social or intimate relationships with former patients.

Malpractice lawsuits are often filed when there is suspicion of a negligent or improper diagnosis. In the case of psychologists, the claim of improper diagnosis is often the result of child custody evaluation decisions. The purpose of child custody evaluations is to assess the best psychological interests of the child, and the evaluation assesses parenting ability, the needs of the child, and the resulting parent-child fit (American Psychological Association, 1994). Child custody evaluation is a high-risk task for a psychologist. The psychologist must remain neutral, which is very difficult to do in a highly charged situation such as a divorce. Even though joint physical custody is the most common custody decision today (Bow & Quinnell, 2001), granting custody to the mother with visitation rights to the father is second most common. When a parent disagrees with the custody decision, the parent may file a complaint with the state ethics board and/or file a malpractice suit. Among psychologists who conducted custody evaluations, ethics complaints were filed against 35% of the psychologists and 10% were sued for malpractice (Bow & Quinnell, 2001).

Other reasons for malpractice claims include failure to obtain informed consent for treatment, negligent psychotherapy, and negligent release or dangerous acts. For example, grief-stricken family members sometimes blame a mental health professional for not preventing a patient's suicide (a claim of negligent release or dangerous acts), even though predicting this type of behavior can be very difficult. Malpractice claims following a suicide were the sixth most common malpractice complaints in one survey of psychologists who had malpractice insurance (Bongar et al., 1998, cited in Baerger, 2001).

The most common reason that a psychologist is sued for malpractice is as a result of a custody evaluation. It is common for the parent who does not get custody to identify the psychologist as the person responsible for the negative outcome.

malpractice professional misconduct or unreasonable lack of skill

In summary, the practice of psychology requires adherence not only to an ethical code of behavior but also to state laws and regulations. Licensure ensures that the professional has met minimum educational and training standards. However, licensure does *not* guarantee that the therapist will always behave ethically. When unethical behaviors have occurred, a psychologist may be sued for malpractice.

---

concept CHECK

- States regulate the practice of psychology in order to safeguard the public against those who are not qualified to practice therapy.

- The practice of psychology requires a doctoral degree, at least two years of supervised experience, and a licensing examination.

- Malpractice lawsuits against psychologists are uncommon, but when they occur, the reasons include inappropriate sexual behavior and negative child custody decisions.

APPLICATION QUESTION Why do you think that clinical and counseling psychologists need a license but cognitive and social psychologists do not?

Professional Issues

Returning once again to the case of Candace Newmaker, we observe that the people who were conducting the rebirthing therapy were called therapists. When seeking therapy, it is important to understand the educational background of the therapist, because depending on the state, people from many different educational backgrounds may be licensed to provide mental health services. Table 15.2 provides an overview of the providers of mental health services and the educational background of each. As this table illustrates, there is no consistent standard with respect to the level of training

---

TABLE 15.2
Title and Educational Background of Mental Health Clinicians

Title	Educational Background[a]	Type of Service Provided
Psychologist	Five years of graduate study leading to doctoral degree (PhD, PsyD.) in clinical, counseling, or school psychology	Diagnosis, assessment, and treatment from a psychological/psychosocial perspective. May also conduct research on assessment and treatment
Psychiatrist	Four years in medical school leading to a doctoral degree (MD) in medicine followed by 3–4 years of advanced residency training in psychiatry	Diagnosis, assessment, and treatment from a primarily biological perspective, but may use psychosocial procedures May also conduct research
Psychiatric Social Worker	Two years in graduate school leading to a master's degree (MSW) in social work	Assessment and treatment primarily using a family or social perspective
Psychiatric Nurses	Two years in graduate school leading to a master's degree in nursing (MSN)	Treatment usually conducted in a hospital setting as part of a treatment team
Marriage & Family Therapist	Two years leading to a master's degree in marriage and family counseling (MFT)	Treatment directed primarily at marital or family issues
Therapist or Psychotherapist	Two years in graduate school leading to a master's degree (MA, MS, MEd) in psychology, counseling or a similar field	Treatment may be provided independently or in outpatient clinics or hospitals

[a]Represents approximate time to degree completion.

necessary for providing mental health services. In addition to the professions listed in the table, clergy, guidance counselors, substance abuse counselors, and family doctors, among others, at times provide information and services to those suffering from psychological disorders.

THE SCIENTIST-PRACTITIONER MODEL

Throughout this book, we have discussed the scientist-practitioner model, which is identified primarily, but not necessarily exclusively, with psychology. To review, the scientist-practitioner model describes an approach to psychological disorders that values both the science (conducting research) and practice (providing psychological services) of psychology. At a conference in 1990 where this model was developed, the word "scientist" was deliberately placed first to emphasize that treatment strategies needed to be evaluated empirically before they were offered to those with psychological disorders. A commonly accepted definition of the scientist-practitioner model is as follows: "The scientist-practitioner model is an integrative approach to science and practice wherein each must continually inform the other, and represents more than a summation of both parts. Scientist-practitioner psychologists embody a research orientation in their practice and practice relevance in their research. Thus, a scientist practitioner is not defined by a job title or a role, but rather an integrated approach to both science and practice" (Belar, 1990). Not every clinician adheres to the scientist-practitioner model of training, but for psychologists it is the primary model for those who provide clinical services. Yet, even if the goals of treatment are the same, clinicians from different disciplines may use different approaches and methods to achieve the same goal.

PRESCRIPTION PRIVILEGES

A common question the layperson asks is, What is the difference between a psychologist and a psychiatrist? The easy answer used to be, "A psychiatrist is a physician who can prescribe medication, and a psychologist is a doctoral-level health care provider who cannot prescribe medication." That distinction is no longer quite so clear. During the past two decades, some psychologists have sought, and received, the legal right to prescribe medication for psychological disorders. As we have noted throughout this book, medications are an important part of the treatment of many psychological disorders, and in some cases, such as schizophrenia, they are the primary treatment. Although psychiatrists have always been free to use both psychotherapy and medication, traditionally, psychologists provide only psychological treatment. When their patients need medication, most psychologists arrange for treatment by a physician. Some psychologists believe that splitting treatment in this way is not in the best interest of the patient, as different providers may provide the patient with different, and sometimes conflicting, viewpoints. With the ability to prescribe medications, some psychologists believe that they would be able to provide comprehensive treatment, as is the case for psychiatry. Prescription privileges, the legal right to prescribe medication, is a contentious issue throughout the psychological community (e.g., Heiby, 2002).

Psychologists propose several reasons for prescription privileges. First, many psychologists have hospital admitting privileges, treating the emotional features or reactions that accompany or are the result of physical health problems such as stress, cancer, and heart disease. These psychologists view the ability to write prescriptions as a natural extension of their practice (Norfleet, 2002; Welsh, 2003). Second, graduate programs in clinical psychology already offer courses in psychophysiology and psychopharmacology, courses that are necessary, but not sufficient, for prescribing medication. Therefore, psychologists already have some of the training necessary for prescribing medications. Third, because medications are the treatment of choice for some disorders, such as schizophrenia, prescription privileges would allow psychologists to treat patients who might not have access to treatment. Many people lack access to psychiatrists and get their medication from general practitioners, who are much less knowledgeable about psychological disorders than psychologists. Allowing psychologists to prescribe medications would guarantee treatment by someone with specialized knowledge of abnormal behavior.

Other psychologists (Albee, 2002) suggest that prescribing medication undermines psychology's unique contributions to understanding behavior, such as the role of learning and the importance of the environment. From this perspective, seeking prescription privileges suggests that psychologists no longer value psychology's contributions and deemphasizes the efficacy of highly effective psychological treatments. Psychologists would also need additional training to prescribe medications safely and would require an undergraduate education such as that found in a premedicine curriculum (Sechrest & Coan, 2002). Providing appropriate biological training at the graduate level would extend the length of training (Wagner, 2002), which already averages about 6 years.

The issue of prescription privileges is a very contentious one for psychology. Over the past few years, psychologists have gained the right to prescribe medication in New Mexico, Louisiana, and the island of Guam (Stambor, 2006). In mid-2006, there were 31 medical psychologists in Louisiana (the term used in the Louisiana statute) and 4 psychologists in New Mexico who could prescribe medication (Stambor, 2006).

If prescription privileges become part of the treatment armamentarium for psychologists, medication providers will face the controversial issues that relate to the marketing and funding of pharmacological treatment. Medications used to treat psychological disorders constitute a substantial percentage of all pharmaceutical sales (22% in the year 2003; Brodkey, 2005), and they are among the industry's most profitable drugs. Their use is increasing, both among adults and children (see Figure 15.1). The potential influence of the pharmaceutical industry extends far beyond public media advertisements. In one survey, 60% of published medication trials in psychiatry received funding from a pharmaceutical company (Perlis et al., 2005), although having pharmaceutical company support did not guarantee a positive outcome for the medication. Until recently, pharmaceutical companies provided promotional materials (pens, mouse pads, etc.) to potential medication prescribers. Unfortunately, these gifts were more influential than one might think. Medical students, for example, rated the information that they receive from gift-bringing pharmaceutical representatives as more valuable and helpful than information they received from non–gift-bearing representatives (Sandberg, 1997). Although such gifts are no longer allowed, health professionals must always be careful to guard against marketing influences when deciding on forms of therapy.

FIGURE 15.1

Changes in Rates of Psychoactive Medication Use For Adults (1988–1994) and Children (1987 and 1996) in the United States

The use of psychoactive medication has increased dramatically over time. In the United States, there has been a substantial increase in the percentage of adults using any type of psychoactive medication and in the percentage using antidepressants, and a smaller increase in the percentage using anti-anxiety medications. The number of children who are prescribed any type of psychoactive medication has also increased, and there have been specific increases in the use of antidepressants and stimulants (for ADHD). Anti-anxiety drugs are less often prescribed for children because of the potential for addiction.

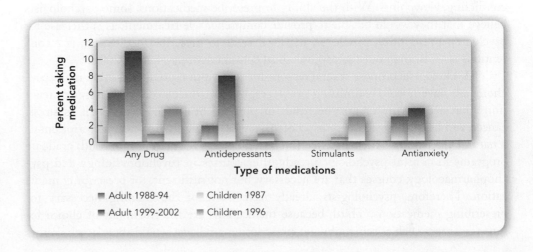

- People with many different types of educational backgrounds provide mental health services to those with psychological disorders. The goal is always the same—to alleviate psychological distress. However, depending on the background and training of the clinician, the type of therapy provided (medication, psychotherapy, family therapy, marriage therapy) may be different.

- The scientist-practitioner approach may be utilized by clinicians with different types and levels of education, but the approach is characterized by a scientific/empirical approach to clinical work and a clinical relevance to research.

- Psychologists in two states and one territory now have laws allowing them to prescribe medications for psychological disorders, although permitting prescription privileges continues to be controversial.

APPLICATION QUESTION   The ability to prescribe medication leads to potentially vulnerable exposure to pharmaceutical marketing campaigns, all of which aim at having their drug prescribed to patients. Do you think that psychologists, given their extensive background in research training, would be able to resist this influence more than physicians?

Research and Clinical Trials

This book has approached the study of abnormal behavior from a scientist-practitioner perspective. Throughout, we have highlighted how designing, conducting, and understanding research in abnormal behavior contributes to theories of etiology and approaches to treatment. If you had any doubts about the need to conduct research in order to understand behavior, the case of Candace Newmaker should be sufficient to convince you. When treatments are not based on science, serious or even life-threatening consequences may result. Although the Newmaker case was extreme, the use of unscientific theories and unsubstantiated treatments can result in the waste of time and money and public mistrust of therapy. But research itself comes with its own ethical issues. Although there are many issues to consider when examining clinical research, in this section we will focus on four important areas: the rights of research participants, special rights and issues for children and adolescents, the use of placebo controls, and the importance of conducting research that reflects the diversity of the United States population.

RIGHTS OF PARTICIPANTS IN RESEARCH

On December 9, 1946, the American military initiated a tribunal against 23 German physicians and administrators for war crimes and other crimes against humanity. During World War II, some German physicians conducted a euthanasia program, systematically killing people that they deemed unworthy of life. In a second program, physicians conducted pseudoscientific medical experiments on thousands of concentration camp prisoners (Jews, Poles, Russians and Gypsies) without their consent (http://www/ushmm.prg/research/doctors). Most participants died or were permanently injured as a result of this inhumane experimentation. Sixteen doctors were found guilty; seven of these were executed.

The horrific and senseless nature of these "experiments" prompted the development of the **Nuremberg Code** (1947), which established directives for experimentation with human subjects. This code specifies that voluntary consent is absolutely essential for clinical research. Consent must not be coerced, and participants should know the nature, duration, and purpose of the research, together with its methods and means

Nuremberg Code   directives for experimentation with human subjects, which specify that voluntary consent is absolutely essential for clinical research and all inconveniences and hazards that could be reasonably expected as a result of participation. The experiment must be conducted by qualified individuals, and the participant must be allowed to discontinue participation at any time (Trials of War Criminals before the Nuremberg Military Tribunals, 1949).

A second document developed as a result of Nazi atrocities is the **Declaration of Helsinki**, first adopted by the World Medical Assembly in 1964 and reaffirmed on subsequent occasions (http://ohsr.od.nih.gov/helsinki.php3). This document also sets forth basic guidelines for the conduct of research, including the need for clearly formulated experimental procedures, a careful assessment of risks compared with benefits, and the provision of adequate information to the participants including the aims, methods, benefits and risks, and the freedom to withdraw. It is important to note that the Declaration of Helsinki does not specifically state how these principles are to be implemented; that is left to federal, state, and local governments and professional organizations.

A third document important for research conducted in the United States is the **Belmont Report**, which created the National Commission for the Protection of Human Subjects of Biomedical and Behavioral Research in 1979. The Belmont Report identified three basic principles to guide behavioral and biomedical research with human subjects. The first is *respect for persons*, including the beliefs that (a) individuals should be treated as autonomous agents, capable of independent thought and decision-making abilities; and (b) persons who have limited or diminished autonomy (such as prisoners or those with limited cognitive ability) are entitled to special protections, and should not be coerced or unduly influenced to participate in research activities.

The second principle is *beneficence*, meaning that researchers (a) do no harm (as in the Hippocratic Oath) and (b) maximize potential benefits and minimize possible harm. In other words, the study's potential benefits must be greater than the perceived risks (Striefel, 2001), not only the risks and benefits to the individual but also those to society at large.

The third and final principle is *justice*: both the benefits and burdens of research must be imposed equally. For example, for many years, all research on heart disease (much of it funded by the federal government) was conducted using male subjects. It was only many years later that researchers began to study heart disease and its treatment in women. This example illustrates how the *benefits* of research were not being equally distributed; only one sex benefited from the efforts of scientists. Other instances where one might question whether the principle of justice was violated are the Tuskegee Experiment and the Baltimore Lead Paint Study (see below). In general, the recruitment of research subjects must consider whether some classes of participants (welfare patients, specific racial or ethnic minorities, or persons confined to institutions) are selected simply because they are easily accessible or easily manipulated. In short, no one group should be selected as research participants because of their availability, lack of power, or the possibility of easy manipulation (Striefel, 2001).

An important aspect of the research process is the issue of **informed consent**. Potential subjects must understand the aims and methods of the research, what they will be asked to do, and what types of information they will be asked to provide. In addition, they must understand the risks and benefits of research participation. Before starting a research study, the psychologist, or anyone else who wishes to conduct research with human participants, submits the research plan to an **Institutional Review Board (IRB)**, which is charged by the researcher's institution with reviewing and approving the research using the guidelines described above. An informed consent form is part of the submission, and this form presents all aspects of the study in layperson's

Declaration of Helsinki a document that sets forth basic guidelines for the conduct of research, including the need for clearly formulated experimental procedures, a careful assessment of risks compared with benefits, and the provision of adequate information to the participants

Belmont Report a document that sets forth three basic principles to guide behavioral and biomedical research with human subjects: respect for persons, beneficence, and justice

informed consent the concept that all people who participate in research must understand the aims and methods of the research, what they will be asked to do, and what types of information they will be asked to provide. In addition, they must understand the risks and benefits of research participation, and based on that information, have the right to agree or refuse to participate in the any research project

Institutional Review Board (IRB) committee charged by the researcher's institution with reviewing and approving scientific research

language. You may have signed a consent form if you participated in research in your introductory psychology class.

Informed consent is based on the idea that providing enough information will allow cognitively competent people to understand the research process and make a voluntary and rational decision about participation. However, this assumption is not necessarily true. In one study examining the effects of a treatment, 62% of people who read the consent form and agreed to participate in the study failed to understand that treatment would be applied in a standard fashion and not individualized to their needs, or they overestimated the benefit of study participation based on a lack of understanding of the study methodology (e.g., use of a placebo control group that would provide little to no therapeutic benefit; Appelbaum et al., 2004). When it came to understanding the disclosed risk, 25% failed to recall any risk listed in the informed consent document, whereas 45.8% understood the risks of the experimental *treatment* but not risks of the experimental *design* (Lidz, 2006), such as the possibility of being assigned to the placebo control group. Therefore, despite continuing efforts to ensure that research participants are fully informed, participants often agree to research participation without sufficient understanding.

CONSIDERATIONS WITH CHILDREN AND ADOLESCENTS

Jeff, 14 years old, was extremely anxious in social situations. His parents brought him to the clinic to participate in a research study to treat social phobia. His parents signed the consent form for Jeff's participation. Jeff refused, and his father asked the investigator to leave the room, guaranteeing that Jeff would sign the form "in the next 10 minutes."

Although parental or guardian consent is necessary for children and adolescents to participate in research, ethical guidelines require that whenever they are able to do so, children and adolescents should be allowed to *assent* to their own participation. Although the ability to give assent will vary with the individual child, by age 14, adolescents can understand and make decisions that are similar to adults (Caskey & Rosenthal, 2005). In Jeff's case, the investigator could not enroll him in the study because it was clear that Jeff did not wish to participate, even though his parents wanted him to do so.

To honor the principle of beneficence, investigators who study adolescents must protect their welfare. Researchers, like clinicians, must violate confidentiality when there is evidence of sexual or physical abuse. In certain instances, they must report alcohol or substance abuse to parents (Caskey & Rosenthal, 2005). Finally, justice in this case means that adolescents deserve the opportunity to participate in and benefit from research important to the adolescent population. Some adults believe that asking adolescents whether they have thought about committing suicide will instill such thoughts and urges in people who have never considered this behavior. Psychologists know that this is simply not true, yet many school districts will not allow research that includes questions about suicide. This denies treatment opportunities to adolescents who are seriously depressed and contemplating suicide. In this case, the principle of justice is not fulfilled because adolescents are denied an opportunity to participate in potentially important and helpful research.

Many of the same considerations surrounding the ability of children to consent to participate in research also apply to older adults who have cognitive difficulties and to prisoners who may feel coerced to participate because of their incarcerated status. When the research involves people from racial or ethnic minority groups, additional considerations include making sure that (a) assessments are culturally valid; (b) group differences are not attributed to race or ethnicity when they may be just as likely to result from other demographic variables such as socioeconomic status or level of education;

(c) behaviors or developmental patterns of the white majority are not considered the "normal" standard for mental health; (d) research is not coercive; and (e) research teams include someone who is culturally competent (Fisher et al., 2002). For other issues regarding research with racial or ethnic minority groups, see the section Cultural Perceptions Regarding Research later in this chapter.

THE ETHICS OF PLACEBO CONTROL

In Chapter 2, you learned that the most rigorous types of scientific research have designs that involve the use of a control group. There are different types of control groups, including a wait list or no-treatment control group, a pill placebo or psychological placebo control group, or another active treatment group. Placebo control groups are used to understand the effects of time (some conditions, such as a cold, resolve with the passage of time) and/or the effects of clinical attention or education (for example, people are relieved to know that their response to a traumatic event is typical and not a sign of pathology; see Chapter 4). However, questions often arise as to how and when the use of control groups is ethical (see the box "Research Hot Topic: The Use of Placebo in Clinical Research").

Sometimes the use of a placebo control condition is not clinically acceptable. The possibility of denying treatment to a suicidal patient cannot be justified when efficacious treatments are available. Among children, the ethical use of a placebo is

---

Research HOT Topic

The Use of Placebo in Clinical Research

Placebo-controlled trials are considered a rigorous test by which to determine the effectiveness of a new treatment. Deep brain stimulation (DBS), for example, has shown preliminary effectiveness for depression that does not respond to medication. However, its effectiveness has not been demonstrated compared with placebo. Imagine that a researcher proposes to conduct a randomized, controlled trial in which one group receives DBS and the second group undergoes the surgical procedure in the brain but the wire is not connected to the stimulator. Is the use of a placebo ethical?

■ **Argument in Favor of the Surgical Placebo** Article II.3 of the Declaration of Helsinki states: "In any medical study, every patient—including those of a control group, if any— should be assured of the best proven diagnostic and therapeutic method. This does not exclude the use of inert placebo in studies where no proven diagnostic or therapeutic method exists." The study that the researcher proposes might provide some additional support for the use of DBS, particularly in a group of patients who have not responded to standard medication treatments. However, the researchers must consider the potentially harmful consequences from surgery that has no benefit.

■ **Argument against the Use of the Surgical Placebo** Surgical placebo for DBS involves actual neurosurgery, an invasive procedure. In addition to potential complications of the procedure itself, consequences of the placebo implant include reaction to anesthesia and postoperative infection (La Vaque & Rossiter, 2001). Does the potential for symptom remission in a group with medication-resistant depression outweigh the potential for harm from surgical placebo?

■ **Conclusion** When there is no known standard, effective treatment, using a placebo as a control condition might be appropriate until the efficacy of a new intervention is known and available to the public. In the case of DBS or other invasive medical procedures, the risks associated with neurosurgery are the same whether or not the device is operative. In fact, those in the placebo condition have brain surgery for no therapeutic reason, a very substantial medical risk with no benefit. Of course, if participants in the placebo group are later allowed to have the implant activated, *then* the benefits may outweigh the risks for people whose depressive symptoms have not responded to any currently accepted conventional treatment.

becoming increasingly complex. Scientifically, we know that placebo effects are larger in children than in adults; specifically, more children than adults have a positive (therapeutic) response to placebo medication (Fisher & Fisher, 1996; Malone & Simpson, 1998). One reason for this difference may be that children may not understand the concept of a placebo (i.e., that it is an inactive treatment). Children, who are accustomed to getting medication from a physician for physical illness, may believe that the placebo pill will also make them well. When they take a pill for a bacterial infection, the elimination of the bacteria can be determined by a blood test that reveals the absence of infection. However, the outcome of most psychological research is based on the patient's report of changed feelings; there is no "psychological blood test" to independently determine symptom improvement. Therefore, children's reports may be biased, based on their belief that they took a pill and therefore should be feeling better. We should note that adult reports also may be biased by taking a pill but an adult's greater cognitive maturity increases the likelihood that the concept of a placebo is understood. In order to control the assumption (at any age) that taking a pill will make you better, it is clear that placebo controls are necessary, especially for children (March et al., 2004). In summary, placebo controls are necessary for valid scientific research, but ethical issues continue to challenge scientist-practitioners interested in providing effective treatments to children.

CULTURAL PERCEPTIONS REGARDING RESEARCH

An interesting and little known fact about the world's mental health database is that the vast majority of research has been conducted in the United States using white college students (Sue, 1999), who in turn represent less than 5% of the world's population. The National Institutes of Health have recognized this inequity and now mandate that study samples recruited for federally funded research be representative of the United States population. However, when researchers, particularly white researchers, try to recruit a diverse sample, they often find that historical events have created a climate of cultural mistrust. Some members of minority populations fear participating in research studies, and history explains why. One infamous historical event is known as the **Tuskegee Experiment**, in which each of the three core values of research (respect for persons, beneficence, and justice) was violated.

In 1932, the Public Health Service, working with the Tuskegee Institute, began a study to determine the long-term effects of syphilis. Nearly 400 poor African American men with syphilis from Macon County, Alabama, were enrolled. They were never told that they had syphilis, nor were they ever treated for it. According to the Centers for Disease Control, the men were told that they were being treated for "bad blood," a local term that described several illnesses, including syphilis, anemia, and fatigue. For participating in the study, the men were given free medical exams, free meals, and free burial insurance. When the study began, there was no proven treatment for syphilis. But even after penicillin became a standard cure in 1947, the medicine was withheld from these men. The Tuskegee scientists wanted to continue to study how the disease spread through the body. Of course, in some cases, the disease killed the patient. The experiment lasted four decades, until public health workers leaked the story to the media in 1972. Dozens of the men had died, and many wives and children had been infected. In 1973, the National Association for the Advancement of Colored People (NAACP) filed a class-action lawsuit. A $9 million settlement was divided among the study's participants. Free health care was given to the men who were still living and to infected wives, widows, and children.

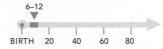

Tuskegee Experiment infamous historical study in which core values of research (respect for persons, beneficence, and justice) were violated

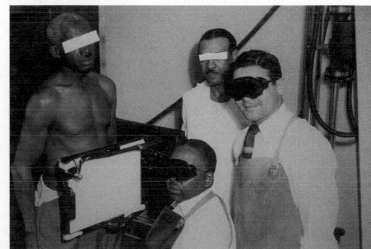

In the Tuskegee Experiment, medical treatment was knowingly withheld from patients who suffered from a deadly disease—so that the disease could be studied. This unethical experiment on human beings was one factor that led to the development of review boards for institutional research.

But it wasn't until 1997 that the government formally apologized for the unethical study. President Clinton delivered the apology, saying that what the government had done was profoundly and morally wrong. "To the survivors, to the wives and family members, the children and the grandchildren, I say what you know: No power on Earth can give you back the lives lost, the pain suffered, the years of internal torment and anguish. What was done cannot be undone. But we can end the silence. We can stop turning our heads away. We can look at you in the eye and finally say, on behalf of the American people: what the United States government did was shameful. And I am sorry." (From *Bad Blood: The Tuskegee Syphilis Experiment*, James H. Jones, expanded edition, New York: Free Press, 1993).

Although it may seem that the current regulation of research activities would prevent another Tuskegee Experiment, some research studies still provoke controversy, particularly when the subjects are children. From 1993 to 1995, the Kennedy-Krieger Institute (KKI) in Baltimore, Maryland, conducted a study to determine the short- and long-term effects of environmental lead in older homes. Lead is a natural element in the environment, but concentrations of lead in the blood are naturally quite low. In the United States, higher than acceptable lead levels usually result from two sources: lead in gasoline and leaded paint chips and dust associated with deteriorating lead paint. The elimination of lead from gasoline and paint decreased blood-level concentrations in children dramatically, although older homes with lead paint remain a source of concern. High lead levels lead to cognitive impairment (low IQ scores), inattention, hyperactivity, aggression, and delinquency (Committee on Environmental Health, American Academy of Pediatrics, 2005). In Baltimore, attempts to remove lead paint through lead abatement procedures reduced lead dust levels by 80%. However, there was interest in further abatement, and KKI agreed to conduct a study to examine three different abatement procedures (some representing only partial abatement). In addition to these three experimental groups, there were two control groups, one in which no further abatement occurred and one in which the homes were newer and presumably lead-free.

Some of the homes were occupied at the start of the study. In other instances, "inner city families who likely had no choice but to rent non-abated properties elsewhere in Baltimore" were recruited to live in the study houses (Lead Based Paint Study Fact Sheet, cited in Nelson, 2002). This resulted in two groups of children: those already living in a study home and those recruited to move into these homes. Inducements to move into the houses and participate in the study included T-shirts, food stamps, and $5–10 payments. For most of the children in the homes, the additional abatement procedures lowered levels of lead in the children. However, the study had some negative effects; lead levels increased in some children. In one instance, parental notification was delayed by 9 months. Mothers of two study participants later filed lawsuits, stating that they had not been fully informed about the goals of the study and were not promptly notified of the high levels of lead in their children's blood. If they had had this information, they would not have agreed to participate in the study.

This study raises many ethical and moral issues (see the box "Examining the Evidence: Children and Nontherapeutic Research"). One is the issue of *justice* set forth in the Belmont Report. Was the research unethical if the family's only alternative was to live in other homes that had not undergone any abatement procedures? Should social deprivation be a reason for conducting a "natural experiment," or are researchers taking advantage of the subject's social predicament? (Spriggs, 2006). In other words, is it acceptable to induce low-income children to live in partially lead-abated houses because the alternative might have been worse?

In both the Tuskegee Experiment and the Baltimore Lead Paint Study, groups with limited or diminished autonomy were put at risk. Poorly designed experiments such as these have led to grave mistrust among certain minority populations. This cultural mistrust, however, is not the only challenge facing those who wish to conduct sensitive, cross-cultural research. Some members of minority groups are unfamiliar with aspects of the research process, such as telephone interviews about psychological disorders (Okazaki & Sue, 1995). Uncomfortable telephone interviews about personal issues such as anxiety and depression may interfere with valid data collection. Another challenge occurs when survey instruments constructed in English are translated into other languages. For example, English cultural expressions such as "shake off the blues" have no literal Spanish translation, making the phrase meaningless to Hispanic populations. Without cultural sensitivity, any data collected will be meaningless (Rogler, 1999). Issues of cultural diversity affect all aspects of the research process from the initial development of the project to recruitment of participants, to the study design and selection of assessment methods, and to how the data are collected and interpreted. All result in scientific data that can be biased and not appropriate to much of the world's population (Turner & Beidel, 2003). There are probably many aspects of human behavior where there are no differences among racial and ethnic groups.

examining the evidence

Children and Nontherapeutic Research

Before gaining approval, all proposed research must be reviewed to ensure that the study provides benefit and does not subject participants to undue risk or harm. In the case of the KKI lead-based paint study, concerns were raised that this study did not provide sufficient benefit and exposed children to undue risk. Do parents have the right to enroll their children in "nontherapeutic" research?

Let's examine the evidence

■ **Was There a Direct Benefit for the Children Who Participated in the Study?** The research project offered monitoring of blood levels and notification to the parents if the blood level exceeded a certain standard. But testing is not treatment, and the study did not provide treatment if living in the house resulted in high blood levels in the child (Nelson, 2002).

Recall that there were two groups of children: those already living in the targeted houses and those who were recruited to live in the houses. Enticing someone to move into a house that contains lead can hardly be viewed as providing a benefit. For children already living in such homes, the research project offered the benefit of lead abatement. Therefore, the research offered a benefit only to those already living in a house known to contain lead (Spriggs, 2006).

■ **Did the Procedure Present Greater than Minimal Risk to the Subjects?** Monthly blood testing to determine the level of lead exposure presents only minimal risk. However,

living in a home while lead removal occurs involves more than minimal risk, because lead levels may increase when the lead is being removed. Parents were not informed that the three different methods might not have equal benefit. Is intentionally recruiting families to move into homes that have had potentially ineffective methods of lead exposure only minimal risk? Do parents deserve the right to know that there was uncertainty about the benefits of these different procedures? Would your answer be different if the researchers told you that it was the best available option for these children?

■ **Did the Consent Form Allow Parents to Make a Fully Informed Decision?** The consent document did not inform the parents (a) about the primary aim of the study (to examine the effectiveness of three different methods of lead removal); (b) about the different methods used; (c) about the importance of blood monitoring and the impact of high lead levels on the development of young children; and (d) about the risks of inadequate lead removal (Nelson, 2002). Without this information, did parents have the opportunity to give fully informed consent?

■ **Conclusion** The court noted that the Institutional Review Board did not adequately consider the risks to the participants. Would you agree? Because removing lead from homes is an important societal goal, how could you change the study to address the issues raised above?

However, until scientists begin to adequately address these issues, our understanding of abnormal behavior, indeed of all human behavior, will be limited.

---

concept CHECK

- Three universal documents—the Nuremberg Code, the Declaration of Helsinki, and the Belmont Report—set forth important ethical standards for conducting clinical research.

- Respect for persons, beneficence, and justice are important cornerstones of clinical research, and of clinical treatment as well.

- Informed consent implies that the researcher provides a complete explanation of the research project: the aims and methods of the study, what subjects will be asked to do, and what type of information subjects will be asked to provide.

- When children are research participants, both the child's assent and the parent's consent are needed before the study begins.

- Use of placebo controls is a controversial area of clinical research. They are necessary when no established treatments exist or when there is a suspicion that time or attention alone may change behavior. Once an effective treatment is established, comparing a new treatment to an established one, rather than a placebo, may be the most ethical approach.

APPLICATION QUESTION   A state-affiliated medical school that provides treatment to almost exclusively poor populations is concerned about the number of expectant mothers who are addicted to cocaine. The newborns suffer greatly and drain already limited state resources. The treatment team institutes a policy of drug testing for all pregnant mothers but tells patients that it is just "routine blood work." Those who test positive are given the choice of entering a drug abuse program or being reported to the police, whereupon they will be arrested and go to jail. The program's policy becomes known, and there is public outrage. The treatment team defends the program by calling it a research study to determine whether mothers who are informed of their drug addiction will choose to receive treatment during their pregnancy. How do the principles of respect, beneficence, and justice apply to this situation?

THE WHOLE STORY: GREGORY MURPHY—PSYCHIATRY AND THE LAW

On April 19, 2000, 8-year-old Kevin Shifflett was playing in the front yard of his great-grandmother's house in northern Virginia with some other children when he was stabbed 18 times by a stranger in an unprovoked attack. The suspect, Gregory D. Murphy, had been paroled from prison only 12 days earlier, after a conviction for an unprovoked assault. A note found in Murphy's hotel room said "Kill them racess whiate kidd's anyway".

As the killer headed toward Kevin, he yelled something about hating white people. Kevin was white and Murphy is African American.

First, it is important to consider whether Gregory Murphy's actions meet the criterion for abnormal behavior. At one court hearing soon after his arrest, Murphy was verbally explosive in the court room, calling the judge a racist. At a later hearing, he attacked his lawyer,

knocking him unconscious. It took at least five deputies to subdue Murphy. The new defense attorney asked for a competency hearing to determine whether Murphy was mentally competent to stand trial for the murder of Kevin Shifflett. If incompetent, Murphy could be forced to take medication to restore his sanity, after which he would be tried for murder. Relying on a 1992 U.S. Supreme Court ruling, the state would have to show that it had considered less intrusive alternatives and that those drugs were medically appropriate for his safety and the safety of others, or that treatment would be necessary to adjudicate Murphy's guilt or innocence.

The court had to determine whether Gregory Murphy was competent. By December 2000, the competency evaluation determined that Murphy suffered from psychosis, exhibiting both paranoia and delusions. His defense team suggested that the symptoms resulted from an organic brain disorder. An electroencephalogram (EEG) test, which measures brain waves, would be needed to confirm or rule out an organic cause for his unpredictable and aggressive behavior.

An important issue to consider was whether abnormal EEG activity would prove an organic cause. An EEG requires placing electrodes on a person's head to record his or her brain activity. The irony was that Murphy's delusions included beliefs that he had been attached to a machine since age 5, that the machine had influenced him for many years, and that he had arranged for "legal assistance" to turn off the machine. Murphy allowed the electrodes to be placed on his scalp, but then refused to allow the machine to be turned on. He was transferred to a state psychiatric facility.

Murphy's defense team learned that during his previous incarcerations, he had tested positive for syphilis, but no records existed regarding his treatment. It is important to consider if issues of race and culture may have played a role in the defendant's lack of treatment. If Murphy had advanced neurosyphillis, this could explain his psychotic behavior. A spinal tap would be needed to confirm the diagnosis. However, the information that Murphy may have suffered delusions from age 5 would discount the idea that his abnormal behavior was the result of untreated syphilis. Furthermore, Murphy refused to submit to a spinal tap.

Prosecution attorneys petitioned the court to force Murphy to take medication—not only for his safety and the safety of others, but to treat his illness and restore him to competency. The defense team argued that because the defendant might suffer from neurosyphillis, antibiotic medication, not antipsychotic medication, was appropriate. However, the court ruled that antipsychotic medication was appropriate.

Several months later, a forensic psychiatrist testified that a spinal tap was not necessary to rule out neurosyphillis because Murphy's condition had not deteriorated over the past several months, as would be expected if he had a progressive organic illness. The defense team argued that antipsychotic medications could have dangerous and permanent side effects and should not be used until the possible organic illness was ruled out. However, the judge would not vacate the order.

Finally, a spinal tap determined that Murphy did not have neurosyphillis. Murphy continued to receive antipsychotic medications, and his behavior became less aggressive. At one point, he asked the judge to appoint Johnnie Cochran as his attorney if he was tried on a capital murder charge. The request for representation by Johnnie Cochran would confirm some level of contact with reality since he knew the name of a famous defense attorney. However, he continued to be found incompetent to stand trial.

Since the murder, Murphy has had five competency evaluations but remains incompetent to stand trial. Although the psychologist found that his psychotic symptoms were largely in remission, the evaluations revealed that Murphy has a low intellect and puts facts together in simplistic ways. Murphy remains in custody and will never be released without going to trial.

The parents of Kevin Shifflett filed a wrongful death suit against the state of Virginia and a parole officer based on documents indicating that state officials were warned that Murphy "has the ingredients of a high degree of future dangerousness." The lawsuit faulted the state for failing to civilly commit Murphy because "prison officials knew or should have known" that he suffered from a mental illness. The suit further charged that as a condition of Murphy's release, he had to stay with his parents and be monitored electronically. Installation of the electronic monitoring requirement was delayed. However, the monitoring system would not have notified anyone where Murphy was, only that he had left home. The parents of Kevin Shifflet finally withdrew their suit once government lawyers clarified that the electronic monitoring was not required.

Information on this case was drawn from articles in the *Washington Post* filed by reporters Patricia Davis, Josh White, Brooke A. Masters, and Tom Jackman.

CRITICAL ISSUES to remember

1. The work of psychologists is regulated by various entities including federal and state governments, as well as codes of ethics adopted by professional organizations. These codes are developed by professional societies and dictate how members will behave when engaged in their profession. Some of the most important concepts governing the treatment of people with psychological disorders include beneficence, fidelity, integrity, justice, and respect for people's rights and dignity.

2. The goal of deinstitutionalization was to allow people with psychological disorders to be treated in the least restrictive environment. Although deinstitutionalization has allowed many individuals with psychological disorders to live in the community, a substantial number have not been successful in achieving community integration, resulting in homelessness or return to other state facilities such as jail.

3. Civil commitment is a legal process that mandates treatment for people when there is concern that they may be a danger to themselves or others. Patients may be committed to inpatient treatment or outpatient treatment, which is far more common. Criminal commitment occurs when someone commits a crime and may result from jury decisions of not guilty by reason of insanity or guilty but mentally ill. Criminal commitment involves removal from society; the person is committed to a psychiatric ward within a penal institution.

4. Involuntary commitment for treatment is considered appropriate when a person is a danger to self or to another person. Therefore, a person who threatens to commit suicide or threatens to harm another person may be committed against his or her will to a psychiatric care facility. Similarly, a person may be committed if he or she is so disabled as to be unable to take care of basic needs (does not eat or drink or take care of other activities of daily living).

5. Participation in research must be a choice; potential participants should never be coerced or misled. The Nuremberg Code, the Declaration of Helsinki, and the Belmont Report are important documents that set standards (rights of participants, beneficence, and justice) that must be met by any research project.

6. Lack of attention to these issues is reflected in the maltreatment of research participants in cases such as the Tuskegee Experiment and the Baltimore Lead Paint Study. In turn, these experiments, as well as cultural insensitivity, have left many racial and ethnic minority groups mistrustful of research and research participation.

TEST yourself

For more review plus practice tests, flashcards, and Speaking Out: DSM in Context videos, log onto www.MyPsychLab.com

1. Psychologists assume ethical responsibilities for individuals when they
   a. provide clinical services or conduct research
   b. provide services for a fee
   c. represent themselves to the media as psychologists
   d. provide clinical services but not when they conduct research

2. Before the 1970s, severely mentally ill patients were typically confined to hospitals because
   a. large numbers of untreated patients overwhelmed community programs
   b. available psychosocial treatments were best provided in an institutional setting
   c. effective treatments and medications had yet be discovered
   d. too few psychiatrists provided services in a community setting

3. The effects of deinstitutionalization include
   a. contributions to society by some people who would otherwise not have had the opportunity
   b. fewer psychiatric hospital beds and more community-based care
   c. greater rates of incarceration for mentally disabled individuals
   d. all of the above

4. The deinstitutionalization movement failed because
   a. health insurance never adequately covered the true cost of care
   b. state governments gave up on the movement and reopened the hospitals
   c. the new outpatient clinics were underfunded and understaffed
   d. the stigma of mental illness led patients to avoid outpatient clinics

5. Outpatient commitment is most successful when it
   a. is sustained and intensive
   b. alternates with inpatient treatment
   c. is provided by a psychologist
   d. includes pharmacologic treatment

6. A person who is judged to be not guilty by reason of insanity, guilty but mentally ill, or incompetent to stand trial
   a. did not commit a crime
   b. is likely to be confined for a definite term
   c. is under criminal commitment
   d. is subject to civil commitment

7. The phrase "not guilty by reason of insanity"
   a. can be applied to individuals with a variety of psychological disorders
   b. is a legal decision, not a psychiatric diagnosis
   c. is not necessarily allowed by every state
   d. all of the above

8. When a person is found guilty but mentally ill (GBMI) or guilty except insane, the person is
   a. considered criminally guilty and is subject to criminal penalties such as incarceration
   b. considered criminally guilty but is assured additional mental health treatment
   c. not subject to criminal incarceration
   d. not subject to judgment in a court of law

9. According to the United States Supreme Court, people can be medicated against their wishes (involuntarily) to restore competency to stand trial only if
   a. important government interests are at stake
   b. the drug is likely to restore their competency
   c. the drug is the least intrusive form of treatment
   d. all of the above

10. Unlike privacy, confidentiality is held by a therapist and patient and
    a. is legally absolute in all jurisdictions
    b. does not apply in some situations
    c. is an ethical ideal but impractical in reality
    d. also applies to organizations

11. Dr. Amanda Stevens, a clinical child psychologist, shares basic diagnostic and treatment information with a 9 year old child's parents and the health insurance company. Dr. Stevens
    a. violated confidentiality
    b. was legally required to tell the insurance company but not the parents
    c. was ethically required to share information with the parents but not the insurance company
    d. was ethically and legally required to share the information with the parents and the insurance company

12. HIPAA was originally designed to protect Americans who were previously ill from losing their health insurance when they changed jobs. However, the law also regulates the
    a. transmission of health care claims forms
    b. reimbursement levels for mental health services
    c. types of treatment available for reimbursement
    d. all of the above

13. John sought treatment from a clinical psychologist to deal with his feelings of depression. At his last therapy session, he revealed that he had a serious plan to harm his boss. The psychologist was obligated to
    a. maintain confidentiality despite the risk
    b. obtain John's promise not to act on his plan
    c. warn John's boss of the threat and inform appropriate law enforcement personnel
    d. consult with her supervisor or another professional practitioner

14. When psychologists are accused of malpractice, the most common cause is
    a. child custody evaluations
    b. disputes during marital and family counseling
    c. inappropriate relationships with former patients
    d. the involuntary hospitalization of a child

15. Professionals who are licensed to provide mental health services have credentials that
    a. require a uniform and standardized training curriculum
    b. can be different depending on the state in question
    c. emphasize training in the scientist-practitioner model
    d. call for a Ph.D. degree and specialized residency

16. Granting prescription privileges to licensed psychologists
    a. will allow any patient who wants medication to get it
    b. will be determined by the laws of each state and territory
    c. will mean that psychologists will now be granted a medical degree
    d. all of the above

17. Both the Nuremberg Code (1947) and the Declaration of Helsinki (1967) set forth early specific directives for
    a. conducting valid and well controlled experiments with human subjects
    b. analyzing and reporting the results of placebo research with human subjects
    c. performing involuntary experiments with prisoners and other vulnerable populations
    d. protecting human subjects in all experiments

18. The Belmont Report (1979) identified three basic principles to guide behavioral and biomedical research with human subjects. Which of the following is not one of those principles?
    a. respect for persons
    b. justice
    c. beneficence
    d. informed consent

19. Conducting psychological research with children in most circumstances and jurisdictions requires parental or guardian consent and
    a. cooperation from the local school district
    b. each child's assent, when possible
    c. no use of placebos
    d. monitoring by state authorities

20. People who are members of racial and ethnic minority groups are often reluctant to participate in research because
    a. they are not aware of the value of research studies
    b. in the past, researchers mistreated members of these groups
    c. they are more sensitive to privacy issues
    d. research studies take a lot of time

Answers: 1 a, 2 c, 3 d, 4 c, 5 a, 6 c, 7 d, 8 a, 9 d, 10 b, 11 d, 12 a, 13 c, 14 a, 15 b, 16 b, 17 d, 18 d, 19 b, 20 b.

GLOSSARY

abnormal behavior: behavior that is inconsistent with the individual's developmental, cultural, and societal norms, creates emotional distress, or interferes with daily functioning

abstinence violation effect: the core feature of relapse prevention, which focuses on a person's cognitive and affective responses to re-engaging in a prohibited behavior

acute stress paradigm: a procedure in which short-term stress is created in the laboratory and its impact on physiological, neuroendocrine, and psychological responses is measured

ageism: tendency to attribute a multitude of problems to advancing age

agonist substitution: a type of therapy that substitutes a chemically similar medication for the drug of abuse

agoraphobia without history of panic: fear and/or avoidance of public places without any past occurrence of a panic attack

alcohol cirrhosis: a liver disease that occurs in about 10 to 15% of people with alcoholism

alogia: decreased quality and/or quantity of speech

Alzheimer's disease (AD): the most common form of dementia, characterized by a gradual onset and continuing cognitive decline, which includes memory loss, difficulties with language and decision making, and ultimately inability to care for self

amenorrhea: the absence of menstruation for at least three consecutive months

amnesia: inability to recall important information that usually occurs after a medical condition or event

amnestic MCI: mild cognitive impairment in which cognitive complaints focus on memory difficulties

amphetamines: stimulant drugs that prolong wakefulness and suppress appetite

analgesic medications: medications that reduce pain

anhedonia: a lack of capacity for pleasure; the person does not feel joy or happiness

animal magnetism: a force that Mesmer believed flowed within the body and, when impeded, resulted in disease

anorexia nervosa: a serious condition marked by an inability to maintain a normal healthy body weight

antabuse: aversive medication that pairs the ingestion of a drug with a noxious physical reaction

antidepressants: medications designed to alter mood-regulating chemicals in the brain and body that are highly effective in reducing symptoms of depression

antipsychotics: a class of medications that block dopamine receptors at neuron receptor sites

antisocial personality disorder: a pervasive pattern of disregard for and violation of the rights of others

anxiety disorders: a group of disorders characterized by heightened physical arousal, cognitive/subjective distress, and behavioral avoidance of feared objects/situations/events

anxiety: a common emotion characterized by physical symptoms, future-oriented thoughts, and escape or avoidance behaviors

appraisal process: a person's assessment of whether he or she has the resources or coping skills to meet the demands of a situation

Asperger's disorder: qualitative impairment in social interaction, restricted and stereotyped behaviors, interests, and activities, but no deficits in communication and at least average intellectual functioning

attention-deficit/hyperactivity disorder: a common childhood disorder characterized by inattentiveness, hyperactivity, and impulsivity

atypical antipsychotics: medications that effectively treat positive symptoms, are much less likely to produce tardive dyskinesia, and have some effect on negative symptoms and cognitive impairments

autism spectrum disorders: a group of disorders consisting of autistic disorder, Asperger's disorder, and pervasive developmental disorder not otherwise specified

autistic disorder: disorder characterized by qualitative impairment in social interactions and communication, and a pattern of restricted and stereotyped behaviors, interests, and activities

aversion therapy: a treatment approach in which drug or alcohol use is paired repeatedly with an aversive stimulus or images

avoidant personality disorder: a pervasive pattern of social inhibition, feelings of inadequacy, and hypersensitivity to negative evaluation

avolition: an inability to initiate or follow through on plans

barbiturates: sedatives that act on the GABA system in a manner similar to alcohol

behavioral avoidance tests: behavioral assessment strategies used to assess phobias and related avoidance behavior by asking a patient to approach a feared situation as closely as possible

behavioral genetics: field of study that explores the role of genes and environment in the transmission of behavioral traits

behavioral inhibition: a temperamental feature characterized by withdrawal from (or failure to approach) novel people, objects, or situations

behavioral medicine: an interdisciplinary field that studies the relation between behavioral and biomedical science

behavioral observation: the measurement of behavior as it occurs by someone other than the person whose behavior is being observed

behaviorism: the theory that the only appropriate objects of scientific study are behaviors that can be observed and measured directly

Belmont Report: a document that sets forth three basic principles to guide behavioral and biomedical research with human subjects: respect for persons, beneficence, and justice

benzodiazepines: sedatives that can be used responsibly and effectively for short-term treatment of anxiety and insomnia but have addictive properties

binge eating disorder (BED): a disorder characterized by regular binge eating behavior, but without the compensatory behaviors that are part of bulimia nervosa

binge eating: eating an unusually large amount of food in a short period of time and feeling out of control

biofeedback: process in which patients learn to modify physical responses such as heart rate, respiration, and body temperature

biological scarring: the process whereby years of living with a disorder causes changes in the brain

biomedical model: a perspective that explains illnesses solely by biological processes

biopsychosocial model: a theoretical perspective that suggests that health is determined by complex interactions among biological, psychological, and social factors

biopsychosocial perspective: the idea that biological, psychological, and social factors probably contribute to the development of abnormal behavior and different factors are important for different individuals

bipolar disorder: both episodic depressed mood and episodic mania

bipolar I: full-blown mania alternates with episodes of major depression

bipolar II: hypomania alternates with episodes of major depression

blunted affect: diminished or immobile facial expressions and a flat, monotonic vocal tone that does not change even when the topic of conversation becomes emotionally laden

body dysmorphic disorder: an overwhelming concern that some part of the body is ugly or misshapen

body mass index or BMI: weight, in kilograms, divided by height, in meters squared (kg/m^2)

borderline personality disorder: a pervasive pattern of instability in interpersonal relationships, self-image, and affect, with marked impulsive features such as frantic efforts to avoid real or imagined abandonment

brain stem: part of the brain, located at its base, which controls fundamental biological functions such as breathing

brief psychotic disorder: the sudden onset of any psychotic symptom that may resolve after one day and does not last for more than one month

bulimia nervosa: a disorder characterized by recurrent episodes of binge eating in combination with some form of compensatory behavior aimed at undoing the effects of the binge or preventing weight gain

caffeine: a central nervous system stimulant that boosts energy, mood, awareness, concentration, and wakefulness

candidate gene association study: compares one or a few genes in a large group of individuals who have a specific trait or disorder with a well-matched group of individuals who do not have the trait or disorder

case study: comprehensive description of an individual (or group of individuals) that focuses on assessment or description of abnormal behavior or its treatment

catatonia: condition in which a person is awake but is nonresponsive to external stimulation

central nervous system: one part of the human nervous system that includes the brain and the spinal cord

cerebral cortex: the largest part of the forebrain; contains structures that contribute to higher cognitive functioning including reasoning, abstract thought, perception of time, and creativity

cerebral senile plaques: deposits of beta-amyloid protein that form between the cells found in the brains of patients with Alzheimer's disease

civil commitment: a state-initiated procedure that forces involuntary treatment on people who are judged to have a mental illness, who present a danger to themselves (including an inability to care for themselves) or others

clang associations: speech governed by words that sound alike rather than words that have meaning

classical conditioning: a form of learning in which a conditioned stimulus (CS) is paired with an unconditioned stimulus (UCS) to produce a conditioned response

clinical assessment: the process of gathering information about a person and his or her environment to make decisions about the nature, status, and treatment of psychological problems

clinical interviews: conversations between an interviewer and a patient, the purpose of which is to gather information and make judgments related to assessment goals

clinical significance: observed change that is meaningful in terms of clinical functioning

Cluster A: a group of personality disorders that include behaviors that can be viewed as odd, quirky, or eccentric; includes paranoid, schizoid, and schizotypal personality disorders

Cluster B: a group of personality disorders that include behaviors that can be viewed as exaggerated, inflated, dramatic, emotional, or erratic; includes antisocial, borderline, narcissistic, and histrionic personality disorders

Cluster C: a group of personality disorders that include behaviors that are marked by considerable anxiety or withdrawal; includes avoidant, dependent, and obsessive-compulsive personality disorders

cocaine: a stimulant that comes from the leaves of the coca plant, indigenous to South America

cognitive impairments: impairments in visual and verbal learning and memory, inability to pay attention, decreased speed of information processing, and impaired abstract reasoning, any or all of which may be found in different psychotic disorders

cohort studies: group-based studies in which one group (cohort) shares a common characteristic and moves forward in time as a unit

comorbidity: the co-occurrence of two or more disorders existing in the same person, either at the same time or at some point in the lifetime

compensatory behaviors: any actions that are used to counteract a binge or to prevent weight gain

conduct disorder: continuous and repeated pattern of violating the basic rights of others or breaking societal rules, including aggression toward people or animals, destruction of property, deceitfulness or theft, and serious rule violations

confidentiality: agreement between two parties (in this case, the therapist and patient) that private information revealed during therapy will not be discussed with others

contingency contracting: strategy that relies on setting up a reinforcement program to encourage healthier behavior

contingency management approach: treatment approach in which rewards are provided for specific behaviors, such as treatment compliance

control group: comparison group for an experimental study; in this group, the variable to be studied is absent

controlled group designs: experiments in which groups of participants are exposed to different conditions, at least one of which is experimental and one of which is a control

conventional or typical antipsychotics: medications that effectively reduce the positive symptoms of schizophrenia but produce serious side effects

conversion disorder: pseudoneurological complaints such as motor or sensory dysfunction

correlation coefficient: statistical figure that describes the direction and strength of a correlation

correlations: relationships between variables

covert sensitization: a treatment that uses prolonged, imaginal exposure to engagement in an aversive behavior, such as a sexually deviant act but also imagining the negative consequences that result from it

criminal commitment: a court-ordered procedure that forces involuntary treatment on a person with a psychological disorder who commits a crime

cross-sectional design: a research design in which participants are assessed once for the specific variable under investigation

crystal methamphetamine: a form of methamphetamine that produces longer lasting and more intense physiological reactions than the powdered form

cultural-familial retardation: mild mental retardation that is more common among children in the lower socioeconomic classes and is considered retardation due to psychosocial disadvantage

culture: shared behavioral patterns and lifestyles that differentiate one group of people from another

culture-bound illness: abnormal behaviors that are specific to a particular location or group

cyclothymic disorder: condition characterized by fluctuations that alternate between hypomanic symptoms and depressive symptoms

d-lysergic acid diethylamide (LSD): a synthetic hallucinogen, first synthesized in 1938

Declaration of Helsinki: a document that sets forth basic guidelines for the conduct of research, including the need for clearly formulated experimental procedures, a careful assessment of risks compared with benefits, and the provision of adequate information to the participants

deinstitutionalization: release of inpatients from hospitals to community treatment settings

delirium tremens: a symptom characterized by disorientation, severe agitation, high blood pressure, and fever, which can last up to 3 to 4 days after stopping drinking

delirium: alteration in consciousness that typically occurs in the context of a medical illness or after ingesting a substance

delusion: a false belief

delusional disorder: a condition in which a person has a nonbizarre delusion, no other psychotic symptoms, and few changes in overall functioning other than the behaviors immediately surrounding the delusion

delusions of influence: beliefs that one's thoughts or behaviors are being controlled by others

dementia due to other general medical conditions: cognitive impairment related to HIV, head trauma, Parkinson's disease, and Huntington's disease, or other medical illness

dementia praecox: Kraepelin's name for a psychological disorder characterized by deterioration of mental faculties (now called schizophrenia)

dementia: different syndromes characterized by persistent and multiple cognitive difficulties that create significant impairment in social or occupational functioning

dependent personality disorder: a pervasive and excessive need to be taken care of by others that leads to dependency and fears of being left alone

dependent variable: the variable in a controlled experiment that is assessed to determine the effect of the independent variable

depersonalization disorder: feelings of being detached from one's body or mind, a state of feeling as if one is an external observer of one's own behavior

depression: mood that is abnormally low

detoxification: medically supervised drug withdrawal

developmental trajectory: common symptoms of a disorder may vary depending on a person's age

diagnosis: identification of an illness

Diagnostic and Statistical Manual of Mental Disorders (DSM): a classification originally developed in 1952 to classify mental disorders; revisions have been made over subsequent years, and this document is a standard of care in psychiatry and psychology

diathesis-stress model of abnormal behavior: the idea that psychological disorders may have a biological predisposition (diathesis) that lies dormant until environmental stress occurs and the combination produces abnormal behavior

differential diagnosis: a process in which a clinician weighs how likely it is that a person has one diagnosis instead of another

dissociative amnesia: an inability to recall important information, usually of a personal nature, that follows a stressful or traumatic event

dissociative disorders: a set of disorders characterized by disruption in the usually integrated functions of consciousness, memory, identity, or perception of the environment

dissociative fugue: a disorder involving loss of personal identity and memory, often involving a flight from a person's usual place of residence

dissociative identity disorder: presence within a person of two or more distinct personality states, each with its own pattern of perceiving, relating to, and thinking about the environment and self

dopamine hypothesis: the theory that a cause of schizophrenia is the presence of too much dopamine in the neural synapses

double depression: combination of episodic major depressions superimposed on chronic low mood

Down syndrome: a genetic form of mental retardation caused by the presence of three chromosomes rather than the usual two on the 21st pair

duty to warn: therapists' duty to use reasonable care to protect third parties from dangers posed by patients

dyspareunia: consistent genital pain associated with sexual intercourse

dysthymia: a chronic state of depression; the symptoms are the same as those of major depression, but they are less severe

early-onset schizophrenia (EOS): schizophrenia that develops in childhood or adolescence (usually before age 18)

Eating Disorder Not Otherwise Specified (EDNOS): a residual diagnostic category for people who have eating disorders that do not match the classic profile of anorexia nervosa or bulimia nervosa

echolalia: repeating verbatim what others say

ecstasy: the pill form of *methylenedioxymethamphetamine* (MDMA) a common "club" drug and a frequent trigger for emergency room visits

ego psychology: a form of psychodynamic theory that focuses on conscious motivations and healthy forms of human functioning

electroconvulsive therapy (ECT): the controlled delivery of electrical impulses, which cause brief seizures in the brain and reduce depressed mood

emotional contagion: the automatic mimicry and synchronization of expressions, vocalizations, postures, and movements of one person by those of another

encopresis: repeated elimination of feces on or into inappropriate places such as the floor or clothing by someone over age 4

endocrine system: a system in the body that sends messages to the bodily organs via hormones

enmeshment: overinvolvement of all family members in the affairs of any one member

enuresis: voiding of urine into one's clothing or bedding

epidemiology: a research approach that focuses on the prevalence and incidence of mental disorders and the factors that influence those patterns

ethics: accepted values that provide guidance to make sound moral judgments

executive dysfunction: difficulty planning, thinking abstractly, initiating, and inhibiting actions

exhibitionism: recurrent fantasies, urges, or behaviors involving exposing one's genitals to an unsuspecting stranger

experimental epidemiology: a research method in which the scientist manipulates exposure to either causal or preventive factors

experimental variable: the variable (condition) being tested in an experimental study

exposure: the crucial ingredient in behavior therapy, in which a person learns to overcome fears by actual or imagined contact with the feared object or event

expressed emotion: a concept used to describe the level of emotional involvement and critical attitudes that exist within the family of a patient with schizophrenia

factitious disorder by proxy: a condition in which physical or psychological signs or symptoms of illness are intentionally produced in another person, most often in a child by a parent

factitious disorders: conditions in which physical or psychological signs or symptoms of illness are intentionally produced, in what appears to be a desire to assume a sick role

familial aggregation: process of examining whether family members of a person with a particular disorder are more likely to have that disorder than family members of people without the disorder

female orgasmic disorder: persistent and recurrent delay or absence of orgasm following the normal excitement phase. Sometimes called *anorgasmia*

female sexual arousal disorder: persistent or recurrent inability to maintain adequate vaginal lubrication and swelling response until the completion of sexual activity

fetal alcohol syndrome: a syndrome in babies that occurs when pregnant mothers drink alcohol and it passes through the placenta and harms the developing fetus

fetishism: sexual arousal (fantasies, urges, or behaviors) that involves nonliving objects (not limited to female clothing used in cross-dressing)

fight or flight: a general discharge of the sympathetic nervous system activated by stress or fear that includes increased heart rate, enhanced muscle activity, and increased respiration

forebrain: part of the brain that includes the limbic system, basal ganglia, and cerebral cortex

fragile X syndrome: the most commonly inherited cause of mental retardation; occurs when a DNA series makes too many copies of itself and "turns off" a gene on the X chromosome. When the gene is turned off, cells do not make a necessary protein, and without it, FXS occurs

frontal lobe: one of the four lobes of the brain; seat of reasoning, impulse control, judgment, language, memory, motor function, problem solving, and sexual and social behavior

frotteurism: consistent and intense sexually arousing fantasies, sexual urges, or behaviors involving touching and rubbing against a non-consenting person

functional analysis: also called behavioral analysis or functional assessment; a strategy of behavioral assessment in which a clinician attempts to identify causal links between problem behaviors and environmental variables

gender identity disorder: strong and persistent cross-gender identification and persistent discomfort with one's own biological sex

gene–environment correlation: the same person who provides a patient's genetic makeup also provides the environment in which that person lives

General Adaptation Syndrome (GAS): a three-stage process of stress adaptation, including alarm, resistance, and exhaustion

generalized anxiety disorder: excessive worry about future events, past transgressions, financial status, and the health of oneself and loved ones

genomewide association study: unbiased search of the human genome comparing cases and controls on genes scattered across the genome for evidence of association

genomewide linkage analysis: a technique that uses samples of families with many individuals who are ill with the same disorder or large samples of relatives who have the same disorder to identify genomic regions that may hold genes that influence a trait

geropsychology: a subdiscipline of psychology that addresses issues of aging, including normal development, individual differences, and psychological problems unique to older persons

goodness-of-fit: the idea that behavior is problematic or not problematic depending on the environment in which it occurs

guilty but mentally ill: a legal decision in which a person is considered criminally guilty and is subject to criminal penalties. The addition of the phrase "but mentally ill" acknowledges the presence of a psychological disorder when the offense was committed, but does not change the person's criminal responsibility

hallucination: a false sensory perception

hallucinogens: drugs that produce altered states of bodily perception and sensations, intense emotions, detachment from self and environment, and, for some users, feeling of insight with mystical or religious significance

Health Insurance Portability and Accountability Act (HIPAA): system of laws and regulations that protect the security and privacy of health information

health psychology: a subfield of psychology that uses its principles and methods to understand how attitudes and behaviors influence health and illness

heritability: the percentage of variance in liability to the disorder accounted for by genetic factors

histrionic personality disorder: a pervasive pattern of excessive emotionality and attention seeking

hormones: chemical messengers that are released into the bloodstream and act on target organs

hypnosis: a procedure for treating pain during which patients relax, a trance-like state is induced, and hypnotic suggestions are used to reduce pain

hypoactive sexual desire disorder: reduced or absent sexual desires or behaviors, either with a partner or through masturbation

hypochondriasis: fears or concerns about having an illness that persist despite medical reassurance

hypomania: mood elevation that is clearly abnormal, yet not severe enough to impair functioning or require hospitalization

hypothalamic-pituitary-adrenocortical (HPA) axis: a physical response to stress in which the hypothalamus produces increased corticotrophin-releasing factor (CRF), which in turn causes increased secretion of adrenocorticotropic hormone (ACTH) and increased cortisol (another hormone)

iatrogenic: a term describing a disease that may be inadvertently caused by a physician, by a medical or surgical treatment, or by a diagnostic procedure

incidence: number of new cases that emerge in a given population during a specified period of time

independent variable: the variable in a controlled experiment that is controlled by the experimenter

informed consent: the concept that all people who participate in research must understand the aims and methods of the research, what they will be asked to do, and what types of information they will be asked to provide. In addition, they must understand the risks and benefits of research participation, and based on that information, have the right to agree or refuse to participate in the any research project

inhalants: vapors from a variety of chemicals that yield an immediate effect of euphoria or sedation and can cause permanent damage to all organ systems including the brain

Institutional Review Board (IRB): committee charged by the researcher's institution with reviewing and approving scientific research

intelligence quotient: a score of cognitive functioning that compares a person's performance to his or her age-matched peers

intelligence tests: tests that measure intelligence quotient (IQ)

International Classification of Diseases (ICD): a classification system for mental disorders developed in Europe that is an international standard diagnostic system for epidemiology and many health management purposes

interrater agreement: the amount of agreement between two clinicians who are using the same measure to rate the same symptoms in a single patient

late-onset schizophrenia: schizophrenia that first appears after age 40

learned helplessness: term meaning that externally uncontrollable environments and presumably internally uncontrollable environments are inescapable stimuli that can lead to depression

learning disorders: conditions involving academic achievement below expectations for age, years in school, and IQ score

life-span developmental diathesis-stress model: considers the role of biological predispositions, stressful life events, and personal protective factors in the etiology of abnormal behavior, such as depression

lithium: a naturally occurring metallic element used to treat bipolar disorder

longitudinal design: a research design in which participants are assessed at least two times and often more over a certain time interval

loose associations: thoughts that have little or no logical connection to the next thought

M'Naghten Rule: a legal principle stating that a person is not responsible for his actions if (a) he did not know what he was doing, or (b) he did not know that his actions were wrong

major depressive disorder: persistent sad or low mood that is severe enough to impair a person's interest in or ability to engage in normally enjoyable activities

male erectile disorder: persistent and recurrent inability to maintain an adequate erection until completion of sexual activity

male orgasmic disorder: sometimes known as delayed ejaculation or retarded ejaculation; the delay of or inability to achieve orgasm despite adequate sexual stimulation

malingering: a condition in which physical symptoms are produced intentionally to avoid military service, criminal prosecution, or work, or to obtain financial compensation or drugs

malpractice: professional misconduct or unreasonable lack of skill

mania: mood that is abnormally high

marijuana: a drug derived from the *Cannabis sativa* plant that produces mild intoxication

mass hysteria: a situation in which a group of people share and sometimes even act upon a belief that is not based in fact (for example, tarantism and lycanthropy)

medical psychology: the study and practice of psychology as it relates to health, illness, and medical treatment

mens rea: Latin term for guilty mind or criminal intent

mental retardation: significantly subaverage intellectual functioning *and* deficits or impairment in at least two areas of life functioning

methadone: the most widely known agonist substitute, used as a replacement for heroin

midbrain: a portion of the brain stem that coordinates sensory information and movement; includes the reticular activating system, the thalamus, and the hypothalamus

mind-body dualism: a belief that the mind and body function independently, associated with the French philosopher René Descartes

mixed state: symptoms of mania and depression that occur at the same time

molecular genetics: the study of the structure and function of genes at a molecular level

mood disorders: syndromes in which a disturbance in mood is the predominant feature

mulitaxial system: a system of diagnosis and classification used by the DSM that requires classifying a patient's behavior on five different dimensions

multi-infarct dementia: cognitive dysfunction that occurs as the result of several small strokes

narcissistic personality disorder: a pervasive pattern of grandiosity, need for admiration from others, and lack of empathy

negative symptoms: behaviors, emotions, or thought processes (cognitions) that exist in people without a psychiatric disorder but are absent (or are substantially diminished) in people with schizophrenia

neuroanatomy: brain structure

neurofibrillary tangles: twisted protein fibers within neurons found in the brains of patients with Alzheimer's disease

neuroimaging: technology that takes pictures of the brain

neurons: nerve cells found throughout the body, including the brain

neuroscience: the study of the structure and function of the nervous system and the interaction of that system and behavior

neurotransmitters: chemical substances that are released into the synapse and relay electrical signals from one neuron to another

nicotine replacement therapy (NRT): a safe and effective therapy used as part of a comprehensive smoking cessation program

nicotine: a highly addictive component of tobacco that is considered to be both a stimulant and a sedative

nightmare disorder: repeated episodes of long, frightening dreams that usually involve a physical threat to survival and produce vivid imagery

nonspecific immune system: a general system that protects against infections and diseases provided by and that includes anatomical barriers, phagocytosis, B-lymphocytes, and inflammation

normative: a comparison group that is representative of the entire population against which a person's score on a psychological test is compared

not guilty by reason of insanity: a legal decision that describes people who commit a crime but who are prevented by a psychological disorder from understanding the seriousness and illegality of their actions

Nuremberg Code: directives for experimentation with human subjects, which specify that voluntary consent is absolutely essential for clinical research

obsessive-compulsive personality disorder: a pervasive preoccupation with orderliness, perfectionism, and mental and interpersonal control to the point of distress

obsessive-compulsive disorder: a condition involving obsessions (intrusive thoughts), often combined with compulsions (repetitive behaviors) that can be extensive, time consuming, and distressful

occipital lobe: one of four lobes of the brain; located at the back of the skull; center of visual processing

olfactory aversion: a treatment pairing an extremely noxious but harmless stimulus (such as ammonia) with either thoughts or behavior, usually of a sexual nature

operant conditioning: a form of learning in which behavior is acquired or changed by the events that happen afterward

opioids: drugs derived form the opium poppy, such as heroin, morphine, and codeine

oppositional defiant disorder: negative, hostile, or defiant behaviors that are less severe than those found in conduct disorder

osteoporosis: decreased bone density

outpatient commitment: a court order that directs a person to comply with a specified, individualized outpatient treatment plan

pain disorder: persistent pain that defies medical explanation

panic attack: a discrete period of intense fear or discomfort (subjective distress) and a cascade of physical symptoms

panic disorder with agoraphobia: panic attacks combined with avoidance of places where escape (in case of a panic attack) may be difficult or impossible

panic disorder without agoraphobia: a disorder in which the person has had at least one panic attack and worries about having more attacks

paranoid personality disorder: a pervasive distrust and suspiciousness of others such that their motives are interpreted as malevolent

paraphilias: intense, persistent, and frequently occurring sexual urges, fantasies, or behaviors that involve unusual situations, objects, or activities

parasomnias: unwanted physical events that happen during sleep

parasympathetic nervous system: part of the autonomic nervous system that counteracts the effects of system activation by slowing down heart rate and respiration, returning the body to a resting state

parietal lobe: one of four lobes of the brain; integrates sensory information from various sources and may be involved with visuospatial processing

pedophilia: consistent and intense sexually arousing fantasies, sexual urges, or behaviors involving sexual activity with a child or children not yet 14 years old. The person is at least 16 years old and at least 5 years older than the child or children

peripheral nervous system: one part of the human nervous system that includes the sensory-somatic nervous system (controls sensations and muscle movements) and the autonomic nervous system (controls involuntary movements) and returns the body to resting levels after these systems have been activated

persecutory delusions: beliefs that someone is persecuting the patient or that the individual is a special agent/individual

personality disorder: an enduring pattern of inner experience and behavior that deviates from the norm, is pervasive and inflexible, has an onset in adolescence or early adulthood, is stable across time, and leads to distress or impairment

personality tests: psychological tests that measure personality characteristics

pervasive developmental disorder not otherwise specified: a diagnosis assigned to children who have *some* but not *all* of the behaviors that characterize autistic disorder

pervasive developmental disorders: a group of disorders characterized by serious impairments in a child's reciprocal social interaction and communication, and the presence of stereotypical behavior, interests, and activities

phenomenology: a school of thought that holds that one's subjective perception of the world is more important than the world in actuality

phenylketonuria: a genetic disorder in which the body cannot break down the amino acid *phenylalanine*; if untreated, leads to the development of mental retardation

pica: recurrent, compulsive consumption of nonnutritive items

placebo control: a control group in which an inactive treatment is provided

placebo effect: a condition in which symptoms of illness diminish or disappear not because of any specific treatment, but because the patient believes that a treatment is effective

plethysmography: a method to measure sexual arousal in men or women

positive symptoms: a group of schizophrenic symptoms including unusual thoughts, feelings, and behaviors that vary in intensity, and in many cases are responsive to treatment

post-traumatic stress disorder: after an event that involved actual or threatened death, serious injury, or a threat to physical integrity, emotional distress leads to avoidance of stimuli associated with the trauma, feelings of emotional numbness, and persistent symptoms of increased sympathetic nervous system arousal

premature ejaculation: consistent ejaculation with minimal sexual stimulation before, immediately upon, or shortly after penetration and before the person wishes it

prevalence: the number of times a given disorder appears in a population at a designated time

primary insomnia: difficulty initiating or maintaining sleep, or nonrestorative sleep, over a period of at least 1 month and with significant distress and/or interference with functioning

primary prevention: intervention programs that focus on increasing healthy behaviors among people without disease

privilege: legal term that prevents a therapist from revealing confidential information during legal proceedings

proband: person with a particular disorder in a familial aggregation study

projective tests: tests derived from psychoanalytic theory in which people are asked to respond to ambiguous stimuli

pseudoseizures: sudden changes in behavior that mimic epileptic seizures but have no organic basis

psychoanalysis: a theory of abnormal behavior originated by Sigmund Freud that was based on the belief that many aspects of behavior were controlled by unconscious innate biological urges that existed from infancy

psychoeducation: patient and families are educated about the disorder in order to reduce familial distress and equip them to work effectively with the patient

psychological autopsy: interviews with family, friends, co-workers, and health care providers in an attempt to identify psychological causes of suicide

psychomotor retardation: slowed mental or physical activities

psychoneuroimmunology: the study of the relations between social, psychological, and physical responses

psychophysiological assessment: assessment strategies that measure brain structure, brain function, and nervous system activity

psychosis: a severe mental condition characterized by a loss of contact with reality

punishment: application of something painful or the removal of something positive

purging: using self-induced vomiting, laxatives, or a diuretic such as a water pill in order to reverse the effects of a binge or to produce weight loss

random assignment: the most critical feature of a randomized controlled design wherein each participant has an equal probability of being assigned to each experimental or control condition

reinforcement: a contingent event that strengthens the response that precedes it

relapse prevention: treatment approach that uses functional analysis to identify the antecedents and consequences of drug use and then develops alternative cognitive and behavioral skills to reduce the risk of future drug use

reliability: how well a psychological assessment instrument produces consistent results each time it is given

reversible dementia: also known as **pseudodementia**, occurs when the full syndrome of dementia appears to be present but resolves after appropriate treatment for another disorder

rumination disorder: regurgitating recently eaten food into the mouth, followed by either rechewing, reswallowing, or spitting it out

satiation: a treatment that uses prolonged, imaginal exposure to arousing sexual stimuli until it no longer produces positive, erotic feelings

schizoaffective disorder: a condition in which, in addition to all of the symptoms of schizophrenia, the patient also suffers from a major depressive, manic, or mixed episode disorder at some point during the illness

schizoid personality disorder: a pervasive pattern of social detachment and a limited expression of emotion in interpersonal contexts

schizophrenia: a severe psychological disorder characterized by disorganization in thought, perception, and behavior

schizophreniform disorder: a condition with symptoms that are identical to those of schizophrenia except that the duration of the illness is shorter (less than 6 months) and there is less impairment in social or occupational functioning

schizotypal personality disorder: a consistent pattern of social problems marked by significant deficits in the ability to maintain close relationships and by idiosyncratic behavior and distortions in thoughts

scientist-practitioner approach: an approach to psychological disorders based on the concept that when providing treatment to people with psychological disorders, the psychologist relies on the findings of research and in turn, when conducting research, the psychologist investigates topics that help to guide and improve psychological care

screening: an assessment process that attempts to identify psychological problems or predict the risk of future problems among people who are not referred for clinical assessment

seasonal affective disorder: subtype of major depression that is characterized by depressive episodes that vary by season

secondary prevention: health-promotion programs for people at increased risk for health problems

sedative drugs: barbiturates and benzodiazepines, which are central nervous system depressants and cause sedation and decrease anxiety

selective serotonin reuptake inhibitors (SSRIs): medications that selectively inhibit the reuptake of serotonin at the presynaptic neuronal membrane, increasing the time that serotonin remains in the synapse, restoring the normal chemical balance

self-monitoring: a procedure within behavioral assessment in which the patient observes and records his or her own behavior as it happens

self-referent comparisons: comparison of responses on a psychological instrument with a person's own prior performance

separation anxiety disorder: severe and unreasonable fear of separation from a parent or caregiver

sex drive: Physical and/or psychological craving for sexual activity and pleasure

sex reassignment surgery: a series of behavioral and medical procedures that matches an individual's physical anatomy to gender identity

sexual aversion disorder: persistent or extreme aversion to, or avoidance of, genital contact with a sexual partner

sexual dysfunctions: absence or impairment of some aspect of sexual response that causes distress or impairment

sexual masochism: consistent intense sexually arousing fantasies, sexual urges, or behaviors involving actual acts of being humiliated, beaten, bound, or otherwise made to suffer

sexual sadism: consistent sexual arousal that occurs when acts of humiliation, beating, bondage, or acts of suffering are inflicted on another person

shared psychotic disorder: a condition in which two or more persons who have a close relationship share the same delusional belief; also known as folie à deux

shenjing shuairuo: loosely translated, nerve weakness, a cultural variation of somatoform disorders found among the Chinese

single-case designs: experimental studies conducted with a single individual

sleep terror disorder: a type of sleep disorder in which the child suddenly sits up, screams, and cannot be consoled

sleepwalking disorder: also known as somnambulism, a disorder that consists of sitting up in bed with eyes open but "unseeing" and sometimes getting out of bed and walking through the house

social phobia: a pervasive pattern of social timidity characterized by fear that the person will behave in a way that will be humiliating or embarrassing

sociocultural models: the idea that abnormal behavior must be understood within the context of social and cultural forces

somatization disorder: the presence of many symptoms that suggest a medical condition, but without a recognized organic basis

somatoform disorders: conditions in which physical symptoms or concerns about an illness cannot be explained by a medical or psychological disorder

specific immune system: protection against specific infections and diseases as a result of natural or artificial processes

specific phobias: severe and persistent fears of circumscribed events, objects, or situations that lead to significant disruption in areas of functioning

stimulus control: modifying behavior by changing the stimuli that bring on the behavior

stress moderators: variables that affect how stress is experienced and how it affects health and other aspects of functioning

stress: any negative emotional experience that is accompanied by biochemical, physiological, cognitive, and behavioral responses that are aimed at changing or adjusting to the stressor

stressor: any event (or stimulus) that produces tension or other negative emotion, such as fear

structured interviews: clinical interviews in which the clinician asks a standard set of questions, usually with the goal of establishing a diagnosis

subcortical dementia: condition involving damage primarily in the inner layers of the brain and found frequently during the later stages of HIV and in Parkinson's disease and Huntington's disease

substance abuse: ingestion of a substance that leads to disruption in social, educational, or occupational functioning

substance dependence: a condition characterized by two distinct factors, tolerance and withdrawal

substance intoxication: the acute effects of substance use

substance use: low to moderate experience with a substance that does not produce problems with social, educational, or occupational functioning

substance-induced dementia: cognitive impairment associated with substance use

suicidal ideation: thoughts of death

sympathetic nervous system: part of the autonomic nervous system that activates the body for the fight-or-flight response. When activated, the sympathetic nervous system increases heart rate and respiration, allowing the body to perform at peak efficiency

sympathetic-adrenomedullary system (SAM): a physical response to stress in which increased adrenal gland stimulation results in the secretion of epinephrine and norepinephrine

synapses: spaces between neurons

synaptic pruning: a process in which weaker synaptic contacts in the brain are eliminated and stronger connections are further strengthened

talking cure: therapy in the form of discussion of psychological distress with a trained professional, leading to the elimination of distressing symptoms

tardive dyskinesia: a neurological condition characterized by abnormal and involuntary motor movements of the face, mouth, limbs, and trunk

temperament: personality components that are biological or genetic in origin, observable from birth (or perhaps before) and relatively stable across time and situations

temporal lobe: one of four lobes of the brain; associated with understanding auditory and verbal information, labeling of objects, and verbal memory

test-retest reliability: how well a test produces similar scores over time when given to the same individual(s)

tetrahydrocannibinol: the active ingredient in marijuana

thought blocking: unusually long pauses in the patient's speech that occur during a conversation

tolerance: diminished response to a drug after repeated exposure to it

trait anxiety: also called anxiety-proneness; a personality trait that exists along a dimension, with those high on this dimension being more "reactive" to stressful events and therefore more likely, given the right circumstances, to develop a disorder

transgender behavior: behavioral attempts to pass as the opposite sex through cross-dressing, disguising one's own sexual genitalia, or changing other sexual characteristics

translational research: a scientific approach that focuses on communication between basic science and applied clinical research

transsexualism: another term for gender identity disorder, commonly used to describe the condition when it occurs in adolescents and adults

transtheoretical model: a five-stage sequential model of behavioral change

transvestic fetishism: sexual arousal in men that results from wearing women's clothing and is accompanied by significant distress or impairment

trephination: process whereby a circular instrument was used to cut away sections of the skull, possibly in an attempt to release demons from the brain

Tuskegee experiment: infamous historical study in which core values of research (respect for persons, beneficence, and justice) were violated

Type A behavior pattern: a personality pattern associated with the onset of coronary heart disease, consisting of consistent strivings for achievement, impatience and time urgency, and aggressiveness toward others

undifferentiated somatoform disorder: one or more physical complaints that are present for at least 6 months and cause distress or functional impairment

unstructured interviews: clinical interviews in which the clinician decides what questions to ask and how to ask them

vaginismus: unwanted involuntary spasms of the vaginal muscles that interfere with intercourse or any attempt at vaginal insertion

validity: the degree to which a test measures what it is intended to assess

vascular dementia: cognitive dysfunction that occurs as the result of cerebrovascular disease

vascular depression: a mood disorder that occurs in the context of cerebrovascular disease

vasovagal syncope: a physiological response consisting of slow heart rate and low blood pressure that sometimes occurs in people with blood-illness-injury phobias

very-late-onset schizophrenia-like psychosis: a schizophrenic-like disorder, but with symptoms that do not include deterioration in social and personal functioning

vicarious conditioning: a distinct type of learning in which the person need not actually do the behavior in order to acquire it

viral infection theory: the theory that during the prenatal period or shortly after birth viral infections could cause some psychological disorders

voyeurism: consistent intense sexually arousing fantasies, sexual urges, or behaviors centered on observing an unsuspecting person who is naked, disrobing, or engaging in sexual activity

waxy flexibility: a condition in which parts of the body (usually the arms) will remain frozen in a particular posture when positioned that way by another person

Wernicke-Korsakoff syndrome: a syndrome caused by deficiencies in thiamine secondary to alcohol dependence

withdrawal: symptoms associated with physical dependence on a drug that occur when the drug is no longer taken

worry: apprehensive (negative) expectations or outcomes about the future or the past that are considered to be unreasonable in light of the actual situation

REFERENCES

AAGP Position Statement: Position Statement: Principles of care for patients with dementia resulting from Alzheimer Disease. (2006). American Association of Geriatric Psychiatry [Online]. Available: www.aagponline.org

Abbass, A. A., Hancock, J. T., Henderson, J., & Kisely, S. (2006). Short-term psychodynamic psychotherapies for common mental disorders. *Cochrane Database Systematic Review,* October 18 (4):CD004687.

Abel, E. L., & Hannigan, J. H. (1995). Maternal risk factors in fetal alcohol syndrome: provocative and permissive influences. *Neurotoxicology and Teratology, 17,* 445–462.

Abel, G. G., & Osborn, C. (1992). The paraphilias: The extent and nature of sexually deviant and criminal behavior. *Clinical Forensic Psychiatry, 15,* 675–687.

Abel, G. G., Becker, J. V., Cunningham-Rathner, J., Mittelman, M., & Rouleau, J. L. (1988). Multiple paraphilic diagnoses among sex offenders. *Bulletin of the American Academy of Psychiatry and the Law, 16,* 153–168.

Abel, G. G., Huffman, J., Warberg, B., & Holland, C. L. (1998). Visual reaction time and plethysmography as measures of sexual interest in child molesters. *Sexual Abuse: A Journal of Research and Treatment, 10,* 81–95.

Abel, G. G., Jordan, A., Rouleau, J. O. L., Emerick, R., Barboza-Whitehead, S., & Osborn, C. (2004). Use of visual reaction time to assess male adolescents who molest children. *Sexual Abuse: A Journal of Research and Treatment, 16,* 255–265.

Abel, G. G., Mittelman, M. S., & Becker, J. V. (1985). Sexual offenders: Results of assessment and recommendations for treatment. In H. W. Ben-Gron (Ed.), *Clinical criminology* (pp. 191–205). Toronto: M. M. Graphics.

Abrahams, P. W., & Parsons, J. A. (1996). Geophagy in the tropics: A literature review. *Geographical Journal, 162,* 63–72.

Abramowitz, J., & Moore, E. L. (2007). An experimental analysis of hypochondriasis. *Behaviour Research and Therapy, 45,* 413–424.

Abramson, L., Alloy, L., & Panzarella, C. (2002). Depression. In *Encyclopedia of cognitive science.* London: Macmillan.

Abramson, L., Seligman, M., & Teasdale, J. (1978). Learned helplessness in humans: Critique and reformulation. *Journal of Abnormal Psychology, 87,* 49–74.

Acocella, J. (1998, April 6). The politics of hysteria. *New Yorker,* 64–79.

Addington, A. M., Gornick, M., Duckworth, J., Spron, A., Gogtayn, N., Bobb, A., Greenstein, D., Lenane, M., Gochman, P., Baker, N., Balissoon, R., Vakkalanka, R. K., Weinberger, D. R., Rapoport, J. L., & Straub R. E. (2005). GAD1 (2q31.1) which encoded glutamic acid decarboxylase (GAD_{67}), is associated with childhood-onset schizophrenia and cortical gray matter volume loss. *Molecular Psychiatry, 10,* 581–588.

Adler, C. M., DelBello, M. P., & Strakowski, S. M. (2006). Brain network dysfunction in bipolar disorder. *CNS Spectrums, 11,* 312–320.

Adler, N. E., Boyce, W. T., Chesney, M. A., Folkman, S., & Syme, S. L. (1993). Socioeconomic inequalities in health. No easy solution. *Journal of the American Medical Association, 269,* 3140–3145.

Agargun, M. Y., Savas Cilli, A., Sener, S., Bilici, M., Ozer, O. A., Selvi, Y., & Karacan, E. (2004). The prevalence of parasomnias in preadolescent school-aged children: a Turkish sample. *Sleep, 47,* 701–705.

Aigner, M., Graf, A., Freidl, M., Prause, W., Weiss, Kaup-Eder, B., Saletu, B., & Bach, M. (2003). Sleep disturbances in somatoform pain disorder. *Psychopathology, 36,* 324–328.

Ainsworth, M. (1982). Attachment: retrospect and prospect. In C. Parkes & J. Stevenson-Hinde (Eds.), *The place of attachment in human behavior.* (pp. 3–30). New York: Basic Books.

Akbarian, S., Viñuela, A., Kim, J. J., Potkin, S. G., Bonney, W. E., Jr., & Jones, E. G. (1993). Distorted distribution of nicotinamide–adenine dinucleotide phosphate–diaphroase neurons in temporal lobe of schizophrenics implies anomalous cortical development. *Archives of General Psychiatry, 50,* 178–187.

Akkerman, R. L., & Ostwald, S. K. (2004). Reducing anxiety in Alzheimer's disease family caregivers: The effectiveness of a nine-week cognitive-behavioral intervention. *American Journal of Alzheimer's Disease and Other Dementias, 19,* 117–123.

Albee, G. W. (2002). Just say no to psychotropic drugs! *Journal of Clinical Psychology, 58,* 635–648.

Alexopoulos, G. S. (2004). Late-life mood disorders. In J. Sadavoy, L. F. Jarvik, G. T. Grossberg, & B. S. Meyers (Eds.), *Comprehensive textbook of geriatric psychiatry.* (pp. 609–653). New York: W.W. Norton & Co.

Alexopoulos, G. S., Kiosses, D. N., Klimstra, S., Kalayam, B., & Bruce, M. L. (2002). Clinical presentation of the depression–executive dysfunction syndrome of late life. *American Journal of Geriatric Psychiatry, 10,* 98–106.

Alexopoulos, G. S., Raue, P., & Arean, P. (2003). Problem-solving therapy versus supportive therapy in geriatric major depression with executive dysfunction. *American Journal of Geriatric Psychiatry, 11,* 46–52.

Alfano, C. A., Beidel, D. C., & Turner, S. M. (2002). Cognition in childhood anxiety: Conceptual, methodological and developmental issues. *Clinical Psychology Review, 22,* 1029–1038.

Alfano, C. A., Beidel, D. C., & Turner, S. M. (2002). Considering cognition in child anxiety: Conceptual, methodological and developmental issues. *Clinical Psychology Review, 22,* 1209–1238.

Ali, Z. (2001). Pica in people with intellectual disability: A literature review of aetiology, epidemiology and complications. *Journal of Intellectual & Developmental Disability, 26,* 205–215.

Allen, K. (1995). Barriers to treatment for addicted African-American women. *Journal of the National Medical Association, 87,* 751–756.

Allen, K., Blascovich, J., & Mendes, W. B. (2002). Cardiovascular reactivity and the presence of pets, friends, and spouses: The truth about cats and dogs. *Psychosomatic Medicine, 64,* 727–739.

Alper, K., Devinsky, O., Perrine, K., Vazquez, B., & Luciano, D. (1993). Nonepileptic seizures and childhood sexual and physical abuse. *Neurology, 43,* 1950–1953.

Althof, S. (2006). The psychology of premature ejaculation: Therapies and consequences. *Journal of Sexual Medicine, 3 Supplement 4,* 324–331.

Alvidrez, J., Arean, P. A., & Stewart, A. L. (2005). Psychoeducation to increase psychotherapy entry for older African Americans. *The American Journal of Geriatric Psychiatry, 13,* 554–561.

Alzheimer's Association (2008). Alzheimer's disease facts and figures. *Alzheimer's & Dementia, 4,* 110–133.

Alzheimer's Association (2009). Alzheimer's disease facts and figures. *Alzheimer's & Dementia,* Vol. 5, Issue 3.

Amaro, H. (1995). Love, sex and power: Considering women's needs in HIV prevention. *American Psychologist, 50,* 437–447.

American Association of Geriatric Psychiatry (2006). Geriatrics and Mental Health [Online]. Available: www.aagponline.org

American Law Institute (1962). *Model penal code: Proposed official draft.* Philadelphia: American Law Institute.

American Psychiatric Association Work Group on Eating Disorders. (2000). Practice guideline for the treatment of patients with eating disorders (revision). *American Journal of Psychiatry, 157,* 1–39.

American Psychiatric Association. (1952). *Diagnostic and statistical manual of mental disorders. First Edition.* Washington, DC: American Psychiatric Association Press.

American Psychiatric Association. (1968). *Diagnostic and statistical manual of mental disorders. Second Edition.* Washington, DC: American Psychiatric Association Press.

American Psychiatric Association. (1980). *Diagnostic and statistical manual of mental disorders. Third Edition.* Washington, DC: American Psychiatric Association Press.

American Psychiatric Association. (1987). *Diagnostic and statistical manual of mental disorders. Edition III-R. Third Edition Revised.* Washington, DC: American Psychiatric Association Press.

American Psychiatric Association. (1994). *Diagnostic and statistical manual of mental disorders: Fourth Edition.* Washington, DC: American Psychiatric Press.

American Psychiatric Association. (2000). *Diagnostic and statistical manual of mental disorders. Fourth edition text revision.* Washington, DC: American Psychiatric Press.

American Psychiatric Association. (2000). Practice guidelines for the treatment of patients with major depressive disorder. *American Journal of Psychiatry, 157* (4 Suppl), 1–45.

American Psychiatric Association. (2005). Practice guidelines for the treatment of patients with bipolar disorder. *American Journal of Psychiatry, 159* (4 Suppl), 1–50.

American Psychiatric Association. (2006). Gay, Lesbian, and Bisexual Issues. Retrieved June 25, 2007, from http://www.healthyminds.org/glbissues.cfm

American Psychological Association (1994). Guidelines for child custody evaluations in divorce proceedings. *American Psychologist, 49,* 677–680.

American Psychological Association (2002). Ethical principles of psychologists and code of conduct. *American Psychologist, 57,* 1060–1073.

American Psychological Association (2004). APA Resolution on Outpatient Civil Commitment.

American Psychological Association (2005). Report of the 2005 Presidential Task Force on Evidence-Based Practice.

American Psychological Association (2006). HIPPA compliance. www.apa.org

American Psychological Association. (2003). *Guidelines for psychological practice with older adults.* Washington, DC.

American Sleep Disorders Association (1997). *International classification of sleep disorders, revised: Diagnostic and coding manual.* Rochester, MN: American Sleep Disorders Association.

Amies, P. L., Gelder, M. G., & Shaw, P. M. (1983). Social phobia: A comparative clinical study. *British Journal of Psychiatry, 142,* 174–179.

Amsterdam, A., Carter, J., & Krychman, M. (2006). Prevalence of psychiatric illness in women in an oncology sexual health population: A retrospective pilot study. *Journal of Sexual Medicine, 3,* 292–295.

Anastasi, A., & Urbina, S. (1997). *Psychological testing* (7th ed.). Englewood Cliffs, NJ: Prentice Hall.

Ancoli-Israel, S., & Cooke, J. R. (2005). Prevalence and comorbidity of insomnia and effect on functioning in elderly populations. *Journal of the American Geriatric Society, 53,* S264–S271.

Andersch, S., Hanson, L., & Haellstroem, T. (1997). Panic disorder: A five-year follow-up study of 52 patients. *European Journal of Psychiatry, 11,* 145–156.

Anderson, C., & Bulik, C. M. M. (2003). Gender differences in compensatory behaviors, weight and shape salience, and drive for thinness. *Eating Behaviors, 5,* 1–11.

Anderson, I. M. (2001). Meta-analytical studies on new antidepressants. *British Medical Bulletin, 57,* 161–178.

Andreasen, N. C., Flashman, L., Flaum, M., et al. (1994). Regional brain abnormalities in schizophrenia measured with magnetic resonance imaging. *Journal of the American Medical Association, 272,* 1763–1769.

Andreasen, N. C., Flaum, M., Swayze, V. W., II, Tyrrell, G., & Arndt, S. (1990). Positive and negative symptoms in schizophrenia: A critical reappraisal. *Archives of General Psychiatry, 47,* 615–621.

Andrews, G., Stewart, G., Allen, R., & Henderson, A. S. (1990). The genetics of six anxiety disorders: A twin study. *Journal of Affective Disorders, 19,* 23–29.

Angold, A., Weissman, M. M., John, K., Wickramaratne, P., & Prusoff, B. (1991). The effects of age and sex on depression ratings in children and adolescents. *Journal of the American Academy of Child and Adolescent Psychiatry, 30,* 67–74.

Annas, J. D. (2004). Forcible medication for courtroom competence—The case of Charles Sell. *New England Journal of Medicine, 350,* 2297–2301.

Anthony, J., & Petronis, K. (1995). Early-onset drug use and risk of later drug problems. *Drug and Alcohol Dependence, 40,* 9–15.

Antoni, M. H., Cruess, D. G., Cruess, S., Lutgendorf, S., Kumar, M., Ironson, G., et al. (2000). Cognitive-behavioral stress management intervention effects on anxiety, 24-hr urinary norepinephrine output, and T-cytotoxic/suppressor cells over time among symptomatic HIV-infected gay men. *Journal of Consulting and Clinical Psychology, 68,* 31–45.

Antony, M. M., & Barlow, D. H. (2002). *Handbook of assessment and treatment planning for psychological disorders.* New York: Guilford Press.

Antony, M. M., & Barlow, D. H. (2004). Specific phobias. In D. H. Barlow, *Anxiety and its disorders* (pp. 380–417). New York: Guilford Press.

Antony, M. M., Downie, F., & Swinson, R. P. (1998). Diagnostic issues and epidemiology in OCD. In R. P. Swinson, M. M. Antony, S. Rachman, & M. A. Richter (Eds.), *Obsessive-compulsive cisorder: Theory, research, and treatment* (pp. 3–32) New York: Guilford Press.

Appelbaum, P. S. (2003). Treating incompetent defendants: The Supreme Court's decision is a tough *sell. Psychiatric Services, 54,* 1335–1341.

Appelbaum, P. S. (2006). Commentary: Psychiatric advance directives at a crossroads—when can PADs be overridden? *Journal of the American Academy of Psychiatry and the Law, 34,* 395–397.

Appelbaum, P. S. (2006). Insanity, guilty minds, and psychiatric testimony. *Psychiatric Services, 57,* 1370–1372.

Appelbaum, P. S., Lidz, C., & Grisso, T. (2004). Therapeutic misconception in clinical research: Frequency and risk factors. *IRB: A Review of Human Subjects Research, 26,* 1–8.

Appelbaum, P. S., Robbins, P. C., & Roth, L. H. (1999). Dimensional approach to delusions: Comparison across types and diagnoses. *American Journal of Psychiatry, 156,* 1938–1943.

Araujo, A., Durante, R., Feldman, H. A., Goldstein, I., & McKinlay, J. B. (1998). The relationship between depressive symptoms and male erectile dysfunction: Cross-sectional results from the Massachusetts Male Aging Study. *Psychosomatic Medicine, 60,* 458–465.

Arean, P. A., Ayalon, L., Hunkeler, E., Lin, E. H., Tang, L., Harpole, L., et al. (2005). Improving depression care for older, minority patients in primary care. *Medical Care, 43,* 381–390.

Armstrong, S. C., Cozza, K. L., & Watanabe, K. S. (1997). The misdiagnosis of delirium. *Psychosomatics, 38,* 433–439.

Arndt, W., Foehl, J., & Good, F. (1985). Specific sexual fantasy themes: A multidimensional study. *Journal of Personality and Social Psychology, 48,* 472–480.

Arnold, I. A., de Waal, M. W., Eekhof, J. A., van Hemert, A. M. (2006). Somatoform disorder in primary care: Course and the need for cognitive-behavioral treatment. *Psychosomatics, 47,* 498–503.

Arnold, L. M., Keck, P. E., Jr., Collins, J., Wilson, R., Fleck, D. E., Corey, K. B., et al. (2004). Ethnicity and first-rank symptoms in patients with psychosis. *Schizophrenia Research, 67,* 207–213.

Arnsten, A. F. (1998). The biology of being frazzled. *Science, 280,* 1711–1712.

Aspberger, H. (1944/1992). "Austistic Psychopathy" in childhood (translated by U. Frith). In U. Frith (Ed.), *Autism and Asperger syndrome* (pp. 37–62). Cambridge: Cambridge University Press.

Atkinson, R. M. (2004). Substance abuse. In J. Sadavoy, L. F. Jarvik, G. T. Grossberg, & B. S. Meyers (Eds.), *Comprehensive textbook of geriatric psychiatry* (3rd ed., pp. 723–761). New York: W.W. Norton & Co.

Atkinson, R. M., & Misra, S. (2002). Further strategies in the treatment of aging alcoholics. In A. M. Gurnack, R. M. Atkinson, & N. J. Osgood (Eds.), *Treating alcohol and drug abuse in the elderly* (pp. 50–71). New York: Springer Verlag.

Atluri, S., Boswell, M. V., Hansen, H. C., Trescot, A. M., Singh, V., & Jordan, A. E. (2003). Guidelines for the use of controlled substances in the management of chronic pain. *Pain Physician, 6,* 233–257.

Attie, I., & Brooks-Gunn, J. (1989). Development of eating problems in adolescent girls: A longitudinal study. *Developmental Psychology, 25,* 70–79.

Author (2004). Studies of capsulotomy, cingulotomy. *Psychiatric News, 39,* 28.

Autism and Developmental Disabilities Monitoring Network Surveillance Year 2002 Principal Investigators; Centers for Disease Control and Prevention. (2007). Prevalence of autism spectrum disorders—Autism and developmental disabilities monitoring network, 14 sites, United States, 2002. *MMWR. Surveillance Summaries: Morbidity and Mortality Weekly Report. Surveillance Summaries / CDC, 56,* 12–28.

Avants, S., Marcotte, D., Arnold, R., & Margolin, A. (2003). Spiritual beliefs, world assumptions, and HIV risk behavior among heroin and cocaine users. *Psychology of Addictive Behaviors, 17,* 159–162.

Averill, P. M., & Beck, J. G. (2000). Post-traumatic stress disorder in older adults: A conceptual review. *Journal of Anxiety Disorders, 14,* 133–156.

Avery, D. H. (1998). A turning point for seasonal affective disorder and light therapy research? *Archives of General Psychiatry, 55,* 863–864.

Ayoub, C. C. (2006). Munchausen by proxy. In T. G. Plante (Ed.), *Mental disorders of the new millennium: Biology and function (Vol. 3)* (pp. 173–193). Westport, CT: Greenwood Publishing Group.

Babulas, V., Factor–Litvak, P., Goetz, R., Schaefer, C. A., & Brown, A. S. (2006). Prenatal exposure to maternal genital and reproductive infections and adult schizophrenia. *American Journal of Psychiatry, 163,* 927–929.

Backman, L., Jones, S., Berger, A. K., Laukka, E. J., & Small, B. J. (2005). Cognitive impairment in preclinical Alzheimer's disease: A meta-analysis. *Neuropsychology, 19,* 520–531.

Badger, T., Segrin, C., Dorros, S. M., Meek, P., & Lopez, A. M. (2007). Depression and anxiety in women with breast cancer and their partners. *Nursing Research, 56,* 44–53.

Badman, M., & Flier, J. (2005). The gut and energy balance: Visceral allies in the obesity wars. *Science, 307,* 1909–1914.

Bae, S. W., & Brekke, J. S. (2002). Characteristics of Korean-Americans with schizophrenia: A cross-ethnic comparison with African-Americans, Latinos, and Euro-Americans. *Schizophrenia Bulletin, 28*, 703–717.

Baerger, D. R. (2001). Risk management with the suicidal patient: Lessons from case law. *Professional Psychology: Research and Practice, 32*, 359–366.

Bailey, J. M., Kirk, K. M., Zhu, G., Dunne, M. P., & Martin, N. G. (2000). Do individual differences in sociosexuality represent genetic or environmentally contingent strategies? *Journal of Personality and Social Psychology, 78*, 537–545.

Bair, M. J., Robinson, R. L., Eckert, G. J., Stang, P. E., Croghan, T. W., & Kroenke, K. (2004). Impact of pain on depression treatment response in primary care. *Psychosomatic Medicine, 66*, 17–22.

Bajos, N., Wadsworth, J., Ducot, B., Johnson, A. M., Le Pont, F., Wellings, K., Spira, A., & Field, J. (1995). Sexual behaviour and HIV epidemiology: Comparative analysis in France and Britain. The ACSF Group. *AIDS, 9*, 735–43.

Baker, D., Hunter, E., Lawrence, E., Medford, N., Patel, M., Senior, C., et al. (2003). Depersonalization disorder: Clinical features. *British Journal of Psychiatry, 182*, 428–433.

Baldessarini, R. J., Tondo, L., Davis, P., Pompili, M., Goodwin, F. K., & Hennen, J. (2006). Decreased risk of suicides and attempts during long-term lithium treatment: A meta-analytic review. *Bipolar Disorders, 8*, 625–639.

Baldwin, R. C., Katona, C., Graham, N., & Chiu, E. (2002). *Guidelines on depression in older people: practising the evidence.* New York: Taylor & Francis.

Ballantyne, J. C., & Mao, J. (2003). Opioid therapy for chronic pain. *New England Journal of Medicine, 349*, 1943–1953.

Baltes, P. B., & Baltes, M. M. (1990). Psychological perspectives on successful aging: The model of selective optimization with compensation. In P. B. Baltes & M. M. Baltes (Eds.), *Successful aging: Perspectives from the behavioral sciences* (pp. 1–34). New York: Cambridge University Press.

Bancroft, J., Loftus, J., & Long, J. S. (2003). Distress about sex: A national survey of women in heterosexual relationships. *Archives of Sexual Behavior, 32*, 193–208.

Bandura, A. (1977a). Self-efficacy theory: Toward a unifying theory of behavioural change. *Psychological Review, 84*, 191–215.

Bandura, A. (1977b). *Social learning theory.* Englewood Cliffs, NJ: Prentice Hall.

Bandura, A. (1986). *Social foundations of thought and action.* Englewood Cliffs, NJ: Prentice Hall.

Bandura, A. (1999). A sociocognitive analysis of substance abuse: An agentic perspective. *Psychological Science, 10*, 214–217.

Banthia, R., Malcarne, V. L., Varni, J. W., Ko, C. M., Sadler, G. R., & Greenbergs, H. L. (2003). The effects of dyadic strength and coping styles on psychological distress in couples faced with prostate cancer. *Journal of Behavioral Medicine, 26*, 31–52.

Barbaree, H. E., & Marshall, W. L. (1989). Erectile responses among heterosexual child molesters, father-daughter incest offenders, and matched non-offenders: Five distinct age preference profiles. *Canadian Journal of Behavioural Science, 21*, 70–82.

Barbaresi, W. J., Katusic, S. K., & Voigt, R. G. (2006). Autism: A review of the state of the science for pediatric primary health care clinicians. *Archives of Pediatrics & Adolescent Medicine, 160*, 1167–1175.

Barbor, T. F., Higgins-Biddle, J. C., Saunders, J. B., & Montero, M. G. (2001). *AUDIT-The Alcohol Use Disorders Identification Test. Guidelines for Use in Primary Care.* Geneva: World Health Organization Department of Mental Health and Substance Dependence. Edition WM 2742001SC, 2nd Ed. Doc # WHO/MSD/MSb/01.6a.

Barez, M., Blasco, T., Fernandez-Castro, J., & Viladrich, C. (2007). A structural model of the relationships between perceived control and adaptation to illness in women with breast cancer. *Journal of Psychosocial Oncology, 25*, 21–43.

Barlow, D. H. (2002). *Anxiety and its disorders: The nature and treatment of anxiety and panic* (2nd ed.). New York: Guilford Press.

Barlow, D. H., & Lehman, C. L. (1996). Advances in the psychosocial treatment of anxiety disorders. Implications for national health care. *Archives of General Psychiatry, 53*, 727–35.

Barnes, A. (2004). Race, schizophrenia, and admission to state psychiatric hospitals. *Administration and Policy in Mental Health, 31*, 241–252.

Barone, J., & Grice, H. (1994). Seventh International Caffeine Workshop, Santorini, Greece June 13–17, 1993. *Food Chemistry and Toxicology, 32*, 65–77.

Barrett, T. R., & Ethridge, J. B. (1992). Verbal hallucinations in normals. I: People who hear voices. *Applied Cognitive Psychology, 6*, 379–387.

Barrios, B. A., Hartman, D. B., & Shigatmoi, C. (1981). Fears and anxieties in children. In E. J. Mash & L. G. Terdal (Eds.), *Behavioral assessment of childhood disorders* (pp. 259–304). New York: Guilford Press.

Barrowclough, C., King, P., Colville, J., Russell, E., Burns, A., & Tarrier, N. (2001). A randomized trial of the effectiveness of cognitive-behavioral therapy and supportive counseling for anxiety symptoms in older adults. *Journal of Consulting and Clinical Psychology, 69*, 756–762.

Barsetti, I., Earls, C. M., Lalumière, M. L., & Bélanger, N. (1998). The differentiation of intrafamilial and extrafamilial heterosexual child molesters. *Journal of Interpersonal Violence, 13*, 275–286.

Barsky, A. J. (1996). Hypochondriasis: Medical management and psychiatric treatment. *Psychosomatics, 37*, 48–56.

Barsky, A. J., & Borus, J. F. (1995). Somatization and medicalization in the era of managed care. *Journal of the American Medical Association, 274*, 1931–1934.

Barsky, A. J., & Klerman, G. L. (1983). Overview: Hypochondriasis, bodily complaints, and somatic styles. *The American Journal of Psychiatry, 140*, 273–283.

Barsky, A. J., Orav, E. J., & Bates, D. W. (2005). Somatization increases medical utilization and costs independent of psychiatric and medical comorbidity. *Archives of General Psychiatry, 62*, 903–910.

Barsky, A. J., Wyshak, G., & Klerman, G. L. (1990b). Transient hypochondriasis. *Archives of General Psychiatry, 47*, 746–752.

Barsky, A. J., Wyshak, G., Klerman, G. L., & Latham, K. S. (1990a). The prevalence of hypochondriasis in medical outpatients. *Social Psychiatry and Psychiatric Epidemiology, 25*, 89–94.

Bartels, S. J., Coakley, E., Oxman, T. E., Constantino, G., Oslin, D., Chen, H., et al. (2002). Suicidal and death ideation in older primary care patients with depression, anxiety, and at-risk alcohol use. *American Journal of Geriatric Psychiatry, 10*, 417–427.

Bartels, S. J. & Smyer, M. A. (2002). Mental disorders of aging: An emerging public health crisis? *Generations, 26*, 14–20.

Bartlett, N. H., Vasey, P. L., & Bukowski, W. M. (2000). Is gender identity disorder in children a mental disorder? *Sex Roles, 43*, 753–785.

Bass, E., & Davis, L. (1988). *The courage to heal.* New York: Harper & Row.

Bassarath, L. (2003). Medication strategies in childhood aggression: A review. *Canadian Journal of Psychiatry, 48*, 367–373.

Bassiony, M. M. (2005). Social anxiety disorder and depression in Saudi Arabia. *Depression and Anxiety, 21*, 90–94.

Basson, R. (2002). Women's sexual desire—Disordered or misunderstood? *Journal of Sex & Marital Therapy, 28*, 17–28.

Basson, R., & Brotto, L. A. (2003). Sexual psychophysiology and effects of sildenafil citrate in oestrogenised women with acquired genital arousal disorder and impaired orgasm: A randomised controlled trial. *International Journal of Obstetrics and Gynaecology, 110*, 1014–1024.

Basson, R., Leiblum, S., Brotto, L., Derogatis, L., Fourcroy, J., Fugl-Meyer, K., Graziottin, A., Heiman, J. R., Laan, E., Meston, C., Schover, L., van Lankveld, J., & Weijmar Schultz, W. (2003). Definitions of women's sexual dysfunction reconsidered: Advocating expansion and revision. *Journal of Psychosomatic Obstetrics and Gynecology, 24*, 221–229

Basson, R., McInnes, R., Smith, M. D., Hodgson, G., & Koppiker, N. (2002). Efficacy and safety of sildenafil citrate in women with sexual dysfunction associated with female sexual arousal disorder. *Journal of Women's Health & Gender-Based Medicine, 11*, 367–377.

Battle, C. L., Shea, M. T., Johnson, D. M., Yen, S., Zlotnick, C., Zanarini, M. C., Sanislow, C. A., Skodol, A. E., Gunderson, J. G., Grilo, C. M., McGlashan, T. H., & Morey, L. C. (2004). Childhood maltreatment associated with adult personality disorders: findings from the Collaborative Longitudinal Personality Disorders Study. *Journal of Personality Disorders, 18*, 193–211.

Baum, A. (1990). Stress, intrusive imagery, and chronic distress. In *Health psychology* (pp. 653–675). New York: Freeman & Co.

Baumeister, R. F. (1989). *Masochism and the Self.* Hillsdale, NJ: Erlbaum.

Baumeister, R. F., Catanese, K. R., & Vohs, K. D. (2001). Is there a gender difference in strength of sex drive? Theoretical views, conceptual distinctions, and a review of relevant evidence. *Personality and Social Psychology Review, 5*, 242–273.

Baxter, L. R. (1992). Neuroimaging studies of obsessive-compulsive disorder. *Psychiatric Clinics of North American, 15*, 871–884.

Baxter, L. R., Schwartz, J. M., Bergman, K. S., Szuba, M. P., Guze, B. H., Maziotta, J. C., Akazraju, A., Selin, C. E., Ferng, H-K., Munford, P., & Phelps, M. E. (1992). Caudate glucose metabolic rate changes with both drug and behavior therapy for obsessive–compulsive disorder. *Archives of General Psychiatry, 49,* 681–689.

Bayles, K. A. & Kim, E. S. (2003). Improving the functioning of individuals with Alzheimer's disease: Emergence of behavioral interventions. *Journal of Communication Disorders, 36,* 327–343.

Beard, G. (1869). *American nervousness.* New York: Putnam.

Beautrais, A. L., Joyce, P. R., & Mulder, R. T. (1997). Precipitating factors and life events in serious suicide attempts among youths aged 13 through 24 years. *Journal of the American Academy of Child and Adolescent Psychiatry, 36,* 1543–1551.

Beautrais, A. L., Joyce, P. R., & Mulder, R. T. (1998). Psychiatric illness in a New Zealand sample of young people making serious suicide attempts. *New Zealand Medical Journal, 111,* 44–48.

Beautrais, A., Joyce, P. R., Mulder, R. T., Fergusson, D. M., Deavoll, B. J., & Nightengale, S. K. (1996). Prevalence and comorbidity of mental disorders in persons making serious suicide attempts: A case-control study. *American Journal of Psychiatry, 153,* 1009–1014.

Beck, A. T. (1967). *Depression: Clinical, experimental and theoretical aspects.* New York: Hoeber.

Beck, A. T. (1979). *Cognitive therapy for depression.* New York: Guilford Press.

Beck, A. T., & Emery, G. (1985). *Anxiety disorders and phobias: A cognitive perspective.* New York: Basic Books.

Beck, A. T., Davis, D. D., & Freeman, A. M. (2003). *Cognitive therapy of personality disorders.* New York: Guilford Press.

Beck, A., & Steer, R. (1993). *Beck Anxiety Inventory Manual* (2nd ed.). San Antonio, TX: Psychological Corporation.

Beck, A., Steer, R., & Brown, G. (1996). *Manual for the Beck Depression Inventory–II.* San Antonio, TX: Psychological Corporation.

Beck, A., Wright, F., Neewman, C., & Liese, B. (1993). *Cognitive therapy of substance abuse.* New York: Guilford Press.

Beck, J. G., & Averill, P. M. (2004). Older adults. In R. G. Heimberg, C. L. Turk, & D. S. Mennin (Eds.), *Generalized anxiety disorder: Advances in research and practice* (pp. 409–433). New York: Guilford Press.

Beck, J. G., Stanley, M. A., & Zebb, B. J. (1996). Characteristics of generalized anxiety disorder in older adults: A descriptive study. *Behavior Research and Therapy, 34,* 225–234.

Beekman, A. T., Bremmer, M. A., Deeg, D. J., van Balkom, A. J., Smit, J. H., de Beurs, E., van Dyck, R., & van Tilburg, W. (1998). Anxiety disorders in later life: A report from the Longitudinal Aging Study Amsterdam. *International Journal of Geriatric Psychiatry, 13,* 717–726.

Beekman, A. T., deBeurs, E., van Balkom, A. J., Deeg, D. J., van Dyck R., & van Tilburg W. (2000). Anxiety and depression in later life: Co–occurrence and communality of risk factors. *American Journal of Psychiatry, 157,* 89–95.

Beidel, D. C. (1988). Psychophysiological assessment of anxious emotional states in children. *Journal of Abnormal Psychology, 97,* 80–82.

Beidel, D. C., & Turner, S. M. (1995). A new inventory to assess childhood social anxiety and phobia: The Social Phobia and Anxiety Inventory of Children. *Psychological Assessment, 7,* 73–79.

Beidel, D. C., & Turner, S. M. (1997). At risk for anxiety: I. Psychopathology in the offspring of anxious parents. *Journal of the American Academy of Child and Adolescent Psychiatry, 36,* 918–924.

Beidel, D. C., & Turner, S. M. (1998). *Shy children, phobic adults: The nature and treatment of social phobia.* Washington, DC: American Psychological Association Books.

Beidel, D. C., & Turner, S. M. (2005). *Childhood anxiety disorders: A guide to research and treatment.* New York: Routledge.

Belar, C. (1990). Proceedings of the Gainesville Conference on the Scientist–Practitioner Model of Training, Gainesville, FL.

Belar, C. D. & Deardorff, W. W. (1995). *Clinical health psychology in medical settings.* (2nd ed.) Washington, DC: American Psychological Association.

Belar, C. D., Perry, N. W., Bielauskas, L. A., Boll, T., Lambert, N., Myers, R., & Ritt, L. (1991). *Proceedings of the National Conference on Scientist-Practitioner Education and Training for the Professional Practice of Psychology.* Sarasota, FL: Professional Resource Press.

Bell, C. C., & Mehta, H. (1980). The misdiagnosis of black patients with manic depressive illness. *Journal of the National Medical Association, 72,* 141–145.

Bell, R. M. (1985). *Holy Anorexia.* Chicago: University of Chicago Press.

Bellack, A. S. (1992). Cognitive rehabilitation for schizophrenia: Is it possible? Is it necessary? *Schizophrenia Bulletin, 18,* 51–57.

Bellack, A. S. (2004). Skills training for people with severe mental illness. *Psychiatric Rehabilitation, 27,* 375–391.

Bellack, A. S., Morrison, R. L., Wixted, J. T., & Mueser, K. T. (1990). An analysis of social competence in schizophrenia. *British Journal of Psychiatry, 156,* 809–818.

Bellino, S., Paradiso, E., & Bogetto, F. (2008). Efficacy and tolerability of pharmacotherapies for borderline personality disorder. *CNS Drugs, 22,* 671–692.

Bellino, S., Zizza, M., Paradiso, E., Rivarossa, A., Fulcheri, M., & Bogetto, F. (2006). Dysmorphic concern symptoms and personality disorders: A clinical investigation in patients seeking cosmetic surgery. *Psychiatry Research, 144,* 73–78.

Bellis, M. D. (2004). Neurotoxic effects of childhood trauma: Magnetic resonance imaging studies of pediatric maltreatment-related posttraumatic stress disorder versus nontraumatized children with generalized anxiety disorder. In J. M. Gorman (Ed.), *Fear and anxiety: The benefits of translational research* (pp. 151–170). Washington, DC: American Psychiatric Publishing.

Bennett, H. A., Einarson, A., Taddio, A., Koren, G., & Einarson, T. R. (2004). Prevalence of depression during pregnancy: systematic review. *Obstetrics and Gynecology, 103,* 698–709.

Benowitz, N. (1988). Pharmacological aspects of cigarette smoking and nicotine addiction. *New England Journal of Medicine, 319,* 1318–1330.

Berenbaum, S. A., Duck, S. C., & Bryk, K. (2000). Behavioral effects of prenatal versus postnatal androgen excess in children with 21-hydroxylase-deficient congenital adrenal hyperplasia. *Journal of Clinical Endocrinology and Metabolism, 85,* 727–733.

Bergen, A. W., van den Bree, M. B. M., Yeager, M., Welch, R., Ganjei, J. K., Haque, K., et al. (2003). Candidate genes for anorexia nervosa in the 1p33-36 linkage region: Serotonin 1D and delta opioid receptor loci exhibit significant association to anorexia nervosa. *Molecular Psychiatry, 8,* 397–406.

Berk, M., & Dodd, S. (2005). Bipolar II disorder: A review. *Bipolar Disorders, 7,* 11–21.

Berman, J. R., Berman, L. A., Toler, S. M., Gill, J. & Haughie, S.; Sildenafil Study Group (2003). Safety and efficacy of sildenafil citrate for the treatment of female sexual arousal disorder: A double-blind, placebo controlled study. *Journal of Urology, 170,* 2333–2338.

Bersoff, D. N. (2003). Confidentiality, privilege, and privacy. In D. N. Bersoff (Ed.), *Ethical conflicts in psychology.* (3rd ed., pp. 155–156).Washington, DC: American Psychological Association.

Bethea, T. C., & Sikich, L. (2007). Early pharmacological treatment of autism: A rationale for developmental treatment. *Biological Psychiatry, 61,* 521–537.

Biederman, J. (2005). Attention-deficit/hyperactivity disorder: A selective overview. *Biological Psychiatry, 57,* 1215–1220.

Biederman, J., & Faraone, S. V. (2005). Attention-deficit hyperactivity disorder. *The Lancet, 366,* 237–248.

Biederman, J., Mick, E., & Faraone, S. V. (1998). Normalized functioning in youths with persistent attention-deficit/hyperactivity disorder. *The Journal of Pediatrics, 133,* 544–551.

Biederman, J., Mick, E., Faraone, S. V., Braaten, E., Doyle, A., Spencer, T., Wilens, T. E., Frazier, E., & Johnson, M. A. (2002). Influence of gender on attention deficit hyperactivity disorder in children referred to a psychiatric clinic. *American Journal of Psychiatry, 159,* 36–42.

Biederman, J., Monuteaux, M. C., Mick, E., Spencer, T., Wilens, T. E., Silva, J. M., et al. (2006). Young adult outcome of attention deficit hyperactivity disorder: A controlled 10-year follow-up study. *Psychological Medicine, 36,* 167–179.

Biederman, J., Petty, C., Faraone, S. V., & Seidman, L. (2004). Phenomenology of childhood psychosis: Findings from a large sample of psychiatrically referred youth. *Journal of Nervous and Mental Disease, 192,* 607–614.

Biederman, J., Petty, C. R., Hirshfeld-Becker, D. R., Henin, A., Faraone, S. V., Fraire, M., et al. (2007). Developmental trajectories of anxiety disorders in offspring at high risk for panic disorder and major depression. *Psychiatry Research, 153,* 245–252.

Bienvenu, O. J., & Eaton, W. W. (1998). The epidemiology of blood-injection-injury phobia. *Psychological Medicine, 18,* 1129–1136.

Bierer, L. M., Yehuda, R., Schmeidler, J., Mitropoulou, V., New, A. S., Silverman, J. M., & Siever, L. J. (2003). Abuse and neglect in childhood: Relationship to personality disorder diagnoses. *CNS Spectrums, 8,* 737–754.

Billy, J. O., Tanfer, K., Grady, W. R., & Klepinger, D. H. (1993). The sexual behavior of men in the United States. *Family Planning Perspectives, 25,* 52–60.

Binks, C. A., Fenton, M., McCarthy, L., Lee, T., Adams, C. E., & Duggan, C. (2006). Psychological therapies for people with borderline personality disorder. *Cochrane Database Systematic Reviews* (1), CD005652.

Binzer, M., & Kullgren, G. (1998). Motor conversion disorder. A prospective 2- to 5-year follow-up study. *Psychosomatics, 39,* 519–527.

Birmingham, C., Su, J., Hlynsky, J., Goldner, E., & Gao, M. (2005). The mortality rate from anorexia nervosa. *International Journal of Eating Disorders, 38,* 143–146.

Bishop, S. R. & Warr, D. (2003). Coping, catastrophizing and chronic pain in breast cancer. *Journal of Behavioral Medicine, 26,* 265–281.

Black, H. (1990). *Black's law dictionary.* St. Paul, MN: West.

Black, M., & Krishnakumar, A. (1998). Children in low-income, urban settings: Interventions to promote mental health and well-being. *American Psychologist, 53,* 635–646.

Blackman, J. A. (1999). Attention-deficit/hyperactivity disorder in preschoolers. Does it exist and should we treat it? *Pediatric Clinics of North America, 46,* 1011–1025.

Blake, D. D., Cook, J. D., & Keane, T. M. (1992). Post-traumatic stress disorder and coping in veterans who are seeking medical treatment. *Journal of Clinical Psychology, 48,* 695–704.

Blake, D. D., Keane, T. M., Wine, P. R., Mora, C., Taylor, K. L., & Lyons, J. A. (1992). Prevalence of PTSD symptoms in combat veterans seeking medical treatment. *Journal of Traumatic Stress, 3,* 15–27.

Blanchard, E. B., Hickling, E. J., Taylor, A. E., Loos, W. R., Forneris, C. A., & Jaccard, J. (1996). Who develops PTSD from motor vehicle accidents? *Behaviour Research and Therapy, 34,* 1–10.

Blanchard, R., & Bogaert, A. F. (2004). Proportion of homosexual men who owe their sexual orientation to fraternal birth order. *American Journal of Human Biology, 16,* 151–157.

Blanchard, R., Cantor, J. M., Bogaert, A. F., Breedlove, S. M., & Ellis, L. (2006). Interaction of fraternal birth order and handedness in the development of male homosexuality. *Hormonal Behavior, 49,* 405–414.

Bland, R. C., Newman, S. C., & Orn, H. (1988). Prevalence of psychiatric disorders in the elderly in Edmonton. *Acta Psychiatrica Scandinavia. Supplementum, 338,* 57–63.

Blashfield, R., & Livesley, W. J. (1999). Classification. In T. Millon, P. H. Blaney, & R. D. Davis (Eds.), *Oxford Textbook of Psychopathology.* (pp. 3–28). New York: Oxford University Press.

Blazer, D. G. (2004). Alcohol and drug problems. In D. G. Blazer, D. C. Steffens, & E. W. Busse (Eds.), *Textbook of geriatric psychiatry* (3rd ed., pp. 351–367). Washington, DC: American Psychiatric Publishing.

Blazer, D. G. (2006). Successful aging. *American Journal of Geriatric Psychiatry, 14,* 2–5.

Blazer, D. G., Hybels, C. F., Simonsick, E. M., & Hanlon, J. T. (2000). Marked differences in antidepressant use by race in an elderly community sample: 1986–1996. *American Journal of Psychiatry, 157,* 1089–1094.

Blazer, D. G., Landerman, L. R., Hays, J. C., Simonsick, E. M., & Saunders, W. B. (1998). Symptoms of depression among community-dwelling elderly African-American and white older adults. *Psychological Medicine, 28,* 1311–1320.

Blazer, D., George, L. K., & Hughes, D. (1991). The epidemiology of anxiety disorders: An age comparison. In C. Salzman & D. Lebowitz (Eds.), *Anxiety in the elderly: Treatment and research* (pp. 17–30). New York: Springer Publishing Company.

Blazer, D., Hughes, D., & George, L. K. (1987). Stressful life events and the onset of a generalized anxiety syndrome. *American Journal of Psychiatry, 144,* 1178–1183.

Bleiberg, K. L., & Markowitz, J. C. (2005). A pilot study of interpersonal psychotherapy for posttraumatic stress disorder. *American Journal of Psychiatry, 162,* 181–183.

Bleuler, E. (1911/1950). *Dementia praecox or the group of schizophrenias* (translated by J. Zinkin). New York: International Universities Press.

Block, J. H., Gjerde, P. F., & Block, J. H. (1991). Personality antecedents of depressive tendencies in 18-year-olds: A prospective study. *Journal of Personality and Social Psychology, 60,* 726–738.

Blum, K., Braverman, E., Holder, J., Lubar, J., Monastra, V., Miller, D., et al. (2000). Reward deficiency syndrome: A biogenetic model for the diagnosis and treatment of impulsive, addictive, and compulsive behaviors. *Journal of Psychoactive Drugs, 32 Suppl: i–iv,* 1–112.

Boggiano, M. M., & Chandler, P. C. (2006). Binge eating in rats produced by combining dieting with stress. *Current Protocols in Neurosciences,* Chapter 9, Unit9 23A.

Boggiano, M. M., Artiga, A. I., Pritchett, C. E., Chandler-Laney, P. C., Smith, M. L., & Eldridge, A. J. (2007). High intake of palatable food predicts binge-eating independent of susceptibility to obesity: An animal model of lean vs obese binge-eating and obesity with and without binge-eating. *International Journal of Obesity (London), 31,* 1357–1367.

Boggiano, M. M., Chandler, P. C., Viana, J. B., Oswald, K. D., Maldonado, C. R., & Wauford, P. K. (2005). Combined dieting and stress evoke exaggerated responses to opioids in binge-eating rats. *Behavioral Neuroscience, 119,* 1207–1214.

Boise, L., Neal, M. B., & Kaye, J. (2004). Dementia assessment in primary care: Results from a study in three managed care systems. *The Journals of Gerontology, Series, A. Biological Sciences and Medical Sciences, 59,* M621–M626.

Boles, S., & Miotto, K. (2003). Substance and violence: A review of the literature. *Aggression and Violent Behavior, 8,* 155–174.

Bonanno, G. A. (2004). Loss, trauma, and human resilience. *American Psychologist, 59,* 20–28.

Bond, G. R., Becker, D. R., Drake, R. E., Rapp, C. A., Meisler, N., Lehman, A. F., Bell, M. D., & Blyler, C. R. (2001b). Implemental supported employment as an evidence-based practice. *Psychiatric Services, 52,* 313–322.

Bond, G. R., Resnick, S. G., Drake, R. E., Xie, H., McHugo, G. J., & Bebout, R. R. (2001a). Does competitive employment improve nonvocational outcomes for people with severe mental illness? *Journal of Consulting and Clinical Psychology, 69,* 489–501.

Bonese, K., Wainer, B., Fitch, F., Rothberg, R., & Schuster, C. (1974). Changes in heroin self-administration by a rhesus monkey after morphine immunisation. *Nature, 252,* 708–710.

Bongar, B., Maris, R. W., Berman, A. L., & Litman, R. E. (1998). Outpatient standards of care and the suicidal patient. In B. Bongar, A. L. Berman, R. W. Maris, M. M. Silverman, E. A. Harris, & W. L. Packman (Eds.), *Risk management with suicidal patients* (p. 4.33). New York: Guilford Press.

Boomsma, D. I. (2005). Exploring female sexuality. *European Journal of Human Genetics, 13,* 696–697.

Bootzin, R. R., & Bailey, E. T. (2005). Understanding placebo, nocebo, and iatrogenic treatment effects. *Journal of Clinical Psychology, 61*(7), 871–880.

Borges, G., Angst, J., Nock, M. K., Ruscio, A. M., Walters, E. E., & Kessler, R. C. (2006). A risk index for 12-month suicide attempts in the National Comorbidity Survey Replication (NCS-R). *Psychological Medicine, 36,* 1747–1757.

Borkovec, T. D. (2002). Psychological aspects and treatment of generalized anxiety disorder. In D.Nutt, K. Rickels, & D. J. Stein (Eds.) (pp. 99–110), *Generalized anxiety disorder: Symptomatology, pathogenesis, & management.* (pp. 99–101) UK: Martin Dunitz, Ltd.

Borkovec, T. D., & Shadick, R. (1989). The nature of normal versus pathological worry. Paper prepared for the DSM-IV Task Force.

Borkovec, T. D., Alcaine, O. M., & Behar, E. (2004). Avoidance theory of worry and generalized anxiety disorder. In R. G. Heimberg, C. L. Turk, and D. S. Mennin (Eds.), *Generalized anxiety disorder: advances in research and practice* (pp. 22–108). New York: Guilford Press.

Borkovec, T. D., Robinson, E., Pruzinsky, T., & DePress, J. A. (1993). Preliminary exploration of worry: Some characteristics and processes. *Behaviour Research and Therapy, 21,* 9–16.

Borowitz, S. M., Cox, D. J., Sutphen, J. L., & Kovatchev, B. (2002). Treatment of childhood encopresis: A randomized trial comparing three treatment protocols. *Journal of Pediatric Gastroenterology and Nutrition, 34,* 378–384.

Borum, R., & Fulero, S. M. (1999). Empirical research on the insanity defense and attempted reforms: Evidence toward informed policy. *Law and Human Behavior, 23,* 117–135.

Bouchard, T. J., Jr., Lykken, D. T., McGue, M., Segal, N. L., & Tellegen, A. (1990). Sources of human psychological differences: The Minnesota Study of Twins Reared Apart. *Science, 250,* 223–228.

Bourgeois, J. A., Seaman, J. S., & Servis, M. E. (2003). Delirium, dementia, and amnesic disorders. In R. E. Hales & S. C. Yudofsky (Eds.), *Essentials of clinical psychiatry* (4th ed., pp. 259–308) Washington, DC: American Psychiatric Publishing.

Bourgeois, M. S., Camp, C., Rose, M., White, B., Malone, M., Carr, J. et al. (2003). A comparison of training strategies to enhance use of external aids by persons with dementia. *Journal of Communication Disorders, 36,* 361–378.

Bow, J. N., & Quinnell, F. A. (2001). Psychologists' current practices and procedures in child custody evaluations: Five years after American Psychological Association Guidelines. *Professional Psychology: Research and Practice, 32,* 261–268.

Bowen, R. C., Offord, D. R., & Boyle, M. H. (1990). The prevalence of overanxious disorder and separation anxiety disorder: Results from the Ontario Child Health Study. *Journal of the American Academy of Child and Adolescent Psychiatry, 29,* 753–758.

Bowman, E. S., & Markand, O. N. (1996). Psychodynamics and psychiatric diagnoses of pseudoseizure subjects. *American Journal of Psychiatry, 153,* 57–63.

Boyle, M. (2000). Emil Kraepelin. In A. Kazdin (Ed.), *Encyclopedia of psychology (Volume 4; pp. 458–460).* Washington, DC: American Psychological Association.

Braam, A. W., Hein, E., Deeg, D. J., Twisk, J. W., Beekman, A. T., & van, T. W. (2004). Religious involvement and 6-year course of depressive symptoms in older Dutch citizens: Results from the Longitudinal Aging Study Amsterdam. *Journal of Aging Health, 16,* 467–489.

Bradley, S. J., & Zucker, K. J. (1997). Gender identity disorder: A review of the past 10 years. *Journal of the American Academy of Child and Adolescent Psychiatry, 36,* 872–880.

Braun, D. L., Sunday, S. R., & Halmi, K. A. (1994). Psychiatric comorbidity in patients with eating disorders. *Psychological Medicine, 24,* 859–867.

Brauner, D. J., Muir, J. C., & Sachs, G. A. (2000). Treating nondementia illnesses in patients with dementia. *Journal of the American Medical Association, 283,* 3230–3235.

Braunstein, G. D., Sundwall, D. A., Katz, M., Shifren, J. L., Buster, J. E., Simon, J. A., et al. (2005). Safety and efficacy of a testosterone patch for the treatment of hypoactive sexual desire disorder in surgically menopausal women. *Archives of Internal Medicine, 165,* 1582–1589.

Brawman–Mintzer, O., Lydiard, R. B., Emmauuel, N., Payeur, R., Johnson, M., Roberts, J., Jarrell, M. P., & Ballenger, J. C. (1993). Psychiatric comorbidity in patients with generalized anxiety disorder. *American Journal of Psychiatry, 150,* 1216–1218.

Brazier, J., Tumur, I., Holmes, M., Ferriter, M., Parry, G., Dent-Brown, K., & Paisley, S. (2006). Psychological therapies including dialectical behaviour therapy for borderline personality disorder: A systematic review and preliminary economic evaluation. *Health Technology Assessment, 10,* iii, ix–xii, 1–117.

Bregman, J. D. (1991). Current developments in the understanding of mental retardation. Part II: psychopathology. *Journal of the American Academy of Child and Adolescent Psychiatry, 30,* 861–872.

Breier, A., Schreiber, J. L., Dyer, J., & Pickar, D. (1991). National Institute of Mental Health longitudinal study of chronic schizophrenia. Prognosis and predictors of outcome. *Archives of General Psychiatry, 48,* 239–246.

Brekke, J. S., Prindle, C., Bae, S. W., & Long, J. D. (2001). Risks for individuals with schizophrenia who are living in the community. *Psychiatric Services, 52,* 1358–1366.

Bremner, J. D. (2007). Neuroimaging in posttraumatic stress disorder and other stress-related disorders. *Neuroimaging Clinics of North America, 17,* 523–538, ix.

Bremner, J. D., Krystal, J. H., Charney, D. S., & Southwick, S. M. (1996). Neural mechanisms in dissociative amnesia for childhood abuse: Relevance to the current controversy surrounding the "false memory syndrome." *American Journal of Psychiatry, 153,* 71–82.

Bremner, J. D., Narayan, M., Staib, L. H., Southwick, S. M., McGlashan, T., & Charney, D. S. (1999). Neural correlates of memories of childhood sexual abuse in women with and without posttraumatic stress disorder. *American Journal of Psychiatry, 156,* 1787–1795.

Bremner, J. D., Randall, P., Scott, T. M., Bronen, R. A., Seibyl, J. P, Southwick, S. M, Delaney, R. C., McCarthy, G., Charney, D. S., & Innis, R. B. (1995). MRI-based measurement of hippocampal volume in patients with combat-related posttraumatic stress disorder [see comments]. *American Journal of Psychiatry, 152,* 973–981.

Bremner, J. D., Randall, P., Vermetten, E., Staib, L., Bronen, R. A., Mazure, C., Capelli, S., McCarthy, G., Innis, R. B., & Charney, D. S. (1997). Magnetic resonance imaging-based measurement of hippocampal volume in posttraumatic stress disorder related to childhood physical and sexual abuse—A preliminary report. *Biological Psychiatry, 41,* 23–32.

Brenes, G. A., Guralnik, J. M., Williamson, J. D., Fried, L. P., Simpson, C., Simonsick, E. M., et al. (2005). The influence of anxiety on the progression of disability. *Journal of the American Geriatrics Society, 53,* 34–39.

Brenes, G. A., Rapp, S. R., Rejeski, W. J., & Miller, M. E. (2002). Do optimism and pessimism predict physical functioning? *Journal of Behavioral Medicine, 25,* 219–231.

Brent, D. A., & Mann, J. J. (2005). Family genetic studies, suicide, and suicidal behavior. *American Journal of Medical Genetics C Seminars in Medical Genetics, 133,* 13–24.

Brent, D. A., Baugher, M., Bridge, J., Chen, T., & Chiappetta, L. (1999). Age- and sex-related risk factors for adolescent suicide. *Journal of the American Academy of Child and Adolescent Psychiatry, 38,* 1497–1505.

Brent, D. A., Bridge, J., Johnson, B. A., & Connolly, J. (1996). Suicidal behavior runs in families. A controlled family study of adolescent suicide victims. *Archives of General Psychiatry, 53,* 1145–1152.

Breslau, J., Aguilar-Gaxiola, S., Kendler, K. S., Su, M., Williams, D., & Kessler, R. C. (2005). Specifying race–ethnic differences in risk for psychiatric disorder in a USA national sample. *Psychological Medicine, 36,* 57–68.

Breslau, J., Kendler, K. S., Su, M., Gaxiola-Aguilar, S., & Kessler, R. C. (2005). Lifetime risk and persistence of psychiatric disorders across ethnic groups in the United States. *Psychological Medicine, 35,* 317–327.

Breslau, N., & Kessler, R. C. (2001). The stressor criterion in DSM-IV posttraumatic stress disorder: An empirical investigation. *Biological Psychiatry, 50,* 699–704.

Bresolin, N., Monza, G., Scarpini, E., Scarlato, G., Straneo, G., Martinazzoli, A., et al. (1988). Treatment of anxiety with ketazolam in elderly patients. *Clinical Therapeutics, 10,* 536–542.

Brestan, E. V., & Eyberg, S. M. (1998). Effective psychosocial treatments of conduct-disordered children and adolescents: 29 years, 82 studies, and 5,272 kids. *Journal of Clinical Child Psychology, 27,* 180–189.

Breton, J. J., Bergeron, L., Valla, J. P., Bertiaume, C., Gauder, N., Lambert, J., et al. (1999). Quebec child mental health survey: Prevalence of DSM–III–R mental health disorders. *Journal of Child Psychology and Psychiatry, 40,* 375–384.

Brewerton, T., & Jimerson, D. (1996). Studies of serotonin function in anorexia nervosa. *Psychiatry Research, 62,* 31–42.

Brewerton, T., Lydiard, R., Herzog, D., Brotman, A., O'Neil, P., & Ballenger, J. (1995). Comorbidity of Axis I psychiatric disorders in bulimia nervosa. *Journal of Clinical Psychiatry, 56,* 77–80.

Bride, B. (2001). Single-gender treatment of substance abuse: Effect on treatment retention and completion. *Social Work Research, 25,* 223–232.

Bridge, J. A., Iyengar, S., Salary, C. B., Barbe, R. P., Birmaher, B., Pincus, H. A., et al. (2007). Clinical response and risk for reported suicidal ideation and suicide attempts in pediatric antidepressant treatment: A meta-analysis of randomized controlled trials. *Journal of the American Medical Association, 297,* 1683–1696.

Briere, J., Weathers, F. W., & Runtz, M. (2005). Is dissociation a multidimensional construct? Data from the Multiscale Dissociation Inventory. *Journal of Traumatic Stress, 18,* 221–231.

Brodkey, A. C. (2005). The role of the pharmaceutical industry in teaching psychopharmacology: A growing problem. *Academic Psychiatry, 29,* 222–229.

Brooks, R. C., Copen, R. M., Cox, D. J., Morris, J., Borowitz, S, & Sutphen, J. (2000). Review of the treatment literature for encopresis, functional constipation, and stool-toileting refusal. *Annals of Behavioral Medicine, 22,* 260–267.

Brooner, R. K., King, V. L., Kidorf, M., Schmidt, C. W., Jr., & Bigelow, G. E. (1997). Psychiatric and substance use comorbidity among treatment-seeking opioid abusers. *Archives of General Psychiatry, 54,* 71–80.

Brosco, J. P., Mattingly, M., & Sanders, L. M. (2006). Impact of specific medical interventions on reducing the prevalence of mental retardation. *Archives of Pediatrics & Adolescent Medicine, 160,* 302–309.

Brothers, L. (1990). The social brain: A project for integrating primate behavior and neurophysiology in a new domain. *Concepts in Neuroscience, 1,* 27–61.

Brotto, L. A., & Klein, C. (2007). Sexual and gender identity disorders. In M. Hersen, S. M. Turner, & D. C. Beidel (Eds.), *Adult psychopathology and diagnosis—Fifth edition* (pp. 504–570). New York: John Wiley and Sons.

Brower, M. C., & Price, B. H. (2001). Neuropsychiatry of frontal lobe dysfunction in violent and criminal behaviour: A critical review. *Journal of Neurology Neurosurgery & Psychiatry, 71,* 720–726.

Brown, A. S., Begg, M. D., Gravenstein, S., Schaefer, C. A., Wyatt, R. J., Brenahan, M., Babulas, V. P., & Susser, E. S. (2004). Serological evidence of prenatal influenza in the etiology of schizophrenia. *Archives of General Psychiatry, 61*, 774–780.

Brown, E. M. (1994). French psychiatry's initial reception of Bayle's discovery of general paresis of the insane. *Bulletin of the History of Medicine, 68*, 235–253.

Brown, G. W., Harris, T. O., & Eales, M. J. (1996). Social factors and comorbidity of depressive and anxiety disorders. *British Journal of Psychiatry Supplement* (30), 50–57.

Brown, J. D. & Siegel, J. M. (1988). Exercise as a buffer of life stress: A prospective study of adolescent health. *Health Psychology, 7*, 341–353.

Brown, K. W., Levy, A. R., Rosberger, Z., & Edgar, L. (2003). Psychological distress and cancer survival: a follow-up 10 years after diagnosis. *Psychosomatic Medicine, 65*, 636–643.

Brown, M. J., McLaine, P., Dixon S., & Simon, P. (2006). A randomized, community-based trial of home visiting to reduce blood lead levels in children. *Pediatrics, 117*, 147–153.

Brown, R. J., Schrag, A., & Trimble, M. R. (2005). Dissociation, childhood interpersonal trauma, and family functioning in patients with somatization disorder. *American Journal of Psychiatry, 162*, 899–905.

Brown, S., Inskip, H., & Barraclough, B. (2000). Causes of the excess mortality of schizophrenia. *British Journal of Psychiatry, 177*, 212–217.

Brown, T. A., Campbell, L. A., Lehman, D. L., Grisham, J. R., & Mancill, R. B. (2001). Current and lifetime comorbidity of the DSM–IV anxiety and mood disorders in a large clinical sample. *Journal of Abnormal Psychology, 110*, 585–599.

Brownley, K. A., Berkman, N. D., Sedway, J. A., Lohr, K. N., & Bulik, C. M. (2007). Binge eating disorder treatment: A systematic review of randomized controlled trials. *International Journal of Eating Disorders, 40*, 337–348.

Bruce, B., & Wilfley, D. (1996). Binge eating among the overweight population: A serious and prevalent problem. *Journal of the American Dietetic Association, 96*, 58–61.

Bruce, M. L., & McNamara, R. (1992). Psychiatric status among the homebound elderly: an epidemiologic perspective. *Journal of American Geriatrics Society, 40*, 561–566.

Bruce, M. L., McAvay, G. J., Raue, P. J., Brown, E. L., Meyers, B. S., Keohane, D. J., et al. (2002). Major depression in elderly home health care patients. *American Journal of Psychiatry, 159*, 1367–1374.

Bruce, M. L., Seeman, T. E., Merrill, S. S., & Blazer, D. G. (1994). The impact of depressive symptomatology on physical disability: MacArthur Studies of Successful Aging. *American Journal of Public Health, 84*, 1796–1799.

Bruce, S. E., Machan, J. T., Byck, I., & Keller, M. B. (2001). Infrequency of "pure" GAD: Impact of psychiatric comorbidity on clinical course. *Depression and Anxiety, 14*, 219–225.

Bruch, H. (1973). *Eating Disorders*. New York: Basic Books.

Bruch, H. (1978). *The golden cage*. Cambridge, MA: Harvard University Press.

Brunello, N., Davidson, J.R.T., Deahl, M., Kessler, R. C., Mendloewicz, J., Racagni, G., Shalev, A. Y., & Zohar, J. (2001). Posttraumatic stress disorder: Diagnosis and epidemiology, comorbidity and social consequences, biology and treatment. *Neuropsychobiology, 43*, 150–162.

Brush, J. A., & Camp, C. J. (1998). A therapy technique for improving memory: Spaced retrieval. Presented in Beachwood, OH: Menorah Park Center for the Aging.

Bryant, K. (2006). Making gender identity disorder of childhood: Historical lessons for contemporary debates. *Sexuality Research & Social Policy, 3*, 23–38.

Buchwald, D., Herrell, R., Hartman, S., Belcourt, M., Schmaling, K., Sullivan, P. F., et al. (2001). A twin study of chronic fatigue. *Psychosomatic Medicine, 63*, 936–943.

Budney, A., Hughes, J., Moore, B., & Novy, P. (2001). Marijuana abstinence effects in marijuana smokers maintained in their home environment. *Archives of General Psychiatry, 58*, 917–924.

Budney, A., Moore, B., Vandrey, R., & Hughes, J. (2003). The time course and significance of cannabis withdrawal. *Journal of Abnormal Psychology, 112*, 393–402.

Buhrich, N., & McConaghy, N. (1985). Preadult feminine behaviors of male transvestites. *Archives of Sexual Behavior, 14*, 413–419.

Buka, S. L., Tsuang, M. T., & Lipsett, L. P. (1993). Pregnancy/delivery complications and psychiatric diagnosis: a prospective study. *Archives of General Psychiatry, 50*, 151–156.

Bulik, C. M. (2002). Eating disorders in adolescents and young adults. *Child and Adolescent Psychiatric Clinics of North America, 11*, 201–218.

Bulik, C. M., Berkman, N. D., Brownley, K. A., Sedway, J. A., & Lohr, K. N. (2007). Anorexia nervosa treatment: A systematic review of randomized controlled trials. *International Journal of Eating Disorders, 40*, 310–320.

Bulik, C. M., Devlin, B., Bacanu, S. A., Thornton, L., Klump, K. L., Fichter, M. M., et al. (2003). Significant linkage on chromosome 10p in families with bulimia nervosa. *American Journal of Human Genetics, 72*, 200–207.

Bulik, C. M., Prescott, C. A., & Kendler, K. S. (2001). Features of childhood sexual abuse and the development of psychiatric and substance use disorders. *British Journal of Psychiatry, 179*, 444–449.

Bulik, C. M., Sullivan, P. F., & Kendler, K. S. (2002). Medical and psychiatric morbidity in obese women with and without binge-eating. *International Journal of Eating Disorders, 32*, 72–78.

Bulik, C. M., Sullivan, P., Carter, F., & Joyce, P. (1995). Temperament, character, and personality disorder in bulimia nervosa. *Journal of Nervous and Mental Disease, 183*, 593–598.

Bulik, C. M., Sullivan, P., Fear, J., & Joyce, P. (1997). Eating disorders and antecedent anxiety disorders: A controlled study. *Acta Psychiatrica Scandinavica, 96*, 101–107.

Bulik, C. M., Sullivan, P., Fear, J., Pickering, A., & Dawn, A. (1999). Fertility and reproduction in women with anorexia nervosa: A controlled study. *Journal of Clinical Psychiatry, 2*, 130–135.

Bulik, C. M., Sullivan, P., Wade, T., & Kendler, K. (2000). Twin studies of eating disorders: A review. *International Journal of Eating Disorders, 27*, 1–20.

Bulik, C., Sullivan, P., Fear, J., & Pickering, A. (1997). Predictors of the development of bulimia nervosa in women with anorexia nervosa. *Journal of Nervous and Mental Disease, 185*, 704–707.

Burgio, L. D., Len-Burge, R., Roth, D. L., Bourgeois, M. S., Dijkstra, K., Gerstle, J., et al. (2001). Come talk with me: Improving communication between nursing assistants and nursing home residents during care routines. *Gerontologist, 41*, 449–460.

Burgio, L. D., Stevens, A., Burgio, K. L., Roth, D. L., Paul, P., & Gerstle, J. (2002). Teaching and maintaining behavior management skills in the nursing home. *Gerontologist, 42*, 487–496.

Burke, J. D., Loeber, R., & Birmaher, B. (2002). Oppositional defiant disorder and conduct disorder: A review of the past 10 years, part II. *Journal of the American Academy of Child and Adolescent Psychiatry, 41*, 1275–1293.

Burke, P. M., Meyer, V., Kocoshis, S., Orenstein, D. M., Chandrea, R., Nord, D. J., Sauer, J., & Cohen, E. (1989). Depression and anxiety in pediatric inflammatory bowel disease and cystic fibrosis. *Journal of the American Academy of Child and Adolescent Psychiatry, 28*, 525–527.

Bushnell, J. A., Wells, E., McKenzie, J. M., Hornblow, A. R., Oakley-Browne, M. A., & Joyce, P. R. (1994). Bulimia comorbidity in the general population and in the clinic. *Psychological Medicine, 24*, 605–611.

Buss, D. M. (1999). Social adaptation and five major factors of personality. In J. S. Wiggins (Ed.), *The five-factor model of personality: Theoretical perspectives* (pp. 180–207). New York: Guilford Press.

Buster, J. E., Kingsberg, S. A., Aguirre, O., Brown, C., Breaux, J. G., Buch, A., Rodenberg, C. A., Wekselman, K., & Casson, P. (2005). Testosterone patch for low sexual desire in surgically menopausal women: A randomized trial. *Obstetrics and Gynecology, 105*, 944–952.

Butcher, J. N., Dahlstrom, W. G., Graham, J. R., Tellegen, A. M., & Kaemmer, B. (1989). Minnesota Multiphasic Personality Inventory-2. In *Manual for Administration and Scoring*. Minneapolis: University of Minnesota Press.

Butler, A. C., Chapman, J. E., Forman, E. M., & Beck, A. T. (2006). The empirical status of cognitive–behavioral therapy: A review of meta-analyses. *Clinical Psychology Review, 26*, 17–33.

Butler, R. J., & Gasson, S. L. (2005). Enuresis alarm treatment. *Scandinavian Journal of Urology and Nephrology, 39*, 349–357.

Butterfield, M. I., Forneris, C. A., Feldman, M. E., & Beckham, J. C. (2000). Hostility and functional health status in women veterans with and without posttraumatic stress disorders: a preliminary study. *Journal of Traumatic Stress, 13*, 735–741.

Butzlaff, R. L., & Hooley, J. M. (1998). Expressed emotion and psychiatric relapse: A meta-analysis. *Archives of General Psychiatry, 55*, 547–552.

Buwalda, F. M., Vouman, T. K., & van Duijn, M. A. J. (2006). Psychoeducation for hypochondriasis: A comparison of a cognitive-behavioural approach and a problem-solving approach. *Behaviour Research and Therapy, 45*, 887–899.

Byers, E. S., & Grenier, G. (2003). Premature or rapid ejaculation: Heterosexual couples' perceptions of men's ejaculatory behavior. *Archives of Sexual Behavior, 32*, 261–270.

Bynum, J. P., Rabins, P. V., Weller, W., Niefeld, M., Anderson, G. F., & Wu, A. W. (2004). The relationship between a dementia diagnosis, chronic illness, medicare expenditures, and hospital use. *Journal of American Geriatrics Society, 52*, 187–194.

Cain, V. S., Johannes, C. B., Avis, N. E., Molte, B., Shocken, M., Skurnick, J., & Ory, M. (2003). Sexual functioning and practices in a multi-ethnic study of midlife women: Baseline results from SWAN. *Journal of Sex Research, 40*, 266–277.

Callahan, C. M., Hui, S. L., Nienaber, N. A., Musick, B. S., & Tierney, W. M. (1994). Longitudinal study of depression and health services use among elderly primary care patients. *Journal of American Geriatrics Society, 42*, 833–838.

Campinha-Bacote, J. (1988). Culturological assessment: An important factor in psychiatric consultation–liaison nursing. *Archives of Psychiatric Nursing, 2*, 244–250.

Campinha-Bacote, J. (1992). Voodoo illness. *Perspectives in Psychiatric Care, 28*, 11–17.

Canino, G. J., Bird, H. R., Shrout, P. E., Rubio-Stipec, M., Bravo, M., Martinez, R., Sesman, M., & Guevara, L. M. (1987). The prevalence of specific psychiatric disorders in Puerto Rico. *Archives of General Psychiatry, 44*, 727–735.

Canino, G., Shrout, P. E., Rubio-Stipec, M., Bird, H. R., Bravo, M., Ramirez, R., Chavez, L., Alegria, M., Bauermeister, J. J., Hohmann, A., Riberta, J., Garcia, P., & Martinez-Taboas, A. (2004). The DSM-IV rates of child and adolescent disorders in Puerto Rico. *Archives of General Psychiatry, 61*, 85–93.

Cannon, M., Jones, P. B., & Murray, R. M. (2002). Obstetric complications and schizophrenia: Historical and meta-analytic review. *American Journal of Psychiatry, 159*, 1080–1092.

Cannon, W. B. (1932). *The wisdom of the body* (2nd ed.) New York: W.W. Norton & Co.

Cannon, W. B. (1929). *Bodily changes in pain, hunger, fear and rage.* New York: Appleton.

Cano, A., Mayo, A., & Ventimiglia, M. (2006). Coping, pain severity, interference, and disability: The potential mediating and moderating roles of race and education. *Journal of Pain, 7*, 459–468.

Caprioli, D., Celentano, M., Paolone, G., & Badiani, A. (2007). Modeling the role of environment in addiction. *Progress in Neuro-Psychopharmacology & Biological Psychiatry, 31*, 1639–1653.

Capron, A. M. (1999). Ethical and human-rights issues in research on mental disorders than may affect decision-making capacity. *New England Journal of Medicine, 340*, 1430–1434.

Cardno, A., Marshall, E., Coid, B. et al. Heritability estimates for psychotic disorders: the Maudsley twin psychosis series. *Archives of General Psychiatry, 56*, 162–168.

Carlson, G. A., & Kashani, J. H. (1988). Phenomenology of major depression from childhood through adulthood: Analysis of three studies. *American Journal of Psychiatry, 145*, 1222–1225.

Carnes, P., Delmonico, D. L., & Griffin, E. (2001). *In the shadows of the net: breaking free of compulsive online sexual behavior.* Center City, MN: Hazelden.

Carney, C. P., Jones, L., Woolson, R. F., Noyes, R., Jr., & Doebbeling, B. N. (2003). Relationship between depression and pancreatic cancer in the general population. *Psychosomatic Medicine., 65*, 884–888.

Carpintero, H. (2004). Watson's *Behaviorism*: A comparison of the two editions (1925 and 1930). *History of Psychology, 7*, 183–202.

Carrigan, M. H., & Randall, C. L. (2003). Self-medication in social phobia: A review of the alcohol literature. *Addictive Behavior, 28*, 269–284.

Carrillo, J., & Benitez, J. (2000). Clinically significant pharmacokinetic interactions between dietary caffeine and medications. *Clinical Pharmacokinetics, 39*, 127–153.

Carroll, R. T. (2003). *The skeptic's dictionary.* New York: John Wiley and Sons.

Carter, C. S. (1998). Neuroendocrine perspectives on social attachment and love. *Psychoneuroendocrinology, 23*, 779–818.

Caruso, S., Intelisano, G., Lupo, L., & Agnello, C. (2001). Premenopausal women affected by sexual arousal disorder treated with sildenafil: A double-blind, cross-over, placebo-controlled study. *British Journal of Obstetrics and Gynaecology, 108*, 623–628.

Caskey, J. D., & Rosenthal, S. L. (2005). Conducting research on sensitive topics with adolescents: Ethical and developmental considerations. *Developmental and Behavioral Pediatrics, 26*, 61–67.

Casper, R. C., Eckert, E. D., Halmi, K. A., Goldberg, S. C., & Davis, J. M. (1980). Bulimia: Its incidence and clinical importance in anorexia nervosa. *Archives of General Psychiatry, 37*, 1030–1035.

Caspi, A., Sugden, K., Moffitt, T., Taylor, A., Craig, I., Harrington, H., et al. (2003). Influence of life stress on depression: Moderation by a polymorphism in the 5-HTT gene. *Science, 301*, 386–389.

Castellanos, F. X., Lee, P. P., Sharp, W., Jeffries, N. O., Greenstein, D. K., Clasen, L. S., Blumenthal, J. D., James, R. S., Ebens, C. L., Walter, J. M., Zijdenbos, A., Evans, A. C., Giedd, J. N., & Rapoport, J. L. (2002). Developmental trajectories of brain volume abnormalities in children and adolescents with attention-deficit/hyperactivity disorder. *Journal of the American Medical Association, 288*, 1740–1748.

Castles, A., Datta, H., Gayan, J., & Olson, R. K. (1999). Varieties of developmental reading disorder: Genetic and environmental influences. *Journal of Experimental Child Psychology, 72*, 73–94.

Cather, C., Penn, D., Otto, M. W., Yovel, I., Mueser, K. T., & Goff, D. C. (2005). A pilot study of functional Cognitive Behavioral Therapy (fCBT) for schizophrenia. *Schizophrenia Research, 74*, 201–209.

Cavanaugh-Johnson, T. (1988). Child perpetrators: Children who molest children. *Child Abuse and Neglect, 12*, 219–229.

Ceballos, N. A., Houston, R. J., Hesselbrock, V. M., & Bauer, L. O. (2006). Brain maturation in conduct disorder versus borderline personality disorder. *Neuropsychobiology, 53*, 94–100.

Cederlof, R., Rantasalo, I., Floderus-Myrhed, B., Hammar, N., Kaprio, J., Koskenvuo, M., Langinvainio, H., & Sarna, S. (1982). A cross-national epidemiological resource: The Swedish and Finnish cohort studies of like-sexed twins. *International Journal of Epidemiology, 11*, 387–390.

Center for Disease Control and Prevention (2007). Fruit and vegetable consumption among adults—United States, 2005. *Morbidity and Mortality Weekly Report, 56*, 213–217.

Centers for Disease Control & Prevention (2003). Prevalence of current cigarette smoking among adults and change in prevalence of current and some day smoking—United States, 1996–2001. *Morbidity and Mortality Weekly Report, 52*, 303–307.

Centers for Disease Control and Prevention (2006). Youth Risk Behavior Surveillance—United States, 2005. *MMWR (Morbidity and Mortality Weekly Report) Surveillance Summary, 55* (No. SS–5), 1–108.

Centers for Disease Control and Prevention. (1994). Cigarette smoking among adults—United States, 1993. *Morbidity and Mortality Weekly Reports, 43*, 925–930.

Centers for Disease Control and Prevention. (2002). Annual smoking-attributable mortality, years of potential life lost, and economic costs—United States, 1995–1999. *Morbidity and Mortal Weekly Report, 51*, 300–303.

Centers for Disease Control and Prevention. (2004a). Prevalence of cigarette use among 14 racial/ethnic populations—United States, 1999–2001. *Morbidity and Mortality Weekly Reports, 53*, 49–52.

Centers for Disease Control and Prevention. (2004b). Youth Risk Behavior Surveillance United States, 2003. *Morbidity and Mortality Report Weekly, 53*, 1–96.

Centers for Disease Control and Prevention. National Center for Injury Prevention and Control. Web-based Injury Statistics Query and Reporting System (WISQARS) www.cdc.gov/ncipc/wisqars).

Centerwatch. (1995–2007). www.centerwatch.com.

Cerletti, U., & Bini, L. (1938). Un nuovo metodo di shockterapia: "L'elettroshock". *Bollettino ed Atti della Reale Accademia Medica di Roma, 64*, 136–138.

Chalkley, A. J., & Powell, G. E. (1983). The clinical description of forty-eight cases of sexual fetishism. *British Journal of Psychiatry, 142*, 292–295.

Chambless, D. L., & Williams, K. E. (1995). A preliminary study of African Americans with agoraphobia: Symptom severity and outcome of treatment with in vivo exposure. *Behavior Therapy, 26*, 501–515.

Chambless, D. L., Fydrich, T., & Rodebaugh, T. L. (2008). Generalized social phobia and avoidant personality disorder: Meaningful distinction or useless duplication? *Depression and Anxiety, 25*, 8–19.

Chang, D. F., Myers, H. F., Yeung, A., Zhang, Y., Zhao, J., & Yu, S. (2005). Shenjing shuairuo and the DSM-IV: Diagnosis, distress, and disability in a Chinese primary care setting. *Transcultural Psychiatry, 42*, 204–218.

Chapman, C. R., & Gavrin, J. (1999). Suffering: The contributions of persistent pain. *The Lancet, 353*, 2233–2237.

Chapman, D. P., Williams, S. M., Strine, T. W., Anda, R. F., & Moore, M. J. (2006). Dementia and its implications for public health. *Preventing Chronic Disease, 3*, 1–13.

Chapman, T. R., Mannuzza, S., & Fyer, A. J. (1995). Epidemiology and family studies of social phobia. In R. G. Heimberg, M. R. Liebowitz, D. A. Hope, & F. R. Schneier (Eds.), *Social phobia: diagnosis, assessment and treatment* (pp. 21–40). New York: Guilford Press.

Charman, T., Taylor, E., Drew, A., Cockerill, H., Brown J. A., & Baird, G. (2005). Outcome at 7 years of children diagnosed with autism at age 2: Predictive validity of assessments conducted at 2 and 3 years of age and pattern of symptom change over time. *Journal of Child Psychology and Psychiatry, 46*, 500–513.

Charney, D., Heninger, G., & Jatlow, P. (1985). Increased anxiogenic effects of caffeine in panic disorders. *Archives of General Psychiatry, 42*, 233–243.

Chassin, L., Presson, C. C., Rose, J. S., & Sherman, S. J. (2001). From adolescence to adulthood: age-related changes in beliefs about cigarette smoking in a midwestern community sample. *Health Psychology, 20*, 377–386.

Chavira, D., Grilo, C. M., Shea, M. T., Yen, S., Gunderson, J. G., Morey, L. C., Skodol, A. E., Stout, R. L., & McGlashan, T. H. (2003). Ethnicity and four personality disorders. *Comprehensive Psychiatry, 44*, 483–491.

Chen, E. Y., Matthews, L., Allen, C., Kuo, J. R., & Linehan, M. M. (2008). Dialectical behavior therapy for clients with binge-eating disorder or bulimia nervosa and borderline personality disorder. *International Journal of Eating Disorders, 41*, 505–512.

Cheng, T. (1989). Symptomatology of minor psychiatric morbidity: A crosscultural comparison. *Psychological Medicine, 19*, 697–708.

Chenneville, T. (2000). HIV, confidentiality, and duty to protect: A decision-making model. *Professional Psychology: Research and Practice, 31*, 661–670.

Chess, S., & Thomas, A. (1977). Temperamental individuality from childhood to adolescence. *Journal of the American Academy of Child and Adolescent Psychiatry, 116*, 218–226.

Chess, S., & Thomas, A. (1991). Temperament and the concept of goodness of fit. In J. Strelau and A. Angleitner (Eds.), *Explorations in temperament: International perspectives on theory and measurement* (pp. 15–28). New York: Plenum Press.

Cheyne, J. (2005). Sleep paralysis episode frequency and number, types, and structure of associated hallucinations. *Journal of Sleep Research, 14*, 319–324.

Chial, H. J., Camilleri, M., Williams, D. E., Litzinger, K., & Perrault, J. (2003). Rumination syndrome in children and adolescents: Diagnosis, treatment, and prognosis. *Pediatrics, 111*, 158–162.

Chiesa, M., Fonagy, P., & Holmes, J. (2006). Six-year follow-up of three treatment programs to personality disorder. *Journal of Personality Disorders, 20*, 493–509.

Chiesa, M., Fonagy, P., Holmes, J., & Drahorad, C. (2004). Residential versus community treatment of personality disorders: A comparative study of three treatment programs. *American Journal of Psychiatry, 161*, 1463–1470.

Chiu, S. W., Gervan, S., Fairbrother, C., Johnson, L. L., Owen-Anderson, A. F., Bradley, S. J., & Zucker, K. J. (2006). Sex-dimorphic color preference in children with gender identity disorder: A comparison to clinical and community controls. *Sex Roles, 55*, 385–395.

Chockroverty, S. (1999). An overview of sleep. In S. Chokroverty (Ed.), *Sleep disorder medicine: Basic science, technical considerations, and clinical aspects* (pp. 7–20). Boston: Butterworth-Heinemann.

Chodoff, P. (2002). The medicalization of the human condition. *Psychiatric Services, 53*, 627–628.

Chorvinsky, M. (2000). The haunted boy of Cottage City. *Strange Magazine.* (http://www.strangemag.com/exorcistpage1.html).

Chronis, A. M., Chacko, A., Fabiano, G. A., Wymbs, B. T., & Pelham, W. E., Jr. (2004). Enhancements to the behavioral parent training paradigm for families of children with ADHD: Review and future directions. *Clinical Child and Family Psychology Review, 7*, 1–27.

Chronis, A., Jones, H. A., & Raggi, V. L. (2006). Evidence-based psychosocial treatments for children and adolescents with attention-deficit/hyperactivity disorder. *Clinical Psychology Review, 26*, 486–502.

Chung, Y. B., & Harmon, L. W. (1994). The career interests and aspirations of gay men: How sex-role orientation is related. *Journal of Vocational Behavior, 45*, 223–239.

Ciechanowski, P., Wagner, E., Schmaling, K., Schwartz, S., Williams, B., Diehr, P., et al. (2004). Community-integrated home-based depression treatment in older adults: A randomized controlled trial. *Journal of the American Medical Association, 291*, 1569–1577.

Cintron, A. & Morrison, R. S. (2006). Pain and ethnicity in the United States: A systematic review. *Journal of Palliative Medicine, 9*, 1454–1473.

Clarfield, A. M. (2003). The decreasing prevalence of reversible dementias: An updated meta-analysis. *Archives of Internal Medicine, 163*, 2219–2229.

Clark, C. W. (1997). The witch craze in 17th-Century Europe. In W. G. Bringman, H. E. Lück, R. Miller, & C. Early (Eds.), *A pictorial history of psychology* (pp. 23–29). Carol Stream, IL: Quintessence Publishing Co.

Cloninger, C. R., Svrakic, D. M., & Przybeck, T. R. (1993). A psychobiological model of temperament and character. *Archives of General Psychiatry, 50*, 975–990.

Clum, G. (1989). Psychological interventions versus drugs in the treatment of panic disorder. *Behavior Therapy, 20*, 429–457.

Cochran, S. D. (1984). Preventing medical noncompliance in the outpatient treatment of bipolar affective disorders. *Journal of Consulting and Clinical Psychology, 52*, 873–878.

Cohen, P., Cohen, J., & Brook, J. (1993). An epidemiological study of disorders in late childhood and adolescence—II. Persistence of disorders. *Journal of Child Psychology and Psychiatry, 34*, 869–877.

Cohen, S., Doyle, W. J., Turner, R. B., Alper, C. M., & Skoner, D. P. (2003). Emotional style and susceptibility to the common cold. *Psychosomatic Medicine, 65*, 652–657.

Cohen, S., Frank, E., Doyle, W. J., Skoner, D. P., Rabin, B. S., & Gwaltney, J. M., Jr. (1998). Types of stressors that increase susceptibility to the common cold in healthy adults. *Health Psychology, 17*, 214–223.

Cohen-Bendahan, C. C., van de Beek, C., & Berenbaum, S. A. (2005). Prenatal sex hormone effects on child and adult sex-typed behavior: Methods and findings. *Neuroscience and Biobehavioral Reviews, 29*, 353–384.

Cohen-Kettenis, P. T., Owen, A., Kaijser, V. G., Bradley, S. J., & Zucker, K. J. (2003). Demographic characteristics, social competence, and behavior problems in children with gender identity disorder: A cross-national, cross-clinic comparative analysis. *Journal of Abnormal Child Psychology, 31*, 41–53.

Colapinto, J. Gender Gap. *Slate Magazine (posted June 3, 2004).* Retrieved on 1/1/2008.

Coldwell, H., & Heather, N. (2006). Introduction to the special issue. *Addiction Research and Theory, 14*, 1–5.

Collins, R., & Lapp, W. (1991). Restraint and attributions: Evidence of the abstinence violation effect in alcohol consumption. *Cognitive Therapy and Research, 15*, 69–84.

Combs, D. R., & Mueser, K. T. (2007). Schizophrenia. In M. Hersen, S. Turner, and D. Beidel (Eds.), *Adult psychopathology and diagnosis.* New York: John Wiley and Sons.

COMMIT. (1991). Community Intervention Trial for Smoking Cessation (COMMIT): Summary of design and intervention. COMMIT Research Group. *Journal of the National Cancer Institute, 83*, 1620–1628.

COMMIT. (1995a). Community Intervention Trial for Smoking Cessation (COMMIT): I. Cohort results from a four-year community intervention. *American Journal of Public Health, 85*, 183–192.

COMMIT. (1995b). Community intervention trial for smoking cessation (COMMIT): II. Changes in adult cigarette smoking prevalence. *American Journal of Public Health, 85*, 193–200.

Committee on Environmental Health. Lead exposure in children: Prevention, detection, and management. *Pediatrics, 116*, 1036–1046.

Compas, B. E., & Gotlib, I. H. (2002). *Introduction to Clinical Psychology: Science and Practice.* New York: McGraw-Hill.

Compton, S. N., March, J. S., Brent, D., Albano, A. M., Weersing, R., & Curry, J. (2004). Cognitive-behavioral psychotherapy for anxiety and depressive disorders in children and adolescents: An evidence-based medicine review. *Journal of the American Academy of Child and Adolescent Psychiatry, 43*, 930–959.

Compton, W., Grant, B., Colliver, J., Glantz, M., & Stinson, F. (2004). Prevalence of marijuana use disorders in the United States: 1991–1992 and 2001–2002. *Journal of the American Medical Association, 291,* 2114–2121.

Conn, D. K. (2004). Other dementias and mental disorders due to general medical conditions. In J. Sadavoy, L. F. Jarvik, G. T. Grossberg, & B. S. Meyers (Eds.), *Comprehensive textbook of geriatric psychiatry* (3rd ed., pp. 545–577). New York: W.W. Norton & Co.

Conners, C. K., Epstein, J. N., March, J. S., Angold, A., Wells, K. C., Klaric, J., et al. (2001). Multimodal treatment of ADHD in the MTA: An alternative outcome analysis. *Journal of the American Academy of Child and Adolescent Psychiatry, 40,* 159–167.

Conwell, Y., Duberstein, P. R., & Caine, E. D. (2002). Risk factors for suicide in later life. *Biological Psychiatry, 52,* 193–204.

Coolidge, F. L., Thede, L. L., & Young, S. E. (2002). The heritability of gender identity disorder in a child and adolescent twin sample. *Behavior Genetics, 32,* 251–257.

Cooper, A., Delmonico, D. J., Griffin-Shelley, E., & Mathy, R. M. (2004). Online sexual activity: An examination of potentially problematic behaviors. *Sexual Addiction & Compulsivity, 11,* 120–143.

Copolov, D.L., Mackinnon, A., & Trauer, T. (2004). Correlates of the affective impact of auditory hallucinations in psychotic disorders. *Schizophrenia Bulletin, 30,* 163–171.

Corkin, S. (1968). Acquisition of motor skill after bilateral medial temporal-lobe excision. *Neuropsychologia 6,* 255–265.

Coryell, W., & Norten, S. (1981). Briquet's syndrome (somatization disorder) and primary depression: Comparison of background and outcome. *Comprehensive Psychiatry, 22,* 249–255.

Costello, E. J., Angold, A., Burns, B. J., Stangl, D. K., Tweed, D. L., Erkanli, A., et al. (1996). The Great Smoky Mountains Study of Youth. Goals, design, methods, and the prevalence of DSM-III-R disorders. *Archives of General Psychiatry, 53,* 1129–1136.

Costello, E. J., Farmer, E. M. Z., Angold, A., Burns, B. J., & Erkanli, A. (1997). Psychiatric disorders among American Indian and white youth in Appalachia: The Great Smoky Mountains Study. *American Journal of Public Health, 87,* 827–832.

Costello, E. J., Keeler, G. P., & Angold, A. (2001). Poverty, race/ethnicity, and psychiatric disorder: A study of rural children. *American Journal of Public Health, 91,* 1494–1498.

Costello, E. J., Mustillo, A., Erkanli, A., Keeler, G., & Angold, A. (2003). Prevalence and development of psychiatric disorders in childhood and adolescence. *Archives of General Psychiatry, 60,* 837–844.

Costello, E. J., Mustillo, S., Erkanli, A., Keeler, G., & Angold, A. (2003). Prevalence and development of psychiatric disorders in childhood and adolescence. *Archives of General Psychiatry, 60,* 837–844.

Cottler, L. B., Nishith, P., & Compton, W. M., 3rd. (2001). Gender differences in risk factors for trauma exposure and post-traumatic stress disorder among inner-city drug abusers in and out of treatment. *Comprehensive Psychiatry, 42,* 111–117.

Cougnard, A., Grolleau, S., Lamarque, F., Beitz, C., Brugère, S., & Verdoux, H. (2006). Psychotic disorders among homeless subjects attending a psychiatric emergency service. *Social Psychiatry and Psychiatric Epidemiology, 41,* 904–910.

Courchesne, E., & Pierce, K. (2005). Brain overgrowth in autism during a critical time in development: Implications for frontal pyramidal neuron and interneuron development and connectivity. *International Journal of Developmental Neuroscience, 23,* 153–170.

Covington, E. C. (2000). Psychogenic pain—What it means, why it does not exist, and how to diagnose it. *Pain Medicine, 1,* 2878–2894.

Cox, B. J., Direnfeld, D. M., Swinson, R. P., & Norton, G. R. (1994). Suicidal ideation and suicide attempts in panic disorder and social phobia. *American Journal of Psychiatry, 151,* 882–887.

Cox, D. J., & Maletzky, B. M. (1980). Victims of exhibitionism. In D. J. Cox & R. J. Daitzman (Eds.), *Exhibitionism: Description, Assessment and Treatment* (pp. 289–293). New York: Garland.

Cox, D. J., Morris, J. B. Jr., Borowitz, S. M., & Sutphen, J. L. (2002). Psychological differences between children with and without chronic encopresis. *Journal of Pediatric Psychology, 27,* 585–591.

Cox, D. J., Sutphen, J. L., Borowtiz, S. Kovatchev, B., & Ling, W. (1998). Contribution to behavior therapy and biofeedback to laxative therapy in the treatment of pediatric encopresis. *Annals of Behavioral Medicine, 20,* 70–76.

Crabtree, F. A. (2000). Mesmer, Franz Anton. In A. Kazdin (Ed.), *Encyclopedia of psychology (Volume 4;* pp. 200–201). Washington, DC: American Psychological Association.

Craig, T. J., Siegel. C., Hopper, K., Lin, S., & Sartorius, N. (1997). Outcome in schizophrenia and related disorders compared between developing and developed countries: A recursive partitioning re-analysis of the WHP SOSMD data. *British Journal of Psychiatry, 170,* 229–233.

Craig, T. K., Bialas, I., Hodson, S., & Cox, A. D. (2004). Intergenerational transmission of somatization behaviour: 2. Observations of joint attention and bids for attention. *Psychological Medicine, 34,* 199–209.

Craighead, W. E., & Miklowitz, D. J. (2000). Psychosocial interventions for bipolar disorder. *Journal of Clinical Psychiatry, 61*(Suppl 13), 58–64.

Crane, C., Martin, M., & the ALSPAC Study Team. (2004). Illness-related parenting in mothers with functional gastrointestinal symptoms. *American Journal of Gastroenterology, 99,* 694–702.

Craske, M. G., Golinelli, D., Stein, M. B., Roy-Byrne, P., Bystritsky, A., & Grebourne, C. (2005). Does the addition of cognitive-behavioral therapy improve panic disorder treatment outcome relative to medication alone in the primary care setting. *Psychological Medicine, 35,* 1645–1654.

Crawford, D. C., Meadows, K. L., Newman, J. L., Taft, L. F., Scott, E., Leslie, M., Shubek, L., Holmgreen, P., Yeargin-Allsopp, M., Boyle, C., & Sherman, S. L. (2002). Prevalence of the fragile X syndrome in African-Americans. *American Journal of Medical Genetics, 110,* 226–233.

Creed, F., & Barsky, A. (2004). A systematic review of the epidemiology of somatisation disorder and hypochondriasis. *Journal of Psychosomatic Research, 56,* 391–408.

Crimlisk, H. L., Bhatia, K., Cope, H., David, A., Marsden, C. D., & Ron, M. A. (1998). Slater revisited: 6 year follow up study of patients with medically unexplained motor symptoms. *British Medical Journal, 316,* 582–586.

Croen, L. A., Grether, J. K., & Selvin S. (2001). The epidemiology of mental retardation of unknown cause. *Pediatrics, 107,* E86.

Cronbag, H. F. M., Wagenaar, W. A., & van Koppen, P. J. (1996). Crashing memories and the problem of "source monitoring." *Applied Cognitive Psychology, 10,* 95–104.

Cross National Collaborative Panic Study Second Phase Investigation. (1992). Drug treatment of panic disorder: Comparative efficacy of alprazolam, imipramine, and placebo. *British Journal of Psychiatry, 160,* 191–202.

Cruess, D. G., Schneiderman, N., Antoni, M. H., & Penedo, F. (2004). Biobehavioral bases of disease processes. In T. J. Boll, R. G. Friedman, A. Baum, & J. L. Wallander (Eds.), *Handbook of clinical health psychology.* (pp. 31–79). Washington, DC: American Psychological Association.

Cruess, S., Antoni, M., Cruess, D., Fletcher, M. A., Ironson, G., Kumar, M. et al. (2000). Reductions in herpes simplex virus type 2 antibody titers after cognitive behavioral stress management and relationships with neuroendocrine function, relaxation skills, and social support in HIV-positive men. *Psychosomatic Medicine, 62,* 828–837.

Cuffe, S. P., McKeown, R. E., Addy, C. L., & Garrison, C. Z. (2005). Family and psychosocial risk factors in a longitudinal epidemiological study of adolescents. *Journal of the American Academy of Child and Adolescent Psychiatry, 44,* 121–129.

Cully, J. A., Graham, D. P., Stanley, M. A., Ferguson, C. J., Sharafkhanch, A., & Souchek, J. K. M. E. (2006). Quality of life in patients with chronic obstructive pulmonary disease and comorbid anxiety or depression. *Psychosomatics, 47,* 312–319.

Cully, J. A., Graham, D. P., Stanley, M. A., Ferguson, C. J., Sharafkhanch, A., Souchek, J., & Kunik, M. E. (2006). Quality of life in patients with chronic obstructive pulmonary disease and comorbid anxiety or depression. *Psychosomatics, 47,* 312–319.

Cummings, J. L. (1986). Organic psychoses: Delusional disorders and secondary mania. *Psychiatric Clinics of North America, 9,* 293–311.

Cunningham-Owens, D. G., Miller, P., Lawrie, S. M., & Johnstone, E. C. (2005). Pathogenesis of schizophrenia: A psychopathological perspective. *British Journal of Psychiatry, 186,* 386–393.

Curry, S., Marlatt, G., & Gordon, J. (1987). Abstinence violation effect: Validation of an attributional construct with smoking cessation. *Journal of Consulting and Clinical Psychology, 55,* 145–149.

Curtis, G. C., Magee, W. J, Eaton, W. W., Witchen, H. U., & Kessler, R. C. (1998). Specific fears and phobias. Epidemiology and classification. *British Journal of Psychiatry: The Journal of Mental Science, 173,* 212–217.

Cyranowski, J. M., Bromberger, J., Youk, A., Matthews, K., Kravitz, H. M., & Powell, L. H. (2004). Lifetime depression history and sexual function in women at midlife. *Archives of Sexual Behavior, 33,* 539–548.

Cyranowski, J., Frank, E., Young, E., & Shear, M. (2000). Adolescent onset of the gender difference in lifetime rates of major depression. *Archives of General Psychiatry, 57,* 21–27.

Czarnetzki, A., Blin, N., & Pusch, C. M. (2003). Down's syndrome in ancient Europe. *The Lancet, 362,* 1000.

Daley, D. (2006). Attention deficit hyperactivity disorder: A review of the essential facts. *Child: Care, Health & Development, 32,* 193–204.

Dalman, C., & Cullberg, J. (1999). Neonatal-hyperbilirubinemia—A vulnerability factor for mental disorder? *Acta Psychiatrica Scandinavica, 100,* 469–471.

Damon, W., & Simon Rosser, B. R. (2005). Anodyspareunia in men who have sex with men: Prevalence, predictors, consequences and the development of DSM diagnostic criteria. *Journal of Sex & Marital Therapy, 31,* 129–141.

Daneback, K., Cooper, A., & Månsson, S. A. (2005). An internet study of cybersex participants. *Archives of Sexual Behavior, 14,* 321–328.

Dare, C., le Grange, D., Eisler, I., & Rutherford, J. (1994). Redefining the psychosomatic family: Family process of 26 eating disorder families. *International Journal of Eating Disorders, 16,* 211–226.

Daubenmier, J. J., Weidner, G., Sumner, M. D., Mendell, N., Merritt-Worden, T., Studley, J. et al. (2007). The contribution of changes in diet, exercise, and stress management to changes in coronary risk in women and men in the multisite cardiac lifestyle intervention program. *Annals of Behavioral Medicine, 33,* 57–68.

Daughters, S., Bornovalova, M., Correia, C., & Lejuez, C. (2007). Psychoactive Substance Use Disorders: Drugs. In M. Hersen, S. Turner & D. Beidel (Eds.), *Adult psychopathology and diagnosis: Fifth edition.* (pp. 201–233) Hoboken, NJ: John Wiley & Sons.

Davidson, J. R. T. (1993, March). Childhood histories of adult social phobics. Paper presented at the Anxiety Disorders Association of America Annual Convention, Charleston, SC.

Davidson, J. R. T., Foa, E. B., Huppert, J. D., Keefe, F. J., Franklin, M. E., Compton, J. S., Zhao, N., Connor, K. M., Lynch, T. R., & Gadde, K. M. (2004). Fluoxetine, comprehensive cognitive behavioral therapy, and placebo in generalized social phobia. *Archives of General Psychiatry, 61,* 1005–1013.

Davidson, J. R. T., Potts, N. L. S., Richichi, E., Krishnan, R., Ford, S. M., Smith, R., & Wilson, W. (1993). Treatment of social phobia with clonazepam and placebo. *Journal of Clinical Psychopharmacology 13,* 423–428.

Davidson, J. R. T., Potts, N., Ruchichi, E., Krishnan, R., Ford, S. M., Smith, R., & Wilson, W (1993). Treatment of social phobia with clonazepam and placebo. *Journal of Clinical Psychopharmacology, 13,* 423–428.

Davis, K. L., Kahn, R. S., Ko, G., & Davidson, M. (1991). Dopamine in schizophrenia: A review and reconceptualization. *American Journal of Psychiatry, 148,* 1474–1486.

Dawood, K., Kirk, K. M., Bailey, J. M., Andrews, P. W., & Martin, N. G. (2005). Genetic and environmental influences on the frequency of orgasm in women. *Twin Research and Human Genetics, 8,* 27–33.

Dawson, D. (2000). Drinking patterns among individuals with and without DSM-IV alcohol use disorders. *Journal of Studies on Alcohol, 61,* 111–120.

Dawson, D., & Grant, B. (1993). Gender effects in diagnosing alcohol abuse and dependence. *Journal of Clinical Psychology., 49,* 298–307.

De Beurs, E., Beekman, A. T., van Balkom, A. J., Deeg, D. J., van, D. R., & van, T. W. (1999). Consequences of anxiety in older persons: Its effect on disability, well-being and use of health services. *Psychological Medicine, 29,* 583–593.

De Clercq, B., & De Fruyt, F. (2007). Childhood antecedents of personality disorder. *Current Opinions in Psychiatry, 20,* 57–61.

de Kruiff, M. E., ter Kuile, M. M., Weijenborg, P. T., & van Lankveld, J. J. (2000). Vaginismus and dyspareunia: Is there a difference in clinical presentation? *Journal of Psychosomatic Obstetrics and Gynaecology, 21,* 149–155.

De Leon, J., Dadvanc, M., Canuso, C., White, A. O., Stanilla, J. K., & Simpson, G. M. (1995). Schizophrenia and smoking: An epidemiological survey at a state hospital. *American Journal of Psychiatry, 152,* 453–455.

de Zwaan, M., Mitchell, J., Seim, H., Specker, S., Pyle, R., Raymond, N., & Crosby, R. (1994). Eating related and general psychopathology in obese females with binge-eating disorder. *International Journal of Eating Disorders, 15,* 43–52.

Dean, C. E. (2006). Antipsychotic-associated neuronal changes in the brain: Toxic, therapeutic, or irrelevant to the long-term outcome schizophrenia? *Progress in Neuro-Psychopharmacology and Biological Psychiatry, 30,* 174–189.

DeBeurs, E., van Balkom, A. J. L. M., Lange, A., Koele, P., & van Dyck, R. (1995). Treatment of panic disorder with agoraphobia: Comparison of fluvoxamine, placebo, and psychological panic management combined with exposure and of exposure in vivo alone. *American Journal of Psychiatry, 152,* 683–691.

DeBuono, B. A., Zinner, S. H., Daamen, M., & McCormack, W. M. (1990). Sexual behavior of college women in 1975, 1986, and 1989. *New England Journal of Medicine, 22,* 821–825.

Decker, H. S. (2004). The psychiatric works of Emil Kraeplein: A many faceted story of modern medicine. *Journal of the History of the Neurosciences, 13,* 248–276.

Deichert, N. T., Fekete, E. M., Boarts, J. M., Druley, J. A., & Delahanty, D. L. (2008). Emotional Support and Affect: Associations with Health Behaviors and Active Coping Efforts in Men Living with HIV. *AIDS and Behavior, 12,* 139–145.

Dein, S. (2003). Psychogenic death: Individual effects of sorcery and taboo violation. *Mental Health, Religion, & Culture, 6,* 195–202.

deJong, J. T. V. M. (2005). Cultural variation in the clinical presentation of sleep paralysis. *Transcultural Psychiatry, 42,* 78–92.

Delahanty, D. L., Wang, T., Maravich, C., Forlenza, M., & Baum, A. (2000). Time-of-day effects on response of natural killer cells to acute stress in men and women. *Health Psychology, 19,* 39–45.

Delemarre-van de Waal, H. A., & Cohen-Kettenis, P. T. (2006). Clinical management of gender identity disorder in adolescents: A protocol on psychological and paediatric endocrinology aspects. *European Journal of Endocrinology, 155,* S131–S137.

Delgado, P. L., Charney, D. S., Price, L. H., Aghajanian, G. K., Landis, H., & Heninger, G. R. (1990). Serotonin function and the mechanism of antidepressant action. *Archives of General Psychiatry, 47,* 411–418.

Dell, P. F., & Eisenhower, J. W. (1990). Adolescent multiple personality disorder: A preliminary study of eleven cases. *Journal of the American Academy of Child and Adolescent Psychiatry, 29,* 359–366.

Delvenne, V., Goldman, S., De Maertelaer, V., & Lotstra, F. (1999). Brain glucose metabolism in eating disorders assessed by positron emission tomography. *International Journal of Eating Disorders, 25,* 29–37.

Depp, C. A., & Jeste, D. V. (2006). Definitions and predictors of successful aging: A comprehensive review of larger quantitative studies. *American Journal of Geriatric Psychiatry, 14,* 6–20.

Depression and Bipolar Support Alliance. (2006, January 26, 2007). Signs and Symptoms of Mood Disorders. Retrieved February 24, 2007, from www.DBSAlliance.org.

Derogatis, L. R., & Lynn, L. L. (1999). Psychological tests in screening for psychiatric disorders. In M. E. Maruish (Ed.), *The Use of Psychological Testing for Treatment Planning and Outcomes Assessment* (2nd ed.) (pp. 41–79). Mahwah, NJ: Lawrence Erlbaum Associates.

Desrosiers, A., & St. Fleurose, S. (2002). Treating Haitian patients: Key cultural aspects. *American Journal of Psychotherapy, 56,* 508–521.

Devlin, B., Bacanu, S., Klump, K., Bulik, C. M., Fichter, M., Halmi, K., et al. (2002). Linkage analysis of anorexia nervosa incorporating behavioral covariates. *Human Molecular Genetics, 11,* 689–696.

Deyo, R. A., Mirza, S. K., & Martin, B. I. (2006). Back pain prevalence and visit rates: estimates from U.S. national surveys, 2002. *Spine, 31,* 2724–2727.

Diamond, M. (1993). Homosexuality and bisexuality in different populations. *Archives of Sexual Behaviour, 22,* 291–310.

Diamond, M., & Sigmundson, K. (1977). Sex reassignment at birth: Long-term review and clinical implications. *Archives of Pediatric and Adolescent Medicine, 151,* 298–304.

Dickens, C., McGowan, L., & Dale, S. (2003). Impact of depression on experimental pain perception: A systematic review of the literature with meta-analysis. *Psychosomatic Medicine, 65,* 369–375.

Didie, E. R., Tortolani, C., Walters, M., Menard, W., Fay, C., & Phillips, K. A. (2006). Social functioning in body dysmorphic disorder: Assessment considerations. *Psychiatric Quarterly, 77,* 223–229.

Diefenbach, G. J., Robison, J. T., Tolin, D. F., & Blank, K. (2004). Late-life anxiety disorders among Puerto Rican primary care patients: impact on well-being, functioning, and service utilization. *Journal of Anxiety Disorders, 18,* 841–858.

DiMatteo, M. R., & Martin, L. R. (2002). *Health psychology.* Boston: Allyn & Bacon.

Dinan, T. G., Quigley, E. M., Ahmed, S. M., Scully, P., O'Brien, S., O'Mahony, L., O'Mahony, S., Shanahan, F., & Keeling, P. W. (2006). Hypothalamic-pituitary-gut axis dysregulation in irritable bowel syndrome: Plasma cytokines as a potential biomarker? *Gastroenterology, 130,* 304–311.

Ding, K., Torabi, M. R., Perera, B., Jun, M. K., & Jones–McKyer, E. L. (2007). Inhalant use among indiana school children, 1991–2004. *American Journal of Health Behavior, 31*, 24–34.

DiScala, C., Lescohier, I., Barthel, M., & Li, G. (1998). Injuries to children with Attention Deficit Hyperactivity Disorder. *Pediatrics, 102*, 1415–1421.

Diwadkar, V. A., Montrose, D. M., Dworakowski, D., Sweeney, J. A., & Keshavan, M. S. (2006). Genetically predisposed offspring with schizotypal features: An ultra high-risk group for schizophrenia. *Progress in Neuro–Psychopharmacology & Biological Psychiatry, 30*, 230–238.

Docter, R. F., & Prince, V. (1997). Transvestism: A survey of 1032 cross-dressers. *Archives of Sexual Behavior, 26*, 589–605.

Doi, T. (1973). *The anatomy of dependence.* Tokyo: Kodansha International.

Dolan, B. M., Warren, F., & Norton, K. (1997). Change in borderline symptoms one year after therapeutic community treatment for severe personality disorders. *British Journal of Psychiatry, 171*, 274–279.

Dolan, R., Mitchell, J., & Wakeling, A. (1988). Structural brain changes in patients with anorexia nervosa. *Psychological Medicine, 18*, 349–353.

Domes, G., Heinrichs, M., Michel, A., Berger, C., & Herpertz, S. C. (2007). Oxytocin improves "mind-reading" in humans. *Biologicall Psychiatry, 61*, 731–733.

Domjan, M. (2005). Pavlovian conditioning: A functional perspective. *Annual Review of Psychology, 56*, 179–206.

Done, D. J, Crow, T. J., Johnestone, E. C., & Sacker, A. (1994). Childhood antecedents of schizophrenia and affective illness: social adjustment at ages 7 and 11. *British Medical Journal, 309*, 699–703.

Donegan, N. H., Sanislow, C. A., Blumberg, H. P., Fulbright, R. K., Lacadie, C., Skudlarski, P., et al. (2003). Amygdala hyperreactivity in borderline personality disorder: Implications for emotional dysregulation. *Biological Psychiatry, 54*, 1284–1293.

Donohue, B., Thevenin, D. M., & Runyon, M. K. (1997). Behavioral treatment of conversion disorder in adolescence. *Behavior Modification, 21*, 231–251.

Doolan, D., & Froelicher, E. (2006). Efficacy of smoking cessation intervention among special populations: Review of the literature from 2000 to 2005. *Nursing Research, 55 (Suppl)*, S29–S37.

dos Santos, L. L., de Castro Magalhãs, M., Januário, J. N., Burle de Agular, M. J. & Santos Carvalho, M. R. (2006). The time has come: a new scene for PKU treatment. *Genetics and Molecular Research, 5*, 33–44.

Dougherty, D. D., Baer, L., Cosgrove, G. R., Cassem, E. H., Price, B. H., Nierenberg, A. A., Jenike, M. A., & Rausch, S. L. (2002). Prospective long-term follow-up of 44 patients who received cingulotomy for treatment-refractory obsessive-compulsive disorder. *American Journal of Psychiatry, 159*, 269–275.

Doust, J., & Del Mar, C. (2004). Why do doctors use treatments that do not work? *British Medical Journal (Clinical research ed.), 328*, 474–475.

Downing, A., Prakash, K., Gilthorpe, M. S., Mikeljevic, J. S., & Forman, D. (2007). Socioeconomic background in relation to stage at diagnosis, treatment and survival in women with breast cancer. *British Journal of Cancer, 96*, 836–840.

Drake, R. E., & Brunette, M. F. (1998). Complications of severe mental illness related to alcohol and drug use disorders. In M. Galanter (Ed.), *Recent developments in alcoholism, volume 14: The consequences of alcoholism* (pp. 285–299). New York: Plenum Press.

Driessen, M., Herrmann, J., Stahl, K., Zwaan, M., Meier, S., Hill, A., et al. (2000). Magnetic resonance imaging volumes of the hippocampus and the amygdala in women with borderline personality disorder and early traumatization. *Archives of General Psychiatry, 57*, 1115–1122.

Driscoll, J. W. (2006). Postpartum depression: The state of the science. *Journal of Perinatal and Neonatal Nursing, 20*, 40–42.

Drossman, D. A., Talley, N., Leserman, J., Olden, K., & Barreiro, M. (1995). Sexual and physical abuse and gastrointestinal illness: Review and recommendations. *Annual Internal Medicine, 123*, 782–789.

Drummond, K. D., Bradley, S. J., Peterson-Badall, M., & Zucker, K. J. (2008). A follow-up study of girls with gender identity disorder. *Developmental Psychology, 44*, 34–45.

Dubbert, P. A. M., King, A. C., Marcus, B. H., & Sallis, J. F. (2004). Promotion of physical activity through the life span. In T. J. Boll, J. M. Raczynski, & L. C. Leviton (Eds.), *Handbook of clinical health psychology* (pp. 147–181). Washington, DC: American Psychological Association.

Duits, A. A., Boeke, S., Taams, M. A., Passchier, J., & Erdman, R. A. (1997). Prediction of quality of life after coronary artery bypass graft surgery: A review and evaluation of multiple, recent studies. *Psychosomatic Medicine, 59*, 257–268.

Dulit, R. A., Fye, R. M. R., Miller, F. T., Sacks, M. H., & Frances, A. J. (1993). Gender differences in sexual preference and substance abuse of inpatients with borderline personality disorder. *Journal of Personality Disorders, 7*, 182–185.

Dunlop, D. D., Song, J., Lyons, J. S., Manheim, L. M., & Chang, R. W. (2003). Racial/ethnic differences in rates of depression among preretirement adults. *American Journal of Public Health, 93*, 1945–1952.

Dunn, G. E., Paolo, A. M., Ryan, J. J., & Van Fleet, J. N. (1994). Belief in the existence of multiple personality disorder among psychologists and psychiatrists. *Journal of Clinical Psychology, 50*, 454–457.

Durrence, H. H., & Lichstein, K. L. (2006). The sleep of African Americans: A comparative review. *Behavioral .Sleep Medicine, 4*, 29–44.

Dutra, L., Stathopoulou, G., Basden, S., Leyro, T., Powers, M., & Otto, M. (2008). A meta-analytic review of psychosocial interventions for substance use disorders. *American Journal of Psychiatry, 165*, 179–187.

Dyck, D. G., Short, R., & Vitaliano, P. P. (1999). Predictors of burden and infectious illness in schizophrenia caregivers. *Psychosomatic Medicine, 61*, 411–419.

Eagles, J., Johnston, M., Hunter, D., Lobban, M., & Millar, H. (1995). Increasing incidence of anorexia nervosa in the female population of northeast Scotland. *American Journal of Psychiatry, 152*, 1266–1271.

Eaton, W. W. (1975). Marital status and schizophrenia. *Acta Psychiatrica Scandinavica. 52*, 320–329.

Eaves, L. C., & Ho, H. H. (2008). Young adult outcome of autism spectrum disorders. *Journal of Autism and Developmental Disabilities, 38*, 739–747.

Ebersole, J. S., Pedley, T. A. (2002). *Current practice of clinical electroencephalography.* 3rd Edition. New York: Lippincott Williams & Wilkins.

Ebmeier, K. P., Donaghey, C., & Steele, J. D. (2006). Recent developments and current controversies in depression. *Lancet, 367*(9505), 153–167.

Eckert, E. D., Halmi, K. A., Marchi, P., Grove, W., & Crosby, R. (1995). Ten-year follow-up of anorexia nervosa: Clinical course and outcome. *Psychological Medicine, 25*, 143–156.

Edginton. B. (1997). Moral architecture: the influence of the York Retreat on asylum design. *Health & Place, 3*, 91–99.

Edwards, R., Telfair, J., Cecil, H., & Lenoci, J. (2001). Self-efficacy as a predictor of adult adjustment to sickle cell disease: One-year outcomes. *Psychosomatic Medicine, 63*, 850–858.

Egeland, J. A., & Sussex, J. N. (1985). Suicide and family loading for affective disorders. *Journal of the American Medical Association, 254*, 915–918.

Eggers, C., & Bunk, D. (1997). The long-term course of childhood-onset schizophrenia: A 42 year follow-up. *Schizophrenia Bulletin, 23*, 105–117.

Eggert, L. L., Thompson, E. A., Herting, J. R., & Nicholas, L. J. (1995). Reducing suicide potential among high-risk youth: Tests of a school-based prevention program. *Suicide Life Threatening Behaviors, 25*, 276–296.

Ehlers, C. L., Frank, E., & Kupfer, D. J. (1988). Social zeitgebers and biological rhythms: A unified approach to understanding the etiology of depression. *Archives of General Psychiatry, 45*, 948–952.

Ehlert, U., Gaab, J., & Heinrichs, M. (2001). Psychoneuroendocrinological contributions to the etiology of depression, posttraumatic stress disorder, and stress-related bodily disorders: The role of the hypothalamus-pituitary-adrenal axis. *Biological Psychology, 57*, 141–152.

Ehrensaft, M. K. (2005). Interpersonal relationships and sex differences in the development of conduct problems. *Clinical Child and Family Psychology Review, 8*, 39–63.

Ehrhardt, A. A., & Meyer-Bahlburg, H. F. (1981). Effects of prenatal sex hormones on gender-related behavior. *Science, 211*, 1312–1318.

Eidlitz-Markus, T. Shuper, K., & Amir, A. (2000). Secondary enuresis: posttraumatic stress disorder in children after car accidents. *Israeli Medical Association Journal, 2*, 135–137.

Einat, H., Yuan, P., & Manji, H. K. (2005). Increased anxiety-like behaviors and mitochondrial dysfunction in mice with targeted mutation of the Bel-2 gene: further support for the involvement of mitochondrial function in anxiety disorders. *Behavior and Brain Research, 165*, 172–180.

Eisen, A. (1999). *Recommendations for the Practice of Clinical Neurophysiology.* Amsterdam: Elsevier.

Eisendrath, S. J., & Young, J. Q. (2005). Factitious physical disorders: A review. In M. Maj, H. S. Akiskal, J. E. Mezzich, & A. Okasha (Eds.). *Somatoform disorders* (pp. 325–351). Hoboken, NJ: John Wiley & Sons.

Eldh, J., Berg, A., & Gustafsson, M. (1997). Long-term follow up after sex reassignment surgery. *Scandinavian Journal of Plastic and Reconstructive Surgery and Hand Surgery, 31*, 39–45.

Elzinga, B. M., van Dyck, R., & Spinhoven, P. (1998). Three controversies about dissociative identity disorder. *Clinical Psychology and Psychotherapy, 3,* 13–23.

Emslie, G. J., Ryan, N. D., & Wagner, K. D. (2005). Major depressive disorder in children and adolescents: Clinical trial design and antidepressant efficacy. *Journal of Clinical Psychiatry, 66,* Suppl 7, 14–20.

Endicott, N. A. (1999). Chronic fatigue syndrome in private practice psychiatry: Family history of physical and mental health. *Journal of Psychosomatic Research, 47,* 343–354.

Erkiran, M., Özünalan, H., Evren, C., Aytaçlar, S., Kirisci, L., & Tarter, R. (2006). Substance abuse amplifies the risk for violence in schizophrenia spectrum disorder. *Addictive Behaviors, 31,* 1797–1805.

Ernst, C., Földényi, M., & Angst, J. (1993). The Zurich Study: XXI. Sexual dysfunctions and disturbances in young adults. *European Archives of Psychiatry and Clinical Neuroscience, 243,* 179–188.

ESEMed/MHEDEA 2000 Investigators. (2004). Prevalence of mental disorders in Europe: Results from the European Study of the Epidemiology of Mental Disorders (ESEMeD). *Acta Psychiatrica Scandinavia, 109 (Suppl 420),* 21–27.

Essau, C. A., Conradt, J., & Peterman, F. (1999). Frequency of panic attacks and panic disorder in adolescents. *Depression and Anxiety, 9,* 10–26.

Essau, C. A., Conradt, J., & Peterman, F. (2000). Frequency, comorbidity and psychosocial impairment of specific phobia in adolescents. *Journal of Clinical Child Psychology, 29,* 221–231.

Essau, C. A., Conradt, J., & Petermann, F. (2000). Frequency, comorbidity, and psychosocial impairment of anxiety disorders in German adolescents. *Journal of Anxiety Disorders, 14,* 263–279.

Evans, J. D., Heaton, R. K., Paulsen, J. S., McAdams, L. A., Heaton, S. C., & Jeste, D. V. (1999). Schizoaffective disorder: A form of schizophrenia or affective disorder. *Journal of Clinical Psychiatry, 60,* 874–882.

Evans, J. D., Heaton, R. K., Paulsen, J. S., Palmer, B. W., Patterson, T., & Jeste, D. V. (2003). The relationship of neuropsychological abilities to specific domains of functional capacity in older schizophrenia patients. *Biological Psychiatry, 53,* 422–430.

Evans, J., Heron, J., Lewis, G., Araya, R., & Wolke, D. (2005). Negative self-schemas and the onset of depression in women: Longitudinal study. *British Journal of Psychiatry, 186,* 302–307.

Evengard, B., Jacks, A., Pedersen, N. L., & Sullivan, P. F. (2005). The epidemiology of chronic fatigue in the Swedish Twin Registry. *Psychological Medicine, 35,* 1317–1326.

Exner, J. E. (2005). "A Rorschach Workbook for the Comprehensive System." Paper presented at the Rorschach Workshops, Asheville, NC.

Eyler Zorrilla, L. T., Heaton, R. K., McAdams, L. A., Zisook, S., Harris, M. J., & Jeste, D. V. (2000). Cross-sectional study of older outpatients with schizophrenia and healthy comparison subjects: No differences in age-related cognitive decline. *American Journal of Psychiatry, 157,* 1324–1326.

Eysenck, H. J. (1991). Dimensions of personality: 16, 5, or 3?—Criteria for a taxonomic paradigm. *Personality and Individual Differences, 12,* 773–790.

Eysenck, H. J., & Eysenck, M. W. (1985). *Personality and individual differences: A natural science approach.* New York: Plenum.

Fagan, P. J., Wise, T. N., Schmidt, C. W., Jr., & Berlin, F. S. (2002). Pedophilia. *Journal of the American Medical Association, 288,* 2458–2465.

Fairbrother, N. (2002). The treatment of social phobia—100 years ago. *Behaviour Research and Therapy, 40,* 1291–1305.

Fairburn, C. G. (1981). A cognitive-behavioural approach to the treatment of bulimia. *Psychological Medicine, 11,* 707–711.

Fairburn, C. G. (1993). Interpersonal psychotherapy for bulimia nervosa. In G. Klerman & M. Weissman (Eds.), *New applications of interpersonal psychotherapy* (pp. 355–378). Washington, DC: American Psychiatric Press.

Fairburn, C. G., & Walsh, B. (2002). Atypical eating disorders (eating disorders not otherwise specified). In C. Fairburn & K. Brownell (Eds.), *Eating disorders and obesity: A comprehensive handbook,* (2nd ed., pp. 171–177). New York: Guilford Press.

Fairburn, C. G., Cooper, Z., Doll, H. A., Norman, P., & O'Connor, M. (2000). The natural course of bulimia nervosa and binge eating disorder in young women. *Archives of General Psychiatry, 57,* 659–665.

Fairburn, C. G., Jones, R., Peveler, R. C., Carr, S. J., Solomon, R. A., O'Connor, M. E., et al. (1991). Three psychological treatments for bulimia nervosa: A comparative trial. *Archives of General Psychiatry, 48,* 463–469.

Fairburn, C. G., Welch, S. L., & Hay, P. J. (1993). The classification of recurrent overeating: The "binge eating disorder" proposal. *International Journal of Eating Disorders, 13,* 155–159.

Fairburn, C. G., Welch, S. L., Doll, H. A., Davies, B. A., & O'Connor, M. E. (1997). Risk factors for bulimia nervosa: A community-based case-control study. *Archives of General Psychiatry, 54,* 509–517.

Fairburn, C., Jones, R., Peveler, R., Hope, R., & O'Connor, M. (1993). Psychotherapy and bulimia nervosa: Longer-term effects of interpersonal psychotherapy, behavior therapy, and cognitive-behavioral therapy. *Archives of General Psychiatry, 50,* 419–428.

Faison, W. E., & Armstrong, D. (2003). Cultural aspects of psychosis in the elderly. *Journal of Geriatric Psychiatry and Neurology, 16,* 225–231.

Faraone, S. V., Perlis, R. H., Doyle, A. E., Smoller, J. W., Goralnick, J. J., Holmgren, M. A., & Sklar, P. (2005). Molecular genetics of attention-deficit/hyperactivity disorder. *Biological Psychiatry, 57,* 1313–1323.

Faravelli, C., & Pallanti, S. (1989). Recent life events and panic disorder. *American Journal of Psychiatry, 146,* 622–626.

Faravelli, C., Salvatori, S., Galassi, F., Aiazzi, L., Drei, C., & Cabras, P. (1997). Epidemiology of somatoform disorders: A community survey in Florence. *Social Psychiatry and Psychiatric Epidemiology, 32,* 24–29.

Farmer, E. M., Compton, S. N., Burns, B. J., & Robertson, E. (2002). Review of the evidence base for treatment of childhood psychopathology: Externalizing disorders. *Journal of Consulting and Clinical Psychology, 70,* 1267–1302.

Farr, C. B. (1994). Benjamin Rush and American Psychiatry. *American Journal of Psychiatry, 151,* 65–73.

Farrer, L. A., Cupples, L. A., Haines, J. L., Hyman, B., Kukull, W. A., Mayeux, R. et al. (1997). Effects of age, sex, and ethnicity on the association between apolipoprotein E genotype and Alzheimer disease. A meta-analysis. APOE and Alzheimer Disease Meta Analysis Consortium. *Journal of the American Medical Association, 278,* 1349–1356.

Fassino, S., Amianto, F., Gramaglia, C., Facchini, F., & Abbate Daga, G. (2004). Temperament and character in eating disorders: Ten years of studies. *Eating and Weight Disorders, 9,* 81–90.

Fatemi, S. H., Emamian, E. S., Kist, D., Sidwell, R. W., Nakajima, K., Akhter, P., et al. (1999). Defective corticogenesis and reduction in immunoreactivity in cortex and hippocampus of prenatally infected neonatal mice. *Molecular Psychiatry, 4,* 145–154.

Fava, G. A., Bartolucci, G., Rafanelli, C., & Mangelli, L. (2001). Cognitive-behavioral management of patients with bipolar disorder who relapsed while on lithium prophylaxis. *Journal of Clinical Psychiatry, 62,* 556–559.

Fava, G. A., Grandi, S., Rafanelli, C., Ruini, C., Conti, S., & Belluardo, P. (2001). Long-term outcome of social phobia treated by exposure. *Psychological Medicine, 31,* 899–905.

Federoff, J. P., Fishell, A., & Federoff, B. (1999). A case series of women evaluated for paraphilic sexual disorders. *Canadian Journal of Human Sexuality, 8,* 127–140.

Fein, G., & Calloway, E. (1993). Electroencephalograms and event-related potentials in clinical psychiatry. In D. L. Dunner (Ed.), *Current Psychiatric Therapy* (pp. 18–26). Philadelphia: W. B. Saunders.

Felder, C., Dickason-Chesterfield, A., & Moore, S. (2006). Cannabinoids biology: The search for new therapeutic targets. *Molecular Interventions, 6,* 149–161.

Feldman, H. A., Goldstein, I., Hatzichristou, D. G., Krane, R. J., & McKinlay, J. B. (1994). Impotence and its medical and psychosocial correlates: Results of the Massachusetts Male Aging Study. *Journal of Urology, 151,* 54–61.

Fenton, W. S., & McGlashan, T. H. (1991). Natural history of schizophrenia subtypes: II. Positive and negative symptoms and long term course. *Archives of General Psychiatry, 48,* 978–986.

Fenton, W. S., Blyler, C. R., & Heinssen, R. K. (1997). Determinants of medication compliance in schizophrenia: Empirical and clinical findings. *Schizophrenia Bulletin, 23,* 637–651.

Ferber, R. (1985). *Solve your child's sleep problems.* New York: Simon & Schuster.

Ferguson, J. M. (2001). The effects of antidepressants on sexual functioning in depressed patients: A review. *Journal of Clinical Psychiatry, 62 (supplement 3),* 22–34.

Fergusson, D. M., Horwood, L. J., & Shannon, F. T. (1990). Secondary enuresis in a birth cohort of New Zealand children. *Pediatrics and Perinatal Epidemiology, 4,* 53–63.

Fichter, M., & Quadflieg, N. (1997). Six-year course of bulimia nervosa. *International Journal of Eating Disorders, 22,* 361–384.

Fichter, M. M., Quadflieg, N., & Brandl, B. (1993). Recurrent overeating: An empirical comparison of binge eating disorder, bulimia nervosa, and obesity. *International Journal of Eating Disorders, 14,* 1–16.

Fichter, M. M., Quadflieg, N., & Gnutzmann, A. (1998). Binge eating disorder: Treatment outcome over a 6-year course. *Journal of Psychosomatic Research, 44*, 385–405.

Finkenbine, R., & Miele, V. J. (2004). Globus hystericus: A brief review. *General Hospital Psychiatry, 26*, 78–82.

Fiore, M. (2000). Treating tobacco use and dependence: an introduction to the US Public Health Service Clinical Practice Guideline. *Respiratory Care, 45*, 1196–1199.

Fisher, C. B., Hoagwood, K., Boyce, C., Duster, T., Frank, D. A., Grisso, T., Levine, R. J., Macklin, R., Spencer, M. B., Takanishi, R., Trimble, J. E., & Zayas, L. H. (2002). Research ethics for mental health science involving ethnic minority children and youths. *American Psychologist, 57*, 1024–1040.

Fisher, E. B., Brownson, R. C., Heath, A. C., Luke, D. A., & Summer II, W. (2004). Cigarette smoking. In T. J. Boll, J. M. Raczynski, & L. C. Leviton (Eds.), *Handbook of Clinical Health Psychology* (pp. 75–120). Washington, DC: American Psychological Association

Fisher, R. A., (1936) Has Mendel's work been rediscovered? *Annals of Science, 1*, 115–137.

Fisher, R. L., & Fisher, S. (1996). Antidepresssants for children. Is scientific support necessary? *Journal of Nervous and Mental Disease, 184*, 99–102.

Fitzgerald, P. B., deCastella, A. R., Filia, K. M., Filia, S. L., Benitez, J., & Kulkarni, J. (2005). Victimization of patients with schizophrenia and related disorders. *Australian and New Zealand Journal of Psychiatry, 39*, 169–174.

Flament, M. F., Whitaker, A., Rapoport, J. L., Davies, M., Zaemba Berg, C., Kalikow, K., Sceery, W., & Shaffer, D. (1988). Obsessive compulsive disorder in adolescence: An epidemiological study. *Journal of the American Academy of Child and Adolescent Psychiatry, 27*, 74–771.

Flavell, J. H., Flavell, E. R., & Green, F. L. (2001). Development of children's understanding of connections between thinking and feeling. *Psychological Science, 12*, 430–432.

Flavell, J. H., Green, F. L., Flavell, E. R., & Grossman, J. B. (1997). The development of children's knowledge about inner speech. *Child Development, 68*, 39–47.

Fleischhacker, W. W., & Widschwendter, C. G. (2006). Treatment of schizophrenia patients: comparing new-generation antipsychotics to each other. *Current Opinions in Psychiatry, 19*, 128–134.

Fleming, M. F., Manwell, L. B., Barry, K. L., Adams, W., & Stauffacher, E. A. (1999). Brief physician advice for alcohol problems in older adults: A randomized community-based trial. *The Journal of Family Practice, 48*, 378–384.

Flint, A. J. (2004). Anxiety disorders. In J.Sadavoy, L. F. Jarvik, G. T. Grossberg, & B. S. Meyers (Eds.), *Comprehensive textbook of geriatric psychiatry* (3rd ed., pp. 687–699). New York: W.W. Norton & Co.

Flint, J. (2002). Genetic effects on an animal model of anxiety. *FEBS Letters, 529*, 131–134.

Foley, D. L., Pickles, A., Maes, H. M., Silberg, J. L., & Eaves, L. J. (2004). Course and short-term outcomes of separation anxiety disorder in a community sample of twins. *Journal of the American Academy of Child and Adolescent Psychiatry, 43*, 452–460.

Folstein, M. F., Bassett, S. S., Romanoski, A. J., & Nestadt, G. (1991). The epidemiology of delirium in the community: The Eastern Baltimore Mental Health Survey. *International Psychogeriatrics, 3*, 169–176.

Folstein, S. E., & Rosen-Sheidley, B. (2001). Genetics of autism: Complex aetiology for a heterogeneous disorder. *Nature Reviews Genetics, 2*, 943–955.

Fombonne, E. (2005). The changing epidemiology of autism. *Journal of Applied Research in Intellectual Disabilities, 18*, 281–294.

Fonagy, P., Steele, M., & Moran, G. (1991). The capacity for understanding mental states: The reflective self in parent and child and its significance for security of attachment. *Infant Mental Health Journal, 12*, 200–217.

Foote, B., Smolin, Y., Kaplan, M., Legatt, M. E., & Lipschitz, D. (2006). Prevalence of dissociative disorders in psychiatric outpatients. *American Journal of Psychiatry, 163*, 623–629.

Ford, C. V. (2005). Deception syndrome: Factitious disorders and malingering. In J. L. Levenson (Ed.), *The American psychiatric publishing textbook of psychosomatic medicine* (pp. 297–309). Washington, DC: American Psychiatric Press.

Forsythe, W. I., & Redmond, A. (1974). Enuresis and spontaneous cure rate: Study of 1129 enuretics. *Archives of Disorders in Childhood, 49*, 259.

Fortuna, L., Perez, D., Canino, G., Sribney, W., & Alegria, M. (2007). Prevalence and correlates of lifetime suicidal ideation and attempts among Latino subgroups in the United States. *Journal of Clinical Psychiatry, 68*, 572–581.

Foxman, B., Valdez, R. B., & Brook, R. H. (1986). Childhood enuresis: Prevalence, perceived impact, and prescribed treatments. *Pediatrics, 77*, 482–487.

Foxx, R. M., & Martin, E. D. (1975). Treatment of scavenging behavior (coprophagy and pica) by overcorrection. *Behaviour Research and Therapy, 13*, 153–162.

Franco, K., Litaker, D., Locala, J., & Bronson, D. (2001). The cost of delirium in the surgical patient. *Psychosomatics, 42*, 68–73.

Frank, E., Hlastala, S., Ritenour, A., Houck, P., Tu, X. M., Monk, T. H., et al. (1997). Inducing lifestyle regularity in recovering bipolar disorder patients: Results from the maintenance therapies in bipolar disorder protocol. *Biological Psychiatry, 41*, 1165–1173.

Frank, E., Kupfer, D. J., Thase, M. E., Mallinger, A. G., Swartz, H. A., Fagiolini, A. M., et al. (2005). Two-year outcomes for interpersonal and social rhythm therapy in individuals with bipolar I disorder. *Archives of General Psychiatry, 62*, 996–1004.

Frank, E., Kupfer, D. J., Wagner, E. F., McEachran, A. B., & Corner, C. (1991). Efficacy of interpersonal psychotherapy as a maintenance treatment of recurrent depression: Contributing factors. *Archives of General Psychiatry, 48*, 1053–1059.

Frank, E., Swartz, H. A., Mallinger, A. G., Thase, M. E., Weaver, E. V., & Kupfer, D. J. (1999). Adjunctive psychotherapy for bipolar disorder: Effects of changing treatment modality. *Journal of Abnormal Psychology, 108*, 579–587.

Frank, G. K., Bailer, U. F., Henry, S. E., Drevets, W., Meltzer, C. C., Price, J. C., et al. (2005). Increased dopamine D2/D3 receptor binding after recovery from anorexia nervosa measured by positron emission tomography and raclopride. *Biological Psychiatry, 58*, 908–912.

Frary, C., Johnson, R., & Wang, M. (2005). Food sources and intakes of caffeine in the diets of persons in the United States. *Journal of the American Dietetic Association, 105*, 110–113.

Frattola, L., Piolti, R., Bassi, S., Albizzati, M. G., Cesana, B. M., Bottani, M. S., et al. (1992). Effects of alpidem in anxious elderly outpatients: A double-blind, placebo-controlled trial. *Clinical Neuropharmacology, 15*, 477–487.

Freeman, A. M. (2002). Cognitive-behavioral therapy for severe personality disorders. In S. G. Hofman & M. Tompson (Eds.), *Treating chronic and severe mental disorders: A handbook of empirically supported interventions* (pp. 382–402). New York: Guilford Press.

Fremont, W. P. (2004). Childhood reactions to terrorism-induced trauma: A review of the past 10 years. *Journal of the American Academy of Child and Adolescent Psychiatry, 43*, 381–392.

Freud, S. (1917). Mourning and melancholia. In J. Strachey & A. Freud (Eds.), *The standard edition of the complete psychological works of Sigmund Freud, 1953–1974* (Vol. 14, p. 248). London: Hogarth Press.

Fridell, S. R., Owen-Anderson, A., Johnson, L. L., Bradley, S. J., & Zucker, K. J. (2006). The playmate and play style preferences structured interview: A comparison of children with gender identity disorder and controls. *Archives of Sexual Behavior, 35*, 729–737.

Friedl, M. C., & Draijer, N. (2000). Dissociative disorders in Dutch psychiatric inpatients. *American Journal of Psychiatry, 157*, 1012–1013.

Friedman, M., & Rosenman, R. H. (1974). *Type A behavior and your heart*. New York: Alfred A. Knopf.

Friedman, S., Hatch, M., Paradis, C. M., Popkin, M., & Shalita, A. R. (1995). Obsessive compulsive disorders in two black ethnic groups: Incidence in an urban dermatology clinic. *Journal of Anxiety Disorders, 7*, 343–348.

Frierson, R. L. (1991). Suicide attempts by the old and the very old. *Archives of Internal Medicine, 151*, 141–144.

Froguel, P. (1998). The genetics of complex traits: From diabetes mellitus to obesity. *Pathologie Biologie (Paris), 46*, 713–714.

Frohlich, P., & Meston, C. (2002). Sexual functioning and self–reported depressive symptoms among college women. *Journal of Sex Research, 39*, 321–325.

Fugl-Meyer, A. R., & Sjögren Fugl-Meyer, K. (1999). Sexual disabilities, problems and satisfaction in 18–74 year old Swedes. *Scandinavian Journal of Sexology, 2*, 79–105.

Fyer, A. J., Mannuzza, S., Gallops, M. S., Martin, L. Y, Aaronson, C., Gorman, J. M., Liebowitz, M. R., & Klein, D. E. (1990). Familial transmission of simple phobias and fears: A preliminary report. *Archives of General Psychiatry, 47*, 252–256.

Gaab, J., Engert, V., Heitz, V., Schad, T., Schürmeyer, T. H., & Ehlert, U. (2004). Associations between neuroendocrine responses to the Insulin Tolerance Test and patient characteristics in chronic fatigue syndrome. *Journal of Psychosomatic Research, 56,* 419–424.

Gallacher, J. E., Sweetnam, P. M., Yarnell, J. W., Elwood, P. C., & Stansfeld, S. A. (2003). Is type A behavior really a trigger for coronary heart disease events? *Psychosomatic Medicine, 65,* 339–346.

Gallagher-Thompson, D., Coon, D. W., Solano, N., Ambler, C., Rabinowitz, Y., & Thompson, L. W. (2003). Change in indices of distress among Latino and Anglo female caregivers of elderly relatives with dementia: site-specific results from the REACH national collaborative study. *Gerontologist, 43,* 580–591.

Gallagher-Thompson, D., Shurgot, G. R., Rider, K., Gray, H. L., McKibbin, C. L., Kraemer, H. C. et al. (2006). Ethnicity, stress, and cortisol function in Hispanic and non-Hispanic white women: A preliminary study of family dementia caregivers and noncaregivers. *American Journal of Geriatric Psychiatry, 14,* 334–342.

Gallo, D. A., & Finer, S. (2000). The power of a musical instrument: Franklin, the Mozarts, Mesmer, and the glass armonica. *History of Psychology, 3,* 326–343.

Gallo, J. J., Ryan, S. D., & Ford, D. E. (1999). Attitudes, knowledge, and behavior of family physicians regarding depression in late life. *Archives of Family Medicine, 8,* 249–256.

Gallo, L. C., & Matthews, K. A. (2003). Understanding the association between socioeconomic status and physical health: Do negative emotions play a role? *Psychological Bulletin, 129,* 10–51.

Ganzini, L., McFarland, B. H., & Cutler, D. (1990). Prevalence of mental disorders after catastrophic financial loss. *The Journal of Nervous and Mental Disease, 178,* 680–685.

Garattini, S. (1993). *Caffeine, coffee, and health.* New York: Raven Press.

Garb, H. N., Wood, J. M., Lilienfeld, S. O., & Nezworski, M. T. (2005). Roots of the Rorschach controversy. *Clinical Psychology Review, 25,* 97–118.

Garbutt, J., Kranzler, H., O'Malley, S., Gastfriend, D., Pettinati, H., Silverman, B., Loewy, J. W., Ehrich, E. W. and the Vivitrex Study Group. (2005). Efficacy and tolerability of long-acting injectable naltrexone for alcohol dependence: A randomized controlled trial. *Journal of the American Medical Association, 293,* 1617–1625.

Garbutt, J., West, S., Carey, T., Lohr, K., & Crews, F. (1999). Pharmacological treatment of alcohol dependence: a review of the evidence. *Journal of the American Medical Association, 281,* 1318–1325.

Gardner, W., Lidz, C. W., Mulvey, E. P., & Shaw, E. C. (1996). Clinical versus actuarial predictions of violence in patients with mental illness. *Journal of Consulting and Clinical Psychology, 64,* 602–609.

Gartlehner, G., Hansen, R. A., Carey, T. S., Lohr, K. N., Gaynes, B. N., & Randolph, L. C. (2005). Discontinuation rates for selective serotonin reuptake inhibitors and other second-generation antidepressants in outpatients with major depressive disorder: A systematic review and meta-analysis. *International Clinical Psychopharmacology, 20,* 59–69.

Gartner, J. (2005). *The hypomanic edge: The link between (a little) Craziness and (a Lot of) Success in America.* New York: Simon & Schuster.

Gatchel, R. J., & Maddrey, A. M. (2004). The biopsychosocial perspective of pain. In T. J. Boll, J. M. Raczynski, & L. C. Leviton (Eds.), *Handbook of clinical health psychology* (pp. 357–403). Washington,DC: American Psychological Association.

Gatz, M. (2000). Variations on depression in later life. In S. H. Qualls & N. Abeles (Eds.), *Psychology and the aging revolution: How we adapt to longer life.* Washington, DC: American Psychological Association.

Gaudiano, B. A. (2006). Is symptomatic improvement in clinical trials of cognitive-behavioral therapy for psychosis clinically significant? *Journal of Psychiatric Practice, 12,* 11–23.

Geldmacher, D. S., Provenzano, G., McRae, T., Mastey, V., & Ieni, J. R. (2003). Donezapil is associated with delayed nursing home placement in patients with Alzheimer's disease. *Journal of the American Geriatrics Society, 51,* 937–944.

Gelernter, J., Liu, X., Hesselbrock, V., Page, G., Goddard, A., & Zhang, H. (2004). Results of a genomewide linkage scan: Support for chromosomes 9 and 11 loci increasing risk for cigarette smoking. *American Journal of Medical Genetics B Neuropsychiatr Genetics, 128,* 94–101.

Geller, B., & Luby, J. (1997). Child and adolescent bipolar disorder: A review of the past 10 years. *Journal of the American Academy of Child and Adolescent Psychiatry, 36,* 1168–1176.

Geller, D., Biederman, J., Jones, J., Park, K., Schwartz, S., Shapiro, S., & Coffey, B. (1998). Is juvenile obsessive-compulsive disorder a developmental subtype of the disorder? *Journal of the American Academy of Child and Adolescent Psychiatry, 40,* 773–779.

Geller, J. L. (1992). An historical perspective on the role of state hospitals viewed from the "revolving door." *American Journal of Psychiatry, 149,* 1526–1535.

Geller, J. L., & Morrissey, J. P. (2004). Asylum within and without asylums. *Psychiatry Services, 55,* 1128–1130.

Gendall, K., Joyce, P., Carter, F., McIntosh, V. V., Jordan, J., & Bulik, C. (2006). The psychobiology and diagnostic significance of amenorrhea in patients with anorexia nervosa. *Fertility and Sterility, 85,* 1531–1535.

Gerald, C., Walker, M., Criscione, L., Gustafson, E., Batzl-Hartmann, C., Smith, K., et al. (1996). A receptor subtype involved in neuropeptide-Y-induced food intake. *Nature, 382,* 168–171.

Gerbasi, J. D., Bonnie, R. B., & Binder, R. L. (2000). Resource document on mandatory outpatient treatment. *Journal of the American Academy of Psychiatry and Law, 28,* 127–144.

Gibbons, L. E., Teri, L., Logsdon, R., McCurry, S. M., Kukull, W. A., Bowen, J. D., et al. (2002). Anxiety symptoms as predictors of nursing home placement in patients with Alzheimer's disease. *Journal of Clinical Geropsychology, 8,* 335–342.

Gijs, L., & Gooren, L. (1996). Hormonal and psychopharmacological interventions in the treatment of paraphilias: An update. *Journal of Sex Research, 33,* 273–290.

Giles, D. E., Dahl, R. E., & Coble, P. A. (1994). Childbearing, developmental, and familial aspects of sleep. In J. M. Oldham and M. B. Riba (Eds.), *Review of psychiatry* (pp. 621–650). Washington, DC: American Psychiatric Press.

Gillcrot, Y., Koulischer, L., Yasse, B., & Wetzburger, C. (1989). The geneticist and the so-called "socio cultural" familial mental retardation. *Journal de Génétique Humaine, 37,* 103–112.

Ginsberg, G. S., & Silverman, W. K. (1996). Phobic and anxiety disorders in Hispanic and Caucasian youth. *Journal of Anxiety Disorders, 10,* 517–528.

Gitlin, M. (2006). Treatment-resistant bipolar disorder. *Molecular Psychiatry, 11,* 227–240.

Gladstone, G., Parker, G., Mitchell, P., Wilhelm, K., & Malhi, G. (2005). Relationship between self-reported childhood behavioral inhibition and lifetime anxiety disorders in a clinical sample. *Depression & Anxiety, 22,* 103–113.

Glaister, B. (1985). A case of auditory hallucination treated by satiation. *Behaviour Research and Therapy, 23,* 213–215.

Glance, L. G., Wissler, R., Glantz, C., Osler, T. M., Mukamel, D. B., & Dick, A. W. (2007). Racial differences in the use of epidural analgesia for labor. *Anesthesiology, 106,* 19–25.

Glaser, R., Kiecolt-Glaser, J. K., Speicher, C. E., & Holliday, J. E. (1985). Stress, loneliness, and changes in herpesvirus latency. *Journal of Behavioral Medicine, 8,* 249–260.

Gleaves, D. H., May, M. C., & Cardeña, E. (2001). An examination of the diagnostic validity of dissociative identity disorder. *Clinical Psychology Review, 21,* 577–608.

Glick, I. D., Clarkin, J. F., Haas, G. L., & Spencer, J. H., Jr. (1993). Clinical significance of inpatient family intervention: Conclusions from a clinical trial. *Hospital and Community Psychiatry, 44,* 869–873.

Gochman, P. A., Greenstein, D., Sporn, A., Gogtay, N., Keller, B., Shaw, P., & Rapoport, .L. (2005). IQ stabilization in childhood-onset schizophrenia. *Schizophrenia Research, 77,* 271–277.

Godart, N., Flament, M., Perdereau, F., & Jeammet, P. (2002). Comorbidity between eating disorders and anxiety disorders: A review. *International Journal of Eating Disorders, 32,* 253–270.

Goisman, R. M., Warshaw, M. G., Peterson, L. G., Rogers, M. P., Cuneo, P., Hunt, M. E., et al. (1994). Panic, agoraphobia, and panic disorder with agoraphobia: Data from a multicenter anxiety disorders study. *Journal of Nervous and Mental Disease, 182,* 72–79.

Gokalp, P. G., Turkel, R., Solmaz, D., Demir, T., Kizillan, E., Demir, D., et al. (2001). Clinical factors and comorbidity of social phobics in Turkey. *European Psychiatry, 16,* 115–121.

Gold, L. (2005). American Psychiatric Association honors Dorothea Dix with first posthumous fellowship. *Psychiatric Services, 56,* 502.

Goldberg, D. P., & Hillier, V. F. (1979). A scaled version of the General Health Questionnaire. *Psychological Medicine, 9,* 139–145.

Goldberg, J. H., Breckenridge, J. N., & Sheikh, J. I. (2003). Age differences n symptoms of depression and anxiety: Examining behavioral medicine outpatients. *Journal of Behavioral Medicine, 26*, 119–132.

Goldberg, P. D., Peterson, B. D., Rosen, K. H., & Sara, M. L. (2008). Cybersex: The impact of a contemporary problem on the practices of marriage and family therapists. *Journal of Marital and Family Therapy, 34*, 469–480.

Golden, C. J., Purisch, A. D., & Hammeke, T. A. (1980). *The Luria-Nebraska Neuropsychological Battery: Manual (Revised Edition)*. Los Angeles: Western Psychological Services.

Goldstein, A. J., & Chambless, D. L. (1978). A reanalysis of agoraphobia. *Behavior Therapy, 9*, 47–59.

Goldstein, R. B., Dawson, D. A., Saha, T. D., Ruan, W. J., Compton, W. M., & Grant, B. F. (2007). Antisocial behavioral syndromes and DSM-IV alcohol use disorders: Results from the National Epidemiologic Survey on Alcohol and Related Conditions. *Alcoholism Clinical and Experimental Research, 31*, 814–828.

Goldston, D. B., Molock, S. D., Whitbeck, L. B., Murakami, J. L., Zayas, L. H., & Nagayama Hall, G. C. (2008). Cultural considerations in adolescent suicide prevention and psychosocial treatment. *American Psychologist, 63*, 14–31.

Gonzalez, H. M., Haan, M. N., & Hinton, L. (2001). Acculturation and the prevalence of depression in older Mexican Americans: Baseline results of the Sacramento Area Latino Study on Aging. *Journal of the American Geriatrics Society, 49*, 948–953.

Gonzalez, J. S., Penedo, F. J., Antoni, M. H., Duran, R. E., Pherson-Baker, S., Ironson, G. et al. (2004). Social support, positive states of mind, and HIV treatment adherence in men and women living with HIV/AIDS. *Health Psychology, 23*, 413–418.

Goodman, M., New, A. S., & Siever, L. J. (2004). Trauma, genes, and the neurobiology of personality disorders. *Annals of the New York Academy of Sciences, 1032*, 104–116.

Goodman, Y., Bruce, A. J., Cheng, B., & Mattson, M. P. (1996). Estrogens attenuate and corticosterone exacerbates excitotoxicity, oxidative injury and amyloid beat-peptide toxicity in hippocampal neurons. *Journal of Neurochemistry, 5*, 1836–1844.

Goodwin, J. L., Kaemingk, K. L., Fregosi, R. F., Rosen, G. M., Morgan, W. J., Smith, T., & Quan, S. F. (2004). Parasomnias and sleep disordered breathing in Caucasian and Hispanic children—The Tucson children's assessment of sleep apnea study. *Biomedcentral (BMC) Medicine, 2*, 14.

Gooren, L. (2006). The biology of human psychosexual differentiation. *Hormonal Behavior, 50*, 589–601.

Gottesman, I. I. (2001). Psychopathology through a life span-genetic prism. *American Psychologist, 56*, 867–878.

Gottfredson, L. S. (1997). Why g matters: The complexity of everyday life. *Intelligence, 24*, 79–132.

Gould, M. S. (1990). Teenage suicide clusters. *Journal of the American Medical Association, 263*, 2051–2052.

Gould, R., Buckminster, S., Pollack, M., Otto, M., & Yap, L. (1997). Cognitive-behavioral and pharmacological treatment for social phobia: A metaaanalysis. *Clinical Psychology: Science and Practice, 4*, 291–306.

Grabe, H. J., Meyer, C., Hapke, U., Rumpf, H. J., Freyberger, H. J., Dilling, H., & John, U. (2003). Specific somatoform disorder in the general population. *Psychosomatics, 44*, 304–311.

Graetz, B. W., Sawyer, M. G., Hazell, P. L., Arney, F., & Baghurst, P. (2001). Validity of DSM-IV ADHD subtypes in a nationally representative sample of Australian children and adolescents. *Journal of the American Academy of Child and Adolescent Psychiatry, 40*, 1410–1417.

Graham, J. R. (2000). *MMPI-2: Assessing personality and psychopathology* (3rd ed.). New York: Oxford University Press.

Graham, S., Furr, S., Flowers, C., & Burke, M. T. (2001). Religion and spirituality in coping with stress. *Counseling and Values, 46*, 2–13.

Grandin, L. D., Alloy, L. B., & Abramson, L. Y. (2006). The social zeitgeber theory, circadian rhythms, and mood disorders: Review and evaluation. *Clinical Psychology Review, 26*, 679–694.

Granholm, E., McQuaid, J. R., McClure, F. S., Auslander, L. A., Perivoliatis, D., Pedrelli, P., et al. (2005). A randomized, controlled trial of cognitive–behavioral social skills training for middle-aged and older outpatients with chronic schizophrenia. *American Journal of Psychiatry, 162*, 520–529.

Grant, B. F., Dawson, D. A., Stinson, F. S., Chou, S. P., Dufour, M. C., & Pickering, R. P. (2004). The 12-month prevalence and trends in DSM-IV alcohol abuse and dependence: United States, 1991–1992 and 2001–2002. *Drug and Alcohol Dependence, 74*, 223–234.

Grant, B. F., Hasin, D. S., Stinson, F. S., Dawson, D. A., Chou, S. P., Ruan, W. J., & Pickering, R. P. (2004). Prevalence, correlates, and disability of personality disorders in the United States: results from the national epidemiologic survey on alcohol and related conditions. *Journal of Clinical Psychiatry, 65*, 948–958.

Grant, B. F., Hasin, D. S., Stinson, F. S., Dawson, D. A., Patricia Chou, S., June Ruan, W., & Huang, B. (2005). Co-occurrence of 12-month mood and anxiety disorders and personality disorders in the US: results from the national epidemiologic survey on alcohol and related conditions. *Journal of Psychiatric Research, 39*, 1–9.

Grant, B. F., Stinson, F. S., Hasin, D. S., Dawson, D. A., Chou, S. P., Ruan, W. J., et al. (2005). Prevalence, correlates, and comorbidity of bipolar I disorder and axis I and II disorders: Results from the National Epidemiologic Survey on Alcohol and Related Conditions. *Journal of Clinical Psychiatry, 66*, 1205–1215.

Grant, B., Dawson, D., Stinson, F., Chou, S., Dufour, M., & Pickering, R. (2004). The 12-month prevalence and trends in DSM-IV alcohol abuse and dependence: United States, 1991–1992 and 2001–2002. *Drug and Alcohol Dependence, 74*, 223–234.

Gray, R., Parr, A. M., & Robson, D. (2005). Has tardive dyskinesia disappeared? *Mental Health Practice, 8*, 20–22.

Green, M. F. (1996). What are the functional consequences of neurocognitive deficits in schizophrenia? *American Journal of Psychiatry, 153*, 321–330.

Green, M. F., Nuechterlein, K. H., Gold, J. M., Barch, D. M., Coehen, J., Essock, S., et al. (2004). Approaching a consensus battery for clinical trials in schizophrenia: The NIMH-MATRICS conference to select cognitive domains and test criteria. *Biological Psychiatry, 56*, 30–307.

Green, R. (1987). *The "Sissy Boy Syndrome" and the development of homosexuality*. New Haven, CT: Yale University Press.

Green, R., & Money, J. (1969). *Transsexualism and sex reassignment*. Baltimore, MD: Johns Hopkins University Press.

Greenberg, B., Malone, D., Friehs, G., Rezai, A., Kubu, C., Malloy, P., et al. (2006). Three-year outcomes in deep brain stimulation for highly resistant obsessive-compulsive disorder. *Neuropsychopharmacology, 31*, 2384–2393.

Greenberg, P. E., Sisitsky, T., Kessler, R. C., Finkelstein, S. N., Berndt, E. R., Davidson, J. R., et al. (1999). The economic burden of anxiety disorders in the 1990's. *Journal of Clinical Psychiatry, 60*, 427–35.

Greene, R. W., Biederman, J., Faraone, S. V., Monuteaux, M. C., Mick, E., Fine, C. S., et al. (2001). Social impairment in girls with ADHD: patterns, gender comparisons, and correlates. *Journal of the American Academy of Child and Adolescent Psychiatry, 40*, 704–710.

Greeven, A., van Balkom, A. J. L. M., Merkelbach, J. W., van Rood, Y. R., van Dyck, R., Wan der Does, A. J. W., et al. (2007). Cognitive behavior therapy and paroxetine in the treatment of hypochondriasis: A randomized controlled trial. *American Journal of Psychiatry, 164*, 91–99.

Gregory, R. J. (1999). *Foundations of intellectual assessment*. Needham Heights, MA: Allyn & Bacon.

Grenard, J., Ames, S., Pentz, M., & Sussman, S. (2006). Motivational interviewing with adolescents and young adults for drug-related problems. *International Journal of Adolescent Medical Health, 18*, 53–67.

Grenier, G., & Byers, E. S. (2001). Operationalizing premature or rapid ejaculation. *Journal of Sex Research, 38*, 369–378.

Grice, D. E., Halmi, K. A., Fichter, M. M., Strober, M., Woodside, D. B., Treasure, J. T., et al. (2002). Evidence for a susceptibility gene for anorexia nervosa on chromosome 1. *American Journal of Human Genetics, 70*, 787–792.

Grigsby, R. K., Thyer, B. A., Waller, R. J., & Johnston, G. A. Jr. (1999). Chalk eating in middle Georgia: A culture-bound syndrome of pica? *Southern Medical Journal, 92,* 190–192.

Grilo, C. M., & Masheb, R. M. (2000). Onset of dieting vs binge eating in outpatients with binge eating disorder. *International Journal of Obesity and Related Metabolic Disorders, 24,* 404–409.

Grob, G. N. (1994). *The mad man among us: A history of the care of America's mentally ill.* Cambridge, MA: Harvard University Press.

Grob, G. N. (1994). The history of the asylum revisited: Personal reflections. In M. S. Micale & R. Porter (Eds.), *Discovering the history of psychiatry* (pp. 260–281). New York: Oxford University Press.

Grootens, K. P., & Verkes, R. J. (2005). Emerging evidence for the use of atypical antipsychotics in borderline personality disorder. *Pharmacopsychiatry, 38,* 20–23.

Grove, W. M. (2005). Clinical versus statistical prediction: The contribution of Paul E. Meehl. *Journal of Clinical Psychology, 61,* 1233–1243.

Grove, W. M., Zald, D. H., Lebow, B. S., Snitz, B. E., & Nelson, C. (2000). Clinical versus mechanical prediction: A meta-analysis. *Psychological Assessment, 12,* 19–30.

Grucza, R., & Beirut, L. (2007). Co-occurring risk factors for alcohol dependence and habitual smoking: Update on findings from the Collaborative Study on the Genetics of Alcoholism. *Alcohol Research & Health, 29,* 172–177.

Grunhaus, L., Schreiber, S., Dolberg, O. T., Polak, D., & Dannon, P. N. (2003). A randomized controlled comparison of electroconvulsive therapy and repetitive transcranial magnetic stimulation in severe and resistant nonpsychotic major depression. *Biological Psychiatry, 53,* 324–331.

Grunseit, A., Richters, J., Crawford, J., Song., A., & Kippax, S. (2005). Stability and change in sexual practices among first-year Australian university students (1990–1999). *Archives of Sexual Behavior, 34,* 557–568.

Guarnaccia, P. J., De La Canela, V., & Carrillo, E. (1989). The multiple meanings of ataques de nervios in the Latino community. *Medical Anthropology, 11,* 47–62.

Guilleminault, C., Palombini, L., Pelayo, R., & Chervin, R. D. (2003). Sleepwalking and sleep terrors in prepubertal children: What triggers them? *Pediatrics, 111,* e17–e25.

Gull, W. W. (1874). Anorexia nervosa (apepsia hysterica, anorexia hysterica). *Transactions of the Clinical Society of London, 7,* 22–28.

Gum, A. M., Arean, P. A., Hunkeler, E., Tang, L., Katon, W., & Hitchcock, P., et al. (2004). Depression treatment preferences in older primary care patients. *The Gerontologist, 46,* 14–22.

Gunderson, J. (1984). *The borderline patient.* Washington, DC: American Psychiatric Press.

Gupta, A. R., & State, M. W. (2007). Recent advances in the genetics of autism. *Biological Psychiatry, 61,* 429–437.

Gur, R. C., Ragland, J. D., Moberg, P. J., Turner, T. H., Bilker, W. B., Kohler, C., et al. (2001). Computerized neurocognitive scanning: I. Methodology and validation in healthy people. *Neuropsychopharmacology, 25,* 766–776.

Gureje, O., Simon, G. E., Ustun, T. B., & Goldberg, D. P. (1997). Somatization in cross-cultural perspective: A World Health Organization study in primary care. *American Journal of Psychiatry, 154,* 989–995.

Gurland, B. J. (1980). *Handbook of mental health and aging.* Englewood Cliffs, NJ: Prentice-Hall.

Gurland, B. J. (2004). Epidemiology of psychiatric disorders. In J. Sadavoy, L. F. Jarvik, G. T. Grossberg, & B. S. Meyers (Eds.), *Comprehensive textbook of geriatric psychiatry* (3rd ed., pp. 3–37). New York: W.W. Norton & Co.

Gurvits, T. V., Shenton, M. E., Hokama, H., Hirokazu, O., Lasko, N. B., Gildertson, M. W., et al. (1996). Magnetic resonance imaging study of hippocampal volume in chronic, combat-related posttraumatic stress disorder. *Biological Psychiatry, 40,* 1091–1099.

Gurwitch, R. J., Kees, M., & Becker, S. M. (2002). In the face of tragedy: Placing children's reactions to trauma in a new context. *Cognitive and Behavioral Practice, 9,* 286–295.

Gustafson, K. E., & McNamara, J. R. (1987). Confidentiality with minor clients: Issues and guidelines for therapists. *Professional Psychology: Research and Practice, 18,* 503–508.

Haas, L. F. (1993). Benjamin Rush (1745–1813). *Journal of Neurology Neurosurgery and Psychiatry, 56,* 741.

Haas, L. F. (2001). Jean Martin Charcot (1825–93) and Jean Baptise Charcot (1867–1936). *Journal of Neurology Neurosurgery and Psychiatry, 71,* 524.

Haas, L. F. (2003). August von Wassermann (1866–1925). *Journal of Neurology Neurosurgery and Psychiatry, 74,* 1104.

Hagedoorn, M., Kuijer, R. G., Buunk, B. P., DeJong, G. M., Wobbes, T., & Sanderman, R. (2000). Marital satisfaction in patients with cancer: Does support from intimate partners benefit those who need it the most? *Health Psychology, 19,* 274–282.

Hakala, M., Karlsson, H., Kurki, T., Aalto, S., Koponen, S., Vahlberg, et al. (2004). Volumes of the caudate nuclei in women with somatization disorder and healthy women. *Psychiatry Research: Neuroimaging, 131,* 71–78.

Hall, A., & Hay, P. J. (1991). Eating disorder patient referrals from a population region 1977–1986. *Psychological Medicine, 21,* 697–701.

Hall, W. D. (2006). How have the SSRI antidepressants affected suicide risk? *Lancet, 367,* 1959–1962.

Halmi, K., Eckert, E., Marchi, P., Sampugnaro, V., Apple, R., & Cohen, J. (1991). Comorbidity of psychiatric diagnoses in anorexia nervosa. *Archives of General Psychiatry, 48,* 712–718.

Handen, B. L., & Gilchrist, R. (2006). Practitioner review: Psychopharmacology in children and adolescents with mental retardation. *Journal of Child Psychology and Psychiatry, 47,* 871–882.

Haney, M., Ward, A., Comer, S., Foltin, R., & Fischman, M. (1999). Abstinence symptoms following smoked marijuana in humans. *Psychopharmacology, 141,* 395–404.

Hanna, G. H. (2000). Clinical and family-genetic studies of childhood obsessive-compulsive disorder. In W. K. Goodman, M. V. Rudofer, and J. D. Maser (Eds.), *Obsessive-compulsive disorder: Contemporary issues in treatment* (pp. 87–103). Mahwah, NJ: Lawrence Erlbaum Associates.

Hansen, C. J., Stevens, L. C., & Coast, J. R. (2001). Exercise duration and mood state: How much is enough to feel better? *Health Psychology, 20,* 267–275.

Hansen, R. A., Gartlehner, G., Lohr, K. N., Gaynes, B. N., & Carey, T. S. (2005). Efficacy and safety of second-generation antidepressants in the treatment of major depressive disorder. *Annals of Internal Medicine, 143,* 415–426.

Hanson, R. K., & Slater, S. (1988). Sexual victimization in the history of sexual abuses: A review. *Annals of Sex Research, 1,* 485–499.

Hanssen, M., Bak, M., Bijl, R., Vollebergh, W., & van Os, J. (2005). The incidence and outcome of subclinical psychotic experiences in the general population. *British Journal of Clinical Psychology, 44,* 181–191.

Harasty, J., Couble, K. L., Hallliday, G.M., Kril, J. J., & McRitchie, D. A. (1997). Language-associated cortical regions are proportionally larger in the female brain. *Archives of Neurology, 54,* 171–176.

Hare, R. D., Hart, S. D., & Harpur, T. J. (1991). Psychopathy and the DSM-IV criteria for antisocial personality disorder. *Journal of Abnormal Psychology, 100,* 391–398.

Harris, M. G., Henry, L. P., Harrigan, S. M., Purcell, R., Schwartz, O. S., Farrelly, S. E., et al. (2005). The relationship between duration of untreated psychosis and outcome: An eight-year prospective study. *Schizophrenia Research, 70,* 85–93.

Harris, M. J., & Jeste, D. V. (1988). Late-onset schizophrenia: An overview. *Schizophrenia Bulletin, 14,* 39–45.

Harrison, P. J., & Owen, M. J. (2003). Genes for schizophrenia: Recent findings and their pathophysiological implications. *The Lancet, 361,* 417–419.

Hartung, C. M., Willcutt, E. G., Lahey, B. B., Pelham, W. E., Loney, J., Stein, M. A., & Keenan, K. (2002). Sex differences in young children who meet criteria for attention deficit hyperactivity disorder. *Journal of Clinical Child and Adolescent Psychology, 31,* 453–464.

Hartwell, C. E. (1996). The schizophrenogenic mother concept in American psychiatry. *Psychiatry, 59,* 274–297.

Hasin, D., Grant, B., & Endicott, J. (1990). The natural history of alcohol abuse: Implications for definitions of alcohol use disorders. *American Journal of Psychiatry, 147,* 1537–1541.

Hatfield, E., Cacioppo, J. T., & Rapson, R. L. (1993). Emotional contagion. *Psychological Science, 2,* 96–99.

Haugaard, J. J. (2004). Recognizing and treating uncommon behavioral and emotional disorders in children and adolescents who have been severely maltreated: Somatization and other somatoform disorders. *Child Maltreatment, 9,* 169–176.

Hawkley, L. C., & Cacioppo, J. T. (2003). Loneliness and pathways to disease. *Brain Behavior, Immunity, Suppl. 1,* S98–105.

Hawton, K. (1995). Treatment of sexual dysfunctions by sex therapy and other approaches. *The British Journal of Psychiatry, 167,* 307–314.

Hayden, E. P., & Nurnberger, J. I., Jr. (2006). Molecular genetics of bipolar disorder. *Genes Brain and Behavior, 5*, 85–95.

Haynes, S. N., Keuthen, N. J., Wagener, P. D., & Stanley, M. A. (2006). *Principles and practice of behavioral assessment.* New York: Kluwer Academic/Plenum Press.

Hayward, C., Killen J. D., Kraemer, H. C., & Taylor, C. B., 2000, Predictors of panic attacks in adolescents, *Journal of the American Academy of Child and Adolescent Psychiatry, 39*, 1–8.

Hayward, C., Killen, J., Kraemer, H., & Taylor, C. (1998). Linking self-reported childhood behavioral inhibition to adolescent social phobia. *Journal of the American Academy of Child and Adolescent Psychiatry, 37*, 1308–1316.

Heathcote, A., Popiel, S. J., & Mewhort, D. J. K. (1991). Analysis of response time distributions: An example using the Stroop Task. *Psychological Bulletin, 109*, 340–347.

Heather, N. (1995). The great controlled drinking consensus: Is it premature? *Addiction, 90*, 1160–1163.

Heaton, R. (2003). Computerized Wisconsin Card Sort Task Version 4: Psychological Assessment Resources. Lutz, FL.

Hechtman, L., & Greenfield, B. (2003). Long-term use of stimulants in children with attention deficit hyperactivity disorder. *Paediatric Drugs, 5*, 787–794.

Heckman, T. G., Anderson, E. S., Sikkema, K. J., Kochman, A., Kalichman, S. C., & Anderson, T. (2004). Emotional distress in nonmetropolitan persons living with HIV disease enrolled in a telephone-delivered, coping improvement group intervention. *Health Psychology, 23*, 94–100.

Hegel, M. T., Ravaris, C. L., & Ahles, T. A. (1994). Combined cognitive-behavioral and time-limited alprazolam treatment of panic disorder. *Behavior Therapy, 25*, 183–195.

Heiby, E. M. (2002). Concluding remarks on the debate about prescription privileges for psychologists. *Journal of Clinical Psychology, 58*, 709–722.

Heim, C., & Nemeroff, C. (1999). The impact of early adverse experiences on brain systems involved in the pathophysiology of anxiety and affective disorders. *Biological Psychiatry, 46*, 1509–1522.

Heim, C., Ehlert, U., & Hellhammer, D. H. (2000). The potential role of hypocortisolism in the pathophysiology of stress-related bodily disorders. *Psychoneuroendocrinology, 25*, 1–35.

Heim, C., Newport, D. J., Heit, S., Graham, Y. P., Wilcox, M., Bonsall, R. et al. (2000). Pituitary-adrenal and autonomic responses to stress in women after sexual and physical abuse in childhood. *Journal of the American Medical Association, 284*, 592–597.

Heiman, J. R. (2002). Sexual dysfunction: Overview of prevalence, etiological factors, and treatments. *Journal of Sexual Research, 39*, 73–78.

Heiman, J., & LoPiccolo, J. (1987). *Become orgasmic: A sexual and personal growth program for women.* New York: Simon & Schuster.

Hellekson, K. L. (2001). NIH consensus statement on phenylketonuria. *American Family Physician, 63*, 1430–1432.

Henderson, B. N., & Baum, A. (2004). Neoplasms. In T. J. Boll, S. Bennett Johnson, N. W. Perry, & R. H. Rozensky (Eds.), *Handbook of clinical health psychology* (pp. 37–64). Washington, DC: American Psychological Association.

Henggeler, S. W., Rowland, M. D., Randall, J., Ward, D. M., Pickrel, S. G., Cunningham, P. B., et al. (1999). Home-based multisystemic therapy as an alternative to the hospitalization of youths in psychiatric crisis: Clinical outcomes. *Journal of Clinical Child Psychology, 38*, 1381–1389.

Henggeler, S. W., Schoenwald, S. K., Borduin, C. M., Rowland, M. D., & Cunningham, P. B. (1998). *Multisystemic treatment of antisocial behavior in children and adolescents.* New York: Guilford Press.

Henningsen, P., Jakobsen, T., Schiltenwolf, M., & Weiss, M. G. (2005). Somatization revisited: Diagnosis and perceived causes of common mental disorders. *The Journal of Nervous and Mental Disease, 193*, 85–92.

Hepp, U., Kraemer, B., Schnyder, U., Miller, N., & Delsignore, A. (2005). Psychiatric comorbidity in gender identity disorder. *Journal of Psychosomatic Research, 58*, 259–261.

Hepp, U., Wittmann, L., Schnyder, U., & Michel, K. (2004). Psychological and psychosocial interventions after attempted suicide: An overview of treatment studies. *Crisis, 25*, 108–117.

Herbert, J. D., Hope, D. A., & Bellack, A. S. (1992). Validity of the distinction between generalized social phobia and avoidant personality disorder. *Journal of Abnormal Psychology, 101*, 332–339.

Herbert, T. B., & Cohen, S. (1993). Depression and immunity: A meta-analytic review. *Psychological Bulletin, 113*, 472–486.

Herd, D., & Grube, J. (1996). Black identity and drinking in the US: A national study. *Addiction, 91*, 845–857.

Herek, G. M., Capitanio, J. P., & Widaman, K. F. (2003). Stigma, social risk, and health policy: Public attitudes toward HIV surveillance policies and the social construction of illness. *Health Psychology, 22*, 533–540.

Heres, S., Davis, J., Maino, K., Jetzinger, E., Kissling, W., & Leucht, S. (2006). Why olanzapine beats risperidone, risperidone beats quetiapine, and quetiapine beats olanzapine: An exploratory analysis of head-to-head comparison studies of second-generation antipsychotics. *American Journal of Psychiatry, 163*, 185–194.

Herman, J. L., Perry, J. C., & van der Kolk, B. A. (1989). Childhood trauma in borderline personality disorder. *American Journal of Psychiatry, 146*, 490–495.

Herpertz, S. C., Dietrich, T. M., Wenning, B., Krings, T., Erberich, S. G., Willmes, K., Thron, A., & Sass, H. (2001). Evidence of abnormal amygdala functioning in borderline personality disorder: A functional MRI study. *Biological Psychiatry, 50*, 292–298.

Herzog, D., Dorer, D., Keel, P. K., Selwyn, S., Ekeblad, E., Flores, A., et al. (1999). Recovery and relapse in anorexia and bulimia nervosa: a 7.5-year follow-up study. *Journal of the American Academy of Child and Adolescent Psychiatry, 38*, 829–837.

Hettema, J. M., Prescott, C. A., Myers, J. M., Neale, M. C., & Kendler, K. S. (2005). The structure of genetic and environmental risk factors for anxiety disorders in men and women. *Archives of General Psychiatry, 62*, 182–189.

Hettema, J., Prescott, C., & Kendler, K. (2001). A population-based twin study of generalized anxiety disorder in men and women. *Journal of Nervous and Mental Disease, 189*, 413–420.

Hibbard, S. (2003). A critique of Lilienfeld et al.'s (2000) "The scientific status of projective techniques." *Journal of Personality Assessment, 80*, 260–271.

Hickie, I., Kirk, K., & Martin, N. (1999). Unique genetic and environmental determinants of prolonged fatigue: A twin study. *Psychological Medicine, 29*, 259–268.

Hiday, V. A., Swartz, M. S., Swanson, J. W., Borum, R., & Wagner, H. R. (2002). Impact of outpatient commitment on victimization of people with severe mental illness. *American Journal of Psychiatry, 183*, 233–238.

Hill, E. L., & Frith, U. (2003). Understanding autism: Insights from mind and brain. *Philosophical Transactions of the Royal Society* B: *Biological Sciences, 358*, 281–289.

Hill, J. W., Futterman, R., Duttagupta, S., Mastey, V., Lloyd, J. R., & Fillit, H. (2002). Alzheimer's disease and related dementias increase costs of comorbidities in managed Medicare. *Neurology, 58*, 62–70.

Hill, M. L., Banks, P. D., Handrich, R. R., Wehman, P. H., Hill, J. W., & Shafer, M. S. (1987). Benefit-cost analysis of supported competitive employment for persons with mental retardation. *Research in Developmental Disabilities, 8*, 71–89.

Hill, T. D., Burdette, A. M., Angel, J. L., & Angel, R. J. (2006). Religious attendance and cognitive functioning among older Mexican Americans. *Journal of Gerontology B Psychological Scences and Social Sciences, 61*, 3–9.

Hillebrand, J. J., Koeners, M. P., de Rijke, C. E., Kas, M. J., & Adan, R. A. (2005). Leptin treatment in activity-based anorexia. *Biological Psychiatry, 58*, 165–171.

Hiller, W., Leibrand, R., Rief, W., & Fichter, M. M. (2002). Predictors of course and outcome in hypochondriasis after cognitive–behavioral treatment. *Psychotherapy and Psychosomatics, 71*, 318–325.

Himmelfarb, S., & Murrell, S. A. (1984). The prevalence and correlates of anxiety symptoms in older adults. *Journal of Psychology, 116*, 159–167.

Hines, M., Brook, C., & Conway, G. S. (2004). Androgen and psychosexual development: core gender identity, sexual orientation and recalled childhood gender role behavior in women and men with congenital adrenal hyperplasia (CAH). *Journal of Sex Research, 41*, 75–81.

Hinney, A., Ziegler, A., Nöthen, M., Remschmidt, H., & Hebebrand, J. (1997). 5-HT2a receptor gene polymorphisms, anorexia nervosa and obesity. *The Lancet, 350*, 1324–1325.

Hinshaw, S. P. (1994). Conduct disorder in childhood: conceptualization, diagnosis, comorbidity, and risk status for antisocial functioning in adulthood. *Progress in Experimental Personality & Psychopathology Research, 15*, 3–44.

Hirshfeld, D. R., Rosenbaum, J. F., Biederman, J., Bolduc, E. A., Faraone, S. V, Snidman, N., et al. (1992). Stable behavioral inhibition and its association with anxiety disorder. *Journal of the American Academy of Child and Adolescent Psychiatry, 31*, 301–311.

Hirshfeld, D. R., Rosenbaum, J. F., Biederman, J., Bolduc, E. A., Faraone, S. V., Snidman, N., et al. (1992). Stable behavioral inhibition and its relationship with anxiety disorders. *Journal of the American Academy of Child and Adolescent Psychiatry, 31,* 103–111.

Hodgins, S., Mednick, S. A., Brennan, P. A., Schulsinger, F., & Engberg, M. (1996). Mental disorder and crime: Evidence from a Danish birth cohort. *Archives of General Psychiatry, 53,* 489–496.

Hoek, H., & van Hoeken, D. (2003). Review of the prevalence and incidence of eating disorders. *International Journal of Eating Disorders, 34,* 383–396.

Hoek, H., Bartelds, A., Bosveld, J., van der Graaf, Y., Limpens, V., Maiwald, M., & Spaaij, C. (1995). Impact of urbanization on detection rates of eating disorders. *American Journal of Psychiatry, 152,* 1272–1278.

Hoffman, G. W., Ellinwood, E. H., Jr., Rockwell, W. J., Herfkens, R. J., Nishita, J. K., & Guthrie, L. F. (1989). Cerebral atrophy in bulimia. *Biological Psychiatry, 25,* 894–902.

Hoffman, M. D., & Hoffman, D. R. (2007). Does aerobic exercise improve pain perception and mood? A review of the evidence related to healthy and chronic pain subjects. *Current Pain and Headache Reports, 11,* 93–97.

Hoffman, R. E., Hawkins, K. A., Gueorguieva, R., Boutros, N. N., Rachid, F., Carroll, K., & Krystal, J. H. (2003). Transcranial magnetic stimulation of left temporoparietal cortex and medication-resistant auditory hallucinations. *Archives of General Psychiatry, 60,* 49–56.

Hoffman, R. E., Hawkins, K. A., Gueorguieva, R., Boutros, N. N., Rachid, F., Carroll, K., & Krystal, J. Y. H. (2006). Transcranial magnetic stimulation of left temporoparietal cortex and medication-resistant auditory hallucinations. *Archives of General Psychiatry, 60,* 49–56.

Hoge, C., Terhakopian, A., Castro, C., Messer, S., & Engel, C. (2007). Association of posttraumatic stress disorder with somatic symptoms, health care visits, and absenteeism among Iraq war veterans. *American Journal of Psychiatry, 164,* 150–153.

Hollander, E., Friedberg, J. P., Wasserman, S., Yeh, C. C., & Iyengar, S. (2005) The case for the OCD spectrum. In J. Abramowitz & A. C. Houts (Ed.), *Concepts and controversies in obsessive compulsive disorder* (pp. 95–118). New York: Springer Publishing.

Hollander, E., Phillips, A., Chaplin, W., Zagursky, K., Novotny, S., Wasserman, S., & Iyengar, R. (2005). A placebo controlled crossover trial of liquid fluoxetine on repetitive behaviors in childhood and adolescent autism. *Neuropsychopharmacology, 30,* 582–589.

Hollis, C. (2000). Adult outcomes of child- and adolescent-onset schizophrenia: Diagnostic stability and predictive validity. *American Journal of Psychiatry, 157,* 1652–1659.

Hollon, S. D., DeRubeis, R. J., Evans, M. D., Wiemer, M. J., Garvey, M. J., Grove, W. M., et al. (1992). Cognitive therapy and pharmacotherapy for depression: Singly and in combination. *Archives of General Psychiatry, 49,* 774–781.

Holmes, A. J., MacDonald, A., Career, C. S., Barch, D. M., Stenger, V. A., & Cohen, J. D. Prefrontal functioning during context processing in schizophrenia and major depression: An event-related fMRI study. *Schizophrenia Research, 76,* 199–206.

Holmes, E. A., Brown, R. J., Mansell, W., Fearon, R. P., Hunter, E. C., Frasquilho, F., et al. (2005). Are there two qualitatively distinct forms of dissociation? A review and some clinical implications. *Clinical Psychology Review, 25,* 1–23.

Holmes, T. H., & Rahe, R. H. (1967). The Social Readjustment Rating Scale. *Journal of Psychosomatic Research, 11,* 213–218.

Holmgren, P., Norden-Pettersson, L., & Ahlner, J. (2004). Caffeine fatalities—Four case reports. *Forensic Science International, 139,* 71–73.

Holt, C. S., Heimberg, R. G., & Hope, D. A. (1992). Avoidant personality disorder and the generalized subtype of social phobia. *Journal of Abnormal Psychology, 101,* 318–325.

Honda, H., Shimizu, Y., & Rutter, M. (2005). No effect of MMR withdrawal on the incidence of autism: A total population study. *Journal of Child Psychiatry and Psychology, 46,* 572–579.

Honig, A., Romme, M., Ensink, B., Escher, S. D., Pennings, M. H. A., Devries, M. W. (1998). Auditory hallucinations: A comparison between patients and nonpatients. *Journal of Nervous and Mental Disease, 186,* 646–651.

Honigman, R. J., Phillips, K. A., & Castle, D. J. (2004). A review of psychosocial outcomes for patients seeking cosmetic surgery. *Plastic and Reconstructive Surgery, 113,* 1229–1237.

Hope, D. A., Heimberg, R. G., & Bruch, M. A. (1995). Dismantling cognitive-behavioral therapy for social phobia. *Behaviour Research and Therapy, 33,* 637–650.

Hopfer, C., Mendelson, B., & Van Leeuwen, J. (2006). Club drug use among youths in treatment for substance abuse. *The American Journal on Addictions, 15,* 94–99.

Hopko, D. R., Lejuez, C. W., Ruggiero, K. J., & Eifert, G. H. (2003). Contemporary behavioral activation treatments for depression: Procedures, principles, and progress. *Clinical Psychology Review, 23,* 699–717.

Horacek, J., Cubenikova-Balesova, V., Kopecek, M., Palenicek, T., Dockery, C., Mohr, P., & Hoschl, C. (2006). Mechanism of action of atypical antipsychotic drugs and the neurobiology of schizophrenia. *CNS Drugs, 20,* 389–409.

Horner, A. (1974). Early object relations and the concept of depression. *International Journal of Psychoanalysis, 1,* 337–340.

Hornstein, N. L., & Putnam, F. W. (1992). Clinical phenomenology of child and adolescent dissociative disorders. *Journal of the American Academy of Child and Adolescent Psychiatry, 31,* 1077–1085.

Houy, E., Debono, B., Dechelotte, P., & Thibaut, F. (2007). Anorexia nervosa associated with right frontal brain lesion. *International Journal of Eating Disorders, 40,* 758–761.

Howard, M., Elkins, R., & Rimmele, C. (1991). Chemical aversion treatment of alcohol dependence. *Drug and Alcohol Dependence, 29,* 107–143.

Howard, R., Rabins, P. V., Seeman, M. V., & Jeste, D. V. (2000). Late-onset schizophrenia and very-late-onset schizophrenia-like psychosis: An international consensus. The International Late-Onset Schizophrenia Group. *American Journal of Psychiatry, 157,* 172–178.

Hser, Y., Huang, Y., Teruga, C., & Anglin, M. (2004). Gender differences in treatment outcomes over a three-year period: A path model analysis. *Journal of Drug Issues, 34,* 419–440.

Hsu, L. K., Rand, W., Sullivan, S., Liu, D. W., Mulliken, B., McDonagh, B., & Kaye, W. H. (2001). Cognitive therapy, nutritional therapy and their combination in the treatment of bulimia nervosa. *Psychological Medicine, 31,* 871–879.

Hucker, S., Langevin, R., Dickey, R., Handy, L., Chambers, J., Wright, S., et al. (1988). Cerebral damage and dysfunction in sexually aggressive men. *Annals of Sex Research, 1,* 33–47.

Hudson, J. I., Hiripi, E., Pope, H. G., & Kessler, R. C. (2006). The prevalence and correlates of eating disorders in the National Comorbidity Survey Replication. *Biological Psychiatry, 61,* 348–358.

Hudson, J. I., Pope, H. G., Jonas, J. M., Yurgelun-Todd, D., & Frankenburg, F. R. (1987). A controlled family history study of bulimia. *Psychological Medicine, 17,* 883–890.

Hudson, J., Lalonde, J., Pindyck, L., Bulik, C. M., Crow, S., McElroy, S., et al. (2006). Familial aggregation of binge-eating disorder. *Archives of General Psychiatry, 63,* 313–319.

Hudson, S., Ward, T., & Marshall, W. (1992). The abstinence violation effect in sexual offenders: A reformulation. *Behavior Research and Therapy, 30,* 435–441.

Hunt, G., & Azrin, N. (1973). A community-reinforcement approach to alcoholism. *Behaviour Research and Therapy, 11,* 91–104.

Hunter, E. C. M., Sierra, M., & David, A. S. (2004. The epidemiology of personalization and derealisation: A systematic review. *Social Psychiatry and Psychiatric Epidemiology, 39,* 9–18.

Hunter, E. C., Baker, D., Phillips, M. L., Sierra, M., & David, A. S. (2005). Cognitive-behaviour therapy for depersonalization disorder: An open study. *Behaviour Research and Therapy, 43,* 1121–1130.

Huppert, J. D., Strunk, D. R., Ledley, D. R., Davidson, J. R., & Foa, E. B. (2008). Generalized social anxiety disorder and avoidant personality disorder: Structural analysis and treatment outcome. *Depression and Anxiety, 25,* 441–448.

Hurwitz, T. A., & Prichard, J. W. (2006). Conversion disorder and fMRI. *Neurology, 67,* 1914–1915.

Husain, M. M., Rush, A. J., Fink, M., Knapp, R., Petrides, G., Rummans, T., et al. (2004). Speed of response and remission in major depressive disorder with acute electroconvulsive therapy (ECT): A Consortium for Research in ECT (CORE) report. *Journal of Clinical Psychiatry, 65,* 485–491.

Ickovics, J. R., Hamburger, M. E., Vlahov, D., Schoenbaum, E. E., Schuman, P., Boland, R. J., et al. (2001). Mortality, CD4 cell count decline, and depressive symptoms among HIV-seropositive women: Longitudinal analysis from the HIV Epidemiology Research Study. *Journal of the American Medical Association, 1466–1474.*

Ilott, R. (2005). Does compliance therapy improve use of antipsychotic medication? *British Journal of Community Nursing, 10,* 514–519.

Inouye, S. K., & Charpentier, P. A. (1996). Precipitating factors for delirium in hospitalized elderly persons. Predictive model and interrelationship with baseline vulnerability. *Journal of the American Medical Association, 275,* 852–857.

Inouye, S. K., Viscoli, C. M., Horwitz, R. I., Hurst, L. D., & Tinetti, M. E. (1993). A predictive model for delirium in hospitalized elderly medical patients based on admission characteristics. *Annals of Internal Medicine, 119,* 474–481.

Insel, T. R., & Winslow, J. T. (1992). Neurobiology of obsessive-compulsive disorder. *Psychiatric Clinics of North America, 15,* 813–824.

Inskip, H. M., Harris, E. C., & Barraclough, B. (1998). Lifetime risk of suicide for affective disorder, alcoholism, and schizophrenia. *British Journal of Psychiatry, 172,* 35–37.

International Society for the Study of Dissociation. (2005). Guidelines for treating dissociative identity disorder in adults. *Journal of Trauma & Dissociation, 6,* 69–149.

Ironson, G., Balbin, E., & Schneiderman, N. (2002). Health psychology and infectious diseases. In T. J. Boll, S. Bennett Johnson, & N. W. Perry (Eds.), *Handbook of clinical health psychology* (pp. 5–36). Washington, DC: American Psychological Association.

Irwin, M. R., Cole, J. C., & Nicassio, P. M. (2006). Comparative meta-analysis of behavioral interventions for insomnia and their efficacy in middle-aged adults and in older adults 55+ years of age. *Health Psychology, 25,* 3–14.

Isidori, A. M., Giannetta, E., Gianfrilli, D., Greco, E. A., Bonifacio, V., Aversa, A., et al. (2005). Effects of testosterone on sexual function in men: Results of a meta-analysis. *Clinical Endocrinology, 63,* 381–394.

Issenman, R. M., Filmer, R. B., & Gorski, P. A. (1999). A review of bowel and bladder control development in children: How gastrointestinal and urological conditions relate to problems in toilet training. *Pediatrics, 103,* 1346–1352.

Jablensky, A. (1989). Epidemiology and cross-cultural aspects of schizophrenia. *Psychiatric Annals, 19,* 516–524.

Jablensky, A. (2000). Epidemiology of schizophrenia: The global burden of disease and disability. *European Archives of Psychiatry & Clinical Neuroscience, 250,* 274–285.

Jackson-Triche, M. E., Greer Sullivan, J., Wells, K. B., Rogers, W., Camp, P., & Mazel, R. (2000). Depression and health-related quality of life in ethnic minorities seeking care in general medical settings. *Journal of Affective Disorders, 58,* 89–97.

Jacobson, N. S., & Truax, P. (1991). Clinical significance: A statistical approach to defining meaningful change in psychotherapy research. *Journal of Consulting and Clinical Psychology, 59,* 12–19.

Jalkut, M. W., Lerman, S. E., & Churchill, B. M. (2001). Enuresis. *Pediatric Urology, 48,* 1461–1488.

James, K. (1997). *Understanding caffeine: A biobehavioral analysis.* Thousand Oaks, CA: Sage Publications.

Jamison, K. (1993). *Touched with fire: Manic-depressive illness and the artistic temperament.* New York: Free Press/Macmillan.

Jamison, K. (1995). Manic-depressive illness and creativity. *Scientific American, 272,* 62–67.

Jang, K. L., Livesley, W. J., & Vernon, P. A. (1996). Heritability of the big five personality dimensions and their facets: A twin study. *Journal of Personality, 64,* 577–591.

Janicak, P. G., Dowd, S. M., Martis, B., Alam, D., Beedle, D., Krasuski, J., et al. (2002). Repetitive transcranial magnetic stimulation versus electroconvulsive therapy for major depression: Preliminary results of a randomized trial. *Biological Psychiatry, 51,* 659–667.

Jankowsi, K. (2006). PTSD and physical health. U.S. Department of Veterans Affairs, National Center for Post-Traumatic Stress Disorder [Online]. Available: http://www.ncptsd.va.gov/facts/specific/fs_physical_health.html

Jarvik, L., & Mintzer, J. (2000). Expert panel summary. Paper presented at Genetics, Response and Cognitive Enhancer: Implications for Alzheimer's Disease (GRACE), December 2003, Bethesda, MD.

Jenike, M. A., Baer, L., Minichiello, W. E., Schwartz, C. E., & Carey, R. J. (1986). Concomitant obsessive-compulsive disorder and schizotypal personality disorder. *American Journal of Psychiatry, 143,* 530–532.

Jenkins, E. J., & Bell, C. C. (1994). Violence among inner city high school students and posttraumatic stress disorder. In S. Friedman (Ed.), *Anxiety disorders in African Americans* (pp. 76–88). New York: Springer.

Jerrell, J., & Wilson, J. (1997). Ethnic differences in the treatment of dual mental and substance disorders. *Journal of Substance Abuse Treatment, 14,* 133–140.

Jeste, D. V., & Finkel, S. I. (2000). Psychosis of Alzheimer's disease and related dementias. Diagnostic criteria for a distinct syndrome. *American Journal of Geriatric Psychiatry, 8,* 29–34.

Jeste, D. V., Alexopoulos, G. S., Bartels, S. J., Cummings, J. L., Gallo, J. J., Gottlieb, G. L., Halpain, M. C., Palmer, B. W., Patterson, T. L., Reynolds, C. F. 3rd, & Lebowitz, B. D. (1999). Consensus statement on the upcoming crisis in geriatric mental health: Research agenda for the next 2 decades. *Archives of General Psychiatry, 56,* 848–853.

Jeste, D. V., Dunn, L. B., & Lindamer, L. A. (2004b). Psychoses. In J. Sadavoy, L. F. Jarvik, G. T. Grossberg, & B. S. Meyers (Eds.), *Comprehensive textbook of geriatric psychiatry* (3rd ed., pp. 655–685). New York: W.W. Norton & Co.

Jeste, D. V., Twamley, E. W., Eyler Zorrilla, L. T., Golshan, S., Patterson, T. L., & Palmer, B. W. (2003). Aging and outcome in schizophrenia. *Acta Psychiatrica Scandinavia, 107,* 336–343.

Jeste, D. V., Wetherell, J. L., & Dolder, C. R. (2004a). Schizophrenia and paranoid disorders. In D. G. Blazer, D. C. Steffens, & E. W. Busse (Eds.), *Textbook of geriatric psychiatry* (3rd ed., pp. 269–281). Washington, DC: American Psychiatric Publishing.

Jimerson, D. C., Wolfe, B. E., Metzger, E. D., Finkelstein, D. M., Cooper, T. B., & Levine, J. M. (1997). Decreased serotonin function in bulimia nervosa. *Archives of General Psychiatry, 54,* 529–534.

Joe, G., Simpson, D., & Broome, K. (1999). Retention and patient engagement models for different treatment modalities in DATOS. *Drug and Alcohol Dependence, 57,* 113–125.

Johns, L. C., & van Os, J. (2001). The continuity of psychotic experiences in the general population. *Clinical Psychology Review, 21,* 1125–1141.

Johnson, E. O., Roth, T., Schultz, L., & Breslau, N. (2006). Epidemiology of DSM–IV insomnia in adolescence: lifetime prevalence, chronicity, and an emergent gender difference. *Pediatrics, 117,* e247–e256.

Johnson, J. G., Cohen, P., Chen, H., Kasen, S., & Brook, J. S. (2006). Parenting behaviors associated with risk for offspring personality disorder during adulthood. *Archives of General Psychiatry, 63,* 579–587.

Johnson, J. G., Cohen, P., Kasen, S., & Brook, J. S. (2006). Dissociative disorders among adults in the community, impaired functioning, and axis I and II comorbidity. *Journal of Psychiatric Research, 40,* 131–140.

Jones, J. F., & Reeves, W. C. (2005). GBV-C-a virus without a disease: We cannot give it to chronic fatigue syndrome. *Biomedcentral (BMC) Infectious Diseases, 5,* 78.

Jones, K., & Smith, D. (1973). Recognition of the fetal alcohol syndrome in early infancy. *The Lancet, 2,* 999–1001.

Jones, P., Rodgers, B., Murray, R., & Mormot, M. (1994). Child development risk factors for adult schizophrenia in the British 1946 birth cohort. *The Lancet, 344,* 1398–1402.

Jones, T. F., Craig, A. S., Hoy, D., Gunter, E. W., Ashley, D. L., Barr, D. B., et al. (2000). Mass psychogenic illness attributed to toxic exposure at a high school. *New England Journal of Medicine, 342,* 96–100.

Josefsson, A., Larsson, C., Sydsjo, G., & Nylander, P. O. (2007). Temperament and character in women with postpartum depression. *Archive of Women's Mental Health, 10,* 3–7.

Joseph, R. (2000). The evolution of sex differences in language, sexuality, and visual-spatial skills. *Archives of Sexual Behavior, 29,* 35–66.

Judd, L. L., Akiskal, H. S., Maser, J. D., Zeller, P. J., Endicott, J., Coryell, W., et al. (1998). A prospective 12-year study of subsyndromal and syndromal depressive symptoms in unipolar major depressive disorders. *Archives of General Psychiatry, 55,* 694–700.

Junginger, J., Phelan, E., Cherry, K., & Levy, J. (1993). Prevalence of psychopathology in elderly persons in nursing homes and in the community. *Hospital and Community Psychiatry, 44,* 381–383.

Kabakçi, E., & Batur, S. (2003). Who benefits from cognitive behavioral therapy for vaginismus? *Journal of Sex & Marital Therapy, 29,* 277–288.

Kagan, J. (1982). Heart rate and heart rate variability as signs of a temperamental dimension in infants. In E. D. Izard (Ed.), *Measuring emotions in infants and children* (pp. 38–66). Cambridge, England: Cambridge University Press.

Kagan, J. (1994). *Galen's prophecy.* New York: Basic Books.

Kagan, J., Reznick, J. S., & Snidman, N. (1987). The physiology and psychology behavioral inhibition in children. *Child Development, 58,* 1459–1473.

Kaltenbach, K., Berghell, V., & Finnegan, L. (1998). Opioid dependence during pregnancy. *Obstetrics and Gynecology Clinics of North America, 25,* 151.

Kamali, M., Kelly, B. D., Clarke, M., Browne, S., Gervin, M., Kinsella, A., Lane, A., Larkin, C., & O'Callaghan, E. (2006). A prospective evaluation of adherence to medication in first episode schizophrenia. *European Psychiatry, 21,* 29–33.

Kampov-Polevoy, A., Garbutt, J., & Khalitov, E. (2003). Family history of alcoholism and response to sweets. *Alcoholism Clinical and Experimental Research, 11,* 1743–1749.

Kandel, D., & Davies, M. (1992). Progression to regular marijuana involvement: Phenomenology and risk factors for near-daily use. In M. Glantz & R. Pickens (Eds.), *Vulnerability to drug abuse* (pp. 211–253). Washington, DC: American Psychological Association.

Kanner, A. D., Coyne, J. C., Schaefer, C., & Lazarus, R. S. (1981). Comparison of two modes of stress measurement: daily hassles and uplifts versus major life events. *Journal of Behavioral Medicine, 4,* 1–39.

Kaplan, H. S. (1974). *The new sex therapy.* New York: Brunner Mazel.

Kaplan, H. S. (1979). *Disorders of sexual desire.* New York: Brunner Mazel.

Kaplan, S. A., Reis, R. B., Kohn, I. J., Ikeguchi, E. F., Laor, E., Te, A. E., et al. (1999). Safety and efficacy of sildenafil in postmenopausal women with sexual dysfunction. *Urology, 53,* 481–486.

Kara, H., Aydin, S., Yücel, M., Agargün, M. Y., Odabaş, O., & Yilmaz, Y. (1996). The efficacy of fluoxetine in the treatment of premature ejaculation. A double-blind placebo controlled study. *The Journal of Urology, 156,* 1631–1632.

Karavidas, M. K., Tsai, P. S., Yucha, C., McGrady, A., & Lehrer, P. M. (2006). Thermal biofeedback for primary Raynaud's phenomenon: A review of the literature. *Applied Psychophysiology and Biofeedback, 31,* 203–216.

Karlsson, H. (2003). Viruses and schizophrenia, connection or coincidence? *NeuroReport, 14,* 535–542.

Karno, M., Golding, J. M., Sorenson, S. B., & Burnham, A. B. (1988). The epidemiology of obsessive-compulsive disorder in five U.S. communities. *Archives of General Psychiatry, 45,* 1094–1099.

Karno, M., Hough, R. L., Burnam, M. A., Escobar, J. I., Timbers, D. M., Santana, F., & Boyd, J. H. (1987). Lifetime prevalence of specific psychiatric disorders among Mexican Americans and non-Hispanic whites in Los Angeles. *Archives of General Psychiatry, 44,* 695–701.

Kas, M. J., Van Elburg, A. A., Van Engeland, H., & Adan, R. A. (2003). Refinement of behavioural traits in animals for the genetic dissection of eating disorders. *European Journal of Pharmacology, 480,* 13–20.

Kashner, T. M., Rodell, D. E., Ogden, S. R., Guggenheim, F. G., & Karson, C. N. (1992). Outcomes and costs of two VA inpatient treatment programs for older alcoholic patients. *Hospital and Community Psychiatry, 43,* 985–989.

Kass, F., Skodol, A. E., Charles, E., Spitzer, R. L., & Williams, J. B. (1985). Scaled ratings of DSM-III personality disorders. *American Journal of Psychiatry, 142,* 627–630.

Katon, W. J., & Walker, E. A. (1998). Medically unexplained symptoms in primary care. *Journal of Clinical Psychiatry, 59 [suppl 20],* 15–21.

Katz, I. R., Reynolds, C. F., III, Alexopoulos, G. S., & Hackett, D. (2002). Venlafaxine ER as a treatment for generalized anxiety disorder in older adults: pooled analysis of five randomized placebo-controlled clinical trials. *Journal of the American Geriatrics Society, 50,* 18–25.

Kaufman, A. S. (1999). *Essentials of WAIS-III Assessment.* New York: John Wiley.

Kaufman, J., & Charney, D. (2001). Effects of early stress on brain structure and function: Implications for understanding the relationship between child maltreatment and depression. *Development and Psychopathology, 13,* 451–471.

Kaufman, M. R., & Heiman, M. (1964). *Evolution of psychosomatic concepts: Anorexia Nervosa: A paradigm.* New York: International Universities Press.

Kaur, S., Stechuchak, K. M., Coffman, C. J., Allen, K. D., & Bastian, L. A. (2007). Gender differences in health care utilization among veterans with chronic pain. *Journal of General Internal Medicine, 22,* 228–233.

Kauth, M. R. (2005). Revealing assumptions: Explicating sexual orientation and promoting conceptual integrity. *Journal of Bisexuality, 5,* 81–105.

Kawachi, I., Sparrow, D., Vokonas, P. S., & Weiss, S. T. (1994). Symptoms of anxiety and risk of coronary heart disease. The Normative Aging Study. *Circulation, 90,* 2225–2229.

Kawakami, N., Takeskima, T., Ono, Y., Uda, H., Hata, Y., Nakane, Y., et al. (2005). Twelve-month prevalence, severity, and treatment of common mental disorders in communities of Japan: Preliminary finding from the World Mental Health Survey 2002–2003. *Psychiatry and Clinical Neuroscience, 59,* 441–452.

Kaye, W. (1997). Anorexia nervosa, obsessional behavior, and serotonin. *Psychopharmacology Bulletin, 33,* 335–344.

Kaye, W. H., Bailer, U. F., Frank, G. K., Wagner, A., & Henry, S. E. (2005). Brain imaging of serotonin after recovery from anorexia and bulimia nervosa. *Physiology and Behavior, 86,* 15–17.

Kaye, W. H., Bulik, C. M., Thornton, L., Barbarich, B. S., Masters, K., & The Price Foundation Collaborative Group. (2004). Comorbidity of anxiety disorders with anorexia and bulimia nervosa. *American Journal of Psychiatry, 161,* 2215–2221.

Kaye, W. H., Greeno, C. G., Moss, H., Fernstrom, J., Fernstrom, M., Lilenfeld, L. R., et al. (1998). Alterations in serotonin activity and psychiatric symptoms after recovery from bulimia nervosa. *Archives of General Psychiatry, 55,* 927–935.

Kaye, W. H., Gwirtsman, H. E., George, D. T., & Ebert, M. H. (1991). Altered serotonin activity in anorexia nervosa after long-term weight restoration. Does elevated cerebrospinal fluid 5-hydroxyindoleacetic acid level correlate with rigid and obsessive behavior? *Archives of General Psychiatry, 48,* 556–562.

Kaye, W. H., Klump, K. L., Frank, G. K., & Strober, M. (2000). Anorexia and bulimia nervosa. *Annual Review of Medicine, 51,* 299–313.

Kazdin, A. (2003). *Research design in clinical psychology, 4th edition.* Boston: A Pearson Education Company.

Keck, P. E., Jr., McElroy, S. L., & Arnold, L. M. (2001). Bipolar disorder. *Medical Clinics of North America, 85,* 645–661, ix.

Keck, P., McElroy, S., & Arnold, L. M. (2002). Bipolar disorder. *Medical Clinics of North America, 85,* 645–661.

Keel, P. K., & Klump, K. (2003). Are eating disorders culture-bound syndromes? Implications for conceptualizing their etiology. *Psychological Bulletin, 129,* 747–769.

Keel, P. K., & Mitchell, J. (1997). Outcome in bulimia nervosa. *American Journal of Psychiatry, 154,* 313–321.

Keel, P. K., Haedt, A., & Edler, C. (2005). Purging disorder: An ominous variant of bulimia nervosa? *International Journal of Eating Disorders, 38,* 191–199.

Keel, P. K., Mitchell, J. E., Miller, K. B., Davis, T. L., & Crow, S. J. (1999). Long-term outcome of bulimia nervosa. *Archives of General Psychiatry, 56,* 63–69.

Keenan, K., & Wakschlag, L. S. (2002). Can a valid diagnosis of disruptive behavior disorder be made in preschool children? *American Journal of Psychiatry, 159,* 351–358.

Keenan, K., Loeber, R., & Green, S. (1999). Conduct disorder in girls: A review of the literature. *Clinical Child and Family Psychology Review, 2,* 3–19.

Kelder, S., Prokhorov, A., Barroso, C., Murray, N., Orpinas, P., & McCormick, L. (2003). Smoking differences among African American, Hispanic, and White middle school students in an urban setting. *Addictive Behaviors, 28,* 513–522.

Keller, M. B. (2003). The lifelong course of social anxiety disorder: a clinical perspective. *Acta Psychiatrica Scandinavia, 108,* 85–95.

Keller, M. B., Hirschfeld, R. M., & Hanks, D. (1997). Double depression: A distinctive subtype of unipolar depression. *Journal of Affective Disorders, 45,* 65–73.

Kenardy, J., Smith, A., Spence, S. H., Lilley, P. R., Newcombe, P., Dob, R., & Robinson, S. (2007). Dissociation in children's trauma narratives: An exploratory investigation. *Journal of Anxiety Disorders, 21,* 456–466.

Kendall, P. C., & Norton-Ford, J. D. (1982). *Clinical psychology: Scientific and professional dimensions.* New York: John Wiley and Sons.

Kendler, K. (1996). Major depression and generalized anxiety disorder: Same genes, (partly) different environments: Revisited. *British Journal of Psychiatry, 168,* 68–75.

Kendler, K., & Karkowski-Shuman, L. (1997). Stressful life events and genetic liability to major depression: Genetic control of exposure to the environment? *Psychological Medicine, 27*, 539–547.

Kendler, K., & Prescott, C. (1999). A population-based twin study of lifetime major depression in men and women. *Archives of General Psychiatry, 56*, 39–44.

Kendler, K., Gardner, C., & Prescott, C. (1997). Religion, psychopathology, and substance use and abuse: A multimeasure, genetic-epidemiologic study. *American Journal of Psychiatry, 154*, 322–329.

Kendler, K., Gardner, C., Gatz, M., & Pedersen, N. (2007). The sources of comorbidity between major depression and generalized anxiety disorder in a Swedish national twin sample. *Psychological Medicine, 37*, 453–462.

Kendler, K., Kessler, R. C., Walters, E. E., MacLean, C., Neale, M. C., Heath, A. C., et al. (1995). Stressful life events, genetic liability, and onset of an episode of major depression in women. *American Journal of Psychiatry, 152*, 833–842.

Kendler, K. S. (2005). Toward a philosophical structure for psychiatry. *American Journal of Psychiatry, 162*, 433–440.

Kendler, K. S., Aggen, S. H., Czajkowski, N., Roysamb, E., Tambs, K., Torgersen, S., et al. (2008). The structure of genetic and environmental risk factors for DSM-IV personality disorders: A multivariate twin study. *Archives of General Psychiatry, 65*, 1438–1446.

Kendler, K. S., Hettema, J. M., Butera, F., Gardner, C. O., & Prescott, C. A. (2003). Life event dimensions of loss, humiliation, entrapment, and danger in the prediction of onsets of major depression and generalized anxiety. *Archives of General Psychiatry, 60*, 789–796.

Kendler, K. S., Karkowski, L. M., & Prescott, C. A. (1998). Stressful life events and major depression: Risk period, long-term contextual threat, and diagnostic specificity. *Journal of Nervous and Mental Disease, 186*, 661–669.

Kendler, K. S., MacLean, C., Neale, M. C., Kessler, R. C., Heath, A. C., & Eaves, L. J. (1991). The genetic epidemiology of bulimia nervosa. *American Journal of Psychiatry, 148*, 1627–1637.

Kendler, K. S., McGuire, M., Gruenberg, A. M., O'Hare, A., Spellman, M., & Walsh, D. (1993). The Roscommon family study III: Schizophrenia-related personality disorders in relatives. *Archives of General Psychiatry, 50*, 781–788.

Kendler, K. S., Myers, J., Prescott, C. A., & Neale, M. C. (2001). The genetic epidemiology of irrational fears and phobias in men. *Archives of General Psychiatry, 58*, 257–265.

Kendler, K. S., Myers, J., Torgersen, S., Neale, M. C., & Reichborn–Kjennerud, T. (2007). The heritability of cluster A personality disorders assessed by both personal interview and questionnaire. *Psychological Medicine, 37*, 655–665.

Kendler, K. S., Neale, M. C., Kessler, R. C., Heath, A. C., & Eaves, L. J. (1992). Major depression and generalized anxiety disorder: Same genes, (partly) different environments? *Archives of General Psychiatry, 49*, 716–722.

Kendler, K. S., Thornton, L. M., & Gardner, C. O. (2000). Stressful life events and previous episodes in the etiology of major depression in women: An evaluation of the "kindling" hypothesis. *American Journal of Psychiatry, 157*, 1243–1251.

Kendler, K. S., Thornton, L. M., Gilman, S. E., & Kessler, R. C. (2000). Sexual orientation in a U.S. national sample of twin and in-twin sibling pairs. *American Journal of Psychiatry, 157*, 1843–1846.

Kent, D. A., Tomasson, K., & Coryell, W. (1995). Course and outcome of conversion and somatization disorders. A four-year follow-up. *Psychosomatics, 36*, 138–144.

Kenyon, P. (1994–2007). Depression and learned helplessness. *Study and Learning Materials ONline*, from http://salmon.psy.plym.ac.uk/year2/psy221depression/psy221depression.htm#learnedhelplessnesstheory

Keppel-Benson, Ollendick, T. H., & Benson, M. J, (2002). Post-traumatic stress in children following motor vehicle accidents. *Journal of Child Psychology & Psychiatry, 43*, 203–212.

Kerker, B. D., Owens, P. L., Zigler, E., & Horwitz, S. M. (2004). Mental health disorders among individuals with mental retardation: Challenges to accurate prevalence estimates. *Public Health Reports, 119*, 409–417.

Kernberg, O. (1975). *Borderline Conditions and Pathological Narcissism.* NY: Jason Aronson.

Kerr, L. R., Hundal, R., Silva, W. A., Emerman, J. T., & Weinberg, J. (2001). Effects of social housing condition on chemotherapeutic efficacy in a Shionogi carcinoma (SC115) mouse tumor model: influences of temporal factors, tumor size, and tumor growth rate. *Psychosomatic Medicine, 63*, 973–984.

Kerrigan, S., & Lindsey, T. (2005). Fatal caffeine overdose: Two case reports. *Forensic Science International, 153*, 67–69.

Kessler, R. (1994). The National Comorbidity Survey of the United States. *International Review of Psychiatry, 6*, 365.

Kessler, R. C. (2003). The impairments caused by social phobia in the general population: Implications for intervention. *Acta Psychiatricia Scandinavica, 108* (Suppl. 417), 19–27.

Kessler, R. C., Berglund, P., Demler, O., Jin, R., Koretz, D., Merikangas, K. R., et al. (2003). The epidemiology of major depressive disorder: Results from the National Comorbidity Survey Replication (NCS-R). *Journal of the American Medical Association, 289*, 3095–3105.

Kessler, R. C., Berglund, P., Demler, O., Jin, R., Merikangas, K. R., & Walter, E. E. (2005). Lifetime prevalence and age-of-onset distributions of DSM-IV disorders in the National Comorbidity Survey Replication. *Archives of General Psychiatry, 62*, 593–602.

Kessler, R. C., Birnbaum, H., Demler, O., Falloon, I. R. H., Gagnon, E., Guyer, M., et al. (2005). The prevalence and correlates of nonaffective psychosis in the National Comorbidity Survey Replication (NCS-R). *Biological Psychiatry, 58*, 668–676.

Kessler, R. C., Chiu, W. T., Demler, O., Merikangas, K. R., & Walters, E. E. (2005). Prevalence, severity, and comorbidity of 12-month DSM-IV disorders in the National Comorbidity Survey Replication. *Archives of General Psychiatry, 62*, 617–627.

Kessler, R. C., Chiu, W. T., Jin, R., Ruscio, A. M., Shear, K., & Walters, E. F. (2006). The epidemiology of panic attacks, panic disorder, and agoraphobia in the National Comorbidity Survey Replication. *Archives of General Psychiatry, 63*, 415–424.

Kessler, R. C., Chiu, W., Demler, O., & Walters, E. (2005). Prevalence, severity, and comorbidity of twelve-month DSM-IV disorders in the National Comorbidity Survey Replication (NCS-R). *Archives of General Psychiatry, 62*, 617–627.

Kessler, R. C., Crum, R. M., Warner, L. A., Nelson, C. B., Schulenberg, J., & Anthony, J. C. (1997). Lifetime co-occurrence of DSM-III-R alcohol abuse and dependence with other psychiatric disorders in the National Comorbidity Survey. *Archives of General Psychiatry, 54*, 313–321.

Kessler, R. C., Foster, C. L., Saunders, W. B., & Stang, P. E. (1995). Social consequences of psychiatric disorders, I: Education attainment. *The American Journal of Psychiatry, 152*, 1026–1032.

Kessler, R. C., McGonagle, K. A., Zhao, S., Nelson, C. B., Hughes, M., Eshleman, S., et al. (1994). Lifetime and 12-month prevalence of DSM-III-R psychiatric disorders in the United States. *Archives of General Psychiatry, 51*, 8–19.

Kessler, R. C., Walters, E. E., & Wittchen, H. U. (2004). Epidemiology. In R. G. Heimberg, C. L. Turk, & Mennin, D. S. (Eds.), *Generalized anxiety disorder: Advances in research and practice* (pp. 29–50). New York: Guilford Press, pp. 29–50.

Khan, A., Leventhal, R. M., Kahn, S., & Brown, W. A. (2002). Suicide risk in patients with anxiety disorders: A meta-analysis of the FDA database. *Journal of Affective Disorders, 63*, 183–191.

Khanna, S. Rajendra. P. N., & Channabasavanna, S. M. (1988). Life events and onset of obsessive compulsive disorder. *International Journal of Social Psychiatry, 34*, 305–309.

Khantzian, E. D. (1987). The self-medication hypothesis of addictive disorders: Focus on heroin and cocaine dependence. In D. Allen (Ed.), *The cocaine crisis* (pp. 65–74). New York: Plenum Press.

Kiecolt-Glaser, J. K., Garner, W., Speicher, C., Penn, G. M., Holliday, J., & Glaser, R. (1984). Psychosocial modifiers of immunocompetence in medical students. *Psychosomatic Medicine, 7*–14.

Kiecolt-Glaser, J. K., Glaser, R., Cacioppo, J. T., & Malarkey, W. B. (1998). Marital stress: Immunologic, neuroendocrine, and autonomic correlates. *Annals of the New York Academy of Sciences, 840*, 656–663.

Kieseppa, T., Partonen, T., Haukka, J., Kaprio, J., & Lonnqvist, J. (2004). High concordance of bipolar I disorder in a nationwide sample of twins. *American Journal of Psychiatry, 161*, 1814–1821.

Kihlstrom, J. F. (2001). Dissociative disorders. In H. E. Adams & P. B. Sutker (Eds.), *Comprehensive handbook of psychopathology* (pp. 259–276). New York: Academic/Plenum Publishers.

Kihlstrom, J. F., & Frankle, F. H. (2000). In memoriam: Martin T. Orne, 1927–2000. *International Journal of Clinical and Experimental Hypnosis, 48,* 355–360.

Killen, J., Hayward, C., Hammer, L., Wilson, D., Miner, B., Taylor, C., Varady, A., & Shisslak, C. (1992). Is puberty a risk factor for eating disorders? *American Journal of Diseases of Children, 146,* 323–325.

Killen, J., Taylor, C., Hayward, C., Wilson, D., Haydel, K., Hammer, L., et al. (1994). Pursuit of thinness and onset of eating disorder symptoms in a community sample of adolescent girls: A three-year prospective analysis. *International Journal of Eating Disorders, 16,* 227–238.

Kim, H. F., Kunik, M. E., Molinari, V. A., Hillman, S. L., Lalani, S., Orengo, C. A., et al. (2000). Functional impairment in COPD patients: The impact of anxiety and depression. *Psychosomatics, 41,* 465–471.

Kim, S. J., Lee, H. S., & Kim, C. H. (2005). Obsessive-compulsive disorder, factor-analyzed symptom dimensions and serotonin transporter polymorphism. *Neuropsychobiology, 52,* 176–182.

Kimhy, D., Goetz, R., Yale, S., Corcoran, C., & Malaspina, D. (2005). Delusions in individuals with schizophrenia: Factor structure, clinical correlates, and putative neurobiology. *Psychopathology, 38,* 338–344.

Kindermann, S. S., Kalayam, B., Brown, G. G., Burdick, K. E., & Alexopoulos, G. S. (2000). Executive functions and P300 latency in elderly depressed patients and control subjects. *American Journal of Geriatric Psychiatry, 8,* 57–65.

King, N. J., Ollendick, T. H., & Montgomery, I. M. (1995). Obsessive-compulsive disorder in children and adolescents. *Behaviour Change, 12,* 51–58.

King, S., Laplante, D., & Joober, R. (2005). Understanding putative risk factors or schizophrenia: Retrospective and prospective studies. *Journal of Psychiatry and Neuroscience, 30,* 342–348.

Kingsberg, S. (2007). Testosterone treatment for hypoactive sexual desire disorder in postmenopausal women. *Journal of Sexual Medicine, 4 Suppl 3,* 227–234.

Kinney, A. Y., Bloor, L. E., Dudley, W. N., Millikan, R. C., Marshall, E., Martin, C., et al. (2003). Roles of religious involvement and social support in the risk of colon cancer among Blacks and Whites. *American Journal of Epidemiology, 158,* 1097–1107.

Kinsey, A. C., Pomeroy, W. R., & Martin, C. E. (1948). *Sexual behavior in the human male.* Philadelphia: W. B. Saunders.

Kinsey, A. C., Pomeroy, W. R., & Martin, C. E. (1953). *Sexual behavior in the human female.* Philadelphia: W. B. Saunders.

Kirchner, J. E., Zubritsky, C., Cody, M., Coakley, E., Chen, H., Ware, J. H., Oslin, D. W., Sanchez, H. A., Durai, U. N., Miles, K. M., Llorente, M. D., Costantino, G., & Levkoff, S. (2007). Alcohol consumption among older adults in primary care. *Journal of General Internal Medicine, 22,* 92–97.

Kirk, K. M., Bailey, J. M., Dunne, M. P., & Martin, N. G. (2000). Measurement models for sexual orientation in a community twin sample. *Behaviour Genetics, 30,* 345–356.

Kirmayer, L. (2001). Cultural variations in the clinical presentation of depression and anxiety: Implications for diagnosis and treatment. *Journal of Clinical Psychiatry, 62,* 22–28.

Kirmayer, L. J., & Looper, K. J. (2007). Somatoform disorders. In M. Hersen, S. M. Turner, & D. C. Beidel (Eds.), *Adult psychopathology and diagnosis,* 5th ed. (pp. 410–472). Hoboken, NJ: John Wiley & Sons.

Kirmayer, L. J., & Robbins, J. M. (1991). Three forms of somatization in primary care: Prevalence, co-occurrence, and sociodemographic characteristics. *Journal of Nervous and Mental Disease, 179,* 647–655.

Kirmayer, L. J., & Robbins, J. M. (1996). Patients who somatize in primary care: A longitudinal study of cognitive and social characteristics. *Psychological Medicine, 26,* 937–951.

Kirmayer, L. J., & Santhanam, R. (2001). The anthropology of hysteria. In P. W. Halligan, C. Bass, & J. C. Marshall (Eds.), *Contemporary approaches to the study of hysteria: Clinical and theoretical perspectives* (pp. 251–270). Oxford: Oxford University Press.

Kirmayer, L. J., Groleau, D., Looper, K. J., & Dao, M. D. (2004). Explaining medically unexplained symptoms. *Canadian Journal of Psychiatry, 49,* 663–672.

Kirmayer, L., Young, A., & Hayton, B. (1995). The cultural context of anxiety disorders. *Psychiatric Clinics of North America, 18,* 503–521.

Kirschbaum, C., Kudielka, B. M., Gaab, J., Schommer, N. C., & Hellhammer, D. H. (1999). Impact of gender, menstrual cycle phase, and oral contraceptives on the activity of the hypothalamus-pituitary-adrenal axis. *Psychosomatic Medicine, 61,* 154–162.

Klackenberg, G. (1987). Incidence of parasomnias in children in a general population. In C. Guilleminault (Ed.), *Sleep and its disorders in children* (pp. 99–13). New York: Raven Press.

Klein, R. G. (1995). Is panic disorder associated with childhood separation anxiety disorder? *Clinical Neuropharmacology, 18* (Suppl 2), S7–S14.

Klein, R. G., & Mannuzza, S. (1988). Hyperactive boys almost grown up. III. Methylphenidate effects on ultimate height. *Archives of General Psychiatry, 45,* 1131–1134.

Klerman, G. L., & Weissman, M. M. (1989). Increasing rates of depression. *Journal of the American Medical Association, 261,* 2229–2235.

Klerman, G. L., Weissman, M. M., Rounsaville, B. J., & Chevron, E. S. (1984). *Interpersonal psychotherapy for depression.* New York: Basic Books.

Klin, A. (2006). Autism and Asperger syndrome: An overview. *Revista Brasileira de Psiquiatria, 28 Suppl. 1,* S3–11.

Kluft, R. P. (1993). Multiple personality disorder. In D. Spiegel (Ed.), *Dissociative disorders: A clinical review* (pp. 17–44). Lutherville, MD: Sidran Press.

Klump, K. L., Gobrogge, K. L., Perkins, P. S., Thorne, D., Sisk, C. L., & Marc Breedlove, S. (2006). Preliminary evidence that gonadal hormones organize and activate disordered eating. *Psychological Medicine, 36,* 539–546.

Koenig, H. G., George, L. K., & Siegler, I. C. (1988). The use of religion and other emotion-regulating coping strategies among older adults. *Gerontologist, 28,* 303–310.

Koepke, H. H., Gold, R. L., Linden, M. E., Lion, J. R., & Rickels, K. (1982). Multicenter controlled study of oxazepam in anxious elderly outpatients. *Psychosomatics, 23,* 641–645.

Koessler, L., Maillard, L., Benhadid, A., Vignal, J. P., Braun, M., & Vespignani, H. (2007). Spatial localization of EEG electrodes. *Neurophysiology Clinics, 37,* 97–102.

Kogan, J. N., Edelstein, B. A., & McKee, D. R. (2000). Assessment of anxiety in older adults: Current status. *Journal of Anxiety Disorders, 14,* 109–132.

Kohler, C. L., Fish, L., & Greene, P. G. (2002). The relationship of perceived self-efficacy to quality of life in chronic obstructive pulmonary disease. *Health Psychology, 21,* 610–614.

Kolb, B., & Whishaw, I. (1996). *Fundamentals of human neuropsychology, 4th edition.* New York: W. H. Freeman.

Kolevzon, A., Mathewson, K. A., & Hollander, E. (2006). Selective serotonin reuptake inhibitors in autism: A review of efficacy and tolerability. *Journal of Clinical Psychiatry, 67,* 407–414.

Kopelman, M. D. (1987). Amnesia: Organic and psychogenic. *British Journal of Psychiatry, 150,* 428–442.

Kosfeld, M., Heinrichs, M., Zak, P. J., Fischbacher, U., & Fehr, E. (2005). Oxytocin increases trust in humans. *Nature, 435,* 673–676.

Kovacs, M. (1992). *The Children's Depression Inventory (CDI) Manual.* Toronto, ON: Multi-Health Systems.

Kovacs, M., Obrosky, D. S., & Sherrill, J. (2003) Developmental changes in the phenomenology of depression in girls compared to boys from childhood onward. *Journal of Affective Disorders, 74,* 33–48.

Kozlowska, K., Nunn, K. P., Rose, D., Morris, A., Ouvrier, R. A., & Varghese, J. (2007). Conversion disorder in Australian pediatric practice. *Journal of the American Academy of Child and Adolescent Psychiatry, 46,* 68–75.

Kraepelin, E. (1919/1971). *Dementia praecox and paraphrenia* (translated by R. M. Barclay). New York: Robert E. Krieger Publishing Co.

Krahn, L. E., Li, H., & O'Connor, M. K. (2003). Patients who strive to be ill: Factitious disorder with physical symptoms. *American Journal of Psychiatry, 160,* 1163–1168.

Kranzler, H. N., Kester, H. M., Gerbino-Rosen, G., Henderson, I. N., Youngerman, J., Beauzile, G., Ditkowsky, K., & Kumra, S. (2006). Treatment-refractory schizophrenia in children and adolescents: An update on clozapine and other pharmacological interventions. *Child and Adolescent Psychiatric Clinics of North America, 15,* 135–159.

Kraus, C. A., Kunik, M., Rhoades, H., Novy, D. M., Wilson, N., Weiss, B. J., et al. (2005, November). Cross Cultural Differences in Older Adults with GAD. Presented at the 39th Annual Convention of the Association for Advancement of Behavior Therapy, Washington, DC.

Kraus, C. A., Seignourel, P., Balasubramanyam, V., Snow, A. L., Wilson, N. L., Kunik, M. E., Schultz, P. E., & Stanley, M. A. (2008). Cognitive behavioral treatment for anxiety in patients with dementia: Two case studies. *Journal of Psychiatric Practice, 14,* 186–192.

Krause, N., Liang, J., Shaw, B. A., Sugisawa, H., Kim, H. K., & Sugihara, Y. (2002). Religion, death of a loved one, and hypertension among older adults in Japan. *Journal of Gerontology B Psychological Sciences and Social Sciences, 57,* S96–S107.

Krauthammer, C., & Klerman, G. L. (1978). Secondary mania: Manic syndromes associated with antecedent physical illness or drugs. *Archives of General Psychiatry, 35,* 1333–1339.

Krem, M. M. (2004). Motor conversion disorders reviewed from a neuropsychiatric perspective. *Journal of Clinical Psychiatry, 65,* 783–790.

Krieg, J. C., Lauer, C., & Pirke, K. M. (1989). Structural brain abnormalities in patients with bulimia nervosa. *Psychiatry Research, 27,* 39–48.

Kroenke, K., & Mangelsdorff, A. D. (1989). Common symptoms in ambulatory care: Incidence, evaluation, therapy, and outcome. *American Journal of Medicine, 86,* 262–266.

Kroenke, K., & Spitzer, R. L. (1998). Gender differences in the reporting of physical and somatoform symptoms. *Psychosomatic Medicine, 60,* 150–155.

Kronenberger, W. G., & Dunn, D. W. (2003). Learning disorders. *Neurological Clinics of North America, 21,* 91–952.

Krueger, R. B., & Kaplan, M. S. (2001). The paraphilic and hypersexual disorders: An overview. *Journal of Psychiatric Practice, 7,* 391–403.

Krueger, R. B., & Kaplan, M. S. (2002). Behavioral and psychopharmacological treatment of the paraphilic and hypersexual disorders. *Journal of Psychiatric Practice, 8,* 21–32.

Krueger, R. F., Watson, D., & Barlow, D. H. (2005). Introduction to the special section: toward a dimensionally based taxonomy of psychopathology. *Journal of Abnormal Psychology, 114,* 491–493.

Kubzansky, L. D., Sparrow, D., Vokonas, P., & Kawachi, I. (2001). Is the glass half empty or half full? A prospective study of optimism and coronary heart disease in the normative aging study. *Psychosomatic Medicine, 63,* 910–916.

Kuhn, T. S. (1962). *The structure of scientific revolutions.* Chicago: University of Chicago Press.

Kumar, R., Marks, M., Wieck, A., Hirst, D., Campbell, I., & Checkley, S. (1993). Neuroendocrine and psychosocial mechanisms in post-partum psychosis. *Progress in Neuropsychopharmacology and Biological Psychiatry, 17,* 571–579.

Kunik, M. E., Roundy, K., Veazey, C., Souchek, J., Richardson, P., Wray, N. P., & Stanley, M. A. (2005). Surprisingly high prevalence of anxiety and depression in chronic breathing disorders. *Chest, 127,* 1205–1211.

Kunik, M. E., Snow, A. L., Molinari, V. A., Menke, T. J., Souchek, J., Sullivan, G., et al. (2003). Health care utilization in dementia patients with psychiatric comorbidity. *Gerontologist, 43,* 86–91.

Kunik, M. E., Veazey, C., Cully, J. A., Souchek, J., Graham, D. P., Hopko, D., et al. (2008). COPD education and cognitive behavioral therapy group treatment for clinically significant symptoms of depression and anxiety in COPD patients: A randomized controlled trial. *Psychological Medicine, 38,* 385–396.

Kupelian, V., Link, C. L., Rosen, R. C., & McKinlaym, J. B. (2008). Socioeconomic status, not race/ethnicity, contributes to variation in the prevalence of erectile dysfunction. *Journal of Sexual Medicine, 5,* 1325–1333.

Kurtz, M. M., Seltzer, J. C., Ferrand, J. L., & Wexler, B. E. (2005). Neurocognitive function in schizophrenia at a 10-year follow-up: A preliminary investigation. *CNS Spectrums, 10,* 277–280.

Kushner, M. G., Sher, K. J., & Beitman, B. D. (1990). The relationship between alcohol problems and the anxiety disorders. *American Journal of Psychiatry, 147,* 685–695.

Kuwabara, H., Shioiri, T., Nishimura, A., Abe, R., Nushida, H., Ueno, Y., et al. (2006). Differences in characteristics between suicide victims who left notes or not. *Journal of Affective Disorders, 94,* 145–149.

La Greca, A. M., Silverman, W. K., Vernberg, E. M., & Prinstein, M. J. (1996). Symptoms of posttraumatic stress in children after Hurricane Andrew: A prospective study. *Journal of Consulting and Clinical Psychology, 64,* 712–723.

La Vaque, T. J., & Rossiter, T. (2001). The ethical use of placebo controls in clinical research: The Declaration of Helsinki. *Applied Psychophysiology and Biofeedback, 26,* 23–37.

Laberge, L., Tremblay, R. E., Vitaro, F., & Montplaisir, J. (2000). Development of parasomnias from childhood to early adolescence. *Pediatrics, 106,* 67–74.

Lackner, J. M., Gudleski, G. D., & Blanchard, E. B. (2004). Beyond abuse: The association among parenting style, abdominal pain, and somatization in IBS patients. *Behaviour Research and Therapy, 42,* 41–56.

Ladouceur, R., Gosselin, P., & Dugas, M. J. (2000). Experimental manipulation of uncertainty. *Behaviour Research and Therapy, 38,* 933–941.

Lahey, B. B., Pelham, W. E., Loney, J., Kipp, H., Ehrhardt, A., Lee, S. S., Willcutt, E. G., Hartung, C. M., Chronis, A., & Massetti, G. (2004). Three-year predictive validity of DSM-IV attention deficit hyperactivity disorder in children diagnosed at 4–6 years of age. *American Journal of Psychiatry, 161,* 2014–2020.

Lahey, B. B., Pelham, W. E., Stein, M. A., Loney, J., Trapani, C., Nugent, K., Kipp, H., Schmidt, E., Lee, S., Cale, M., Gold, E., Hartung, C. M., Willcutt, E., & Baumann, B. (1998). Validity of DSM-IV attention-deficit/hyperactivity disorder for younger children. *Journal of the American Academy of Child and Adolescent Psychiatry, 37,* 695–702.

Lai, H., Lai, S., Krongrad, A., Trapido, E., Page, J. B., & McCoy, C. B. (1999). The effect of marital status on survival in late-stage cancer patients: An analysis based on surveillance, epidemiology, and end results (SEER) data, in the United States. *International Journal of Behavioral Medicine, 6,* 150–176.

Lake, C. R., & Hurwitz, N. (2006). Schizoaffective disorders are psychotic mood disorders: There are no schizoaffective disorders. *Psychiatry Research, 143,* 255–267.

Lake, J. (2007, September–October). Emerging paradigms in medicine: Implications for the future of psychiatry. *Explore (NY), 3,* 467–477.

Lakin, K. C., Prouty, R., Polister, B., & Coucouvanis, K. (2004). States' initial response to the President's New Freedom Initiative: Slowest rates of deinstitutionalization in 30 years. *Mental Retardation, 42,* 241–244.

Lalonde, J. K., Hudson, J. I., Gigante, R. A., & Pope, H. G., Jr. (2001). Canadian and American psychiatrists' attitudes toward dissociative disorders diagnoses. *Canadian Journal of Psychiatry, 46,* 407–412.

Lalumière, M. L., & Quinsey, V. L. (1994). The discriminability of rapists from non-sex offenders using phallometric measures. A meta-analysis. *Criminal Justice and Behavior, 21,* 150–157.

Lam, R., & Levitt, A. (1999). *Canadian consensus guidelines for the treatment of seasonal affective disorder.* Vancouver, B.C., Canada: Clinical & Academic Publishing.

Lamb, D. H., Catanzaro, S. J., & Moorman, A. S. (2003). Psychologists reflect on their sexual relationships with clients, supervisees, and students: Occurrence, impact, rationales and collegial intervention. *Professional Psychology: Research and Practice, 34,* 102–107.

Lamb, H. R., & Bachrach, L. I. (2001). Some perspectives on deinstitutionalization. *Psychiatric Services, 52,* 1039–1045.

Lamb, H. R., & Weinberger, L. E. (2005). One-year follow-up of persons discharged from a locked intermediate care facility. *Psychiatric Services, 56,* 198–201.

Lamb, H. R., & Weinberger, L. E. (2005). The shift of psychiatric inpatient care from hospitals to jails and prisons. *Journal of the American Academy of Psychiatry and the Law, 33,* 529–534.

Lambert, M. J., & Lamber, J. M. (1999). Use of psychological tests for assessing treatment outcome. In M. E. Maruish (Ed.), *The Use of Psychological Testing for Treatment Planning and Outcomes Assessment* (2nd ed.) (pp. 115–151). Mahwah, NJ: Lawrence Erlbaum Associates.

Lambert, M. V., Sierra, M., Phillips, M. L., & David, A .S. (2002). The spectrum of organic depersonalization: A review plus four new cases. *Journal of Neuropsychiatry and Clinical Neurosciences, 14,* 141–154.

Landén, M., Wålinder, J., Hambert, G., & Lundsström, B. (1998). Factors predictive of regret in sex reassignment. *Acta Psychaitrica Scandinavia, 97,* 284–289.

Landen, M., Eriksson, E., Agren, H., & Fahlen, T. (1999). Effect of buspirone on sexual dysfunction in depressed patients treated with selective serotonin reuptake inhibitors. *Journal of Clinical Psychopharmacology, 19,* 268–271.

Laney, C., & Loftus, E. F. (2005). Traumatic memories are not necessarily accurate memories. *Canadian Journal of Psychiatry, 50,* 823–828.

Langer, L., Warheit, G., & Zimmerman, R. (1992). Epidemiological study of problem eating behaviors and related attitudes in the general population. *Addictive Behaviors, 16,* 167–173.

Langle, G., Egerter, B., Albrecht, F., Petrasch, M. & Buchkremer, G. (2005). Prevalence of mental illness among homeless men in the community—Approach to a full census in a southern German university town. *Social Psychiatry and Psychiatric Epidemiology, 40,* 382–390.

Larimer, M., Palmer, R., & Marlatt, G. (1999). Relapse prevention: An overview of Marlatt's cognitive-behavioral model. *Alcohol Research & Health, 23,* 151–160.

Larsson, C., Sydsjo, G., & Josefsson, A. (2004). Health, sociodemographic data, and pregnancy outcome in women with antepartum depressive symptoms. *Obstetrics and Gynecology, 104,* 459–466.

Lasègue, E.-C. (1873). On hysterical anorexia. *Medical Times and Gazette,* 265–266, 367–369.

Lask, B., & Bryant-Waugh. (2000). *Anorexia nervosa and related eating disorders in children and adolescence.* Hove, East Sussex, UK: Psychology Press.

Last, C. G., Perrin, S., Hersen, M., & Kazdin, A. E. (1996). A prospective study of childhood anxiety disorders. *Journal of the American Academy of Child and Adolescent Psychiatry, 35,* 1502–1510.

Laumann, E. O., Gagnon, J. H., Michale, R. T., & Michales, S. (1994). *The social organization of sexuality: Sexual practices in the United States.* Chicago: University of Chicago Press.

Laumann, E. O., Nicolosi, A., Glasser, D. B., Paik, A., Gingell, C., Moreira, E., et al.; GSSAB Investigators' Group. (2005). Sexual problems among women and men aged 40–80 years: Prevalence and correlates identified in the Global Study of Sexual Attitudes and Behaviors. *International Journal of Impotence Research, 17,* 39–57.

Laumann, E. O., Paik, A., & Rosen, R. C. (1999). Sexual dysfunction in the United States. *The Journal of the American Medical Association, 281,* 537–544.

Law, S., & Kirmayer, L. J. (2005). Inuit interpretations of sleep paralysis. *Transcultural Psychiatry, 12,* 93–112.

Lawrence, A. A. (2003). Factors associated with satisfaction or regret following male-to-female sex reassignment surgery. *Archives of Sexual Behavior, 32,* 299–315.

Laws, D. R. (2001). Olfactory aversion: Notes on procedure, with speculations on its mechanism of effect. *Sexual Abuse: A Journal of Research and Treatment, 13,* 275–287.

Lawson, W. B., Hepler, N., Holiday, J., & Cuffel, B. (1994). Race as a factor in inpatient and outpatient admissions and diagnosis. *Hospital and Community Psychiatry, 45,* 72–74.

Lawton, M. P., Kleban, M. H., & Dean, J. (1993). Affect and age: Cross-sectional comparisons of structure and prevalence. *Psychology and Aging, 8,* 165–175.

Lay, B., Blanz, B., Hartmann, M., & Schmidt, M. H. (2000). The psychosocial outcome of adolescent-onset schizophrenia: A 12-year follow-up. *Schizophrenia Bulletin, 26,* 801–816.

Lazarus, R. S. (1999). *Stress and emotion: A new synthesis.* New York: Springer.

Lazarus, R. S., & Folkman, S. (1984). Coping and adaptation. In W. D. Gentry (Ed.), *The handbook of behavioral medicine* (pp. 282–325). New York: Guilford Press.

le Grange, D., Crosby, R. D., Rathouz, P. J., Leventhal, B. L. (2007) A randomized controlled comparison of family-based treatment and supportive psychotherapy for adolescent bulimia nervosa. *Archives of General Psychiatry, 64,* 1049–1056.

Le Roux, H., Gatz, M., & Wetherell, J. L. (2005). Age at onset of generalized anxiety disorder in older adults. *American Journal of Geriatric Psychiatry, 13,* 23–30.

Lecrubier, Y., Wittchen, H. U., Faravelli, C. Bobes, J., Patel, A., & Knapp, M. (2000). A European perspective on social anxiety disorder. *European Psychiatry, 15,* 5–16.

Lee, B., & Newberg, A. (2005). Religion and health: A review and critical analysis. *Journal of Religion and Science, 40,* 443–468.

Lee, R. E., & King, A. C. (2003). Discretionary time among older adults: How do physical activity promotion interventions affect sedentary and active behaviors? *Annals of Behavioral Medicine, 25,* 112–119.

Lee, S. (1998). Estranged bodies, simulated harmony and misplaced cultures: Neurasthenia in contemporary Chinese society. *Culture, Medicine and Psychiatry, 60,* 448–457.

Lee, S. H., Kim, W., Chung, Y. C., Jung, K. H., Bahk, W. M., Jun, T. Y., et al. (2005). A double blind study showing that two weeks of daily repetitive TMS over the left or right temporoparietal cortex reduces symptoms in patients with schizophrenia who are having treatment-refractory auditory hallucinations. *Neuroscience Newsletters, 376,* 177–181.

Leff, J., Tress, K., & Edwards, B. (1988). The clinical course of depressive symptoms in schizophrenia. *Schizophrenia Research, 1,* 25–30.

Lehman, J., & Phelps, S. (2004). *West's Encyclopedia of American Law* (2nd ed.). Gale Group.

Leiblum, S. R. (2000). Vaginimus: A most perplexing problem. In S. R. Leiblum & R. C. Rosen (Eds.). *Principles and practice of sex therapy* (3rd ed.) (pp. 181–202). New York: Guilford Press.

Leichsenring, F. (2005). Are psychodynamic and psychoanalytic therapies effective? *International Journal of Psychoanalysis, 86,* 841–868.

Leigh, B. C., Temple, M. T., & Trocki, K. F. (1993). The sexual behavior of US adults: Results from a national survey. *American Journal of Public Health, 83,* 1400–1408.

Lejuez, C. W., Hopko, D. R., & Hopko, S. D. (2001). A brief behavioral activation treatment for depression: Treatment manual. *Behavior Modification, 25,* 255–286.

LeMarquand, D., Pihl, R., & Benkelfat, C. (1994). Serotonin and alcohol intake, abuse, and dependence: clinical evidence. *Biological Psychiatry, 36,* 326–337.

Lenze, E. J., Karp, J. F., Mulsant, B. H., Blank, S., Shear, M. K., Houck, P. R., et al. (2005). Somatic symptoms in late-life anxiety: Treatment issues. *Journal of Geriatric Psychiatry and Neurology, 18,* 89–96.

Lenze, E. J., Mulsant, B. H., Shear, M. K., Dew, M. A., Miller, M. D., Pollock, B. G., et al. (2005). Efficacy and tolerability of citalopram in the treatment of late-life anxiety disorders: Results from an 8-week randomized, placebo-controlled trial. *American Journal of Psychiatry, 162,* 146–150.

Lenze, E. J., Mulsant, B. H., Shear, M. K., Schulberg, H. C., Dew, M. A., Begley, A. E., et al. (2000). Comorbid anxiety disorders in depressed elderly patients. *American Journal of Psychiatry, 157,* 722–728.

Lenze, E. J., Rogers, J. C., Martire, L. M., Mulsant, B. H., Rollman, B. L., Dew, M. A., et al. (2001). The association of late-life depression and anxiety with physical disability: a review of the literature and prospectus for future research. *American Journal of Geriatric Psychiatry, 9,* 113–135.

Lenze, E. J., Rollman, B. L., Shear, M. K., Dew, M. A., Pollock, B. G., Ciliberti, C., et al. (2009). Escitalopram for older adults with generalized anxiety disorder: A randomized controlled trial. *Journal of the American Medical Association, 301,* 295–303.

Lenze, E. J., Rollman, B. L., Shear, M. K., et al. (2009). Escitalopram for older adults with generalized anxiety disorder: A randomized controlled trial. *Journal of the American Medical Association, 301,* 295–303.

Leon, G., Fulkerson, J., Perry, C., & Cudeck, R. (1993). Personality and behavioral vulnerabilities associated with risk status for eating disorders in adolescent girls. *Journal of Abnormal Psychology, 102,* 438–444.

Leonard, D., Brann, S., & Tiller, J. (2005). Dissociative disorders: Pathways to diagnosis, clinical attitudes and their impact. *Australian and New Zealand Journal of Psychiatry, 39,* 940–946.

Leonard, H., & Wen, X. (2002). The epidemiology of mental retardation: Challenges and opportunities in the new millennium. *Mental Retardation and Developmental Disabilities Research Reviews, 8,* 117–134.

Lerner, A. J., Hedera, P., Koss, E., Stuckey, J., & Friedland, R. P. (1997). Delirium in Alzheimer disease. *Alzheimer Disease and Associated Disorders, 11,* 16–20.

Lesaca, T. (2001). Executive functions in parents with ADHD. *Psychiatric Times, 18.*

Leserman, J., Petitto, J. M., Golden, R. N., Gaynes, B. N., Gu, H., Perkins, D. O., et al. (2000). Impact of stressful life events, depression, social support, coping, and cortisol on progression to AIDS. *American Journal of Psychiatry, 157,* 1221–1228.

Leung, A. K. C., & Robson, W. L. M. (2007). Tuberous sclerosis complex: A review. *Journal of Pediatric Health Care, 21,* 108–114.

Levinson, D. F. (2005). Meta-analysis in psychiatric genetics. *Current Psychiatry Reports, 7*, 143–151.

Levkoff, S. E., Evans, D. A., Liptzin, B., Cleary, P. D., Lipsitz, L. A., Wetle, T. T., et al. (1992). Delirium: The occurrence and persistence of symptoms among elderly hospitalized patients. *Archives of Internal Medicine, 152*, 334–340.

Lewinsohn, P. M. (1974). A behavioral approach to depression. In R. J. Friedman & M. M. Katz (Eds.), *Psychology of depression: Contemporary theory and research*. Oxford: Wiley.

Lewinsohn, P. M., & Graf, M. (1973). Pleasant activities and depression. *Journal of Consulting and Clinical Psychology, 41*, 261–268.

Lewinsohn, P., Seeley, J., Moerk, K., & Striegel-Moore, R. H. (2002). Gender differences in eating disorder symptoms in young adults. *International Journal of Eating Disorders, 32*, 426–440.

Lewis, C. M., Levinson, D. F., Wise, L. H., DeLisi, L. E., Straub, R. E. Hovatta I., et al. (2003). Genome scan meta-analysis of schizophrenia and bipolar disorder, part II:Schizophrenia. *American Journal of Human Genetics, 73*, 34–48.

Lewis, D. O., Yeager, C. A., Swica, Y., Pincus, J. H., & Lewis, M. (1997). Objective documentation of child abuse and dissociation in 12 murderers with dissociative identity disorder. *American Journal of Psychiatry, 143*, 1703–1710.

Lewis, R. W., Sadovsky, R., Eardley, I., O'Leary, M., Seftel, A., Wang, W. C., et al. (2005). The efficacy of tadalafil in clinical populations. *Journal of Sexual Medicine, 2*, 517–531.

Lewis, T. T., Everson-Rose, S. A., Powell, L. H., Matthews, K. A., Brown, C., Karavolos, K., et al. (2006). Chronic exposure to everyday discrimination and coronary artery calcification in African-American women: The SWAN Heart Study. *Psychosomatic Medicine, 68*, 362–368.

Lewis-Fernandez, R., (1998). A cultural critique of the DSM-IV dissociative disorders section. *Transcultural Psychiatry, 35*, 387–400.

Libbey, J. E., Sweeten, T. L., McMahon, W. M., & Fujinami, R. S. (2005). Autistic disorder and viral infections. *Journal of Neurovirology, 11*, 1–10.

Libow, J. A. (2000). Child and adolescent illness falsification. *Pediatrics, 105*, 336–342.

Liddell, A., & Lyons, M. (1978). Thunderstorm phobias. *Behaviour Research and Therapy 16*, 306–308.

Lidz, C. W., Mulvey, E. P., & Gardner, W. (1993). The accuracy of predictions of violence to others. *Journal of the American Medical Association, 269*, 1007–1011.

Lidz, C.W. (2006). The therapeutic misconception and our models of competency and informed consent. *Behavioral Sciences and the Law, 24*, 535–540.

Lieb, R., Wittchen, H., Höfler, M., Fuetsch, M., Stein, M., & Merikangas, K. (2000). Parental psychopathology, parenting styles, and the risk of social phobia in offspring: A prospective-longitudinal community study. *Archives of General Psychiatry, 57*, 859–866.

Liebowitz, M. R., Gorman, J. M., Fyer, A. J., & Klein, D. R. (1985). Social phobia. *Archives of General Psychiatry, 42*, 729–736.

Liebowitz, M. R., Salman, E., Jusino, C. M., Garfinkel, R., Street, L., Cardenas, D. L., Libbey, J. E., Sweeten, T. L., McMahon, W. M., & Fujinami, R. S. (2005). Autistic disorder and viral infections. *Journal of Neurovirology, 11*, 1–10. (1994). *Ataque de nervios* and panic disorder. *American Journal of Psychiatry, 151*, 871–875.

Lilenfeld, L., Kaye, W. H., Greeno, C., Merikangas, K., Plotnikov, K., Pollice, C., Libbey, J. E., Sweeten, T. L., McMahon, W. M., & Fujinami, R. S. (2005). Autistic disorder and viral infections. *Journal of Neurovirology, 11*, 1–10. (1998). A controlled family study of restricting anorexia and bulimia nervosa: Comorbidity in probands and disorders in first-degree relatives. *Archives of General Psychiatry, 55*, 603–610.

Lilienfeld, A. M., & Lilienfeld, D. E. (1980). *Foundations of epidemiology, 2nd edition*. New York: Oxford University Press.

Lilienfeld, S. O., Lynn, S. J., Kirsch, I., Chaves, J. F., Sarbin, T. R., & Ganaway, G. K. (1999). Dissociative identity disorder and the sociocognitive model: Recalling the lessons of the past. *Psychological Bulletin, 125*, 507–523.

Lilienfeld, S. O., Wood, J. M., & Garb, H. N. (2000). The scientific status of projective techniques. *Psychological Science in the Public Interest, 1*, 27–66.

Limosin, F., Rouillon, F., Payan, C., Cohen, J-M., & Strub, N. (2003). Prenatal exposure to influenza as a risk factor for adult schizophrenia. *Acta Psychiatrica Scandinavica, 107*, 331.

Lin, K. M., Poland, R. E., & Silver, B. (1993). The interface between psychobiology and ethnicity. In K. M. Lin, R. E. Poland, and G. Nakasaki (Eds.), *Psychopharmacology and psychobiology of ethnicity* (pp. 11–35). Washington, DC: American Psychiatric Press.

Linaker, O. M. (2000). Dangerous female psychiatric patients: Prevalence and characteristics. *Acta Psychiatrica Scandinavia, 101*, 67–72.

Linden, W., Lenz, J. W., & Con, A. H. (2001). Individualized stress management for primary hypertension: A randomized trial. *Archives of International Medicine, 161*, 1071–1080.

Lindwall, M., Rennemark, M., Halling, A., Berglund, J., & Hassmen, P. (2007). Depression and exercise in elderly men and women: Findings from the Swedish national study on aging and care. *Journal of Aging and Physical Activity, 15*, 41–55.

Linehan, M. M., Comtois, K. A., Murray, A. M., Brown, M. Z., Gallop, R. J., Heard, H. L., Korslund, K. E., Tutek, D. A., Reynolds, S. K., & Lindenboim, N. (2006). Two-year randomized controlled trial and follow-up of dialectical behavior therapy vs therapy by experts for suicidal behaviors and borderline personality disorder. *Archives of General Psychiatry, 63*, 757–766.

Linehan, M. M., Heard, H., & Armstrong, H. (1993). Naturalistic follow-up of a behavioral treatment for chronically parasuicidal borderline patients. *Archives of General Psychiatry, 50*, 971–974.

Linet, O. I., & Ogrinc, F. G. (1996). Efficacy and safety of intracavernosal alprostadil in men with erectile dysfunction. The Alprostadil Study Group. *New England Journal of Medicine, 334*, 873–877.

Linton, S. J. (2002). A prospective study of the effects of sexual or physical abuse on back pain. *Pain, 96*, 347–351.

Lipsitz, J. D., Gur, M., Miller, N. L., Forand, N., Vermes, D., & Fyer, A. J. (2006). An open pilot study of interpersonal psychotherapy for panic disorder (IPT-PD). *Journal of Nervous and Mental Disease, 194*, 440–445.

Lipsitz, J. D., Markowitz, J. C., Cherry, S., & Fyer, A. J. (1999). Open trial of interpersonal psychotherapy for the treatment of social phobia. *American Journal of Psychiatry, 156*, 1814–1816.

Liptzin, B. (2004). Delirium. In J. Sadavoy, L. F. Jarvik, G. T. Grossberg, & B. S. Meyers (Eds.), *Comprehensive Textbook of Geriatric Psychiatry* (3rd ed., pp. 525–544). New York: W.W. Norton & Co.

Lock, J., le Grange, D., Agras, W. S., & Dare, C. (2002). *Treatment manual for anorexia nervosa: A family based approach*. New York: Guilford Press.

Lockwood, K. A., Alexopoulos, G. S., Kakuma, T., & van Gorp, W. G. (2000). Subtypes of cognitive impairment in depressed older adults. *American Journal of Geriatric Psychiatry, 8*, 201–208.

Loeber, R., Burke, J. D., Lahey, B. B., Winters, A., & Zera, M. (2000). Oppositional defiant and conduct disorder: a review of the past 10 years, part I. *Journal of the American Academy of Child and Adolescent Psychiatry, 39*, 1468–1484.

Loewenstein, R. J. (2005). Psychopharmacologic treatments for dissociative identity disorder. *Psychiatric Annals, 35*, 666–673.

Loftus, E. F. (1993). The reality of repressed memories. *American Psychologist, 48*, 518–537.

Loftus, E. F., & Pickrell, J. E. (1995). The formation of false memories. *Psychiatric Annals, 25*, 720–725.

Long, D. N., Wisniewski, A. B., & Migeon, C. J. (2004). Gender role across development in adult women with congenital adrenal hyperplasia due to 21-hydroxylase deficiency. *Journal of Pediatric Endocrinology & Metabolism, 17*, 1367–1373.

Looper, K. J., & Kirmayer, L. J. (2002). Behavioral medicine approaches to somatoform disorders. *Journal of Consulting and Clinical Psychology, 70*, 810–827.

Lopez, O. L., Jagust, W. J., DeKosky, S. T., Becker, J. T., Fitzpatrick, A., Dulberg, C., Libbey, J. E., Sweeten, T. L., McMahon, W. M., & Fujinami, R. S. (2005). Autistic disorder and viral infections. *Journal of Neurovirology, 11*, 1–10. (2003). Prevalence and classification of mild cognitive impairment in the Cardiovascular Health Study Cognition Study: part 1. *Archives of Neurology and Psychiatry, 60*, 1385–1389.

Lopez, S. R. & Guarnaccia, P. J. J. (2000). Cultural psychopathology: Uncovering the social world of mental illness. *Ammual Review of Psychology, 51*, 571–598.

Lord, C., Risi, S., DiLavore, P. S., Shulman, C., Thurn, A., & Pickles, A. (2006). Autism from 2 to 9 years of age. *Archives of General Psychiatry, 63*, 694–701.

Lott, I. T., & Head, E. (2005). Alzheimer disease and Down syndrome: Factors in pathogenesis. *Neurobiology of Aging, 26,* 383–389.

Lovaas, O. I. (1987). Behavioral treatment and normal educational and intellectual functioning in young children. *Journal of Consulting and Clinical Psychology, 55,* 3–9.

Luber, M. P., Hollenberg, J. P., Williams-Russo, P., DiDomenico, T. N., Meyers, B. S., Alexopoulos, G. S., & Charlson, M. E. (2000). Diagnosis, treatment, comorbidity, and resource utilization of depressed patients in a general medical practice. *International Journal of Psychiatry in Medicine, 30,* 1–13.

Luchins, A. S. (2001). Moral treatment in asylums and general hospitals in 19th-century *American Journal of Psychiatry, 123,* 585–607.

Ludwig, A. (1995). *The price of greatness.* New York: Guilford Press.

Lugo Steidel, A., & Contreras, J. (2003). A new familism scale for use with Latino populations. *Hispanic Journal of Behavioral Sciences, 25,* 312–330.

Lundgren, L., Amodeo, M., Ferguson, F., & Davies, K. (2001). Racial and ethnic differences in drug treatment entry of injection drug users in Massachusetts. *Journal of Substance Abuse Treatment, 21,* 145–153.

Lykken, D. (1982). Fearlessness: Its carefree charms and deadly risks. *Psychology Today, 16,* 20–28.

Lyness, J. M., Caine, E. D., King, D. A., Cox, C., & Yoediono, Z. (1999). Psychiatric disorders in older primary care patients. *Journal of General Internal Medicine, 14,* 249–254.

Lynn, K. S. (1987). *Hemingway.* New York: Simon & Schuster.

Lyons, A. P., & Lyons, H. D. (2006). The new anthropology of sexuality. *Anthropologica, 48,* 153–157.

Mackin, R. S., & Arean, P. A. (2005). Evidence-based psychotherapeutic interventions for geriatric depression. *Psychiatric Clinics of North America, 28,* 805–820.

Mackintosh, M. A., Gatz, M., Wetherell, J. L., & Pedersen, N. L. (2006). A twin study of lifetime Generalized Anxiety Disorder (GAD) in older adults: Genetic and environmental influences shared by neuroticism and GAD. *Twin Research and Human Genetics, 9,* 30–37.

Macy, R. D., Behar, L., Paulson, R., Delman, J., Schmid, L., & Smith, S. F. (2004). Community-based, acute posttraumatic stress management: A description and evaluation of a psychosocial-intervention continuum. *Harvard Review of Psychiatry, 12,* 217–228.

Magee, W. J. (1999). Effects of negative life experiences on phobia onset. *Social Psychiatry and Psychiatric Epidemiology, 34,* 343–351.

Magee, W. J., Eaton, W. W., Wittchen, H. U., McGonagle, K. A., & Kessler, R. C. (1996). Agoraphobia, social phobia and simple phobia in the National Comorbidity Survey. *Archives of General Psychiatry, 53,* 159–168.

Magill, F. (1983). Ernest Hemingway. In F. Magill (Ed.), *The critical survey of long fiction.* New York: Salem Press.

Magno Zito, J., Derivan, A. T., & Greenhill, L. L., for the Pediatric Psychopharmacology Initiative. (2004). Making research data available: An ethical imperative demonstrated by the SSRI debacle. *Journal of the American Academy of Child and Adolescent Psychiatry, 43,* 512–514.

Magno Zito, J., Safer, D. J., dosReis, S., Gardner, J. F., Magder, L., Soeken, K., Boles, M., Lynch, F., & Riddle, M. A. (2003). Psychotropic practice patterns for youth. *Archives of Pediatrics & Adolescent Medicine, 157,* 17–25.

Magno Zito, J., Safer, D. J., dosReis, S., Gardner, J. F., Boles, M., & Lynch, F. (2000). Trends in the prescribing of psychotropic medications to preschoolers. *Journal of the American Medical Association, 283,* 1025–1030.

Magruder, K., Frueh, B. C., Knapp, R., Davis, L., Hamner, M. B., Martin, R. H., et al. (2005). Prevalence of posttraumatic stress disorder in Veterans Affairs primary care clinics. *General Hospital Psychiatry, 27,* 169–79.

Maher, W. B., & Maher, B. A. (1985). Psychopathology: I. From ancient times to the 18th century. In G. A. Kimble & K. Schlesinger (Eds.), *Topics in the history of psychology* (Vol.2). Hillsdale, NJ: Erlbaum.

Maier, W., Gansicke, M., Freyberger, H. J., Linz, M., Heun, R., & Lecrubier, Y. (2000). Generalized anxiety disorder (ICD-10) in primary care from a cross-cultural perspective: a valid diagnostic entity? *Acta Psychiatrica Scandinavica, 101,* 29–36.

Maj, M. (2005). "Psychiatric comorbidity": An artifact of the current diagnostic system? *British Journal of Psychiatry, 186,* 182–184.

Malhotra, A., Murphy, G., & Kennedy, J. (2004). Pharmacogenetics of psychotropic drug response. *American Journal of Psychiatry, 161,* 780–796.

Malla, A. K., & Payne, J. (2005). First-episode psychosis: Psychopathology, quality of life, and functional outcome. *Schizophrenia Bulletin, 31,* 650–671.

Malla, A. K., Mittal, C., Lee, M., Scholten, D. J., Assis, L., & Normak, R. M. (2002). Computed tomography of the brain morphology of patients with first-episode schizophrenic psychosis. *Journal of Psychiatry & Neuroscience, 27,* 350–358.

Mallinger, J. B., Fisher, S. G., Brown, T., & Lamberti, J. S. (2006). Racial disparities in the use of second-generation antipsychotics for the treatment of schizophrenia. *Psychiatric Services, 57,* 133–136.

Malone, R. P., & Simpson, G. M. (1998). Use of placebos in clinical trials involving children and adolescents. *Psychiatric Services, 49,* 1413–1414, 1417.

Mangweth-Matzek, B., Rupp, C. I., Hausmann, A., Assmayr, K., Mariacher, E., Kemmler, G., et al. (2006). Never too old for eating disorders or body dissatisfaction: A community study of elderly women. *International Journal of Eating Disorders, 39,* 583–586.

Mann, J. J., Brent, D. A., & Arango, V. (2001). The neurobiology and genetics of suicide and attempted suicide: A focus on the serotonergic system. *Neuropsychopharmacology, 24,* 467–477.

Mann, J. J., Stanley, M., McBride, P. A., & McEwen, B. S. (1986). Increased serotonin2 and beta-adrenergic receptor binding in the frontal cortices of suicide victims. *Archives of General Psychiatry, 43,* 954–959.

Marano. L. (1982). Windigo psychosis: The anatomy of an emic-etic confusion. *Cultural Anthropology, 23,* 385–412.

March, J. S., Franklin, M. E., Leonard, H. L., & Foa, E. B. (2004). Obsessive-compulsive disorder. In T. L. Morris & J. S. March (Eds.), *Anxiety disorders in children and adolescents* (pp. 212–240). New York: Guilford Press.

March, J. S., Parker, J. D., A., Sullivan, K., Stallings, P., & Conners, K. (1997). The Multidimensional Anxiety Scale for Children (MASC): Factor structure, reliability and validity. *Journal of the American Academy of Child and Adolescent Psychiatry, 36,* 554–565.

March, J., Kratochvil, C., Clarke, G., Beardslee, W., Derivan, A., Emslie, G., Green, E. P., Heiligenstein, J., Hinshaw, S., et al. (2004). ACAAP 2002 research forum: placebo and alternatives to placebo in randomized controlled trials in pediatric psychopharmacology. *Journal of the American Academy of Child and Adolescent Psychiatry, 43,* 1046–1056.

Marcos, L. R., & Cancro, R. (1982). Pharmacotherapy of Hispanic depressed patients: Clinical observations. *American Journal of Psychotherapy, 36,* 505–512.

Marcus, M. D., Moulton, M. M., & Greeno, C. G. (1995). Binge eating onset in obese patients with binge eating disorder. *Addictive Behaviors, 20,* 747–755.

Marcus, M. D., Wing, R. R., & Hopkins, J. (1988). Obese binge eaters: affect, cognitions and response to behavioral weight control. *Journal of Consulting and Clinical Psychology, 56,* 433–439.

Margolese, H. W., & Ferreri, F. (2007). Management of conventional antipsychotic-induced tardive dyskineisa. *Journal of Psychiatry & Neuroscience, 32,* 72.

Markus, H. R., & Kitayama, S. (1991). Culture and the self: Implications for cognition, emotion and motivation. *Psychological Review, 98,* 244–253.

Marlatt, G. A., & Gordon, J. R. (1985). *Relapse prevention: Maintenance strategies in the treatment of addictive behaviors.* New York: Guilford Press.

Marlatt, G., Larimer, M., Baer, J., & Quigley, L. (1993). Harm reduction for alcohol problems: Moving beyond the controlled drinking controversy. *Behavior Therapy, 24,* 461–504.

Marshall, W. L., & Eccles, A. (1991). Issues in clinical practice with sex offenders. *Journal of Interpersonal Violence, 6,* 68–93.

Martin, L. R. & Brantley, P. J. (2004). *Stress, coping, and social support in health and behavior.* (vols. 2) Washington, DC: American Psychological Association.

Martin, N., Boomsma, D., & Machin, G. (1997). A twin-pronged attack on complex traits. *Nature Genetics, 17,* 387–392.

Martinez-Barrondo, S., Saiz, P. A., Morales, B., Garcia-Portilla, M. P., Coto, E., Alvarez, Y., & Bobes, J. (2005). Serotonin gene polymorphisms in patients with panic disorder. *Actas España Psiquiatrica, 33,* 215–215.

Marucha, P. T., Kiecolt-Glaser, J. K., & Favagehi, M. (1998). Mucosal wound healing is impaired by examination stress. *Psychosomatic Medicine, 60,* 362–365.

Maruish, M. E. (1999). Introduction. In M. E. Maruish (Ed.), *The use of psychological testing for treatment planning and outcomes assessment* (2nd ed.) (pp. 1–39). Mahwah, NJ: Lawrence Erlbaum Associates.

Maruta, T., Colligan, R. C., Malinchoc, M., & Offord, K. P. (2002). Optimism-pessimism assessed in the 1960s and self-reported health status 30 years later. *Mayo Clinic Proceedings, 77,* 748–753.

Marzuk, P., Leon, A., Tardiff, K., Morgan, E., Stajic, M., & Mann, J. (1992). The effect of access to lethal methods of injury on suicide rates. *Archives of General Psychiatry, 49,* 451–458.

Mashour, G. A., Walker, E. E., & Martuza, R. L. (2005). Psychosurgery: Past, present, and future. *Brain Research Reviews, 48,* 409–419.

Masi, G., Millipiedi, S., Mucci, M., Poli, P., Bertini, N., & Milantoni, L. (2004). Generalized anxiety disorder in referred children and adolescents. *Journal of the American Academy of Child and Adolescent Psychiatry, 38,* 916–922.

Masi, G., Mucci, M., Favilla, L., Romano, R., & Poli, P. (1999). Symptomatology and comorbidity of generalized anxiety disorder in children and adolescents. *Comprehensive Psychiatry, 40,* 210–215.

Mason, T. B., II, & Pack, A. I. (2005). Sleep terrors in childhood. *Journal of Pediatrics, 147,* 388–392.

Massey, L. (1998). Caffeine and the elderly. *Drugs and Aging, 13,* 43–50.

Masters, W. H., & Johnson, V. E. (1966). *Human sexual response.* Boston: Little, Brown.

Masters, W. H., & Johnson, V. E. (1970). *Human sexual inadequacy.* Boston: Little, Brown.

Matson, J. L., & Nebel-Schwalm, M. S. (2006). Comorbid psychopathology with autism spectrum disorder in children: An overview. *Research in Developmental Disabilities, 28,* 341–352.

Matson, J. L., Benavidez, D. A., Compton, L. S., Paclawskyj, T., & Baglio, C. (1996). *Research in Developmental Disabilities, 17,* 433–465.

Matthews, K. A., Owens, J. F., Allen, M. T., & Stoney, C. M. (1992). Do cardiovascular responses to laboratory stress relate to ambulatory blood pressure levels? Yes, in some of the people, some of the time. *Psychosomatic Medicine, 54,* 686–697.

Mattik, R., & Newman, C. (1991). Social phobia and avoidant personality disorder. *International Review of Psychiatry, 3,* 163–173.

Mattis, S. (2001). *Dementia Rating Scale-2: Professional Manual.* Psychological Asssessment Resources. Odessa. FL

Maurice, W. L. (2005). Male hypoactive sexual desire disorder. In R. Balon & R. T. Segraves (Eds.). *Handbook of sexual dysfunction* (pp. 76–109). Boca Raton, FL: Taylor & Francis.

Maxwell, J. (2001). Deaths related to the inhalation of volatile substances in Texas: 1988–1998. *American Journal of Drug and Alcohol Abuse, 27,* 689–697.

Mayberg, H. S., Lozano, A. M., Voon, V., McNeely, H. E., Seminowicz, D., Hamani, C., et al. (2005). Deep brain stimulation for treatment-resistant depression. *Neuron, 45,* 651–660.

Mayer, E. A., Naliboff, B. D., Chang, L., & Coutinho, S. V. (2001). V. Stress and irritable bowel syndrome. *American Journal of Physiology Gastrointestinal and Liver Physiology, 280,* G519–G524.

Mayes, L. C. (2000). A developmental perspective on the regulation of arousal states. *Seminars in Perinatology, 24,* 267–279.

Mayes, R., & Horwitz, A. V. (2005). DSM-III and the revolution in the classification of mental illness. *Journal of the History of the Behavioral Sciences, 41,* 249–267.

Mayne, T. J., Vittinghoff, E., Chesney, M. A., Barrett, D. C., & Coates, T. J. (1996). Depressive affect and survival among gay and bisexual men infected with HIV. *Archives of Internal Medicine, 156,* 2233–2238.

McAlearney, A. S., Reeves, K. W., Tatum, C., & Paskett, E. D. (2007). Cost as a barrier to screening mammography among underserved women. *Ethnicity and Health, 12,* 189–203.

McCabe, E. B., & Marcus, M. D. (2002). Is dialectical behavior therapy useful in the management of anorexia nervosa? *Eating Disorders, 10,* 335–337.

McCabe, R., & Priebe, S. (2004). Explanatory models of illness in schizophrenia: Comparison of four ethnic groups. *British Journal of Psychiatry, 185,* 25–30.

McCaughrin, W. B., Ellis, W. K., Rusch, F. R., & Heal, L. W. (1993). Cost-effectiveness of supported employment. *Mental Retardation, 31,* 41–48.

McCaul, M., Svikis, D., & Moore, R. (2001). Predictors of outpatient treatment retention: Patient versus substance use characteristics. *Drug and Alcohol Dependence, 62,* 9–17.

McClellan, J., Breiger, D., McCurry, C., & Hlastala, S. A. (2003). Premorbid functioning in early-onset psychotic disorders. *Journal of the American Academy of Child and Adolescent Psychiatry, 42,* 666–673.

McCloskey, M. S., Phan, K. L., & Coccaro, E. F. (2005). Neuroimaging and personality disorders. *Current Psychiatry Reports, 7,* 65–72.

McConaghy, N. (1993). *Sexual behavior: Problems and management.* New York: Plenum.

McCracken, J. T., McGough, J., Shah, B., Cronin, P., Hong, D., Aman, M. G., et al. Research Units on Pediatric Psychopharmacology Autism Network. (2002). Risperidone in children with autism and serious behavioral problems. *New England Journal of Medicine, 347,* 314–321.

McCrae, R. R., Yang, J., Costa, P. T., Dai, X., Yao, S., Cai, T., & Gao, B. (2001). Personality profiles and the prediction of categorical personality disorders. *Journal of Personality, 69,* 155–174.

McCusker, C. (2001). Cognitive biases and addiction: An evolution in theory and method. *Addiction, 96,* 47–56.

McDonald, C., Grech, A., Touloupoulou, T., Schulze, K., Chapple, B., Sham, P., et al. (2002). Brain volumes in familial and non-familial schizophrenic probands and their unaffected relatives. *American Journal of Medical Genetics and Neuropsychiatric Genetics, 114,* 616–625.

McDougle, C. J., Scahill, L., Aman, M. G., McCracken, J. T., Tierney, E., Davies, M., et al. (2005). Risperidone for the core symptom domains of autism: Results from the study by the Autism Network of the Research Units on Pediatric Psychopharmacology. *American Journal of Psychiatry, 162,* 1142–1148.

McElroy, S. L., Soutullo, C. A., Taylor, P., Jr., Nelson, E. B., Beckman, D. A., Brusman, L. A., et al. (1999). Psychiatric features of 36 men convicted of sexual offenses. *Journal of Clinical Psychiatry, 60,* 414–420.

McGough, J. J., & Barkley, R. A. (2004). Diagnostic controversies in adult attention deficit hyperactivity disorder. *American Journal of Psychiatry, 161,* 1948–1956.

McGrath, E., Keita, G. P., Stickland, B. R., & Russo, N. F. (1990). *Women and depression: Risk factors and treatment issues.* Washington, DC: American Psychological Association.

McGuffin, P., Owen, M. J., & Farmer, A. E. (1995). Genetic basis of schizophrenia. *The Lancet, 346,* 678–682.

McIntosh, J. L., Santos, J. F., Hubbard, R. W., & Overholser, J. C. (1994). *Elder suicide: Research, theory, and treatment.* Washington, DC: American Psychological Association.

McIntosh, V. V., Bulik, C. M., McKenzie, J. M., Luty, S. E., & Jordan, J. (2000). Interpersonal psychotherapy for anorexia nervosa. *International Journal of Eating Disorders, 27,* 125–139.

McIntosh, V. V., Jordan, J., Carter, F., Luty, S., McKenzie, J., Bulik, C. M., et al. (2005). Three psychotherapies for anorexia nervosa: A randomized controlled trial. *American Journal of Psychiatry, 162,* 741–747.

McKenna, M. C., Zevon, M. A., Corn, B., & Rounds, J. (1999). Psychosocial factors and the development of breast cancer: a meta-analysis. *Health Psychology, 18,* 520–531.

McKnight Investigators. (2003). Risk factors for the onset of eating disorders in adolescent girls: Results of the McKnight longitudinal risk factor study. *American Journal of Psychiatry, 160,* 248–254.

McLaren, J., & Bryson, S. E. (1987). Review of recent epidemiological studies of mental retardation: prevalence, associated disorder, and etiology. *American Journal of Mental Retardation, 92,* 243–254.

McMahon, C. G., Althof, S., Waldinger, M. D., Porst, H., Dean, J., Sharlip, I., et al. International Society for Sexual Medicine Ad Hoc Committee for Definition of Premature Ejaculation. (2008). An evidence-based definition of lifelong premature ejaculation. *BJU International, 102,* 338–350.

McMahon, F. J. (2004). Genetics of mood disorders and associated psychopathology. In J. Sadavoy, L. F. Jarvik, G. T. Grossberg, & B. S. Meyers (Eds.), *Comprehensive textbook of geriatric psychiatry* (3rd ed., pp. 85–104). New York: W.W. Norton & Co.

McNally, R. J. (1995). Automaticity and the anxiety disorders. *Behaviour Research and Therapy, 33,* 747–754.

McNally, R. J. (1999). EMDR and Mesmerism: A comparative historical analysis. *Journal of Anxiety Disorders, 13,* 225–236.

McNally, R. J. (2001). Vulnerability to anxiety disorders in adulthood. In R. E. Ingram & J. M. Price (Eds.), *Vulnerability to psychopathology: Risk across the lifespan* (pp. 304–321). New York: Guilford Press.

McNally, R. J. (2005). Debunking myths about trauma and memory. *Canadian Journal of Psychiatry, 50,* 817–822.

Meadows, M. (2004). Institute of Medicine Report: No link between vaccines and autism. http://www/fda.gov/fdac/features/2004/504_iom.htm.

Medina-Moira, M. E., Borges, G., Lara, C., Benjet, C., Blanco, J., Fleiz, C., Villatoro, J., Rojas, E., & Zambrano, J. (2005). Prevalence, service use, and demographic correlates of 12–month DSM–IV psychiatric disorders in Mexico: Results from the Mexican National Comorbidity Survey. *Psychological Medicine, 35,* 1773–1783.

Mednick, S. A., Machon, R. A., Huttunen, M. O., & Bonett, D. Adult schizophrenia following prenatal exposure to an influenza epidemic. *Archives of General Psychiatry, 45,* 189–192.

Mehta, K. M., Simonsick, E. M., Penninx, B. W., Schulz, R., Rubin, S. M., Satterfield, S., & Yaffe, K. (2003). Prevalence and correlates of anxiety symptoms in well-functioning older adults: Findings from the health aging and body composition study. *Journal of the American Geriatrics Society, 51,* 499–504.

Meijler, M., Matsushita, M., Wirsching, P., & Janda, K. (2004). Development of immunopharmacotherapy against drugs of abuse. *Current Drug Discovery Technology, 1,* 77–89.

Meilman, P. W., & Hall, T. M. (2006). Aftermath of tragic events: The development and use of community support meetings on a university campus. *Journal of American College Health, 54,* 382–384.

Mendlowicz, M. V., & Stein, M. B. (2000). Quality of life in individuals with anxiety disorders. *American Journal of Psychiatry, 157,* 669–682.

Mennin, D. S., Heimberg, R. G., & Turk, C. L. (2004). Clinical presentation and diagnostic features. In R. G. Heimberg, C. L. Turk, & D. S. Mennin (Eds.), *Generalized anxiety disorder: Advances in research and practice* (pp. 3–28). New York: Guilford Press.

Merck & Co. (1995–2006). Drug Use and Dependence Accessed on the web at http://www.merck.com/mmpe/sec15/ch198/ch198a.html?qt=drug%20use%20and%20dependence&alt=sh

Meston, C. M., & Ahrold, T. (2007). Ethnic, gender, and acculturation influences on sexual behaviors. *Archives of Sexual Behavior, 33,* 223–234.

Meston, C. M., Trapnell, P. D., & Gorzalka, B. B.(1996). Ethnic and gender differences in sexuality: Variations in sexual behavior between Asian and non-Asian university students. *Archives of Sexual Behavior, 25,* 33–72.

Metz, M. E., Pryor, J. L., Nesvacil, L. J., Abuzzahab, F., Sr., & Koznar, J. (1997). Premature ejaculation: A psychophysiological review. *Journal of Sex & Marital Therapy, 23,* 3–23.

Meyer, G. J., Finn, S. E., Eyde, L. D., Kay, G. G., Moreland, K. L., Dies, R. R., Eisman, E. J., Kubiszyn, T. W., & Reed, G. M. (2001). Psychological testing and psychological assessment: A review of evidence and issues. *American Psychologist, 56,* 128–165.

Meyer, R. G. (2003). *Case studies in abnormal behavior* (6th ed.). Boston: Allyn and Bacon.

Meyer, W. J., III (2004). Comorbidity of gender identity issues. *American Journal of Psychiatry, 161,* 934–935.

Meyer, W., III, Bockting, W. O., Cohen-Kettenis, P., Coleman, E., DiCeglie, D., Devor, H., et al. (2001). The Harry Benjamin International Gender Dysphoria Association's Standards of Care for Gender Identity Disorders, 6th edition. *Journal of Psychology & Human Sexuality, 13,* 1–30.

Meyers, L (2008, April). The lingering storm. *American Psychological Association Monitor,* 50–52.

Meyers, R., Smith, J., & Lash, D. (2003). The community reinforcement approach. In M. Galanter (Ed.), *Recent developments in alcoholism, Volume 16: Research on alcoholism treatment* (pp. 183–195). New York: Kluwer Academic/Plenum Publishers.

Michel, A., Mormont, C., & Legros, J. J. (2001). A psycho-endocrinological overview of transsexualism. *European Journal of Endocrinology, 145,* 365–376.

Migneault, J., Adams, T., & Read, J. (2005). Application of the transtheoretical model to substance abuse: Historical development and future directions. *Drug and Alcohol Review, 24,* 437–438.

Mikkelsen, E. J. (2001). Enuresis and encopresis: Ten years of progress. *Journal of the American Academy of Child and Adolescent Psychiatry, 40,* 1146–1158.

Milak, M. S., Parsey, R. V., Keilp, J., Oquendo, M. A., Malone, K. M., & Mann, J. J. (2005). Neuroanatomic correlates of psychopathologic components of major depressive disorder. *Archives of General Psychiatry, 62,* 397–408.

Miller, E. R., III, Pastor-Barriuso, R., Dalal, D., Riemersma, R. A., Appel, L. J., & Guallar, E. (2005). Meta-analysis: High-dosage vitamin E supplementation may increase all-cause mortality. *Annals of Internal Medicine, 142,* 37–46.

Miller, G. E., Chen, E., & Zhou, E. S. (2007). If it goes up, must it come down? Chronic stress and the hypothalamic-pituitary-adrenocortical axis in humans. *Psychological Bulletin, 133,* 25–45.

Miller, J. G. (1997). Theoretical issues in cultural psychology. In J. W. Berry, Y. H. Poortinga, & J. Pandey (Eds.), *Handbook of cross-cultural psychology* (2nd ed.). Boston: Allyn and Bacon.

Miller, W. (1983). Motivational interviewing with problem drinkers. *Behavioural Psychotherapy, 11,* 147–172.

Miller, W., & Rollnick, S. (1991). *Motivational interviewing: Preparing people to change addictive behavior.* New York: Guilford Press.

Milos, G., Spindler, A., Schnyder, U., Martz, J., Hoek, H., & Willi, J. (2004). Incidence of severe anorexia nervosa in Switzerland: 40 years of development. *International Journal of Eating Disorders, 36,* 118–119.

Mineka, S., & Cook, M. (1986). Immunization against the observational conditioning of snake fear in rhesus monkeys. *Journal of Abnormal Psychology, 95,* 307–318.

Mineka, S., & Zinbarg, R. (2006). A contemporary learning theory perspective on the etiology of anxiety disorders: It's not what you thought it was. *American Psychologist, 61,* 10–26.

Minsky, s., Vega, W., Miskimen, T., Gara, M., & Escobar, J. (2003). Diagnostic patterns in Latino, African American, and European American psychiatric patients. *Archives of General Psychiatry, 60,* 637–644.

Minuchin, S., Rosman, B. L., & Baker, L. (1978). *Psychosomatic families. Anorexia nervosa in context.* Cambridge, MA: Harvard University Press.

Miranda, A. O., & Fraser, L. D. (2002). Culture-bound syndromes: Initial perspectives from individual psychology. *Journal of Individual Psychology, 58,* 422–433.

Mischel, W. (1973). Toward a cognitive social learning reconceptualization of personality. *Psychology Review, 39,* 351–364.

Mischel, W., & Shoda, Y. (1995). A cognitive-affective system of personality: Reconceptualizing situations, dispositions, dynamics and invariance in personality structure. *Psychology Review, 102,* 246–268.

Mitchell, J. E. (1990). *Bulimia nervosa.* Minneapolis: University of Minnesota Press.

Mitchell, J., Specker, S., & De Zwaan, M. (1991). Comorbidity and medical complications of bulimia nervosa. *Journal of Clinical Psychiatry, 52,* 13–20.

Moeller, F. G., Chen, Y. W., Steinberg, J. L., Petty, F., Ripper, G. W., Shah, N., et al. (1995). Risk factors for clozapine discontinuation among 805 patients in the VA hospital system. *Annals of Clinical Psychiatry, 7,* 167–173.

Mohammed, I., Cherkas, L. F., Riley, S. A., Spector, T. D., & Trudgill, N. J. (2005). Genetic influences in irritable bowel syndrome: A twin study. *American Journal of Gastroenterology, 100,* 1340–1344.

Mojtabai, R. (2005). Perceived reasons for loss of housing and continued homelessness among homeless persons with mental illness. *Psychiatric Services, 56,* 172–178.

Moller, J., Hallqvist, J., Diderichsen, F., Theorell, T., Reuterwall, C., & Ahlbom, A. (1999). Do episodes of anger trigger myocardial infarction? A case-crossover analysis in the Stockholm Heart Epidemiology Program (SHEEP). *Psychosomatic Medicine, 61,* 842–849.

Monahan, J. (2001). Major mental disorders and violence: Epidemiology and risk assessment. In G. F. Pinard & L. Pagani (Eds.), *Clinical assessment of dangerousness: Empirical contributions* (pp. 89–102). New York: Cambridge University Press.

Monahan, J., Bonnie, R. J., Appelbaum, P. S., Hyde, P. S., Steadman, H. J., & Swartz, M. S. (2001). Mandated community treatment: Beyond outpatient commitment. *Psychiatric Services, 52,* 1198–1205.

Money, J. (1994). The concept of gender identity disorder in childhood and adolescence after 39 years. *Journal of Sex and Marital Therapy, 20,* 163–177.

Money, J., & Ehrhardt, A. (1972) *Man and woman, boy and girl.* Baltimore, MD: Johns Hopkins University Press.

Money, J., & Ehrhardt. A. A. (1972). Gender dimorphic behavior and fetal sex hormones. *Recent Progress in Hormonal Research, 28,* 735–763.

Monohan, J., Steadman, H. J., Silver, E., Appelbaum, P. S., Robbins, P. C., Mulvey, E. P., et al. (2001). *Rethinking risk assessment: The MacArthur study of mental disorder and violence.* New York: Oxford University Press.

Monroe, S. M., Harkness, K., Simons, A. D., & Thase, M. E. (2001). Life stress and the symptoms of major depression. *Journal of Nervous and Mental Disease, 189,* 168–175.

Moore, D. B., & Bona, J. R. (2001). Depression and dysthymia. *Medical Clinics of North America, 85,* 631–644.

Moore, H., West, A. R., & Grace, A. A. (1999). The regulation of forebrain dopamine transmission: Relevance to the pathophysiology and psychopathology of schizophrenia. *Biological Psychiatry, 46,* 40–55.

Moore, K., & McLaughlin, D. (2003). Depression: The challenge for all healthcare professionals. *Nursing Standard, 17,* 45–52.

Moos, R. (2008). Active ingredients of substance use-focused self-help groups. *Addiction, 103,* 387–396.

Moradi, B., Dirks, D., & Matteson, A. V. (2005). Roles of sexual objectification experiences and internalization of standards of beauty in eating disorder symptomatology: A test and extension of objectification theory. *Journal of Counseling Psychology, 51,* 420–428.

Morales, A., Heaton, J. P., & Carson, C. C. (2000). Andropause: A misnomer for a true clinical entity. *Journal of Urology, 163,* 705–712.

Moreira, E. D., Brock, G., Glasser, D. B., Nicolosi, A., Laumann, E. O., Paik, A., et al., & GSSAB Investigators' Group. (2005). Help-seeking behaviour for sexual problems. The global study of sexual attitudes and behaviors. *International Journal of Clinical Practice, 59,* 6–16.

Morgan, D., & Morgan, R. (2001). Single-participant research design: Bringing science to managed care. *American Psychologist, 56,* 119–127.

Morin, C. M., & Espie, C. A. (2003) *Insomnia: A clinical guide to assessment and treatment.* New York: Kluwer Academic/Plenum.

Morin, C. M., Bastien, C., Guay, B., Radouco-Thomas, M., Leblanc, J., & Vallieres, A. (2004). Randomized clinical trial of supervised tapering and cognitive behavior therapy to facilitate benzodiazepine discontinuation in older adults with chronic insomnia. *American Journal of Psychiatry, 161,* 332–342.

Morin, C. M., LeBlanc, M., Daley, M., Gregoire, J. P., & Merette, C. (2006). Epidemiology of insomnia: Prevalence, self-help treatments, consultations, and determinants of help-seeking behaviors. *Sleep Medicine, 7,* 123–130.

Morin, C. M., Vallieres, A., Guay, B., Ivers, H., Savard, J., Merette, C., Bastien, C., et al. (2009). Cognitive behavioral therapy, singly and combined with medication, for persistent insomnia: A randomized controlled trial. *Journal of the American Medical Association, 301,* 2005–2015.

Moritz, S., Fricke, S., Jacobsen, D., Kloss, M., Wein, C., Rufer, M., et al. (2004). Positive schizotypal symptoms predict treatment outcome in obsessive-compulsive disorder. *Behaviour Research and Therapy, 42,* 217–227.

Morris, J. C. (2005). Dementia update 2005. *Alzheimer Disease and Associated Disorders, 19,* 100–117.

Morris, J. C. (2005). Early-stage and preclinical Alzheimer disease. *Alzheimer Disease and Associated Disorders, 19,* 163–165.

Morris, J. C. (2006). Mild cognitive impairment is early-stage Alzheimer disease: Time to revise diagnostic criteria. *Archives of Neurology, 63,* 15–16.

Morrison, J. (1989). Childhood sexual histories of women with somatization disorder. *American Journal of Psychiatry, 146,* 239–241.

Moscicki, E. (1999). Epidemiology of suicide. In D. Jacobs (Ed.), *The Harvard Medical School guide to suicide assessment and intervention* (pp. 40–51). San Francisco: Jossey-Bass.

Moscicki, E. (2001). Epidemiology of completed and attempted suicide: Toward a framework for prevention. *Clinical Neuroscience Research, 1,* 310–323.

Moses-Kolko, E. L., & Roth, E. K. (2004). Antepartum and postpartum depression: Healthy mom, healthy baby. *Journal of the American Medical Women's Association, 59,* 181–191.

Mossakowski, K. N. (2003). Coping with perceived discrimination: Does ethnic identity protect mental health? *Journal of Health and Social Behavior, 44,* 318–331.

Motlova, L., Dragomirecka, E., Spaniel, F., Goppoldova, E., Zalesky, R., Selepova, P., et al. (2006). Relapse prevention in schizophrenia: Does group family psychoeducation matter? One year prospective follow-up field study. *International Journal of Psychiatry in Clinical Practice, 10,* 38–44.

Moynihan, R. (2006). Scientists find new disease: Motivational deficiency disorder. *British Medical Journal, 332,* 745.

Mrvos, R., Reilly, P., Dean, B., & Krenzelok, E. (1989). Massive caffeine ingestion resulting in death. *Veterinary and Human Toxicology, 31,* 571–572.

MTA Cooperative Group (1999). A 14-month randomized clinical trial of treatment strategies for attention-deficit/hyperactivity disorder. *Archives of General Psychiatry, 56,* 1073–1086.

Mueser, K. T., & McGurk, S. R. (2004). Schizophrenia. *The Lancet, 363,* 2063–2072.

Mueser, K. T., Bellack, A. S., & Brady, E. U. (1990). Hallucinations in schizophrenia. *Acta Psychiatrica Scandiavica, 82,* 26–29.

Mueser, K. T., Rosenberg, S. D., Goodman, L. A., & Trumbetta, S. L. (2002). Trauma, PTSD, and the course of schizophrenia: An interactive model. *Schizophrenia Research, 53,* 123–143.

Mufson, L., Moreau, D., Weissman, M., Wickramaratne, P., Martin, J., & Samoilov, A. (1994). Modification of interpersonal psychotherapy with depressed adolescents (IPTA-A): Phase I and II studies. *Journal of the American Academy of Child and Adolescent Psychiatry, 33,* 695–705.

Muhlau, M., Gaser, C., Ilg, R., Conrad, B., Leibl, C., Cebulla, M. H., et al. (2007). Gray matter decrease of the anterior cingulate cortex in anorexia nervosa. *American Journal of Psychiatry, 164,* 1850–1857.

Munk-Jorgensen, P. (1987). First-admission rates and marital status of schizophrenics. *Acta Psychiatrica Scandinavica, 76,* 210–216.

Muratori, F., Salvadori, F., D'Arcangelo, G., Viglione, V., & Picchi, L. (2005). Childhood psychopathological antecedents in early onset schizophrenia. *European Psychiatry, 20,* 309–314.

Muris, P., Schmidt, H., & Merckelbach, H. (1999). The structure of specific phobia symptoms among children and adolescents. *Behaviour Research and Therapy, 37,* 863–868.

Murphy, D., & Peters, J. M. (1992). Profiling child sexual abusers. Psychological considerations. *Criminal Justice and Behavior, 19,* 24–37.

Muse, L., Harris, S., & Field, H. (2003). Has the inverted-U theory of stress and job performance had a fair test? *Human Performance, 16,* 349–364.

Musselman, D. L., Evans, D. L., & Nemeroff, C. B. (1998). The relationship of depression to cardiovascular disease: Epidemiology, biology, and treatment. *Archives of General Psychiatry, 55,* 580–592.

Mutrie, N., Campbell, A. M., Whyte, F., McConnachie, A., Emslie, C., Lee, L., et al. (2007). Benefits of supervised group exercise programme for women being treated for early stage breast cancer: Pragmatic randomised controlled trial. *British Medical Journal, 334,* 517.

Myers, J. K., Weissman, M. M., Tischler, G. L., Holzer, C. E., III, Leaf, P. J., Orvaschel, H., et al. (1984). Six-month prevalence of psychiatric disorders in three communities 1980 to 1982. *Archives of General Psychiatry, 41,* 959–967.

Naik, A. D., Concato, J., & Gill, T. M. (2004). Bathing disability in community-living older persons: Common, consequential, and complex. *Journal of the American Geriatrics Society, 52,* 1805–1810.

Namanzi, M. R. (2001). Avicenna, 980–1037. *American Journal of Psychiatry, 158,* 1796.

Nanda, S. (1985). The hijras of India: Cultural and individual dimensions of an institutionalized third gender role. *Journal of Homosexuality, 11,* 35–54.

Nathan, P. E., & Langenbucher, J. W. (1999). Psychopathology: Description and classification. *Annual Review of Psychology, 50,* 79–107.

Nation, M., Crusto, C., Wandersman, A., Kumpfer, K., Seybolt, D., Morrisey-Kane, E., et al. (2003). What works in prevention: Principles of effective prevention programs. *American Psychologist, 58,* 449–456.

National Institute of Clinical and Health Excellence. (2004). http://www.nice.org.uk/page.aspx?o=101239.

National Institute of Health (2005). State-of-the-Science Conference Statement on Manifestations and Management of Chronic Insomnia in Adults.

National Institute of Mental Health. (2000). *Depression* (No. 00-3561). Bethesda, MD: National Institute of Mental Health, National Institutes of Health, U.S. Department of Health and Human Services.

National Institute of Mental Health. (2001). *Bipolar disorder*, from http://www.nimh.nih.gov/publicat/bipolar.cfm

National Institute of Mental Health. (2003). Older adults: Depression and suicide facts. *Depression*. Retrieved January 21, 2006, from http://www.nimh.nih.gov/publicat/elderlydepsuicide.cfm

National Institute of Mental Health. (2005, December 5, 2006). Antidepressant medications for children and adolescents: Information for parents and caregivers. Retrieved February 24, 2007, from http://www.nimh.nih.gov/healthinformation/antidepressant_child.cfm

National Institute of Mental Health. (2007). *Suicide in the U.S.: Statistics and prevention* (No. NIH Publication No. 06-4594). National Institutes of Health, U.S. Department of Health and Human Services.

National Institute on Drug Abuse. (2001). *Nicotine Addiction*. Bethesda, MD: National Institutes of Health.

National Institute on Drug Abuse. (2004a). *Inhalant Abuse*. Bethesda, MD: National Institutes of Health.

National Institute on Drug Abuse. (2004b). *Research Report Series: Cocaine abuse and addiction*: National Institute of Drug Abuse, National Institutes of Health, U.S. Department of Health and Human Services.

National Institute on Drug Abuse. (2005a). *Hallucinogens and Dissociative Drugs*. Bethesda, MD: National Institutes of Health.

National Institute on Drug Abuse. (2005b). *Marijuana*. Bethesda, MD: National Institutes of Health.

National Survey on Drug Use and Health: Substance use among older adults: 2002 & 2003 update (2006). www.oas.samhsa.gov [Online].

Nau, S. D., McCrae, C. S., Cook, K. G., & Lichstein, K. L. (2005). Treatment of insomnia in older adults. *Clinical Psychology Review., 25*, 645–672.

Nay, M. (1994, September). Beliefs and practices about food during pregnancy. *Economic and Political Weekly*, 2427–2438.

Neaton, J. D., & Wentworth, D. (1992). Serum cholesterol, blood pressure, cigarette smoking, and death from coronary heart disease: Overall findings and differences by age for 316,099 white men. Multiple Risk Factor Intervention Trial Research Group. *Archives of Internal Medicine, 152*, 56–64.

Needleman, H. L., & Gatsonis, C. A. (1990). Low-level lead exposure and the IQ of children. A meta-analysis of modern studies. *Journal of the American Medical Association, 263*, 673–678.

Needleman, H. L., Schell, A., Bellinger, D., Leviton, A., & Allred, E. N. (1990). The long-term effects of exposure to low doses of lead in childhood: An 11-year follow-up report. *New England Journal of Medicine, 322*, 83–88.

Neighbors, H. W (1985). Seeking help for personal problems: Black Americans' use of health and mental health services. *Community Mental Health Journal, 21*, 156–166.

Neisser, U., & Harsch, N. (1992). Phantom flashbulbs: False recollections of hearing the news about Challenger. In E. Winograd & U. Neisser (Eds.), *Affect and accuracy in recall: studies of flashbulb memories* (pp. 9–31). Cambridge, MA: Cambridge University Press.

Nelson, E. C., Grant, J. D., Bucholz, K. K., Glowinski, A., Madden, P. A. F., Reich, W., et al. (2000). Social phobia in a population-based female adolescent twin sample: Co-morbidity and associated suicide-related symptoms. *Psychological Medicine, 30*, 797–804.

Nelson, E. C., Heath, A. C., Madden, P. A., Cooper, M. L., Dinwiddie, S. H., Bucholz, K. K., et al. (2002). Association between self-reported childhood sexual abuse and adverse psychosocial outcomes. *Archives of General Psychiatry, 59*, 139–145.

Nelson, R. M. (2002). Appropriate risk exposure in environmental health research. The Kennedy-Krieger lead abatement study. *Neurotoxicology and Teratology, 24*, 445–449.

Nestadt, G., Bienvenu, O. J., Cai, G., Samuels, J., & Eaton, W. W. (1998). Incidence of obsessive-compulsive disorder in adults. *Journal of Nervous and Mental Disease, 186*, 401–406.

Nestadt, G., Romanoski, A. J., Chahal, R., Merchant, A., Folstein, M. F., Gruenberg, E. M., et al. (1990). An epidemiological study of histrionic personality disorder. *Psychological Medicine, 20*, 413–422.

Nestoriuc, Y., & Martin, A. (2007). Efficacy of biofeedback for migraine: A meta-analysis. *Pain, 128*, 111–127.

Newcomb, M., & Richardson, M. A. (1995). Substance use disorders. In M. Hersen & R. Ammerman (Eds.), *Advanced abnormal child psychology* (pp. 411–431). Hillsdale, NJ: Lawrence Erlbaum Associates.

Newton, E., Landau, S., Smith, P., Monks, P. N., Sherrill, S., & Wykes, T. (2005). Early psychological intervention for auditory hallucinations. *Journal of Nervous and Mental Disease, 193*, 58–61.

Nicolosi, A., Laumann, E. O., Glasser, D. B., Brock, G., King, R., & Gingell, C. (2006). Sexual activity, sexual disorders and associated help-seeking behavior among mature adults in five Anglophone countries from the Global Survey of Sexual Attitudes and Behaviors (GSSAB). *Journal of Sex & Marital Therapy, 32*, 331–342.

Nicolosi, A., Laumann, E. O., Glasser, D. B., Moreira, E. D. Jr., Paik, A., & Gingell, C., for the Global Study of Sexual Attitudes and Behaviors Investigators' Group. (2004). Sexual behavior and sexual dysfunctions after age 40: The Global Study of Sexual Attitudes and Behaviors. *Urology, 64*, 991–997.

Niedermeyer, E. (1999). Historical aspects. In *Electroencephalography: Basic principles, clinical applications and related fields* (pp. 1–13). New York: Lippincott Williams & Wilkins.

Nieto, J. A. (2004). Children and adolescents as sexual beings: cross-cultural perspectives. *Child and Adolescent Psychiatric Clinics of North America, 13*, 461–477.

NIH consensus conference (1992). Diagnosis and treatment of depression in late life. *Journal of the American Medical Association, 268*, 1018–1024.

Nolen-Hoeksema, S. (2001). Gender differences in depression. *Current Directions in Psychological Science, 10*, 173–176.

Nordhus, I. H., & Pallesen, S. (2003). Psychological treatment of late-life anxiety: An empirical review. *Journal of Consulting and Clinical Psychology, 71*, 643–652.

Norfleet, M. A. (2002). Responding to society's needs: Prescription privileges for psychologists. *Journal of Clinical Psychology, 58*, 599–610.

Norris, F. H., & Kaniasty, K. (1994). Psychological distress following criminal victimization in the general population: Cross-sectional, longitudinal, and prospective analysis. *Journal of Consulting and Clinical Psychology, 62*, 111–124.

North, C. S., Ryall, J. E. M., Ricci, D. A., & Wetzel, R. D. (1993). *Multiple personalities, multiple disorders*. New York: Oxford University Press.

Norton, N., Williams, H. J., & Owen, M. J. (2006). An update on the genetics of schizophrenia. *Current Opinion in Psychiatry, 19*, 158–164.

Novy, D. M., Stanley, M. A., Averill, P., & Daza, P. (2001). Psychometric comparability of English- and Spanish-language measures of anxiety and related affective symptoms. *Psychological Assessment, 13*, 347–355.

Noyes, R., Woodman, C., Garvey, M. J., Cook, B. L., Suelzer, M., Clancy, J., et al. (1992). Generalized anxiety disorder versus panic disorder: Distinguishing characteristics and patterns of comorbidity. *Journal of Nervous and Mental Disease, 180*, 369–378.

Nusbaum, M. R., Gamble, G., Skinner, B., & Heiman, J. (2000). The high prevalence of sexual concerns among women seeking routine gynecological care. *Journal of Family Practice, 49*, 229–232.

Nydegger, R. V. (1972). The elimination of hallucinatory and delusional behavior by verbal conditioning and assertive training: A case study. *Journal of Behavior Therapy and Experimental Psychiatry, 3*, 225.

O'Brien, C., Woody, G., & McLellan, A. (1995). Enhancing the effectiveness of methadone using psychotherapeutic interventions. *NIDA Research Monograph, 150*, 5–18.

O'Brien, M. D., Bruce, B. K., & Camilleri, M. (1995). The rumination syndrome: Clinical features rather than manometric diagnosis. *Gastroenterology, 108*, 1024–1029.

O'Carroll, R. (1989). A neuropsychological study of sexual deviation. *Sexual and Marital Therapy, 4*, 59–63.

O'Connor, K., & Roth, B. (2005). Finding new tricks for old drugs: An efficient route for public-sector drug discovery. *Nature Reviews Drug Discovery, 4*, 1005–1014.

O'Hara, M., & Swain, A. (1996). Rates and risk of postpartum depression: A meta-analysis. *International Review of Psychiatry, 8*, 37–54.

O'Leary, T., & Monti, P. (2002). Cognitive-behavioral therapy for alcohol addiction. In S. Hofmann & M. Tompson (Eds.), *Treating chronic and severe mental disorders: A handbook of empirically supported interventions* (pp. 234–257). New York: Guilford Press.

O'Malley, P. G., Jackson, J. L., Santoro, J., Tomkins, G., Balden, E., & Kroenke, K. (1999). Antidepressant therapy for unexplained symptoms and symptom syndrome. *Journal of Family Practice, 48*, 980–990.

Odendaal, J. S., & Meintjes, R. A. (2003). Neurophysiological correlates of affiliative behaviour between humans and dogs. *Veterinary Journal, 165*, 296–301.

Office of the U.S. Surgeon General. (2004). *The Health Consequences of Smoking: A Report of the Surgeon General.* Retrieved. from http://www.surgeongeneral.gov/library/smokingconsequences/. Accessed February 5, 2008.

Ogata, S. N., Silk, K. R., Goodrich, S., Lohr, N. E., Westen, D., & Hill, E. M. (1990). Childhood sexual and physical abuse in adult patients with borderline personality disorder. *American Journal of Psychiatry, 147*, 1008–1013.

Ohara K., Sato, Y., Tanabu, S., Yoshida, K., & Shibuya, H. (2006). Magnetic resonance imaging study of the ventricle-brain ratio in parents of schizophrenia subjects. *Progress in Neuro-Psychopharmacology & Biological Psychiatry, 30*, 89–92.

Okazaki, S., & Sue, S. (1995). Methodological issues in assessment research with ethnic minorities. *Psychological Assessment, 7*, 367–375.

Oleseon, O. F., Bennike, B., Hansen, E. S., Koefoed, P., Woldbye, D. P., Bolwig, T. G., & Mellerup, E. (2005). The short/long polymorphism in the serotonin transporter gene prooter is not associated with panic disorder in a Scandinavian sample. *Psychiatric Genetics, 15*, 159.

Olfsen, M., Guardino, M., Struuning, E., Schneier, F. R., Hellman, F., & Klein, D. F. (2000). Barriers to treatment of social anxiety. *American Journal of Psychiatry, 15*, 521–527.

Olfson, M., Marcus, S. C., Weissman, M. M., & Jensen, P. D. (2002). National trends in the use of psychotropic medications by children. *Journal of the American Academy of Child and Adolescent Psychiatry, 41*, 514–521.

Olfson, M., Mechanic, D., Hansell, S., Boyer, C. A., & Walkup, J. (1999). Prediction of homelessness within three months of discharge among inpatients with schizophrenia. *Psychiatric Services, 50*, 667–673.

Olin, J. T., Schneider, L. S., Katz, I. R., Meyers, B. S., Alexopoulos, G. S., Breitner, J. C., et al. (2002). Provisional diagnostic criteria for depression of Alzheimer disease. *American Journal of Geriatric Psychiatry, 10*, 125–128.

Ollendick, T. H., & King, N. J. (1991). Origins of childhood fears: An evaluation of Rachman's theory of fear acquisition. *Behaviour Research and Therapy, 29*, 117–125.

Ollendick, T. H., King, N. J., & Muris, P. (2004). Phobias in children and adolescents. In M. Maj, H. S. Akiskal, J. J. Lopez-Ibor, & A. Okasha (Eds.), *Phobias* (pp. 245–279). London: John Wiley & Sons.

Ollendick, T. H., Matson, J. L., & Helsel, W. I. (1985). Fears in children and adolescents: Normative data. *Behaviour Research and Therapy, 23*, 465–467.

Olson, L., & Houlihan, D. (2000). A review of behavioral treatments used for Lesch-Nyhan syndrome. *Behavior Modification, 24*, 202–222.

Opler, M. G. A., & Susser, E. S. (2005). Fetal environment and schizophrenia. *Environmental Health Perspectives, 113*, 1239–1242.

Osborn, T. (2007). The psychosocial impact of parental cancer on children and adolescents: a systematic review. *Psycho-oncology, 16*, 101–126.

Osby, U., Correia, N., Brandt, L., Ekbom, A., & Sparen, P. (2000). Mortality and causes of death in schizophrenia in Stockholm County, Sweden. *Schizophrenia Research, 45*, 21–28.

Oslin, D. (2005a). Brief interventions in the treatment of at-risk drinking in older adults. *Psychiatric Clinics of North America, 28*, 897–911.

Oslin, D. W. (2004). Late-life alcoholism: Issues relevant to the geriatric psychiatrist. *American Journal of Geriatric Psychiatry, 12*, 571–583.

Oslin, D. W. (2005). Evidence-based treatment of geriatric substance abuse. *Psychiatric Clinics of North America, 28*, 897–911, ix.

Oslin, D. W., Liberto, J. G., O'Brien, J., Krois, S., & Norbeck, J. (1997). Naltrexone as an adjunctive treatment for older patients with alcohol dependence. *The American Journal of Geriatric Psychiatry 5*, 324–331.

Oslin, D. W., Pettinati, H., & Volpicelli, J. R. (2002). Alcoholism treatment adherence: older age predicts better adherence and drinking outcomes. *American Journal of Geriatric Psychiatry, 10*, 740–747.

Ost, L. G. (1996). Long-term effects of behavior therapy for specific phobia. In M. Mavissakalian and R. R. Prien (Eds.), *Long-term treatments of anxiety disorders* (pp. 121–170). New York: Plenum.

Osterloh, I. H., & Riley, A. (2002). Clinical update on sildenafil citrate. *British Journal of Clinical Pharmacology, 53*, 219–223.

Oswald, D. P., Countinho, M. J., Best, A. M., & Nguyen, N. (2001). Impact of sociodemographic characteristics on the identification rates on minority students as having mental retardation. *Mental Retardation, 39*, 351–367.

Otto, M. W., Pollack, M. H., Sachs, G. S., Reiter, S. R., Meltzer-Brody, S., & Rosenbaum, J. R. (1993). Discontinuation of benzodiazepine treatment: Efficacy of cognitive-behavioral therapy for patients with panic disorder. *American Journal of Psychiatry, 150*, 1485–1490.

Otto, M. W., Pollack, M. H., Maki, K. M., Gould, R. A., Worthington, J. J., III, Smoller, J. W., et al. (2001). Childhood history of anxiety disorders among adults with social phobia. *Depression and Anxiety, 14*, 209–213.

Ouimette, P. C., Finney, J. W., & Moos, R. H. (1997). Twelve-step and cognitive-behavioral treatment for substance abuse: A comparison of treatment effectiveness. *Journal of Consulting and Clinical Psychology, 65*, 230–240.

Overall, J., & Gorham, D. (1988). The Brief Psychiatric Rating Scale (BPRS): Recent developments in ascertainment and scaling. *Psychopharmacology Bulletin, 24*, 97–99.

Owens, D. G., Miler, P., Lawrie, S. M., & Johnstone, E. C. (2005). Pathogenesis of schizophrenia: A psychopathological perspective. *British Journal of Psychiatry, 186*, 386–393.

Ozer, E. J., Best, S. R., Lipsey, T. L., & Weiss, D. S.(2003). Predictors of posttraumatic stress disorder and symptoms of adults: A meta-analysis. *Psychological Bulletin, 129*, 52–75.

Padma-Nathan, H., Brown, C., Fendl, J., Salem, S., Yeager, J., & Harning, R. (2003). Efficacy and safety of topical alprostadil cream for the treatment of female sexual arousal disorder (FSAD): A double-blind, multicenter, randomized, and placebo-controlled clinical trial. *Journal of Sex & Marital Therapy, 29*, 329–344.

Padma-Nathan, H., Hellstrom, W. J., Kaiser, F. E., Labasky, R. F., Lue, T. F., Nolten, W. E., et al. (1997). Treatment of men with erectile dysfunction with transurethral alprostadil. Medicated Urethral System for Erection (MUSE) Study Group. *New England Journal of Medicine, 336*, 1–7.

Palazzoli, M. (1978). *Self-starvation: From individual to family in the treatment of anorexia nervosa.* New York: Jason Aronson.

Palmer, B. W., Pankrantz, V. S., & Bostwicdk, J. M. (2005). The lifetime risk of suicide in schizophrenia: A reexamination. *Archives of General Psychiatry, 62*, 247–253.

Pande, N., & Naidu, R. K. (1992). Anasaki and health: A study of non-attachment. *Psychology and Developing Societies, 4*, 91–104.

Pandina, G. J., Aman, M. G., & Findling, R. L. (2006). Risperidone in the management of disruptive behavior disorders. *Journal of Child and Adolescent Psychopharmacology, 16*, 379–392.

Paradis, C. M., & Friedman, S. (2005). Sleep paralysis in African-Americans with panic disorder. *Transcultural Psychiatry, 42*, 123–134.

Paris, J. (2002). Chronic suicidality among patients with borderline personality disorder. *Psychiatric Services, 53*, 738–742.

Parker, G. (1982). Re-searching the schizophrenogenic mother. *Journal of Nervous and Mental Disease, 170*, 452–462.

Parker, G. B., & Brotchie, H. L. (2004). From diathesis to dimorphism: The biology of gender differences in depression. *Journal of Nervous and Mental Disease, 192*, 210–216.

Parker, J. C., Smarr, K. L., Buckelew, S. P., Stucky–Ropp, R. C., Hewett, J. E., Johnson, J. C., et al. (1995). Effects of stress management on clinical outcomes in rheumatoid arthritis. *Arthritis and Rheumitism, 38*, 1807–1818.

Pasewark, R., & McGinley, H. (1986). Insanity plea: National survey of frequency and success. *Journal of Psychiatry and Law, 13*, 101–108.

Patel, V. (2001). Cultural factors and international epidemiology. *British Medical Bulletin, 57*, 33–45.

Patterson, G. R., & Gullion, M. E. (1968). *Living with children: New methods for parents and teachers.* Champaign, IL. Research Press.

Patterson, T. L., & Jeste, D. V. (1999). The potential impact of the baby-boom generation on substance abuse among elderly persons. *Psychiatric Services, 50*, 1184–1188.

Paulose-Ram, R., Safran, M. A., Jonas, B. S., Fu, Q., & Orwig, D. (2007). Trends in psychotropic medication use among U.S. adults. *Pharmacoepidemiology and Drug Safety, 16*, 560–570.

Pauls, D. L., Alsobrook, J. P., Goodman, W, Rasmussen, S., & Leckman, J. F. (1995). A family study of obsessive-compulsive disorder. *American Journal of Psychiatry, 152*, 76–84.

Paulson, G. (2006). Death of a president and his assassin—Errors in their diagnosis and autopsies. *Journal of the History of the Neurosciences, 15,* 77–91.

Pedersen, N. L., McClearn, G. E., Plomin, R., & Friberg, L. (1985). Separated fraternal twins: Resemblance for cognitive abilities. *Behavior Genetics, 15,* 407–419.

Pegram, G. V., McBurney, J., Harding, S. M., & Makris, C. M. (2004). Normal sleep and sleep disorders in adults and children. In T. J. Boll, J. M. Raczynski, & L. C. Leviton (Eds.), *Handbook of clinical health psychology* (pp. 183–230). Washington, DC: American Psychological Association.

Pelham, W. E., Fabiano, G. A., Gnagy, E. M., Greiner, A. R., & Hoza, B. (2004). Intensive treatment: Summer treatment program for children with ADHD. In E. D. Hibbs, & P. S. Jensen (Eds.), *Psychosocial treatment for child and adolescent disorders: Empirically based strategies for clinical practice,* 2nd ed. Washington, DC: American Psychological Association Press.

Pelham, W. E., Jr., Gnagy, E. M., Greiner, A. R., Hoza, B., Hinshaw, S. P., Swanson, J. M., Simpson, S., Shapiro, C., Bukstein, O., Baron-Myak, C., & McBurnett, K. (2000). Behavioral versus behavioral and pharmacological treatment in ADHD children attending a summer treatment program. *Journal of Abnormal Child Psychology, 28,* 507–525.

Pelham, W. E., Jr., Wheeler, T., & Chronis, A. (1998). Empirically supported psychosocial treatments for attention deficit hyperactivity disorder. *Journal of Clinical Child Psychology, 27,* 190–205.

Pence, B. W., Miller, W. C., Whetten, K., Eron, J. J., & Gaynes, B. N. (2006). Prevalence of DSM-IV-defined mood, anxiety, and substance use disorders in an HIV clinic in the Southeastern United States. *Journal of Acquired Immune Deficiency Syndrome, 42,* 298–306.

Pendery, M., Maltzman, I., & West, L. (1982). Controlled drinking by alcoholics? New findings and a reevaluation of a major affirmative study. *Science, 217,* 169–175.

Penn, D. L., Combs, D. R., & Mohamed, S. (2001). Social cognition and social functioning in schizophrenia. In P. W. Corrigan & D. L. Penn (Eds.), *Social Cognition and Schizophrenia* (pp. 97–122). Washington, DC: APA Press.

Peplau, L. A. (2003). Human sexuality: How do men and women differ? *Current Directions in Psychological Science, 12,* 37–40.

Perkins, D. O., Johnson, J. L., Hamer, R. M., Zipursky, R. B., Keefe, R. S., Centorrhino, F., et al. (2006). Predictors of antipsychotic medication adherence in patients recovering from a first psychotic episode. *Schizophrenia Research, 83,* 53–63.

Perkonigg, A., Kessler, R. C., Storz, S., & Wittchen, H. U. (2000). Traumatic events and post-traumatic stress disorder in the community: Prevalence, risk factors and comorbidity. *Acta Psychiatric Scandinavia, 101,* 46–59.

Perlis, R. H., Brown, E., Baker, R. W., & Nierenberg, A. A. (2006). Clinical features of bipolar depression versus major depressive disorder in large multicenter trials. *American Journal of Psychiatry, 163,* 225–231.

Perlis, R. H., Perlis, C. S., Wu, Y., Hwang, C., Joseph, M., & Nierenberg, A. A. (2005). Industry sponsorship and financial conflict of interest in the reporting of clinical trials in psychiatry. *American Journal of Psychiatry, 162,* 1957–1960.

Perry, A., Tarrier, N., Morriss, R., McCarthy, E., & Limb, K. (1999). Randomised controlled trial of efficacy of teaching patients with bipolar disorder to identify early symptoms of relapse and obtain treatment. *British Medical Journal, 318,* 149–153.

Peters, M. L., Godaert, G. L., Ballieux, R. E., van, V. M., Willemsen, J. J., Sweep, F. C., et al. (1998). Cardiovascular and endocrine responses to experimental stress: Effects of mental effort and controllability. *Psychoneuroendocrinology, 23,* 1–17.

Petersen, R. C., Doody, R., Kurz, A., Mohs, R. C., Morris, J. C., Rabins, P. V., et al. (2001). Current concepts in mild cognitive impairment. *Archives of Neurology, 58,* 1985–1992.

Petersen, R. C., Smith, G. E., Ivnik, R. J., Tangalos, E. G., Schaid, D. J., Thibodeau, S. N. et al. (1995). Apolipoprotein E status as a predictor of the development of Alzheimer's disease in memory-impaired individuals. *Journal of the American Medical Association, 273,* 1274–1278.

Petrila, J., Ridgely. M. S., & Borum, R. (2003). Debating outpatient commitment: Controversy, trends and empirical data. *Crime and Delinquency, 49,* 157–172.

Pfiffner, L. J., & McBurnett, K. (1997). Social skills training with parent generalization: Treatment effects for children with attention deficit disorder. *Journal of Consulting and Clinical Psychology, 65,* 749–757.

Phelan, E. A., & Larson, E. B. (2002). Successful Aging: Where next? *Journal of the American Geriatrics Society, 50,* 1306–08.

Philips, K. A., Menard, W., Pagano, M. E., Fay, C., & Stout, R. L. (2006c). Delusional versus nondelusional body dysmorphic disorder: Clinical features and course of illness. *Journal of Psychiatric Research, 40,* 95–104.

Phillips, K. A., & Dufresne, R. G. (2002). Body dysmorphic disorder: A guide for primary care physicians. *Primary Care, 29,* 99–110.

Phillips, K. A., & Menard, W. (2006). Suicidality in body dysmorphic disorder: A prospective study. *American Journal of Psychiatry, 163,* 1280–1282.

Phillips, K. A., & Taub, S. L. Skin picking as a symptom of body dysmorphic disorder. *Psychopharmacology Bulletin, 31,* 279–288.

Phillips, K. A., Coles, M. E., Menard, W., Yen, S., Fay, C., & Weisberg, R. B. (2005). Suicidal ideation and suicide attempts in body dysmorphic disorder. *Journal of Clinical Psychiatry, 66,* 717–725.

Phillips, K. A., Didie, E. R., Menard, W., Pagano, M. E., Fay, C., & Weisberg, R. B. (2006a). Clinical features of body dysmorphic disorder in adolescents and adults. *Psychiatry Research, 141,* 305–314.

Phillips, K. A., Pagano, M. E., & Menard, W. (2006b). Pharmacotherapy for body dysmorphic disorder: Treatment received and illness severity. *Annals of Clinical Psychiatry, 18,* 251–257.

Pickens, R., & Fletcher, B. (1991). Overview of treatment issues. In R. Pickens, C. Leukefeld, & C. Schuster (Eds.), *Improving Drug Abuse Treatment (pp. 1–19). National Institute on Drug Abuse (NIDA) Research Monograph No. 106.* Rockville, MD: NIDA.

Pierce, K., Haist, R., Sedaghat, F., & Courchesne, E. (2004). The brain response to personally familiar faces in autism: findings of fusiform activity and beyond. *Brain, 12,* 2703–2716.

Pierce, K., Muller, R. A., Ambrose, J., Allen, G., & Courchesne, E. (2001). Face processing occurs outside the fusiform "face area" in autism: Evidence for functional MRI. *Brain, 124,* 2059–2073.

Pike, K., Loeb, K., & Vitousek, K. (1996). Cognitive-behavioral therapy for anorexia nervosa and bulimia nervosa. In J. Thompson (Ed.), *Eating disorders, obesity, and body image: A practical guide to assessment and treatment.* Washington, DC: APA Books.

Piotrowski, C. (1995). A review of the clinical and research use of the Bender-Gestalt Test. *Perceptual and Motor Skills, 81,* 1272–1274.

Piper, A., & Merskey, H. (2004a). The persistence of folly: A critical examination of dissociative identity disorder. Part I. The excesses of an improbable concept. *Canadian Journal of Psychiatry, 49,* 592–600.

Piper, A., & Merskey, H. (2004b). The persistence of folly: Critical examination of dissociative identity disorder. Part II. The defence and decline of multiple personality or dissociative identity disorder. *Canadian Journal of Psychiatry, 49,* 678–683.

Pitschel-Walz, G., Leucht, S., Bauml, J., Kissling, W., & Engel, R. R. (2001). The effect of family interventions on relapse and rehospitalization in schizophrenia—A meta-analysis. *Schizophrenia Bulletin, 27,* 73–92.

Plassman, B. L., & Steffens, D. C. (2004). Genetics. In D. G. Blazer, D. C. Steffens, & E. W. Busse (Eds.), *Textbook of geriatric psychiatry* (3rd ed., pp. 109–120). Washington, DC: American Psychiatric Publishing.

Plomin, R., DeFries, J. C., McClearn, G. E., & Rutter, M. (1994). *Behavioral genetics, 3rd edition.* New York: W. H. Freeman & Co.

Politi, P., Minoretti, P., Falcone, C., Martinelli, V., & Emanuele, E. (2006). Association analysis of the functional Ala111Glu polymorphism of the glyoxalase I gene in panic disorder. *Neuroscience Letter, 396,* 163–166.

Pollack, M. H., & Marzol, P. C. (2000). Panic: Course, complications, and treatment of panic disorder. *Journal of Psychopharmacology, 14 (Suppl. 1),* S25–30.

Poortinga, Y. H., & Van Hemert, D. A. (2001). Personality and culture: Demarcating between the common and the unique. *Journal of Personality Disorders, 69,* 1033–1060.

Pope, H. G., Jr., Barry, S., Bodkin, A., & Hudson, J. I. (2006). Tracking scientific interest in the dissociative disorders: A study of scientific publication output 1984–2003. *Psychotherapy and Psychosomatics, 75,* 19–24.

Pope, H. G., Lalonde, J. K., Pindyck, L. J., Walsh, T., Bulik, C. M., Crow, S. J., et al. (2006). Binge eating disorder: A stable syndrome. *American Journal of Psychiatry, 163,* 2181–2183.

Pope, H. G., Olivia, P. S., Hudson, J. I., Bodkin, J. A., & Gruber, A. J. (1999). Attitudes to DSM-V-TR dissociative disorders among Board-certified American psychiatrists. *American Journal of Psychiatry, 156,* 321–323.

Pope, H. G. Jr., Poliakoff, M. B., Parker, M. P., Boynes, M., & Hudson, J. I. (2006). Is dissociative amnesia a culture-bound syndrome? Findings from a survey of historical literature. *Psychological Medicine, 37,* 225–233.

Popper, C. W., Gammon, G. D., West, S. A., & Bailey, C. E. (2004). Disorders usually first diagnosed in infancy, childhood, or adolescence. In R. E. Hales and S. G. Yudofsky (Eds.), *Essentials of clinical psychiatry second edition* (pp. 591–735). Washington, DC: American Psychiatric Publishing.

Porst, H., Rosen, R., Padma-Nathan, H., Goldstein, I., Giuliano, F., Ulbrich, E., & Bandel, T. (2001). The efficacy and tolerability of vardenafil, a new, oral, selective phosphodiesterase type 5 inhibitor, in patients with erectile dysfunction: The first at-home clinical trial. *International Journal of Impotence Research, 13,* 192–199.

Porter, V. R., Buxton, W. G., Fairbanks, L. A., Strickland, T., O'Connor, S. M., Rosenberg-Thompson, S., et al. (2003). Frequency and characteristics of anxiety among patients with Alzheimer's disease and related dementias. *The Journal of Neuropsychiatry and Clinical Neuroscience, 15,* 180–186.

Post, R. M., Speer, A. M., Weiss, S. R., & Li, H. (2000). Seizure models: Anticonvulsant effects of ECT and rTMS. *Progress in Neuropsychopharmacology and Biological Psychiatry, 24,* 1251–1273.

Potvin, S., Sepehry, A. A., & Stip, E. (2006). A meta-analysis of negative symptoms in dual diagnosis schizophrenia. *Psychological Medicine, 36,* 431–440.

Powell, L. H., Shahabi, L., & Thoresen, C. E. (2003). Religion and spirituality. Linkages to physical health. *American Psychologist., 58,* 36–52.

Pratt, H. D., & Patel, D. R. (2007). Learning disorders in children and adolescents. *Primary Care: Clinics in Office Practice, 34,* 361–374.

Prendergast, M., Podus, D., & Finney, J. (2006). Contingency management for treatment of substance use disorders: A meta-analysis. *Addiction, 101,* 1546–1560.

Prescott, C. (2001). The genetic epidemiology of alcoholism: Sex differences and future directions. In D. Agarwal & H. Seitz (Eds.), *Alcohol in health and disease* (pp. 125–149). New York: Marcel Dekker.

Prien, R. F., & Kupfer, D. J. (1986). Continuation drug therapy for major depressive episodes: How long should it be maintained? *American Journal of Psychiatry, 143,* 18–23.

Prochaska, J., & DiClemente, C. (1983). Stages and processes of self-change of smoking: Toward an integrative model of change. *Journal of Consulting and Clinical Psychology, 51,* 390–395.

Putnam, F. W. (1989). *Diagnosis and treatment of multiple personality disorder.* New York: Guilford Press.

Putnam, F. W. (1993). Dissociative disorders in children: Behavioral profiles and problems. *Child Abuse & Neglect, 17,* 39–45.

Putnam, F. W., Guroff, J. J., Silberman, E. K., Barban, L., & Post, R. M. (1986). The clinical phenomenology of multiple personality disorder: Review of 100 recent cases. *Journal of Clinical Psychiatry, 47,* 285–293.

Qin, P., & Nordentoft, M. (2005). Suicide risk in relation to psychiatric hospitalization: Evidence based on longitudinal registers. *Archives of General Psychiatry, 62,* 427–432.

Qin, P., Agerbo, E., & Mortensen, P. B. (2002). Suicide risk in relation to family history of completed suicide and psychiatric disorders: A nested case-control study based on longitudinal registers. *Lancet, 360,* 1126–1130.

Qualls, S. H., Segal, D. L., Benight, C. C., & Kenny, M. P. (2005). Geropsychology training in a specialist geropsychology doctoral program. *Gerontology and Geriatrics Education, 25,* 21–40.

Quay, H. C. (1965). Psychopathic personality as pathological stimulation-seeking. *American Journal of Psychiatry, 122,* 180–183.

Rachal, F., & Kunik, M. E. (2006). Treating aggression in patients with dementia. *Psychiatric Times, 23,* 90–95.

Rachman, S. J. (1977). The conditioning theory of fear-acquisition: A critical examination. *Behaviour Research and Therapy, 15,* 375–387.

Rachman, S. J., & Hodgson, R. J. (1980). *Obsessions and compulsions.* Englewood Cliffs, NJ: Prentice-Hall.

Radloff, L. S. (1977). The CES-D scale: A self report depression scale for research in the general population. *Applied Psychological Measurements, 1,* 385–401.

Rahim–Williams, F. B., Riley, J. L., III, Herrera, D., Campbell, C. M., Hastie, B. A., & Fillingim, R. B. (2007). Ethnic identity predicts experimental pain sensitivity in African Americans and Hispanics. *Pain, 129,* 177–184.

Rahman Q., & Wilson, G. D. (2003). Born gay? The psychobiology of human sexual orientation. *Personality and Individual Differences, 34,* 1337–1382.

Raikkonen, K., Matthews, K. A., Flory, J. D., Owens, J. F., & Gump, B. B. (1999). Effects of optimism, pessimism, and trait anxiety on ambulatory blood pressure and mood during everyday life. *Journal of Personality and Social Psychology, 76,* 104–113.

Raimundo Oda, A. M. G., Banzato, C. E. M., & Dalgalarrondo, P. (2005). Some origins of cross-cultural psychiatry. *History of Psychiatry, 16,* 155–169.

Raju, T. N. K. (1998). The Nobel Chronicles—Julius Wagner-Jauregg. *The Lancet, 352,* 1714.

Ramchandani, P. G., Hotopf, M., Sandhu, B., Stein, A. and the ALSPAC Study Team. (2005).The epidemiology of recurrent abdominal pain from 2 to 6 years of age: Results of a large, population-based study. *Pediatrics, 116,* pp. 46–50.

Ran, M. S., Chan, C.L.W., Chen, E.Y.H., Xiang, M. Z., Caine, E. D., & Conwell, Y. (2006). Homelessness among patients with schizophrenia in rural China: A 10-year cohort study. *Acta Psychiatrica Scandinavica, 114,* 118–123.

Raney, T. J., Thornton, L. M., Berrettini, W., Brandt, H., Crawford, S., Fichter, M. M., Centers for Disease Control and Prevention. (2008). Influence of overanxious disorder of childhood on the expression of anorexia nervosa. *International Journal of Eating Disorders, 41,* 326–332.

Raphael, K. G., Widom, C. S., & Lange, G. (2001). Childhood victimization and pain in adulthood: A prospective investigation. *Pain, 92,* 283–293.

Rapoport, J. L., Addington, A. M., Frangou, S., & Psych, M. R. (2005). The neurodevelopmental model of schizophrenia: Update 2005. *Molecular Psychiatry, 10,* 434–449.

Rapoport, M. H., Pollack, M. H., Clary, C. M., Mardekian, J., & Wolkow, R. (2001). Panic disorder and response to sertraline: The effect of previous treatment with benzodiazepines. *Journal of Clinical Psychopharmacology, 21,* 104–107.

Raskind, M., Bonner, L. T., & Reskind, E. R. (2004). Cognitive disorders. In D. G. Blazer, D. C. Steffens, & E. W. Busse (Eds.), *Textbook of geriatric psychiatry* (3rd ed., pp. 207–229). Washington, DC: American Psychiatric Publishing.

Rasmussen, S. A., & Tsuang, M. T. (1986). Clinical characteristics and family history in DSM-III obsessive-compulsive disorder. *American Journal of Psychiatry, 143,* 317–322.

Raynor, K., Forman, B. R., Perfetti, C. A., Pesetsky, D., & Seidenberg, M. S. (2001). How psychological science informs the teaching of reading. *Psychological Science in the Public Interest, 2,* 31–74.

Razali, S. M. (2000). Help-seeking pathways among Malay psychiatric patients. *International Journal of Social Psychiatry, 46,* 281–289.

Read, J., Kahler, C., & Stevenson, J. (2001). Bridging the gap between alcoholism treatment research and practice: Identifying what works and why. *Professional Psychology: Research and Practice, 32,* 227–238.

Reagan, P., & Hersch, J. (2005). Influence of race, gender, and socioeconomic status on binge eating frequency in a population-based sample. *International Journal of Eating Disorders, 38,* 252–256.

Rebach, H. (1992). Alcohol and drug use among ethnic minorities. In J. Trimble, C. Bolek, & S. Niemcryk (Eds.), *Ethnic and multicultural drug abuse: Perspective on current research* (pp. 23–57). New York: Haworth Press.

Regeser López, S., & Guarnaccia, P. J. J. (2000). Cultural psychopathology: Uncovering the social world of mental illness. *Annual Review of Psychology, 51,* 571–598.

Regier, D. A., Boyd, J. H., Burke, J. D., Jr., Rae, D. S., Myers, J. K., Kramer, M., et al. (1988). One-month prevalence of mental disorders in the United States: Based on five Epidemiologic Catchment Area sites. *Archives of General Psychiatry, 45,* 977–986.

Regier, D. A., Farmer, M. E., Rae, D. S., Locke, B. A., Keith, S. J., Judd, L. L., & Centers for Disease Control and Prevention. (1990). Comorbidity of mental disorders with alcohol and other drug abuse. *Journal of the American Medical Association, 264,* 2511–2518.

Reichborn-Kjennerud, T., Czajkowski, N., Neale, M. C., Orstavik, R. E., Torgersen, S., Tambs, K., Centers for Disease Control and Prevention. (2007). Genetic and environmental influences on dimensional representations of DSM-IV cluster C personality disorders: A population-based multivariate twin study. *Psychological Medicine, 37*, 645–653.

Reichborn-Kjennerud, T., Bulik, C. M., Sullivan, P., Tambs, K., & Harris, J. (2004). Psychiatric and medical symptoms in binge eating in the absence of compensatory behaviors. *Obesity Research, 12*, 1445–1454.

Reichborn-Kjennerud, T., Bulik, C. M., Tambs, K., & Harris, J. (2004). Genetic and environmental influences on binge eating in the absence of compensatory behaviours: A population-based twin study. *International Journal of Eating Disorders, 36*, 307–314.

Reichenberg, A., Gross, R., Weiser, M., Bresnahan, M., Silverman, J., Harlap, S., Centers for Disease Control and Prevention. (2006). Advance paternal age and autism. *Archives of General Psychiatry, 63*, 1026–1032.

Reisberg, B., Doody, R., Stoffler, A., Schmitt, F., Ferris, S., & Mobius, H. J. (2003). Memantine in moderate-to-severe Alzheimer's disease. *New England Journal of Medicine, 348*, 1333–1341.

Reissing, E. D., Binik, Y. M., Khalifé, Cohen, D., & Amsel, R. (2004). Vaginal spasm, pain and behavior: An empirical investigation of the diagnosis of vaginismus. *Archives of Sexual Behavior, 33*, 5–17.

Reitan, R. L., & Davidson. (1974). *Halstead-Reitan Neuropsychological Battery*: Reitan Neuropsychology Laboratories, University of Arizona.

Rekers, G. A., & Lovaas, O. I. (1974). Behavioral treatment of deviant sex-role behaviors in a male child. *Journal of Applied Behavior Analysis, 7*, 173–190.

Rekers, G. A., & Mead, S. (1979). Early intervention for female sexual identity disturbance: Self-monitoring of play behavior. *Journal of Abnormal Child Psychology, 7*, 405–423.

Rekers, G. A., Lovaas, O. I., & Low, B. (1974). The behavioral treatment of a "transsexual" preadolescent boy. *Journal of Abnormal Child Psychology, 2*, 99–116.

Remschmidt, H., & Theisen, F. M. (2005). Schizophrenia and related disorders in children and adolescents. *Journal of Neural Transmission [Suppl.], 69*, 121–141.

Repetti, R. L., Taylor, S. E., & Seeman, T. E. (2002). Risky families: Family social environments and the mental and physical health of offspring. *Psychological Bulletin, 128*, 230–266.

Reschly, D. J., & Jipson, F. W. (1976). Ethnicity, geographic locale, age, sex, and urban–rural residence as variables in the prevalence of mild retardation. *American Journal of Mental Deficiency, 81*, 154–161.

Research Units on Pediatric Psychopharmacology (RUPP) Autism Network. (2005). Randomized, controlled, crossover trial of methylphenidate in pervasive developmental disorders with hyperactivity. *Archives of General Psychiatry, 62*, 1266–1274.

Research Units on Pediatric Psychopharmacology Autism Network. (2002). Risperidone in children with autism and serious behavioral problems. *New England Journal of Medicine, 347*, 314–321.

Rettew, D. C. (2000). Avoidant personality disorder, generalized social phobia, and shyness: Putting the personality back into personality disorders. *Harvard Review of Psychiatry, 8*, 283–297.

Rettew, D. C., Rebollo-Mesa, I., Hudziak, J. J., Willemsen, G., & Boomsma, D. I. (2008). Non-additive and additive genetic effects on extraversion in 3314 Dutch adolescent twins and their parents. *Behavior Genetics, 38*, 223–233.

Revell, W. G., Wehman, P., Kregel, J., West, M., et al. (1994). Supported employment for persons with severe disabilities: Positive trends in wages, models and funding. *Education & Training in Mental Retardation & Developmental Disabilities, 29*, 256–264.

Reynolds, K. J., Vernon, S. D., Bouchery, E., & Reeves, W. C. (2004). The economic impact of chronic fatigue syndrome. *Cost Effectiveness and Resource Allocation, 2*, 4.

Rheaume, J., Freeston, M. H., Leger, E., & Ladouceur, R. (1998). Bad luck: An underestimated factor in the development of obsessive-compulsive disorder. *Clinical Psychology & Psychotherapy, 5*, 1–12.

Rice, M. E., & Harris, G. T. (2002). Men who molest their sexually immature daughters: Is a special explanation required? *Journal of Abnormal Psychology, 111*, 329–339.

Richardson, S. A., Katz, M., & Koller, H. (1986). Sex differences in number of children administratively classified as mildly mentally retarded: An epidemiological review. *American Journal of Mental Deficiency, 91*, 250–256.

Rickels, K., Downing, R., Schweizer, E., & Hassman, H. (1993). Antidepressants for the treatment of generalized anxiety disorder: A placebo-controlled comparison of imipramine, trazodone, and diazepam. *Archives of General Psychiatry, 50*, 884–895.

Rickels, K., Pollack, M. H., Sheehan, D. V., & Haskins, J. T. (2000). Efficacy of extended-release venlafaxine in nondepressed outpatients with generalized anxiety disorder. *American Journal of Psychiatry, 157*, 968–974.

Rickels, K., Zaninelli, R., McCafferty, J., Bellew, K., Iyengar, M., & Sheehan, D. (2003). Paroxetine treatment of generalized anxiety disorder: A double-blind, placebo-controlled study. *American Journal of Psychiatry, 160*, 749–756.

Rief, W., Hessel, A., & Braehler, E. (2001). Somatization symptoms and hypochondriacal features in the general population. *Psychosomatic Medicine, 63*, 595–602.

Rief, W., Hiller, W., Geissner, E., & Fichter, M. M. (1995). A two-year follow-up study of patients with somatoform disorders. *Psychosomatics, 36*, 376–386.

Rigotti, N., Neer, R., Skates, S., Herzog, D., & Nussbaum, S. (1991). The clinical course of osteoporosis in anorexia nervosa: A longitudinal study of cortical bone mass. *Journal of the American Medical Association, 265*, 1133–1137.

Rimmele, C., Howard, M., & Hilfrink, M. (1995). Aversion therapies. In R. Hester & W. R. Miller (Eds.), *Handbook of alcoholism treatment approaches: Effective alternatives* (2nd ed.) (pp. 134–147). Needham Heights, MA: Allyn & Bacon.

Riolo, S. A., Nguyen, T. A., Greden, J. F., & King, C. A. (2005). Prevalence of depression by race/ethnicity: Findings from the National Health and Nutrition Examination Survey III. *American Journal of Public Health, 95*, 998–1000.

Robbins, J. M., & Kirmayer, L. J. (1996). Transient and persistent hypochondriacal worry in primary care. *Psychological Medicine, 26*, 575–589.

Roberts, R. E., Roberts, C. R., & Chan, W. (2006). Ethnic differences in symptoms of insomnia among adolescents. *Sleep, 29*, 359–365.

Robertson, E., Jones, I., Haque, S., Holer, R., & Craddock, N. (2005). Risk of puerperal and non-puerperal recurrence of illness following bipolar affective puerperal (post-partum) psychosis. *British Journal of Psychiatry, 186*, 258–259.

Robins, L. (1994). How recognizing "comorbidities" in psychopathology may lead to an improved research nosology. *Clinical Psychology: Science and Practice, 1*, 93–95.

Robins, L. N., & Regier, D. A. (1991). *Psychiatric disorders in America: The Epidemiologic Catchment Area Study*. New York: Free Press.

Robins, L. N., Helzer, J. E., Weissman, M. M., Orvaschel, H., Gruenberg, E., Burke, J. D., Jr., & Regier, D. A. (1984). Lifetime prevalence of specific psychiatric disorders in three sites. *Archives of General Psychiatry, 41*, 949–958.

Robins, L., & Slobodyan, S. (2003). Post-Vietnam heroin use and injection by returning US veterans: Clues to preventing injection today. *Addiction, 98*, 1053–1060.

Roccatagliata, G. (1997). Classical Psychopathology. In W. G. Bringman, H. E. Lück, R. Miller, & C. Early (Eds.), *A pictorial history of psychology* (pp. 383–390). Carol Stream, IL: Quintessence Publishing Co.

Rode, S., Salkovskis, P. M., & Jack, T. (2001). An experimental study of attention, labeling and memory in people suffering from chronic pain. *Pain, 94*, 193–203.

Rodebaugh, T. L., Holaway, R. M., & Heimberg, R. G. (2004). The treatment of social anxiety disorder. *Clinical Psychology Review, 24*, 883–908.

Rogler, L. H. (1999). Methodological sources of cultural insensitivity in mental health research. *American Psychologist, 54*, 424–433.

Rohan, K. J., Lindsey, K. T., Roecklein, K. A., & Lacy, T. J. (2004). Cognitive-behavioral therapy, light therapy, and their combination in treating seasonal affective disorder. *Journal of Affective Disorders, 80*, 273–283.

Rohde, L. A., Szobot, C., Polanczyk, G., Schmitz, M., Martins, S., & Tramontina, S. (2005). Attention-deficit/hyperactivity disorder in a diverse culture: Do research and clinical findings support the notion of a cultural construct for the disorder? *Biological Psychiatry, 57*, 1436–1441.

Rohde, P., Lewinsohn, P., Kahler, C., Seeley, J., & Brown, R. (2001). Natural course of alcohol use disorders from adolescence to young adulthood. *Journal of the American Academy of Child and Adolescent Psychiatry, 40*, 83–90.

Rohleder, N., Schommer, N. C., Hellhammer, D. H., Engel, R., & Kirschbaum, C. (2001). Sex differences in glucocorticoid sensitivity of proinflammatory cytokine production after psychosocial stress. *Psychosomatic Medicine, 63*, 966–972.

Rohsenow, D., Niaura, R., Childress, A., Abrams, D., & Monti, P. (1990). Cue reactivity in addictive behaviors: Theoretical and treatment implications. *International Journal of the Addictions, 25*, 957–993.

Roid, G. H., & Miller, L. J. (1997). *Examiner's Manual: Leiter International Performance Scale-Revised.* Wood Dale, IL: Stoelting Co.

Roll, J., Petry, N., Stitzer, M., Brecht, M., Peirce, J., McCann, M., Blaine, J., et al. (2006). Contingency management for the treatment of methamphetamine use disorders. *American Journal of Psychiatry, 163*, 1993–1999.

Rosario-Campos, M. C., Leckman, J. F., Mercadante, M. R., Shavitt, R. G., Prado, H. D., Sada, P., et al. (2001). Adults with early-onset obsessive-compulsive disorder. *American Journal of Psychiatry, 158*, 1899–1903.

Rose, E. A., Porcecelli, J. H., & Neale, A. V. (2000). Pica: Common but commonly missed. *Journal of the American Board of Family Practice, 13*, 353–358.

Rosen, J. C., Reiter, J., & Orosan, P. (1995). Cognitive-behavioral body image therapy for body dysmorphic disorder. *Journal of Consulting and Clinical Psychology, 63*, 263–269.

Rosenberg, S. D., Goodman, L. A., Osher, F. G., Swartz, M. S., Essock, S. M., Butterfield, M. I., et al. (2001). Prevalence of HIV, hepatitis B and hepatitis C in people with severe mental illness. *American Journal of Public Health, 91*, 31–37.

Rosenfarb, I. S., Bellack, A. S., & Aziz, N. (2006). Family interactions in the course of schizophrenia in African-American and white patients. *Journal of Abnormal Psychology, 115*, 112–120.

Rosenvinge, J. H., Martinussen, M., & Ostensen, E. (2000). The comorbidity of eating disorders and personality disorders: a meta-analytic review of studies published between 1983 and 1998. *Eating and Weight Disorders, 5*, 52–61.

Ross, C. A. (1997). *Dissociative identity disorder: Diagnosis, clinical features and treatment of multiple personality.* New York: John Wiley & Sons.

Roth, B., & Shapiro, D. (2001). Insights into the structure and function of 5-HT2 family serotonin receptors reveal novel strategies for therapeutic target development. *Expert Opinion on Therapeutic Targets, 5*, 685–695.

Rothbaum, B. O., Hodges, L, Anderson, P. L., Price, L., & Smith, S. (2002). Twelve-month follow-up of virtual reality and standard exposure therapies for the fear of flying. *Journal of Consulting and Clinical Psychology, 70*, 428–432.

Rotosky, S. S., Wilcox, B. L., Wright, M. L. C., & Randall, B. A. (2004). The impact of religiosity on adolescent sexual behavior: A review of the evidence. *Journal of Adolescent Research, 19*, 677–697.

Roubertoux, P. L., & Kerdelhúe, B. (2006). Trisomy 21: From chromosomes to mental retardation. *Behavior Genetics, 36*, 346–354.

Roundy, K., Cully, J. A., Stanley, M. A., Veazey, C., Souchek, J., Wray, N. P., et al. (2005). Are anxiety and depression addressed in primary care patients with chronic obstructive pulmonary disease? A chart review. *Primary Care Companion to the Journal of Clinical Psychiatry, 7*, 213–218.

Routtenberg, A., & Kuznesof, A. (1967). Self-starvation of rats living in activity wheels on a restricted feeding schedule. *Journal of Comparative Physiology and Psychology, 64*, 414–421.

Rowland, D., Perelman, M., Althof, S., Barada, J., McCullough, A., Bull, S., et al. (2004). Self-reported premature ejaculation and aspects of sexual functioning and satisfaction. *Journal of Sexual Medicine, 1*, 225–232.

Roy, A., & Linnoila, M. (1986). Alcoholism and suicide. *Suicide and Life Threatening Behaviors, 16*, 244–273.

Roy, A., Segal, N. L., Centerwall, B. S., & Robinette, C. D. (1991). Suicide in twins. *Archives of General Psychiatry, 48*, 29–32.

Roy-Byrne, P. P., Craske, M. G., Stein, M. B., Sullivan, G., Bystritsky, A., Katon, W., Golinelli, D., & Sherbourne, C. D. (2005). A randomized effectiveness trial of cognitive-behavioral therapy and medication for primary care panic disorder. *Archives of General Psychiatry, 62*, 290–298.

Roy-Byrne, P. P., Sherbourne, C. D., Craske, M. G., Stein, M. B., Katon, W., Sullivan, G., et al. (2003). Moving treatment research from clinical trials to the real world. *Psychiatric Services, 54*, 327–332.

Röpcke, B., & Eggers, C. (2005). Early-onset schizophrenia. *European Child & Adolescent Psychiatry, 14*, 341–350.

Rösler, A., & Witztum, E. (2000). Pharmacotherapy of paraphilias in the next millennium. *Behavioral Sciences and the Law, 18*, 43–56.

Ruchlin, H. S. (1997). Prevalence and correlates of alcohol use among older adults. *Prevention Medicine, 26*, 651–657.

Ruitenberg, A., van Swieten, J. C., Witteman, J. C., Mehta, K. M., van Duijn, C. M., Hofman, A., et al. (2002). Alcohol consumption and risk of dementia: The Rotterdam Study. *Lancet, 359*, 281–286.

Russell, G. F. M. (1979). Bulimia nervosa: An ominous variant of anorexia nervosa. *Psychological Medicine, 9*, 429–448.

Russell, G. F. M., Szmukler, G. I., Dare, C., & Eisler, I. (1987). An evaluation of family therapy in anorexia and bulimia nervosa. *Archives of General Psychiatry, 44*, 1047–1056.

Rutter, M. (1978). Diagnosis and definitions of childhood autism. *Journal of Autism and Developmental Disorders, 8*, 139–161.

Rutter, M. (1989). Isle of Wight revisited: Twenty-five years of child psychiatric epidemiology. *Journal of the American Academy of Child and Adolescent Psychiatry, 28*, 633–653.

Rutter, M. (2005). Incidence of autism spectrum disorders: Changes over time and their meaning. *Acta Pediatrica, 94*, 2–15.

Rutter, M., Tizard, J., Yule, W., Graham, P., & Whitmore, K. (1976). Research report: Isle of Wight Studies, 1964–1974. *Psychological Medicine, 6*, 313–332.

Rybarczyk, B., Stepanski, E., Fogg, L., Lopez, M., Barry, P., & Davis, A. (2005). A placebo-controlled test of cognitive-behavioral therapy for comorbid insomnia in older adults. *Journal of Consulting and Clinical Psychology, 73*, 1164–1174.

Sánchez, M. M., Ladd, C., & Plotsky, P. (2001). Early adverse experience as a developmental risk factor for later psychopathology: Evidence from rodent and primate models. *Development and Psychopathology, 13*, 419–449.

Saba, G., Verdon, C. M., Kalalou, K., Rocamora, J. F., Dumortier, G., Benadhira, R., et al. (2006). Transcranial magnetic stimulation in the treatment of schizophrenic symptoms: A double blind sham controlled study. *Journal of Psychiatric Research, 4*, 147–152.

Sadeh, A. (2005). Cognitive-behavioral treatment for childhood sleep disorders. *Clinical Psychology Review, 25*, 612–628.

Safer, D. J., Magno Zito, J., & dosReis, S. (2003). Concomitant psychotropic medication for youths. *American Journal of Psychiatry, 160*, 438–449.

Safer, D. L., Telch, C. F., & Agras, W. S. (2001). Dialectical behavior therapy for bulimia nervosa. *American Journal of Psychiatry, 158*, 632–634.

Sagan, C. (1996). *The demon-haunted world: Science as a candle in the dark.* New York: Ballantine Books.

Saha, S., Chant, D., Welham, J., & McGrath, J. (2005). A systematic review of the prevalence of schizophrenia. *Public Library of Science, 2*, e141.

Sakauye, K. (2004). Ethnocultural aspects of aging in mental health. In J. Sadavoy, L. F. Jarvik, G. T. Grossberg, & B. S. Meyers (Eds.), *Comprehensive textbook of geriatric psychiatry* (pp. 225–250). New York: W.W. Norton & Co.

Salaberria, K., & Echeburua, E. (1998). Long-term outcome of cognitive therapy's contribution to self-exposure in vivo to the treatment of generalized social phobia. *Behavior Modification, 22*, 262–284.

Salkovskis, P. M. (1989). Somatic problems. In K. Hawton, P. M. Salkovskis, J. Kirk, & D. M. Clark (Eds.), *Cognitive-behavior therapy for psychiatric problems* (pp. 235–276). Oxford: Oxford University Press.

Salleh, A. (2005). Female orgasm is in the genes. http://www.abc.net.au/science/news/health/HealthRepublish_1305742.htm.

Sallet, P. C., Elkis, H., Alves, T. M., Oliveria, J. R., Sassi, E., de Castro, C. C., et al. (2003). Reduced cortical folding in schizophrenia: An MRI morphometric study. *American Journal of Psychiatry, 160*, 1606–1613.

Salmon, P. (2001). Effects of physical exercise on anxiety, depression, and sensitivity to stress: A unifying theory. *Clinical Psychology Review, 21*, 33–61.

Samuels, J. F., Riddle, M. A., Greenberg, B. D., Fyer, A. J., McCracken, J. T., Rauch, S. L., et al. (2006). The OCD collaborative genetics study: Methods and sample description. *American Journal of Medical Genetics Part B: Neuropsychiatric Genetics, 143B*, 201–207.

Sanchez, J., Ladd, C., & Plotsky, P. (2001). Early adverse experiences as developmental risk factor for later psychopathology: Evidence from rodent and primate models. *Development and Psychopathology, 13*, 419–449.

Sandberg, D. E., Meyer-Bahlburg, H. F., Ehrhardt, A. A., & Yager, T. J. (1993). The prevalence of gender-atypical behavior in elementary school children. *Journal of the American Academy of Child and Adolescent Psychiatry, 32*, 306–314.

Sandberg, W. S. (1997). The effect of education gifts from pharmacological firms on medical students' recall of company names or produces. *Academic Medicine, 72*, 916–918.

Sands, J. R., & Harrow, M. (1999). Depression during the longitudinal course of schizophrenia. *Schizophrenia Bulletin, 25,* 157–171.

Şar, V., Akyüz, G., & Doğan, O. (2007). Prevalence of dissociative disorders among women in the general population. *Psychiatry Research, 149,* 169–176.

Şar, V., Unal, S. N., Kiziltan, E., Kundakci, T., & Ozturk, E. (2001). HMPAO SPECT study of regional cerebral blood flow in dissociative identity disorder. *Journal of Trauma & Dissociation, 2,* 5–25.

Sartorium, N., Jablensky, A., Gulbinat, W., & Ernberg, G. (1980). WHO Collaborative Study: Assessment of depressive disorders. *Psychological Medicine, 10,* 739–779.

Sartorius, N., Jablensky, A., & Shapiro, R. (1978). Cross-cultural differences in the short-term prognosis of schizophrenic psychosis. *Schizophrenia Bulletin, 4,* 102–113.

Scammell, T., & Saper, C. B. (2005). Orexin, drugs and motivated behaviors. *Nature Neuroscience, 8,* 1286–1288.

Scarborough, H. S. (1990). Very early language deficits in dyslexic children. *Child Development, 61,* 1728–1743.

Schaffer, A., Cairney, J., Cheung, A., Veldhuizen, S., & Levitt, A. (2006). Community survey of bipolar disorder in Canada: Lifetime prevalence and illness characteristics. *Canadian Journal Psychiatry, 51,* 9–16.

Schaffer, D. (1996). A participant's observations: Preparing DSM-IV. *Canadian Journal of Psychiatry, 41,* 325–329.

Scheeringa, M. S. (2001). The differential diagnosis of impaired reciprocal social interaction in children. *Child Psychiatry and Human Development, 32,* 71–89.

Scheier, M. F., Matthews, K. A., Owens, J. F., Magovern, G. J., Sr., Lefebvre, R. C., Abbott, R. A. et al. (1989). Dispositional optimism and recovery from coronary artery bypass surgery: The beneficial effects on physical and psychological well-being. *Journal of Personality and Social Psychology, 57,* 1024–1040.

Scheier, M. F., Weintraub, J. K., & Carver, C. S. (1986). Coping with stress: Divergent strategies of optimists and pessimists. *Journal of Personality and Social Psychology., 51,* 1257–1264.

Schellenberg, G. D., Dawson, G., Sung, Y. J., Estes, A., Munson, J., Rosenthal, E., et al. (2006). Evidence for multiple loci from a genome scan of autism kindreds. *Molecular Psychiatry, 11,* 1049–1060.

Schiffman, J., Walker, E., Ekstrom, M., Schulsinger, F., Sorensen, H., & Mednick, S. (2004). Childhood videotaped social and neuromotor precursors of schizophrenia: A prospective investigation. *American Journal of Psychiatry, 161,* 2021–2027.

Schneider, J. P. (2003). The impact of compulsive cybersex behaviours on the family. *Sexual and Relationship Therapy, 18,* 329–354.

Schneider, L. S. (1996). Pharmacologic considerations in the treatment of late-life depression. *American Journal of Geriatric Psychiatry, 4,* S51–S65.

Schneider, L. S., Dagerman, K. S., & Insel, P. (2005). Risk of death with atypical antipsychotic drug treatment for dementia: Meta-analysis of randomized placebo-controlled trials. *Journal of the American Medical Association, 294,* 1934–1943.

Schneider, L. S., Dagerman, K., & Insel, P. S. (2006). Efficacy and adverse effects of atypical antipsychotics for dementia: Meta-analysis of randomized, placebo-controlled trials. *American Journal of Geriatric Psychiatry, 14,* 191–210.

Schoevers, R. A., Deeg, D. J., van, T. W., & Beckman, A. T. (2005). Depression and generalized anxiety disorder: co occurrence and longitudinal patterns in elderly patients. *American Journal of Geriatric Psychiatry, 13,* 31–39.

Schooler, N. R., Keith, S. J., Severe, J. B., Matthews, S. M., Bellack, A. S., Glick, I. D., et al. (1997). Relapse and rehospitalization during maintenance treatment of schizophrenia: The effects of dose reduction and family treatment. *Archives of General Psychiatry, 54,* 453–63.

Schotte, C.K.W., Van Den Bossche, B., De Doncker, D., Claes, S., & Cosyns, S. (2006). A biopsychosocial model as a guide for psychoeducation and treatment of depression. *Depression and Anxiety, 23,* 312–324.

Schulman, K. A., Berlin, J. A., Harless, W., Kerner, J. F., Sistrunk, S., Gersh, B. J., et al. (1999). The effect of race and sex on physicians' recommendations for cardiac catheterization. *New England Journal of Medicine, 340,* 618–626.

Schulsinger, F., Kety, S., Rosenthal, D., & Wender, P. (1979). A family study of suicide. In M. Schou & E. Stromgren (Eds.), *Origin, prevention and treatment of affective disorders* (pp. 277–287). New York: Academic Press.

Schultz, R. T., Grelotti, D. J., Klin, A., Levitan, E., Cantey, T., Gore, J. C., et al. (2001). An fMRI study of face recognition, facial expression detection, and social judgment in autism spectrum disorders. *International Meeting for Autism Research,* San Diego, CA.

Schultz, R., & Heckhausen, J. (1996). A life span model of successful aging. *American Psychologist, 51,* 702–717.

Schultz, S. K., Hoth, A., & Buckwalter, K. (2004). Anxiety and impaired social function in the elderly. *Annals of Clinical Psychiatry, 16,* 47–51.

Schulz, R., Bookwala, J., Knapp, J. E., Scheier, M., & Williamson, G. M. (1996). Pessimism, age, and cancer mortality. *Psychology of Aging, 11,* 304–309.

Schulz, R., Visintainer, P., & Williamson, G. M. (1990). Psychiatric and physical morbidity effects of caregiving. *Journal of Gerontology, 45,* 181–191.

Schuurmans, J., Comijs, H. C., Beekman, A. T., de Beurs, E., Deeg, D. J., Emmelkamp, P. M., et al. (2005). The outcome of anxiety disorders in older people at 6-year follow-up: results from the Longitudinal Aging Study Amsterdam. *Acta Psychiatrica Scandinavia, 111,* 420–428.

Schuurmans, J., Comijs, H., Emmelkamp, P. M., Gundy, C. M., Weijnen, I., van denHout, M., et al. (2006). A randomized, controlled trial of the effectiveness of cognitive-behavioral therapy and sertraline versus a waitlist control group for anxiety disorders in older adults. *American Journal of Geriatric Psychiatry, 14,* 255–263.

Schwartz, C., Wright, C., Shin, L., Kagan, J., & Rauch, S. (2003). Inhibited and uninhibited infants "grown up": adult amygdalar response to novelty. *Science, 300,* 1952–1953.

Scull, A. (2004). The insanity of place. *History of Psychiatry, 15,* 417–436.

Seal, K., Bertenthal, D., Minor, C., Sen, S., & Marmar, C. (2007). Bringing the war back home: Mental health disorders among 103,788 US veterans returning from Iraq and Afghanistan seen at Department of Veterans Affairs facilities. *Archives of Internal Medicine, 167,* 476–482.

Sechrest, L., & Coan, J. (2002). Preparing psychologists to prescribe. *Journal of Clinical Psychology, 58,* 649–658.

Sedlak, A. J., & Broadhurst, D. D. (1996). *Executive Summary for the Third National Incidence Study of Child Abuse and Neglect.* Washington, DC: U.S. Department of Health and Human Services: Administration for Children and Families; Administration on Children, Youth and Families; National Center on Child Abuse and Neglect.

Seeman, M. V. (1996). The role of estrogen in schizophrenia. *Journal of Psychiatry and Neuroscience, 21,* 123–127.

Seftel, A. D., & Althof, S. E (2000). Rapid ejaculation. *Current Urological Reports, 1,* 302–306.

Seignourel, P. J., Kunik, M. E., Snow, L., Wilson, N., & Stanley, M. A. (2008). Anxiety in dementia: A critical review. *Clinical Psychology Review, 28,* 1071–1082.

Seligman, M. (1975). *Helplessness: On depression, development, and death.* San Francisco: W. H. Freeman.

Selling, L. S. (1940). *Men against madness.* New York: Greenberg.

Sellwood, W, & Tarrier, N. (1994). Demographic factors associated with extreme non-compliance in schizophrenia. *Social Psychiatry and Epidemiology, 29,* 172–177.

Selye, H. (1956). *General adaptation syndrome (GAS).* New York: McGraw-Hill.

Semans, J. H. (1956). Premature ejaculation: A new approach. *Southern Medical Journal, 49,* 353–358.

Sergeant, J. A., Geurts, H., & Oosterlaan, J. (2002). How specific is a deficit of executive functioning for attention-deficit/hyperactivity disorder? *Behavioural Brain Research, 130,* 3–28.

Seto, M. C. (2001). The value of phallometry in the assessment of male sex offenders. *Journal of Forensic Psychology Practice, 1,* 65–75.

Severeijns, R., Vlaeyen, J. W., van den Hout, M. A., & Picavet, H. S. (2004). Pain catastrophizing is associated with health indices in musculoskeletal pain: a cross-sectional study in the Dutch community. *Health Psychology, 23,* 49–57.

Shaffer, D., Gould, M. S., Fisher, P., Trautman, P., Moreau, D., Kleinman, M., et al. (1996). Psychiatric diagnosis in child and adolescent suicide. *Archives of General Psychiatry, 53,* 339–348.

Shanmugham, B., Karp, J., Drayer, R., Reynolds, C. F., III, & Alexopoulos, G. (2005). Evidence-based pharmacologic interventions for geriatric depression. *Psychiatric Clinics of North America, 28,* 821–835.

Shannon, M. P., Lonigan, C. J., Finch, A. J., Jr., & Taylor, C. M. (1994). Children exposed to disaster: I. Epidemiology of post-traumatic symptoms and symptom profiles, *Journal of the American Academy of Child and Adolescent Psychiatry, 33,* 80–93.

Shapiro, J. R., Berkman, N. D., Brownley, K. A., Sedway, J. A., Lohr, K. N., & Bulik, C. M. (2007). Bulimia nervosa treatment: A systematic review of randomized controlled trials. *International Journal of Eating Disorders,* 321–336.

Sharma, B. R. (2007). Gender identity disorder and its medico-legal considerations. *Medicine, Science, and the Law, 47,* 31–40.

Shavers, V., Lynch, D., & Burmeister, L. (2002). Racial differences in factors that influence the willingness to participate in medical research. *Annals of Epidemiology, 12,* 248–256.

Shaywitz, S. E., Gruen, J. R., & Shaywitz, B. A. (2007). Management of dyslexia, its rationale, and underlying neurobiology. *Pediatric Clinics of North America, 54,* 609–623.

Sheikh, A. (2006). Why are ethnic minorities under-represented in US research studies? *PLOS Medicine, 3,* e49.

Sheikh, J. I., & Swales, P. J. (1999). Treatment of panic disorder in older adults: A pilot study comparison of alprazolam, imipramine, and placebo. *International Journal of Psychiatry in Medicine, 29,* 107–117.

Sheikh, J. I., & Yesavage, J. A. (1986). Geriatric depression scale (GDS): Recent evidence and development of a shorter version. *Clinical Gerontologist, 5,* 165–173.

Sher, K. (2006). Towards a cognitive theory of substance use and dependence. In R. Wiers & A. Stacy (Eds.), *Handbook on implicit cognition and addiction.* (pp. 273–276). New York: Guilford Press.

Sheridan, M. S. (2003). The deceit continues: An updated literature review of Munchausen Syndrome by Proxy. *Child Abuse & Neglect, 27,* 431–451.

Sherman, C. (2005). Dopamine Enhancement Underlies a Toluene Behavioral Effect. *NIDA Notes, 19,* 4–5.

Sheth, D. N., Bhagwate, M. R., & Sharma, N. (2005). Curious clicks—Sigmund Freud. *Journal of Postgraduate Medicine, 51,* 240–241.

Shiffman, S., Hickcox, M., Paty, J., Gnys, M., Kassel, J., & Richards, T. (1997). The abstinence violation effect following smoking lapses and temptations. *Cognitive Therapy and Research, 21,* 497–523.

Shin, L. M., Wright, C. I., Cannistraro, P. A., Wedig, M. M., McMullin, K., Martis, B., et al. (2005). A functional magnetic resonance imaging study of amygdala and medial prefrontal cortex responses to overtly presented fearful faces in posttraumatic stress disorder. *Archives of General Psychiatry, 62,* 273–281.

Shiren, J. L., Braunstein, G. D., Simon, J. A., Casson, P. R., Buster, J. E., Redmond, G. P., et al. (2000). Transdermal testosterone treatment in women with impaired sexual function after oophorectomy. *New England Journal of Medicine, 343,* 682–688.

Shulman, K. I., Tohen, M., Satlin, A., Mallya, G., & Kalunian, D. (1992). Mania compared with unipolar depression in old age. *American Journal of Psychiatry, 149,* 341–345.

Shuttleworth-Edwards, A. B., Kemp, R. D., Rust, A. L., Muirhead, J. G., Hartman, N. P., & Radloff, S. E. (2004). Cross-cultural effects on IQ test performance: A review and preliminary normative indications on WAIS-III test performance. *Journal of Clinical and Experimental Neuropsychology, 26,* 903–920.

Siegel, K., & Schrimshaw, E. W. (2007). The stress moderating role of benefit finding on psychological distress and well-being among women living with HIV/AIDS. *AIDS and Behavior, 11,* 421–433.

Siegel, S., Baptista, M., Kim, J., McDonald, R., & Weise-Kelly, L. (2000). Pavlovian psychopharmacology: The associative basis of tolerance. *Experimental and Clinical Psychopharmacology, 8,* 276–229.

Siever, L. J., Koenigsberg, H. W., Harvey, P., Mitropoulou, V., Laruelle, M., Abi-Dargham, A., et al. (2002). Cognitive and brain function in schizotypal personality disorder. *Schizophrenia Research, 54,* 157–167.

Sigerist, H. E. (1943). *Civilization and disease.* Ithaca, NY: Cornell University Press.

Sigusch, V. (2004). Richard von Krafft-Ebing (1980–1902). In memory of the 100th anniversary of his death. *Nervenartz, 75,* 92–96.

Sikdar, S., Kulhara, P., Avasthi, A., & Singh, H. (1994). Combined chlorpromazine and electroconvulsive therapy in mania. *British Journal of Psychiatry, 164,* 806–810.

Silagy, C., Lancaster, T., Stead, L., Mant, D., & Fowler, G. (2004). Nicotine replacement therapy for smoking cessation. *Cochrane Database Systematic Reviews* (3):CD000146.

Silveira, J. M., & Seeman, M. V. (1995). Shared psychotic disorder: a critical review of the literature. *Canadian Journal of Psychiatry, 40,* 389–395.

Silverman, J. M., Smith, C. J., Marin, D. B., Mohs, R. C., & Propper, C. B. (2003). Familial patterns of risk in very late-onset Alzheimer disease. *Archives of General Psychiatry, 60,* 190–197.

Silverman, K., Evans, S., Strain, E., & Griffiths, R. (1992). Withdrawal syndrome after double blind cessation of caffeine consumption. *New England Journal of Medicine, 327,* 1109–1114.

Silverman, W. K., & Dick-Niederhauser, A. (2004). Separation anxiety disorder. In T. L. Morris & J. S. March (Eds.), *Anxiety disorders in children and adolescents* (pp. 164–188). New York: Guilford Press.

Simansky, K. J. (2005). NIH symposium series: Ingestive mechanisms in obesity, substance abuse and mental disorders. *Physiology and Behavior, 86,* 1–4.

Simeon, D., Guralnik, O., Knutelska, M., Hollander, E., & Schmeidler, J. (2001). Hypothalamic-pituitary-adrenal axis dysregulation in depersonalization disorder. *Neuropsychopharmacology, 25,* 793–795.

Simeon, D., Guralnik, O., Schmeidler, J., Sirof, B., & Knutelska, M. (2001). The role of childhood interpersonal trauma in depersonalization disorder. *American Journal of Psychiatry, 158,* 1027–1033.

Simeon, D., Knutelska, M., Nelson, D., & Guralnik, O. (2003). Feeling unreal: A depersonalization disorder update of 117 cases. *Journal of Clinical Psychiatry, 64,* 990–997.

Simon, G. E., VonKorff, M., Piccinelli, M., Fullerton, C., & Ormel, J. (1999). An international study of the relation between somatic symptoms and depression. *New England Journal of Medicine, 341,* 1329–1335.

Simoni–Wastila, L. (2000). The use of abusable prescription drugs: The role of gender. *Journal of Women's Health & Gender-Based Medicine, 9,* 289–297.

Simoni–Wastila, L., Ritter, G., & Strickler, G. (2004). Gender and other factors associated with nonmedical use of abusable prescription drugs. *Substance Use & Misuse, 39,* 1–23.

Simpson, D., Joe, G., Rowan–Szal, G., & Greener, J. (1997). Drug abuse treatment process components that improve retention. *Journal of Substance Abuse Treatment, 14,* 565–572.

Singh, A. N. (1999). Shamans, healing and mental health. *Journal of Child and Family Studies, 8,* 131–134.

Singh, S. P. & Lee, A. S. (1997). Conversion disorders in Nottingham: Alive, but not kicking. *Journal of Psychosomatic Research, 43,* 425–430.

Sink, K. M., Covinsky, K. E., Newcomer, R., & Yaffe, K. (2004). Ethnic differences in the prevalence and pattern of dementia-related behaviors. *Journal of the American Geriatrics Society, 52,* 1277–1283.

Sitzer, D. I., Twamley, E. W., & Jeste, D. V. (2006). Cognitive training in Alzheimer's disease: A meta-analysis of the literature. *Acta Psychiatrica Scandinavia, 114,* 75–90.

Sivec, H. J., & Lynn, S. J. (1995). Dissociative and neuropsychological symptoms: The question of differential diagnosis. *Clinical Psychology Review, 15,* 297–316.

Sjögren Fugl-Meyer, K., & Fugl-Meyer, A. R. (2002). Sexual disabilities are not singularities. *International Journal of Impotence Research, 14,* 487–493.

Skeem J. L., Schubert, C., Odgers, C., Mulvey, E. P., Gardner, W., & Lidz, C. (2006). Psychiatric symptoms and community violence among high-risk patients: A test of the relationship at the weekly level. *Journal of Consulting and Clinical Psychology, 74,* 967–979.

Skeem, J. L., Mulvey, E. P., & Lidz, C. W. (2000). Building mental health professionals' decisional models into tests of predictive validity: The accuracy of contextualized predictions of violence. *Law and Human Behavior, 24,* 607–628.

Skeem, J., Schubert, C., Stowman, S., Beeson, S., Mulvey, E., Gardner, W., et al. (2005). Gender and risk assessment accuracy: Underestimating women's violence potential. *Law and Human Behavior, 29,* 173–186.

Skinner, B. (1953). *Science and human behavior.* New York: Free Press.

Skodol, A. E., Oldham, J. M., & Gallaher, P. E. (1999). Axis II comorbidity of substance use disorders among patients referred for treatment of personality disorders. *American Journal of Psychiatry, 156,* 733–738.

Slagboom, P., & Meulenbelt, I. (2002). Organisation of the human genome and our tools for identifying disease genes. *Biological Psychology, 61,* 11–31.

Small, J. G., Klapper, M. H., Kellams, J. J., Miller, M. J., Milstein, V., Sharpley, P. H., et al. (1988). Electroconvulsive treatment compared with lithium in the management of manic states. *Archives of General Psychiatry, 45*, 727–732.

Smith, B. H., Waschbusch, D. A., Willoughby, M. T., & Evans, S. (2000). The efficacy, safety, and practicality of treatments for adolescents with attention deficit/hyperactivity disorder (ADHD). *Clinical Child and Family Psychology Review, 3*, 243–267.

Smith, D. E., Marcus, M. D., Lewis, C. E., Fitzgibbon, M., & Schreiner, P. (1998). Prevalence of binge eating disorder, obesity, and depression in a biracial cohort of young adults. *Annals of Behavioral Medicine, 20*, 227–232.

Smith, E., & Kosslyn, S. (2007). *Cognitive psychology: Mind and brain, 1st edition*. Upper Saddle River, NJ: Pearson/Prentice Hall.

Smith, M. T., Perlis, M. L., Park, A., Smith, M. S., Pennington, J., Giles, D. E., et al. (2002). Comparative meta-analysis of pharmacotherapy and behavior therapy for persistent insomnia. *American Journal of Psychiatry, 159*, 5–11.

Smith, Y. L., van Goozen, S. H., & Cohen-Kettenis, P. T. (2001). Adolescents with gender identity disorder who were accepted or rejected for sex reassignment surgery: A prospective follow-up study. *Journal of the American Academy of Child and Adolescent Psychiatry, 40*, 472–481.

Smith, Y. L., van Goozen, S. H., Kuiper, A. J., & Cohen-Kettenis, P. T. (2005). Sex reassignment: Outcomes and predictors of treatment for adolescent and adult transsexuals. *Psychological Medicine, 35*, 89–99.

Smith-Bell, M., & Winslade, W. J. (1994). Privacy, confidentiality, and privilege in psychotherapeutic relationships. *American Journal of Orthopsychiatry, 64*, 180–193.

Smolak, L., Levine, M. P., & Thompson, J. K. (2001). The use of the sociocultural attitudes towards appearance questionnaire with middle school boys and girls. *International Journal of Eating Disorders, 29*, 216–223.

Soares, J. C., & Mann, J. J. (1997). The anatomy of mood disorders—Review of structural neuroimaging studies. *Biological Psychiatry, 41*, 86–106.

Sobell, M., & Sobell, L. (1973). Alcoholics treated by individualized behavior therapy: One year treatment outcomes. *Behavior Research and Therapy, 11*, 599–618.

Sobell, M., & Sobell, L. (1978). *Behavioral treatment of alcohol problems: Individualized therapy and controlled drinking*. New York: Plenum Press.

Sobell, M., & Sobell, L. (1995). Controlled drinking after 25 years. How important was the great debate? *Addiction, 90*, 1149–1153.

Sobin, C., Blundell, M. L., & Karayiorgou, M. (2000). Phenotypic differences in early- and late-onset obsessive-compulsive disorder. *Comprehensive Psychiatry, 41*, 373–379.

Somerfield, M. R., Curbow, B., Wingard, J. R., Baker, F., & Fogarty, L. A. (1996). Coping with the physical and psychosocial sequelae of bone marrow transplantation among long-term survivors. *Journal of Behavioral Medicine, 19*, 163–184.

Song, Y., Shiraishi, Y., & Nakamura, J. (2001). Digitalis intoxication misdiagnosed as depression-revisited (Letter). *Psychosomatics, 42*, 369–370.

Southern, S. (2008). Treatment of compulsive cybersex behavior. *Psychiatric Clinics of North America, 31*, 697–712.

Soykan, I., Chen, J., Kendall, B., & McCallum, R. W. (1997). The rumination syndrome: Clinical and manometric profile, therapy, and long-term outcome. *Digestive Diseases and Sciences, 42*, 1866–1872.

Spanos, N. P. (1994). Multiple identity enactments and multiple personality disorder: A sociocognitive perspective. *Psychological Bulletin, 116*, 143–165.

Specker, S., de Zwaan, D., Raymond, N., & Mitchell, J. (1994). Psychopathology in subgroups of obese women with and without binge eating disorder. *Comprehensive Psychiatry, 35*, 185–190.

Spencer, T. J., Biederman, J., & Mick, E. (2007). Attention-deficit/hyperactivity disorder: Diagnosis, lifespan, comorbidities, and neurobiology. *Ambulatory Pediatrics, 7*, 73–81.

Spencer, T., Biederman, J., & Wilens, T. (2004). Stimulant treatment of adult attention-deficit/hyperactivity disorder. *Psychiatric Clinics of North America, 27*, 361–372.

Spitzer, R. L., Devlin, M., Walsh, T. B., Hasin, D., Wing, R., Marcus, M. D., et al. (1992). Binge eating disorder: A multisite field trial of the diagnostic criteria. *International Journal of Eating Disorders, 11*, 191–203.

Spitzer, R. L., Stunkard, A., Yanovski, S., Marcus, M. D., Wadden, T., Wing, R., et al. (1993). Binge eating disorder should be included in DSM-IV: a reply to Fairburn et al.'s "the classification of recurrent overeating: the binge eating disorder proposal" [comment]. *International Journal of Eating Disorders, 13*, 161–169.

Spitzer, R. L., Yanovski, S., Wadden, T., Wing, R., Marcus, M. D., Stunkard, A. et al. (1993). Binge eating disorders: Its further validation in a multisite study. *International Journal of Eating Disorders, 13*, 137–153.

Spriggs, M. (2006). Canaries in the mines: Children, risk, non-therapeutic research, and justice. *Journal of Medical Ethics, 30*, 176–181.

Springer, M. V., McIntosh, A. R., Winocur, G., & Grady, C. L. (2005). The relation between brain activity during memory tasks and years of education in young and older adults. *Neuropsychology, 19*, 181–192.

Stafford, J., & Lynn, S. J. (2002). Cultural scripts, memories of childhood abuse, and multiple identities: A study of role-played enactments. *International Journal of Clinical and Experimental Hypnosis, 50*, 67–85.

Stafford, K. P., & Wygant, D. B. (2005). The role of competency to stand trial in mental health courts. *Behavioral Sciences and the Law, 23*, 245–258.

Stambor, Z. (2006). Psychology's prescribing pioneers. *APA Monitor on Psychology, 37*, 30.

Stanford, J. L., Feng, Z., Hamilton, A. S., Gilliland, F. D., Stephenson, R. A., Eley, J. W., Albertsen, P. C., Harlan, L. C., & Potosky, A. L. (2000). Urinary and sexual function after radical prostatectomy for clinically localized prostate cancer: The Prostate Cancer Outcomes Study. *Journal of the American Medical Association, 283*, 354–60.

Stanley, M. A. & Novy, D. M. (2000). Cognitive-behavior therapy for generalized anxiety in late life: An evaluative overview. *Journal of Anxiety Disorders, 14*, 191–207.

Stanley, M. A. (2003). Generalized anxiety disorder in late life. In D. J. Nutt, K. Rickels, & D. J. Stein (Eds.), *Generalized anxiety disorder: Symptomatology, pathogenesis, and management*. London: Martin Dunitz Limited.

Stanley, M. A., Hopko, D. R., Diefenbach, G. J., Bourland, S. L., Rodriguez, H., & Wagener, P. (2003). Cognitive-behavior therapy for late-life generalized anxiety disorder in primary care: preliminary findings. *American Journal of Geriatric Psychiatry, 11*, 92–96.

Stanley, M. A., Roberts, R. E., Bourland, S. L., & Novy, D. M. (2001). Anxiety disorders among older primary care patients. *Journal of Clinical Geropsychology*, 105–116.

Stanley, M. A., Wilson, N., Novy, D. M., Rhoades, H., Wagener, P., Greisinger, A. J., Cully, J. A., & Kunik, M. E. (2009). Cognitive behavior therapy for older adults with generalized anxiety disorder in primary care: A randomized clinical trial. *Journal of the American Medical Association, 301*, 1460–1467.

Stanley, M., Veazey, C., & Hopko, D. (2005). Anxiety and depression in chronic obstructive pulmonary disease: A new intervention and case report. *Cognitive and Behavioral Practice, 12*, 424–436.

Stanley, S. (1999). Science, ethnicity, and bias: Where have we gone wrong? *American Psychologist, 54*, 1070–1077.

Starcevic, V. (2006). Somatoform disorders and DSM-V: Conceptual and political issues in the debate. *Psychosomatics, 47*, 277–281.

Starkstein, S. E., Jorge, R., Petracca, G., & Robinson, R. G. (2007). The construct of generalized anxiety disorder in Alzheimer disease. *American Journal of Geriatric Psychiatry, 15*, 42–49.

Statham, D. J., Heath, A. C., Madden, P. A., Bucholz, K. K., Bierut, L., Dinwiddie, S. H., et al. (1998). Suicidal behaviour: An epidemiological and genetic study. *Psychological Medicine, 28*, 839–855.

Steadman, H. J. (1983). Predicting dangerousness among the mentally ill: Art, magic, and science. *International Journal of Law and Psychiatry, 6*, 381–390.

Steadman, H. J., Gounis, K., Dennis, D., Hopper, K., Roche, B., Swartz, M., et al. (2001). Assessing the New York City involuntary outpatient commitment pilot program. *Psychiatric Services, 52*, 330–381.

Steadman, H., & Braff, J. (1983). Defendants not guilty by reason of insanity. In J. Monahan & H. Steadman (Eds.), *Mentally disordered offenders: Perspectives from law and social science*. New York: Plenum.

Steffen, P. R., Hinderliter, A. L., Blumenthal, J. A., & Sherwood, A. (2001). Religious coping, ethnicity, and ambulatory blood pressure. *Psychosomatic Medicine, 63*, 523–530.

Steffens, D. C., Hays, J. C., & Krishnan, K. R. (1999). Disability in geriatric depression. *American Journal of Geriatric Psychiatry, 7*, 34–40.

Steffens, D. C., Skoog, I., Norton, M. C., Hart, A. D., Tschanz, J. T., Plassman, B. L., et al. (2000). Prevalence of depression and its treatment in an elderly population: The Cache County study. *Archives General Psychiatry, 57*, 601–607.

Steiger, H., Gauvin, L., Israel, M., Kin, N., Young, S., & Roussin, J. (2004). Serotonin function, personality-trait variations, and childhood abuse in women with bulimia-spectrum eating disorders. *Journal of Clinical Psychiatry, 65,* 830–837.

Steiger, H., Joober, R., Israël, M., Young, S., Ng Ying Kin, N., Gauvin, L., et al. (2005). The 5HTTLPR polymorphism, psychopathological symptoms, and platelet paroxetine binding in bulimic syndromes. *International Journal of Eating Disorders, 37,* 57–60.

Stein D. J. (2002). Obsessive-compulsive disorder. *Lancet, 360,* 397–405.

Stein D. J., Seedat, S., van der Linden G. J. H., & Zungu-Dirway, N. (2000). Selective serotonin reuptake inhibitors in the treatment of post-traumatic stress disorder: A meta-analysis of randomized controlled trials. *International Clinical Psychopharmacology, 15,* SUP 2, S31–S39.

Stein, D. J., & Hugo, F. J. (2004). Neuropsychiatric aspects of anxiety disorders. In S. C. Yudofsky and R. E. Hales (Eds.), *Essentials of neuropsychiatry and clinical neurosciences* (pp. 1049–1068). Washington, DC: American Psychiatric Association.

Stein, D. J., Westenberg, H. G. M., Yang, H., Li, D., & Barbato, L. M. (2003). Fluvoxamine CR in the long-term treatment of social anxiety disorder: The 12- to 24-week extension phase of a multicentre, randomized, placebo-controlled trial. *International Journal of Neuropsychopharmacology, 6,* 317–325.

Stein, M. B., Koverola, C., Hanna, C., Torchia, M. G., & McClarty, B. (1997). Hippocampal volume in women victimized by childhood sexual abuse. *Psychological Medicine, 27,* 951–960.

Stein, M. B., Roy-Byrne, P. P., Craske, M. G., Bystritsky, A., Sullivan, G., Pyne, J. M., Katon, W., & Sherbourne, C. D. (2005). Functional impact and health utility of anxiety disorders in primary care outpatients. *Medical Care, 43,* 1164–1170.

Stein, S., Chalhoub, N., & Hodes, M. (1998). Very early-onset bulimia nervosa: Report of two cases. *International Journal of Eating Disorders, 24,* 323–327.

Steinberg, M., Cicchetti, D., Buchanan, J., Hall, P., & Rounsaville, B. (1993). Clinical assessment of dissociative symptoms and disorders: The Structured Clinical Interview for DSM-IV Dissociative Disorders (SCID-D). *Dissociation, 6,* 3–15.

Steketee, G., & Barlow, D. H. (2002). Obsessive compulsive disorder. In D. H. Barlow, *Anxiety and its disorders: The nature and treatment of anxiety and panic,* 2nd ed. (pp. 516–550). New York: Guilford Press.

Stemberger, R. L, Turner, S. M., Beidel, D. C., & Calhoun, K. (1995). Social phobia: An analysis of possible developmental factors. *Journal of Abnormal Psychology, 104,* 526–531.

Stern, Y., Gurland, B., Tatemichi, T. K., Tang, M. X., Wilder, D., & Mayeux, R. (1994). Influence of education and occupation on the incidence of Alzheimer's disease. *Journal of the American Medical Association, 271,* 1004–1010.

Sternberg, R. J., Grigorenko, E. L., & Kidd, K. K. (2005). Intelligence, race, and genetics. *American Psychologist, 60,* 46–59.

Stice, E., Agras, W., & Hammer, L. (1999). Risk factors for the emergence of childhood eating disturbances: A five-year prospective study. *International Journal of Eating Disorders, 25,* 375–387.

Stiegler, L. N. (2005). Understanding pica behavior: A review for clinical and education professionals. *Focus on Autism and Other Developmental Disabilities, 20,* 27–38.

Stilley, C. S., Sereika, S., Muldoon, M. F., Ryan, C. M., & Dunbar-Jacob, J. (2004). Psychological and cognitive function: Predictors of adherence with cholesterol lowering treatment. *Annals of Behavioral Medicine, 27,* 117–124.

Stinson, F. S., Dawson, D. A., Chou, S. P., Smith, S., Goldstein, R. B., Ruan, W. J., et al. (2007). The epidemiology of DSM-IV specific phobia in the USA: Results from the National Epidemiological Survey on Alcohol and Related Conditions. *Psychological Medicine, 37,* 1047–1059.

Stone, A. A., Neale, J. M., Cox, D. S., Napoli, A., Valdimarsdottir, H., & Kennedy-Moore, E. (1994). Daily events are associated with a secretory immune response to an oral antigen in men. *Health Psychology, 13,* 440–446.

Strakowski, S. M., Adler, C. M., & DelBello, M. P. (2002). Volumetric MRI studies of mood disorders: Do they distinguish unipolar and bipolar disorder? *Bipolar Disorders, 4,* 80–88.

Strassberg, D. S., de Gouveia Brazao, C. A., Rowland, D. L., Tan, P., & Slob, K. (1999). Clomipramine in the treatment of rapid (premature) ejaculation. *Journal of Sex & Marital Therapy, 25,* 89–101.

Straub, R. E., Sullivan, P. F., Ma, Y., Myakishev, M. V., Harris-Kerr, C., Wormley, B., Kadambi, B., Sadek, H., Silverman, M. A., Webb, B. T., Neale, M. C., Bulik, C. M., Joyce, P. R., & Kendler, K. S. (1999). Susceptibility genes for nicotine dependence: A genome scan and followup in an independent sample suggest that regions on chromosomes 2, 4, 10, 16, 17 and 18 merit further study. *Molecular Psychiatry, 4,* 129–144.

Striefel, S. (2001). Ethical research issues: Going beyond the Declaration of Helsinki. *Applied Psychophysiology and Biofeedback, 26,* 39–59.

Striegel-Moore, R. H., & Bulik, C. M. (2007). Risk factors for eating disorders. *American Psychologist, 62,* 181–198.

Striegel-Moore, R. H., Cachelin, F. M., Dohm, F. A., Pike, K. M., Wilfley, D. E., & Fairburn, C. G. (2001). Comparison of binge eating disorder and bulimia nervosa in a community sample. *International Journal of Eating Disorders, 29*(2), 157–165.

Striegel-Moore, R. H., Dohm, F., Kraemer, H., Taylor, C., Daniels, S., Crawford, P., & Schreiber, G. (2003). Eating disorders in white and black women. *American Journal of Psychiatry, 160,* 1326–1331.

Striegel-Moore, R. H., Fairburn, C. G., Wilfley, D. E., Pike, K. M., Dohm, F. A., & Kraemer, H. C. (2005). Toward an understanding of risk factors for binge-eating disorder in black and white women: A community-based case-control study. *Psychological Medicine, 35,* 907–917.

Striegel-Moore, R. H., Silberstein, L., & Rodin, J. (1986). Toward an understanding of risk factors for bulimia. *American Psychologist, 41,* 246–263.

Strober, M., Freeman, R., Lampert, C., Diamond, J., & Kaye, W. (2000). Controlled family study of anorexia nervosa and bulimia nervosa: Evidence of shared liability and transmission of partial syndromes. *American Journal of Psychiatry, 157,* 393–401.

Stromme, P., & Magnus, P. (2000). Correlations between socioeconomic status, IQ and aetiology in mental retardation: a population-based study of Norwegian children. *Social Psychiatry and Psychiatric Epidemiology, 35,* 12–18.

Stuart, S. (1995). Treatment of postpartum depression with interpersonal psychotherapy. *Archives of General Psychiatry, 52,* 75–76.

Studer, L. H., & Aylwin, A. S. (2006). Pedophilia: The problem with diagnosis and limitations of CBT in treatment. *Medical Hypotheses, 67,* 774–781.

Substance Abuse and Mental Health Services Administration. (2003). *Results from the 2002 National Survey on Drug Use and Health: National Findings* (No. NHSDA Series H-22: DHHS Publication No. SMA 03-3836). Rockville, MD: Substance Abuse and Mental Health Services Administration, Office of Applied Studies.

Substance Abuse and Mental Health Services Administration. (2005). *Results from the 2004 National Survey on Drug Use and Health: National Findings* (No. Office of Applied Studies, NSDUH Series H-28, DHHS Publication No. SMA 05-4062). Rockville, MD: Substance Abuse and Mental Health Services Administration.

Substance Abuse and Mental Health Services Administration. (2006). *Results from the 2006 National Survey on Drug Use and Health: National Findings.* Rockville, MD: Substance Abuse and Mental Health Services Administration.

Sue, S. (1999). Science, ethnicity and bias. *American Psychologist, 54,* 1070–1077.

Sullivan, J. R., Ramirez, E., Rae, W. A., Pena Razo, N., & George, C. A. (2002). Factors contributing to breaking confidentiality with adolescent clients: A survey of pediatric psychologists. *Professional Psychology: Research and Practice, 33,* 396–401.

Sullivan, P. F., Evengard, B., Jacks, A., & Pedersen, N. L. (2005). Twin analyses of chronic fatigue in a Swedish national sample. *Psychological Medicine, 35,* 1327–1336.

Sullivan, P. F. (1995). Mortality in anorexia nervosa. *American Journal of Psychiatry, 152,* 1073–1074.

Sullivan, P. F. (2005). The genetics of schizophrenia. *PLoS Medicine, 2,* e212.

Sullivan, P. F. (2008). Schizophrenia genetics: The search for a hard lead. *Current Opinions in Psychiatry, 21,* 157–160.

Sullivan, P. F., & Kendler, K. S. (1999). The genetic epidemiology of smoking. *Nicotine and Tobacco Research, 1 Suppl 2,* S51–57; discussion S69–70.

Sullivan, P. F., Bulik, C. M., Fear, J. L., & Pickering, A. (1998). Outcome of anorexia nervosa. *American Journal of Psychiatry, 155,* 939–946.

Sullivan, P. F., Kovalenko, P., York, T. P., Prescott, C. A., & Kendler, K. S. (2003). Fatigue in a community sample of twins. *Psychological Medicine, 33,* 263–281.

Sullivan, P. F., Neale, M. C., & Kendler, K. S. (2000). Genetic epidemiology of major depression: Review and meta-analysis. *American Journal of Psychiatry, 157,* 1552–1562.

Sullivan, P., Joyce, P., & Mulder, R. (1994). Borderline personality disorder in major depression. *Journal of Nervous and Mental Disease, 182,* 508–516.

Summerfeldt, L. J., & Antony, M. M. (2002). Structured and semistructured diagnostic interviews. In M. M. Antony & D. H. Barlow (Eds.), *Handbook of assessment and treatment planning for psychological disorders* (pp. 3–37). New York: Guilford Press.

Sundaram, S. K., Chugani, H. T., & Chugani, D. C. (2005). Positron emission tomography methods with potential for increased understanding of mental retardation and developmental disabilities. *Mental Retardation and Developmental Disabilities Research Reviews, 11,* 325–330.

Susser, E. S., Naugebauer, R., Hoek, H. W., Brown, A. S., Lin, S., Labovitz, D., et al. (1996). Schizophrenia after prenatal famine: Further evidence. *Archives of General Psychiatry, 53,* 25–31.

Sussman, S. (1998). The first asylums in Canada: A response to neglectful community care and current trends. *Canadian Journal of Psychiatry, 43,* 260–264.

Sutherland, A. J., & Rodin, G. M. (1990). Factitious disorders in a general hospital setting: Clinical features and a review of the literature. *Psychosomatics, 31,* 392–399.

Suzuki, L. A., Ponterotto, J. G., & Meller, P. J. (2001). *Handbook of multicultural assessment (Clinical, Psychological, and Educational Applications)* (2nd ed.). San Francisco: Jossey-Bass.

Swanson, J. W., Swartz, M. S., Van Dorn, R. A., Elbogen, E. B., Wagner, R., Rosenheck, R. A., Stroup, T. S., McEvoy, J. P., & Lieberman, J. A. (2006). A national study of violent behavior in persons with schizophrenia. *Archives of General Psychiatry, 63,* 490–499.

Swartz, C. (2001). Misdiagnosis of schizophrenia for a patient with epilepsy (Letter). *Psychiatric Services, 52,* 109.

Swartz, M. S., & Monahan, J. (2001). Special section on involuntary outpatient commitment: Introduction. *Psychiatric Services, 52,* 323–324.

Swartz, M. S., Swanson, J. W., Hiday, V. A., Wagner, H. R., Burns, B. J., & Borum, R. (2001). A randomized controlled trial of outpatient commitment in North Carolina. *Psychiatric Services, 52,* 325–329.

Swartz, M. S., Swanson, J. W., Wagner, H. R., Burns, B. J., Hiday, V. A., & Borum, R. (1999). Can involuntary outpatient commitment reduce hospital recidivism? Findings from a randomized trial with severely mentally ill individuals. *American Journal of Psychiatry, 156,* 1968–1975.

Swartz, M., Blazer, D., George, L., & Winfield, I. (1990). Estimating the prevalence of borderline personality disorder in the community. *Journal of Personality Disorders, 4,* 257–272.

Swartz, M., Landerman, R., George, L. K., Blazer, D. G., & Escobar, J. (1991). Somatization disorder. In L. N. Robins, & D. A. Fegier (Eds.), *Psychiatric disorders in America: The Epidemiological Catchment Area Study* (pp. 220–257). New York: Free Press.

Swedo, S. E., Rapoport, J. L., Leonard, H., Lenane, M., & Cheslow, D. (1989). Obsessive-compulsive disorder in children and adolescents. *Archives of General Psychiatry, 46,* 335–341.

Swerdlow, N. (2001). Obsessive-compulsive disorder and tic syndromes. *Medical Clinics of North America, 85,* 735–755.

Symonds, C. S., Taylor, S., Tippens, V., & Turkington, D. (2006). Violent self-harm in schizophrenia. *Suicide and Life-Threatening Behavior, 36,* 44–49.

Symonds, T., Roblin, D., Hart, K., & Althof, S. (2003). How does premature ejaculation impact a man's life? *Journal of Sex & Marital Therapy, 29,* 361–370.

Szmukler, G., Brown, S., Parsons, V., & Darby, A. (1985). Premature loss of bone in chronic anorexia nervosa. *British Medical Journal, 290,* 26–27.

Szymanski, L., & King, B. H. (1999). Summary of the Practice Parameters for the Assessment and Treatment of Children, Adolescents, and Adults with Mental Retardation and Comorbid Mental Disorders. *Journal of the American Academy of Child and Adolescent Psychiatry, 38,* 1606–1610.

Tabert, M. H., Manly, J. J., Liu, X., Pelton, G. H., Rosenblum, S., Jacobs, M., Zamora, D., Goodkind, M., Bell, K., Stern, Y., & Devanand, D. P (2006). Neuropsychological prediction of conversion to Alzheimer disease in patients with mild cognitive impairment. *Archives of General Psychiatry, 63,* 916–924.

Taher, N. S. (2007). Self-concept and masculinity/femininity among normal male individuals and males with gender identity disorder. *Social Behavior and Personality, 35,* 469–478.

Tait, R., & Hulse, G. (2003). A systematic review of the effectiveness of brief interventions with substance using adolescents by type of drug. *Drug and Alcohol Review, 22,* 337–346.

Talbott, J. A. (2004). Care of the chronically mentally ill—Still a national disgrace. *Psychiatric Services, 55,* 1116–1117.

Talbott, J. A. (2004). Deinstitutionalization: Avoiding the disasters of the past. *Psychiatric Services, 55,* 1112–1115.

Tan, S. Y., & Yeow, M. E. (2003). Paracelsus (1493–1541): The man who dared. *Singapore Medical Journal, 44,* 5–7.

Tan, S. Y., & Yeow, M. E. (2004). Philippe Pinel (1745–1826): Liberator of the insane. *Singapore Medical Journal, 45,* 410–412.

Tanielian T., & Jaycox L. H. (2008). *Invisible wounds of war: Psychosocial and cognitive injuries, their consequences, and services to assist recovery.* Santa Monica, CA: RAND Corporation.

Tanofsky-Kraff, M., Cohen, M. L., Yanovski, S. Z., Cox, C., Theim, K. R., Keil, M., et al. (2006). A prospective study of psychological predictors of body fat gain among children at high risk for adult obesity. *Pediatrics, 117,* 1203–1209.

Tariot, P. N., Farlow, M. R., Grossberg, G. T., Graham, S. M., McDonald, S., & Gergel, I. (2004). Memantine treatment in patients with moderate to severe Alzheimer disease already receiving donepezil: A randomized controlled trial. *Journal of the American Medical Association, 291,* 317–324.

Tarrier, N., Haddock, G., Lewis, S., Drake, R., & Gregg, L. (2006). Suicide behavior over 18 months in recent onset schizophrenic patients: The effects of CBT. *Schizophrenia Research, 83,* 15–27.

Tarsy, D., & Baldessarini, R. J. (2006). Epidemiology of tardive dyskinesia: Is risk declining with modern antipsychotics? *Movement Disorders, 21,* 589–598.

Tartaro, J., Luecken, L. J., & Gunn, H. E. (2005). Exploring heart and soul: effects of religiosity/spirituality and gender on blood pressure and cortisol stress responses. *Journal of Health Psychology, 10,* 753–766.

Tarter, R. E., Hegadus, A. M., Alterman, A. I., & Katz-Garris, L. (1983). Cognitive capacities of juvenile, violent, nonviolent, and sexual offenders. *Journal of Nervous and Mental Disease, 171,* 564–567.

Tarter, R., Vanyukov, M., & Kirisci, L. (2006). Predictors of marijuana use in adolescents before and after licit drug use: Examination of the gateway hypothesis. *American Journal of Psychiatry, 163,* 2134–2140.

Taylor, B. (2006). Vaccines and the changing epidemiology of autism. *Child Care Health and Development, 32,* S11–19.

Taylor, M. J., Freemantle, N., Geddes, J. R., & Bhagwagar, Z. (2006). Early onset of selective serotonin reuptake inhibitor antidepressant action: Systematic review and meta-analysis. *Archives of General Psychiatry, 63,* 1217–1223.

Taylor, S. (1995). Anxiety sensitivity: Theoretical perspectives and recent findings. *Behaviour Research and Therapy, 33,* 243–258.

Taylor, S. (1996). Meta-analysis of cognitive-behavioral treatments for social phobia. *Journal of Behavior Therapy and Experimental Psychiatry, 27,* 1–9.

Taylor, S. E. (2006). *Health psychology* (6th ed.). Boston: McGraw-Hill.

Taylor, S. E., Klein, L. C., Lewis, B. P., Gruenewald, T. L., Gurung, R. A., & Updegraff, J. A. (2000). Biobehavioral responses to stress in females: tend-and-befriend, not fight-or-flight. *Psychological Review, 107,* 411–429.

Taylor, S. E., Welch, W. T., Kim, H. S., & Sherman, D. K. (2007). Cultural differences in the impact of social support on psychological and biological stress responses. *Psychological Science, 18,* 831–837.

Taylor, S., & Asmundson, G. J. G. (2004) *Treating health anxiety.* New York: Guilford Press.

Teipel, S. J., Alexander, G. E., Schapiro, M. B., Moller, H. J., Rapoport, S. I., & Hampel, H. (2004). Age-related cortical grey matter reductions in non-demented Down's syndrome adults determined by MRI with voxel-based morphometry. *Brain, 127,* 811–824.

Tempelman, T. L., & Stinnett, R. D. (1991). Patterns of sexual arousal and history in a "normal" sample of young men. *Archives of Sexual Behavior, 20,* 137–150.

ter Kuile, M. M., van Lankveld, J. J., de Groot, E., Melles, R., Neffs, J., & Zandbergen, M. (2007). Cognitive-behavioral therapy for women with life-long vaginismus: Process and prognostic factors. *Behaviour Research and Therapy, 45,* 359–373.

Teri, L., Ferretti, L. E., Gibbons, L. E., Logsdon, R. G., McCurry, S. M., Kukull, W. A., et al. (1999). Anxiety of Alzheimer's disease: prevalence, and comorbidity. *The Journals of Gerontology, Series A, Biological Sciences and Medical Sciences, 54,* M348–M352.

Teri, L., Gibbons, L. E., McCurry, S. M., Logsdon, R. G., Buchner, D. M., Barlow, W. E., et al. (2003). Exercise plus behavioral management in patients with Alzheimer disease: A randomized controlled trial. *Journal of the American Medical Association, 290,* 2015–2022.

Teri, L., Logsdon, R. G., Peskind, E., Raskind, M., Weiner, M. F., Tractenberg, R. E., et al. (2000). Treatment of agitation in AD: A randomized, placebo-controlled clinical trial. *Neurology, 55,* 1271–1278.

Teri, L., Logsdon, R. G., Uomoto, J., & McCurry, S. M. (1997). Behavioral treatment of depression in dementia patients: A controlled clinical trial. *The Journals of Gerontology, Series B, Psychological Sciences and Social Sciences, 52,* 159–166.

Tevyaw, T., & Monti, P. (2004). Motivational enhancement and other brief interventions for adolescent substance abuse: Foundations, applications and evaluations. *Addiction, 99,* 63–75.

Thase, M. E., & Friedman, E. S. (1999). Is psychotherapy an effective treatment for melancholia and other severe depressive states? *Journal of Affective Disorders, 54,* 1–19.

Thase, M. E., & Kupfer, D. J. (1996). Recent developments in the pharmacotherapy of mood disorders. *Journal of Consulting and Clinical Psychology, 64,* 646–659.

The Association for Applied Psychophysiology and Biofeedback. (2007). Biofeedback and Psychophisiology. from http://www.aapb.org

The National Commission for the Protection of Human Subjects of Biomedical and Behavioral Research (1979). The Belmont Report. http://ohrp.osophs.dhhs.gov/humansubjects/guidance/belmont.htm.

Thiedke, C. C. (2001). Sleep disorders and sleep problems in childhood. *American Family Physician, 63,* 277–284.

Thomas, J., & Reddy, B. (1982). The treatment of mania: A retrospective evaluation of the effects of ECT, chlorpromazine, and lithium. *Journal of Affective Disorders, 4,* 85–92.

Thomason, J. W., Shintani, A., Peterson, J. F., Pun, B. T., Jackson, J. C., & Ely, E. W. (2005). Intensive care unit delirium is an independent predictor of longer hospital stay: A prospective analysis of 261 non-ventilated patients. *Critical Care, 9,* R375–R381.

Thompson, C. M., & Durrani, A. J. (2007). An increasing need for early detection of body dysmorphic disorder by all specialties. *Journal of the Royal Society of Medicine, 100,* 61–62.

Thompson, E. A., & Eggert, L. L. (1999). Using the suicide risk screen to identify suicidal adolescents among potential high school dropouts. *Journal of the American Academy of Child and Adolescent Psychiatry, 38,* 1506–1514.

Thompson, E. A., Eggert, L. L., & Herting, J. R. (2000). Mediating effects of an indicated prevention program for reducing youth depression and suicide risk behaviors. *Suicide and Life Threatening Behaviors, 30,* 252–271.

Thompson, R. J., & VanLoon, K. J. (2002). Mental disorders. In T. J. Boll, S. Bennett Johnson, N. W. Perry, & R. H. Rozensky (Eds.), *Handbook of clinical health psychology* (pp. 143–172). Washington, DC: American Psychological Association.

Thorp, S. R., Ayers, C. R., Nuevo, R., Stoddard, J. A., Sorrell, J. T., & Wetherell, J. L. (2009). Meta-analysis comparing different behavioral treatments for late-life anxiety. *American Journal of Geriatric Psychiatry, 17,* 105–115.

Tiefer, L. (2001). A new view of women's sexual problems. Why new? *Journal of Sex Research, 38,* 89–96.

Tienari, P., Wynne, L. C., Läksy, K., Moring, J., Nieminen, P., Sorri, A., Lahti, I., & Wahlberg, K. E. (2003). Genetic boundaries of the schizophrenia spectrum: Evidence from the Finnish adoptive family study of schizophrenia. *American Journal of Psychiatry, 160,* 1587–1594.

Tienari, P., Wynne, L. C., Sorri, A., Lahti, I., Laksy, K., Morning, J., Naarala, M., Nieminen, P., & Wahlberg, K. E. (2004). Genotype–environment interaction in schizophrenia-spectrum disorder. *British Journal of Psychiatry, 184,* 216–222.

Tierney, M. C., Szalai, J. P., Snow, W. G., Fisher, R. H., Nores, A., Nadon, G., et al. (1996). Prediction of probable Alzheimer's disease in memory-impaired patients: A prospective longitudinal study. *Neurology, 46,* 661–665.

Tirupati, S. N., Padmavati, R., Thara, R., & McCreadie, R. G. (2006). Psychopathology in never-treated schizophrenia. *Comprehensive Psychiatry, 47,* 1–6.

Tolin, D. F., Robison, J. T., Gatzambide, S., Horowitz, S., & Black, K. (2007). *Ataques de nervios* and psychiatric disorders in older Puerto Rican primary care patients. *Journal of Cross Cultural Psychology, 38,* 659–669

Tolin, D. F., Robison, J. T., Gaztambide, S., & Blank, K. (2005). Anxiety disorders in older Puerto Rican primary care patients. *American Journal of Geriatric Psychiatry, 13,* 150–156.

Tolman, D. L., & Diamond, L. M. (2001). Desegregating sexuality research: Cultural and biological perspectives on gender and desire. *Annual Review of Sex Research, 12,* 33–74.

Torgersen, S. (1983). Genetic factors in anxiety disorders. *Archives of General Psychiatry, 40,* 1085–1089.

Torgersen, S. (2002). Genetics and somatoform disorders. *Tidsskrift for den Norske Laegeforening, 122,* 1385–1388.

Torgersen, S., Kringlen, E., & Cramer, V. (2001). The prevalence of personality disorders in a community sample. *Archives of General Psychiatry, 58,* 590–596.

Tozzi, F., Thornton, L., Klump, K., Bulik, C. M., Fichter, M., Halmi, K., Kaplan, A., Strober, M., Woodside, D., Crow, S., Mitchell, J., Rotondo, A., Mauri, M., Cassano, C., Keel, P. K., Plotnicov, K., Pollice, C., Lilenfeld, L., Berrettini, W., & Kaye, W. H. (2005). Symptom fluctuation in eating disorders: Correlates of diagnostic crossover. *American Journal of Psychiatry, 162,* 732–740.

Tracey, S. A., Chorpita, B. F., Doubn J., & Barlow, D. H. (1997). Empirical evaluation of DSM-IV Generalized Anxiety Disorder criteria in children and adolescents. *Journal of Child Clinical Psychology, 26,* 404–414.

Trevisan, L., Boutros, N., Petrakis, I., & Krystal, J. (1998). Complications of alcohol withdrawal: Pathophysiological insights. *Alcohol Health & Research World, 22,* 61–66.

Trials of War Criminals before the Nuremberg Military Tribunals under Control Council Law No. 10, Nuremberg, October 1946–April 1949. Washington, DC: U.S. Government Printing Office, 1949–1953.

Trivedi, M. (1996). Functional neuroanatomy of obsessive-compulsive disorder. *Journal of Clinical Psychiatry, 57,* 26–36.

Troutman, B. R., & Cutrona, C. E. (1990). Nonpsychotic postpartum depression among adolescent mothers. *Journal of Abnormal Psychology, 99,* 69–78.

Trudel, G., Marchand, A., Ravart, M., Aubin, S., Turgeon, L., & Fortier, P. (2001). The effect of a cognitive-behavioral group treatment program on hypoactive sexual desire in women. *Sexual and Relationship Therapy, 61,* 145–164.

Trull, T. J., Sher, K. J., Minks–Brown, C., Durbin, J., & Burr, R. (2000). Borderline personality disorder and substance use disorders: A review and integration. *Clinical Psychology Review, 20,* 235–253.

Trzepacz, P. T. (2000). Is there a final common neural pathway in delirium? Focus on acetylcholine and dopamine. *Seminars in Clinical Neuropsychiatry, 5,* 132–148.

Trzepacz, P. T., Meagher, D. J., & Wise, M. G. (2002). Neuropsychiatric aspects of delirium. In R. E. Hales & S. C. Yudofsky (Eds.), *The American psychiatric publishing textbook of neuropsychiatry and clinical neurosciences* (4th ed) (pp. 525–564). Washington, DC: American Psychiatric Publishing Press

Tsai, G., Curbow, B., & Heinberg, L. (2003). Sociocultural and developmental influences on body dissatisfaction and disordered eating attitudes and behaviors of Asian women. *Journal of Nervous and Mental Disease, 191,* 309–318.

Tsai, J. L., Butcher, J. N., Muñoz, R. F., & Vitousek, K. (2001). Culture, ethnicity, and psychopathology. In P. B. Sutker and H. E. Adams, *Comprehensive Handbook of Psychopathology* (3rd ed.) (pp. 105–127). New York: Kluwer Academic/Plenum Publishers.

Tschanz, J. T., Corcoran, C., Skoog, I., Khachaturian, A. S., Herrick, J., Hayden, K. M., Welsh-Bohmer, K. A., Calvert, T., Norton, M. C., Zandi, P., & Breitner, J. C. (2004). Dementia: the leading predictor of death in a defined elderly population: the Cache County Study. *Neurology, 62,* 1156–1162.

Tseng, W. S. (2003). *Clinician's guide to cultural psychiatry.* San Diego, CA: Academic Press.

Tsoi, Y. F., & Kok, L. P. (1995). Mental disorders in Singapore. In T. Y. Lin, W. S. Tseng, & E. K. Yeh (Eds.), *Chinese societies and mental health* (pp. 266–278). Hong Kong: Oxford University Press.

Tsuang, D. W., & Bird, T. D. (2004). Genetics of dementia. In J. Sadavoy, L. F. Jarvik, G. T. Grossberg, & B. S. Meyers (Eds.), *Comprehensive textbook of geriatric psychiatry* (3rd ed., pp. 39–84). New York: W.W. Norton & Co.

Tsuang, M. T., Stone, W. S., & Faraone, S. V. (2000). Toward reformulating the diagnosis of schizophrenia. *American Journal of Psychiatry, 157,* 1041–1050.

Tukel, R., Ertekin, E., Batmaz, S., Alyanak, F., Sozen, A., Aslantas, B., et al. (2005). Influence of age of onset on clinical features in obsessive-compulsive disorder. *Depression & Anxiety, 21,* 112–117.

Turk, D. C., & Monarch, E. S. (2002). Biopsychosocial perspective on chronic pain. In D. C. Turk & R. J. Gatchel (Eds.), *Psychological approaches to pain management* (pp. 3–29). New York: Guilford Press.

Turner, H., & Bryant-Waugh, R. (2003). Eating disorders not otherwise specified (EDNOS): Profiles of clients presenting at a community eating disorders service. *European Eating Disorders Review, 12*, 18–26.

Turner, J. A., Holtzman, S., & Mancl, L. (2007). Mediators, moderators, and predictors of therapeutic change in cognitive-behavioral therapy for chronic pain. *Pain, 127*, 276–286.

Turner, S. M. (1998). Expressed emotional and the development of new treatments for substance abuse. *Behavior Therapy, 4*, 647–654.

Turner, S. M., & Beidel, D. C. (2003). The enriching experience. In J. D. Robinson and L. C. James (Eds.), *Diversity in human interactions* (pp. 195–205). New York: Oxford University Press.

Turner, S. M., Beidel, D. C., & Frueh, B. C. (2005). Multicomponent behavioral treatment for chronic combat-related posttraumatic stress disorder: Trauma management therapy. *Behavior Modification, 29*, 39–69.

Turner, S. M., Beidel, D. C., & Townsley, R. M. (1992). Social phobia: A comparison of specific and generalized subtypes and avoidant personality disorder. *Journal of Abnormal Psychology, 101*, 326–331.

Tyron, W. W. (1998). Behavioral observation. In A. S. Bellack & M. Herson (Eds.), *Behavioral Assessment: A Practical Handbook* (pp. 79–103). Boston: Allyn & Bacon.

Uchino, B. N., Cacioppo, J. T., & Kiecolt-Glaser, J. K. (1996). The relationship between social support and physiological processes: A review with emphasis on underlying mechanisms and implications for health. *Psychological Bulletin, 119*, 488–531.

Uhde, T. W., & Singareddy, R. (2002). Biological research in anxiety disorders. *Psychiatry as a neuroscience* (pp. 237–285). New York: John Wiley and Sons.

UK ECT Review Group. (2003). Efficacy and safety of electroconvulsive therapy in depressive disorders: A systematic review and meta-analysis. *Lancet, 361*, 799–808.

United States Surgeon General's Report. (1988). *The Health Consequences of Smoking: Nicotine Addiction.* Washington, DC: U.S. Department of Health and Human Services.

Unutzer, J., Katon, W., Callahan, C. M., Williams, J. W., Jr., Hunkeler, E., Harpole, L., et al. (2002). Collaborative care management of late life depression in the primary care setting: A randomized controlled trial. *Journal of the American Medical Association, 288*, 2836–2845.

Unutzer, J., Patrick, D. L., Diehr, P., Simon, G., Grembowski, D., & Katon, W. (2000). Quality adjusted life years in older adults with depressive symptoms and chronic medical disorders. *International Psychogeriatrics, 12*, 15–33.

Upadhyaya, H., & Deas, D. (2008). Pharmacological interventions for adolescent substance use disorders. In Y. Kaminer & O. Bukstein (Eds.), *Adolescent substance abuse: Psychiatric comorbidity and high-risk behaviors* (pp. 145–161). New York: Routledge/Taylor & Francis Group.

U.S. Department of Health and Human Services (2001). *Mental Health: Culture, Race and Ethnicity—A Supplement to Mental Health: A Report of the Surgeon General.* Department of Health and Human Services, Substance Abuse and Mental health Services Administration, Center for Mental Health Services.

U.S. Department of Health and Human Services. (2003). Major depression in children and adolescents. http://mentalhealth.samhsa.gov/publications/allpubs/CA-0011/default.asp

U.S. Preventive Services Task Force (2004). Screening and behavioral counseling interventions in primary care to reduce alcohol misuse: Recommendation statement, *Annals of Internal Medicine, 140*, 554–556.

Valdimarsdottir, H. B., & Bovbjerg, D. H. (1997). Positive and negative mood: Association with natural killer cell activity. *Psychology and Health, 12*, 319–327.

Valdovinos, M. G. (2007). Brief review of current research in FXS: implications for treatment with psychotropic medication. *Research in Developmental Disabilities, 28*, 539–545.

Valleni-Basile, L. A., Garrison. C. Z., Jackson, K. L., Waller, J. L., McKeown, R. E., Addy, C. L., et al. (1994). Frequency of obsessive-compulsive disorder in a community sample of young adolescents. *Journal of the American Academy of Child and Adolescent Psychiatry, 33*, 782–791.

van Balkom, A. J., Beekman, A. T., de, B. E., Deeg, D. J., van, D. R., & van, T. W. (2000). Comorbidity of the anxiety disorders in a community-based older population in The Netherlands. *Acta Psychiatrica Scandinavia, 101*, 37–45.

Van Citters, A. D., Pratt, S. I., Bartels, S. J., & Jeste, D. V. (2005). Evidence-based review of pharmacologic and nonpharmacologic treatments for older adults with schizophrenia. *Psychiatric Clinics of North America, 28*, 913–939, ix.

van den Wiel, N., Matthys, W., Cohen-Kettenis, P. C., & van Engeland, H. (2002). Effective treatments of school-aged conduct disordered children: Recommendations for changing clinical and research practices. *European Child and Adolescent Psychiatry, 11*, 79–84.

van Dijk, M., Benninga, M. A., Grootenhuis, M., Nieuwenhuizen, A. M., & Last, B. F. (2007). Chronic childhood constipation: A review of the literature and the introduction of a protocolized behavioral intervention program. *Patient Education and Counseling, 67*, 63–77.

Van Duijl, M., Cardeña, & De Jong, J. T. (2005). The validity of DSM–IV dissociative disorders categories in south-west Uganda. *Transcultural Psychiatry, 42*, 219–241.

Van Gerpen, M. W., Johnson, J. E., & Winstead, D. K. (1999). Mania in the geriatric patient population: A review of the literature. *American Journal of Geriatric Psychiatry, 7*, 188–202.

van Hout, H. P., Beekman, A. T., de Beurs, E., Comijs, H., van Marwijk, H., de Haan, M., et al. (2004). Anxiety and the risk of death in older men and women. *British Journal of Psychiatry: The Journal of Mental Science, 185*, 399–404.

van Melle, J. P., de Jonge, P., Spijkerman, T. A., Tijssen, J. G., Ormel, J., van Veldhuisen, D. J., et al. (2004). Prognostic association of depression following myocardial infarction with mortality and cardiovascular events: A meta-analysis. *Psychosomatic Medicine, 66*, 814–822.

van Ojen, R., Hooijer, C., Bezemer, D., Jonker, C., Lindeboom, J., & van Tilburg, W. (1995). Late-life depressive disorder in the community. II. The relationship between psychiatric history, MMSE and family history. *British Journal of Psychiatry: The Journal of Mental Science, 166*, 316–319.

van, E. M., Berkhof, H., Nicolson, N., & Sulon, J. (1996). The effects of perceived stress, traits, mood states, and stressful daily events on salivary cortisol. *Psychosomatic Medicine, 58*, 447–458.

Vandenberg, B. (1993). Fears of normal and retarded children. *Psychological Reports, 72*, 473–474.

Varon, S. R., & Riley, A. W. (1999). Relationship between maternal church attendance and adolescent mental health and social functioning. *Psychiatric Services, 50*, 799–805.

Vatz, R. E., & Weinberg, L. S. (1994). The rhetorical paradigm in psychiatric history: Thomas Szasz and the myth of mental illness. In M. S. Micale & R. Porter (Eds.), *Discovering the history of psychiatry* (pp. 311–330). New York: Oxford University Press.

Velicer, W., Redding, C., & Sun, X. (2007). Demographic variables, smoking variables, and outcome across five studies. *Health Psychology, 26*, 278–287.

Velligan, D., Bow-Thomas, C. C., Mahurin, R. D., Miller, A. L., & Halgunseth, L. C. (2000). Do specific neurocognitive deficits predict specific domains of community function in schizophrenia? *Journal of Nervous and Mental Disease, 188*, 518–524.

Verheul, R., & Widiger, T. A. (2004). A meta-analysis of the prevalence and usage of the personality disorder not otherwise specified (PDNOS) diagnosis. *Journal of Personality Disorders, 18*, 309–319.

Verheul, R., Bartak, A., & Widiger, T. (2007). Prevalence and construct validity of Personality Disorder Not Otherwise Specified (PDNOS). *Journal of Personality Disorders, 21*, 359–370.

Verma, S., & Gallagher, R. M. (2000). Evaluating and treatment co-morbid pain and depression. *International Review of Psychiatry, 12*, 103–114.

Vermetten, E., Schmahl, C., Lindner, S., Loewenstein, R. J., & Bremner, J. D. (2006). Hippocampal and amygdala volumes in dissociative identity disorder. *American Journal of Psychiatry, 163*, 630–636.

Vesga-López, O., Schneier, F. R., Wang, S., Heimberg, R. G., Liu, S. M., Hasin, D. S., et al. (2008). Gender differences in generalized anxiety disorder: Results from the National Epidemiologic Survey on Alcohol and Related Conditions (NESARC). *Journal of Clinical Psychiatry*. November 18 Epub ahead of print

Vickers, K., & McNally, R. J. (2004). Panic disorder and suicide attempt in the National Comorbidity Survey. *Journal of Abnormal Psychology, 113*, 582–591.

Vidal, C. N., Rapoport, J. L., Hayashi, K. M., Geafa, J. A., Sui, Y., McLemore, L. E., et al. (2006). Dynamically spreading frontal and cingulated deficits mapped in adolescents with schizophrenia. *Archives of General Psychiatry, 63*, 25–34.

Vincent, M., & Pickering, M. R. (1988). Multiple personality disorder in childhood. *Canadian Journal of Psychiatry, 33*, 524–529.

Vita, A., De Peri, L., Silenzi, C., & Dieci, M. (2006). Brain morphology in first-episode schizophrenia: A meta-analysis of quantitative magnetic resonance imaging studies. *Schizophrenia Research, 82,* 75–88.

Vloet, T. D., Konrad, K., Huebner, T., Herpertz, S., & Herpertz-Dahlmann, B. (2008). Structural and functional MRI-findings in children and adolescents with antisocial behavior. *Behavior Science Law, 26,* 99–111.

Vogel, W., Young, M., & Primack, W. (1996). A survey of physician use of treatment methods for functional enuresis. *Journal of Developmental and Behavioral Pediatrics, 17,* 90–93.

von Gontard, A., Schaumburg, H., Hollmann, E., Eiberg, H., & Rittig, S. (2001). The genetics of enuresis: A review. *Journal of Urology, 166,* 2438–2443.

Von Korff, M., Dworkin, S. F., LeResche, L., & Kruger, A. (1990). An epidemiological comparison of pain complaints. *Pain, 32,* 173–183.

Von Krafft-Ebing, R., & McCorn, W. A. (1900). The etiology of progressive paralysis. *American Journal of Insanity, 61,* 645–668.

Vowles, K. E., Zvolensky, M. J., Gross, R. T., & Sperry, J. A. (2004). Pain-related anxiety in the prediction of chronic low-back pain distress. *Journal of Behavioral Medicine, 27,* 77–89.

Wade, T. D., Bulik, C. M., Neale, M., & Kendler, K. S. (2000). Anorexia nervosa and major depression: Shared genetic and environmental risk factors. *American Journal of Psychiatry, 157,* 469–471.

Wade, T. D., Martin, N., Neale, M., Tiggemann, M., Trealor, S., Heath, A., et al. (1999). The structure of genetic and environmental risk factors for three measures of disordered eating characteristic of bulimia nervosa. *Psychological Medicine, 29,* 925–934.

Wadsworth, M. E., & Achenbach, T. M. (2005). Exploring the link between low socioeconomic status and psychopathology: Testing two mechanisms of the social causation hypothesis. *Journal of Consulting and Clinical Psychology, 73,* 1146–1153.

Wagner, A., Greer, P., Bailer, U., Frank, G., Henry, S., Putnam, K., Meltzer, C., Ziolko, S., Hoge, J., McConaha, C., & Kaye, W. (2006). Normal brain tissue volumes after long-term recovery in anorexia and bulimia nervosa. *Biological Psychiatry, 59,* 291–293.

Wagner, M. K. (2002). The high cost of prescription privileges. *Journal of Clinical Psychology, 58,* 677–680.

Wakefield, A. J. (1999). MMR vaccinations and autism. *The Lancet, 354,* 949–950.

Waldinger, M. D. (2002). The neurobiological approach to premature ejaculation. *Journal of Urology, 168,* 2359–2367.

Waldinger, M. D., Rietschel, M., Nöthen, M. M., Hengeveld, M. W., & Olivier, B. (1998). Familial occurrence of primary premature ejaculation. *Psychiatric Genetics, 8,* 37–40.

Walker, E. F., Savoie, T., & Davis, D. (1994). Neuromotor precursors of schizophrenia. *Schizophreia Bulletin, 20,* 441–451.

Walker, W. O., Jr., & Johnson, C. P. (2006). Mental retardation: Overview and diagnosis. *Pediatrics in Review, 27,* 204–212.

Wallace, J. M., Jr., & Forman, T. A. (1998). Religion's role in promoting health and reducing risk among American youth. *Health Education & Behavior, 25,* 721–741.

Waller, J., Kaufman, M., & Deutsch, F. (1940). Anorexia nervosa: A psychosomatic entity. *Psychosomatic Medicine, 11,* 3–16.

Wallien, M. S. C., & Cohen-Kettenis, P. T. (2008). Psychosexual outcome of gender-dysphoric children. *Journal of the American Academy of Child and Adolescent Psychiatry, 47,* 1413–1423.

Walsh, B. (1992). Diagnostic criteria for eating disorders in DSM-IV: Work in progress. *International Journal of Eating Disorders, 11,* 301–304.

Walsh, C. M., Zainal, N. Z., Middleton, S. J., & Paykel, E. S. (2001) A family history study of chronic fatigue syndrome. *Psychiatric Genetics, 11,* 123–128.

Walsh, E., Moran, P., Scott, C., McKenzie, K., Burns, T., Creed, F., et al. (2003). Prevalence of violent victimization in severe mental illness. *British Journal of Psychiatry, 183,* 233–238.

Walters, E. E., & Kendler, K. S. (1995). Anorexia nervosa and anorexic-like syndromes in a population-based female twin sample. *American Journal of Psychiatry, 152,* 64–71.

Walters, G. (2000). Behavioral self-control training for problem drinkers: A meta-analysis of randomized control studies. *Behavior Therapy, 31,* 135–149.

Wang, A., Peterson, G., & Morphey, L. (2007). Who is more important for early adolescents' developmental choices? Peers or parents? *Marriage & Family Review, 42,* 95–122.

Wang, P. S., Berglund, P., Olfson, M., Pincus, H. A., Wells, K. B., & Kessler, R. C. (2005). Failure and delay in initial treatment contact after first onset of mental disorders in the National Comorbidity Survey Replication. *Archives of General Psychiatry, 62,* 603–613.

Wang, W., Barratt, B., Clayton, D., & Todd, J. (2005). Genome-wide association studies: Theoretical and practical concerns. *Nature Review Genetics, 6,* 109–118.

Ward, A. & Mann, T. (2000). Don't mind if I do: Disinhibited eating under cognitive load. *Journal of Personality and Social Psychology, 78,* 753–763.

Ward, T., & Hudson, S. (1996). Relapse prevention: A critical analysis. *Sexual Abuse: A Journal of Research and Treatment, 8,* 177–200.

Warheit, G., Langer, L., Zimmerman, R., & Biafora, F. (1993). Prevalence of bulimic behaviors and bulimia among a sample of the general population. *American Journal of Epidemiology, 137,* 569–576.

Warshaw, M. G., Dolan, R. T., & Keller, M. B. (2000). Suicidal behavior in patients with current or past panic disorder: Five years of prospective data from the Harvard/Brown Anxiety Research Program. *American Journal of Psychiatry, 157,* 1876–1879.

Watson, D. (2005). Rethinking the mood and anxiety disorders: A quantitative hierarchical model for DSM-V. *Journal of Abnormal Psychology, 114,* 522–536.

Watson, J. B., & Rayner, R. (1920). Conditioned emotional reactions. *Journal of Experimental Psychology, 3,* 1–14.

Watson, T., & Andersen, A. (2003). A critical examination of the amenorrhea and weight criteria for diagnosing anorexia nervosa. *Acta Psychiatrica Scandinavica, 108,* 175–182.

We, E. Q., Birnbaum, H. G., Shi, L., Ball, D. E., Kessler, R. C., Moulis, M., & Affarwal, J. (2005). The exonomic burden of schizophrenia in the United States in 2002. *Journal of Clinical Psychiatry, 66,* 1122–1129.

Weber, J. B., Coverdale, J. H., & Kunik, M. E. (2004). Delirium: Current trends in prevention and treatment. *Internal Medicine Journal, 34,* 115–121.

Webster, L. R. & Webster, R. M. (2005). Predicting aberrant behaviors in opioid-treated patients: preliminary validation of the Opioid Risk Tool. *Pain Medicine, 6,* 432–442.

Webster-Stratton, C., Kolpacoff, M., & Hollinsworth, T. (1988). Self-administered videotape therapy for families with conduct-problem children: Comparison with two cost-effective treatments and a control group. *Journal of Consulting and Clinical Psychology 56,* 558–566.

Wechsler, D. (2008). *Wechsler Adult Intelligence Scale: Administration and Scoring Manual.* San Antonio: Psychological Corporation.

Weijmar Schultz, W. C. M., & Van de Wiel, H. B. M. (2005). Vaginismus. In R. Balon & R. T. Segraves (Eds.), *Handbook of sexual dysfunction* (pp. 43–65). Boca Raton, FL: Taylor and Francis.

Weiller, E., Bisserbe, J. C., Boyer, P., Lepine, J. P., & Lecrubier, Y. (1996). Treatment of anxiety disorders with comorbid depression. *British Journal of Psychiatry: The Journal of Mental Science, 168,* 169–174.

Weiner, D. B. (1992). Philippe Pinel's "Memoir on Madness" of December 11, 1794: A fundamental text of modern psychiatry. *American Journal of Psychiatry, 725–732.*

Weiner, S. K. (2003). First person account: Living with the delusions and effects of schizophrenia. *Schizophrenia Bulletin, 29,* 877–879.

Weinhardt, L. S., Carey, M. P., Johnson, B. T., & Bickham, N. L. (1999). Effects of HIV counseling and testing on sexual risk behavior: a meta-analytic review of published research, 1985–1997. *American Journal of Public Health, 89,* 1397–1405.

Weintraub, D., & Katz, I. R. (2005). Pharmacologic interventions for psychosis and agitation in neurodegenerative diseases: Evidence about efficacy and safety. *Psychiatric Clinics of North America, 28,* 941–983.

Weiss, D. S., Marmar, C. R., Schlenger, W. E., Fairbank, J. A., Jordan, B. K., Hough, R. L., & Kulka, R. A. (1992). The prevalence of lifetime and partial post-traumatic stress disorder in Vietnam theater veterans. *Journal of Traumatic Stress, 5,* 365–376.

Weissman, M. M. (1994). Psychotherapy in the maintenance treatment of depression. *British Journal of Psychiatry Supplement* (26), 42–50.

Weissman, M. M., Bland, R., Ganino, G., Greenwald, S., Hwo, H., Lee, C., et al. (1994). The cross national epidemiology of obsessive compulsive disorder. *The Journal of Clinical Psychiatry, 55,* 5–10.

Weissman, M. M., Myers, J. K., Tischler, G. L., Holzer, C. E., III, Leaf, P. J., Orvaschel, H., et al. (1985). Psychiatric disorders (DSM-III) and cognitive impairment among the elderly in a U.S. urban community. *Acta Psychiatrica Scandinavia, 71*, 366–379.

Weissman, M. M., Wolk, S., Goldstein, R. B., Moreau, D., Adams, P., Greenwald, S., et al. (1999). Depressed adolescents grown up. *Journal of the American Medical Association, 281*, 1707–1713.

Weisz, J. R. (1990). Cultural-familial mental retardation: A developmental perspective on cognitive performance and "helpless" behavior. In R. M. Hodapp, J. A. Burack, & E. Zigler (Eds.), *Issues in the developmental approach to mental retardation* (pp. 137–168). New York: Cambridge University Press.

Weisz, J. R., McCarty, C. A., Eastman, K. L., Chaiyasir, W., & Suwanlert, S. (1997). Developmental psychopathology and culture: Ten lessons from Thailand. In S. S. Lothan, J. A. Burnack, D. Cicchetti, & J. R. Weisz. *Developmental psychopathology: Perspectives on Adjustment, Risk and Disorder* (pp. 568–592). Cambridge: Cambridge University Press.

Weller, E., Weller, R., & Fristad, M. (1995). Bipolar diagnosis in children: Misdiagnosis, underdiagnosis, and future directions. *Journal of the American Academy of Child and Adolescent Psychiatry, 34*, 709–714.

Wellings, K., Field, J., Johnson, A. M., & Wadsworth, J. (1994). *Sexual behavior in Britain: The National Survey of sexual attitudes and lifestyles.* Harmondsworth, England: Penguin.

Wells, K. C., Pelham, W. E., Kotkin, R. A., Hoza, B., Abikoff, H. B., Abramowitz, A., et al. (2000). Psychosocial treatment strategies in the MTA study: Rationale, methods, and critical issues in design and implementation. *Journal of Abnormal Child Psychology, 28*, 483–505.

Welsh, R. S. (2003). Prescription privileges: Pro or con. *Clinical Psychology: Science and Practice, 10*, 371–372.

Wentzel, A., Statler-Cowen, T., Patton, G. K., & Holt, C. S. (1998). *A comprehensive meta-analysis of psychosocial and pharmacological interventions for social phobia and social anxiety.* Poster presented at the 19th Annual Conference of the Anxiety Disorders Association of America, San Diego, CA.

Weschler, D. (1939). *The measurement of adult intelligence* (1st ed.). Baltimore, MD: Waverly Press.

West, D. S., Harvey Berino, J., & Raczynski, J. M. (2004). Behavioral aspects of obesity, dictary intake, and chronic disease. In T. J. Boll, J. M. Raczynski, & L. C. Leviton (Eds.), *Handbook of clinical health psychology* (pp. 9–41). Washington, DC: American Psychological Association.

West, J. R., & Blake, C. A. (2005). Fetal alcohol syndrome: An assessment of the field. *Experimental Biology and Medicine, 230*, 354–356.

Westen, D., & Arkowitz–Westen, L. (1998). Limitations of axis II in diagnosing personality pathology in clinical practice. *American Journal of Psychiatry, 155*, 1767–1771.

Westermeyer, J., & Boedicker, A. (2000). Course, Severity, and Treatment of Substance Abuse among Women Versus Men. *American Journal of Drug Alcohol Abuse, 26*, 523–535.

Wetherell, J. L., Gatz, M., & Pedersen, N. L. (2001). A longitudinal analysis of anxiety and depressive symptoms. *Psychology of Aging, 16*, 187–195.

Wetherell, J. L., Kaplan, R. M., Kallenberg, G., Dresselhaus, T. R., Sieber, W. J., & Lang, A. J. (2004). Mental health treatment preferences of older and younger primary care patients. *International Journal of Psychiatry in Medicine, 34*, 219–233.

Wetherell, J. L., Lenze, E. J., & Stanley, M. A. (2005). Evidence-based treatment of geriatric anxiety disorders. *Psychiatric Clinics of North America, 28*, 896.

Weyers, S., Elaut, E., De Sutter, P., Gerris, J., T'sjoen, G., Heylens, G., et al. (2008). Long-term assessment of the physical, mental, and sexual health among transsexual women. *Journal of Sexual Medicine, Nov 17.* [Epub ahead of print)

Whaley, A. L. (1998). Cross-cultural perspective on paranoia: A focus on the Black American experience. *Psychiatric Quarterly, 69*, 325–343.

Wheeler, J., George, W., & Marlatt, G. (2006). Relapse prevention for sexual offenders: Considerations for the "abstinence violation effect." *Sexual Abuse, 18*, 233–248.

White, F., & Wolf, M. (1991). Psychomotor stimulants. In J. Pratt (Ed.), *The Biological bases of drug tolerance and dependence* (pp. 153–197). London: Academic Press.

Whitehead, W. E., Crowell, M. D., Heller, B. R., Robinson, J. C., Schuster, M. M., & Horn, S. (1994). Modeling and reinforcement of the sick role during childhood predicts adult illness behavior. *Psychosomatic Medicine, 56*, 541–550.

Widiger, T. A. (1992). Generalized social phobia versus avoidant personality disorder: A commentary on three studies. *Journal of Abnormal Psychology, 101*, 340–343.

Widiger, T. A., & Lowe, J. R. (2008). A dimensional model of personality disorder: proposal for DSM-V. *Psychiatric Clinics of North America, 31*, 363–378, v.

Widiger, T. A., & Samuel, D. B. (2005). Diagnostic categories or dimensions? A question for the *Diagnostic and Statistical Manual of Mental Disorders—Fifth Edition. Journal of Abnormal Psychology, 114*, 494–504.

Wilbert, J. R., & Fulero, S. M. (1988). Impact of malpractice litigation on professional psychology: Survey of practitioners. *Professional Psychology: Research and Practice, 4*, 379–382.

Wilens, T. E., Biederman, J., Brown, S., Tanguay, S., Monuteaux, M. C., Blake, C., & Spencer, T. J. (2002). Psychiatric comorbidity and functioning in clinically referred preschool children and school-age youths with ADHD. *Journal of the American Academy of Child and Adolescent Psychiatry, 41*, 262–268.

Wilfley, D., Agras, W., Telch, C., Rossiter, E., Schneider, J., Golomb Cole, A., Sifford, L., & Raeburn, S. (1993). Group cognitive-behavioral therapy and group interpersonal psychotherapy for the nonpurging bulimic individual: A controlled comparison. *Journal of Consulting and Clinical Psychology, 61*, 296–305.

Willcutt, E. G., Doyle, A. E., Nigg, J. T., Faraone, S. V., & Pennington, B. F. (2005). Validity of the executive function theory of attention-deficit/hyperactivity disorder: A meta-analytic review. *Biological Psychiatry, 57*, 1336–1346.

Wille, S. (1994). Functional bladder capacity and calcium creatinine quota in enuretic patients, former enuretic and non enuretic controls. *Scandinavian Journal of Urology and Nephrology, 28*, 353–357.

Willi, J., & Grossman, S. (1983). Epidemiology of anorexia nervosa in a defined region of Switzerland. *American Journal of Psychiatry, 140*, 564–567.

Williams White, S., Keonig, K., & Scahill, L. (2007). Social skills development in children with autism spectrum disorders: A review of the intervention research. *Journal of Autism and Developmental Disorders, 37*, 1858–1868.

Williams, P. G. (2004). The psychopathology of self-assessed health: A cognitive approach to health anxiety and hypochondriasis. *Cognitive Therapy and Research, 28*, 629–644.

Wills, T., Sandy, J., & Yaeger, A. (2001). Coping dimensions, life stress, and adolescent substance use: A latent growth analysis. *Journal of Abnormal Psychology, 110*, 309–323.

Wilson, G. (1993). Relation of dieting and voluntary weight loss to psychological functioning and binge-eating. *Annals of Internal Medicine, 119*, 727–730.

Wilson, M. (1993). DSM-III and the transformation of American psychiatry: A history. *American Journal of Psychiatry, 150*, 399–410.

Winzelberg, A., Eppstein, D., Eldredge, K., Wilfley, D., Dasmahapatra, R., Dev, P., et al. (2000). Effectiveness of an Internet-based program for reducing risk factors for eating disorders. *Journal of Consulting and Clinical Psychology, 68*, 346–350.

Wisner, K. L., Peindl, K. S., Gigliotti, T., & Hanusa, B. H. (1999). Obsessions and compulsions in women with postpartum depression. *Journal of Clinical Psychiatry, 60*, 176–189.

Witkiewitz, K., & Marlatt, G. (2006). Overview of harm reduction treatments for alcohol problems. *International Journal of Drug Policy, 17*, 285–294.

Wittchen, H. U., & Hoyer, J. (2001). Generalized anxiety disorder: Nature and course. *Journal of Clinical Psychiatry, 62*, 15–19.

Wittchen, H. U., Kessler, R. C., Beesdo, K., Krause, P., Hofler, M., & Hoyer, J. (2002). Generalized anxiety and depression in primary care: Prevalence, recognition, and management. *Journal of Clinical Psychiatry, 63 Suppl 8*, 24–34.

Wittchen, H. U., Nelson, C. B., & Lachner, G. (1998). Prevalence of mental disorders and psychosocial impairments in adolescents and young adults. *Psychological Medicine, 28*, 109–126.

Wittchen, H. U., Stein, M. B., & Kessler, R. C. (1999). Social fears and social phobia in a community sample of adolescents and young adults: prevalence, risk factors and co-morbidity. *Psychological Medicine, 29*, 309–323.

Wittchen, H. U., Zhao, S., Kessler, R. C., & Eaton, W. W. (1994). DSM-III-R generalized anxiety disorder in the National Comorbidity Survey. *Archives of General Psychiatry, 51*, 355–364.

Wolpe, J. (1952). *Psychotherapy by reciprocal inhibition.* Stanford, CA: Stanford University. Press.

Wolraich, M. L., Hannah, J. N., Baumgaertel, A., & Feurer, I. D. (1998). Examination of DSM-IV criteria for attention deficit/hyperactivity disorder in a county-wide sample. *Journal of Developmental and Behavioral Pediatrics, 19,* 162–168.

Woo, E. (2000, February 18). Dr. Martin Orne: Hypnosis expert detected Hillside strangler ruse. *Los Angeles Times,* A28.

Wood, J. M., Nezworski, M. T., Garb, H. N., & Lilienfeld, S. O. (2006). The controversy over Exner's Comprehensive System for the Rorschach: The critics speak. *The Independent Practitioner.* www.division42.org/MembersArea/IPfiles/Spring06/practitioner/rorschach.php.

Woodman, C. L., Noyes, R., Black, D. W., Schlosser, S., & Yagla, S. J. (1999). A 5-year follow-up study of generalized anxiety disorder and panic disorder. *Journal of Nervous and Mental Disease, 187,* 3–10.

Woodman, C. L., Stout, L., Hardardottir, H., & Hartz, A. (2001). Chronic fatigue syndrome and psychiatric illness: A family study. *Psychosomatic Medicine, 63,* 94–95.

Woodside, D. B., Garfinkel, P. E., Lin, E., Goering, P., Kaplan, A. S., Goldbloom, D. S., Wilfley, D., Agras, W., Telch, C., Rossiter, E., Schneider, J., Golomb Cole, A., Sifford, L., & Raeburn, S. (2001). Comparisons of men with full or partial eating disorders, men without eating disorders, and women with eating disorders in the community. *American Journal of Psychiatry, 158,* 570–574.

Woolfenden, S. R., Williams, K., & Peat, J. K. (2002). Family and parenting interventions for conduct disorder and delinquency: a meta-analysis of randomised controlled trials. *Archives of Disease in Childhood, 86,* 251–256.

World Health Organization (1948). *World Health Organization, Constitution of the World Health Organization.* Geneva, Switzerland.

World Health Organization (Ed.). (1992). *International statistical classification of diseases and related health problems, Tenth Revision.* Geneva: World Health Organization.

World Health Organization (WHO) (1973). *The international study of schizophrenia* Geneva: WHO.

World Health Organization. (2007). International Classification of Disease. Retrieved June 18, 2007, from http://www.who.int/classifications/icd/en/

World Medical Association (1964). Declaration of Helsinki. http://ohsr.od.nih.gov/helsinki.php.

Wright, J. C., Rabe-Hesketh, S., Woodruff, P. W., David, A. S., Murray, R. M., & Bullmore, E. T. (2000). Meta-analysis of regional brain volumes in schizophrenia. *American Journal of Psychiatry, 157,* 16–25.

Wright, L., Clipp, E., & George, L. (1993). Health consequences of caregiver stress. *Medicine, Exercise, Nutrition and Health 2,* 181–195.

Wright, P., Takei, N., Murray, R. M., & Sham, P. C. (1999). Seasonality, prenatal influenza exposure, and schizophrenia. In E. S. Susser, A. S. Brown, and J. M. Gorman (Eds.), *Prenatal exposures in schizophrenia* (pp. 89–112). Washington, DC: American Psychiatric Press.

Wykes, T., Hayward, P., Thomas, N., Green, N., Surguladze, S., Fannon, D., Wilfley, D., Agras, W., Telch, C., Rossiter, E., Schneider, J., Golomb Cole, A., Sifford, L., & Raeburn, S. (2005). What are the effects of group cognitive behaviour therapy for voices? A randomized trial. *Schizophrenia Research, 77,* 201–210.

Wykes, T., Parr, A. M., & Landau, S. (1999). Group treatment of auditory hallucinations. *British Journal of Psychiatry, 175,* 180–185.

Yamada, K., Watanabe, K., Nemoto, N., Fujita, H., Chikaraishi, C., Yamauchi, K., Wilfley, D., Agras, W., Telch, C., Rossiter, E., Schneider, J., Golomb Cole, A., Sifford, L., & Raeburn, S. (2006). Prediction of medication noncompliance in outpatients with schizophrenia: 2-year follow-up study. *Psychiatry Research, 141,* 61–69.

Yanovski, S., Nelson, J., Dubbert, B., & Spitzer, R. (1993). Association of binge eating disorder and psychiatric comorbidity in obese subjects. *American Journal of Psychiatry, 150,* 1472–1479.

Yap, P. M. (1967). Classification of the culture-bound reactive syndromes. *Australia and New Zealand Journal of Psychiatry, 1,* 172–179.

Yehuda, R. (2002, Current concepts: Posttraumatic stress disorder, *New England Journal of Medicine, 346,* 108–114.

Yerkes, R. M., & Dodson, J. D. (1908). The relation of strength of stimulus to rapidity of habit-formation. *Journal of Comprehensive Neurology and Psychology, 18,* 459–482.

Yeung, C. K., Sreedhar, B., Sihoe, J. D., Sit, F. K., & Lau, J. (2006). Differences in characteristics of nocturnal enuresis between children and adolescents: A critical appraisal from a large epidemiological study. *British Journal of Urology International, 97,* 1069–1073.

Yorbik, O., Birmaher, B., Axelson, D., Williamson, D. E., & Ryan, N. D. (2004). Clinical characteristics of depressive symptoms in children and adolescents with major depressive disorder. *Journal of Clinical Psychiatry, 65,* 1654–1659.

Young, L. J., & Wang, Z. (2004). The neurobiology of pair bonding. *Nature Neuroscience, 7,* 1048–1054.

Young, R. C. (2005). Evidence-based pharmacological treatment of geriatric bipolar disorder. *The Psychiatric Clinics of North America, 28,* 837–869.

Yule, W., Bolton, D., Udwin, O., Boyle, S., O'Ryan, D., & Nurrish, J. (2000). The long-term psychological effects of a disaster experienced in adolescence: I: The incidence and course of PTSD. *Journal of Child Psychology and Psychiatry, 41,* 503–511.

Yurgelun-Todd, D. A., & Ross, A. J. (2006). Functional magnetic resonance imaging studies in bipolar disorder. *CNS Spectrums, 11,* 287–297.

Zahl, D. L., & Hawton, K. (2004). Repetition of deliberate self-harm and subsequent suicide risk: Long-term follow-up study of 11,583 patients. *British Journal of Psychiatry, 185,* 70–75.

Zaider, T. I., & Heimberg, R. G. (2003). Non-pharmacologic treatments for social anxiety disorder. *Acta Psychiatrica Scandinavica, 108 (Suppl. 417),* 72–85.

Zanarini, M. C., Frankenburg, F. R., Hennen, J., & Silk, K. R. (2003). The longitudinal course of borderline psychopathology: 6-year prospective follow-up of the phenomenology of borderline personality disorder. *American Journal of Psychiatry, 160,* 274–283.

Zanarini, M. C., Gunderson, J. G., Marino, M. F., Schwartz, E. O., & Frankenburg, F. R. (1989). Childhood experiences of borderline patients. *Comprehensive Psychiatry, 30,* 18–25.

Zaretsky, A. E., Segal, Z. V., & Gemar, M. (1999). Cognitive therapy for bipolar depression: A pilot study. *Canadian Journal of Psychiatry, 44,* 491–494.

Zeiss, A. M., & Steffens, A. (1996). *A guide to psychotherapy and aging: Effective clinical interventions in a late-stage context.* Washington, DC: American Psychological Association.

Zhang, W., Ross, J., & Davidson, J. R. (2004). Social anxiety disorder in callers to the Anxiety Disorders Association of America. *Depression and Anxiety, 20,* 101–107.

Zhou, J. N., Hofman, M. A., Gooren, L. J., & Swaab, D. F. (1995). A sex difference in the human brain and its relation to transsexuality. *Nature, 378,* 68–70.

Zhu, A., & Walsh, B. (2002). Pharmacologic treatment of eating disorders. *Canadian Journal of Psychiatry, 47,* 227–234.

Zirpolo, K (as told to Debbie Nathan) (2005). A long delayed apology from one of the accusers in the notorious McMartin Pre-school molestation case. *Los Angeles Times,* October 30.

Zohar, A. H., & Felz, L. (2001). Ritualistic behavior in young children. *Journal of Abnormal Child Psychology, 29,* 121–128.

Zubenko, G. S., Henderson, R., Stiffler, J. S., Stabler, S., Rosen, J., & Kaplan, B. B. (1996). Association of the APOE epsilon 4 allele with clinical subtypes of late life depression. *Biological Psychiatry, 40,* 1008–1016.

Zucker, K. J. (2004). Gender identity development and issues. *Child and Adolescent Psychiatric Clinics of North America, 13,* 551–568.

Zucker, K. J. (2008). On the "natural history" of gender identity disorder in children. *Journal of the American Academy of Child and Adolescent Psychiatry, 47,* 1361–1363.

Zucker, N., Ferriter, C., Best, S., & Brantley, A. (2005). Group parent training: A novel approach for the treatment of eating disorders. *Eating Disorders: The Journal of Treatment & Prevention, 13,* 391–405.

CREDITS

PHOTO CREDITS

Chapter 1

Page 2 (center) Image Source, Getty Images Inc. RF; Page 2 (left) Orion, Jupiter Images; Page 2 (right) istockphoto.com: Page 5 (center) Richard Haughton, Lebrecht Music & Arts Photo Library; Page 5 (left) Richard Carson, CORBIS-NY; Page 5 (right) © Douglas Kirkland, CORBIS, All Rights Reserved; Page 7 AP Wide World Photos; Page 13 Neg. no. 283253 (Photo by Bierwert), Courtesy Dept. of Library Services-Special Collection, American Museum of Natural History; Page 14 Stock Montage, Getty Images Inc.-Hulton Archive; Page 15 Museo Real Academia de Medicina, Madrid, Spain/The Bridgeman Art Library; Page 17 Charles Ciccione, Photo Researchers, Inc.; Page 18 The Granger Collection; Page 19 Image Works/Mary Evans Picture Library Ltd.; Page 20 (bottom) Archives of the History of American Psychology; Page 20 (top) © CORBIS; Page 28 Ken Heyman, Woodfin Camp & Associates, Inc.; Page 29 Bonnie Kamin, PhotoEdit Inc.; Page 32 Allan Tannenbaum, The Image Works; Page 33 Robert Sullivan, Getty Images, Inc./Agence France Presse; Page 34 Jeff Greenberg, PhotoEdit Inc.

Chapter 2

Pages 40–41 istockphoto.com, Page 41 John Madden, istockphoto.com, Page 41 Robyn Mackenzie, istockphoto.com; Page 49 (left) Geoff Tompkinson, Photo Researchers, Inc.; Page 49 (right) Philippe Plailly/Science Photo Library/Photo Researchers, Inc.; Page 52 Thomas Wanstall, The Image Works; Page 54 CORBIS-NY; Page 56 David Young-Wolff, PhotoEdit Inc.; Page 60 Ryan McVay, Getty Images/Digital Vision; Page 62 Damien Lovegrove/SPL/Photo Researchers, Inc.; Page 64 (top) Bill Bachmann, Photolibrary.com; Page 64 (bottom) Jeff Greenberg, Peter Arnold, Inc.; Page 65 Spencer Grant, PhotoEdit Inc.

Chapter 3

Page 74 Zentilia, Shutterstock, Greg Nicholas, istockphoto.com, Christopher Robbins, Getty Images/Photodisc; Page 75 Elena Schweitzer, Shutterstock; Page 77 Pearson Education/PH College; Page 79 Matthew Simmons, Getty Images; Page 83 Bob Daemmrich, Stock Boston; Page 85 Spencer Grant, PhotoEdit Inc.; Page 86 University of Minnesota; Page 92 Pearson Education/PH College; Page 97 Deep Light Productions/Photo Researchers, Inc.; Page 102 Pearson Education/PH College.

Chapter 4

Page 110 istockphoto.com, Oliver Blondeau. istockphoto.com; Page 111 Jupiter Images Royalty Free, istockphoto.com; Page 120 Spencer Platt, Getty Images; Page 123 AP Wide World Photos; Page 126 Rick Wilking, CORBIS-NY; Page 131 Dorling Kindersley, Dorling Kindersley Media Library; Page 132 Comstock Images, Getty Images Inc. RF; Page 137 Archives of General Psychiatry, © 2006 Citation 63:25-34. Figures 4, 5, American Medical Association. All rights reserved; Page 147 Charles Vandermas, Delft University of Technology.

Chapter 5

Pages 152–153 Heather Laing, istockphoto.com, Caspar Benson, Getty Images Inc. RF, Roman Sigaev, istockphoto.com, Krechet, Shutterstock, Caspar Benson, Getty Images Inc. RF; Page 155 The Granger Collection; Page 159 The Cartoon Bank; Page 160 Tony Freeman, PhotoEdit Inc.; Page 161 J. LL. Banus, SuperStock, Inc.; Page 168 Michael Newman, PhotoEdit Inc.; Page 171 Lois Bernstein, Lois Bernstein; Page 172 Shutterstock: Page 181 Mike Gunnill, AP Wide World Photos.

Chapter 6

Page 186 Getty Images-Digital Vision; Pages 186–187 Vectoria, Shutterstock; Page 189 Frank Herholdt, Getty Images Inc.-Stone Allstock; Page 194 Lockyer, Romilly, Getty Images Inc.- Image Bank; Page 196 Dorling Kindersley Media Library; Page 197 Getty Images-Stockbyte; Page 200 Philip James Corwin, CORBIS-NY; Page 202 (top) Loomis Dean/Time Life Pictures/Getty Images/Time Life Pictures; Page 202 (middle) Dave Allocca, Getty Images/Time Life Pictures; Page 202 (bottom) Gemeente Museum, The Hague, Netherlands/SuperStock, Inc.; Page 204 Mary Kate Denny, PhotoEdit Inc. Page 210 Mark Richards, PhotoEdit Inc.; Page 212 National Institute of Mental Health; Page 216 James Wilson, Woodfin Camp & Associates, Inc.; Page 217 John Griffin, The Image Works.

Chapter 7

Page 224 Image Source, Getty Images Inc. RF; Pages 224–225 Veer Inc., Royalty Free; Page 225 Ethan Boisvert, Shutterstock: Page 226 The Bridgeman Art Library International; Page 228 Spencer Grant, PhotoEdit Inc.; Page 230 (top) Getty Images Inc. Hulton Archive; Page 230 (bottom) AP Wide World Photos; Page 235 AP Wide World Photos; Page 236 Tim Graham Picture Library, AP Wide World Photos; Page 241 Russell A. Dewey; Page 242 Mary M. Boggiano; Page 246 Salvador Minuchin; Page 247 (top) Shannon Stapleton, CORBIS-NY; Page 247 (bottom) Lawrence Jackson, AP Wide World Photos.

Chapter 8

Pages 256–257 Compassionate Eye Foundation/Siri Stafford/Getty Images/Digital Vision; Page 257 Shutterstock; Page 258 (top) Bert_Garai, Getty Images Inc. Hulton Archive Photos; Page 258 (bottom) Art Phillips, CORBIS-NY; Page 261 (top) Kevin Dodge, CORBIS-NY; Page 261 (bottom) Kazuyoshi Nomachi, CORBIS-NY; Page 266 CORBIS-NY; Page 267 Rob Elliott, Getty Images; Page 281 vaginismus.com; Page 282 Rune Hellestad, CORBIS-NY.

Chapter 9

Pages 294–295 Ray Torino, Shutterstock, Thomas Northcut, Getty Images, Inc.-Lifesize Royalty Free, Nicholas Eveleigh, Getty Images-Iconica, C Squared Studios, Getty Images, Inc. Photodisc.; Page 296 (top) David Young-Wolff, PhotoEdit Inc.; Page 296 (bottom) William Fritsch, Jupiter Images-PictureArts Corporation/Brand X Pictures Royalty Free; Page 299 (top) Cathy Melloan, PhotoEdit Inc.; Page 299 (bottom) George Steinmetz, CORBIS-NY; Page 300 Bill Barksdale, CORBIS-NY; Page 303 Susan J. Astley, Ph.D./Professor of Epidemiology/Pediatrics; Page 308 C. Sherburne/Photolink, Getty Images Inc. RF; Page 311 Frank Micelotta, Getty Images; Page 313 Yves Gellie, CORBIS-NY; Page 319 Jean Marc Giboux/Liaison Getty Images; Page 324 John Boykin, PhotoEdit Inc.; Page 325 B. Boissonnet, CORBIS-NY.

Chapter 10

Pages 332–333 Gino Crescoli, istockphoto.com, Olga Ekaterincheva, istockphoto.com, David Freund, istockphoto.com, Koksharov Dmitry, Shutterstock; Page 334 Gideon Mendel, CORBIS-NY; Page 336 Bonnie Kamin, PhotoEdit Inc.; Page 337 Grunnitus, Photo Researchers, Inc.; Page 339 CHARLES REX ARBOGAST, AP Wide World Photos; Page 342 Petteri Kokkonen/Impact/HIP The Image Works; Page 346 (both) Archives of General Psychiatry, © 2006 Citation 63:25 34. Figures 4,5 American Medical Association. All rights reserved; Page 347 Brett Coomer, Getty Images; Page 350 Monte S. Buchsbaum, M.D.; Page 357 Ted Streshinsky, CORBIS-NY; Page 359 George Ruhe/The New York Times Redux Pictures.

Chapter 11

Pages 364–365 Selahattin BAYRAM, istockphoto.com, Vasko Miokovic, istockphoto.com; Page 366 Scott Cunningham, Merrill Education; Page 369 Picture Desk, Inc./Kobal Collection; Page 371 Isabella Vosmikova/FOX Photofest; Page 373 Jim Smith, Photo Researchers, Inc.; Page 375 Mark Elias, AP Wide World Photos; Page 377 Dr. P. Marazzi, Photo Researchers, Inc;. Page 383 (top) John Greim, Photo Researchers, Inc.; Page 383 (bottom) Laimute Druskis,

Pearson Education/PH College; Page 386 R.R. Jones; Page 388 Laura Dwight, Peter Arnold, Inc.; Page 389 Ellen Senisi; Page 390 Karen Struthers, iStockPhoto; Page 392 (top) Ryan McVay, Getty Images, Inc. - fStop; Page 392 (bottom) Kelly, John P., Getty Images Inc. Image Bank; Page 394 Courtesy of Dr. Marsha Linehan.

Chapter 12
Pages 398–399 Getty Images, Inc. Photodisc, Yunus Arakon, istockphoto.com, Sudhir Karnataki, istockphoto.com, Veer Inc., Royalty Free; Page 402 Laura Dwight, Laura Dwight Photography; Page 403 L. Willatt/East Anglian Regional Genetics Service Photo; Researchers, Inc.; Page 414 Rosalie Winard, Rosalie Winard Photography; Page 416 Brain, Journal of Neurology; Page 422 Ken Lax, Photo Researchers, Inc.; Page 424 Ellen B. Senisi, Ellen Senisi; Page 428 J. Allan Hobson, Photo Researchers, Inc.; Page 430 Bryan Mercer.

Chapter 13
Pages 434–435 Jim Jurica, istockphoto.com, istockphoto.com, Carl Hebert, istockphoto.com, Shutterstock; Page 436 Ken Chernus, Getty Images; Page 437 (top) David Young-Wolff, Getty Images Inc.-Stone Allstock; Page 437 (bottom) Michael Newman, PhotoEdit Inc.; Page 442 Jim Noelker, The Image Works; Page 445 Robert Harbison, Robert Harbison; Page 447 Bonnie Kamin, PhotoEdit Inc.; Page 449 (left) David Young-Wolff, PhotoEdit Inc.; Page 449 (center) Hill Street Studios/Stock This Way/CORBIS-NY; Page 449 (right) Michael Newman, PhotoEdit Inc.; Page 452 Will Hart; Page 456 Michal

Heron, Pearson Education/PH College; Page 458 A. Pakieka, Photo Researchers, Inc.; Page 459 (top) CORBIS-NY; Page 459 (bottom) ISM, Phototake NYC; Page 463 Bronwyn Kidd, Getty Images, Inc. Photodisc.

Chapter 14
Pages 468–469 Wolfgang Amri, Shutterstock, Feng Yu, Shutterstock; Page 472 Marta Lavandier, AP Wide World Photos; Page 473 Getty Images Stockbyte; Page 474 Chad Ehlers, Stock Connection; Page 476 Juergen Berger, Photo Researchers, Inc.; Page 478 Tom Hood, AP Wide World Photos; Page 479 Robert Harbison; Page 481 Mary Kate Denny, PhotoEdit Inc.; Page 483 Rufus F. Folkks, CORBIS-NY; Page 484 Joe Raedie, Getty Images, Inc. Liaison; Page 486 Bob Daemmrich, The Image Works; Page 490 Doug Menuez, Getty Images, Inc. PhotoDisc; Page 493 CORBIS-NY; Page 494 Lynn Johnson/ Sports Illustrated/Getty Images.

Chapter 15
Pages 498–499 Sashkin, Shutterstock; Page 502 Jerry Cooke/Time Life Pictures/Getty Images/Time Life Pictures; Page 503: Jim Whitmer Photography; Page 504 Andrew Lichtenstein, The Image Works; Page 506 (top) Barry Thumma, AP Wide World Photos; Page 506 (bottom) Ron Edmonds, AP Wide World Photos; Page 508 (top) CORBIS-NY; Page 508 (bottom) Emily Carota Orne; Page 509 Ravell Call, Getty Images; Page 511 John Neubauer, PhotoEdit Inc.; Page 512 Michael Newman, PhotoEdit Inc;. Page 515 Michael Newman, PhotoEdit Inc.; Page 523 CORBIS-NY.

NAME INDEX

589

DSM-IV-TR Classification: Axes I and II

AXIS I

DISORDERS USUALLY FIRST DIAGNOSED IN INFANCY, CHILDHOOD, OR ADOLESCENCE

Mental Retardation (See Axis II)
Learning Disorders
 Reading Disorder
 Mathematics Disorder
 Disorder of Written Expression
 Learning Disorder NOS (Not Otherwise Specified)
Motor Skills Disorder
 Developmental Coordination Disorder
Communication Disorders
 Expressive Language Disorder
 Mixed Receptive-Expressive Language Disorder
 Phonological Disorder
 Stuttering
 Communication Disorder NOS
Pervasive Developmental Disorders
 Autistic Disorder
 Rett's Disorder
 Childhood Disintegrative Disorder
 Asperger's Disorder
Attention-Deficit and Disruptive Behavior Disorders
 Attention-Deficit/Hyperactivity Disorder
 Attention-Deficit/Hyperactivity Disorder NOS
 Conduct Disorder
 Oppositional Defiant Disorder
 Disruptive Behavior Disorder NOS
Feeding and Eating Disorders of Infancy or Early Childhood
 Pica
 Rumination
 Feeding Disorder of Infancy or Early Childhood
Tic Disorders
 Tourette's Disorder
 Chronic Motor or Vocal Tic Disorder
 Transient Tic Disorder
 Tic Disorder NOS
Elimination Disorders
 Encopresis
 Enuresis (Not Due to a General Medical Condition)
Other Disorders of Infancy, Childhood, or Adolescence
 Separation Anxiety Disorder
 Selective Mutism
 Reactive Attachment Disorder of Infancy or Early Childhood
 Stereotypic Movement Disorder
 Disorder of Infancy, Childhood, or Adolescence NOS

DELIRIUM, DEMENTIA, AND AMNESTIC AND OTHER COGNITIVE DISORDERS

Delirium
 Delirium Due to [Indicate the General Medical Condition]
 Substance Intoxication/Withdrawal Delirium
 Delirium Due to Multiple Etiologies
 Delirium NOS
Dementia
 Dementia of The Alzheimer's Type, with Early Onset
 Dementia of The Alzheimer's Type, with Late Onset
 Vascular Dementia
 Dementia Due to Other General Medical Conditions [Specify Condition]
Amnestic Disorders
 Amnestic Disorder Due to [Indicate the General Medical Condition]
 Substance-Induced Persisting Amnestic Disorder
 Amnestic Disorder NOS
Other Cognitive Disorders
 Cognitive Disorder NOS

MENTAL DISORDERS DUE TO A GENERAL MEDICAL CONDITION NOT ELSEWHERE CLASSIFIED

Catatonic Disorder Due to [Indicate the General Medical Condition]
Personality Change Due to [Indicate the General Medical Condition]
Mental Disorder NOS Due to [Indicate the General Medical Condition]

SUBSTANCE-RELATED DISORDERS

Alcohol-Related Disorders
Amphetamine (or Amphetamine-Like)-Related Disorders
Caffeine-Related Disorders
Cannabis-Related Disorders
Cocaine-Related Disorders
Hallucinogen-Related Disorders
Inhalant-Related Disorders
Nicotine-Related Disorders
Opioid-Related Disorders
Phencyclidine (or Phencyclidine-Like)-Related Disorders
Sedative-, Hypnotic-, or Anxiolytic-Related Disorders
Polysubstance-Related Disorder

SCHIZOPHRENIA AND OTHER PSYCHOTIC DISORDERS

Schizophrenia
 Paranoid Type
 Disorganized Type
 Catatonic Type
 Undifferentiated Type
 Residual Type
Schizophreniform Disorder
Schizoaffective Disorder
Delusional Disorder
Brief Psychotic Disorder
Shared Psychotic Disorder
Psychotic Disorder Due to [Indicate the General Medical Condition]
Substance-Induced Psychotic Disorder
Psychotic Disorder NOS

MOOD DISORDERS

Depressive Disorders
 Major Depressive Disorder
 Dysthymic Disorder
 Depressive Disorder NOS
Bipolar Disorders
 Bipolar I Disorder
 Bipolar II Disorder
 Cyclothymic Disorder
 Bipolar Disorder NOS
Mood Disorder Due to [Indicate the General Medical Condition]
Substance-Induced Mood Disorder
Mood Disorder NOS

ANXIETY DISORDERS

Panic Disorder
 Without Agoraphobia
 With Agoraphobia
Agoraphobia Without History of Panic Disorder
Specific Phobia
Social Phobia (Social Anxiety Disorder)
Obsessive-Compulsive Disorder
Posttraumatic Stress Disorder
Acute Stress Disorder
Generalized Anxiety Disorder
Anxiety Disorder Due to [Indicate the General Medical Condition]
Substance-Induced Anxiety Disorder
Anxiety Disorder NOS

SOMATOFORM DISORDERS

Somatization Disorder
Undifferentiated Somatoform Disorder
Conversion Disorder
Pain Disorder
Hypochondriasis
Body Dysmorphic Disorder
Somatoform Disorder NOS